YOU AND YOUR RIGHTS

YOU AND YOUR RIGHTS

AN A TO Z GUIDE TO THE LAW IN SCOTLAND

PUBLISHED BY THE READER'S DIGEST ASSOCIATION LIMITED
London · New York · Montreal · Sydney · Cape Town

in association with
T. & T. CLARK LIMITED
Edinburgh

YOU AND YOUR RIGHTS (SCOTLAND EDITION)
was edited and designed by
The Reader's Digest Association Limited, London
and
T. & T. Clark Limited, 36 George Street, Edinburgh EH2 2LQ

Typesetting: Vantage Photosetting Co. Ltd.,
Eastleigh and London
Separations: Aero Offset Reproductions Ltd.,
Eastleigh
Cover marble design: Mitchell and Malik Ltd.,
Mere, Wiltshire
Paper: Bowater Paper Co. Ltd.,
Sittingbourne, Kent
Printing: Blantyre Printing & Binding Co. Ltd.,
Glasgow
Binding: Hazell Watson & Viney Ltd., Aylesbury

The main text of YOU AND YOUR RIGHTS
is typeset in 9 on 10 point Times New Roman

Printed in Scotland

GENERAL EDITORS

Robert A. McCreadie LLB, PhD
Lecturer in Scots Law, University of Edinburgh

Ian D. Willock MA, LLB, PhD
Professor of Jurisprudence, University of Dundee

CONSULTANT EDITOR

Robert Black LLB, LLM
Professor of Scots Law, University of Edinburgh

PRINCIPAL CONTRIBUTORS

Robert A. McCreadie LLB, PhD
Lecturer in Scots Law, University of Edinburgh

John MacLean LLB,
Lecturer in Scots Law, University of Edinburgh

Ian D. Willock MA, LLB, PhD
Professor of Jurisprudence University of Dundee

CONTRIBUTORS

John W. G. Blackie BA, LLB, *Lecturer in Scots Law, University of Edinburgh*

Lynda Clark LLB, PhD, *Advocate*

Victor Craig LLB, Dip. Eur. Int., *Lecturer, Heriot Watt University, Edinburgh*

W. C. H. Ervine BA, LLB, LLM, *Lecturer, University of Dundee*

Keith D. Ewing LLB, PhD, *Fellow of Trinity Hall, Cambridge, University Assistant Lecturer in Law*

David J. Field BA, *Solicitor, Head of Department of Law, Napier College, Edinburgh*

Wilson W. Finnie LLB, *Lecturer in Constitutional and Administrative Law, University of Edinburgh*

A. D. M. Forte MA, LLB, FSA Scot, *Lecturer, University of Dundee*

Chris Himsworth BA, LLB, *Lecturer in Constitutional and Administrative Law, University of Edinburgh*

Ian C. Maclure MA, LLB, *Solicitor*

James J. McManus LLB, *Lecturer in Jurisprudence, University of Dundee*

David I. Nichols MA, PhD, Writer to H. M. Signet, *Scottish Law Commission, Edinburgh*

Alan A. Paterson LLB, DPhil, *Solicitor, Lecturer in Scots Law, University of Edinburgh*

Fiona E. Raitt LLB, *Solicitor*

Kenneth G. C. Reid BA, LLB, *Lecturer in Scots Law, University of Edinburgh*

W. D. H. Sellar BA, LLB, *Senior Lecturer in Scots Law, University of Edinburgh*

Elaine E. Sutherland LLB, *Lecturer in Scots Law, University of Edinburgh*

Colin J. Tyre LLB, DESU, *Solicitor*

Robin M. White LLB, LLM, Cert. Soc. Anth., *Lecturer in Law, University of Dundee*

Eric S. Young MA, LLB, *Solicitor, Senior Lecturer in Law, University of Strathclyde*

Cartoons by David Langdon

Picture sequences drawn by Jim Gorman (Forth Studios Limited) and Barbara Walker (Saxon Artists)

Other artwork by Forth Studios Limited and Hayward and Martin Limited

The publishers gratefully acknowledge the works of the Consultant Editor and Contributors to the England and Wales edition of *You and Your Rights*. This publication formed the basis from which the Scotland edition has been prepared.

CONSULTANT EDITOR

The late HARRY STREET CBE, LLM, PhD, LLD, FBA
Professor of English Law, Manchester University

Contributors: *F. E. Adams* LLB, *Solicitor, Professor of Law, Queen Mary College, University of London; Geoffrey Bindman, Solicitor; C. D. Brandreth* MA (Oxon), *Solicitor; Margaret Brazier* LLB, *Lecturer in Law, Manchester University; Rodney Brazier* LLB, *Barrister-at-Law, Senior Lecturer in Law, Manchester University; A. L. Diamond, Professor of Law in the University of London; Frank Eaglestone* LLB, FCII, FCIArb, *Barrister-at-Law; Terence Flanagan* LLM, *Solicitor; J. F. Garner* LLD, *Solicitor, Professor of Public Law, University of Nottingham; E. R. Hardy Ivamy* LLB, Phd, LLD, *Barrister-at-Law, Professor of Law in the University of London; Diana M. Kloss* LLM, *Senior Lecturer in Law, Manchester University; Sarah Leigh, Solicitor; Tony Lynes; Andrew J. Martin* MA, *Barrister-at-Law; Dr. Vincent Powell-Smith* LLB (Hons), LLM, DLitt, FCIArb, FRSA, FSA *Scotland; John Pritchard, Solicitor; W. E. Pritchard* BA, FTII, *Lecturer and consultant in taxation; Margaret Puxon* QC, MD, FRCOG, *Barrister-at-Law; Paul Puxon, Barrister-at-Law; Bert Raisbeck* TD, LLB, ACIS, *Principal Lecturer in Law, Lanchester Polytechnic, Coventry; Alec Samuels* JP, *Barrister-at-Law, Reader in Law in the University of Southampton; Michael F. Saunders* FCII; *Felicity Taylor; Bobbie Vincent-Emery; Mary Vitoria* PhD, *Barrister-at-Law; Charles Webster* LLB, *Solicitor, Lecturer in Law, Manchester University; David W. Williams* LLM, PhD, ATII, *Solicitor, Senior Lecturer in Law, Manchester University; Carol Wilson* PSW, CQSW, *Assistant area officer, Social Services Department, London Borough of Hammersmith and Fulham; David Yates* MA, *Professor of Law, University of Essex.*

The laws described in this book are those of Scotland at the time of printing

There are substantial differences in the laws of England and Wales, Northern Ireland, the Republic of Ireland, the Isle of Man and the Channel Islands.

Inevitably some of the figures used in this book change from year to year, especially tax rates and social security levels. The tax figures are for the tax year April 6, 1984 to April 5, 1985. To obtain up to date figures, ask at a local tax office.

The social security figures are for November 1983 to November 1984. To obtain up to date figures, ask at a social security office for the following free leaflets:
NI 196 (Social Security benefit rates and earnings rules)
NI 208 (national insurance contribution rates and statutory sick pay rates)
MPL 154 (rates of war pensions and allowances)

Foreword

by

The Rt Hon. THE LORD KILBRANDON LLD, DSc

HOUSE OF LORDS,
SW1A 0PW

It is a common saying that everyone is presumed to know the law. The law does indeed set up some rather unrealistic presumptions, but this is not one of them. What the saying is intended to mean is that ignorance of a law cannot be pleaded as a defence to a charge of breaking it, but that is a very different thing. No-one knows all the law, even judges of the highest rank. The Law Reports disclose that in many of the most important cases there were judicial differences of opinion. No doubt if there were a court to which appeals could be taken from the House of Lords, that court would often decide that their Lordships had been wrong. And so on ad infinitum.

Nevertheless we are all under a duty to obey the law and this is something in which the citizen will need help. The law surrounds each one of us with the most detailed and complex rules and enactments. If we don't have the means of knowing what rights are conferred on us by the law, we may be much the poorer. If we don't know the duties the law has imposed on us, we may get into trouble. This is why access to a clear, simplified, accurate legal encyclopedia – as I believe this to be – is so essential. Of course people who have a legal problem should get advice from a solicitor, which nowadays may cost us very little. But it is only when you have some idea where you stand that you realise you need advice. This book does not pretend to take the place of a legal adviser, but it does help you to know whether you ought to consult one.

The book does more than that. Quite often in the normal transactions of everyday life you are wise to know something of what the law says about what you are going to do. So many ordinary things are regulated by the law. Insurance of one's home is one of them. There are plenty of them arising out of buying and running a car. Domestic relations, also relations with your neighbours, are controlled by legal rules. Do you want to put up a greenhouse? Is your employer treating you fairly and are you treating your employer fairly? One could multiply instances, as in fact this book does. It is also very easy, and indeed enjoyable, to read.

I will add, if my colleagues in the law will forgive me, that, when they are consulted, they would be wise to glance (surreptitiously) at this book before giving their advice. I know I would.

Kilbrandon

ABANDONED VEHICLE

When the local council is responsible

If you believe that a vehicle has been abandoned, complain to your district or islands council. The council must remove the vehicle, unless it is on private property and the cost would be unreasonably high.

A council official will inspect the vehicle and decide either to sell or destroy it.

If he decides to sell, he can remove the vehicle immediately but cannot carry out the sale until some attempt has been made to find the owner. If he decides to destroy, he must put a notice on the vehicle giving a date by which its owner must reclaim it. If the vehicle is not reclaimed by that date then the council official can remove it.

The owner is liable for the council's expenses, but is entitled to the proceeds of any sale if he claims within a year.

Anyone who abandons a vehicle or part of a vehicle on a public road or on someone else's property is committing an offence.

Maximum penalty A £400 fine or 3 months' imprisonment, or both.

ABDUCTION

Carrying off a person against his will

It is a crime to carry off any person by force, or to detain someone against his or her will, without lawful authority. The crime is committed when a person is illegally deprived of personal liberty, and an offender can be sent to prison or ordered to pay an unlimited fine.

Abduction is often carried out to extort a ransom from relatives or business friends of the victim. But abduction for any purpose is criminal. A man who forcibly removes his wife from the place where she wishes to be can be guilty of abduction.

The carrying away of a child below the age of puberty (girls 12, boys 14) from its parents is an example of the crime of THEFT.

Child snatched by parent

Parents who are parting, or who are already separated or divorced, may disagree over CUSTODY of their children and one may try to take away the children from the other, possibly to a location outside the jurisdiction of the courts.

A parent probably cannot be accused of abducting his or her own child. But if a court has granted one parent custody of a child and the other parent takes the child away, without the consent of the one with custody, that parent is guilty of CONTEMPT OF COURT and can be sent to prison.

If no custody order exists and the child has been taken away by one parent, the other parent can apply to a court for custody and an order for delivery of the child.

A parent who fears that his or her child may be taken away by the other parent can apply to the court for an INTERDICT, whether or not the child is in his or her custody. The interdict prohibits the taking away of the child and any subsequent removal of the child will be contempt of court.

Laws that protect women and girls

It is an offence punishable by up to 2 years' imprisonment to detain any woman or girl against her will in any premises with intent that she have unlawful sexual intercourse – that is sex outside marriage – with a man or men.

It is also an offence to take an unmarried girl under the age of 18 away from her parents (or other person in charge of her) without their consent, with the intention that she have sexual intercourse with her abductor or someone else. A charge can be brought whether or not intercourse has actually taken place. The offence is punishable by up to 2 years' imprisonment.

The girl must have been 'taken' from her parents. The fact that she agreed to be taken is not a defence. But the accused must have played an active part in the girl's leaving. He is not guilty if he passively consented to her own suggestion that she should leave.

ABORTION

When a woman wishes to end her pregnancy

Causing an abortion is a crime unless it is carried out under the Abortion Act 1967.

A woman does not have an automatic right to an abortion under the 1967 Act, but she can usually get one if she is determined not to have a child. It is not always possible, however, to arrange one free under the National Health Service.

If a woman wants her pregnancy to be terminated, she should see her own doctor as soon as possible. In early pregnancy the operation is usually quite simple but it becomes more difficult and dangerous as the pregnancy advances.

In Scotland, under the 1967 Act, an abortion is in theory possible at any stage of the pregnancy. But in practice the operation will only be possible up to the 24th – 28th week of pregnancy; and doctors may be unwilling to perform it after the 20th – 24th week.

The 1967 Act allows an abortion on

any one of the following grounds:
1. That continuation of the pregnancy would involve a greater risk to the mother's life than an abortion would.
2. That the pregnancy is a greater risk to her physical or mental health, or the health of her existing children, than an abortion. The woman's social circumstances can be taken into account.
3. That there is a risk that the child would be born with a physical or mental abnormality.

It is illegal for anyone other than a doctor to end a pregnancy, although a nurse may give drugs to cause abortion under the direct supervision of a doctor.

The consent of the father of the unborn child is not necessary, and he has no legal power to prevent the mother having an abortion.

If a doctor considers an abortion is appropriate, he refers the woman to a gynaecologist who may agree to perform the operation. (Two doctors have to certify the grounds for the abortion.)

If a place is not available under the National Health Service, private treatment can usually be arranged, but in this case the woman may have to travel to England for the operation.

If the doctor refuses

A doctor may be opposed to an abortion because he thinks there are no legal grounds for it or because of a personal conviction that abortions are wrong. No doctor or nurse can be compelled to be a party to an abortion if it is against his or her moral principles, unless there is an emergency and the woman's life is in danger.

If a woman does not accept her doctor's decision, she can try to find another general practitioner who takes a different view. That can be difficult and may cause dangerous delay. She is more likely to get immediate help and advice through the Brook Advisory Centre in Edinburgh or Pregnancy Advisory Service (fee payable) in Glasgow, or at one of the family planning clinics throughout Scotland.

ABSOLUTE DISCHARGE

When an offender may not be punished

If a court does not think that it would be appropriate to punish an accused person who has been found to have committed an offence – for example, if he was found guilty on a technicality and was not blameworthy in any way – it may grant an absolute discharge. The fact that the person committed the offence is nevertheless recorded.

An absolute discharge cannot be granted in cases where the penalty is fixed by law – as, for instance, with the crime of murder. *See:* SENTENCE

ACCESS TO CHILDREN

When separated parents cannot agree

When separated parents, whether married or unmarried, cannot agree on the conditions under which one of them may see or visit their child or children, the parent with whom the child is not living can apply to the sheriff court or Court of Session for an access order.

The courts, however, are concerned less with the parents' rights than with the right of the child to enjoy and benefit from contact with both parents. Generally the courts refuse access only when they think it could cause real harm.

They would also be unlikely to grant access when the child had never known the parent applying because the parents had never lived together during the child's lifetime.

The arrangements can cover either regular visits and outings or quite long stays – for instance, for part of the school holidays.

The judge listens to both parents or their lawyers and decides what seems to be the most reasonable arrangement in the interests of the child. If it seems appropriate, he may ask a social worker, an advocate or a solicitor to see both parents and the child, and make recommendations. *See:* CUSTODY OF CHILDREN

ACCIDENT

Collect evidence if you can

Whenever you are involved in an accident, try to make sure that someone collects evidence on your behalf. Make sure, particularly, that the names of any witnesses are taken and a drawing is made of the scene. *See:* ACCIDENT AT WORK; AIR ACCIDENT; ROAD TRAFFIC ACCIDENT

ACCIDENT AT SCHOOL

A teacher's duty to look after the children

A school is responsible for the safety and well-being of its pupils during the time they are in its charge. If a child is harmed in some way and the parents can show that it happened because a teacher or some other school employee did not take reasonable care, the child can take legal action to recover damages for his or her suffering and for the consequences of any disablement that results – for example, the cost of medical care.

If an accident involves a private school, the action must be taken against the body running the school – often a limited company; in a state school it is taken against the local EDUCATION AUTHORITY.

The basic issue is always whether reasonable care was taken of the child in the circumstances.

When the teacher is responsible

Usually it is a question of supervision. If a child is burned in a chemistry experiment or in cookery class, the parents would need to find out if the teacher had the class under proper control and had taken commonsense precautions to try to stop such an accident happening. If the teacher can show that he or she gave proper instruction and warnings but one member of the class behaved quite unpredictably, the court would probably dismiss a claim.

In some circumstances, a teacher is held to have an added responsibility because of his or her specialist training. For example, a chemistry teacher is expected to be aware of the potential danger of various substances in the laboratory. Likewise, a physical education teacher is expected to have a special understanding of safety problems in a gymnasium.

When an accident is caused by another child in the school – for example, when one child throws a dart that hits another in the eye – the injured child could sue the other, but there

THE SCHOOLGIRL WHO INJURED AN EYE

Although in principle the law does not expect a child to behave as responsibly as an adult, there may be instances where the court will decide that a teacher is not to blame for an accident to a pupil.

A pupil at a Highland primary school received an eye injury from a knitting needle. She alleged that a 10-year-old classmate had poked her with one of four needles on a half-knitted sock while they were drinking from a playground fountain.

The school, however, maintained that the accident occurred because the girls were using their knitting needles to try to extract a coin from a drain.

DECISION

The court took the view that whatever version of the story was true, the knitting teacher could not be held to be at fault.

Knitting needles are not dangerous in themselves, but their potential danger should be obvious to a 10-year-old. Moreover it would be unreasonable to expect the teacher to provide protective covering for the 8 needle ends on every sock.

would usually be little to gain.

The culprit would be unlikely to have money to meet a successful claim, and his or her parents would have no liability since they were not present and the child was in the charge of the school. *See:* PARENTAL OBLIGATIONS

If it could be shown, however, that the children were not properly supervised at the time of the accident, the injured child would succeed in a claim against the education authority which runs the school. The authority is liable for any negligence by teachers in the course of their employment.

Outside school hours

A school's responsibilities are not limited to school hours. If, for example, children are allowed to leave school before their parents are due to collect them and one is run over, the school could be held responsible for the accident. Similarly, children travelling to and from school on a school bus must be properly supervised – although not necessarily by a teacher. One court held that two senior pupils were sufficient.

When the premises are dangerous

In some cases it is not the staff of the school who are at fault but the premises. One school was found liable when a school gate fell on a child, because the gate had defective hinges. The possibility that the child had been swinging on it did not affect this finding.

When the school is not to blame

On other occasions, however, it has been established that the child was at fault in some way and helped to bring about his or her own misfortune. Yet the law does not expect the same standard of conduct from a child that it would from an adult. Usually the contributory negligence of the child does not entirely invalidate the claim for damages, although the amount awarded would be reduced.

A school is not responsible for the conduct and actions of its employees when they are acting outside the terms of their employment.

If, for example, a teacher sends a child on a personal errand outside the school and the child is injured as a result, any claim has to be made against the teacher personally rather than the school. That can be unsatisfactory as the teacher may have neither the means nor the insurance to pay any award that a court may make. *See:* EMPLOYER'S LIABILITY

ACCIDENT AT WORK

How to get compensation if you are injured

More than 700,000 people are injured at work in Britain every year. In a great many cases, the employer has to pay compensation (or his insurers do).

If you have an accident at work, you may be entitled to compensation on one of three grounds:

1. Your employer's negligence.

2. Your employer's failure (or that of someone for whom he is responsible) to carry out safety measures ordered by Parliament.

3. A fellow employee's negligence.

When the employer is to blame

An employer has a legal duty to take reasonable care for the safety of all his workers. That duty may be neglected in three ways:

1. The employer may have engaged an unqualified or incompetent person, with the result that another worker, whose safety depends on that person's skill and competence, is injured.

2. The employer may have failed to provide safe premises and plant – by not installing necessary equipment, such as a safety guard on a machine; by installing defective equipment or not maintaining the premises or plant properly.

3. The employer may have failed to do enough to make a job safe.

For example, if the job involves a risk of skin disease, it is not enough for the employer to provide a protective cream. He must also make sure that his employees know when and how to use the cream – and he must put up notices warning of the health risk involved.

If you make a claim against your employer, alleging that he was negligent, he cannot evade liability by showing that unsafe equipment was the fault of the manufacturer who supplied it or the contractor who installed it.

When another employee is to blame

If you are injured as a result of some wrongdoing by someone who is carrying out his job, you are entitled to claim against his employer. The employer's indirect responsibility is known as vicarious liability.

Many injury claims arise from accidents at work caused by the carelessness of the victims' fellow-employees.

For example, a fork-lift truck driver may have stacked a load so carelessly that part of it falls and injures an employee. The accident is not the employer's personal fault – but he is still liable for the negligence of the person who stacked the load.

When safety laws are broken

Regulations laid down by Parliament set out in great detail safety precautions that an employer must take. These include fencing and guarding machinery, making sure that ladders are securely fixed and ensuring that roofs – in coal-mines, for example – are properly supported.

Any employer who is found breaking a safety law is liable to criminal prosecution as well as to pay compensation to anyone injured because of his neglect.

If you are injured at work, check whether the safety regulations were being broken at the time of your accident. A safety officer at your workplace may be able to help. Many injured employees have won compensation from their employers, even though they could not prove that anyone had been negligent, simply by showing that at the time of the accident, safety regulations were being broken on the premises. *See:* HEALTH AND SAFETY AT WORK

Claiming benefit

When an accident forces you to stay away from work, you may be entitled to statutory sick PAY from your employer. After 8 weeks you can claim SICKNESS BENEFIT.

Thousands of people lose part of their benefit claim every year because they have not claimed within the time allowed – 6 days if you have made a claim for sickness benefit or non-contributory invalidity pension before, 1 month if it is your first claim.

Deciding whether to sue your employer

Your employer is legally bound to insure against the risk of an unlawful accident to an employee. This makes it possible for him to pay compensation if you make a successful claim for accidental injury at work.

If you are injured, do not just seek sick pay or social security benefit. Take advice about the possibility of suing the employer for direct or indirect negligence or breach of his duty under the safety laws.

If your injuries are serious enough to consider suing, you should consult a solicitor. If you are a member of a trade union which handles such claims, you can ask the union to take up the matter through its own legal advisers.

If your legal claim succeeds, the damages awarded are likely to be much more than the amount of your sick pay and sickness benefit – although you should still claim that.

When damages are assessed, the court will deduct half the value of any sickness, invalidity or disablement benefit (less any constant attendance increase) which you receive in the first 5 years after your accident.

THE MAN WHO TRIPPED PEOPLE UP

Many injury claims arise from accidents at work that are caused by the carelessness, foolishness or negligence of the victim's fellow employees.

Harold Chadwick had indulged himself for years in horseplay at the expense of workmates – tripping them up and other 'jokes'. This went on for 4 years, despite a reprimand from his employers.

Then one of the workmates he tripped broke a wrist.

DECISION

A court decided that the employers were not liable indirectly for Harold Chadwick's negligence, because tripping people up was not in the course of his employment. However, the firm was ordered to pay compensation for its own direct negligence – failing to make sure that Chadwick stopped his horseplay.

THE SEAMAN WHO FELL DOWN A HATCH

Even where there is no specific legislation stating that certain safety precautions are necessary, the courts are likely to award damages to any employee who is injured through no direct fault of his own, if he can show that the environment in which he was expected to work was inherently unsafe and likely to cause an accident.

Robert Morris, a young seaman, fell down a 40 ft deep hatch on his ship. The accident happened as he was making his way along a 12 ft wide way beside the open hatch. There was no guard rail.

The shipowners claimed it was common practice to have such unfenced hatches when ships were at sea.

DECISION

The seaman's claim for damages, because of negligence, was upheld by the House of Lords.

WHAT TO DO AFTER AN ACCIDENT

Many working accidents seem trivial at the time, but produce more serious effects later on – perhaps even making it impossible for the employee to go on earning a living.

1 As soon as you have an accident at work, take steps to protect your right to compensation: report the incident immediately to someone in authority.

2 If you work for a company that employs 10 or more people on the premises, or in a factory, mine or quarry, your employer must by law keep a special 'accident book'.

Make sure that your employer records your accident in the book – and unless you are too badly injured, make sure that you see the entry for yourself. It may be crucial evidence if you eventually have to claim compensation.

3 If you have to rely on a workmate, union steward or supervisor to check the accident entry, you must write as soon as possible to your employer (or ask someone to do so on your behalf) setting out details of your accident. Keep a copy. Do not just telephone the company: you will have no proof that the message was received.

4 Even if your injury has been treated by your employer's first-aid staff, and you feel fit to carry on working, see your own doctor as soon as possible.

5 The doctor may think that there is a risk of later complications from the injury. If so, safeguard your right to claim SICKNESS BENEFIT and DISABLEMENT BENEFIT by immediately applying to have your mishap declared an industrial accident. Use form BI 95, available from your social security office.

6 Then – whether you are actually claiming benefit, considering suing your employer or just taking precautions in case your injury leads to complications – you should collect evidence about the accident.

7 If possible, get signed statements from people who saw the accident, while the details are still fresh in their minds. Make sure that you have their home addresses, in case they have left the company by the time you need your witnesses again.

ACCIDENT INSURANCE

Protecting yourself against the risk of personal injury

Most insurance companies offer policies giving cover against the possibility that you could be injured in an accident. *See:* PERSONAL ACCIDENT INSURANCE

ACCOMMODATION AGENCY

Paying for home-finding

One way of finding a rented house or flat is through an accommodation agency. If you go to one, you need pay a fee only when you become tenant of one of the properties on its lists.

It is illegal for the agency to charge a fee simply for registering your name and requirements, or for providing you with a list of addresses. It is also illegal for it to ask for a deposit in advance, even if returnable. Refuse to pay if such a payment is required.

The proprietors of an agency which acts illegally can be fined up to £400 or imprisoned for 3 months, or both. You are also entitled to recover the fee which you have paid, by taking court action if necessary.

ACT OF PARLIAMENT

When a Bill becomes the law of the land

The legislation that governs us becomes law through an Act of Parliament which binds all who come within its terms and which all courts are bound to enforce. An Act remains valid until it is repealed or amended; only Parliament has the power to change its laws.

The process of creating an Act of Parliament or 'statute' involves the House of Commons, the House of Lords and – in a symbolic way – the Queen. It begins with a draft of the legislation required – known as a Bill. *See:* PARLIAMENTARY BILL

137 Acts of the Scottish Parliament which was abolished in 1707 still survive – for example, Acts of 1621 and 1696 preventing an insolvent person from favouring a relative, business partner or one creditor at the expense of others. Such Acts, unlike those of today's Parliament, can become invalid through mere disuse.

ACT OF SEDERUNT

Laws made by judges

Soon after the COURT OF SESSION was founded in 1532 the judges were given authority by the King to make rules of procedure for the conduct of the Court's business. These are now published as Rules of Court. Sometimes in past centuries the judges went further and modified the law itself.

Many later statutes have given the judges power to make rules of procedure for other civil courts too. All these enactments are called Acts of Sederunt. Since 1946 they have been classified as STATUTORY INSTRUMENTS.

Since its foundation in 1672, the HIGH COURT OF JUSTICIARY has exercised a similar power to regulate the procedure of all criminal courts. Such rules are known as Acts of Adjournal.

ADMONITION

A warning from the court

When a person is convicted of an offence the court might not impose a sentence. Instead the court may dismiss the offender with a warning, or admonition, which reproves him for his behaviour, reminds him of his duty not to break the law, and warns of a more substantial punishment if he should be convicted of a further offence in the future.

ADOPTION

The legal process by which a child obtains new parents

If you are considering adopting a child, contact an adoption agency – a regional or islands council, or an approved adoption society. It is an offence for anyone other than an agency or a relative to make *arrangements* for a child's adoption.

There are far fewer babies available for adoption that there are people who want to adopt. But there are many school-age children, and young children with physical or mental handicaps, who would benefit enormously from adoption.

WHO MAY BE ADOPTED

A child can be adopted once he or she is at least 19 weeks old. No one who is aged 18 or over can be adopted. Nor can anyone who is or has been married, even if still under 18.

A child can be adopted more than once.

Freeing a child for adoption

From September 1, 1984, an agency which intends to place a child for adoption will be able to apply to the sheriff court (or Court of Session) for an order declaring the child to be free for adoption.

Under a freeing order the agency takes over parental rights and duties from the natural parents, normally with their agreement. The child can then be placed with prospective adopters without the risk that the parents will later change their minds and be able to prevent the adoption.

The application needs the consent of at least one parent (or guardian), and of the child if a MINOR – except when the agency is caring for the child and is asking the court to dispense with the parents' agreement, or the child is incapable of consenting.

If the child is in the agency's care, it is an offence for a parent who does not consent to the application to take the child back while the application is pending. The maximum penalty is 3 months' imprisonment or a £2,000 fine, or both.

The hearing The application is heard by the judge in private. The parents will be notified of the time and place. They do not need to attend unless they want to, or the court requires it.

The court will make a freeing order if satisfied that each parent knows what adoption involves, and freely and unconditionally agrees to it. A mother cannot validly agree until her child is 6 weeks old – though she can consent to the making of application at any time before then.

The court can dispense with a parent's agreement if the child is already placed with prospective adopters – or is likely to be – and the parent:

WHO IS ELIGIBLE TO ADOPT A CHILD

A married couple can adopt a child jointly if each is at least 21 years old. A single person can also adopt if he or she is at least 21 years old. However restrictions exist in practice.

If the child to be adopted is a baby, many adoption agencies and local authorities will only consider applicants who are under 35 (for a woman) or 40 (for a man). This is to ensure that the parents will still be active and vigorous when the child is growing up.

Single people are rarely allowed to adopt babies or very young children. However it is becoming more common for them to be allowed to adopt older children, or those with special needs.

Two people who are living together but not married cannot jointly adopt a child.

A married person cannot adopt without his or her spouse being a party to the adoption, unless the court is satisfied that the spouse:

1. Cannot be found, by the usual processes involved in attempting to serve notice of legal proceedings.

2. Lives apart from the applicant and the separation is likely to be permanent.

3. Is incapable of joining in the application because of physical or mental illness.

- Is withholding agreement unreasonably.
- Has persistently failed without good reason to act as a proper parent.
- Has abandoned or neglected the child.
- Has persistently or seriously ill-treated the child.
- Is incapable of giving agreement.
- Cannot be found.

Illegitimate children Where the child is illegitimate, the father's agreement is only necessary if a court has given him custody of the child. However, before making a freeing order the court must be satisfied that he does not intend to apply for custody or that his application is likely to be refused.

Progress reports Before making the freeing order, the court must give each parent the opportunity to declare that he or she prefers not to be involved in any future questions concerning the child's adoption.

A parent who does not make a declaration must be told, after a year, whether the child has been adopted or placed for adoption. If there has been no adoption, that parent must be told about any subsequent placement or adoption.

If neither placement nor adoption has occurred, the parent can apply to court to end the freeing order and resume parental rights and duties. The court's decision will depend on what is best for the child.

Starting an application

When a couple apply to an agency to adopt a child, it will need to make extensive inquiries into their background and suitability. Some agencies put applicants on a waiting list before they begin their inquiries.

A worker from the agency meets both partners several times – separately, together and often with other prospective adopters. Both must have full medical examinations and provide character references for themselves.

Adoption by relatives

A relative can adopt a child without approaching an adoption agency – though it is still necessary to apply to court for an adoption order (see below).

For instance, a married couple can adopt the child of one partner's previous marriage – whether it ended through death or divorce. They can also adopt one partner's illegitimate child.

Where there has been a divorce, a court will not usually allow a couple to adopt a child if the other parent has a legal right of access. This is because adoption would exclude that other parent from any right to see the child.

A father or mother, acting alone, can adopt his or her illegitimate child. The child can then be treated like a legitimate child. But adoption will only be allowed if the court is satisfied that the other parent is dead or cannot be found – or that there is some other good reason for excluding that parent.

Other relatives – such as aunts, uncles or grandparents – can also apply to court to adopt a child.

CHILDREN IN LONG-TERM CARE

If a child has been living for at least 5 years with someone – such as a relative or foster parent – who has applied for an adoption order, the child cannot be taken away from that person unless a court or other authority so directs.

Anyone who takes the child away – for instance, a parent who opposes adoption – against the wishes of the applicant, commits an offence.

If a child has lived with the applicant for less than 5 years, it is an offence for a parent who has agreed to adoption to take the child away unless a court so directs.

The maximum penalty for both these offences is 3 months' imprisonment or a £2,000 fine, or both.

If a child is taken away illegally, the court can order premises to be searched and the child to be returned to the applicants.

Placing a child

No adoption order can be made until a child has lived with prospective adopters for 13 weeks (and, if a baby, is at least 19 weeks old). This applies not only to children placed by agencies, but also to children who are to be adopted by relatives.

In all other cases – for instance, where foster parents want to adopt – no adoption order can be made until the child has lived with the prospective adopters for a year (and is at least 1 year old).

An agency which places a child for adoption must prepare a report on the proposed adoption for the court which will consider the matter.

If the child was not placed by an adoption agency – as when relatives or foster parents are adopting, or the child is from overseas – the adopters must notify the regional (or islands) council, in writing, that they intend to adopt. A social worker will then visit regularly to monitor the child's welfare and to prepare a report for the court.

Making the application

Adoption requires a formal application, called a 'petition', to be made to court – normally the sheriff court, but occasionally the Court of Session.

As soon as the court receives the

REGISTERING THE ADOPTION OF A CHILD

The documents which confirm the new parents' status and provide the child with his proof of identity

Only the new name of the child is given on the Extract Entry and on the Certificate of Birth. The Certificate of Birth does not give the names either of the child's natural parents or of its new ones. The adopting couple are named in the Extract Entry.

Only the names and occupations of the new parents are given on the Extract Entry. The natural parents are not mentioned. The court order, containing details of the child's original name and date of birth, is kept by the General Register Office in Edinburgh. Information about natural parents can be obtained from the General Register Office only by order of a court, or by the adopted person when he or she reaches the age of 17.

EXTRACT of an IN DEFENS **ENTRY in the**

ADOPTED CHILDREN REGISTER

000053

Vol. 114	Entry No. 2	Year 1980	N.H.S. No. 5 5 0 8 0 0 6 2

1. Surname: MacDonald
   Name(s): Fiona
2. Sex: F
3. When born: 1979 February Third
4. Country of birth: Scotland
5. Name(s), surname, occupation and address of adopter(s): Alistair MacDonald, Heavy Goods Vehicle Driver, Ruby Wallace MacDonald m.s. Munro, 521 Hailes Gardens, Edinburgh
6. ADOPTI[ON] Date: 1980 March 30th. Made by: Sheriff Court of Lothian and Borders at Edinburgh
7. Date of registration: 1980 April 22nd. F J Edwards for the REGISTRAR GENERAL

Form B19/72

[...] General Register Office, New Register House, Edinburgh, under the [...] Office, this ....Twentyfourth.................... March......19.82.....

[...] only if it has been authenticated by the seal of the General Register Office. If the particulars in [...]e statutory register have been reproduced by photography, xerography or some other similar process [...]en impressed after the reproduction has been made. The General Register Office will authenticate [...]ons which have been produced by that office.

[...]ection 53(3) of the Registration of Births, Deaths and Marriages (Scotland) Act 1965 for any person to [...] copy or reproduction of this extract which has not been made and authenticated by the General

[...]ies or forges any of the particulars on this extract or knowingly uses, gives or sends as genuine any [...] is liable to prosecution under section 53(1) of the said Act.

THE SEAL OF THE GENERAL REGISTER OFFICE • SCOTLAND •

IN DEFENS

ABBREVIATED CERTIFICATE OF BIRTH 000027

REGISTRATION OF BIRTHS, DEATHS AND MARRIAGES (SCOTLAND) ACT 1965, S.40

Vol. 114	Entry No. 2	Year 1980	N.H.S. No. 5 5 0 8 0 0 6 2

(*) Surname: MacDonald
Name(s): Fiona
(*) Sex: F
(*) When Born: 1979 February Third
(*) Country of Birth: Scotland

B5/72

IT IS HEREBY CERTIFIED that the above particulars are extracted from a register kept in the General Register Office.

Given under the Seal of the General Register Office, New Register House, Edinburgh on the...Twentyfourth....day of...March..........................1982.

This certificate is valid only if it has been authenticated by the seal of the General Register Office. If the particulars in the relevant entry in the statutory register have been reproduced by photography, xerography or some other similar process the seal must have been impressed after the reproduction has been made. The General Register Office will authenticate only those reproductions which have been produced by that office.

It is an offence under section 53(3) of the Registration of Births, Deaths and Marriages (Scotland) Act 1965 for any person to pass as genuine any copy or reproduction of this certificate which has not been made and authenticated by the General Register Office.

Any person who falsifies or forges any of the particulars on this certificate or knowingly uses, gives or sends as genuine any false or forged certificate is liable to prosecution under section 53(1) of the said Act.

THE SEAL OF THE GENERAL REGISTER OFFICE • SCOTLAND •

When a court finally approves the adoption of a child, it sends an adoption order to the General Register Office at Edinburgh, where it is entered in the Adopted Children Register. A full copy of the Extract Entry (illustrated above) can be obtained on request. So can an abbreviated Certificate of Birth (left). A fee is payable for each document. Neither the entry nor the birth certificate discloses who the natural parents are, and the birth certificate does not say that the child is adopted.

petition, it appoints a person known as a curator *ad litem* – usually a social worker or solicitor – to look after the child's interests.

The curator's job is to prepare a report for the court on all the circumstances relevant to the adoption – including the applicants' home, family, means, health and religion, and whether they understand what adoption means.

If the child is old enough to understand, the curator will try to find out how he or she feels about the proposed adoption.

The curator will also interview those who have taken part in the adoption arrangements – including, if necessary, the natural parents.

Getting agreement to the adoption

A court cannot make an adoption order unless each parent (or guardian) has agreed to it. However no agreement is needed if the child is already free for adoption (see above).

Agreement is usually given in a formal document, witnessed by a JP, but it can also be given orally at the adoption hearing. If the child is a baby, the mother cannot give any valid agreement until 6 weeks after the birth.

If the parents are not married, the father is not legally regarded as a parent, and his agreement is not needed unless a court has given him legal custody of the child.

If necessary, the court can dispense with a parent's agreement. The grounds for doing so are the same as for a freeing order (see above).

The adoption hearing

The adoption petition is considered by the judge in private. He will have before him the report of the curator *ad litem* and of the adoption agency (or local authority).

If the child has not been freed for adoption, the parents must be notified of the time and place of the hearing. They do not need to attend unless they want to, or the court requires them to.

Unless the petition is disputed, neither applicants nor parents normally attend. If there is a dispute, the parents will give evidence. The judge may also interview the applicants – particularly if there is doubt about their suitability.

The judge will then decide whether to make the adoption order. In reaching a decision, the child's welfare must be his first priority.

When the order has been granted

If the application succeeds the applicants are normally informed by post.

The order, which gives the child his or her new parents' surname and records the date of the adoption, is sent to the Registrar General in Edinburgh. He enters the adoption in the Adopted Children Register.

An abbreviated birth certificate, or a full copy of the entry in the Adopted Children Register – called an 'extract' – will be sent on request. A small fee is payable. Neither the birth certificate nor the extract gives the names of the natural parents; nor does the certificate disclose that the child is adopted.

Appealing against an order

Once an adoption order has been made, or refused, a person who wishes to appeal against the decision can do so within 3 months. The appeal is usually to the sheriff principal.

An appeal against the decision of the sheriff principal must be made to the Court of Session within 3 months.

The effect of adoption

Once adopted, a child has the same legal rights as any natural child born to the adoptive parents, except that he or she cannot inherit a title.

There is no restriction on the right to inherit the adoptive parents' money or property, whether or not they leave a will. *See:* INHERITANCE

An adopted child loses any right to inherit unwilled property belonging to a natural parent – except where the adoptive parents died before September 10, 1964. *See:* INTESTACY

Marriage restrictions An adopted child cannot marry his or her natural parent or adoptive parent. Even if a child is adopted for a second time, by a different couple, the bar against marrying the first adoptive parent remains. Prohibitions on marriage with other members of the natural family also still apply. *See:* INCEST; MARRIAGE

However an adopted child can legally marry a brother or sister by adoption, or any other relative of his adopted parents.

Tracing natural parents

At the age of 17 an adopted person is legally entitled to information about his or her natural parents.

The information can be obtained from the Registrar General for Scotland. The Registrar must first advise the adopted person about the counselling services available from the local authority social work department.

The job of a counsellor is to discuss with the adopted person the implications of obtaining information concerning his or her origins – including the possible effect this might have on a natural parent.

The information which an adopted person can obtain includes:

1. His or her original name before the adoption order was made by the court.

2. The name and address of the natural mother at the time of birth; and perhaps the name of the natural father.

3. The name of the court where the adoption order was made.

To obtain access to your birth records write for an application form to the General Register Office, New Register House, Edinburgh. You will need to produce evidence of identity.

FOREIGN ADOPTIONS

At present, if a foreigner living in Britian temporarily – for instance, a foreign serviceman – wants to take a child out of the country and adopt him under the laws of his own country, he must ask the court to make a 'provisional' adoption order.

The court will only make the order if satisfied that he genuinely intends to adopt the child. Once made, it is sufficient authority for the child to be taken out of the country.

From September 1, 1984, there will be a new procedure. Instead of making a provisional adoption order, the court will make an order transferring parental rights and duties to the applicant. It must still be satisfied that he intends to adopt the child. He can then take the child out of the country.

Recognition Scottish courts recognise adoptions made in some foreign countries – including most of the Commonwealth and countries which are members of the European Economic Community.

ADULTERY

When a husband or wife is unfaithful

Voluntary sexual intercourse between someone who is married and a member of the opposite sex other than the marriage partner is called adultery. A married man who commits RAPE is an adulterer; a married woman who is raped is not. Sexual activity short of intercourse is not adultery.

Artificial insemination by a donor other than the husband is not adultery, nor is it adultery for a husband to act as an insemination donor for a woman other than his wife.

Adultery and divorce

A DIVORCE can be obtained by a marriage partner on the ground of the other partner's adultery. Whether or not the other partner – called the defender – denies the adultery, it is necessary to prove that it took place.

Direct evidence of sexual intercourse is not necessary; indirect evidence is sufficient. For instance, if the defender is living with the person with whom adultery is alleged – called the paramour – or shares a hotel room with that person, the court will normally infer that adultery took place.

If the partner seeking the divorce – called the pursuer – knows who the paramour is, he or she should name that person. The paramour must be given official notice of the action but cannot be made to appear in court. A paramour can defend a charge of adultery even if the defender decides not to do so: it is possible for adultery by the defender to be proved but for the case against the paramour to be dismissed for lack of evidence.

If the paramour decides to defend the case and is unsuccessful, the court may order him or her to pay the pursuer's divorce costs. If successful, the court may order his or her costs to be paid by the pursuer.

A defender or paramour may admit the adultery but evidence of another witness will be required to prove it in court. *See:* EVIDENCE

If the pursuer has continued to live with the defender (although without necessarily resuming sexual intercourse) for more than 3 months after finding out about the adultery, and the adultery has ceased, the court will not regard the adultery as a reason for a divorce. If the partners separate after the pursuer learns of the adultery, but then live together again for more than 3 months, the adultery will not be treated as a reason for a divorce.

Sometimes a pursuer who has been found entitled to a divorce on any ground is proved to have committed adultery himself in an action brought by the defender. The court will then give a divorce decree to both the pursuer and the defender.

ADVERTISING

Protection against misleading claims

An advertisement must always state the truth, whether it appears in a newspaper or magazine, on television or radio, on a poster or a packet, or simply in a shop window. If it is untruthful, or if it is illegal or offensive, there are several courses of action open to the public.

Code of advertising practice

The standards of newspaper, magazine and cinema advertising and of promotional leaflets delivered door-to-door are governed by the British Code of Advertising Practice. Strict standards are applied to advertisements concerning credit, drugs and alcohol.

If you believe that an advertisement is misleading, illegal or offensive, you should write to the Advertising Standards Authority, Brook House, 2-16 Torrington Place, London WC1E 7HN, providing full details of your complaint. The advertiser will then have to satisfy the authority that your complaint is unjustified. If he cannot, the authority will recommend that the advertisement no longer be displayed or delivered and will publish a report of the matter.

If a complainer has suffered some loss because of false claims made in the advertisement, the advertiser may decide to offer compensation. The Authority has no power to demand such a payment, however.

Standards for television and radio

The Independent Broadcasting Authority's Code of Advertising Standards and Practice is basically the same as the British Code of Advertising Practice, but it also bans entirely the advertising of certain products, such as cigarettes (but not cigars), and does not allow subliminal advertising – where the 'message' is flashed on a TV screen for fractions of a second so that the viewer is not aware of seeing it, yet his brain absorbs the message.

If you have a complaint, write to the Authority's advertising control department, 70 Brompton Road, London.

Posters and handbills

Posters are also governed by the British Code of Advertising Practice, unless they are political advertisements.

If you have a complaint about a poster, write to the Advertising Standards Authority.

Local posters and handbills – advertising, for example, a sale of carpets or a Scout concert, are not subject to the strict standards of the British Code of Advertising Practice. But they are still governed by the general laws on advertising and must not contain incorrect statements or prices, or be offensive.

When an advertiser can be prosecuted

If an advertisement contains a false or misleading description of the goods it advertises, there is another channel of complaint open to a member of the public: a criminal prosecution can be brought against the person or company responsible for the advertisement. The prosecution will be brought by the procurator fiscal, but as he will rely on the regional council's trading standards department to investigate the complaint, it is best to complain directly to that department. *See:* TRADE DESCRIPTIONS

For a criminal offence to have been committed, the description in the advertisement must have been false 'to a material degree'. Some legal authorities maintain that people are sensible enough not to believe everything they read in advertisements.

If the court finds the advertiser guilty, it may order the payment of compensation to the person who complained to the council if this person suffered some loss, damage or personal injury as a result of believing the claims made by

THE 'CURE' FOR GREY HAIR

If a court finds an advertiser guilty of breaking a definite promise in his advertisement it can award compensation to the pursuer at the hearing

Mr Wood read the following advertisement for a comb which contained a small battery: *Great news for hair sufferers. What is your trouble? Is it grey hair? In 10 days not a grey hair left. £500 guarantee.*

Mr Wood bought the comb and used it for 10 days. His greying hair remained grey. He sued for the £500.

The defence argued that the claim in the advertisement was obviously impossible and could deceive no one.

DECISION

The court disagreed with the argument put by the defence. It ordered payment of the £500 to Mr Wood.

the advertiser about the goods being advertised.

It is also possible to bring a civil action against an advertiser, but the complainer then has to prove misrepresentation or breach of contract and show what loss or injury he has actually suffered.

ADVISORY, CONCILIATION AND ARBITRATION SERVICE (ACAS)

The government-backed way to settle disputes at work

ACAS is a free service – set up by the Government to help to prevent or settle industrial disputes and individual employer/employee disagreements. It is not a government agency, however; trade unions and employers are represented equally on its council.

It issues codes of general practice to improve industrial relations and also specific advice to employers and employees, collectively or individually, on such matters as union recognition, redundancy and dismissal.

If an employee thinks he has been dismissed unfairly, he can ask ACAS to discuss his case with his employer and, perhaps, reach a satisfactory solution without having to wait to go to an INDUSTRIAL TRIBUNAL. However, any claim to an industrial tribunal ought to be made within 3 months of dismissal. A claim made after 3 months will probably not be heard, even if ACAS has been discussing the case in the meantime.

A complaint made to an industrial tribunal will automatically be notified to ACAS. If a settlement is reached through ACAS the employee can then withdraw the complaint. The service can be contacted through the local job centre or office of the Department of Employment. *See:* UNFAIR DISMISSAL

ACAS conciliation officers have no official powers, and seeking their help does not prevent an employee or employer from pursuing other courses of action later.

The conciliation officers try to find common ground between the two sides and to get them talking. In major disputes, they can, if both sides agree, arrange to have the case heard by the CENTRAL ARBITRATION COMMITTEE.

ADVOCATE

A specialist in pleading cases in any court

Advocates form the senior branch of the Scottish legal profession and are the equivalent of barristers in England. All are members of the Faculty of Advocates, which has existed since at least the early 17th century.

The Faculty has about 390 members, of whom about 170 practise as advocates, the rest being judges, sheriffs, teachers of law and so on. The practising advocates have their base in the Advocates' Library at Parliament House, in Edinburgh, where there are facilities for consultations with clients.

The principal duty of advocates is to represent clients in court, and before comparable bodies such as tribunals and public inquiries. They have the sole right to represent people in the Court of Session, the High Court and other courts of the same rank.

They are entitled to appear in the House of Lords and any court in Scotland. But in the lower courts they share this right with SOLICITORS, who in practice provide most representation in these courts.

Advocates work independently and are forbidden to form partnerships. Unlike English barristers they do not share office expenses. Advocates can only be approached to take a case through a solicitor. The solicitor, acting for a client, instructs the advocate in writing and he in turn is bound to accept any instructions tendered with a reasonable fee, unless he is otherwise committed. A client may ask for a particular advocate, but will usually leave the choice to his solicitor. At all meetings with the advocate the client will be accompanied by his solicitor.

The more senior advocates are appointed Queen's Counsel (also known as seniors or silks). They command higher fees than juniors (non-Q.C.s) and are entitled to insist that they be supported by a junior before accepting instructions to appear in court.

Advocates are also consulted by solicitors to clear up doubts as to the applicable law, to advise on the prospects of a court action, or to propose a settlement of a dispute and so avoid the need to take it to court. The solicitor draws up a document called a Memorial to Counsel, which sets out in numbered paragraphs the points at issue. The advocate replies to each point in an Opinion.

An advocate owes a higher duty to the courts than to his client and for that reason cannot be sued for negligence or any other fault short of fraud in his court work. Once he has been instructed he is entitled to conduct the case as he thinks right and proper and to agree a settlement if he thinks fit. This will be binding on his client (unless the advocate has been instructed not to settle). The client can however withdraw the authority he has given the advocate to act for him. It is probable that an advocate can be sued for negligence in giving advice.

AFFIDAVIT

When it is necessary to put legal evidence down in writing

An affidavit is a written statement of some fact or facts. It is made on oath or affirmation before someone entitled to administer oaths, such as a sheriff, justice of the peace or notary public.

The most common use of affidavits occurs in undefended DIVORCE actions. The person seeking the divorce has to state in an affidavit, sworn before a notary public, sufficient facts to justify the granting of a decree of divorce. At least one other person must testify to the same facts in a similar affidavit.

Affidavits are also used in bankruptcy proceedings by creditors who are asking for someone to be declared bankrupt or making a claim to a share of the bankrupt's property.

Statements on oath are also made by executors seeking the right to deal with the estate of a deceased person, although they are not usually called affidavits. *See:* CONFIRMATION

To swear a false affidavit does not amount to perjury except in bankruptcies, but it is nevertheless a serious criminal offence.

AFFILIATION AND ALIMENT

A single woman's claim on the father of her child

Where a single woman is pregnant or has given birth to an ILLEGITIMATE CHILD, she may seek to enter into an agreement with the child's father that he is to pay her a regular amount of money to maintain the child.

WHEN A MOTHER AND FATHER AGREE

The father and mother of an illegitimate child may agree that the father should maintain the child by paying the mother a regular sum of money.

Ideally the agreement should be drafted in writing by a solicitor. Then if the father later refuses payment, the mother will more easily be able to get the agreement enforced by a court.

If the solicitor registers the agreement in the Books of Council and Session (an official register), and obtains a warrant for execution (giving permission to enforce the agreement) the mother will be able to obtain payment without going to court.

Such an agreement does not prevent the mother from later applying to a sheriff court for a decree of affiliation and aliment – even if the agreement states that the father cannot be required to make any other payment. The court would take into account the amount that the father was already paying.

If the father will not agree, or disputes that the child is his, the mother can apply to a sheriff court for an order of affiliation and aliment – an order that declares him to be the father and makes him share in the responsibility of maintaining the child.

If the court grants the application it will fix the amount which the father must pay for the support of his child. The payment will be treated as income if the mother makes a claim for SUPPLEMENTARY BENEFIT.

If the father falls into arrears with his payments, the mother can take legal action to recover the arrears.

Who else can apply?

The application is usually made by the mother. However if she is unwilling to do so, and is in receipt of supplementary benefit, the Department of Health and Social Security can itself raise an action of affiliation and aliment against the father to recover some of the cost of paying benefit for the child. So can a local authority which is caring for an illegitimate child.

How to apply

You should consult a solicitor if you wish to raise an action of affiliation and aliment. Your local CITIZENS ADVICE BUREAU will have a list of local solicitors offering LEGAL ADVICE and LEGAL AID. *See:* BLOOD TEST

AGE OF MAJORITY

When a child becomes an adult

Children come of age on their 18th birthday. Until then, a child is treated as a MINOR or, if under 12 (girls) or 14

THE SIGNIFICANT AGES OF HUMAN LIFE

From the moment of birth until the age of 80 there are many legal milestones

Age	Rights and responsibilities
From birth	Can have a deposit or current account with a bank or building society Can hold premium bonds Can own property Can be sued (along with tutor)
0–3 years	Parent can claim £9 death grant on child's death
2 years	Can receive attendance allowance
3–5 years	Parent can claim £15 death grant on child's death
5 years	Must start full-time education Can receive mobility allowance Can have own passport

Age	Rights and responsibilities
6–17 years	Parent can claim £22.50 death grant on child's death
7 years	Can have a deposit account with National Savings or Trustee Savings Bank and draw money on own signature
8 years	Can be found guilty of a crime or offence
12 years (girl) 14 years (boy)	Can make a contract or will Can sue (with the consent of curator, if any) or be sued in a court Can be a trustee Can witness a deed
13 years	Can do light work as permitted under regulations – not

Age	Rights and responsibilities
13 years continued	before 7 a.m. or after 7 p.m., not during school hours or for more than 2 hours on a school day or Sunday, not involving heavy lifting or carrying
14 years	Can have with him an airgun or ammunition for an airgun. An airgun can be used under the age of 14 but only under the supervision of someone aged 21 or over, or at a rifle club or shooting gallery Can be taken into a bar but must not consume any alcoholic drink there
15 years	Can see a '15' film Can have with him a shotgun and ammunition (under 15 if supervised by someone aged 21 or over)
16 years	Can marry Girl can legally consent to sexual intercourse Parent loses right to child benefit unless child is receiving full-time education Can nominate a person to take over, in the event of death, money deposited with National Savings or Trustee Savings Bank Can fly a glider solo Can buy wine, beer, cider or perry in a restaurant, but cannot buy it in a bar, off-licence or supermarket Can apply for a passport without parental consent if married or in the armed forces Can join a trade union Can buy tobacco Boy can work underground in a mine Can ride a moped of up to 50 cc and drive an invalid carriage Can leave school and take a full-time job after the Christmas following 16th birthday or at the end of May if 16 between March 31 and September 30. Must pay national insurance contributions if employed Can apply for supplementary benefit, and for sickness and unemployment benefits once sufficient contributions have been paid Can buy fireworks Must pay National Health Service prescription charges, and National Health Service dental charges if no longer at school Can open a giro account Can collect on behalf of a charity Cannot be brought before a children's hearing unless already under supervision Can change name with consent of parent or guardian Can be sent to detention centre or young offenders institution
17 years	Can drive a car and fly an aircraft solo Can buy or hire any gun Can have an airgun in public Can get information about natural parents if adopted
18 years	Can vote Can apply for a passport without parental consent Can go abroad as a performer without a licence

Age	Rights and responsibilities
18 years continued	Can change name without parental consent Can serve on jury Can donate blood Can buy alcoholic drink in a bar Can bet in a betting shop Can be tattooed Cannot be kept in care by a local authority Can submit a football pool coupon Can see any film Cannot be adopted
19 years	Parent loses right to child benefit for child who has been receiving full-time education
21 years	Can adopt Can stand for council or Parliament Can drive a lorry or bus Can be licensed to sell alcoholic drinks Males can lawfully consent to homosexual acts in private Can be a bookmaker Can be sent to prison
24 years	A male charged with unlawful sexual intercourse with a girl of 13 and over, and under 16 can no longer rely on the defence that he had reasonable cause to believe she was 16 or over
41 years	Widow over 40 when her husband dies can claim age-related widow's pension on her late husband's contributions Widow over 40 when she ceases to draw an allowance for her child is entitled to higher rate of industrial death benefit
51 years	Widow over 50 when her husband dies can claim standard widow's pension on her late husband's contributions, or where appropriate the higher rate of industrial death benefit
60 years	Women no longer have to pay national insurance contributions, or National Health Service prescription charges A woman is entitled to retirement pension if she has paid sufficient national insurance contributions.
65 years	Men no longer have to pay national insurance contributions, or National Health Service prescription charges Retirement pension for man who has paid sufficient contributions, and for his wife. No earnings limit for woman receiving retirement pension on her own contributions No longer qualified for jury service
70 years	No earnings limit for man receiving retirement pension
80 years	May be entitled to non-contributory retirement pension if resident in UK during 10 of preceding 20 years

(boys), a PUPIL, with special legal protections but without all the rights and duties of adults.

In general, people of 18 and over are considered capable of making decisions in all legal matters and of accepting liability for the consequences. They can vote in parliamentary and local elections and serve on a jury. But they cannot stand for ELECTION until the age of 21.

If the age of majority is mentioned in a legal document drawn up before January 1, 1970 (when the legal age was lowered) then it means 21.

AGE OF SEXUAL CONSENT

When a girl can say 'yes' to a man

It is an offence to have sexual intercourse with a girl under 16, or to use lewd (indecent) behaviour towards her, even if she consents. A girl must be 16 before a man charged with a sexual offence can use her consent as a defence. Sexual activity short of intercourse may be indecent assault.

Maximum penalty For full intercourse with a girl under 13, life imprisonment; with a girl between 13 and 16, 2 years' imprisonment. For lewd behaviour towards a girl under 12, at the court's discretion; towards a girl between 12 and 16, 2 years' imprisonment. For indecent assault, at the court's discretion.

AIDING AND ABETTING

Helping somebody to commit a crime

Someone who encourages or helps someone else to commit a crime can be charged with aiding and abetting the criminal – the legal phrase is being 'art and part' in the crime – if the encouragement or help given was important.

For example, if a man keeps watch while others rob a bank he is guilty of aiding and abetting the robbers; or, put another way, he is art and part guilty of robbery. But if he is only a bystander he cannot be prosecuted, even if he does nothing to prevent the robbery.

Maximum penalty Can be the same as for committing the offence, but it may be less heavy than that imposed on the principal criminals.

RESPONSIBILITY FOR UNINTENDED CONSEQUENCES

When a group of persons commits a crime, each group member is responsible for everything done by any of the others in pursuit of the group purpose, but not for something beyond that purpose.

Two men broke into a house in Glasgow to commit a theft. The noise awakened the occupant, a feeble old woman. One of the men lifted a crowbar and assaulted the woman so violently that she died. The prosecutor argued that the act of the man who used the crowbar should be regarded as the act also of the man who did not use it, because they were acting together.

DECISION

The judge rejected this argument. He said so unexpected an attack on an old woman incapable of resistance would not have been reasonably expected by anyone other than the man who did it. Therefore only the man who struck the blow could be convicted of murder.

AIR ACCIDENT

When you can claim compensation for an injury

If you are injured on board an airliner, or while boarding or disembarking, you are entitled to some compensation without having to prove that the airline or its staff were at fault.

Compensation for injuries suffered in an air accident is governed by international agreements or conventions which set out what maximum payments can be made. These limits depend on the nationality of the airline involved, whether the flight was international or domestic and whether the journey began or ended in the United States.

An airline can avoid paying compensation even within these agreed limits, if it can prove that all necessary measures were taken to avoid your injury, or that it was not possible to take such measures.

On the other hand, you can get compensation above the agreed limits if you can prove that your injury resulted from something that the airline or its staff did (or failed to do) recklessly, or with intent to cause damage, or knowing that damage would probably result.

A case brought on this ground failed even though a passenger was seriously hurt when in foreseeable conditions of serious turbulence the pilot did not advise passengers to fasten their seatbelts.

If there is evidence that the accident was caused by careless design or manufacture of the aircraft, you can overcome the compensation limits by suing the manufacturers, who are not covered by the airline agreements.

Where an accident is caused by the negligence of a third party – for example, the pilot of another aircraft, or air-traffic control staff, or perhaps both – the international limits do not apply, and you can sue the culprit or his employers for negligence.

However, there are serious practical difficulties in pursuing claims outside the agreements.

It will be expensive to assemble the expert evidence needed to prove negligence. Your claim may have to be fought in a foreign court and according to foreign law, and you get no legal aid for actions abroad.

In pursuing a claim your solicitor may need to seek the advice of a specialist aviation lawyer, especially if the accident was abroad.

If you are one of many victims of an accident, try to get publicity for your claim: others may join you in making similar claims through the same lawyer, and so share the heavy legal costs.

The most practical way to make sure of getting adequate compensation after an air accident is to take out insurance, before the flight, against personal injury or death.

Any money paid out on an insurance policy is in addition to compensation from the airline.

Hovercraft are covered by similar rules. The maximum compensation payable for personal injury or death is £30,000. The maximum for lost or damaged luggage is £236.

If an aircraft crashes or crash-lands on your property, or if something falls on to it from an aircraft, you can sue for damages even though the pilot may not be to blame.

AIR POLLUTION

Laws that keep the air fit to breathe

The emission of any kind of smoke from a chimney other than one on a private dwelling is prohibited if it causes a NUISANCE. The ban also applies to smoke caused in other ways. For instance it can be an offence to have bonfires, if they cause a nuisance.

KEEPING THE AIR FREE FROM POLLUTION

It can be an offence to have a bonfire in the garden if it causes a nuisance to other people.

Causing 'dark smoke' by, for example, burning tyres or plastic is an offence, even if not a nuisance, when the smoke is emitted from chimneys or business premises.

Many local councils have declared smoke-control areas where it is an offence to use any fuel other than those authorised by government regulations – for example, oil, gas, electricity, and smokeless solid fuels. Most coal merchants can give advice on what can be used in your area. If you are in doubt, contact your nearest Solid Fuel Advisory Service branch (listed in the telephone directory).

It is illegal for a trader to sell unauthorised fuel – for example wood or ordinary coal – in a smoke-controlled area, but the responsibility for burning it is nevertheless the householder's and he can be fined up to £400 for breaking the law.

If a council decides to impose smoke-control regulations it must advertise its intention in the Edinburgh Gazette, in local newspapers and in notices posted in the area affected. If you want to object, write within 6 weeks to the council, which is legally obliged to consider your objection before confirming the order. You have no right to appeal against an order.

The order will come into effect on a date fixed by the council, which must be at least 6 months after it is made.

If your house is in an area covered by an order and you need to adapt your chimney, fireplace or water supply, apply to the council for a grant to help with the cost. At least 70% of any reasonable cost is allowable if the council approves your proposed changes.

AIR SPACE

A landowner's protection against intrusion

If you own a house or land then you also own the air space immediately above. This means that if, for example, the branches of a neighbour's tree reach over the boundary into your garden and he refuses to remove them, you can apply to court for an order requiring him to do so.

THE BUILDERS' CRANE

An owner can protect the air space above his house from intrusions even where they are temporary and do not cause damage.

Builders began to develop the empty site next to Mr Brown's house. They erected a tower crane with a jib, the arc of which passed over all of Mr Brown's garden. Mr Brown sued.

DECISION

Mr Brown was entitled to protection even although the crane was only a temporary erection and might not be dangerous. The court granted an INTERDICT to prevent the builders from using the crane in any way that would involve any part of it passing over Mr Brown's property.

You cannot, however, legally stop aircraft flying over your land at a reasonable height. For passenger airliners this is generally 2,000 ft or more, and for light aircraft 1,000 ft.

AIR TRAVEL

Compensation for hitches and delays

If you travel by air and your flight is delayed, you may be entitled to claim compensation for any loss that you suffer. But that loss must be something an airline could foresee arising from a delay – for example, the cost of staying overnight at a hotel.

Compensation cannot be claimed for 'unforeseeable' damage, such as loss of profit through missing a valuable business contract because of the delay.

The airline is not liable if it can show that all necessary measures were taken to avoid your loss, or that such measures could not be taken. If your flight is delayed by bad weather or by a strike outside the airline's control, for example, the airline would not be liable. However, if the delay is caused by repairs to an aircraft that had not been properly maintained, the airline could not claim that it had taken all necessary measures, and so would be liable to pay compensation.

In practice, delayed passengers are often accommodated in hotels at the airline's expense.

When a flight is overbooked

To allow for the non-appearance of passengers who have reservations, most airlines book more passengers for a flight than the aircraft can carry. If everyone does check in, some would-be passengers have to be turned away – normally on a first come first served basis.

Some airlines, including British Airways, now offer compensation agreements for passengers turned away because of overbooking. They generally undertake to get the passenger to his destination within 2 hours (on a domestic flight) or 4 hours (overseas flights) of the arrival time of the original flight. If that cannot be done the passenger is entitled to:

1. Reasonable expenses for accommodation, meals, telephone calls and so on while awaiting alternative transport.

2. A refund of half the fare for the leg of the flight that was overbooked, with a minimum of £10 and a maximum of £100.

The passenger has to sign a receipt giving up any other rights he may have to compensation for the delay, but the uncertainties of legal action make it worthwhile to accept the offer.

Luggage difficulties

Compensation can also be claimed for luggage that is delayed, although an airline's liability is limited to about £12 for each kilogram (2.2 lb.).

If your suitcase is flown to the wrong place, the airline will probably be liable for the cost of spare nightclothes and toilet articles such as toothbrush and razor – and also the cost of any extra journey you have to make to the airport to collect the case when it is available.

When luggage is lost If luggage is lost while it is in the airline's care, you can claim compensation to a maximum of about £12 per kilogram. The airline, however, has a defence if it can show that all necessary measures were taken to avoid the loss.

When luggage is damaged If your luggage is damaged when it is in the care of the airline, complain at once. If you accept it without complaint, it is assumed in law to have been delivered back to you in good condition.

There may, however, be damage that is not obvious from the outside. If so, you should claim compensation, in writing, as soon as the damage is discovered – and not later than 7 days after you have collected the luggage. If you do not, the airline is no longer liable.

PURSUING A COMPLAINT

If you are not satisfied with an airline's response to a complaint, you can write to the Air Transport Users' Committee, set up by the Civil Aviation Authority to investigate complaints by air travellers.

The committee can investigate a wide variety of complaints about airlines, including complaints about overbooking, wrong booking and lost luggage. However it cannot deal with complaints about hotels. Nor can it handle claims for compensation.

AIRCRAFT NOISE

When you may be able to have something done about it

If you live near an airport and are disturbed by aircraft noise, find out from the nearest office of the Civil Aviation Authority whether the airport is governed by legally enforceable regulations.

These may control the level of noise permitted during taxiing, take-off and landing; they may also state the hours during which jet aircraft can operate. It is an offence for aircraft to disregard these regulations.

Specified airports can be required to make grants towards the cost of soundproofing homes – schemes have been introduced for Aberdeen, Edinburgh, Glasgow and Prestwick airports.

If physical damage – such as broken windows – is caused by aircraft noise or vibration, you may be able to sue the operator of the aircraft for compensation.

However, if there is no physical damage, and flying regulations are being complied with, you will not normally be able to claim for NUISANCE merely on the ground that aircraft noise interferes with your enjoyment of your home.

But if the value of your home has gone down because of noise resulting from a new or altered airfield, you may be able to claim compensation. *See:* PLANNING BLIGHT

If aircraft noise has increased, a householder might also be justified in seeking a reduction in the rateable value of his property. *See:* RATES

AIRPORT INSURANCE

Short-term insurance cover for a single flight

Insurance against death or injury while travelling by air can be taken out at most airports.

There is usually a maximum amount (often £100,000) for which you can insure yourself and the cover is usually available from the time you board the aircraft to the time you disembark after your journey – and again for the return flight.

By paying an extra premium, you can insure against the risk of hi-jacking or terrorist attacks.

To take out insurance, go to the airport desk marked 'Flight Insurance'. You will be given a form to complete on the spot and you will need to show your flight ticket. In some airports you can buy insurance from automatic vending machines.

ALIBI

When an accused person claims he was elsewhere

Anyone accused of a crime who claims that he was not at the scene when it was committed can plead an alibi – the Latin word for 'elsewhere' – as his defence.

If the defence is to succeed, some evidence in support of the alibi must be given at the trial by either the accused or any defence or prosecution witnesses. If that evidence creates a reasonable doubt as to the guilt of the accused he must be acquitted.

For example, if a man is charged with committing a theft in Edinburgh but claims to have been staying at a hotel in Dundee on the day of the crime, he can plead that alibi as his defence.

If he proves not only that he was in Dundee on the day in question but also that he could not have been in Edinburgh at or near the time of the theft, the prosecution case fails. If he cannot prove that conclusively, with witnesses to support his claim, it is for the jury or court to decide whether it believes the alibi evidence.

In summary CRIMINAL PROCEEDINGS an accused person cannot plead alibi unless he gives notice of the defence to the prosecutor before the first prosecution witness gives evidence. When notice is given the prosecutor, if he wishes, can ask for an adjournment of the case to check the alibi.

In solemn criminal proceedings the accused must lodge written notice of the alibi at least 10 days before the date of the trial. If he fails to do so, but for a good reason, the court may allow the notice to be lodged before the oath is administered to the jury.

The notice of alibi must contain particulars about time and place and about the witnesses by whom it is proposed to prove the alibi.

Unless due notice is given the court may refuse to allow the accused to give evidence in support of the alibi.

ALIEN

The position of foreigners in the UK

Aliens are people who are neither COMMONWEALTH CITIZENS (including British Citizens) nor IRISH CITIZENS. They have most of the legal rights of citizens, though in war-time these are liable to be curtailed.

They must pay NATIONAL INSURANCE CONTRIBUTIONS and taxes if at work, and are eligible for most health and welfare benefits. Aliens owe allegiance to the Queen while in the UK (so can commit TREASON) and may, under some conditions, join the ARMED FORCES.

But aliens cannot vote, serve on a JURY, be MPs or councillors or policemen, nor hold certain Civil Service jobs. They may be required to report to the police.

In general, aliens have no legal right to enter the UK but are admitted only under whatever conditions the Government imposes. However citizens of EEC countries have considerable rights of entry for the purpose of work. *See:* EUROPEAN COMMUNITIES; IMMIGRATION

ALIMENT

Supporting your spouse and children

Married partners are legally obliged to support each other and their children. However a wife need only support her husband if she is reasonably well off and he cannot support himself.

If one married partner does not receive adequate support from the other, she (or he) can apply to the SHERIFF COURT for a decree – a court order – requiring that other partner to pay a regular sum of money, called aliment, to her. Aliment can also be claimed for the support of a child.

When deciding how much money to award, the court will look not only at the needs of the person applying but also at the ability of the other partner to pay.

Thus a working wife will not get decree against her husband unless he is earning substantially more than she. But a husband who is not working because of unemployment or disability can get decree against his wife if she is earning a good wage.

A sheriff court claim for aliment can be combined with other legal proceedings when the marriage has broken down. Thus one partner may raise an action of SEPARATION and aliment against the other, seeking judicial separation as well as money. When one partner is in DESERTION the other can raise an action of adherence and aliment, asking the court to order the deserting partner to return and to pay aliment if he or she fails to do so. (Actions of adherence are to be abolished during 1984.)

A married couple who decide to separate amicably can agree between themselves on the amount of aliment to be paid, and then put it into a written agreement. This agreement is legally binding and court proceedings can be taken to recover any arrears of aliment. The payments are eligible for tax relief.

Financial support on divorce

In DIVORCE proceedings either partner can claim payment from the other of:

- A periodical allowance (a fixed amount to be paid at regular intervals) and/or
- A lump sum of money.

If a marriage is ended by a declaration of NULLITY, neither partner is entitled to claim a payment from the other.

Children, relatives and cohabitees

Legitimate children have a legal right to be supported by their parents, even when they are adults. Adopted children have the same right to be supported by their adoptive parents. However legal proceedings by adult children against their parents are rare. To obtain aliment, an adult would have to be in need and his parents reasonably well off.

An Act of Parliament gives illegitimate children the right to be supported by their parents until the age of 16, or 21 if undergoing education or training. But they have the same right as legitimate children to claim aliment from their parents after reaching this age.

Legitimate children have a legal duty to support their parents. Grandparents and legitimate grandchildren may even have a legal duty to support each other. However the existence of social security has made these duties unimportant; there have been very few such proceedings for aliment in recent years.

Brothers and sisters have no legal duty to support each other.

A woman who lives with a man to whom she is not married has no legal right to be supported by him. However she can claim aliment for their children through an action of AFFILIATION AND ALIMENT. *See:* COHABITATION

The 'liable relative'

Under social security law there is no limitation on a wife's legal duty to support her husband and children.

A person may receive SUPPLEMENTARY BENEFIT because his or her wife, husband or parent is failing to provide support. The Department of Health and Social Security can attempt to recover some of the cost of paying benefit by taking sheriff court proceedings against the person – called the 'liable relative' – who is failing to provide support. The court will decide how much the liable relative can afford to pay to the Department.

ALLOTMENT

Council land for local gardeners

Allotments are small portions of land which can be rented cheaply for cultivation. Some are organised privately, but district and islands councils have a statutory duty to provide a sufficient number where private organisation is too expensive, and in practice most allotments are owned by the councils.

The tenant of an allotment should always obtain a written agreement from the council stating the terms of his lease. This may include conditions about keeping the allotment tidy, what can be grown and what animals kept.

Ending the lease

If the tenant does not keep its terms, the agreement usually allows the council to end the lease. The council always has this right, on a month's notice, where the rent is 40 days or more in arrears. The tenant has to pay for any deterioration caused by his failure to keep the allotment clean, well-cultivated and fertile. Both the council and the tenant can end the lease providing they give a certain amount of notice.

Where the allotment is used mainly for growing vegetables for the tenant's family and is not bigger than ¼ acre, it is technically an 'allotment garden'. This means that, whatever the agreement may say, the council must give at least

ALLOTMENT LAND FOR LOCAL RESIDENTS

To end the lease of a council-owned allotment the council must give the tenant reasonable notice.

12 months' notice, to end on or before May 1 or on or after November 1, so that the tenant does not lose his allotment in the middle of the growing season. If the council ends the lease, the tenant is entitled to compensation for crops lost and fertiliser wasted.

ALL-RISKS INSURANCE

Protection for valuables and goods in transit

All-risks insurance gives wider cover than a normal indemnity policy.

In all-risks policies insuring household effects, for example, cover is provided for a whole range of accidental loss or damage, wherever the effects are at the time of loss. Such cover is popular in the case of valuables such as fur coats, cameras or jewellery.

Despite its name, such insurance does not always cover *all* risks. For example, a policy covering 'goods in transit' will not protect the items concerned from inherent defects in the articles themselves, nor from risks commonly excluded from all policies – such as civil commotion, riot and war.

The exclusion of inherent defects means that the insurance company would not be liable if the colours in a painting faded with the passage of time, or if a clock spring broke because of a mechanical fault. There is no liability if goods in transit are damaged because they were not properly packed.

In making a claim, the insured person has to show that the goods concerned were damaged or lost by accident. But he does not have to prove exactly how they were lost. *See:* INSURANCE

AMBULANCE

Sometimes a doctor's authority is needed

In Scotland, the ambulance service is a national service administered by the Common Services Agency of the Scottish Health Service. There are eleven ambulance areas in Scotland: Highland and Islands, Grampian, Orkney and Shetland, Tayside, Fife, Lothian and Borders, Forth and Lanark, Argyll and Clyde, Ayr, Dumfries and Galloway, and Greater Glasgow – each of which is administered by a Chief Ambulance Officer.

People do not have a right to an ambulance to take them to hospital. However, an ambulance will attend emergencies when a 999 call is received.

In all other cases, a doctor must normally decide whether an ambulance should be summoned.

If someone falls ill at home, the ambulance service will usually insist that the family doctor is called first. They will help to trace him or his deputy if he is difficult to locate. Where the doctor cannot be found and the patient seems to need urgent help, most services will agree to send an ambulance.

People attending hospital as outpatients may require transport. If the GP in charge of the case considers an ambulance is necessary, he will tell the local health board. Where the patient has been discharged from hospital, but is returning as an outpatient, the hospital doctor will arrange for an ambulance if he feels one is needed.

There is no right of appeal against a doctor's decision not to recommend providing an ambulance – although he could be sued if it could be established that he had been negligent.

Road accidents Where a person requires emergency treatment at a hospital or by a doctor as the result of a road traffic accident, the person using the vehicle involved in the accident may be liable to pay a fee – even though in no way to blame. The fee is payable to the hospital or doctor and currently is £10.90 for each person who requires treatment and 21p for each mile or part of a mile in excess of two miles which the doctor must travel to give emergency treatment.

The fee can be reclaimed by the motorist from his insurance company, without affecting his no-claim bonus, if he was not to blame for the accident.

When the ambulance service is negligent

If a patient dies or suffers greater injuries as a result of delay in the arrival of an ambulance, and this appears to be due to negligence on the part of either the ambulance crew or controller, an action for damages could be brought against the Common Services Agency.

If a service is disrupted or withdrawn because of industrial action, it is unlikely that there would by any legal redress available to anyone harmed as a result.

ANCIENT MONUMENT

Protecting the nation's heritage

Any structure or site that the Secretary of State for Scotland considers to be of national historical importance can be scheduled as an ancient monument. There is no right to object.

If the site is owned by the Secretary of State or a local authority the public must be allowed access, subject to local regulations on hours and admission charges. If the site is on private ground the owner may agree with the Secretary of State or local authority that it should be taken under their guardianship. In the absence of an agreement, the owner remains liable for the site's upkeep and cannot be forced to allow the public access.

The Secretary of State can compulsorily acquire any ancient monument to secure its preservation.

It is an offence to carry out demolition, removal or repair work on a scheduled monument without permission.

Maximum penalty: unlimited fine.

History underground Where remains of historical importance are believed to be underground, the Secretary of State or a local authority now have powers to designate the land an area of archaeological importance.

This will mean that anyone who plans flooding or tipping operations or other work that could disturb the ground will have to give the local authority at least 6 weeks' notice, or run the risk of an unlimited fine.

Metal detectors It is an offence to use a metal detector without the Secretary of State's consent on a scheduled monument site or an area designated as being of archaeological importance.

Maximum penalty: £1,000 fine.

ANIMAL

Protecting people from animals and animals from people

The law protects people from animals by imposing certain duties on those responsible for them. Some animals have to be licensed and sometimes payment has to be made for damage done by them.

The law protects animals from people by restricting their right to kill or be cruel to them.

Responsibility for domestic pets

Most domestic pets except dogs can be kept without a licence. However a licence is required for certain wild animals listed in the Dangerous Wild Animals Act 1976.

The list includes poisonous snakes, alligators, bears and chimpanzees. The licence is issued by the district or islands, who must be satisfied, among other things, that the person applying for one is a responsible adult. The council will also inspect the premises where the animal is to be kept. The licence will only cover these premises.

Animals imported from abroad – including cats and dogs – are also subject to QUARANTINE restrictions.

Since you may become liable for injury and damage caused by your animal, you should insure against the possibility. Your house or house contents insurance policy may provide cover for this. It is wise to check with the company which issued the policy if you are in doubt.

To succeed in legal proceedings for damage caused by domestic animals, you normally need to show that the owner or person in charge of the animal failed to take reasonable care in the circumstances. For example, you may be able to get compensation if someone's horse runs out of an open gate into the road and kicks your car. But you may not succeed if his cat runs out and scratches the paintwork. This is because it is usually considered reasonable to let a cat wander.

However if an animal injures you, or an animal belonging to you, its owner will be liable if you can prove that it is more inclined to attack than normal animals of that type. Whatever the circumstances, therefore, pet owners will be liable, for instance, for the bite of a dog particularly giving to biting, or for the damage caused by a cat which is very fond of poultry.

If a dog kills or injures cattle, sheep, poultry and certain other types of livestock, its owner is automatically liable for the damage even if the dog has no particular tendency to kill.

PROTECTION AGAINST OTHER PEOPLE'S PETS

Anyone who owns or is in charge of an animal has a legal duty to take reasonable care that the animal does not cause injury or damage. But with some dangerous animals there is automatic liability.

THE KILLER CAT

Anyone whose animal has an abnormal tendency to damage others will be liable for its actions.

A man kept a pet cat. His neighbour kept ducks, pigeons and rabbits. The cat had tried to get at the birds and the neighbour had complained.

One day the cat got into the neighbour's poultry house and pigeon loft even though they were locked. There it killed 6 Minorca pullets, 3 Aylesbury ducklings and 31 swallow-tumbler pigeons. It then went on to the rabbit hutch, where it killed 8 rabbits.

DECISION

The owner of the cat had to pay compensation to his neighbour. The fact that the cat had tried to get at the birds before indicated a peculiar fondness for poultry and the extent of one day's killing suggested that too. So the owner was automatically liable.

When a dangerous wild animal is kept as a pet, the owner is automatically liable for any damage it does to another person or animal. Bears, lions, tigers – and even monkeys – are covered by this rule.

The owner cannot escape liability by showing that his tiger was normally friendly, or that his monkey meant well. Nor is he likely to be able to excuse himself by showing that someone else let the animal loose. However, if the injured person did something stupid – such as putting his hand in the tiger's mouth – his compensation might be reduced. Indeed in an extreme case he might get nothing at all.

If someone's pets are noisier, smellier or more dangerous than is reasonable for the area where they are kept, you may be able to get a court order stopping him from keeping them there, on the ground that they are a legal NUISANCE.

Animals on the farm

A farmer whose animals cause damage will be liable for that damage in the same way as people are liable for their pets.

For instance, if his horse bolts out of the farm gate and causes a collision, he will be liable if he failed to take reasonable care to stop it. On the other hand, it may be perfectly reasonable for him to allow his sheep to wander on the road in open country such as moorland. Whether or not he is liable will always depend on the circumstances.

Even the farmer who owns a dangerous animal such as a bull will not always be automatically liable if it injures people or other animals. He will only be liable if it tends to be more vicious than other bulls of that type and he ought to have known this.

However the fact that a bull is likely to be dangerous will be relevant in deciding whether or not the farmer took reasonable care to prevent injury.

For instance, he could find himself liable for injuries caused to one of his workers who was required to work with the bull in a place without an escape route.

Since bulls are normally a hazard it will usually be possible to obtain a court order stopping a bull being allowed to wander in a public place, such as a right of way.

Farmers, like other dog owners, are automatically liable for damage done by their dogs to cattle, sheep, poultry and certain other types of livestock. However farmers can kill other people's dogs which are attacking (or seem very likely to attack) their animals.

Farmers are also automatically liable for damage done to gardens, tree plantations and fields by straying horses, sheep, cattle, pigs or goats.

The owner of the damaged land can hold onto the straying animals if he catches them on his land. He does not need to tell their owner, but while he has them he must feed and look after them.

He can claim the cost back from the owner; and he can also claim, according to an old law, one half mark Scots money (about 3p) as a nominal payment for each beast.

However, as there is a risk that the owner might not be found, or will not pay, it is probably safer to try to find out straightaway who he is, get him to take the animals back and then seek only the cost of putting right any damage.

Animals as a business

People who keep animals as a business – for instance, in a zoo, in a circus, or for transport – are liable in the same way as pet-owners.

To get compensation for damage or injury caused by such an animal, you will have to show that its owner took insufficient care, or that the animal was wild and dangerous (as is likely in a zoo) or that it was known to be particularly prone to attack.

Some animals in zoos and circuses require special licences before they can be kept. These licences are issued to owners by local authorities and have more stringent conditions than licences issued under the Dangerous Wild Animals Act.

Licences are also required for kennels, catteries and pet shops. The local authority issuing the licences can lay down particular conditions about hygiene and about the measures to be taken to deal with any emergency that might arise.

Many businesses use guard dogs for security purposes. It is an offence to have a guard dog that is neither tied up nor in the control of a handler. A notice must be exhibited at every entrance to premises on which there is a guard dog.

How the law protects animals

Certain wild animals which are in danger of extinction are given special protection under the Wildlife and Countryside Act 1981. They include most bats, certain butterflies, moths, crickets and spiders, some species of newt, natterjack toad, smooth snake, red squirrel, otters, dolphins and porpoises.

It is an offence to deliberately kill, injure or take any such wild animal except for humane reasons or to prevent serious damage to property and livestock. It is also an offence to damage or destroy its shelter, or to disturb it there, unless the shelter is in a private house. The maximum penalty is a fine of £2,000 for each animal affected.

Badgers are covered by special rules. It is an offence to kill them at any time except to prevent suffering, the spread of disease (for example, bovine tuberculosis) or serious damage to land or animals.

It is possible to get a licence to kill badgers from the Scottish Office's Department of Agriculture and Fisheries to prevent the spread of disease.

Some wild animals which are classed as game cannot be killed at certain times of the year. The species protected include hares, rabbits and pheasants. Protection is necessary to allow stocks to regenerate. *See:* GAME

Deer, can only be killed at certain times of the year. At other times it is generally only legal to kill them to prevent suffering. Farmers can legally kill deer at any time if they get into their crops, or into gardens, fenced-off trees or grassland.

Control of the red deer population is the responsibility of the Red Deer Commission. They may allow killing outside the normal permitted periods where this is necessary to control the level of the deer population.

THE TIMES OF THE YEAR WHEN DEER CAN BE KILLED

Red and Sika Deer Red/Sika Deer Hybrids	
Males	July 1 – October 20
Females	October 21 – February 15
Roe Deer	
Males	April 1 – October 20
Females	October 21 – March 31
Fallow Deer	
Males	August 1 – April 30
Females	October 21 – February 15

Cruelty to wild animals is not an offence unless they are taken captive. They are then protected in the same way as domestic animals (see below). But certain cruel methods of killing animals in the wild are prohibited.

It is an offence to use a self-locking snare to catch any wild animal. It is also an offence to use traps, snares, poison or gas to catch certain animals – including badgers, otters, hedgehogs and red squirrels. The maximum penalty is £1,000 for each animal affected (£2,000 if a self-locking snare is used).

Domestic animals can be lawfully killed. However cruelty to domestic and captive wild animals is an offence, and any killing carried out by an unskilled person may well constitute cruelty. This could apply, for instance, to the drowning of unwanted kittens. Domestic animals should be put down by a vet using humane methods. The SSPCA will be able to give guidance on this.

It is not necessary to kill an animal in a cruel manner in order to commit the offence of cruelty to animals. Convictions have been obtained for unreasonable beating, inadequate feeding and failure to treat a sick animal.

It is no defence that the cruel practice is widely found in the community. The penalties can be severe: a fine of up to £400 or 6 months' imprisonment. The court can also deprive the person of ownership of the animal involved.

It is generally only legal to kill a domestic animal for human consumption if you use the services of a licensed slaughter house.

APPRENTICESHIP

An ancient way to start a new career

Apprenticeship is a special kind of practical training that gives young people the skills of a trade or craft.

An apprenticeship is usually regarded as the best qualification for a trade, and those who have completed one generally command good wages. But the pay during apprenticeship is low and the training period – usually 4 years – is long compared with other methods of job entry.

A person entering an apprenticeship must usually be over 16 years old. Theoretically there is no upper age limit, but in practice there often is. Older women seeking training who have problems should get in touch with the Equal Opportunities Commission. *See:* EQUAL OPPORTUNITIES

Training is governed by a written contract, often called an indenture, in which the apprentice's 'master' – an individual, a partnership or a company – promises to teach the apprentice his or her trade, and the apprentice agrees to learn it and to obey the master's instructions.

Under an apprenticeship contract the trainee has no legal right to even a low wage, for the master, in theory and occasionally in practice, can demand a premium or fee for giving instruction.

If the apprentice-to-be is under 18, a parent or guardian must normally sign the contract along with him or her.

STARTING WORK AS AN APPRENTICE

An apprentice's training is governed by a contract in which an employer promises to teach the apprentice his or her craft and the apprentice agrees to learn it and to obey the 'master's' instructions.

When an apprentice is dismissed

Employers have greater powers to discipline apprentices than other employees, but may find it more difficult to dismiss them. An apprentice dismissed before the end of his or her apprenticeship could probably sue for damages to compensate for lost earnings and training during the rest of the contract period, and for lost opportunity and reduced status in the future.

An apprentice can also normally claim UNFAIR DISMISSAL before an INDUSTRIAL TRIBUNAL if he or she has been in the job for at least 1 year. If the dismissal is for trade union reasons, the apprentice can apply to an industrial tribunal, within 7 days of dismissal, for 'interim relief' – irrespective of how long he or she has been in the job. *See:* TRADE UNION

Some grounds for dismissing an apprentice – for example, stubborn refusal to learn, habitual neglect of studies, persistent illness or behaviour which interferes with instruction – are not unfair in law, provided the employer had given previous warnings.

But employers are traditionally expected to suspend and discipline apprentices who misbehave, rather than dismiss them, particularly if the contract is nearing its end.

THE APPRENTICE WHOSE MANNER CHANGED

An employer has greater powers to discipline apprentices than he has over other workers; but his rights to dismiss an apprentice are more restricted. He must be able to show that he gave the apprentice several warnings and chances to mend his or her ways.

When Mr Smedley was first apprenticed to his horticultural firm, he proved a very capable worker – the best apprentice to date, according to his employers. He passed proficiency exams, and after a while was paid a craftsman's wage.

But then his behaviour changed. He challenged instructions, would not work in a group and declined to do overtime.

He was given warning after warning verbally, and finally a warning in writing. Eventually, he was dismissed.

DECISION

The dismissal was fair, the Employment Appeal Tribunal ruled.

When an apprentice is made redundant

Apprentices made redundant during their contract term can claim redundancy payment only if they have reached the age of 20 and have completed at least 2 years' service.

They might win a claim for unfair dismissal if their employer did not find a new master for them, or did not give enough warning.

When an apprenticeship is over, no redundancy payment is due if the employer refuses to take on the newly qualified journeyman under a fresh contract. Nor can the apprentice claim unfair dismissal, unless the employer had previously promised him a job, or unless, as in some sections of engineering, it is a well-known custom of the trade to offer continued employment. *See:* REDUNDANCY

National insurance contributions

From the age of 16, apprentices must pay NATIONAL INSURANCE CONTRIBUTIONS if they earn more than the qualifying weekly wage – that was £34 in 1984–5.

APPROVAL, Goods on

When goods can be sent back without payment

Goods are sometimes advertised for sale 'on approval', which means that after sending for them you need keep and pay for them only if you like them; if not, you can return them.

The goods are usually on approval for a limited period – 10 days, for example. If you do not want them and fail to tell the seller this within the time limit, you will have to keep and pay for them.

If no time limit is mentioned, the law states that you must decide to keep or return them within a reasonable time. In fact, if you do not want the goods it is best not to delay returning them by even a day or two. You could find yourself liable to pay for them.

If you use the goods as though you owned them, before the stipulated or reasonable time expires, you are likely to be regarded in law as having 'adopted the transaction' – that is, agreed to buy the goods.

A person who pawned jewellery which he had received on approval was held to have adopted the transaction. Even if you simply lend someone a book sent to you on approval, this could be interpreted in the same light.

ARBITRATION

An informal way of settling a dispute

The usual way to settle a civil dispute – for example, over faulty goods or an unpaid bill – is to start proceedings in a court and let the judge settle the matter.

A more informal, faster and sometimes cheaper, way is to refer it to an independent person – called an arbiter – to decide. Going to an arbiter may be agreed upon by the parties once they are in dispute. But insurance companies often insist in advance that any complaint by a policyholder that cannot be settled amicably must be referred to an arbiter.

By law, disputes between landlords and farm tenants must be settled this way. Many commercial organisations, usually under pressure from the Office of Fair Trading, have set up arbitration schemes which dissatisfied customers can make use of. These include:

- Scottish Motor Trade Association
  3 Palmerston Place
  Edinburgh.
- Association of British Travel Agents
  53/54 Newman Street
  London WIP 4AH.
- Scottish House Furnishers' Association
  203 Pitt Street
  Glasgow G2 4DB.
- Association of Manufacturers of Domestic Appliances
  593 Hitchin Road
  Stopsley,
  Luton LU2 7UN.

Rather than go to arbitration under one of these schemes, you can go to court – but only one or the other. Some trade associations will first try to get you and their member to agree through conciliation. There will usually be an initial fee to pay, but it may be returned by the arbiter to the successful side. If there is no agreement in advance about a fee, each party has to pay half.

In general once an arbiter has taken up a dispute it cannot be raised in court. But a court can be asked to overrule his award if it turns out that he showed bias, had an interest in the result, or did not give both sides an equal chance to state their case. If he goes beyond the subject referred to him, or was mistaken as to what he was supposed to be deciding, he may also be overruled by a court.

Arbiters are usually not named in advance but chosen from among people with some knowledge of the point in dispute – for instance a chartered surveyor might be asked where an owner of a new home and the builder fall out. Sometimes the head of the appropriate professional body is asked to name a suitable arbiter. The Chartered Institute of Arbiters, at 85 Claremont Street, Glasgow G3 7RF provides training and maintains lists of suitable arbiters.

The arbiter decides on his own procedure. He has no power, as a court does, to summon witnesses or have documents produced, but he can ask a court to give him the right to do so.

He can decide on matters of fact or law. Sometimes he will issue his proposed findings and ask the parties to comment on them before finalising his decision. If the decision is not complied with the arbiter can have it registered in the court registers: it then becomes as enforceable as a court decree. Except on the grounds mentioned above, there is no appeal to a court.

ARMED FORCES

The rights of servicemen often differ from those of civilians

Members of the armed forces – including reservists in training and, in some cases, members of Service families – are subject not only to ordinary law but also to military law. Its purpose is to maintain discipline, and the officers who administer it – in all 3 Services – do so by the authority of Parliament.

How military law works for Service personnel

Most serious offences – whether they are crimes in civilian life, such as theft, or are purely military offences, such as desertion – can be tried by a COURT MARTIAL. Someone who committed a crime during his service can be tried by court martial even after he has returned to civilian life.

However, if a civilian court has tried a serviceman, he cannot be tried again by his Service for 'substantially' the same offence. For example, a serviceman who steals from a shop while on leave and is dealt with by a civilian court, cannot be tried again for the theft by a court martial.

Usually a serviceman who has committed a crime will be prosecuted by whoever finds him first – the civil authority or the military. The two cooperate closely and sometimes the military authority will hand over the case to the civilian authority even if the military authority made the arrest.

If the serviceman who stole was a deserter or absent without leave, however, he could still be prosecuted by the Service for desertion or his absence.

Serious crimes The most serious offences – murder, treason, culpable homicide or rape – cannot be tried by military courts if they are committed in the United Kingdom.

Outside the United Kingdom the Services have power to try all cases against anyone who is subject to military law. But this right is often waived, especially if the local police have made the arrest.

How families are affected by Service rules

A serviceman's wife and children normally live with him in married quarters, for which he pays rent even if he is sent elsewhere for a while. He can choose to arrange his own accommodation and many servicemen are home-owners.

Medical treatment A serviceman's family in married quarters overseas is treated by the unit medical officer. In the UK, they generally register with a National Health Service family doctor, and receive army treatment only in an emergency.

Overseas and in Britain, a Service family can go to a local doctor and pay for private treatment if they want.

Education In the United Kingdom, servicemen's children go to civilian schools. If the family go abroad, the children can attend a school provided by the British Forces Education Service and, if the father's base is not near enough to such a school for the children to go there every day, they can become boarders.

When the children reach secondary-school age, their father is entitled to a special allowance to enable him to send them to boarding school in the United Kingdom. Even if the father is moved back to the United Kingdom from time to time, he is still entitled to the allowance to ensure that the children's education is not disrupted.

Reserve forces

Members of the reserve forces are subject to military law like full-time servicemen when they:

- Are in training.
- Have been called out on permanent service.
- Are helping the civil authorities – for example, the police.

WHO MAY BE SUBJECT TO MILITARY LAW

In some circumstances, civilians are subject to military law, just as if they were members of the armed forces.

Civilian workers who accompany a forces unit on active service are subject to military law. So are certain civilians on official duty outside the United Kingdom even if not on active service.

Those affected include some civil servants, NAAFI staff, members of their families living abroad with them, and members of any Service family living abroad with the serviceman.

A serviceman's employee – for example, a nanny – is also subject to military law and so are any members of the employee's family who are living abroad with the serviceman if they are British subjects. But if the employee is a national of the country where she is living, she will then be subject to the local civil law.

A visiting relative who does not reside with the serviceman – someone who for example stays with him overnight or merely visits him from time to time – is not subject to military law.

If a serviceman is injured while on duty

If a serviceman is injured on duty and is discharged as a result, he is entitled to a DISABILITY PENSION.

Where a superior officer or authority causes damage or injury by abusing or exceeding his powers, the serviceman can obtain damages in the civil courts – but only if the court is satisfied that the officer or authority was motivated by malice, cruelty or oppression. That restriction means that a serviceman has fewer rights than a civilian in such circumstances.

A serviceman who is injured through the negligence of a fellow-serviceman while on duty cannot sue his comrade or his employer, the Ministry of Defence. Nor can he sue if he is injured by an enemy at a time when the United Kingdom is formally at war. But he can sue a civilian who injures him by an act of terrorism.

He cannot sue the Ministry for injuries caused by any defects in premises, ship, aircraft, vehicle, equipment or Service supplies.

The only right he can rely on, in such circumstances, is his right to a disability pension.

Criminal injury A serviceman who is injured by a criminal act – such as by a terrorist bomb – is entitled to seek CRIMINAL INJURIES COMPENSATION. It does not matter whether he was on or off duty at the time.

If a serviceman dies

When a member of the forces dies as a result of being injured on duty or from an illness contracted because of his service, his dependants are entitled to a pension.

Dependants are normally a wife and children, not a girl-friend. More than one pension can be paid – for example, to a wife and a widowed mother who had been partly supported from a serviceman's pay.

The amount depends on the applicant's degree of dependency.

Leaving the Service

Full-time servicemen cannot usually leave the forces before they have served the period for which they signed on. However, if they are serving for the first time they can claim a discharge in the early months of service, by paying a fee – the amount depends on the length of service and the unit served in – or without fee in the case of boys recruited

SOCIAL SECURITY FOR THE FORCES

Members of the armed forces pay a reduced rate for Class I NATIONAL INSURANCE CONTRIBUTIONS, but they are not eligible for unemployment, sickness or invalidity benefit or non-contributory invalidity pension.

Servicemen are normally entitled to full social security benefits immediately they leave the forces.

If someone is dismissed after a court martial or civilian court case, however, he cannot claim unemployment benefit for the first 6 weeks. But if he is discharged at his own request or if he is invited to resign, he is eligible at once.

SERVICEMEN AND POLITICS

A full-time regular serviceman is not allowed to become a Member of the House of Commons. Nor can he campaign for a politician – whether in or out of uniform.

If a serviceman wants to stand for Parliament, he must apply for a discharge. He is not allowed to run a campaign until the application is approved by a special Home Office committee which has to be satisfied that he is a genuine candidate.

Any serviceman is allowed to vote in parliamentary or local elections by post or by proxy.

under the age of 17½. Female recruits have a right to free discharge in the first 3 weeks.

Arranging early retirement

Early retirement may be allowed, but only with the consent of the Service. A serviceman who tried to walk out of his job would face trial by his commanding officer, or by court martial. If found guilty a soldier could be imprisoned. An officer could also be imprisoned and would be dismissed.

ARREST

When a citizen can be deprived of his freedom

A person who is arrested by the POLICE is thereby deprived of his right to freedom and may have CRIMINAL PROCEEDINGS taken against him.

Although an arrest is usually carried out by a policeman, every citizen has the right under certain circumstances to make a CITIZEN'S ARREST of another. If he does so he may run the risk of being sued later for WRONGFUL ARREST.

Even the police have to have good grounds for arrest and they can be sued for arresting maliciously and without good reason.

Before a person can be arrested there must be enough evidence to charge him with an offence. The police cannot arrest him for questioning – although they can detain him temporarily. *See:* DETENTION

When a warrant for arrest is not required

If a policeman sees someone committing an offence – or trying to – he may arrest without a warrant. He may also do so if a credible person points out to him someone else who he claims he saw commit an offence.

But even in these circumstances a policeman is not supposed to arrest unless he thinks it necessary. It would be necessary, for instance, if the person he arrests is unknown to him and might escape, or is drunk, or is acting in an obscene way or is threatening violence.

A person found in suspicious circumstances in possession of property he cannot account for may also be arrested without a warrant.

Many Acts of Parliament also give power to the police to arrest without a warrant – for example, those dealing with PUBLIC ORDER offences such as BREACH OF THE PEACE (under the Public Order Act 1936), OBSTRUCTION or possessing an OFFENSIVE WEAPON.

When a warrant is issued

A warrant is obtained by the PROCURATOR FISCAL, who applies for it to a magistrate, usually the local sheriff. He gives written details of the case (name, address, designation of accused, the criminal charge involved) and states why a warrant is required. The sheriff decides whether to issue a warrant, but he usually takes the procurator fiscal's word and issues one as a matter of course.

If a warrant is issued, the police are entitled to arrest the person named in it at any time of the day or night.

A policeman does not have to take the warrant with him when he makes the arrest, though he usually does so. However, the person being arrested is entitled to see the warrant on request, or as soon as it can be produced.

If the person believes that the warrant is incorrect or does not refer to him, he may refuse to be arrested. If the warrant does not refer to him, but he is arrested, he can sue the police for wrongful arrest.

If the warrant is itself illegal – for example, because it has no date – then the person arrested can also sue the magistrate who issued it for wrongful arrest. However he will have to prove not only that it was illegal but also that the magistrate who issued it was acting out of malice, or had a grudge against him.

When the police make an arrest

When a person is arrested he must be told by a policeman why the arrest is being made. If he is not, and is later acquitted, he can sue the police for wrongful arrest.

The arrested person may also be cautioned that he does not need to say anything but that anything he says will be noted and may be used in evidence.

Sometimes – for example, where a person being arrested is struggling violently – it may not be possible for a policeman to deliver the caution or tell him why he is being arrested. He must, however, be told as soon as possible.

The explanation need only be general and no specific charge is necessary. For example, a policeman may say 'I am arresting you for unlawfully killing Mary McLeod', but he need not say whether the charge will be murder or culpable homicide.

The police are entitled to use reasonable force to arrest a person. They may use handcuffs if they believe an arrested person might escape without them, or if they think he might try to harm himself or someone else.

If the police use excessive force, or employ handcuffs for any other reason, they can later be sued for ASSAULT or be the subject of a complaint to the procurator fiscal.

A person who refuses to be arrested or struggles with a policeman may be charged with resisting arrest or obstructing the policeman in the exercise of his duty.

An arrested person has the right to have his solicitor informed of his arrest. The police are obliged to inform him of this right.

Helping the police with their inquiries

A person who has not been arrested may still be asked to go to a police station. He is usually said to be 'helping the police with their inquiries'. He is entitled to refuse to go unless told that he is being taken into DETENTION for questioning.

If he agrees to go with the policeman,

he can leave the police station at any time, provided that he is not subsequently arrested or is not detained for questioning.

Sometimes it is not clear whether a person in the police station is there voluntarily or has been arrested without warrant. The test is whether the police have used such words as 'you are under arrest' or have physically restrained him (or said they will do so).

If they have done either of these then there has been an arrest. If they had the right to arrest, the arrest is lawful. If they did not, there is a wrongful arrest and the person arrested may sue.

What happens at the station

After a person is arrested he is taken to a police station.

At the station the arrested person must be cautioned and charged. The caution is that he need not say anything in answer to the charge, but that anything which is said will be noted and may be used in evidence.

The charge is a statement of the law which he is accused of breaking. Sometimes the procurator fiscal later decides that the person should be charged with a different offence.

The arrested person should be told of his right to inform his solicitor, if he was not told at the time of arrest. He must also be told of his right to inform a reasonably-named person of his arrest – though notification can be delayed for as long as necessary in the interests of justice (for example to prevent a warning being given to another suspect).

The police may take photographs and fingerprints of anyone who has been arrested. They may also search him for evidence connected with the suspected crime and may seize anything they find. They will remove anything with which the suspect can cause injury to himself or others, or damage to the police station.

They may also take away anything that could be used as a weapon or as a means of escape. If they think a person may try to take his own life, they will probably remove items such as tie, belt and shoelaces.

If the police take away a person's belongings, they:

- List all the items taken.
- Ask the person to check the list.
- Package the items and seal them with a label signed by witnesses.

The police are entitled to keep any item for use as evidence in court. When a person is released, or after he is tried – even if he has been convicted – the police must usually return all the items they have taken unless they were used in committing an offence. If they fail to do so, he can apply to the sheriff to have the items returned.

When a convicted person is sent to prison, his belongings are transferred there, and will be returned to him only when he is released at the end of his sentence.

However any of his belongings used as evidence at the trial may be given to a relative for safekeeping.

Once someone has been charged with an offence which is not too serious, the police may decide to release him on BAIL.

UNFAIR PRESSURE TO MAKE A STATEMENT

Statements made under pressure cannot be used at the trial.

Mr Law was arrested at 8 a.m. on 24th December and charged with stealing 16½ stones of fish. He asked the police to contact his solicitor. They did but the solicitor was busy at that moment. Time wore on and a policeman remarked to Mr Law that if they did not get a statement soon the case would not be disposed of by that morning's court. Mr Law might then have to be kept in custody awaiting trial over Christmas. As a result Mr Law made a confession and was convicted.

DECISION

The appeal court decided that the confession was obtained through unfair pressure and that the lower court should neither have accepted it nor convicted Mr Law.

Questioning

Once an accused person is arrested and charged he should no longer be questioned by the police. By then the police should have sufficient information to report the accused for prosecution.

However the accused may volunteer to make a statement, and the police can question him in order to remove any ambiguity in it. If the police do continue to question the accused after arrest, he is not obliged to reply. Anything he does say will be held by a court to be inadmissible as evidence if it has been unfairly obtained. *See:* CONFESSION

Although an accused person is not obliged to say anything to the police, inferences can be drawn at his trial if he does not mention certain defences to the sheriff at any JUDICIAL EXAMINATION that may be held.

It is an offence not to reveal to the police information about TERRORISM.

RESISTING POLICE ARREST

Even someone who knows that he is innocent, and genuinely believes that the police have no grounds for arresting him, should go quietly – he will have an opportunity later to contact a lawyer.

If he does not, he may be charged with resisting arrest, or with obstructing a police officer in the execution of his duty, or with assaulting a police officer. The penalty for these offences may be imprisonment.

The proper place for disputing the correctness of an arrest is at the police station or in court, not at the scene of the arrest. In the rare case where a person can prove that an arrest was illegal, he may do two things. He can complain to the Chief Constable as it is a breach of police discipline to make an unnecessary or unlawful arrest; or he can sue for wrongful arrest.

Bringing the accused to court

After a person has been arrested and charged, what happens next depends on the charge. If it is serious enough for a jury trial, he is first taken before a sheriff for JUDICIAL EXAMINATION.

This must be done as soon as possible, and at most 48 hours after the arrest. The accused is entitled to speak with his solicitor before the examination. Unless he is given BAIL, he is then committed to prison to await trial.

If the offence is a minor one, to be tried without a jury in the DISTRICT COURT or SHERIFF COURT, the accused must be brought before the court as soon as possible – normally on the morning after the arrest. Since the courts do not usually sit at weekends, an accused arrested on a Friday evening may not appear in court until Monday morning. The accused is entitled to an interview with a solicitor before his appearance in court. *See:* LEGAL AID

An accused person who pleads guilty may be dealt with immediately by the court. If he pleads not guilty a trial date will be fixed. He will then be either sent to prison to await trial, granted bail or ordered to appear on the trial date. *See:* CRIMINAL PROCEEDINGS

The time limits do not apply to people detained for questioning on suspicion of being involved in TERRORISM.

ARRESTMENT

A legal way to recover debts

If a debtor fails to pay a debt when a court orders him to, his creditor can ask a SHERIFF OFFICER to 'freeze' money or property belonging or due to the debtor, to the value of the debt. The money or property must be held by a third party.

This procedure – called arrestment – is normally used against wages due from an employer or money held in a savings or current account.

If the debtor still fails to pay, the money or property frozen can be made over to the creditor. *See:* DEBT

ARTIFICIAL INSEMINATION

When nature is helped to take its course

A woman can be made pregnant artificially by the injection of a man's semen or by the implanting of a fertilised ovum (egg).

When the husband's semen is used (artificial insemination by husband, or AIH) there is no legal problem. The child has exactly the same status in law as one conceived normally.

If the semen comes from a man other than the woman's husband, however (artificial insemination by donor, or AID), the child is illegitimate, although the woman is not held to have committed ADULTERY.

If the husband were to leave the mother before the child was born and then refused to accept it as his own, he could not legally be made to maintain the child.

When the donor can be made to pay

The donor of the semen, on the other hand, could be made responsible for the child, but his identity is usually known only to the doctor who carried out the insemination. The mother is rarely, if ever, told his identity because the code of medical ethics dictates that the doctor should not disclose any names.

In practice, doctors make sure that the husband approves the use of AID. They may be reluctant to approve AID for single women.

The child will have the usual rights to inherit the mother's property, but will have no rights to inherit her husband's property; unless adopted by him.

But as a 'child of the family' – that is a child who has been accepted in a household, like a step-son or step-daughter – he or she could claim ALIMENT.

Registering the birth of an AID child

It is a criminal offence when registering an AID birth to show the mother's husband as the father of the child, although a prosecution would be extremely unlikely.

ASSAULT

Violence against the person

An assault is any deliberate attack on another person.

The attack may be indirect – for example, setting a dog on someone. Substantial violence is not necessary – it is assault to spit or throw dirt at someone. Nor need the victim actually be touched. It is assault to aim a blow at someone and it does not matter if the blow misses the intended target. In practice, however, a prosecution is unlikely unless there is serious violence or injury.

Assault can also consist of threatening gestures which put the victim in fear of personal injury: to present a toy gun at someone can be assault if the victim believes it to be real and loaded.

HAVING A 'SQUARE GO'

Consent can be a defence to assault where there is no intention to injure – as in, for example, a lawful surgical operation or in sports like football and boxing where participants consent to the use of force within the rules of the game.

But sometimes a court will refuse to accept a defence of consent.

William Smart and Isaac Wilkie were having an argument. Smart invited Wilkie to have a 'square go' and Wilkie consented to this. During their fight Smart inflicted a number of injuries on Wilkie and he was charged with assault.

Smart's defence was that he was not guilty because Wilkie had consented to fight and therefore no assault had been committed.

DECISION

The defence failed and Smart was convicted. On appeal, it was held that consent to a 'square go' was not a defence to a charge of assault based on that agreed combat. The High Court emphasised that evil intent to injure is essential to assault and that if there is an attack on a person, done with intent to harm, the attitude of the victim is irrelevant.

If someone accused of assault proves he was acting in self-defence, he will be acquitted, provided he used what is considered to be reasonable force in the circumstances.

Assault is a DELICT, which means that a victim can sue for compensation in a civil action if he thinks his attacker has enough money to pay damages. *See also:* CRIMINAL INJURIES COMPENSATION

ASSESSMENT CENTRE

Examining children with problems

Assessment centres are run by regional councils. Their purpose is to examine the problems of children who have been brought before a court or CHILDREN'S HEARING because of difficulties at home, or offences they have committed or failure to attend school regularly.

The staff of an assessment centre includes social workers, teachers, and sometimes psychologists and psychiatrists. They work with the child and recommend to the court or hearing what should be done for the child's educational, social and emotional welfare.

A child who is sent to an assessment centre will have to live there in the care of the local authority while the case is being examined. But in rare circumstances there can be exceptions to this rule. For example it may be thought in the child's interests for him or her to stay at home. In this case the child would probably be required to attend the centre daily during assessment.

Certain specialist centres provide facilities for very difficult children, and those facing major criminal charges who have been remanded by a court. *See:* REMAND

ATTEMPTED CRIME

Failure carries the same penalties as success

The law makes no distinction between a person who sets out to commit a crime but fails and one who succeeds. In practice, however, it is often more difficult to prove an attempted crime than a completed one. The prosecution will usually have to prove that the accused intended to commit a crime and had a serious try at doing so.

The legal test is: has the accused passed from the stage of preparation to that of perpetration?

The court normally needs to be satisfied that there is no other reasonable explanation of the accused's behaviour.

ATTENDANCE ALLOWANCE

Financial help for the severely handicapped

An attendance allowance is a weekly payment to people who have been severely disabled, physically or mentally, for at least six months and who need a lot of personal attention at home or in a private institution. It is tax-free, non-means tested and non-contributory and is paid by the Department of Health and Social Security.

HOW A DISABLED PERSON QUALIFIES

To qualify for attendance allowance a person must have been, for at least 6 months, so severely disabled, physically or mentally, as to need:

- Continual supervision by day or by night to avoid substantial danger to himself or herself or to others; or
- Frequent attention by day, or prolonged or repeated attention by night, to help with bodily functions. That includes seeing, speech and hearing but not cooking, shopping or housework.

Spells of treatment for the disability as a hospital in-patient count towards the 6 months qualifying period, but payment of the allowance will stop after the first 4 weeks if the disabled person is maintained in hospital or other accommodation at public expense.

In addition the disabled person:

- Must be at least 2 years old.
- Must live in Great Britain, be present there and have been so present for at least 26 weeks out of the previous 12 months.
- Must, if under 16, require considerably more personal attention than that normally given to a child of the same age and sex.

Entitlement to attendance allowance is assessed by the Attendance Allowance Board, which comprises mainly doctors, and every applicant must be examined – usually at home – by a doctor nominated by the Board. The claimant does not have to prove that attendance is actually being provided; to qualify, it is enough to show that it is required.

There are two rates of allowance. The lower one (£18.15 a week in 1983–4) is paid to those who need attention or supervision either by day or by night. The higher rate (£27.20 a week in 1983–4) is paid to those who require attention both day and night.

How to claim

To claim the benefit, complete form NI 205, 'Attendance Allowance', obtainable from any office of the Department of Health and Social Security.

A disabled person should complete the form if he or she is able. Otherwise someone else can do it. The mother should generally make the claim for a child who is under 16.

Help and assistance in claiming attendance allowance, or in finding out more about the benefit generally, may be obtained by writing to the local office of the DHSS or to the Attendance Allowance Unit, DHSS, Norcross, Blackpool, Lancs, FY5 3TA.

If the disabled person has met the medical requirements for 6 months or more, the claim should be made immediately. The allowance cannot be backdated to a date before the claim.

If the disabled person meets the medical requirements, but has not done so for 6 months, the claim should be submitted after 4 months of disability. This allows sufficient time for a decision to be reached before the end of the 6 months and for payment to be made immediately.

A claim for a young child should not be made before he or she is 22 months old.

The examining doctor usually submits his report to another doctor authorised by the Board to take a final decision.

How to appeal

If a claimant is dissatisfied, either because he has been refused an allowance or because only the lower rate has been granted, he may apply in writing to the DHSS office or the Attendance Allowance Unit for a review of the Board's decision. He has 3 months in which to do this.

A claimant may ask his doctor to submit a report; and written evidence from relatives about the personal attention that is required should also accompany the request for a review.

The claimant may appeal to the SOCIAL SECURITY COMMISSIONERS, on a question of law only, against the decision of the Board on review, or any refusal to review. An appeal form is obtainable from offices of the DHSS.

How payment is made

The allowance is normally made payable to the claimant, unless he or she cannot manage his or her own affairs. If this is the case, the allowance is paid to the person who is legally responsible for administering them. Payment is made by books of orders which can be cashed in a named post office, chosen by the recipient.

AU PAIR

When a foreign girl joins a British family

A girl from abroad who wants to come to Britain for a limited period can stay for up to 2 years, living with a family as an 'au pair'. She does not need a work permit, provided that the immigration officer at her port of arrival or the Home Office approves the arrangement. This arrangement is available only for girls who come from Western European countries, Malta, Cyprus and Turkey.

If she is from an EEC country, she is not subject to the 2 year limit, as EEC nationals are guaranteed the complete right to live and work in Britain. *See:* EUROPEAN COMMUNITIES

An au pair must be between 17 and 27 years old and must be unmarried and have no dependants. The Home Office has sometimes objected even to an au pair who has been married in the past. There is no official au pair arrangement for boys.

She is not a domestic servant, but a temporary member of the host family (which must be English-speaking). A domestic servant would have to have a work permit (unless she was an EEC national).

The au pair is expected to do some of the housework and/or help with the children in return for her keep and pocket money. The Home Office recommends that she should not be asked to do more than 5 hours' work a day. She should be able to enter into family life, have a room of her own and have time for her own recreation, study and any religious observance.

It is advisable to settle in writing details of duties, pocket money, time off and travel expenses to and from her own country before she arrives.

Immigration formalities An au pair should not need a VISA or other entry clearance to enter the UK, unless she is a national of a country whose citizens need a visa to enter the UK for any purpose. Normally an immigration officer will want to see only a letter from the host family inviting her.

If she is coming to the United Kingdom from Turkey or Cyprus, however, it might be wise for her to apply for an entry clearance before travelling, and for the host family to arrange to meet her at the airport.

The immigration officer should admit the au pair for 12 months, and he will stamp the time limit on her passport, together with a notice forbidding her to take employment within the UK.

An au pair has no claim to remain here when her 2 years expire and she will not be allowed to transfer to another job, unless she is a citizen of an EEC country.

An au pair who has been here before on an au pair basis will have the earlier period taken into account in calculating the 2 years she is allowed here. Someone who is already in Britain – for example, as a student – and who wants to stay on as an au pair, must apply to the Home Office, either in person or by writing. The same procedure applies when the first 12 months' leave expires.

The application must be made and received by the Home Office before the leave stamped in her passport runs out, otherwise she commits a criminal offence by remaining, and has no right of appeal if the Home Office refuses her application.

In that case the notice refusing her application is served on her by the local police, who notify her that she will be prosecuted for over-staying her leave if she does not go within 14 days.

Otherwise, if the application was made in time, and they do refuse, she does have a right of appeal to an adjudicator. *See:* IMMIGRATION

National insurance contributions

An au pair is not required to pay national insurance contributions, provided that her income in Britain is not above the lower earnings limit for such contributions – £34 in 1984–5. The value of an au pair's keep is not taken into account.

However, girls from countries which have social security agreements with Britain and who are paying contributions in their own countries may benefit by continuing to pay in Britain.

When the arrangements break down

If an au pair has trouble settling in or falls out with her host family, the Home Office will allow her to be an au pair with another family, but not to take a regular job.

AUCTION

Practices and pitfalls of the salerooms

Sales at an auction are binding only when the auctioneer brings his hammer down. Until that point the bidder can withdraw his bid and the auctioneer can withdraw the lot.

Goods up for auction may be subject to an upset price which is made public as the price at which the bidding will start. A reserve price is known only to the auctioneer, and if it is not reached, the goods will not be sold. Upset prices are common in Scotland, reserve prices in England.

If no upset price is specified and the goods are not subject to a reserve price then the highest bid secures them, even though it may not be as high as the seller hoped for.

If a seller notifies other bidders that he is bidding for his own goods, or that he has employed somebody else to bid for him, the bidding is legal. If he does not give notice and bids or gets someone, called a 'whitebonnet', to bid for him – so forcing up the price – the sale is fraudulent, and the buyer can purchase the goods for the amount of the last bid he made before fraudulent bidding started.

The highest bidder may in fact be the seller or his whitebonnet: in this case the other bidders may have the right to demand that the whole sale be declared void.

When auctions are illegal

Auction rings One fraudulent practice, which affects the seller but not the buyer, is that operated by a ring or group of dealers who agree that only one of their number will bid for the goods being auctioned.

By eliminating any competitive bidding, they can buy the goods for less than their worth and auction them privately among themselves later.

Rings are illegal, but prosecutions are rare because it is difficult to obtain proof of their operations.

Mock auctions Auctions that attract customers by pretending that all the goods are on offer at extremely low prices, or are even being given away, are illegal under the Mock Auctions Act 1961.

Maximum penalty: £2,000 fine.

BAIL

Freeing an accused person pending trial

A person charged with a criminal offence and taken into custody may be given bail. This means that he or she is released from custody until the trial.

Release by the police

The officer in charge of a police station may release a person arrested and charged with an offence, provided it is one which is likely to be tried in the DISTRICT COURT, or in the SHERIFF COURT without a jury. The police have no power to release a person who is likely to be tried before a jury in the sheriff court or HIGH COURT OF JUSTICIARY because of, for instance, the seriousness of the offence or a previous criminal record.

An arrested person who is released by the police will usually have to sign a written undertaking to appear at court at a stated time. Failure to appear in court in breach of a written undertaking may amount to an offence.
Maximum penalty £400 fine and 60 days' imprisonment (3 months' imprisonment if convicted in the sheriff court).

Release of children

The police have wider powers to release children who have been arrested. Generally, where a child or his parent undertakes that the child will attend at the hearing of the charge, the police should release the child. However they may keep the child in custody if the charge is homicide or some other grave crime, or if they consider it is in the child's interests to be protected from criminals or prostitutes, or if release would defeat the ends of justice.

Unless there are special circumstances – for example, unruly behaviour – a child who is not released should be removed from the police station to a place of safety (for example, a children's home) until he or she can be brought before a sheriff. Thereafter the child will generally be dealt with by a special procedure, rather than by the criminal courts. *See:* CHILDREN'S HEARING

Bail by a court

A person who has been arrested and charged must be brought before a court without delay – usually within 24 hours. There may be a longer delay at weekends and during court holidays. *See:* ARREST

Anybody in custody will have the opportunity of a free consultation with a defence solicitor on duty at the court. If a person in custody intends to plead not guilty, the defence solicitor will provide free representation at the first court appearance. In almost all cases the solicitor will ask the court to grant release on bail before the trial. *See:* LEGAL AID

The court is likely to refuse bail if, for example, the person has no fixed address, or has a serious criminal record, or is likely to interfere with witnesses.

Where the court grants bail, it usually attaches conditions requiring the person to appear in court and forbidding any interference with witnesses. Other conditions may also be imposed by the court.

The former practice of depositing bail money no longer occurs except in special circumstances. It is almost unknown for a person to be asked to act as a cautioner (a guarantor) or to deposit money in court in order to obtain another person's release.

If a person released on bail fails to appear in court without good reason, or breaches any other condition of bail, he may be guilty of an offence and can be arrested without a warrant. For instance, a person on bail who makes threats against a witness may be arrested and brought before a court charged with breaching a bail condition. As a result the court may recall or vary the original order of bail.
Maximum penalty As stated above. Where bail has been granted in relation to a jury trial, the maximum penalty is increased to an unlimited fine and two years' imprisonment. There is a right of appeal to the High Court of Justiciary.

The court before which an accused is first brought will generally have the power to grant bail. However, where the accused is charged with murder or treason, only the High Court of Justiciary or the Lord Advocate has the power to grant bail.

Review and appeal

If a court refuses bail, or fixes unacceptable conditions, the accused can ask it to review its decision. He can do so on the fifth day after the bail decision and thereafter on the 15th day after any subsequent decision of the court.

The court may be persuaded to change its decision if circumstances have changed significantly – for example, if an accused without a fixed address is subsequently offered accommodation by friends.

Both the PROCURATOR FISCAL and the accused may appeal to the High Court of Justiciary against the granting or refusal of bail or any conditions imposed. There is no time limit for appealing but an accused who is to be tried before a jury cannot appeal until he has been fully committed (usually 7 days after the first court appearance). The accused may be able to obtain LEGAL AID for the appeal. If the procurator

MAKING AN APPLICATION FOR BAIL

How an accused may be able to regain his freedom, pending trial

1 After arrest an accused will have the opportunity to speak to a duty solicitor. The duty solicitor will advise the accused – for example, about his plea. If the accused is pleading not guilty, the solicitor will obtain information from him about his circumstances. This will enable the solicitor to apply for bail on behalf of the accused in court.

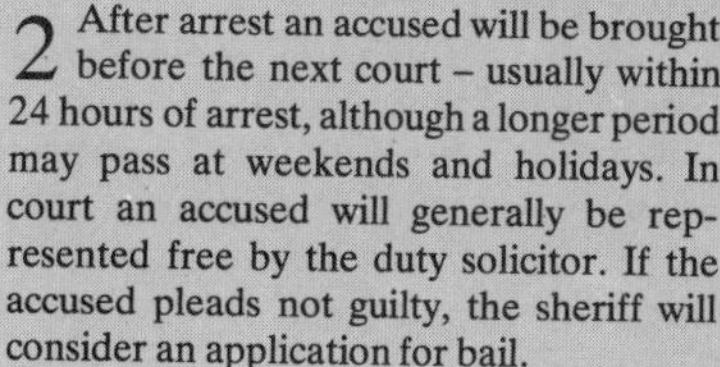

2 After arrest an accused will be brought before the next court – usually within 24 hours of arrest, although a longer period may pass at weekends and holidays. In court an accused will generally be represented free by the duty solicitor. If the accused pleads not guilty, the sheriff will consider an application for bail.

3 If bail is refused by a sheriff, the accused may obtain legal aid to appeal the decision to a judge of the High Court. Bail appeal will take place in chambers. The accused will not generally be present and he will be represented by an advocate, who will be instructed by a solicitor on behalf of the accused.

4 If the accused is freed, he must observe all the bail conditions. If he fails to do so he may be re-arrested and be prosecuted for breach of the bail conditions.

fiscal appeals against the granting of bail, the accused will generally remain in custody for up to 72 hours, until the appeal is decided.

Appeals are heard before a judge of the HIGH COURT OF JUSTICIARY sitting in Edinburgh. They are usually heard in chambers (his private office) rather than in court. The accused will not generally be present but will be represented by a solicitor and an advocate. The appeal procedure is relatively quick and inexpensive.

Release during or after trial

During a trial – or after the trial when, for example, a medical or social enquiry report is requested before sentence – the court may agree to an application by the accused or his legal representative for bail pending the final outcome.

A person who is appealing against conviction or sentence may apply to the High Court for bail. Legal aid may be granted for such an application.

Such bail is usually only granted in special circumstances – for example, where a very short custodial sentence is imposed.

BANK ACCOUNT, Joint

Sharing the management of money

Any two people can open a joint bank account, on which each may draw cheques. It is commonly used by married couples as a simple way of pooling their income and allowing either to pay household bills. But neither husband nor wife can insist on such an arrangement. Each is entitled by law to sole ownership of his or her property.

A joint account depends on mutual trust. In the case of business partners, for example, one could draw out large sums without the other's knowledge, and both would be equally liable to pay off any overdraft. Either party in any joint bank account can sue the other for any loss.

If a husband or wife dies or becomes bankrupt, or if the marriage ends in divorce or separation, a court will usually regard the balance of any joint account as held in equal shares, whatever the individual contributions might have been. However there may be evidence of a contrary intention – letters between the two people, or specific instructions to the bank – indicating how the account is to be shared.

WHEN MORE THAN ONE SIGNATORY IS NOT NEEDED

A joint bank account, which depends on mutual trust, is commonly used by married couples so that either can easily write cheques to pay the bills.

BANK LOAN

Borrowing money in the High Street

Ordinary High Street banks lend money to individual customers in three main ways: by overdraft, personal loan or bridging loan (for a property transaction).

Arranging an overdraft

A bank overdraft is an arrangement by which the customer is allowed to draw more money than he has in his current account – up to an agreed limit.

The bank manager may set a date by which the overdraft is to be cleared. But the bank is also entitled to call in the overdraft at any time, without notice.

If the overdraft is large, the bank may require some type of security – for example, the deposit of share certificates, or national savings or unit trust certificates.

Interest charged will be higher than for a personal loan, and an individual cannot normally claim overdraft interest as an expense against income tax. *See:* INCOME TAX

An overdraft, under the Consumer Credit Act, is running-account credit. Even when the loan limit has been reached, the customer by reducing his debt – for example, by paying in a salary cheque – can restore the state of his account and resume borrowing, up to the agreed limit.

A bank overdraft is normally arranged by word of mouth and does not require the special documents called for in other types of CONSUMER CREDIT agreement.

Since it is a debtor-creditor agreement, in which the lender has no business arrangement with any supplier, the bank is not liable for the quality of goods or services bought with the money borrowed.

However, an overdraft is still subject to some of the Consumer Credit Act rules for making and ending a credit agreement.

Going over the limit

If an overdraft limit set by the bank manager exceeds £5,000, the overdraft will not normally be covered by the Consumer Credit Act. However, if the overdraft was not expected to exceed £5,000 – or if it goes over that figure only temporarily – the arrangement is covered by the Act.

That situation could arise, for example, if you draw a cheque that takes you over the limit and the bank – to protect your reputation of being credit-worthy – decides to honour the cheque on condition that you take prompt steps to reduce your debt.

If you exceed the limit of an overdraft without permission, the bank is entitled to refuse to honour the cheque and also to suspend your overdraft without notice – although normally the bank manager will write or telephone, telling you of his action.

The bank is also entitled to demand full repayment of an overdraft loan, without notice, so long as the demand complies with the terms of the agreement – for example, if the time limit has run out.

As a last resort, the bank can sue for the money, but will be subject to the controls of the Consumer Credit Act.

Arranging a personal loan

Another way of borrowing from the bank is by personal loan – a fixed sum, borrowed over a fixed period and usually cleared by regular payments from a current account to cover the loan plus a proportion of the interest.

A personal loan is arranged with

more formality than an overdraft: you are normally required to sign an agreement. Unlike an overdraft, it cannot be suddenly called in at any time.

If the loan is taken out for certain purposes, the interest is tax-deductible.

When you can save tax Interest paid on a loan to an individual is tax-deductible if the loan is to be used to buy or improve property or land that is or will be your main residence, or occupied by a dependent relative (or a former or separated spouse), or let to someone else.

Tax relief can also be claimed if the loan is to buy a life annuity, pay capital transfer tax, acquire an interest in a partnership or buy plant or machinery to be used in a partnership or employment.

Provided that your personal loan does not exceed £5,000 you are protected by the Consumer Credit Act. *See:* CREDIT AGREEMENT

Arranging a bridging loan

If you are buying a house or other property and need to raise most of the price by a MORTGAGE, you may need to complete the deal before the mortgage lender is ready to hand over the money. In that case, you may raise a bridging loan, to avoid the risk of losing the property to someone else.

A bridging loan is usually provided by a bank – probably for 3 to 6 months – to tide you over the delay.

You may also need a bridging loan if you are buying a house and selling another and need to pay for the new house before the other one is sold.

Provided that a bridging loan does not exceed £5,000, it is covered by the protection of the Consumer Credit Act. For example, the sheriff court can be asked to grant relief if you are in difficulty in repaying.

Because of the need to avoid delay in many property transactions, however, there is no need for an unsigned advance copy of the loan agreement to be sent to you – as normally required for loans not exceeding £5,000 secured on property for purposes other than house purchase or improvement.

With a bridging loan, there is also no cooling-off period in which you may cancel the agreement. But the bank cannot suddenly call in a bridging loan, unless the borrower defaults.

The £5,000 limits mentioned above will increase to £15,000 on May 20, 1985. *See also:* INTEREST CHARGE

BANK REFERENCE

When a bank may give information about clients

Banks are generally obliged to keep details of their customers' accounts secret. But when a customer gives the name of his bank as a reference, he voluntarily lifts that condition of secrecy.

In giving a reference, the bank will not reveal the details of a customer's financial affairs, but it will make general comments – 'without responsibility'. This means that if you think you have been misled by a reference you may not be able to sue the bank for negligent misrepresentation. The law here is not very clear and until a court gives a definitive ruling the matter must remain in doubt.

If you are seeking a bank reference about someone, ask first for written permission to obtain it and for the name and address of the bank concerned. Then ask your own bank to secure the reference on your behalf: most banks will not provide references to individual inquirers.

The bank's reply may be informative, such as: 'respectable, and considered good for your figures'. It may be noncommittal: 'we believe he would not undertake any commitment he was unable to fulfil'. If the reply is: 'the sum quoted is larger than we are accustomed to see', or 'we cannot speak for your figures', be warned. *See also:* REFERENCE

BANKRUPTCY

What happens when debts cannot be paid

When someone – who may be in business – owes money to a number of creditors, he may not be able to pay them all at once. As a result the creditors may find themselves competing for a share of his assets.

The difficulties facing the debtor may be increased if he is being constantly pressed for payment by different people. Sometimes one creditor may be trying to get a share of some particular asset against which another creditor is taking enforcement proceedings. Taking such action does not necessarily benefit all the creditors and does nothing to help the debtor.

There are various ways of bringing about a bankruptcy, depending on the nature of the debtor's problem. Their purpose is to share the debtor's assets – money and property, including intangible property such as insurance policies – amongst his creditors on a fair basis and then to enable the debtor to be free of his former debts even if he has not paid them in full.

A bankruptcy can take the relatively informal form of some sort of agreement between the debtor and his creditors with a view to his assets being shared amongst them. Alternatively it can be a more formal procedure involving the courts. With a limited company only a formal procedure, called 'liquidation', is possible.

Informal bankruptcy

There are two ways in which a bankruptcy can take place without involving the courts:

1. The debtor may make an agreement with his creditors that they will accept only a part of what he owes them. In return they agree that he will then be free from his debts. This method, known as a 'composition contract', is cheap to administer. However it is little used because no independent third party is involved and it is therefore likely to be difficult to get all of the creditors to agree.

2. The debtor may hand over his assets to an independent third party to hold them in trust on behalf of all his creditors. The debtor signs a document called a trust deed, which is nearly always a standard form. *See:* TRUST

It will be necessary to look at the words of the form to know its exact effect. They will provide for a trustee to be appointed – normally an accountant or solicitor. They generally also provide for the assets to be transferred to him and for the debtor to co-operate in the transfer. In return the debtor will be free from the debts of those creditors willing to go along with the arrangement.

The amount of his debt that any one

creditor will get will depend on the rules for a formal bankruptcy involving the courts, since these rules are invariably included in the trust deed.

This method is efficient and relatively cheap (although the trustee has to be paid). But it depends for its effectiveness on enough creditors going along with it. Creditors who are not prepared to do so can bring about a formal bankruptcy involving the court. In case of this or any other difficulty, the trustee will be given power to apply to the court himself.

Debtors who are subject to these arrangements are usually banned from being company directors by their companies.

Formal bankruptcy

Bankruptcy involving a court is called 'sequestration'. The court which deals with this is normally the sheriff court for the area where the debtor lives or has his business.

An application for sequestration can be made in different ways:

- The debtor can apply on his own if his assets are worth £4,000 or less. The court has power to refuse the application but this rarely happens.
- The debtor can apply with the agreement of a creditor to whom he owes at least £200 or with the agreement of a number of creditors whose debts together add up to that amount. The court cannot refuse this kind of application.
- One or more creditors can apply without the debtor's agreement. The amount owed to the applicant(s) must be at least £200. Here too the court cannot refuse the application. The £200 limit is designed to stop some minor creditor forcing a bankruptcy on others who may not want it.

When can an application be made? If the debtor is involved in the application, it can be made at any time. If creditors apply on their own, one of them must have taken steps within the previous 4 months to recover his debt by using certain legal enforcement procedures – excluding ARRESTMENT – set out in the Bankruptcy (Scotland) Act 1913.

There are technical rules about how far each of the possible enforcement procedures must have gone. This requirement is most commonly satisfied when any creditor has obtained a court order requiring the debtor to pay within a specified time and no payment has been made.

When such steps have taken place the debtor is said to be 'notour bankrupt'. The idea behind this procedure is that a debtor should only be faced with bankruptcy against his will if a creditor has fairly recently tried to get him to pay.

Bankruptcy proceedings

An application involving the debtor results in an immediate award of sequestration. An application by creditors only results in a warrant being issued informing the debtor that he can appear at a hearing 14 days later. He can produce evidence at this hearing that the creditors are not owed anything. If he fails to do so, an award of sequestration is then made.

A meeting of the creditors is fixed to take place within 10 to 16 days to elect a trustee – normally an accountant – to administer the bankruptcy. The trustee's election is confirmed by the court within a week. It is possible for creditors to object to the person chosen but only rarely does a court heed the objection and reject that person.

What a trustee does The trustee must first find out what the debtor's assets are. He then takes these assets over, assesses the creditors' claims and pays them according to priorities laid down in the Bankruptcy (Scotland) Act 1913.

Finding out the debtor's assets The debtor is bound to reveal his assets; and within 15 to 29 days of the trustee's appointment being confirmed the debtor may be formally examined about his affairs. This examination takes place before the sheriff, usually in private.

The debtor may, for example, be asked how he ran his business (if he had one). He may also be asked why he became insolvent or whether he has recently disposed of any assets. If the debtor refuses to answer any relevant questions he can be imprisoned immediately by the sheriff.

If the debtor has given away some asset, the trustee can often get it back by raising an action against the person who holds it. The trustee must prove that at the time the asset was given away, the debtor had insufficient assets to pay all his creditors. This is easier to show if the asset was land or a house given to a close associate of the debtor: in such a case it is up to the recipient to show that the debtor did have adequate assets.

The trustee cannot challenge a reasonable transfer of assets to someone with a claim to be looked after by the debtor. Nor, in general, can he challenge where the debtor gets something adequate in return for the asset. This rule has been applied to money given to a fiancée to buy the marital home.

A debtor may have insufficient assets to pay all his creditors, but there is nothing to stop him paying one in full before the others. However he cannot allow that creditor an easier way of getting payment than originally agreed.

If, for example, the debtor gave one creditor his gold watch in lieu of payment, the trustee could get it back. If the transaction took place when the debtor was 'notour bankrupt', it is up to the recipient to show that there were sufficient assets. That is also so if the transaction took place within the 6 months before the debtor became 'notour bankrupt.'

Taking over the assets The trustee automatically becomes the legal owner of most assets on confirmation of his appointment by the court.

He is then looked on as having been the owner from the first step in the procedure. This stops creditors carrying out enforcement procedures for their own benefit.

The trustee becomes legal owner of land and houses when he records his confirmation by the court in the Register of Inhibitions and Adjudications (a public register).

If the debtor continues to earn, a proportion of his wages normally goes automatically to the trustee.

An asset may look like the debtor's but actually belong to someone else. This would include not only something borrowed or hired by the debtor but also anything which a person can show was held in TRUST for him by the debtor. Thus the clients of a bankrupt solicitor can take the money held by him in accounts in their name.

It is not safe to assume that any deposit which you have paid will be found to be held in trust for you. The safest thing to do is to keep the money on deposit receipt in a bank.

The Newspaper Publishers' Association runs a voluntary scheme to reimburse readers for deposits lost through answering mail order advertisements placed by insolvent traders.

Assessing the creditors' claims The creditors must produce sufficient evidence to show that they have a genuine claim. Unpaid invoices would be sufficient for an ordinary debt; a written undertaking would be sufficient for a loan. A creditor whose claim is rejected by the trustee can appeal to the court.

The trustee can make a payment after 4 months but he is not bound to do so until 6 months have elapsed. The normal timetable for payment may be shortened if a sufficient number of creditors are prepared to accept only a stated proportion of their debt, or some other specially devised arrangement. For this to become binding on all the creditors, at least half of them with debts amounting in total to three quarters of all that is owed must agree. The court must also give its approval.

Paying the creditors Some creditors may have safeguarded themselves against a possible bankruptcy by obtaining some security from the debtor as part of their original deal with him. For example, the creditor may be a building society with a security over the debtor's house.

A creditor in this position can sell the thing over which he has security and is only entitled to payment from the trustee if the sale does not cover his debt.

People who are owed money by the bankrupt and who in turn owe him some, can hold on to what they owe in so far as it covers what is owed to them.

Creditors are paid on the basis of priorities, and fall into different groups for this purpose. All of those in a group must be paid in full before those in the next group down get anything at all.

If there is not enough to pay every member of the group in full, then each gets part payment in proportion to the size of their claim. These part payments are called dividends and are expressed as so many pence in the pound.

For example, if the dividend is 10p in the pound, a creditor owed £100 will get £10 and a creditor owed £1,000 will get £100. Even if there is eventually enough to pay all the members of the group in full, they will usually be paid by instalments on this dividend basis.

The groups (disregarding some very uncommon classes of creditor) are given priority over each other as follows:

First The trustee must be paid for his administration costs, and any creditor involved in the application for his costs arising from the application.

Second The appropriate authorities are entitled to up to one year's unpaid taxes, rates and social security contributions. Employees are entitled to unpaid wages. *See:* PAY

Third 'Ordinary creditors'. This includes everyone else except those in the fourth group (below). Also included are creditors in the second group in so far as they are owed more than they have been given priority for – for example, the Inland Revenue if they are owed more than one year's taxes.

Fourth 'Postponed creditors'. The only significant member of this group would be the bankrupt's wife who claims that some of her money was mixed in with his assets.

If everyone is paid in full, the bankrupt can keep the surplus.

WHAT IT MEANS TO BE BANKRUPT

A bankrupt may be permitted by the trustee to continue in business for the benefit of the creditors, but this is difficult. It is an offence for him to obtain credit of more than £50 without revealing that he is a bankrupt. Most companies ban a bankrupt from being a director; and even if he escapes such a ban he still needs the court's permission.

A bankrupt cannot hold certain public positions – for instance, he cannot be a local councillor or MP.

Ceasing to be bankrupt

A bankrupt can get a discharge at any time if all his creditors have been paid in full. He can also get a discharge if the normal course of the sequestration has been ended by a creditors' agreement to accept only part of their debts, or by some other special arrangement.

Alternatively the debtor can apply to the court for a discharge. Until 2 years have passed this requires the agreement of a specified number of creditors. If all the creditors have been paid one quarter of what was due, the court will normally discharge the bankrupt.

The court can also discharge the bankrupt, even though the creditors have received less than this amount, when satisfied that the bankrupt was an innocent victim of events rather than actively responsible for his own failure.

BATTERED WOMAN

Getting protection against violence in the home

A woman can call in the police if she is assaulted by her husband or the man she lives with. The police will arrest him if they think there is enough evidence for a prosecution. The woman can act as a witness.

Apart from calling in the police, a woman who is assaulted can try to protect herself by applying to court for an INTERDICT ordering the man not to assault or molest her, or an order excluding him from the home entirely even if he is the owner or tenant.

If the man defies an interdict or exclusion order he may be arrested. He may also face proceedings for CONTEMPT OF COURT.

If the home is rented by the man, or jointly, the woman can ask the court to transfer it into her name alone. *See:* MATRIMONIAL PROPERTY

Obtaining accommodation

Housing authorities must provide permanent accommodation for women with dependent children if satisfied that they were forced to leave home through fear of violence. Temporary accommodation will usually be provided while the case is being investigated.

The Scottish Office has urged housing authorities to give similar help to women without children. *See:* HOMELESSNESS

Temporary shelter may also be available in a refuge for battered women. Refuges, which also offer information and advice, are run by voluntary organisations such as Women's Aid. Your housing or social work department, the police or local CITIZENS' ADVICE BUREAU can help you get in touch with a refuge. Their addresses are kept secret but their telephone numbers should be in the phone book.

Before providing permanent accommodation, housing authorities usually require evidence of separation. *See:* ALIMENT; CRIMINAL INJURIES COMPENSATION; OCCUPANCY RIGHTS

BEACHCOMBING

Who owns the pebbles on the beach?

Your right to keep something you find at the seaside depends on whether or not it is likely to be – or have been – the property of someone else.

If you are sure the object has never belonged to anyone else, you can keep it as your own. For this reason you can take most kinds of fish and shellfish from the sea and foreshore (but not from fixed nets) whether they are alive or already dead. You can also keep attractive pebbles or seaweed. Sand belongs to the owner of the beach or FORESHORE on which it is found and cannot usually be removed.

If the object once belonged to someone else, it still belongs to that person unless – as with for example buried TREASURE TROVE – it has been abandoned. Abandoned property belongs to the Crown. You are not obliged to pick up objects of this class, but if you do you must treat them as LOST PROPERTY and deliver them to the police, otherwise you may be guilty of theft. Special rules apply for wrecks, and cargo washed ashore from wrecks. If you come across either of these, you must report this to the local Receiver of Wrecks.

BETTING

How the law controls the lucrative business of betting and gambling

All public betting is strictly controlled by law. *See:* GAMBLING

BETTING TAX

When the Government takes part of your winnings

Her Majesty's Customs and Excise levies duty on all forms of commercially operated GAMBLING, except a LOTTERY.

The tax is payable by the people or organisations taking the bets – that is, bookmakers, casinos, bingo clubs or pools companies. They may or may not attempt to recover their duty liability by deducting a percentage from individual gambler's winnings.

Bookmakers and the Tote

The duty payable on bets laid at the racecourse (when both bookmaker and client are present) is 4 per cent – 4p in the £. Off-course, bets are taxed at the rate of 8p in the £. Both on-course bookmakers and the Tote deduct the whole amount from the client's winnings.

In addition, off-course bookmakers deduct the horserace betting levy of about 0.5p to 1p in the £, plus a small charge for running costs. The off-course customer, therefore, usually loses a total of 9p in the £ on his winnings.

Betting-shop and off-course gamblers often have a choice of paying the tax only on their stake before the race is run. If they win, they pay no further tax.

This is called betting 'tax-on' and can make a substantial difference to winnings. For example, a winning bet of £1 at odds of 10 to 1 would normally make the gambler liable for tax of 8 per cent of £11 – 88p. If he bets 'tax-on', he is liable only for 8 per cent of £1 – 8p.

Gaming clubs

Individual gamblers in a gaming club pay no betting tax.

Any club or casino that has a licence to run games of unequal chance must pay a gaming licence duty. This comprises an initial payment of £250 and a second payment based on gross gaming yield – that is, a percentage of the value of stakes less players' winnings.

Private members' clubs, bridge and whist clubs and clubs running equal chance games, without a banker, are exempt.

Bingo

Bingo duty is not payable on games played as an activity of a club provided that:

- The annual subscription is not more than £3.
- The admission charge is not more than 15p.
- No other payment is required and no deduction is made from stakes (e.g. for club funds).

Bingo promoted otherwise than for private gain, and small-scale bingo in amusement arcades, can qualify for exemption on certain conditions.

All other bingo is liable to duty at 10% and additional duty may be due if the promoter subsidises prize money. The duty may be passed directly to players by deducting it from the total stake before the prizes are paid. *See:* BINGO CLUB

Pool betting

The duty on POOL BETS – for example a football pool – is normally 42½ per cent, deducted by the promoters from the stake money before it is redistributed as winnings. The client pays nothing.

In the case of charity pools, the amount that actually goes to the charity – usually less than 10 per cent of the total stake – is exempt from betting tax. Seven charity pools, registered before the 1971 Pools Competitions Act, pay tax of only 33⅓ per cent.

Gaming machines

Gaming machines, other than penny machines provided at travelling pleasure fairs, are subject to a licence duty. The amount per machine depends on the cost to play it and the type of premises. The players pay nothing directly.

BIGAMY

When the law forbids more than one spouse

A person who marries while knowingly married to someone else commits the crime of bigamy. The bigamous second 'marriage' is void.

The children of such a 'marriage' are illegitimate only if both parties knew it was bigamous.

Even if only one of the partners believed the 'marriage' was valid, the children are legitimate.

When the facts are known

If both partners in a bigamous 'marriage' are already married, both are guilty of bigamy. If only one is married and the other does not know this, only the first is guilty. But if the unmarried partner knows of the bigamy he or she can be prosecuted for aiding and abetting the bigamist in the crime.

Similarly, any other person – for example, celebrant or witness – who knowingly takes part in a bigamous marriage ceremony is art and part guilty of bigamy. *See:* AIDING AND ABETTING

The legal wife or husband may be called to give prosecution evidence in a bigamy case, even without the consent of the other spouse.

Possible defences It is a defence to a bigamy charge that the legal spouse was absent for 7 years continuously before the second 'marriage', so long as the accused proves that there was no reason to believe he or she was alive. It is also a defence that the first marriage has been dissolved.

Maximum penalty In practice, bigamy prosecutions are rare. The penalty is at the discretion of the court, subject to the maximum sentencing power of the court in which the prosecution is brought. *See:* CRIMINAL PROCEEDINGS

BILL-POSTING

When permission is needed to advertise

Advertisements cannot be displayed on the outside of a building anywhere without the consent of the local authority which is responsible for planning control in the particular area. *See:* LOCAL AUTHORITY. A fee is payable to the planning authority when an application is made for consent.

Anyone who puts up a poster or other advertisement without consent can be ordered to take it down and may be prosecuted.

There are, however, certain exceptions. These include:

- Election notices.
- Notices advertising property for sale or to let.
- Advertisements appropriate to business premises on which they are displayed.
- Advertisements on hoardings that have existed since 1948.

It is a criminal offence to post an advertisement on someone else's property without his permission. This applies to posters stuck on fences, walls and even lamp-posts.

A planning authority can refuse an application to display an advertisement only on the grounds that it would injure the amenities of the area or would be a threat to public safety. It could, for example, decide that an advertisement showing a girl in a bikini could be a danger to motorists at a road junction.

An applicant can appeal against refusal to the Secretary of State for Scotland. He will usually decide the appeal on the basis of letters from the applicant and the planning authority, but he has the power to call a public inquiry.

BINGO CLUB

Playing the modern version of housey-housey

Bingo is a game played for money or – in the case of prize bingo – for goods. It is generally played for money in the commercial clubs, where the total stake from the participants is redistributed as winnings. The players have no enforceable legal contract with the promoter. Neither side can sue in a dispute.

Unlike with other pool systems, however, the proprietor of a commercial bingo club cannot deduct his profits or running costs from the stake money. All he can deduct is the bingo duty that he has to pass on to Customs and Excise. *See:* BETTING TAX

A bingo club derives its income in two ways: from an admission fee – usually about 20p per session – and a participation fee – from 5p a game to about £1 for a two-hour session. The players pay these amounts in addition to their stake money for each game. Games of bingo must not start before 2 p.m. on weekdays or 7 p.m. on Sundays, and must be ended by 11 p.m. On Saturdays, or on New Year's Eve, games are allowed to continue until midnight.

Players' rights

No one can play bingo in a commercial club until he has been a member of it, or one of its branches, for at least 24 hours. People under 18 can watch but not play.

The club needs the consent of the Gaming Board and a licence from the local licensing board before it can start operating. Anyone with good reason to object to the club can write to the Board to oppose the granting or renewal of the licence. An application for renewal must be made annually and it must be advertised in the local press.

Limits on winnings

There is no limit on the prize money in normal bingo, except that the club itself cannot donate more than £1,000 towards it in any one week.

In 'linked' bingo – when a game is played simultaneously by landline in several clubs in the same area – there is a weekly limit of £2,000 in the total prize money.

Prize bingo

Because the winnings are in the form of household goods, for example, or food and drinks, prize bingo is regarded as an amusement rather than serious gaming.

It may be operated on premises open to the public, like a fairground, with a permit from the local authority, and the promoter can keep as much of the stake money as he wants.

BIRDS

Wild birds are stringently protected by law

In general, it is an offence to deliberately kill, injure or take any wild bird, take or damage its nest or take or destroy even one of its eggs. It is also generally an offence to be in possession of any such bird or egg – whether it is dead or alive. The penalty is a fine of up to £400 for each bird, nest or egg.

However, at certain times of the year, or under certain conditions, some species are not protected in this way.

How birds are classified

Except on Sundays and Christmas Day, the following species can be killed, and their nests or eggs taken or destroyed, but only by a landowner or someone acting for him, or by a person authorised by the local authority, certain fishing bodies or the Nature Conservancy Council. Certain methods of killing are outlawed – for example, using poison, pole traps or bird lime – and a fine of up to £2,000 can be imposed.

Collared dove	House sparrow
Crow	Jackdaw
*Domestic pigeon turned wild	Jay
Gull (great and lesser black-backed and herring)	Magpie
	Rook
	Starling
	*Woodpigeon

*Dead pigeons can be sold at any time

All other wild birds, except GAME birds, are protected throughout the year as stated in the first paragraph. Some receive special protection: it is a particularly serious offence to kill or interfere with the following species, their eggs or their nests. The penalty is a fine of up to £2,000 for each bird, nest or egg.

Avocet	Long-tailed duck
Bee-eater	Merlin
Bittern and little bittern	Osprey
Black redstart	Owl (barn and snowy)
Black-tailed godwit	Peregrine
Black-winged stilt	*Pintail
Bluethroat	Plover (Kentish and little ringed)
Brambling	Purple heron
Bunting (cirl, Lapland and snow)	Red kite
Chough	Red-backed shrike
Common quail	Red-necked phalarope
Corncrake	Redwing
Crossbills (all species)	Ruff
Divers (all species)	Sandpiper (green, purple and wood)
Dotterel	Scarlet rosefinch
Eagle (golden and white tailed)	Scaup
Fieldfare	Scoter (common and velvet)
Firecrest	Serin
Garganey	Shorelark
*Goldeneye	Short-toed treecreeper
Golden oriole	Spoonbill
Goshawk	Spotted crake
Grebe (black-necked and Slavonian)	Stone curlew
*Greylag goose (in Outer Hebrides, Caithness, Sutherland and Wester Ross)	Swan (Bewick's and Whooper)
Greenshank	Temminck's stint
Gull (little and Mediterranean)	Tern (black, little and roseate)
Gyr falcon	Tit (bearded and crested)
Harriers (all species)	Warbler (Cetti's, Dartford, Marsh and Savi's)
Hobby	Whimbrel
Honey buzzard	Woodlark
Hoopoe	Wryneck
Kingfisher	
Leach's petrel	

*Specially protected during close season only

However it is not an offence to kill, injure or take some protected species outside their close season (see diagram), unless the Secretary of State has imposed a ban – which he may do during bad weather.

Exceptions

It is not an offence to kill any seriously disabled wild bird for humane reasons, nor to keep and care for it until it is well, so long as the person concerned did not inflict the injury unlawfully.

Certain authorised persons – for example, landowners – can kill any birds, except those specially protected, in order to prevent damage to crops or property, the spread of disease or danger to the public (for example, at airports).

Wild birds' eggs

It is an offence to sell, or offer for sale, the eggs of a wild bird except under the terms of an official licence. The penalty is a fine of up to £400, or £2,000 if the bird is specially protected.

WHEN PROTECTED BIRDS MAY LEGALLY BE KILLED IN SCOTLAND

Some species can be lawfully shot outside their close season

Aug 12–Jan 31	Sept 1–Jan 31	Sept 1–Jan 31 (Sept 1–Feb 20 at sea or on the foreshore)	Oct 1–Jan 31
Common snipe	Coot	Gadwall	Capercaillie
	Golden plover	Goldeneye	
	Moorhen	*Goose, Canada, greylag and pink-footed	
	Woodcock	Mallard	
		Pintail	
		Pochard	
		Shoveler	
		Teal	
		Tufted duck	
		Wigeon	

*All these birds, except geese, can be sold dead from Sept 1 to Feb 28.

BIRTH CERTIFICATE

Proof of identity that is always needed

A birth certificate has to be produced whenever you are required to prove your age or place of birth – for example, to get a passport or claim a pension.

There are two kinds: short and full. The short one records only the name of the child, the date of birth, the sex and the place of birth. The full certificate also records details of the father and mother of the child, including the date and place of their marriage. So if a child is illegitimate this may be evident because the father's name is likely to be absent.

If you have lost your birth certificate, you can get a replacement from the registrar of the district where you were born. When applying, give your full name (maiden surname if you are a married woman), date and place of birth and your mother's maiden surname. Alternatively you can get the certificates from the General Register Office in Edinburgh.

At the time of registration a short certificate is supplied free. A full certificate is available then and for the next month at £2. Thereafter it costs £5. *See also:* BIRTH REGISTRATION

BIRTH REGISTRATION

Your duty to record the birth of a child

Every child born in Scotland must be registered, normally by a parent, with the registrar of births, deaths and marriages for the district in which the child was born, or in which the mother usually resides if that is in Scotland.

The registrar records the place, date and hour of birth, name and sex of the child, the full name and occupation of the father, the full name, maiden name and usual place of residence of the mother and the date and place of their marriage. He gives the parents, free of charge, a short certificate of the registration, omitting details about the parents. Full certificates can be obtained

TWO KINDS OF BIRTH CERTIFICATE

The circumstances in which the names of a child's parents need not be shown

The shortened form of birth certificate, which does not disclose whether a child is illegitimate or adopted, is sufficient for virtually all later purposes, like obtaining a passport or joining a pension fund – any instance where proof of identity has to be provided. Either sort can be obtained from the register office where the birth was originally recorded or from the General Register Office in Edinburgh.

Abbreviated CERTIFICATE of BIRTH AB 000010

Registration of Births, Deaths and Marriages (Scotland) Act 1965, Ss. 19 and 40

District No. 550	Year 1980	Entry No. 62	N.H.S. No. 5 5 0 8 0 0 6 2

Birth registered in the district of Isle of Bute

1. Surname MacDonald
   Name(s) Ailsa
2. Sex F
3. When born 1980 February Third 0715 hours.
4. Where born 13 Harbour Street Rothesay

certify that the above particulars are extracted from a Register of Births in my

der my hand this ... Third ... day of February ... 19 80

... A. B. Smart ... Registrar

District of ... Isle of Bute ...

particulars incorporate any subsequent corrections or amendments to the original entry made uthority of the Registrar General.

ffence under section 53(3) of the Registration of Births, Deaths and Marriages (Scotland) Act ny person to pass as genuine any copy or reproduction of this certificate which has not been district registrar or assistant registrar and authenticated by his signature.

n who falsifies or forges any of the particulars on this certificate or knowingly uses, gives or nuine any false or forged certificate is liable to prosecution under section 53(1) of the said Act.

XB3R

Extract of an entry in a REGISTER of BIRTHS BE 000010

Registration of Births, Deaths and Marriages (Scotland) Act 1965

District No. 550	Year 1980	Entry No. 62	N.H.S. No. 5 5 0 8 0 0 6 2

Birth registered in the district of Isle of Bute

1. Surname MacDonald
   Name(s) Ailsa
2. Sex F
3. When born 19 80 February Third 0715 hours
4. Where born 13 Harbour Street Rothesay
5. Mother's name(s) and surname Mary Ann MacDonald
6. Maiden surname Robertson
7. Mother's usual residence (if different from 4 above) —
8. Father's name(s) and surname Angus Stuart MacDonald
9. Occupation Private, The King's Own Scottish Borderers
10. Date and place of parents' marriage: Year 19 68 Month 4 Day 1 Place Helmstadt, West Germany
11. Informant's signature and qualification (Signed) Angus S. MacDonald Father
12. When registered: Year 19 80 Month 2 Day 3
13. (Signed) A. B. Smart Registrar
14.

Extracted from the Register of Births for the District of Isle of Bute.

on Third February 1980

A. B. Smart. Registrar

The above particulars incorporate any subsequent corrections or amendments to the original entry made with the authority of the Registrar General.

Warning

It is an offence under section 53(3) of the Registration of Births, Deaths and Marriages (Scotland) Act 1965 for any person to pass as genuine any copy or reproduction of this extract which has not been made by a district registrar or assistant registrar and authenticated by his signature.

Any person who falsifies or forges any of the particulars on this extract or knowingly uses, gives or sends as genuine any false or forged extract is liable to prosecution under section 53(1) of the said Act

XB4(R)

The short birth certificate, which is supplied free when a baby's birth is registered, gives no details about the parents. The fuller standard certificate always gives the mother's name and usually the father's, unless the child is illegitimate

Either the mother or father of a legitimate child can register the birth. If they are unable to do so a close relative, or the occupier of the house where the child was born – or a person present at the birth or whoever is in charge of the child – should register it for a fee. *See:* BIRTH CERTIFICATE

Still-births Any child born after the 28th week of pregnancy must be registered, even if there is no sign of life after birth. A still-birth is recorded in a separate register, and no certificate is given.

Illegitimate children The mother must register the birth of an illegitimate child: the father alone cannot. The father's name can only be recorded if:

- both parents sign the register, or
- a statutory declaration acknowledging paternity, signed by the father before a J.P. or notary public, is produced; and the mother signs a declaration naming him as the father.

If the father's name is not recorded in the original registration, it can be added if he signs a declaration within 12 months of the birth, and also in certain other circumstances. *See:* ILLEGITIMATE CHILD

Time limit All the details about the child and the parents must be given to the registrar, by the father or the mother in person, within 21 days of the child's birth.

If both parents (or the mother of an illegitimate child) are dead, or unable to register the child, a close relative should do so. Failing that, the occupier of the house in which the child was born, or anyone who was present at the birth, for instance a relative, doctor, nurse or midwife, or the person in charge of the child, can register the birth. If necessary the registrar is empowered to summon people to his office to provide relevant information.

Details of the child's birth are sent by the registrar to the area Health Board.

Inspection If you wish to inquire into someone's birth and parentage, all records are kept at the General Register Office in Edinburgh. The records are indexed and the index can be searched for a fee. The indexes of registrations in all local registrars' offices are also open to inspection for any period covering five years at a fee of £1.60.

BLASPHEMY

Legal protection for Christianity

At one time it was an offence in Scotland to publish writings which vilified the Christian religion and brought it into ridicule and contempt. The last reported prosecution for blasphemy in Scotland was 1843. It is very unlikely that any such prosecution would now be brought and it may even be the case that the crime of blasphemy no longer exists in Scots law.

However, conduct which previously may have been charged as blasphemy will almost always give rise to some other criminal charge. A blasphemous publication expressed in indecent terms may be prosecuted as an indecent publication, and a blasphemous statement made in circumstances likely to cause a BREACH OF THE PEACE may be prosecuted as a breach of the peace.

BLINDNESS

Help that is available for people with defective sight

Someone who is wholly or partly blind may be entitled to a wide range of benefits and services. To qualify for them, he must register as blind or partially sighted.

The first step is to ask the family doctor to arrange an outpatient appointment with an ophthalmologist under the National Health Service or contact the office of the local social work department to arrange an appointment for a medical examination. That examination can be carried out by an ophthalmic surgeon in the applicant's home or at a hospital or clinic.

If the doctor is satisfied that the person is technically blind – so blind as to be unable to do work for which eyesight is essential – or seriously and permanently handicapped by defective vision, he completes a confidential document recommending registration (form BP1) and sends it to the social work department.

Once the doctor's recommendation arrives, the council arranges for a social worker to visit the blind person and explain the benefits of registration – from direct financial help to opportunities for training in new skills.

What financial help is available

Direct financial help is provided for people registered as technically blind but not for the partly sighted. The assistance includes:

Income tax An extra personal allowance (£360 in 1984–5) can be claimed.

Supplementary benefit A blind person already eligible for SUPPLEMENTARY BENEFIT is entitled to an additional £1.25 per week to meet his special needs. A partially sighted person will also be entitled to this, if unable to do any work for which eyesight is essential. If 18 or over and a non-householder, he gets the full householder rate of benefit.

Attendance allowance A blind person may be entitled to an ATTENDANCE ALLOWANCE. If an application is rejected, the Royal National Institute for the Blind may help an applicant with an appeal against the decision.

Cash help Local and national voluntary organisations may also provide small weekly pensions or make grants for specific purposes.

Applications to such organisations are normally made on behalf of blind people by council social workers, but a voluntary worker or a relative can apply.

What other help is available

Blind and partially sighted people are eligible for special services and facilities provided by local authorities and by state and voluntary organisations.

Travel Registered blind people are often entitled to free bus travel, although the concession may apply only outside peak hours.

Blind people can also get free concessions for business travel on the railways and on a number of domestic airline routes.

White sticks Local authorities issue white walking sticks to the technically blind and to partially sighted people whose sight is likely to get worse. The stick has no legal significance but it is universally recognised as a warning symbol.

Sticks – for which the recipient may have to pay a small charge – can also be obtained from the Royal National Institute for the Blind and other voluntary societies.

Holidays Local authorities may arrange holidays – free of charge or partly subsidised – for blind and partially sighted people. Voluntary societies may also make such arrangements.

Housing Both councils and voluntary organisations provide housing for many blind people who are also elderly and/or infirm. In many cases, special facilities are needed for the blind residents. Inquiries about special housing arrangements should be made to the local authority housing department.

Postage Articles for the blind – up to 7 kg – are carried post free in the mail. Special labels are sometimes supplied by blind people's organisations but it is enough to mark a package or letter 'Blind Material'.

Radio VHF radio sets are issued – and maintained – free to registered blind people by the British Wireless for the Blind Fund.

Television Any registered blind person is entitled to a slight reduction in the price of the broadcasting licence. At present it amounts to £1.25 for both colour and monochrome. The concession is obtained by producing evidence of registration when renewing the licence.

Guide dogs A small number of blind people – mainly young and active – are supplied with guide dogs. There is no charge but a voluntary donation is expected. Most such dogs are provided by the Guide Dogs for the Blind Society, which trains the dogs. Their owners may contribute to feeding and veterinary expenses. No licence is needed for a dog supplied by the society.

The dog becomes the property of the blind person, but the society reserves the right to buy it back if it ceases to work properly or if there is maltreatment.

PEOPLE BLINDED IN WAR

People whose sight was damaged or destroyed on war service can get special help from St Dunstan's.

That help covers not only members of the armed forces and merchant seamen but also civil defence workers such as air raid wardens and auxiliary firemen. Troops and civilian workers – for example, policemen and firemen – serving in the Northern Ireland emergency are similarly covered.

St Dunstan's provides rehabilitation and training and advises on possible pension claims. For example, a man receiving a small pension for war-service damage to one eye can apply for full pension if the sight of his other eye deteriorates later in life, even though the deterioration is not caused by war service.

Aftercare visits to the blind person's home are made about once a year so that the dog's abilities can be assessed. When a guide dog is nearing the end of its working life, probably at about 8 years of age, the blind person may be given a new young dog. The old dog is not generally taken away.

A guide dog with its owner is usually allowed in public places even where an ordinary dog is not. However, it may be prohibited in – for example – a food shop or restaurant, or where there is an escalator on which dogs must be carried to avoid risk of being injured.

Education and training

Local authorities have the same duty to educate children with defective sight as they have for other children. They provide specially trained teachers and special teaching facilities for registered blind children – starting before the normal school age of 5 and continuing beyond the minimum leaving age of 16.

Some partially sighted children do better if they can attend an ordinary school, helped by special facilities. Others benefit more at a special school among other children who have sight problems. Parents have the right to be consulted as to which sort of school they think is best for their child's future.

School leavers For children who do not seek higher education, special guidance and assessment centres can advise on choice of skills in which they can be trained.

Courses are available, for example, in light engineering, shorthand and typing, telephone work, physiotherapy and piano-tuning.

Adults Someone who is born with normal sight, but who loses it through accident or illness, can be helped by a social worker to choose the right training for a new livelihood. Courses can be taken at home or in residential units.

It may be possible to train the person to continue in his previous job – particularly with office or professional work. If that is not possible, contact the disablement resettlement officer at the local Department of Employment to arrange employment or training.

Books and tape recordings for the blind

Books printed in the Braille and Moon blind-reading systems are provided by most councils, which also arrange to teach blind people to read by those systems.

Local councils also normally arrange for blind people in their area to become members of the National Library for the Blind – based in London and Manchester – which has a wide range of books, fiction and non-fiction. The Scottish Braille Press, Craigmillar Park, Edinburgh, publishes paperback books in Braille.

Tape-recorded books and playback machines can be obtained from the British Talking Book Service, with the rental fee paid by the local authority.

Weekly papers, monthly magazines and sheet music in Braille are available from the Royal National Institute for the Blind.

All Braille publications are carried free of charge in the post.

For partially sighted people, books in specially large print are on loan from local libraries.

BLOOD TEST

Medical evidence in paternity and other disputes

A man's blood can show whether he might be the father of a child whose paternity is in dispute, if it is studied along with samples of the mother's and child's blood. Such a blood test can never establish that he is definitely the father, but it can prove that he is not.

Blood tests may be asked for in actions of AFFILIATION AND ALIMENT and in actions involving ADULTERY, rights of inheritance and claims to titles. The parties do not have to supply blood samples if they do not want to. The courts will not draw any adverse inference from a refusal to submit to a blood test. *See:* DRINK AND DRIVING

BORROWING

Neighbourly rights and obligations

Borrowing and lending, even on the most friendly basis, involve legal rights and obligations. If, for example, someone borrows a lawnmower and it breaks down because he does not take proper care while using it, he is obliged to pay for the repairs. And if he is asked to return the machine and fails to do so, he is held liable if anything happens to it later, unless he can show that he was not to blame.

If someone lends his property and it is not returned, he can sue the borrower for its return.

BOUNDARIES, WALLS AND FENCES

Settling disputes with your neighbours

Boundaries can be the source of various disputes. Neighbours may quarrel over which of them owns the hedge separating their properties, over whose duty it is to repair a wall, or whether a new fence erected by one of them encroaches on the other's land.

In many cases there is simply no way of arriving at a clear answer. If there is an answer, it will usually be contained in the title deeds of the property. If there is a MORTGAGE on the property, the title deeds are kept by the building society or other lender. The solicitor who acted in the purchase often has a note of what the deeds contain, and, if necessary, he can also arrange to borrow the deeds for a period.

Finding the boundary

The title deeds often contain a written description of the boundaries. There are special rules for interpreting this description: for example, if your house is said to be 'bounded by' a wall, this means that your property stops just before the wall. If the description is in an old deed it is sometimes impossible to identify the boundaries because the landmarks referred to no longer exist.

The title deeds sometimes contain a plan, and this is usual for new houses. Under the new system of REGISTRATION OF TITLE all properties will be plotted on an Ordnance Survey map. Even if there is a plan, it may not make the boundary clear: it may not be drawn to scale or may be too small in scale.

If there is both a plan *and* a written description, and they disagree with each other, the written description is usually taken as correct.

Quite frequently, though, the title deeds do not give the information you need, and in that case you probably own the area that has actually been 'possessed' by you and your predecessors as owners over the past ten years.

You may also want to know whether you own any fence or wall that runs round your boundaries, or whether you and your neighbour have CO-OWNERSHIP. Again, if the title deeds are not helpful it may well be impossible to find out the answer.

Repairing the boundary

The local authority has power to require you to carry out repairs to boundary walls and fences attached to your house. In practice, the authority will usually choose not to exercise this power and you are free to neglect the walls and fences as you wish. Even if part of your wall collapses, your neighbour cannot force you to rebuild it but can only sue you for any damage he might have sustained.

SEARCHING THE TITLE DEEDS

The best hope for sorting out problems about boundaries is often to study the title deeds of the property.

There are, however, two situations where you must repair walls and fences. One is where your title deeds contain a provision requiring you to do so. The other is where you share ownership of the walls or fences with a neighbour and he insists on carrying out necessary repairs.

There are special rules about boundaries in flats. *See:* FLAT

BREACH OF PROMISE

Breaking off an engagement

A couple who get engaged to marry enter into an agreement that is legally binding. If one of them breaks off the engagement without the agreement of the other – that is, commits what is known as breach of promise – he or she can be sued for DAMAGES.

Damages are not restricted to any financial loss sustained – for example, the cost of a reception or wedding invitations. Compensation can also be awarded for hurt feelings.

A person whose engagement is broken off has a right to recover whatever he or she has contributed to property acquired for the marriage. This contribution can be tangible – for example, a washing machine – or can be the value of any work done. For example, if a woman decorates some rooms of the house which her fiancé has bought as the future matrimonial home, and the engagement is then broken off, she can claim for the proportion of the property's value represented by her work.

Breach of promise actions are extremely rare and in 1984 a Bill was before Parliament to abolish them. *See:* ENGAGEMENT

BREACH OF THE PEACE

Enforcing public order

There is no precise definition of what constitutes a breach of the peace. The typical breach of the peace is the creation of a public disturbance, such as shouting and bawling in public or putting people in a state of alarm by disorderly behaviour.

But the offence is wider than this, and the police can arrest not only someone who is actually causing a breach of the peace but also anyone whose behaviour they consider likely to provoke a breach. For example, it is an offence to use abusive or insulting words if these are considered likely to lead to a breach of the peace.

The High Court has said that there is no limit to the kind of conduct which may give rise to a charge of breach of the peace, providing the conduct in question actually creates a disturbance or gives rise to a belief that a disturbance will occur.

The offence is so wide that a man who made indecent remarks in private to two women, neither of whom was alarmed or annoyed and only one of whom was 'embarrassed', was convicted of a breach of the peace. The same happened to another man who refused to 'move on' when requested to do so by the police.

The charge can be used against demonstrators who may have had no intention of causing a breach of the peace.
See: PUBLIC ORDER

BREAKDOWN OF MARRIAGE

The only ground for divorce

Since 1977, irretrievable breakdown of marriage has been the only ground on which the courts in Scotland may grant a decree of DIVORCE or a judicial SEPARATION.

For the breakdown to qualify as irretrievable, the person asking for the decree must prove one of five facts:

- ADULTERY
- Behaviour which makes it unreasonable to expect him or her to go on with the marriage.
- DESERTION by the other spouse for at least 2 years.
- That for at least 2 years immediately before the action is raised the couple have not lived together as man and wife. Both partners must consent to the divorce.
- That for at least 5 years the couple have not lived together as man and wife (in which case no consent is required).

BREATH TEST

Police powers to arrest a motorist

When the police stop a driver because they believe he has committed some moving traffic offence, or he has been involved in an accident, or they have reason to believe that he has alcohol in his body, they have the right to ask him to take a breath test – at the roadside, if necessary.

If the crystals in one type of testing device turn green, or the lights in another type change colour, the motorist must accompany the police to a police station.

At the police station

There, the police use a special breath-test machine which gives an instant reading. An offence has been committed if the reading exceeds 35 microgrammes of alcohol per 100 millilitres of breath.

If the reading is between 35 and 50 microgrammes, the motorist may insist upon a blood or urine test at the police station.

A motorist who refuses the breath test can be arrested and may be prosecuted for refusing.
See: DRINK AND DRIVING

BRIBERY

When a kindness can be corrupt

Bribery is offering a gift or favour to a public employee in an attempt to influence him in carrying out his public duties. The person receiving the bribe is also guilty of the offence, even if he does nothing to earn it.
See: CORRUPT GIFT

BRIDGING LOAN

When you need a substantial sum to 'tide you over' for a few weeks

Not all loans are long term. You may need a substantial sum of money for only a short period – say, between having to pay for a new house and actually getting the money from the person who is buying your old one.

The rules about such a loan, called a bridging loan, are similar to those governing any other BANK LOAN, except that the need to avoid delay in many property transactions results in a relaxation in the rules over the supply of copies.

There is no need for the bank to send you an unsigned advance copy of the loan agreement for your consideration, as would normally be the case if you were borrowing less than £5,000 on the security of property for purposes other than specifically for house purchase or improvement.
See: CONSUMER CREDIT

BRITISH EMBASSY

Guardians of the interests of British citizens living abroad

An embassy represents its country abroad. Its headquarters are almost always situated in the capital of the host country, with local representation, known as consulates, in other major towns.

The British Government maintains an embassy or its equivalent (in Commonwealth countries it is known as a High Commission) in almost every other country.

The exceptions are Britain's dependent territories and colonies, such as Gibraltar, and those countries with which we have broken off diplomatic relations.

The dependencies are ruled by a British governor or commissioner and have no need of an embassy; and in the countries where embassies have been withdrawn, British interests are handled by the embassy of a friendly foreign state.

How to obtain advice or assistance abroad

The consular department of the British embassy in a foreign capital and the individual British consulates in the country's major towns are there to advise, help and protect the rights of British Citizens living in or visiting that country. They also have a duty to assist the master of any British ship who seeks their help.

The consular department is generally run by consuls and vice-consuls, but in less-important towns, British interests may be represented by a single, honorary consul – often a British businessman. An honorary consul has the same powers as a full-time official.

Sickness and death The consul will provide 'help in cases of illness and death'. Consuls may also act as guardian for any British Citizen suffering mental illness and as executor of the local ESTATE of any British person who dies abroad.

Lack of money If a British Citizen runs out of money the consul may agree to obtain tickets for him to take the cheapest convenient form of transport back to Britain. The money for this passage home is provided as a loan, and to ensure that the debt is repaid to the Foreign Office, the consul endorses the visitor's passport, which is then held by immigration officials at the British port of entry. It will not be released, nor will a new passport be issued, until the loan has been repaid.

After an arrest When a British Citizen is arrested abroad, the foreign police usually have a duty to inform the British consul without delay. By international agreement, the consul then has the right to visit the arrested person within a reasonable time of his arrest and to obtain legal help for him.

If there is a trial, the consul may attend as an observer, though this is not a right in all countries. And if the penalty for the offence is imprisonment, the consul will visit the prisoner from time to time to ensure that he is being treated properly.

If a consul's rights are denied, the Foreign Office in London can use high-level diplomatic pressure to influence events.

Property seized When a British Citizen's property is seized by a foreign government or authority, the local British embassy will make representations to have it returned, but in most cases where official policy is involved the Foreign Office in London will have to pursue any claim for compensation.

If you need help in those circumstances contact your MP.

Marriage Some consuls are authorised to conduct marriage ceremonies between British subjects.

Children born abroad Under the British Nationality Act 1981 (which came into force in January, 1983), a child born abroad is automatically a British Citizen if *either* parent is a British Citizen and

1. was born, naturalised or registered in the U.K., *or*

2. is in Crown Service or other approved employment, *or*

3. works for the EUROPEAN COMMUNITIES.

If either parent is a British Citizen, but does not fulfil any of those three conditions, then under certain conditions the child may be registered by the local British Consul, as a British Citizen. *See:* CITIZENSHIP

Help for businesses The commercial department of the embassies provides information, facilities and contacts for British exporters doing business in the host country. Contact the Overseas Trade Division of the Department of Trade and Industry, or your nearest British Overseas Trade Board Regional Office.

BROADCASTING

Legal checks on television and radio programmes

If you have a complaint about a television or radio programme, the way you go about making it must depend on the nature of the complaint and whether the programme was broadcast by the BBC, an Independent Broadcasting Authority company or the Fourth Channel.

Programmes produced by the BBC

The BBC transmits its programmes under government licence. But the Government does not control or supervise broadcasts – although the licence gives it the right to forbid or order a particular broadcast.

Apart from a duty not to express a BBC opinion in any broadcast, there are few specific rules. Instead, the BBC has its own voluntary set of guidelines on decency, quality and accuracy.

General complaints If you feel that a BBC programme has offended against a general principle, write to or telephone the Director-General, Broadcasting House, London W1A 4AA or BBC Scotland, Broadcasting House, Queen Margaret Drive, Glasgow G12 8DG.

Alternatively, write to the producer whose name appears on the screen or Radio Times – or telephone the duty officer (in London) or information department (in other regions).

Unfair treatment Complaints about unfair broadcasts or infringements of your privacy may be made to the Broadcasting Complaints Commission.

IBA programmes

The rules that are self-imposed by the BBC are imposed by law on independent broadcasting.

Programmes transmitted by the independent television and radio companies, under the Independent Broadcasting Authority, must not offend against good taste or decency or be likely to lead to crime or disorder or be offensive to public feelings.

In addition, all news bulletins and current affairs programmes must be accurate and impartial.

Programmes must also comply with the IBA Code on Violence, which limits the portrayal of violence on the screen, and the Family Viewing Policy, which ensures that all programmes shown before 9 p.m. must be suitable for viewers of any age.

The IBA has power to prevent the showing of any programme that does not meet any of the requirements.

Similar rules apply to ADVERTISING on television.

Making a complaint If you have a complaint about a programme, write to the Programme Controller of your independent television company.

If your complaint involves some aspect of IBA supervision – for example, if you feel that a particular programme was of a kind that should not have been shown before 9 p.m. – complain direct to the IBA, 70 Brompton Road, London SW3 1EY.

If you feel the broadcast is unfair to you, or infringes your privacy, you may complain to the Broadcasting Complaints Commission.

Complaints about ADVERTISING are dealt with separately.

The Fourth Channel

Channel 4 is under the control of the IBA, which must ensure that a substantial proportion of the programmes broadcast are supplied by independent programme producers.

The IBA must also ensure that some programmes are of an educational nature and that the channel caters for tastes and interests not generally provided for by ITV.

Teletext and cable services

The Ceefax service (run by the BBC) and Oracle (run by the IBA) are subject to the same general controls as other programmes. You need no special licence to receive them. But Prestel (run by British Telecom through your telephone) is the responsibility of each person who provides a 'page'. You may be charged a small fee (on your telephone bill) for each page viewed.

Cable television services can operate only with a government licence. Government proposals will allow multi-

AN INDEPENDENT COMPLAINTS BODY

The Broadcasting Complaints Commission (20 Albert Embankment, London SE1 7TL) was set up in 1981 to deal with complaints about any television or radio broadcast.

The commission will investigate any complaint that a programme actually transmitted was unjust or unfair to any participant, to anyone who has died in the previous 5 years or anyone else directly interested in the topic covered.

It will also look into any complaint that a programme actually broadcast involved an unwarranted infringement of the privacy of a person, or that privacy was infringed in obtaining material for the broadcast.

Complaints must be made in writing by those subjected to the unfairness or invasion of privacy, or someone authorised by them (such as a neighbour). They must be made within a reasonable time of the broadcast.

The commission will ask the broadcasters to provide a repeat of the broadcast and for comments. If the complaint is upheld, the broadcasting company may be required to broadcast or publish details of the complaint and the commission's decision. But the commission need not deal with a complaint if it could be dealt with in the courts or is frivolous.

channel cable services under licences to be controlled by a Cable Authority.

Controls over use of equipment

It is a criminal offence to transmit a radio or television signal, or to receive a television signal, without a licence or Home Office consent.

Licences to broadcast are issued by the Home Office to the BBC, independent broadcasting companies, and amateur radio operators. To apply for a licence write to the Home Office Radio Regulatory Department.

Amateur applicants must pass an examination controlled by British Telecommunications to make sure they are proficient in the use of a transmitter.

You need both a Home Office and a British Telecom licence to run a programme distribution system – that is, any cable relaying service either for your own programmes or for broadcasts.

However, a licence is not required for such a system if it is contained entirely within one building, if it is a hospital programme, if it carries education programmes for education institutions only, if it carries business information within one business, or if it is a news agency service, such as Reuters.

Anyone making unauthorised broadcasts can be imprisoned for 3 months, fined up to £400 and ordered to surrender his equipment.

Citizens' Band Radio The Government legalised Citizens' Band radio in 1981. Anyone using approved equipment can broadcast and receive messages on the set frequencies – 27MHz and 934MHz. An annual licence is required and can be obtained from a main post office.

A radio receiver does not need a licence, but it is an offence to listen to certain broadcasts, such as police or fire service messages, which are not intended for public reception.

Pirate broadcasting It is a criminal offence to broadcast unauthorised 'pirate' programmes either from a land-based station or from a ship or aircraft.

Anyone who takes part in such a broadcast, or buys advertising time on it or supplies the station with goods or services, also commits a crime.

The maximum penalties are 2 years' imprisonment and an unlimited fine plus seizure of equipment.

Improving reception If your television or radio is being interfered with from some outside source, ask the Post Office to investigate. There is no charge.

The Home Office has power to prevent the sale or use of any machine or apparatus likely to cause accidental interference with reception of broadcasts.

Deliberate interference with broadcasts – 'jamming' – is illegal.

BUDGET ACCOUNT

Buying by easy instalments

A budget account is an arrangement by which a customer can have permanent credit with a retailer. The customer will buy, say, clothes on credit and pay monthly instalments off the debt but he is not required to clear the debt altogether. As long as the customer pays the agreed instalments, he can continue to have goods, up to an agreed limit.

That arrangement, like a bank overdraft, is running account credit and the agreement will be covered by the CONSUMER CREDIT Act.

If you have a budget account you are entitled to a statement of account whenever any movement is recorded in it – an instalment paid, or a charge made for goods or interest. However much or little you use a budget account, you are entitled to a statement at least once a year.

If a lender fails to supply the required statements, he cannot sue you, repossess goods, suspend the account or demand repayment of the entire sum owed, instead of instalments. If he is more than a month late with a statement, he commits an offence for which he can be fined up to £1,000.

The lender is bound by any figures supplied in a statement of account. If a mistake is made, and the statement shows that the borrower owes less than he really does, the lender must stand by the mistaken figure.

The reverse does not apply: a borrower is not bound by what the statement shows if it is wrong.

However, a sheriff court can waive that rule if a lender has made a genuine, honest and excusable mistake which is being taken advantage of by an unscrupulous borrower.

If you have a credit account with a shop, but are required to settle it in full each month, the arrangement is exempt from the Consumer Credit Act and the shopkeeper does not have to supply statements. *See also:* INTEREST CHARGE

BUILDING PRESERVATION

The protection of historic architecture

Buildings of special architectural or historic interest (such as Hopetoun House, Glasgow City Chambers, and many Georgian or Victorian buildings) may be 'listed' – that is, designated as being worth preserving – by the Secretary of State for Scotland. The owner and occupier are then notified. They have no statutory right to object.

Once a building is listed it is a criminal offence to demolish it, or to alter or

HOW TO SAVE A HISTORIC BUILDING

If you know of a building that you think should be preserved because it is of special architectural or historic interest, ask the Historic Buildings branch of the Scottish Development Department to consider listing it. It will help if you can enclose an up-to-date photograph and any relevant information about the building – for example, its date, historical associations, the architect, and details of any interior features of interest.

If the building is in danger of being demolished, or altered in such a way as to affect its historic character, there may not be time to try to have it listed. In that case you can approach the local planning authority, which can serve a building preservation notice on the owner and the occupier.

The preservation notice protects the building, as if it were listed, for 6 months. The planning authority will use this period to ask the Secretary of State for Scotland to consider listing the building.

If the Secretary of State decides not to list the building, the conservation notice ceases to have effect even though the 6 months have not expired, and the planning authority is barred from issuing a fresh notice for 12 months. In addition, if the owner or someone else connected with the building has suffered any loss or damage as a result of the notice, compensation can be claimed from the planning authority.

extend it in a way that would affect its architectural or historic interest, without obtaining listed building consent from the local planning authority (usually the district council).

If consent is refused, an appeal can be made to the Secretary of State for Scotland. If consent is given, and the work involves demolition, the Royal Commission on the Ancient and Historical Monuments of Scotland must be given the opportunity to photograph and make records of the building.

The owner of a listed building, or of an unlisted building which is nevertheless of architectural or historic interest, may be able to obtain a grant towards its maintenance from the local authority or the Secretary of State for Scotland.

Similar rules apply to buildings within a CONSERVATION AREA. There are also special rules for buildings that are ANCIENT MONUMENTS – for example, parts of the Antonine Wall.

BUILDING REGULATIONS

Legal duties as you improve your home

Planning is concerned with the way land is developed and the effect that buildings have on their surroundings. Building regulations, on the other hand, deal with precise standards of construction, detailed choice of materials and safe design. Planning permission and building regulations approval – 'building warrant' – are entirely distinct: approval of an application for one does not automatically confer a grant of the other.

Generally, building regulations approval is required for all structural work and alterations. You should apply for approval to your local district or islands council. (If your property is in the Highland, Borders, or Dumfries and Galloway Regions jurisdiction lies with the regional council.)

To take some examples, approval is required for: erection of new buildings; alterations and additions to existing buildings, including new staircases or extended habitable rooms; new or altered external and internal drainage; installation of certain heating and sanitary appliances; and installation and alteration of flue pipes.

Approval would not be required for: general repairs; fitting electric heating appliances; fitting gas appliances provided the work is done by the gas board and complies with building regulations; replacing heating and sanitary appliances, provided the work complies with the regulations; fitted furniture; fences and garden walls under a certain height (though you may need planning permission); erection of certain small buildings such as greenhouses and garden sheds.

It is an offence to start works requiring building regulations approval if no approval has been granted. The owner of the building could be prosecuted for this.

Procedure and requirements

1. The first step will be to find out whether your proposed works require approval. If you are in any doubt, the building inspector at the Building Control Department of your local authority will assist you. Alternatively, you should be able to obtain a copy of the current regulations from your library or Her Majesty's Stationery Office, 13a Castle Street, Edinburgh. The regulations will give you details of the type of materials and specifications for any given job.

2. The local authority will give you an application form to complete and this has to be accompanied by a full set of working drawings, plans and elevations. You may be asked to submit the plans and other documents in duplicate. For each application there is a fee which varies according to the estimated cost of the work.

It is not essential to seek the professional advice of an architect or builder, but if your proposals are complex this may be advisable. It will certainly help to secure approval of your proposals if you discuss them at the outset with the building inspector who can suggest improvements before your application is formally considered by the local authority.

3. Since 1982 there is no longer any need to notify a neighbour of an application for a building warrant, as such notification is now covered by the planning legislation.

4. The local authority cannot refuse your application without first telling you the reason for refusal and allowing you to put your case either in person or in writing.

5. Provided your application complies with the regulations the local authority must grant approval. Even if your application does not meet the building standards it may be possible to obtain a relaxation of the regulations if, for example, you plan to use unusual but nonetheless reasonable construction methods or materials. The local authority have this power in appropriate circumstances, though certain types of relaxation can only be granted by the Secretary of State for Scotland. You can appeal to the Secretary of State against a refusal by the local authority to relax a regulation. In such a case it may be desirable to ask the assistance of a building specialist in presenting your case.

6. Once a building warrant has been granted it remains valid for 3 years though extensions of this period can be granted. You must notify the local authority, first, that works have started, within 7 days of doing so; and second, of the date on which the operations are completed. You may also have to give notice during various stages of the work, depending on its nature. For example, you must give notice of the laying or covering-up of any drain.
7. If the works involve the construction of a building (or any part) you must obtain a Certificate of Completion and it is an offence to use a building without such a Certificate. The local authority must grant the Certificate if the conditions of the building warrant have been complied with.

The maximum penalties for offences under the building regulations are £200 plus £25 for each day the offence continues after conviction.

BUILDING SOCIETY

Investing in other people's homes

Building societies are the major source of loans for people buying their own homes. The loans are secured on the property being bought.

A building society has two classes of member: borrowing and investing. Borrowers pay a higher interest charge than is paid to investors. The difference covers the society's running costs and provides the small surplus it needs as reserve.

Borrowing

Borrowers are normally expected to find part of the price of the property – often 10 to 20 per cent – from their own resources. If you are already an investor, you will often be given priority over non-investors. If you are not already an investor you may be required to become a member of the society by the technicality of buying one nominal share. *See:* MORTGAGE

Investing

Investors are paid interest net, income tax at the basic rate being deducted automatically at source. This means that:

- If you pay income tax at the basic rate on the rest of your income, there is no further liability to tax unless you have a high proportion of INVESTMENT INCOME.
- If you do not otherwise pay income tax, you cannot claim back the amount deducted at source, and a building society account is therefore a poor investment for you.
- If you pay income tax at more than the basic rate, you will still be liable for the difference between what is automatically deducted and what you would be charged on the entire amount of interest at your highest tax rate.

Example: Mr A, whose highest tax rate is 40 per cent, receives £140 interest from his building society (£200 less £60 tax already deducted).

Mr A's liability on full £200 at 40%..	£80
minus	
Tax already deducted at 30%.........	£60
Net tax liability is therefore.............	£20

Building society collapse

In the rare event that a building society could not meet its obligations, it would be wound up. Societies usually reserve the right to demand the repayment of all loans at short notice, and so borrowers would have to repay their mortgages.

Investors are not liable for the debts of societies. They would be entitled to a share of the remaining assets in proportion to the investment held at the time of the collapse, but this share could be less than the investment.

BUSES AND COACHES

Your rights as a passenger

Your rights when you travel by bus or coach are usually governed, at least in part, by the operator's conditions of carriage.

In some cases, however, those conditions may not be binding on you, since they do not have the force of law and take effect as terms in a contract only if the operator has taken reasonable steps to draw them to your attention. Even then, if they are not fair and reasonable they may be invalid under the Unfair Contract Terms Act. *See:* UNFAIR CONTRACT

Tickets and seats

If you make a firm booking for a seat on a coach, you have a contract with the operator even before you pay for the ticket. That means that you have certain rights. If by mistake the same seat is allocated to two people and one passenger has to travel on a later coach, he would in most cases be able to claim that there has been a breach of contract and demand compensation – for example, the cost of overnight accommodation.

BOOKING A SEAT ON A BUS OR COACH

If you make a firm booking for a seat on a bus or coach, even if you have not paid for the ticket at the time, you have a contract with the operator which gives you certain rights to that seat.

The ticket conditions may say that no liability is accepted in such cases, but under the Unfair Contract Terms Act 1977 such a condition would be invalid in law if it could be proved in court not to be fair and reasonable.

Cancellation and delays

Timetables usually say that there is no guarantee or undertaking on the part of the operators that buses or coaches will run on time – or at all. Under the Unfair Contract Terms Act it may be possible to win an action for damages on the grounds that such a stipulation is unreasonable. In the first years of the Act's operation, no cases on this issue had been reported.

When there is an accident

If there is an accident, the operator of the bus or coach is not necessarily bound to pay compensation for injuries. His liability will depend on whether there has been a failure on his own part or that of his staff to take reasonable care.

For example, if the accident was caused by a failure to maintain the vehicle properly, the operator will be liable. If the driver negligently tries to drive the bus under a bridge that is too low, there will again be liability on the operator. Similarly, if there is a collision caused in part by the driver's negligence, the operator will have to pay compensation if a passenger sues.

THE BURST TYRE THAT KILLED FOUR

When a driver is found to have been even partly responsible for an accident that led to injury, his company will be held liable to pay damages to the victims.

Mr Barkway was on his way to work in a double-decker bus when a front tyre burst. The bus veered across the road, went through iron railings and fell over an embankment on to a railway line. Mr Barkway and three other passengers were killed.

Mr Barkway's widow sued the bus company for damages. The company denied negligence. It said the tyres were inspected twice a week and the impact fracture which caused the blow-out could not have been detected by visual examination.

DECISION

The House of Lords thought the fracture had probably been caused by a heavy blow against a kerb. The driver should have reported any such blow. His failure to do so was negligence and the bus company was liable. So Mrs Barkway was awarded £2,000 damages.

No conditions on tickets can exclude or limit liability in such cases.

But if the accident is caused solely by the negligence of another driver or of a pedestrian, the bus or coach operator is not liable to the passengers. They will have the right only to sue the person whose negligence caused the accident. If that person was driving a motor vehicle, insurance is compulsory and a claim should be worth making; but a claim against a pedestrian would be worth making only if he or she had the financial resources to meet it. In rare cases accidents happen without anyone being to blame. In such cases there is no one against whom to claim.

Hiring a coach

If you hire a coach, the hiring company is obliged to take reasonable care to see that the vehicle is fit for the journey. This is so even if you drive the coach yourself. So if the coach subsequently breaks down, the company will be liable for breach of contract unless the fault was one that inspection would not have revealed and proper maintenance would not have prevented.

Any clause in the hire agreement stating that the company is not liable for any breakdowns may be void under the Unfair Contract Terms Act. *See:* UNFAIR CONTRACT

Complaining about the service

If you have a complaint about local, excursion or express bus services take it up first with the operating company.

However, if the operator seems unable or unwilling to do anything, send the complaint to the Traffic Commissioners for your area, and ask them to look into it.

The Traffic Commissioners supervise all bus services on behalf of the Department of Transport. They issue licences for every operator and driver. They also license all local bus services and routes, but, under the Transport Act 1980, express coach services are no longer licensed.

In the last resort the local Commissioners have the power to refuse or revoke licences, which could stop a service.

The Commissioners will consider any serious complaint about a service – such as fare staging, routes, frequency, unsafe driving or rudeness of staff.

Any new bus route or fare increase also needs approval by the Commissioners: so does alteration of an existing service. Licences for each service must be renewed every 5 years. If you have grounds for objecting to the service (for instance, that a proposed alteration is against the public interest), write to the Commissioners. At the Commission chairman's discretion you will probably be able to put your objection in person at the licence hearing.

BUSINESS, Starting a

How different kinds of firms have different legal responsibilities

Anyone setting up a business has a choice of three ways of conducting it: as a sole trader, in a partnership or through a company. Each form has its advantages and disadvantages.

Trading on your own

You can carry on a business under your own name without any legal formalities whatsoever. You simply start trading and retain sole ownership of the assets and goodwill of the business. You can employ staff and buy or lease property and equipment in connection with the business. You must, however, keep books recording all financial transactions so that you can be assessed for income tax and value added tax. For income tax you will be assessed under Schedule D as a self-employed person; similarly, you will have to pay class 2 and possibly also class 4 NATIONAL INSURANCE CONTRIBUTIONS.

If you want to trade under a name other than your own, you will have to disclose your own name to your customer. *See:* BUSINESS NAME.

The main advantages of being a sole trader are the freedom and independence it gives and the fact that all profits accrue to the trader. The main disadvantage is that the trader also has unlimited personal responsibility for any losses. If your business fails you may lose not only all your business assets but also your home, your car, your personal savings and anything else you own. *See:* BANKRUPTCY

Creating a partnership

Two or more people can start a business as partners in just the same way as a sole trader. No legal formalities are necessary.

The business relationship between the partners is regulated by the Partnership Act 1890, unless the partners agree otherwise. Under the Act, each is entitled to an equal share of the profits and has an equal responsibility for any losses. If the partnership is dissolved, each partner is entitled to take out the amount of capital he has put in. The rest of the assets are then divided equally.

In most businesses, 20 is the maximum number of partners allowed. But many professional people, such as lawyers, accountants, architects and surveyors, are allowed to form partnerships with as many partners as they like.

Partners usually have a partnership agreement or deed drawn up by a solicitor to define their relationship and prevent possible disagreement if only the general terms of the Partnership Act were relied on.

The partnership deed should cover such points as the aims and scope of the partnership, how decisions are to be made, how financial matters are to be arranged, and how a partner can withdraw without causing the dissolution of the partnership.

Whatever arrangements are made, however, each partner remains personally responsible to any outside creditors for the whole of the partnership's liabilities. However, creditors must sue the firm or the whole body of partners in the first instance. If one partner pays off a firm debt he has a right to be compensated by the other partners.

Forming a company

It is possible for a partner to limit his liability for the firm's debts by forming a limited partnership. These are rare, however and the best way to limit the personal responsibility that sole traders and partners have for business liabilities it to form a limited liability company.

A limited liability company is a legal entity quite separate from its owners with many of the same rights as an individual. It owns all the assets of the business and it is responsible for any liabilities. The people who formed and run it are not personally liable.

In order to form such a company it is necessary to submit various documents to the Registrar of Companies, the most important of which are:

Memorandum of association The memorandum is the 'constitution' of the company and must state the name of the company, whether its registered office will be in Scotland, England or Wales, the business purpose for which it is formed and the maximum amount of capital which may be put into the company (the authorised capital). The authorised capital must be divided into fixed portions called shares.

Each share has a nominal value and may be sold by the company for that value – or more. It is not necessary for all shares in the company to be sold. The nominal value of shares sold is the issued capital.

Articles of association The articles lay down the rules that are to govern the day-to-day running of the company – such as the appointment and powers of directors, and the rights and responsibilities of shareholders.

If you do not register your own set of articles, the law assumes that a model laid down in the Companies Acts applies. But it is better to use your own.

The price of limited liability

Having formed a limited liability company, a businessman has achieved the major advantage of limited liability for himself. However, there are also disadvantages. Besides the cost of forming the company (more than £100), there is annual expenditure on having the accounts audited and filing these and other documents with the Registrar of Companies. Accounts and other documents filed with the Registrar are open to public inspection. Privacy is therefore lost; competitors and employees are able to see how well or how badly the business is doing.

Buying a company 'off the peg'

The process of forming a company from scratch usually takes several weeks. If you urgently require a company, it is possible to buy one that has already been registered. The disadvantages are that the business purposes stated in the memorandum may not be appropriate, and the name of the company will almost certainly not be. Such matters can be altered subsequently, but that involves further expense and inconvenience.

Private and public companies

A private company cannot offer to sell its shares to the public. A public company may do so, but must have an authorised capital of at least £50,000. Before it starts to carry on business, a public company must also have an *issued* capital of at least £50,000.

The names of all public companies now have to end with the words 'public limited company' or 'p.l.c.'.

Every company – private and public – must have at least two shareholders, one director and one secretary. There need be no limit on the number of members, although private companies do usually limit their numbers to 50.

COMPANIES ARE SEPARATE FROM PEOPLE

One of the most fundamental rules of company law is that every company is a legal unit, an individual quite distinct from its owners or shareholders.

Mr Woolfson owned some units in a shop, the remainder of which belonged to Solfred Holdings Ltd, a company in which Mr Woolfson owned the majority of shares. The actual business in the shop was carried out by M & L Campbell (Glasgow) Ltd, which had 1,000 issued ordinary shares, of which Mr Woolfson had 999 and his wife 1.

The shop was acquired by Glasgow Corporation under a compulsory purchase order. Under the legislation then in force no compensation for disturbance was payable other than to the occupier of the premises, namely M & L Campbell (Glasgow) Ltd.

Mr Woolfson argued that in reality he was these 2 companies and claimed over £175,000 as compensation. This was refused by the court.

DECISION

The House of Lords held that these companies were in law quite separate and distinct from Mr Woolfson. Only M & L Campbell (Glasgow) Ltd, which was in law a separate person, could obtain compensation. His appeal was therefore dismissed.

Most public companies raise money by issuing shares which are quoted on the Stock Exchange. It is a criminal offence for a director of a public company or someone with similar access to 'inside information' to deal on the Stock Exchange in the shares of any company with which he is connected if he is making use of such information. If an 'insider' gives a tip to someone else, knowing that the other will deal in the shares, both commit an offence. The maximum penalty in each case is 2 years' imprisonment and an unlimited fine.

BUSINESS NAME

Restrictions on the names that businesses can use

A business can trade under any name it chooses provided that it does not use the name of another business in the same field.

Duplicate names

The owner of a business is prohibited from using a trading name that is likely to confuse the public into believing that his business is the same as another. That applies even if the name is the trader's own. It is a civil, not a criminal matter, however, and the responsibility for seeking redress lies with the person or company whose name has been copied. He has to take civil action, by seeking an INTERDICT against the offender in the sheriff court or Court of Session.

Disclosing business ownership

It is no longer necessary for a business which wants to trade under a name other than that of its owner or owners to register that name. The Register of Business Names was abolished on 26 February 1982.

THE TWO KELVINS

A new company can use a name similar to that of a competitor if people are not likely to be confused.

James Meikle had once been the managing director of the Kelvindale Chemical Co. He left it and started the Kelvinside Chemical Co. Both companies were in the same line of business in the same area. The Kelvindale Chemical Co. tried to interdict Meikle from using the name Kelvinside as it would cause confusion.

DECISION

The interdict was not granted because the Court felt that the public would not confuse the two companies.

However the name and address of each owner must be displayed legibly on all business letters, orders, invoices and receipts. This information must also be displayed prominently in any business premises.

BYELAWS

Rules which are made locally

Local authorities and some other public bodies (such as the British Railways Board) are authorised by Parliament to make byelaws. These are rules which apply only in an authority's own area. Although they are frequently made to govern behaviour on land subject to the authority's control – such as public parks – they may also extend more widely for the prevention and suppression of nuisances. It is usually a criminal offence to break a byelaw.

How to oppose a new byelaw

Before submitting a new byelaw to the Secretary of State for Scotland for confirmation, an authority must give the public one month's notice of its intention to do so by advertising in a local newspaper that a copy of the draft byelaw can be inspected at the council offices.

Anyone wishing to oppose the making of the byelaw, perhaps because he thinks the new rule will be unfair, may write to the Secretary of State for Scotland explaining his objections. The Secretary of State is bound to consider all objections before making a decision and he may order a public inquiry. The validity of a confirmed byelaw may still be challenged in the courts if it can be shown to be unreasonable or illegally made.

An important change recently made is the introduction of new 'management rules' to be drawn up by local authorities. These will resemble byelaws but will not need ministerial confirmation. Publicity will still be required and objections will be directed to the authority itself. At the same time many rules formerly contained in local byelaws have been put into the Civic Government (Scotland) Act 1982.

CAPITAL GAINS TAX

When you pay for making a profit

When any property (including goods which have been damaged) is disposed of, capital gains tax may have to be paid.

The tax, which applies to personal as well as business assets, is levied on any increase in the value of an item between its acquisition and its disposal.

There are, however, many types of assets and circumstances when tax is not payable or can be postponed, or when the gross liability can be reduced.

Gains that are always exempt

Capital gains tax is never payable on the disposal of:

1. Any motor vehicle suitable for private use, including vintage and veteran cars.

2. Cash acquired for your own use – although other forms of tax, such as capital transfer tax, may apply.

3. Betting, gambling and lottery winnings.

4. Compensation for personal injuries or wrongs – although compensation for damage to property or goods can be taxable, unless the whole of the money is spent on restoring or replacing the asset, when the tax can be partly or wholly postponed.

5. Moveable objects – including coins, old furniture and paintings – if no individual item is sold for more than £3,000 and if you are not buying and selling so frequently as to be considered a trader. Krugerrands, and gold sovereigns minted after 1936, are not exempt.

6. 'Wasting assets' which are also tangible, moveable objects with a useful life of not more than 50 years – except for business plant and machinery.

7. Life assurance policies when they mature or are cashed in.

8. A private house which has been your family's main or only home throughout the time you have owned it.

9. Medals and other decorations for valour, as long as you did not buy them, but won or inherited them.

10. Government securities and securities in quoted companies, if you inherited them, or if you bought them but do not sell for at least 12 months.

Assets partly exempt Other assets may be partly exempt. For example, assets acquired before April 6, 1965, will be taxed only on any gain made after that date.

There are two ways in which you can choose to have the taxable gain worked out, but special rules apply to quoted shares.

One is to divide the overall gain in proportion to the periods for which the assets were held before and after April 6, 1965. If they were held for 5 years before that date and sold 2 years after it, the taxable gain would be two-sevenths of the total profit.

The other is to take the value as at April 6, 1965 and deduct it from the value at the time of disposal.

The second method would be an advantage if, for example, the assets made a big gain before April 6, 1965, and grew more slowly thereafter.

For example, if the total gain was £700, of which £500 was made before April 6, 1965, the taxable amount would be £200 as with the first method. However, if the gain before the relevant date was £650, it would benefit you to adopt the second method, because that would leave only £50 on which to pay tax.

If the greatest gain was made after April 6, 1965, under the second method of assessment you would have to pay more tax.

If you wish the second method to apply, you must tell the Inland Revenue in writing within 2 clear years after the date of disposal. However, if a large sum is involved, take specialist advice from an accountant.

RATES AT WHICH CAPITAL GAINS ARE TAXED

For individuals – not companies or trustees – there is a special exemption from capital gains on the first £5,600 of net gains in each tax year. This figure applies in the year 1984–5.

For example, if a man made net gains of £6,600 in a year, he would pay tax of £300 (£1,000 × 30 per cent). A husband and wife qualify for only one exemption per year between them.

Capital gains tax is payable 9 months after the end of the tax year (on or before December 1).

Taking account of inflation

From April 1982, allowance is made for the fact that many apparent gains are the result of inflation and are not true gains at all. Account is taken only of increases due to inflation since April 1982, and no account is taken of inflation during the first year of ownership of the asset.

Gains on which some tax relief is given

If the total gains made by an individual or married couple in a year do not exceed a certain amount – £5,600 a year from 1984–5 – they are entirely free of capital gains tax. There are also special reliefs for those selling a business on retirement.

Unit Trusts If you sell units in unit trusts, you are liable to pay capital gains tax on any profit you make.

Until April 5, 1980, there was given a

'tax credit' of 10 per cent which could be offset against your tax liability on the units, but that was abolished for sales on or after April 6, 1980.

Shares There may be special relief on the sale of quoted shares if they have been the subject of a takeover bid and if no cash was received on the takeover. New shares issued in exchange for old, at the same cost, are not liable for tax until they are sold.

Shares in a private, unquoted company are subject to the same general rules, but valuing them is a matter for a specialist.

If you invested in the shares of an unquoted trading company on its formation and you eventually dispose of them at a loss, you may be able to offset that loss against your taxable income.

The 'roll-over' facility

When an individual makes a gift to someone else (an individual or trustees) the gain can be 'rolled over' if the donor and the recipient make a joint claim. That means the recipient receives the asset at the value at which the donor originally acquired it. Thus the donor pays no tax on any increase in its value during his ownership. Tax is postponed and paid by the recipient when he eventually disposes of the gift.

If any CAPITAL TRANSFER TAX is paid on the gift, it is added to the original cost of the asset and therefore reduces the taxable profit on any subsequent sale.

For example, Mr George Forrest acquired a holiday home for £15,000 in 1972. In 1981, he gives it to his son, David Forrest, when it is worth £60,000, and £2,000 of capital transfer tax is paid on the gift. David sells it in 1985 for £80,000. The taxable gain is:

Sale price		80,000
Father's original cost	15,000	
Capital transfer tax paid on gift	2,000	17,000
David's taxable gain		63,000

When you make a loss

If an asset is sold at a loss – or otherwise disposed of when the value has dropped – the loss can be set off against gains in the same tax year or carried forward to another tax year.

The loss cannot be used to offset gains in a previous tax year or to reduce liability for income tax as opposed to capital gains tax.

A self-employed person cannot set off a business trading loss against a capital gain, but someone who lends or guarantees money to a trader and does not get repaid can claim a loss.

The relationship between losses and the annual exemption limit is difficult. Losses of the current year must be offset against capital gains of the same year, even if that reduces the net gains to less than £5,600 (thus exempt from tax), but losses brought forward need be used only to the extent that they reduce the gains to the exemption level.

For example, a man has unused losses of £2,000 from a previous year, and in the current year losses of £600 and gains of £6,700.

Gains of year		6,700
Losses of current year fully offset		600
		6,100
Losses brought forward	2,000	
Partly used	500	500
Carry forward	1,500	
Net gains (exempt)		5,600

Special rules for husbands and wives

In assessing capital gains tax, a husband and wife are treated as one person. Any transfer of property between them is not taxable. Losses made by one can be set against gains made by the other.

If a couple get divorced, capital gains tax can be charged on property transferred after the decree is pronounced. But the matrimonial home is exempt, if it is transferred as part of a divorce settlement.

Selling the family home

Normally the profit on selling your home is exempt from capital gains tax. However, in certain circumstances you should take steps to avoid becoming liable.

Business use If you use part of your home for business and intend to claim part of the running costs against your income tax liability, try to assess what the effect would be if you later sold your home for a good profit.

It is possible for capital gains tax on a house that greatly increases in value to outweigh the benefit of expenses claimed against income tax.

Capital gains tax is charged on part of the profit, in proportion to the amount of it used for business purposes.

For example, if the owner of a 5-roomed house has claimed the use of a room as a study, he may face capital gains tax on one-fifth of any profit, when he eventually sells.

However, if he buys another home and again uses a room in it for business he can postpone paying capital gains until he eventually sells the second home.

If you sell a house that you use partly for business and re-invest in another property, you will not be liable for capital gains tax on any profit relating to the business part – provided that you spend it all on the business part of the new property.

You can 'roll over' on every such sale and purchase: tax is not payable even on death.

When only part is used If you use part of your home for business only occasionally and that part is also sometimes used for private purposes, you are not liable for capital gains tax, even though you can claim for its business use against income tax.

When part of your home is let

If part of your home is exclusively let – say, as a bedsitter – you may, when you sell it, have to pay capital gains tax on the let part.

In order to ascertain whether this is the case, you must calculate the proportion of the gain attributable to the let part. If this is greater than the proportion attributable to the unlet part (or alternatively greater than £20,000) then you will have to pay capital gains tax on the excess.

For example, a widow lets off the top floor of her house as a self-contained flat. She bought the house for £20,000 and sells it for £70,000 several years later.

Assuming that her flat and the flat that she lets are of equal value, the capital gains that she will pay is as follows:

Sale price		70,000
Cost		20,000
Total gain		50,000
Exempt:		
Gain on her own flat	25,000	
Gain on let flat	25,000	

The gain on the let flat does not exceed the gain on her own flat, but it does exceed £20,000. She pays tax on £25,000 minus £20,000: £5,000.

When you have a lodger If part of the house is used by a lodger or paying guest, make sure that he has no exclusive use of it – by reserving your right to enter and inspect it, for example, and by allowing your own family to use it when there is no lodger or guest.

If the garden is very large Tax may be levied if the garden of your home is more than 1 acre – unless you can show that its size is reasonable for the size and character of the house, or that it is required for the reasonable enjoyment of the house as a private home.

If you have to pay tax, it will be charged on the excess area of garden as a proportion of the value of the entire property.

If you sell part of your garden to be built on, but keep the house, it may be against your interests to apply for planning permission for the proposed buildings yourself.

If you do apply, you may be required to pay capital gains tax on any profit from the sale. If is often advisable to leave the planning application to the purchaser.

When you are away from home for long periods

If you leave your house unoccupied for long periods, you may be liable for capital gains tax on part of the profit when you sell.

The taxable gain is worked out according to the proportion of absence to occupation during your period of ownership.

There are, however, exemptions. You can be absent from the house throughout the last 2 years before selling. That allows a period of grace in which to dispose of the property after moving elsewhere.

You also escape tax if your periods of absence do not total more than 3 years during ownership. But you must have lived in the house before and after those absences, unless that is impracticable – for example, if you have emigrated.

If you work away from home, elsewhere in the United Kingdom, you are entitled in addition to a total of 4 years' absence. If you are employed overseas, you are entitled to be absent as much as you like without becoming liable to capital gains tax.

If you buy a plot of land on which to build a private home for yourself, any absence does not begin to be calculated until you have built the house and moved in.

If you own two homes

Only one home at a time can normally be exempt from capital gains tax. If you own two homes, the one that you choose as your main residence is exempt.

To establish which home you wish to be considered tax exempt, notify the Inland Revenue in writing within 2 years of buying the second home.

Otherwise the question will be decided according to which home is in fact your main residence, at the time when you sell one or other of the properties. If that question cannot be agreed between you and the tax inspector, it will be decided by the Inland Revenue Appeal Commissioners.

When a second home is exempt A second home is exempt from capital gains tax if it is occupied, rent-free, throughout your ownership, by a dependent relative – a widowed mother or mother-in-law, or by a relative who is over 65 or unable to look after himself or herself because of mental or physical disability.

But if the dependent relative pays rent at any time the property will be immediately liable to capital gains tax.

Selling a business

Profit on the sale of land, buildings and goodwill in a business are all liable to capital gains tax.

Profit on stock-in-trade, cash and debts owed to the business are exempt.

If machinery or fixtures sell at a profit, capital gains tax may be charged.

Putting off the tax When a business asset is sold, the capital gains tax on any profit can be postponed if the entire sale price is reinvested in another business asset. That is known as 'roll-over relief'.

The replacement asset need not be of the same type as the old one. You can use the profit from the sale of a shop to buy machinery for an entirely different kind of business.

However, roll-over relief is restricted to land, buildings (including furnished holiday accommodation), goodwill and fixed plant and machinery.

The replacement asset must be bought not more than 1 year before and not more than 3 years after the sale of the other asset.

If only part of the sale money is spent on the new asset, tax will be assessed on the amount retained.

Retirement relief Someone over retiring age who is in business can sometimes claim retirement relief on profits made by disposing of business assets or by selling shares in a family trading company.

To qualify for the full relief you have to be over 60 and to have worked continuously in the business for at least 10 years before disposing of it. If you worked for less than 10 years the relief to which you are entitled is reduced. You need only dispose of assets to qualify for relief: you are not obliged to retire.

Relief begins at £20,000 one year after the 60th birthday and increases by £20,000 each year – with proportionate increases for parts of a year – to a maximum of £100,000.

If the relief is being claimed on the sale of shares in a family company, the person claiming must have been a full time working director for the previous 10 years, with restricted relief for shorter periods.

Furthermore he must own no fewer than 25 per cent of the voting shares himself, or his immediate family must have more than 51 per cent of which he must have 5 per cent.

Relief on such shares may be due only on a proportion of the profit.

When someone dies

Capital gains tax is not chargeable on accrued gains in the value of items in a person's estate at death. These gains are wiped out. The person inheriting the property is treated as acquiring it at its value at the date of the owner's death, and tax is chargeable on gains in value thereafter.

For example, if a man buys a painting for £4,000, and dies five years later when it is worth £7,000, this gain is not chargeable.

If his son inherits it and later sells it for £10,500, then capital gains tax will be chargeable only on the £3,500 by which the value has risen since his father's death.

CAPITAL TRANSFER TAX

When giving generously has its penalties

Capital transfer tax is really two taxes in one:

1. A tax on gifts which a person makes during his or her lifetime.

2. A death duty on the value of the estate of a person at the date of death.

Both these cases involve a transfer from one person's estate to another's. The tax is on the loss in value to the donor's estate.

Lifetime gifts are subject to lower rates of tax than transfers on death or within 3 years before death. There are a number of exemptions and reliefs which exclude or reduce any tax liability.

How much tax is payable

Like income tax, capital transfer tax is progressive: the amount of the gift is treated in slices, and the greater it is, the higher the rate of tax on the upper slice. Rates of tax on lifetime gifts go up to 30%, while the top rate which may apply to your estate after death is 60%. These rates however are only payable on the top slices of very large transfers.

At the bottom of the scale, there is a 0% rate band for the first £64,000 transferred, which means that many people will not be troubled by capital transfer tax at all. This figure is raised periodically: £64,000 has been the tax threshold since March 1984.

Capital transfer tax is progressive in another sense: in calculating the tax on a gift or on death, you have to take account of certain previous gifts which you have made. So if you make a gift of £30,000 to your son today and a further gift of £40,000 to your daughter tomorrow, your cumulative total of gifts is £70,000. Since only £64,000 of this is free of tax, you will pay tax on the remaining £6,000 of the second gift. If you then make a further gift of £20,000 to your nephew, this whole amount will be taxable.

In calculating your cumulative total of gifts for this purpose, you must take account only of gifts within the previous 10 years. You also ignore gifts made before March 1974, when capital transfer tax was introduced.

Gifts made less than 3 years before the death of the donor are subject to the higher death rates. (The idea is to prevent avoidance of tax by means of so-called 'deathbed' gifts.) Thus if a donor dies within 3 years of making a taxable gift, extra tax is due, and must be paid by the recipient of the gift.

In many circumstances – for example, where a donor is elderly, or the gift is very large – it will be wise to insure against this possible extra tax bill. Insurance companies offer appropriate single-premium insurance policies: seek the advice of a broker.

RATES OF CAPITAL TRANSFER TAX

The rates apply to transfers made on or after March 13, 1984. The lifetime rates are half those on death.

Gross cumulative total	Lifetime rate of tax (%)	Rates applicable on or within 3 years before death (%)
£0 to 64,000	Nil	Nil
64,001 to 85,000	15	30
85,001 to 116,000	17½	35
116,001 to 148,000	20	40
148,001 to 185,000	22½	45
185,001 to 232,000	25	50
232,001 to 285,000	27½	55
Over 2,850,000	30	60

Tax on lifetime gifts

Capital transfer tax is chargeable on all occasions when there is a loss to the donor's estate. Thus tax is payable when you make a gift to someone, and also when you sell property to someone at a price below market value with the intention that it should be in part a gift.

So if you sell a painting worth £2,500 to a friend for £1,000, you will be liable for tax on the element of gift: £1,500.

However you are not liable for tax if you sell something for less than its value without intending to benefit the recipient. Capital transfer tax is not payable on bad bargains.

For example, you have a car worth £5,000 and you sell it to a friend for £3,000. If you intend to benefit him to the extent of the balance of £2,000, then you are liable to tax. If on the other hand you are under the mistaken impression that the car is only worth £3,000, then you are not liable to tax.

Tax is calculated on the loss to the donor's estate. In some circumstances this will not be the same as the increase in value of the recipient's estate.

For instance, if you own a pair of candlesticks worth £1,000, and give away one of them, so that each is worth only £300 on its own, then the loss to your estate is £700, and this is the value transferred for tax purposes. The situation most often arises where a controlling shareholding (i.e. more than 50%) in a private company is divided up so that no-one has control any longer.

Because tax is payable on the overall loss to your estate, there is a difference in the amount of tax payable depending on whether you pay tax in addition to the gift, or else out of the gift itself.

If tax is to be paid out of the gift itself, the calculation is straightforward. If A gives B £1,000, on condition that B pays the tax, and according to A's cumulative total tax is payable at 20%, then the tax due is £200, and B receives £800.

The position is more complicated if A wishes B to receive the full £1,000. The loss to A's estate is the total of gift plus tax, and this is the figure upon which tax is payable at 20%. Thus more tax is payable than if the total loss to the

HOW TO PAY CAPITAL TRANSFER TAX

Lifetime gifts of cash or property which may be liable to capital transfer tax must be reported to the Capital Taxes Office in Edinburgh within 12 months from the end of the month in which the gift took place. Tax falls due 6 months after the end of the month of the gift, unless the gift was made between April 6 and September 30, in which case payment falls due on the following April 30. The significance of the date on which tax falls due is that interest is payable on unpaid tax after that date, at a rate of 8 per cent.

The gift must be reported on form C-5, available from the Capital Taxes Office. There is space on the form to state who will be responsible for paying the tax: the person giving or the person receiving. If the form is not submitted, or if there is no arrangement about payment, the donor is legally responsible. The Inland Revenue will work out any tax due and send you a demand.

In the case of transfers on death, any capital transfer tax due must be paid before the person's executors can obtain CONFIRMATION. Adjustment of the amount can be made later if any valuations have to be amended. The same periods for payment apply as for lifetime gifts, but interest on overdue tax on death is only at 6 per cent.

Tax can be paid in ten annual instalments where the transfer is on death, or where the recipient is paying the tax on a lifetime gift, and the property is land or buildings, business assets, a controlling shareholding or in some circumstances a minority holding in an unquoted company.

HOW THE TAX ON NET GIFTS IS CALCULATED

David makes a gift to his son Eric of a painting worth £1,000. There are no exemptions to be taken into account. David agrees to pay the tax on the gift. Because of previous gifts, the rate of tax applicable to this one is 20 per cent.

The total loss to David's estate is the value of the picture plus tax. Thus the value of the picture is only 100 per cent less 20 per cent – that is, 80 per cent – of the total value transferred.

Tax payable	= 20% of the total loss.
Value of the picture	= 80% of the total loss.
Thus tax payable	= 20/80 of the value of the picture
	= 20/80×£1,000.

The tax payable is therefore £250, representing 20% of the total loss to David's estate of £1,250.

HOW THE CUMULATIVE PRINCIPLE WORKS

Gordon is a wealthy businessman who makes the following gifts:

1. In 1981 he gives £8,000 to his son.

2. In 1982 he gives £15,000 to his wife and £20,000 to his daughter.

3. In 1984 he gives £50,000 to his son and £100 to each of his three grandchildren.

4. In 1986 he gives £24,000 to his daughter and £5,000 to Cancer Research.

In 1988 he dies leaving £15,000 to each of his two children, and the residue of his estate to his wife. Assume that all gifts and legacies to Gordon's children are to bear their own tax.

1. Gift of £8,000 to son:
Annual exemption £3,000
Tax on balance at 0% = 0
Cumulative total = £5,000.

2. Gift of £15,000 to wife exempt
Gift of £20,000 to daughter:
Annual exemption £3,000
Tax on balance at 0% = 0
Cumulative total = £22,000.

3. Gift of £50,000 to son
Annual exemption £3,000
Tax: £42,000 at 0%
£5,000 at 15% = £750
Cumulative total = £69,000

Gifts to grandchildren exempt (less than £250).

4. Gift of £24,000 to daughter
Annual exemption £3,000
Tax: £16,000 at 15% = £2,400
£5,000 at 17½% = £875
£3,275
Cumulative total = £90,000

£5,000 gift to Cancer Research exempt.

Tax on Gordon's death:
Residue to wife exempt
Tax on £30,000 at death rates.

Cumulative total

£90,000 (Lifetime)		
£116,000	£26,000 at 35%	= £9,100
£120,000	£4,000 at 40%	= £1,600
		£10,700

estate were merely the value of the gift. You have to calculate the amount which, once tax is taken off at 20%, leaves £1,000.

There may in addition be a CAPITAL GAINS TAX liability on a lifetime gift of certain assets.

Tax on a person's estate at death

Capital transfer tax is payable on the value of a person's estate immediately before his death. It is thus necessary to ascertain the net value of his estate, after deduction of all liabilities. For example, a house worth £35,000 subject to a mortgage with £15,000 still outstanding has a value of £20,000. A deduction may also be made for funeral expenses.

To this figure must be added the value of any life policy maturing on the person's death, unless the rights under the policy were assigned during the person's lifetime (which would have been a taxable gift, of a value normally equal to the sum of premiums paid so far).

If the person had been entitled to any benefit under a trust, such as the right to receive income, or the use of a house or other property during his lifetime, then this too must be taken into consideration in determining the tax payable on his death. In such a situation the tax bill will be shared between his own estate (payable by his executors) and the trust fund (payable by the trustees).

Exemptions and reliefs from capital transfer tax

The following are exempt from liability to capital transfer tax:

- Transfers between husband and wife whether they are lifetime gifts or take place on the death of one of them. However if the recipient is living outside the United Kingdom, only the first £55,000 of any transfer is exempt.

Transfers from one partner to another as a result of marital breakdown are exempt only if they are made before divorce is granted or under a court order. In other circumstances the transfer will be taxable.

- Gifts and bequests for the maintenance of a former spouse or the maintenance and education of the donor's child, which are made to the former spouse or child. So are gifts and bequests to dependent relatives for their maintenance.

- Lifetime gifts in favour of any person in one tax year (6th April – 5th April) if they amount to £250 or less.
- Lifetime gifts to a couple getting married, up to a limit which varies according to the relationship between the donor and the recipient.

Each parent can give the couple up to £5,000 without tax consequences. Each grandparent can give up to £2,500, as can one partner to the other before marriage. Anyone else can give up to £1,000 without attracting tax.

- Normal expenditure out of income during one's lifetime. This includes, for example, life assurance premiums, or payments under a deed of covenant. The word 'normal' excludes one-off gifts, and also means that the payments must be made out of the donor's income without affecting his capital wealth or standard of living.
- Lifetime gifts, up to an annual maximum of £3,000 (in addition to the exemptions mentioned above).

Any unused balance of this exemption may be carried forward for one year only. So if you made £2,000 of chargeable gifts in 1983–84, you could carry the balance of £1,000 forward and make £4,000 of gifts tax-free in 1984–85. If in fact you made no gifts that year, you would carry forward that year's exemption of £3,000 (but not the £1,000 left from 1983–84) giving you a total of £6,000 exempt in 1985–86.

- Gifts to charities.
- Lifetime gifts to political parties which had at least two members of parliament elected, or which had one member elected and attracted 150,000 votes, at the general election preceding the gift. Gifts on or within one year of death are exempt only up to a limit of £100,000.
- Gifts for national purposes and public benefit, such as gifts to universities, museums, and the like.
- Gifts and bequests of property outside the United Kingdom, made by a person domiciled outside the United Kingdom.

Any gifts and bequests not falling within these statutory exemptions are added to the donor's cumulative total, although the first £64,000 of this total is not taxed.

In addition to these exemptions there are certain reliefs which result in a percentage reduction in the value of a transfer or in the amount of tax payable:

- The value of an interest in a business (including the value of the business assets) is reduced by 50% if the interest is that of a sole trader, a partner or the controlling shareholder of a company. The value of business assets owned by the donor but used by his partnership or by a company controlled by him, is reduced by 30%. The value of a minority shareholding in a private company is also reduced by 30%.

For example, Margaret is a grocer whose business, including the fixed assets, is worth £80,000. She dies leaving the business to her son, Brian. The transfer attracts business relief of 50%; thus the value transferred for capital transfer tax purposes is £40,000. If she has made no other taxable gifts, no tax is due now.

- Agricultural land and buildings also attract relief. Provided the farm is not subject to a tenancy continuing after the transfer, the value transferred is reduced by 50%. If there is a sitting tenant, the relief is only 30%.
- Relief is given where the recipient of a gift or bequest dies soon afterwards. This is known as 'quick succession relief', and is a way of softening the blow of two tax charges on the same property within a short period of time.

Relief is given by a percentage reduction in the tax payable on the second transfer, that is, the death of the recipient of the first gift. This percentage varies from 100% where the recipient dies less than a year after receiving the gift, down to 20% where the intervening period is less than 5 years.

Valuation of assets for capital transfer tax

The value of property is taken to be its open market value at the time of the transfer.

In many circumstances valuation of an asset is a highly specialised matter. In the case of land or buildings you will have to estimate what you could expect to get by selling the property on the open market, and agree a figure with the District Valuer acting on behalf of the Inland Revenue. A house or farm with a sitting tenant will be worth a lot less than it would be if it were vacant.

The value of shares quoted on the Stock Exchange can be ascertained by consulting the Official List for the date on which the transfer took place. Unquoted shares are much harder to value: many factors – for example, the size of the shareholding, the health of the company and its future business prospects – must be taken into account. Specialist advice will usually be essential.

CAR DEALER

When a code of practice may protect you

If you buy a new or used car, or if you have to have repairs made to your own car, and then have cause to complain, you may choose to exercise your rights under the law. *See:* DEFECTIVE GOODS; REPAIRER

But if the car dealer belongs to a trade association you can also pursue your complaint through it. Such a course of action is simpler, quicker and generally cheaper than starting court proceedings. It does not, however, jeopardise your legal rights. If you are dissatisfied with the trade association's response to your complaint, you can still take legal action later.

Dealers who belong to an association generally exhibit the symbol at the en-

WHEN YOUR NEWLY BOUGHT CAR BREAKS DOWN

A customer with a complaint about his car should first approach the dealer, then the dealer's trade association and finally, if all else fails, should consider taking legal action.

trance to the garage and may reproduce it on letter headings and invoices.

Voluntary codes of practice

The four main motor trade associations – the Motor Agents' Association Ltd (MAA), the Society of Motor Manufacturers and Traders Ltd (SMMT), the Scottish Motor Trade Association Ltd (SMTA) and the Vehicle Builders and Repairers Association Ltd – have produced voluntary codes of practice after negotiations with the Office of Fair Trading.

These codes cover the sale of new cars, the sale of used cars and repairs and servicing. Although their provisions are not usually binding in law, the associations try to see that their members observe the rules. The codes also provide an ARBITRATION scheme for disputes which reach deadlock. Arbitration is not, however, compulsory.

CODE OF PRACTICE

The motor trade associations' code of practice lays down the following rules:

Buying a new car

- Every customer should be given a maker's handbook for the car and should be shown a copy of the dealer's pre-delivery inspection check-list.

Buying a secondhand car

- Used cars are given a pre-sales inspection in accordance with an approved checklist which must be displayed in a prominent place in the car. A copy of the checklist must be given to the customer. If the customer has reason to complain about the condition of the car after the sale, the list could be produced as evidence although it would not be conclusive.
- All documents provided by previous owners – for example, service records, repair invoices and inspection reports – should be passed to the customer.
- The dealer should take reasonable steps to verify the mileage shown on the car. *See:* TRADE DESCRIPTIONS

LICENSING DEALERS

Dealers in new cars need no licence. But district councils can now require used car dealers to be licensed, and to observe licence conditions. It is an offence for a licensed dealer not to record a car's mileage when he acquires it.

Making a complaint

Under the basic code agreed by the four main associations, a customer must first ensure that the dealer has been made aware of his complaint. It should be addressed to a senior executive or to the person appointed by the dealer to handle complaints.

If the customer is still dissatisfied he should find out to which trade association the dealer belongs and refer the complaint to it in writing. Each association promises to use its 'best endeavours' to try to resolve the complaint. If those efforts fail, the dealer will agree to go to arbitration, unless his trade association advises him that would be unreasonable. If there is an arbitration clause in the contract between the dealer and the customer, the dealer would be bound to go to arbitration.

Main agents and manufacturers

Some car dealers call themselves agents or main agents for a particular manufacturer. That does not mean that they are agents in the legal sense that they act on a manufacturer's behalf. It is a business term to describe an outlet for a particular manufacturer's goods.

The distinction is important, for if you decide to make a claim under the Sale of Goods Act, it is the dealer not the manufacturer you must sue.

In addition, however, you may have rights under the manufacturer's warranty. *See:* GUARANTEE; MANUFACTURERS' LIABILITY

CAR HIRE

Your right to be hired a car in good condition

If you hire a car to drive, the company which hires it to you is legally responsible for making sure that it is roadworthy.

Any clause in your hire agreement making you responsible is of no effect, unless you hire the car for business use. Even if you do, you can challenge the clause under the UNFAIR CONTRACT Terms Act.

Nevertheless, if you drive the vehicle when it is in an unroadworthy condition or when there are other illegal faults – such as a bald tyre – you could be in breach of the Motor Vehicles (Construction and Use) Regulations.

That could mean that both you and the owner could be liable to prosecution under the Road Traffic Act 1972, which says that it is an offence to drive a car that does not comply with those regulations. *See:* GOODS RENTAL; MOTOR VEHICLE

CAR INSURANCE

The duty imposed on every motorist to insure against accidents

It is a criminal offence to drive a motor vehicle on a public road or in a public place without being insured.

Driving while disqualified means that any insurance a driver might have had is invalid. If he is involved in an accident, and negligently causes injury or damage, he is liable to pay the damages himself.

The insurance companies operate a scheme, known as the Motor Insurers' Bureau (MIB), which pays damages due by uninsured drivers and then tries to recover the money from them. *See:* MOTOR INSURANCE

CAR PARK

The risks you run when you leave your car

When you use a car park your rights depend on the responsibilities accepted by the car park operators. Normally they will merely have agreed to permit you to leave your car on their property, even though you pay a charge. This means that you are not entitled to expect the car to be supervised.

Theft or damage to the car or its contents

You will generally be unable to claim against the operators of the car park if your car or any of its contents are stolen – even if the thief is one of their employees.

The employee would usually be considered to be acting for his own benefit and not for that of the car park operators. However his employers could be liable if they knew that he had stolen cars from them before.

The car park operators would also be liable if you handed over the keys and they failed to take reasonable care to secure the car from theft.

WHEN CONDITIONS CAN EXCLUDE LIABILITY FOR THEFT OR DAMAGE TO PROPERTY

Conditions referred to in tickets and notices which exclude liability for theft or property damage will only be effective if your attention is sufficiently drawn to them so that you have a reasonable opportunity to reject them. Otherwise you cannot be said to have agreed to them.

In one case a court did not give effect to a condition referred to on the back of a ticket dispensed by an automatic machine. The ticket was issued in a way that offered the motorist no opportunity to reject it, and the full conditions could only be found in the office where payment was made on leaving the car park.

Since this case many car parks have their conditions prominently displayed in large, easy to read letters, so that drivers have a chance to read them before accepting a ticket. But whether this provides a reasonable opportunity to refuse is still a question of circumstances – for example, if you are caught in a stream of cars queuing for a car park you may not be able to refuse to enter.

Even if the conditions are part of the agreement, they will only be effective if they are sufficiently clear to apply to a particular situation and are also fair and reasonable. The courts will give you the benefit of the doubt if there is any ambiguity in the condition which the car park operator tries to rely on.

The courts have not yet made clear what sort of conditions would be fair and reasonable. It is unlikely, however, that a condition excluding liability for damage arising from negligence would be. But if the car was parked on a long-term basis – perhaps by a businessman for the whole of every working day – such a condition might be held to be fair and reasonable. In such a case the car owner might be expected to take the risk and insure himself.

THE JEWELS THAT VANISHED FROM A ROLLS-ROYCE

Written conditions – on the car park ticket, for example – do not always free the operators from liability for loss or damage.

Mr Mendelssohn parked his friend's Rolls-Royce on the 1st floor of a car park. When the attendant told him he could not lock the car, Mr Mendelssohn explained that there was a suitcase of jewellery on the back seat under a rug. The attendant agreed to lock the car as soon as he had moved it.

An hour later Mr Mendelssohn came back and paid his fee. The car door was unlocked and the key was in the ignition. The rug was still on the back seat.

Mr Mendelssohn drove away and only later moved the rug. He found the suitcase was missing. He returned to the car park and made enquiries, but the suitcase was never found. He sued the car park proprietors.

DECISION

The court found that the suitcase had been stolen from the car park. Although the printed ticket contained a condition that the proprietors were not responsible for loss of vehicle contents, the judge ruled that the attendant's promise to lock the car took priority over this. The proprietors were held responsible.

If the car is damaged the operators of the car park would be liable if they or one of their employees have been negligent. For example, there might be negligence if a part of the building fell on the car because the operators failed to carry out reasonable maintenance, or if an attendant caused an accident by giving a driver misleading directions when parking.

But even in situations where the car park operators could be liable, they may have attempted to exclude their liability by conditions referred to on the ticket or in a notice. A court will only accept this exclusion if the conditions are fair and reasonable. *See:* UNFAIR CONTRACT

THE BOGUS FRIEND WHO DROVE AWAY A CAR

To use a car park is normally merely to pay for or borrow space on someone else's premises. You cannot expect the car to be supervised or looked after continuously.

Mr Ashby parked his car in a seaside car park. He paid the fee, and the attendant handed him a ticket.

When he came back a few hours later the car had gone. Mr Ashby asked the attendant why he had let someone without the ticket drive away. The attendant explained he had been told that the person who took the car was the owner's friend. Mr Ashby sued the operators of the car park.

DECISION

The court said the operators were under no obligation to take care of the car. Mr Ashby's fee simply allowed him to leave the car on their premises.

Injury or death

Car park operators are liable to pay compensation for any death or injury caused by unsafe premises or the negligence of an employee. In such cases they cannot under any circumstances exclude their liability by any condition on a ticket or notice.

CAR REPAIR

Your right to satisfactory workmanship

When you have your car repaired or serviced, you are entitled to expect the repairer to use reasonable care in the work, and to ensure that any spare parts supplied are reasonably fit for their purpose.

A code of practice, drawn up by the Motor Agents' Association Ltd, the Society of Motor Manufacturers and Traders Ltd, and the Scottish Motor Trade Association Ltd, although not legally binding, recommends:

Cost Wherever possible, a garage should give a firm quotation for the cost of major repairs, and state whether the amount shown includes VAT. When the customer accepts a quotation, both sides are bound by it.

If the garage has to dismantle parts before giving an estimate, the customer should be warned about the dismantling costs in advance, and there should be a clear understanding on whether he has to pay these costs if he rejects the estimate. If, during the progress of any work, it appears that the estimate will be exceeded by a significant amount, then the customer should be notified and asked for permission to continue the work. *See:* QUOTATION

Guarantees Repair work and servicing must always be guaranteed against failure due to faulty workmanship, for a specified mileage or length of time after the work is done.

The repairer should be adequately insured against any claim for loss arising out of bad workmanship – for example, damage to the customer's vehicle, or other vehicles, in an accident caused by the faulty repair or servicing.

Parts Spare parts should be readily available from the time a new model is offered for sale. When a model is going out of production, the manufacturer should indicate the minimum time during which parts will remain generally available to the trade.

When new parts are fitted, the old ones should be made available for the customer to collect, if he wishes, for a 'reasonable period'. Dealers should display notices showing how long they will keep such parts available.

Damage or loss Dealers should take adequate care to protect customers' cars and possessions and should be insured against loss or damage. They are legally responsible (unless the loss or damage was not through their negligence) and must not try to avoid that responsibility by posting notices disclaiming liability.

If your repairer is a member of one of the trade associations mentioned, and does not follow the code of practice or deal satisfactorily with your complaint, complain to the association.

CAR SHARING

When you can charge

Under the Transport Act 1980, motorists may use their cars on a regular basis for shared journeys and collect a contribution from the passengers, without breaking the Public Service Vehicle licensing laws.

How insurance is affected

Although private motor insurance policies exclude use of the car for payment, even if it includes no element of profit, the insurance will remain effective in situations where motorists receive contributions from passengers for car-sharing arrangements, provided that:

- The vehicle is not adapted to carry more than eight passengers.
- Arrangements were made before the journey began for the payment of fares by the passengers.
- The total contributions received for the journey concerned do not involve an element of profit.

Public advertising by would-be car sharers in newspapers and shops, for example, is allowed.

CARAVANS

When you may need permission to park

You do not need PLANNING PERMISSION simply to store your holiday caravan in your garden. Nor is permission normally necessary if the caravan is merely used as an adjunct to your house, perhaps to provide additional accommodation for members of your household.

If, however, a caravan parked in your garden is used as a separate residence, providing accommodation independent of your house, planning permission will be required.

If you own a piece of land not connected with your home and you want to store a caravan on it for more than 28 days in the year, planning permission will normally be necessary.

Before land is used as a site for any caravan or caravans in which people are to live, not only will it generally be necessary to obtain planning permission, but a caravan site licence will also be required. District and island councils are responsible for the issue of site licences. There are, however, several minor exemptions from the site licensing requirements.

If you use your caravan as your main home, the Mobile Homes Acts will protect your right to remain on a site you have rented. *See:* MOBILE HOME

On holiday You should be careful where you park your caravan while touring. You have no right to park in lay-bys or on private land without the owner's consent.

CARELESS DRIVING

A motorist must be alert and considerate

The term careless driving covers two offences: driving without due care and attention, and driving without reasonable consideration for other users of the road, including passengers in the accused driver's vehicle and pedestrians. The offences are equally serious and are treated in law as the same, with the same maximum penalty. *See:* ROAD TRAFFIC OFFENCES

Driving without due care and attention

Every driver is legally obliged to be constantly alert to the situation on the road, including traffic and weather conditions, speed limits and road signs. When a court considers a charge of driving without due care it compares the evidence of the accused driver's behaviour with how a prudent driver would have driven. The standard is the same for everyone, including a learner driver.

An error of judgment, or momentary inattention, can amount to driving without due care and attention. A court, however, does not expect a driver to react perfectly in all situations.

Accident or not Most cases arise because of accidents, but there need not be an accident for there to be a prosecution. For example, turning a corner without giving a proper signal may be judged careless driving.

However, if there has not been an accident the driver must either be warned at the time of the offence of the possibility of a prosecution or be served with a SUMMARY COMPLAINT within 14 days of the offence; or the procurator fiscal must send a NOTICE OF INTENDED PROSECUTION to the driver or the registered owner of the vehicle within 14 days of the offence.

It can be a defence for the motorist to show that an accident was caused by a mechanical defect of which he or she had no knowledge. In such a case the vehicle may be inspected to see if it had been maintained properly and whether a prudent motorist could reasonably have suspected the defect.

It may also be a defence for the accused person to prove that he is a diabetic and at the time of the incident he was suffering from hypoglycaemia.

Driving without reasonable consideration

The alternative charge under the general heading careless driving is less a matter of inattention than of deliberate bad manners – for example, driving at night with undipped headlights; cutting in after overtaking; blocking traffic by turning right from the inside lane; or splashing pedestrians by driving through a visible puddle at speed.

Maximum penalties The maximum fine for either offence is £1,000. Licence endorsement is automatic unless there are special reasons. The offences carry up to 5 points under the totting-up rules. Disqualification can also be imposed and the court can order anyone convicted to take a driving test. *See:* DRIVING DISQUALIFICATION

A motorist who by driving carelessly injures another or damages his vehicle may have to pay compensation to his victim if he is sued for NEGLIGENCE.

CARRIAGE OF GOODS

The significance of the small print

A carrier who transports goods, including house removals, by road or rail may try to avoid his basic legal liability to make good any loss or damage suffered by his customers by the way he words his conditions of carriage.

You are not bound by such conditions, however, if you did not know of them and did not sign them when you sent the goods.

If the carrier can show that he took reasonable steps to draw your attention to the conditions before the contract is made, you may be bound.

On the other hand, under the Unfair Contract Terms Act 1977, the carrier cannot be immune against a claim for negligence if his conditions are unfair or unreasonable.

WHEN GOODS GET DAMAGED OR LOST IN TRANSIT

A commercial carrier or transporter must take reasonable care of the goods in his possession if he wants to avoid a claim against him for loss or damage.

If you have to make a claim, it is important to do so within any time limit laid down in your agreement – probably 7 to 28 days after loss or damage is discovered. *See:* UNFAIR CONTRACT

Care of the goods The basic legal rule for carriers is that they must take reasonable care of goods in their possession. A carrier is not liable for loss or damage if it is not his fault, but he must prove that he did take reasonable care.

However, some carriers – known as common carriers – are liable even where they are not at fault. A common carrier is one who makes public his desire to carry for anyone willing to hire him. Not surprisingly, many carriers state in their contracts that they are not to be regarded as common carriers.

If goods perish by fire during the course of carriage, then the carrier is always obliged to pay compensation, whether he is a common carrier or not.

Insuring against loss

To avoid uncertainty about the carrier's liability for your goods, it is advisable to insure them yourself independently. The carrier may arrange the insurance for you.

Railway risk One carrier, British Rail, carries goods either at 'owner's risk' or at 'carrier's risk'.

Conditions for 'owner's risk' exempt the railway from most responsibility. 'Carrier's risk' conditions mean that British Rail accepts responsibility.

It is usually advisable to choose owner's risk – and insure the goods yourself, separately, because any claim against the railway is likely to be more restricted than one against your own insurers.

If goods are delayed

You are entitled to have goods delivered within a reasonable time, even if no fixed delivery date is specially agreed.

However, you cannot get compensation from the carriers for loss caused by delay if they did not know (and could not reasonably foresee) that delay would cause you loss. So you should always specify fast delivery when promptness is necessary, and also explain to a senior official of the company why it is necessary.

Sending goods abroad

Carriers handling international traffic are governed by special rules. The rules for international carriers apply even while the transporting vehicle is in the United Kingdom, so long as it is engaged in international carriage.

Road transport When goods are sent

THE SPARE PART THAT ARRIVED TOO LATE

When prompt delivery is required, tell the carriers so, and tell them also the reason for the urgency. Otherwise, they cannot be held responsible for any delay.

A firm of carriers agreed to deliver a broken piece of machinery to repairers. They delivered it several days late. As a result, the machine was out of action for several days longer than it should have been.

The owners of the machine claimed damages for loss of profits which would have been made if the machinery had been working earlier.

DECISION

The carrier was not liable for the customer's loss of profits because it did not know that the machinery was going to be out of action and so could not have foreseen the loss of profits.

abroad by road, the carrier is liable, under international agreement, for loss of goods or damage from the time he takes charge of the goods until they are delivered. He is also liable for any delay in delivery.

However, the carrier can avoid these liabilities if he can show that the loss, damage or delay was caused by circumstances he could not foresee or avoid – for example, if weather conditions stop a ferry, or if a ship sinks.

A carrier's liability is generally limited, under the agreement, to about £4 per kg. (£1.80 per lb.) for loss or damage, and to the total of the carriage charges in case of delay.

Those limits do not apply when you have declared the value of the goods or stated your special interest in delivery by a fixed date.

Sea transport When goods go by sea, there is usually a limit to the carrier's liability – about £460 for each package or £1.40 per kg. (63p per lb.), whichever is the higher.

Air transport When goods go by air, the airline will be liable for loss, damage or delay unless it can prove that it and its servants took all necessary measures to avoid loss or damages or that such measures were impossible.

Airline liability for loss, damage or delay is limited to a maximum of about £12 per kg. (£5.44 per lb.) of goods, regardless of their value.

THE CARRIER WHO LOST THE GARMENTS

Common carriers have to pay for customers' losses even if they are not to blame.

A firm of carriers specialised in transporting hanging garments. Their calendars, advertisements and circulars stated that they would carry for anybody at standard rates regardless of the attractiveness of the offer of business. But goods sent were hijacked.

DECISION

The carriers were found automatically liable to make compensation without proof of negligence because they were common carriers.

CARRIAGE OF PASSENGERS

Damages for passenger injury

If you are injured while being carried by inland public transport – including taxis or hired cars – you are entitled to sue the carriers for any negligence by their employees.

Any conditions printed on your ticket cannot take away or limit this right.

See also: AIR ACCIDENT
BUSES AND COACHES
RAIL TRAVEL

CASINO

Controlling the growth of gambling houses in Britain

There are strict laws governing the setting up and running of any club that allows gaming on its premises. People who want to operate such clubs, called casinos, must have a licence from the local licensing board, and they are liable to have their premises inspected at any time by officials of the Gaming Board. *See:* GAMBLING

CASUAL WORKER

The rights of those whose work is irregular

Although the term 'casual worker' is widely used, it has never been legally defined and it may describe several types of worker whose hours are short or irregular.

Most commonly, casual workers are those who are employed for fewer than 16 hours a week and who do not generally qualify for certain statutory EMPLOYMENT PROTECTION rights. *See:* PART-TIME WORKER

Someone who undertakes several short jobs for different people during a week – for example, a window-cleaner or jobbing gardener – may be regarded by his various employers as casual labour, but in law he will normally be regarded as SELF-EMPLOYED.

Another type of casual worker may work long hours during a short period – for example, as a fruit-picker. He may or may not be classed as an employee. *See:* SEASONAL WORKER

Casual employees, like all other employed people, have an EMPLOYMENT CONTRACT, though often it is not in writing and its terms may therefore be unclear. Self-employed people who do casual work have a contract for services which also may not be in writing.

Rights and obligations

A casual worker is liable for INCOME TAX and also NATIONAL INSURANCE CONTRIBUTIONS on his earnings.

If employed, his employer is also obliged to pay national insurance contributions for him if his wages from the employment are more than the LOWER EARNINGS LIMIT.

A casual worker has the same right as permanent staff to compensation for industrial injury and, if he is an employee, he can also claim sick PAY and SICKNESS BENEFIT.

CAVEAT EMPTOR

Advice to the buyer

'Let the buyer beware' – in Latin *caveat emptor* – is sound advice if you are buying from anyone who does not have an established business. There is, for example, little legal redress against a doorstep salesman who never reappears after taking your money. Nor can the law greatly help if you buy defective goods at a one-day sale from a seller who moves on.

Otherwise, the buyer is well protected in modern law. If he buys goods from someone who sells in the course of business, and those goods prove to be unfit for their purpose, he can demand his money back or, if necessary, sue the seller for its return. That is a right that cannot be taken away by small print in the seller's literature or by a notice saying 'No money returned'. *See:* DEFECTIVE GOODS

CENSUS

Taking a survey of the population

The Government has power, under the Census Act 1920, to carry out a census (the word comes from the Latin *censere*, to rate) not more than once every 5 years. Parliament must give its approval before each census is taken, normally once every 10 years. The last census was in April, 1981.

The Census Act also empowers the Government to hold a selective census, subject to Parliament's approval.

When a census is conducted, a questionnaire has to be completed for every household. Normally one member of the household is required to complete the questionnaire to the best of his or her ability with details of all the people in the household on census day or night. This is usually done by the head – or joint heads – of the household. If no head exists, household members over 16 are responsible. It is an offence not to answer all the questions asked or to give false information.

If you do not wish the person completing the questionnaire for your household to know your personal details, ask a census official for a separate form and complete it yourself.

If you do not answer

Anyone who refuses to give information required in the census can be fined up to £400.

Everyone involved in taking a census is bound to secrecy. For census officials, including the collector to whom the forms are given, the maximum penalty for disclosing census information to an unauthorised person is an unlimited fine and 2 years' imprisonment. The person who completes the questionnaire for the household can be fined up to £400 for divulging information which the other members of the household have given to complete the form.

When you need not answer

The word 'census' is sometimes used by local authorities and private market research organisations when they conduct their own surveys. Such surveys are voluntary, and no one is obliged to answer the questions.

CENTRAL ARBITRATION COMMITTEE

Settling disputes between unions and employers

The Central Arbitration Committee, which replaced the Industrial Arbitration Board in 1976, is an independent body which has power to settle certain disputes between unions and employers.

The Committee consists largely of union representatives and employers' representatives. They are appointed by the Secretary of State for Employment on the recommendation of the ADVISORY, CONCILIATION AND ARBITRATION SERVICE.

The Committee's role includes hearing complaints by unions against employers who refuse to provide them with the information needed for effective COLLECTIVE BARGAINING.

It can also change collective agreements, pay structures and wages orders to remove unfair differences in treatment between men and women. *See:* SEX DISCRIMINATION

Apart from its statutory role, the Committee will also attempt to settle an industrial dispute if a party to it asks – via ACAS – for its assistance.

CHARITIES

Rules for collecting from the public

If you want to run a charity collection in Scotland you need written permission from the Scottish Home and Health Department or the local authority – depending on the type of collection you want to make.

House-to-house collections

For a house-to-house collection you need the permission of the Scottish Home and Health Department. If you also intend to run the collection in England and Wales, you will need to register with the Charities Commissioners and get permission from the Home Office. However, if you plan a purely local collection which will be over quickly, you need only a certificate from your local district or islands council.

Before issuing a certificate, the council will want to establish that you are a fit and proper person to hold a collection. Someone who has a criminal record will not be considered suitable.

The certificate may also be refused if the organiser proposes to pass on too small a percentage of the collection to the charity, after expenses, or if collecting agents are to receive 'excessive' payments.

In making your application, you will be asked to state the scale of any such proposed payments.

Rules for collectors

Every charity collector should wear a badge – obtainable from HM Stationery Office – and carry a certificate of authority from the organisers. Failure to do so is an offence carrying a maximum fine of £50.

If a collector calls at your home, you are entitled to ask to see both badge and certificate. If you do not wish to give a donation to his or her particular charity, the collector is not entitled to annoy you, or to stay on your doorstep after being asked to leave. A collector who does either of those things can be punished by a small fine.

Collections in the street

If you want to organise a street collection for charity, you must get permission from the local authority and all collectors should wear badges and carry certificates of authority.

The authority may set conditions about when and where collectors can operate, and you are obliged to conform to those conditions. Anyone who does not do so can be fined up to £50.

Setting up a charity

A group raising funds or collecting materials for a worthy cause is more likely to attract support from the public (and donations from other charitable bodies) if it has charitable status. In addition, income by way of donations or investment may qualify for exemption from INCOME TAX, CORPORATION TAX and CAPITAL GAINS TAX, and the charity will be able to recover tax deducted on payments under a deed of COVENANT in its favour. If it has its own premises, it is entitled to a 50% reduction in RATES. Some local authorities exercise a discretion in favour of charitable organisations and allow remission of all or part of the remaining 50%.

To obtain charitable status, the group's constitution must be submitted, together with a copy of the latest accounts, to the local Inspector of Taxes for approval. It is advisable, when setting up a new charity, to submit a draft of the proposed constitution for approval before adopting it.

The Inspector will approve a constitution if it meets the following requirements:

1. The 'objects' of the organisation must be charitable. This means in law that they must fall into one of four categories: relief of poverty; advancement of education; advancement of Christianity or another religion; or other purposes beneficial to the community (for example, disaster relief or the rehabilitation of former prisoners). So far as the last three categories are concerned, it must be shown that a 'substantial proportion' of the community will benefit, and not just a single section.

Projects to protect animals qualify only if they benefit humans as well. That condition may be met by declaring that the aim is 'to safeguard public morality' by preventing cruelty to animals.

2. Membership of the organisation must be open to any individual over 18 interested in supporting the objects of the body concerned.

3. The 'finance clause' of the constitution should make it clear that monies must be devoted to the objects of the body, and not distributed among the membership.

4. The constitution must also provide that on dissolution of the organisation, any funds left over will be used for similar charitable purposes. No further registration of the charity is needed in Scotland.

The Scottish Council of Social Service, 18/19 Claremont Crescent, Edinburgh, can supply model constitutions which have been agreed in principle by the Inland Revenue as being in charitable form. It will also advise any community or voluntary group with problems connected with charitable status.

Even if application for charitable status for a project is not desirable, it is a good idea to appoint trustees and to have clearly written rules regarding the use of funds collected.

CHECK TRADING

Credit for consumers on a low income

Trading checks, paid for by instalments, allow the customer to buy goods on credit at shops that have agreed to deal in the checks.

They are a comparatively easy way for someone on a low income to get credit. Because the sums borrowed are not large, the check company is not bearing a big risk on any one transaction.

A check trading or finance company which issues checks is just as liable as a retailer for DEFECTIVE GOODS or MISREPRESENTATION if the goods or services bought with the checks are faulty in some way. If you agree to buy checks, you must be given a copy of the written agreement, signed on behalf of the company issuing the checks, before or when you receive them.

Legally, you accept trading checks when you sign them on the front, sign a receipt for them, use them at a shop – or merely tell the trader who issues the checks that you accept them.

Checks are usually sold by a doorstep salesman.

If he does not have a canvassing licence, he is committing a criminal offence for which he can be imprisoned for up to two years and be fined up to £2,000. *See:* DOORSTEP CREDIT

If you receive trading checks that you have not asked for and do not want, complain to your local trading standards department. It is an offence to give anyone trading checks which have not been ordered unless an existing agreement is being renewed. *See also:* INTEREST CHARGE

CHEQUE

Telling your bank to hand over your money

A cheque is simply an instruction to a bank to pay money out of your account and pass it to someone else. Legally you do not need to use the bank's printed cheque form: a bank has been known to pay out on all sorts of 'cheques', from those written on plain paper to one written on the side of a cow. However, it is as well to keep to the prescribed form, except in an emergency.

If you have more than one account, do not mix your cheques. A cheque normally has the branch and account numbers printed in magnetic computer characters: the cheque you use is likely still to find its way to the account for which it was issued even though you alter the details in ink.

For the same reason, it is unwise to use someone else's cheque form, or let him have one of yours.

Most cheques have the customer's name printed on them. That does not, by itself, enable someone else to steal from you by forging your signature. It is up to your bank to recognise your signature and not to pay out on a forged one.

If money is lost as a result of your carelessness, however, the bank may try to make you bear the loss.

You have a duty to make it difficult for someone to alter a cheque. You should make sure there is no room for a word or a figure to be added to what you write (for example, by altering 'twenty pounds' to 'one hundred and twenty pounds' and changing £20 to £120).

If what you write does not take up all the space, draw lines to fill the rest.

Crossed or uncrossed There are two types of cheque form – 'crossed' and 'open'. A crossed cheque has two parallel lines across the face – up and down, or diagonally – or in some cases a broad tinted band which serves the same purpose.

It cannot be exchanged for cash, even at the bank named on the cheque: a crossed cheque can only be paid into a bank account and it is therefore difficult for a thief to avoid detection.

Banks supply whichever type you ask for, but it is generally safer to use the crossed type.

An open cheque has no crossing lines and can be cashed at the bank branch named on it. The open cheque carries a greater risk of theft and fraud, but can be turned into a crossed cheque simply by drawing in the two parallel lines. Even if someone gives you an open cheque, you can cross it yourself as a security measure until you can pay it into your bank.

If you lose your cheque book

When a cheque book is lost or stolen, and someone manages to obtain money from the bank by using it, the bank must bear the loss – as long as the customer has not been negligent.

For example, if you discover that your cheque book is missing, you should warn the bank immediately – especially if you lose your CHEQUE GUARANTEE CARD at the same time.

You should also warn the bank at once if you ever suspect that someone

CHEQUES SHOULD BE WRITTEN CAREFULLY TO AVOID PROBLEMS

Legal safeguards to protect you, the payer and the bank when you pay by cheque

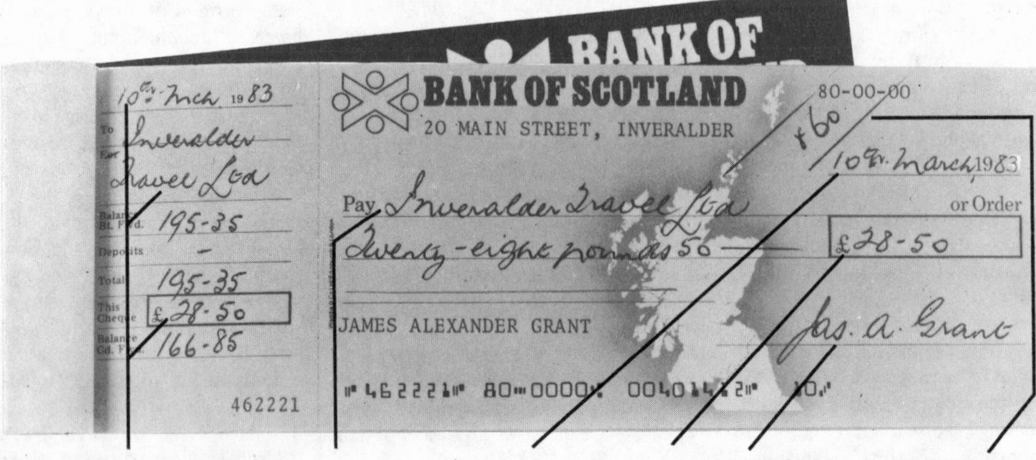

1 As a record of cheques drawn, note the date, payee, and amount on the cheque stub (or a separate record folder). It helps when there is a query.

2 Starting at the end of the upper line, write the amount in words without gaps between them. Draw a line to fill the remaining space. If the figures are not clear the sum can be verified from the words. The drawn line makes it difficult to alter the total.

3 A cheque should be dated with the date on which you draw it, though this is not essential. You may put in a later date. If the bank cashes the cheque too soon it must re-credit your account and hold the cheque until the right date.

4 Write the amount in figures in the box. Start close to the £ sign and draw a line between the pounds and the pence.

5 Sign the cheque with your usual signature, of which the bank will have a copy.

6 For greater security a cheque should be crossed. Then it can only be paid into a bank account.

A cheque must be signed on the back – that is, endorsed – by the person to whom it is made payable. When you endorse a cheque, use the name on the front even if that is not your normal signature.

may have forged your signature on a cheque, or tampered with it in any way. The bank will 'stop' the cheque on your instructions, if it has not already paid it.

If you lose a signed cheque

Warn your bank as soon as you discover that any cheque has gone astray, and ask it to stop payment.

A crossed cheque which has been properly made out to someone and signed should be of no value to anyone else who finds or steals it – although if the cheque is not crossed, he may be able to cash it at the branch on which it is drawn.

The only risk with a crossed cheque is that a thief may persuade someone to exchange it for cash, in the belief that he is the person to whom it is made out.

Anyone who accepts the cheque cannot pay it into his bank account unless it is endorsed – signed on the back by the person to whom it is made out. Therefore he must get the thief to endorse it.

When a theft or forgery comes to light, the person likely to lose money is whoever gave the thief cash for the stolen cheque. His own bank will not be liable because they are not expected to recognise the signature of people who are not their customers. (If a branch on which a cheque was drawn paid out cash for a crossed cheque, it would lose its protection, but that is unlikely to happen.)

If you find that someone has cashed a stolen cheque belonging to you, you are entitled to claim the money from him: he has no legal right to it.

A cheque may be lost or stolen on its way to you. If that happens, there is no question of you having been paid. You still have the legal right to the payment: you do not lose that right simply because a cheque has been put in the post.

THE COST OF CARELESSNESS

When drawing a cheque make sure it cannot be easily altered.

A clerk made out a cheque for £2 for his employer's signature. He did not write the sum in words and left a space in front of the figure '2'. After the cheque was signed the clerk altered the figure to £120 and wrote in that amount in words. He obtained the money. His employer sued the bank for repayment of the £118 debited from his account.

DECISION

The claim failed and the court said that when drawing a cheque the customer must take reasonable care to see that the bank cannot be misled.

Even if you receive the cheque but then lose it, you will not lose your money if you have not endorsed it on the back. However, if for some reason you have endorsed it, you are likely to lose your money.

In any case you should immediately warn the person who wrote the cheque to stop payment on it.

If the cheque is paid into a bank, you should be able to trace the person who paid it in. All banks keep records of cheques that are banked or paid out. After that, your right to claim the money from him will depend on whether or not you endorsed the cheque.

If it was not endorsed when you lost it, you are entitled to claim from him. If it was endorsed, you cannot claim unless you can prove that he knew the cheque had been stolen (or possibly that he obtained it without giving full cash value for it).

Blank cheques

If you want to make a payment but are not sure what the exact amount will be, do not simply sign a blank cheque, leaving details to be filled in by the other person once the figure is known. Your bank might make you stand any loss if the cheque is stolen.

Instead, fill in everything but the amount and write across the face of the cheque the largest amount you want the other person to draw. If the sum is £15, write 'Not exceeding £15'.

If a stranger asks you to cash a cheque for him, you run no risk as long as the cheque is made out by him and made payable to you, he has a CHEQUE GUARANTEE CARD and the cheque is not for an amount greater than the card limit.

The cheque should be signed in your presence and should have the same code number as appears on the card. Check that the card has not expired and that the signatures compare. Write the card number on the back of the cheque yourself.

Do not take more than one cheque for any one transaction: if there are no funds, the bank may refuse to honour the guarantee if the card's cash limit has been exceeded.

The cheque card is useless as a guarantee for a cheque written by a third party. If you cash such a cheque for someone who says he is the person to whom the cheque is payable, the bank can refuse to pay it.

If you know the other person, you may be willing to cash the cheque. If so, get him to endorse it on the back, signing exactly as he is named on the front. Then get him to write, above the endorsement, an instruction: 'Pay . . .' (with your name).

When you pay the cheque into your bank, you will have to endorse it yourself.

THE WIFE WHO FORGED HER HUSBAND'S CHEQUES

A bank normally has to stand the loss of any money paid out on a forged cheque – but not if the account holder has been negligent by failing to warn the bank.

Mr Greenwood, a dairyman, discovered that his wife had been drawing money from his bank account by forging his signature. When challenged, she said she did it to raise money for her sister, who was having legal problems.

Mrs Greenwood implored her husband not to tell the bank about her forgeries, and he agreed. Later, he found out that the story about the sister was a lie.

After Mrs Greenwood died, Mr Greenwood tried to get the bank to repay him the money his wife had obtained with forged cheques. Eventually, he sued.

DECISION

Mr Greenwood lost his claim, because he had failed to tell the bank as soon as he discovered what his wife had been doing.

Stopping a cheque when there is a dispute

If you decide to stop payment on a cheque that you have written, the bank must obey your instruction, unless the cheque was backed by a cheque guarantee card – in which case it must be paid.

Otherwise, once you have given the instruction, if the bank mistakenly pays, it must bear the loss.

When a cheque has been stopped the bank must retain enough money to meet it. This means that the money will not be available to you until the problem is sorted out.

In a dispute The most common reason for stopping a cheque is dissatisfaction with something you have bought.

If you stop a cheque because goods you have bought are faulty and the shopkeeper will not replace them (perhaps insisting on repair, instead), give him your reason in writing – and keep a copy of the letter. You should see that the goods are returned or collected by the seller.

The shopkeeper can sue you for the money but it is a good defence that the goods are so faulty that you were entitled to reject them.

When issuing a cheque may be an offence

If a person obtains goods by writing a cheque, knowing that he does not have the money in his bank account to meet it, then he commits the offence of FRAUD.

It is probably not an offence to write a cheque in ignorance of the fact that your account is overdrawn.

CHEQUE GUARANTEE CARD

The token that says the bank will meet your cheque

A cheque guarantee card is a token by which your bank promises to meet any of your cheques, up to a limit shown on the card.

The limit must not be exceeded for any one transaction, otherwise the bank's guarantee does not apply. For example, if the limit is £50 and you buy something costing £60, the shopkeeper must not accept two cheques – one for £50, say, and one for £10. You will have to pay the excess in cash.

If someone exceeds his limit by writing two cheques and has not enough money in his account to meet either of them, the bank can refuse to honour both.

Some cheque cards, such as Barclaycard, are also a CREDIT CARD and can be used to obtain goods or cash without a cheque, as well as to guarantee a cheque.

Even a straightforward cheque card, however, is covered by the Consumer Credit Act. That is because the card represents potential credit: even if you do not expect ever to write a cheque that could not be met from your own funds at the bank, in theory you could withdraw all your money and then write a cheque which someone accepts on the strength of the card. If you did so, the bank would have to honour the cheque and try to recover the money from you.

An agreement covering the issue of a cheque guarantee card has to comply with most of the Consumer Credit Act rules protecting borrowers. *See:* CREDIT AGREEMENT

If you lose your cheque card

You should tell the bank at once if your cheque card is lost or stolen. The bank will cancel the old card, issue a new one and circularise other branches with the number of the cancelled card, so that it cannot be used to draw cash.

Provided that you are not negligent, reporting the loss as soon as it is realised, you will not be liable for unauthorised use of the lost card – for example, if someone finds or steals your cheque book as well as your card. *See:* CHEQUE

Sign your cheque card on the front with a ball-point pen as soon as you receive it. Keep a note of its number. Keep it separate from your cheque book.

CHILD ABUSE

Special protection for children under 16

It is a criminal offence for a person aged 16 or over to neglect or ill-treat a child under 16 in a way which is likely to cause unnecessary suffering or injury to health. The offence can only be committed by a person who has custody, charge or care of the child – for example, a parent, guardian or child minder.

Inflicting very minor suffering on a child – for example, by smacking the child as a punishment – would not amount to an offence.

Anyone who is convicted of this offence can be sentenced to up to 2 years' imprisonment and an unlimited fine.

When ill-treatment is suspected

Anyone who suspects that a child is being ill-treated should inform the local authority social work department, the RSSPCC, the reporter to the children's panel or the police.

Once this is done the case will be investigated. The organisations involved may meet together to consider the best course of action. If the child is thought to be in need of compulsory care the case will be passed to the reporter, who may decide to refer the child to a CHILDREN'S HEARING. The procurator fiscal may also decide to prosecute.

When a child is thought to be in immediate danger an application can be made to a justice of the peace or sheriff for a PLACE OF SAFETY ORDER. If this is granted, the child can be removed immediately to a children's home, foster home or other safe place – perhaps the home of a relative – for up to 7 days.

The reporter must arrange for a children's hearing to consider the place of safety order within 7 days. However the child can be held for a further 21 days if the hearing cannot make a speedy decision. If necessary, detention can be continued for three more 21-day periods (the last two must be authorised by a sheriff).

Parents' rights

If parents do not admit what is alleged about the child's treatment, or if a child is too young to understand the proceedings, the case must be passed to the sheriff (unless the children's hearing decides to drop it). He will decide whether there are legal grounds for referring the child to the hearing.

A parent can appeal to the sheriff within 3 weeks against the decision of a children's hearing, including any decision to detain a child for longer than 7 days in a place of safety.

CHILD BENEFIT

The state's weekly allowance payable to every young family

If you have a child under 16 you are entitled to child benefit – a non-taxable weekly cash payment, which in 1983–4 amounted to £6.50 per child. It is normally paid to the mother but can be claimed by anyone who is responsible for maintaining a child.

Someone with whom the child is living has a prior claim to child benefit over someone who merely contributes towards the child's upkeep – and who therefore is not responsible for the child's immediate needs.

If your child is over 16

Benefit is paid for any child over 16, but under 19, who is receiving full-time education at a school or other officially recognised educational establishment

It is not paid if the child is taking an advanced course for a degree, diploma of higher education, higher technical or business diploma, or teaching qualifications – or any other course certified as above ordinary or national diploma level, SCE Higher Grade or SYS level.

The benefit continues during school holidays or if education is interrupted due to any other reasonable cause (for example, temporary school closure, illness, or exposure to infectious disease), up to a maximum absence of 6 months.

Awaiting exam results If your child is awaiting examination results before deciding whether to continue full-time education, you can still draw benefit for the time being. But you must write to the social security office, explaining the circumstances – and also notify it as soon as you have decided whether the child is to continue his or her education.

If you do not keep in touch, the social security department may ask you to repay any benefit received since the end of the child's last term at school.

When a child is in hospital

You are entitled to child benefit for up to 12 weeks if your child is admitted to hospital or a home for the handicapped or mentally ill.

After that time, a parent may draw child benefit only if he or she is regularly spending money on the child – for example, paying fares to visit him or her.

CLAIMING CHILD BENEFIT

You should claim child benefit as soon as you realise you are entitled to it: it cannot be back-dated more than a year from the day you apply.

Go to the nearest social security office and ask for the necessary forms (CH2 and CH3). You will also receive a prepaid addressed envelope in which to send off the claim. Make sure that you enclose the child's birth or adoption certificate.

If your claim is accepted, you will receive a letter telling you the amount of benefit you will get, how this is worked out and how you will be paid.

If for some reason your claim is not accepted, you will receive a letter setting out the reasons and telling you how to appeal to an independent tribunal, if you wish to.

Collecting the money

Benefit is *due* once a week, but, for mothers who claim for the first time after January 1982, it is *paid* every four weeks – either by a book of orders, which can be cashed at a post office, or direct into a bank or building society account.

In an emergency, such as illness, the person named in the order book can nominate someone else to collect the money.

Mothers who were getting child benefit before January 1982 were given a choice of weekly payments if they wished. Single parents and people receiving SUPPLEMENTARY BENEFIT or FAMILY INCOME SUPPLEMENT can have the money weekly or four-weekly. You are not allowed to cash any order more than three months after the date shown on it.

Someone who has been drawing benefit because he or she contributes to the support of a child who was not living with him or her is entitled to continue to draw it while the child is in hospital, for however long, providing he or she continues to support the child.

Children 'in care'

When a child is in the care of a local authority – in a children's home, boarded out with foster parents or placed with a voluntary organisation by the council – the parents will still receive benefit for up to 8 weeks. After that time, benefit may be drawn only if the local authority has agreed to allow the child to live at home for at least seven consecutive days. *See:* CHILDREN IN CARE

Going abroad temporarily

If you and your child go abroad for a time, you can continue to claim for 26 weeks.

If you go abroad by yourself, you are absolutely entitled to benefit for 8 weeks, but only entitled to it for the remaining 18 weeks if you intend to return and if you contribute to the child's support – at least the amount of benefit – while you are away.

Special arrangements with certain countries allow payment of child benefit in those countries for more than 26 weeks or payment of the country's equivalent benefit. The countries include the Isle of Man, Northern Ireland, the Channel Islands, Common Market countries, Australia, New Zealand, Austria, Finland, Norway and Sweden.

If your child goes abroad by himself, you can draw the benefit for 26 weeks, again depending on your own contribution to his support. Benefit can be paid beyond the 26 weeks if the child is going abroad for full-time education or for his health.

If you and/or your child move abroad permanently, benefit stops on the day you leave Britain.

Returning from abroad

Parents who have just returned to Britain from abroad, and intend to stay for at least 6 months, are eligible for child benefit at once, if either husband or wife received it at any time in the previous 3 years.

Anyone who has not drawn the benefit within that time, or who has not lived in Britain before, becomes entitled to the payments only after the husband or wife starts a job. In those circumstances, benefit is paid from the first week after the job is started.

Other people arriving from abroad can normally claim benefit only after spending 26 out of 52 weeks in Britain.

There are, however, special arrangements allowing benefit even if the usual requirements have not been met. These apply to people arriving from Common Market countries, Australia, Austria, Canada, the Channel Islands, Finland, Gibraltar, Northern Ireland, Isle of Man, New Zealand, Portugal, Spain, Switzerland or Yugoslavia.

One-parent increase

A single parent – a widow, if she is not receiving any widow's benefit, widower, divorcee or unmarried or separated person – may be entitled to a one-parent increase, provided that he or she is not living with someone as husband or wife. *See:* COHABITATION

The increase is paid for the first child only and is not taxable. In 1983–4, the one-parent increase was £4.05 a week.

In the case of separation, the claim can be made once husband and wife have lived apart for 13 weeks unless legal separation or divorce takes place before then. In all other circumstances the benefit can be claimed immediately.

If your spouse is absent only temporarily or is in hospital, but you are not otherwise living apart, you cannot claim one-parent benefit.

If you are receiving supplementary benefit, this will be reduced by the amount of the one-parent increase.

How to claim To claim the increase, fill in the form attached to leaflet CH11, available from your local social security office.

Retirement pension protection

The amount of retirement pension to which working people are entitled is calculated on reckonable working years. The government's 'home responsibilities protection' scheme is designed to compensate people who have not been able to complete the full number of working years, because they have stayed at home to look after a child under 16 for whom they receive child benefit. The scheme ensures that when your pension is being calculated, the years for which you get child benefit count as if they were years when you were working and paying national insurance contributions. You can get a full pension if the number of years that count towards your pension does not fall below 20. *See:* RETIREMENT PENSION

To qualify, a mother must have paid full-rate national insurance contributions when at work (the married women's lower rate does not qualify). A father who is out of work and looking after the children (while his wife is working) can get protection if the child benefit, with his wife's agreement, is paid to him. You do not need to apply for home responsibilities protection – it is given automatically until child benefit stops or your youngest child reaches 16, whichever is the earlier.

When a child's special allowance can be claimed

A mother whose marriage has been dissolved or annulled and whose former husband dies may be entitled to a child's special allowance. The allowance is not paid to a father whose ex-wife dies. Certain conditions must be satisfied:

- The mother must be eligible for child benefit for the child.
- Either she or her ex-husband must have been entitled to child benefit immediately before his death.
- The mother must not have remarried nor be living with a man as his wife.
- Her ex-husband must have been paying at least 25p a week towards the child's support, or have been obliged to do so under a court order or maintenance agreement which she tried to enforce.
- Her ex-husband must have paid a minimum amount of national insurance contributions amounting to at least 50 times the weekly LOWER EARNINGS LIMIT (£34 in 1984–5) in any income tax year.

Child's special allowance, £7.60 a week for each child in 1983–4, can be drawn in addition to child benefit. But if the mother is a single parent getting the one-parent increase, she will lose her right to that.

If the mother is already receiving a £7.60 child increase with invalidity, retirement or widow's benefit, non-contributory invalidity pension/severe disablement allowance, or invalid care allowance, she will not get child's special allowance.

How to claim To claim child's special allowance, get form CS1 from the social security office. You will need to produce your marriage certificate, evidence of divorce or annulment, or a death certificate, and details of your ex-husband's payments towards the child's support.

Even if all the documents are not immediately available, it is advisable to claim at once. The allowance will not be back-dated more than 3 months unless you can show good cause for delay in claiming – and it will never be back-dated more than 12 months.

CHILD GUIDANCE

Help for children with problems

Children with special difficulties can be helped by the child guidance service which each local education authority must provide. Help and advice are given by specially trained psychologists, teachers and social workers.

The service works with children who have many different problems – including withdrawn and aggressive behaviour, over-activity, bed-wetting, truancy, stealing and learning difficulties.

The child guidance service also helps to assess the needs of children who are physically and mentally handicapped. Once this has been done, the service will assist with placing such children so that their needs can be met.

Child guidance staff will usually work with children at school or in the home. Other members of the family may also need help and advice if the child's problem originates in the home. However a child who needs special attention may be asked to attend a child guidance centre.

Special education

The education authority must give a child a medical and psychological examination before deciding that SPECIAL EDUCATION is necessary. It is an offence for a parent of a school-age child to refuse to allow this without good reason – but the parent has the right to be present at any such examination.

You cannot prevent the education authority deciding that your child needs special education. But you have the right to refer the matter to an appeal committee set up by the education authority. You should do this within 28 days of the decision being issued.

The education authority can reconsider the need for special education from time to time. A parent can request the authority to do this at least once a year.

Special education may be given in ordinary schools or in day and residential special schools and units.

CHILD MINDER

Looking after other people's children in your own home

If you want to be paid – in cash or kind – for looking after other people's children in your home, you may have to observe certain legal rules.

It is an offence for a person to receive payment for looking after a child under 5 years of age for more than 2 hours a day unless she or he has registered with the local authority's social work department.

The department's job is to ensure that a child will be properly cared for in safe conditions. The maximum penalty is a fine of £400.

When an application is received, the authority sends someone to assess the applicant and inspect her (or his) home. Registration can be refused if the applicant or the premises seem unfit for children. Electrical wiring must be up-to-date and sound and there must be a satisfactory fire exit and other safety precautions.

The premises may be inspected at any time, without notice.

The applicant must be in good health and may be asked to have a chest X-ray. This will be done free of charge at a clinic or hospital. References may also be required: if any member of the household has ever been convicted of any offence against a child, the application will be refused.

A child minder may be held liable for NEGLIGENCE and have to pay compensation if any child in her or his care is injured through careless supervision. The child minder should insure against that liability.

Limit on numbers

The local authority will decide how many children a child minder can register for. The law does not fix a limit but in practice the child minder will not be allowed to look after more than three children under 5 years of age, including any children of her or his own.

Once registered, the child minder must keep a written record of the children left in her or his care, including names, addresses and ways of contacting parents in an emergency. The child minder must also allow the local authority to make regular visits to ensure that the children are being properly cared for.

Benefits for child minders

A registered child minder is entitled to a milk allowance for children in her or his care at the rate of one-third of a pint per child per day. The benefit comes as a cash allowance, which can be claimed on a form available from the Scottish Home and Health Department, St. Andrew's House, Edinburgh. Local authorities may also provide safety equipment such as fireguards and fire blankets.

Minders on supplementary benefit

A child minder who draws SUPPLEMENTARY BENEFIT, or whose husband does, should report any child-minding payments to the social security office, as benefit may be affected.

Only one-third of the child-minding payments is treated as earnings. Any reasonable expenses incurred in looking after the children can be deducted from that one-third.

For example, if a woman is paid £30 a week as a child minder and has no other earnings, and her child-minding expenses amount to £3 a week, her earnings will be £10 (one-third of £30) less £3 expenses, leaving £7 a week.

Of that amount, the first £4 is ignored (or £5.50 if she is a single parent). The balance of £3 a week (£1.50 for a single parent) is deducted from supplementary benefit.

CHILDREN IN CARE

How a local authority protects children's welfare

A child can come into the care of a regional or islands council – in practice its social work department – in a number of different ways.

If a child is orphaned, abandoned or lost, or if a parent or guardian is unable to look after him or her, the local authority must take the child into its care where this is necessary for the child's welfare. This is often called 'voluntary care'.

When a parent is seeking CUSTODY of a child, either as part of divorce proceedings or in a separate action, the court may decide that it is in the child's best interests to be put into the care of the local authority.

A CHILDREN'S HEARING can make a SUPERVISION REQUIREMENT in respect of a child who has committed an offence; or a child who is truanting, at risk or very difficult to control. When the supervision requirement is made, the child is treated in law as being in the care of the local authority – even though still living at home.

A local authority must review the cases of all children in its care (except those in care under supervision requirements) at least every 6 months.

Voluntary care

A child under 17 can be received into care without a court or hearing being involved if he or she:

- Has no parent or guardian.
- Is lost or has been abandoned by a parent or guardian.
- Has a parent or guardian who is temporarily or permanently unable to care for the child properly – perhaps because of illness or family crisis.

The local authority has a duty to receive such a child into care where this is necessary to protect the child's welfare. Sometimes a parent who feels unable to cope will ask the authority to care for his or her child.

When a child is taken into care and the parents' whereabouts are unknown, the local authority must take reasonable steps to find them and (if appropriate) return the child to them. If the parents cannot be found, a relative or friend may be asked to care for the child. The authority may consider paying an allowance to such a person so the child does not have to be taken into care.

If this does not happen, or is inappropriate, the child will be placed in a children's home or with foster parents. *See:* FOSTERING

During the first 6 months of voluntary care a parent or guardian can demand that the local authority return the child immediately. It is an offence to remove a child who has been in care for longer than 6 months, unless the local authority agrees or the parent or guardian gives it at least 28 days' written notice that the child will be removed.

A child can remain in voluntary care until the age of 18. The parents can be required to contribute to the child's upkeep until the age of 16 (but not if they receive supplementary benefit or family income supplement). Thereafter the child can be made to contribute.

If a child has been in care at any time after the age of 16, the authority can help pay the cost of accommodation and maintenance until the age of 21.

When a child is taken into care, the authority will usually ask the parents to give written consent to medical treatment, including vaccinations, which the child may need.

Taking away the parents' rights

If a child has come into care the local authority has power to go further and pass a resolution to take over virtually all the rights and duties of the parents. This is called 'assuming parental rights'. Parental rights can be assumed whether the child is in care voluntarily or by order of a court or children's hearing.

A resolution can be passed on any of the following grounds:

- The parents are dead and the child has no guardian.
- The child has been in care for 3 years or more.
- The child has been abandoned.
- The parents or guardian have persistently failed without good reason to take proper care of the child.
- The parents or guardian are unable to care for the child because of mental illness or handicap or permanent disability.
- The parents' or guardian's way of life makes them unfit to care for the child.

The local authority does not need to tell parents that it intends making a resolution. But often parents will be told and asked whether they will consent to this.

Once the resolution is passed the parents (unless they object to it) lose their rights over the child, except the right to refuse agreement to an ADOPTION. The child must continue to be brought up in his or her existing religion.

The child's parents, however, will still be liable to contribute to the child's upkeep.

Objecting to the resolution After passing the resolution the authority must notify the parents and tell them of their right to object to it. They must do this even if parents have previously given written consent to the resolution.

A parent who objects must give written notice to the authority, objecting to the resolution, within a month of being notified about it. The resolution will then cease to have effect unless the authority applies to the sheriff within 14 days and asks him to uphold it.

The sheriff will uphold the resolution if one of the above-mentioned grounds is made out, and it is in the child's interests to do so. If he refuses, the resolution will automatically lapse.

The resolution, if upheld or unchallenged, normally remains in force until the child is 18. However the parents are entitled to apply to the sheriff at any time for the resolution to be ended. The local authority can itself decide to end the resolution – thereby giving the parents back their rights.

An authority must give written notice

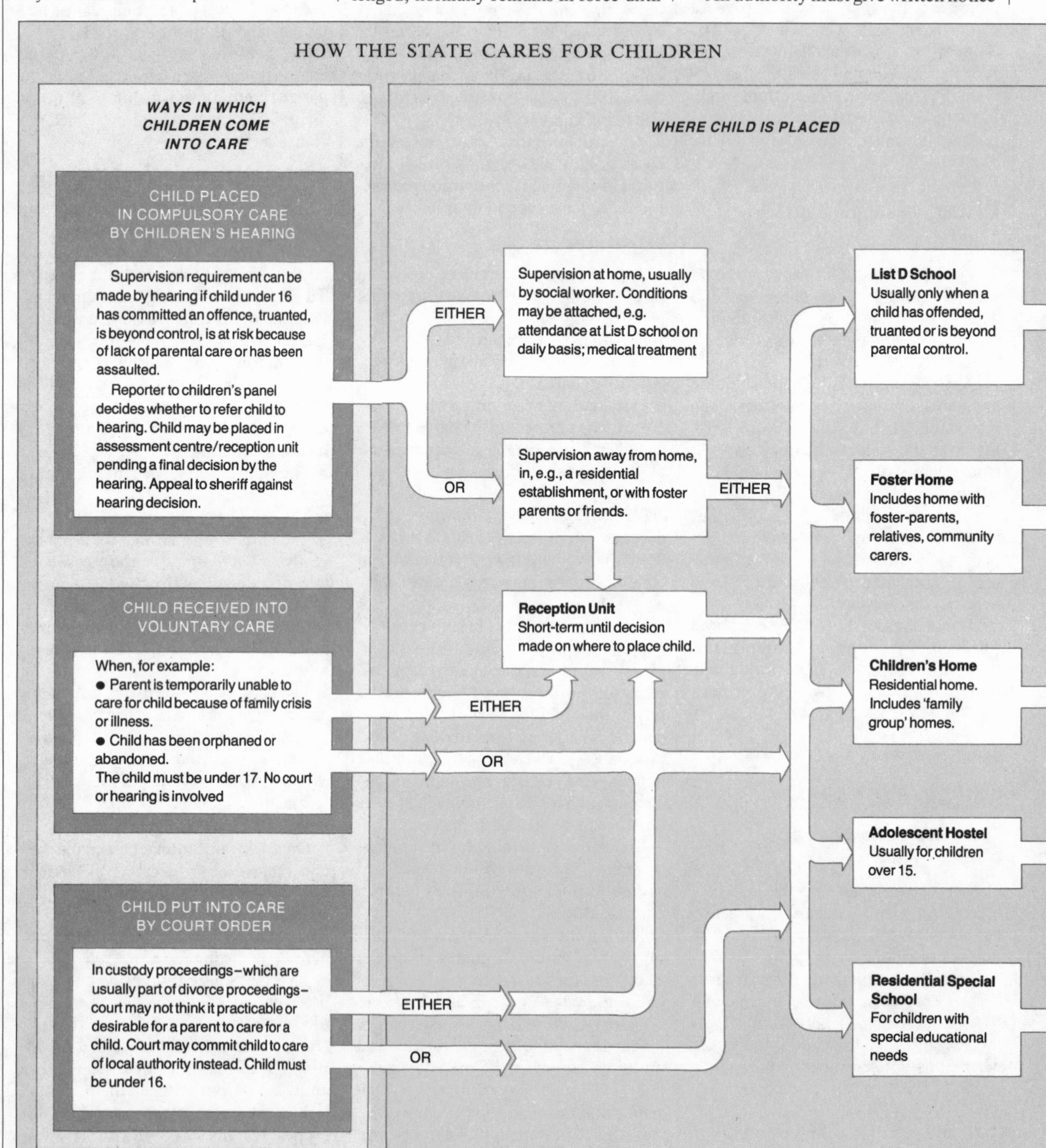

if it intends to refuse a parent access to a child subject to a resolution. The parent can appeal to a sheriff against the refusal.

The resolution ceases to have effect if the child is adopted or if a permanent guardian is appointed by a court.

CHILDREN'S HEARING

Coping with children in trouble

A children's hearing is a form of tribunal which deals with children up to the age of 16. Most of them have committed offences; some have not been attending school regularly or are beyond parental or local authority control. Others are neglected, at risk, or the victims of offences.

Whatever brings them before a hearing, the question to be decided is

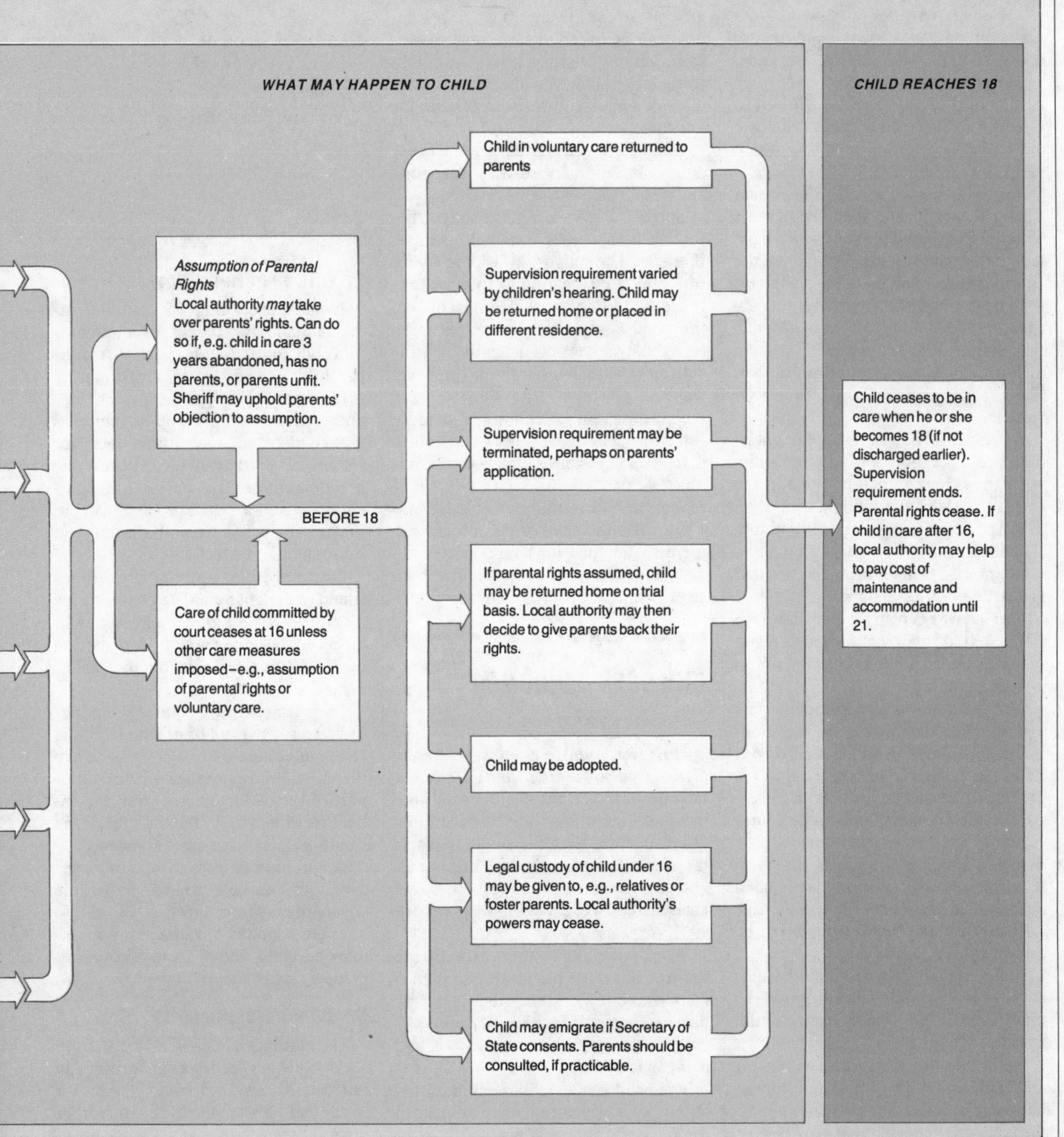

whether they are in need of 'compulsory measures of care'.

The hearing consists of a chairman and two members from a CHILDREN'S PANEL.

The parents and anyone acting as a parent are obliged to attend the sitting. The atmosphere is kept deliberately informal and everyone taking part sits round one table to help discussion. Normally the only other people present are the REPORTER, who acts as clerk, and a social worker.

Members of the press are allowed to attend, but very rarely do so. The case must not be reported in a way which identifies the child.

The case begins with the chairman asking the child and then the parents whether they admit the facts which have led to the child being brought to the hearing. If they all agree, a discussion then begins in which the child is encouraged to talk about his life, and the family's relationships are explored. To help in this a social background report will have been prepared by the social worker.

After about half an hour the chairman will try to find out from the family what they think should be done in the best interests of the child. He will then ask his colleagues what they think. Finally he will give his own opinion and announce what the hearing has decided and its reasons for doing so.

The hearing can do three things:

- The child may be removed from home to live in a LIST D SCHOOL for an indefinite period.
- The child may be placed under supervision while still living in the community. Usually this will mean living at home, with visits by or to a social worker. But it may mean living with foster-parents or attending an activity centre regularly while staying at home.
- The hearing may decide that the family situation is now such that it need make no order. However it may give advice as to how future trouble can be avoided.

If the child or a parent denies the facts at the outset (or the child is too young to understand) the case is sent to the sheriff.

He listens (in private) to witnesses and legal argument in the same way as he would in court, and decides whether the facts – or some of them – are true.

If they are found not to be true, that is the end of the case. If they are true in whole or part, then the case goes back to the reporter to make arrangements for another hearing. LEGAL AID is available to employ a solicitor at this stage.

The child or parents are entitled to appeal to the sheriff against any decision of a children's hearing on any ground. From the sheriff a further appeal can be taken to the Court of Session, but only about a legal point or an irregularity in the way the case was conducted. Legal aid is also available for appeals.

Children's hearings have some other duties. In emergencies they may continue a PLACE OF SAFETY ORDER.

Some children are still brought before criminal courts, usually for serious offences. The judge may ask the advice of a children's hearing as to what sentence, if any, to impose. He must do so if the child is already under supervision ordered by a hearing. Then the hearing will meet with the family in the usual way.

An order of a children's hearing (known as a SUPERVISION REQUIREMENT) expires after a year if it is not reviewed. Because of this the progress of the child is assessed at least once a year. But the child or parents can call for a review hearing more frequently, and the social work department can do so at any time.

CHILDREN'S INCOME

Managing a young person's money

However young a child is, he or she can receive both earned and investment income in his or her own name. If the income, excluding any educational grant, is more than the single person's tax-free allowance, the balance is taxable. The rate of single person's allowance increases every year. *See:* INCOME TAX

When a child's income exceeds the tax-free limit, the parent or guardian is responsible for ensuring that a tax return is completed – provided that the child is unmarried and under 18 and living at home.

The child's income is assessed for tax in the same way as that of an adult, and the same allowances apply.

ALL HIS OWN WORTH

No matter how young a child is, he is entitled to his own investment and earned income – say, from a paper round.

Effects on parents' tax

Income exceeding £5 from investments made by a parent for an unmarried child under 18 is taxed as part of the parent's income. If the investment is made by someone else – for example, a grandparent – the income is treated as the child's and may attract less tax. However, any advantage is lost if the grandparent or other person not a parent invests in a BUILDING SOCIETY, as the tax deducted from the interest at source cannot be reclaimed.

One of the best ways for a relative or friend to benefit a child not his own is by a COVENANT, an agreement to pay or invest a fixed sum annually for a period of more than 6 years on the child's behalf.

The arrangement requires the donor to deduct tax at the basic rate from the covenanted sum. The balance is given to the child, who may then recoup all or part of the deducted sum from the Inland Revenue, up to the amount of the single person's tax-free allowance. If the child has other taxable income, the sum that can be recouped under the covenant may be reduced.

There is no tax advantage for an unmarried child under 18 in a covenant made by a parent.

Supplementary benefit

The earnings of a child under 16 from a part-time job such as a paper round do not affect any parental claim for SUPPLEMENTARY BENEFIT. But other income received by a dependent child of any age living with his or her parents, including children over 16 and still at school, is treated as the parents' income and may reduce the benefit.

Invested capital is regarded as belonging to the parents, but they will not lose their entitlement to benefit simply because a child's capital puts them above the £3,000 limit.

CHILDREN'S PANEL

People who take decisions about children in trouble

Every regional and islands authority in Scotland has a children's panel, a list of people from whom members of CHILDREN'S HEARINGS are drawn. Applications for membership are invited from the general public towards the end of each year by a Children's Panel Advisory Committee.

Anyone between 18 and 55 (normally) may apply. There are no other qualifications, but an interest in the problems of children and an ability to communicate with them and their parents is looked for. The Committee has also to ensure that the panel as a whole is evenly-balanced in respect of sex and age, and is representative of occupations and districts within its area.

The appointments are made by the Secretary of State for Scotland on the recommendation of the Committee. They are for 5 years and may be renewed.

Members of panels are unpaid, but can apply for allowances for travelling, subsistence and loss of earnings. They go through an initial training course and also have opportunities to widen their knowledge of children and their problems while serving as members of the panel.

CHILDREN'S RIGHTS

The duties of society towards its future citizens

In general, children under the AGE OF MAJORITY – that is, under 18 – cannot exercise their rights of citizenship, for example by voting, standing for election, or serving on a jury. But they do have many of the legal rights of adults, although they themselves cannot always take steps to enforce them in law.

Pupil children

PUPIL children – boys under 14 and girls under 12 – cannot make legally binding contracts. But their TUTOR – usually a parent - can make contracts, and sue for breach of contract on their behalf.

Since pupil children who have a tutor cannot start court proceedings, they cannot themselves sue for injury caused by someone's negligence.

But their tutor can sue on their behalf. A child who negligently causes injury can be sued, along with any tutor.

Minors

MINORS – boys aged 14 to 17 and girls aged 12 to 17 – can generally only make legally binding contracts with the consent of their CURATOR – usually a parent.

However the curator's consent is probably not necessary when entering into a contract of employment or apprenticeship.

Minors can sue someone who injures them negligently, and can be sued themselves if they are negligent. Their curator may have to join with them in the action.

Protecting and educating

If children are not supported by parents, guardians or relatives, they will be cared for by the state. If the parent or guardian is killed in an accident caused by someone else's negligence, the child can sue that person for damages. The court will appoint a person – called a curator ad litem – to protect the child's interests.

A regional or islands council must provide education for children in its area. It must also care for a child who is neglected, abandoned or ill-treated by parents. *See:* CHILD ABUSE; CHILDREN IN CARE

The child's own money

Any child, however young, may have a bank account and can also inherit property and titles. A pupil child cannot make a valid WILL but a minor can.

When a child under 16 takes a job, he or she has special rights to protection. A child is also liable to income tax and can be made bankrupt. *See:* MINOR

Rights before birth

An UNBORN CHILD has no legal right to life, but it is still a criminal offence to terminate a pregnancy except within the limits of the ABORTION Act 1967.

A child who is born disabled or deformed as a result of someone's negligence can – through his or her tutor – sue that person for damages. For example, if a doctor gives a pregnant woman drugs which he knows, or ought to know, can cause deformity in the child, the doctor can be sued if the child is in fact born deformed or disabled.

A child can sue his or her parent for negligence. If, for example, a child is born deformed because the mother smoked or drank to excess during pregnancy, the child can sue the mother. Similarly a child can, for instance, sue his father if injured by the father's negligent driving, whether before or after birth.

A child probably has no right to sue a health board or doctor for failing to advise the mother to have an abortion and thereby allowing him or her to be born deformed or handicapped.

CITIZENS ADVICE BUREAU

A network of trained advisers

The Citizens Advice Bureau service provides free information and advice about almost any personal problem, especially in the fields of law and social welfare rights.

Most of Scotland is covered by a network of bureaux supported by the Scottish Association of Citizens Advice Bureaux. Each bureau is staffed mainly by trained volunteers. Some offices have solicitors and financial experts who attend to give free advice on one day or evening each week.

Advice is offered at each office or by telephone. To find your nearest office, check the local telephone directory under 'Citizens Advice Bureau'.

CITIZEN'S ARREST

What the man in the street can do

A citizen is bound to make an arrest in two situations:

1. If a magistrate (that is to say, a justice of the peace, a sheriff or a senior judge) orders him to do so, he must arrest the person indicated by the magistrate. If it turns out that the arrest should not have been made, the magistrate is the person who must answer for the mistake.

2. If a policeman is attempting to make an arrest, but cannot overpower the person he is trying to arrest, he can order bystanders to assist. It is not clear what the penalty is for failing to give assistance.

Apart from that, every citizen has certain powers of arrest himself. However they are not as wide as police powers of arrest, and must be exercised with great care.

> *AN ERROR OF JUDGMENT*
>
> *You may have to pay compensation if you arrest a person wrongfully*
>
> Mr Young ran a pawnbroker's shop. One day Mr Mackenzie came in to pawn a set of bagpipes. Mr Young thought they were stolen and locked Mr Mackenzie in a back room for 3 hours before he called a policeman.
>
> Mr Mackenzie gave a satisfactory explanation to the policeman of how he had come by the bagpipes and was released. He then sued Mr Young for keeping him locked up for 3 hours instead of handing him over to the police immediately.
>
> DECISION
>
> At the hearing the judge accepted that it was possible to obtain damages in such circumstances.

You can arrest someone only if you know for certain that an offence has been committed (by, for example, seeing it or being the victim), and if the offence is a serious one.

For example, you cannot arrest people who are only committing a breach of the peace, although you are obliged to help the police break up riots if they request you to do so.

You cannot arrest someone on suspicion of a crime that you are not certain has been committed. Nor can you arrest someone who is attempting a crime but who has not yet committed it.

So you cannot arrest someone you find prowling outside your house wearing gloves and carrying a bag, just because you suspect him of planning a theft.

The police, on the other hand, are entitled to arrest someone they reasonably suspect of having committed some crime or having attempted to commit one. Even if they turn out to have made a mistake, they still cannot be sued for damages.

Making an arrest

If you arrest someone, you must tell him why you are doing so. If he resists, you are entitled to use reasonable force. You must take him to a police station within a reasonable time for the arrest to be legal.

Private citizens – including store detectives – who arrest people may lay themselves open to claims for WRONGFUL ARREST or charges of ASSAULT if they had no power to arrest, or if a court decides that no offence was committed.

CITIZENSHIP

Right of entry, claim to a passport and diplomatic protection, and gateway to Commonwealth citizenship.

The law has been considerably changed recently. Until the British Nationality Act 1981 (which came into force at the beginning of 1983) everybody – apart from a couple of unimportant exceptions – born in the UK, the Channel Islands, the Isle of Man or any British colony had the status of Citizen of the United Kingdom and Colonies (a status now abolished). So had anybody born in a foreign country with a father born in the UK, the Channel Islands, the Isle of Man or a British colony.

Indeed, subject to the requirement of registration at a UK Consulate, so had further generations born outside the Commonwealth. There is, for example, in South America, a small 'British colony' of people registered in this way.

When a colony became independent, the citizens belonging to it acquired citizenship of the new country, and lost UK citizenship, except in a few cases where they had UK ancestry, or failed to acquire the new citizenship.

However not all citizens of the UK and Colonies had the right to enter the UK.

The right was limited by the IMMIGRATION Act 1971 to the following – known as patrials:

- Citizens born, adopted, naturalised, or registered in the UK, the Channel Islands, or the Isle of Man (but not those naturalised or registered elsewhere).
- Citizens with a patrial parent.
- Citizens with a citizen parent who was not patrial, but who himself had a patrial parent.
- Citizens not born, adopted, etc. in the UK, but 'settled' in the UK for 5 years or more.
- COMMONWEALTH CITIZENS who, though not citizens of the UK and Colonies, had a UK born parent.

Thus citizens of the UK and Colonies who acquired that citizenship by a connection with a colony (or a former colony) in general did not have a right to enter the UK.

The new law

Under the new law, if you are a citizen of the UK and Colonies who had a right of entry to the UK under the old law, you take a newly invented status called British Citizenship. (Falkland Islanders can now claim this status.)

But children born in the UK after the Act came into effect will only become British Citizens if one of a number of conditions is fulfilled:

- Either parent is a British Citizen, or is 'settled' in the UK.
- Either parent becomes a British Citizen, or is 'settled' in the UK while the child is still under 18 years of age.
- The child is resident in the UK for the first 10 years of his or her life (though 3 months a year abroad are allowed, and the Home Secretary can reduce the number of years required, or increase the allowed absences in special circumstances). His or her parents' nationality, or status in immigration law, is irrelevant in this case.

In the last two cases, registration is also necessary before the child becomes a British Citizen.

A child adopted by an order of a UK court becomes a British Citizen from the date of adoption, and a foundling is assumed to be entitled to be a British

THE WIFE WHO WOULD NOT JOIN A 21 MONTH QUEUE

If unreasonable delay by officials abroad forces an immigrant with a right of entry to land in Britain without a certificate of entitlement, the immigrant cannot be denied the right to enter.

Maimuna Phansopkar's husband was a UK citizen by registration in Britain. That gave him a right of entry so she acquired a right of entry when she married him.

In 1975 she applied for a certificate of entitlement so that she could travel to Britain with her husband. They were told at the British High Commission in Bombay that she would have to wait a year and 9 months for an interview.

The couple decided to leave immediately. Mrs Phansopkar arrived in Britain without even an entry certificate. She was refused entry by an immigration officer. In appeals to an adjudicator and to the immigration appeals tribunal, the officer's decision was upheld.

The case went to the English Court of Appeal which had to decide whether in the circumstances Mrs Phansopkar was entitled to expect the immigration officer to issue a certificate of entitlement.

DECISION

The court ruled that her right to enter Britain could not be taken away by administrative delay. Because the High Commission had been wrong to defer her application, the immigration officer was wrong to refuse her a certificate on arrival.

Citizen. An ILLEGITIMATE CHILD inherits citizenship from the mother.

What 'settled' means

'Settled' means that the person has been accepted by the Home Office for permanent settlement in the UK – in other words has a right to work and live in the UK (though a person accepted for settlement could still be deported on certain grounds, such as conviction of a major criminal offence) – and is ordinarily resident there. Whether a person is ordinarily resident depends on a number of factors, such as intention to stay, purpose in staying, and number and length of absences from the UK.

So a child born in the UK, whose father is here on a work permit (*See:* IMMIGRATION) and whose mother is here as a dependant of the father, will not be a British Citizen unless the parents apply for settlement later, are accepted, and considered to be ordinarily resident. It is not clear how this affects the child of a citizen of one of the member states of the EUROPEAN COMMUNITIES who is working here, since he or she does not need a work permit and has the right to stay as long as he or she likes, with his or her immediate family, while working.

Citizenship by descent

Anybody born abroad after the Act came into force will be a British Citizen if either of his or her parents (or if illegitimate, his or her mother) is a British Citizen and the parent satisfies one of the following conditions:

- Was born, adopted or naturalised in the UK (or the Falkland Islands).
- Is in Crown service; service abroad for the European Communities; or other service approved by the Home Secretary and Parliament.
- Has at least 3 years' residence in the UK or Falkland Islands before the child's birth (with a possible 9 months of absences) and had a parent who was UK (or Falklands) born, adopted or naturalised.

In this last case the child must be registered before the age of 1, though the Home Secretary can extend this period up to the age of 6. Also the need for the parent to have 3 years' residence is automatically dropped if the child would otherwise be stateless.

A child who does not qualify under these conditions is entitled to be registered at any time before he or she is 18 if the following apply:

- Either parent was a British Citizen when the child was born.
- The child and both parents reside in the UK for 3 years (with again a possible 9 months of absences).
- Both parents consent to the registration.

If the parents are divorced or separated at the time of registration, the 3 years' residence is not required of both parents, but both must still consent. An illegitimate child cannot rely on his or her father's status, but the father's consent to registration is not required.

Naturalisation

A person can apply to become a British Citizen by naturalisation if he or she:

- Has been accepted by the Home Office for settlement.
- Has at least 5 years' residence in the UK (with 3 months' absences permitted in the year before applying, and 15 months' absences over the 5 years before applying) *or* is in Crown service for the UK Government outside the UK (this would include, for instance, employment in a UK HIGH COMMISION).
- Can pass a simple language test (in English, Welsh, or Gaelic).
- Is considered to be 'of good character'.
- Has not breached an immigration law in the 5 years before applying.
- Has taken an oath of allegiance to the Queen (unnecessary if he holds one of the other citizenships created by the Act, or is a citizen of a Commonwealth country of which the Queen is Head of State).

There is also a fee.

Naturalisation is completely at the discretion of the Home Secretary, and there is no appeal against refusal. The Home Secretary can however reduce or waive some of the requirements. For instance the language test can be waived on the grounds of age or medical condition.

YOU MUST SPEAK THE LANGUAGE TO BE NATURALISED

The language test for naturalisation can now be taken in Gaelic

A person seeking naturalisation who has a British Citizen husband or wife has to satisfy easier conditions. Only 3 years' residence is required, and there is no language test. Wives married before the Act came into force keep the right they used to have to register without any conditions at all, for 5 years. But in the case of widows and divorcees, the right is now at the discretion of the Home Secretary.

Marriage to a British Citizen has no effect by itself, but marriage to an ALIEN might, depending upon the law of his or her country. Also the Home Secretary can register any child under 18 at his discretion.

Some old forms of registration phased out

There are also several forms of registration akin to naturalisation.

A Commonwealth Citizen or Irish Citizen accepted for settlement and ordinarily resident in the UK since before 1st January 1973 can be registered as a British Citizen. So a Jamaican or a New Zealander who made his home here over 20 years ago may be entitled to register.

Equally a Commonwealth Citizen who had a right of entry to the UK before the new Act on account of a UK born parent or marriage to a person with a UK born parent, plus 5 years' ordinary residence in the UK, is entitled to register. So a Canadian or a Malaysian with a father born in one of those countries, but with a UK born mother, can register after a suitable period of living in the UK.

Any of the following can take the place of ordinary residence:

- Employment in Crown service for the UK Government.
- Employment in an international organisation to which the UK belongs.
- Employment in a UK based company.
- A mixture of residence and employment.

However in all these cases there is no right to register. The Home Secretary must consider the registration 'fitting' because of the applicant's 'close connection with the UK'. So employment with the United Nations, or in a High Commission can be used, but cannot be relied upon.

These two Commonwealth Citizen's rights run out in 1988.

So does the old right for children born to citizen fathers outside the Commonwealth.

Some new forms of registration

Gibraltarians now have the right to be registered as British Citizens. This is because Gibraltar is part of the EUROPEAN COMMUNITIES, within which there is free movement of workers and businessmen. *See:* IMMIGRATION

Also, any British Dependent Territories Citizen or British Overseas Citizen can register as a British Citizen on the strength of 5 years' residence in the UK (with up to 15 months' absences allowed) and acceptance for settlement by the Home Office. In certain special circumstances the Home Secretary can waive those conditions. All these registrations are subject to a fee.

British Dependent Territories Citizens and British Overseas Citizens

These titles are given to those who, before the new Act, were citizens of the UK and Colonies, without a right of entry to the UK. It is possible, though, to have more than one of the three citizenships created by the Act.

> ### *A CITIZEN'S CLAIM TO CROWN PROTECTION*
>
> *A Citizen can claim, but not demand, Crown protection.*
>
> The China Navigation Company traded in Chinese waters in the 1920's. At that time they were infested with pirates who sometimes attacked in the usual fashion, and sometimes came aboard as passengers, then overpowered the crew on the high seas.
>
> The Crown provided some armed guards, but took the view that protection was the ship-owners' responsibility, and withdrew the soldiers unless the ship-owners agreed to pay the full cost of them.
>
> The court decided that the Crown had no obligation to protect British ships in foreign waters or indeed to protect citizens anywhere abroad, and that if it did do so, it might be able to charge for its services.

British Dependent Territories Citizens are:

- Those who were born before the Act in one of the remaining colonies, or to a father born in one; or a woman married to such a person (or who is connected with a colony in a number of other ways).
- Those born after the Act in a colony, with a parent who is a British Dependent Territories Citizen or who is 'settled' in a colony.

Most inhabitants of Britain's dozen or so remaining dependencies will have this citizenship.

British Overseas Citizens are those who were citizens of the UK and Colonies before the Act and who do not qualify for either of the other two citizenships.

They are chiefly people born in a country which was a colony or other dependency but which has since achieved independence, and who did not get the citizenship of the newly independent country (such as the East African Asians).

This citizenship will not usually be acquired by anyone after the Act has come into force, but a few people may acquire it – for instance, by marriage to a British Overseas Citizen.

There is not much difference in practice between these two citizenships. However British Dependent Territories Citizens will usually have a right of entry to a colony (depending on that colony's immigration rules), and a British Overseas Citizen will not (although the East African Asians will usually be eligible to queue for a special voucher giving entry to the UK).

Effects of citizenship

While only British Citizenship carries a full legal right – that of entry to the UK – all three types of citizen can claim a PASSPORT from the UK Government (or a colonial government) and claim UK diplomatic protection when abroad.

However these claims cannot be enforced in court. All three will be liable for TREASON, and possibly for some other crimes, like murder and bigamy, even when committed outside British territory.

All three citizenships are also gateways to Commonwealth Citizenship and the rights that it carries.

Loss of citizenship

Any of the three citizenships can be renounced by means of a declaration, registered by the Home Office, as long as it does not result in the person becoming stateless. Also, in wartime the Home Secretary can refuse to register a declaration for any reason.

After renunciation, British Citizenship and British Dependent Territories Citizenship (but not British Overseas Citizenship) may be resumed.

Resumption is at the discretion of the Home Secretary except where the renunciation was made in order to obtain another citizenship, in which case there is a right to resumption. This takes account of the fact that many countries (for example, India and the United States) frown upon a person taking their citizenship without renouncing all others.

British Citizens and British Dependent Territories Citizens who acquired citizenship by naturalisation or registration may be deprived of citizenship by the Home Secretary if he believes it is for the public good, for one of the following reasons:

- The naturalisation or registration was obtained by fraud.
- The citizen has been disloyal.
- The citizen has received a prison sentence of more than a year within 5 years of obtaining citizenship.

However the Home Secretary may not deprive a person of citizenship in certain cases if it would make him or her stateless. In all cases, the citizen must be told the grounds for deprivation, and can require a committee of inquiry to be set up with a judge as chairman.

Other statuses under the act

Two other statuses exist, both of them rare. These are British Subject (*See:* COMMONWEALTH CITIZENS) and British Protected Person. Most of the latter are citizens of countries which were British Protectorates and which still have some special relationship with the UK – for example Brunei.

Statelessness

Since children may be born in the UK or a colony without acquiring any of the citizenships or statuses under the Act, and may have no other citizenship, special provisions exist for them. These are complicated, but in general, if a parent of the child has one of the citizenships or statuses, then the child will inherit that, even though the normal provisions of the Act do not permit it. If neither parent has such a citizenship or status, the child acquires that normally held by people in the territory he or she is born in.

Multiple citizenships

It is perfectly possible to hold more than one citizenship. For instance a second citizenship may be acquired as a result of marriage.

As mentioned before, many countries dislike multiple citizenship, but the UK has not objected to this for many years.

UK National and other terms

Some statutes and treaties refer to UK Nationals. For instance, free movement in the European Communities is granted to UK Nationals. The definition used here will have to be changed to take account of the new law, but will no doubt cover British Citizens and Gibraltarians. UK National has, however, no general meaning, and will be defined in any treaty or statute for its own purposes.

Terms like British National are also sometimes used, but have no legal meaning at all except perhaps in INTERNATIONAL LAW.

CLOAKROOM

When you are entitled to compensation for theft

If the staff of a restaurant or meeting place take charge of your coat or other belongings, whether or not they charge you for doing so, you are entitled to expect the management to take reasonable care of your property.

The management will be liable for any loss unless they can prove that they took reasonable care.

Special conditions

Cloakroom conditions, on signs or tickets, which seek to exclude or limit the management's liability have no effect unless you are given reasonable notice of them before you deposit the article, and unless they are fair and reasonable as required by the UNFAIR CONTRACT Terms Act.

LEAVING BELONGINGS IN A CLOAKROOM

The management of any establishment which accepts charge of people's coats or other property may be held liable for any loss or damage, unless they can prove that they took reasonable care.

When you are liable If you hang up your own coat in a restaurant or meeting hall, without help from the staff, the management will not normally be responsible for looking after it. *See:* UNFAIR CONTRACT

CLOSE SEASON

The time when hunting is illegal

There are certain times during the year when hunting of particular kinds of animals or birds and fishing for certain fresh-water fish is forbidden by law.
See: ANIMALS; BIRDS; FISHING; GAME

CLUB

There are, in law, two types of club – members' and proprietary

A members' club may be formed by any group of people who get together for some social purpose and who each contribute towards running expenses. A members' club is not primarily operated to make a profit, so it is not a partnership. But it can be turned into a company to give it legal advantages, particularly that of being able to sue in its own

THE IMPORTANCE OF THE CLUB'S RULES

Always read the club rules carefully before you join. They form a contract between you and the other members.

name – which a club cannot do in the Court of Session. Members' clubs may have property of their own – for example, a golf course or tennis courts – or may meet by agreement in someone else's premises – like a chess or bridge club.

A proprietary club is run for profit. The proprietor owns it and charges the members fees for whatever privileges the club provides. The entertainment clubs which have supplanted music halls are usually proprietary clubs.

The importance of club rules

Clubs of both types are governed by their rules, which form part of the contract between the members, in the case of members' clubs, or between the members and the proprietor in proprietary clubs.

Membership

Generally, clubs are free to make whatever rules they like, although those with 25 or more members may not practise RACIAL DISCRIMINATION in admission, exclusions, allocation of club privileges or use of the facilities.

SEX DISCRIMINATION is at present allowed in a club that is genuinely a member's club, but it is not permitted in proprietary clubs.

A person who has the right qualifications to join a particular club, but who is refused membership, cannot compel the club to make him a member.

Expulsion

However, a member who is expelled may be able to get a court to declare that the expulsion was not valid if he can show he was denied a fair hearing in accordance with NATURAL JUSTICE, or if the club broke its own rules over the expulsion. But even if the expelled member can show this, the court will hold the expulsion to be void only if the club has property which is jointly owned by the members and which the member would be deprived of if he were expelled.

Club debts

Always read the club rules carefully before joining. You may find that they commit you to liabilities that you would not normally expect. If a members' club obtains goods on credit, for example, the person liable for the debt is usually the one who placed the order, together with anyone who authorised him to place it.

Debts incurred by proprietary clubs are treated in law in the same way as those of any other business. The proprietor is liable for what his agents do on his behalf.

If someone is injured

If someone is injured on club premises, anyone whose fault contributed to the injury may be sued. In addition, anyone who employs the person to blame may be liable. So if a club waiter spills scalding soup on someone, the waiter and the club as his employer could be sued. In the Court of Session (but not in the sheriff court) the club would have to be sued along with its office bearers or committee members.

Members held liable for damages cannot demand financial help from other members unless the club rules specifically say so.

Changing club rules

Members of proprietary clubs have no control over the proprietor, and if they dislike the way he runs things there is little they can do. But those belonging to members' clubs may be able to secure changes. The first step is to study the club rules.

These may contain procedures for amending the rules themselves, if enough members agree. They also commonly lay down the way in which members must be notified of club meetings. If proper notice was not given, decisions taken at a meeting may be anulled.

If the committee is at fault it can be replaced, usually at an annual meeting.

However, there is nothing in law to prevent a club giving the power to make decisions to only a few members, if its rules say so.

JOINING AN ENTERTAINMENT CLUB

Entertainment clubs may make anyone a member without going through the formalities of nomination and written application if their rules permit.

The proprietor is permitted to sell liquor to members and guests under an 'entertainment licence' from the local licensing board, and subject to such conditions as the board may impose.

When liquor is sold

A club cannot supply intoxicating liquor to members or guests unless it has either a registration certificate from the sheriff or a liquor licence from the local licensing board. Clubs are usually required to observe the general licensing hours of the area, but they may obtain an extension if meals are served, or on some special occasion.

CODICIL

Alteration to a will

A codicil is a document altering a will. It may, for example, appoint a new EXECUTOR or increase or cancel a legacy.

A codicil should be used only for simple alterations: for major changes it is better to start afresh with a new will.

The document must be dated, signed and witnessed by 2 witnesses, unless it is a HOLOGRAPH writing, in which case witnesses are unnecessary. The witnesses need not be the same as for the will.

A codicil should refer to the will (or a previous codicil) which it alters, set out the changes clearly, and confirm that the unaltered provisions remain valid.

A will often contains a clause stating that it can be altered by later documents which are neither witnessed nor holog-

AN EXAMPLE OF A CODICIL

I, Ian Macdonald of 53 Marchmont Avenue, Edinburgh hereby make this codicil to my will dated 15 May 1979:

First. I revoke the appointment of James Smith as executor and I appoint Henry Irvine of 27 George Avenue, Edinburgh as executor.

Second. I increase to £500 the legacy of £300 bequeathed to my sister Margaret in my will.

Third. Subject to the above amendments I hereby confirm my will.

IN WITNESS WHEREOF this codicil is signed by me at Edinburgh on 6 December 1981 before the following witnesses:

Ian Macdonald.

Thomas Fairgrieve, Witness
27 Richard Street
Edinburgh

Philip Green, Witness
2 Napier Loan
Edinburgh

raph. A codicil would then be valid if simply signed.

COHABITATION

Living with a man who is not your husband

A woman who lives with a man without being legally married to him is known as a cohabitee. She has few of the rights of a lawful wife.

She cannot draw a RETIREMENT PENSION through her partner's contributions, nor widow's benefit, as a widow can. The couple are taxed as single people and any children of the union are illegitimate.

The man is not legally liable to ALIMENT (maintain) the woman, yet, because they will be regarded as living together as husband and wife, she may lose social security benefits that would otherwise be available.

The woman, however, does have some rights. For instance, where a partner is violent she can seek a sheriff court order banning him from their home even though he owns or rents it. *See:* BATTERED WOMAN

If a man leaves his cohabitee with children he has fathered, she can claim for their support. *See:* AFFILIATION AND ALIMENT

In certain circumstances, one partner of an unmarried couple who have lived together as if they were husband and wife can get a court declaration that they are legally married. *See:* COMMON LAW MARRIAGE

Social security

Unmarried couples living together lose the right to a number of social security benefits through what is known as the cohabitation rule – under which the DHSS can decide that the couple are living as man and wife although they have no legal obligation to maintain each other.

Under the rule, a widow can lose her widow's benefit, including any increase for children, so long as she is cohabiting. However, the rule does not affect the

WIDOW ORDERED TO PAY BACK £5,000

The Department of Health and Social Security is likely to consider a couple to be cohabiting if they share a home for a long time and if the woman takes the man's name.

An anonymous telephone caller told a local social security office that a woman had been drawing widow's benefit while living with a man for years. The widow was ordered to repay £5,000.

The couple insisted that the man was only a lodger, but the woman cooked for him. They denied any sexual relationship, and the woman said she had taken the man's name only to stop gossip.

DECISION

The tribunal ruled that because of the length of time they had lived together and because the woman had habitually taken the man's name, they must be considered to be behaving as man and wife. Therefore, under the cohabitation rule, the widow's benefit had to be repaid.

COHABITATION *continued on p. 92*

MARRIAGE OR COHABITATION

The advantages and disadvantages of living together without being married

		Married	Unmarried
Names			
	Choice of name	Wife or husband can use each other's surname, provided no fraud intended.	Woman or man may use other's surname, provided no fraud intended.
	Business name	Wife may retain 'maiden' name for business or professional purposes.	No restriction if woman or man uses the name by which she or he is currently known.

Continued overleaf

MARRIAGE OR COHABITATION *continued*

	Married	Unmarried
Sexual relationship		
Marriage	Marriage possible only between two people of different sexes, both 16 or over, both unmarried and not more closely related by blood than first cousins (adoptive parents and children, step-parents and step-children, parents-in-law and children-in-law also prohibited).	Sexual relations permitted with partner of the opposite sex, if female aged 16 or over, whether or not married to someone else. Sexual relations forbidden between parents and children, grandparents and grandchildren, brothers and sisters, aunts and nephews, uncles and nieces, parents-in-law and children-in-law and step-parents and step-children.
Refusing sexual intercourse	Refusal of intercourse by either partner can be ground for annulling marriage if it amounts to impotency. It can be a ground for divorce if it amounts to unreasonable behaviour. Husband can be charged with raping wife, if she does not want intercourse (although this may be difficult to prove).	Woman or man has no obligation to take part in sexual intercourse. It is rape if the man has intercourse with his woman partner against her will.
Contraception	Husband's consent not needed for: ● Fitting or supplying contraceptives for wife. ● Wife's abortion. ● Wife's sterilisation. (Husband's consent not needed in law, but usually required in practice before the surgeon agrees to operate.) Wife's consent not needed for husband's vasectomy. Depriving either husband or wife of a child might be ground for divorce, so doctor might not act without consent of both.	No restriction.
Money		
Buying on credit	Wife is assumed to have husband's permission to buy food and other necessaries on his credit. Unless he gives notice to the shops with which she has been dealing that she is not his agent, he may have to pay. (In 1984 a Bill was before Parliament to abolish this rule.)	Woman living with a man has no right to buy food and necessaries on his credit.
Household expenses	Wife can apply for court order if husband fails to support her and their children. Husband may also apply.	Neither party can apply for court order if other fails to give financial support.
Housekeeping allowance	Wife has right to half-share in any savings from housekeeping allowance made by husband or in things bought from savings. Husband has right to other half.	Neither party has any right to share in savings from housekeeping unless in joint account to which both have contributed.
Loss of services	If husband is killed because of someone else's wrong-doing, wife can claim damages for loss of financial support and for loss of unpaid personal services. She can also claim for loss of his companionship. Husband can make same claim if wife killed.	Same rules apply.
Income tax		
Basic principle	While husband and wife live together incomes are assessed together for income tax and treated as husband's. He must fill in tax return and pay any tax not collected under PAYE. Husband can set married man's allowance and, if wife earning, wife's earned income allowance against joint income. Even if wife is sole earner, both allowances are available.	Incomes separately taxed. Each can set off single person's allowance against own income. If only one income, only one allowance. If children, parent can claim extra allowance.

MARRIAGE OR COHABITATION *continued*

	Married	Unmarried
Income tax *continued*		
Separate assessment	Wife can choose to complete own tax return and be responsible for paying her share of their joint tax. Husband need not know her income, but income still added together. Allowances shared roughly in proportion to income, and total tax bill not affected. Higher tax rates payable if joint taxable income more than £15,400.	Always assessed separately. Each can have £15,400 taxable income before paying higher rates.
Wife's earnings election	Couple can elect not to have wife's earnings added to husband's, avoiding higher tax rates. Each spouse can only claim one single person's allowance.	Income never added together for tax.
	Choice not possible for wife's investment income, which is always added to husband's total income and taxed at his higher rate. If joint investment income more than £7,100, investment income surcharge must be paid.	Investment income not added together. Each partner can have up to £7,100 before paying surcharge.
Business expenses	Husband or wife wishing to deduct other's salary – for example as secretary or chauffeur – as business expense must prove the expense is reasonable for duties performed.	Inland Revenue more likely to accept that employment genuine.
Additional personal allowance	Married man with child can claim extra allowance if wife totally incapacitated. Age relief if self or wife is over 65. Blind person's relief for self or wife.	No extra allowances on behalf of partner. Single parent can, however, claim additional personal allowance.
Covenants	One spouse cannot save tax by arranging covenanted payments to the other.	Tax can be reclaimed on deeds of covenant between partners.
Property		
Right to a home	Wife or husband has right to live in matrimonial home owned or rented by other, unless evicted by court order.	Either party can apply to the court for the right to live, for a limited time, in a home owned or rented by the other.
Home in spouse's name or joint names	Husband or wife who buys property and puts it in spouse's name is assumed to have given it to spouse. By putting it in joint names, husband or wife is assumed to have given spouse half.	Same rule applies.
Mortgage relief	Relief is obtainable only once on joint mortgage.	Both man and woman can obtain relief on joint mortgage.
Part ownership	Neither can prevent sale or mortgage of matrimonial home even if part owner, but can continue to live in home once sold.	Neither can prevent sale or mortgage of home even if part owner, but may be able to continue to live in home for limited time.
Selling a home	Where home is in husband's name, wife has no automatic right to share in proceeds of eventual sale – even if she has helped in purchase by paying mortgage instalments, deposit or household bills.	Same rule applies.
Second home	If husband and wife own two homes, capital gains tax must be paid on the profit from the sale of the second home.	Each partner can own a home and dispose of it without being charged capital gains tax.
Sale to other	If one spouse disposes of property to the other, capital gains tax not payable unless other spouse also disposes of it immediately.	Capital gains tax payable when unmarried partner passes property to the other.

Continued overleaf

MARRIAGE OR COHABITATION *continued*

	Married	Unmarried
Properties *continued*		
Gift of property	If one spouse gives property to the other, whether during life or at death or under court order on divorce, capital transfer tax not payable.	Capital gains tax may be avoided by a joint election for 'gifts relief' but capital transfer tax may be due.
Rates	Wife occupying house liable for rates, but may apply to court to have all or part paid by husband living elsewhere.	Only the occupier is liable for rates.
Rent arrears	Sheriff officer cannot poind goods belonging to wife unless she is tenant.	Same rule applies.
Social security		
Increase for women and children	Husband receiving national insurance benefit can claim extra allowance for wife and children. Wife receiving national insurance benefit in her own right can claim extra allowances for husband and children. From November, 1984, she can claim for children regardless of husband's earnings.	Man cannot get extra allowance for woman alone, but he can for children plus woman if she looks after them. Woman receiving benefit in her own right can get extra for another woman (but not a man) looking after children.
Ex-spouse's pension	Divorced or widowed woman or man can use ex-spouse's contribution record to help establish right to retirement pension.	Neither man nor woman can claim pension on other's contributions.
Widower's pension	Retired widower can claim retirement pension on contributions of wife who died over 60, if hers are better than his.	Man cannot claim pension on woman's contributions.
Wife's and widow's benefits	Wife who does not pay full contributions can claim some benefits from husband's contributions – for example, retirement pension and child's special allowance. Widow's benefits paid only on husband's contributions.	Woman can claim only benefits from own contributions.
Invalid's pension	Non-contributory invalidity pension payable only to wife incapable of work and substantially incapable of normal household duties. Invalid care allowance not payable to wife living with husband.	Same rules apply.
Supplementary benefit	If husband and wife living together, either can claim supplementary benefit for family. Partner who claims will normally have to sign on as available for work, unless 60 or over.	Same rules apply.
Duty to family	Spouse may be prosecuted for any deliberate failure to maintain his or her own family and ordered to repay some or all of the cost of supplementary benefit paid to other spouse.	Man or woman can be prosecuted for deliberate failure to maintain his or her own children. Partner cannot be ordered to repay cost of supplementary benefit paid to other partner.
Children		
Child allowances	Child benefit, family income supplement and child's special allowance available.	Child benefit, family income supplement, but not child's special allowance available.
Child benefit	Wife has prior claim to child benefit even if children not hers.	Child's parent has prior claim to benefit.
Family income supplement	Husband or wife can claim if either is in full-time work (at least 30 hours a week), they have at least one child and their income is low.	Man or woman can claim if either in full-time work. Income of both taken into account.

MARRIAGE OR COHABITATION *continued*

	Married	Unmarried
Children *continued*		
Child increases	Husband receiving national insurance benefits can claim extra allowance for dependent children. From November, 1984, wife receiving benefits can claim regardless of husband's earnings.	Either can claim.
Child's special allowance	If ex-husband maintaining children after divorce dies, ex-wife may be entitled to child's special allowance on his contributions.	No state benefit if father dies.
Child maintenance	Either parent may be ordered to provide for the children, depending on incomes.	Father can be ordered to provide for children if paternity proved in affiliation and aliment proceedings.
Upbringing	Mother and father have equal powers over upbringing, e.g. religion, education, medical treatment, foreign travel.	Mother has parental powers, unless father obtains custody order.
Name of child	Parents must agree on choice and any change of child's surname.	Mother can choose and change child's surname, and is entitled to give it the father's surname if paternity is admitted or proved.
Marriage of child	Person over 16 may marry without parent's agreement.	Same rule applies.
Adoption of child	Agreement of both parents required for adoption of their child, unless there are grounds for dispensing with it, e.g. abandonment, ill-treatment or neglect.	Only mother's agreement required unless father has custody order.
Custody	Both parents have joint custody rights. If parents separate, court can decide who shall have custody. Parent without custody will normally be allowed reasonable access.	Mother automatically has custody unless father obtains court order. Father may be allowed access.
Guardianship	Each parent can appoint guardian to act after his or her death.	Neither parent can appoint guardian to act after death.
Inheritance	Legitimate children have automatic succession rights if relatives die without making a will.	Illegitimate children have automatic succession rights only from mother and father, not from grandparents, brothers and sisters, uncles and aunts.
	If succession rights or provision in will are inadequate, legitimate children can apply to court for reasonable maintenance from parents' estate.	Illegitimate children have same right.
Students		
Grants	If both spouses claim student grants, marriage reduces the total grant only if they have other income. If one spouse is mature student and other is working, the earner may have to make contributions normally made by parents.	Earnings for working partner do not affect assessment of other's grant. If both are students, total grant will not be affected by living together.
Extra grants	Married mature student can claim extra grant for dependent spouse and children.	Can claim for children, not usually for other adult.
Breaking up		
Eviction from home	Husband or wife cannot evict spouse who is joint or sole owner or tenant, or has OCCUPANCY RIGHTS. To do so is an offence.	If sole owner or tenant tries to evict partner, partner can apply to court for right to remain for limited time.

Continued overleaf

MARRIAGE OR COHABITATION *continued*

	Married	Unmarried
Breaking up *continued*		
Maintenance payments	Either husband or wife may be ordered to pay maintenance to spouse on separation or divorce. Wife unlikely to be made to support husband unless cannot support himself and wife is much better off.	Neither can be ordered to support the other after parting, although a father can be ordered to support a child of the relationship.
Sharing property	Each entitled to his or her own property. On divorce either spouse may be ordered to pay lump sum to the other.	Each entitled to own property, including share in joint property.
New relationship		
Widow's benefit	Widow who remarries loses widow's benefit permanently.	Widow living with man loses benefit for period of cohabitation only.
Private pension	Widow who remarries likely to lose private pension.	Woman unlikely to lose any private pension.
Maintenance	Divorced person who remarries automatically loses right to maintenance payments.	Maintenance not automatically lost through cohabitation, but may be reduced or stopped if partner receiving maintenance is supported by the other.
Death and insurance		
Share of estate	If either dies without leaving a will, the other is automatically entitled to the home (up to £50,000), furniture (up to £10,000), money (up to £25,000, or £15,000 if there are children) and to a share in the remainder of the estate.	No automatic share in other's estate.
Life insurance	Either can hold insurance policy on own life payable to other. Survivor then gets the money, even if dead partner's estate is insolvent. Either can take out insurance policy on other's life.	No such possibility, unless one has an 'insurable interest' in the other, for example, if they are business partners.
Accidental death	If either is killed in an accident, the survivor can claim compensation for loss of the breadwinner or housekeeper from person responsible.	Same rule applies.
Private pension	Occupational pension schemes normally provide for a widow's and sometimes for a widower's pension.	Less likely to provide for survivor even if he or she is a dependant.
Widow's national insurance	Woman married before April 6, 1977 or widowed before April 6, 1978 may be able to pay reduced national insurance contributions.	Woman who is earning must pay full contributions.
Widow's benefits	Widow may be entitled to widow's allowance, widowed mother's allowance and widow's pension on husband's national insurance contributions.	Woman entitled to no benefit when man dies, unless COMMON LAW MARRIAGE exists.

COHABITATION *continued from p. 87*

woman's right to benefits for which she has paid contributions herself.

If a couple have been living together without being legally married and the man dies, the woman is usually not entitled to widow's benefits or, if he is killed at work, to industrial injury death benefits, as a widow would be. However, benefit may be payable if the Department decides that a COMMON LAW MARRIAGE exists.

The cohabitation rule also affects supplementary benefits. A couple's needs and resources are added together as if they were married, and only one of them is entitled to claim benefit on behalf of both. An unmarried, separated or divorced woman who begins to live with a man as his wife may therefore lose any supplementary benefit being paid for her or her children.

If a woman does lose her benefit – for instance, because the man is working – a temporary allowance may be payable for her children if the man is not their father. Payment for the children's needs can continue for a 4 week 'adjustment' period if cutting off the benefit completely would reduce the household's income 'disproportionately'. This adjustment period can be extended for another 6 weeks if the income is expected to increase.

If the couple's net income (after deducting the normal disregards, any maintenance payments the man may be making to a wife and children elsewhere and any hire purchase payments for essential furniture and household equipment) is below supplementary benefit level, the woman's benefit payments are continued indefinitely as if the couple were not living as husband and wife. However she will not get more than is needed to bring them up to supplementary benefit level.

The woman can also continue to receive supplementary benefit on grounds of urgent need, whether there are children or not, if the man refuses to support her. But she may have to repay the money if she is later in a position to do so.

See: SUPPLEMENTARY BENEFIT

COLLECTIVE BARGAINING

When employers and trade unions get round the table

Collective bargaining between trade unions and employers directly affects the pay and working conditions of about 15 million people in Britain, nearly 65 per cent of the employed population.

There are hundreds of 'bargaining units'. The simplest, which involve only two people – a shop steward representing the employees and a foreman or supervisor appointed by the management – cover one section or department of a company. Such bargaining is not normally concerned with wages, but is confined to purely local matters such as the allocation of overtime work.

At the highest bargaining level, where national negotiations affect an entire industry, an employers' association usually represents the individual companies in that sector, and employees are represented by confederations of unions.

When agreements conflict

The number of levels at which bargaining can take place may lead to a conflict between the provisions of two or more agreements.

For example, a national agreement covering an entire industry may say that the normal working week is 40 hours, while a plant agreement for one factory may state that it is 50 hours.

A former employee from the factory who is claiming REDUNDANCY would get more money if the 50 hour provision were applied. But if neither agreement stated which of the two took precedence, and if collective bargaining could not resolve the specific case, only a court or industrial tribunal could decide whether the normal work-week in the factory was 40 or 50 hours.

When agreements are enforceable

A collective agreement is not a legally enforceable contract between the collective parties who sign it – the employer or employers on one hand and the union or unions on the other – unless they expressly agree that it is.

If an agreement does not include a clause stating that it is legally enforceable, an employer is not entitled to sue a union, as an organisation, for breach of its terms. Similarly, the union cannot, in its own right, sue the employer.

However, many of the terms of collective agreements become legally binding on the employer and on his employees as individuals by being incorporated in each employee's EMPLOYMENT CONTRACT.

How individual contracts are affected

Collectively agreed provisions which deal with working terms and conditions – such matters as wages, hours, holidays, sick pay, pensions and maternity leave – can become incorporated into individual contracts explicitly or implicitly. They then affect all employees, whether members of a union or not.

In explicit cases, the terms may be written into an individual contract or the contract may simply refer to the collective agreement so that it incorporates the terms of the agreement automatically.

If an individual contract says nothing about the incorporation of collective agreement provisions dealing with terms and conditions, they will become incorporated into it implicitly if they have been accepted to the point of becoming custom and practice in the company or industry concerned.

STRIKING A BARGAIN BETWEEN BOSS AND WORKER

The simplest form of collective bargaining involves only two people – the shop floor representative of the employees and a management spokesman, representing the employer.

Unions' right to information

The law gives recognised trade unions the right to obtain from an employer non-confidential information about an employer's affairs if it is needed for collective bargaining. *See:* TRADE UNION

The information is that which would normally be given 'in accordance with good industrial practice' and which, if not given, would materially impede the conduct of negotiations.

If the employer refuses to provide such information to a recognised trade union, the union can ask the CENTRAL ARBITRATION COMMITTEE to intervene.

The CAC cannot compel an employer to comply, but he is legally obliged to abide by any terms and conditions of employment that it may fix for the employees concerned.

COMMON LAW MARRIAGE

When living together can result in marriage

Usually a couple can only get married by going through either a civil ceremony before a registrar or a religious ceremony.

Before 1940 there were three other ways to get married in Scotland. Two of these have now been abolished. The third – cohabitation with habit and repute – is still possible.

The first way was for the couple to exchange consent to be married. The second way was for one party (usually the man) to promise to marry the other party and, once this promise was accepted, for sexual intercourse to take place because of it.

Since 1940 it has not been possible to get married by these two methods. However marriages that took place in these ways, before 1940, are still valid. In cases of doubt the COURT OF SESSION can be asked to declare that there is a valid marriage.

Cohabitation with habit and repute

If a couple live together as husband and wife for some time and friends, relatives and neighbours believe they are married, one of them can ask the Court of Session for a declaration that they are legally married. This is called marriage by 'cohabitation with habit and repute'. They must have lived together for a fairly lengthy period (which can be as little as a year) and they can only count the years that they were free to marry (that is, single and over 16).

If one partner has died, the surviving partner can still ask the Court for a declaration. If both partners have died, their children can apply.

A declaration of marriage will be necessary, for example, where one partner is seeking a legal right to part of the ESTATE of a deceased partner.

A declaration can also be sought if a woman's claim for widow's benefits fails because the social security authorities decide that there was no common law marriage between her and the man she lived with. *See:* WIDOW'S ALLOWANCE; WIDOWED MOTHER'S ALLOWANCE; WIDOW'S PENSION

COMMONWEALTH CITIZENS and BRITISH SUBJECTS

What it means to be a Commonwealth Citizen

The term Commonwealth Citizen means anyone who is a citizen of a Commonwealth country, including the United Kingdom itself.

You must normally be a Commonwealth Citizen to get a job in the Civil Service. You must be either a Commonwealth Citizen or an IRISH CITIZEN to vote in a parliamentary or local ELECTION or to serve on a JURY, or to be an MP or a privy councillor.

Whether you are a Commonwealth Citizen may in some circumstances determine whether you can be found guilty of TREASON.

Commonwealth Citizenship no longer has much relevance in immigration, as the right to enter the UK is largely confined to British Citizens.

But some Commonwealth Citizens still have a right of entry. *See:* IMMIGRATION

Commonwealth Citizens used to be called British Subjects. Many Acts of Parliament use that term, and have not been amended. Confusingly, the term British Subject now refers in law only to a small group of people previously called British Subjects Without Citizenship. *See:* CITIZENSHIP

COMMUNITY SERVICE ORDER

When an offender can be sentenced to work for the community

If a person aged 16 or over is convicted the court may, instead of imposing a fine, imprisonment or detention, give the offender the choice of doing unpaid part-time work under a community service order. This applies only to offences punishable by imprisonment or detention.

A community service order is usually made in less serious cases and in cases where there are mitigating circumstances. The kind of work involved can vary widely – from decorating and labouring to visiting the old and disabled.

Before making the order the court will assess the offender's suitablility for community service, with the help of a report from a local authority social worker. The court cannot impose community service on someone who is unwilling to accept it.

Community service can be ordered for not less than 40 and not more than 240 hours altogether. The work will be supervised by a local authority social worker. The hours usually have to be completed within 12 months of the order being made.

Work not done If the offender fails to carry out the work ordered, or if he does not do it properly, he can be brought back to court, fined up to £400 and again ordered to do the work. Alternatively he can be given a different sentence altogether – such as imprisonment – for the original offence.

Probation When imposing a probation order on an offender aged 16 or over, a court can include a requirement that the offender perform unpaid work (not less than 40 and not more than 240 hours) for the community. This requirement is not a community service order.

However, if an offender is in breach of a probation requirement - including a requirement to do unpaid work – the court can impose a community service order for that breach. The offender then becomes subject to both the probation order and the community service order. *See:* PROBATION

COMPENSATION

Financial award when you have suffered

If a person suffers through an action of another, he may be entitled to receive compensation for any injury or loss incurred.

For example, if he is the victim of a crime and is injured, he may be entitled to CRIMINAL INJURIES COMPENSATION.

He may also be entitled to compensation in the civil courts if he is injured through someone else's negligence.

Compensation may also be payable by order of an industrial tribunal to a person who is out of work through REDUNDANCY or UNFAIR DISMISSAL. *See:* CRIMINAL COMPENSATION ORDER; DAMAGES; GOLDEN HANDSHAKE; PERSONAL INJURY

COMPULSORY PURCHASE

Safeguards when an authority decides to buy land

Public bodies such as local authorities and government departments often find it necessary to purchase land for such purposes as road construction or house building.

In order to enable public authorities to carry out their functions, Parliament has given many of them the power to acquire land or buildings by compulsory purchase. This means that land or buildings can be taken from owners in spite of their opposition.

A compulsory purchase can take effect only if it is approved by a government minister – generally the Secretary of State for Scotland. Anyone who would be affected by the proposed purchase has the opportunity to object to it.

The first stage in the process is for the authority to make a compulsory purchase order. The order cannot be acted upon immediately. It must be advertised in the local press, and every owner, occupier and tenant (except tenants for a month or less) must be notified.

Opposing the order

If you wish to oppose a compulsory purchase order – either because you own the land involved or because you object to the use proposed for it – start your campaign as soon as possible.

You must send your objection to the government department named in the notice of the order within 21 days of the notice first being advertised. Objections about compensation are not relevant at this stage.

Contact your local councillors. If it is the council which has made the order, try to persuade the councillors to have it withdrawn. If some other authority has made the order, try to persuade the council to oppose it.

Enlist help from your neighbours and from local organisations such as civic societies and other pressure groups. If the land involved is a beauty spot or part of a green belt, or if an attractive building is at risk, ask for support from national bodies such as the Scottish Civic Trust. Write to your Member of Parliament. A petition may help – but make sure all signatures are genuine.

Public inquiry

If the initial campaign fails to get the compulsory purchase order withdrawn, be prepared to fight at a public inquiry.

If an owner, tenant or occupier who is directly affected lodges a formal objection, the Secretary of State will order one of his reporters to hold a local inquiry into the objections. Unless there is an objection by someone directly affected, there need not be an inquiry.

If an inquiry is to be held it will be advertised. Everyone directly affected by the order is entitled to attend the inquiry and explain his or her objections to the order. Groups of protesters may find it useful to engage a solicitor or advocate to present their objections.

It is generally up to the authority which made the order to justify the proposed compulsory purchase. It may be possible to oppose the order by arguing, for example, that there is no strong need for the purchase or that some acceptable alternative exists. Modifications to the original proposal might be suggested.

After an inquiry

After the inquiry the reporter makes a report of his findings to the Secretary of State for Scotland. The Secretary of State decides whether or not to confirm the order. He can vary it. Everyone directly involved is informed and can ask for a copy of the inquiry report. The decision is also advertised.

If an order is confirmed, it takes effect when notice of its confirmation is first published, but it is possible to appeal to the Court of Session. Such an appeal is, of course, expensive.

The only grounds on which an appeal can be made are that it is not within the power of the authority to make the order or that the proper procedure was not observed. An appeal has to be lodged within 6 weeks of the confirmation of the order being first published.

Compensation

An owner, a tenant or any other person who has had some right compulsorily taken from him as a result of an order is entitled to compensation.

The rules on assessment of compensation are intended to ensure that a fair price is paid for property taken. The rules are, however, very complex and anyone entitled to compensation would be wise to obtain professional guidance.

Compensation should match the amount that the property would have fetched on the open market if no compulsory purchase had been made. However, full market value is sometimes not payable in the case of a house that is below a certain standard.

Expenses can also be claimed – for example, money spent on professional advice, or removal expenses.

Agreement on compensation is often reached by negotiation, but if you believe you have not been offered enough, you can appeal to the Lands Tribunal for Scotland.

When part of your property is acquired – for example, for road widening – you are entitled to be compensated not only for the land taken, but also for any loss in the value of the property you are left with.

Even if no property has been taken from you, you can – as a neighbour – claim compensation if new public works cause noise, smell, fumes or some other physical factor that reduces the value of your property. *See:* PLANNING BLIGHT

Losing your home

If an order results in an owner-occupier or tenant losing the home where he has lived for at least 5 years,

CHALLENGING AUTHORITY

Where a public authority has decided to lay a pipeline or overhead cable across your land you can object but it may be best to try to reach agreement by negotiation.

he is entitled to an extra sum known as a 'home loss payment'. In 1983 the payment was equivalent to $2\frac{1}{4}$ times the rateable value of the house. The payment cannot be less than £150 or more than £1,500.

If suitable alternative housing on reasonable terms is not otherwise available to you, you may also be able to insist on being rehoused by the local housing authority.

Limited right to cross land

Public bodies, such as gas, electricity and local authorities have powers to lay cables, pipes and other apparatus in or across privately-owned land. Private companies sometimes have similar powers to lay pipelines. You have a right to object to such a proposal, but a public inquiry need not always be held. You are entitled to compensation for any loss suffered.

COMPUTER RECORD

The ever-increasing threat to privacy

Although many organisations, including government agencies, keep computerised records on you, your right to know what is recorded is at present very limited. You have no legal right to check such records, except those held by a CREDIT REFERENCE AGENCY or, in certain circumstances, a housing authority. *See:* COUNCIL TENANCY

However, in 1984 the government's Data Protection Bill was before Parliament. Under the Bill you will have a right of access to personal data held in many computer files – for instance, school, medical (subject to exceptions), employment and housing records. The Bill will not apply to manual records.

What the Bill does

The Data Protection Bill requires those who hold or process computer data on individuals to register with a Data Protection Registrar. Failure to do so is an offence. Registered users must say what kind of information they hold, what they do with it, where they obtain it and to whom they disclose it.

Data users must observe certain principles. For instance, personal data must be obtained and processed fairly and lawfully; be accurate and up-to-date; be secure; and be no more than is required for the user's stated purposes.

The Bill gives you the right to know about, and get a copy of, personal data held on you. If the data are wrong, or wrongly disclosed, and you suffer damage as a result, you can claim compensation. You can also ask a court to order the data to be corrected.

The requirements of registration and access do not apply to personal data if non-disclosure is necessary to safeguard national security; or to personal data held by the police or by tax officials, if disclosure would prejudice their work.

CONDITIONAL SALE

Agreeing to purchase by instalments

A conditional-sale agreement is one in which a customer agrees to buy goods by instalments, but will not own the goods until all instalments are paid.

It differs from HIRE PURCHASE in that the customer agrees to buy, and the trader agrees to sell, at the start of the transaction, whereas in a hire-purchase contract the customer exercises an option to buy only at the end.

Someone who buys goods that are still subject to a conditional-sale agreement cannot keep them, except in the case of a private individual purchasing a motor vehicle who is unaware of the agreement, or unaware that some of the instalments have still to be paid.

Conditional sale also differs from CREDIT SALE. With the latter, the goods become the buyer's property at the start of the agreement and he can legally sell them before they are paid for – unless his agreement forbids this.

A conditional-sale agreement has the same protection under the Consumer Credit Act as a hire-purchase contract. *See:* CREDIT AGREEMENT; INTEREST CHARGE

CONFESSION

When a confession may be used in evidence

An accused person may confess to a crime by pleading guilty to the criminal charge in court. A plea of guilty is a judicial confession and if accepted by the prosecutor will result in an immediate conviction.

However, an accused person may confess to a crime before appearing in court – for example in a statement made to the police – but then plead not guilty

UNFAIR PRESSURE FROM A FAMILIAR FACE

In deciding whether incriminating statements made by a suspect to the police are to be accepted as evidence, the court will ask the question: "Is what has taken place fair or not?".

A 17 year old boy was brought to trial on a charge of assault with intent to rob. The prosecution tried to lead evidence of incriminating statements made by the boy to the police. The defence objected that these statements had been unfairly obtained.

Two police officers had called at the boy's home at 5.30 in the morning and he had agreed to accompany them to the police station. At first the boy said nothing to the officers. However he agreed to wait in the station in order to take part in an identification parade later in the day.

At about 8.15 a.m. another police officer not involved in the inquiry saw the boy sitting in the C.I.D. room. He knew the boy, who played football with his own son, and asked him why he was in the police station. The boy told him.

The officer then asked the boy along to his room, and questioned him about his involvement in the crime. Another policeman was present. The boy made certain incriminating remarks. The boy's parent was not present in the police station and he did not have the services of a solicitor.

In court, the police officer agreed that the accused had been pleased to see a friendly face and had obviously been willing to speak to him. He also agreed that he had spoken to the accused only because he knew him and that the procedure followed had been unusual.

DECISION

The judge decided that the accused's statements had been obtained unfairly and he refused to accept them as evidence.

in court. In such a case the accused cannot be convicted on proof of his confession alone.

To justify conviction there must also be other evidence which links the accused with the crime. Proof of incriminating behaviour by the accused after a crime has occurred – for example, the accused leading the police to the victim's body – would be enough to support a confession.

The court will not accept as evidence a confession made by an accused person to the police if it has been unfairly obtained. Unfairness includes forms of physical and mental pressure. A confession freely made by an accused without pressure by the police can never be said to have been obtained unfairly.

Confessions obtained unfairly

Anyone reasonably suspected of having committed an offence punishable by imprisonment may be detained by the police for up to 6 hours and questioned about the offence. The suspect does not need to provide any information other than his name and address. *See:* DETENTION

If the police interrogate or cross-examine the suspect in order to obtain a statement or confession damaging to him, the court will hold that such a statement or confession has been obtained unfairly and will refuse to accept it as evidence. While the police may question a suspect, it is not their job to obtain a confession. So anything said or done by the police which induces a suspect to make a confession may result in the court rejecting it as evidence.

Once a suspect has been arrested, cautioned and charged, all police questioning should stop. Any confession obtained by the police after the accused has been cautioned and charged will be inadmissible as evidence. *See:* ARREST

If the criminal charge brought against an accused is serious enough to be prosecuted before a judge and jury, the accused will have to attend a JUDICIAL EXAMINATION.

At this examination the prosecutor can question the accused about any confession he has allegedly made to or in the hearing of a police officer. If the prosecutor proposes to do this he must, before the examination, ensure that the accused has been given a written record of the alleged confession.

The accused can refuse to answer any question put by the prosecutor. However the prosecutor may, at the trial, comment to the jury about such a refusal. He can do so if the accused challenges the confession on a ground which he could have disclosed in answer to a question asked at the judicial examination.

Confessions need not be made to the police

A confession is not necessarily a statement made to the police. It can be made to a friend, relative, acquaintance or any member of the public. If the prosecution wishes, such a person can be ordered to attend court to give evidence.

With one exception, it makes no difference if the confession was given in professional confidence – for example, to a doctor, a social worker or a priest. All the witness can do in such a case is to ask the judge's permission to decline to answer. If he is ordered to answer, but refuses, he is guilty of CONTEMPT OF COURT.

The only person who has an absolute right not to give evidence of a confession is a solicitor or an advocate acting for an accused person. Statements made to them are confidential and cannot be admitted as evidence without the accused's consent.

THE INNOCENT SOLDIER WHO CONFESSED TO ARMED ROBBERY

If an accused person pleads not guilty to a criminal charge, proof of a confession made by the accused will not result in a conviction unless there is other evidence available to link him with the crime. This corroboration of a confession is not necessary if the accused pleads guilty at his trial and that plea is accepted by the prosecutor.

Private Boyle was a soldier in the Scots Guards. He went absent without leave. He was caught and detained by the Glasgow police, who released him into the custody of a military escort.

While being returned to his army base Boyle fell into conversation with the sergeant in charge of the escort. During this conversation conditions in military and civilian prisons were compared. Boyle produced a newspaper cutting of a bank robbery in Glasgow and told the sergeant that he was responsible for it. Because of this confession Boyle was returned to the Glasgow police, to whom he made a further and detailed confession to the crime.

Boyle was charged with the armed robbery of the bank in Glasgow. He pled guilty and as no further evidence was required in such a case, he was convicted and sentenced to 9 years' imprisonment.

On appeal Boyle said that he had confessed and pled guilty to a charge of which he was completely innocent.

He said he had confessed to the armed robbery because he thought that a civilian prison would be preferable to a military one. He mistakenly thought that he would not get too long a sentence from the civilian court.

DECISION

The Appeal Court quashed his conviction and sentence after the prosecutor said there was not enough evidence to support Boyle's confession. He should never have been prosecuted in the first place.

CONFIRMATION

Authority to act as an executor

An EXECUTOR may be appointed by a will or by a court order. In both cases the executor must be officially confirmed in his appointment before he can collect the estate, sell whatever is necessary and divide it according to the will or the rules of INTESTACY.

The document which confirms him is called a confirmation. It is issued by the sheriff court and sets out the names and addresses of the deceased and his executor(s) and an itemized list of the estate.

The confirmation is evidence of the executor's right to demand and receive payments due to the estate – for instance, money due under a life insurance policy. Organisations or people will not usually make payments to executors who have not been confirmed, although there are exceptions – for example, the National Savings Bank,

Trustee Savings Bank and Friendly Societies may pay up to £1,500.

Confirmation only authorises an executor to deal with property in the United Kingdom. Where the deceased had assets situated abroad, the executor has to take legal proceedings in the countries concerned.

How to obtain confirmation

The executor sets out on a special form (obtainable from the Capital Taxes Office in Edinburgh or main post offices) an itemized list of the deceased's estate. The names and addresses of the deceased and his executor(s) and details of the will or court order appointing the executor(s) are also shown.

The executor must swear before a notary public or a justice of the peace that the information contained in the form is complete and accurate to the best of his knowledge.

HOW TO OBTAIN CONFIRMATION

What executors must do to obtain authority to wind up an estate

PAGE 4

(This is a binding margin—please leave it blank)

INVENTORY of heritable estate in Scotland, belonging to the said deceased or the destination of which he had power to and did evacuate, of the moveable estate of the said deceased in Scotland of the real and personal estate of the said deceased situated in England and Wales and in Northern Ireland and of the personal or moveable estate of the said deceased situated elsewhere, including property over which he had, and exercised, an absolute power of disposal.

The estate should appear under these headings and in this order:
Estate in Scotland (Heritable property first)
Estate in England and Wales
Estate in Northern Ireland
Summary for Confirmation

NB: Further subdivisions fall to be made on Page 8.

No. of Item			Prices of Shares	£
	Heritable Estate in Scotland			
1.	House and garden at 10 Napier Avenue, Edinburgh.	£40,000.00		
	Less sum due to Forthview Building Society (loan incurred on August, 4, 1978)	15,000.00		25,000.00
	Moveable Estate in Scotland			
2.	Furniture and plenishings £4,000 as valued by Arnotts, Auctioneers			
	Personal effects belonging to deceased £1,000			5,000.00
3.	Royal Bank of Scotland plc., 36 St. Andrew Square, Edinburgh, Sum at credit of account No. 230556			145.56
4.	Income tax rebate estimated			1.00
	Estate in England and Wales			
5.	Imperial Chemical Industries plc., 200 Ordinary Shares of £1		300p	600.00
				£30,746.56
	Summary for Confirmation			
	Estate in Scotland	£30,146.56		
	Estate in England and Wales	600.00		
	Estate in Northern Ireland	0.00		
		£30,746.56		

NOTE: If space for heritage is insufficient, continue on page 5. If there is no heritable estate in Scotland or if its description does not occupy the whole page, proceed on this page to the next heading of the estate.

This part of the confirmation is called the 'grant page'. This confirms the executors, giving them the authority to deal with the deceased's estate.

This is the 'Inventory' page of the form sent (if tax is payable) to the Inland Revenue's Capital Taxes Office in Edinburgh. On this page the executor should list all the items in the deceased's estate.

These are the names of the executors who are entitled to deal with the estate.

This document is sealed and signed by the Clerk of the appropriate Sheriff Court.

Executors must obtain confirmation before administering an estate. To do this they complete an Inland Revenue form, giving a full inventory of the deceased's possessions, pay any tax due and send or take the form to the appropriate sheriff court.

Any CAPITAL TRANSFER TAX due must be paid before confirmation can be obtained. The completed form is sent to the Capital Taxes Office together with the amount due.

The executor may have to obtain a short-term loan to pay the tax, since the estate is "frozen" until he has been confirmed. This loan is best obtained from the deceased's bank (if he has one) or from the executor's bank. If the deceased left premium bonds or National Savings funds or certificates, the executor can apply to use that money to pay the tax.

Finally the form is delivered to the sheriff court of the district in which the deceased lived, together with the will (if any) and the appropriate fee.

An executor appointed by the court must obtain a bond of caution – a guarantee that he will carry out his duties properly. This is not needed if the executor is the widow(er) entitled to all his or her late spouse's estate. A bond can be obtained from most insurance companies for a modest premium.

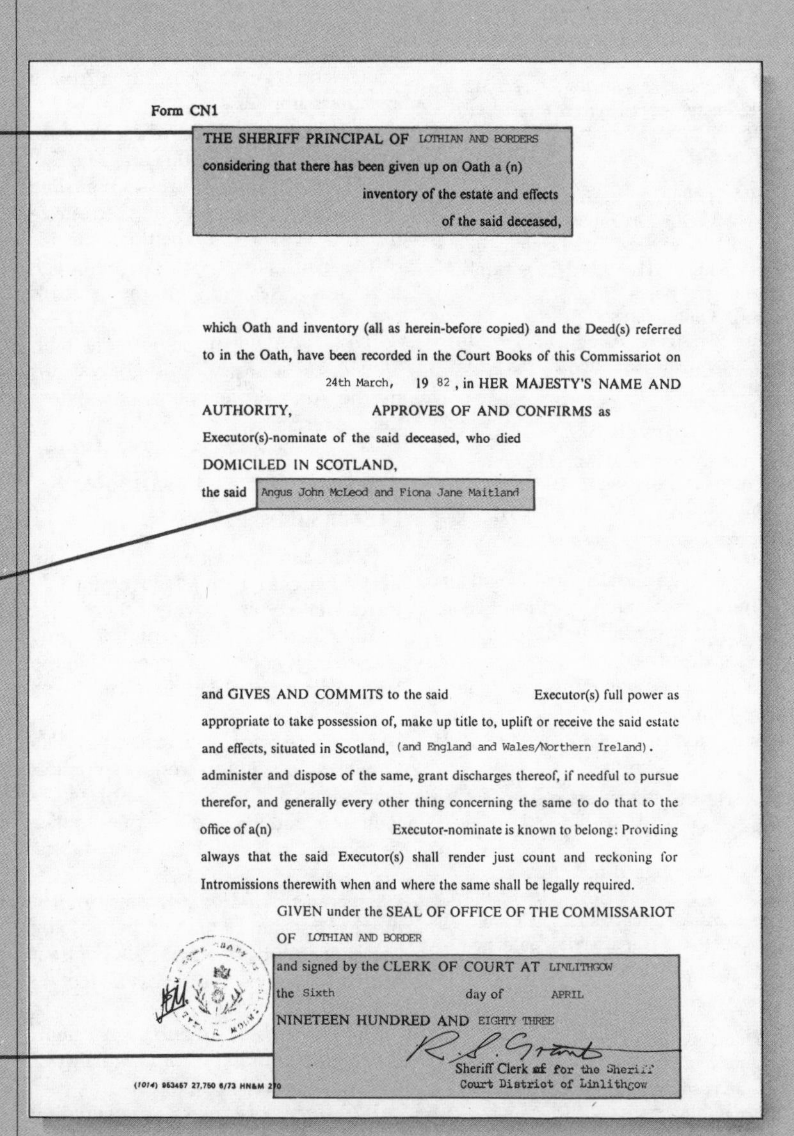

Form CN1

THE SHERIFF PRINCIPAL OF LOTHIAN AND BORDERS considering that there has been given up on Oath a (n) inventory of the estate and effects of the said deceased,

which Oath and inventory (all as herein-before copied) and the Deed(s) referred to in the Oath, have been recorded in the Court Books of this Commissariot on 24th March, 19 82, in HER MAJESTY'S NAME AND AUTHORITY, APPROVES OF AND CONFIRMS as Executor(s)-nominate of the said deceased, who died DOMICILED IN SCOTLAND, the said Angus John McLeod and Fiona Jane Maitland

and GIVES AND COMMITS to the said Executor(s) full power as appropriate to take possession of, make up title to, uplift or receive the said estate and effects, situated in Scotland, (and England and Wales/Northern Ireland). administer and dispose of the same, grant discharges thereof, if needful to pursue therefor, and generally every other thing concerning the same to do that to the office of a(n) Executor-nominate is known to belong: Providing always that the said Executor(s) shall render just count and reckoning for Intromissions therewith when and where the same shall be legally required.

GIVEN under the SEAL OF OFFICE OF THE COMMISSARIOT OF LOTHIAN AND BORDER and signed by the CLERK OF COURT AT LINLITHGOW the Sixth day of APRIL NINETEEN HUNDRED AND EIGHTY THREE

R. S. Grant
Sheriff Clerk of for the Sheriff Court District of Linlithgow

(1014) 963457 27,750 6/73 HN&M 270

The confirmation consists of a photocopy of parts of the form (including the inventory) together with the 'grant page' confirming the executors. Confirmation is usually granted within 1 to 2 weeks.

Confirmation to small estates

For small estates – total gross value £10,000 or less – a simplified procedure can be used. The executor sends an itemized list of the deceased's estate and the will to the appropriate sheriff court. The sheriff clerk prepares the necessary forms for the executor to sign and will then issue confirmation.

If the deceased died without a will, the person claiming to be executor must provide evidence from two people of his identity and relationship to the deceased.

CONSERVATION AREA

Protecting a treasured place

An area of special architectural or historic interest may be protected against unsuitable development by being declared a conservation area. This is done by the LOCAL AUTHORITY responsible for planning control in the particular area.

You cannot object to the designation of an area as a conservation area. But if no such designation has been made, you can suggest it to the planning authority. Declaring an area a conservation area may well increase the value of property in the area.

The planning authority must submit their proposals for preservation and improvement of a conservation area to a public meeting in the area.

Once a conservation area has been declared, the planning authority must give publicity to any application for PLANNING PERMISSION that might affect the character of the area. This is done by means of newspaper advertisement and a notice on the site. All comments made within 21 days must be considered by the authority before they decide the application.

In a conservation area, the consent of the planning authority is usually required before a building can be demolished or a tree can be cut down. If you go ahead without obtaining such consent, you can be fined. *See:* PRESERVATION ORDER

CONSPIRACY

The crime of planning a crime

If two or more people agree to do something which will involve them in crime, they are guilty of conspiracy – even if they do not carry out the crime. The crime of conspiracy is created by the agreement alone.

Where the conspiracy is to commit a particular crime, and it is committed or attempted, the conspirators may be prosecuted for the completed or ATTEMPTED CRIME and not the conspiracy.

There must be at least two people charged with conspiracy, even if one of them is a 'person unknown to the prosecutor' or is dead or uncaught.

If one conspirator is acquitted it does not necessarily follow that his co-accused will also be acquitted. For example, the conspirator may be acquitted because of the lack of admissible evidence against him; but there may be sufficient evidence against the co-accused to establish that he is guilty. Only if it would be inconsistent to convict one and not the other(s) must they all be acquitted.

THE CONSPIRACY THAT WAS IMPOSSIBLE BUT CRIMINAL

Conspiracy is still a crime even though its object or intended result is impossible to achieve at the time of the conspiracy.

In January 1978 four men were accused of conspiracy to bribe members of Glasgow Licensing Board to approve the transfer of a gaming licence to premises owned by their company.

However, at that date the power to transfer the gaming licence was out of the hands of the licensing board. This was because a decision made by the board in May 1977 on that particular licence was under appeal to the sheriff, who had not yet decided the case.

The defence argued that the accused men should be found not guilty of the charge because agreement to achieve a result which was impossible could not amount to a criminal conspiracy.

DECISION

The defence failed and the accused were convicted.

The court said that it was the criminal purpose and not the result which made the agreement in this case a criminal conspiracy. The purpose of the agreement was to corrupt public officials and such an agreement was a criminal conspiracy under Scots law.

CONSTRUCTIVE DISMISSAL

When resigning is the same as getting the sack

An employee who leaves his job because his employer's behaviour is a serious breach of the employment contract is said in law to have been 'constructively' dismissed.

MACHINE OPERATOR WHOSE PAY WAS CUT

If an employee quits his job because his firm proposes to reduce his pay, he may be treated as having been dismissed.

Mr Gillon, a machine operator, was asked by his firm to accept a pay cut. This was because the amount he was being paid breached the government's pay policy.

Mr Gillon refused to accept the cut and resigned. A colleague agreed to the cut and lost only 73p over 10 weeks as a result.

DECISION

The Employment Appeal Tribunal held that reducing Mr Gillon's pay amounted to constructive dismissal.

An employee should obtain legal advice before resigning. If there is no breach, or it is not serious, he will not be treated as dismissed.

The employee has the same right as other dismissed employees to claim compensation for UNFAIR DISMISSAL. If he is also redundant, he can claim a REDUNDANCY payment.

CONSUMER CREDIT

The different ways to buy now and pay later

There are many ways in which you can obtain goods or services wholly or partly on credit. You may borrow money to spend as you wish, or obtain a loan that is tied to the purchase of particular goods or services, often from a specified supplier.

As long as the sum borrowed does not exceed £5,000 (£15,000 from May 20, 1985) – excluding interest, credit and installation charges – all credit arrangements are covered by the tight controls of the Consumer Credit Act, although in a few cases, not all the controls apply.

If the sum borrowed is more than £5,000, the transaction is still covered by the Act's protection against extortionate terms.

Two types of credit available to the consumer

Credit can be divided into two main kinds: 'purchaser' and 'loan' credit.

Purchaser credit covers the type of lending in which the person borrowing money buys goods or services from the lender or from a supplier who has a business arrangement with the lender.

A contract for such a loan is also known as a 'debtor-creditor-supplier' agreement. Under that type of agreement the lender, as well as the supplier of goods, can be sued if they are faulty. *See:* DEFECTIVE GOODS

Loan credit is a straightforward loan of money, not tied to the purchase of any particular goods or services. A contract of that type is also known as a 'debtor-creditor' agreement.

Under a debtor-creditor agreement, the lender is not liable for the quality of goods or services bought.

Both types of credit are covered by similar rules for making, conducting and ending the contract. They are treated differently, however, in some circumstances – for example, in the rules that control canvassing. *See:* DOORSTEP CREDIT

Help for the jobless A sick or jobless person on SUPPLEMENTARY BENEFIT can sometimes have his HIRE PURCHASE commitments paid for by the Department of Health and Social Security.

Help, in the form of an additional weekly payment, is given only for certain items of essential furniture or household equipment – for example, beds, chairs, dining table or curtains. In very limited circumstances a washing machine, refrigerator and vacuum cleaner can be paid for.

Such help will only be given if:

- The hire purchase commitment was entered into before benefit began to be paid; and
- The goods are not used solely or mainly by someone other than a member of the 'assessment unit'; and
- There are substantial grounds for believing that benefit will cease to be payable before the commitment ends; and
- The person does not have savings in excess of £500 which could be used to pay off the commitment.

If it is likely that the person will still be on benefit when the commitment ends, help can be given by way of a single payment to clear the debt. A single payment can be made even if the commitment was entered into when the person was receiving benefit.

CONSUMER GROUP

Forming a group to act for local consumers

Consumer groups are voluntary, independent associations formed to promote the interests of consumers in their own locality.

Most groups publicise the results of their research work in magazines, newsletters or on local radio. Some act as pressure groups, concentrating on one particular topic of local concern at any one time.

The fields covered by consumer groups include:

- Comparing prices of goods in local shops.
- Expressing dissatisfaction with bus services or refuse collection.
- Explaining simply how new legislation passed by Parliament affects consumers.

How to start a group

Contact the National Federation of Consumer Groups, 12 Mosley Street, Newcastle-upon-Tyne NE1 1DE, which will put you in touch with your nearest area organiser or group.

The Federation can certainly advise on the best tactics to use in a particular district, but the usual way is to form a small working party. Sound out friends, put leaflets in libraries and on noticeboards, inform the local newspaper and radio station.

When you have gathered some support, plan and hold a public meeting to draw in members, form a group and decide on priorities for action.

CONSUMER PROTECTION

A wealth of protective legislation that is still evolving

Any customer buying goods or services is entitled to a wide range of protection by law – much of which can be enforced by public officials at public expense.

Trading standards officers (or consumer protection officers) are employed by regional councils to administer the Weights and Measures Act, Trade Descriptions Act, Consumer Safety Act and other laws that protect the consumer. Their job is to prevent traders from breaking those laws and to report an alleged offence to the PROCURATOR FISCAL, who will decide whether to prosecute.

A public official, the Director General of Fair Trading, administers the Fair Trading Act and Consumer Credit Act – which also concern criminal offences by traders. If you have a complaint against a trader you should go to your local trading standards officer.

Your right to a fair deal is also supported by pressure groups such as the publicly financed Scottish and National Consumer Councils and the self-supporting Consumers' Association.

If your complaint is over breach of contract by a trader, or breach of the special rules about the sale of goods, you can enforce the civil law which deals with such matters, by going to court if necessary.

See: DEFECTIVE GOODS; FAIR TRADING; TRADE DESCRIPTIONS; TRADING STANDARDS; WEIGHTS AND MEASURES

CONSUMER SAFETY

Making a supplier pay for damage from unfit goods

If something you buy or hire is dangerous, and damage results, the supplier can be sued for compensation – and may also be prosecuted. Your entitlement to compensation is the same, whether you have bought the goods for cash or on credit, obtained them with trading stamps or hired them.

Take your complaint to the local trading standards officer, who will investigate the matter and may decide to ask the PROCURATOR FISCAL to prosecute the supplier. If the supplier is convicted of breaking the safety of goods law, he can be ordered by the sheriff court to pay you compensation.

If no compensation is ordered, you can still sue the supplier in the sheriff court or Court of Session for breach of statutory duty.

As part of your case, you are entitled to give the civil court details of any successful prosecution.

Some goods are not covered by criminal law, but many others, including FOOD, are listed in regulations laying down safety standards.

It is a criminal offence for anyone who supplies goods in the course of a business to fail to comply with safety standards. The maximum penalty is 3 months' imprisonment and a £2,000 fine.

A shopkeeper who is accused can escape conviction, however, if he can show that he took 'all reasonable steps' and exercised 'all due diligence' to avoid committing the offence. For example, a toy-shop owner who makes inquiries to satisfy himself that paint used on the toys complies with safety regulations can claim to have taken the reasonable steps required by law.

However, a manufacturer who uses poisonous paint is likely to be convicted. An importer of foreign toys may also be convicted on the ground that he should take extra precautions when dealing in goods that do not comply with British safety laws.

GOODS COVERED BY CONSUMER SAFETY LAWS

Goods that are subject to special regulations under the Consumer Safety Act 1978 fall into three classes: protection of children, protection against poisons and protection against fire and shock. Upholstered furniture must pass a fire test or bear a warning label.

Protection of children

Anoraks and other outer garments with hoods. The hood must not be adjustable by a cord.

Bags Plastic bags containing toys must have a printed warning about the danger of suffocation.

Carry-cots Stands must comply with size and strength regulations. The underside of the bottom of the carry-cot must be more than 17 in. above floor level and the cot must be retained in position by a guard-rail or rigid stops. The stand must be able to withstand a weight of 60 lb. The stand must have a durable label stoutly fixed to it stating the maximum length and width of carry-cot which it is designed to take.

Babies' dummies All dummies must be made of plastic or rubber, must be resistant to damage and must be sold in a clean condition in a closed container with instructions for use.

Nightdresses must be of material difficult to set alight.

Toys Paint must contain no more than a specified amount of poisonous material – such as lead. Celluloid is prohibited, except in table-tennis balls.

Flammable pile fabric is prohibited.

Mains electricity must be operated through a transformer at 24 volts or less.

Sharp metal points are prohibited.

Thin metal edges must be inaccessible to a child's fingers or be folded back.

Eyes, noses and other features on dolls and other toys should be secured so that they cannot be pulled off and swallowed, or lay bare dangerous points.

Protection against poisons

Pencils, pens, crayons and similar items must contain no more than a stated amount of poisonous materials.

Cooking utensils, vitreous enamel ware and glazed ceramic ware must comply with standards on content of lead or cadmium.

A flameproofing treatment for clothes which could cause cancer is banned.

Protection against fire and shock

Gas, electric and oil fires must always be sold with a fixed fireguard.

Oil heaters burning paraffin must be draught resistant and must carry a notice warning against:

- Using petrol as a fuel.
- Carrying the heater when it is alight.
- Refilling it with fuel when it is alight.
- Using heater in an unventilated place or where it may be exposed to draughts.

They must not be able to be tilted or overturned while they are alight.

Electrical goods must comply with detailed safety standards covering the installation, earthing and accessibility of live parts. They must always be supplied with instructions for safe operation.

All equipment must have wiring coloured according to the official safety code. An explanation must be supplied.

Prohibiting dangerous goods

The supply of certain goods can be prohibited by the government, under the Consumer Safety Act 1978.

The government can make an order prohibiting anyone from supplying specified goods that are considered dangerous.

It can also serve a prohibition notice on a particular supplier, prohibiting him from supplying specified unsafe goods.

The supplier can be compelled to publish, at his own expense, a warning about any unsafe goods he supplies or has supplied in the past.

It is a criminal offence to ignore a prohibition order or notice or to fail to publish a warning when required.

Maximum penalty: 3 months' imprisonment and a £2,000 fine.

Anyone who suffers because a supplier disobeyed a prohibition order can claim compensation from him.

The shopkeeper would escape conviction if he could show that he took all reasonable steps and exercised due diligence to avoid committing the offence.

THE IMPORTER WHO DID NOT KEEP UP WITH THE LAW

Every individual shopkeeper has to make himself responsible for seeing that the goods he sells are not dangerous. Someone else's assurance may not be enough.

A toy sold by an English shopkeeper in 1976 was found to have paint that contained an illegal amount of poisonous lead. The toy had been imported from France in 1971.

The importer was prosecuted under the Toys (Safety) Regulations 1974. The prosecution was brought in 1976.

It had been the importer's practice to make all orders from suppliers subject to a condition that their goods would comply with current British safety regulations. British suppliers and foreign manufacturers all gave such undertakings.

In addition, the importer made a standing invitation to the local trading standards department to take samples of goods for analysis, at any time.

At first, the magistrates dismissed the case on the ground that the importer had taken all reasonable precautions to avoid an offence under the Consumer Protection Act 1961.

The prosecution appealed against the decision, and the appeal was heard in the English High Court.

DECISION

The magistrates were ordered to convict the importer.

The High Court judges held that the importer had no reliable guarantee of safety covering the particular toy involved. Regulations had changed in 1974 and the importer had not taken precautions to make sure that any of his goods complied with the requirements of the new rules.

An adequate precaution would have been to take one or more paint samples from various toys in the relevant consignment and have the paint fully analysed. The importer's 'friendly relations' with the trading standards department did not absolve him from his responsibility for precautions.

The Lord Chief Justice, Lord Widgery, said that there were very few cases in which a company could rely on somebody else's certificate of compliance with the law, if it was possible for the company to have its own analysis made.

Safety standards for vehicles

It is a criminal offence to sell a motor vehicle, privately or by way of business, if it does not comply with the standards laid down in the Motor Vehicles (Construction and Use) Regulations 1978. *Maximum penalty:* £2,000 fine.

The fact that a vehicle has an MOT test certificate is not a sufficient defence.

It is also an offence to supply rear lights and reflectors for any motor vehicle, or crash helmets for motorcyclists, if they do not comply with minimum legal standards.

If a supplier is convicted of breaking the regulations, he may be fined up to £2,000, but the court can also order him to pay compensation to anyone who has suffered injury or damage because of his offence.

However, to obtain compensation in the civil courts, you must be able to show that the supplier was in breach of contract or guilty of negligence.

CONSUMMATION OF MARRIAGE

The legal significance of matrimonial sex

A marriage is legally valid from the moment the couple exchange their vows, whether it is consummated by an act of sexual intercourse or not. However, in law an unconsummated marriage can be declared void if the non-consummation is due to incapacity and not wilful refusal.

Only one or other of the couple can apply to the court to have the marriage declared a NULLITY on this ground.

How the law defines consummation

A marriage is consummated once a single complete act of sexual intercourse has taken place after the marriage ceremony. Ejaculation and orgasm are not regarded in law as essential parts of a complete act of intercourse. Even if a husband practices coitus interruptus, a marriage will be considered consummated. The use of contraceptives is no bar to consummation.

If a child is born

It is possible for a couple to conceive a child without a complete act of intercourse.

Any child born of an unconsummated and nullified marriage is regarded as legitimate in law.

CONTEMPT OF COURT

The powers of a court to prevent any interference with justice

Every criminal and civil court has the power to punish people who are in contempt of it. The purpose of the law is to ensure that the authority of the court is respected, that cases are tried fairly and that there is no interference with justice.

Contempt of court is any of the following:

- Misbehaviour in court.
- Defiance of a court order.
- Publication of comments on a case while it is still before the court.

Misbehaviour Any improper conduct in court may be contempt. For example, it is contempt for anyone to appear drunk in court.

It is also contempt for a witness to refuse to answer a relevant question. It is no defence that the witness (who may be, for instance, a priest, doctor, or journalist) is bound to secrecy by a professional code. If disclosure is necessary in the interests of justice or public safety, they must answer as directed.

Defiance Failure to obey any court order, including a citation to appear in court, is contempt.

Publication Only factual reports of court proceedings are allowed. Any comments on the proceedings might be regarded as an attempt to influence the outcome of a case. It is no excuse that the reporter did not intend to interfere with the course of justice. It is contempt if publication of a report creates a substantial risk that the case will be prejudiced.

This means that freedom of speech is restricted by the right of a citizen to a fair trial. Newspapers and broadcasters

THE NEWSPAPER THAT RECEIVED WRONG LEGAL ADVICE

A court must ensure that a person who is charged with a crime receives a fair and impartial trial. Behaviour that is likely to prejudice a fair trial is a very serious contempt of court and will be dealt with severely. It is no defence that a legal adviser has said that the behaviour would not amount to contempt.

In 1979 four Dutch citizens were arrested in Scotland in connection with the alleged illegal production and possession of drugs. Two days after the arrests an article appeared in the *Glasgow Herald* newspaper with the headline 'Armed raids smash big drugs ring in Scotland'.

The article said that three of the Dutch citizens arrested were thought to have escaped from a Dutch prison and that by their arrest a huge, illegal drugs operation in Scotland had been destroyed. The four persons arrested were not named in the article but it did describe the armed police raids at two addresses near Dundee and Edinburgh. Remarks made by neighbours describing their reactions to the police operations and arrests were quoted in the newspaper.

The LORD ADVOCATE presented a petition to the High Court claiming that publication of the article was contempt of court. In his opinion the article tended to suggest that the people arrested were guilty. He asked that the editor and owners of the newspaper should be prohibited from publishing articles on the case.

In the High Court the *Glasgow Herald* said that they had acted on the advice of their solicitor, who had told them that the article could safely be published.

DECISION

The High Court said that the publication of information which suggested that those arrested were guilty amounted to a substantial interference with the course of justice. In their view it was contempt of court of the most serious kind. The fact that the newspaper had taken the precaution of obtaining legal advice was not sufficient to excuse the contempt.

The court prohibited the newspaper from publishing any further comment about the case. The newspaper owners were fined £20,000 and the editor was fined £750.

THE CONSEQUENCES OF CONTEMPT

The consequences of being in contempt of court can be severe. For example, if a court decides that the publication of comments about a case has prejudiced the trial, the accused may be acquitted – even although there is a convincing case against him.

In such cases the defence would submit that the accused could not expect a fair hearing because of the controversy.

The maximum penalty for contempt of court is 2 years' imprisonment or an unlimited fine, or both.

can be guilty of contempt if they publicly discuss a case while it is still before the court.

They cannot publish interviews with people involved in the case while it is being heard. They cannot speculate on the outcome. They cannot report evidence not given in open court. This is because juries must make their decision only on the evidence they hear.

It is contempt to try to obtain or disclose any part of a jury's deliberations. It is also contempt to use a tape recorder in court without the court's permission.

Contempt of court can be committed in a criminal case even before a person has been charged: comment about a person who is about to be arrested can constitute contempt.

It can be contempt of court to publish a photograph of a person involved in a case in which identification is at issue. This is because a witness seeing the photograph would find it hard to dismiss it from memory in court.

However, if requested to do so by the criminal authorities, newspapers and television can safely publish photographs and identikit pictures of suspects.

All photography or sketching inside a courtroom is forbidden. The publication of an accused person's photograph, or that of anyone else involved in a case (including the judge or an advocate) may also be contempt if it was taken inside the court.

After a verdict has been announced, discussion of the case is allowed. However, if there is an appeal, discussion is prohibited until the appeal is decided.

CONTEMPT OF PARLIAMENT

Parliament itself is prosecutor, judge and jury

Anyone who says or does anything that undermines the authority of, or public respect for, the House of Commons or the House of Lords is guilty of contempt of Parliament.

Allegations of contempt are heard not by the courts but by each House's committee of privileges.

In the Commons, for example, the normal procedure is for an MP to make a complaint to the Speaker, who decides whether to refer the case to the privileges committee. That committee, which consists of MPs appointed at the beginning of every parliamentary session, can if necessary issue a warrant for the accused's arrest.

When he appears before the committee the accused is not allowed to be represented by a lawyer, he is not allowed to ask questions and he has no right of appeal. The hearings are not open to the press or public.

The committee makes a recommendation to the House of Commons, which usually adopts it.

If the offender is found guilty, he is summoned to the Bar of the House where he is expected to apologise. If he does so he is reprimanded by the Speaker and there is no further punishment, if the offence is a minor one. If the offender is an MP he can be expelled from the House for a serious offence.

If someone refused to apologise, he could in theory be sent to prison for an indefinite period.

CONTINUOUS EMPLOYMENT

Many employment protection rights depend on length of service

Your rights as an employee improve the longer you work in any one job.

After 1 month's continuous employment, you become eligible for minimum notice and guaranteed pay; after 1 year, you can claim compensation for UNFAIR DISMISSAL (2 years if your employer employs 20 employees or less), and written reasons for dismissal can be demanded after 6 months. After 2 years you are eligible for REDUNDANCY payment and for MATERNITY rights.

Other periods of employment bring other rights. *See:* EMPLOYMENT PROTECTION

These rights will hold good, in many cases, even when there is a break in your continuity of service, or when there is a temporary reduction in the number of hours you work.

Length of service is assessed in working weeks – in which you work or have a contract to work at least 16 hours. A working week of less than 16 hours does not count towards length of service unless you have worked continuously for 5 years for at least 8 hours per week.

Meal-breaks do not count towards the number of working hours, though coffee and tea breaks may. Stand-by duties can – for example, if you have to remain on call at home or by a telephone elsewhere. Essential work done at home may count.

How long someone has worked is usually calculated backwards from the date when he is actually dismissed.

An employer cannot artificially deprive someone of his unfair dismissal rights by dismissing him without notice just before those rights would have come into effect.

Every employee who has been continuously employed for 1 month is entitled to at least 1 week's notice, and this will count towards his period of continuous employment. *See:* NOTICE

Similarly, a woman who has the right to return to her job after having a baby, but is prevented from doing so, is regarded as having been continuously employed up to the date when she originally said she would return.

When a break does not count

Employment is continuous even when:

- A business changes hands, if the employee stays on in his own job or in some other capacity.
- An employee is transferred to an 'associated' employer. Two employers are associated when one company is under the control of the other or both are controlled by a third.
- An employee changes jobs within a company.
- An employee is absent through sickness or injury or is on MATERNITY leave. (If the employee's contract has ended, continuity is broken after 6

WHEN A CUT IN HOURS DID NOT COUNT

Length of service is assessed by the number of weeks in which you worked or had a contract to work at least 16 hours. But a temporary reduction to less than 16 hours will not affect your rights.

Jane Sheldrake had worked in a department store for more than 3 years. For about 6 weeks before being made redundant, her hours were reduced by her employers from 23 a week to 12. At the industrial tribunal hearing, the store said that trade had fallen off during that 6 week period and it was obliged to pay redundancy compensation only for the previous period when Jane had been working full time.

DECISION

The tribunal ruled that those 6 weeks were a temporary reduction in the hours that were normally worked, and counted towards Jane's weeks of continuous service. She received her full payment.

months' absence.)

- There is a temporary cessation in someone's work, or he is absent through 'arrangement or custom'. Examples of this are when an employee is kept on the books to qualify for a pension, or is lent temporarily to another employer.

A short break between fixed-period contracts may count as a temporary cessation. In 1983 the House of Lords ruled that a college lecturer's employment was continuous even though her contract ended each July and was renewed in September. Whether a break between contracts affects continuity depends on its length relative to the length of both contracts.

- An employer dies – provided that the employee is taken on by the dead employer's representative or trustees.
- An employer re-employs someone after a hearing for unfair dismissal, or by agreement with the official arbitration service, ACAS. An unofficial reinstatement may not guarantee continuity so ACAS should always be involved.

When service is broken

Employment is considered to be not continuous:

- When the employee leaves a company and rejoins later.
- When the employee receives a redundancy payment after a business has been sold or taken over.

If you are laid off or take part in a strike

Going on strike does not break continuity but the weeks you are away from work do not count towards the total served and even a 5 minute strike counts as a whole week lost. So if you work for 51 weeks, but then go on strike for 1 week, you must work a further week to satisfy the 1 year qualifying period for unfair dismissal.

If you are laid off you are still covered by the rules relating to temporary cessation of work or absence by arrangement and continuity is not broken.

WHEN A 30 DAY BREAK DID NOT INTERRUPT SERVICE

Continuity of employment is not broken when a person goes on strike or is temporarily laid off.

After 40 years' service with a Tyneside ship repairer, a riveter was declared redundant and claimed payment based on that length of continuous work. However, his employers pointed out that there had been a gap of 30 days in 1964 when he and others were laid off owing to a shortage of work at the yard.

Although they had been taken on again, there had been no promise at the time that they would be re-employed, and in fact they had been told to seek other work. Had the riveter's service been broken?

DECISION

The court decided it had not. The matter, it said, should be looked at in the light of what actually did happen, not what was expected to happen, when the riveter was laid off. It was a temporary cessation of work which did not break his continuity of service, and he won his fight for full redundancy payment.

CONTRACEPTION

Getting help to prevent unwanted pregnancies

Women are entitled to obtain free contraceptive pills and appliances under the National Health Service. Any female can apply. She does not need to be married, nor to be over 16, nor to have her parents' consent.

If a woman does not want to consult her own GP or if her doctor is not able to offer contraceptive advice, she should consult the Medical List, which contains the names of all general practitioners in the area and indicates which are on the Contraceptive Services List.

Although any GP can prescribe contraceptives the doctors on that list receive extra payment from the NHS for doing so, and are therefore more likely to be available. You will be asked to sign a form confirming that you are to receive contraceptive services from the doctor over the coming year. The list is always available at main post offices and public libraries.

Choosing a contraceptive

Contraceptives that can be prescribed free are the pill, intra-uterine device (coil) and diaphragm (cap), but not the sheath, although the sheath is sometimes provided free of charge by family planning clinics.

The pill, in particular, is prescribed only if the doctor is satisfied that it is safe for the particular patient. Some types of pill, for example, are likely to aggravate certain medical conditions such as high blood pressure. Some are harmful in conjunction with other drugs.

If a doctor refuses to prescribe any pill, the patient is entitled to ask another – but if there are good medical grounds for the first refusal, he is likely to reach the same decision.

A patient's right to confidential treatment

Contraceptive advice and service is confidential between DOCTOR AND PATIENT.

The age of consent for sexual intercourse is 16, and a doctor who supplies contraceptives or prescriptions for a patient under that age may risk prose-

THE WIFE WHO WANTED A BABY

There is no law forbidding a husband or wife from using some means of contraception without the consent of the other – but to do so may be grounds for divorce. There have been no cases in Scotland but there have been in England.

Mr and Mrs Knott lived together for 11 years. Mrs Knott wanted to have children, but Mr Knott practised the withdrawal method of contraception. Full intercourse never took place.

Eventually the couple parted. Mrs Knott sought a divorce on the ground of cruelty by her husband.

The court heard that when the marriage broke up, the wife was in a very nervous condition – although her husband had never been told by doctors that his sexual practice might injure her health.

DECISION

Mrs Knott was granted a divorce. The court held that Mr Knott's refusal to let her have a child and his use of the withdrawal method was 'a deliberate act, contrary to the laws of nature and one which any husband must realise must damage a wife's health'.

cution for AIDING AND ABETTING unlawful intercourse. However a doctor is not obliged to tell the girl's parents that she is seeking contraceptive help or that she has been given it, although many doctors feel that where possible the parents should be consulted.

Husbands and wives

There is no law forbidding a husband or wife from using some means of contraception without the consent of the other. To do so might be grounds for divorce, although there has never been a case in Scotland on this question.

A wife is entitled to take the pill, have a coil inserted, use the cap or be surgically sterilised without her husband's consent – or even his knowledge. A husband can use a sheath or have a vasectomy operation without his wife's consent.

In practice, most doctors insist on a husband's consent for a sterilisation and sometimes even for fitting an intra-uterine contraceptive device, the coil. They will also usually ask for a wife's consent to her husband's vasectomy.

The normal rule of confidentiality applies to a wife or husband who seeks contraceptive help: a doctor who discloses that information to the other spouse against his patient's wishes would be guilty of unprofessional conduct.

Consulting a family planning clinic

Instead of consulting a GP about contraception, you can go to a family planning clinic – usually listed in the Yellow Pages of your local telephone directory under Family Planning.

Informing your GP A family planning clinic would normally inform your GP of any treatment or appliance prescribed – especially if you have been prescribed a contraceptive pill which could have an adverse reaction with some other drug.

You can, however, insist that the clinic does not contact your doctor.

When something goes wrong

A doctor who prescribed a contraceptive pill without carrying out adequate tests, or making enough inquiries about a woman's medical condition could be sued for MEDICAL NEGLIGENCE if the pill caused or aggravated an illness.

The manufacturers who supplied the pill could be liable for negligence to the woman who took it if they failed to give doctors adequate information about the drugs involved – either because insufficient testing had been done or because they feared that sales of their pill would be affected by such disclosure.

If you believe that your health has been affected by a pill negligently prescribed or supplied, you should seek legal advice. If a contraceptive fails to work, or, say, a coil causes serious trouble, a doctor can be sued only where negligence on his part can be proved.

If a contraceptive fails and you obtain damages in a court action for negligence, this can include at least some of the estimated cost of bringing up a child born as a result.

CONTRACT

A legally binding agreement

An agreement does not normally have to be written down to be legally binding. Spoken words are enough to make most contracts enforceable in law, and it is even possible to enter into a contract by actions only, saying nothing.

For example, a housewife, shopping in her local supermarket, enters a legally binding contract when she takes goods from a shelf and pays for them at the check-out.

What matters is that both parties have made an agreement.

A contract is broken where one party fails to do what he has agreed to do. In Scotland the innocent party can normally ask a court to order the party at fault to carry out his part of the bargain. If he wilfully ignores the order he could as a last resort be imprisoned. As an alternative the innocent party can claim damages for breach of contract.

Where the contract has been broken through a failure to pay money, the remedy is to sue for the sum due plus interest.

Compensation can also be claimed if the breach of contract has caused further loss which the person at fault knew might happen or should have foreseen.

If one party has broken the contract in some basic way – such as not delivering goods known to be needed by a certain date – the other party can cancel the contract and claim damages. The

WHEN A CONTRACT MUST BE IN WRITING

Some contracts cannot be legally binding unless there is a signed agreement or other document, such as a letter. They include:

1. A contract for the sale of land and any kind of buildings including houses.
2. A contract to let any such property for more than a year.
3. A contract of apprenticeship or for a job that is agreed to be for a period of more than a year.
4. A contract agreeing to ARBITRATION.
5. A contract to guarantee a debt. *See:* GUARANTOR.
6. Any CONSUMER CREDIT agreement such as HIRE PURCHASE.

CAN A SHOPKEEPER REFUSE TO SELL?

A contract is made only when a genuine offer has been accepted. If a mistake has been made on a price ticket and goods are priced too low, you cannot insist on buying them at the price indicated. A shopkeeper who displays goods in his window with a price on them is not, in law, offering them for sale. He is merely inviting the public to make offers to buy them.

The shopkeeper may, of course, sell the goods at the mistaken low price for the sake of goodwill. But what he cannot do is sell at a higher price than that at which he has advertised the goods. That is an offence under the TRADE DESCRIPTIONS Act for which he can be fined or imprisoned.

alternative is to try to get it carried out and claim damages for any loss due, for instance, to lateness.

When goods are faulty

The terms of a contract do not depend only on the words, spoken or written, of an agreement. For instance, nothing may have been said about the quality of any goods bought, but it is an implied term of any contract of sale that goods will be fit for the purpose for which they are intended. By entering into the contract, the shopkeeper, in effect, guarantees that the goods he is selling are fit for their purpose.

That rule would apply, for example, if a newly bought washing machine did not work. *See:* DEFECTIVE GOODS

If a house owner employs a decorator to paint his house, there is an implied term in the contract that the decorator will take reasonable care and exercise reasonable skill in doing the work, even though nothing has been said about the quality of his workmanship. If the decorator fails to use reasonable care and skill the house owner can sue for breach of contract.

A hotel proprietor can claim damages from you if you fail to take up a booking once you have contracted to do so, unless the hotel was full and he could have re-let the room. The amount awarded would generally be equal to the amount of profit lost. If you have paid a deposit, this sum would be taken into account by the court.

Damages, however, cannot usually be claimed for mere inconvenience or annoyance when a contract is broken – for example, a hotel room is not ready at the time for which it was booked.

Getting out of a contract

It is possible to get out of a contract if you can show that:

- There has been a serious breach of contract by the other party.
- A false statement lured you into a contract which you would not have made if you had been told the full facts.
- There was a complete misunderstanding between you and the other party, so that no agreement existed and there was therefore no contract.

If, through no fault of the parties, performance of a contract becomes impossible, or would be very different from what was agreed, the contract automatically ends. Neither party is then in breach of contract.

SERVING YOURSELF WITH DRUGS

Putting goods on display in a shop constitutes what lawyers call an invitation to treat, not an offer. The offer comes when the customer offers to buy them. There is still no contract until the shopkeeper has accepted that offer – he is quite entitled to refuse.

The Pharmaceutical Society of Great Britain sued Boots the Chemist for selling drugs and medicine without the supervision of a qualified pharmacist as required under the Pharmacy and Poisons Act. Boots ran a self-service shop in which customers helped themselves and paid unqualified staff at a cash desk. Drugs and medicines could be taken from a shelf in an area marked 'Chemists' Department' and paid for at the desk.

The company said that a qualified pharmacist was at the shop and was authorised to stop a customer buying drugs and taking them away if he thought it was necessary to do so. The Society argued that once the drugs had been put in a wire basket and taken to the cash desk the transaction could not be stopped.

DECISION

The court ruled that no contract of sale took place until the customer's offer to buy was agreed to by the acceptance of money at the cash desk. Acceptance took place under a pharmacist's supervision. That constituted supervision under the Act, so the Society lost its case.

THE FAULTY CAR

A minor defect in a purchase does not allow you to get out of the contract

Mr Turpie purchased a new car from a garage. A number of faults appeared which the sellers tried to put right. Mr Turpie tried to treat the contract as ended on account of the defects.

DECISION

The court decided that there was no breach of the implied term that goods should be in proper condition because (1) the defects were small and could be put right fairly cheaply; (2) the sellers were willing to put the car right; and (3) many new cars have such minor faults.

A TALE OF TWO COWS

A false statement intended to make you enter into a contract may not succeed in binding you to the bargain.

Mr Morrison brought his cows to a market where he met Mr Telford, who lied that he was the son of a Mr Wilson with whom Mr Morrison had had business dealings in the past. Mr Telford said that he wished to buy the cows on behalf of his father. Mr Morrison believed him and gave him the cows on credit. Telford then sold them to a Mr Robertson. The question arose whether Mr Robertson could keep the cows.

DECISION

Morrison thought that he was selling the cows to someone he knew to be respectable. It was Telford's fraudulent statement that made him believe that. There was no valid contract between Morrison and Telford nor between Morrison and Wilson. So Telford could not sell the cows to Robertson and Morrison could get them back.

CONTRACTOR'S LIABILITY

What you can expect when you employ an expert

Someone who contracts to do a job for you is bound in law to use reasonable skill and care. If he does the job badly, you can sue him for breach of CONTRACT.

In addition, if someone else is injured or has his property damaged as a result of the bad workmanship, he too can sue the contractor for NEGLIGENCE.

For example, if you pay a contractor to service an electric hedge-trimmer, and he does it badly, you are entitled to sue him for breach of contract.

If his bad workmanship results in injury to someone else using the hedge trimmer, that person can claim damages from the contractor for negligence.

If a garage repairs your car badly, and as a result you have an accident with another vehicle, you can sue the garage for breach of contract – and the other driver can sue it for negligence.

A contractor cannot avoid liability by attempting to contract out of any responsibility for negligence which causes personal injury. *See:* UNFAIR CONTRACT

Using the right materials

A contractor must use materials that are reasonably fit for their purpose. If they are not fit, you can sue him for damages for breach of contract.

The contractor can include a term in the contract excluding or limiting his liability, but if he is acting in the course of a business and you are not – for example, if you are a householder employing him to build a garage – such a condition is invalid.

When you may be liable

Although you are always liable for any harm caused by the negligence of one of your employees in the course of his work, you are not usually held responsible for the wrongful actions of an independent contractor working for you – for example, a taxi driver, garage man or builder.

That is because although in theory you can tell an employee how to do his job, you cannot give detailed instructions to an independent contractor you hire to do a specific task.

In some circumstances, however, you can be made to pay compensation for damage caused by an independent contractor. If you allowed an unqualified person to fit new brakes to your car, and as a result had an accident with another vehicle, you and the repairer would both be liable; you would have been careless in entrusting an important task to someone not qualified to do it.

Even if you are properly careful in choosing a contractor, you may be liable for his negligence if the job he is doing is considered exceptionally hazardous to other people. For example, if you employ a contractor to carry out alterations to a building on a busy street, you will be liable with him for any injury to a passer-by.

In such cases, the victim is entitled to recover damages from either of you, but the court will apportion the damages between you according to what is considered just.

Insurance

If the contractor has no money to pay his share, and is not insured against such liability, you will have to pay the entire sum. Before allowing potentially hazardous work to start, therefore, it is

THE GRAVESTONE THAT FELL ON SOMEONE

When an injury is directly caused by faulty workmanship, the contractor must pay damages.

A 9-year-old boy was taking flowers to his grandmother's grave in a churchyard when a 5 cwt tombstone, recently erected, fell on him. The boy's leg was broken.

After an investigation, it was discovered that the tombstone had not been secured with metal dowels. The monumental mason who erected the tombstone, Mr Cotterill, was sued for negligence.

DECISION

Mr Cotterill, in failing to use metal dowels, had been negligent. He was ordered to pay the boy £117 damages.

THE PAINT THAT KILLED A COW

If you engage a contractor to carry out dangerous work for you, you will be liable for any damage caused to other people or their property. Even ordinary tasks may be dangerous.

Mr Adams, a hotelier, engaged Mr Macpherson, a joiner, to repair his boats, which were in a field by a loch. This involved scraping paint off the boats. No arrangement was made for Mr Macpherson to remove the paint scrapings.

Mr Stewart had the right to graze his cow in the field. While it was browsing near the boats the cow ate some of the paint scrapings. The paint contained white lead and within a week the beast was dead.

DECISION

Mr Adams was held liable for the loss of the cow even though Mr Macpherson was not his employee. Since the job involved leaving poisonous paint scrapings around, the work of repairing the boats was dangerous to the public.

THE BENTLEY WRITTEN OFF BY A SAILOR

If your property is in for repair and is lost or damaged, the repairers will be liable if they failed to take reasonable care of it.

Mr Forbes, the owner of a Bentley car, put it into a garage for repair. When it came back it had a rattle. The garage agreed to put this right and to bring the car to the car park at a hotel where Mr Forbes was doing some business.

When Mr Forbes came out of the hotel to collect his car he found that it was not there. The garage had brought it to the car park but left it unlocked with the keys inside. A sailor coming out of a nearby public house had decided to use it to get back to his base and crashed it on the way.

DECISION

The garage were held liable for the damage caused by the sailor. They had failed to take reasonable care of the car through the action of leaving it unlocked with the keys inside.

advisable to ask to see the contractor's receipt for a current insurance premium.

CONTRIBUTORY NEGLIGENCE

When a victim shares the blame for an accident

If someone crossing a quiet street on a pedestrian crossing is knocked down by a car that suddenly comes round a corner at high speed, it is a clear case of NEGLIGENCE, and the pedestrian is entitled to compensation for any injuries. *See:* PERSONAL INJURY

But if the pedestrian steps off the pavement without looking for traffic, and is hit by a vehicle travelling too fast to stop in time, he himself is guilty of contributory negligence.

Someone whose contributory negligence is partly to blame for his injuries will lose some of the damages which are assessed for his injuries.

The court first assesses the amount that would have been awarded if the accident was entirely the other person's fault and then decides what proportion of the blame can be attributed to the victim.

Damages are then reduced according to that proportion. For example, if the victim is held one quarter to blame for the accident, his compensation will be cut by 25 per cent.

Contributory negligence always makes it difficult to assess what an injured person is likely to be awarded in the end – and therefore it is inevitably difficult to decide whether to accept any out-of-court settlement that may be offered.

If an out-of-court settlement is accepted, expenses are usually paid by the loser.

If a settlement is not accepted, then the injured person must accept what the judge awards, even if it is less than the amount offered in the out-of-court settlement.

If the victim of an accident is under 18, the question of contributory negligence is judged on whether he was taking reasonable care for someone of his age, experience, intelligence and general maturity.

THE PASSENGER WHO DID NOT WEAR A SEAT BELT

Where a person is injured as a direct result of not doing something that a prudent person would do, his or her damages are likely to be reduced accordingly.

Mrs Hanlon was travelling as a passenger in a baker's van. There was a bad accident, which was found to be the fault of the driver of another vehicle.

Mrs Hanlon was seriously injured, particularly because the nerve fibres in one of her arms were damaged. She was not wearing a seat belt. Her reason was that it had flour on it and might have made her clothes dirty.

DECISION

There is a general rule that not wearing a seat belt is contributory negligence if wearing it would have resulted in less serious injury.

Her excuse was held to be inadequate and her damages were reduced by 10 per cent. (Where there are special reasons, judges may deduct up to 20 per cent in such cases).

THE PASSENGER WHO WENT ON A PUB CRAWL WITH THE DRIVER

Mr Dick borrowed his father's car and took two friends to a street containing a number of public houses. After several hours they got drunk and set off home in the car.

A few miles along the road Mr Dick drove into a lamp post. One of the friends, Mr Winnik, was injured and sued Mr Dick for damages.

DECISION

An Act of Parliament prevented him being denied damages altogether on the ground that he had voluntarily run the risk of injury by travelling in the car in such circumstances. But the court still decided that he was one half to blame for his injuries and his damages were reduced from £750 to £375.

DEFINING CONTRIBUTORY NEGLIGENCE

A judge's decision on how damages should be apportioned depends on how serious he thinks an injured person's own actions or omissions were.

For example, a driver who was injured in an accident after he had parked on a bend had his damages reduced by 80 per cent; and a steel erector who was severely injured because he was not wearing safety harness received only 10 per cent of the damages assessed.

The amount deducted by the judge to take account of the victim's own carelessness is rarely less than 10 per cent.

In cases decided by the courts, factors involving contributory negligence have included:

At work

- Worker suffering from dermatitis after refusing to use protective hand cream provided by employer.
- Steel erector not wearing harness.
- Machine operator removing safety guard to increase or speed production.
- Machine operator cleaning moving parts.
- Builder refusing to use crawling board on a fragile roof.
- Railway worker ignoring signal that train was approaching.
- Employee using ladder he knew to be defective.
- Window cleaner not securing sash.
- Dustman not wearing gloves provided when emptying glass from dustbin.

On the road

- Accepting a lift from a driver although realising that he is so drunk as to be unfit to drive.
- Passenger refusing to use a front seat belt.
- Motor cyclist refusing to wear a safety helmet.
- Driving over a white line down the centre of a road.
- Not slowing down at crossroads.
- Ignoring a Stop sign.
- Parking on a bend.
- Not anticipating that a cyclist would move out into path of car.

On foot

- Stepping suddenly off pavement into path of oncoming car.
- Walking into an unfenced hole during daylight.
- Walking with back to traffic at night wearing dark clothing.

CONVEYANCE

Transferring ownership of a house from one person to another

The legal process of transferring ownership of land and buildings from one owner to another is known as conveyancing. The legal document for doing it is called a conveyance.

The kind of conveyance used depends on whether the seller is making an outright transfer of the property, or merely feuing it so that he remains in the feudal chain as SUPERIOR and the buyer becomes his vassal. If the sale is an outright transfer a simple document called a disposition is used. If the property is being feued a feu disposition or feu contract is needed. Nowadays land may sometimes be feued by large building companies or local authorities, but it is extremely unusual for anyone else to do so. *See:* HOUSE BUYING AND SELLING

In a normal sale a draft disposition is drawn up by the buyer's solicitor. The seller's solicitor suggests amendments until both sides agree on the final wording. A fair copy is then signed by the seller and handed over to the buyer on the date of entry. For the transfer of ownership to be complete the buyer must record the disposition in the REGISTER OF SASINES or the LAND REGISTER.

The unbroken chain of conveyances stretching back into the past forms the most essential part of the title deeds, establishing ownership of the property. Under the new system of REGISTRATION OF TITLE, now being slowly introduced, the collection of old conveyances is replaced with a simple title sheet.

Where the property is bought on a mortgage, the building society or other lender takes possession of the new conveyance and the rest of the title deeds until the mortgage is paid off. The buyer can keep the deeds himself if there is no mortgage, but often he gives them to his solicitor for safekeeping. If a conveyance or other deed which has been recorded in the Register of Sasines is lost, a copy can be obtained from the Register. *See:* HOUSE BUYING AND SELLING

GETTING IT RIGHT

The buyer's and seller's solicitors may have to exchange draft conveyances several times before a satisfactory document is agreed.

THE DISPOSITION – THE DOCUMENT WHICH TRANSFERS OWNERSHIP

To complete the transfer this document must be recorded in the Register of Sasines or Land Register

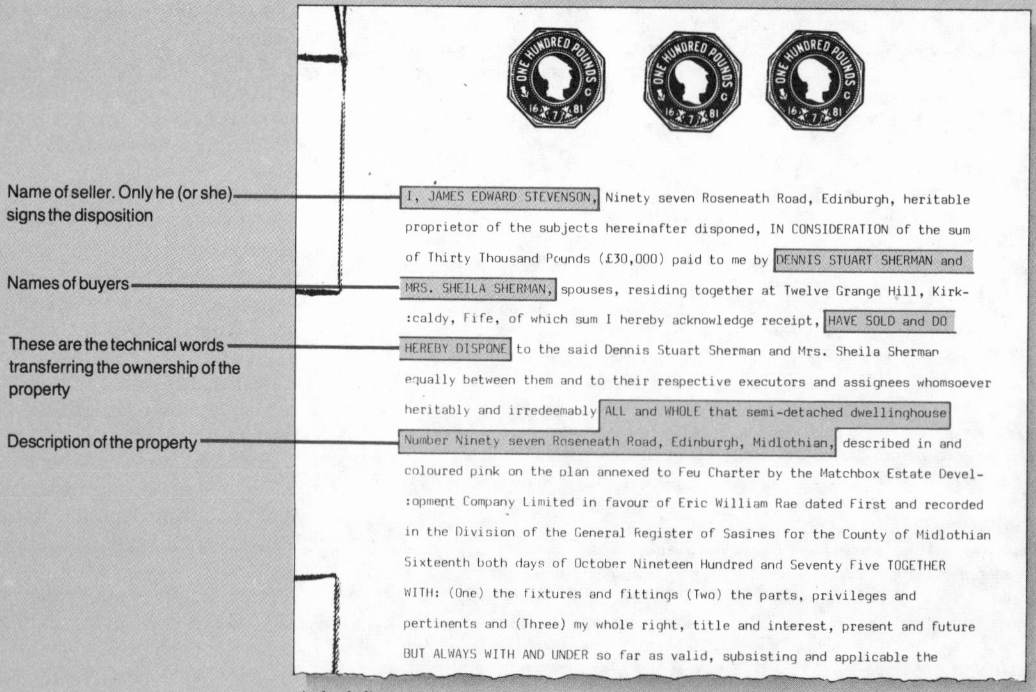

Name of seller. Only he (or she) signs the disposition

Names of buyers

These are the technical words transferring the ownership of the property

Description of the property

ONE HUNDRED POUNDS 16 7 81

I, JAMES EDWARD STEVENSON, Ninety seven Roseneath Road, Edinburgh, heritable proprietor of the subjects hereinafter disponed, IN CONSIDERATION of the sum of Thirty Thousand Pounds (£30,000) paid to me by DENNIS STUART SHERMAN and MRS. SHEILA SHERMAN, spouses, residing together at Twelve Grange Hill, Kirk-:caldy, Fife, of which sum I hereby acknowledge receipt, HAVE SOLD and DO HEREBY DISPONE to the said Dennis Stuart Sherman and Mrs. Sheila Sherman equally between them and to their respective executors and assignees whomsoever heritably and irredeemably ALL and WHOLE that semi-detached dwellinghouse Number Ninety seven Roseneath Road, Edinburgh, Midlothian, described in and coloured pink on the plan annexed to Feu Charter by the Matchbox Estate Devel-:opment Company Limited in favour of Eric William Rae dated First and recorded in the Division of the General Register of Sasines for the County of Midlothian Sixteenth both days of October Nineteen Hundred and Seventy Five TOGETHER WITH: (One) the fixtures and fittings (Two) the parts, privileges and pertinents and (Three) my whole right, title and interest, present and future BUT ALWAYS WITH AND UNDER so far as valid, subsisting and applicable the

A draft disposition is usually drawn up by the buyer's solicitor. He agrees a final version with the seller's solicitor and the document is then signed by the seller.

CO-OWNERSHIP

When an asset belongs to more than one person

One piece of property can be owned by any number of different people as owners in common. Each co-owner usually has an equal share in the property, but this need not always be so. For example, half of a house may be owned by an elderly parent, and one quarter each by her two children.

The owner of a FLAT often co-owns such mutual items as the stairs and roof of the building with his neighbours. Couples married or living together often share the ownership of a house or car or bank account.

If you are married and your house is in your sole name, or that of your wife (or husband), the house belongs to the named partner alone. It makes no difference if the other partner helped pay for the down payment on purchase and may still be contributing to the mortgage repayments.

If your spouse owns the family home, there is nothing you can do about it unless he or she signs a deed of TRUST in your favour. But even if you do not own the house you will usually have a right of occupancy. This means that you have a right to remain in the house. *See:* OCCUPANCY RIGHTS

Management of common property

Owning common property is very much like owning any other kind of property, but there are some special rules:

- All acts of management to do with the property must be agreed by every co-owner. This means that you can stop anything you object to. An exception exists for necessary repairs.
- You can transfer your share in the property at any time, by, for example, selling it or giving it away. You can also bequeath it in your will.
- You can insist that the property is physically divided up amongst the co-owners, or, where this is impracticable or would greatly reduce its value, that the property be sold and the proceeds divided.

Survivorship clauses

When a married couple buy a house together, their solicitor often arranges for the CONVEYANCE to be made out to the couple 'and to the survivor'. This is a survivorship clause, and its effects are rather complicated.

WHEN A COUPLE HAVE EQUAL SHARES IN A HOME

Many homes are bought in joint names of husband and wife. This is because couples recognise the contribution each makes towards the purchase and repayment of the mortgage, and because they wish to share their assets.

As they are co-owners, both husband and wife are free to transfer their share in the house during their lifetimes. But if they have not done so by the time of their death, their share passes automatically to the spouse that survives – unless they have bequeathed it in their will to someone else (and they had power to do so).

A spouse has power to bequeath the share only if he or she alone paid for the house. If both spouses have paid, neither has power to bequeath; if one paid, the other does not have power.

A survivorship clause can tie your hands for many years in the future. If you want to leave your share in the house to your spouse it is better to do so by WILL. Then you are always free to change your mind.

COPYRIGHT

Safeguards for writers, artists and composers

Anyone who writes a book, article, play, poem or words for a song, or who paints, draws or does sculpture, or composes music, is entitled to keep control over the use of his work by others. That entitlement is known as copyright.

The Copyright Act 1956, protects the creator of:

- Literary works, such as books of all kinds, short stories, poems, words of songs, articles and letters.
- Dramatic works, such as plays, mimes, operas and ballets.
- Musical works, such as songs and all forms of music without words.
- Artistic works, such as paintings, drawings, prints, photographs, sculptures, jewellery and pottery.
- Sound and visual recordings, radio and television programmes and films. Specific protection is to be given soon to computer programs and files.

One work can involve more than one copyright. For example, with a record of a song there may be one copyright in the words, another in the music and a third in the sound recording. Each of those may be owned by a different person.

Copyright protection is given only to an original work, not one copied from someone else. Furthermore, the protection applies only to the form in which an idea is expressed, not to the idea itself.

For example, if someone makes a speech explaining his theory for doubling the world's food supply, he cannot prevent others from repeating his ideas, even if he is not given the credit for them. But if he sets out his ideas in writing, the written version is protected by copyright and cannot be copied without his permission.

If you invent a valve that works in a new way, your drawing of the valve is copyright, but not the invention itself. To protect an invention, a PATENT must be obtained.

A work does not usually have to possess literary or artistic worth to be protected by copyright: the protection extends to such items as football pool coupons and trade directories.

Making sure of your copyright

In most countries, including the UK, an original work is protected by copyright as soon as it is created or in some way recorded. There is no need to register copyright, but you should indicate your claim to protection by marking your work with the international copyright symbol © and the date of publication or creation. For example © Reader's Digest Association Ltd, 1984.

By international agreement, copyright created in one country is usually effective in others. So copying a book here may infringe copyright even if the book was written, printed, published and bought in, say, Sweden. There are also special rules in the European Communities.

How long copyright lasts

The length of time that your protection lasts depends on the type of work you have created. For most published works, copyright lasts for the author's lifetime and for 50 years after his death.

If a work is first published after the author's death, copyright lasts for 50 years after the publication.

For photographs, prints, records and films, copyright protection lasts for 50 years from the date of first publication, whether or not the creator of the work is alive at that time.

Where a design is exploited commercially the copyright may expire 15 years after the design's first commercial use.

When the creator does not own copyright

Although copyright usually belongs to the creator of the work, there are exceptions.

Someone who creates a work for an employer – for example, a photographer on the staff of a newspaper or magazine, or a staff poster-designer – is not entitled to the copyright. It belongs to his employer.

If you engage a freelance photographer to take pictures of you – for example, at a wedding – you will own the copyright of the photographs. However, if the photographs have not been commissioned – for example, if a friend takes them without payment – the photographer retains the copyright.

When a copyright work is performed

Anyone who creates a work that can be performed – whether dramatic or musical – has a right to prevent other people performing it in public without his permission. *See also:* PERFORMING RIGHT

However, it is not a breach of copyright to perform the work in private – for example, in a school drama production to which outsiders are not admitted. But if parents were admitted, the performance would be public and be subject to copyright restrictions.

A performance to a private members' club or society – for example, a women's institute – is a public performance. So is playing records or radio music to workers in a factory.

Seeking permission A licence to perform a play in public should normally be obtained from the publisher of the printed version of the work. For music or records, the licence can be obtained from the Performing Right Society and Phonographic Performance Ltd.

Live performances A performer however has no copyright in his live performance. If someone else imitates it, that person cannot be sued for breach of copyright.

Nevertheless it is a criminal offence to make a recording or film of a live performance for commercial purposes, without the written consent of the performer. But it is not illegal to make a recording or film purely for private purposes.

If the recording or film has been made commercially, a crime is committed only by the maker, not by anyone who buys a copy, even if he knows it was illegally produced.

Taping an existing recording If you

WHO OWNS 'POPEYE'?

A businessman who admires a rival product must get permission to copy it.

A British toy manufacturer, O. M. Kleeman Ltd, applied to the American copyright holders for a licence to produce 'Popeye the Sailor' toys and dolls.

The copyright holders, King Features Syndicate Incorporated, had given permission to other British companies, but could not agree on terms with Kleeman's. Instead, Kleeman's imported a batch of 'Popeye' dolls, brooches and toys from a foreign manufacturer and produced copies of them.

King Features sued for breach of copyright. Kleeman's claimed that they had not infringed copyright. They said that they had copied, not from the original sketch but from a product not protected by a registered design – and as the designs should have been registered under the Patents and Designs Act, and were not, they were not entitled to protection.

The case was pursued through several courts and ended as an appeal to the House of Lords.

DECISION

The House of Lords granted an injunction to stop O. M. Kleeman infringing copyright by import and manufacture.

It was ruled that a model could infringe the copyright of a sketch. In this case, it had done so by adopting the essential features of Popeye from the sketches. The Patents and Designs Act did not affect author's copyright. *See also:* PATENT

THE EXAM PAPERS THAT WERE COPIED

Original work is protected by copyright – it does not have to possess literary merit.

Examination papers published by the University of London Press were copied and published by a rival company, University Tutorial Press Ltd.

UTP, who had obtained 16 of the 42 test papers from a student who sat the exams, were sued by the University of London Press and by two freelance examiners, Professor Lodge and Mr Jackson, some of whose questions had been used in the plagiarised papers.

In their defence, University Tutorial Press argued that the exams were not protected by copyright because they were neither literary nor original – the questions being fairly standard. They also claimed that the original publishers did not own the papers properly as they did not have authority in writing from the University Senate, only in an oral resolution.

DECISION

The English High Court ruled: 'What is worth copying is worth protecting.'

The questions set were the product of someone's original skill and labour and were therefore protected by copyright. Since the papers were in print, they were protected as being 'literary'.

However, the court said University of London Press did not have written authority and found in favour of only Professor Lodge and Mr Jackson.

ALL MY OWN WORK

The international copyright symbol helps to protect your work by advising copyists that you are aware of your rights.

make a tape recording of an existing record, you infringe copyright, even if the taped copy is for private use only.

Recording television programmes If an event is broadcast live on television – for example, a cricket match or state ceremony – you are entitled to record it on video tape without permission.

You are not entitled to record any type of programme that includes copyright material, such as a film that is less than 50 years old or a concert or variety show in which any music played was written by someone who has been dead less than 50 years.

Using a photo-copying machine If you use a photo-copying machine to copy someone else's work for private research and study, you are not normally breaking the copyright law, provided you observe the rules of 'fair dealing'.

It is fair dealing, for example, to copy a few pages of a book for research purposes, but it would not be considered fair to copy the whole book, or to copy extracts to be circulated to an entire class of pupils.

Fair dealing has not been legally defined, but the Publishers Association and the Society of Authors have said that no permission is needed for an extract of up to 3,000 words, or a series of extracts totalling 8,000 words, provided that the total amount copied does not exceed 10 per cent of the entire work.

A librarian in an educational institution is entitled to make a copy of a complete article in a periodical, or of an extract from a book, for private study by any reader.

Copyright in a letter

The copyright in a letter belongs to the person who writes it. The person to whom it is sent is entitled to retain the letter itself, but not to publish the text without the writer's permission.

If you write to a newspaper or other publication the letter is assumed to be intended for publication and therefore not subject to copyright restrictions, unless you make it clear that publication is not intended.

THE SUPPORTERS' CLUB THAT BREACHED COPYRIGHT

Copyright is infringed if music is performed in public without the permission of the person who owns the copyright. A performance may be public even though it takes place in a private members' club.

Rangers F.C. Supporters Club in Greenock was a non-profit-making members club. Supporters of Rangers football team were able to join the club for a small annual subscription. No charge was made for entry, and members had a limited right to bring guests. The club had a bar and also provided music and dancing.

On three successive Fridays inspectors from the Performing Right Society – who act as a 'watchdog' on behalf of authors and composers – visited the club. On each occasion music over which the Society held the copyright was being performed before around 150 members and guests. The club had not obtained the Society's permission to perform the music.

The Society alleged that the club had breached their copyright, because the Copyright Act 1956 allowed performance 'in public' only if the Society's permission was obtained. The club argued that the performance was private, so copyright had not been broken.

The Society applied to the Court of Session for an interdict to prevent the club infringing their copyright. They also sued for damages.

DECISION

The appeal court decided that the music had been played 'in public' and the Society's copyright had therefore been breached. The judges were influenced by the numbers in the club, as well as the entertainment which it provided. In their view it was much the same as going to a place of public entertainment.

The court granted the interdict and awarded the Society £150 damages for the breach of their copyright.

THE NYMPH WHO APPEARED WITHOUT WINGS

Copyright is infringed not only by the copier but by anyone who sells or imports the copy.

The August 1905 issue of 'Munsey's Magazine', an American periodical on sale at W. H. Smith bookstalls, contained an advertising competition. Readers were offered a 6 month subscription to 'The American Illustrator' if they could identify 40 per cent of some famous advertisements.

One of the illustrations was a picture, 'Nature's Mirror' by a German artist, Paul Thumann. The picture had been licensed to The White Rock Mineral Spring Company for use in its publicity.

On seeing this reproduction in a copy of the magazine bought from Smith's, the owner of the copyright of 'Nature's Mirror' – a fine art publisher named Hanfstaengl – complained to the booksellers.

He pointed out that where the original showed a draped female with butterfly wings – the goddess Psyche – gazing into a reflecting pool of water, the reproduction showed no wings and no reflections, and had no artistic merit.

W. H. Smith told its agents to tear the offending page from all outstanding issues of the magazine. Mr Hanfstaengl was not satisfied and sued Smith.

In the English High Court, he claimed that the picture had been vulgarised in the magazine and would therefore damage his sale of fine reproductions. W. H. Smith maintained that the picture in the magazine was not a copy of the original.

DECISION

The court ruled that copyright had been infringed.

The judge said the picture in the magazine 'came so near to the original as to suggest the original in the mind of anyone seeing it.'

Mr Hanfstaengl was awarded a nominal one farthing damages, and costs.

Quotations from copyright material

An extract from a copyright work can be reproduced without a breach of copyright if it is done as part of a criticism or review of that work or another work, and is accompanied by an acknowledgment. Similarly, a series of illustrations, reproduced to show how an artist's style has changed, would not infringe his copyright.

Titles and slogans

The title of a work cannot be copyrighted, nor can a slogan, for the law considers very short phrases too insubstantial or trivial to be protected under the copyright law.

However, if someone copies the title of a well-known book, play or film, or an advertising slogan, it is possible to sue him for 'passing off' his work. *See:* TRADE MARK

When copyright is infringed

A private individual who infringes someone else's copyright is not likely to be sued. But someone in business who does so risks an action for damages and a court order to prevent any further infringement.

It is good business practice to keep all the drawings relating to the products you manufacture. If your products are copied you may be able to sue for infringement of the drawing. If you are accused of copying, your drawings may prove that you designed the product independently. All drawings should ideally be dated and signed by the draughtsman.

A businessman who admires a rival product or advertisement, therefore, should seek legal advice before deciding to copy it.

Copyright may sometimes be infringed innocently – for example, when a publisher prints material which, unknown to him, has been copied by the supposed author from someone else's work. Publishers usually safeguard themselves by making the author responsible, in his contract, for any expense caused by an accidental infringement of copyright.

Copyright is infringed not only by the person who copies someone else's work, but also by anyone who sells or imports that copy, provided that he knows the material infringes copyright.

Copyright law is highly specialised, and anyone who considers that his copyright has been infringed should consult a solicitor. Do not delay before seeking legal advice as the law provides better remedies for those who act quickly. In most clear cases, a court will grant an interim INTERDICT to stop the infringer from carrying out further infringements.

If you have been accused of infringing someone's copyright you should seek legal advice as there may be many technical defences available to you. If you are in the wrong, stop copying at once. The successful pursuer is always entitled to some damages.

CORPORATION TAX

The levy that some clubs and all companies have to pay

Corporation tax is a tax on the net profits of all companies. Social, sports and political clubs and associations are also liable to pay it on some of their profits.

Companies pay corporation tax at a fixed percentage rate on their net profits. The actual rate depends on how much profit they make.

There are two rates: the small company rate (in 1983–84, 30 per cent, for companies with profits of less than £100,000); and the full rate (in 1983–84, 50 per cent for companies with profits of more than £500,000). A tapering relief ensures that companies with profits between these two figures pay tax at a rate somewhere between 30 and 50 per cent.

An unincorporated association – that is an organisation that is not a company or a partnership – such as a cricket club, dancing club or business association, pays corporation tax only on investment profits or unearned profits. Those would include earnings from bank interest, building-society deposits or rent from letting property.

Earnings from bars, social events or other functions are exempt from corporation tax provided that the money is received from the members and the profits are used only for the benefit of the members and the organisation.

But a club that allows outsiders to use its facilities – without, for instance, being signed in only as a guest – is liable to pay corporation tax on all its profits from outsiders and members.

Money raised for charity

Charities do not pay corporation tax on their earnings. Any money raised by a club or organisation for charity would not be subject to corporation tax, even if the club has to pay corporation tax on some of its income.

CORRUPT GIFT

How the law tackles the use of bribes

A gift becomes a bribe in law if it is made with the intention of weakening the recipient's loyalty to his employer or to a public body for which he works or acts.

It does not matter whether a bribe is successful or not: it is the intention that makes the gift illegal. The person offering the bribe is guilty of corruption, and so is the receiver if the bribe is accepted.

A bribe need not be cash. It can be anything of value: a free holiday, the use of a car, theatre tickets, meals, drinks or the chance to buy goods at a specially low price.

Public corruption

The law is particularly concerned with bribery and corruption in public bodies. There are extremely strict controls on people in public life.

WHO BELONGS TO A PUBLIC BODY

A wide interpretation is given to the term 'public body' when the question of bribery arises.

It includes any publicly owned body which has public or legally imposed duties and which is intended to benefit the public rather than make a private profit.

The list of people involved includes all civil servants and local authority employees including teachers, social workers and traffic wardens

It also includes anyone working for a nationalised industry or the National Health Service; police, court officers and staff; MPs, local councillors and justices.

A BRIBE IS ILLEGAL – EVEN WHEN REFUSED

It is an offence for anyone to offer a bribe to someone who holds public office or works for a public body, in the hope that he will do, or not do, something connected with his job or office. It makes no difference if the offer is rejected.

It is an offence for anyone to offer a bribe to someone who holds public office or works for a public body, in the hope that he will do, or refrain from doing, anything connected with his job or office.

If the offered bribe is accepted then the receiver will also be guilty. It is also a crime for a person involved with a public body to solicit a bribe.

The law presumes that any gift to an employee or officer of a public body is a bribe. It is up to the suspected person, either the donor or the receiver, to prove that it is not a bribe.

As a result, anyone who is involved in a public body should be very careful about accepting gifts from business acquaintances.

The gift may not even be intended as a bribe, or accepted as one, but that may be hard to prove later. If a gift is offered or given, it is wise to consult a senior official.

Private corruption

Bribery is also an offence in private business, but when corruption is alleged, the prosecution has to prove that any gift was intended to be a bribe when it was handed over.

Penalties for corruption

The maximum penalty for taking or giving bribes in a public body is 7 years' imprisonment and an unlimited fine. The bribe can be confiscated by the court and the convicted person prevented from holding any public office for 5 years (or forever in the case of a second or subsequent offence). A convicted public servant may have to forfeit all or part of his pension rights.

Corruption in private business carries less severe penalties: the maximum is 2 years' imprisonment and an unlimited fine. *See:* COUNCILLORS

COUNCIL HOUSE SALE

When a tenant can buy his home

Most public sector tenants have the right to buy their homes at a discount on their market value. Those who do are tenants of district and islands councils, development corporations, the Scottish Special Housing Association (but not a HOUSING ASSOCIATION) and some housing co-operatives.

Those with no right to buy include police authority, health board, and Forestry Commission tenants; and also tenants of sheltered housing for the elderly or disabled. Tenants of non-sheltered housing specially adapted for the elderly can be refused the right to buy.

Joint tenants can buy jointly. A tenant can also buy jointly with one or more family members who are over 18 and have lived in the house for at least 6 months. (The landlord can waive these conditions.)

To exercise the right to buy, an applicant (or one of them) must have occupied the house or a series of houses provided by public authorities, for a continuous period of at least 3 years.

The minimum discount is 33 per cent of the market value. One per cent is added for each year of continuous occupation beyond the first 3, up to a maximum of 60 per cent after 30 years.

Occupation of a parent's house after the age of 16, or as a tenant's spouse, counts. Breaks in occupation of under a year are ignored. Breaks of between 1 and 2 years *may* be ignored.

Council loans

Tenants who buy are also entitled to a council loan (or a SSHA or development corporation if one of these is the landlord). The tenant may be able to borrow the entire purchase price – the amount depends upon his age, income and whether he is buying jointly.

The tenant must serve a loan application on the council within a month of receiving its offer to sell. He will need to enclose evidence of his income and evidence that he has been unable to obtain a sufficient loan from a building society.

If the tenant is offered a smaller loan than he applied for, he can still exercise his right to buy provided he can pay the balance himself. Alternatively he can pay a deposit of £100 to the landlord within 2 months of receiving the loan offer. He then has 2 years to complete his purchase, at the original price.

The tenant can appeal to the sheriff court if the loan is refused because he is alleged to have given incorrect information. He can also appeal against the calculation of his loan. The appeal must be brought within 2 months.

The legal formalities

If you decide that you want to buy your home, you have to serve a statutory application on the council (or other authority), telling it of your wish to buy. Unless it refuses your application, the council must send you an offer to sell within 2 months. This should tell you the purchase price, and how that figure was arrived at. The council must also give you information about the terms it will insist on in the CONVEYANCE.

Once everything has been agreed you must notify your acceptance to the council within 2 months of the final offer to sell, or of any later loan offer. The contract of sale is then completed. If you do not do so, the sale is off (unless you have paid your deposit of £100, in which case you have 2 years in which to complete the purchase).

If the council tries to impose a condition in the offer which you think is unreasonable, or refuses to add a new one, you can apply to the Lands Tribunal for Scotland, 1 Grosvenor Crescent, Edinburgh. It can strike out or alter conditions and add new ones.

If the council disputes your right to purchase, you can appeal to the Lands Tribunal within one month.

If the council refuses to consider your request to buy your house or is deliberately slow or obstructive in dealing with your application to buy, you may complain to the Secretary of State for Scotland, New St. Andrews House, Edinburgh. He can investigate and if necessary take proceedings in the Court of Session to make the council carry out its duties. Alternatively you can go to the Court of Session direct.

Selling the house

If a person who has bought his house sells it within five years, he will be liable to pay a percentage of his discount back to the council. If he sells in the first year he will have to pay the whole discount. But the amount to be refunded will be reduced by 20% for each completed year, until the five years have elapsed.

The council can recover the repayment due even from someone who has bought the house from the former tenant. When you buy a former public sector house, your solicitor should check in the Land Registers whether repayment has been made.

COUNCIL MEETING

How elected representatives deal with local affairs

All local authorities must hold a meeting within three weeks of their election. *See:* LOCAL AUTHORITY

Thereafter, a council may hold as many meetings as it likes, but in practice councils meet once every three or four weeks on a regular schedule. The chairman of a council can call a special meeting at any time – on his own responsibility or at the written request of a quarter of the council members.

How meetings can be called

All council meetings must be advertised by a notice put up at the council's offices at least 3 clear days in advance.

Apart from the public notices, each councillor must be given formal warning of a meeting. He must be sent a summons to attend, stating the business to be transacted, at least 3 clear days in advance.

If for some reason a councillor does not receive his summons to attend, the meeting is nevertheless valid.

No councillor can be excluded from a council meeting. The only exception is when the chairman orders a councillor to leave on the ground that he is causing a disturbance which disrupts the council's business.

The public's right to attend council meetings

All council and committee meetings – though not sub-committee meetings – must be open to the public and the press. They should be held in a room big enough to accommodate a reasonable number of spectators.

However, if the council or committee decides that particular business should be conducted in private, the public and the press can be ordered to leave – but the council or committee must first pass a resolution to that effect.

The chairman of the meeting is also empowered to order the removal of any member of the public who causes a disturbance. This, in his opinion, must be preventing the council carrying on its business in an orderly manner.

After a meeting, the minutes of the proceedings must be recorded in a book, kept specially for that purpose. The minutes must be amended, if necessary, in the light of any members' objections and be signed at the next meeting.

Once the minutes are signed, any local government elector in the area is entitled to inspect them at the council's offices and make a copy of all or part of them. Minutes are also frequently available for inspection at public libraries, but this is not a legal requirement.

COUNCIL TENANCY

Renting a home from a local authority

Every citizen can approach a district or islands council and ask to be put on the waiting list for a council house or flat. However most councils have rules for deciding who should be admitted to their waiting lists. These rules must be made available to the public.

A council cannot refuse to admit an applicant to its waiting list on the ground of his or her age – except when the applicant is under 18. Nor can it refuse admission because the applicant does not reside in its area, so long as he or she

- Is, or will be, employed in the area.
- Wishes to move into the area to look for work.
- Is over 60 and wants to move into the area to be near a younger relative.
- Has special social or medical reasons for being housed in the area.

A council cannot refuse to admit a tenant's spouse, or ex-spouse, to the waiting list on the ground that the tenant is in arrears with rent.

How priorities are decided

Councils allocate houses on a priority basis to applicants on their waiting lists. Any rules concerning priorities must be made available to the public.

A council cannot take the following circumstances into account when allocating houses:

- The applicant's age – unless he or she is under 18.
- Length of residence in the council's area.
- The income of the applicant and his or her family.
- Rent arrears owed by the applicant's spouse.

Nor can a council impose a minimum waiting period during which an applicant cannot be considered for a house.

Someone whose home is being compulsorily purchased – for example, if it is in an improvement or HOUSING ACTION AREA – may be given priority for a council house, if he can find no other suitable accommodation, such as a private flat. Priority is also given to people whose homes are unfit for habitation, and to certain homeless people. *See:* HOMELESSNESS

In other cases, councils generally decide priorities by some kind of 'points' system – which means that applicants do not simply move up the list according to the length of time they have been waiting.

The speed at which a person reaches the top of the list, and is offered a home, depends on the number of points his family can tot up, taking into account present housing conditions, and other circumstances, such as age and health.

Even after points have been allocated, some councils may take other factors into account. For instance, an applicant who has not paid his rent regularly in his present home may be pushed back on the waiting list.

A person who feels that his housing application has not been dealt with fairly, for whatever reason, is entitled to lodge a complaint with the local government OMBUDSMAN.

An applicant for a council house has a right to check the information supplied by him to the housing department to make sure that it is accurate.

Keeping in touch

Councils may require applicants to re-register their application every year and to notify them of any change of address and circumstances. Failure to do so may lead to their being dropped from the waiting list.

One-way transfers

In some cases a council may allow a tenant to move to another council house even when no exchange has been arranged with another tenant – for example, when the children grow up and the house becomes too big for the parents.

Exchanging council homes

The tenant of a council house will normally be allowed to exchange it for another – either in the same local authority area or in another. He will probably have to make his own arrangements, some councils advertise requests for exchanges in their office.

Many councils have joined the National Mobility Scheme. Under the Scheme, each council agrees to make at least 1 per cent of its annual lets available to applicants from areas other than its own.

Rules for landlords and tenants

A council tenant is entitled to a written lease containing all the terms of the tenancy except those implied by law – such as, for example, the implied term requiring the council to keep the house in a habitable condition. The written lease, which is a legally binding CONTRACT, is sometimes described as a missive of let or tenancy agreement.

The terms of the lease cannot be varied unless both council and tenant agree. Any agreed variation must be put in a formal document prepared by the council. This rule does not apply to rent increases – these take effect automatically so long as the council gives at least 4 weeks' notice in writing.

The council can apply to the sheriff court if the tenant refuses to agree to a variation. The tenant can also apply if the council refuses to vary a term which the tenant claims is unreasonable and restricts his use or enjoyment of the house. The sheriff can order the variation to be made.

Rent payments Council house rents are normally payable in advance. Failure to pay is usually a breach of the lease and may result in eviction proceedings.

Tenants who find themselves in financial difficulties should inform the housing department at an early stage. They should also find out whether they are entitled to any assistance with housing costs. *See:* HOUSING BENEFITS

Withholding rent A tenant can lawfully withhold rent if the council is in serious breach of the lease – for example, if it fails to maintain the house properly or to remedy a dangerous defect.

A tenant should take legal advice before withholding rent – there may well be doubt as to whether the council has broken the terms of the lease. If he decides to go ahead he should inform the council and put his unpaid rent in a deposit account – he may have to pay it over to the council eventually.

Maintenance Under common law the council must keep the house in a reasonably habitable condition – which includes keeping it 'wind and watertight'. However the council will only be in breach of this duty when a tenant reports a relevant defect and the council then fails to put it right within a reasonable time.

Under the Housing (Scotland) Act 1966 every council is legally responsible for repairing the structure and exterior of its houses. That includes repairing doors and windows, replacing broken window glass and unblocking drains – whether or not caused by vandalism.

The council is also legally responsible for repairing and maintaining water and gas pipes, electrical wiring, boilers, baths, toilets and sinks.

A tenant cannot be charged for any such repairs unless they were necessary because of his fault or neglect. Any term in his lease making him responsible for such repairs is invalid.

The responsibilities of councils and tenants for maintenance and repair are often detailed in schedules to the lease. The tenant should first consult this document to see what his responsibilities are.

The tenant is usually responsible for inside decoration and for minor repairs such as mending fuses. He is also responsible for repairing damage caused through his fault. If the housing department fails to carry out essential repairs, the tenant can:

1. Complain to his local COUNCILLOR.

2. Give the council notice of his intention to do the repairs himself. He should first allow a reasonable period for the council to do the repairs. He is then entitled to deduct the cost of the repairs from his next rent payment, although he should keep receipted accounts to prove that the repairs have been done.

3. Complain to the council's Environmental Health Department if he thinks the disrepair amounts to a NUISANCE under the Public Health (Scotland) Act 1897. If the council fails to remedy the nuisance, 10 ratepayers can petition the sheriff court to order it to do so.

4. Start a court action for damages arising from the council's neglect and seek a court order enforcing work that is needed. The tenant should first seek the advice of a solicitor.

A council is not liable for any damage or injury caused by a defect in its buildings unless it is at fault – such as when one of its maintenance staff was told of the defect or it was something which the council ought reasonably to have known about anyway.

The council ought, for example, to be aware of faults such as leaking tanks or loose roof tiles, if its workmen should have found them in routine inspections.

WAITING FOR A
COUNCIL HOME

Local councils usually decide priorities by some kind of 'points' system, which means that applicants do not simply move up the list according to the length of time they have been waiting.

5. Complain to the local government OMBUDSMAN.

New rules Under a statutory repairs scheme to be introduced soon, tenants will be able to carry out repairs which are the landlord's responsibility and then recover some or all of the cost from the landlord.

Improving your home

You may carry out improvements at your own expense to your council house, provided you have the council's consent. This consent must not be unreasonably withheld.

If consent is refused you can ask the sheriff to order the council to consent. You can also ask the sheriff to strike out any unreasonable conditions which the council imposes.

The council cannot increase your rent because of improvements you have carried out at your own expense. Provided you had council consent you may be able to obtain compensation when the tenancy ends, to take account of the amount by which the value of the property has been increased.

Restrictions on sub-letting

A council tenant must not transfer his tenancy to anyone, or sub-let part of his home, or take in a lodger, without the council's written consent. This consent must not be unreasonably withheld.

A council refusing consent must tell the tenant in writing why it is doing so. If the tenant thinks consent has been unreasonably refused, he can ask the sheriff to order the council to consent.

The rent charged by a tenant cannot be increased without the council's agreement.

Business use

A council house or flat can be used only as a place to live; business use, such as hairdressing or car hire, is generally forbidden.

Causing a nuisance

A tenant who has been convicted of using his home for illegal or immoral purposes, or who causes a nuisance to neighbours – for example, by being noisy, keeping animals or storing refuse – is liable to be evicted.

A council tenant is usually specifically forbidden to obstruct a common driveway, park without permission, cut down trees and shrubs, or make alterations to the property, without permission.

Keeping animals

A tenant may be forbidden to keep animals and birds without the council's permission. He should look at the terms of his lease to find out what his rights are.

If the council wants to evict a tenant

Most council tenants now have some security of tenure as a result of the Tenants' Rights (Scotland) Act 1980. A tenant who pays his rent regularly and does not cause damage or a nuisance is usually entitled to live in his council home without interference.

Some council tenants do not have security of tenure. They include:

- Council employees who are required to live in a council house as a condition of their employment.
- Homeless persons who have been given temporary accommodation under the Housing (Homeless Persons) Act 1977. *See:* HOMELESSNESS
- Tenants who are given another house while work is carried out on their usual home.
- Tenants who have moved into the area to take a job and have been given a temporary house so that they can look for permanent accommodation.

A council which wants to evict a tenant must first serve a written notice of possession on the tenant. This notice tells the tenant that the council may start sheriff court proceedings to evict him.

The notice also states:

- The date after which proceedings can be started. This must be at least 4 weeks after the date on which the notice was served.
- The grounds on which possession may be sought.

The notice becomes invalid 6 months after the date on which eviction proceedings can be started. The council must then serve a new notice if it still wishes to evict the tenant.

To obtain an eviction order against a secure tenant the sheriff must be satisfied that it is reasonable to make such an order and that at least one of the following grounds applies:

- The tenant is in arrears with the rent or has broken some other important term of his lease.
- The tenant or someone living with him has been convicted of using the house for immoral or illegal purposes.
- The tenant and his spouse have not lived in the house for over 6 months, without good reason, or have ceased to occupy it as their main home.
- The tenant or someone living with him has caused nuisance or annoyance to other people.
- The tenant or someone living with him has damaged or neglected the house, or any furniture provided by the council.

However in some circumstances a council can obtain an eviction order against a secure tenant without the sheriff having to be satisfied that it would be reasonable to make such an order. In these cases the sheriff must be satisfied that other suitable accommodation is available. The circumstances are that:

- The house is overcrowded.
- The council intends, in the near future, to demolish, reconstruct or carry out major works involving the house, and cannot do so without gaining possession.
- The house has been specially designed or adapted for use by a physically disabled person, and the council needs the house for such a person. In this case there must not be a disabled person living there when possession is sought.
- The house is one of a group which the council normally lets to people with special needs that are catered for in the immediate locality (for example, special schooling for deaf or subnormal children or a social service facility). Again, there must no longer be a person with these special needs living in the house – and the council must need it for occupation by such a person.
- The tenant, or someone living with him, has caused nuisance or annoyance to other people and the council thinks it right to move him to other accommodation.

In deciding whether there is other suitable accommodation available for the tenant, the court will consider:

- Whether the accommodation is similar in character to his existing accommodation.
- How the terms offered compare with

those of his existing tenancy.

- How accessible places of work and schools are for the tenant and his family.
- The needs of the tenant's family – including any that are special.
- If furniture was provided under the old tenancy, whether adequate furniture is to be provided with the new one.

If the sheriff does make an eviction order, the council can only evict after the date set out in the order.

Adjournment

The sheriff can adjourn eviction proceedings for a few weeks in cases where he must be satisfied that it is reasonable to evict a tenant. If he does so, he can impose conditions – such as payment of rent arrears or a guarantee of future good behaviour.

Adjournment is much more likely if the tenant appears in court and offers to pay arrears or to behave properly. If his case is then adjourned and he keeps to his word, there will be no eviction.

Inheriting a council tenancy

It is possible to inherit a council tenancy automatically when the tenant dies.

The person wishing to inherit the tenancy must have been using the house as his only or main home at the time of the tenant's death and be either:

- The deceased tenant's spouse.
- A joint tenant.
- Another member of the deceased tenant's family. He or she must be at least 16 and have lived with the tenant for at least 12 months immediately before the tenant's death. A family member can only inherit where there is no spouse or joint tenant.

If there are two or more members of the tenant's family who qualify, they should agree between them who should succeed to the tenancy (they can all be joint tenants). If they cannot agree, the council will choose the successor(s).

It is not possible for a tenancy to be inherited more than once.

When marriage problems arise

Some councils let their houses to husband and wife jointly. In such cases, when a marriage breaks down both partners are entitled to possession and both are liable for any rent arrears. So if a husband leaves and fails to pay the rent, the wife will be responsible for arrears as well as the current rent.

If a wife is not a tenant, but her husband is, she can apply to the sheriff court (either separately or as part of divorce proceedings) to have the tenancy transferred to her. The sheriff must consider all the circumstances – including her husband's behaviour and the council's opinion, if any – when deciding whether to order the transfer.

A wife who is not a tenant cannot be forced to pay her husband's rent arrears – not even when his tenancy is transferred to her by court order.

COUNCILLORS

Getting elected to serve the community

Most Commonwealth citizens (or citizens of the Irish Republic) who are at least 21 years old are eligible to stand for election to a regional, district or islands council.

To qualify, however, a candidate must also have:

- Ensured that his or her name is on the local electoral roll, or
- Occupied land – even a field so long as it is used – in the area for the whole of the 12 months before being nominated for election, or
- Worked or lived in the area for the whole of that time.

To stand for election, the candidate must be nominated on the appropriate form (available from the council) and be proposed and seconded by two local electors, with eight others also signing. A person can be nominated for more than one council at a time, provided he or she qualifies. It is usual for a candidate to stand as the representative of a political party but this is not required.

WHEN A PERSON CANNOT BECOME A COUNCILLOR

The following are not allowed to stand as councillors:

- Employees of the council for which the election is being held.
- Persons who are undischarged bankrupts.
- Anyone who within the past 5 years has been sentenced to at least 3 months' imprisonment.
- Certain persons who have previously been found guilty of corrupt or illegal election practices.

What a councillor can do

Once a person becomes a councillor – whether by winning an election or by being returned unopposed – he or she is entitled to attend council meetings and take part in council business, and to sit on any committees to which fellow-councillors elect him or her.

Most councillors will attend at least one meeting per week. Committee chairmen have extra duties – such as office work, advising officials and seeing people – and some of them are virtually full-time councillors. All councillors may claim an allowance (£15.07 in 1984) for every day they do council work, and they are also entitled to expenses. Special responsibility payments can be made to certain councillors (to a maximum of over £4,000 per annum in a few cases).

A councillor will generally deal with matters arising in his or her own ward or division but is not obliged to confine himself or herself to that area.

He or she is entitled to see correspondence between the council and other persons if it contains information which is necessary for the performance of his or her duties as a councillor.

No councillor, not even a committee chairman, is entitled to give instructions to any council staff unless the council has given that person express permission to do so.

Conflict of interests If a council or committee is to discuss a matter in which a councillor (or a spouse, if they are living together) has a financial interest, that councillor must disclose that interest and take no part in the discussion or in any subsequent vote.

A conflict of interests would arise, for example, if an application for planning permission were made by a property owner for whom the councillor was acting as solicitor or estate agent.

Spending public money

Local authorities may spend money only where they have legal authority to do so. In cases where an audit (supervised by the Commission for Local Authority Accounts in Scotland) reveals that individual councillors have authorised an illegal payment (by voting for it), they may be held personally responsible for making good the loss.

Dishonest claims Any councillor or official who dishonestly obtains council money to which he or she is not entitled – for example, by making a false claim for travel expenses – can face criminal charges in court and can be ordered to repay the money.

Any councillor who accepts a gift as bribery is guilty of a criminal offence. It is an offence to accept a gift even when not carrying out the promise made in return for the bribe. *See:* CORRUPT GIFT

Giving up office

A councillor's term of office normally lasts 4 years. When the term expires he or she must stand for re-election in order to remain on the council.

Resigning office A councillor who wishes to leave the council before the end of his or her term can do so by giving notice in writing to that effect.

Resignation by absence A councillor who misses all meetings of the council and its committees for a period of 6 months will lose his or her seat on the council. The council may, however, approve a reason given for the absence, in which case he or she will not lose office.

COURT MARTIAL

How servicemen can be tried for their crimes

A common code of service law exists for all the forces. This code is based on the criminal law of England and Wales.

Some offences committed by servicemen and women or by their families when overseas are dealt with by Service court martial.

An offence may be purely military (such as mutiny or desertion), or committed abroad; or it may be committed in the United Kingdom but the civilian authorities decide not to bring a charge. In all these instances the serviceman or woman may be charged under military law and tried by court martial.

A serviceman who has left the forces can be court martialled for an offence committed while he was still under military law – but only if proceedings are brought within 3 years of his discharge. That same rule applies to a member of his family who has committed an offence whilst abroad.

A court martial has no jury. It consists of a panel of serving officers who are not connected with the accused person or his unit. They are advised on legal points, procedure and evidence by a judge advocate, who is a trained lawyer in the forces. Rules of evidence and procedure are based on the law of England and Wales and are similar to those in a civilian court.

A serviceman facing a court martial can be represented by a Service lawyer if the charge is serious enough – such as mutiny. Otherwise he can be represented by an officer.

If the charge is one that is considered to warrant representation by an officer only, the accused can insist on being represented by a lawyer, but he must pay the cost.

What a court martial can do

The sentencing powers of a court martial are extensive. They range from a mere reprimand for lesser offences to the death penalty for mutiny, treason, or for desertion in war.

A court martial will not usually impose more than one punishment for one offence – except in the case of an officer sentenced to imprisonment who must automatically be dismissed.

Both verdict and sentence are subject to confirmation by a confirming officer. After confirmation, they may be reviewed by the Defence Council which can quash one or both – or uphold the verdict but alter the sentence.

A serviceman cannot be tried twice for the same offence. He may be tried by court martial or by a civilian court, but not both.

Appealing against the decision

A serviceman can appeal against his conviction – but not his sentence alone – to the Courts-Martial Appeal Court, which consists of not less than three judges of the HIGH COURT OF JUSTICIARY. However, he must first obtain that court's permission to appeal.

For this appeal he may be allowed LEGAL AID.

When a reservist commits a crime

Volunteer reservists are subject to military law, including court martial, when carrying out military training or when called out for permanent Service.

Even if a reservist who has committed an offence has resigned he can be dealt with by military law. However, proceedings must be brought within 3 years of his resignation, and he must be reasonably suspected of offending whilst subject to military law.

In practice, a volunteer reservist who seriously offends against civilian or military law is invited to resign and does so. If the offence is a civil one he may then be prosecuted in a civilian court. If it was against military law, no further action is taken.

When civilians are involved

If martial law is declared, all civilians can be tried by court martial – informal committees or tribunals of serving officers. When normal conditions are resumed the military authorities may be held liable to a civilian for unnecessary use of force or abuse of authority. However an Act of Indemnity is usually passed to exonerate the military personnel from liability.

COURT OF SESSION

The highest civil court in Scotland

The Court of Session sits in Edinburgh, at Parliament House, and has been in existence since 1532. It hears all kinds of civil claims, including actions for damages for PERSONAL INJURY or breach of CONTRACT, with no limit as to their value.

DIVORCE and SEPARATION cases may be heard there – or in the sheriff courts. But NULLITY actions must be heard by the Court of Session. So must actions alleging marriage by cohabitation. *See:* COMMON LAW MARRIAGE.

The Court of Session is divided into an Outer House and an Inner House. The Outer House consists of 14 judges. They sit singly and hear most cases coming to the Court for the first time.

The Inner House consists of two benches of appeal judges, called the First and Second Divisions. There are 4 judges in each Division. They hear appeals from Outer House judges, from the sheriff courts and, in some circumstances, from tribunals.

The judges of the Court of Session also act as the judges of the HIGH COURT OF JUSTICIARY.

COURT REPORTING

When public and press may be excluded

It is a fundamental principle that court proceedings are public. Courts of law are open to the public and the press, and broadcasters are free to report their proceedings – but not from inside the court. *See:* CONTEMPT OF COURT

However there are exceptions in which publicity is prevented because it might be harmful.

Matrimonial cases

In actions of divorce, nullity of marriage and judicial separation the press can report only the names, addresses and occupations of the parties and witnesses; a short statement of the charges and defences in support of which evidence has been given; submissions on points of law (and the court's decision on them); and the judgment. These details may be published so long as they do not contain anything indecent (see below).

Cases involving children

Any child under the age of 16 who appears in a Scottish criminal court (whether as the accused, or as the victim or a witness) must not be publicly identified. This means that journalists and broadcasters in the United Kingdom must not, unless the court so directs, reveal the child's name, address or school, or publish any identifying picture.

It is also forbidden to disclose any other information that could enable the child to be identified – for example, that his father is a local headteacher.

However information about a child under 16 can be published – unless the court directs otherwise – if the child is a witness (and not a victim of the alleged crime) and the accused persons are 16 or over.

In a civil (meaning non-criminal) case a court can order a ban on publication of information about a person under 17 who is involved. For example, this may be done in a CUSTODY dispute to protect a child from undesirable publicity.

Indecent material

The press cannot publish any indecent matter, or indecent medical or surgical details, arising in court proceedings, if publication of such material would be likely to injure public morals.

Other cases

A court has the power to sit in private if justice cannot otherwise be done, or if publicity is not in the public interest. For example, a court may be cleared in the interests of national security or where publicity would prejudice other proceedings.

Where a child is called as a witness in a trial for an offence against decency or morality, the judge can order anyone not directly involved in the case to leave the courtroom while the child is giving evidence.

Where evidence is being given in a trial for RAPE, or some similar crime, the judge can order the public to leave. However the press are usually allowed to stay on the understanding that they do not disclose the identity of the victim of the alleged rape.

The press will usually not publish information about the identity of victims of alleged blackmail.

Proceedings in private

Some court proceedings are held in private and the press are excluded. They include:

- Any hearing in chambers – meaning the judge's rooms.
- Bail appeals heard by the High Court in chambers.
- Adoption proceedings.
- The JUDICIAL EXAMINATION held in serious criminal cases.

Old convictions

There are reporting restrictions on some old or 'spent' convictions. *See:* REHABILITATION

COVENANT

Enhancing cash gifts by tax rebate

A written undertaking to do something, or to refrain from doing something, is sometimes referred to as a covenant. This is an English legal term, simply meaning an undertaking, or promise.

A common example is a written promise by one person to pay another (or perhaps a charity) a fixed amount of money each year.

If the undertaking, or deed, is properly drawn up the recipient can claim back from Inland Revenue all or part of the tax that the donor has paid on the covenanted sum.

The Inland Revenue treats the reclaimed tax and the net sum paid as part of the income of the person receiving money under a covenant. If he or she has other significant income, the covenanted money may bring his or her income above the tax-free amount allowed by the Inland Revenue and then the advantages of the arrangement would disappear.

Such covenants, therefore, are of most benefit to people with low incomes – children, the chronically sick and the elderly. Charities also benefit.

To be effective under the tax rules, a covenant must be:

1. Capable of lasting for over 6 years. There is no tax penalty if the donor fails to maintain the payments for the whole period.

2. A legally enforceable deed, expressed in writing and signed and dated in the presence of two witnesses by the person making the payments. A copy must be given to the recipient.

3. Paid out of earned or investment income.

4. Freely made, not in payment for goods or services received.

If a parent makes investments for an unmarried child of his or hers under 18, the income they produce is treated by the tax authorities as income of the parent. Therefore, there is no advantage in setting up a covenant for your own child under 18.

However, if the covenant is established by a grandparent or other relative or friend, the tax benefits remain. But you cannot get tax relief by giving a covenant to a friend's child, while your friend gives one to your child. A son or daughter over 18, or under 18 and married – for example, a student – may reclaim tax on sums paid by a parent.

Payments under a covenant

A person making payments under a covenant must deduct from them an amount equivalent to income tax at the basic rate before transferring them to the recipient.

So, if you want an elderly aunt to receive £1,000 a year and the basic tax rate is 30%, you covenant to give her 'such sum as after deduction of income tax at the basic rate amounts to £700' – that is, £1,000 less 30%.

You retain the other £300. If you are paying income tax at the basic rate or at higher rates, you will not have to do any more, because it is assumed that you have already paid income tax on the covenanted sum.

Your aunt can then apply to the Inland Revenue for repayment of the tax when completing her tax return. She must send with it form R185(AP), obtainable from any tax office, filled in and signed by you as the donor.

If she has no other source of income, she will receive the full amount up to the value of the tax-free allowance to which she is entitled. After that, any outstanding balance will be taxed. If she has other taxable income, she will get back only that amount which brings her income up to the tax-free limit.

Whether or not you pay income tax at higher rates, you may only deduct tax at 30% when making payments under the covenant. This obviously limits the scope for avoidance of tax.

For instance, tax cannot be saved by a person who pays tax at rates up to, say, 60% granting a covenant in favour of a basic-rate taxpayer. The only exception to this rule is that payments to charity under a covenant are deductible for higher rate (as well as basic rate) tax purposes so long as they do not exceed £5,000 per annum.

To be valid for tax purposes, covenants to charity need be capable only of exceeding three annual payments (and not the 6 years applied to other covenants).

A WAY OF AVOIDING TAX ON CASH GIFTS

Making your gift by means of a deed of covenant can result in it being worth more

I, DONALD MACLEAN, of 46 Tay Street, Stirling, do hereby bind and oblige myself to make annual payment to my daughter KIRSTY MACLEAN, of 12 Henderson Gardens, Edinburgh, for a period of seven years, or during such period as the said Kirsty Maclean is undergoing full-time education, or during the residue of our joint lives, whichever period shall be the shorter, of such sum as after deduction of Income Tax at the basic rate in force at the time of payment amounts to Eight Hundred Pounds (£800) to be payable on such dates as I deem appropriate, such sums to be paid out of my general fund of taxed income: IN WITNESS WHEREOF I have subscribed these presents at Stirling on the Twenty-sixth day of March, 1983, before these witnesses:

Alexander Taylor, Witness
Parkview
Fairway Crescent
Stirling

Alison Macrae, witness
3 High Street
Dunblane

Donald McLean

For a covenant to have financial advantage over a simple banker's order it must be capable of lasting for a period exceeding 6 years.

This deed of covenant is designed for payments to a person engaged in full-time education. For a covenant in favour of anyone else, you would omit the words '... or during such period as the said (name) is undergoing full time education'.

Alternatively: 'by quarterly instalments' or 'by weekly instalments'

Two witnesses are required by Scots law. The person receiving the gift should not act as one of the witnesses

If the covenantee has no other income he will receive the amount of tax up to the value of the tax-free allowance to which he is entitled. If he has other taxable income he will get back only the amount that brings his income up to the tax-free limit. Inland Revenue will repay any tax paid on money promised as a regular gift over a minimum of 6 years. The amount shown on the deed of covenant is the gross amount. Tax is recovered by sending form R185(AP), signed by the donor, to the convenatee's tax office, with his tax return.

CRASH HELMET

Safety rule for motor-cyclists

All motor-cyclists and their pillion passengers – except followers of the Sikh religion wearing a turban – must wear crash helmets. Helmets must conform to one of the British Standards for helmets, and imported helmets must match these standards. The chin strap must be worn in the proper position.

If a motor-cyclist or his passenger is injured through the fault of another road user and suffers serious head injuries as the result of not wearing a helmet, the damages will be reduced. *See:* CONTRIBUTORY NEGLIGENCE

CREDIT ADVERTISING

How a lender can describe his offer

Most advertisements offering credit must conform to rules laid down in the Consumer Credit Act. Only private advertisements – for example, in a shop window, newspaper or bargains magazine – are exempt. Anyone who advertises credit in connection with a business cannot be exempt.

It is a criminal offence for anyone to advertise credit facilities in a false or misleading way.

The rules cover all forms of advertising – in newspapers, magazines and other publications, on television or radio, in notices, signs, labels, showcards and price-lists, on display models or goods and so on.

Anyone who advertises credit for goods or services – either direct from himself or through a third party, such as a finance company – must be prepared to tell the borrower the total costs of such an arrangement including interest, and the true interest rate.

An advertisement which contains any financial details such as 'credit up to 20 times your monthly payment' or 'only 2 per cent interest' must also give the true interest rate (expressed as a percentage-per-year), the total cost of the transaction, and the cash price of the goods. A trader cannot advertise goods or services on credit only. He must also be prepared to sell them for cash.

If you feel that a credit advertisement is false or misleading or may be breaking the rules, report the advertiser to your trading standards department.

Advertising to minors

People under the age of 18 are protected by law against touting by people who offer credit.

It is a criminal offence to send to anyone under 18 – with a view to financial gain – any document that invites him or her to borrow money, obtain anything on credit or hire or even apply for information about such facilities.

The sender has a defence if he can prove that he had no reasonable ground to suspect that the recipient was under 18.

However, if such material is sent to someone under 18 at a school or other educational establishment for minors, it is presumed that the sender knew the recipient's age.

CREDIT AGREEMENT

Safeguards for customers who borrow to buy

When you buy something on credit, or borrow money to make the purchase independently – even from a friend or relative – you have legal rights and wide protection whatever the type of credit arrangement you enter into.

Whether the deal is described as BUDGET ACCOUNT, CHECK TRADING, CONDITIONAL SALE, CREDIT SALE, HIRE PURCHASE or personal loan, the same legal safeguards, set out in the Consumer Credit Act 1974, will generally cover you – provided that the total amount borrowed is not more than £5,000 (£15,000 from May 20, 1985).

Even if you borrow more than £5,000, if interest rates are extortionate, you are entitled to ask a sheriff court to alter the agreement in your favour.

If you borrow money to be used for a specific purchase from a supplier who has a business arrangement with the lender, the person or company who lends the money is just as liable as the supplier if the goods are defective. *See:* DEFECTIVE GOODS

Even a hiring agreement, in which you do not agree to buy the goods hired, may come under the 1974 Act. *See:* GOODS, Rental of

Making a credit agreement

The type of protection the law gives you depends largely on the stage you have reached in the contract and the way in which you made it.

Before you enter into any credit agreement, you must be given the following information:

- The total cost of your loan, including interest.
- The true rate of interest, set out as a yearly rate-per-cent of the money you owe. *See* INTEREST CHARGE
- The cash price of any goods or services being bought by hire purchase or credit sale.

It is not enough for the lender to give this information in the credit agreement itself. The details must be set out in a formal price quotation, or an advertisement, notice, catalogue or price ticket. *See:* CREDIT ADVERTISING

Unless you are given the information in one of those ways, the lender cannot sue you or seek to repossess goods without a court order overriding his breach of the rules.

Reading the agreement

The agreement itself must contain a good deal more besides. Read it carefully before you sign. If possible take it home to study at greater length before you commit yourself.

The agreement form or document should be clear and legible. Regulations coming into force specify the information which should be included in an agreement. This varies according to the type of agreement.

However an agreement must state, on the front, what kind of agreement it is – a hire purchase, conditional sale or other credit agreement – and also the parties' names and addresses. The agreement should also include:

- Clear statements of your rights and duties in the transaction.
- The total cost of the loan, and true yearly rate of interest.
- Clear statements of the protection to which you are entitled and the remedies that you can obtain if you are dissatisfied.
- Notice of whether, at what stage and how you can legally cancel.
- All the terms of the deal, apart from those that the law considers 'implied terms' – for example, the assumption

that any goods will be fit to sell.

Do not sign simply on the basis of an assurance given by a salesman about the obligations being undertaken – for example, a verbal statement of the interest rate that you will be paying. All the terms, except those implied, must be stated in the written agreement.

If they are not – or if the agreement does not comply with other legal requirements – the lender cannot normally enforce the contract against you.

A court would allow a lender to sue a borrower over such a defective agreement only if the lender has been completely honest and open and the borrower appeared to have been dishonest.

Signing the agreement

When you are given a copy of the agreement to sign, it is generally not yet signed by the lender. At that stage, the 'agreement' is still merely an offer by you to enter into the contract: the lender, for example, will probably wish to make inquiries about your creditworthiness before he signs.

When you have signed, you must be given a copy to keep.

When the lender does accept your offer to borrow and signs the agreement, you must be given or sent – within 7 days of the lender posting or telephoning notification of his acceptance – a copy containing both your signature and his.

If you have not received that copy within 7 days, the lender cannot sue you or repossess goods. If you have still not received it after a full month, the sender may have committed a criminal offence for which he can be prosecuted.

If, after you have inquired about the copy, it still is not sent, tell the local council's trading standards department.

The lender's acceptance of your offer to borrow, which marks the start of the credit agreement, takes effect when he posts his letter of acceptance or signed form – not when you receive it. The contract is then legally binding.

In some cases, the contract can be completed simply by a telephone call. If the lender informs you by telephone that he has agreed to lend the money you want, the agreement is legally effective even though you have not received his signed copy of the agreement form. The 7 day period during which he must send your second copy will start on the day of the telephone call.

You cannot be sued over the agreement, however, until you have received that form.

If the agreement has already been signed by the lender before you are asked to sign it, you are entitled to only one copy – but it must bear both parties' signatures, and the agreement will be binding the moment you sign.

Pulling out of an agreement

Once you have signed a credit agreement, there are three ways in which you may still pull out: by cancelling, withdrawing or terminating.

When you can cancel If you have signed a credit agreement of any sort at home rather than in a trader's or lender's place of business, you may be entitled to cancel it during a 5 day 'cooling-off' period – provided that the negotiations that led you to sign the agreement were conducted orally and in your presence.

The 'cooling-off' period begins on the day after you receive your copy of the agreement signed by the lender.

You can send your notice of cancellation to the dealer or his agent, or directly to the lender.

If you cancel, the lender must give back any deposit and any part-exchange goods. You must return any goods already obtained under the agreement as soon as the lender gives back your deposit and part-exchange goods (or the part-exchange allowance in cash). Any cash loan must also be returned. But if you have borrowed money and spent it, and cannot repay at once, you may still be entitled to cancel. *See:* BORROWING

If you cancel an agreement for 'unrestricted use' credit – not tied to a specific purchase – the loan, and any interest due while any part of it is still outstanding, must be paid.

If you can arrange to pay off the whole debt within 1 month of giving notice of cancellation – perhaps by borrowing elsewhere at a lower interest rate – you need pay no interest at all under the credit agreement.

If you pay part of the sum within a month, you can pay the rest by instalments over the period originally agreed – and pay interest only on that balance.

When you cannot cancel If you sign a credit agreement at a lender's or dealer's business premises, you cannot cancel it; there is no 'cooling-off' period. However, you may be able to withdraw – as opposed to cancel – before the contract becomes binding.

Even if you sign at your own home – or somewhere else, other than the business premises involved – you cannot cancel if negotiations which led you to sign were not conducted orally and in your presence.

If the agreement was made solely as a result of your reading advertising literature – for example, a mail-order catalogue – and there were no oral negotiations, you cannot cancel.

If there were oral negotiations but these were conducted by telephone, they were not carried on in your presence, so you cannot cancel.

However, if you feel that you have been misled by advertising or by telephone sales-talk, you can sue for MISREPRESENTATION and inform the trading standards department, who may ask the procurator fiscal to prosecute the advertiser. *See:* CREDIT ADVERTISING

In any case, you cannot cancel if the credit is for £50 or less.

When you can withdraw Even if you sign a loan or hire-purchase agreement on business premises, you are not legally bound to go through with the transaction.

You can withdraw either by word of mouth or in writing, before the lender

TIME TO CHANGE YOUR MIND

If you sign a credit agreement of any sort at home after discussing it orally with the salesman, you are given a 5 day 'cooling-off' period during which you can cancel the deal.

IF YOU CANNOT KEEP UP THE INSTALMENTS

If you find that you can no longer afford to pay the hire-purchase or conditional sale instalments, but do not wish to hand back the goods, it may sometimes be in your interest to wait for the lender to make the first move.

As long as you have paid one-third of the total price, the company cannot take back the goods without a court order (it is probably unwise for the lender ever to take back goods without a court order.) Even if you have not yet paid one-third, the lender has no right to enter your property to take back goods without your permission or a court order. If he does so, you are entitled to sue him for damages.

If a car is kept on the buyer's property, the lender cannot seize the vehicle without risking an action for damages.

Even if the car is left in a public street, the lender cannot repossess it without first serving a default notice and obtaining a court order.

If you agree to hand back goods without a court order being made, you will be considered to have terminated the agreement voluntarily and must finish paying one-half of the total price.

However, if you believe that you will be able to pay within a reasonable time – or could cope with easier instalments – but the lender is not willing to depart from the strict terms of the agreement, it may be advisable to wait for him to take sheriff court action.

If the matter goes to court, the judge can rearrange the credit terms in your favour, enabling you to keep the goods and pay by easier instalments – smaller sums, spread over a longer period. He may also order you to hand back the goods, but suspend the order for as long as you pay a specified amount of the arrears in a specified time.

A court may even, in rare cases, order a reduction in credit charges.

On the other hand, the court can decide against you and allow the lender to repossess the goods without giving you an opportunity to pay more instalments. It may order you to pay the lender's expenses and any other money he is owed.

When a default notice is needed

A creditor is not allowed to begin court action or try to enforce the agreement in any other way, without first serving a default notice – even if less than one-third of the total price has been paid.

The default notice warns the buyer that he has done wrong – for example, failed to pay the instalments, or perhaps unlawfully sold the goods which are not yet his to sell – and what steps he must take – pay the arrears, return the goods, or both. The notice will also say how much money the lender expects as compensation, as an alternative to having the goods returned.

Once you receive a default notice, you are allowed 7 days to act on it. If you fail to do so, the lender can sue.

WHEN TRANSACTIONS ARE LINKED

When the law says that you can cancel or withdraw from a credit agreement, it also allows you to pull out of secondary deals related to the main agreement – called linked transactions.

For example, you have the right to cancel an agreement for the insurance or maintenance of a piece of equipment bought on credit, insurance against sickness leading to cancellation of a package holiday being paid for on credit, or the cash purchase of food for a freezer that is the subject of the main credit agreement.

Except for HIRE PURCHASE, any agreement by which the lender has a business connection with the seller of the goods automatically involves a linked transaction. The loan is the main agreement and the purchase is the secondary one. The borrower-buyer can sue the lender for defects in any goods bought under a linked transaction, as with the main contract.

Even if a linked deal is agreed before the customer signs the main agreement – for example, if frozen food is ordered before the agreement to buy a freezer is signed – it is still a linked transaction which can be cancelled if the customer pulls out of the main contract.

Even if the two contracts name different companies, your protection is not affected, as long as those companies have a business arrangement with each other.

completes his side of the deal by posting or handing to you his signed copy.

If you do it by word of mouth, take someone with you as a witness. If you withdraw in writing, the withdrawal does not take effect until the lender receives it, so it is advisable to send the letter by first-class recorded delivery.

If you arranged the credit agreement through a retailer or the lender's agent – for example, a CREDIT BROKER – it is enough to notify the agent of your withdrawal.

Once you withdraw, any goods that you handed over in a part-exchange deal must be returned to you, within 10 days, in substantially the condition they were in when you parted with them. Otherwise you are entitled to the equivalent part-exchange allowance in cash.

If you are not promptly given back any deposit, part-exchange goods or cash allowance, you can sue the lender for the money and/or the value of goods in the sheriff court.

When you cannot withdraw If you sign an agreement that has already been signed by the lender, it is binding on you immediately; you cannot pull out unless the contract includes a clause allowing you to cancel. In most hire purchase or conditional sale agreements, however, you may be able to terminate your contract later.

When you can terminate A hire purchase or conditional sale agreement can be terminated before the final payment, but, if you have not already done so, you will usually have to pay at least half the total price plus the cost of any extras, such as installation charges.

If you have paid half the price and then return the goods, you need pay no more. If you have paid more than half, you cannot get anything back.

If you have paid half, but are behind with further instalments when you decide to terminate, you must still pay off the instalments due up to the date of termination.

When the credit charges are too high

If you feel that you are paying excessive credit charges, you can ask a sheriff court to alter the terms of the agreement. You do not have to prove that the charges are extortionate: the lender must prove that they are not.

If the judge decides that the charges are extortionate, he can rearrange the agreement to make them fairer – provided that the borrower is an individual, not a company – even if the sum involved exceeds the normal limit, under the Consumer Credit Act, of £5,000.

Agreements made before the Act came into force are covered in the same way.

What is extortionate To decide whether a borrower's payments are extortionate, the court will need to look at the interest rates that were generally being charged when the agreement was made. The judge will also consider whether apparently low-interest payments in fact disguise an inflated selling price.

Some of the borrower's personal circumstances will be taken into account – for example, his age, general ability to do business (including his degree of business experience), state of health when the agreement was made and any pressure that he might have been under, from any source, at that time.

On the lender's side, the court will consider the amount of risk which he accepted in making the loan, his relationship to the borrower – for example, if a family dispute is involved – and any other matter that the judge thinks relevant.

If a lender sues you for repossession, arrears or damages for breach of the credit agreement, and you consider his interest charges extortionate, you can respond by asking the court to intervene on your behalf and alter the terms.

What the court can do If a credit agreement is ruled to be extortionate the court can do one of several things: set aside part of the contract, order money to be repaid to the borrower, alter the terms of the agreement and/or order the return of any security which has been paid to the lender by a GUARANTOR.

When you settle early

You are entitled to cut short a credit agreement by settling the debt before the agreed date – and to get some rebate of credit charges, because you will not be borrowing the money for as long as had been expected.

To arrange an early settlement, simply write to the lender saying that you wish to complete the agreement ahead of time.

Do not expect a large rebate: the lender is still entitled to a reasonable profit on the deal. You can check the amount you are entitled to by inspecting special credit-rebate tables at a consumer advice centre, council trading standards department or Citizens Advice Bureau.

Borrowing less than £50

A loan of not more than £50 – called a small agreement – is exempt from some of the rules of the Consumer Credit Act.

The formalities of making a credit agreement are not required and there is no 'cooling-off' period for the borrower. The lender in such a small agreement is not required to provide periodic statements of account, or copies of the agreement where new credit tokens are being issued.

However, no HIRE PURCHASE or CONDITIONAL SALE agreement can be classed as a 'small agreement'. Neither can any loan for which security has been taken in goods – for example, a PAWNBROKER agreement – or in cash. But a CREDIT SALE, or an arrangement in which the security is a written guarantee or indemnity against failure to pay as opposed to goods or money deposited with the lender – can be regarded as a small agreement.

Short-term credit

Some agreements, by which a fixed sum is borrowed and is to be repaid in not more than four instalments, are also exempt. The exemption applies if the money is to be spent with the lender or with someone who has a business arrangement with him.

Under that rule, ordinary monthly trade credit – for example, the milkman's or newsagent's bill – will not be covered by the Consumer Credit Act.

Running account credit

Running account credit is an arrangement whereby the creditor usually obtains goods or services on credit, paying regular instalments off the debt, but not clearing the debt off altogether. As long as the agreed instalments are paid, the creditor can continue to have goods or services up to an agreed limit, as in a shop BUDGET ACCOUNT.

If the credit is running account credit, and the creditor must clear the entire debt each period (say monthly) in one payment, the arrangement is exempt from the Consumer Credit Act.

It will also be exempt if the money is

WHEN THERE IS AN INSTALLATION CHARGE

If your credit agreement includes a charge for installing the goods – for example, plumbing in a dishwasher or putting up a television aerial – that charge must be treated separately if you decide to terminate the agreement or if the lender wishes to repossess the goods without a court order.

Terminating an agreement

To work out how much you have to pay before terminating, deduct the installation charge from the total and divide the balance by two. Then add the whole installation charge. The result is the minimum to be paid when terminating the agreement.

Example A dishwasher is bought for £300 including interest and a £60 installation charge.

Deduct £60 from £300	£240
Termination payment 50% of £240	£120
plus	
100% of installation charge	£60
Minimum payment to terminate	£180

Repossession of goods

The lender can repossess his goods without a court order only if you have not yet paid one-third of the loan. (Even if this is so, it is probably unwise for him to do so.)

To work out whether that proportion has been paid, deduct the installation charge, divide the balance by three, then add the whole installation charge.

If you have paid the resulting amount, the lender cannot repossess his goods without a court order.

Example A central-heating system costs £840 plus £120 installation charge.

Total price	£960
minus	
Installation charge	£120
equals	£840
Divide £840 by three	£280
plus	
Installation charge	£120
One-third payment for repossession purposes is therefore	£400

borrowed from the lender who has no business arrangement with the person with whom the money is spent, provided the interest does not exceed the greater of 13 per cent or 1 per cent above the highest of the clearing banks' base rates 28 days previously.

CREDIT BROKER

Introducing borrowers to lenders

Anyone who earns money by introducing customers to a money-lending company must have a credit broker's licence issued by the Office of Fair Trading, but he is not obliged to display this licence.

A licence is needed not only when credit broking is the main business – for example, mortgage broking – but also when it is secondary, as when a car dealer arranges hire purchase or when a solicitor, estate agent or accountant arranges a mortgage for a client.

If the credit broker has no licence, he is committing a criminal offence, and whoever lends the money is not legally entitled to make the borrower keep to the credit agreement, unless he can get an order to that effect from the Director General of Fair Trading. Without such an order the borrower is entitled to keep the cash and refuse to pay. However, if goods are being bought on HIRE PURCHASE, the lender can recover the goods if the buyer parts with possession of them – if, for example, he sells them.

If an introduction by a credit broker does not result in a credit or hire agreement within 6 months, no fee or commission of more than £3 is payable to him, whichever side decides not to proceed.

Under the Consumer Credit Act, the broker's client can sue in the sheriff court to recover any commission of more than £3 already paid.

CREDIT CARD

Paying for your purchases without having to carry cash

If you have a credit card issued by a bank or credit-card company, you are entitled to certain legal protection in your transactions with the bank or the lender of the money used for your purchases. Some credit-card agreements are fully protected under the Consumer Credit Act. Others are only partly protected.

Fully protected agreements

A credit-card agreement – such as Barclaycard and Access – by which you are allowed running account credit, paying only an agreed proportion of your total debt each month, has the full protection of the Consumer Credit Act.

The credit-card company, within 7 days of agreeing to issue you with a card, must send you a copy of your agreement.

When your card is renewed – probably once a year – a further signed copy of your agreement must be sent to you. If the company fails to send one, it cannot in theory recover any money you obtain or spend by using the card until you have been sent the copy agreement.

Furthermore, if a copy of the agreement is not sent to you within a month, the company commits a criminal offence, and can be fined up to £400.

When a credit-card agreement is fully protected, anything you buy becomes the subject of a linked transaction, and the card-issuing company becomes as liable as the supplier for unsatisfactory goods or services.

Agreements partly protected

If your credit-card agreement does not automatically allow running account credit, so that you are required to clear your debt in full every month – as with American Express and Diners Club cards – the agreement is not fully covered by the Consumer Credit Act. The credit-card company is not then liable for the quality of any goods you buy.

If you pay interest Although your agreement may say that you have to clear your debt every month, if you fail to do so, and are then charged interest or a 'service charge' on the money owed, the agreement becomes protected under the Consumer Credit Act. The credit-card company then becomes liable for the quality of goods bought after the interest charge is imposed.

If a credit-card company does not allow a customer to go into debt and pay interest, but cancels the card and adds a penalty payment to the closing account, the penalty counts as interest and the agreement becomes fully protected.

The added interest will be subject to the controls of the Consumer Credit Act and the ex-card holder will be entitled to receive statements of what he owes, as well as to ask a court to decide at what rate he should pay the debt.

If you lose a credit card

Until you accept a card – by signing it, or by signing a receipt for it – you cannot be made liable for any use made of it. The receipt signed must be for the card itself, not just for the envelope in which it was sent.

Once you have accepted the card, you still cannot be made liable for debts totalling more than £30 (£50 from May 20, 1985) which arise as a result of theft or unauthorised use. Even that maximum £30 liability applies only until you have given the credit-card company notice that you have lost your card.

In many cases, it may be enough to telephone the company as soon as you discover that the card is lost. If your agreement calls for the notice to be in writing, you can still give oral notice, for the sake of speed, and it will be effective

HOW THE CREDIT-CARD SYSTEM WORKS

The main difference between a credit and cheque guarantee card is that a credit card can be used to buy goods or services from traders who have agreed to accept it, but a CHEQUE GUARANTEE CARD can be used only to guarantee that your cheque, up to a stated amount, will be paid by your bank.

A credit card cannot be used to guarantee cheques, except at specified banks. The exception is the dual-purpose card, such as Barclaycard, that can be used for this and to get credit.

Some cards, such as Barclaycard and Access, are issued free. Others including American Express and Diners Club, charge a membership fee.

With certain cards, such as Access and Barclaycard, cash can be drawn at a bank without a cheque – but you start paying interest from the day you draw cash, whereas no interest would be payable on a cashed cheque.

With others, such as American Express and Diners Club, cash cannot be drawn without a cheque.

at once, as long as you confirm it in writing within 7 days.

If you owe money on the account when your card is lost or stolen, you are entitled to have any membership fee you have paid set off against any debt for which you are liable through unauthorised use.

For example, if you lose your credit card and someone uses it to run up a £20 debt, you may be liable for that debt because it is less than £30. But if you did not owe money when the card was lost, your membership fee of, say, £10 can be deducted from your £20 liability.

If you give or lend your card to someone else, you are liable for all the debts incurred with it, provided that the original agreement gives a name, address and telephone number for notifying the company of a lost or stolen card.

When credit is stopped

The credit-card company, without warning you, can stop the use of your card by telling suppliers not to accept it.

However, unless the original agreement reserves the right to do so, or you have broken the agreement yourself by exceeding a credit limit or failing to pay your debts, the company will have broken its contract with you and you can sue in the sheriff court for anything you have lost – for example, by having to go elsewhere for credit and pay higher interest.

CREDIT NOTE

When you want to return goods you have bought

If you take goods back to a shop, you may be offered a credit note rather than your money back. However, you may be entitled to a full cash refund: that will depend on your reason for returning the goods.

Changing your mind If you return the goods because you decide you do not want them after all – for example, because the colour does not match something else – you have no rights at all against the shop. It can refuse to take the goods even if you have not unpacked them, and it does not even have to offer a credit note.

Defective goods You are legally entitled to a full money refund, however, if the goods are defective and you return them promptly. You need not take a credit note.

Do not be deterred if a shop assistant says that it is not the company's policy to give cash refunds. *See:* DEFECTIVE GOODS

CREDIT REFERENCE AGENCY

Finding out what has been said about you

Anyone who tries to obtain credit is entitled to know what information about him has been filed away by a credit-checking agency, whether the credit is allowed or not.

To get the information, write to the company from whom you sought credit, asking for the name and address of any credit reference agency it has consulted about your financial standing. The request must be made within 28 days of the end of the credit negotiations.

The company must supply the information. The time limit for doing so is 7 days (excluding Saturday and Sunday). If it fails to do so, it commits a criminal offence for which the maximum penalty is a £1,000 fine.

If a credit reference agency has not been used by the company, you are not entitled to find out what information it holds itself about you.

Checking your file Next, write to the agency asking to see your file. You must enclose a cheque or postal order for £1, which is not recoverable even if the agency has no information about you.

If there is a file, the agency must send you a copy of all the information in it.

If the file is wrong You may discover that your file contains incorrect information. If so, you are entitled to insist that the incorrect information is put right or removed.

Within 28 days of your request for a correction or deletion, the agency must tell you in writing either that it has complied or that it has not.

If the agency says it has not complied, or if it fails to reply, you have a further 28 days in which to submit your own form or rewritten correction, which must not exceed 200 words.

If the agency says that it does not accept your correction, or if it fails to reply within 28 days, you can apply in writing to the Director General of FAIR TRADING, who can make such order as he thinks fit. He could, for example, order the agency to include your amendments.

A credit-reference agency can also ask the Director to intervene if it does not accept your suggested correction.

If you and the agency cannot agree, the Director can decide what should be done about the entry. If the agency fails to comply with the Director's orders, he can revoke the agency's licence.

Licence to trade A credit-reference agency must have a licence from the Office of Fair Trading. The penalty for trading without a licence can be 2 years' imprisonment for the company secretary or managing director and/or an unlimited fine on the company.

If a customer suspects that an agency is trading without a licence he can report the agency to the trading standards department. There is no penalty for a customer who uses an unlicensed agency. *See also:* COMPUTER RECORD

CREDIT SALE

A more 'secure' alternative to hire purchase

If you buy goods on credit sale they become your property as soon as the agreement is made, not when the final instalment is paid – as with conditional sale – or when the customer takes up an option to buy – as at the end of a HIRE PURCHASE agreement.

The seller cannot repossess the goods at any stage. If a buyer fails to pay the instalments, the seller can only sue for what is owed. *See:* CREDIT AGREEMENT

The rules governing formation, cancellation, termination and interest rates are the same as those applying to any other credit arrangement governed by the Consumer Credit Act. *See:* INTEREST CHARGE

CREDIT UNION

Getting together to save and lend

A credit union is a self-help financial co-operative. It is formed and run by people who have a common bond – such as living in the same area or belonging to the same organisation. Members of a union pool their savings and use them to lend money to each other at a very reasonable rate of interest.

Credit unions are part of a large world-wide movement. The first British union was established in London in 1964 and the first Scottish union was established in the Drumchapel district of Glasgow in 1970. There are now a number of Scottish unions – so far all of them are in the Strathclyde area.

Registering a union

Credit unions are regulated by the Credit Unions Act 1979, and must be registered with the Chief Registrar of Friendly Societies. To obtain registration a union must include amongst its objects encouraging saving, providing credit and educating members in money management.

The members of the union must have a common bond – for instance:

- Living or working in the same area.
- Working for the same employer or in the same occupation.
- Belonging to the same club or organisation.

A credit union must have at least 21 members and normally not more than 5,000 members. The union is run by its members, each of whom has one vote.

Depositing savings

Members create a pool of income by buying £1 shares in the union. Each share can be paid for by instalments.

A member must hold at least one share but the union's rules cannot require him to hold more than five. The maximum shareholding is £2,000. At least 60 days' notice is necessary to cash in shares.

If a person qualifies as a member through a common bond, his family and relatives can also join. Children of members can deposit up to £250 only.

Providing credit

A union can lend money to a member for a 'provident or productive' purpose. This can include buying household goods, paying for a holiday and meeting an unexpectedly large fuel bill.

The maximum amount of credit which a member can have is £2,000 plus the value of his shares. The maximum repayment period is five years for secured loans and two years for unsecured loans.

A credit union cannot charge an interest rate of more than 1 per cent per month on the reducing monthly balance of the loan – an annual rate of interest of approximately 12⅔ per cent.

Unions are expected to deal sympathetically with members who get into financial difficulties – perhaps because of sickness, redundancy or unexpected expenditure. The union may agree to reduce the repayments, extend the repayment period or temporarily require interest only to be repaid.

Paying out profits

A credit union makes a profit through banking or investing savings and receiving interest on loans. To begin with, a union must transfer 20% of its annual surplus to a reserve fund until that equals 10% of its total assets. The fund must then be maintained at between 10–20% of total assets.

At least 90% of any net annual profit must be distributed to members in the form of a share dividend – at up to 8% interest – or in the form of an interest rebate on loans. No income tax will be payable on dividends until at least the 1985–6 tax year.

Union members can decide to donate all or part of the net profit for social, cultural or charitable purposes.

Insurance

Credit unions offer insurance through their own insurance agency. This includes life insurance, and loan protection insurance to clear loans which are outstanding when a borrower dies. The premiums are paid by the union.

For more information about credit unions, contact the Credit Union League of Great Britain, Ecumenical Centre, Firbeck, Skelmersdale, Lancashire WN8 6PN.

CRIMINAL COMPENSATION ORDER

Compensation for victims

A person who is injured or suffers loss or damage to his property as the result of a crime may be awarded compensation by the court hearing the case, after the accused has been convicted.

A compensation order is made at the court's initiative and without any application by the victim – though he will usually be asked to fill in a form detailing his loss.

See: CRIMINAL INJURIES COMPENSATION

CRIMINAL INJURIES COMPENSATION

How the victim of a crime is financially recompensed

The victim of a crime may obtain compensation for his injuries and losses in 3 ways:

- He can sue the criminal for DAMAGES in a civil court action
- He can be granted a compensation order by a criminal court, which compels the criminal to make some compensatory payment to him – either immediately or in instalments.
- He can apply to the Criminal Injuries Compensation Board for an award to be paid out of state funds.

Granting a compensation order

Criminal courts can award compensation for personal injury, loss or damage resulting from the offence. If someone's property is misappropriated, and is damaged while out of the owner's possession, the damage is treated as having resulted from the offence – regardless of how it was in fact caused. This includes damage to motor vehicles.

But apart from this no compensation order can be made for personal injury or damage caused by a ROAD TRAFFIC ACCIDENT – although in this case the victim may obtain compensation from his insurers or the Motor Insurers' Bureau. The criminal courts cannot make awards to dependants of someone killed as a result of a crime.

In solemn CRIMINAL PROCEEDINGS there is no limit to the amount which may be awarded under a compensation order.

In summary criminal proceedings a sheriff or stipendiary magistrate can award up to £2,000 compensation for each offence; and a justice in the district court can award up to £1,000 for each offence.

Making a compensation order

If the accused is convicted the court may make a compensation order. The court alone decides whether or not to make a compensation order – no application is made by the victim. However the victim will have provided details of his loss to the prosecution.

In deciding whether to make an order – or how much compensation should be paid – the court must take into account the offender's means – the whole of his assets, capital and income (including state benefits).

The offender may be ordered to pay an immediate lump sum to the court, or be given time to pay, or be ordered to pay by instalments.

The figure assessed will take account of the physical and psychological suffering caused to the victim by his injuries. Loss of earnings and expenses are added. The offender's lack of means may make it impossible for the court to order the full amount of compensation due to the victim, but the court can make an order compensating part of the victim's loss.

The payment of compensation always takes precedence over the payment of any fine. If the offender defaults in payment of a compensation order he may be sent to prison.

The award of compensation by the court does not prevent the victim from pursuing a civil claim for further compensation. The civil courts will take into account any sums awarded by the criminal court or the Criminal Injuries Compensation Board.

Compensation orders are not restricted to the victims of violence. Anyone who suffers loss or damage may be awarded compensation, provided the person responsible is convicted.

For example, a person may be misled by a tour operator's brochure into taking a holiday which turns out to be well below the advertised standard. If the tour operator is prosecuted under the TRADE DESCRIPTIONS Act and convicted, the court can award compensation to the disappointed holiday maker.

Criminal Injuries Compensation Board

An application may be made to the Criminal Injuries Compensation Board for compensation for personal injury which is the direct result of a crime of violence that has been reported without delay to the police.

An application may also be made by anyone injured while arresting a suspect or helping a police officer to discharge his duties; and by dependants of people killed as the result of a crime.

The Board will only consider claims that it believes deserve compensation of at least £400 (£500 for cases of family violence). It excludes all claims for injuries resulting from traffic offences – unless the crime was deliberately running someone down or attempting this.

Compensation for loss of society (companionship) is payable to the relatives of a victim who has been killed.

How to apply First you must write to the Board's London office (10–12 Russell Square, WC1B 5EN) requesting the standard form on which you will need to supply full particulars of the case. Once you have completed and returned the form, one of the Board's members will decide whether or not the claim should be accepted in the first instance.

If the claim is accepted by the board A successful claimant can be awarded an amount similar to that which it is estimated would have been given if he had decided to sue the criminal in the civil courts for damages. *See:* PERSONAL

A GUIDE TO THE COMPENSATION A COURT CAN ORDER FOR CRIMINAL INJURIES

In deciding how much compensation to order a criminal to pay, the court will usually be able to take into account details of loss (including loss of earnings) provided by the victim to the prosecution. District courts, however, do not hear civil cases and lack experience in assessing compensation in cases involving personal injury.

The following table – prepared by the English Magistrates Association – was therefore issued for the guidance of the district courts. This version was published in October 1980, so the courts will need to bear in mind the effects of inflation.

The guidelines are designed to give no more than a rough and ready basis for the courts to work on in order that a victim may receive compensation and receive it quickly.

They are starting points only, and – for example in the case of scarring – the compensation might well be much higher.

Compensation for pain is increased when the injury is in a particularly sensitive area of the body and when the victim is elderly and infirm.

Compensation may be reduced when the injury is slight or if the victim provoked the offender.

Type of injury	Assessment of physical or mental suffering	Compensation suggested
Graze	Considerable pain for a few days; little after a week.	£20
Bruise	The closer the bruise to the bone, the greater the pain usually; pain likely for 2 weeks.	£40
Cut	Depending on size of cut and whether stitched; pain likely to have gone in 2 weeks.	£30–£100
Loss of tooth	Variable mental suffering, depending upon position of lost tooth and on sex and age of victim. Compensation greatest for front tooth of young female.	£50–£100
Sprain	Pain likely to last 3 weeks	£60–£100
Head injuries	Variable pain lasting, on average, for one month. Possibility of severe headaches.	£60–£200
Fractures	Depending on where; pain likely for 4 to 6 weeks.	£100–£200
Permanent scarring on face	Variable mental suffering, depending on position of scar, on sex and age of victim. Compensation greatest for young female.	£150–£300

INJURY

Compensation for loss of earnings is paid as a lump sum. If the claimant was earning more than twice the national average of industrial earnings, the excess is ignored in calculating the compensation.

Any social security payments received – such as disablement benefit – are deducted from the compensation payable.

If the effect of an injury is prolonged, the board may make an interim payment. When the victim has recovered, the case will be reviewed and a final award made.

If the claim is rejected at first Anyone whose claim is at first rejected by the single member appointed by the Board is entitled to have it reconsidered by 3 members of the Board and, at that stage, to produce witnesses in support of the claim.

After such a hearing, there is no further appeal against the board's decision except by judicial review on a point of law.

CRIMINAL PROCEEDINGS

How the court system works when a crime is alleged

Criminal proceedings in Scotland start in either of the two following ways.

Arrest The first way is when a person is arrested and charged by the POLICE. Such a person will be either kept in custody and detained in the police cells overnight or released by the police after providing a written undertaking to appear in court at a stated time. *See:* BAIL

The police submit a report on the case to the PROCURATOR FISCAL (the public prosecutor) who decides whether or not to proceed against the accused. If no proceedings are to be taken the fiscal will authorise the accused's release.

If proceedings are to be taken the fiscal will first decide on the crime to be charged. The police charge may be confirmed or a different one substituted. The fiscal will then decide whether the prosecution is to be taken on INDICTMENT or SUMMARY COMPLAINT – this depends upon the seriousness of the crime charged.

All serious crimes (for example, murder, rape, armed robbery, serious assault) are tried on indictment. This means that the trial will be heard by a judge and jury in the High Court or the sheriff court. Less serious crimes are tried on summary complaint before a judge alone, either in the sheriff court or district court. Once the decision to proceed is made the accused must be brought before either the sheriff or district court – which one it is depends upon the seriousness of the crime charged – on the morning after his arrest (excluding weekends and holidays). What happens next depends upon whether the proceedings are on indictment or summary complaint, and whether the accused wishes to plead guilty or not guilty.

Citation The second way criminal proceedings start is by the issue by the prosecutor of a document called a citation. This happens in two situations:

1. When the police have not arrested the person charged with a crime.

2. When the police have arrested the person charged but then released him without obtaining a written undertaking that he will appear in court at a stated time.

These situations can occur when the crime involved is not very serious (for example, minor ROAD TRAFFIC OFFENCES) and the accused has a known residence.

In these cases the police submit a report to the procurator fiscal. If he decides to proceed with the case he will order, or cite, the accused to appear in either the sheriff or district court at a stated time. The citation naming the accused, and ordering him to appear, will usually be sent through the post by recorded delivery. All cited cases proceed on summary complaint.

What happens next depends upon whether the accused wishes to plead guilty or not guilty. In cited cases there is the possibility of pleading by letter and the accused may not have to appear in court personally.

Employing a solicitor

A person who has been arrested and kept in custody has the right to an interview with a solicitor before his appearance in court. This can be his own solicitor, but if he is unavailable (or the accused does not have one) the duty solicitor is available.

The duty solicitor The Law Society of Scotland administers a scheme under which duty solicitors are in attendance at each sheriff and district court. All persons in custody will be interviewed (free of charge) by the duty solicitor who will represent each prisoner (again free of charge) on his first appearance in court. Where appropriate, the duty solicitor will also apply to the court for LEGAL AID on behalf of the prisoner.

EMPLOYING A LAWYER

An accused person is entitled to defend himself without a lawyer. Most accused, however, do the job badly and would be better advised to employ a lawyer to act on their behalf.

If the accused is not in custody, but attends court because of his written undertaking to the police or because he has been cited by the procurator fiscal, he may bring his own solicitor. If he does not, and he wishes to be represented in court, he should see the duty solicitor who can advise on applying for legal aid. If the matter is serious it is advisable to approach the duty solicitor for initial advice at least. Any court official will tell you how and where to find him.

An accused person is allowed to appear in court without a solicitor, and some do so – particularly if they are going to plead guilty. However it is always advisable to consult a solicitor about the case before appearing in court, whether you intend to plead guilty or not guilty.

Deciding how to plead

If you are accused of an offence you should get legal advice. It is in your interests to know whether – on the basis of what you admit to having done – you

THE CRIMINAL COURTS OF SCOTLAND AND THEIR PROCEDURE

In Scotland there are three criminal courts: the High Court of Justiciary, the sheriff court and the district court.

An accused person does not have the right to choose the court in which his case will go to trial or the right to opt for trial by jury. It is the prosecutor who decides the court in which a trial is to proceed. That decision will be governed by the seriousness of the crime involved.

Broadly speaking, the High Court deals with very serious crimes, the sheriff courts with less serious crimes, and the district courts with the least serious crimes.

The selection of court to prosecute in will also determine whether the trial will be under solemn procedure or summary procedure.

Solemn procedure

Under solemn procedure the trial takes place before a judge sitting with a jury of 15 persons. The charge against the accused is set out in a document called an INDICTMENT.

The judge decides questions of law (for example, 'Is there enough evidence to let this case go to the jury?') and the jury decides questions of fact (for example, 'Is the evidence which we have heard believable evidence?').

There are three possible verdicts open to a jury – guilty, not guilty and not proven. A not proven verdict has the same effect as a not guilty verdict – both verdicts are acquittals and mean that the accused cannot be tried again on the same charge.

Jury verdicts are by a simple majority, but a guilty verdict can only be reached if at least 8 of the jury are in favour of it.

Summary procedure

Under summary procedure the trial takes place before a judge alone. No jury is involved. The charge against the accused person is set out in a document called a SUMMARY COMPLAINT. The judge decides questions of both fact and law. The three possible verdicts of guilty, not guilty and not proven are also available in summary procedure.

High Court of Justiciary

The High Court is the supreme criminal court in Scotland. There is no appeal from it to the House of Lords.

The High Court is both a trial court and an appeal court. It is based in Edinburgh but when hearing trials it goes on circuit to other cities and major towns. Appeals are always heard in Edinburgh.

When it sits as a court of appeal it consists of at least three judges, and hears appeals from the High Court sitting as a trial court, and from the sheriff and district courts.

When the High Court sits as a trial court there is usually only one judge and the procedure is always solemn. The High Court has jurisdiction over the whole of Scotland, and over all categories of crime not specially reserved by Act of Parliament to another court. Only the High Court can deal with cases of treason, murder, rape and incest. As a general rule, it has unlimited powers of imprisonment and fine.

Sheriff court

The sheriff court is a local court. Scotland is divided into six sheriffdoms, which are sub-divided into 49 sheriff court districts. The authority of each sheriff court is limited to its own district.

The sheriff court is exclusively a trial court and can sit under either solemn or summary procedure.

A sheriff sitting with a jury may impose a sentence of not more than 2 years' imprisonment, an unlimited fine or both. But where the sheriff thinks someone convicted under solemn procedure merits more severe penalties, he can send the accused to the High Court for sentence.

Under summary procedure a sheriff may impose up to 3 months' imprisonment (in some cases 6 months), a fine up to £2,000 or both.

District court

The district court is the lowest criminal court in Scotland. It is a local court and one is usually to be found in each district and islands area.

The district court judge is a lay justice. He is not legally qualified and is advised on points of law by the clerk of court or by a legal assessor who sits on the bench with the judge. It is possible, however, to have a legally qualified judge in the district court. He is called a stipendiary magistrate and sits without a legal assessor. There are presently three stipendiary magistrates in Scotland, who all sit in Glasgow District Court.

The district court is exclusively a trial court and the procedure is always summary. The maximum sentences it can usually impose are 60 days' imprisonment, £1,000 fine or both.

However, when the judge is a stipendiary magistrate the district court has the same sentencing powers as a sheriff under summary procedure.

are in law guilty or not guilty. If you believe yourself innocent you should never plead guilty, nor allow yourself to be persuaded to plead guilty to a charge, even a trivial one.

A charge is never so trivial that it is not worth an innocent person's while to contest it.

If you are guilty you should admit your offence in the first place to your solicitor. If you plead not guilty and then lie on oath at your trial you commit the crime of PERJURY. This can result in you being given an additional punishment.

In most cases, however, an accused person is unlikely to be prosecuted for perjury simply because the court did not believe his evidence.

Indictment: High Court and sheriff court

If the procurator fiscal has decided that the arrested person is to be prosecuted on indictment, he brings the charge firstly in a petition, a copy of which is given to the accused. The accused (on the day after his arrest) will then appear before a sheriff for JUDICIAL EXAMINATION in private. The fiscal and the solicitor for the accused will be present.

At the end of the examination the fiscal will ask the sheriff to commit the accused to prison for further examination or to await trial. A committal for further examination is for not more than 8 days, after which the accused must be committed for trial.

The sheriff will grant the fiscal's application unless the accused has applied for and been granted bail by the sheriff at the judicial examination. The accused may apply for bail (unless charged with treason or murder) at later stages also.

Prevention of delay in trials If bail is not granted the '110-day rule' operates to prevent the accused being kept in custody for an undue length of time without trial.

This rule states that when a person is committed to prison to await trial his trial usually must begin within 110 days from that committal. If it does not the accused will be freed and be immune from further prosecution for the crime charged. The rule is strictly applied unless the delay is not the fault of the prosecution – for example, where it is due to the accused being ill or an industrial strike by court staff.

The 110-day rule does not apply where the accused is on bail awaiting trial. In that case the trial usually must begin within 12 months from his first appearance on petition. If it does not, the accused will be immune from further prosecution for the crime charged unless the delay is not the fault of the prosecution.

Preparing the prosecution case Whether the accused is in prison or on bail, the procurator fiscal continues with preparing the prosecution case by interviewing witnesses and gathering other evidence. He then reports the case to Crown Counsel in Edinburgh, who decide if there is enough evidence for the case to go to trial.

If there is enough evidence, Crown Counsel also decide (according to the seriousness of the charge) whether the accused is to be sent for trial by the High Court, or by a sheriff and jury, or before a judge alone on summary complaint.

If the trial is to be by the High Court or by a sheriff and jury, an indictment setting out the crimes charged must be prepared and served on the accused. The indictment cites the accused to appear at a trial 'diet' (a sitting of the court). It contains a list of any documents (like medical reports) and articles (like offensive weapons), and also the names and addresses of witnesses whom the prosecution intends to produce and examine at the trial.

A list of any previous convictions which the prosecutor intends to lay before the court in the event of a guilty verdict will also be served along with the indictment.

If no indictment has been served on an accused who has been in custody for 80 days awaiting trial, he must be released – but he can still be prosecuted.

Pleading not guilty The indictment served on the accused must give him at least 29 clear days' notice of the date of the trial. The accused should not wait until he knows the trial date before preparing the defence case.

He – or his solicitor on his behalf – should already have applied for legal aid. His solicitor should have been provided with details of possible defence witnesses and may also apply to the procurator fiscal for a preliminary list of prosecution witnesses. If any of these refuse to give a statement to the defence, an application can be made to the sheriff. He can order them to appear in court in private to give a statement on oath.

If the accused intends to put forward a defence of self-defence, ALIBI, insanity, or that the crime was committed by another person (who must be named), then a notice to that effect must be lodged in court 10 clear days before the trial. Lists of defence witnesses and productions (unless they already appear on the prosecutor's lists) should be lodged in court 3 clear days before the trial. *See:* INSANITY AS A DEFENCE.

In some cases there may be a preliminary meeting of the court before the trial date. For example, the defence may claim that the indictment does not charge the accused with any known crime. If written notice of the claim is given to the trial court within 15 days of the indictment being served, the court will then hold a preliminary meeting to deal with the matter.

Being ready in time If the defence is not likely to be ready to defend the case on the date set for the trial – possibly because an important defence witness is on holiday – then an application can be made to the trial court for an adjournment.

The court is not obliged to grant an adjournment. However, if the prosecutor is given early notice he is not likely to oppose a defence application for more time.

Procedure at the trial A jury of 15 is chosen by ballot and sworn in unless the accused changes his plea to guilty. The indictment is read to the jury.

There are no opening speeches by either side and the case starts immediately with the prosecution examining its witnesses.

The accused is not allowed to interrupt the witnesses, but each witness in turn can be questioned – 'cross-examined' – by the defence.

If the cross-examination raises new matters of evidence, the prosecutor can put further questions to the witness to clarify the points raised.

When the prosecution has closed its case the defence may submit to the court that in law there is no case to answer on all or any of the charges. If this plea succeeds the accused will be acquitted. If it fails, the defence can then put forward its evidence.

The defence witnesses, including the accused if he so wishes, are examined by the defence, cross-examined by the prosecutor and, if appropriate, re-examined by the defence.

All the evidence is recorded by a shorthand writer.

Closing speeches to the jury, sum-

THE SYSTEM OF PROSECUTION

Criminal prosecutions in Scotland are conducted by full-time prosecutors acting in the public interest. PRIVATE PROSECUTION (for example, by the victim of a crime) is very rare and would only be allowed in exceptional circumstances. The police in Scotland *never* prosecute.

The system of public prosecution is under the control of the Lord Advocate. He is assisted by the Solicitor General for Scotland and a number of advocates-depute (who are ADVOCATES employed by the Crown). They are known collectively as 'Crown Counsel' and work with the Crown Office in Edinburgh.

The Crown Office is the administrative headquarters of the public prosecution system. It is staffed by full-time civil servants headed by the Crown Agent. The Crown Office is concerned with the preparation of prosecutions in the High Court and with the direction and control of the prosecutors in the sheriff and district courts.

Although the Lord Advocate is responsible for all public prosecutions the actual conduct of such prosecutions is delegated to others.

In the High Court, prosecutions are conducted by the advocates-depute. In the sheriff and district courts the public prosecutors are called procurators fiscal, and are under the control of the Lord Advocate. Fiscals are full-time civil servants who must either be advocates or solicitors (they are usually solicitors).

In all cases of crime the police report the details to the procurator fiscal for the local area. He has complete freedom to decide whether or not to prosecute, subject to the general direction and control of the Crown Office.

ming up the case for each side, are made by the prosecutor and then the defence – so the defence has the benefit of the last word.

The judge then 'charges' the jury, instructing them on the law, on the evaluation of the evidence and on their duties. He will tell them, for example, that the burden of proving guilt is on the prosecution, which must prove its case beyond all reasonable doubt.

The jury usually retires to consider its verdict, although it can give it at once. If the verdict is 'not guilty' or 'not proven', the accused is discharged. If the verdict is guilty, the prosecutor will ask the judge to pass sentence and put before him any notice of previous convictions.

An accused who wishes to object to any of the convictions listed must already have given notice of this to the prosecutor. The prosecutor must then prove the convictions.

The defence is given the opportunity to make a plea in mitigation of sentence, asking the judge to take certain factors into account when passing sentence. The speech in mitigation should not dispute the substance of the case which has been proved against the accused but it may include such factors as the following:

- Mitigating circumstances in the offence itself (for example, if the offence was a serious assault, the fact that the accused had committed the assault 'in hot blood' in response to extreme provocation from the victim).
- Any family commitments and the accused's financial circumstances.
- Previous good character.

The judge then passes SENTENCE, either immediately or after a period of adjournment to enable a social background or other report on the accused to be obtained.

Pleading guilty An accused who intends to plead guilty can have his case dealt with quickly by giving written notice of his intention to the Crown Office in Edinburgh. He is then served immediately with an indictment and a notice to appear in either the High Court or sheriff court (depending upon the seriousness of the charge) at an early date. A notice of any previous convictions of the accused will also be sent to him.

It is not necessary for the prosecution to provide a list of witnesses or productions with such an indictment.

The accused is given at least 4 days' notice of the court appearance.

The accused must actually plead guilty in court. When he does so the prosecutor gives a short summary of the facts and presents any list of previous convictions to the judge. After any defence plea in mitigation of penalty, sentence will be passed.

If the accused changes his mind, goes against his letter to the Crown Office, and pleads not guilty in court, that particular court sitting will be abandoned. A date for trial will be arranged in due course.

APPEALING AGAINST COURT DECISIONS

A person who is dissatisfied with his conviction or sentence may appeal against it whether the case was conducted under solemn or summary procedure.

Under summary procedure, but not solemn procedure, the prosecutor is entitled to appeal on a point of law against an accused person's acquittal or the sentence passed by the court.

All appeals go to the High Court sitting as a Criminal Appeal Court. Each appeal is heard by at least 3 judges.

Appeal against conviction

A person who is convicted after pleading not guilty is entitled to appeal against the conviction on the ground that there has been a miscarriage of justice.

An appeal will not succeed merely because an error was made during the trial. It must be shown that the error amounted to a miscarriage of justice. Malice or oppression by the trial judge would amount to such a miscarriage.

A successful appeal may not be the end of the matter as the appeal court has power to authorise the bringing of a new prosecution.

Appeal against sentence

Whether he pleaded guilty or not guilty, a person is entitled to appeal against the sentence imposed by the court. He can do so provided the sentence is not one fixed by law. For example, it is not possible to appeal against a sentence of life-imprisonment for murder.

The ground of appeal is that the sentence is excessive or inappropriate. The appeal court has power to increase or reduce the sentence.

Prosecutor's appeal against acquittal or sentence

Under summary procedure the prosecutor has the right to appeal against a finding of not guilty, or not proven, or against the sentence imposed by the court. The ground of appeal is that the trial judge has made a mistake on a point of law.

For an appeal against acquittal to succeed the appeal court must be satisfied that there has been a miscarriage of justice. If the appeal is successful, the appeal court can itself convict and sentence the accused person, or it can send the case back to the original court for this purpose.

Summary complaint: sheriff court and district court

When the procurator fiscal takes the decision to proceed by summary complaint in the sheriff or district court, the accused will be served with a citation unless he is under arrest and in custody.

If citation is required, a summary complaint stating the charges and the place and time of the court will be served on the accused, normally by recorded delivery post. A notice will also be sent of any previous convictions which the prosecutor has decided to lay before the court in the event of the accused pleading or being found guilty.

The fiscal will also send to the accused together with the citation:

- A form to be completed and returned by him stating whether he pleads guilty or not guilty.
- A means form to be completed and returned, setting out the accused's financial circumstances.
- A form containing directions to the accused as to how the summary complaint may be answered.
- A form to be completed and returned by him stating whether he intends to appear personally or be represented.
- A notice of the penalties which can be imposed (only if the offence is statutory).

The case will be heard in court on the date stated on the complaint. If the accused indicates that he intends to plead not guilty, a date will be fixed for the trial.

If the accused is in custody, the complaint and any notice of previous convictions will be served on him while in custody. He will then appear in court as soon as possible – usually the day after his arrest. He will have been interviewed by the duty solicitor, who will represent him in court on his first appearance unless the accused refuses his services.

If he pleads not guilty a trial date will be fixed. The accused will then either be kept in custody, granted bail, or ordained (that is ordered under penalty) to appear at the trial diet.

Prevention of delay in trials Where the accused is kept in custody, his trial on summary complaint must normally begin within 40 days of the complaint first being brought in court. If it does not, the accused will be released and be immune from further prosecution for the offence.

Preparing the prosecution and defence cases The procurator fiscal, if requested, will usually give the defence a list of prosecution witnesses in exchange for a promise to provide a list of defence witnesses.

Before the date of the trial the court may fix a hearing to discover the state of preparation of the prosecution and defence cases, and whether the accused intends to continue with his plea of not guilty. If he changes his plea to guilty he may be sentenced.

If the prosecution or the defence case is unlikely to be ready by the date of the trial, an application can be made to the court for an adjournment. If both sides apply jointly the court must grant the adjournment unless it thinks there has been undue delay in the preparation of the cases.

Procedure at the trial If the defence is alibi, the accused must give notice and details of the defence to the prosecutor before the examination of the first prosecution witness. The prosecutor is then entitled to an adjournment of the case to investigate the defence.

Apart from this, and the fact that there is no jury, a trial on summary complaint follows the same procedure as a trial on indictment. The prosecution leads its evidence, after which the defence may plead 'no case to answer'. If this is unsuccessful the defence witnesses will be examined, cross-examined and, if appropriate, re-examined.

The fiscal and the defence then address the judge, who will usually give his verdict immediately. If the accused is found guilty, the defence may submit a plea in mitigation before sentence is passed.

Pleading guilty An accused may plead guilty to the charges in a summary complaint when the case is heard in court.

An accused who is in custody will be present in court when the plea is offered. An accused who is cited to appear can plead guilty by returning the appropriate form or by stating the plea in court either personally or through a representative (for example a solicitor).

Where the guilty plea is made in writing, the accused is understood to admit any previous conviction set out in any notice served with the summary complaint – unless he expressly denies this in his written plea.

Sentence can be passed there and then. If the accused is absent and unrepresented the court will use the information provided on the means form in order to assess any fine.

If the court decides the accused should be present before being sentenced it will adjourn the case to another date and order the accused's personal appearance. Custodial sentences cannot be passed in the absence of the accused.

CRIMINAL RECORD

How the police compile and keep information

Details of every person convicted of crime by a court in Britain are recorded and kept permanently under the supervision of the Scottish Criminal Record Office, 173 Pitt Street, Glasgow. In England the same information is kept by the English Criminal Record Office at New Scotland Yard, London. Only the police have access to these records.

When someone is charged with a crime the police supply the PROCURATOR FISCAL with a report on the incident giving rise to the charge. They also supply details of any previous convictions against the person charged.

If the procurator fiscal decides to prosecute, a notice of any previous conviction will be served on the accused person. If he or she is found guilty, this notice will be laid before the judge so that it may be taken into account in passing sentence.

The provisions for REHABILITATION of offenders, which require most convictions to be forgotten in normal life after various periods of time have elapsed, do not apply to police records or criminal proceedings. Previous convictions can be brought to the attention of the court if a person is convicted again, no matter when.

Other information on file

There is no legal restriction on the amount and type of other information which the police can record. Details of people suspected of crimes or who associate with criminals are recorded.

A citizen has no right to know what information is recorded about him. Police regulations, however, seek to confine the use of such information strictly to the prevention or detection of crime. *See:* COMPUTER RECORD

CRIMINAL RESPONSIBILITY

When a child can be prosecuted

A child under the age of 8 cannot be found guilty of a crime, in any circumstances. This is because the law presumes that anyone so young cannot know what is legally right or wrong.

However a child under 8 who is involved in an offence can be brought before a CHILDREN'S HEARING and may be put in the care of the local authority. *See:* SUPERVISION REQUIREMENT

A child aged 8 to 15 who is alleged to have committed an offence may be prosecuted in the criminal courts or referred to a children's hearing. However no child can be prosecuted for any crime except on the instructions of the LORD ADVOCATE. Only the HIGH COURT OF JUSTICIARY or the SHERIFF COURT can try a child for an offence – a DISTRICT COURT cannot do so.

In practice the police report most offences involving children to the REPORTER to the CHILDREN'S PANEL, not to the PROCURATOR FISCAL. Only certain serious offences – murder, rape, serious assault, road traffic offences involving motor vehicles – will usually be considered for prosecution. Such cases are reported to the procurator fiscal who may prosecute the child or refer the case to the reporter. Children under the age of 13 may be prosecuted only on the specific instructions of the Lord Advocate.

Children aged 16 and over may be prosecuted in court in the usual way. *See:* CRIMINAL PROCEEDINGS

CROFTING

Statutory protection for crofters and their families

Since 1886 many small agricultural tenancies in the Highlands have been protected and regulated by Acts of Parliament. These tenancies are known as crofts and their tenants as crofters.

In 1980 there were nearly 18,000 crofts in Scotland. More than 2 million acres of land were subject to crofting tenure in the seven 'crofting counties' – Shetland, Orkney, Caithness, Sutherland, Ross and Cromarty, Inverness-shire and Argyll.

A typical croft consists of a few acres (usually less than 50) of arable (or 'inbye') land together with a right to graze animals on common ground (called a Common Grazing).

Any permanent improvements made to the bare land – for example, drainage, walls and buildings (including the croft house itself) will usually be the result of the crofter's own labour, or of his predecessors.

Basic legal rights

The crofter is guaranteed several basic rights. He has security of tenure (meaning that he cannot be evicted) so long as he pays his rent and observes certain statutory conditions. These include:

- Cultivating his croft, with or without hired help, and not allowing the soil to deteriorate.
- Keeping the croft house and buildings in good repair.
- Observing any reasonable conditions contained in any written lease or missive of let.

The crofter is entitled to a 'fair rent'. If he and his landlord cannot agree, either can apply to the Scottish Land Court for a fair rent to be fixed. Thereafter the rent cannot be changed for 7 years unless both parties agree.

If the crofter has made any permanent improvements to the croft, he is entitled to compensation for these when his tenancy comes to an end. The improvements must be suitable and have been carried out or paid for by the crofter or his predecessors.

A crofter can assign (transfer) his tenancy to a member of his family so long as he obtains written agreement from his landlord. He can also bequeath the tenancy to any one person – usually a family member – subject to various safeguards. That person must notify the landlord that he has inherited the croft within 2 months of the crofter's death.

If the crofter dies without leaving a WILL the normal rules of succession apply. *See:* INHERITANCE

The right to buy

Since 1976 a crofter has had an absolute right to buy the site of his croft house, and a qualified right to buy his croft land, on generous terms. However if he disposes of his newly-purchased croft land within 5 years to someone other than a family member, he must share any profits with his ex-landlord.

Statutory bodies

The Crofters Commission (based in Inverness) keeps crofting matters under review, maintains a Register of Crofts and administers schemes of financial assistance to crofters. It also has various legal powers – for example, a landlord must get the Commission's consent before re-letting a vacant croft.

The Scottish Land Court is primarily a judicial body. It can, for example, decide disputes about rent and compensation for improvements, or order a reluctant landlord to sell a croft. *See:* LAND COURT

Other agricultural tenants

In the non-crofting counties of Scotland, small agricultural tenants – known as landholders or statutory small tenants – have rights similar to those enjoyed by crofters, with the exception of the right to buy.

CROSS-ACTION

When counter-allegations are made in a divorce

When a marriage partner raises an action for divorce, nullity or judicial separation, the other partner will usually either not defend the action or will submit answers denying the allegations made and ask for the case to be dismissed.

In some cases, however, the other partner will raise his or her own action, making counter-allegations that the pursuer caused the breakdown of the marriage, and asking that he or she, rather than the pursuer, should be granted a decree of divorce. These counter-allegations are known as the cross-action.

CROWN

The symbol of the power of the state

The term 'Crown' means more than the sovereign: in law it includes all central government departments and their agents. The term Crown liability, therefore, covers the action of civil servants, servicemen and other government employees.

The legal liability of the Crown is in practice much the same as that of companies and individual people. So if the chauffeur of a Royal or official car knocks someone down, the injured person can sue for damages in much the same way as against any other person.

There are, however, a very few exceptions. A soldier who is hurt through the negligence of another serviceman or who is injured on Crown property cannot claim damages in the ordinary courts. *See:* ARMED FORCES

A member of the armed forces who is dismissed does not have the same right to claim for unfair DISMISSAL as a worker in industry.

CROWN OFFICE

Controlling public prosecutions

The Crown Office in Edinburgh is the headquarters of the public prosecution system of Scotland. There decisions are taken by the Crown Counsel – who are ADVOCATES – about whether to prosecute serious cases of alleged crime, whether in the HIGH COURT OF JUSTICIARY or SHERIFF COURT. Such prosecutions are conducted in the name of the LORD ADVOCATE.

The permanent staff of the Crown Office is headed by a legally qualified civil servant called the Crown Agent. Prosecutions in the High Court are prepared in the Crown Office. Certain suspicious deaths, including all apparent suicides, are reported by procurators fiscal to the Crown Office for consideration by Crown Counsel. *See:* CRIMINAL PROCEEDINGS

CULPABLE HOMICIDE

An unlawful killing that does not amount to murder

Culpable homicide is the killing of a person:

- Without the state of mind necessary for MURDER, or
- In circumstances where certain excusing factors reduce the quality of the crime from murder to culpable homicide.

A killing would be culpable homicide if committed through:

- PROVOCATION.
- An unlawful act – such as assault – where death was not intended or probable.
- Gross or criminal negligence in carrying out a lawful act, such as driving a car.

Culpable homicide covers a wide range of killings, from those not far removed from murder to those which are almost accidents. The penalties imposed are at the court's discretion and depend on the type of killing. They range from substantial periods of imprisonment to a fine or even admonition.

DEATH CAUSED BY MINOR ASSAULT IS CULPABLE HOMICIDE

If death has been caused by an assault, but there was no intention to kill and death was not likely to occur, the crime is culpable homicide. The assailant cannot be convicted of assault only, even if the violence used was very slight.

Bird, a petty officer in the navy, got drunk. While in this condition he formed the impression that a woman had stolen money from him. He followed her along a road, shouting and swearing at her.

The woman became very alarmed and flagged down a passing car. As she was getting into the car Bird grabbed hold of her to prevent her doing so. The woman, who had a weak heart, collapsed and died from shock. Bird was charged with culpable homicide.

DECISION

The judge told the jury that it did not matter that the degree of violence used had been very slight. If death resulted from it then the accused person was guilty of culpable homicide and could not be convicted of assault only. The jury found Bird to be guilty as charged.

GUILTY OF CULPABLE HOMICIDE BUT ADMONISHED

Culpable homicide covers different types of killing, ranging from those which fall just short of murder to those which are not much more than accident or misfortune. The sentence passed by the court will reflect the nature of the killing.

Myra Meechan came out of a dancehall in Glasgow with another young woman. As they crossed the road they argued about whether to get a taxi to their next destination. Distracted, they stopped on a traffic island in the middle of the road and continued arguing.

In the heat of the dispute Meechan pushed her friend, who fell into the path of a passing car and was killed.

Meechan had no intention to kill and death was not likely to result from her very minor assault – but for the fact that her companion was caught off-balance.

DECISION

Meechan was convicted of culpable homicide. However the court then admonished her and ordered her release. It considered this to be a just decision in the circumstances.

Voluntary culpable homicide

A person may be charged with murder because it is alleged that he deliberately intended to kill the victim. He may also be charged with murder on the ground that he killed the victim recklessly, not caring whether he lived or died. In both cases he may be able to have the verdict reduced to culpable homicide if there was provocation.

For example, a father who sees his daughter raped, and immediately kills the rapist, has killed under extreme provocation and would be found guilty of culpable homicide. However, if his daughter has gone home and told him of the rape, and as a result he has then gone out and killed the rapist, that would be murder. This is because the father had time to calm down and did not act in the heat of the moment.

The survivor of a genuine SUICIDE pact, in which one person agrees to kill another person and then himself, would probably be guilty of voluntary culpable homicide rather than murder. For this to happen the survivor must have made a serious attempt to take his own life.

A person who successfully pleads that he killed while suffering from DIMINISHED RESPONSIBILITY is guilty of voluntary culpable homicide.

Involuntary culpable homicide

When someone causes the death of another person through a criminal act, which was neither intended nor likely to be fatal, he is guilty of involuntary culpable homicide.

For example, an escaping thief pushes a policeman who, as a result of this minor assault, falls, hits his head on the ground and dies. The thief is guilty of involuntary culpable homicide. Parents are guilty of involuntary culpable homicide if their child dies after they abandon it in circumstances where death is not intended or probable.

A motorist who drives with criminal negligence and causes a pedestrian to die is guilty of involuntary culpable homicide.

In all these cases the death is more than just an accident.

Culpable homicide involving motor vehicles is usually prosecuted under the Road Traffic Act 1972 as the offence of causing death by reckless driving.

CURATOR

Protecting children and the mentally ill

In Scotland the guardian of a MINOR – a child of at least 12 (if a girl) or 14 (if a boy), but under 18 – is known as a curator. Parents are usually the curators of legitimate children. A father and mother have equal guardianship rights and each may act without the other. *See:* GUARDIAN.

An ILLEGITIMATE CHILD who is a minor has no curator unless one is appointed by a court.

Protecting a child's interests in court

It is sometimes necessary for a court to appoint a guardian to protect the interests of a minor or a PUPIL child in legal proceedings – for instance, an action to recover DAMAGES for injury. Such as guardian is known as a curator *ad litem* and is normally an ADVOCATE or, in the sheriff court, a SOLICITOR.

A court may appoint a curator *ad litem* to a pupil child if he or she has no guardians or if their whereabouts are unknown. A curator can also be appointed if the child's guardians refuse to act or if the child is taking legal proceedings against them.

A minor can sometimes raise a court action in his or her own name, but in practice the consent of a guardian is required. When a minor is defending an action, his or her guardian must also usually be called as a defender. The court can appoint a curator *ad litem* to safeguard a minor's interests in the same circumstances as for a pupil child.

In ADOPTION proceedings the sheriff court will appoint a curator *ad litem* – usually a solicitor – to protect the child's interests and to prepare a report on the proposed adoption.

Protecting people who are mentally disordered

A person may be unable to manage his or her property and affairs because of MENTAL DISORDER. The problem often arises when a previously normal person becomes senile or suffers severe brain damage in an accident.

In these circumstances an application can be made to a sheriff court or the Court of Session for the appointment of a guardian known as a curator *bonis*. The job of such a curator is to administer the mentally disordered person's property and affairs.

The MENTAL WELFARE COMMISSION, which exists to protect the interests of the mentally disordered in Scotland, will usually recommend the appointment of a curator *bonis* where the value of a person's estate is more than £4,000.

The petition for appointment of a curator *bonis* is usually made by a relative. However if nobody petitions the court the local authority – or the Mental Welfare Commission – may do so where satisfied that the person is incapable of managing his or her property and affairs adequately.

The petition must normally be accompanied by 2 medical certificates testifying to the person's incapacity.

The curator *bonis* will usually be a solicitor or accountant, although it is possible for a relative to be appointed. The curator has the same powers as a JUDICIAL FACTOR and manages the estate as the agent of the disordered person (who is called a ward).

If the ward's incapacity is due to someone's negligence – for instance, a car accident caused by bad driving – the curator *bonis* can sue that person for damages on the ward's behalf.

Divorce protection If the defender in a divorce or separation action appears to be suffering from mental disorder the Court of Session can appoint a curator *ad litem* (normally an advocate) to protect the defender's interests.

The curator has the power to defend the action. Even if he does not do so, he can still intervene in the case on the defender's behalf. *See:* TUTOR

CUSTODY OF CHILDREN

When courts decide who should control a child's upbringing

A mother and father have equal rights to the legal custody of their legitimate or adopted children. Only the mother has the right to legal custody of an ILLEGITIMATE CHILD, but the father can ask a court to give him custody.

A parent who has legal custody of a child has the right to control the child's upbringing, residence and education. He or she retains legal custody even if the child is living with someone else – for instance, a grandparent. Except as mentioned below, only a court can remove a parent's right to custody.

A parent still has legal custody of a child in local authority care – but not if the authority assumes parental rights. The right to custody is then lost, and cannot be recovered in court proceedings – such as a divorce action – while the authority retains parental rights. *See:* CHILDREN IN CARE

A dispute about custody may eventually have to be settled by the courts. In court neither parent has a greater claim to custody than the other. In reaching a decision the judge must regard the welfare of the child as the first and most important consideration.

When parents separate

When a married couple separate, one parent – usually the mother – normally continues to look after the children. But both parents continue to have custody rights. So if a mother has the children living with her, the father is legally entitled to take them from her – she has no more right to them than he has.

Agreeing to custody Parents who separate often agree that one should care for the children and the other should have regular access. They may also agree that joint custody should continue; or that one should seek sole custody (see below), and the other access. Agreement is always preferable to a bitter court dispute.

Even if custody is disputed by the parents in court proceedings, they can still come to an agreement at any time before their case is finally heard by the court. A joint minute, or written statement, recording their plans for the child can be put before the judge for his approval.

Taking legal proceedings

A parent who wishes to have sole custody of a child must apply to a court – normally the sheriff court. The application is usually made as part of legal proceedings for DIVORCE, judicial SEPARATION or NULLITY. The child must be under 16.

It is also possible for a parent who does not wish to raise such proceedings to apply to court for an order giving sole custody rights. The child concerned must be under 16.

The court can also be asked to award ALIMENT for the child's maintenance.

Taking preventive action A parent who starts court proceedings for divorce, separation or nullity can ask the

WHEN SOMEONE ELSE MAY BE GIVEN CUSTODY

In proceedings for divorce, nullity or separation, the court can give custody to someone other than the parents – for instance, a grandparent, aunt or foster parent who is actually looking after the child.

That person is entitled to be told if a parent is seeking custody in marital proceedings; and can claim custody by intervening in these proceedings.

A third party seeking custody can also apply to court independently of any marital proceedings.

In all cases the court must put the child's welfare first when deciding whether to award custody.

court to grant certain interim (temporary) orders before the case is finally heard.

The court can grant one parent an interim INTERDICT to prevent the other parent removing a child from that parent's control. Interdict will be granted if the judge thinks removal is likely.

The court can also award interim custody to one parent and order interim aliment to be paid until the case is finally decided. If one parent obtains interim custody, the other can ask for interim access. *See:* ACCESS TO CHILDREN

Before making an interim custody or access order the court may ask for a report on the child and on the suitability of each parent.

The final decision The court cannot generally grant decree of divorce (or of nullity or separation) until it is satisfied about the arrangements made for the care and upbringing of the children. This is so even if the parents have already agreed on custody.

Before deciding who should have custody of a child, the judge may ask for a report to be prepared on the child and on the proposed arrangements for his or her care and upbringing.

The report is usually prepared by an ADVOCATE named by the judge, but it may occasionally be done by a solicitor or local authority social worker. He or she will usually talk to the child and both parents, the child's teachers and doctor and perhaps relatives or a cohabitee of either parent. The home proposed for the child will also be inspected. A written report is then presented to the judge.

The judge must do what is in the best interests of the child. In deciding who should have custody he is likely to consider some or all of the following:

- The character of each parent.
- Their behaviour towards each other and towards the child.
- What each can offer the child – for instance the kind of home or education offered.
- Their financial circumstances.
- The age and sex of the child.
- The wishes of the child about which parent he or she would prefer to live with. The judge may want to interview the child privately to find out what these wishes are.

The courts usually give sole custody rights to the parent who has looked after the child since the separation. This is because they are reluctant to uproot a child from his or her home, friends and school except where the child's welfare requires it.

The court will consider giving sole custody to the other parent if, for instance, the parent who has cared for the child is an alcoholic or has failed to provide adequate food and clothing.

When one parent is given custody, the other parent can ask to be given the right to visit the child and to take him or her away at set times. *See:* ACCESS TO CHILDREN

In a recent case the judge took the unusual step of granting custody of a girl to her father, but granting her mother the right to provide day-to-day care – as she was already doing. The court thought that the father was a more suitable person to control the child's upbringing and education, but did not

DIVIDING CUSTODY AND CARE

In a custody dispute the court normally awards custody to one parent and gives access rights to the other. The parent with custody then has day-to-day care of the child. But in a recent case the court emphasised that custody and care can be split.

A couple were in dispute about the custody of their 8 year old daughter. The mother had committed adultery and was living with the man concerned. Her daughter had lived with her since the marriage broke down.

The judge felt that the girl's father was likely to provide the more secure and stable background. However he was reluctant to remove the girl from her mother's home because of the dependence which she was likely to have on her mother.

DECISION

The judge decided that the father should have the final decision concerning the girl's upbringing and awarded custody to him. However he then gave her mother the right to continue to look after her, so as not to uproot her from her home and surroundings.

COURT ORDER VERSUS SUPERVISION REQUIREMENT

Where a court awards custody of a child to one parent, but a children's hearing requires the child to live with the other parent, the decision of the hearing will have priority.

A wife was given interim (temporary) custody of her 3 children by the Court of Session. Her mental health deteriorated and the children were referred to a children's hearing by the local authority on the ground that they needed compulsory care.

Her husband then applied to the Court of Session for interim custody of the children. He was given custody, subject to the children being supervised by the local authority.

The children's hearing then considered the case and decided to make a supervision requirement with a condition that the children should live with the mother.

The local authority asked the Court of Session for guidance on whether they could give effect to the hearing's decision.

DECISION

The court said that they could. Although the husband had eventually been given custody of the children, that did not mean that he therefore had the right to care for them. In this case the hearing had decided that it was in the children's interests that they should remain in the care of their mother. The court's decision on custody did not invalidate this decision.

want to remove her from her mother.

It is possible for a court to grant both parents joint custody of a child if they apply for this by way of a joint minute.

Refusing custody In exceptional cases the court may decide that neither parent is fit to have custody of a child. This may happen, for instance, where the child has been in the care of the local authority for some time.

In such a case the court can refuse custody to either parent and put (or keep) the child in the care of the local authority. It can also give care of the child to some other person – for example, a grandmother or foster parent. The court, if it wishes, can go even further and award custody of the child to such a person if he or she applies for this.

Sometimes, while prepared to grant one parent custody, the court may be unhappy about the arrangements made by that parent for the child's care. In such a case the court can grant custody to the parent but require the child to be supervised by the local authority.

Custody and aliment

In an action for custody, whether on its own or as part of other legal proceedings, the parent seeking custody can ask the court to order the other parent to pay maintenance for the child. *See:* ALIMENT

Varying a custody order

A custody order made by a court can be altered or terminated on application by either parent. The application can be made to a sheriff court even if the custody order was made by the Court of Session.

A parent with custody may seek a variation to prevent the other parent having access to a child. Also, if a parent who has custody dies, the other parent can ask to be given custody. The court must give first consideration to the child's welfare when reaching a decision.

A custody order ends automatically when the child becomes 16.

Enforcing custody orders

The court can order a child to be returned if he or she is taken from a parent or other person who has the right to custody. The court can authorise court officers – called messengers-at-arms or sheriff officers – to search for and remove the child.

Failure to obey the court's order amounts to a CONTEMPT OF COURT, punishable by a fine or imprisonment.

Foreign custody orders

If one parent obtains a custody order from a foreign court, that order is not directly enforceable in Scotland. If the parent applies to the Scottish courts for a custody order, they will usually follow a recent foreign order unless the foreign court had no jurisdiction or the child's welfare would be adversely affected.

However the Scottish courts are not *bound* to follow the foreign order. They can decide to award custody to the other parent if they think this is in the child's best interests. *See:* DIVORCE

CUSTOMS DUTY

The tax a traveller pays on goods brought home

A traveller returning to Britain with foreign goods worth more than the permitted amount may have to pay customs duty on the excess goods.

Notices at the port or airport inform travellers what value of goods are duty-free, and a customs officer may ask a traveller if he has goods other than those to declare.

It is a criminal offence, carrying severe penalties, not to declare goods that are subject to duty. If you are in any doubt about goods you are carrying, ask the customs officer. The maximum penalty for fraudulent evasion of customs duty is an unlimited fine and/or imprisonment for 2 years.

Duty-free allowance The duty-free allowance for each traveller in 1984 was:

From non-EEC countries or if goods are bought in a duty-free shop:

1. 200 cigarettes; or 100 cigarillos (cigars weighing not more than 3 grammes); or 50 large cigars: or 250 grammes of smoking tobacco.

2. 1 litre of alcoholic drink more than 22% by volume; or 2 litres of drink of 22% by volume or less; or 2 litres of fortified wine (such as sherry) or sparkling wine; plus, in addition to any of these, 2 litres of unfortified, still (ordinary table) wine.

3. 50 grammes of perfume and 0.25 litre of toilet water.

4. Articles of any other description up to a value of £28; but not goods in commercial quantities.

PAYING DUTY ON GOODS BROUGHT BACK FROM ABROAD

A traveller caught trying to bring undeclared goods into Britain can be heavily fined or even imprisoned. He cannot refuse to be searched by customs officers.

From EEC countries, and goods not bought in a duty-free shop:

1. 300 cigarettes; or 150 cigarillos; or 75 large cigars; or 400 grammes of smoking tobacco.

2. 1.5 litres of alcoholic drink more than 22% by volume; or 3 litres of drink of 22% by volume or less; or 3 litres of fortified wine or sparkling wine; plus, in addition to any of these, 4 litres of unfortified, still wine.

3. 75 grammes of perfume and 0.375 litre of toilet water.

4. Articles of any other description up to a value of £120; but not goods in commercial quantities.

These allowances apply also to day trippers abroad, but not if you do not set foot on foreign soil.

There are no tobacco and alcohol allowances for travellers under 17.

Search and seizure A customs officer, policeman, member of the armed forces or coastguard can stop and search a vehicle or vessel if he believes it may be carrying goods subject to duty. If undeclared goods are found, the vehicle or vessel containing them can be forfeited as well as the goods.

A customs officer can also search a person suspected of possessing undeclared goods. But the suspect can ask to be taken before a justice of the peace or the Chief Customs Officer, who must then decide whether there are sufficient grounds for a search. There is no legal right simply to refuse to be searched by a customs officer.

CYCLING

Rules for taking a bicycle on the road

Although a court cannot imprison or disqualify a cyclist for a cycling offence, it can fine him as much as it does a motorist for certain offences. For example, a cyclist who disobeys a traffic sign or light is liable to the same maximum fine as a motorist – £400.

Cycling offences A cyclist must not hold on to motor vehicles in order to be towed. Nor must he carry a passenger – unless the bicycle is specially built or adapted to carry another person safely.

It is an offence to cycle recklessly, carelessly or inconsiderately – for example, to pull out from a kerb or line of traffic without signalling, to ride too far from the kerb or to have insufficient control of the bicycle – perhaps through carrying something heavy.

Cyclists do not need to obey yellow 'no parking' lines, but it is an offence to leave a bicycle in a dangerous position on a road.

The law treats a dismounted cyclist as a rider, not as a pedestrian. Therefore he cannot ignore a TRAFFIC SIGN or wheel his bicycle through traffic lights that are against him. A dismounted rider, however, is entitled to wheel his bicycle over a pedestrian crossing.

Lights Bicycles must be fitted at the back with a red light and reflector and at the front with a white light. The cyclist must have the lights on when riding at night or in poor visibility during the day. There is no need to have the lights on if the bicycle is stationary or if it is simply being wheeled along beside the kerb.

Brakes Bicycles with maximum safe saddle heights of 635 mm. or more – or, if made before August 1, 1984, with wheels that are more than 460 mm. in diameter – must have a brake for each wheel. Smaller bicycles need only one braking system.

It is an offence to sell a bicycle with an inadequate braking system or inefficient brakes – but not if the seller can prove that he had good reason to believe that the bicycle would not be used until the brakes were repaired.

Drunkenness It is an offence for anyone to ride a bicycle while he is incapable of controlling it properly because of drunkenness or the effect of drugs. It is also an offence to be in charge of a bicycle while drunk.

The police can arrest a drunken cyclist but they cannot test him with a breathalyser or take a sample of his blood or urine. They may call a doctor to pronounce on the cyclist's fitness to ride, but if the doctor asks for a specimen of blood or urine, the cyclist has the right to refuse.

However if the cyclist does supply a sample, it may be used in evidence against him. An alcohol level in a cyclist's blood above the legal level for a motorist is not considered necessarily to render a cyclist unfit to ride. The court's decision on whether the cyclist was unfit to ride will be made on all the available evidence.

Child cyclists A child of any age is legally allowed to ride a bicycle on a public road. However, the parents of child cyclists are responsible for ensuring that the child can ride properly.

If a child causes an accident because he or she is unfit to ride on a public road, the parent can be held liable. Parents are also responsible for ensuring that the brakes and lights on a child's bicycle work efficiently.

PENALTIES FOR CYCLING OFFENCES

What it can cost to ride carelessly or unlawfully

	Offence	Maximum fine
Brakes	Riding or permitting use with defective brake.	£400
	Selling or offering for sale bicycle with defective brakes.	£400
Lights	Riding or permitting use of bicycle with defective lights at night.	£400
	Riding or permitting use of bicycle with defective lights in poor visibility.	£400
Parking	Leaving bicycle in a dangerous position on road.	£400
Riding	Careless or inconsiderate riding.	£50
	Reckless riding.	£400
	Riding whilst unfit.	£400
	Taking hold of another vehicle.	£50
	Carrying a passenger.	£50
	Unauthorised racing.	£50
Signs and signals	Disobeying signal given by police constable or traffic warden.	£400
	Disobeying traffic signs, traffic lights or white lines.	£400
	Failing to accord precedence to pedestrian, or overtaking on approach to zebra crossing.	£400

DAMAGES

Compensation for loss

If you suffer loss – including injury or damage – as a result of someone else's action or failure to act, you may be able to obtain compensation from that person in legal proceedings. The legal term for compensation is damages.

To obtain damages you will have to show that the defender has committed a legal wrong against you. For example, he may have broken a CONTRACT with you – as when a shop sells you a washing machine which does not work. Or he may have failed in his duty to take reasonable care not to injure you or damage your property.

To obtain damages, the loss which you suffer must:

- Be of a kind which is recognised by the law.
- Have been caused by the defender's actions.
- Be a reasonably foreseeable consequence of his actions.
- Be of a kind that the court can evaluate financially.

What losses does the law recognise?

There are many obvious kinds of loss which are recognised by the courts and may result in an award of damages.

For example, if you pay someone £20 to repair your vacuum cleaner, but it still does not work, you have suffered a clear loss of £20. And if you are permanently disabled by a negligent motorist, you will suffer loss if your earning capacity or the quality of your life is affected. These are both losses for which damages can be paid.

You may even be able to get damages if someone causes you disappointment and inconvenience. For instance, if you contract with a package tour operator for a holiday with 'full entertainment' laid on, and there is no entertainment, you may be able to claim damages for loss of enjoyment.

However there are some losses which the law does not recognise. For example, you cannot get compensation for any worry or upset you suffer because a negligent motorist runs over your dog or cat. The law does not concern itself with that. But you would be able to get damages for the cost of veterinary treatment, or the cost of replacing the animal.

Loss must be caused by defender

Often it will be clear that the loss is directly linked to the defender's actions. For example, if a motorist knocks you down and breaks your leg, that injury is undoubtedly caused by the motorist's actions and you will be able to claim damages.

But sometimes the connection between the loss and the defender's actions is much less direct. Suppose that the hotel at which you booked your holiday tells you at the last minute that it has no accommodation. While looking for another hotel you are injured in a road accident. The accident would not have happened had it not been for the hotel's breach of contract. However the hotel owners cannot be held liable as their actions were not a sufficiently direct cause of your accident.

Even loss which seems to be directly caused by the defender may not be treated as such by the law.

For instance, a woman whose husband is killed by someone's negligence may be able to get damages for loss of his companionship. But if he becomes permanently unconscious she cannot obtain damages, since the connection between her loss and the defender's negligent behaviour is not treated as sufficiently direct.

An action can be brought on her husband's behalf, however, even though he is unconscious.

Similarly if the hotel you wanted to go to for your holiday has to close because a negligent builder has made it dangerous, you could not recover from him the cost of staying in a more expensive hotel. The courts would only be interested in the loss (of trade) suffered directly by the hotel owner, if he sued.

Loss must be foreseeable

Not every kind of loss that a defender causes will entitle you to damages. The

> *THE BOXER WHO SAID HE COULD HAVE BEEN WORLD CHAMPION*
>
> ***Damages are only recoverable for a loss if the court is able to assess it.***
>
> Mr Neill, a professional boxer, alleged that he had been injured by a bus. Before the accident he had beaten the British featherweight champion in a non-title fight. He claimed that one result of his injury was that he was no longer able to challenge the champion in a title fight.
>
> Mr Neill claimed damages for the loss of his chance to become British featherweight champion and ultimately world featherweight champion.
>
> DECISION
>
> The court refused to give him damages for the lost opportunity. The judge said that the chance of someone winning a sporting contest was not something the courts should be asked to put a value on.

loss must also be one which a reasonable person would have foreseen as a consequence of the defender's actions.

For instance, if a worker is struck on the head in an accident at work caused by a fellow employee's negligence, and suffers anxiety and depression, he can be awarded damages for that. But if his depression causes him to attempt suicide and he suffers further injury, he might not get damages for this – the court may decide that a reasonable person would not have foreseen that this would result from the original blow on the head.

Valuing the loss

The court must be able to put a value on the loss. Sometimes this will be quite easy. For example, if you buy a car which subsequently turns out to be completely unroadworthy, your loss is the price which you paid less the scrap value of the car.

But on other occasions the assessment will be more difficult – such as when a court has to put a value on pain and suffering arising out of injury caused by the defender.

It is possible for a court to put a value on most types of loss – even the loss of a chance. So you may be able to get damages from a solicitor who negligently fails to bring your case to court within the time allowed, even though you would have lost the case. This is because the solicitor's behaviour lost you the chance to settle the case.

There are some chances, however, which are so difficult to assess that no damages can be got for their loss. If you are deprived of the chance of passing an examination, for instance, you cannot obtain damages.

Assessing damages

The court, when assessing the amount of damages:

1. Tries to assess what the claimant's position would have been if the defender had not committed the wrong against him.

2. Looks at what his position actually is now that the wrong has happened.

The damages awarded are the best estimate that the court can make of the differences in money value between 1 and 2.

See: CONTRACT; FATAL INJURY; PERSONAL INJURY; SALE OF GOODS

DANGEROUS ANIMAL

A licence is required before you can keep certain wild animals. These are listed in the Dangerous Wild Animals Act 1976.

The owner of a dangerous wild animal is automatically liable for any damage which it causes to other persons or animals. *See:* ANIMAL

DANGEROUS GOODS

Claiming from seller or manufacturer

Some goods are dangerous because they are unfit for their purposes. For example, if a child's cuddly toy has dangerous wires sticking out of it, the toy is not suitably made, and the buyer can claim his money back from the seller. Someone who is injured because of a defect can sue the manufacturer for damages. *See:* CONSUMER SAFETY; DEFECTIVE GOODS

Other goods may be dangerous because they carry insufficient warning about their potential harmful effects. A consumer who suffers injury or loss, as a result of using such goods, can sue the manufacturer.

THE LABORATORY THAT EXPLODED

In 1969 B.D.H. Chemicals supplied Vacwell Engineering Co. with a chemical in glass vessels. The vessels were labelled 'Harmful Vapour' but were not marked with any reference to the violent reaction of the chemical to water.

A physicist who was washing the full vessels in a sink dropped one.

There was an explosion, which killed the physicist and destroyed the laboratory.

The engineering company sued the chemical manufacturers for supplying dangerous goods; it claimed £375,000 including £300,000 for lost profits.

DECISION

The court awarded the engineering company the damages claimed. However, the chemical manufacturers appealed and the matter was settled on agreed terms.

UNSUITABLE FOR CHILDREN

A dangerous article may be one either unfit for its purpose or offering a potential hazard.

For example, a kitchen knife can be dangerous if used carelessly, but there is no cause for complaint to retailer or manufacturer just because the knife has a sharp blade or point. However, if the top edge of the blade is also sharp, and the knife carries no warning, anyone injured by the top edge could sue the supplier or manufacturer.

DAY CARE CENTRE

Daily companionship, therapy and care for people in need

Local authorities and voluntary organisations run day care centres for the old, the disabled, the mentally ill or mentally handicapped, people recovering from alcoholism or drug addiction and others in need.

The centres vary considerably in their activities. Those for the very old and frail provide meals and care for people unable to look after themselves adequately and who would otherwise need full-time care in a residential home. They also offer support, advice and social activities. The centres usually provide transport from and to home.

Centres for the disabled provide, in addition to companionship and cooked meals, occupational therapy and sometimes light industrial work for pocket money.

A small charge may be made for meals and drinks.

Day care is also provided by adult

training centres – specialised, work-orientated training centres for adult mentally handicapped people.

To discuss the possibility of someone attending a local authority centre, contact the authority's social work department. Attendance at centres run by voluntary organisations is also usually arranged through the same department. However, you can approach such an organisation direct: addresses can be obtained from the local authority or a CITIZENS ADVICE BUREAU

DAY NURSERIES

Day care for the under fives

Day nurseries (sometimes called children's centres) provide care for children under 5 – particularly those whose parents are facing problems at home. The demand for a place in a nursery is heavy and no child has an automatic right to a place.

Local authority nurseries cater for children whose parents are in very difficult circumstances. Other nursery places are provided privately by voluntary organisations and sometimes employers.

Rules for local authority nurseries

Most are open from 8 a.m.–6 p.m., 5 days a week, including school holiday periods. Children must be at least 6 weeks old before admission but some nurseries can only accept children over 2 years of age.

Places in all these nurseries are allocated by the local social work department in co-operation with health visitors, doctors and nursery staff. Priority is given to children at risk of abuse, children or parents with health problems, and children who have only one parent bringing them up.

Charges vary in these nurseries but parents will be asked to pay according to their income. Charges can range from 30p a day to £25 per week. A few authorities make no charges.

Private nurseries These are nurseries run by someone other than the local authority. The local authority social work department has to register a private nursery and supervise it regularly.

The local authority will insist that there is an adequate staff/child ratio. This will usually be one member of staff to between 8 to 10 children.

Staff will need to be suitably experienced. Health and safety aspects are also considered and regulations about fire precautions must be observed.

Private nurseries may make a flat-rate charge for all children. Each nursery can decide how much it will charge.

Lists of private nurseries are available at social work department offices.

Employers' nurseries Some companies run nurseries at work. These must be supervised in exactly the same way as private nurseries. The same regulations apply to both kinds of nursery.

SETTING UP A NURSERY

Anyone wishing to set up a nursery must apply to the local authority social work department. The department will check the premises for safety and health risks. They will also arrange for a firemaster to visit in order to make recommendations about any fire precautions which may be necessary.

DEAFNESS

Help and training for those who cannot hear

Someone who becomes deaf or hard of hearing should ask his doctor to refer him to a specialist, called an audiologist. All treatment, including the provision of a hearing aid, is available free under the National Health Service.

Deaf or partially deaf people may be entitled to DISABLEMENT BENEFIT and to additional disablement allowances if their disability is caused by their work. Ask at the local social security office for claim form BI 100(OD).

A person must suffer a minimum hearing loss before being entitled to disablement benefit. In addition, the deafness must have occurred while working at a limited number of jobs – such as a job involving a pneumatic drill. For more information, ask at the social security office for leaflet NI 207.

To find out about the special facilities for deaf people in your area, contact the local social work department.

Volunteers who help

Few authorities have social workers specially trained to help the deaf, but in most areas voluntary organisations such as the Royal National Institute for the Deaf (RNID) are available to help. If there is no local office in your area contact the office of the Royal National Institute for the Deaf at 9a Claremont Gardens, Glasgow.

When a child is affected

To enable a deaf child to learn to speak, his hearing impairment must be diagnosed as early as possible. Local child health clinics test babies' hearing from 6 weeks old as part of their regular checks on the development of infants. There is a second test at the age of 6 months and a third, more comprehensive, examination at the age of 8 months.

Advice and guidance for parents of deaf babies are available from health visitors and the child health clinic. If no qualified social worker is available, the parents can be referred to organisations such as the National Deaf Children's Society, 31 Gloucester Place, London, which provides information, advice, financial help, holidays and special toys and equipment. They also arrange local groups so that parents can meet and support one another.

Education

The regional or islands council education department is responsible for the education of deaf children. If it does not provide special facilities in its own schools, it can pay for children for whom it is responsible to attend schools run by voluntary organisations for the deaf (such as Donaldson's School for the Deaf, Edinburgh). Children who live in rural areas may have to become boarders.

Some schools for the deaf have nursery units, and accept children from the age of 2. *See:* SPECIAL EDUCATION

When an adult is deaf

Some local authorities run free lip-reading classes and social clubs for the deaf, but in most areas the services for adults are provided by the voluntary organisations such as the RNID, Tayside Highland and Islands Association for the Deaf, and Edinburgh and

East of Scotland Society for the Deaf.

These organisations offer information and advice on finding employment and all the other problems of deafness, as well as arranging many social activities.

The address of the nearest branch of these organisations can be found in the telephone directory, or obtained from the local authority social work department.

Special help for the elderly

Local authorities must provide residential accommodation for the elderly, including those who are deaf. Such homes have staff specially trained in communicating with the deaf, and many run social activities aimed at improving communication.

For details of the help available in your area, contact the council's social work department.

If the person concerned prefers to enter a special home run by a voluntary organisation – for example, if he or she is Jewish and wants to be in the care of others of the same faith – the local authority, subject to a means test, may contribute towards the cost.

DEATH

What must be done when a life ends

Only a registered doctor is legally entitled to decide that someone has died.

A doctor who finds neither pulse nor breathing in a body can normally safely decide that the person is dead. However, if the doctor fails to carry out the tests, or if he does them inadequately, he may wrongly decide that a live patient is dead, and necessary medical treatment may be ended.

If he does so, and the patient dies or suffers damage, the doctor can be sued for MEDICAL NEGLIGENCE – either by the patient's dependants or by the patient, if he survives.

Certifying a death When someone dies, the death and its cause must be certified by a doctor and reported to the Registrar.

If the doctor is suspicious about the cause of death it must be reported to the PROCURATOR FISCAL for investigation. *See:* DEATH, Registration of

WHEN A BRITON DIES ABROAD

When a British citizen dies abroad, the death must be registered in accordance with the laws of the country in which he dies. It should also be registered with the BRITISH EMBASSY or consul.

Some countries require immediate burial or cremation. Otherwise, the executors or next-of-kin may decide to bring the body back to Britain. To make local arrangements abroad, ask the British consul.

If the death occurs in the Isle of Man or the Channel Islands or anywhere else abroad, and there is to be a cremation in Scotland, permission must be obtained from the Scottish Home and Health Department, St Andrew's House, Edinburgh. The undertaker may arrange this for you, but you will have to be able to produce a death certificate in English, showing the cause of death, as well as the usual cremation forms. *See:* FUNERAL. If the death occurs in England or Wales, the local coroner's permission must be obtained before the body can be removed to Scotland or anywhere else.

When a foreigner dies in Britain

The death of a foreigner in Britain must be registered by the Registrar of Deaths here like any other death. If the relatives wish to take the body out of the country, the procurator fiscal should be informed in case he has any objection. Some countries will also require a medical certificate stating that the body is free from infection and that certain diseases are not prevalent at the place of death. The remains are then embalmed and put in a sealed container to which the death certificate and any other documents are attached.

What happens to property

When someone dies, all that he possesses – even his body – passes to his personal representatives. If he has left a will, he may have appointed one representative to act as his EXECUTOR-nominate. If there is no will, or no appointment of an executor in it, anyone with an interest in the estate, such as a beneficiary or creditor, can apply to the sheriff court to be appointed executor-dative.

The executors have the right to decide what is to happen to the body – whether it will be cremated; if not, where it will be buried, with what funeral rite, and whether any organs can be donated to a hospital *See:* TRANSPLANT

However where a sudden or suspicious death has been reported to the procurator fiscal, the body may not be disposed of without his consent. He may wish to hold a POST-MORTEM examination or retain certain organs as evidence in any trial that may be held.

Any wishes expressed in the will, as to the disposal of the body and any transplant, are generally carried out, but the personal representatives are not obliged to do so.

If the dead person carried a card permitting organs to be used in transplants, or made such a provision in his will, the relative or other person responsible for the body may give permission for the organs to be removed. He may also do so if, after making enquiries, he has no reason to think either that the dead person would have objected or that a widow, widower or close relative objects.

Claims and contracts

Death has many legal consequences. Some contracts continue after a person's death and bind his executors, but those contracts which depend on being fulfilled by a particular person are automatically ended when that person dies.

An action of DIVORCE or SEPARATION ends if one or other party to the proceedings dies. A widow living with her husband at his death is entitled to a temporary allowance from his estate while she is awaiting settlement of any claims she may have against it.

HELP IN THE HOME WHEN SOMEONE IS DYING

When someone is dying and being nursed at home by the family, a wide range of services is provided by the local council and the health board.

Assistance may include visits by social workers, health visitors, nurses and home helps. Special beds, back rests, bed tables and hoists may also be supplied, as well as incontinence pads and an incontinence laundry service.

If the defender in an action for damages dies, his estate remains liable for any damages awarded. If the person bringing (or entitled to bring) the action dies, his executor can continue (or begin) it for the benefit of his estate. But they cannot claim for the pain and suffering of the dead person.

If someone is killed through another person's fault, his relatives can claim for loss of support: this claim must usually be made within 3 years. Close relatives may also claim for loss of the dead person's society and guidance. These claims must be made in one joint action. *See:* FATAL INJURY

When someone dies financially insolvent, a JUDICIAL FACTOR may be appointed to distribute whatever assets are available from the estate.

Death after an assault

When a criminal assault results in the victim's death, the person responsible can be charged with MURDER or CULPABLE HOMICIDE.

If someone dies alone

Sometimes the district or islands council must take responsibility for arranging the burial or cremation of a person who dies while living alone. This happens when the dead person has no known relatives, and no-one has arranged burial or cremation. The council can recover the cost from any estate left by the deceased.

The regional or islands council may arrange the burial or cremation if its social work department was caring for the deceased or was giving help at the time of the death.

DEATH, Presumption of

Declaring a person dead

If someone vanishes without trace or is thought to have died in some accident or natural disaster, but his body is never found, problems can arise for his relatives. Who is to look after his property or draw benefit from it? Does his marriage still exist? Can claims be made on any insurance policies on his life?

To settle all such questions a simple form of action has been available in the sheriff courts or the Court of Session since 1978. Anyone with an interest in the matter (including the LORD ADVOCATE) can raise the action. LEGAL AID is available.

Evidence has to be brought to satisfy the judge that the missing person died on a certain date or within a certain period, or that he has not been known to be alive for at least 7 years.

If the judge is satisfied he will issue a decree (a court order). This dissolves the missing person's marriage and allows the surviving partner to re-marry. It also enables any will to operate or claims to be made on the estate. Claims by relatives for social security benefits, private pensions, and life insurance can be made. *See:* INTESTACY

If the missing person turns up, the ending of his marriage still stands. However he will still be liable for any crime he may have committed.

The missing person or anyone else with an interest can ask for the decree to be withdrawn or corrected. This could mean that property which has been transferred will have to be returned. Insurance cover may be taken out against the possibility of the missing person returning.

DEATH, Registration of

Legal procedures when someone dies

Any death must be reported within 8 days to the registrar of births, deaths and marriages for the area where it occurs or the dead person resided.

Four certificates must be obtained:

1. A medical certificate of death, issued free, stating the cause of death and completed and signed by a doctor who attended the deceased person during his or her last illness.

If for any reason the doctor does not issue a certificate of death immediately, a relative who was present at the death or during the last illness – or who lives in the same registration district as the dead person did – has a right to insist on one.

If someone dies in hospital, the hospital staff generally arrange for a doctor to prepare the certificate. When someone dies outside hospital, a doctor should be called immediately – preferably one who has treated the dead person in his or her last illness, or his or her usual doctor.

2. A disposal certificate allowing the body to be buried or cremated, issued free of charge by the registrar for the district where the death occurred.

Without the disposal certificate, an undertaker cannot legally carry out a funeral. The certificate will not be issued without a medical certificate.

3. A death certificate, also issued by the registrar on production of a medical certificate.

The full death certificate is a copy of the entry in the official Register of Deaths, and is needed, for example, to claim life-insurance benefits. It costs £2 on registration and for a month after, then £5.

4. A short death certificate (BD8), issued free, which is needed to claim DEATH GRANT or widow's benefit.

Finding the registrar The address of the local registrar should be supplied by the doctor who issues the medical certificate of death. It can also be found in the telephone directory, under 'Registration of Births, Deaths and Marriages'.

Whoever is responsible for registering the death must do so in person. If that is not possible within 8 days – for example, because the responsible person is ill – send the registrar written notice of the death, with the medical certificate issued by a doctor.

What the registrar requires

If you go to get a death registered you must take the medical certificate with you. The registrar will ask you the full names of the dead person, his or her place and date of birth, occupation, place and date of death and the address where the person normally lived.

WHO SHOULD INFORM THE REGISTRAR

The following people are legally obliged to have a death registered.

- Any relative of the dead person.
- Any person present at the death.
- The dead person's EXECUTOR or other legal representative.
- The occupier of the premises where the death took place.
- Any other person having the information necessary for registration.

Once the required information has been provided by some qualified person, no-one else is under any obligation to do so.

You will also be asked for details of his or her father and mother and of his or her marriage, if any. It is helpful if you can bring with you the dead person's birth and marriage certificates.

The registrar will need to know whether the person was receiving a pension or allowance from public funds and – if he or she was married – the date of birth of the surviving widow or widower.

Once he has that information, he will register the death and issue the disposal certificate. Take this to the undertaker.

When a death is investigated

If the death is sudden, unexpected or suspicious, the PROCURATOR FISCAL must be given the opportunity to investigate it and take whatever action may be necessary, including criminal pro-

WRITTEN EVIDENCE OF THE CAUSE OF DEATH

A doctor's duty to examine a person who has died and state the reasons for his death

MEDICAL CERTIFICATE OF CAUSE OF DEATH **FORM 11** D2(R) 780

This certificate is intended for the use of the Registrar of Births, Deaths and Marriages, and all persons are warned against accepting or using this certificate for any other purpose.

To the Registrar of Births, Deaths and Marriages. *See note overleaf*

I hereby certify that Alexander MacDonald

died at 0100 (time) hours on 27 December (date) 1980

at 26 Sycamore Street, Broughty Ferry (place of death)

and that to the best of my knowledge and belief, the cause of death and duration of disease were as stated below.

Registrar to enter:
Dist No. 350
Entry No. 1079
Year 1980

CAUSE OF DEATH (Please print clearly)			Not to be entered in register — Approximate interval between onset and death: years	months	days
I **Disease or condition directly leading to death***	a	Myocardial Infarction	Immediate		
Antecedent causes Morbid conditions, if any, giving rise to the above cause, the underlying condition to be stated last	b	*due to (or as a consequence of)*			
	c	*due to (or as a consequence of)*			
II **Other significant conditions** contributing to the death, but not related to the disease or condition causing it		Pneumonia			5
		Epilepsy	25		

This does not mean the mode of dying such as heart failure, asthenia, etc.; it means the disease, injury or complication which caused death.

Please ring appropriate letter and appropriate figure:—
Certified cause takes account of post-mortem information .... A
Information from post-mortem may be available later .... B
Post-mortem not proposed .... (C)

Seen after death by me .... (1)
Seen after death by another medical practitioner but not by me 2
Not seen after death by a medical practitioner 3

If deceased was a married woman and death occurred during pregnancy, or within six weeks thereafter, write 'Yes' [crossed out]

Signature Lewis O'Flaherty
Date 27 December 1980
Name in BLOCK CAPITALS LEWIS O'FLAHERTY
Registered medical qualifications MB ChB
Address Main Street Broughty Ferry

If a doctor signs the medical certificate without the procurator fiscal being informed, the registrar of births, deaths and marriages issues a certificate for disposal straight away unless he has doubts about the circumstances of death.

If the doctor or the registrar is not satisfied about the cause of death, the procurator fiscal must be informed. In that case the registrar registers the death only after the procurator fiscal authorises him to do so.

THE CERTIFICATE WHICH RECORDS THAT THE DEATH HAS BEEN REGISTERED

When a dead person's particulars are entered in the official Register of Deaths and a copy of the entry issued

IN DEFENS

Extract of an entry in a REGISTER of DEATHS DE 000009

Registration of Births, Deaths and Marriages (Scotland) Act 1965

District No. 350 — Year 1980 — Entry No. 1079

Death registered in the district of Dundee

1. Surname: MacDonald
Name(s): Alexander
2. Sex: M
3. Occupation: Plumber (Master)
4. Marital status: Married
5. Date of birth: Year 1946, Month 4, Day 4
6. Age: 34 years
7. Name(s), surname and occupation of spouse(s): Jean Paterson.
8. When and where died: 19 80 December Twenty-seventh 0100 hours, 26 Sycamore Street, Broughty Ferry
9. Usual residence (if different from 8 above)
10. Name(s), surname and occupation of father: Robert Edward MacDonald, Coal Miner (Brusher)
11. Name(s), surname(s) and maiden surname of mother: Elizabeth Simpson MacDonald m.s. Brown
12. Cause of death
I (a) Myocardial Infarction
(b)
(c)
II Pneumonia, Epilepsy

Certifying registered medical practitioner: Lewis O'Flaherty

13. Informant's signature, qualification and address: (Signed) J MacDonald — Widow, 26 Sycamore Street, Broughty Ferry
14. When registered: Year 19 80, Month 12, Day 29
15. (Signed) Wm. Blacklock, Registrar
16.

Extracted from the Register of Deaths for the District of Dundee

on Twenty-ninth December 1980 — Wm. Blacklock, Registrar

The above particulars incorporate any subsequent corrections or amendments to the original entry made with the authority of the Registrar General.

Warning

It is an offence under section 53(3) of the Registration of Births, Deaths and Marriages (Scotland) Act 1965 for any person to pass as genuine any copy or reproduction of this extract which has not been made by a district registrar or assistant registrar and authenticated by his signature.

Any person who falsifies or forges any of the particulars on this extract or knowingly uses, gives or sends as genuine any false or forged extract is liable to prosecution under section 53(1) of the said Act

XD3 (R)

The cause of death is taken from the medical certificate issued by the doctor who attended the deceased

The 'informant' is the person who registers the death, usually a relative who has been close to the deceased during his final illness and death

Someone who is responsible for registering a person's death must give particulars of that person, including his or her full name, place and date of birth, occupation, place and date of death and where that person lived, to the local registrar. He notes the details in the official Register of Deaths and provides a copy of that entry as a death certificate before issuing a certificate for burial or cremation.

ceedings or the holding of a public inquiry. *See:* FATAL ACCIDENT INQUIRY

The procurator fiscal usually gets his information from the police. But the registrar is also obliged to report to him any unusual deaths which come to his notice. These include deaths by accident, poisoning, violence or drowning; deaths of newborn babies and of foster children; deaths under anaesthetic; deaths through neglect.

In such cases the procurator fiscal is entitled to delay the burial or cremation until satisfied as to the cause of death. He may arrange for a POST-MORTEM to be performed and parts of the body to be retained. He may summon relatives or witnesses and take confidential statements from them. Such inquiries will be carried out as speedily as possible.

If death happens abroad

If a British Citizen dies abroad, the death must be registered in compliance with the local law. But it can also be registered with the nearest British Consul or, in some Commonwealth countries, the High Commissioner. The following year, certified copies of these registered deaths are sent to the Registrar General in Edinburgh. Copies are then obtainable on payment of a set fee.

When a body has not been found

In some deaths – for example, an air crash or shipwreck – a body may not be found. Therefore no medical certificate of death can be issued.

In such cases there is a court procedure for establishing that death has occurred. The decree of the court is sent to the Registrar General, who registers the death and may issue a certificate. *See:* DEATH, Presumption of

The death can sometimes be registered in other ways: in the Marine Register, by the Civil Aviation Authority or following a fatal accident inquiry.

If a baby is born dead

Stillborn children, born after the 28th week of pregnancy, must be reported to the registrar within 21 days. The doctor or midwife present should supply a certificate of still-birth.

If neither was present the registrar will ask the parents to sign an appropriate form. He then gives them a certificate which can be used to obtain burial or cremation.

DEATH GRANT

How the state helps people to meet the cost of a funeral

A death grant is a lump sum paid by the Government to whoever pays, or has agreed to meet, someone's funeral expenses. If the dead person left a will, the grant is usually paid to the executor. If the cost is met by the armed services or a burial society, the grant can still be paid to the dead person's next of kin.

The amount of the grant varies with the age of the deceased. In 1983–4 it ranged from £9 for a child aged under 3 to a maximum of £30.

Qualification for the death grant depends on NATIONAL INSURANCE CONTRIBUTIONS paid by, or credited to, the dead person or a close relative. Contributions paid abroad are sometimes taken into account.

If a hospital or local authority arranges the funeral for someone who has no relatives, or none willing to pay for the funeral, it is paid any grant for which the dead person was eligible.

The Department of Health and Social Security makes special payments, equivalent to the full death grant, towards the funeral expenses for anyone who received a war disablement pension but is not eligible for the death grant.

The department will, alternatively, arrange a simple funeral for anyone receiving a war disablement pension who dies as a result of the disablement. Next-of-kin should inquire at the local war pensions office.

Supplementary benefit

A claimant of SUPPLEMENTARY BENEFIT may be able to claim a single payment of a lump sum to meet the funeral expenses of a member of his household or a close relative. If such a payment is made the amount of the death grant will normally be deducted.

When someone dies abroad

A grant is payable for a death outside the United Kingdom if it happens in another EEC country or in Austria, Cyprus, Jamaica, Jersey, Guernsey, Norway, Portugal, Spain, Turkey or Yugoslavia.

If it occurs elsewhere abroad and the deceased was receiving United Kingdom social security benefit – such as retirement pension – at the time of death, or if he was ordinarily resident in Great Britain and died within 13 weeks of going abroad, the death grant is also payable.

How to claim

A person claiming death grant must do so within 6 months after the death. This period may be extended if there was good cause for a failure to claim in time. He or she should take along to any social security office the death certificate, the marriage certificate, if the claimant is the widow or widower of the deceased, and the undertaker's account or estimate, if the claimant's claim is based on the fact that he has paid, or has agreed to pay the funeral expenses.

Even when those documents cannot be obtained within the 6 months, the claim form should still be filled in.

WHO CAN AND CANNOT GET A DEATH GRANT

The lump sum death grant is given to whoever is paying for the funeral.

Full grant payable

- For death of man or woman who has paid (or been credited with) 25 national insurance contributions between July 25, 1948 and April 5, 1975, or who actually paid contributions in one tax year on at least 25 times the lower earnings limit for that year.
- For death of spouse, widow, widower of someone with similar insurance record.
- For death of handicapped person unable to work but living with close relative with similar insurance record (or whose husband had such a record).

Half grant payable

- For death of man born between July 5, 1883 and July 4, 1893; woman born between July 5, 1888 and July 4, 1898.

Reduced grant payable

- For death of child of someone with the appropriate insurance record:

Age under 3, grant £9
Age 3–5, grant £15
Age 6–17, grant £22.50.

Grant not payable

- For death of man born before July 5, 1883; woman born before July 5, 1888; stillborn child.

A PAYMENT TOWARDS THE UNDERTAKER'S BILL

How a person can claim death grant from the state towards the expenses of a funeral

The grant is normally payable if the dead person qualified while he was alive for some kind of national insurance benefit

As payment of a death grant is usually based on the dead person's national insurance contributions, the number helps to establish eligibility

If the claim is made for a dependant, the person on whose national insurance contributions the claim is based must be eligible

Reduced grants are payable when a child has died. Claims can be made for newly born children who did not survive, but not for a stillbirth

The grant is also payable for the funeral expenses of people who, because they were children or disabled, were unable to work

Particulars of the Deceased

1 Full name (BLOCK CAPITALS PLEASE) *Surname last*

Mr/~~Mrs/Miss~~ ROBERT EDWARD MacDONALD

His/her National Insurance number, if any — Letters: ZZ; Figures: 00 00 00; Letter: AA

State whether single, married, widowed or divorced — MARRIED

Last home address — 14 ASH STREET, BROUGHTY FERRY

2 Date of death THIRD (day) OCTOBER (month) 1982 (year)

3 Date of birth FIRST (day) FEBRUARY (month) 1916 (year)

If the date of birth is not known, please state the approximate age of the deceased

4 Was any benefit, pension or allowance (including war pension or allowance) being paid to the deceased by this Department or by the Department of Employment, or was payment for the deceased as a dependant being made to you or to any other person or is any such claim currently under consideration? (Yes or No) YES

If YES, (1) give particulars STATE RETIREMENT PENSION *Please return any order book or Girocheque still held*

(2) say whether you wish to claim any outstanding arrears. (Yes or No) YES

Particulars of claim

5 Did the deceased leave a Will? (Yes or No)

If YES, give the name and address of the Executor(s)

WILLIAM MASON
C/o MASON & BLACKWOOD, SOLICITORS
6 TAY RD. DUNDEE

6 IF THERE IS NO WILL, have Letters of Administration (in Scotland, Confirmation) been obtained or are they being obtained? (Yes or No)

If YES, give the name and address of the person(s) in whose name the Letters, etc are being taken out

7 IF YOU ARE NOT THE NEXT OF KIN and if you have answered NO to both questions 5 and 6 give the name and address of the next of kin. The order of priority is normally: widow/widower (but not if a decree of judicial separation was in force), children, father or mother, brothers or sisters, other relatives.

Relationship of next of kin to the deceased

8 If the funeral expenses have been (or will be) paid by someone other than yourself, or if a local authority or hospital authority is arranging (or has arranged) the burial, give the following information

Name and address of authority or person

To be completed only if the deceased was a child

9 Were you receiving Child Benefit for any child up to the date of the death? (Yes or No)

If YES, please send all order books covering payment of Child Benefit unless the deceased was a newly-born child for whom you have not claimed Child Benefit.

If you are not receiving Child Benefit, please send the child's birth certificate (if you have it) or give the following information

Place of the child's birth

Names of parents (BLOCK CAPITALS PLEASE) *Surname last*

Father

Mother

To be completed only if the claim is based on the contributions of someone other than the deceased

10 Particulars of person on whose contribution record the claim is based

11 **If you have any of the following documents please send them with this form, but if they are not available do NOT delay making your claim: please tick the box for any which you send with this form.**

- ☑ Any order book or Girocheque issued by this Department for the deceased (Any Girocheque issued by the Department of Employment should be returned to the Unemployment Benefit Office)
- ☑ Any contribution card, certificate of age exception/earner's non-liability or certificate of election/reduced liability of the deceased
- ☑ Marriage Certificate (if claim is made by widow or widower)
- ☐ Undertaker's receipted account
- ☐

If the deceased was a child:

- ☐ All order books covering payment of Child Benefit (but see item 9)
- ☐ Any Welfare Foods Service Books for the child

When there is no will give the name and address of any person acting as administrator of the deceased's estate

If the deceased left a will, the claimant should supply the name and address of the executor(s)

The grant can be paid to someone who did not pay the funeral expenses. But the claimant must state who paid the expenses

If there is no executor and you are not the next of kin, give his or her name and address

Even if relevant documents such as NHS cards are not available, you should send the completed claim form within 6 months

The undertaker usually helps bereaved relatives to make an application for the death grant, as well as with the registration formalities. He normally supplies a copy of form BD 1 on which the application is made, but it can also be obtained from the local office of the Department of Health and Social Security, to which it should be returned when completed and signed. Application can also be made on the back of the free certificate of registration of death along with the undertaker's account or estimate.

DEBT

How a creditor can lawfully recover money from a debtor

It is not a crime to owe money and therefore a debtor cannot be prosecuted for failing to pay up.

However a creditor can raise an action for payment of a debt in a civil (non-criminal) court, and that court may order the debtor to pay. If the debtor still fails to do so, the creditor then has to use certain legal procedures to enforce payment.

A debtor can be sent to prison for up to 6 weeks by a civil court if he fails to pay the following:

- **Rates** – but only if payment cannot be obtained by selling some of the debtor's possessions.
- **Aliment** for a spouse or child. Failure to pay must be wilful.

What a creditor should not do

It is not a crime for a creditor or someone acting on his behalf – such as a DEBT COLLECTOR – to harass a debtor by demanding payment or by threatening publicity or civil court proceedings.

However it is a crime for a creditor to threaten violence or damage to property in order to obtain payment. It is also a crime to threaten the debtor with criminal proceedings.

If you get into debt

If you owe money, you should try to come to a voluntary arrangement with your creditor as soon as possible. Delay may result in the debt increasing, as you will have to pay the cost of any legal action which the creditor may eventually take to recover the money.

Ignoring some debts can have particularly serious consequences. For example, if you fail to pay your gas or electricity bill, your supply may be disconnected. If you fail to pay rent, your landlord may decide to take eviction proceedings against you. If you owe rates, an extra 10 per cent will be added to your bill when the local authority applies to the sheriff for authority to collect the arrears.

Your name will also be recorded on a debtors' 'black list' if a court order for debt is obtained against you. You will then find it very difficult to get credit.

Help and advice on debt problems can be obtained from a CITIZENS ADVICE BUREAU.

SUING FOR A DEBT OF NOT MORE THAN £1,000

How a sheriff court case proceeds according to the course taken by the debtor

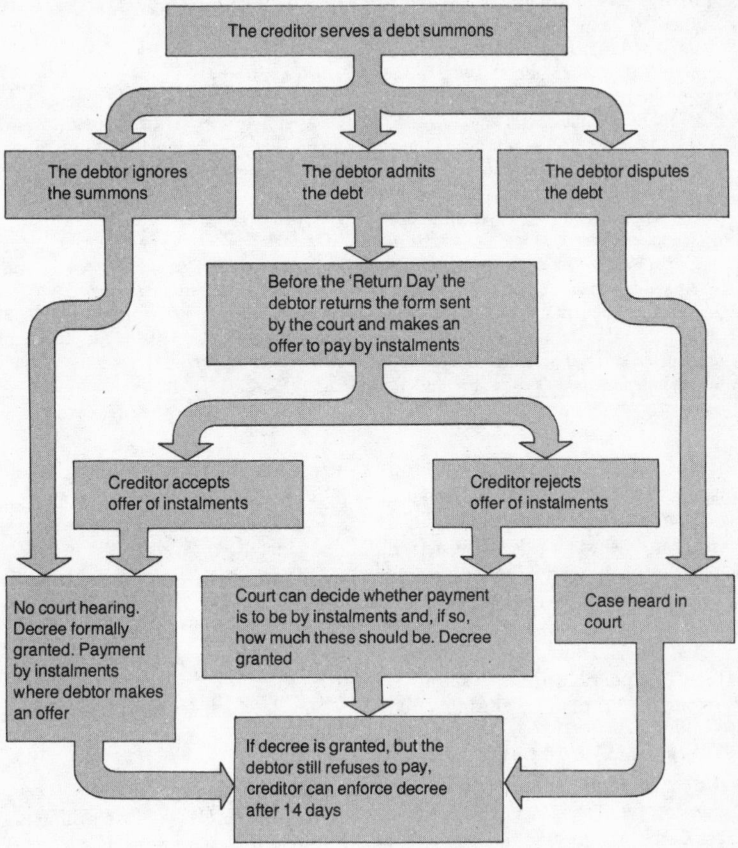

If you are sued

Most debt cases are heard in the sheriff court. Claims for debts up to £1,000 are dealt with there under a special 'summary cause' procedure. *See:* SUMMONS

To start legal proceedings, a document called a summons must be served on the alleged debtor. If the debt is more than £1,000, the document is called an INITIAL WRIT.

Debts up to £1,000 The summons will state how much is alleged to be owing. It will also state:

1. The 'Return Day'. This is the date by which the alleged debtor must tell the court whether he intends to defend the action or to admit the debt.

He should also make any offer to pay by instalments before this date. If he does make such an offer, he should ensure that he can afford to keep up the payments, otherwise the whole amount will become due at once.

2. The 'Calling Day'. This is the date when the action will be heard in court. It must be 7 days after the Return Day. If the alleged debtor does not reply to the summons on the form provided, the creditor can obtain a court decree, ordering him to pay, without a hearing.

Where decree is granted, the sheriff will normally allow the debtor to pay by instalments if he has made an offer to pay in this way. The sheriff can allow payment by instalments even if the creditor objects.

The debtor can appeal to the sheriff principal within 14 days, but only on a point of law.

Debts over £1,000 An initial writ is

HELP FOR A DEBTOR ON SUPPLEMENTARY BENEFIT

If a debtor who is receiving SUPPLEMENTARY BENEFIT, or who would be entitled to supplementary benefit if he claimed it, is in danger of eviction because he cannot pay his rent, or of having his fuel supply cut off because he has not paid the bill – he may be able to get help.

If he has got into debt through failing to claim supplementary benefit earlier, or failing to claim an additional allowance or lump-sum payment he was entitled to under the supplementary benefit scheme, a payment can be made towards the debt. The payment will not exceed the amount of unclaimed benefit.

A payment must also be made if the amount he has put aside for a fuel bill is less than the actual bill either because of a spell of exceptionally severe weather or because he has recently acquired an unfamiliar heating system.

Hire purchase

A debtor on supplementary benefit can also get help with HIRE PURCHASE payments for some essential items of furniture and household equipment.

Health and safety

In other cases, help can be given, either in the form of a payment towards the debt or, if it is for fuel, by supplying an alternative source, but only if it is the only way of preventing serious risk to the health or safety of the claimant or members of his family. *See:* FUEL BILL

more formal than a summons. It sets out how the debt is said to have arisen and asks the alleged debtor to indicate whether he wishes to defend the action. If he does nothing, decree will usually be granted in his absence. If he decides to defend, he must notify the sheriff clerk within a set time.

It is not possible for the sheriff to allow the debtor to pay by instalments.

Forcing a debtor to pay

If decree is granted, the creditor can obtain a copy, or 'extract', of it after 14 days. Once he does so he can ask a SHERIFF OFFICER to use legal procedures to force the debtor to pay. These procedures are called 'diligence'. The creditor's expenses in using diligence are charged to the debtor.

Two procedures are normally used to enforce payment. One – called poinding (pronounced pinnding) and sale – allows the creditor to lay claim to some of the debtor's possessions and sell them if necessary. The other – called arrestment – allows the creditor to obtain property, usually money, belonging to the debtor but in someone else's hands.

Poinding and sale The creditor can ask a sheriff officer to poind, or select and value, some of the debtor's possessions to the amount of the debt. The debtor must be given 14 days' formal warning that a poinding will take place if he does not pay up.

The sheriff officer is legally entitled to break into the debtor's house, when he cannot otherwise gain entry, to select items for sale.

Some possessions cannot be poinded. They include:

- Goods which are jointly owned or belong to another member of the debtor's family.
- Goods which are being bought on HIRE PURCHASE
- Goods which are hired – for example, a rented television.
- Beds, bedding, chairs, tables, equipment for heating and for eating, cooking or storing food – unless selling them would not cause undue hardship. The debtor can appeal to the sheriff within 7 days if any such item is poinded.
- Clothes (except items far in excess of the debtor's needs) and working tools.

It is a criminal offence for a debtor to dispose of any item which has been poinded. The sheriff officer leaves a list of all such items with the debtor.

The sheriff officer can ask the sheriff to authorise a warrant sale if the poinding fails to produce payment. If the request is granted, the sale – usually by public auction at the debtor's house – is then advertised locally.

The debtor, or someone acting on his behalf, can buy back his own possessions. Items which are not sold become the property of the creditor and the debt is reduced by the value put on them.

Arrestment Where the debtor is working, the creditor will usually enforce payment by arresting, or 'freezing', part of the debtor's wages due to him from his employer.

The debtor does not have to be given any advance warning. The sheriff officer will serve a document called an arrestment on the debtor's employer. This instructs the employer not to pay over to the debtor a stated amount of wages.

The creditor can arrest up to half the gross wages of certain employees – mainly manual workers – over £4 per week. However when the debt is unpaid aliment, rates or taxes the whole weekly wages can be arrested – though this is arguably subject to the common law rule that the debtor should be left enough for his subsistence.

The debtor will then be asked to sign a mandate allowing the money to be paid to his creditor. Even at this stage it may be possible for the debtor to make a voluntary arrangement with the creditor to pay by weekly instalments.

Further arrestments can be served on subsequent payments of wages if the first arrestment does not produce enough to clear the debt.

The same procedure can be used against money which the debtor has in, for example, a bank or building society account. However social security benefits cannot be arrested. Nor, generally, can alimentary payments – such as ALIMENT or a periodical allowance payable on DIVORCE.

Unpaid rates and taxes Rating and tax authorities can recover arrears by using the ordinary court procedure, but usually only do so when liability is disputed. If it is not, they can recover arrears (plus a 10 per cent surcharge in rates cases) by obtaining a summary warrant from a sheriff in respect of a list of defaulters. This allows them to poind goods or – for rates only – to arrest sums of money.

DEBT COLLECTOR

The rules which must be observed

It is not illegal for a person or company employed to collect unpaid debts to harass a debtor by making frequent demands for payment, threatening publicity or threatening to sue for payment.

However a debt collector must obey the criminal law. Threats of violence against the debtor, his family or his property are illegal. So is the recovery of a debt by false pretences – for instance, by someone deliberately pretending to be a SHERIFF OFFICER.

It is also illegal for a debt collector to threaten criminal proceedings to obtain payment of a debt. *See:* EXTORTION

The debt collector should make a polite request for payment. This is usually done by letter. If the debt is still not paid the debt collector will normally inform the debtor that court proceedings will be started. The case may then be passed to a solicitor.

Anyone who wishes to act as a debt collector must obtain a licence from the Director General of Fair Trading. The Director General will only issue the licence if he is satisfied that the applicant is a suitable person – for example, he has not been convicted of fraud or dishonesty.

The Director General keeps a public register containing details of people holding or applying for licences. The register also lists licences which have been suspended or revoked. To get information write to the Office of Fair Trading, Field House, 15–25 Bream's Buildings, London, EC4A 1PR.

Any debt collector convicted of working without an Office of Fair Trading licence can be fined up to £2,000 in summary CRIMINAL PROCEEDINGS. In solemn proceedings he can be fined an unlimited sum or imprisoned for up to 2 years (or both). *See:* DEBT

DEFAMATION

When writing or speaking too freely can be dangerous

Everyone is entitled to protect his or her reputation against unfair or malicious attacks. Anyone who accuses or criticises another person to the damage of his or her character, credit or reputation risks being sued for defamation.

In Scotland, anyone who offers another person a personal insult or affront may be sued for defamation for injured feelings.

A statement can be defamatory even if it is not made public to third parties.

Defamation usually takes the form of a statement, written or spoken – although action, without words, can also be defamatory. Scots law draws no particular distinction between defamation by the written word (called libel) and by the spoken word (called slander).

To succeed in a defamation action the person bringing the case (the pursuer) must prove that the statement or action complained of was defamatory. He must also show that it referred to him or was taken to refer to him. Even then the action may fail if the defender succeeds in a defence such as *veritas* (meaning that the statement is true), fair comment or privilege (see below).

A person who circulates a slander can be sued in the same way as the original author of the slander.

What makes a statement defamatory

It is not possible to give a complete definition of what constitutes a defamatory statement. Much will depend on the circumstances of each case. In general, however, a statement will be defamatory if it:

- Damages the reputation of the pursuer; or
- Tends to lower him or her in the esteem of ordinary men or women; or
- Is a calculated insult or affront.

Some types of comment are more risky than others. For example, it is particularly dangerous to criticise someone's morals or honesty, or to accuse him or her of criminal behaviour or professional incompetence.

So it may be safe to write that a television actor's performance was unsatisfactory, and even to write the same about his subsequent performances. But it is defamatory to suggest that he is generally incompetent as an actor.

Defamation by innuendo An apparently innocent statement may still lead to a defamation action if people reading

WIFE OR MISTRESS?

If a man is already married and his engagement is announced in the newspaper his wife can sue because the innuendo is that she is only his mistress.

THE AFFRONTED ACTOR

Publication to third parties is not necessary for an action for defamation to succeed

An actor was engaged for 3 theatre performances. After the first 2 performances the theatre manager cancelled the third one.

He then wrote to the actor. 'You made your engagement under false pretences. You advertise what you are not capable of performing.'

Although there had been no publication to third parties, the actor raised an action for defamation.

DECISION

The court decided that on the face of it the letter was actionable. The fact that it had been sent to the pursuer himself, and had not been communicated to third parties, did not mean there were no grounds for defamation.

THE IMAGINARY TWINS

A statement which appears to be quite innocent may still lead to an action for defamation if people are able to draw a defamatory inference from it

On August 11, 1901, the *Scotsman* printed a birth notice stating that George Morrison's wife had given birth to twins. This was not true. Worse still, the couple had only married on July 12, 1901.

Mr Morrison sued for defamation on the ground that there was a clear suggestion that he and his wife had indulged in pre-marital intercourse.

DECISION

The court decided that it was possible for people to draw such an inference and as a result the action was allowed to proceed.

POSSIBLE DEFENCES AGAINST AN ACTION FOR DEFAMATION

Three main defences are open to someone accused of defamation: *veritas* (truth), fair comment and privilege.

Veritas The best defence against an action for defamation is to prove that the statement complained of is true. However it is often difficult to establish the truth of a defamatory statement. The law assumes that such a statement is false unless the defender can prove that it is substantially true.

Fair comment Anyone making a defamatory statement that consists of comment, rather than allegation of fact, can defend himself by showing that the comment was made honestly.

He must also show that the comment was made on a matter of public interest, and without any improper motive, such as malice.

His defence can only concern itself with comment, not statements of fact. The facts on which the comment is based must be accurate.

It is not easy to define a matter of public interest. In general terms the matter must be one in which the public is entitled to take an interest because it is of genuine public concern. Comments on the private lives of private citizens would clearly not be regarded as being on a matter of public interest. Nor would some comments on the private lives of public figures.

A local newspaper may write that the rates are unnecessarily high because the chairman of the local authority finance committee is incapable of controlling the budget. If the chairman sues, the newspaper must prove that it was an honest comment on his performance as chairman of a public body. This defence will not succeed if the chairman can show that the newspaper editor, or the reporter, was motivated by malice.

The defence of fair comment still applies even if most people disagree with the comment. The comment can even be intemperate, one-sided and exaggerated, so long as it is honestly made.

For example, a critic is entitled to write a scathing review of a book, so long as it represents his honest opinion and he does not have an improper motive – such as a personal vendetta against the author.

Privilege There are two types of privilege: absolute and qualified.

A statement covered by absolute privilege is always protected against an action for defamation. For example, a member of the House of Commons or House of Lords can say whatever he likes during a parliamentary debate. Witnesses giving evidence in court are similarly protected. So are newspapers and broadcasters who make fair reports of parliamentary and judicial proceedings. Judges acting in their judicial capacity are also protected, as are advocates or solicitors addressing the courts.

If a statement is covered by absolute privilege, ill-will, spite or malice is irrelevant even although it can be proved.

The defence of qualified privilege also protects someone who has made a defamatory statement, but only if:

- He has a legally recognised interest or duty to make the statement.
- The person to whom he makes the statement has a corresponding right, duty or interest.
- He is not motivated by malice – that is, by any dishonest or improper motive.

Whether qualified privilege applies or not depends largely on the occasion. For example, a litigant has qualified privilege in respect of statements he makes in court or in his written pleadings. A solicitor may also have qualified privilege when he makes a statement to third parties in his client's interest.

An employer has privilege when he writes a reference for an employee. So does a teacher or lecturer when writing a reference for a pupil or student. Doctors usually have privilege in relation to medical reports.

Broadcasters and journalists have qualified privilege in a number of cases laid down by statute.

Any member of the public has privilege when reporting a crime or suspicious circumstances to the police, so long as no ulterior or improper motive is involved.

Many meetings – for example, council meetings, kirk session meetings and university court meetings – will be regarded as privileged occasions.

Other defences There are other possible defences to an action for defamation. For example, it can be a defence that the words complained of were spoken in the heat of the moment, or that the defamation was unintentional. However these defences are generally of limited application.

or hearing it think that it is defamatory.

For example, it may seem harmless for a newspaper to publish a photograph of a man and a woman, with a caption announcing their engagement. But if the man is already married, his wife can sue if people who know her infer from the caption that she is merely the man's mistress and has been pretending to be his wife.

Identifying the person defamed

The pursuer cannot succeed unless he can show that he is the person defamed. It is not essential that he should actually be named in the statement concerned, so long as he can show that people thought the statement referred to him.

For example, a writer on food may say that every restaurant in town cheats on its bills. If he is writing about a large town with many restaurants this is unlikely to be held to be defamatory. But if he is writing in the local paper of a small town with only two restaurants, such a statement may well be regarded as defamatory.

If a group of people are defamed, each must normally sue as an individual and be able to show that he or she was clearly the subject of the defamatory statement. However, a company or a partnership can sue in its own name.

Defaming the dead

Only a living person, or a company that is still trading, can sue for defamation.

A dead person is regarded as being beyond damage, and as a result his surviving friends or relatives cannot sue on his behalf.

What to do if you are defamed

Never enter into a defamation action lightly. Defamation proceedings can be expensive and you cannot get LEGAL AID.

If you feel very hurt or annoyed about what you believe to be a defamatory statement, consult a solicitor at once. If he agrees that you have a good case, he may suggest that you should seek only a written or printed apology. A newspaper or other publication which agrees to make a suitable apology will normally also pay your legal expenses.

However, if the matter is too serious to be dealt with in that way your solicitor may seek not only an apology but also DAMAGES. Usually such cases are settled out of court between lawyers acting for both sides.

Going to court If the action is not settled out of court it will go to trial, usually before a single judge. If the pursuer proves defamation, he is entitled to damages. These may range from a nominal amount to thousands of pounds. Damages are intended to compensate the person defamed rather than to punish the defamer.

Another possible remedy is to apply to the court for an INTERDICT (court order) prohibiting further publication or circulation of the defamatory material.

Verbal injury

Some statements which are not in law defamatory may still give rise to an action for verbal injury. These include statements which hold a person up to public hatred and contempt, or slander his property or business and cause him loss.

In such cases, however, the pursuer must be able to prove that the statements were false and made with intent to injure, and that damage or injury has resulted.

Criminal libel

Libel can also be a criminal offence in England, but in Scotland this is no longer the case.

DEFECTIVE GOODS

Knowing what a 'defect' is and how to claim for it

A trader who sells a customer goods that are defective, faulty or otherwise unsatisfactory must refund his money in full or pay compensation if:

- The goods do not match the seller's description.
- The goods are not fit for their common, everyday usage.
- The goods do not do the specific job for which they were bought.

The customer does not need to prove that the trader was in any way to blame. All that has to be shown is that the goods had a defect.

When goods are not as described

Goods are defective if they do not match any oral or written description attached to them at the time of the sale.

If, for example, a ring described as 'solid gold' turns out to be gold-plated, the trader has broken a term of his contract with the buyer and is liable to compensate him.

Similarly, if goods are chosen from a sample – for example, wallpaper or carpets – they must conform to the sample in style, colour and texture. *See:* GUARANTEE; SALE OF GOODS; TRADE DESCRIPTIONS

Goods not fit for their purposes

Any article you buy must be reasonably fit for the purpose to which people usually put goods of that kind – what the law calls of 'merchantable quality'. In addition, if you have told the trader you want an article for a specific purpose or job, it must be suitable for that.

Merchantable quality Goods need not be perfect or without blemish to satisfy the 'merchantable quality' condition. The test is whether a reasonable person, knowing their condition and their normal, everyday usage, would still buy them for the price.

But a trader cannot escape his obligations to provide goods of merchantable quality simply by labelling them 'seconds' or 'defective'. They must still be as suitable for their general purpose as it is reasonable to expect 'seconds' to be.

If they turn out to be less than suitable, the trader can escape liability to pay compensation only if he pointed out, at the time of the sale, the particular defect that later caused complaint.

Specific suitability An article can be of merchantable quality but be unfit for the specific purpose you have in mind. A length of material, for example, could be used to make curtains or a skirt or cover an armchair.

If you wanted to use it for upholstery, and it proved unsatisfactory for that though it was suitable for its other purposes, you would have no claim against the trader unless you had told him why you wanted the material.

When a trader need not pay

When you take goods back to a shop on the ground that they are not of merchantable quality, your claim will not succeed if:

- The trader pointed out the specific defect before you bought the article.
- You noticed the defect or examined the article closely enough to have been able to notice it.
- You claim that the goods are unfit for a specific purpose but the trader can show that you ignored his recommendations and bought something he had advised against.

Asking for your money back

Assuming that the trader *has* broken one of the conditions of sale, you must still act quickly if you want to return defective goods and get your money back.

- Do not keep the goods longer than is reasonably necessary to discover the defect.
- Do not tell the trader that the goods

THE BOY WHO LOST AN EYE

A customer can claim compensation from a trader for any damage or injury caused by defective goods.

Nigel Godley, aged 6, bought a plastic toy catapult from Mr Perry's newsagent's shop in 1958.

Three days later the catapult broke as Nigel was firing a stone from it. The elastic snapped back and a sharp piece of plastic hit his left eye. As a result he lost the eye.

Nigel, through his father, sued the newsagent – claiming that the catapult was not fit for its normal purpose and was therefore not of merchantable quality. In evidence, a chemist said the toy was dangerous because of the plastic's fragility and tendency to 'dogtooth' fracture.

DECISION

The court held that, even although the newsagent could not reasonably have known about the catapult's defects, he was liable to pay compensation. Nigel was awarded damages of £2,500.

The newsagent in turn sued the wholesalers who had supplied him, and they sued the company that had imported the toys. Both claims succeeded, so ultimately it was the importers who paid for Nigel's injury.

are satisfactory and that you are keeping them.

- Do not consume any of the goods.

You are entitled to some delay, however, if the goods you bought – tinned food, for example – could not be fully examined until you came to use them.

Claiming compensation

Even if you do not reject the goods promptly and get your money back, you have the right to claim compensation for up to 5 years from the date of purchase – unless you are claiming compensation for personal injury caused by the goods. In that case the limit is normally 3 years.

There are two main types of compensation, both of which are intended to put a claimant in the same financial position as if the goods had not been defective:

- If the defect can be put right by having the goods repaired, the trader must pay any reasonable repair cost. You are not obliged to give the goods back to the retailer or manufacturer. You can have the repair work done anywhere.
- If the goods cannot be repaired, you can ask the trader to pay you compensation in the form of a partial refund. In effect, he pays you the difference between the true value of the defective goods and the amount you originally gave him for them. *See:* MANUFACTURERS' LIABILITY

DEFECTIVE PREMISES

Avoiding injury to others

The law expects the occupier of any premises, private or commercial, to take care to keep them in good repair. Otherwise he may be liable to pay damages to a person who is injured as a result of the defect. *See:* OCCUPIERS' LIABILITY; PROPERTY INSURANCE

DEFERRED SENTENCE

Delaying the punishment of an offender

After a person has been convicted the court need not pass SENTENCE immediately. Instead it may defer, or delay, passing sentence until a later date. There is no restriction on the length of time for which a sentence can be deferred. A sentence can also be deferred more than once for the same conviction.

The court is unlikely to defer sentence if the crime is serious and the offender has a bad criminal record.

Attaching conditions

A condition is often attached to a deferred sentence – for example, the offender must be of good behaviour or pay for the cost of repairing property damaged by him when committing the offence.

Strictly speaking, the court has no power to enforce a condition. However, if it is observed, the court will usually be more lenient with the offender when he returns for sentence. The court, for instance, can order PROBATION when imposing sentence at the end of the period of deferment.

The court may also defer passing sentence if it wishes to see the outcome of a matter which may be relevant to the sentence.

For example, if the offender has a chance of obtaining a job, or if he is an alcoholic or drug addict undergoing or about to undergo treatment, his sentence may be deferred until the result of the job application or treatment is known.

When another offence is committed

When a sentence is deferred, the offender usually cannot be dealt with until the end of the period of deferment. But if the offender is convicted of another offence by any court in Great Britain during this period, the court which deferred sentence can issue a warrant for his ARREST. The offender can then be brought before the court and immediately sentenced for the original offence.

If the court which deferred sentence convicts the offender of another offence during the period of deferment, it can immediately sentence him for both the original offence and the other offence.

A deferred sentence is different from the suspended sentence used in England and Wales, where an actual sentence is pronounced and may be brought into effect later.

DELICT

A loss that can be prevented or compensated

If another person's action causes you loss – or threatens to – the law may give you the right to obtain compensation or to have the action stopped.

For this to be so the person's action must amount to a delict – meaning that it must be wrongful in law. Examples of delicts are injury by a negligent motorist, DEFAMATION by an article in a newspaper or pollution of your garden by sewage from your neighbour's house.

Sometimes a delict may also amount to a breach of CONTRACT. For example, your employer commits a delict if you are injured at work through his failure to take reasonable care to maintain machinery. But he has also broken your contract of employment. However, a delict gives rights irrespective of whether there has been a breach of contract.

If you wish to claim for your loss, you must raise an action for DAMAGES.

If you want the wrongful action stopped you can apply to a court for an INTERDICT. *See:* ANIMAL; CONTRACTOR'S LIABILITY; CONTRIBUTORY NEGLIGENCE; DEFAMATION; FATAL INJURY; MEDICAL NEGLIGENCE; NUISANCE; PERSONAL INJURY

DEMONSTRATION

How to go about organising a protest

Freedom of speech is a basic right, and in principle anyone can hold a demonstration or organise a procession in the streets.

However, demonstrations may give rise to various offences – for example, BREACH OF THE PEACE, obstructing the police, obstructing the highway, using threatening, abusive, or insulting words or behaviour, and mobbing and rioting. It is also against Britain's race discrimination laws for any demonstrator, speaker or banner to incite people to racial hatred. *See:* RACIAL DISCRIMINATION; RIOT

Some parts of the law concerning demonstrations differ from town to town. You should always check with the administration department of your district council before you organise a demonstration.

Restrictions on marching

If you are organising a demonstration and, for example, intend to hold a procession in Aberdeen, you must give 48 hours' notice to the district council. In Edinburgh, you must give seven days' notice. In both cases, failure to do so is an offence.

In other towns you do not have to give notice, but it is advisable to consult the district council as it can forbid processions or order changes of route.

You should also find out whether there are any byelaws to be observed in the streets through which you plan to walk.

When the Civic Government Act, 1982, comes into force (on July 1, 1984), anyone organising a procession anywhere will have to give 7 days' notice to the regional or islands council. The council may forbid the procession or impose conditions, though there will be an appeal to the sheriff. Holding a procession without giving notice will be punishable by up to a £1,000 fine or 3 months' imprisonment. Taking part in one after being told to stop doing so by a policeman will be punishable by a fine of up to £400.

The local police sometimes have the right to regulate your route, so you should consult them first.

The local police chief can impose whatever restrictions he feels necessary if he believes that the march could give rise to public disorder. He may, for example, forbid the use of flags, banners and emblems. No particular march can be forbidden by the police, but the Secretary of State for Scotland can give the regional council permission to prohibit certain types of procession in their area for up to 3 months.

Anyone who disobeys lawful police instructions about a demonstration can be fined £100 and imprisoned for 3 months.

Restrictions on meetings

If your demonstration is to include a PUBLIC MEETING, you should ask the district council whether there are any local Acts or byelaws that have to be observed.

Many places open to the public – parks and public squares, for example – are owned and controlled by the local authority and in many of them meetings are banned altogether or at certain times.

It is advisable to tell the police when and where your meeting is to be held, even if you are not legally obliged to do so – especially if you expect any opposition or a large attendance.

The police have very limited powers to prohibit a meeting in advance. The fact that it may amount to TRESPASS or cause obstruction is not sufficient reason. The police or local authority may refuse permission for the meeting to take place only if their permission is required under a byelaw or if the authority owns the site. The police have wider powers covering processions.

Who is responsible for what happens

An organiser of a demonstration cannot be punished for any offence that happens during the demonstration, unless he was personally responsible for the incident. Anyone taking part in the demonstration must be careful to obey lawful police instructions. Anyone who causes a breach of the peace by using threatening, abusive or insulting words or behaviour is liable to be arrested.

Using a loudspeaker

The law about loudspeakers varies from town to town. In some towns, it is an offence to use loudspeakers without getting permission. You should ask your district council about this.

When property is damaged

A property owner may be able to claim compensation from the regional council if his premises are damaged during a demonstration. He will have to show that the damage was done by an unlawful riotous or tumultuous assembly, or by members of that assembly.

However a businessman who for safety's sake decides to close premises on a demonstration route cannot claim compensation for any resulting loss of trade.

Most private house insurances specifically exclude compensation for damage caused by mobbing and rioting.

A person who is injured during or because of a demonstration may be able to obtain CRIMINAL INJURIES COMPENSATION.

Putting up posters

Planning permission from the local authority is not required for putting up posters announcing a local, non-commercial event of a religious, educational, cultural, political, social or recreational character. However the posters must be not more than 6 ft square and must not obstruct the highway.

DENTIST

Your rights to dental treatment

A dentist, whether working privately or within the National Health Service, is under no obligation to accept a new patient.

If he has begun a course of treatment, he must finish it. Otherwise he is not obliged to continue treating any particular patient.

How to find a dentist

Not all dentists accept National Health patients. Those who do can be found on a list at any main post office or at the offices of the health board for your area, the address of which is on your medical card. *See:* DOCTOR AND PATIENT

Once you find a dentist, establish at the outset whether he is taking you as a private or health service patient. Legally, it is his choice as well as yours.

If he accepts you as a health service patient, he will ask you to sign a form stating that you want treatment under the health service. That enables him to claim payment from the state for the treatment he gives you.

A patient's right to treatment

Under the Health Service, most dentists take the patient's wishes into account, but you have no right to demand any specific treatment. The dentist has the final say, although you are entitled to refuse any treatment.

With the most common types of work – X-rays, fillings, extractions, dentures and one or perhaps two crowns – the dentist can proceed at once.

In the case of more expensive forms of treatment – a gold filling, inlay or

WHEN YOU HAVE TO PAY FOR NHS DENTAL TREATMENT

The most a NHS patient need pay for any necessary treatment is £110, if it includes dentures, bridges, crowns, inlays or gold fillings. If not, the maximum is £14.50. Typical charges are:

- Fillings and extractions, including local anaesthetic, up to £14.50.
- Dentures and bridges – from £24 for a synthetic resin denture or bridge with one tooth, to £92 for more than one denture or bridge in metal or porcelain.

There is no charge for an initial check-up, for stopping bleeding, for repairs to dentures, for the dentist's travelling time and expenses if he has to come to your home, for treatment in a dental hospital, or for opening the surgery in an emergency.

Those who need not pay

- People who are receiving some measure of SUPPLEMENTARY BENEFIT or FAMILY INCOME SUPPLEMENT.
- People getting free prescriptions or free milk and vitamins because of low income.
- Children under 16.
- Young people aged under 18 who are in full-time education; those who are not must pay for dentures and bridges.
- Students under 19.
- Expectant mother or a woman who has had a baby in the last 12 months.

Other exemptions and refunds

Anyone with a net income just above supplementary benefit level may claim exemption or reclaim the charges he has paid. Others with a slightly higher income may pay a reduced charge or reclaim part of the charges.

Claim forms can be obtained from the dentist or social security office.

crown, or a more costly denture or bridge – he must first have the approval of the Scottish Dental Estimates Board and you will have to pay for the extra work up to a maximum of £110.

If the Estimates Board refuses to approve more expensive work, or sets a price which you or the dentist regard as excessive, write to the Board at Trinity Park House, South Trinity Road, Edinburgh, asking for the decision to be reconsidered, or to the Secretary of State, or to your MP. (See the Scottish Home and Health Department leaflet, *Your Guide to Dental Treatment.)*

How to complain

If you think a dentist has been guilty of unprofessional behaviour – for example, misusing drugs, working while drunk or making sexual advances to a patient – write to the General Dental Council at 37 Wimpole Street, London W.1.

If your complaint is about negligence – for example, if the dentist pulled out the wrong tooth – you can either complain to the Dental Council in a serious case or sue for DAMAGES or both.

If you are treated in a dental hospital, you may be able to sue the hospital as well as the dentist.

If you are a health service patient and think that the dentist's general service has been poor – for example, that conditions were unhygienic, treatment inadequate, or the dentist was rude, write to your local health board. Give them full details of your name, your dentist and the date when the treatment was carried out and ask them to investigate.

Dentists are entitled to charge patients for appointments that they do not keep.

When dentures do not fit You have the right to reject NHS false teeth that do not fit. If a denture causes you any prolonged, unreasonable pain or injury, you may also sue the dentist for negligence.

Under private treatment only, the dentist has a contract with you that is covered by the SALE OF GOODS Act, and you can claim against him in the same way as anyone who buys DEFECTIVE GOODS.

DEPENDANT

When extra social security benefits can be claimed for a family

Anyone who is eligible for a social security benefit may receive more money if he has dependants.

There are three categories of dependants: children, wives and husbands, and child carers. A fourth – certain adult relatives being maintained by a claimant – was abolished in November, 1983.

Children

A person entitled to CHILD'S SPECIAL ALLOWANCE, DISABLEMENT BENEFIT (if accompanied by unemployability supplement), INVALID CARE ALLOWANCE, INVALIDITY PENSION, MATERNITY allowance, non-contributory INVALIDITY PENSION, RETIREMENT PENSION, SICKNESS BENEFIT, UNEMPLOYMENT BENEFIT, WIDOW'S ALLOWANCE, or WIDOWED MOTHER'S ALLOWANCE, can claim extra for any child or children for whom CHILD BENEFIT is payable.

If the father of an illegitimate child is living with the mother of that child, or if he can prove that he has been paying at least half the cost of maintaining the child during the preceding 6 months, he is entitled to extra social security benefit, even if child benefit is not payable.

Anyone who has a child who is not living with him but for whom child benefit is being paid, qualifies for an increase only if his contribution to the child's support equals or exceeds the increase and child benefit combined.

For example, to qualify for a 15p increase in unemployment benefit for a dependent child, he must, as child benefit is £6.50 a week, have been regularly contributing at least £6.65 a week to the child's support.

A married woman who is living with her husband, and receiving one of the above benefits, can claim an increase for dependent children. However she can only do so if she is also entitled to an increase for her husband.

She can claim an increase for her husband provided that he does not earn more than the amount of that increase.

From November, 1984, she will be able to claim an increase for her children regardless of whether she is entitled to an increase for her husband.

The 15p child dependency increase at present (1983–4) paid with unemployment benefit, sickness benefit and maternity benefit is to be abolished from November, 1984.

Overlapping benefits When a husband and wife who are living together are both receiving a benefit, and can both claim an increase for dependent children, the wife's claim has priority.

Wife or husband

Any man entitled to DISABLEMENT

BENEFIT (if accompanied by unemployability supplement), INVALID CARE ALLOWANCE, INVALIDITY PENSION, non-contributory INVALIDITY PENSION, RETIREMENT PENSION, UNEMPLOYMENT BENEFIT or SICKNESS BENEFIT can claim extra benefit for a wife provided that she is living with him or, if not, that the amount he pays for her support equals or exceeds the increase in benefit. A husband cannot claim extra for a wife if she is earning more than the increase.

A woman receiving one of the above benefits (except retirement pension), or maternity allowance, can claim an increase for her husband if he is not earning more than the amount of the increase.

Child carers

A claiment of either sex can get an increase for a woman if she is over 18; looks after a child or children for whom the claimant is entitled to draw child benefit; lives with the claimant, or costs the claimant at least the amount of that increase in wages or maintenance; and is not earning more than that increase from another job. Cohabitees, female relatives and housekeepers, for example, can be claimed for.

From November 1984, the rule will be extended to cover men (including cohabitees) who are caring for a claimant's children.

DEPORTATION

When someone is ordered to leave the country

No one who is a British Citizen can be deported to another country (though he may be extradited to face trial for crimes committed abroad).

If a person who has been deported returns without permission he can be fined £500 and imprisoned for 6 months.

Deportation can be ordered by the Home Secretary if:

1. Someone breaks the IMMIGRATION rules.

2. Someone aged 17 or over is convicted of an offence punishable by imprisonment and the court recommends deportation. (The Home Secretary has to consider all the circumstances, particularly the person's age and domestic circumstances; the strength of his links with and length of his residence in the UK; his character, conduct and employment record; the nature of the offence of which he has been convicted and any compassionate circumstances.)

3. The Home Secretary thinks it conducive to the public good.

4. Someone in the person's immediate family is to be, or has been, deported. For example, if a man is being deported, his wife and children under 18 will also be told to leave; if the person being deported is a woman, only her children under 18 are also affected.

A wife who is no longer living with her husband is not treated as a member of his family.

Before deporting a dependent relative, the Home Secretary takes into account whether a wife can support herself and her children in Britain even if her husband is deported; and whether she has ties with Britain quite separately from her husband.

If children are involved, the Home Secretary considers what effect deportation might have on their education and whether realistic plans have been made to support them.

A child approaching 18, or one who has left the family home and is financially independent, is not normally deported. If deported in this way, he or she can apply for readmission when 18.

A deportation order cannot be made against a family member if more than 8 weeks have passed since his relative was deported from the country.

5. The Secretary of State for Scotland considers it to be in the interests of an ALIEN who is a mental patient in a Scottish hospital. Proper arrangements must be made for his travel and his care and treatment on arrival.

When an order will not be made

A deportation order is not enforced if the only country to which a person can be deported is one to which he would be unwilling to go because of a well-founded fear of being persecuted for reasons of race, religion, nationality or political opinion.

No Commonwealth citizen or IRISH CITIZEN is liable to deportation if he has been ordinarily resident in Britain since January 1, 1973 and for at least 5 years since then. That rule does not apply if he has become a Commonwealth citizen only since then.

His immunity from deportation is not affected by his having left the country during this period so long as he did so for some temporary reason, such as holidays, business or family illness. But a person who obtained readmission to the UK by giving the immigration officer false information about his status in the UK would run the risk of being regarded as an illegal entrant.

There is one pitfall. If a decision to deport is made with or without the person's knowledge within the 5 year period, he has no immunity even though he has since completed the 5 years' residence.

No alien – except a citizen of Pakistan who is regarded by the Home Office as a Commonwealth citizen for these purposes – is immune from deportation, no matter how long he lives in the UK.

In practice, the Home Office gives indefinite leave to remain in the UK to those immune from deportation, but that is not a legal right.

Appealing against deportation

If the Home Office serves a notice of intention to deport, the individual usually has the right of appeal to an adjudicator on the question of whether it is right to deport him. He also has the right to object to being deported to the country that the Home Office has specified.

If the deportation is recommended by a court, he can appeal to a higher court against the recommendation. He can also appeal against the choice of country to which he is to be sent.

Anyone threatened with deportation should contact the Joint Council for the Welfare of Immigrants or the United Kingdom Immigrants Advisory Service. *See:* IMMIGRATION

If all else fails, he can ask his MP to intervene on his behalf, and put forward any claims he might have to be allowed to remain in Britain – such as being married to a woman settled here.

Arrest and detention

The Home Office can authorise the arrest and detention in prison of anyone on whom notice of intention to deport has been served. After a deportation order has been made, moreover, the person named may be detained until he

WHEN YOU HAVE NO CHOICE

Someone on whom a deportation order has been served can be kept in prison or police custody until he leaves the country if there is a risk he may disappear.

eventually leaves Britain, or is allowed to stay – a process that may take several months. While an immigration appeal is pending, there is the right to apply for bail to an appeals adjudicator.

But a recommendation by a court that someone be deported does not automatically mean that he is kept in prison until the Home Office decides. Judges are expected to grant bail unless there is a serious risk that the person to be deported will disappear.

Where can a deportee be sent?

The Home Secretary must direct that the person being deported should be sent either to a country of which he is a citizen, or one to which there is reason to believe he would be admitted. Someone who wishes to go to another country will have to show good reason and will also have to prove that he will be admitted to the country of his choice.

The cost of the deportation is paid by the Government.

The status of diplomats

Foreign diplomats have a special status under our immigration laws, and can come and go freely so long as they are members of a diplomatic mission. This applies also to any member of the diplomat's family who forms part of his household. Domestic servants of such households are given permission to remain by the Home Office without the necessity to apply for work permits, but only for 12 months at a time; they will be given further extensions of stay only if they remain members in the diplomat's employment.

DEPOSIT AND PART-PAYMENT

Whose is the money when there is no sale?

If you put money down on goods – for example when they are temporarily out of stock – make clear to the shop or trader that you are making a part payment, not paying a deposit. To be sure of your rights, ask the trader to mark the receipt 'cash returnable if no sale'.

When it is clearly understood by both sides that the money was intended as a part-payment, and the buyer then pulls out of a sale, he may be able to have his money refunded in full, if it is acceptable to the trader for him to pull out.

When money is paid as a deposit, it is immediately the property of the shop or trader. If the buyer later withdraws from the sale, he is not entitled to have the deposit refunded, although the trader may be prepared to give a refund for goodwill.

If the sale goes through, however, the deposit counts as a part-payment which is deducted from the total price to be paid. The customer is not entitled to interest on money held as part-payment unless it is agreed that he should be.

If goods have been specially made for you, and you reject them without good reason, the trader is entitled to sue you for breach of contract. You in turn are entitled to sue to get your money back if you reject the goods because they were not properly made.

A deposit paid under a CREDIT AGREEMENT must be returned in full if you cancel or withdraw from the contract within the time allowed.

DESERTION

A husband and wife have a duty to share their lives

A partner who, without consent or good reason, withdraws from the sharing arrangements of a marriage – with the intention of being apart permanently – is in desertion.

That does not necessarily mean leaving a particular place. It would probably be desertion for one partner to insist on living in a separate part of the same house and refusing to eat meals together or to share household tasks.

When the 'deserter' stays

A husband or wife who causes the other to leave unwillingly – by force, say, or by order – or prevents the other from entering the home can be held to have deserted.

Causing a spouse to live apart is not desertion if there is justification for it – such as a reasonable belief that the spouse is committing adultery.

An unwilling departure caused, for example, by imprisonment, illness or war is not desertion. Nor is a SEPARATION to which both parties agree. If both sign a separation agreement, neither is guilty of deserting the other while it is in force.

Desertion and divorce

Desertion for at least 2 years is a ground for DIVORCE. The pursuer must prove that the parties have separated, and that his or her partner intended to end their living together.

The defender can oppose the action by showing that the pursuer consented, or behaved in such a way that the defender was justified in leaving.

If the defender makes a genuine and reasonable offer to return, and this is refused, the defender's desertion comes to an end. It is then the pursuer who is in desertion after the refusal.

Separation for 2 years must be strictly proved. But to encourage reconciliation attempts, a couple may resume their life together during that time for periods totalling not more than 6 months.

Those periods are added to the 2 years apart. So if a couple live together for a total of 3 months, a divorce action cannot be raised until 27 months after the original desertion.

Application to a sheriff court

Desertion is one of the grounds for applying for a decree of adherence – seeking the defender's return – and ALIMENT, separation and aliment or interim aliment. (Actions of adherence will be abolished during 1984.)

Decrees of adherence and aliment

and interim aliment can be granted even if desertion has not continued for 2 years: the desertion need only exist when the action is raised and at the time of the hearing.

DETENTION

Police powers to restrict liberty

For many years the judges said that in Scotland the police could not hold a person for questioning against his will merely for the purpose of helping with their enquiries.

The police could only restrict liberty by making an ARREST – and a person under arrest had to be charged with committing a crime and brought before a court without delay. A person who was not arrested was free to go about his business.

This rule, however, is now subject to a number of important exceptions created by Parliament:

1. When a policeman has reason to suspect that an offence has been committed, he can detain a person without arresting him. There must be some circumstance which is clearly suspicious; but the policeman need not have any proof, and the offence in question may have been committed a long time before the detention.

Detention can occur in the following circumstances:

- If the policeman thinks that you are guilty of the suspected offence, then he is entitled to know your name and address. You are obliged to remain for a reasonable time while he checks this information. He may also ask you to explain the suspicious circumstances, but you need not reply.
- The policeman can detain you for questioning on reasonable suspicion that you have committed an offence punishable by imprisonment. This covers not only the most serious crimes but also some trivial ones like BREACH OF THE PEACE.

Even if you think there are no grounds for detaining you, you should not resist. You can complain when you arrive at the police station.

The police have the right to detain you for up to 6 hours. They must tell you of what you are suspected. They must usually tell a solicitor and any friend or member of your family that you name that you are being detained, and where. However, you may not talk to these people.

After 6 hours you are free to leave – unless you have been arrested. You cannot be detained twice on suspicion of the same offence.

You can be questioned while you are being detained, but you do not have to say anything. You can also be searched and your fingerprints can be taken.

If you are illegally detained and you protest, you can sue for WRONGFUL ARREST.

You may also be able to sue for ASSAULT if the police use force to overcome any resistance on your part.

2. The police may have the power to SEARCH someone without arresting him and can detain him while they do so. For example, the police can detain and search someone who is reasonably suspected of possessing controlled DRUGS.

3. Following a series of IRA bomb attacks, the police now have power to arrest without warrant someone whom they reasonably suspect of being involved in the use of violence for political purposes. They can then detain such a person for 48 hours without charging him. *See:* TERRORISM

If they want to detain him any longer, they may ask the Secretary of State for Scotland's permission to do so. The Secretary of State can allow detention for up to five more days.

A person arrested and detained in this way has the right to have a solicitor informed about the arrest and the place where he is being held. He also has the right to have another person reasonably named by him informed.

DEVELOPMENT LAND TAX

Rates of taxation on the sale of developed land

If you sell land or buildings the value of which has increased as a result of property development potential, you may have to pay Development Land Tax.

It is charged in addition to any CAPITAL GAINS TAX and INCOME TAX or CORPORATION TAX for which the seller may be liable, but credit is given against any or all of those taxes.

The tax is levied as follows:

- The first £75,000 of development value in a financial year exempt (though one or more of the other taxes will still have to be paid).
- Profit above £75,000 taxed at 60%.

The tax is assessed by the Development Land Tax Office, a branch of the Inland Revenue.

There are several exemptions from the tax. If the developed house was the main home of the seller, or his wife, or was occupied rent-free by a dependent relative, it will be free of the tax provided that the size of the house and garden combined is not more than 1 acre.

Houses with larger gardens may also be exempt if the garden is 'in character with the house'.

DIMINISHED RESPONSIBILITY

Defence to a charge of murder

A person charged with murder may be able to avoid being convicted by pleading a mental condition described as 'diminished responsibility'.

If the plea succeeds – and medical evidence will be very important – he will be acquitted of murder. However, he will then be convicted of the lesser crime of CULPABLE HOMICIDE.

DIPLOMAT

The immunities granted to official representatives

An embassy in Britain is rather like a small part of the country it represents being deposited on British soil.

Only its own staff are automatically entitled to enter it. It cannot be searched by the police. Its post and telephone calls are protected by international law from interception, and its diplomats and other staff stand almost entirely outside British law.

The same privileges apply to consuls and to representatives of international organisations.

Diplomatic immunity

A foreign diplomat in Britain cannot be arrested or prosecuted for any criminal offence. His person and property, including his car, cannot be searched; and he or his chauffeur can disregard parking and other regulations. If the car is not showing CD plates to indicate a diplomatic car, a diplomatic pass may have to be shown to prove immunity if questioned.

A civil action can be brought against him only if it concerns land he owns privately in Britain, his entitlement or assumed entitlement to a dead person's estate, or professional or commercial activities outside his official functions. However, a diplomat still remains subject to his own country's law, and a claimant might be able to take civil action against him in the courts of that country. *See:* INTERNATIONAL PRIVATE LAW

Diplomatic privileges

Apart from such cases, a diplomat does not have to give evidence in court and he is exempt from jury service. He does not have to pay British income tax, customs duties or national insurance contributions.

Members of a foreign diplomat's family have the same privileges if they are not British Citizens. So do administrative and technical staff of an embassy, except that their immunity from civil actions only extends to acts done in the course of their duties. If British Citizens are members of the administrative and technical staff they are normally also immune.

The foreign domestic staff at an embassy have immunity for acts done in the course of their duties. In addition, they do not have to pay tax or national insurance contributions.

A diplomat does not have a free hand to act as he wants, however. If he seriously abuses his privileged status, the Government can demand his removal from Britain. If he is suspected of being a spy, he is declared persona non grata, and made to leave the country, perhaps within 24 hours. No reason need be given for the suspicion.

A diplomat's privileged status can be waived by his ambassador or head of mission.

International officials

Some officials of certain international organisations also have similar privileges and immunities while carrying out their duties. These include the Secretary-General of the United Nations and judges of the European Court of Justice.

Consuls and honorary consuls

Many of the privileges granted to diplomats extend also to consuls and honorary consuls, but in addition to the civil actions that can be brought against diplomats, consuls may also be sued in connection with traffic accidents or contracts signed by them otherwise than on behalf of their state.

Consuls can also be prosecuted for criminal offences and they can be called to give evidence in court. If they refuse to attend, they cannot be penalised, however.

British diplomats abroad

British diplomats abroad have the same privileges and immunities as foreign diplomats in Britain. If Britain went to war with the foreign country, the diplomat would be withdrawn immediately.

If there were any delay, the country would protect the diplomat. *See also:* FOREIGN EMBASSY

PROTECTION OF DIPLOMATS

It is a serious offence to interfere with a diplomat, whether by attacking him or by taking him hostage. Under the Internationally Protected Persons Act 1978, British courts can deal with not only offences occurring in Britain, but also offences against diplomats anywhere in the world.

It is the duty of the host state to protect all foreign diplomats against such attacks. In 1980 the International Court of Justice and the United Nations Security Council ruled that Iran was in breach of international law in allowing the American Embassy in Teheran to be seized and the diplomats to be taken and kept hostage.

A host state cannot enter an embassy without the permission of the foreign state. For example, when the British authorities wanted to send the Special Air Service into the Iranian Embassy in London to seize the hostage-takers and free their hostages, the permission of the Iranian government had to be obtained.

THE CLERK WHO TRIED TO GIVE UP HIS IMMUNITY

Diplomatic immunity does not belong to an individual and a person employed as a diplomat in a foreign country has no power to waive it.

Mr Madan was a clerk on the staff of the Indian High Commission in London when police arrested him for trying to get a railway ticket by false pretences.

He told police that he waived the diplomatic immunity that went with his job, and was put on trial.

At the trial his lawyer tried to stop the case, saying that Madan's diplomatic immunity still prevailed.

The court overruled the argument and convicted Mr Madan. He appealed as a result.

DECISION

The English Appeal Court ruled that diplomatic immunity belongs to a country, not an individual. Madan had no power to waive it and was therefore immune at the time of his trial. The conviction was quashed.

DIRECTOR

Employers who may also be employees of a company

Both private and public companies must have at least one director. *See:* BUSINESS, Starting a

There can be two types of director in a company: full-time and part-time. A part-time director receives a relatively small fee and is expected merely to appear at occasional board meetings.

A full-time director will almost always be an employee, and be entitled to the same protection as other employees against unfair dismissal and redundancy.

All directors have legal responsibilities to their companies. They must perform their duties with reasonable care, exercising the degree of skill which can be expected of a person with their knowledge and experience.

Directors must act honestly in the

best interests of the company at all times. They must also have regard to the interests of the company's employees.

If the company fails If a company becomes insolvent and ceases to trade, an employee-director becomes entitled to a redundancy payment which is met entirely by the State. *See:* REDUNDANCY

If a director is dismissed

An employee-director who is dismissed is entitled to seek compensation through an industrial tribunal. *See:* UNFAIR DISMISSAL

However, the sum he can claim is subject to a maximum and it may be better to sue through the courts for WRONGFUL DISMISSAL instead.

National insurance contributions

Employee-directors have to pay Class 1 NATIONAL INSURANCE CONTRIBUTIONS. The percentage contribution depends on whether, as a member of his company's occupational pension scheme, a director is contracted out of the additional provisions of the state scheme.

Income tax

A director who receives any FRINGE BENEFIT is taxed on what it costs his company to provide the benefit unless he is a full-time employee owning no more than 5 per cent of the share capital and earning less than the relevant amount. Those few directors who fall within the exception are taxed on the amount of money they could get by selling the benefit at its second-hand value.

DISABILITY PENSION

Regular payment awarded to disabled ex-servicemen and women

Anyone who is disabled or is unable to take normal work because of injury or damage suffered during military service is entitled to a special disability pension. *See also:* WAR PENSIONS

How to make a claim

If you think you are entitled to a pension, ask for form MPB 214 at your local social work department, or obtain one from your services welfare officer, complete and send it to the Department of Health and Social Security.

If your application is rejected, you must be told why, and you have the right to appeal to a pension appeal tribunal. But you must do so within 12 months.

The local office of the Department of Health and Social Security will tell you how to make an appeal and where to find the tribunal.

If you are awarded a pension but disagree with the amount awarded you can ask the tribunal to review the award – within 12 months. If your condition worsens, you may apply for a review of the amount awarded.

When contributory negligence is alleged

If the Secretary of State agrees that the disability was caused by the applicant's military service, but that the serviceman was wholly or partly responsible for his injury because of negligence or misconduct, an award can be refused or reduced. The applicant can appeal to the pensions appeal tribunal within 12 months.

Appealing to a tribunal

A pensions appeal tribunal must have at least three members, all of them appointed by the Lord President of the Court of Session. At least one member must be of the same sex, status and rank and have served in the same arm of the Services as the claimant.

If the appeal is against refusal of a pension, the tribunal must include an advocate or solicitor and a doctor. If the appeal is against the assessment of disability, the tribunal must include two doctors.

When an appeal is heard, the tribunal may pay the applicant's travelling expenses and any expenses incurred by him in obtaining medical reports and certificates and the attendance of expert medical witnesses.

The decision of a tribunal is usually final, but if the appellant considers that a decision as to entitlement is wrong on a point of law, he may ask the tribunal for leave to appeal to the Court of Session.

If such an appeal is heard, the tribunal may pay any costs incurred by the appellant – for example, if he cannot afford to pay.

The right to a pension

Once a pension has been awarded to an ex-serviceman, payment continues as of right unless the Secretary of State varies or revokes the award. The Secretary is allowed, by law, to do this – under powers granted to him by Royal Warrant or Order in Council. If that happens, the pensioner can appeal to the pensions appeal tribunal.

DISABLEMENT

Help available to disabled and chronically sick people

A disabled person is someone who, because of physical or mental impairment, or loss of limbs, experiences difficulty in functioning properly in a society that is largely designed to suit the needs of fit people.

A disabled person does not have to be formally registered to qualify for the welfare services that are available. If he is permanently or severely disabled he should approach the social work department of his regional or islands council to find out what help he can get.

When you contact your council, the social work department will arrange for a social worker or occupational therapist to visit you. Your disability and needs will be assessed and you can be put in touch with any voluntary organisation concerned with your particular handicap.

Many of the services for the disabled – disability benefits, artificial limbs, home nursing, for example – come from central government or the National Health Service and depend upon the assessment of a family doctor or hospital doctor and not a local government social worker.

The Chronically Sick and Disabled Persons Act 1970 says that every Scottish local authority, when considering the housing needs of its area, must take into account the special needs of chronically sick and disabled people. It also requires both private developers and local authorities to provide access, parking facilities and sanitary conveniences for disabled people in buildings and institutions to which the public have access.

Getting advice Most disabled people qualify for more than one benefit or service, so you should check your rights carefully. Your local social security office, social work department, hospital social worker or Citizens Advice Bureau will help you to do this.

Leaflets HB 1 *Help for handicapped people in Scotland* and HB 2 *Aids for the disabled* – obtainable from your local social security office or DHSS Leaflets Unit, PO Box 21, Stanmore, Middlesex HA7 1AY – will also help you to know what is available.

The Scottish Council on Disability has an Information Service for the Disabled at Princes House, 5 Shandwick Place, Edinburgh (tel. 031-229-8632).

Services available through the National Health Service

Your health needs – such as treatment by a GP, hospital doctor, chiropodist or district nurse – or any necessary health aids and appliances such as hearing aids, incontinence pads or artificial limbs, are generally covered by the National Health Service.

Your doctor If you need advice about your general health, consult your family doctor. He will see that you get treatment and will also tell you what services are available.

Hospital treatment If your doctor thinks that you need hospital treatment he will refer you to a hospital or ask the specialist to visit you at home. You are not entitled to demand hospital treatment or the services of a specialist. *See:* HOSPITAL

Prescriptions If you need continuous drug treatment or other items on prescription, such as bandages, or if you are on a low income, you may be able to get your prescriptions free or at a reduced rate. For information about such concessions get leaflet P 11 (low-income or medical exemption) or EC 95 (season ticket) from a social security office.

Health visitor If you are suffering from a long illness, or if you have a handicapped child, a health visitor can visit you regularly, to advise on health matters and nursing aids and equipment.

District nurse Your family doctor can arrange for you to be visited by a district nurse. The nurse will also give you any injections you need, help you with bathing, bandages and other nursing requirements and arrange for you to get special nursing aids – such as a bedpan or lifting hoist.

Chiropody treatment If you have foot trouble, ask your doctor or district nurse to arrange for you to see a chiropodist – who can visit you at home, if necessary. If you cannot afford a chiropodist's fee, or if you are a pensioner, you can be treated free of charge.

Artificial limbs and appliances Some surgical appliances are supplied, maintained and replaced free of charge through the National Health Service on the recommendation of a hospital consultant. The hospital will make arrangements for you to visit the nearest limb fitting or artificial limb and appliance centre where you can be fitted with a limb or appliance and taught how to cope with it.

Other needs The National Health Service can supply most of your medical needs – sometimes free – so if you need a hearing aid, wig, artificial eye or anything else to help you to lead a fuller life, ask your doctor to refer you to a specialist.

A wig is supplied free usually only if the patient is prematurely bald or has extensive head scars – caused, for example, by an accident or illness.

Social work services

Every regional or islands council has a social work department that provides a wide range of non-medical services – in and outside the home – for the disabled. These services may vary from area to area so contact your local office to see what is available to you.

Home help If you cannot cope with your housework, washing or shopping, ask your GP or hospital to contact your regional or islands council. Some authorities provide such help free. Others make a charge according to the disabled person's income.

Hot meals Housebound people can get meals from a meals on wheels service – run either by the council itself or by a voluntary organisation such as the Women's Royal Voluntary Service.

People who can get about can go to a day centre or lunch club if there is one in their area. Transport may be provided if necessary. A small charge is made for all meals.

Telephone Some local authorities pay for the installation of a telephone for handicapped people or for the parents of handicapped children. They may also pay the telephone rent – but you must pay for the calls yourself.

Cheap travel Bus passes are issued by some councils entitling registered disabled people to cheap or free travel. British Rail offers a number of fare concessions, including a Railcard that allows seriously disabled people to travel at half-fare.

Parking badge If you are blind (or have very bad sight), or have a permanent and substantial disability that causes very considerable difficulty in walking, or receive MOBILITY ALLOWANCE, and you use a car – either as driver or passenger – you are entitled to an orange badge which allows you to ignore certain parking rules. You can use a meter without a time limit and without paying; park on a yellow 'no parking' line, provided you do not obstruct traffic; or park without a time limit in a street that has one. The badge is valid for 3 years and costs £2.

Holidays Some local authorities may provide holidays for mobile disabled people and people in wheelchairs who do not need nursing care. The holidays are usually provided at holiday centres run by voluntary organisations and you may have to pay a charge for such a holiday. Transport to and from the holiday centre is provided. Day outings, particularly for people living alone, may also be provided.

Home aids Councils lend aids – such as raised lavatory seats, hoists, alarm signals, geriatric chairs and commodes. They also carry out adaptations to the home – for example, fitting handrails or ramps. Minor alterations are usually provided free.

If major adaptations are required, the disabled person may be asked to meet part of the cost.

Other services In some areas, voluntary agencies may assist with adapted radio and T.V. sets. Some voluntary organisations may also provide a home library service. Some local authorities have free laundry services, usually run in co-operation with health boards. Other authorities run day centres to provide social contact and recreation. Transport to and from the centres is usually provided. Most areas have visiting occupational therapists for

ADAPTING A HOME TO HELP A DISABLED PERSON

How to find out about the hundreds of aids and appliances that are available

Getting out of bed
Getting in and out of bed can be made easier by using an electrically operated hoist which slides along tracking fixed to a gantry or to the ceiling. Alternatively, a 3-position bed enables an invalid or disabled person to sit in a chair without the problem of getting out of bed

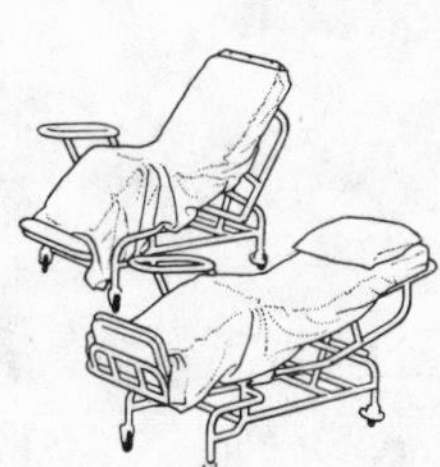

Raised lavatory seat
A removable seat, held in the desired position by plastic pads, raises the lavatory to a comfortable height. The surround which is portable enables the handicapped person to help pull himself on and off the seat

Taking a bath in private
An automatic chair lift is one of the many ways in which a handicapped person can lift himself in and out of a bath

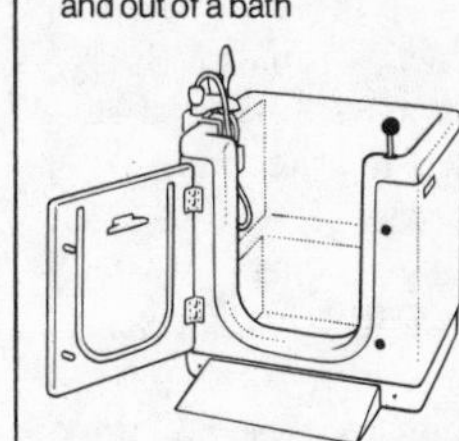

In a portable bath closet the disabled person can take a bath in a sitting position in waist-high water

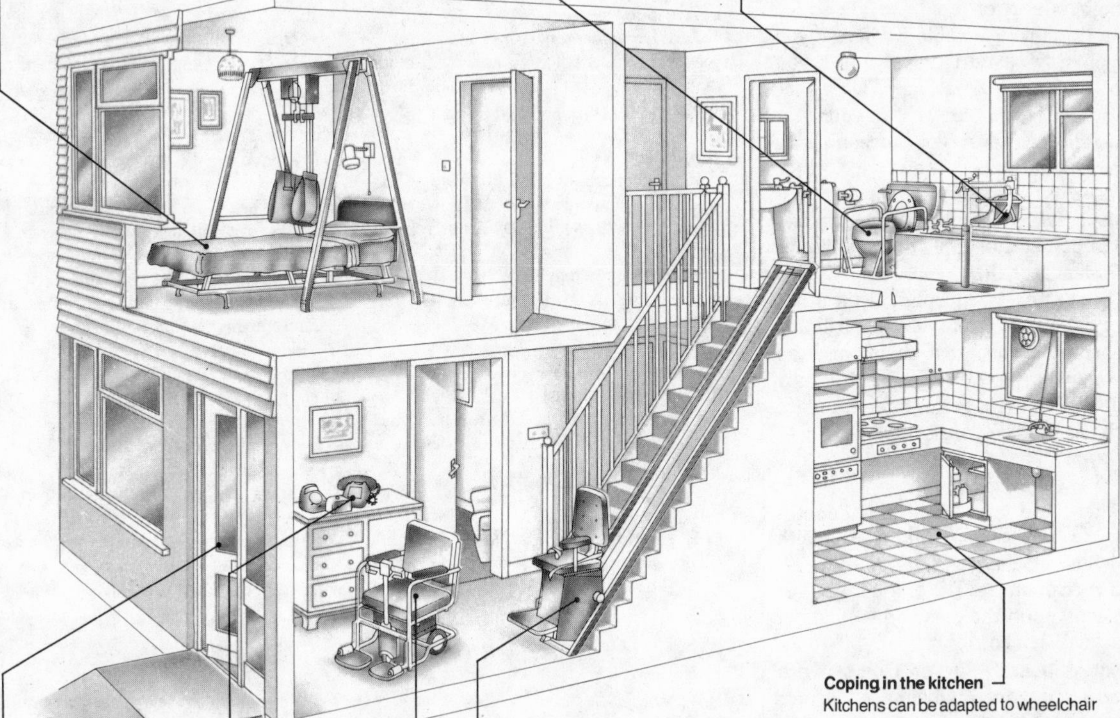

Coping in the kitchen
Kitchens can be adapted to wheelchair users with the help of built-in and low-level equipment

Making a ramp
A wheelchair can be manoeuvred easily into a house with the aid of a wooden ramp

Indoor wheelchair
A battery-operated indoor wheelchair allows the user to move freely around the house

Travelling upstairs
A chairlift, on which the handicapped person can sit or stand, can be fitted to an existing staircase

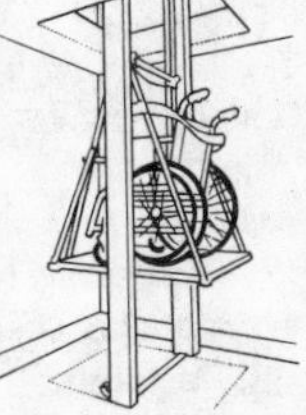

An electrically operated hoist carries a handicapped person in a wheelchair through a trap door to a higher or lower floor level without him leaving the chair

Widening a doorway
If an existing doorway is too narrow for a wheelchair to pass through, it can be widened and a wider door fitted

Adapted telephone
The Post Office has a large range of specially designed equipment for adapting a telephone to suit any type of disability

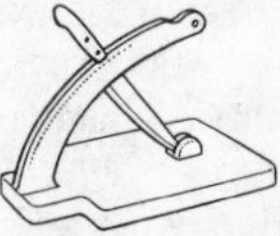

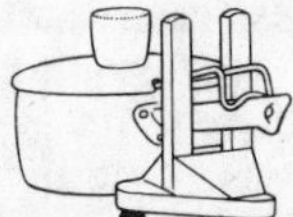

Gadgets, such as the one on the left with which to guide a knife, and the saucepan clamp on the right, help those with limited use of their hands

The long-handled helping hand grips items which would normally be beyond reach of the handicapped person

disabled people who cannot get to a day centre.

Local housing help

Local councils have several types of housing specially designed for disabled people. They also have IMPROVEMENT GRANT schemes to help those who need to adapt their own homes. Such schemes cover only part of the cost. There is no means test for the grant.

Rent and rate rebates If you are a disabled person and your income is limited, you may be entitled to a rent rebate or allowance, and a rate rebate. People who are handicapped can claim a higher level of rebate or allowance than those who are able-bodied. If you are on SUPPLEMENTARY BENEFIT, you can claim a rebate or allowance amounting to the full cost of your rent and rates. Apply to your local housing department. *See:* RATES; RENT ALLOWANCE; RENT REBATE

Rate relief Regardless of means, disabled people can apply to the Director of Finance of their regional or islands authority for a reduction in the rates they have to pay, provided their home has some facility that their handicap makes necessary. It might be a therapy room or an extra bathroom, or a place for a car used by the disabled person.

Financial help

There are many financial benefits payable by the Department of Health and Social Security to disabled people and their families. The amount you get depends upon the cause and effects of your disablement.

Sickness benefit If you cannot work because of your disablement you are usually entitled to claim statutory sick PAY from your employer for the first 8 weeks. Then you can claim SICKNESS BENEFIT for up to 20 weeks provided you have paid the qualifying number of insurance contributions.

If you are still unable to work after 28 weeks, your sickness benefit automatically becomes an INVALIDITY PENSION and an INVALIDITY ALLOWANCE is usually added to the benefit.

If you do not have enough national insurance contributions you can claim a non-contributory invalidity pension (due to be phased out from November 1984 and replaced by severe disablement allowance. *See:* INVALIDITY PENSION).

If you are a married woman of working age and incapable of both paid work and your normal household duties you may be entitled to a housewife's non-contributory invalidity pension.

Disablement benefit If you are disabled because of an accident at work or an industrial disease, you may be entitled to DISABLEMENT BENEFIT. Disablement benefit can be paid even if you are able to work.

Attendance allowance An ATTENDANCE ALLOWANCE is payable for anyone over the age of 2 who is severely disabled – physically or mentally – and has needed a lot of looking after for at least 6 months. Anyone – other than a wife living with or supported by her husband – who stays at home to look after such a person may be entitled to an INVALID CARE ALLOWANCE.

Mobility allowance If you are under pension age and unable to walk – or can walk only with help – you may be entitled to a MOBILITY ALLOWANCE.

When a disabled person is capable of working

If you are capable of working but have difficulty in finding a job, contact the disablement resettlement officer at your local employment office or job centre. He will help you to find suitable employment or recommend a course at

WHEN SUPPLEMENTARY BENEFIT IS PAYABLE

Special rules governing extra financial help for the disabled

Any disabled person over the age of 16 can claim SUPPLEMENTARY BENEFIT if his or her income is below a certain level. Although benefit is not normally paid to people who are still at school or in full-time employment, there are some exceptions for the disabled.

Still at school

Anyone who is still at school, and is so severely handicapped as to be unlikely to get a job, can claim benefit from their 16th birthday.

In full-time work

A self-employed person whose earning power is substantially reduced by disablement, compared with other people doing similar work, can claim benefit.

If you can work

If you are able to work but have no job you must sign on as available for work. If you do not do so, you will not receive benefit.

However, you may not have to sign on if your disability makes it unlikely that you will be able to find a job.

If you cannot work

If you are unable to work, you do not have to sign on as available for work, but you must submit medical certificates to the social security office.

Rates of benefit

The amount of benefit you receive depends upon what other income you have.

If you are getting an ATTENDANCE ALLOWANCE or MOBILITY ALLOWANCE your supplementary benefit will not be affected.

Up to £4 of a DISABILITY PENSION can also be ignored, but the rest of a disability pension and any other national insurance benefits will be deducted in full from your entitlement.

If you received a lump sum payment as compensation for an injury it will be treated as capital, but you are allowed £3,000 savings (excluding the value of your own home). If you have more, you cannot claim supplementary benefit.

If the money is held in trust it will be treated as yours if the trustees are empowered to make payments to you or for your benefit.

Extra benefit

If you have additional expenses because of your disablement – you may have abnormally heavy wear and tear on clothing or shoes, for instance, or you may need a special diet, extra heating or domestic help – ask your social security office if you qualify for either occasional lump sum special payments, or additions to your weekly benefit.

If you are getting an attendance or mobility allowance, you will automatically be assumed to need extra heating.

If you receive supplementary benefit, or a long-term invalidity benefit, for longer than 1 year without being required to be available for work, you will qualify for the long-term rate of supplementary benefit. If you (or your partner) are over 60, you will get that rate automatically.

an employment rehabilitation centre if he thinks you need to regain your confidence to work.

The courses usually last for 6 weeks. You will not receive wages during your training, but you will be paid a tax-free living allowance and all your expenses.

If you show potential for training for a particular job, the resettlement officer will arrange for you to take a course at a skill centre or other training establishment and will tell you what allowances you get during training.

Disabled register If you are severely handicapped, the resettlement officer will invite you to register as a disabled person. Registration is voluntary, but it does have advantages. For instance, employers of 20 or more people are legally bound to employ registered disabled people to make up at least 3 per cent of their total payroll.

Sheltered employment If someone is too handicapped to work under ordinary conditions the resettlement officer may be able to arrange 'sheltered' employment for him. Sheltered employment means that the individual competes only with other handicapped people, and does not have to cope with the work standards of people with no disability. The main sources of sheltered employment are Remploy, who have 87 factories throughout Britain, local authorities and voluntary organisations, subsidised by the Government.

Help with fares If you are severely disabled you may be able to claim a proportion of the cost of getting to and from work – for instance, the cost of taxi fares.

To qualify, you must be registered as a disabled person and you must be physically unable to use public transport for all or part of your journey.

People who are getting MOBILITY ALLOWANCE will not normally qualify for this kind of assistance also. If they do qualify, the allowance will be partly reduced. But those who are waiting for a decision on a claim for mobility allowance can often benefit.

How mentally handicapped people can be helped

Mentally handicapped people are entitled to many of the same benefits and services as the physically handicapped. *See:* MENTAL HANDICAP

SPECIAL HELP FOR DISABLED CHILDREN

Some health boards keep a register of 'at risk' children who could become handicapped – that is children whose mothers have had illnesses in pregnancy, babies who have shown abnormal reactions or babies born to families who already have a handicapped child.

When a child is on the register, the authorities keep a check on its development and advise the parents on where to get treatment for the child.

If you are concerned about your child's development ask your GP to refer the child to a specialist at a hospital. If your doctor is unsympathetic, contact the local hospital or area health board direct. You can find the address in the telephone book.

Health clinics All health boards have child health clinics which treat disabled children. They will also give advice to parents.

Nursery care Many social work departments run day-care nurseries which also offer day care for disabled children.

Financial help Children over the age of 2 who need a lot of looking after are entitled to an attendance allowance. Children over 5 who are unable to walk, or can walk only with help, can be paid a mobility allowance.

If you are the parent of a disabled child ask the social work department of your regional council to explain what services and financial help you are entitled to receive. *See:* FAMILY FUND

Education Under the Education (Sc) Act 1980, it is the duty of every regional education authority to find out which children in its area need special education. Any education authority will arrange a medical examination for a handicapped child over the age of 2 and advise the parents on its educational needs.

The authority must arrange where the child is to be sent – either to a special class in an ordinary school or to a special school devoted to a particular handicap. If a child is severely handicapped, home tuition may be provided.

The education authority may also be in a position to provide aids for education, For example, it may be able to supply Braille equipment for a blind child or an interpreter for a child who is deaf and dumb.

DISABLEMENT BENEFIT

Compensation for injury at work

If, as a result of an ACCIDENT AT WORK or a prescribed INDUSTRIAL DISEASE, you suffer a personal injury that means you can no longer enjoy a normal life to the full – called 'loss of faculty' – you are entitled to disablement benefit.

Your entitlement is not governed by your earning capacity – disfigurement, for example, even although it caused no bodily handicap, would qualify.

You do not need to have paid any national insurance contributions to be eligible, but you must have sustained the injury or industrial disease in the course of your employment.

Self-employed people do not qualify for disablement benefit.

Even if the accident or disease makes you incapable of work, you cannot draw disablement benefit until 15 weeks after the date of the accident or of the onset of the disease.

During that time you can claim statutory sick pay from your employer for the first 8 weeks, and then SICKNESS BENEFIT. *See:* SICKNESS

If you are still incapable of work when your entitlement to sickness benefit ends, you may be entitled to an INVALIDITY PENSION as well as disablement benefit.

If you are still disabled 9 weeks after the date of the accident or onset of the disease, claim disablement benefit straightaway. If you delay for longer than 6 months, you will lose benefit.

Benefit supplements

If you receive disablement benefit you may be entitled to the following supplements:

- Special hardship allowance – payable if you are likely to be permanently unable to return to your job or to equivalent work.
- Unemployability supplement – payable if you are permanently unable to work or to earn more than a limited amount.
- Hospital treatment allowance – payable while you are receiving treatment for your injury as a hospital in-patient.
- Constant attendance allowance – payable if you are receiving full disablement benefit and need constant care

and attention.

- Exceptionally severe disablement allowance – payable if you are exceptionally severely disabled and your need for constant care and attention is likely to be permanent.

However, the Government propose to abolish these supplements, with the exception of special hardship allowance (to be renamed reduced earnings allowance) and exceptionally severe disablement allowance.

How to claim

Claim at your local social security office, using:

- Form BI.100A for accidents.
- BI.100 (Pn) for pneumoconiosis and byssinosis.
- BI.100 (OD) for deafness.
- BI.100 (OA) for occupational asthma.
- BI.100B for other industrial diseases.

If your injury or disease is accepted by the DHSS as an industrial one, one or more adjudicating doctors appointed by it decide whether you have suffered a loss of faculty as a result and assess the degree and duration of your disablement.

If you can travel, you are told where and when to go for a private medical examination, and your expenses are reimbursed. If someone is unfit to travel alone, a companion's expenses are paid as well.

If you are not fit to travel you are examined at home or in hospital.

It would be useful to you to have a report about your disablement, so you should ask your GP or hospital doctor to make one for you.

The doctors express the degree of disablement as a percentage. If it is less than 20 per cent the benefit will be paid in a lump sum. If it is 20 per cent or above it is paid as a weekly pension.

Not all cases are straightforward. The

HOW AN APPLICANT'S DEGREE OF DISABLEMENT IS CLASSIFIED

Working out the level of compensation that should be awarded for the loss of limbs or faculties

Injury	% degree of disablement
Very severe facial disfiguration	100
Absolute deafness	100
Loss of:	
both hands	100
a hand and a foot	100
both legs or a leg and other foot	100
sight	100
Amputation:	
through shoulder joint	90
at hip	90
of both feet	80–90
below hip and above knee	70–80
below shoulder	60–80
at knee	60–70
Loss of:	
a hand, or of the thumb and four fingers of one hand	60
four fingers of one hand	50
Amputation:	
below knee	40–50
Loss of:	
one eye	40
thumb	30–40
all toes of both feet	20–40

Injury	% degree of disablement
Amputation:	
of one foot	30
Loss of:	
vision of one eye	30
three fingers of one hand	30
two fingers of one hand or of thumb end	20
all toes of one foot	20
whole great toe	14
whole index finger	14
whole middle finger	12
part of index finger	5–11
four toes of one foot, excluding great toe	9
part of middle finger	4–9
whole ring or little finger	7
three toes of one foot excluding great toe	6
part of ring or little finger	2–6
two toes of one foot excluding great toe	5
part of great toe	3
any other toe	3
part of four toes of one foot, excluding great toe	3
part of three toes of one foot, excluding great toe	3
part of two toes of one foot, excluding great toe	2
part of any other toe	1

A percentage tariff is used by the independent adjudicating doctors to decide an applicant's degree of disablement. For example, loss of both hands rates 100 per cent, loss of one hand is 60 per cent and the amputation of a little finger tip without loss of bone rates 2 per cent. An applicant is compensated according to the tariff of compensation rates unless the nature of his injury makes this unreasonable.

claimant may have had a congenital defect or some pre-existing injury which made the effects of the accident more serious. He may suffer multiple injuries or have a succession of accidents. These cases – which are not covered by the tariff – are dealt with under separate regulations.

How to appeal

Anybody who is dissatisfied with the decision of the adjudicating doctors can appeal to a medical appeal tribunal. If you wish to do so you should inform your local social security office in writing within 3 months of the doctor decision and state your reasons for doing so.

The tribunal consists of two doctors and a lawyer chairman. You can be represented by anyone you choose, but if a lot of money is at stake it would be advisable to get a solicitor who specialises in industrial injury claims. He would be best able to assemble the necessary medical evidence and he would know whether it was worthwhile getting a specialist's report. It may be possible to get assistance from your trade union.

DISAFFECTION

The law against inciting members of the forces to rebel

It is an offence to attempt to seduce any member of the armed forces either verbally or otherwise, from his duty or allegiance, or even to possess a document that, if distributed, would constitute such an attempt.

It is not an offence to distribute a leaflet that merely gives information – for example, you are entitled to tell a soldier how he can lawfully obtain his discharge. But you are not allowed to encourage him to desert or to neglect his duty in some other way. A member of the armed forces is forbidden to join a trade union.

Anyone convicted of incitement to disaffection can be sentenced to 2 years' imprisonment and/or fined an unlimited amount.

PACIFIST LITERATURE IS FORBIDDEN

You may give propaganda literature to a member of the armed forces but you must not encourage him to neglect his duty.

DISCIPLINE AT WORK

A worker who misbehaves may be punished

Employees must behave themselves at work, take care in what they do and conduct themselves in a reasonable manner. All of those obligations are imposed by common law. If an employee fails to observe one of them, his employer can discipline him.

Dismissal is the only punishment that is recognised under common law. Others – for example, fines or a period of suspension without pay – will be unlawful unless they are included as part of the EMPLOYMENT CONTRACT. If they are not in the contract, but are imposed, the employee can sue for breach of CONTRACT. If he resigns in protest, he may be entitled to claim CONSTRUCTIVE DISMISSAL.

The Employment Protection (Consolidation) Act 1978 requires an employer to give every employee details of his employment contract in writing within 13 weeks of his starting work. These should include information about disciplinary rules.

Both employer and employee can benefit from having disciplinary rules and procedures written down rather than relying on custom and practice. An employer is more likely to resist claims for breach of contract or UNFAIR DISMISSAL if he can show that the grounds for disciplinary action were clearly set out in writing and accepted by the employee when he joined the company. In particular, the right to suspend an employee without pay is not likely to be upheld by a court or an industrial tribunal unless it is specifically written into the contract.

If an employee is sacked for a trivial offence, he can claim unfair dismissal. Even if the offence is serious, the employee may succeed in an unfair dismissal claim if he can show that the employer acted unreasonably. That may occur in several circumstances, of which the most common are:

- If disciplinary rules and procedures were not properly followed.
- If the employee was not given an adequate chance to explain his version of events.
- If the employee could not be reasonably expected to know that the offence could lead to dismissal.

In such cases, the compensation will be reduced if the employee's behaviour contributed to his dismissal.

Following the ACAS code

Even when disciplinary rules and procedures are clearly stipulated in a written employment contract, accepted by both parties, they can be discounted by an industrial tribunal if it decides they are unreasonable.

The tribunal will judge an employer's disciplinary rules by the standard laid down in the ADVISORY, CONCILIATION AND ARBITRATION SERVICE (ACAS) Code of Practice No. 1, *Disciplinary Practice and Procedures in Employment*, available from Her Majesty's Stationery Office, 13a Castle Street, Edinburgh.

The code is not legally binding on employers, but an industrial tribunal must take it into account when deciding if an employer has acted reasonably.

When dismissal is justified

Misconduct may not always justify dismissal. For example, the use of bad language at work may be unacceptable in a department store, but of less concern on a building site.

Drinking at work Drinking or being under the influence of alcohol does not generally justify dismissal for a first offence unless the job is hazardous – for example, construction work – or the employee is a pilot, a nurse or a public transport worker.

If an employer wants to be able to sack an employee who is not in a posi-

DISCIPLINARY RULES THAT SHOULD BE OBSERVED

The ACAS code recommends that disciplinary rules should be:

1. Reasonable and adequate for both employer and employees.
2. Drawn up only after consultation with the employees, if possible through their trade union representatives.
3. Clear and concise – capable of being understood by employees and not written in legal jargon, or expressed so generally as to be meaningless.
4. Precise in their statement of penalties, with a clear indication of the type of conduct that may lead to summary DISMISSAL.
5. Known and understood by the employees. (ACAS says that the employer must not only ensure that employees are aware of the rules, but should explain what they mean.)

The code further suggests that disciplinary procedures should allow:

- Careful and prompt investigation by a manager or supervisor before any action is taken, even in serious cases where misconduct would justify summary dismissal.
- The suspension of the employee on full pay to allow an investigation into any allegation that could lead to summary dismissal.
- Both sides to put their cases fully.

The employee should be informed of the complaint against him and be allowed to defend himself, in person or through a union representative or fellow employee, before any decision on disciplinary action is reached. (Failure to allow a worker to present his side of a complaint is one of the most common reasons that employers lose claims for unfair dismissal.)

- A clear and unmistakable written warning to offenders.

It is not enough for a manager to write 'further conduct of this sort may lead to your dismissal'. He should write 'further conduct of this sort will lead to your dismissal'.

Only those guilty of the most serious offences should be dismissed without a previous written warning.

- An agreed procedure for appeals against disciplinary measures.

ACAS says it is the duty of the employer, when an employee is disciplined, to inform him that he can appeal and to tell him how to do it.

- Full disciplinary records to be kept.

Employers should make written records of the nature of any breach of discipline, the action taken, the reason for it, whether an appeal was lodged and, if so, the outcome of the case.

The code does not suggest that employers should make copies of disciplinary records available to the employees concerned, but there is nothing to prevent an employee asking to read or take notes from his disciplinary file.

- A period of limitation, negotiated between management and staff, after which a warning becomes 'spent' if the employee concerned has behaved satisfactorily in the intervening period.

Once a warning is spent, it should not be used to justify further disciplinary action. The ACAS code does not suggest how long the period of limitation should be, but in some companies it is 1 year and sometimes longer, depending upon the nature of the offence.

- Special attention to certain cases.

Such cases could include the disciplining of trade union officials, in which the employer might be accused of hampering union activity, or of staff on night shifts or in remote depots, when senior managers are not available to take part in the disciplinary procedures.

tion of such responsibility for a first drinking offence, he should write a provision into the disciplinary rules.

Disobeying safety rules A serious breach of safety rules justifies summary dismissal – that is, immediate dismissal without notice or warnings – although the employee must normally be given a chance to explain himself. It makes no difference whether the safety rules are laid down by the Government or by the employer. But if the infringement is not serious, or if its consequences are not obvious, the employee may succeed in claiming unfair dismissal.

Falsifying time-sheets If there have been clear warnings to staff that dishonest completion of time-sheets will be punished by dismissal, an employer can dismiss offenders fairly provided that the allegations are thoroughly investigated and that the employees are given the chance to explain.

If an employee tried to justify his behaviour by claiming that 'everyone is doing the same thing', he must be able to show that the claim is true. If it were, and the employer turned a blind eye to other offenders, a dismissal would be unfair unless the person sacked had already been given written warnings.

Lateness for work Employees are legally obliged to work the hours stipulated in their employment contracts. But in practice some leeway is allowed.

If an employer is concerned about someone's persistent lateness for work, and is considering dismissal, he should warn the employee of the consequences of continued lateness – in writing if possible. An industrial tribunal may not regard general comments about timekeeping or even specific requests to arrive on time as sufficient warning to justify dismissal.

Absenteeism Persistent or prolonged absence from work without informing the employer or without proper reason may be grounds for dismissal. However, the employer risks having to pay compensation for unfair dismissal if he does not ask the employee concerned for an explanation, or if he fails to follow the disciplinary rules, before dismissing him.

THE WORKER WHO WAS FOUND IN THE PUB

An employer who wants to be able to dismiss employees for a specific offence – for example, drinking at work – must ensure that they have been given clear warning that it is an offence. He must follow proper disciplinary rules and procedures, and must be consistent in his treatment of offenders.

Mr Beverstock was summarily dismissed after his employer found that he had been drinking in a pub when he should have been working. He applied to an industrial tribunal for a finding that he had been unfairly dismissed.

DECISION

The dismissal was unfair. The employer had previously fined employees who drank when they should have been at work.

If the employer now wished to dismiss employees, he had to state this clearly in the employment contract.

AN ERROR AT THE CHECKOUT

In any case involving dishonesty, an employer must give the employee a chance to defend himself or herself before a decision on dismissal is taken.

Mrs Hill, who worked at a supermarket checkout, failed to ring up 18 items, worth a total of £7, in a large quantity of goods bought by a customer. Asked about the incident by a checkout controller, she replied she had felt unwell. The police were called, and they took Mrs Hill away to the police station for questioning. Later the same day, the company decided to dismiss her from her post.

The police decided not to bring charges against Mrs Hill, and she claimed unfair dismissal.

DECISION

The dismissal was unfair. Mrs Hill had been unwell when questioned by the controller. She should have been given a further chance to explain a few days later. The proper disciplinary procedures had not therefore been fulfilled.

THE MAN WHO CLOCKED OFF EARLY

It is quite possible that an industrial tribunal will overlook an employer's failure to follow dismissal procedure if the dismissal is for a clocking offence

Mr Stewart was in the habit of clocking off early and submitting false time-sheets. Without being told, he was watched by company inspectors and was eventually dismissed. The company rules stated that he should have been given a warning that he was suspected of clocking offences. He claimed unfair dismissal.

DECISION

The tribunal held the dismissal to be fair.

False clocking is a matter which justifies instant dismissal because it is regarded as a serious form of dishonesty.

THE NIGHT WATCHMAN SACKED FOR VANDALISM

If an alleged theft or act of vandalism is being investigated by the police, an employer does not need to wait until the end of the inquiries or for the outcome of the trial before deciding to dismiss the employee concerned. Provided the employer has good grounds for suspecting that the person concerned is guilty, the dismissal is not unfair, even if no criminal charges are brought or if a court eventually acquits the employee.

Mr Conway, a part-time night watchman at a factory, was charged by the police with malicious damage after windows in the premises were broken. Several weeks later, Mr Conway's employer asked the police if the charge still stood. He was told that it did and, as a result, he dismissed Mr Conway at once.

When the charge was eventually dropped, Mr Conway claimed unfair dismissal.

DECISION

The dismissal was fair. Although the charges were eventually dropped, the employer had, on the evidence, reasonable grounds to believe that Mr Conway had broken the windows.

HOW EMPLOYEES MAY BE DISCIPLINED

An employer has the choice of several disciplinary methods even within the recommended rules and procedures.

In ascending order, the most usual forms are:

1. An oral warning. By itself, an oral warning carries little legal weight and, alone, it cannot be relied upon to justify a later dismissal, although it is often the first step in formal disciplinary procedures. A summary of the conversation in which a verbal warning has been given should be kept in the company's disciplinary records.

2. A written warning. A copy of the letter to the employee, and of the employee's reply, should be filed in the employer's disciplinary records.

3. Suspension with full pay. An employer is usually allowed to suspend an employee on full pay for disciplinary reasons – perhaps while the case against him is being investigated. However, in some jobs, for example, acting or piloting an aircraft, the EMPLOYMENT CONTRACT says or implies that the employee is entitled to be given work to do, and suspension, even with full pay, might be unlawful.

4. Fines or suspension on reduced pay or without pay. None of these measures is lawful unless it is specifically authorised in the employment contract or by disciplinary rules that can be said to form part of the contract.

5. Demotion. Unless demotion for disciplinary reasons is authorised by the employment contract, the employee may be able to claim CONSTRUCTIVE DISMISSAL if he decides to resign. However, an employer and employee may agree upon demotion, with or without a reduction in pay, as an alternative to sacking.

6. Dismissal. The DISMISSAL of a worker for disciplinary reasons is justified only in the most serious cases, and may be held to be unfair unless the offence is grave or unless the employee has received previous written warnings for similar misconduct.

A dismissed worker who has completed 1 year's service with his employer (2 years in the case of employers with no more than 20 employees during that period) can claim for UNFAIR DISMISSAL. The employer must then prove that the dismissal was fair and that the proper rules and procedures were followed.

If an employee is sacked before he has served 1 year, he can claim damages for WRONGFUL DISMISSAL if his employer has broken the employment contract.

Fighting at work An employee should know that fighting at work cannot be allowed, but he cannot know the consequences unless they are pointed out to him.

So if an employer intends that fighting should lead to dismissal – in particular to summary dismissal – he should make this clear in his disciplinary rules.

The status of the person who is attacked may affect a decision whether a dismissal for fighting is fair. An attack on a foreman or supervisor is more likely to justify dismissal than a similar attack on an equal.

Theft and damage If a worker can be proved to have stolen from his employer or workmates, or to have deliberately damaged his employer's property, he can be dismissed without notice.

Even when an employer has no direct proof, only suspicion, he can sack a worker if there are 'reasonable grounds' for believing he committed theft or vandalism, and the evidence shows he is guilty 'on a balance of probabilities'.

If the dismissed worker takes the case to an industrial tribunal, the employer will have to be able to show the evidence he had and prove that proper

THE FITTER WHO CAME TO BLOWS WITH A WORK-MATE

Although fighting will often justify dismissal, this is not always so. Much will depend on the circumstances of each case

Mr Taylor, a bench fitter, was dismissed for fighting with another employee. He had been employed for 20 years and had a previously unblemished record. The company's policy was that fighting would lead to dismissal.

DECISION

The tribunal decided that the dismissal was unfair.

A reasonable employer would have taken Mr Taylor's long service and good conduct into account, and would not have dismissed him.

However Mr Taylor's compensation was reduced by 25 per cent because he was partly to blame.

THE RADIOGRAPHER WHO REFUSED TO WORK OVERTIME

Persistent failure to do what the employment contract requires can justify dismissal.

Mr Martin had been employed as a radiographer for five years. He was dismissed when he refused to work overtime on a Saturday morning. He claimed unfair dismissal.

DECISION

The dismissal was fair. Mr Martin had signed a contract which said that he would be expected to work overtime when necessary. He was therefore legally obliged to do so.

The facts that the employer had overlooked his previous refusals to work overtime and that he was not warned that he could be dismissed were held to be irrelevant.

There comes a time when it is reasonable to dismiss an employee determined to go his own way.

disciplinary procedures were followed.

Offences outside work If an employee is convicted of a crime committed outside the workplace, his employer may be entitled to dismiss him, depending mainly on the nature of the crime and the nature of the job.

Dismissal is fair if the conviction undermines the employer's confidence in the employee's suitability for the post he holds, or if it adversely affects the employer's own reputation. For example, a shopfitting company was held by an industrial tribunal to be justified in sacking a fitter who stole goods from a client's shop.

Financial crimes by employees regularly handling sums of money are generally grounds for dismissal. So, in many circumstances, are sexual offences.

Local and national government employees, and those who work for public corporations such as the Post Office, are more likely to be dismissed for a conviction than their counterparts in private industry – particularly if it involves dishonesty.

Lack of co-operation An employee has a duty to co-operate with his employer and to do his job in accordance with his contract. If he does not – for example, by refusing to work overtime when he is obliged to do so by his contract – he can be disciplined.

But he is under no obligation to like his employer, or even to be friendly towards him. Surliness or deliberate awkwardness may fall short of disciplinary offences. In such cases, the employer should attempt to discover and, if possible, remove the causes of the employee's attitude.

If the surliness develops into rudeness and the awkwardness into a refusal to carry out orders, the employer can follow the disciplinary rules, giving the worker a chance to discuss the problem. Any warning should be in writing and make the consequences of continued misbehaviour clear.

An employer can also operate his disciplinary rules against an employee whose personality is creating serious unrest among staff.

DISCOUNT

If a store or manufacturer offers reduced prices, you have a right to demand the discount as advertised. However, the supplier is not obliged to sell to you – though if he does, it should be at the discount price. *See:* FAIR TRADING; PRICE REDUCTION

DISINHERITANCE

When a will does not provide properly for the family

If a person leaves a will which makes no, or inadequate, provision for his immediate family, they can claim their 'legal rights' – so long as the person was domiciled in Scotland at the date of his death. *See:* DOMICILE

If there is no will, the deceased's estate is divided among his relatives according to the rules of INTESTACY laid down by Act of Parliament.

Claims for legal rights out of a person's estate may be made at any time up to 20 years after his death. A claimant is entitled to a sum of money but not to any specific items which belonged to the deceased.

Who can claim?

The following can claim legal rights:

- The surviving spouse. An ex-wife or husband cannot claim. A person who lived with the deceased can claim if he or she could be regarded as married to the deceased by cohabitation with habit and repute. *See:* COMMON LAW MARRIAGE
- A legitimate, illegitimate or adopted child of the deceased – unless later adopted by someone else. A stepchild or foster child cannot claim.
- Legitimate or adopted descendants of a child who has died before the deceased.

How much legal rights are worth

The surviving spouse has a legal right to one-third of the deceased's net moveable ESTATE – that is, the moveable estate after all liabilities have been met. (Moveable estate is roughly everything except land and buildings.) This is increased to one-half if there are no children or their legitimate or adopted descendants surviving.

The children have a legal right to one-third of the net moveable estate, or one-half if there is no surviving spouse. This is divided among all the children equally.

Each child's share remains the same

whether or not the others claim. The descendants of a dead child can claim the share the child would have been entitled to claim had he survived.

The value of a child's claim is reduced if he was given money by the deceased on marriage or to set him up in business.

The surviving spouse or any of the children may have renounced (given up) their legal rights while the deceased was alive – perhaps in return for lifetime gifts. A person who renounces is treated as not surviving. If a child does so, his descendants cannot claim in his place.

Legal rights are often not worth very much because they are claimable only out of moveable property. Many estates nowadays consist mainly of the deceased's house with little in the way of moveable property. *See:* ESTATE

Legacy or legal rights?

A person who benefits under the will must choose between his legacy (that is, a bequest) or his legal rights – he cannot have both. Before making a choice, the value of the legacy and the legal rights should be ascertained. Other factors – such as family feelings – also affect the choice. It is wise to get independent legal advice before making any decision.

A person who claims legal rights loses his legacy, but the rest of the will remains valid. That person remains entitled to any unwilled property which comes to him through intestacy.

Claiming legal rights

The claimant should contact the deceased's EXECUTOR or the lawyer acting for him. Provided the executor is satisfied that the claimant is related to the deceased, the claim should be met. It is necessary to go to court only if payment is refused or the relationship has to be established. *See:* INHERITANCE

> CLAIMING YOUR RIGHTS
>
> *The following example illustrates how legal rights are worked out.*
>
> Ian is survived by his wife Morag and his two children Alexander and Fiona. His net estate amounts to £35,000 – house £29,000; furniture, car, money in bank and building society accounts £6,000.
>
> In his will, Ian leaves everything to a local charity.
>
> Morag can claim £2,000 ($\frac{1}{3}$ of the moveable estate of £6,000) as her legal rights. Alexander and Fiona can each claim £1,000.
>
> The rest – the house and £2,000 – goes to the charity.

DISMISSAL

What happens when an employee is sacked

An employer can end an employee's contract at any time, simply by sacking him. But if the employer does not give proper notice or follow certain procedures, or if he does not have valid reasons for the sacking, he may face a claim for UNFAIR DISMISSAL or perhaps WRONGFUL DISMISSAL.

Dismissal with notice

The procedures for dismissing an employee are generally stated or implied in his EMPLOYMENT CONTRACT. They provide for a period of notice, from the time the employee is informed of his dismissal to the time it takes effect.

Minimum notice periods are laid down by law for most categories of workers, but not for all. The main exceptions are: those who have been in the job for less than 1 month; part timers; and people who perform their duties abroad. *See:* EMPLOYMENT PROTECTION

The statutory minimum notice period for an employee with more than 1 month's service, but less than 2 years', is 1 week. After 2 years' service, the notice period increases by 1 week for each complete year of service, up to a maximum of 12 weeks after 12 years or more in the job. Those minimum periods may be increased by the employment contract, which may also grant a right to notice to employees excluded from the statutory provisions. *See:* NOTICE

The employer must continue to pay wages during the notice period. The employee may be required to continue to work, but if he is not he must still be paid wages 'in lieu of notice'.

An employee can leave while under notice so long as he gives his employer some notice, no matter how short. He has no right to wages for the notice period that he does not work, but he can still claim unfair dismissal. However, he may lose his right to a redundancy payment if he fails to give notice in the proper way. *See:* REDUNDANCY

Giving notice Some individual employment contracts and most collective agreements require notice of dismissal to be given in writing. If there is no such requirement, oral notice of dismissal is just as valid as written notice. But it is in the interests of an employer to write the notice down in case of a future dispute.

Some employers send dismissal notices by recorded delivery, or require the employee to sign and return a copy of the letter as proof of receipt. However, an employee cannot be compelled to sign the letter.

Written notice should state clearly the date from which it takes effect and the length of the notice period or the date by which the employee is expected to leave. The notice period cannot start until the employee has been informed that he is under notice. If payment is to be made in lieu of notice, that should be stated.

Getting written reasons for dismissal

An employer who dismisses someone is not always obliged to give his reasons for doing so at the time. But most employees are entitled to be given the reasons in writing, and should insist on this when considering a claim for unfair dismissal or redundancy.

The main groups of workers who are not entitled to written reasons are:

1. Those who have been employed continuously by an employer for less than 6 months at the time the employment contract ended. The statutory notice period is taken into account in calculating the 6 months. For example, an employee who works for 25 weeks and is then given 1 week's pay in lieu of notice can demand a written explanation for his dismissal. But if he had worked for only 24 weeks, he would have no such right.

2. Part-timers working fewer than 16 hours per week. *See:* PART-TIME WORKER

3. People who normally work outside Great Britain. *See:* EMPLOYMENT PROTECTION

An employee who is entitled to ask for written reasons for his dismissal should put his request in writing. Once the employer has received it, he has 14 days in which to reply. If he fails to do so and there is no good reason for his failure, or if the reasons for dismissal appear untrue or incomplete, the employee can complain to an industrial tribunal.

The employer's reply does not have to be completely exhaustive, but it must be self-explanatory, so that anyone reading it can understand from it the essential reasons for dismissal. Provided that the reply meets that condition, it can refer to other documents – for example, previous written warnings – as well.

The employee's complaint must be submitted to the industrial tribunal on form IT1, obtainable from any local job centre, within 3 months of the end of the employment contract, or the tribunal will almost certainly refuse to consider it. If the tribunal upholds the complaint it declares what it considers to be the reasons for dismissal, and orders the employer to pay 2 weeks' extra wages to the employee.

Dismissal without notice

An employer is entitled to dismiss an employee summarily – on the spot, without notice – if he is guilty of gross misconduct clearly amounting to a fundamental breach of his contract.

The employee is entitled to demand the reasons for dismissal in writing, provided that he is qualified to do so. He retains the right to claim wrongful dismissal, to try to obtain his notice pay and to claim compensation for unfair dismissal or redundancy if he disputes his employer's action.

Only the gravest offences justify summary dismissal. They include embezzlement, deliberate vandalism, theft at the workplace and violent assault upon a superior. Isolated misbehaviour, or a breach of discipline which, while serious, cannot be described as gross misconduct, is not enough.

When dismissal is not clear

If notice of dismissal is given in writing, it is generally clear to the employee that he is being dismissed. But sometimes notice is given orally and it may not be immediately obvious whether the employee has been sacked – and therefore may claim unfair dismissal – or has resigned, when he may forfeit his rights to legal redress. Industrial tribunals consider all the circumstances surrounding a possible dismissal before determining whether it is one or not.

An employee who stopped work arguing that he had been dismissed, simply because his employer had told him angrily to 'get lost', would be unlikely to have a claim upheld by an industrial tribunal. It is in the employee's interest to wait for confirmation of dismissal before stopping work.

If an employee is, or thinks he may have been, dismissed orally, he is entitled to demand written reasons in exactly the same way as if the dismissal notice were in writing.

When dismissal is wrongful

If an employer fails to give proper notice, the employee may claim wrongful dismissal to secure compensation for the breach of contract. Compensation in cases of wrongful dismissal is normally restricted to the amount of money to which the employee is entitled under the employment contract had proper notice been given. Further damages are rarely awarded.

For example, if the employee were entitled to 6 months' notice, but his employer gave only 3 months' notice, the employee could claim wrongful dismissal to obtain the remaining 3 months' money.

Wrongful dismissal claims may be heard in the sheriff court or in the Court of Session. The employee can apply for LEGAL AID.

An employee who sues for wrongful dismissal may, if justified by circumstances, also bring a separate claim for unfair dismissal before an industrial tribunal, which may take into account the lack of notice in awarding compensation.

If an employee is dismissed because the company is reducing its activities and he is not to be replaced, he may be entitled to claim REDUNDANCY.

Constructive dismissal

If an employee decides to resign from his job because of some act by his employer that amounts to a serious breach of the employment contract, he may be able to claim he has been 'constructively' dismissed and obtain compensation from a tribunal for unfair dismissal.

For example, if an employer decides arbitrarily to cut an employee's wages, or to switch him to work entirely different from what he was employed to do, the employee would have a good chance of winning compensation.

He would not be likely to succeed if the change was provided for in the employment contract.

When outside circumstances end a contract

Sometimes an employment contract is ended as the result of outside circumstances.

Death The death of the employer or of the employee automatically ends their contract. If the employer dies and the employee is not kept on by whoever carries on the business, he can claim redundancy, but not unfair dismissal unless he was under notice or had left the job before his employer's death. *See:* EMPLOYEE, Death of; EMPLOYER, Death of

Bankruptcy If an employer goes bankrupt or into liquidation and the employees are dismissed as a result, they can claim redundancy, but not unfair dismissal.

They are entitled to claim, as preferential creditors, up to £800 of any unpaid wages due in the 4 months before the employer's insolvency; and to claim any balance as ordinary creditors. They can also submit the claim for unpaid wages (including holiday pay, maternity pay and unfair dismissal compensation), to the Department of Employment. *See:* PAY

When a contract is 'frustrated'

An employer may decide that he cannot continue to employ an employee because of his prolonged absence from work – for example, through illness or accident. In such a case he may be able to show that the employment contract has been 'frustrated' – automatically ended – by the employee's inability to fulfil his contractual duties.

A contract is not frustrated if the employee's inability is due to his own deliberate conduct, or fault.

Courts and tribunals are reluctant to accept frustration of contract as grounds for ending someone's employment, because the principle would, if too broadly interpreted, greatly undermine employees' legal rights. If a court or tribunal does decide that a contract has been frustrated, the employee cannot claim unfair dismissal because, legally, he has not been dismissed.

Illness An employee who is absent for a long time because of illness may lose his job through frustration of contract.

Many employers define the maximum period during which they will grant sick pay in the written particulars of employment that they give to employees. If they do so, they are unlikely to be able to claim frustration of contract during the period specified. But once that period has expired, the argument that the contract has been frustrated may be upheld.

Imprisonment An employee who is imprisoned cannot perform his duties. But his employment contract is not frustrated since non-performance is due to his own fault. So if his employer dismisses him, he can claim unfair dismissal.

Fixed-term contracts

When a fixed-term contract expires, without either side giving notice, the contract is automatically renewed for the same period – or for one year if the fixed term was longer than a year.

However, if the contract is not renewed the employee can claim unfair dismissal where he has been continuously employed for 1 year or more (2 years in the case of employers with no more than 20 employees during that period). After 2 years he can also make a redundancy claim. An employer offering a contract of at least 1 year (2 years for redundancy) can insist that the employee waives his right to claim unfair dismissal or redundancy. *See:* EMPLOYMENT CONTRACT

An employee on a fixed-term contract who has been continuously employed for at least 6 months is usually entitled to written reasons if he is dismissed.

When contract provisions still apply

Some employers require employees to sign a written agreement that, after leaving, they will not set up in competition with their former company, or reveal trade secrets to rivals.

THE GARDENER WHO USED BAD LANGUAGE

Even if an employee has been guilty of misconduct, his summary dismissal may not be upheld if the incident was an isolated one, unrelated to his general behaviour and performance. A single act is rarely ground for summary dismissal unless it involves a serious crime – for example, embezzlement or large-scale theft.

Mr Wilson was employed as a gardener by Mr Racher. He was diligent and efficient, but Mr Racher criticised him for trivial reasons. One day, Mr Wilson turned his back on his employer to avoid unjustified criticism. But the criticism continued. Mr Wilson retorted with obscene language, which was heard by Mr Racher's wife and children. Mr Racher sacked him on the spot, without notice. Mr Wilson contested the dismissal.

DECISION

Summary dismissal was not justified by one use of obscene language, particularly as Mr Wilson was diligent and efficient.

THE WORKER WHO EXPECTED A 6 MONTH SENTENCE

If an employee cannot perform his job due to his own fault, his employment contract is not frustrated.

Mr Norris was employed as a local authority cleaner. In 1981 he was convicted of assault, reckless driving and driving while disqualified. He was kept in custody pending sentence.

The woman that he lived with told the local authority that he expected to get at least 6 months' imprisonment. The next day, they sent him a notice of dismissal.

Mr Norris claimed unfair dismissal. However, the industrial tribunal said that his contract had been frustrated and therefore he had not been dismissed. So he could not get any compensation. Mr Norris appealed against the decision.

DECISION

The Employment Appeal Tribunal said that a contract could only be frustrated if there was no fault. So Mr Norris had been dismissed. They sent the case back to an industrial tribunal to decide whether the dismissal was unfair.

WHEN THE REASONS WERE A DAY LATE

Industrial tribunals strongly uphold the rights of employees to receive written statements of the reasons for dismissal.

Mr Keen was dismissed from his job as regional sales manager. He asked his employer for written reasons, and they were posted to him 12 days after he made the request.

However, they took 3 days to reach Mr Keen, arriving on the 15th day. He asked an industrial tribunal to award him 2 weeks' pay because of his employer's 'unreasonable refusal' to supply the written information within 14 days of his request.

DECISION

Mr Keen was awarded 2 weeks' pay.

THE EMPLOYEE WHO WAS TOLD 'DON'T BOTHER TO GIVE NOTICE'

Industrial tribunals take into account the underlying intention of the employer when determining whether an employee's departure from his job is resignation by him or dismissal by the employer.

Mr Bishop was a foreman who got into dispute with his employer about the length of his lunchbreak.

During their arguments, Mr Bishop said he wanted to leave, giving a week's notice. His employer retorted: 'Don't bother to give notice. Leave now!' Mr Bishop did, and claimed unfair dismissal.

DECISION

The employer's comments amounted to a dismissal. The claim was upheld.

Such clauses – excluding those which prohibit disclosure of trade secrets – are not enforceable if they unreasonably restrict the former employee's right to earn a living or if the restriction would be against public policy. If the matter is brought to court by either party, the onus is on the employer to prove that the clause is reasonable, but it is not a heavy onus to discharge.

Discipline Employers are expected to follow agreed rules and procedures, outlined in a code drawn up by the ADVISORY, CONCILIATION AND ARBITRATION SERVICE, when disciplining employees. In all disciplinary cases, including those involving summary dismissal, the employer should investigate, and should allow the employee to give his version of events. If the employer does not follow the procedures, he may lessen his chances of successfully defending a claim brought against him by the dismissed employee. *See:* DISCIPLINE AT WORK

Courts and industrial tribunals have come to regard summary dismissal as an extreme punishment, to be used only in exceptional circumstances. Because of the difficulties of knowing whether a particular summary dismissal will be upheld, many employers make a payment in place of notice even though they believe that, legally, they are not obliged to. The employee cannot then claim wrongful dismissal. To help him defend any unfair dismissal claim, the employer should put a note with the wages in place of notice, stating that they are paid 'without prejudice to our view that you are not entitled to your wages because your conduct justifies us in summarily dismissing you'.

DISTRICT COURT

Where minor offences are tried

District courts exist almost everywhere in Scotland. Most of them have justices of the peace as their judges. Justices get some training but are not professional lawyers. Often they are also district councillors. In Glasgow, there are three salaried and legally-trained judges called stipendiary magistrates.

District courts deal with the more trivial offences. For instance, a person who fails to comply with a traffic sign or direction, is drunk and disorderly in public or hits someone without doing serious injury, is likely to be prosecuted in the district court.

A justice can impose a fine of up to £1,000 or send a person to prison for up to 60 days. But some Acts of Parliament allow him occasionally to impose a heavier sentence.

DIVORCE

When a marriage cannot be mended

Irretrievable breakdown of a marriage is the only ground for divorce. The only way it can be proved is by the partner who wants the marriage ended – the pursuer – satisfying a court on one or more of five points:

1. The other partner – the defender – has committed ADULTERY.

2. The defender has deserted the pursuer for 2 years. *See:* DESERTION

3. The couple have lived apart for a total of at least 2 years, and the defender consents to a divorce.

4. The couple have lived apart for 5 years. The defender's consent to a divorce is not required, but the divorce can be opposed on the ground that it would cause grave financial hardship – for example, the loss by a wife of widow's pension rights. In such a case the husband would get his divorce if he made provision to compensate her.

The period of living apart – whether for 2 or 5 years – need not be continuous: the couple may attempt RECONCILIATION for periods totalling not more than 6 months. Living apart usually means living at separate addresses, but a couple might be regarded as conducting separate households under one roof.

5. The defender has behaved in such a way that the pursuer cannot reasonably be expected to live with the defender. In undefended cases the court usually accepts the pursuer's view of what is intolerable behaviour. When an action is opposed, the judge must decide what a reasonable person would expect that particular pursuer to put up with in those particular circumstances. Each case stands on its own facts and on the personalities of the parties.

For example, it may not be reasonable to expect a neurotic woman to put up with overbearing conduct by her husband. But a healthy, well-balanced woman might be expected to cope with exactly the same behaviour.

Persistent drunkenness and violence are typical grounds for complaint. Less obvious objectionable behaviour may also be intolerable if the pursuer is deeply affected. Sometimes nagging might amount to intolerable behaviour. So might habitual refusal of sexual intercourse, or refusal to have children.

When a divorce can be sought

Divorce proceedings cannot be started in Scotland unless *one* partner is domiciled in Scotland or has been living there throughout the 12 months immediately before proceedings are started. *See:* DOMICILE

Divorce proceedings founded on adultery or intolerable behaviour can be started at any time after marriage. Proceedings founded on desertion or separation cannot be started until the 2 or 5 year period has expired.

Getting a divorce

If you want to obtain a divorce, you must apply to your local sheriff court, or to the Court of Session in Edinburgh. Sheriffs have had the power to grant a divorce since May, 1984.

Conciliation The Scottish Family Conciliation Service, an independent voluntary organisation, offers a free, out-of-court service to separating and divorcing couples and their families. It can help to settle disputes about children, finance or property matters, preferably before you apply to court. Contact the Service at 127 Rose Street South Lane, Edinburgh (tel: 031 226 4507).

The different procedures

Two different procedures are available for getting a divorce in the sheriff court or Court of Session:

1. The simplified, or 'do it yourself', procedure. This can only be used for *simple, uncontested* divorces on the ground of 2 or 5 years' separation. You can, if you wish, complete the necessary application forms yourself, without legal help. There is no need to ask a lawyer to start a divorce action in court on your behalf.

2. The ordinary procedure. This must be used for all other divorces. It re-

THE DOCUMENT THAT STARTS A DIVORCE ACTION AND TELLS HOW THE MARRIAGE HAS BROKEN DOWN

The document below – called a summons – starts a divorce action in the Court of Session. A similar document – called an initial writ – starts a divorce action in the sheriff court.

Court of Session, Scotland.

SUMMONS

in causa

MRS. MARY ANN SMITH or BROWN (Assisted Person), 25 Maple Gardens, Falkirk — *Pursuer*

against

JOHN WILLIAM BROWN, 106 Main Street, Edinburgh — *Defender*

ELIZABETH II, by the Grace of God, of the United Kingdom of Great Britain and Northern Ireland and of Her other Realms and Territories Queen, Head of the Commonwealth, Defender of the Faith, To the said

JOHN WILLIAM BROWN

Whereas by this Summons the pursuer craves the Lords of our Council and Session to ....

This sets out the orders that the pursuer is asking the court to make

Conclusions

1. For divorce of the defender from the pursuer in respect that the marriage has broken down irretrievably by reason of non-cohabitation for two years or more and the defender's consent to decree of divorce.
2. For custody of Donald Philip Brown and Susan Jane Brown the children of the marriage under 16 years of age; and for payment to the pursuer by the defender of £2.00 weekly as aliment for each of the said children while in the custody of the pursuer and unable to earn a livelihood; with leave to any person claiming an interest to apply to the Court thereanent until 4th August 1990.
3. For the expenses of the action.

This gives information about the marriage, the breakdown, the arrangements for the children and the pursuer's financial position

CONDESCENDENCE

1. The parties were married at Falkirk on 8th March 1969. There are two children of the marriage, namely Donald Philip Brown born on 28th August 1972 and Susan Jane Brown born on 4th August 1974. Extract certificates of marriage and birth are produced herewith.
2. The defender was born in Scotland of Scottish parents. He has lived all his life in Scotland. He is domiciled in Scotland. To the knowledge of the pursuer no proceedings are continuing in any country outside Scotland which are in respect of the marriage to which this Summons relates or are capable of affecting its validity or subsistence.
3. After the marriage the parties lived together in Falkirk. The defender left the pursuer at or about the beginning of September 1979. The parties have not since lived together nor had marital relations. The defender consents to decree of divorce. The marriage has broken down irretrievably.
4. The said children of the marriage live with the pursuer. They have adequate accommodation. They are happy and well cared for. It is in their best interests to be in the custody of the pursuer. The pursuer is not in employment and devotes all her time to looking after the home and children. She is dependent upon Supplementary Benefit of £60.30 per week. The pursuer believes and avers that the defender is unemployed and is dependent upon state benefits. The pursuer does not seek a periodical allowance. She seeks aliment for the said children. The sums sued for in name thereof are reasonable.

This sets out the legal grounds of the case

PLEAS - IN - LAW

1. The marriage having broken down irretrievably by reason of non-cohabitation for two years or more and the defender's consent to decree of divorce as condescended upon, decree of divorce should be pronounced as concluded for.
2. It being in the best interests of the said children to be in the custody of the pursuer, and the sums sued for as aliment being reasonable, decree of custody and aliment should be pronounced as concluded for.

IN RESPECT WHEREOF

John Cameron

4 McLeod Street,
Edinburgh.

quires a divorce *action* to be started in court. To do this, you will need to use a SOLICITOR.

The corroboration rule

If you apply for a simple, do it yourself divorce, you do not normally need to have a witness to support, or 'corroborate', your case. But if you apply under the ordinary procedure, which requires you to raise a court action, you must have a supporting witness.

In uncontested cases under the ordinary procedure, the witness need only sign a written AFFIDAVIT. But in contested cases where there is a court hearing, the witness must give evidence in court.

Do it yourself divorce

You can only use the do it yourself procedure if *all* the following conditions are met:

1. You and your partner have lived apart for at least 2 years *and* your partner gives his or her written consent to the divorce; OR

You and your partner have lived apart for at least 5 years.

2. There are no children of your marriage under 16. This includes children who are adopted or accepted into the family.

3. Neither you nor your partner applies to the court for a lump sum or periodical allowance (see below).

4. Neither you nor your partner is incapable of managing your affairs because of mental disorder.

5. No other court proceedings have started (in Scotland or elsewhere) which could result in the ending of your marriage.

GETTING A DO IT YOURSELF DIVORCE

This is the main part of the application form that you fill in for a do it yourself divorce on the ground of 2 years' separation.

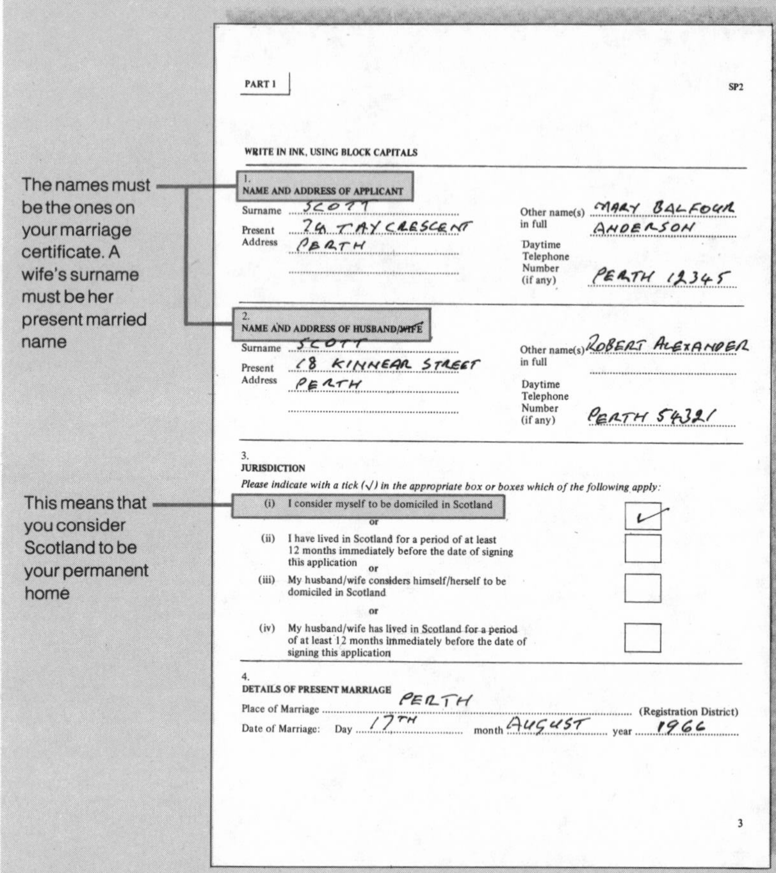

PART 1 SP2

WRITE IN INK, USING BLOCK CAPITALS

1.
NAME AND ADDRESS OF APPLICANT

Surname SCOTT
Present Address 74 TAY CRESCENT PERTH
Other name(s) in full MARY BALFOUR ANDERSON
Daytime Telephone Number (if any) PERTH 12345

2.
NAME AND ADDRESS OF HUSBAND/~~WIFE~~

Surname SCOTT
Present Address 18 KINNEAR STREET PERTH
Other name(s) in full ROBERT ALEXANDER
Daytime Telephone Number (if any) PERTH 54321

3.
JURISDICTION

Please indicate with a tick (√) in the appropriate box or boxes which of the following apply:

(i) I consider myself to be domiciled in Scotland [✓]
or
(ii) I have lived in Scotland for a period of at least 12 months immediately before the date of signing this application [ ]
or
(iii) My husband/wife considers himself/herself to be domiciled in Scotland [ ]
or
(iv) My husband/wife has lived in Scotland for a period of at least 12 months immediately before the date of signing this application [ ]

4.
DETAILS OF PRESENT MARRIAGE

Place of Marriage PERTH (Registration District)
Date of Marriage: Day 17TH month AUGUST year 1966

3

HOW MUCH A DIVORCE ACTION WILL COST

An undefended divorce *action* will usually cost from £290 to £360. A defended action will cost much more. Additional expense will be incurred by disagreements over money or the custody of children.

The pursuer and defender may agree to share the cost of a divorce. If there is no agreement, the husband usually pays for the case. *See:* LEGAL EXPENSES

LEGAL AID may be available to help with or meet the cost of the action.

Getting advice

If you are not sure whether you can use the do it yourself procedure, or if you want advice before you apply, contact your local CITIZENS ADVICE BUREAU or consult a solicitor. Depending on your income, a solicitor can give you free advice under the LEGAL ADVICE and Assistance Scheme.

Making an application

If you decide to use the do it yourself procedure, write for an application form to the Sheriff Clerk at your local sheriff court, or to the Court of Session, Divorce Section (SP), Parliament House, Edinburgh EH1 1RQ (Tel: 031–225–2595, Ext. 316). Say whether you wish to apply for a divorce on the ground of 2 or 5 years' separation – the application forms are different.

Each application form contains detailed instructions about how it is to be filled in. If you have any difficulty, contact a Citizens Advice Bureau, the local sheriff court office or the Court of Session.

If you are applying for a divorce on the ground of 2 years' separation, you

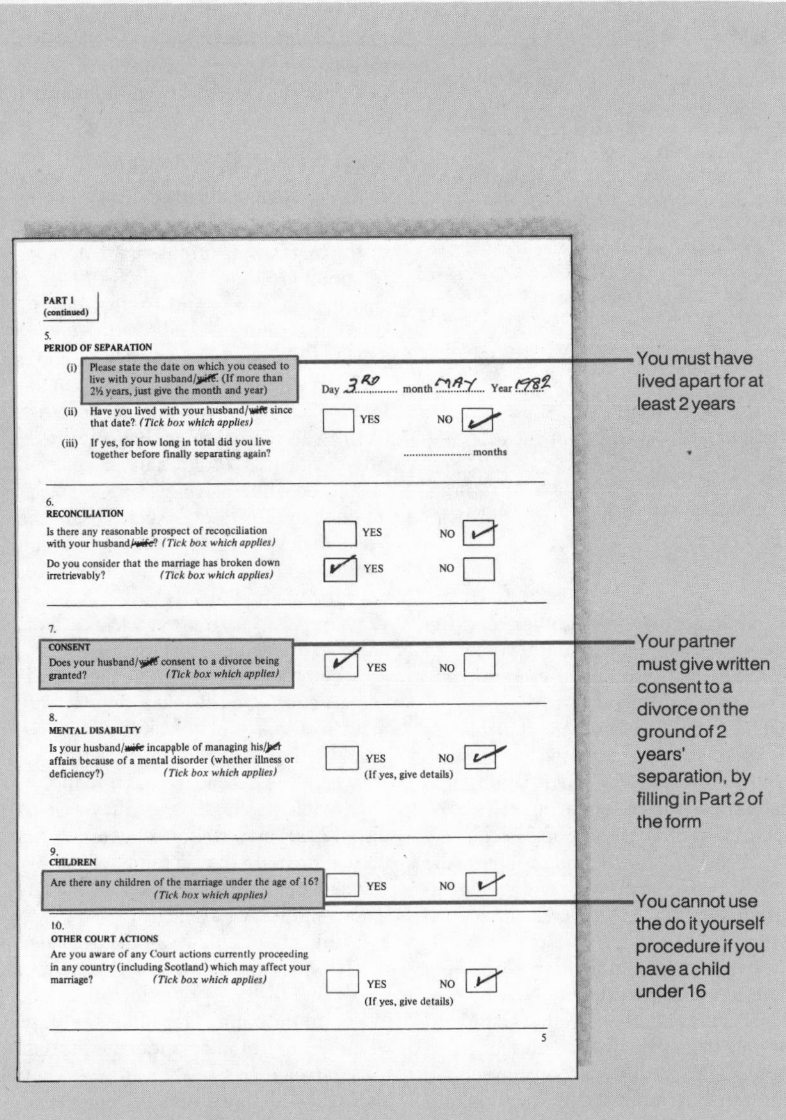

PART 1 (continued)

5.
PERIOD OF SEPARATION

(i) Please state the date on which you ceased to live with your husband/~~wife~~. (If more than 2½ years, just give the month and year) — Day 3RD month MAY Year 1982

(ii) Have you lived with your husband/~~wife~~ since that date? *(Tick box which applies)* — YES [ ] NO [✓]

(iii) If yes, for how long in total did you live together before finally separating again? — .... months

6.
RECONCILIATION

Is there any reasonable prospect of reconciliation with your husband/~~wife~~? *(Tick box which applies)* — YES [ ] NO [✓]

Do you consider that the marriage has broken down irretrievably? *(Tick box which applies)* — YES [✓] NO [ ]

7.
CONSENT

Does your husband/~~wife~~ consent to a divorce being granted? *(Tick box which applies)* — YES [✓] NO [ ]

8.
MENTAL DISABILITY

Is your husband/~~wife~~ incapable of managing his/~~her~~ affairs because of a mental disorder (whether illness or deficiency?) *(Tick box which applies)* — YES [ ] NO [✓] (If yes, give details)

9.
CHILDREN

Are there any children of the marriage under the age of 16? *(Tick box which applies)* — YES [ ] NO [✓]

10.
OTHER COURT ACTIONS

Are you aware of any Court actions currently proceeding in any country (including Scotland) which may affect your marriage? *(Tick box which applies)* — YES [ ] NO [✓] (If yes, give details)

5

will have to send the form to your partner. He or she must give written consent to the divorce by completing and signing Part 2 of the form.

When you have filled in the form, you must complete and swear an affidavit (this is part of the form) before a NOTARY PUBLIC or JUSTICE OF THE PEACE.

A justice of the peace makes no charge for this service. A notary public may charge a small fee. Find out what the fee is first. You will not have to pay it if you qualify for free help under the Legal Advice and Assistance Scheme.

What you must send

When you have completed the form, send (or take) it to the sheriff court, or to the Court of Session at the address above. You must enclose with the form:

- Your MARRIAGE CERTIFICATE (this will be returned to you).
- A cheque or postal order for £40, to cover the court fee. You do not have to pay the fee if you are receiving SUPPLEMENTARY BENEFIT, FAMILY INCOME SUPPLEMENT, or Legal Advice and Assistance in connection with the divorce application. If you want to claim exemption from paying the fee, complete and send form SP 15 (this comes with the application).

LEGAL AID is not available to pay the cost of your divorce application.

What the court does

The court will register your application and post a copy to your partner by recorded delivery. If the copy cannot be delivered, you can pay an additional fee of £4 to enable a court officer to try to make a personal delivery.

If your partner's whereabouts are unknown, the application must be notified to all children of the marriage and to one of your partner's close relatives.

If there are any valid objections to your application, you cannot continue to use the do it yourself procedure. If there are no objections, the court will consider your application. You should hear in about 2 months whether the application has been successful.

If your application is successful, you will be sent a copy of the divorce decree – the court order that ends your marriage.

A change of mind

If you decide not to go ahead with your application – because, for instance, you want to attempt a reconciliation – you can withdraw it at any time before decree is granted. You should contact the court without delay.

If your partner changes his or her mind and refuses to consent to a 2 year divorce, you will not be able to continue with the application.

The court fee cannot be refunded once the application is registered.

Starting a divorce action

If a person wants to take divorce proceedings, but is unable to use the do it yourself procedure, he or she must apply to the court under the ordinary procedure. This requires a divorce *action* to be raised in the court. LEGAL AID may be available to help with or meet the cost of the action.

A person who wants to start a divorce action (the pursuer) should make an appointment to see a solicitor. The local Citizens Advice Bureau has a list of solicitors who can help.

The first meeting with the solicitor is to discuss the facts, the evidence and whether or not a divorce action is likely

GETTING TEMPORARY ALIMENT

Even when a couple agree that they should seek a divorce, getting one can take several months. If one partner opposes the divorce, or contests the financial claims of the other, it can take a lot longer.

During this period either partner can ask the court to order the other partner to pay interim, or temporary, aliment for herself or himself and for any children under 16. Decrees for interim aliment will last until the marriage is legally terminated.

Even if a husband and wife agree on how much aliment should be paid during this period, they should still seek a court decree. This will allow payment to be enforced, if necessary, and also make it eligible for tax relief.

If they do not agree, the partner claiming interim aliment should ask his or her solicitor to apply to the court for interim aliment. The other partner is notified of the application and should consult a solicitor if he or she wants to oppose it.

The application is made by a solicitor or advocate and heard by a judge. The applicant's lawyer gives details of the applicant's financial position – sometimes producing documentary evidence such as pay slips and bank statements – and any information which he has about the other partner's financial position. If the application is being opposed, the other partner's lawyer gives details of his or her client's financial position.

In general, finances are not examined in great detail.

The judge then grants decree for interim aliment to be paid weekly or monthly until the divorce is finalised.

to succeed. The pursuer should bring the MARRIAGE CERTIFICATE and the BIRTH CERTIFICATE of any child under 16 to this meeting.

If the action is to go ahead, the solicitor will then collect the necessary evidence. He or she will interview witnesses to any relevant incidents – for instance, an act of adultery or an assault by the defender.

If the action is to be raised in the sheriff court, the solicitor (or perhaps an advocate) will draw up the initial writ. If the action is to be in the Court of Session, the solicitor must have the summons drawn up by an ADVOCATE. Solicitors whose offices are outside Edinburgh will have to instruct Edinburgh solicitors to do this.

Once the initial writ or summons has been drafted, it is lodged at the court and a copy is then sent to the defender. If the Post Office are unable to deliver the document, it will be served by a sheriff officer or messenger-at-arms (a court official). If a third party – a paramour – is involved in the case, a copy of the document is also sent to him or her. *See:* ADULTERY

When an action is undefended

If a defender decides not to oppose a divorce action, the case can be concluded more quickly. Usually neither party has to go to court.

Once the court has received proof that the initial writ or summons has been served on the defender, and the defender has not given notice that he or she intends to defend the action, the case can usually go ahead.

The exception is where the pursuer seeks a divorce because the couple have been separated for two years, and claims that the defender agrees to the divorce. In this case, the action can only go ahead if the defender signs the Notice of Consent form which accompanies the initial writ or summons and returns it to the court.

The pursuer then signs an affidavit in front of a solicitor who is a Notary Public. This is a statement of the facts about the marriage, the divorce and any children in the family who are under 16. The pursuer must swear – or make a solemn declaration – that these facts are true.

Witnesses who are confirming statements made by the pursuer must also sign an affidavit. They may be providing evidence of the breakdown of the marriage or the welfare of children, or both.

The affidavits are then checked by the pursuer's lawyer. If they are in order they are lodged at the court and a judge considers them along with all the other documents in the case.

If the judge is satisfied that the marriage has broken down irretrievably, decree of divorce is granted. If the judge is not satisfied with the affidavits, the pursuer may be told to produce further evidence or clarification.

A divorce will not normally be granted until the judge is satisfied that satisfactory arrangements have been made for the care of any children under 16.

When an action is defended

It is no defence to a divorce action for the defender to say that the dissolution of the marriage is offensive on moral or religious grounds. Nor is it a defence that the defender wants to stop the pursuer remarrying.

The only way in which the defender can stop a divorce is by showing that the facts relied on by the pursuer to prove irretrievable breakdown have not been proved; or that additional facts proved by the defender give rise to a special defence to the action – such as that the pursuer has forgiven the defender's adultery and lived with him or her after finding out about it. In cases based on 5 years' separation, there is also a defence of grave financial hardship.

A defender who wants to fight a divorce action should make an appointment to see a solicitor as soon as possible.

Even if the defender does not oppose the divorce itself, he or she may wish to dispute the pursuer's arrangements for the children or the amounts of money claimed by the pursuer. Again, the defender should see a solicitor.

Within about 28 days of the defender receiving the initial writ or summons, his or her solicitor should lodge 'defences' at the court. The 'defences' state whether or not the defender admits that the marriage has broken down. They also deal with any orders the pursuer or defender wants the court to make – for example, orders for CUSTODY OF CHILDREN or for a financial award.

If the defender alleges that the pursuer caused the marriage breakdown, he or she may raise a CROSS-ACTION for divorce.

Where there is a CROSS-ACTION, the judge may grant each spouse decree of divorce against the other. For example, the wife may be granted a divorce based on her husband's behaviour, and the husband a divorce based on his wife's adultery.

Once the defences have been lodged, a date is given when the case will be heard in open court by a judge. The parties can conduct the case themselves,

THE DOCUMENT THAT TELLS YOU THAT YOU ARE DIVORCED

You will receive a copy, or extract, of the divorce decree after you are divorced

This is a Court of Session decree granted in a divorce action. The sheriff court decree is similar. Decrees granted under the do it yourself procedure are much shorter.

COURT OF SESSION, SCOTLAND
Extract Decree of Divorce

In Causa

MRS. MARY ANN SMITH or BROWN (Assisted Person) — *Pursuer*
25 Maple Gardens, Falkirk

against

JOHN WILLIAM BROWN, 106 Mein Street, Edinburgh — *Defender*

At Edinburgh the Tenth day of March 19 83 :

SITTING IN JUDGMENT the Lords of Council and Session pronounced Decree:

(1) divorcing the Defender from the Pursuer:
(2) awarding custody to the Pursuer/~~Defender~~ of the following child/children:

DONALD PHILIP BROWN
SUSAN JANE BROWN

(3) ordaining payment:

(a) by the defender to the pursuer of £ 2.00 per week as aliment for each of said ~~child/~~children until sixteen years of age:

~~(b) by the Defender to the Pursuer of a periodical allowance of £ per ---------------- payable until her death or remarriage~~:

~~(c) by the Defender to the Pursuer of a capital sum of £~~

~~(d) by the ------------- to the -------------- of £ -------------- of expenses:~~

~~(4) Finding the Defender liable to the Pursuer in expenses as the same may be subsequently taxed and decerned for:~~

(5) granting leave to any party showing interest to apply to the Court for any order required anent custody and aliment until 4th August 1990 :

And the said Lords Grant Warrant for all lawful execution hereon.

Extracted at Edinburgh this Second day of April, 19 83 by me

Extractor of the Court of Session.

You cannot re-marry until the 21-day period for appeal has expired. The extract copy of the decree will not be sent to you until this period is up

WHEN A WIFE CAN SUPPORT HERSELF

The court may decide not to award any periodical allowance if an applicant is well able to support herself

Mr and Mrs McL married in 1959 and separated 7 years later.

At the time of the separation, Mr McL earned £26 per week and owned the matrimonial home. This was worth £2,800, subject to a loan of £1,500.

After the separation Mrs McL found employment and was able to support herself. By the time of the divorce action, she was earning £2,600 per year and running a car.

Mr McL's assets had increased significantly following the separation. The house increased in value to £20,000 and he had other assets worth £14,500. He earned about £4,500 per year.

DECISION

The judge refused to award Mrs McL either a periodical allowance or a capital sum.

He took into account that Mrs McL was not in need and was capable of supporting herself. He also noted the evidence that the marriage 'had been dead for 13 years' and that all Mr McL's assets had been accumulated by his own efforts since the couple had separated.

but this is rare. Each is normally represented by a solicitor or advocate. Both parties give evidence and call witnesses.

If the defender wants to oppose the action, but has failed to lodge defences within 28 days, his or her lawyers can still ask the court for permission to lodge them. Permission is almost always given.

When decree is granted

Once all the evidence is heard in a defended action, the judge will decide whether to grant decree of divorce. When the action is undefended, he will grant decree if all the documents are satisfactory. The effect of a decree is to end the marriage.

In either case the defender can appeal against a sheriff court decree within 14 days and against a Court of Session decree within 21 days. The pursuer cannot get an 'extract decree' (a certificate confirming the divorce) until that period has elapsed and therefore cannot re-marry until then.

Applying for financial support on divorce

When a divorce action is raised, either partner may apply to the court for a periodical allowance or payment of a lump sum, or both. A periodical allowance is a fixed sum payable at regular intervals – for example, £30 per week. A lump sum is a fixed amount payable on a 'once only' basis.

A pursuer who wishes to claim either or both of these payments should state this in the divorce papers. A defender who wishes to make a claim, or contest the pursuer's claim, should state this in the defences.

The application for a financial award should contain details of the applicant's capital, income and expenses and any information that he or she has about the other spouse's financial position. If an applicant is unsure of the other spouse's financial position, his or her solicitor can apply for a court order to have this information made available. However an order will be granted only in very exceptional cases.

If a husband and wife agree on a periodical allowance, a capital payment, or both, they can draw up a 'joint minute' (written agreement) and ask the court to approve it. Arrangements for payment of ALIMENT for children of the family can be included in this document. The terms of the minute, if approved, will be incorporated by the court into its order.

How the court decides on payment of a financial award

The applications for periodical allowance and/or payment of a capital sum are heard at the same time as the divorce action. The judge listens to evidence from each partner and from witnesses, and examines the documentary evidence – for example, bank statements.

In deciding what financial awards to make, the court tries to reach a fair and reasonable result by considering all the circumstances. These include:

- The respective means of husband and wife.
- The family's standard of living before the marriage broke down.
- The age of the husband and wife and how long the marriage lasted. If the applicant is young and the marriage has lasted only a short time, the award is likely to be smaller.
- Any benefits either partner will lose the chance of acquiring because of the divorce – such as a widow's pension.
- The conduct of both partners. For example, the judge will have regard to whether one partner caused the breakdown of the marriage, but it is for him to decide what weight, if any, to attach to this.

Financial support for children

When there are children of the marriage, the partner who is asking for custody of them can also apply to have aliment paid in respect of each child. *See:* CUSTODY OF CHILDREN

Deciding the level of financial award

Although the courts try to protect the living standards of someone affected by the break-up of a marriage, there is rarely enough money to achieve that. As two households cost much more to run than one, the husband, wife and children usually have to manage on less. In some cases – if the husband is unemployed, for example – there may not even be enough money for an award to be made against him. His ex-wife and children may then have to rely solely on SUPPLEMENTARY BENEFIT.

Generally, the wife – who is usually the partner who requires financial support – receives between one quarter and one third of the family's pre-tax income as a periodical allowance, depending on whether or not there are children of the marriage. She may also receive a capital sum of between one third and one half of the family's capital – again depending on whether or not there are children. This is so whether or not she has made a financial contribution of any kind.

These, however, are only 'rules of

thumb' – the courts will take all the circumstances into account when deciding how much to award.

A husband can apply for a periodical allowance in the same way as his wife, but he is unlikely to succeed unless his wife is much better off than he.

Periodical allowance need not be based on actual earnings, but may take into account the income potential of the husband or wife.

For example, if a husband invested his capital at a low interest rate, say 2 per cent – perhaps in order to thwart a claim for periodical allowance – the court might estimate his income as though the money was earning a realistic rate of, say, 10 per cent. But if it was a reasonable investment – if a farmer bought more land with some spare cash – the court would be unlikely to force him to sell it.

If the husband's real income cannot easily be found out – for example, he may run a small business with many unrecorded cash transactions – the court may make an order based on his standard of living. An expensive car and frequent holidays abroad would give the lie to any claim that he earned only £4,000 per annum.

Appealing against a financial award

Either partner can appeal against a decree for periodical allowance or for payment of a capital sum. The time limit for appealing is 14 days for a sheriff court decree and 21 days for a Court of Session decree. The same procedure applies to appeals against decrees for aliment. Your solicitor will advise on the chance of success.

When periodical allowance can be varied

Any party to a decree for periodical allowance can apply to the sheriff court or Court of Session for it to be changed, or even cancelled, when new circumstances arise.

A man who, for example, loses his job can ask the court to reduce the payments he has to make to his wife. Similarly she can apply for increased payments if she learns that he is earning more than at the time of the divorce, or if it is costing her more to feed and clothe the children.

If a wife who is receiving periodical allowance suddenly inherits a substantial sum of money, her husband can apply for the decree in her favour to be cancelled. However he will usually have to continue to aliment the children.

How re-marriage affects a decree for periodical allowance

Decrees for periodical allowance come to an end when the person receiving the allowance remarries. A woman will not lose her periodical allowance merely by having sexual intercourse with another man after her divorce, even if the man is supporting her financially. However, in that situation her ex-husband can apply for cancellation of the payment.

If a husband continues to pay his wife periodical allowance after she remarries – either because he had not heard of her wedding or because she deceived him about it – he can obtain a court decree to recover excess payments.

If the husband remarries, he is still required to support his former wife. If he applies to the court to reduce the amount of the payments – because he has a new family to support – the court puts the needs of the divorced wife and her family above those of the new wife.

HOW DIVORCE AFFECTS NATIONAL INSURANCE CONTRIBUTIONS AND SOCIAL SECURITY BENEFITS

For national insurance purposes, a woman who gets divorced while under 60 is treated as a single woman from the date of the divorce decree.

So if you are employed and have elected to pay Class 1 national insurance contributions at the married woman's reduced rate, you must then start to pay contributions at the full rate. If you are self-employed and paying no Class 2 contributions, you must start to do so – possibly along with Class 4 contributions.

You do not have to pay any contributions if you continue working after you reach the age of 60. *See* NATIONAL INSURANCE CONTRIBUTIONS

On reaching retirement age (60), a divorced woman can get a retirement pension, based partly on her former husband's national insurance contributions. It works like this.

If your former husband's contribution record is better than your own (it will be if you have not been working, for example) you can take his contributions as your own for either:

- All the tax years of your working life up to the one in which your marriage ended, or
- All the tax years of the marriage.

To that, you add any national insurance contributions of your own – for example, if you work after the divorce. If then both you (for the time after the divorce) and your husband have full contribution records, you should get a full RETIREMENT PENSION. But if, for example, you do not work after the divorce, or your husband does not have a complete contribution record, you may not have enough contributions to qualify for a full pension and will get, therefore, a reduced one instead.

If you remarry before reaching 60, you cannot use your first husband's national insurance contributions any longer. You must rely on your second husband for your pension. In the case of a second divorce, it is the second husband's contributions which are taken into account when you apply for a retirement pension.

Women who were neither working nor paying full national insurance contributions before their divorce can get contribution credits to help them qualify for unemployment benefit, sickness benefit and maternity allowance.

To get credits you must have *paid* Class 1 or Class 2 contributions (or both) on earnings of at least 25 times the lower earning limit. These must have been paid in the tax year *before* the one in which the divorce was granted, or any later tax year.

A woman divorced after age 60 can get a retirement pension immediately using her former husband's contributions. She can get this pension even if her husband has not retired. To do so she can use his contributions in all the tax years of the marriage up to the end of the tax year in which she reached 60, or all the tax years in her working life up to the age of 60, whichever is more favourable to her.

The rules about using a partner's contribution record for a retirement pension also apply to divorced men.

WHEN CHILDREN ARE INVOLVED

In all divorce actions the judge must be satisfied about the arrangements that have been made for children in the family under 16. This is so even where the couple have agreed on the arrangements. If he is not satisfied, he generally cannot grant decree of divorce.

In an undefended action the judge usually makes up his mind on the evidence in the affidavits. In a defended action the evidence is given in court by the spouses and their witnesses. If the judge thinks that more information is required, he can appoint a social worker, solicitor or advocate to report on the arrangements made for the children.

An order is eventually made which decides who should have custody of the children and what the terms of any access should be. *See:* CUSTODY OF CHILDREN; ACCESS TO CHILDREN

The remarriage of either does not affect payment of ALIMENT for their children.

Enforcing a decree for periodical allowance or aliment

When an ex-husband has failed to pay periodical allowance, his ex-wife should inform her solicitor.

If the ex-husband is working, his earnings can be arrested in order to recover the money owed. Even if he is not working, some of his personal possessions can be impounded and eventually sold. *See:* DEBT

As a last resort he can be sent to jail – although this will not produce the money.

An ex-husband can enforce payment of periodical allowance from his ex-wife in the same way. Payment of aliment to children can be similarly enforced.

If a person is left with insufficient income because of non-payment of periodical allowance or aliment, he or she can apply for supplementary benefit.

Foreign decrees for periodical allowance

Decrees for periodical allowance made in foreign countries can be enforced in Britain, but only where we have a mutual agreement with the other country for enforcement of decrees. Consult a solicitor.

Making the best tax arrangements

If a married couple get divorced or become permanently separated, they are no longer treated as one person by the Inland Revenue. The husband keeps his married man's allowance for the full tax year, which starts in April, even if the separation comes near the beginning of that year. In the following year, he reverts to the lower single person's allowance, unless he is still wholly maintaining his wife and she has no other income.

If a wife is working, separation can bring her an immediate tax advantage in the year in which it happens. She qualifies both for a full year's wife's earned-income relief and for a full year's single person's allowance.

The earned-income relief is set against any income she earns up to the date of separation. The single person's allowance is set against income earned after the separation.

So for a wife, the date of separation can be especially important. To gain the maximum tax advantage, she should have earned at least as much as she would be allowed without tax in each part of the tax year.

From the tax point of view, September – halfway through the tax year – is often the best time to separate. However, marriage breakdowns do not always lend themselves to this kind of tax planning.

Allowances for children

If a child lives with one parent after a separation, the parent is entitled to the additional personal allowance.

If the child lives partly with one parent and partly with the other, the allowance can be apportioned between the two. The arrangement can also be made, if the parents agree, whether the child is 'shared' or not. To arrange this, the parents should write a letter to the local Inspector of Taxes.

Maintenance – voluntary or otherwise

The tax treatment of maintenance payments depends on whether the payments are voluntary, or result from a court order or a written agreement between the husband and wife.

Where maintenance is voluntary, the payer does not get any tax relief on the payments and the recipient does not have to pay any tax on them.

The same rule applies to voluntary aliment paid for a child.

However, where the payments are made under a formal agreement or under a court order, the payer can deduct tax at the basic rate before passing on the balance.

For example, if a husband who is paying tax at 30 per cent formally agrees to pay his wife or ex-wife £40 a week, he can deduct £12 (30 per cent of £40) and pay over the balance of £28.

A person who makes the payments from untaxed income or capital must also deduct tax. However, he may not keep the amount deducted but must send it to the Inland Revenue.

In the example above, the wife is treated as having received income of £40 per week, upon which tax has already been paid. But she must, as recipient, declare the maintenance payments as earned income on her tax returns.

At the end of each tax year the person paying maintenance must supply the recipient with an official tax certificate on form R. 185, obtained from the Inland Revenue. This shows the total maintenance payable and the amount of tax deducted. The recipient submits this certificate with her own tax return to the Inland Revenue.

If the recipient has no income other than the maintenance payments, then the amount of tax deducted at source will have been too great, and she can claim some back from the Inland Revenue. This can be done at regular intervals, on a repayment claim form obtainable from the office of the local collector of taxes.

The same rule applies to aliment for a child payable under a formal agreement or a court order.

Small payments Small maintenance payments – that is, payments of less than £33 per week (£143 a calendar month) for a spouse or ex-spouse and £18 a week (£78 a month) for a child – must be paid without deduction of tax.

The payer still gets tax relief on these

THE WIFE WHO WAS TO BLAME

When awarding periodical allowance a court must take account of whether any partner was responsible for the marriage breaking down. However it is for the court to decide whether this should affect the amount of periodical allowance awarded.

Mr L. sued his wife for divorce on the ground of separation for 5 years.

Mrs L. lodged defences seeking custody of their son and periodical allowance for herself.

Mr L. argued that the amount of periodical allowance sought by Mrs L. was too high and ought to be reduced to reflect the fact that she had been responsible for the marriage breaking down.

The judge awarded Mrs L. a periodical allowance of £200 per month. He said that in such a case conduct should have little or no bearing on the amount of periodical allowance awarded.

Mr L. appealed.

DECISION

The appeal court said that a judge always had to have regard to the conduct of the partners when making an order for periodical allowance. However it was for the judge to decide what weight to attach to such conduct.

The appeal court reduced Mrs L.'s allowance to £150 per month because they felt it was unfair to allow her to enjoy the same standard of living as a blameless wife.

payments, and the recipient may still be liable to tax on them.

Foreign orders Tax relief is allowable only on a British court order. Someone paying maintenance under a foreign court order while living in the United Kingdom is not entitled to tax relief on the payments. Anyone who receives maintenance from abroad, while living in Britain, is liable to pay British tax on the amount received.

Paying aliment direct to a child

There may be a tax advantage in having aliment paid direct to a child, instead of to the parent with whom the child is living. As the child is entitled to a tax-free allowance of his own, less tax is due if aliment is paid direct to the child rather than to the parent who already has other taxable income.

Example: A father pays £2,500 a year aliment for a child living with his ex wife, who earns and pays tax herself.

Assume single person's allowance of £2,005 and tax at 30 per cent basic rate.

If aliment is treated as the mother's income,
tax due on £2,500 .... £750

If aliment is child's income and it has no other,
tax is due on £2,500
less
Personal allowance £2,005
Total amount.............................. £495

Tax at 30% on £495................ £148.50

Tax saved by paying as child's income is therefore £601.50

It is advisable that such an arrangement should be incorporated in a court order. This should ensure that an extra single person's allowance is available. Otherwise, the Inland Revenue may argue that the income is the mother's and tax relief may be lost.

DOCTOR AND PATIENT

Your relationship with your general practitioner

If you have moved home and need to find a new doctor, your new neighbours may be able to help. If they cannot, consult the local medical list at your local health board office, public library or main post office. The list gives the names of all GPs in the area and states whether they have agreed to give maternity medical services or contraceptive services, or both, as well as general medical services. *See:* CONTRACEPTION; MATERNITY

When you have chosen a doctor, ask at his surgery whether you can join his list.

The doctor's right of refusal If a GP refuses a new patient, it usually means that his practice already has its permitted quota of patients. In exceptional cases, and when a patient has simply moved from one part of an area to another, the GP may refuse to accept him because he has an unsatisfactory reputation with other doctors. The GP need not give his reason for refusing.

The right to be registered Every citizen in Britain, however, has the right to be registered with a GP. If a patient is unable to find a doctor prepared to accept him, he can obtain one by contacting the local health board. Its address is on the front of the National Health Service MEDICAL CARD, and can also be obtained from the telephone directory or any doctor's surgery.

The local health board must refer the patient's request for a GP to a committee. After looking into the case, the committee arranges for the patient to be allocated to a doctor. The GP must take the patient when instructed, but he can later have that patient removed from his list.

To have a patient removed from his list, the GP must give notice to the health board. Removal then takes effect automatically after 8 days or when the patient is accepted by another GP – whichever is sooner. The patient has no right of appeal, but, if he is undergoing a course of treatment, it must be completed or he must be accepted by another doctor before he can be removed from the list.

Registering as a temporary patient

If you are living temporarily away from home for between 24 hours and 3 months, you are entitled to register with a GP where you are staying.

If you cannot give your National Health Service number, as given on the front of your medical card, the GP is entitled to charge you a fee for treatment – though in practice few GPs do.

If you do have to pay, ask for a receipt so that you can later reclaim the money from the health board for the area in which you are staying.

If registration with the new GP lasts 3 months or more, you should transfer from the list of your previous GP to that of the new one or that of another GP in the area. If you are temporarily away from home and need emergency treatment, any local GP who is summoned must attend you. You will be given a form to sign to enable him to claim payment from the health board. Only if you require further treatment will you be required to register as a temporary patient.

Seeing your doctor

If a GP operates an appointments system, he is entitled to refuse to see any patient who arrives at the surgery without an appointment provided that no appointments are available in the remaining surgery period and he is satisfied that the patient's health will not be at risk. The GP must ensure that the patient is offered an appointment within a reasonable time.

If you do not have an appointment and a receptionist refuses you access to the doctor, you are entitled to insist that he at least knows of your presence so that he can decide for himself whether your health may be jeopardised by delay.

If the receptionist does not inform the GP or if she refuses you an appointment without the GP's knowledge, you have a ground for complaint to the local health board.

If your doctor does not have an appointments system he must designate the times at which he will be available at his surgery. If you arrive at one of those times he must see you, unless he is occupied with an emergency case.

If your doctor refuses to see you during surgery hours, report him to the health board. If harm is suffered as a result of his refusal, you may be able to sue him successfully for damages.

Home visits and emergencies

If you or a relative ask your doctor to see you either outside surgery hours or at your home, the doctor should ask for any information necessary to enable him to decide whether treatment is urgently needed.

He may, after considering the information, decide not to see you until the next convenient surgery, or he may feel that more urgent treatment is called for, in which case he must attend personally or arrange for another doctor to do so or arrange for your admission to hospital.

If a doctor is asked to attend an accident victim he must do so, even if the victim is not his patient, unless the doctor is excused because he is elderly or infirm, or another doctor can attend the accident immediately.

Before a doctor can employ a deputy on a regular basis, he must get the approval of the health board.

If your doctor has handed his practice over to a locum – a replacement – or a deputy, for a holiday or at weekends or during the evenings, you have no right to insist on seeing your own doctor. You have, however, the same right to treatment from the locum or deputy as you would have from your own doctor.

A GP or a locum who fails to attend one of his patients once he has been told that the patient is seriously ill, or the victim of a serious accident, would almost certainly be in breach of his contract with the health board, and you are entitled to complain to it. Make your complaint against the regular doctor because it is his responsibility to provide an adequate locum.

The confidentiality of medical records

Doctors have a professional and a legal duty to respect the confidentiality of the information they acquire about their patients.

A doctor should allow further access only to others involved in treating the patient – and even then, they should receive only the information essential for carrying out their part of the treatment.

For example, if a woman has a child in hospital under the care of an obstetrician and then needs psychiatric treatment because of severe post-natal depression, the obstetrician can pass on to the psychiatrist any confidential information that he believes will help the psychiatrist to help her to recover.

A patient, however, has the right to insist that nothing he or she tells one doctor shall be disclosed to another.

After the doctor has done his duty by pointing out that such rigid confidentiality may hinder treatment, he must respect the patient's wish.

A GP would be entitled to dismiss his receptionist if he discovered that she had wrongly revealed information about patients.

A doctor employed by a company to provide medical examinations for its employees has the same responsibilities to his patients as if they were private or NHS patients. He should limit disclosures of confidential information to the company to stating whether someone is or is not fit for the work he is doing. He should not pass on any clinical information, or anything relating to the general physical or mental health of the employee.

However, the doctor does have to pass on to the Scottish Home and Health Department detailed information on, for example, hospital inpatients or women having smear tests, to help compile medical research statistics. Sometimes this can be done by clerks without the doctor's knowledge.

Also, doctors have to notify cases of suspected drug addiction and certain contagious diseases.

Children's rights A doctor treating a child under 16 normally informs the parents or guardian of everything about the child's condition that he believes they ought to know. However, he can withhold information from them if he thinks fit.

Some doctors will prescribe contraceptives to girls under 16 without informing their parents. If the girl then has sexual intercourse while still under 16 and has made her intentions known to the doctor, he may risk prosecution for AIDING AND ABETTING unlawful intercourse.

A child attains a legal right to refuse or consent to medical treatment at the age of 14, if a boy, and 12, if a girl.

Doctors in court Outside the medical profession, a court of law is the only place where a doctor may disclose confidential information about a patient. Like all witnesses, except a SOLICITOR or ADVOCATE, he must answer fully all questions put to him.

When confidentiality is broken Apart from the circumstances outlined above, a doctor who discloses confidential information about a patient, or whose receptionist does so, can be sued for DAMAGES. In addition, such a breach of confidence is a disciplinary offence, for which the patient or anyone affected can report the doctor to the General Medical Council at 44 Hallam Street, London, W.1.

When you are dissatisfied with your general practitioner

If you are not satisfied with the treatment you are receiving from your GP, first discuss your complaint with the GP. If you remain unconvinced, you can ask him to arrange for a second opinion. However, as the decision involves clinical judgment, it is for the doctors to decide whether referral to hospital is necessary.

Changing your doctor First you must find a GP who is prepared to add your name to his list. This may not be as easy as it sounds. The new GP may find your decision to leave your original GP unreasonable and refuse to accept you. Or professional loyalty may decide him against taking a patient from another doctor's list. His list may already be full. If you find another GP prepared to accept you, ask him to transfer your name to his list.

Suing a doctor If you have suffered injury or a deterioration in health, or if a member of your family has died, because of what you believe to be incompetence on the part of a doctor, you can sue him for MEDICAL NEGLIGENCE.

In the case of negligence by a locum, you can sue your regular doctor, the locum, or both.

But never try to pursue such an action without seeking professional legal advice, for nearly all doctors belong to a medical defence organisation to protect them against actions for negligence. Sometimes the organisation will offer compensation, so that the dispute does not have to go to court.

Making a complaint

There are two ways to complain about a doctor who treats patients under the National Health Service.

Serious professional misconduct A doctor is guilty of serious professional misconduct if, for example:

1. He carries on an 'adulterous or improper' relationship with a patient.
2. He indecently assaults a patient.
3. He shows gross professional negligence – by, for example, failing to attend a sick patient.
4. He performs illegal abortions.
5. He advertises his services.
6. He issues sickness certificates without making sure that the patient is ill.
7. He attends a patient while under the influence of drink or drugs.
8. He makes an unwarranted disclosure of confidential information.

Any complaint of serious professional misconduct must be made to the Registrar of the General Medical Council – the body that supervises the medical profession.

If the council decides to investigate the matter, the complainer has to make a written statement setting out in detail the grounds for his allegation. Eventually, he may be asked to attend a hearing of the council's disciplinary committee and give evidence on oath. He can claim any expenses he incurs.

If his allegations are found to be wrong, he can be sued by the doctor for defamation – but only if it can be shown that he made the complaint maliciously – for example, because of spite.

Poor service or treatment Although National Health Service GPs are not employees, they are bound by contract to provide their patients with a proper medical service. If you believe that your GP's practice falls short of what is required, you can complain to the local health board.

The local HEALTH COUNCIL provides help for anyone who wishes to do so.

A complaint must be made in writing within 6 weeks of the incident that gave rise to the complaint – otherwise it may not be accepted. However, the board takes into account delays caused by absence or illness. If you want to appeal against a refusal to accept a late complaint, you can write to the Secretary of State for Scotland – but an extension is rarely given.

Minor complaints If the complaint is not serious and there is a chance that relations between doctor and patient can be restored, the health board tries to resolve the complaint informally – perhaps by getting doctor and patient together to discuss the problem in the presence of a medical member of the board and an outside chairman.

When you have a serious complaint against a doctor

If the complaint is serious, or if the complainer insists on having it investigated formally, it is referred to a medical service committee. The complaint is first considered by the lay chairman. If he considers there is a case to answer, the complainer is asked to make a fuller written statement.

The lay chairman, another lay member of the board and a general practitioner then hold a formal hearing in private.

The complainer and his doctor attend the hearing and are allowed to produce witnesses. Neither complainer nor doctor can be represented by a paid lawyer but each can be helped by an unpaid adviser. The secretary of the local health council will sometimes help complainers.

The report of that hearing goes to the health board, which decides whether the doctor has broken his contract with the NHS. If he has, the board may deduct money from the doctor's pay to cover the complainer's expenses. Or it may advise the Secretary of State for Scotland to fine him by making such a deduction. It can also recommend that he be struck off the medical list.

Both the complainer and the doctor can appeal against the decision to the Secretary of State for Scotland. *See:* MEDICAL NEGLIGENCE; PRIVATE MEDICINE

DOG CONTROL

How other people can be made to keep their dogs under control

If a dog is not being kept under proper control, and causes nuisance or danger, you can complain to the police.

A criminal prosecution – under Section 2 of the Dogs Act 1871 – may then be brought against the dog-owner in the SHERIFF COURT or the DISTRICT COURT.

When a dog is dangerous

It can be difficult to prove that a dog is dangerous. The court will hear evidence of its known temperament – for example, evidence that it frequently snaps at children. But the court also wants evidence that the animal has been dangerous on some occasion before the one that led to the prosecution.

Where a dog bit a small child who fell on the bone it was eating, the court decided that this single bite, inflicted under provocation, did not make the dog dangerous.

Proper control The prosecutor must prove to the court not only that the dog is dangerous, but also that it has not been kept under proper control. If a dog which was not kept on a lead or muzzled attacked someone, that would be proof of insufficient control.

A dog may be considered dangerous and not under proper control even if it is on the owner's private property, if other persons have a right of access through that property.

There is no need to show that the dog is dangerous to humans: it is enough to prove that it is dangerous to other animals. For example, a dog which has injured cattle or poultry or chased sheep can be dealt with as a dangerous dog. Nor is it necessary to show that the owner knew that his dog was dangerous.

Control order If the owner is convicted of having a dangerous dog not kept under proper control, and the court orders him to keep it under control in future, he has no right of appeal against the order.

Destruction order If the court orders the dog to be destroyed, the owner can appeal to the HIGH COURT of JUSTICIARY.

The appeal must be lodged within 5 days. Until the appeal is heard, the destruction order has only the effect of a control order.

Switching ownership A dog-owner may try to avoid being convicted of owning a dangerous dog by transferring ownership to someone else before the court hearing.

If it is a genuine sale or gift of the dog, the court cannot make a control or destruction order against the owner originally summoned to court. However, an order can be made against the new owner – although a fresh SUMMARY COMPLAINT would need to be issued, naming him as owner.

When a dog is not wearing a collar

If a dog is off the lead and on a highway or in a 'place of public resort' – for example, on a playing field – the owner must ensure that it is wearing a collar bearing the name and address of the owner.

However, this does not apply to a dog while it is being used for sporting purposes or for driving or tending cattle or sheep.

An owner who lets his dog out in public without a collar is committing an offence under an order made under the Diseases of Animals Act 1950, and can be fined up to £1,000.

When a dog is not on a lead

An owner who lets his dog roam in streets that have been designated by the regional or islands council as roads in which dogs must be on leads can be fined up to £50 under the Road Traffic Act 1972.

Although a driver should not swerve because of a dog on the road, it is an understandable reflex action. If an accident and injury or damage results, the owner of the dog can be found wholly or partly to blame, and be liable for damages, if he has not taken proper control of the dog and if he should have foreseen the possibility of an accident – for example, by taking an ill-disciplined dog into a street full of traffic and people.

When dogs foul the footpath

Any person in charge of a dog who allows it to foul a footpath or footway is guilty of an offence and can be fined up to £100. This rule does not apply to a blind person in charge of a guide dog.

The offence relates only to footpaths and footways – that is, ways over which the public have a right of passage or foot entry. It is not an offence for a dog to foul the roadway or gutter. Nor is it an offence for a dog to foul a private garden, as it is not a public place. But the garden-owner could sue the dog-owner for any damage caused if he could show that the dog was encouraged to use his garden.

If a dog worries livestock

An owner whose dog worries sheep, cows, horses or other livestock on agricultural land is guilty of an offence and can be fined up to £400. For the offence to be committed, the dog must attack or chase the livestock in a way which may reasonably be expected to cause injury or suffering – or, in the case of female livestock, abortion or loss or diminution in their produce.

Destruction or control order If a dog can be shown to have injured cattle or poultry, or to have chased sheep, the court can treat it as dangerous and order the owner to keep it under control – or have it destroyed.

If a dog is found straying

Anyone who takes possession of a stray dog must return it to its owner or inform the police station nearest to the place where it was found. There is a maximum fine of £100 for failing to do so.

If you find a stray dog and would like to keep it, you can tell the police so when you take it to them. Unless the owner is traced the dog will be handed back to you, and you must, by law, keep it for at least 1 month afterwards.

If you do not want the stray dog that you have found, the police can sell or destroy it within 7 days of picking it up, unless the owner is traced. The police can also do this if they find the dog. Where the owner is traced, the police can sell or destroy the dog if the owner does not claim it within 7 days of being notified that the police have it.

PROVING A DOG IS DANGEROUS CAN BE DIFFICULT

The court will hear evidence of a dog's known temperament. But the judge often wants proof that the animal has been a danger on some previous occasion.

When a dog is abandoned

Anyone who abandons an animal, including a dog, temporarily or permanently, can be prosecuted if the abandonment is likely to cause the animal unnecessary suffering. The penalty is a fine up to £1,000 or imprisonment for up to 6 months, or both.

A dog-owner convicted of the offence can also be disqualified from owning a dog for a specified period.

What happens if someone is cruel to a dog

The law forbids cruelty to any animal kept as a pet, and there are special rules about keeping dogs.

Anyone convicted of causing a dog unnecessary suffering by ill-treatment can be fined up to £1,000 and/or sentenced to 6 months' imprisonment.

He can also be banned from keeping a dog for a specified period – even for life. If during that period he keeps a dog – or even applies for a dog licence – he commits an offence and can be fined up to £100 or jailed for up to 3 months.

The convicted dog-owner can appeal against disqualification to the High Court of Justiciary. After not less than 6 months, if still disqualified, he can also go back to the original court and ask for review of the disqualification.

If the application for review is rejected, the convicted person must wait at least 3 months before applying again (unless his disqualification expires during that time).

Danger from guard dogs

Guard dogs trained to defend trade premises or building sites against intruders must be kept under strict control.

Under the Guard Dogs Act 1975, a guard dog on commercial premises must either be kept secure – in a kennel or tied or chained up – and unable to roam either inside or outside the premises, or be under the immediate control of a dog handler. There must be a clear warning notice outside the premises. Anyone breaking the law on guard dogs can be fined up to £1,000.

The restrictions do not apply to guard dogs inside people's homes or on farms.

When a dog licence must be obtained

In most cases, anyone who keeps a dog above the age of 6 months must get an annual licence. A licence is needed for each dog. The fee, 37½p, can be paid at any post office.

It is an offence, punishable by a fine of up to £50, to keep a dog without a licence or to fail to produce a licence when asked by a policeman. It is for the accused to prove that the dog is not 6 months old or that it does not belong to the person who is looking after it or on whose premises it is found.

Working sheep dogs and guide dogs kept by blind persons do not require licences.

DOMESTIC HELP

Employing someone to work around the house

The moment you employ someone to work as cleaner, handyman or gardener, you have to pay NATIONAL INSURANCE CONTRIBUTIONS if you pay more than the LOWER EARNINGS LIMIT, no matter how many hours are worked. Contributions must be paid even for workers from overseas.

If someone works for more than one employer, a separate contribution has to be paid for each employment in which the earnings limit is exceeded. No contributions need be paid for any employment in which the lower earnings figure is not reached – even when several separate amounts added together total more than the limit.

No national insurance contributions are payable by the householder when a self-employed window-cleaner, gardener or decorator, for example, is hired to do work.

Who pays for injuries suffered at work?

Anyone employed as a domestic help may be able to claim sick pay and/or SICKNESS BENEFIT if off sick because of injury received at work. Benefit is payable even if no national insurance contributions are paid. *See:* SICKNESS

The householder can be held liable for NEGLIGENCE if dangerous or unsafe equipment has been provided for the employee's work.

For example, a part-time gardener who is injured when trimming a hedge with a faulty electric trimmer could claim damages.

But a domestic help who injures herself by tripping over a vacuum-cleaner cable would probably have no claim against her employer.

Social security help that may be available

If, as a result of old age, illness, disablement or heavy family responsibilities, a person receiving SUPPLEMENTARY BENEFIT needs help with ordinary household tasks such as cleaning or cooking, extra benefit is payable to meet a reasonable charge for essential domestic help. But benefit is not paid to cover the cost of help provided by a close relative who incurs only minimal expenses.

A pensioner or a younger person on the long-term rate of supplementary benefit is expected to pay the first 50p of the cost of domestic help out of the normal weekly benefit. No additional benefit is paid for window cleaning or errands.

DOMICILE

The country, state or province that is your 'legal home'

An individual's marriage status, his liability for certain taxes on capital, even his legitimacy at birth – these and other legal matters are all determined not by where he is permanently resident but by the country in which he is legally domiciled.

A person can be domiciled in Scotland and therefore be subject to Scots law in those matters, yet live elsewhere – for example, England.

How domicile is decided in Scots law

Everyone has a domicile. A child is born with a domicile. A MINOR can decide on a new domicile, but he or she would have to leave home for it to be proved that such a decision has been made. However no one can have more than one domicile at any one time.

Domicile of origin Every child is born with a domicile of origin, which is inherited from one or other of the parents. In Scots law, a child takes the domicile of its father if the father is alive and married to the mother at the time of birth.

If the father is dead, or the child illegitimate, he or she takes the domicile of the mother.

That is so even if a legitimate child is born in another country. A child born, say, in France, has a Scots domicile of origin if the father's domicile at the time of the birth is Scots. It does not matter where the father is living at the time.

Domicile of origin is important, for although a person can change his domicile by choice at any time, he reverts to the original automatically if he abandons a chosen domicile without acquiring another.

Domicile of dependence A child whose parents change their domicile by choice also has his domicile changed. A boy, for example, born to a cook with a Scottish domicile working in Paris would have Scotland as his domicile of origin. If the father moves to London and becomes domiciled there by settling permanently while the boy is still living with him, the boy takes his father's new domicile – England.

If, when he becomes a minor, the boy sets out to travel the world, he immediately reverts to his domicile of origin – Scotland. And if he finally settles to work in Brussels, for example, his domicile becomes Belgian by choice.

Where parents separate or divorce, a PUPIL child living permanently with the mother takes her domicile.

Domicile of choice A person changes his domicile by moving to a new country and deciding to make his permanent home there. He does not have to make any declaration and it does not have the same public recognition as an acceptance of NATIONALITY or CITIZENSHIP.

A court deciding whether someone has changed his domicile has to take into account factors such as:

- The person's permanent home and length of time living there.
- The country where most of his assets are.
- Where most of his family live.
- Where he made his will.
- What impression he has given to other people about where he intends to retire.

For example, a person contesting a claim by the Inland Revenue in the United Kingdom for CAPITAL TRANSFER TAX on a parent's will would have to convince a court that the deceased parent had chosen a domicile in another country.

Under Scots law, a woman who marries keeps her own domicile – which means that it can be different from that of her husband.

The effect of domicile in legal issues

The question of a person's domicile arises only in legal matters, such as disputes in which it is necessary to settle a person's marriage status, and disputes over a person's liability to certain taxes on capital or over inheritance.

The court with jurisdiction over the matter decides the question of domicile. Depending on which country he is in and which domicile he claims, a person may be able to appeal.

Tax liability Someone whose domicile is Scotland has to pay tax on any capital transfers made in Scotland or elsewhere, and his estate is liable to these taxes. Domicile does not, however, make a person liable for income tax. That is determined by residence and a person does not have to be resident in his country of domicile.

Marriage and divorce

Domicile is also important in deciding questions relating to marriage status and divorce.

A woman, for example, married polygamously in a country which recognises polygamy as legal, may have her marriage recognised in a country where polygamy is not legal, provided she can establish the first country as her country of domicile.

That, in turn, can settle the legitimacy of any children born of the marriage and their rights to share in the FAMILY ASSETS.

DOORSTEP CREDIT

How the law controls canvassing of credit

Canvassing – an unsolicited visit to your home by a salesman trying to sell credit facilities – is strictly controlled by the Consumer Credit Act 1974.

A visit is solicited if you ask for it in writing. If you write – or fill in a coupon – merely asking for further details of a credit offer, you are not soliciting a visit. If a salesman calls as a result, he is canvassing.

Such coupons sometimes include an inconspicuous statement that you agree to a visit by a salesman. If you do not wish a visit, do not sign the coupon.

If he telephones to arrange to visit you, any resulting visit will legally be unsolicited, and so he will be canvassing.

On the other hand if he simply telephones, unsolicited, to do business by telephone, he is not canvassing.

A canvasser, or his company, must have a licence from the Office of Fair Trading. A licence will not be granted for soliciting debtor-creditor agreements, in which there is a straightforward loan and the lender has no business connection with the supplier of any goods bought with that loan. *See:* CONSUMER CREDIT

NO FOOT IN THE DOOR

It is illegal for a credit salesman to make unsolicited visits to people's homes. The penalty could be that his company would have its licence revoked by the Office of Fair Trading.

If you receive an unsolicited visit, and a straightforward money loan is made as a result, the lender cannot sue you or make you repay any money borrowed.

Licensed canvassing If the credit being offered is of the debtor-creditor-supplier type – in which the lender has a business connection with the supplier of goods – and the borrower defaults, the lender can sue for the money.

He can also repossess the goods, provided that he is also the supplier of those goods and the agreement is one in which he retains ownership until the debt is paid – as with hire purchase.

However, the borrower will still be protected by the rules allowing him to pull out of a transaction.

Types of business that can legally be canvassed by someone who is licensed include insurance, hire purchase, mail order, check trading, conditional sale agreements and rentals.

Even if the business can legally be canvassed, anyone who does so without a licence cannot sue or repossess goods without an order from the Office of Fair Trading, which is unlikely to be given.

DOORSTEP SELLING

The householder's right to fair dealing and privacy

The door-to-door salesman has the same legal obligations as any other trader. He must make no false claims about his goods and he must refund the money or pay compensation if the goods are defective.

However, a common problem with buying on the doorstep is that later when a complaint arises, the salesman may be difficult to find. Before parting with money or signing an agreement insist on seeing proof of the salesman's identity, his address or the address of his company. *See:* CREDIT AGREEMENT; DEFECTIVE GOODS; SALE OF GOODS; TRADE DESCRIPTIONS

DRAIN

Who has to pay when something goes wrong

The law makes a distinction between drains and sewers. Generally, a drain is a pipe within your property which is only used for the drainage of your property. Once the drain passes out of your property or if it is used for the drainage of any other premises, it is, for legal purposes, a sewer.

A drain is the responsibility of the owner or occupier of the property. All sewers, on the other hand, are the property of the sewerage authority, the regional or islands council, which is solely responsible for their maintenance and renewal.

When you have no main sewer

The sewerage authority has a duty to take public sewers to places where property owners can connect up their drains at reasonable cost. The authority need not, however, do anything that is not practicable at reasonable cost.

If there is a dispute about practicability or reasonable cost, it can be referred for decision to the Secretary of State for Scotland.

Where houses drain to septic tanks, the authority may accept the duty of emptying all such tanks, where practicable, at reasonable intervals, or may, at the request of the owner or occupier of premises, agree to empty a septic tank on appropriate terms.

DRINK AND DRIVING

Penalties for a motorist who takes too much alcohol

The law punishes severely any motorist convicted of a drinking-and-driving offence. A motorist can be prosecuted for any of the following offences:

1. Driving or attempting to drive with excess alcohol in breath, blood or urine.
Maximum penalty 6 months' imprisonment, a £2,000 fine, endorsement of licence and compulsory disqualification for at least 12 months.

2. Being in charge of a motor-vehicle (as opposed to driving or attempting to drive it) with excess alcohol in breath, blood or urine.
Maximum penalty 3 months' imprisonment, a £1,000 fine and licence endorsement. You may also be disqualified at the court's discretion.

3. Failing, without reasonable excuse, to provide a specimen of breath for a preliminary breath test at the roadside.
Maximum penalty £400 fine and licence endorsement. You may also be disqualified at the court's discretion.

4. Failing, without reasonable excuse, to provide a specimen of breath for analysis, or a specimen of blood or urine for a laboratory test.
Maximum penalty 6 months' imprisonment, a £2,000 fine, licence endorsement and compulsory disqualification for at least 12 months.

5. Driving or attempting to drive when unfit through drink or drugs.
Maximum penalty 6 months' imprisonment, a £2,000 fine, licence endorsement and compulsory disqualification for at least 12 months.

6. Being in charge of a motor-vehicle (as opposed to driving or attempting to drive it) when unfit through drink or drugs.
Maximum penalty 3 months' imprisonment, a £1,000 fine and licence endorsement. You may also be disqualified at the court's discretion.

'Driving' Essentially a person is not driving unless he has some control over the direction and movement of the vehicle. A person who is pushing a vehicle along a road while steering it with one arm has been said to be driving the vehicle.

'Attempting to drive' It is irrelevant that the attempt cannot possibly succeed. A motorist who sits in his car trying to make it move forward by accelerating the engine, but who is unable to move off because of a mechanical failure, has been said to be attempting to drive.

'In charge of' A person is only in charge of a vehicle if he has some control over it. The following have been said to be in charge: the supervisor of a learner-driver; a person approaching his vehicle but arrested before he could enter it; and a motorist sleeping off the effects of drink in his car while in possession of his ignition key.

A person in charge of a vehicle has a defence if he can prove that there was no likelihood of his driving it while under the influence of alcohol.

The most frequent charge

Most drinking-and-driving prosecutions are brought under the law that makes it an offence for a person to drive or attempt to drive a vehicle on a road or other public place with an amount of alcohol in his breath, blood or urine which exceeds the prescribed limit.

The prescribed limit is:

- 35 microgrammes of alcohol in 100 millilitres of breath;
- 80 milligrammes of alcohol in 100 millilitres of blood; or
- 107 milligrammes of alcohol in 100 millilitres of urine.

The courts have said that a 'public place' can include the following: a petrol-station forecourt, a public-house car park during licensing hours, a vacant piece of land used as overflow parking ground and the driveway from a public road to a hotel.

The preliminary breath test

If a motorist is suspected of a drinking-and-driving offence, the first step towards possible prosecution is usually a preliminary breath test taken at the roadside.

This test is administered by a police officer, using an Alcotest or similar tube – popularly known as a breathalyser – filled with chemical crystals that react to alcohol. A more modern method is to use a hand-held electronic device in which lights change colour to indicate a positive reading.

This preliminary test is not in itself proof of guilt – it simply allows a police officer to decide whether the motorist should be arrested and required to give a further specimen of breath for analysis, or a specimen of blood or urine for a laboratory test.

The preliminary breath test is not an essential part of the prosecution process. The specimen of breath, blood or urine to be used as evidence can be required without a preliminary breath test.

When a preliminary breath test can be required

The police are entitled to require a preliminary breath test if they reasonably suspect that:

1. The motorist is driving, or attempting to drive, or is in charge of, a motor vehicle with alcohol (not necessarily an excessive amount) in his body.

2. He has been driving, or has been attempting to drive, or has been in charge of, a motor vehicle with alcohol (not necessarily an excessive amount) in his body and he still has alcohol in his body.

3. He has committed a moving traffic offence (for example, speeding or careless driving).

4. He has been involved in a traffic accident.

Although random breath tests are not allowed, the police are entitled to stop any vehicle at random. If they then suspect that the driver has alcohol in his body, a preliminary breath test can be required.

Who can require a preliminary breath test?

Only a constable in uniform – of any rank, and including a special constable – is legally entitled to require a preliminary breath test. He must not be in plain clothes, but his uniform may be incomplete, provided he is easily identifiable as a policeman.

If, for example, a police officer is not wearing his cap, but his uniform is otherwise complete, the demand for a breath test is legal.

The officer who stops a vehicle, for whatever reason, need not be uniformed, but if he wishes to have the motorist breath-tested he must get a uniformed officer to administer the test.

If a suspected motorist has been injured, the police are entitled to require a preliminary breath test from him unless he is actually in hospital – if, for example, he is on his way to hospital by ambulance. The consent of the ambulance crew is not needed, but once he reaches hospital, a breath test cannot be given without the consent of the doctor in charge of the case. The doctor is only allowed to refuse his consent if the breath test would affect the proper care and treatment of the patient.

How soon must a preliminary breath test be given?

The police are not obliged to carry out a preliminary breath test within any time limit. However it will have to be carried out in reasonable time to allow any subsequent specimen of breath, blood or urine to show the level of alcohol as it was at the time when the motorist is alleged to have committed the offence.

It is possible for a motorist to claim that he has consumed alcohol after he has stopped driving. However, he will have to have evidence that he would not have exceeded the prescribed limit but for that later consumption.

Where the preliminary breath test can be given

A preliminary breath test must be given 'at or near' the place where the motorist is stopped. However, if there has been a traffic accident, a breath test may be required at a police station.

It is for the court to decide whether the breath test has been given at or near the place where the motorist is stopped. In an English case the court said that a test administered 160 yards from where the driver had been stopped was too far away to be legal. Each case will depend on the circumstances.

If a driver attempts to put time or distance between the police and himself by rushing away from his vehicle, he can legally be pursued – even onto private property – and still be required to give a breath test when he is caught. In these circumstances he could also be prosecuted for obstructing the police in the execution of their duties.

BLOWING INTO THE BAG

The 'bag-and-tube' preliminary breath-test equipment should be inflated by one breath of between 10 and 20 seconds. But inflation of the bag by several short breaths – for example, by a bronchitic driver – is valid.

Refusing a preliminary breath test

A person who fails to provide a specimen of breath for the preliminary breath test is guilty of an offence. He can be arrested without warrant if the constable reasonably suspects that he has alcohol in his body. Only a person who is in hospital cannot be arrested.

Providing a specimen which is not sufficient to enable the test to operate correctly counts as a failure to provide a specimen. It is a defence if the accused motorist had a reasonable excuse for his failure. But no excuse is reasonable unless the accused was physically or mentally unable to provide a specimen of breath or doing so would have involved a substantial risk to his health. The accused will usually have to produce medical evidence of this.

If the test result is positive

A breath test is positive, indicating excess alcohol in the body, if the crystals turn green beyond a yellow ring marked on the testing tube, or, where the electrónic device is used, the lights change colour from green to red. The motorist is generally allowed to see the test result, but he has no legal right to do so.

A motorist whose breath test is positive will normally be arrested, without a warrant, and taken to a police station.

However, it is not *necessary* for him to be arrested before being required to give a specimen of breath for analysis or a specimen of blood or urine for laboratory test. If the motorist is in hospital, he cannot be arrested.

At the police station

In most cases, the alcohol level will be determined more exactly at the police station, by an electronic breath analysis machine which gives an instant reading.

A police officer must check the machine in the presence of the motorist, using a standard vapour sample equivalent to the prescribed limit, certified by the British Calibration Service. If it is found to be in working order, the motorist must then give two specimens of breath for analysis. A copy of the results is given to the motorist.

When the two specimens have been given, the machine must be checked again, to make sure that it was in proper working order throughout. If the machine is not working properly for any reason, there can be no prosecution based upon evidence from it. A blood or urine specimen will be required instead.

The lower of the two breath readings is taken for the purpose of any prosecution. The higher reading must be disregarded. If one reading is above the limit and the other below, no prosecution will take place. An argument by a motorist that the lower reading was only just over the prescribed limit will not be accepted.

If the lower breath reading does not exceed 50 microgrammes of alcohol, the motorist can insist on having a blood or urine specimen taken for laboratory test. If he then provides such a specimen, the breath analysis will not be used in any prosecution.

If the police consider that the motorist is unable to give a specimen of breath for analysis – for example, because he suffers from severe asthma – a blood or urine specimen will be required.

HOW THE 'BAG-AND-TUBE' BREATHALYSER WORKS

When green is the colour that means a motorist could be a danger to himself and others

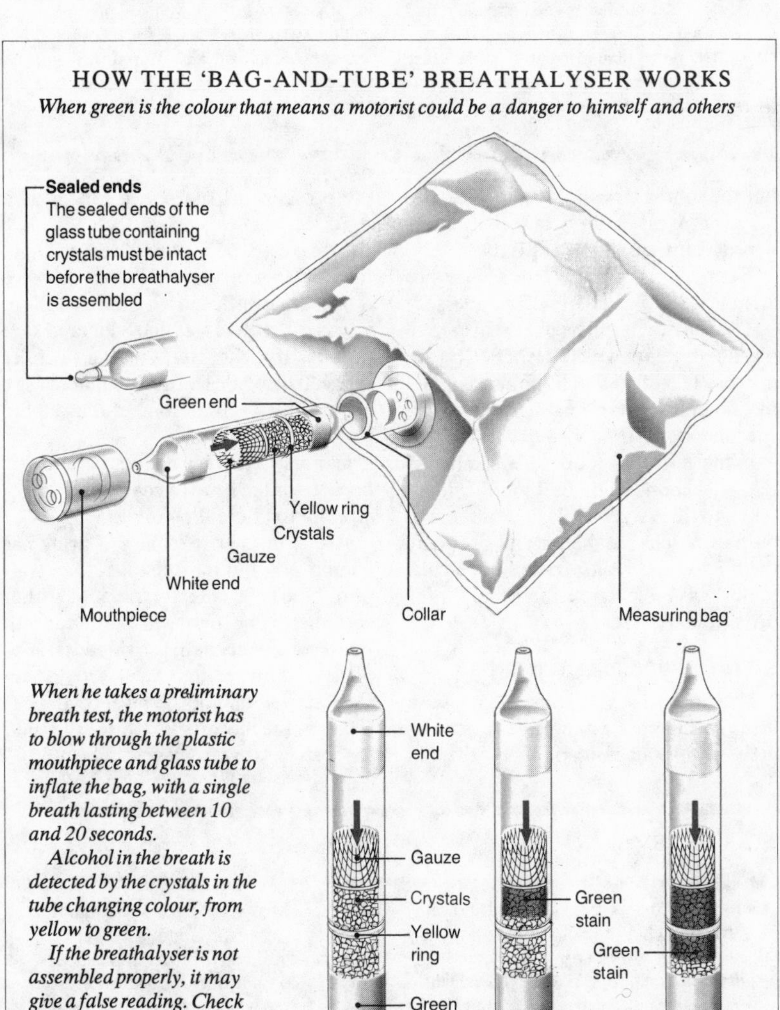

When he takes a preliminary breath test, the motorist has to blow through the plastic mouthpiece and glass tube to inflate the bag, with a single breath lasting between 10 and 20 seconds.

Alcohol in the breath is detected by the crystals in the tube changing colour, from yellow to green.

If the breathalyser is not assembled properly, it may give a false reading. Check that the sealed ends of the tube are undamaged before being snapped off. Also see that the crystals it contains are yellow before the mouthpiece and bag are attached.

The arrow marked on the tube must point from the mouthpiece to the bag.

Blood or urine specimen

Analysis of a breath specimen is the usual way of discovering whether the amount of alcohol in a motorist's body exceeds the prescribed limit. A blood or urine specimen can only be required in limited circumstances.

The police constable, not the motorist, decides whether a specimen should be blood or urine. This is so even where the lower breath reading does not exceed 50 microgrammes of alcohol and the motorist insists on having a blood or urine specimen taken. However, if a doctor advises that a blood specimen should not be taken for medical reasons, the specimen must be urine.

A requirement to provide a specimen of blood or urine can only be made at a police station or hospital. It cannot be made at a police station unless:

- The constable making the requirement reasonably believes that for medical reasons a specimen of breath for analysis cannot be provided or should not be required; or
- No (or no reliable) breath analysis machine is available at the police station; or
- For any other reason it is impracticable to use the breath analysis machine at the police station.

A person who, without reasonable

excuse, fails to provide a blood or urine specimen when required to do so is guilty of an offence. A warning must be given to the motorist by the constable that a failure to provide a specimen may render him liable to prosecution.

The motorist has the right to ask to be supplied with a sample of his blood or urine specimen at the time it is provided. If he does so, the specimen must be divided into at least two parts, with one part supplied to the motorist so that he may have it analysed privately if he so wishes. The part given to the motorist must be large enough to be capable of analysis.

If the motorist asks for part of the specimen, but this is not supplied to him, the specimen cannot be used in court by the prosecution.

THE BREATH-TEST BAG THAT HAD A HOLE IN IT

A motorist does not have to be arrested before being required to give a breath specimen for analysis or a blood or urine specimen for laboratory test. If he is arrested, there must first be a valid *preliminary breath test.*

Mr R, a motorist, was stopped by the police and required to take a breath test. He blew into the bag for several seconds, but it did not inflate. The policeman then realised that there was a hole in it.

The policeman also saw that the crystals had turned green, indicating a positive result, and offered Mr R a second bag to blow into. He refused and was arrested.

DECISION

The court ruled that a motorist cannot be arrested on a result obtained from defective breath test equipment. A bag with a hole in it is not a bag, so the device used to test Mr R was not of the type approved by the Secretary of State.

As a result, the first request for a breath test was not valid. The police could have arrested Mr R for refusing to use the second device offered, but not because the test with the faulty bag proved positive.

Giving a specimen of blood

If the motorist is required to give a specimen of blood, the police will call a doctor. There is no set procedure for providing blood, but it must be taken by a medical practitioner. If it is not, the specimen will be disregarded as evidence.

The police may allow the motorist to call his own doctor, but may call another doctor if the motorist's doctor is not immediately available.

The doctor will tell the motorist where he proposes to take the blood from – normally it is taken from a vein in the left arm.

The motorist himself cannot choose where the blood is taken from, except for some good medical reason. If the doctor asks for a sample from the vein, but the motorist will only allow it to be taken from his finger, this will be considered an unreasonable refusal.

Extracting blood from the vein with a syringe is simple and almost painless.

The specimen will be placed in a small plastic container which is labelled by the doctor. The label will be countersigned by the police officer in charge and the specimen sent for laboratory test.

If the motorist requests a sample of the specimen, enough blood will be taken to fill two small plastic containers, both of which are labelled and signed by the doctor and police officer. One container will be given to the motorist for private analysis.

Giving a specimen of urine

If a motorist is required to give a urine specimen, he must give two specimens within an hour of each other, in the presence of the police officer who requires them.

Normally a policewoman is available for woman motorists. However, if there is no woman officer in the police station, a woman motorist cannot demand that one be brought. But she can lawfully refuse to provide a urine specimen if she is not offered conditions of reasonable propriety and decency.

Complete privacy cannot be allowed because of the need to guard against any attempt to dilute the sample.

After the first specimen of urine has been given, the motorist is told to wait until he or she is ready to pass another specimen. The first will be discarded; the second specimen, provided it is supplied within an hour, will provide an accurate reading of the level of alcohol active in the motorist's body at the time the test was first requested. The motor-

THE PASSENGER WHO WAS CONVICTED

It is an offence for anyone to aid and abet a motorist to drive a motor-vehicle with excess alcohol in his body.

Thomas Mackie and a friend attended a beer festival in Princes Street Gardens, Edinburgh, where they drank a few pints of beer. Later, they had a meal and drank some more beer.

They separated and went to their different homes where the friend consumed another two pints of beer.

Some hours later Mackie called round at his friend's house in his car. After some minutes they both set off together in Mackie's car. Mackie, a qualified driver, sat in the front passenger seat, and allowed his friend, who only had a provisional licence, to drive the car.

The car was stopped by the police, who said it was being driven erratically and had swerved from side to side. The police breathalysed the driver after they noticed that his speech was slurred and that there was a smell of alcohol. The test was positive.

The driver was charged with driving with excess alcohol in his body; and Mackie was charged with aiding and abetting the driver to commit the offence.

DECISION

Mackie was convicted. The sheriff looked at the background of Mackie and his friend drinking together some hours earlier, the opportunity for Mackie to observe his friend when he called round at his house and the erratic manner in which the car was being driven. He said that any reasonable person with Mackie's knowledge would have realised that his friend was likely to have too much alcohol in his body.

Mackie therefore had the necessary knowledge to be guilty of aiding and abetting the driver.

ist is not expected to pass more urine than the small amount required for laboratory test.

When the second specimen is provided, it is put into a container. The procedure is then the same as for a blood specimen. If the motorist requires a sample of the specimen, it will be divided into two parts and one part will be given to him or her for private analysis.

The motorist commits the offence of failing to provide the specimen if the second specimen of urine is not provided within one hour of the first.

Detention of motorists

Once a specimen of breath, blood or urine has been provided, the motorist will be allowed to leave the police station – provided the officer in charge is satisfied that he does not intend to drive or that he is fit to drive. If he is not satisfied, the motorist will be detained until he is fit to drive.

A driver may choose to leave his car keys at the police station and continue his journey by some other means.

When the motorist is in hospital

A motorist who has been taken to hospital after an accident must not be asked to provide a specimen of breath, blood or urine for analysis if the doctor in charge of his case disapproves on medical grounds.

FEAR OF THE NEEDLE

A mental condition or physical injury must be extreme before it can be a reasonable excuse for failing to provide a breath specimen for analysis or a blood or urine specimen for laboratory test.

Mr Lockhart was arrested following a positive breath test. He was taken to Fort William police station.

He was asked by the police to provide a specimen of blood but said: 'I'd rather not. I have reasons'. He was not given an opportunity to explain his position before he was charged with the offence of failing to provide a specimen for laboratory test.

At his trial, Mr Lockhart explained that since childhood he had suffered a deep-seated aversion to the sight of blood and to any effort to use a hypodermic needle on him.

Because of this he became faint to the point of collapse at the sight of blood and upon the use of such needles.

DECISION

The sheriff said that in his view Mr Lockhart's physical and mental reaction to blood and needles was a reasonable excuse for his failure to provide the blood specimen. He was acquitted.

Mr Lockhart, however, was convicted on a further charge of driving while unfit to do so through drink or drugs.

A BIG TOE IS NOT REASONABLE

The doctor who is to take a blood specimen has the right to use his medical skill and experience to choose the part of the body from which blood is to be taken.

Mr Pugh was stopped by the police in his car and asked to take a breath test. He refused. The police had reasonable cause to suspect that Mr Pugh had alcohol in his body, and arrested him.

In the police station Mr Pugh was asked to provide a blood specimen for a laboratory test. He was warned that failure to do so might result in prosecution.

The doctor asked him to roll up his sleeve and provide the specimen from his arm. But Mr Pugh refused and insisted that it be taken only from his big toe. The doctor refused to do so because this was not the normal method of obtaining blood – the normal method being to take it from a vein in the arm – and involved a greater risk of infection.

Mr Pugh was charged with failing to provide a blood specimen.

DECISION

The appeal court said that the doctor had the right to choose the part of the body from which the blood was to be taken. If Mr Pugh had had an infection in his arm, or a plaster over the relevant part, that would have been a reasonable excuse for refusing to comply with the request. Since he had no such excuse, his refusal was unreasonable and he was convicted.

THE ANONYMOUS TIP-OFF

If the police have reasonable cause to suspect that a motorist has been drinking, they are entitled to require a preliminary breath test.

The officer on duty at Kirkcaldy police station received a telephone call from an anonymous informer. He stated that he had nearly been in collision with a Fiat car and that its driver was 'plastered'. He gave the car registration number.

The officer checked the registration number through the police national computer and obtained the car owner's name and address. He passed the information to two uniformed officers on mobile panda patrol in the area.

The two officers decided that if they saw the Fiat car they would stop it and require its driver to take a breath test. While travelling to the address the two officers saw the car, but could find no fault in the way it was being driven.

The suspected driver parked, locked his car and headed towards some nearby houses. The officers followed and asked him to stop. They administered a preliminary breath test – which was positive. The driver was arrested and charged with driving a motor car with excess alcohol in his body.

The accused argued that as the two officers had acted on information from an anonymous informer, they had no reasonable cause to suspect that he had alcohol in his body and that the breath test was therefore unlawful.

DECISION

The argument failed. On appeal, the High Court said that a police officer's reasonable suspicion could be based on information from an anonymous informer alone. The information was such that it merited investigation in the public interest and justified the police taking all necessary steps including administering a breath test.

Getting a private analysis

A motorist has the right, on request, to be given part of his blood or urine specimen for independent analysis. This protects any motorist who fears inaccurate 'official' analysis, or mixed-up specimens.

The police are under no duty to tell the motorist how to store the sample of the specimen given to him, or to give him information about analysts.

Until the analysis can be carried out, the sample should be kept in a refrigerator – but not a freezer. The motorist should immediately contact a solicitor who can arrange for private analysis (which may cost about £30).

The analyst's report will usually give full details of the condition and packing of the sample, as well as the alcohol content found.

Very few police analyses are successfully disputed.

Evidence in court

The prosecution will usually prove the level of alcohol in the motorist's body by means of the printed statement produced by the breath analysis machine. Where a blood or urine specimen is taken instead, the prosecution will rely on a certificate signed by an authorised analyst, containing details of the amount of alcohol in the specimen.

However such a statement or certificate can only be used by the prosecution if a copy has been served on the accused motorist at least 7 days before his trial.

The court will assume that the amount of alcohol in an accused motorist's breath, blood or urine at the time of the alleged offence was not less than in the specimen provided, unless the motorist provides evidence that:

- He consumed alcohol after he had stopped driving, attempting to drive, or being in charge of, a motor-vehicle and before he provided the specimen; and
- The level of alcohol in his body only exceeded the prescribed limit because of that consumption.

What the court can do

The maximum penalty for drunken driving is 6 months' imprisonment, a £2,000 fine, licence endorsement and unlimited disqualification (at least 12 months for a first offence and 3 years for a second offence within 10 years).

Depending upon the gravity of the offence – particularly the level of alcohol – the fine is likely to be several hundred pounds. It will be reduced only if there are any mitigating factors, or if the accused has limited financial means.

Imprisonment is not often imposed, but it may be if, for example:

- Innocent people were put at grave risk.
- One or more people were killed or injured or gravely alarmed.
- The driver has a bad record, especially a previous conviction for drunken driving.

The Department of Transport has indicated that where a driver is convicted within a period of 10 years of two offences of drunken driving with alcohol levels exceeding 87 microgrammes (approximately 200 milligrammes), he will be refused the return or renewal of his licence at the end of the period of disqualification unless he can satisfy the Department that he is not suffering from any disability, such as alcoholism, which would make it dangerous for him to drive.

If refused a licence, he may appeal to the sheriff. The sheriff may make such an order as he thinks fit and it is binding on the Department of Transport. There is no appeal to the Sheriff Principal.

See: DRIVING DISQUALIFICATION

THE ALTERNATIVE CHARGE – DRIVING WHILE UNFIT

A motorist can be prosecuted for driving, attempting to drive or being in charge of a motor vehicle on a road or other public place while unfit to drive through drink or drugs, without taking a preliminary breath test – or even if he takes a test and passes it.

If a motorist's behaviour clearly shows that he is unfit to drive – for example, he may be showing signs of drunkenness, such as unsteady gait or slurred speech – he can be arrested without a warrant and taken to a police station.

A doctor may be called to make sure that there is no medical explanation for the signs of apparent drunkenness. If the motorist consents, the police doctor can examine him and apply traditional tests such as asking him to pick up coins, walk a straight line and answer simple questions.

The motorist does not have to submit to any such examination or may consent only to being examined by a doctor of his own choosing. Such medical evidence is not essential to a prosecution for driving while unfit.

Apart from any preliminary medical examination, the procedure in the police station is the same as where the motorist is charged with an offence involving excess alcohol in the body. The motorist can be required to provide two specimens of breath for analysis or a specimen of blood or urine for a laboratory test. The motorist does not have to be under arrest before being required to provide any such specimens.

If a prosecution takes place, the result of the breath, blood or urine test can be used in evidence by either side. The prosecution must prove not only that the accused motorist had taken drink but that it had actually impaired his ability to drive properly.

If the specimen test result shows that the motorist's level of alcohol was only a little above the prescribed limit, he may be able to convince the court that his ability to drive was not impaired.

This is different from the position of a motorist charged with having excess alcohol in his body (as opposed to being unfit through drink) – he cannot escape conviction if his alcohol level is even marginally over the prescribed limit.

Being unfit through drugs

A motorist can be prosecuted if he drives, attempts to drive or is in charge of a motor vehicle while unfit through any drug, including any type of medicine – for example, an overdose of insulin prescribed for a diabetic. Maximum penalties are the same as for being unfit through drink.

Evidence of unfitness through drugs includes speech or sight difficulties, dilated pupils and sweating.

A motorist who is suspected of being unfit through drugs can be required by the police to provide a blood or urine specimen for a laboratory test.

An accused motorist can plead either that he was not under the influence of a drug or that the drug did not make him unfit to drive or be in charge of a vehicle.

DRIVEWAY

The right of access across a pavement

If you wish to construct a new driveway giving access from your home to a road, you may have to obtain PLANNING PERMISSION from the LOCAL AUTHORITY responsible for planning control in your area.

Planning permission is usually necessary if you have to carry out building or demolition work – such as the removal of part of a garden wall. If you wish to obtain access to a major road, you must have planning permission – it could be refused on grounds of road safety.

In many cases you will also need the consent of the local highway authority (the regional or islands council) before you lower the level of the kerb to form a 'carriage crossing'. The highway authority may require you to construct a crossing at your own expense. The crossing will have to be constructed to standards laid down by the authority.

In exceptional cases, the highway authority can take action to close private accesses – for example, where an access seems likely to endanger or unreasonably interfere with traffic on a highway. You can object to an order stopping up your access.

The highway authority must first be satisfied that an alternative means of access can be provided. They will have to pay compensation for any loss resulting from their action.

The Secretary of State for Scotland can make an order stopping up an access to a trunk road.

PRIVATE DRIVEWAYS

If you require access to a private driveway or garage, it is likely that the local highway authority will insist that the level of the kerb is lowered – at your expense – to make a 'carriage crossing'.

DRIVING DISQUALIFICATION

How a motorist can lose his licence

Disqualification from driving is automatic for some motoring offences and can be imposed at the court's discretion for all endorsable offences. *See:* ROAD TRAFFIC OFFENCES

When a driver is disqualified he must hand his licence over to the court and it is retained by the issuing authority until the period of disqualification expires. For the most serious offences, where disqualification is compulsory, the minimum ban is 12 months, with no upper limit. Discretionary disqualification has no minimum or maximum period.

Disqualification means that a person may not drive at all, and driving includes any form of controlling or steering or propelling a vehicle, including for example pushing it, or steering it down a hill without the engine on. Steering a towed vehicle is driving.

Driving while disqualified is a very serious offence, and heavy penalties are likely to be imposed.

Courts have no power to disqualify for offences that are not endorsable – for example, parking on a yellow line, disobeying a 'one-way street' sign, having a defective silencer or no MoT certificate – regardless of the driver's previous record. If an offence is endorsable, it is also disqualifiable.

When a driver must be disqualified

The offences for which disqualification for a minimum of 12 months is compulsory are:

- Drink-and-driving offences.
- Culpable homicide.
- Causing death by reckless driving.
- Racing on the highway.

Reckless driving on its own involves compulsory disqualification only if the driver has already been convicted of a similar offence within the previous 3 years.

Offences involving DRINK AND DRIVING – including refusal to give a breath, blood or urine specimen – are by far the most common reasons for compulsory disqualification, but if the motorist was only 'in charge' of the vehicle and was not attempting to drive, the court need not disqualify him.

Special reasons against disqualification

In rare cases, the courts need not impose a compulsory disqualification or may reduce the period for 'special reasons'.

In a drink-and-driving case, a motorist can plead special reasons against disqualification if, for example, he can prove that his drink was 'laced' without his knowledge, or if he was affected by a combination of drink and medicinal drugs whose effects he could not be expected to know.

However, the court can still disqualify even if the special reason has been proved. In the case of a laced drink the court may decide that the driver was neglecting his responsibilities by not taking sufficient care to ensure he was given a suitable drink.

A court may also take the view that it is well known that many drugs, particularly sleeping pills and tranquillisers, should never be mixed with drink – and that ignorance of their effects is not an acceptable excuse.

Special reasons have been accepted when a motorist has driven because of an emergency – for example, if he had to take an injured person to hospital. But the rules are strict, and the motorist usually must show that he was unable to obtain an ambulance or taxi or to get someone else to drive.

The distance driven in excess-alcohol cases is normally irrelevant.

Special reasons cannot be pleaded on the ground that driving ability was not impaired, that lack of food affected the alcohol level or that the alcohol level was above the limit only because more alcohol was absorbed after the motorist stopped driving.

When a driver is likely to be disqualified

A court's power to disqualify a motorist for any endorsable offence is rarely used in routine cases of, for example, speeding or minor careless driving. But a motorist who does 60 mph or more in a 30 mph zone and is convicted of speeding may well be disqualified even if he has no previous record of driving offences.

Danger to other people is one of the most important factors when a court is deciding whether to disqualify, so disqualification is regularly imposed for reckless driving and driving without insurance. Disqualification is sometimes imposed in a careless-driving case.

In many endorsable offences the driver can plead guilty by letter, but if the court is considering disqualification it may order his personal attendance in court.

'Totting up' offences for a disqualification

The totting-up law changed in October 1982 with the introduction of a points system graded according to the seriousness of the offence. A driver who collects endorsements totalling 12 points or more in any three-year period will be disqualified for 6 months.

The three-year period is calculated from the date of the first offence to the date of the conviction that brings his total to 12 points.

It is possible for a court not to impose the mandatory 6 months totting disqualification, or not to impose the full 6 months, but only if there are strong mitigating circumstances and they have to be very strong indeed.

It is no argument that the offender will suffer hardship, unless that hardship would be exceptional. Difficulty in getting to work, or even loss of a job, is unlikely to be sufficiently exceptional.

Between October 1982 and October 1985, previous endorsements will count as 3 points.

Most offences have a fixed number of points allocated, but careless driving, failing to stop after an accident, failing to report an accident and driving without insurance have a band or range of points within which the court can fix the appropriate number of points having regard to the gravity of the offence.

Where a number of offences are committed on the same occasion, the number of points to be endorsed on a licence cannot exceed the highest number for any one of those offences. For example, if a person is charged with careless driving, driving without a licence and driving without insurance, all committed on the same occasion, the number of points to be endorsed will be a maximum of 8 (the maximum for driving without insurance).

Offence	Points
• Reckless driving	10
• Careless or inconsiderate driving	2–5
• Being in charge of motor vehicle when unfit through drink or drugs	10
• Being in charge of motor vehicle with alcohol above prescribed limit	10
• Failing to provide specimen for breath test	4
• Failing to provide specimen for analysis	10
• Carrying passenger on motor cycle contrary to section 16	1
• Failing to comply with traffic directions	3
• Leaving vehicle in dangerous position	3
• Failing to stop after accident	5–9
• Failing to give particulars or report accident	4–9
• Contravention of construction and use regulations	3
• Driving without licence	2
• Failing to comply with conditions of licence	2
• Driving with uncorrected defective eyesight	2
• Refusing to submit to test of eyesight	2
• Driving while disqualified as under age	2
• Driving while disqualified by order of court	6
• Using, or causing or permitting use of, motor vehicle uninsured and unsecured against third-party risks	4–8
• Taking a motor vehicle without consent or lawful authority, or driving, or allowing oneself to be carried in, a motor vehicle so taken	8
• Contravention of traffic regulations on special roads	3
• Contravention of pedestrian crossing regulations	3

THE INVALID WHO DRANK AND DROVE

Personal hardship and similar mitigating circumstances are not 'special reasons' for not disqualifying a driver

Mr Mullarkey, who had artificial legs, was convicted of driving his invalid car after drinking. He said that disqualification would cause appalling hardship because he could walk only a very short distance.

DECISION

The court ruled that, despite his disability, Mr Mullarkey's circumstances did not amount to a special reason and he was disqualified.

THE PREGNANT WIFE WHO WAS A SPECIAL REASON

Circumstances which show that the safety of the public would not be endangered can be 'special reasons' for not ordering disqualification

In 1978 Mr Graham was disqualified from driving for 18 months. He made formal arrangements for others to drive him on business and social outings during his period of disqualification.

In 1979 Mr Graham was travelling home in a car being driven by his wife, who was 7 months pregnant. His wife began to feel unwell and was forced to stop the car to get out and be sick. She felt faint and was unfit to drive.

Mr Graham did not know why his wife had suddenly fallen ill, and because of her condition he did not wish to leave her and seek help. He decided that he would drive the car home and take a route which went near a hospital in case his wife's condition got worse. While driving, Mr Graham was seen by police officers who knew he was a disqualified driver. There was no question of the car being driven in an unsafe manner.

He was charged and convicted of driving while disqualified. The judge disqualified him from driving for a further 18 months.

DECISION

On appeal, the High Court quashed the order for disqualification on the ground that there were special reasons for not imposing disqualification.

The court indicated that the decision whether or not to disqualify depended on the risk to public safety and the likelihood of the offence being repeated. The crisis which lead Mr Graham to drive the car was unexpected and repetition was extremely unlikely.

- Failure to obey sign exhibited by school crossing patrol..3
- Contravention of order prohibiting or restricting use of street playground by vehicles..2
- Exceeding a speed limit 3
- Stealing or attempting to steal motor vehicle 8

Having served his 6 months disqualification, the driver starts with a clean slate – there is no carry forward. But a second totting disqualification within 3 years carries a 1 year disqualification and a third totting disqualification carries a 2 year disqualification.

When a driving test may be ordered

A motorist convicted of an endorsable offence can be disqualified until he passes a driving test again. For example, a motorist convicted of reckless driving may be disqualified for 12 months and ordered to take a driving test. He must not drive at all for 12 months. Thereafter he can drive only as a provisional driver, displaying L-plates and accompanied by a qualified driver.

Appealing against a disqualification

A motorist can appeal against disqualification even if he has pleaded guilty – and even if the offence involved a compulsory or totting-up disqualification. The period of disqualification takes effect immediately but the motorist can ask the court to suspend it until his appeal is heard. Such applications are rarely successful.

Getting a disqualification removed

Disqualification need not last for the full period imposed by the court. After a time the motorist can apply to the court that disqualified him to have the ban lifted. Normally, he will need some very good reason – for example, a new job that requires him to drive.

If the disqualification was for between 2 and 4 years he can apply to end it after 2 years – the minimum time that must elapse before any such application. If disqualified for between 4 and 10 years, he can apply after half the period has elapsed. If the disqualification is for more than 10 years, he can apply after 5 years.

A motorist cannot apply for the disqualification to be removed if it was for less than 2 years.

The clerk of the court notifies the prosecutor of every application, so that he can oppose it if he wishes. The court considers the circumstances of the original offence, and the present position of the offender, especially whether he requires his licence for work.

If an application is refused, it can be renewed every 3 months. If granted, the disqualification can be ended at once, or at a future date fixed by the court.

DRIVING INSTRUCTION

Standards of teaching required by law

Anyone with a full driving licence can legally give lessons to a learner. But no one can charge for such lessons unless he is registered as a Department of Transport approved driving instructor, or holds a special licence issued by the Department to trainee instructors.

A car dealer is not allowed to give free lessons unless he is registered as an instructor. That is to prevent him including 'free' lessons as part of the purchase price of a vehicle, and then giving unqualified instruction to the purchaser.

A learner should ask to see the instructor's certificate of registration – or, if the instructor is a trainee, the special licence.

Anyone who takes payment for giving driving lessons while unregistered can be fined £1,000 and, if not paid, sentenced to 60 days' imprisonment.

DRIVING LICENCE

Who can drive what, and what happens when the rules are broken

No one may drive a motor vehicle on British roads without a valid licence. The type of licence needed, and your entitlement to it, depends on:

- The vehicle you want to drive.
- Whether you have passed a driving test.
- Your age.
- Your health.
- Your nationality.
- Your driving record.

How to go about applying for a driving licence

All licences are issued – and all drivers' records kept – by the Driver and Vehicle Licensing Centre in Swansea.

But do not apply to the licensing centre immediately. First, you must obtain a driving licence application form from any post office.

The form, which covers all cases except heavy goods or public-service driving, asks for information about yourself, the type of licence you want, the details of your last licence, if any, and whether you have been, and remain, disqualified or convicted of any 'endorsable' motoring offences.

Giving false information or failing to reveal a current endorsement or disqualification is an offence, carrying a maximum penalty of up to £1,000.

BEING MEDICALLY FIT TO DRIVE

You should tell the licensing centre about any medical or physical illness that could make you a danger to other road users – not only when you first apply for a licence, but also later on, if you become aware of a potentially dangerous condition.

Any illness that causes fainting, giddiness or blackouts, or which severely restricts a driver's use of his arms and legs, should be reported.

Examples are epilepsy, diabetes, a stroke, multiple sclerosis, Parkinson's disease, heart disease, high blood pressure, arthritis, drug addiction, alcoholism and any mental illness.

If you report such an illness, this does not necessarily mean that you will be refused a licence. The licensing centre will accept advice from your doctor about your physical competence to drive, but it may decide to grant a licence for a limited period of 1, 2 or 3 years.

You need not report an illness or injury which is not expected to last more than 3 months. If in doubt, consult your doctor.

Standard of eyesight

Every driver must be able to read a standard number plate from a distance of 75 ft in good daylight. If you need spectacles or contact lenses to do so, you should wear them every time you drive.

When you have completed the form, send it to the Centre – the address is on the form – with the appropriate fee, and your previous licence or pass certificate from your driving test.

Getting a provisional licence to start driving

A provisional driving licence is issued to enable a learner to drive a motor vehicle before passing a test. It is valid for any vehicle except heavy goods and large passenger vehicles. Like a full licence, it normally runs until a driver's 70th birthday.

If you already have a full licence to drive one type of vehicle, you may not need a provisional licence to drive another type. A qualified car driver, for example, does not need a provisional licence to learn to ride a motor cycle. Nor will a qualified motor cyclist require a provisional licence if he decides to learn to drive a car.

All provisional licence holders and anyone driving a vehicle for which he has not passed the test, must display 'L' plates at the front and back.

He must also be accompanied by a qualified driver unless it is a vehicle built to carry only one person, or a motor cycle with or without a sidecar.

A learner motor cyclist must not carry anyone on his pillion except a qualified motor cyclist.

Since February, 1983, learner motor cyclists have been restricted to machines:

- Not exceeding 125 cc.
- With maximum output of engine not exceeding 9 kilowatts.
- With power-to-weight ratio not exceeding 100 kilowatts per metric tonne.

The test for motor cyclists is two-part:

- A machine-handling test off the road on a large flat area, normally conducted by an approved training organisation.
- The traditional road test.

Learner motor cyclists can hold a provisional licence for only 2 years unless they already hold a full licence for a motor car, tricycle or moped. If they have not become qualified by then, they are not allowed to ride motor cycles for the next 12 months.

Getting a full licence when you have passed the test

A driver may apply for a full licence provided that he has held one at any time in the past 10 years or has passed the test for the vehicle he wants to drive, and is not disqualified. The fee for a full licence is usually £10.

A full licence normally runs until your 70th birthday. But if you are 67 or older, it will be issued for 3 years or less – depending on your state of health.

The employer's responsibility for his drivers

An employer must ensure that his driver holds a valid licence and is accordingly insured. Otherwise the employer commits an offence, even if he honestly believed that the driver did hold a valid licence.

Getting a duplicate licence

If you lose your licence, or it is destroyed or defaced, you may apply for a duplicate. A £3 fee is payable.

If the original licence is later found, and is still valid, you must return it to the licensing centre and keep the duplicate. Do not return the duplicate and keep the original.

How to go about exchanging a licence

If you pass a test, or become qualified by age, to drive additional groups of vehicles, you can obtain an exchange licence. The fee is £3.

WHAT YOUR LIFE-LONG DRIVING LICENCE QUALIFIES YOU TO DRIVE

Understanding the legal restrictions on drivers who have even a 'full' licence

'Code letters refer to the types of vehicle you are licensed to drive. For example, 'A' authorises you to drive any vehicle except one in group 'D' (motor cycle), 'E' (road roller), 'G' (vehicle steered by its tracks), 'H' (invalid carriage) or 'J' (trolley vehicle)'.

When you have a full licence to drive, say, a moped only – letter 'E' – and want to drive a motor-cycle – letter 'D' – you will be regarded as a learner driver on the motor-cycle and must carry 'L' plates

Type of licence FULL

valid from 01.10.1983 to 30.06.2022 inclusive

Date last licence expired 30. 9.1983

The person named is hereby licensed to drive motor vehicles of groups

A ************************************

This licence has the effect of a Provisional Licence to drive motor vehicles of all other groups: see relevant conditions overleaf.

all subject to reaching the minimum ages for driving specified overleaf

You are required by law to inform Drivers Medical Branch, DVLC, Swansea, SA99 1AT at once if you have any disability (includes any physical or mental condition), which is or may become likely to affect your fitness as a driver, unless you do not expect it to last for more than 3 months.

A driving licence expires on the day before the holder's 70th birthday. For anyone who has reached 67, renewal is possible for only 3 year periods, but there is no age beyond which a licence is not issued – unless there are medical reasons for stopping someone driving.

RULES FOR DISABLED DRIVERS

A full licence to drive an invalid carriage or specially constructed vehicle does not entitle a disabled person to drive any other type of vehicle. If he wants to learn to drive something else, he must take out a provisional licence for it.

However, a licence issued to a disabled driver often stipulates that the driver must be able to operate all the controls effectively at all times. The stipulation applies to any vehicle that the driver wants to learn to drive.

For example, if a qualified motor cyclist passes a test to drive a road roller, he is entitled to an exchange licence that records the new information. So is a fully licensed car driver who, at the age of 18, becomes automatically entitled to drive other types of vehicle.

The other reason for applying for an exchange licence is to have previous endorsements removed. That can be done only 4 years after the date of an endorsement – or 11 years, if the endorsement was for a drink-and-driving offence.

What you need if you are planning to drive abroad

A full British driving licence is enough for most Western and several Eastern European countries. Elsewhere, you need an international driving permit, which can be obtained from the Automobile Association, the Royal Automobile Club or the Royal Scottish Automobile Club. You do not have to be a member.

You can apply in person at one of their local offices – taking your full British licence and a passport-sized photograph – or you can send a completed application form and a photograph. If you apply in writing you do not need to produce your driving licence, but you must give its number. The permit costs £2 and lasts for a year.

The motoring organisation will also tell you the specific licence requirements of any country you intend to visit.

It is an offence for a British driver whose licence has expired, or who has been disqualified, to use an international permit to drive in Britain. But it is not illegal for him to use one to drive abroad.

Rules for drivers from abroad

A tourist coming to Britain can use his own national licence or an international permit for up to a year. He must then take out a provisional licence and pass the appropriate test to qualify for a full British licence.

A full licence can be issued to new residents in Britain who hold a licence issued within the EEC. It can also be issued to anyone who has held a full licence issued within the past 10 years in Northern Ireland, the Isle of Man or the Channel Islands.

Endorsements for driving offences

Many motoring offences carry an automatic endorsement which is recorded in code on the driver's licence.

For example, someone convicted of exceeding a 30 mph speed limit will have the fact stamped on his licence with the dates of offence and conviction, the penalty and a code number identifying the court.

There are more than 50 endorsable offences, each with its own code reference. The full list is to be found on form INS1, available from DVLC, Swansea.

Under a 'totting-up' system, endorsements totalling 12 points or more within 3 years brings an automatic 6 month DRIVING DISQUALIFICATION.

If someone commits a motoring offence, but has no current licence or is too young to obtain one, the details of any endorsement or disqualification are recorded at the licensing centre and will appear on any licence he later obtains.

When the police stop a driver

Anyone driving a vehicle or supervising a learner is obliged to show his licence when asked to do so by a police officer. When there has been an accident or motoring offence, the police can also demand to see the licence of anyone they believe to have been driving at the time.

If a driver does not have his licence with him, he must produce it, in person, at a police station of his choice within 5 days of being asked to show it, including Sundays. He must go to the police station that he has named.

The police may stop a driver to check that his documents are in order, if they do so in good faith.

DRUGS

How the law controls their use and abuse

Unlawful drugs – that is, drugs whose use and distribution are 'controlled' under the Misuse of Drugs Act 1971 – are divided into three groups, A, B and C, indicating their degree of danger. Those in group A are regarded as the most dangerous and those in group C as the least dangerous.

Possession of drugs

It is an offence to possess or take any controlled drug except by doctor's prescription. The maximum penalty is 7 years' imprisonment. However, penalties of up to 14 years can be imposed for trafficking – producing, supplying, importing or exporting drugs.

When a blood or urine test reveals a controlled drug in someone's body, he is regarded as being 'in possession', just as if the drug were in his pocket. If a person pleads that he did not know he was in possession of a controlled drug, or that he had taken it, it is for the prosecution to prove that he did know.

What the police can do

The police can stop and search anyone they reasonably suspect of possessing a controlled drug – without a warrant. But to search a person's home, or any other premises, a SEARCH warrant is needed.

Vehicles can be stopped and searched for drugs – without warrant – and the police and Customs and Excise officers can search all ships and aircraft.

Substances suspected of containing a controlled drug can be seized for analysis.

If someone is found with drugs on your premises – for example, a lodger who has a room to himself – you are not involved in the offence provided that you were unaware of it. The prosecutor must prove that you did know.

When someone is an addict

Anyone who knows or suspects that someone is a drug addict – for example, a son or daughter – should urge the person to seek medical help, but is under no obligation to report the matter, or to report suspected possession of drugs whether legal or illegal.

However, if a doctor has reasonable cause to believe that a person is addicted to a controlled drug, he has a legal obligation to inform the Home Office, in writing, within 7 days.

Some doctors are licensed by the Home Office to prescribe controlled drugs for registered addicts. A doctor who is not so licensed, and who cannot treat a patient by any means apart from prescribing controlled drugs, can refer the patient to a specialist drug clinic. An addict can go directly to such a clinic without consulting a doctor.

There are about 70 drug clinics in Britain (18 of them in the London area). Addresses of the clinics can be obtained from family doctors, hospitals, local authority social work departments, or the police.

When prescribed medicine causes harm

If you have been harmed by a prescribed drug, you may be able to seek compensation by suing the doctor who prescribed it, the chemist who dispensed it, the company which manufactured it, or all three – depending on the circumstances.

If the doctor prescribed the wrong drug for your illness, or if there were medical reasons why you should not have been given the prescribed drug, or if he gave the wrong dosage, you can sue him on grounds of MEDICAL NEGLIGENCE. You can also complain against him to your local health board and the General Medical Council. *See:* DOCTOR AND PATIENT

If you were given a harmful drug in hospital, you should sue both the doctor who prescribed it and his employer, the local health board.

If you have been harmed by drugs issued on prescription, the pharmacist can be sued only if he was at fault – for example, if he dispensed a drug other than the one prescribed, or wrote incorrect instructions on the label, or stored or prepared the medicines in such a way that they were damaged.

If you have been harmed by drugs sold without a prescription – if, for example, you asked the pharmacist to recommend an ointment for a rash, but found it caused the irritation to spread – you may be able to sue the chemist for selling faulty or incorrect goods. You might also be able to sue for negligence. *See:* DANGEROUS GOODS; DEFECTIVE GOODS

If you were harmed as a result of incorrect manufacture of the drug, or if you can prove that it had been inadequately tested, you could sue the manufacturer for negligence.

In general, however, negligence by a manufacturer would be difficult to ascertain as drug companies test their products extensively and must satisfy stringent government safeguards before the drugs can be marketed.

Never pursue an action against a doctor, pharmacist, health board or manufacturer without taking professional legal advice. If you lose the case, your legal costs will be heavy, while those you are suing will usually have insured themselves against claims of this nature. *See:* LEGAL ADVICE

HOW DRUGS ARE CLASSIFIED

Class A 101 drugs including heroin, morphine, dextromoramide, medicinal opium, dipipanone, levorphanol, cocaine, LSD, injectable amphetamines and mescaline.

Class B 15 drugs including purple hearts, cannabis, cannabis resin and benzedrine.

Class C 6 drugs including several amphetamine-type substances and Mandrax.

DRUNK AND DISORDERLY

When someone is 'incapable' in public

When the police charge someone with being drunk and incapable (of taking care of himself) in public, they do not need the evidence of a breath test. It is enough for the police officers to tell the court that the accused showed 'the typical symptoms of being drunk' – for example, inability to stand up straight, slurred speech and drowsiness. In fact, the police cannot insist on breathalysing a non-motorist and do not, in practice, try to do so.

The maximum penalty for being drunk and incapable is a £100 fine. It is a defence to the charge that the accused was under the care or protection of a suitable person – for example, a sober friend or relative.

It is also an offence to be drunk and disorderly (that is, behaving in a noisy or unruly manner) in public, or to use obscene or indecent language while drunk to the annoyance of any person. The maximum penalty is a £100 fine.

DRUNKENNESS AS A DEFENCE

Drinking is usually no excuse

The law draws a distinction between someone who gets drunk occasionally and the chronic alcoholic who has drunk himself into a state of insanity.

Generally, the actions of someone who is drunk are judged in law by the same standards as would be applied to the actions of a sober person. His drunkenness would be no defence to a criminal charge.

Someone who deliberately makes himself drunk to give himself courage to commit a crime cannot successfully argue later that he did not know what he was doing when he committed the crime.

However the chronic alcoholic who commits a crime may be able to plead INSANITY AS A DEFENCE.

DRY CLEANER

Who is responsible for damaged clothes

When a dry cleaner accepts clothes for cleaning or pressing he accepts a responsibility to take all reasonable care of them. If they are lost or damaged the cleaner is liable to pay compensation unless he proves that the loss was not the result of negligence or lack of skill.

To guard against such claims some cleaners issue receipts with printed conditions limiting their liability.

These conditions may not always be legally enforceable. A condition that says that no liability at all is accepted for loss or damage may well be held to be unreasonable. On the other hand, a condition limiting liability to a fixed amount would probably be said to be reasonable if that condition had been brought to the customer's attention.

Dry cleaners do not generally promise to remove all stains.

Conditions printed on the receipt may give the cleaner power to sell clothes if they are not collected within a reasonable time, such as 6 months. He is entitled to keep the cost of cleaning and the cost of selling the clothes out of the price he receives, but any surplus must be kept available for the customer if he eventually demands it. *See:* LAUNDRY

EARNED INCOME

Defining income for tax purposes

For income tax, earned income is strictly defined in law:

1. PAY (including statutory sick pay and maternity pay) from a job and any taxable benefits from it – such as free medical insurance, a suit or a car.
2. Any earnings from self-employment in a trade or profession, including any partnership in which you are actively engaged.
3. Income from most pensions or any retirement annuity from a scheme approved by the Inland Revenue.
4. Certain social security benefits that are taxable. *See:* INCOME TAX
5. Sums of money paid to a person after leaving a job – for example, taxable compensation for loss of office.
6. Any income from the creation of a copyright or patent.
7. Maintenance payments made by a marriage partner to the other partner, for his or her benefit or that of a child – or by a natural father to his child.

EDUCATION AUTHORITY

How schools are run and paid for

The education authorities in Scotland are the nine regional councils – Highland, Grampian, Tayside, Fife, Lothian, Borders, Central, Strathclyde, Dumfries and Galloway – and the three islands councils – Orkney, Shetland, and the Western Isles. These councils must provide 'adequate and efficient' school and further education for their areas. They carry out this duty through an education committee and a team of professional officers headed by a Director of Education.

Education is compulsory for children between the ages of 5 and 16.

The education authority must educate children in accordance with the wishes of their parents, unless the cost of doing so would be unreasonably high or the children would not receive what the authority considers to be a suitable education.

With a few exceptions, no fees are payable at local authority schools. The education authority must supply without charge any books, writing materials, mathematical instruments and other articles necessary to allow pupils to take full advantage of the education provided.

An education committee consists mainly of elected regional councillors. It must also include at least two teachers employed by the authority and at least three people appointed because of their interest in the promotion of religious education.

Like other local authority committee meetings, the education committee meetings are open to the public, including the press – except on the occasions when the committee decides that publicity on a particular subject under discussion would be harmful to the public interest. Advance notice giving the time and place of meetings open to the public is displayed at the council's offices.

The press have a right to receive copies of the agenda and other papers for a meeting but other members of the public do not. However, you will generally be given these papers if you ask for them before the meeting.

Your right as a member of the public to attend a committee meeting does not allow you to take part in the committee's discussions or ask questions – unless, of course, you are asked to do so.

Although education authorities have extensive powers, they cannot do more than is allowed by the relevant Acts of Parliament. Because around two thirds of their money comes from central government as rate support grant, the Government can exercise control over their total expenditure.

Choice of school

The education authority will normally designate a particular school for attendance by children living in the area of that school. If you want your child to attend another school, you can make a written request to the authority asking for a placing at that other school.

The education authority is legally bound to comply with your request and can only refuse if one or more of certain statutory grounds for objection apply – for example, if:

- Placing the child in that school would force the authority to employ another teacher.
- The authority would have to spend a significant amount of money on extending the school.
- Education provided at the school specified in the request is not suited to the age, ability or aptitude of the child.

If your request is refused by the education authority and you feel that its reason is not a good one, you can refer the question to an appeal committee set up by the education authority. If you are dissatisfied with the decision of the appeal committee, there is a further right of appeal to the sheriff court. *See:* SCHOOL

Problems at school

Problems about your child's schooling should be discussed with the class teacher or the head teacher, who has overall responsibility for the day-to-day running of the school. If that does not resolve the difficulty you should get in touch with the Director of Education, or with the divisional education officer if there are divisional education offices in your region. It may help to tell the regional councillor for your area about the difficulty. He should be in a good position to find out the facts. Your local MP may also be able to help.

If you believe that the regional council has been guilty of maladministration, you can ask your regional councillor to forward your written complaint to the local government 'Ombudsman' – officially known as the Commissioner for Local Administration in Scotland. *See:* OMBUDSMEN

Further education

The education authority has to make arrangements for education after school age. This may be in further education colleges where part-time or full-time courses of education are provided; or in further education centres – usually in schools – running vocational or non-vocational evening classes.

Student grants

The education authority is responsible for the payment of student grants for: preliminary or foundation courses taken before a degree or other further education course; courses in SCE/GCE subjects; courses leading to the Ordinary National Diploma; courses leading to Ordinary or Higher National Certificates; courses leading to Certificates of the City and Guilds of London Institute; and courses of part-time study, including Open University courses.

Grants for full-time courses at universities or colleges of education and for advanced full-time and sandwich courses at other establishments are the responsibility of the Scottish Education Department in Edinburgh.

Influencing the authority

If you want to influence the policies of the education authority – for example, to provide nursery education in your area or to improve its careers service to pupils – you should first take the matter up with the elected regional councillors.

Most councillors hold regular sessions or 'surgeries' to meet members of the public who wish to raise particular questions with them. The regional council offices will tell you the name of the councillor for your area.

ADMISSION TO MEETINGS

Admission to meetings does not entitle a member of the public to speak.

Regional councils are organised on political lines and it may be that one or other of the political groups will be willing to support your argument.

The education authority is legally obliged to consult parents on some matters before taking action. These include proposals to:

- Close a school or a part of it.
- Change the site of a school.
- Provide a new school.
- Change the residential area laid down as the zone for a particular school.
- Change a school which admits one sex of pupils only to one admitting both sexes or vice versa.
- Alter the authority's guidelines on priorities for school admissions.

ELDERLY PEOPLE

Help available to the retired

Elderly people are generally considered to be those who have reached retirement pension age – that is, 65 for men and 60 for women.

Services available to elderly people fall into six main categories: money, health, housing, help in the home, outside activities, work and leisure.

Financial help

Most elderly people are entitled to a state RETIREMENT PENSION, to which they have contributed during their working lives. But that pension by itself is not normally sufficient. Anyone whose income is below a certain level – decided from time to time by the Government – may claim a supplementary pension from the local social security office.

If you have any capital, such as savings, worth more than £3,000 in all, you will not usually qualify for a supplementary pension.

To claim, the pensioner should obtain form SB1 from any post office or social security office, and send it completed to the local social security office. You should say if you would prefer to call at the local office rather than have an officer to call on you to discuss your claim.

The supplementary pension is paid with your retirement pension. One pension book covers both.

Anyone receiving a supplementary pension will also qualify for other benefits, such as free dental treatment and free spectacles. *See:* SUPPLEMENTARY BENEFIT

Medical help

Apart from the usual National Health Service treatments, and help with the cost of spectacles, hearing aids and dental treatment, elderly people are entitled to free medicine on prescription.

To get free medicines complete the appropriate section on the back of the prescription form. In some areas a free chiropody service is provided by the regional or islands council.

Elderly people often suffer from more than one complaint at the same time and some general hospitals have special geriatric units, which allow an elderly person to be treated without having to be transferred from one department to another.

In some areas, day hospitals provide medical treatment, physiotherapy and occupational therapy to enable elderly people to continue to live at home despite their disabilities.

Transport between home and hospital is generally available free by hospital car or ambulance. Otherwise, people on low incomes can claim a refund of fares, by completing form H11 – obtainable at the hospital – or by showing the supplementary benefit or Family Income Supplement order book at the hospital.

Health visitors call on some elderly

people at home, giving advice on such matters as health, nutrition and keeping warm. The district nurse also visits patients and gives any nursing attention required – including injections, surgical dressings and bathing.

Help with housing

Most elderly people are able to continue to live in their own homes. Even the disabled can usually do so with the help of family and friends who live near by, and with practical aids provided by the regional or islands council.

To help to meet the cost of maintaining a home, HOUSING BENEFITS are available to people who are on low incomes. Details can be obtained from the district or islands council offices.

If an elderly person becomes too infirm to continue to live alone, or if his house is too large to heat or keep clean, he should apply to the district or islands council for a pensioner's house or a house in a scheme where there is a resident warden. (Houses may be scarce and there is usually a waiting list.)

If an elderly person is living in insanitary conditions, and is not being properly cared for, a sheriff can order his removal to a hospital or home.

Residential houses

Also available are residential homes, where people may have to share a bedroom – although more and more separate rooms are being provided.

Councils provide a wide range of services that may enable the person to remain in his or her own home – for example, home helps, walking and bathing aids. These possibilities should all be investigated before a residential home is considered.

Other accommodation available to the elderly are homes – owned usually by charities and let free or for a very small sum, to people who have followed a particular religion, trade or profession, – residential homes provided by local authorities and voluntary organisations, and flats or bed-sitting-room units provided by voluntary housing associations such as Abbeyfield Societies.

Details can be obtained from the local authority housing or social work department or from the local Citizens Advice Bureau.

Help in the home

Many services and appliances are available from the regional or islands council to help elderly people to retain their independence in their own homes. Applications should be made to the social work department.

Those who cannot cope with housework or washing and shopping may be provided with a home help, and housebound people who find cooking for themselves difficult can receive meals on wheels. A charge may be made for both these services, depending on the applicant's financial circumstances. No charge is made for a home help to people who are receiving a supplementary pension. *See:* SUPPLEMENTARY BENEFIT

Many councils provide linen and a free laundry service for people who cannot cope with soiled sheets. Application for those services should be made by the family doctor, or the hospital if the elderly person has recently been receiving hospital treatment.

Among the aids and appliances available are handrails on stairs and in bathrooms and lavatories, seats, rails and grip-mats for baths and 'helping hands' (long-handled grips for reaching high).

Councils may provide telephones for some elderly housebound people or, if a telephone is already installed, pay the rental. But they do not pay for calls.

Regional and islands councils have a duty to publish information about the services which they provide and to make sure that anybody using one of them is told of any others he may need.

If in doubt about your rights, consult a Citizens Advice Bureau, Age Concern branch or disabled people's organisation.

If you are severely disabled and someone stays off work to look after you, he or she may be entitled to claim certain benefits, such as INVALID CARE ALLOWANCE and SUPPLEMENTARY BENEFIT. If so, their pension rights will be protected, at least in part, by 'home responsibilities protection'.

If you are over 65 and a relative looks after you, even though you are not an invalid, he will be able to claim a dependent relative's income tax allowance.

Taking part in outside activities

One of the main fears of the elderly, especially those who live alone, is isolation from the social life of the community. Being cut off from the mainstream of activity can lead to depression and an avoidable general decline in health.

To avoid that, many local authorities and voluntary organisations, such as churches, the Red Cross and WRVS, organise clubs and day centres that provide a variety of social activities.

Day centres Many local councils provide or support clubs for elderly people living in their area. Members take part in a wide range of social activities for all or part of the day. *See:* DAY CARE CENTRE

Lunch is sometimes provided, for a small charge, and free transport is generally available for those who cannot make their own way to the club.

For the elderly infirm, many day centres provide bathing, chiropody and laundering facilities as well.

Luncheon clubs Regional and islands councils, sometimes in conjunction with voluntary organisations, run luncheon clubs to provide a well-balanced meal

SPECIAL CONCESSIONS FOR THE ELDERLY

Pensioners qualify automatically for many cost concessions. Those most commonly available include:

- *Transport* Reduced fares are charged for travel by British Rail and most publicly owned bus services.
- *Holidays* Many travel organisations allow pensioners rates for holidays in Britain or abroad. But you should make sure that the saving offered is not cancelled out by a demand for a specially high medical insurance premium.
- *Entertainment* Many cinemas and theatres offer reduced charges or special performances for pensioners. Museum and exhibition charges may also be reduced.
- *Services* Pensioners often benefit from price concessions at hairdressers, dry-cleaners, swimming baths, leisure centres, libraries and so on.
- *Investment* Some finance houses and insurance societies offer special terms for the elderly.

for people who can get about, but who might not cook for themselves. Often there is some social function after the meal.

A small charge is usually made, and the clubs generally have a waiting list.

To join a day centre or luncheon club, apply to the local social work department.

Holidays Some councils provide a limited number of holidays each year for old people who can get about. The holidays in seaside guest houses or houses run by voluntary organisations may be free or greatly subsidised.

Apply as early in the year as possible to the local social work department. Priority is often given to people who have not had a holiday for a long time.

Infirm elderly people may be considered for a holiday for the disabled. For those recovering from physical or mental illness a convalescent holiday may be available.

A family doctor or local social worker is the best source of detailed information.

Work and leisure

Many people who reach retirement age choose to carry on working, sometimes on a part-time basis. Others even decide to begin a new career. Up to the age of 70 – 65 for women – their pension is reduced if they earn more than a certain amount a week (£65 in 1984–85). After those ages, there is no earnings limit.

In some areas, pre-retirement courses are organised by the regional council or by a local branch of the Workers' Educational Association. These courses provide information about, for example, budgeting, nutrition and hobbies.

For pensioners who wish to follow their hobbies, or take up new interests, the council's education department or a local branch of Worker's Educational Association may run classes for pensioners at reduced rates.

ELECTION

Your right to choose a government

British people have a legal right to choose their own national and local government in free elections. Voting for district, regional and islands councils normally takes place separately from a general election when Members of Parliament are chosen, but the principles are the same. People casting their vote must be able to do so in secret and candidates must be prevented from using bribery or unfair means to influence the result.

Who can vote?

Anyone over the age of 18 who is on the ELECTORAL REGISTER can vote unless he or she is a peer (who can vote in local government elections only), an alien, a person serving a prison sentence or a person certified as being of unsound mind. But it is up to each person to check that his name is on the local electoral roll.

Parliamentary election rules

A general election must be held at least every 5 years, but the Prime Minister can ask the Queen to dissolve Parliament at any time during its 5 year life – even if he or she still has the support of the majority of members.

When Parliament has been dissolved, writs, or orders, to hold a general election are issued to the returning officer – usually the chief executive – at each constituency. Each constituency must return one member to Parliament, but there can be any number of candidates.

How candidates are nominated

When a returning officer receives a parliamentary election writ he must publish the date of the election by putting up posters at public places such as town halls and libraries within 2 days. A time is fixed during which nominations for candidates can be accepted by the returning officer. Polling must by law take place on the tenth day after nominations have closed.

Candidates can be nominated only with their consent. Each must be supported by at least 10 registered electors, including a proposer and a seconder.

The candidate does not have to belong to any political party, nor does he have to live in the constituency where he is seeking election. Nominations must be made on a special form obtainable from the returning officer.

Every nomination must be backed by a deposit of £150, returnable only if the candidate polls more than one-eighth of the total vote at the election.

Every candidate must appoint an agent, usually unpaid. The amount of expenses they can spend during their election campaign is limited by law.

In a county constituency the expenses limit is £2,700 plus 3.1p for every elector; in towns it is £2,700 plus 2.3p for every elector. The candidate's personal expenses are not limited, but he can only pay up to £100 of these himself – the election agent must pay the rest.

It is an offence for anyone to bribe or attempt to bribe a voter, to attempt to intimidate a voter, or to impersonate a voter. Any person found guilty could be imprisoned and the election could be declared void.

ELECTING YOUR EUROPEAN MP

Since 1979, members of the European Parliament have been elected by the voters of the countries of the European Community. Britain, France, Italy and West Germany each return 81 members. Holland returns 25, Belgium and Greece 24, Denmark 16, the Irish Republic 15 and Luxembourg 6.

In Britain, the normal parliamentary constituencies have been grouped into larger European constituencies, each with about 500,000 voters – 66 in England, 8 in Scotland, 4 in Wales and 3 in Northern Ireland.

Candidates must be aged at least 21 years, of sound mind and must not have spent more than 3 months in prison during the 5 years before nomination.

Bankrupts and employees of the Crown cannot stand, but peers, clergymen and members of the House of Commons can do so. Candidates pay a £600 deposit, which they forfeit if they poll less than 12½ per cent of the total number of votes cast.

Everyone on the normal electoral roll can vote, as well as peers and citizens of the Irish Republic resident in Britain. The voting procedure is the same as in a national election.

In England, Scotland and Wales the candidate in each constituency who polls the most votes is elected. In Northern Ireland the province as a whole elects all three members, using the system of a single transferable vote, a form of proportional representation.

Rules for local elections

The rules for parliamentary elections apply generally to local elections. No one can vote unless he is registered on the current electoral roll for the parliamentary constituency in which he lives.

Scotland has 9 regional councils, and 53 district councils. The two kinds of council have different responsibilities. The islands councils – Orkney, Shetland and the Western Isles – are all-purpose authorities. *See:* LOCAL AUTHORITY

When elections are held

Polling for regional and islands councils takes place every 4 years from 1974. Polling for district councils takes place every four years from 1980. The election is held on the first Thursday in May.

Local councils are elected for 4 years and cannot be dissolved during that term. If any members resign they can be replaced in by-elections. At the end of the 4 years a councillor can, if he wishes, submit himself for re-election.

Casting your vote

Before polling day at an election each registered voter receives by post from the local returning officer a note of his voting number and the polling station at which he should vote.

Polling stations must be open from 7 a.m. until 10 p.m. on the day of the election (8 a.m. to 9 p.m. for local elections). At the station, each voter is given a ballot paper, and his name must be crossed off the list of registered voters so that it is impossible for him to vote a second time.

The ballot paper contains the names of all the candidates in alphabetical order and a description of their politics in not more than six words, such as the party to which they belong.

The voter should put an X against the name of the candidate he wishes to see elected. He should then fold the paper and place it in the sealed ballot box.

If any other mark is put on a ballot paper it can be discredited as a 'spoiled paper'. The voter can, however, ask for a second paper, provided he has not already put the first into the ballot box.

Every voter must leave the polling station as soon as he has deposited his paper in the box.

Secrecy Voting in Britain has been secret since 1872 and the returning officer, the presiding officer, who supervises the poll, and all poll clerks must make a declaration of secrecy.

Postal voting Some electors are allowed to vote by post in both parliamentary and local elections:

1. Anyone likely to be unable to vote because of physical disability, blindness or religion. Applications made by people who are disabled, or not registered as blind, must be supported by a doctor – or, if the registration officer agrees, by someone else, such as a nurse or J.P.

2. Anyone who moves permanently to another electoral division – for instance, another division in the same regional council area. This applies to parliamentary elections only.

3. Anyone likely to be unable to vote because of their (or their spouse's) job.

4. Anyone likely to be unable to vote without making an air or sea journey.

5. Service voters – members of the armed forces, Crown and British Council staff employed abroad, and their spouses – who move within the UK.

6. Police and counting staff involved in the election; and, at general elections only, a candidate (and spouse) standing in another constituency.

7. Voluntary patients in mental hospitals. To stay on the register they can complete a special declaration form. *See:* MENTAL DISORDER

If a postal vote is allowed on grounds 1 to 4 (except for religious grounds), it is valid for as long as the elector's name remains on the electoral roll at the same address. If it is allowed on grounds 5 to 7, or on religious grounds, it is valid for a particular election only.

No voter is allowed a postal vote if he is away on holiday (but the government plans to allow this by 1986). Nor is anyone who has emigrated, but is still on the electoral roll.

To get an application form, write to the electoral registration officer at your regional or islands council. Say why you want a postal vote, so that you get the correct form.

Your form must be returned to the registration officer by noon on the eleventh day before the election (not counting Saturdays, Sundays, and Christmas, Easter and bank holiday breaks). If you are refused a postal vote, you can appeal to the sheriff court.

Voting by proxy Service voters stationed outside the U.K., and people whose job is likely to take them abroad on election day, can apply to vote by proxy – that is, to have someone else vote for them. So can their spouses.

An application for a proxy vote is made in the same way as for a postal vote. The time limit for returning the application is also the same.

On the application form the voter must say why he wants to appoint a proxy, and give the names of a first and second choice. If the first-choice proxy refuses to act, the registration officer will contact the second choice.

You can change your mind about having your vote cast by proxy – but not after the vote has been cast.

Counting votes After polling has ended, the votes in an election must be counted as soon as practicable. Apart from the clerks officially conducting the poll, the candidates' spouses, their agents and counting agents nominated by the candidates, no one is allowed in the counting room.

The returning officer supervises the count and he decides whether a paper is spoiled, but his decision is subject to review on an election petition.

If a poll ends in a tie, with two candidates having exactly the same number of votes, lots are drawn to decide who is the winner. After the returning officer announces the result, he must send it to the Clerk of the Crown in London.

Challenging an election

Any elector has the right to challenge an election result if he alleges corrupt or illegal practices, or that the winner was not qualified or properly elected.

The procedure is complicated and varies between local and Parliamentary elections. If you wish to challenge an election, consult a lawyer quickly.

If the appeal is successful, the elected candidate can be disqualified and the person who came second can be declared elected in his stead, or the election can be declared void and a new election ordered.

Illegal voting

The maximum fine for voting twice in a general election is £200. An offender can also be barred from voting for 5 years. The maximum penalty for claiming to be someone else in order to vote is 2 years' imprisonment.

ELECTORAL REGISTER

How to register to vote

The right to vote in a parliamentary or local council election in Britain is open, with certain exceptions, to people over the age of 18. In order to use that right, however, your name must appear on the electoral register of the constituency in which you live.

Each autumn the electoral registration officer visits, or sends a form to, every house in his constituency. The householder or occupier has a legal duty to write on it the name of every person over the age of 16 years and 8 months living in the house on October 10 – including the name of someone who is temporarily away from home – and to return it to the registration officer.

It is an offence not to fill in the form properly. The penalty is a fine of up to £100.

THE FORM THAT SECURES YOUR RIGHT TO VOTE

How the head of a household lists the eligible voters of his premises

If a merchant seaman lives in your house between voyages, he should be registered. He will then be invited to vote by post or to appoint a proxy to vote for him

The form allows for someone aged 16 or 17 to be enrolled in advance if he or she will be eligible to vote in the *following* year

Please complete Parts 1, 2 and 3 and sign the declaration (Part 4)

Part 1. Address:— Full Postal Address. (Where applicable state street, name and number of house and postcode.)

47 GLASGOW ROAD, EDINBURGH EH4 2LP

Part 2. Residents eligible to be included (see notes 1 and 2 on the left)
If there are none, please write "None"

Surname (Block Letters) (Enter Householder's name first, if resident)	**Full Christian Names or Forenames (Block Letters)**	If aged 18 on or before 16th February 1982 enter a √ in this column	**16/17 year olds** If 18th birthday is after 16th February 1982 and on or before the following 15th February, give date of birth (see Note 1)	If a Merchant seaman enter "M" See note 1 (f)
McINTOSH	DAVID COLIN	✓		
McINTOSH	CYNTHIA GRACE	✓		
McINTOSH	FIONA MARY	✓		
REID	THOMAS JAMES		3·3·64	

Part 3. Other residents

(1) Is any part of your house or flat separately occupied by persons whose names are not entered in Part 2? State "YES" or "NO" ....NO.......

(2) If "YES" give names of separate occupiers ....

Part 4. Declaration:

I declare that to the best of my knowledge and belief the particulars given above are true and accurate, that all those whose names are entered in Part 2 above are British subjects or citizens of the Irish Republic and will be 18 or over on 15th February, 1983.

SIGN HERE *David Colin McIntosh* Date *21st Oct 1981*

If others live in a separate household on your premises – not just as guests or lodgers – they are sent a registration form of their own

The head of the household is responsible for ensuring that the people listed are entitled to vote. 'British subjects' includes Commonwealth Citizens.

Electoral registration forms are sent to every known household in Britain, addressed to 'occupier'. It is the duty of the head of each household – usually the husband in a married relationship, or the main breadwinner in other groups – to see that it is completed correctly. The form must be returned to the local Electoral Registration Officer.

Who qualifies

The electoral register comes into force on February 16 each year and should include all names sent to the registration officer the previous autumn.

Your name should be on the electoral register if you are:

- A citizen of the United Kingdom or the Republic of Ireland, or a citizen of an independent country in the Commonwealth.
- Resident in the constituency (occupying business premises is not enough).

OBTAINING A POSTAL VOTE

The form you fill in if you are unable to get to the polls

R.P.F. 7 (Scotland)

REPRESENTATION OF THE PEOPLE ACTS
EUROPEAN ASSEMBLY ELECTIONS ACT 1978
APPLICATION TO BE TREATED AS AN ABSENT VOTER
FOR AN INDEFINITE PERIOD OWING TO OCCUPATION
OR PHYSICAL INCAPACITY

1. I, *(Surname, block letters)* ......GRANT......
(Other names, block letters) ......ROBERT......
am registered as an elector for *(Address in full, in block letters)*
......16 FORTH STREET......
......EDINBURGH EH2 2LQ......
....

2. I apply to be treated as an absent voter at parliamentary, European Assembly and local government elections because I am likely to be unable to go in person to the polling station (or, where *(c)* or *(d)* below applies, to vote unaided)—
**(a)* by reason of the general nature of my occupation/service/employment as ....
......JOURNALIST......
because ....
(Give full reasons for application)
....
**(b)* by reason of the general nature of the occupation, service or employment of my *husband/wife as ....
and my resulting absence from my qualifying address until ......INDEFINITE...... *(insert likely date of return)* to be with my *husband/wife
**(c)* by reason of blindness† (in respect of which I have been registered as a blind person by the ....
.... Council)
**(d)* by reason of physical incapacity (see note 2).
Signed ......Robert Grant...... Date......30th 1981......
Address in the United Kingdom, in block letters, to which ballot paper is to be sent (if different from the address given above)
....
....

**Delete whichever is inapplicable*
†*If the applicant is not registered as a blind person delete the words in brackets and ask a medical practitioner to complete the certificate or a Christian Science practitioner to complete the declaration (see back of form).*

A medical certificate given by a doctor will ensure that a disabled or frail person can vote by post. A blind person may also need one

The husband or wife of someone entitled to vote by post, because of employment, can also vote by post

If, when you register your name for voting, you know that your occupation will keep you away from your home area at election time, you should ask for form RPF7, on which you can claim your right to vote by post. People who are blind or disabled are also entitled to vote by post.

Who does not qualify

Certain people do not qualify for a vote and would not normally appear on an electoral roll:

- Aliens.
- People of unsound mind.
- Anyone serving a prison sentence or convicted of corrupt or illegal electoral practices.

Peers, who cannot vote in a parliamentary election, are included on the electoral roll but are listed as local government electors only.

The rights of teenagers A person is entitled to vote immediately he or she becomes 18, so a teenager's name should appear on the electoral roll for the year in which the 18th birthday falls. If an election is held before the 18th birthday, however, he or she is not entitled to vote then.

When a name is omitted from the register

However long a person has lived in the same house, he or she should complete and return a registration form for the electoral roll every year. The names of all people eligible to vote should be included, even if they are the same names year after year.

Failure to return the form is not only an offence, but may also lead to your name being left off the electoral roll. That does not automatically happen, however: even if you do not send in a form, provided that your name continues to appear on the electoral roll, you are still entitled to vote.

On November 28 each year, a provisional list of electors is available for inspection in each constituency at public libraries and local post offices. If your name does not appear on the list for your street or area, and you believe it should, you have until December 16 to ask the local registration officer to add it to the list.

It may be that the householder where you live accidentally left your name off his form, or that the form has been lost. If the registration officer refuses to add your name to the list, he must give his reasons. You can appeal to the sheriff.

Special rules for students

Someone studying at a college away from his home constituency is entitled to be registered on the electoral rolls of two constituencies – the one where he lives and the one where his college is.

He can vote in both constituencies in local elections and parliamentary by-elections, but for a parliamentary general election he can vote only once.

Working away from home

People working temporarily away from home, including merchant seamen, can register for a vote at the address where they would usually live – even if the house is sub-let to someone else while they are away.

When a voter moves People who move home remain on the electoral roll in their former constituency until new rolls are drawn up, the following February. Then they qualify for inclusion in the electoral roll of their new constituency.

In any intervening election, local or parliamentary, they can vote – either by post, or personally – only in the constituency in which they are registered. *See:* ELECTION

ELECTRIC WIRING

Safety laws to protect users

When the electric wiring on domestic equipment that works on mains electricity has an earth wire, the three wires must be coloured differently. The mains lead must have attached to it when it is bought a label or tag of the type shown below.

It is a criminal offence to sell electrical equipment without such a notice or to sell equipment that is not correctly wired.

Maximum penalty: Fine of £2,000 and 3 months' imprisonment under the CONSUMER SAFETY Act 1978.

A DOWN-TO-EARTH LAW ON ELECTRICAL APPLIANCES

When equipment must carry instructions on correct fitting

WARNING—THIS APPLIANCE MUST BE EARTHED

IMPORTANT The wires in this mains lead are coloured in accordance with the following code:—

Green-and-Yellow: Earth **Blue: Neutral**

Brown: Live

As these colours may not correspond with the coloured markings sometimes used to identify the terminals in a plug, connect as follows:—

The wire coloured green-and-yellow must be connected to the terminal marked E or by earth symbol ⏚ or coloured green or green-and-yellow.

The wire coloured blue must be connected to the terminal marked N or coloured black.

The wire coloured brown must be connected to the terminal marked L or coloured red.

RH4

To protect the public, retailers selling electrical equipment have a duty to see that any articles they sell carry clear instructions on how to fit or change plugs so that they will be earthed safely. Second-hand goods are not covered by the law, however.

ELECTRICITY SUPPLY

Your right to have power in your house

Anyone who owns or occupies a property connected to an electricity main is entitled to be supplied with electricity by the electricity authority, provided he has paid all his previous electricity bills and the electrical installation is safe. There are two electricity authorities in Scotland: the South of Scotland Electricity Board (SSEB) and the North of Scotland Hydro-Electric Board (NSHEB).

To obtain a supply of electricity, get an application form from your local board office. On it you must indicate generally the sort of appliances that you expect to use, so that the appropriate tariff can be applied.

A leaflet containing details of the amount of electricity used by different appliances is available on request.

A board is entitled to ask an applicant for security by way of a deposit or otherwise – for example, by asking for a GUARANTOR or a credit reference. Deposits are not often requested, but they may be asked for if, for instance, the applicant has previously got into arrears. The amount of the deposit required by the SSEB is the value of a winter two-monthly bill. Interest on the deposit is payable to the consumer.

Any dispute about the amount of a deposit can be referred to the local sheriff court for determination.

If you buy a house or flat, particularly if it is old, arrange a survey of the electricity circuits by a qualified electrician. The SSEB (but not the NSHEB) will also carry out a survey on request. It is your responsibility to make sure that your system meets the standard laid down in the Electricity Regulations.

Getting connected

If your house is not connected to a distribution main, but is within 50 yards of one, you can require the board to connect your property to it.

The board may ask you to pay the cost of providing any cable longer than 20 yards between your land and the main, as well as the cost of any cables that have to be laid on your land – for example, the line from your front gate to the house. However the usual practice of the SSEB is to make a standard connection charge instead. If the cost to the board of providing a supply is greater than an 'economic level', which is fixed from time to time, the excess over that level will be charged to the consumer in addition to the standard connection charge.

Paying for your electricity

Electricity is paid for either on credit – with bills submitted every 2 months (3 months in the case of the NSHEB) according to the total units of electricity shown on the credit meter – or by putting coins in a slot, or prepayment, meter (for which the consumer pays a separate rental).

A credit meter is installed without additional expense to the consumer.

Domestic electricity bills in the NSHEB area include a basic quarterly charge, which is a standing charge for using electricity, as well as a charge for the number of electricity units used by the consumer during that quarter. The standing charge will not exceed 50 per cent of a consumer's bill.

The SSEB does not make a standing charge. However a minimum two-monthly charge is payable if a consumer uses no electricity or an amount of electricity costing less than the charge.

If the board's meter reader finds no one at home, he will usually leave a card so that the consumer can make his own meter reading. Otherwise an estimated bill will be issued, based on your bill for the equivalent two-monthly period or quarter of the previous year.

The SSEB now operates an 'Immediate Billing System'. The meter reader carries a portable computer and can issue actual or estimated bills.

If anyone fills in his card incorrectly and over or undercharges himself, or if an estimate is low or high, the error will be adjusted on the bill following the next official meter reading.

The boards will require access at least once a year to read the meter, so that actual consumption can be recorded.

Challenging a meter reading

A meter may sometimes register more or less electricity than has in fact been used. If you suspect such a fault, ask your local electricity office to have the meter tested.

An electricity meter is deemed to be accurate if it runs fast by no more than 2½ per cent or slow by no more than 3½ per cent. If your meter is found to be running too fast, and is outwith the limit, you will be repaid the amount of the over-run, if this can be checked. Otherwise you will be repaid a reasonable estimate. If the meter is running too slow, you may be asked to make up the underpayment.

The board will send an official to check your appliances and meter. He will test your meter with his own portable ammeter, which clips on to your credit meter and checks the current used against the registration on the dial. If the consumer still insists that there is something wrong with a meter after this initial test, a check meter will be installed to run alongside the meter.

No charge is made for the initial test. The boards make a charge for a check meter installation if the meter is found to be accurate, but not if it is found to be inaccurate.

If after a test you are still not satisfied that your meter is working properly, you can apply to the Department of Energy for an independent meter examiner to be appointed. He will check the meter and issue a certificate showing its degree of accuracy. There is normally no charge.

The same inspection and payment system operates if you have a prepayment meter in your home.

Changing your meter If a consumer wishes to change from a credit meter to a prepayment meter, he can make a request to the local electricity board office. A prepayment meter will be installed provided that it is safe and practical to do so. The NSHEB (but not the SSEB) makes a charge for installing such a meter.

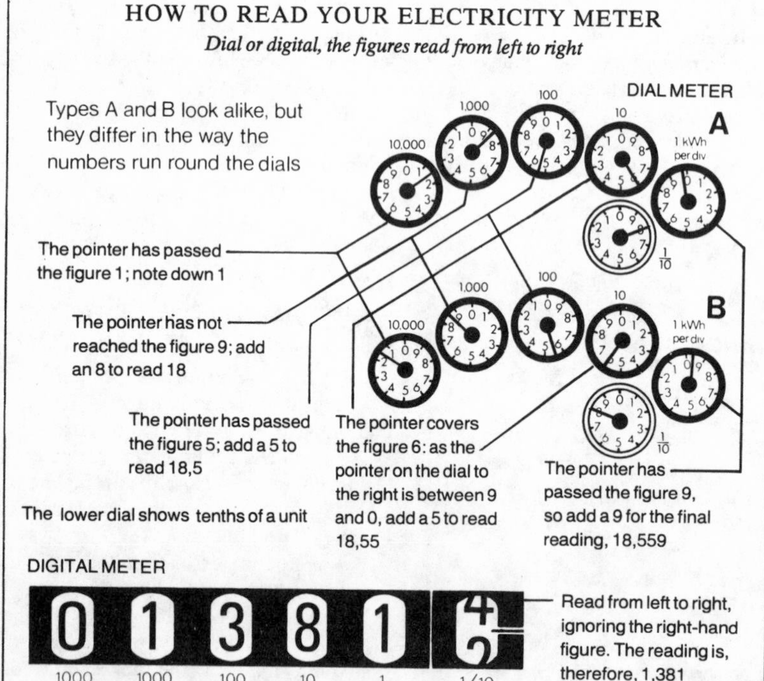

All types of meter show the total number of electricity units used since the meter was installed. To find out how much you have consumed and still have to pay for, deduct the total of units already charged for, shown on your last bill, from the new reading.

Electricity offences

No one should ever tamper with a meter or attempt to alter a reading or feed it foreign coins.

Anyone who, with intent to avoid paying, diverts an electricity supply so that it is not registered by the meter, commits THEFT.

Anyone who deliberately damages or interferes with a meter, or any electric lines or other fittings belonging to a board, commits an offence. The penalty is a fine of up to £400.

When your home can be entered by an electricity official

An electricity board official has power to enter homes for a wide range of purposes connected with the supply of electricity.

However, such an official is not entitled to enter your home, or to try to use force to enter it, without your consent, unless he has obtained a warrant authorising the entry from a justice of the peace.

The board must inform the justice why entry is required – for example,

- To enable an official to inspect apparatus.
- To disconnect the supply.
- To check how much electricity has been used by the consumer.
- To remove apparatus thought to be dangerous.

A warrant cannot be issued unless the

AVOIDING POWER BILLS CAN BE AN OFFENCE

Any person who tries to avoid paying for electricity by diverting the supply so that it cannot be registered by a meter is committing the crime of theft and can be prosecuted.

justice is satisfied that the admission was sought after giving the consumer at least 24 hours' notice, except when:

- Entry has been refused in an emergency.
- Giving notice would defeat the purpose of the entry.
- The premises are unoccupied.

It is an offence to obstruct an electricity official who has a warrant and seeks entry.

An official who enters your home, whether under a warrant or otherwise, must leave your home as secure as he found it. If he leaves it insecure and someone else then enters and steals something belonging to you, you can sue the electricity board for the loss arising from his negligence.

If the official causes any damage by entering the property, he must make it good. If he does not do so, claim compensation from the board – or sue it.

When the supply can be cut off

Electricity boards have the right to disconnect a supply, or to refuse to connect a new supply, if:

- The consumer has not paid his bills for electricity used.
- The consumer has made an arrangement to repay arrears and has then failed to keep to the arrangement.
- The consumer has failed to give security by way of a deposit or otherwise.
- The electrical installation is unsafe and the supply to others is affected.
- The consumer is using electricity dishonestly, or has deliberately damaged board equipment.

The supply cannot be disconnected on the ground that the consumer has failed to pay for equipment obtained from the electricity board.

Non-payment of bills Under a code of practice on disconnection, agreed between the electricity and gas industries and the Department of Energy, neither board should disconnect any consumer's supply for non-payment of arrears if he or she makes a firm arrangement to repay any arrears within a reasonable period and agrees to pay future bills regularly. The board will make an offer of a repayment arrangement.

When the consumer cannot pay, or the supply has already been cut off for non-payment, he can consider contacting the council social work department or the local social security office. One or other of them *may* be able to help pay the bill or make arrangements for it to be paid. *See:* FUEL BILL

If the consumer who is in arrears is a retirement pensioner, and all the people in the house with incomes are also pensioners, the supply will not be disconnected between October 1 and March 31 – unless it is clear that they can pay, but have not done so.

Landlord and tenant

A landlord is entitled to resell electricity to his tenant. He can do so by using his own prepayment meter or credit meter or fitting a prepayment meter for his tenant, or by including the cost of electricity in the rent. If he includes it in the rent, a special section should be set aside in the rent book stating the rates charged for electricity.

If a tenant is supplied through the landlord's meter, any money due at the end of the tenancy belongs to the landlord and not to the electricity board.

A tenant can ask his local board to be supplied direct, provided that he has not made an oral or written agreement with the landlord to pay the landlord for electricity.

A tenant who is supplied by his landlord, and who has difficulty in paying, will receive the same consideration from the local social security office or social work department as if he were supplied direct by the electricity board.

What a landlord can charge

A landlord who resells electricity to a tenant must not charge more than the maximum resale price fixed by the electricity board. He may make two charges – a small daily 'availability charge' to cover the cost of providing a meter and wiring, and a charge for each unit of electricity used by the tenant.

In 1984, a typical permitted resale price in the SSEB area was the lowest domestic tariff unit rate plus 0.28p per unit, plus a daily charge of 5.8p per day. The NSHEB allowed an extra unit charge of 0.31p, plus a daily charge of 6.25p.

Ask your landlord for a proper bill showing the amount of electricity used, the dates of meter readings and the charges made, and check the charges against the local maximum resale price. You can find out the local maximum resale price from a leaflet obtainable from any electricity board office, or from the boards' published tariffs.

If a tenant discovers that his landlord is overcharging him for his electricity, the electricity board will not help him to recover the money, but he can sue the landlord in the sheriff court for the excess, or he can withhold the amount of overcharge from the rent and tell the landlord he is doing so.

A landlord who disconnects a tenant, or refuses to provide electricity as a

WHEN THE BILL HAS NOT BEEN PAID

Anyone who owns or occupies a house or flat connected to the electricity main is entitled to be supplied with electricity, provided that he has paid all his previous electricity bills and that the electrical installation is safe.

IF A POWER CUT CAUSES LOSS OF BUSINESS

An electricity board cannot be sued for damages if lack of electricity supply causes someone a business loss. A board would not, for example, have to pay for a loss suffered by a factory at which production stopped because the electricity supply had been cut off due to industrial strife. Nor can a householder sue for the inconvenience of not being able to use, say, a washing machine.

means of forcing him to leave the premises, can be prosecuted for HARASSMENT. The tenant can also sue him for breach of contract.

Arranging to end the supply

Anyone leaving a property must give at least 24 hours' notice in writing to the local electricity board office. Failure to do so will make him liable to pay for all the electricity used on the property until the next meter reading, or until the board has been informed by a new occupier requesting a supply that the property has changed hands.

When something goes wrong

If you are dissatisfied with any aspect of the board's supply, charges, goods or service, complain to the manager at your local electricity office.

If that fails to produce a solution, contact the Electricity Consultative Council for the NSHEB area (2 York Place, Perth PH2 8ET, tel. 0738–36669) or the SSEB area (249 West George Street, Glasgow G2 4QE, tel. 041–248–5588). The Councils are independent of the boards, with members appointed by the Secretary of State for Scotland.

Names and addresses of the local representatives on your Council can be obtained from your local board office or from the Consultative Council itself.

EMERGENCY POWERS

When danger threatens society

A state of emergency can be declared at any time if the Government fears that services essential to people's lives are threatened by strikes, civil upheaval or natural causes.

The Government can make regulations and use the armed forces and the police to ensure the supply and distribution of food, water, fuel, electricity and transport.

A state of emergency is proclaimed by the Queen on the advice of the Government and remains in force for 1 month. It can be revoked earlier or be renewed after a month.

Fines of up to £2,000 or sentences of up to 3 months' imprisonment can be imposed on anyone who disobeys new regulations – for example, fixing food prices or requisitioning property – but the right to strike cannot be taken away, conscription cannot be introduced and the right to a trial remains.

In time of war

When Britain is in a state of war, regulations can be imposed to limit a citizen's usual freedom. In modern times they have been authorised by special Acts of Parliament. In theory the ancient measure of martial law could still be enforced, but no one knows its limits.

EMIGRATION

When people want to start a new life abroad

Anyone in Britain has the basic right to leave the country and live elsewhere. No permission is needed from the Government, and there are no controls on the transfer of money. However, a person's normal freedom of movement can be restricted for other legal reasons.

For example, people can be prevented from leaving Britain if they are:

- Subject to criminal proceedings.
- Serving a sentence of detention.
- Required to remain as a condition of bail, probation or parole.
- Compulsorily detained because of mental disorder.
- Serving in the armed forces and travelling without leave.
- Restrained by a court order because their departure would infringe someone else's rights.

Under many of those legal restraints a person can be compelled to give up his or her passport, or can be refused an application for a passport. Someone who has been granted government funds to return to Britain on a previous occasion cannot use his passport until the money is repaid.

FINDING OUT ABOUT WHERE YOU ARE GOING

There are many sources of information about countries to which you might want to emigrate, but in general the diplomatic missions of the country are best.

A passport is not legally necessary to leave Britain – but it is practically impossible to go anywhere else without one. International airlines and shipping companies are unlikely to carry a passenger without a passport, and in most cases they must also be satisfied that a traveller will be allowed to enter his country of destination.

Other countries' rules

No country in the world allows unlimited immigration. Each has its own laws that can keep out non-citizens because of poor health, criminal behaviour or even political activity, and further rules that restrict the flow of people eligible for long residence or permanent settlement.

Emigration to much of Europe is relatively easy because British Citizens have the right to enter any other EEC country to seek or take up work. They are given temporary permission to stay, followed by a residence permit if their work continues. *See:* EUROPEAN COMMUNITIES; CITIZENSHIP

Other countries' immigration restrictions vary, and any country's rules can change at short notice. In general a person's chances of being accepted, assuming that he or she is in good health

THE STEPS YOU MUST TAKE IF YOU DECIDE TO EMIGRATE

The long, painstaking process may daunt all but the most determined families

1 The first need of every would-be emigrant is for information, and making a visit to the embassy of the country of their choice is their first step.

2 From the material produced by governments, the family start to plan their new life, balancing the excitement of the unknown and the reality of their needs and ambitions. Usually they have jobs to go to; if not, it is unlikely that they will be accepted as immigrants. They complete and return the application forms.

3 Eventually – weeks or even months later – the whole family is asked to go to talk to the embassy's migration officer. Meanwhile, their references and histories have been checked carefully; and the officer has made sure that none of them has a criminal record. Their medical examinations are arranged.

4 When the embassy has approved their application, the family begin to wind up their British life, selling their home and settling accounts.

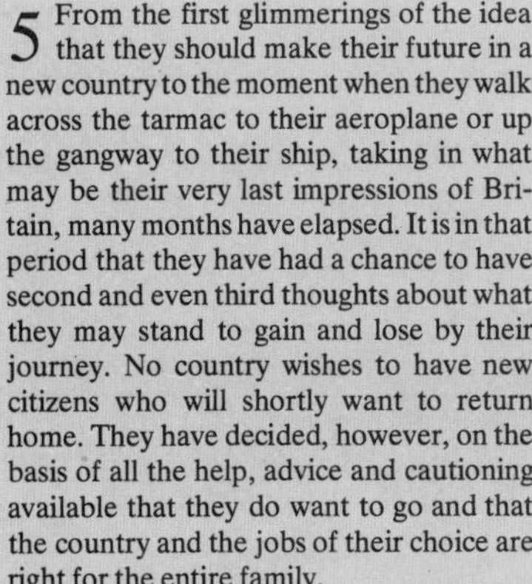

5 From the first glimmerings of the idea that they should make their future in a new country to the moment when they walk across the tarmac to their aeroplane or up the gangway to their ship, taking in what may be their very last impressions of Britain, many months have elapsed. It is in that period that they have had a chance to have second and even third thoughts about what they may stand to gain and lose by their journey. No country wishes to have new citizens who will shortly want to return home. They have decided, however, on the basis of all the help, advice and cautioning available that they do want to go and that the country and the jobs of their choice are right for the entire family.

and has had no serious criminal convictions, depend on:

- Employment prospects.
- Financial means.
- Age.
- Family.

Inquiries about settling in another country should be made to that country's diplomatic mission in Britain. Almost every foreign nation has an embassy or consulate in London, and Commonwealth states have high commissions there. Some countries also have consular offices in other major British cities.

Diplomatic missions usually give general information about conditions in their country, although it is advisable not to rely entirely on that. A country's leading newspapers are a good alternative source of information, and most diplomatic offices have them available.

Diplomatic missions also provide enough explanation of their immigration rules to indicate whether a person could qualify to settle there. If that seems unlikely there is little point in making a formal application, which can be complicated and costly.

Applicants must provide extensive documentary evidence and character references. For example, an application to settle in the United States must include a police report from every country in which the applicant has spent 6 months or more since the age of 16.

Depending on the country to which he hopes to go, a migrant may have to show that he has a job waiting for him. If he is a family man, he may need a guarantee of accommodation. A migrant and any dependants travelling with him will almost certainly have to undergo a medical examination before their final acceptance, which may also be subject to police or security clearance.

A person can be sure of his right to settle in another country only when an immigration entry permit or visa is stamped in his passport. It is unwise to give up a job, sell property or transfer funds before then.

An emigrant's tax position

If an emigrant family's main income was from employment and it stops before the end of the tax year on April 5, the taxpayer is likely to be owed a refund of part of his INCOME TAX deductions. Personal tax allowances are granted for the whole year, even if the income is for only part of a year.

A refund can be claimed by declaring that employment has ceased, on a form obtainable from any tax office. Repayment can be made before the emigrant leaves Britain if he can show proof of his travel arrangements.

A self-employed person is unlikely to be owed a refund of tax. The last half-year's instalment of tax demanded by assessment may be reduced if he produces evidence that his British income is ceasing.

Profit from the sale of an emigrant family's only home is not normally liable to CAPITAL GAINS TAX.

Income from investments left in Britain remains liable to tax, but an emigrant can claim a proportion of the usual personal tax allowance, called the 'world income fraction'. Allowances are granted in the same ratio as the emigrant's British income bears to his total income from all countries.

If the holder of British Government securities becomes a permanent resident abroad, the interest from them ceases to be liable to British income tax. Many emigrants switch to that form of investment to improve their tax situation.

National insurance rights

A person already entitled to a retirement pension or widow's benefit who goes to live abroad, retains the right to receive it. They can normally be paid anywhere abroad. But the recipient will not usually be given any increases in the rate of pensions which are granted after he or she has gone abroad. These increases can only be paid in EEC countries and in other countries with which Britain has reciprocal agreements – Austria, Bermuda, Cyprus, Gibraltar, Israel, Jamaica, Jersey and Guernsey, Malta, Portugal, Spain, Switzerland, Turkey, United States and Yugoslavia.

An emigrant who wishes to maintain his entitlement to a pension on reaching retirement age, or to provide a pension for his widow, may continue to pay contributions voluntarily. He may do this by completing form CF83, obtainable from any social security office. He should state on the form whether he is paying by direct contributions from abroad, by direct debit of an account with a United Kingdom bank, or by arranging for an agent in the UK to pay on his behalf.

Health services abroad

National Health Service treatment is available only in Britain. Emigrants cease to be eligible for treatment because they are not ordinarily resident.

Emigrants must rely on whatever health services are provided in their new country. In most cases that means they must be prepared to buy health insurance, or else pay the full cost of medical attention, drugs or hospital treatment.

A new country's laws

Anyone who settles in a new land is completely bound by its laws and obliged to accept its legal system, which may be altogether different from Britain's.

Behaviour that is acceptable in Britain may be heavily punishable somewhere else – for example, taking an alcoholic drink is an offence for which you can be flogged in some Islamic countries.

An emigrant may be under pressure to acquire local CITIZENSHIP. If he does acquire it, UK law does not require him to renounce British Citizenship, but the law of the new country may do so.

Until an emigrant is granted citizenship of a new country, he is liable to

RECEIVING A PENSION ABROAD

Someone who is already entitled to a retirement pension or widows pension retains the right to receive it even if she or he decides to go to live abroad.

DEPORTATION if he does not comply with that country's law. In many places a court conviction is not necessary to expel a non-citizen.

While an emigrant retains British citizenship he can appeal for help from Britain's diplomatic mission in his new country, or from the Foreign Office. But if an emigrant knowingly breaks the law and is dealt with according to the country's recognised legal system, Britain is unlikely to protest unless the punishment is exceptionally harsh.

British representatives will attempt to aid citizens who appear to be unjustly deprived of their rights – for example, imprisoned without trial. *See:* BRITISH EMBASSY

As long as he retains British citizenship, an emigrant who runs out of money and cannot support himself is entitled to apply to a British diplomatic mission for repatriation as a destitute citizen. That means the Government pays the cost of getting him and his family home. But their passports are confiscated so that they cannot travel abroad again until the money is repaid.

Legal rights in Scotland

If an emigrant wants to deal with a legal problem in Scotland, he must arrange for a Scottish lawyer to act on his behalf. If that is not practicable, his only choice is to return to Scotland. Generally speaking, disputes with a defender who lives in Scotland can only be settled in Scottish courts. (But see INTERNATIONAL PRIVATE LAW)

For that reason it is highly desirable for an emigrant to make sure that arrangements over which there could be a legal dispute – for example, the sale of a house or the shipment of household goods – are completed if possible before he leaves.

He must also be sure that he leaves behind no obligations over which he could be sued, because it is possible that he might be sued in Scotland. It could then be difficult for him to defend himself and whoever sues him could win possession of assets left in Scotland. An emigrant who foresees any legal problem should discuss it with a lawyer before leaving the country.

An emigrant may be subject to EXTRADITION for a serious crime which he is alleged to have committed in the UK.

EMPLOYED PERSON

How the law decides whether someone is an employee

Scots law distinguishes between employed persons, or employees, who work under what is called a 'contract of service', and the self-employed, whose relationship with clients and customers is governed by what is termed a 'contract for services'.

Employees enjoy far wider rights in the course of their work than the self-employed. For example, if they lose their jobs, they may claim UNFAIR DISMISSAL or REDUNDANCY, and are entitled to UNEMPLOYMENT BENEFIT–rights that the self-employed do not have. *See:* EMPLOYMENT PROTECTION

THE SELF-EMPLOYED LECTURER WHO WAS DISMISSED

Although someone pays income tax and national insurance as a self-employed person, he may not be self-employed under the employment protection rules if in most other respects his working terms and conditions are like those of colleagues who are employees.

Mr Davis was a lecturer engaged in 1971 by the New England College of Arundel on an annual lecturing contract. Originally, the college deducted his income tax at source and paid national insurance contributions on his behalf. Later, after appointment, he asked to be treated as self-employed for national insurance and tax purposes, and the college no longer made the deductions.

Eventually, Mr Davis was dismissed and he tried to claim unfair dismissal. The college argued he was self-employed and therefore could not make the claim.

DECISION

The Employment Appeal Tribunal said that Mr Davis was an employee. He asked to be treated as self-employed for tax purposes but that did not alter the relationship. He could claim unfair dismissal.

THE PART-TIME RESEARCHER WHO WORKED TO ORDER

Someone who works from time to time under the detailed control of another is not classed as self-employed simply because the employment is irregular.

Mrs Irving was a market research interviewer who, from time to time, was given work by one particular company. She was free to turn it down or to work for other employers when available. But if she accepted the job, she was expected to follow detailed instructions on how to do it and to complete it by a specified date. The social security authorities claimed that Mrs Irving was an employee and that the company should be paying national insurance contributions for her, which it had not been doing.

DECISION

Whenever Mrs Irving accepted work from the company, she became its employee until the work was finished. She was not self-employed.

THE MANAGER WHO FORMED HIS OWN COMPANY

In deciding whether someone is self-employed or an employee, courts and tribunals may take into account the intentions of both parties to the contract under which he works.

Mr Massey was a branch manager for Crown Life Insurance Company. His accountant told him that he would pay less income tax if he could persuade his employers to treat him in future as self-employed.

Crown Life agreed to the idea. In 1973 Mr Massey formed his own company, John L. Massey Associates, which contracted to supply his services as a branch manager to Crown Life. He paid tax and national insurance as a self-employed person.

But in 1975 Crown Life ended its agreement with Mr Massey. He claimed unfair dismissal.

DECISION

Mr Massey was not an employee of Crown Life and could not claim unfair dismissal. The English Court of Appeal held that both Crown Life and Mr Massey had genuinely intended to change his status from employee to self-employed.

Employees pay income tax under Schedule E, deducted from their wages at source under the Pay As You Earn system. In addition, part of their weekly national insurance contribution is paid by their employers.

Self-employed people pay income tax under Schedule D the year after the income is earned. Because they are allowed to deduct more business expenses when calculating their liability, their tax bills may be lower than those of employees. But they have to meet the whole cost of national insurance contributions themselves and, if their turnover is more than £18,000 a year, are liable for VALUE ADDED TAX as well. *See:* SELF-EMPLOYED; NATIONAL INSURANCE CONTRIBUTIONS

Deciding who is an employee

Most people fall quite clearly into the category either of employee or of self-employed person. But there are borderline cases. When such cases arise – for example, in a claim for unfair dismissal or redundancy, or in a tax dispute – tribunals and courts reach their decisions by looking at all the circumstances surrounding the person's work. They are not always consistent in their conclusions.

There is agreement on one point – the description 'employee' or 'self-employed' adopted by the individual himself, or attached to him by those for whom he works, is not necessarily conclusive in law and may not be upheld in the courts.

However, where the relationship is genuinely in doubt the courts may be prepared to follow the description which the parties have applied to their relationship.

Normally the tribunal or court will look at previous arrangements for paying tax and national insurance to establish whether they have been made for an employee or a self-employed person. It may also examine whether the person gets benefits such as sick pay, holiday pay and the like. If he does, he is likely to be an employee.

The tribunal or court may then ask who controls the way, the manner and the time in which the work is done. If a worker is free to decide how and when to do the job, without specific guidance or control by someone else, he may be self-employed. Otherwise, he is likely to be regarded as an employee.

However, that test does not always provide a satisfactory answer. For example, a hospital surgeon decides how and to some extent when to operate on a patient. His employers do not tell him how to do it. But although the surgeon controls his own work, he is an employee.

The tribunal or court will then consider a number of other issues to determine whether the relationship is generally consistent with a contract of employment. Such issues might include the method of payment for the work done – is it a wage or a commission? Who provides the tools? Who bears any loss made by the business? If such questions suggest that the worker is really an entrepreneur, then he will be regarded as self-employed.

BEING YOUR OWN BOSS BRINGS EXTRA RESPONSIBILITIES

Self-employed people have to record their business expenses, pay all their national insurance contributions, and, if their turnover is £18,000 per annum or more, pay Value Added Tax – with all the extra paperwork and administrative work that that involves.

EMPLOYEE, Death of

When an employee dies

Although the death of an employee automatically ends his EMPLOYMENT CONTRACT with his employer, the employee's executors or a close relative can generally continue to pursue any unsettled claim for REDUNDANCY or UNFAIR DISMISSAL. Wages or other payments to which the employee had become entitled before his death, but which he had not received, form part of the estate. *See also:* ACCIDENT AT WORK

EMPLOYER, Death of

How an employer's death affects employment contracts

When an employer dies, any EMPLOYMENT CONTRACT he has entered into as an individual automatically ends.

However in many cases his employees will be re-employed by someone else who takes over the business. If an employee is re-employed by the deceased's personal representatives or trustees, his employment is treated as continuous for the purpose of EMPLOYMENT PROTECTION rights. *See:* CONTINUOUS EMPLOYMENT

An employee who loses his job as a result of his employer's death – for example, if the business then closes – may be entitled to claim a REDUNDANCY payment from the employer's estate. However, he cannot claim UNFAIR DISMISSAL unless he was already under notice when the employer died.

If the employer is a company, the death of one or more of its officers – for example, the managing director – does not in itself interrupt employment contracts.

In the case of partnerships, the effect of the death of one partner depends on whether the partnership is brought to an end by the death.

EMPLOYER'S LIABILITY

When an employer is liable for the actions of his staff

An employer is liable for any wrong done by a member of his staff if it is done in the course of that person's employment. Anyone who suffers loss as a result of a civil wrong, or DELICT, committed by an employee may therefore be able to recover damages from the employer as well as the employee.

For example, if you are knocked down by a bus, you can sue the bus company for the driver's negligence.

Where the employer is liable, it is usual to sue him and not the employee – this is because, unlike his employee, the employer will normally be insured and able to pay damages.

When the employer is not liable to pay damages

The employer is not liable, however, when an employee commits a wrong outside the normal course of his employment.

If a sales representative goes a mile or so off his business route to buy cigarettes, and while off that route has an accident with his car, through negligence, he will probably be considered to be within the course of his employment: his employer will be liable for any damages. But if he has an accident after driving 20 miles off his route without his employer's permission to visit friends, that will probably be regarded as being outside the course of his employment: if so, he, not his employer, will be liable.

Even when an employer has expressly forbidden an employee to do something but the employee ignores the instruction, the employer may be liable for any accident that results.

If his instruction or prohibition merely told the employee to do his job in a certain way, the employer will still be responsible if the instruction is ignored.

If, however, his instruction or prohibition restricted the scope of the worker's employment, he can avoid liability.

For example, if a garage owner has a young hand, whose job is to push cars around the garage – not drive them, because he is not a qualified driver – the owner will be responsible for any injury or damage caused if the hand ignores an order not to drive.

That is because his order has not sufficiently restricted the scope of the hand's employment, which is moving cars around the garage.

But if an employer made it a condition of a van driver's job that he should not give lifts, and the driver then picks up a passenger, the driver will alone be personally liable if he has an accident through negligence and the passenger is injured.

That is because the employer is seen as having limited the scope of the employee's job.

THE MILKMAN WHO ENGAGED A BOY ASSISTANT

Even when an employer takes precautions – by issuing notices to his staff, for example – he may not evade liability if he is sued.

Mr Plenty was a milkman who agreed to pay Leslie Rose, aged 13, to help him deliver milk. He did so despite notices at the depot which forbade the use of children on rounds.

One day, Mr Plenty drove his milk float too near the kerb. Leslie's leg was dangling over the side, and his foot got trapped between the float and the kerb.

Leslie's father sued Mr Plenty and the dairy company for damages. The court found Mr Plenty liable, but held that the employers were not liable, because of their prohibitory notices about employing children. Mr Rose appealed on his son's behalf, claiming that the company was liable for their roundsmen's acts.

DECISION

The court decided that despite the notices, the employers were liable for Leslie's injuries. The boy had been taken on to carry out the employer's business, and, although prohibited, Mr Plenty's act was done in the course of his employment and for the employer's purposes.

THE LORRY DRIVER WHO WENT OUT OF HIS WAY TO HELP

If an employee is still doing what he is employed to do, the employer will be liable for his negligence even if he is doing other things as well.

Mr Ross, a lorry driver, was engaged to drive a party of boys home to Glasgow from a Boys' Brigade summer camp in Argyll.

On the way home, Mr Ross was persuaded by some of the boys to drive to Stirling railway station – which was not on the direct route to Glasgow – to meet some girls from Dollar who had been camping near the boys. He then agreed to drive to Dollar so that the boys could say goodbye to the girls.

On the way to Dollar, the lorry was involved in an accident and one of the boys, Derek Williams, was gravely injured.

He sued Mr Ross's employers, A. & W. Hemphill Ltd., but they argued that they were not liable because Mr Ross was not acting in the course of his employment.

DECISION

A. & W. Hemphill Ltd., were held liable for the accident.

What one judge called the 'navigational extravagances of the journey' were not sufficient to alter its predominant purpose of getting the boys back to Glasgow. Mr Ross was still doing what he was employed to do and so acting within the course of his employment.

Liability for an independent contractor

In certain circumstances, someone who engages an independent contractor, who is therefore not his employee, will still bear liability for the contractor's actions, as if he were an employer.

For example, if someone hires a taxi and tells the driver to disregard all speed limits and traffic signs to save time, with the result that an accident happens, he will be liable along with the driver. This is because he requested the driver to act illegally.

Similarly if a motorist employs a garage that he knows is not technically qualified to do a brake repair on his car, and subsequent brake failure results in the death of a pedestrian, the motorist is liable for the garage's defective repair, because he was aware of the garage's incompetence.

Anyone who engages a contractor to carry out essentially dangerous work, such as altering the load-bearing walls of a building, may be liable if any damage results. *See:* CONTRACTOR'S LIABILITY

Insuring against liability

Employers are required by law to insure themselves against liability for injuries caused by their employees to other people employed by them. They are not bound to take out insurance against injuries caused by their employees to outsiders. But most employers do so, as do public authorities engaging independent contractors.

EMPLOYMENT AGENCY

How the law protects people who use a private organisation to find – or fill – a vacancy

Privately run employment agencies are strictly controlled by law, to protect people who use them to try to find a job and employers who engage them to fill a staff vacancy.

An employment agency cannot operate without an annual licence from the Department of Employment. It is a criminal offence to run an agency without a licence and offenders may be fined up to £2,000.

The licence must be prominently displayed on the agency's premises. It can be refused if the Department regards the agency proprietor as an 'unsuitable person', or if he or she is under 21, and an application for renewal can be rejected on the same grounds. In such cases, the applicant may appeal to the Secretary of State for Employment, on forms provided by the Department of Employment.

In addition, someone planning to open an employment agency must post a notice on or near the intended premises at least 21 days before the application is submitted. The notice must be in a position that allows it to be read easily by members of the public, and must state the name and address of the proprietor, the address of the proposed agency and a description of the type of work it will do. The proprietor must also advertise in the press his intention of applying, so as to give the public an opportunity to object.

There is no set form for objecting to an application. Objectors should write to the Secretary of State for Employment.

Once a licence application has been granted, the agency's premises and records can be checked by a Department inspector at any time.

Agency fees to job-seekers

Employment agencies are not allowed to charge fees to people looking for jobs. The penalty for doing so is a fine of up to £2,000, and the agency's licence may not be renewed. However, there are two exceptions to that rule:.

1. Fashion models, actors and others in the entertainment industry may be charged fees by their agents, by agreement between the two parties.

2. An agency may charge a fee to an AU PAIR seeking a family with whom to live. The charge may not exceed 1 week of the au pair's payment.

FINDING A JOB

Private employment agencies which people use to try to find a job are strictly controlled by law.

Agency fees to employers

There are no legal restrictions on the fees employment agencies may charge to employers seeking staff. The equivalent of 1 week's wages is common for secretarial or administrative personnel. For executive positions, the fee may be substantially higher, and may include consultancy charges as well.

EMPLOYMENT APPEAL TRIBUNAL

How to lodge an appeal in a case involving employment law

The Employment Appeal Tribunal is a UK court that hears appeals on decisions reached by an INDUSTRIAL TRIBUNAL on matters of employment law such as UNFAIR DISMISSAL, REDUNDANCY payment, equal PAY, RACIAL DISCRIMINATION and SEX DISCRIMINATION at work. In Scotland it sits in Glasgow and Edinburgh. Cases are heard by a Court of Session judge and two laymen – one from a panel nominated by employers and the other from a panel nominated by trade unions.

The tribunal is a court of law, but its procedures are less formal than those of other courts. Nevertheless, it is advisable for anyone who is bringing or facing a case before the tribunal to be represented by a solicitor or advocate.

When you can appeal

An appeal can normally be brought before the tribunal only if it is based on a point of law, not if it is simply a question of fact. The tribunal cannot usually interfere with an industrial tribunal's decision on the facts of a case.

Industrial tribunals are required, however, to give reasons for their decisions, so an appeal may be based on the argument that 'no tribunal, properly directing itself' could come to the decision that it did on the evidence before it. The facts of the case then become relevant, although in theory the appeal is still on a point of law.

Making the appeal

Either side in an employment dispute can appeal to the tribunal against the decision of an industrial tribunal. The appeal must be lodged within 6 weeks of the industrial tribunal's decision being sent to the appellant, using a form obtainable from any office of the Department of Employment.

Who pays for the appeal

Although LEGAL AID is not available to take a case before an industrial tribunal, an appellant can apply for financial help when an appeal is lodged with the Employment Appeal Tribunal. All or part of the costs may be met by legal aid.

Both parties to the appeal have to pay their own attendance expenses, and those of any witnesses they call.

Generally, the tribunal does not award legal expenses to the winner of an appeal. So each side has to pay its own. However, the tribunal can award expenses if the appeal is 'unnecessary, improper or vexatious, or there has been unreasonable delay or other unreasonable conduct'. Someone who makes a completely unjustified appeal can thus be penalised.

There is a further right of appeal to the COURT OF SESSION against the tribunal's decision, but only on a point of law.

EMPLOYMENT CONTRACT

Defining the relationship between employer and employee

Every employed person has a legally binding employment contract that defines his relationship with his employer and their obligations to each other. Under the basic terms of this contract, the employer agrees to pay wages for work performed, to provide a safe work place and to show confidence and trust in the employee. The employee agrees to carry out the work, to co-operate with the employer and to render loyal service.

The contract also defines the terms and conditions of the job – for example, working hours, holiday entitlement and sick-pay arrangements.

An employment contract does not usually have to be in writing to become legally binding. An employer may simply tell the job applicant: 'The pay is £60 a week and you get 3 weeks' holiday a year. You can start on Monday'. If the applicant replies 'I agree', or with some similar phrase, the contract is as valid as if it were written down.

In cases of dispute, a court or INDUSTRIAL TRIBUNAL would then have to work out the terms of the contract, which would generally be implied from the nature of the job, from any collective agreements in the industry concerned or from custom and practice at the place of work.

A written employment contract greatly reduces the chances of a dispute between employer and employee over what exactly has been agreed. In practice, however, most employers do not provide written contracts except to senior or 'professional' employees. But apprentices, merchant seamen on UK registered ships and employees whose contracts are for more than a year must have a written contract.

The Employment Protection (Consolidation) Act 1978 requires employers to provide a written statement of the main terms of an employee's contract within 13 weeks of his starting work. It is important to note that this statement does not have the legal status of a contract – although it will usually be treated as fairly conclusive evidence of a contract's terms. Where the terms of the statement differ from what actually happens in practice, it is the practice and not the statement which may govern the parties' rights.

IF THE CONTRACT IS UNWRITTEN OR INCOMPLETE

Many employers do not provide written employment contracts. Those who do may omit some provisions through oversight. The written statement required by the Employment Protection (Consolidation) Act is not a complete record of the agreement between employer and employee.

If a dispute arises over an unwritten provision of an employment contract, the court or industrial tribunal looks at the surrounding circumstances to determine what, in its view, the contract implied.

Obvious terms Some terms of an employment contract are so obvious that they go almost without saying.

For example, an employer may hire a van driver without specifically stating that it is part of his job to ensure that he holds the appropriate driving licence at all times. If the van driver is found to be disqualified from driving, the employer can dismiss him without being in breach of contract. In such circumstances, a claim for unfair dismissal would be unlikely to succeed.

Custom and practice What is considered the usual practice in a company or industry can help to decide any unwritten provisions of an employment contract.

For example, if a factory customarily closes down entirely during the first 2 weeks of July, it is an implied term of the contract that workers must take 2 weeks of their holiday entitlement then, unless specifically asked not to.

Collective agreements Some written employment contracts state that employees are bound by the terms of collective agreements negotiated between the employer and a trade union. But many do not.

In working out the application of a collective agreement to an individual contract, courts and tribunals generally ask: 'Has the employee accepted the terms of that agreement, or of similar ones, previously?'

If he has, the agreement is usually held to apply, whether the employee concerned is a member of the union or not. So if a non-union member accepts pay rises and other benefits negotiated by the union, he may be in a weak position if he tries to dispute other terms of a collective agreement.

Any employee, whether a union member or not, is entitled to try to prevent a provision in a collective agreement from becoming part of his individual contract. To do so, he must register his objection in writing to his employer immediately he learns of the provision.

However, he stands little chance of success if the employer refuses to accept his objection. If he persists, and his employer dismisses him, or he resigns in protest, he can make a claim of unfair dismissal to an industrial tribunal.

Previous conduct If an employee has previously accepted a reasonable order or decision by his employer without objection, he may be obliged to accept similar future decisions or orders as part of his contract.

For example, if an employer asks an employee to move from one office or factory to another, and the employee does so without objecting, but later declines a second move, he may be in breach of contract. In such circumstances, if he is dismissed for refusing the second move, he might not succeed in a claim for unfair dismissal.

However, one acceptance of a reasonable order or decision is not, by itself, conclusive proof that the employee is obliged under his contract to accept others of the same sort. Courts and tribunals examine all the surrounding circumstances.

Work rules and disciplinary codes

Employers are expected to have comprehensive disciplinary rules and procedures. Provided the rules and procedures are prominently displayed in the workplace, or made easily accessible to employees – for example, as a booklet – they will usually form part of the employment contract, even if they are not referred to in it.

However, in considering disciplinary rules, courts and tribunals take into account whether they are 'reasonable' and whether an employee could be aware of them. *See:* DISCIPLINE AT WORK

An employer who simply pins the rules on the company notice board, but who takes care to point them out to new and existing employees, can assume that they form part of the employment contract.

However, if he pins up new rules at random without mentioning them to all employees, a tribunal might decide that the additions do not form part of the contract unless there is a written provision to the contrary, or unless they had been negotiated with a trade union.

Legal requirements for written statements

In the written statement which he issues under the 1978 Act, the employer can simply refer to other documents, provided that they are easily accessible to the employee.

For example, he may refer an employee to a collective agreement for details of pay, hours and holidays; to a works rulebook for disciplinary rules and procedures; and to a pension booklet for details of the company pension scheme.

There is no criminal penalty for an employer who fails to provide written particulars. But if the information is not set down in writing, the employer may find it more difficult to defend himself against any future claim for breach of contract or unfair dismissal.

The employee may ask an industrial tribunal to give him a correct written statement if his employer has failed to do so.

If the written statement is inaccurate

As the written statement is usually the best evidence of the terms of the employment contract, it must be as accurate as possible.

The employee should check the written statement carefully as soon as he receives it. If there are inaccuracies, he should point them out, in writing, to the employer and ask for them to be corrected. If there are any provisions to which he objects, he should challenge them immediately, writing to the employer and keeping a copy of the letter.

Unless the employee challenges a provision immediately he becomes aware of it – and can produce evidence of having done so – if he later becomes involved in a dispute over that provision, he may be held by a court or tribunal to have accepted it by default.

If an employer refuses to change a provision to which a new employee objects, the employee must decide what further action to take. He may resign or refuse to accept the job. He may pursue the point in other ways – for example, by getting his trade union to take it up. Or he can refer the matter to an industrial tribunal, which can decide what should be included in the statement.

SPECIAL RULES FOR FIXED-TERM CONTRACTS

Employment contracts that last for a pre-arranged period only – fixed-term contracts – are governed by similar rules to those of contracts of indeterminate length.

If a fixed-term contract is not renewed when it expires, the employee will be able to claim UNFAIR DISMISSAL, provided that he has been with the employer at least a year (sometimes two). The only exception is when the contract is for a year or more and the employee has agreed in writing not to make an unfair dismissal claim. A similar agreement in a contract of less than a year is not legally enforceable.

If an employer sacks an employee before the fixed-term contract expires and without good reason, thus breaking the contract, the employee can sue for WRONGFUL DISMISSAL – to obtain damages equal to the wages he would have earned if the contract had run its full term minus any other wages he has been able to earn – and for unfair dismissal.

Some fixed-term contracts include a provision allowing either party to end them at any time by giving notice of, for example, 1 month. Provided that the employee has completed one (or two) year's service, he still has the right to claim unfair dismissal if he is given notice. However, he could not claim wrongful dismissal.

The written statement should include a provision stating when a fixed-term contract is due to expire.

If an employer refuses

If you have been more than 13 weeks in your job and have not received a written statement of the main terms and conditions, either separately or as part of a written employment contract, you are entitled to demand it – unless you are a part-timer or in one of the occupations not covered by the 1978 Act. *See:* EMPLOYMENT PROTECTION

However, if your employer refuses to supply the statement, the law gives you little redress.

You could take the matter to an industrial tribunal and ask it to draft the statement for you. But that takes time, legal aid is not available to pay any lawyer's fees and you risk antagonising your employer. If you have worked for him for less than 1 year, you are not protected by the law on unfair dismissal.

When you have checked that you are entitled to the statement, and that it is not set out in some other document – for example, works rules – to which your employer has already drawn your attention, write to him. Ask for 'the written particulars of my contract of employment, as required by Section 1 of the Employment Protection (Consolidation) Act'. Keep a copy. If you feel that the matter may not be straightforward, send the letter by recorded delivery, so that there is proof that your employer has received it.

If you do not get a satisfactory reply, you could try drafting the statement yourself. Send a copy to your employer, with a covering letter explaining what you have done and why. Say that unless he provides his version of the written statement, you will assume that he accepts yours as correct.

That may persuade him to act. But if he does not, and fails to reply, he will find it difficult to deny the accuracy of your version later.

Changing the contract

Every time an employee gets a pay rise or extra holidays, his terms of employment change. The Employment Protection (Consolidation) Act 1978 obliges employers to give written particulars of changes in a contract – or to direct attention to a document where these changes are to be found – within 1 month of their taking effect. This is not necessary if the employee's written statement tells him that future changes will be contained in such a document.

However, there is no criminal penalty if an employer does not do so, and in practice the rule is often ignored. The alteration simply takes effect by mutual consent between employer and employee.

In some circumstances, an employee might object to a proposed change in the terms and conditions of his employment. Whether he is entitled to do so or not depends upon:

1. Whether the change is provided for in a written contract or in a written statement of employment. For example, if the statement says that the employee 'may be required to work in any of the company's offices in the United Kingdom', he cannot resist a transfer from one place to another. He must either accept or resign and will not normally be able to succeed in a claim of unfair dismissal.

2. Whether, in the absence of a written agreement, the employee has accepted similar changes in the past.

A change not previously provided for, either in writing or by implication, must not, however, be so fundamental that it puts the employer in breach of the employment contract. A reduction in pay, a demotion or a cut in the working week that leads to loss of earnings are all fundamental changes.

An employee facing such a change without any previous expressed or implied condition in his contract can resign, claiming that he has been constructively dismissed. *See:* CONSTRUCTIVE DISMISSAL

Transfers of business ownership

When the ownership of a business is transferred from one employer to another, the employees' contracts of employment continue in force as if no transfer had taken place – except that accrued occupational pension rights are *not* automatically transferred.

If an employee is dismissed because of a transfer of ownership, his dismissal will be automatically unfair. However, if the dismissal is because of 'economic, technical or organisational' reasons which require workforce changes, the dismissal will be fair if an industrial tribunal considers that the employer acted reasonably. *See:* UNFAIR DISMISSAL

EMPLOYMENT PROTECTION

How the law safeguards people's jobs

Many rights aimed at protecting employees from unfair treatment at work and at safeguarding their interests if they lose their jobs have been drawn together in the Employment Protection (Consolidation) Act 1978 – as amended by later legislation.

The main items covered by the Act include: DISMISSAL; the EMPLOYMENT CONTRACT; LAY-OFF and short-time working; MATERNITY leave; NOTICE; PAY; REDUNDANCY; TIME OFF WORK; TRADE UNION rights; and UNFAIR DISMISSAL.

Both men and women have protection under equal PAY and SEX DISCRIMINATION legislation. People of all races are protected, at work as elsewhere, by the law on RACIAL DISCRIMINATION.

Employers who are exempt

All employers, no matter how few people they have working for them, are generally bound by the employment protection rules.

It used to be that, in the case where a husband employed his wife, or a wife her husband, the employed spouse lost many of his or her employment protection rights. But since December, 1982, the legal rule that deprived spouses of these rights has been repealed.

Employers with 5 or fewer employees are exempt from the duty to reinstate an employee after maternity absence where it is not reasonably practicable for them to do so and there is no suitable alternative employment.

Employers with 20 or fewer employees can only be liable for unfair dismissal if they have dismissed an employee with 2 years' continuous service or more (the normal qualifying period is 1 year).

Employees who are excluded

Several categories of employees are excluded from at least *some* of the employment protection rules:

- Part-timers. People employed for fewer than 16 hours a week have little protection. But if they have worked continuously for the same employer for 5 years or more, they are not classed as part-timers unless they work fewer than 8 hours a week. *See:* PART-TIME WORKER
- People who have reached retirement age. Traditionally, retirement age is 65 for men and 60 for women. But if the agreed retirement age for a particular job is lower, the employee has no right to claim unfair dismissal once he has reached it. Conversely, if the agreed age is higher, unfair dismissal rights are not lost at 60 or 65. For instance, a woman teacher with a contract to 65 could claim unfair dismissal if dismissed at 60.
- People on fixed-term contracts of 3 months or less. Someone who is taken

WHAT THE WRITTEN STATEMENT MUST SAY

According to the 1978 Act, the written statement must set out:

1. The names of employer and employee.

2. The date employment began.

3. The rate of PAY and how often wages are paid: if the employee is paid at piece rates or on commission, the basis for calculating payments must be explained.

4. The hours during which the employee is normally expected to work: an employee is not obliged to work overtime unless required to do so under the terms of his employment contract.

5. The holidays to which the employee is entitled, the method of calculating his entitlement and the pay he receives while on holiday. *See:* HOLIDAY ENTITLEMENT

6. The company rules governing absence through illness and sick pay. *See:* SICKNESS

7. The terms of any pension scheme.

If there are no paid holidays, sick pay or pension scheme, the written statement should say so.

8. The period of notice that either employer or employee must give to end the employment contract. If the length of notice stipulated in the written statement is shorter than that required by law, the legal minimum applies. *See:* NOTICE

9. The employee's job title. The employer does not have to describe the employee's duties in writing, but to do so is an added precaution against future disputes.

In particular, if the employee may later be required to do a different job, to do overtime or to move to different premises, it is in the employer's interest to state that fact in the written statement. Otherwise, if the employee later refuses such a change and is dismissed, he might succeed in a claim of unfair dismissal.

10. The disciplinary rules and procedures that apply to the employee and the way in which he can appeal against disciplinary action. *See:* DISCIPLINE AT WORK

11. Any special provisions for defining the employee's length of service. Such provisions most commonly apply to groups of companies, in which an employee may transfer from one subsidiary to another. If service with associated companies is counted for calculating holiday or pension entitlements, it may also be counted in establishing EMPLOYMENT PROTECTION rights – for example, MATERNITY leave, REDUNDANCY payments and awards for unfair dismissal.

HOW THE LAW PROTECTS AN EMPLOYEE'S RIGHTS

Special time limits in some cases

Employee has a right to:	If he or she has worked for:	Employees who are not entitled to protection								
		1	2	3	4	5	6	7	8	9
Written statement of employment terms. *See:* EMPLOYMENT CONTRACT	13 weeks		X	X	X		X	X	X	X
Notice of dismissal. *See:* NOTICE	1 month		X	X	X		X	X	X	X
Written reasons for dismissal. *See:* DISMISSAL	6 months				X		X		X	X
Claim for unfair dismissal. *See:* UNFAIR DISMISSAL	1 year (Employers with 20 employees or less, 2 years)	X			X		X	X	X	X
Redundancy payment. *See:* REDUNDANCY	2 years (provided other conditions are met)	X	X		X	X	X	X	X	X
Transfer of contract in sale of business. *See:* EMPLOYMENT CONTRACT	any time				X					
Maternity pay. *See:* MATERNITY	2 years (provided other conditions are met)						X	X	X	X
Reclaim job after pregnancy. *See:* MATERNITY	2 years (provided other conditions are met)						X	X	X	X
Itemised pay statement. *See:* PAY	Any time			X			X		X	X
Guaranteed pay on short-time or lay-off. *See:* LAY-OFF	1 month (provided other conditions are met)				X		X	X	X	X
Equal pay. *See:* SEX DISCRIMINATION	Any time			X			X			X
Payment on insolvency of employer. *See:* PAY	Any time			X	X		X			
Belong to a trade union and to participate actively. *See:* TRADE UNION	Any time						X			
Time off for union duties. *See:* TRADE UNION	Any time, provided that the union is recognised and independent						X		X	
Time off for public duties. *See:* TIME OFF WORK	Any time but only certain public offices are included			X			X		X	
Time off for training or to look for work. *See:* TIME OFF WORK	2 years (provided other conditions are met)			X	X		X		X	
Time off for ante-natal care. *See:* MATERNITY	Any time.						X			X

1. Retiring age
2. Crown servants
3. Merchant seamen
4. Registered dock workers
5. Domestics who are close relatives
6. Employee ordinarily works outside G.B.
7. Fixed-term contracts for 12 weeks or less
8. Part-timers (usually under 16 hours per week)
9. Share fishermen

The chart summarises employees' rights under employment protection laws.

To qualify for some rights, the employee must have worked for the employer concerned for a specified time. The length of the qualifying period, which starts from the first day of employment, is shown in column 2.

Previous service with another employer will be taken into account in qualifying for some of these employment rights where the business is continued or taken over. Employees of associated employers will be taken into account when calculating the number of employees, where that is relevant.

The rights from which some classes of employee – for example, part-timers – are excluded are listed in the chart according to the type of employment.

on for a specific project that is expected to last for 3 months or less and which is completed within that time is also excluded. A worker whose contract is for longer than 3 months is covered by the employment protection rules.

- People who normally work abroad. If an employee's contract requires him ordinarily to work abroad, he may lose his UK employment protection rights.
- Crown servants. Some employment rights – to a redundancy payment, a written statement and minimum notice – do not apply to Crown servants (who include civil servants and 'industrial' employees). They have their own rules. None of the rights apply to the armed forces.
- Domestic servants. A domestic servant has no right to a redundancy payment if he or she is a close relative of the employer and works only in his private household – not in other premises, such as a family shop. 'Close relative' means a parent, grandparent, step-parent, child, grandchild, brother, sister, half-brother and half-sister.
- Registered dock workers.
- Merchant seamen.
- Share fishermen. The master and crew of a fishing vessel are excluded if paid only by receiving a share of the profits.

Employment abroad

Taking a job abroad with a foreign employer usually results in your rights as an employee being governed by the law of the country concerned. However, some multi-national companies may make express provisions in the EMPLOYMENT CONTRACT as to which laws will operate.

The employment rights of someone working abroad for a British company are often governed by Scots law. The rights given by the employment protection law, however, do not cover those who ordinarily work abroad.

ENGAGEMENT

When a couple decide to marry

A couple who become engaged are entering into a legal contract. If either party calls off the engagement without good reason, the other can sue for BREACH OF PROMISE. (The right to sue will be abolished during 1984).

DAMAGES FOR A JILTED LOVER

If either party calls off an engagement, without good reason, the other person can ask for damages.

What is good reason for calling off an engagement depends on the circumstances. It may be, for example, that one party has concealed the existence of an illegitimate child or has serious fears about his or her health.

If property has been bought out of money provided by both parties and the engagement is then called off, there may be a dispute as to who owns it. If the property has been bought in joint names, it belongs to the parties in equal shares. If it has been bought in the name of one party only, it is presumed to belong to him or her alone. A special standard of proof applies if one party wants to disprove this. A solicitor will be able to give advice on this.

Money spent on wedding preparations – for example, to buy the bridesmaids' dresses or to arrange the wedding reception – can be recovered from one party if he or she called off the engagement without good reason.

Giving back gifts

Wedding presents given to the couple on or during the engagement should be returned to the people who gave them.

Whether or not presents given by one partner to the other should be returned depends on the situation in which they were given. If the present was given without the marriage in mind – for example, it was a birthday present – there is no need to return it. But if the present was conditional on the marriage taking place, it should be returned. It can be difficult to decide whether an engagement ring has been given unconditionally or is conditional on the marriage taking place.

If one party is giving a present – for example, a ring that is a family heirloom – on condition that the marriage takes place, this should be made clear at the outset, either in writing or by saying so before witnesses.

ENTRY, Right of

When an official needs a pass or warrant to enter your home

Thousands of officials have the right – given in Acts of Parliament – to enter your home. However, they must, if you challenge them, produce proof of that right. If they persist in entering against your will, they may commit an ASSAULT and also be liable for TRESPASS if they cause damage.

Checking credentials

If anyone claiming to be an official wishes to enter your home, ask him first to produce his official pass or warrant and then ask him why he claims the right to enter.

If you have any doubt about whether the official is genuine, do not let him in until you have checked his credentials with the office from which he claims to come. If the office cannot satisfy you, call the police.

If you refuse entry to a genuine official who has produced a pass or other document of authorisation, he can usually apply to a justice of the peace or sheriff for a legal warrant to enter your home. If you still refuse to admit him, you may commit an offence.

Landlord's rights

The rights of a landlord to enter a tenant's premises are governed by the lease. Most leases have an express or implied term allowing the landlord to enter and inspect the premises after reasonable notice and at a reasonable time. Where the tenancy is protected by the Rent (Scotland) Act, a condition is read into the lease requiring the tenant to give the landlord reasonable access to inspect and repair the premises. *See:* LANDLORD AND TENANT

WHEN OUTSIDERS CAN ENTER A HOME WITHOUT CONSENT

Understanding the occasions on which any of several thousand people can legally ask to 'come in'

	Grounds	Time	Authorisation needed	Notice required	What happens if the householder refuses entry
British Telecom officials	To check that householders using TV sets have a TV licence	Day or night	Sheriff's warrant	None	Cannot force entry. Refusal is an offence. Up to £400 fine
Local authority housing officials	To inspect premises which may be, for example, dangerous or overcrowded, or subject to compulsory purchase	Reasonable hours	Official carries a letter of authority	Normally 24 hours	Obstruction an offence. Up to £400 fine
	To inspect houses in multiple occupation where entry is refused		J.P.'s or sheriff's warrant	None	Can force entry. Obstruction an offence, up to £400 fine
Local authority building inspectors	To inspect new buildings; buildings where change of use proposed or taken place; dangerous buildings. Also to inspect to ensure compliance with building regulations	Reasonable hours	**1.** Official carries a letter of authorisation	Compliance with building regulations; change of use: 3 days. Otherwise none	Authority can apply for a warrant
			2. J.P.'s warrant	None	Wilful obstruction is an offence
Medical officer	To inspect premises where there is believed to be an infectious disease, or a health hazard	Reasonable hours	**1.** Officer carries a letter of authority	None	Medical officer can apply for a warrant. Wilful obstruction an offence
			2. Sheriff's warrant	None	Can force entry. Wilful obstruction an offence. Up to £400 fine or 6 months' imprisonment
Local authority environmental health inspector	To investigate possible breaches of Public Health (Sc) Acts	Between 9a.m. and 6p.m. (or at any time when any work suspected of causing a health risk is usually carried on)	**1.** None	None	Inspector must apply to J.P. or sheriff for an order. (If no one in house, can force entry without order)
		Day or night	**2.** J.P.'s or sheriff's order	None	Householder commits offence. Up to £50 fine. Application for warrant to force entry. Obstruction an offence. Up to £50 fine
	To enforce court order requiring removal of public health nuisance		J.P.'s or sheriff's warrant	None	Can force entry. Obstruction an offence. Up to £100 fine

Continued on next page

	Grounds	Time	Authorisation needed	Notice required	What happens if the householder refuses entry
Police	To prevent a breach of the peace or make an arrest	Day or night	Officer's warrant card	None	Police may use what force they consider necessary
	To carry out investigations	Day or night	**1.** Officer's warrant card	None	Police usually cannot force entry without magistrate's warrant
			2. Magistrate's warrant	None	Warrant allows police to use force as necessary
	To return children, mental patients, or others subject to special orders, to the appropriate authority	Day or night	Warrant by constable accompanied by medical practitioner	None	Police may use what force they consider necessary
	To seize goods or publications in connection with investigations of offences	Day or night	Magistrate's warrant	None	Warrant allows police to use force as necessary. Must seize goods and show them to magistrate
	To investigate VAT or motor tax offences	Reasonable hours (at night if good reason)	**1.** Official pass	None	Police can apply for warrant
			2. Magistrate's warrant	None	Force can be used as necessary when investigating motor tax offences
Firemen	To put out fire, to protect from fire or to rescue people or property	Day or night	Any fireman on duty	None	Firemen can force entry. Householder liable to a fine of up to £400 if he refuses entry
Customs officers	To search for contraband	Day or night	Magistrate's warrant	None	Doors, windows and containers can be opened by reasonable force. Between 11 p.m. and 5 a.m. a policeman must attend
Court officers (sheriff officers and messengers-at-arms)	To enforce sheriff court and Court of Session orders (for example, to poind goods for debt or non-payment of tax; to evict tenants or squatters; to search for and remove a child)	None specified	Court warrant	None	Can force entry. Offence to prevent officer carrying out warrant. Up to £2,000 fine and 3 months' jail
Valuation officers (Inland Revenue)	To value property for capital transfer tax, income tax or corporation tax	Reasonable hours	Official pass or written authority	None	Liability to £50 fine and demand based on estimate. Forced entry not permitted.
Inland Revenue officers	To collect evidence of tax fraud	None specified	Sheriff's warrant	None	Can force entry
VAT inspectors	Any purpose in connection with administration of VAT (but only if	Reasonable hours	Official pass	None	Can apply for J.P.'s or sheriff's warrant allowing him to use force and remove documents

Continued overleaf

WHEN OUTSIDERS CAN ENTER A HOME WITHOUT CONSENT *continued*

	Grounds	Time	Authorisation needed	Notice required	What happens if the householder refuses entry
VAT Inspectors *continued*	house is also business premises)				
Rating Valuation Assessor	To survey and value for payment of local rates	Any reasonable time of day	Adequate identification	24 hours	Householder commits an offence
Landlords	To inspect property	Reasonable hours	Terms of the lease	According to the lease (usually at least 24 hours' notice)	Landlord can seek court order to gain entry
Electricity board officials	For purposes relating to electricity supply	Reasonable hours	**1.** Official pass	Normally 24 hours' notice	Official can apply for a warrant
			2. J.P.'s or sheriff's warrant	None	Entry by force if necessary; board must repair damage or pay cost
	To deal with an emergency	Day or night	Official pass	None	Official cannot use force; he may ask policeman to accompany him to prevent a breach of the peace
Gas authority officials	To check fittings, read meters, disconnect unsafe fittings or cut off supply because of unpaid bills	Reasonable hours	**1.** Official pass	Normally 24 hours' notice	Official can apply for a warrant
			2. J.P.'s or sheriff's warrant	None	Entry by force if necessary; board must repair damage or pay cost
	To deal with an emergency	Day or night	Official pass	None	Official cannot use force; he may ask policeman to accompany him to prevent a breach of the peace
Water authority officials	To check fittings and to see if water is being wasted, misused or collected	Reasonable hours	Official pass	24 hours	Offence to refuse entry; up to £400 fine
	Urgency, absence of occupiers, refusal of entry by occupier	Day or night	J.P.'s or sheriff's warrant	None	Entry by force if necessary; offence to refuse entry

The landlord will commit an offence if he interferes with the tenant's peace and comfort by forcing his way into the house. *See:* HARASSMENT

The landlord will also be guilty of an offence if he enters a tenant's premises and evicts him by force. If the landlord has lawfully ended the tenancy, but the tenant refuses to leave, the landlord's proper course of action is to obtain an EVICTION order from the sheriff court. A SHERIFF OFFICER can then evict the tenant.

EQUAL OPPORTUNITIES

How the Government monitors its sex equality laws

Anyone who feels unfairly treated because of his or her sex can seek advice from the Equal Opportunities Commission, an independent body set up to promote equality between men and women. It helps people to exercise their rights under the SEX DISCRIMINATION and Equal PAY Acts, and in some cases takes action on its own.

The commission helps to settle disputes, and may provide free legal advice if conciliation fails. If a case is complicated or tests a new point of law, it may provide legal representation if you:

- Sue in a sheriff court over sex discrimination in education, housing, or the provision of goods, facilities or services.
- Take an equal pay or employment claim to an INDUSTRIAL TRIBUNAL.

ESPIONAGE

Spying for enemies of the state

Anyone convicted of espionage or spying may be imprisoned for up to 14 years under the OFFICIAL SECRETS Acts 1911–39.

A person commits such an offence if he approaches, inspects or is in the neighbourhood of a prohibited place for any purposes that are held by a court to be prejudicial to the safety or interests of the state.

The term 'prohibited place' includes military, naval and air force establishments, munitions factories, docks and power stations. The Government may add establishments to the list at any time.

Sketches and notes

Anyone who makes a sketch plan, model or note or who obtains official records or documents which could help an enemy, is also guilty of an offence of spying.

The Acts have been used not only to punish people who are spying but also those who are protesting at a prohibited place. For example, in 1962 nuclear-disarmament demonstrators were convicted under the Official Secrets Act 1911 for planning to enter an air force station in order to prevent aircraft from taking off or landing.

ESTATE

What is left when someone dies

The property of someone who has died – known as his estate – does not pass immediately to those entitled to it. It goes first to the deceased's executors, who divide the estate in accordance with the will or the rules of INTESTACY. *See:* EXECUTOR

If there is only a small amount of cash, and possessions of limited value such as clothes and furniture, the estate can be divided informally.

Assessing the value

The worth of an estate is calculated as its value on the date of death. Interest due on all loans, debts, shares and deposits must be calculated to that date, as must all taxes and rent owed by or to the deceased person.

The executor can estimate the value of property such as cars or houses by, for example, checking newspaper advertisement columns for the price of similar cars or houses. Specialist items, such as antiques, can be professionally valued.

Stocks and shares are valued at their Stock Exchange middle price on the date of death – or, if the Exchange was closed on that date, on the next day that it was open. To find the value of shares in a private company, the executors can ask the company's accountants to certify a figure.

Having assessed the total value of the estate, and all debts and expenses which are due from it, the executors must submit an inventory to the Capital Taxes Office. Any CAPITAL TRANSFER TAX due is payable then, unless postponement can be claimed.

After taxes, debts and the expenses of administration have been paid, the remainder of the estate is divided according to the will or the rules of intestacy.

Valuing the home

The house owned by the deceased is valued as if it had been vacant at the date of death. The widow(er) may become entitled to it by the will or the rules of intestacy. Otherwise he or she may be evicted unless the will gives a right to occupy it.

If the house was jointly owned, the surviving spouse as a joint owner is entitled to stay on. But if he or she does not inherit the deceased's share, the new joint owner may bring legal proceedings to have the house sold. Normally the value of the deceased's half share is taken to be one-half of the value of the whole house with vacant possession.

A house tenanted by the deceased usually has no value to his estate. But the widow(er) or the children may be entitled to take over the tenancy. A tenancy of a croft or a farm may form part of the deceased's estate and should be valued.

Valuing a business

If the deceased owned or was a partner in a business, an accountant will often have to be engaged to value it. His assessment will take into account the stock and property and the goodwill the business has built up.

Valuing personal belongings

The value of personal items is what they would fetch if sold second-hand.

When a beneficiary is not yet 18 years old

A legacy left to a PUPIL should be paid to his parent(s) to administer for him until he becomes a MINOR.

A legacy left to a minor should be paid to him. But the receipt should also be signed by one of his parents, unless the will states that a parent's signature alone is sufficient. The money is the child's, but his parents have a duty to advise him how to look after it. They can refuse their consent to anything they consider ill-advised.

On reaching 18 a child is free to do whatever he likes with his money, unless it has been left in trust for him until he is older.

ESTATE AGENT

Buying and selling property through a third party

An estate agent is a go-between for people buying and selling, or leasing, property.

In Scotland, unlike in England, ordinary houses are often sold by solicitors rather than by estate agents. Some solicitors offer a simple, and therefore cheap, service. Others – they are often estate agents as well – offer a more lavish and expensive service.

If you think your house will be difficult to sell for some reason, it is worth thinking about using an estate agent. He may be able to get you a higher price which would absorb the extra expense of using him.

As well as selling houses, estate agents often deal with more specialised property such as shops or large farms.

Anybody can set up in business as an estate agent, without qualifications of any kind.

If you decide to go to an estate agent, choose one who is also a solicitor or who belongs to another professional body, such as the Royal Institution of Chartered Surveyors, the National Association of Estate Agents or the Incorporated Society of Valuers and Auctioneers. This means that the agent has a code of conduct to observe for your protection.

What an agent does

If you use an estate agent to sell your house, he can help in a number of ways. He can advise on the best method of sale, the right asking price and the best time to sell. He may visit your home to inspect the property and fittings, measure rooms and take photographs for advertising purposes. He can then advertise the property in various ways – on a board outside the property, on a card in his own office window, in a list sent to inquirers, or in the press.

The agent is not legally required to do any of these things. His duties depend on the agreement he has reached with you.

The agency agreement

Some estate agents will ask you to sign a written agreement with them; others will be content with a purely verbal arrangement. If there is a written agreement, you should read it very carefully before signing. Ask about anything you do not understand, and if you are still unhappy, consult your solicitor.

Whether or not the agreement is in writing, make sure that the agent understands what you expect him to do to earn his commission. You should also find out whether he considers himself to be sole selling agent, how much the commission is, and when exactly the commission is payable.

Sole selling agent

An estate agent usually likes to be appointed sole selling agent. This may encourage him to be more active on your behalf. The disadvantage is that you must not employ a second agent unless you have ended the agency agreement with the first. If you do, and the second agent finds a buyer for your home, you will have to pay twice over – once, as commission, to the second agent, and again, as DAMAGES for breach of contract, to the first agent.

A sole agency agreement does not prevent you from trying to find a buyer yourself. If you succeed, you do not have to pay commission.

Agent's commission

Before he enters into an agreement, an estate agent is legally bound to tell you how much you will have to pay to cover his commission and other expenses, and when payment will be due. If he does not do this, he will be unable to recover payment in court if the court feels he acted deliberately and you have suffered as a result. This rule does not apply to estate agents who are also solicitors.

What an agent can charge

There is no uniform commission rate: different agents may charge different amounts. Always ask an estate agent for his scale of charges and compare them with those of other firms in the area before you agree to let him act for you. A typical amount is $1\frac{1}{2}$ per cent of the sale price plus the cost of advertising plus VAT.

When commission is paid

Commission is usually due only if the estate agent has successfully brought about a sale. This means that MISSIVES OF SALE must be completed with the buyer, as this is the point at which neither side can withdraw. If there is a written agency agreement, you should check it carefully to make sure that the agent cannot claim commission without actually bringing about a sale.

Although commission becomes due on completion of the missives of sale, you do not usually have to pay the agent until some weeks later, when the buyer takes possession of the house and you have received the sale price. Do not accept a condition in an agency agreement which requires you to pay earlier than this. Your solicitor will usually pay the estate agent directly on your behalf.

Buying through an estate agent

A prospective buyer may engage an estate agent to find him a suitable house; or may simply ask the agent for a list of available properties. There is no charge for the estate agent's services or for receiving a supply of his property lists, unless you have specifically agreed to pay. This is because the agent is already paid by the seller, and he cannot serve both buyer and seller at the same time.

The estate agent's main duty is to the seller and he is not legally obliged to tell a prospective buyer everything about a property. He need not, for example, point out the defects in a property or answer questions about it.

But anything he does choose to tell the prospective buyer about a property must be true. For example, he need not mention that roof tiles need replacing, but he must not falsely describe the roof as being in good, sound condition.

In England, when a suitable property is found the estate agent sometimes asks the prospective buyer to pay an immediate deposit to demonstrate his genuine interest. In Scotland, such a payment is illegal. *See:* HOUSE BUYING AND SELLING

THE SELLER WHO USED TWO AGENTS

A seller who employs an estate agent as sole selling agent cannot employ a second estate agent without being in breach of contract

In April, 1972, the owners of a pub in Ayrshire employed an estate agent to sell it for them. It was agreed in writing that the agents were 'the sole agents engaged in selling the property'.

Advertising began at the beginning of May, at an asking price of £18,000. Approximately 30 enquiries were received from prospective buyers over the summer, but no-one made an offer.

In September, the owners ran out of patience and engaged the services of a friend who was an estate agent in Ayr. They did not bother terminating the agency of the original estate agent.

Within a few weeks the friend found a buyer willing to pay £17,250. Missives of sale were completed. The first agents then claimed they were entitled to commission at 5% of this amount and sued the owners for £863.75.

DECISION

The sellers were not allowed to employ a second estate agent while they were still under sole agency agreement with another estate agent. They were in breach of that sole agency agreement and were therefore liable for damages. The first agents were entitled to £300 in damages from the sellers.

EUROPEAN COMMUNITIES

How laws made elsewhere affect our lives

Life in Britain is increasingly subject to the laws and regulations of the three European communities to which the United Kingdom belongs. They are:

- The European Economic Community, or Common Market, which was established in 1957, under the Treaty of Rome, to improve and bring into line the economies and living standards of its member countries and to bring the states closer together politically.
- The European Coal and Steel Community, set up in 1951 to establish a common market in coal and steel.
- The European Atomic Energy Community (Euratom), formed in 1957 to develop the peaceful use of nuclear power.

The countries with which Britain is linked in all three European communities are Belgium, Denmark, France, the Federal Republic of Germany (West Germany), Greece, the Irish Republic, Italy, Luxembourg and the Netherlands.

By far the most wide-ranging of the three communities, and the one that has the greatest direct effect on the everyday lives of British citizens, is the European Economic Community.

Under the Treaty of Rome, its governing bodies have power to make laws on trade, agriculture, transport, tax and other economic matters. They also can enforce the free movement of people and goods between member countries and the right of workers from each country to work in any other EEC state.

Abolishing customs duties

Britain's membership of the EEC means that it no longer has the right to impose restrictions – called quotas – on the goods it imports from other member countries: and it no longer charges customs duty on most goods brought into Britain from them. But the new rules do not apply yet to duties and quotas imposed on alcoholic drinks, tobacco, perfumes and other articles bought for private use by citizens from one member state on a visit to another member state.

A step towards abolishing such duties is Britain's two-tier arrangement, under which a British Citizen returning from an EEC country is given a greater duty-free allowance on goods bought in an ordinary shop than on goods bought in a special duty-free shop. For example, a Briton is allowed to bring in 1.5 litres of whisky duty free if he bought it in a French shop, because he has already paid French duty. If he bought the whisky in a duty-free shop – at an airport or on a ferry, for example – he is allowed only 1 litre free of UK duty.

Controlling content and quality

Each member country in the EEC is entitled to make rules controlling the standard of goods sold within its borders. For example, sausages on sale in Belgium must have a higher meat content than is legally necessary in Britain.

Gradually, however, the EEC is harmonising its product quality rules so that all countries will require the same standards. New international standards already govern the quality of cars, crystal glass, textiles, paints and measuring instruments.

Labelling Precise rules about how some dangerous substances are to be labelled in EEC countries have been adopted, and there are also regulations setting out how food is to be labelled if it is made in one member state and sold in another. All such items must carry a list of ingredients and the date by which they must be sold.

Free markets Companies are often prohibited from setting up agreements to divide the European market among themselves – by selling sole trading or manufacturing rights for example – in conflict with the EEC principle of free movement of goods.

THE TYPES OF LAW THAT RULE THE EUROPEAN COMMUNITIES

In the European Economic Community, Euratom and the Coal and Steel Community, EEC laws are more important than those of any single member state. If there is a conflict between Community law and the national law of a member state, Community law prevails.

New Community laws can be made in three ways:

- Regulations passed by the Council of Ministers or the Commission have direct legal effect in all member states and on people and companies in those states, usually once they have been published in the EEC's *Official Journal.*

For example, one regulation says that lorry drivers with vehicles of more than a certain loaded weight may not work more than a stated number of hours during a set period. Member states, companies based in those states and drivers employed by the companies are all obliged to obey those rules.

Regulations passed by the Council do not have to be confirmed by the national parliaments in order to become legally binding in each country. But in Britain, for example, parliamentary committees examine all draft Community law. Where it involves a change in British law, Parliament may decide to cover that change by passing a new Act, or by approving a new ministerial regulation.

The British Government can legally refuse to put a Community regulation into effect, only if it can show that the regulation is against the Community's own rules. The final decision then rests with the European Court of Justice.

- Directives, also passed by the Council of Ministers or the Commission. They are binding on the member states, and *may* apply directly to people or companies in Britain even if not put into effect by a British Act of Parliament or British ministerial order.

A directive outlines a broad aim which member states must achieve by a stated date – usually 2 to 5 years after the directive is passed. Each national government is left free to put a directive into effect in its own way.

A country that fails to meet the deadline for a directive may be brought before the European Court of Justice by the European Commission or by another EEC member, for failing in its obligations.

In such circumstances, the European Court of Justice may also decide that although that country has not introduced the directive into its own law, it does apply directly.

- Decisions, addressed by the Council of Ministers of the European Commission to a member state, a company or even an individual citizen. They are completely binding on whoever they are addressed to.

A decision may be a fine on a company that has broken Community rules on unfair trading, or it may be the setting up of a specialist committee to deal with a particular subject, such as employment.

Travelling in the EEC

All citizens of EEC countries are entitled, under the Treaty of Rome, to travel freely among member countries – for business or for pleasure. In practice, however, there are still restrictions on that right. *See:* CITIZENSHIP

Passports Under EEC rules, a citizen of a member state does not need a passport when travelling to another member state. But he must be able to prove his identity and nationality.

Most EEC countries issue identity cards to their citizens, But Britain does not. For British Citizens, therefore, a Visitors' Passport is normally needed. For a 'no passport' day trip to the Continent from an English Channel port, travel companies arrange temporary identity documents carrying a photograph of the bearer. *See:* PASSPORT

Motor Insurance Checks on motor insurance at national frontiers are eventually to be abolished, and a motor-insurance policy issued by any member state already gives the legal minimum cover in all other EEC countries.

But the main disadvantage is that a UK policy, for example – even if comprehensive – may not provide more than third-party cover in another EEC country. To secure comprehensive protection while motoring in Europe, arrange special cover before you leave Britain.

HOW THE COMMON MARKET IS GOVERNED

The European Economic Community is administered by four institutions set up under the Treaty of Rome:

• **The Council of Ministers** The Community's main body for making major decisions, which consists of government ministers from each of the member states.

It usually meets in Brussels and can make laws and rulings that bind not only the member states but also organisations and individuals in any of those states.

It can decide many issues by majority vote, although the most important decisions – for example, whether a country should be allowed to join the EEC – must be agreed unanimously.

In practice, the majority vote is rarely used, and usually no member state is outvoted on an issue that would affect its own vital interests. If there is a critical disagreement, the Council normally puts off reaching a decision until it can be unanimous, rather than risk driving any member to leave the Community. That practice gives each member a power of veto far wider than any laid down in the Treaty of Rome.

The makeup of the Council of Ministers is not fixed. Each member state sends the government minister most concerned with the topic to be discussed at a particular session. If it is a matter of general policy, for example, the council will consist of the foreign ministers – or, occasionally, the prime ministers – of the member states. If the subject is food, the representatives will be the agriculture ministers.

• **The European Commission** The Community's civil service, which has its headquarters in Brussels. It has two main functions: suggesting how to make the Treaty of Rome work in practice, and carrying out measures approved by the Council of Ministers.

The Commission is also responsible for enforcing EEC rules that forbid unfair trading practices, such as market-sharing agreements, monopolies or price rings. It can order a company to end such arrangements and if the company fails to do so, the Commission can impose a fine.

Commissioners – who must act independently of their home governments – are appointed from all the member nations. Britain, France, Italy and Germany each provide two, and the other members provide one each.

• **The European Court of Justice** Based in Luxembourg, it deals only with matters of Community law. It is not a court of appeal for cases that involve the laws of individual nations. *See:* HUMAN RIGHTS

The court has 11 judges – at least one from each member state – and 5 advocates-general, whose job is to summarise both sides of a case during a hearing and suggest what the Court's decision should be.

The three roles of the European Court of Justice are:

1. To interpret Community law. If a national court cannot decide what an EEC law means, on any particular issue, it may, and sometimes must, ask the European Court for an interpretation which will then become part of that law, for all ten countries in the community.

2. To make sure that the EEC institutions act lawfully. The Council of Ministers, the Commission or any of the member states can challenge a Community law or other decision, on the ground that it conflicts with the principles of the Treaty of Rome. If the court upholds the complaint, it can cancel all or part of the measure complained about.

Individuals and companies can also challenge Community laws or decisions. To do so, however, they must first show that the measure being challenged is of 'direct and individual concern' to them. A company fined by the European Commission for unfair competition, for example, can appeal to the European Court against the decision of the amount of the fine, but someone who merely reads about the fine and is not directly involved has no right to intervene.

3. To ensure that member states respect their obligations to the EEC. If any member state fails to enforce a Community law or other ruling, the European Commission – or another member nation – can draw the court's attention to that failure.

If the court upholds the complaint, it can order the country involved to comply with the law. It cannot impose fines or other penalties on any state. But a Community institution that acts unlawfully can be ordered by the court to pay damages to those who suffer as a result.

No such order has yet been made, and there is no machinery for enforcing payment of damages.

A company or individual disobeying a Community rule can be punished by the courts of the nation concerned, under that nation's laws dealing with EEC matters; or be fined by the Commission.

• **The European Parliament** Meets in Strasbourg and is directly elected by voters in each of the countries of the Community. *See:* ELECTION

It has no power to make laws, but debates laws being prepared by the European Commission and the Council of Ministers.

The Council of Ministers is not bound by the opinions of the European Parliament, but many proposed Community laws have been amended after debate in the Parliament.

The European Commission can be questioned orally or in writing by the Parliament, and is obliged to answer the questions.

The Parliament can – by a two-thirds majority vote – dismiss the whole group of 14 European Commissioners, although the right has never been used. Commissioners cannot be discharged by the Parliament individually.

The European Parliament has power to reject the Community's annual budget. It can only alter 25 per cent of the spending because 75 per cent is obligatory, but it has the power to delay this expenditure if it wishes to.

HOW THE EUROPEAN COMMUNITY MAKES LAWS

Civil servants propose, but governments decide

The main law-making body of the European Economic Community – the Common Market – is the Council of Ministers, in which the governments of the member states, including Britain, are represented.

The European Commission, the Community's civil service, has limited law-making powers delegated to it both by the Council of Ministers and by the treaties setting up the Community.

Most Community laws, other than those dealing with agriculture, follow a procedure of discussion and amendment that may take several years to complete.

EUROPEAN COMMISSION

The heads of the Commission, the European Commissioners, formally adopt draft proposals for new Community laws drawn up by their civil servants after wide consultation. When a draft proposal has been adopted, it is submitted to the Council, which circulates it to other Community bodies. The Commission may withdraw a draft proposal and re-submit it in a revised form

4 Revised proposal

1 Draft proposal

COREPER

The Committee of Permanent Representatives, Coreper, consists of senior officials of ambassador rank representing the governments of the member-states. They do the detailed work of the Council

COUNCIL OF MINISTERS

The Council of Ministers sends the draft proposal to other Community bodies and delegates its own study of the draft to Coreper.

The Council may adopt the draft as Community law, request the Commission to amend it, reject it or simply take no decision.

The Council can adopt its own version, rather than the one proposed by the Commission, only by unanimous agreement

2

3

ECOSOC

The Economic and Social Committee, Ecosoc, consists of representatives of employers and trade unions and a third group that includes other professional interests like farmers and consumers. The Commission is not required to amend proposals for new laws in the light of Ecosoc's comments, but it may do so

EUROPEAN PARLIAMENT

The Parliament is not a law-making body; its role is purely consultative. The European Commission must submit draft proposals to it, and its opinions must be noted – but not necessarily acted upon. However, it has power over part of the budget and can also question the Commission and the Council on their handling of Community matters

5

The Council issues laws in the form of: directives, which the member-states must implement through their national law-making systems; regulations, which automatically have full force in all member-states; and decisions, addressed to a member-state, a company or an individual, which are binding in every respect

National governments or parliaments can influence Community law-making by instructions to their minister at the Council of Ministers

Individuals and groups can influence Community law-making by representation to members of Ecosoc

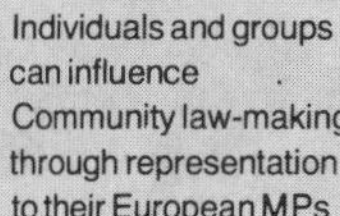

Individuals and groups can influence Community law-making through representation to their European MPs

6

EUROPEAN ECONOMIC COMMUNITY

Most Community laws are applied to people living in the 10 member-states, including Britain, through their national legal system, in the same way as national laws, over which they take precedence

7

EUROPEAN COURT OF JUSTICE

The European Court is the final arbiter on Community law, but it is not an appeal court that can overrule a national court. It may, if requested by a national court, give an interpretation of Community law which the national court is then bound to apply.

The Court may hold Community rules to be invalid if they are imcompatible with Community law. It can hear cases brought by member-states or individuals against the Community institutions and by the institutions against the member-states. It cannot impose fines or prison sentences to reinforce its decisions

If a motorist is involved in an accident in an EEC country, he must provide proof of insurance. The most easily recognisable proof is the International Motor Insurance Card – known as the Green card – although it is no longer compulsory in EEC countries.

Illness Any resident of the United Kingdom who pays NATIONAL INSURANCE CONTRIBUTIONS at the employed person's rate (Class 1) is entitled to medical treatment and medicine in another EEC country on the same basis as a citizen of that country.

Self-employed people are now similarly entitled. Someone who no longer works is also entitled to full medical benefits, provided that he has paid enough UK national insurance contributions to earn a full-rate pension on retirement.

To claim medical benefits in another EEC country, you must produce proof that you are entitled to them. That means in most countries, you must produce your passport and form E111, which you should get from any office of the Department of Health and Social Security before you go abroad.

Form E111 is not needed by British Citizens visiting Denmark or Ireland.

Living and working in Europe

A British Citizen can live and work in any other EEC country without a work permit. However, you must have a valid full passport (not a British Visitors' Passport) endorsed with the words, 'Holder has the right of abode in the United Kingdom' or 'British Citizen'.

If that endorsement is not already printed in your passport, ask a passport office to stamp it in your passport before you move abroad. Without the endorsement, you may not be allowed to stay.

In all EEC countries, except Ireland, you also need a residence permit which is issued after you have arrived. The timing varies from country to country. Consult the London embassy or a consulate in Scotland of the country in which you want to settle.

Reporting to the police

Once abroad, you must register with the police in the area where you will be living – in theory, immediately you arrive, but in practice within a few weeks. You must produce your passport and – if you are an employee – a certificate of employment signed by your employer.

Self-employed people and students must also register with the police, and may be required to produce evidence to justify their stay and to show that they can support themselves. Such evidence may include a certificate of professional qualifications, a client's contract for services, a lease on commercial premises or a note from the university or college where a student is to study.

SOCIAL SECURITY IN THE EEC

A British Citizen who goes to live and work in another Community country must normally pay contributions into the local social security scheme, and stop paying them in the UK.

However, if the employing company has a place of business in the UK, and if the employee knows that he will be working abroad for fewer than 52 weeks, he is normally obliged to continue his UK payments and need not pay into the foreign scheme.

In such circumstances, complete form CF83, available from any office of the Department of Health and Social Security. If your contributions to the UK scheme are not automatically deducted by your employer, you can pay them through an agent, or as a lump sum at the end of the period you are abroad.

Under Community rules, contributions made in any Community country count in any other. So if you return to Britain after 3 or 4 years in, for example, France, you are entitled to benefits as if you had been in Britain all that time.

A British Citizen living and working in another Community country can claim the same social security benefits as citizens of that country, provided that he can show that he would have been entitled to the corresponding benefits at home.

To do so, obtain a certificate from the Department of Health and Social Security, showing that your national insurance contributions were up to date when you left Britain.

Unemployment benefit, however, is not normally paid to a British Citizen in another EEC country unless he can show that he has had a job, and paid social security contributions, in that country. The rule may be waived at the discretion of local social security officials, but this cannot be done without good reason.

For example, if a British Citizen and his wife move to France, where the husband has a job but his wife cannot work because her professional qualifications are not accepted there, benefit may possibly be paid to the wife.

Residence permit

When the police have checked your documents, they issue a residence permit, which is equivalent to the identity card issued to local citizens and which you can use instead of a passport when crossing frontiers within the EEC.

In some areas, you may be given only a temporary permit which you must renew as it expires until your full permit is available.

The police can refuse a permit if they believe an applicant might be a threat to public order or break some local law – for example, if they know that he has a recent criminal record.

Someone who is refused a residence permit can appeal only through the courts of the country concerned. He cannot take legal action in Britain, say, to try to obtain a permit in France.

Taking the family

A British Citizen who goes to live and work in another country is entitled to take with him (or her) his wife (or her husband) and any children under the age of 21, provided that the police of the host country are told of their presence there.

If the children are over 21, their applications for registration with the police are treated separately from those of the other family members.

A child born abroad, one of whose parents is a British Citizen, is entitled to British nationality. To ensure proof of his nationality the parents should register the birth with the British consul, generally within a year. *See:* CITIZENSHIP

Paying taxes in the EEC

A British Citizen who lives and works in another EEC country is liable for all its local taxes, including income tax, capital gains tax (or its local equivalent), property tax, local authority tax and value added tax.

Income tax A British Citizen who becomes liable to income tax in another EEC country may escape British tax on his earnings, even if he sends part of the income back to the United Kingdom.

Provided that you are out of Britain for at least 365 consecutive days – which can be interrupted for short visits home – you do not have to pay any UK tax on your earnings abroad. *See:* FOREIGN INCOME

All EEC countries operate a form of pay-as-you-earn tax system for employed persons, and assess the taxpayer's final liability once a year. Although all the systems are broadly similar to that of the UK, the tax-free allowances have variations from country to country.

Some of the member states – Belgium, France, Ireland and the Netherlands – offer extra allowances to foreign residents at the discretion of the local tax inspector and subject to certain conditions.

Rates of income tax vary throughout the Community. If you go to work in Denmark, you will pay higher rates than in Britain, whatever your income group. In Germany and the Netherlands, tax rates start lower than in Britain, but move sharply upwards for the higher paid worker.

The rights of professionals

Under the Treaty of Rome, all Community citizens have a right to set up in business anywhere in the EEC. However, that rule is not yet in force for all professions, because member states have not yet been able to agree on the relative worth of professional qualifications earned in the various countries.

Doctors, dentists and state-registered nurses can work in all Community countries provided that they can pass a test to satisfy the host country's professional institutions that they are sufficiently familiar with the local language to practise there.

Accountants, teachers, journalists and entertainers are allowed to work in any EEC country without taking a local examination, but cannot expect to be given a job that requires knowledge of the language, if they are not familiar with it.

Advocates and solicitors are entitled to offer legal advice and may appear in court in any Community country.

Engineers' qualifications are not yet formally recognised in EEC countries outside their own.

Rights of workers

Apart from guaranteeing the free movement of workers, the EEC has laid down rules for many aspects of workers' rights.

Equal pay The Treaty of Rome requires all member states to ensure equal PAY for men and women who do similar work. This was put into effect in Britain in 1975, when the Equal Pay Act 1970 came into force.

Redundancy Another directive, put into effect in Britain in the Employment Protection Act 1975, now amended, said that any employer making redundant 10 or more workers within a period of 30 days must give them 30 days' warning, and inform the Department of Employment 30 days ahead. If 100 or more workers are involved, the period is 90 days. *See:* REDUNDANCY

Looking for work

If you go to look for work in another EEC country and you have been receiving UK unemployment benefit in this country, you can continue to get this for up to 3 months elsewhere in the Community. To qualify, you must have been registered as available for work (normally for a period of 4 weeks) at a UK unemployment benefit office or careers office.

Unemployment benefit continues only as long as you register for work in each country in which you are seeking employment.

As long as you register in the new country within 7 days of ceasing to be available for work in the Community country you have just left, benefit can continue to be paid.

After receiving UK unemployment benefit in another EEC country, you are not entitled to it again for another period of unemployment abroad unless you have worked in the UK in the meantime.

If you fall sick while looking for work in another EEC country, you can get UK SICKNESS BENEFIT instead of unemployment benefit as long as the time for which you would have been entitled to the latter has not run out.

You can also get sickness benefit from the UK if you are working in another Community country but have continued to pay contributions to the UK national insurance scheme.

EUTHANASIA

Ending the life of a person who wants to die

Euthanasia, or mercy killing, is the deliberate termination of someone else's life in order to end their suffering. In law, an intentional killing of this nature is MURDER.

However, if the killing was carried out with the genuine and compassionate intention of preventing further physical or mental suffering (particularly in the case of close relations), the prosecutor might restrict the charge to one of CULPABLE HOMICIDE.

In euthanasia cases, the killing may be brought about by:

- An overdose of drugs or withdrawal of life-support treatment.
- Failing to call for essential medical assistance where a duty of care is owed to the person killed – for example, by a private nurse to her patient.

It is no defence to prove that the person who was suffering had pleaded (or consented) to have his or her life ended.

Successfully persuading a person to end his or her life may also amount to murder or culpable homicide.

Pain-killing drugs A doctor who gives a mortally ill patient drugs to relieve extreme suffering is not guilty of any crime, even if the drugs also hasten the patient's death.

EVICTION

When a private tenant can be forced to leave his home

Virtually no one who legally occupies residential property can be forced to leave it except by order of a court. It is an offence to evict a legal occupier unlawfully; or to harass such a person – or other members of the household – in order to make him or her leave. *See:* HARASSMENT

This applies to all house tenants – including tenants of local authorities and other public bodies. It also applies to most occupiers who are not tenants but only have permission, or licence, to occupy their home.

See: COUNCIL TENANCY; LICENCE TO OCCUPY; TIED HOME

Protection under the Rent Act

Many *private* tenants are specially protected against eviction by the Rent (Scotland) Act 1984. If a tenant is protected, the landlord can only evict on a number of statutory grounds. Protected tenants cannot sign away their rights under the Act.

Tenants of local authorities, the Scottish Special Housing Association and housing associations are protected by separate legislation. *See:* COUNCIL TENANCY; HOUSING ASSOCIATION

A private tenancy, whether furnished or unfurnished, is not protected by the Rent (Scotland) Act if:

● The rateable value of the house is above certain limits:

If the house was on the valuation roll on March 23, 1965, or was first entered on the roll between then and March 31, 1978, the tenant will not be protected if the rateable value at that time was more than £200. If the house was first entered on the valuation roll on or after April 1, 1978, the tenant will not be protected if the rateable value at that time was more than £600.

The rateable value can be checked at a main library or at the regional assessor's office.

● No rent is payable; or the rent is less than two-thirds of the rateable value on March 23, 1965, (or the date when the house first appeared on the valuation roll).

Even if these conditions are met, a tenancy will not be protected if any one of the following applies:

1. The landlord – and any successor of his – has resided in the house, or in another flat in a building which has been converted to flats, since the tenancy began – unless the tenancy is being renewed and the tenant was protected immediately before the renewal date. This rule applies to tenancies granted after August 14, 1974. It also applies to furnished, but not to unfurnished, tenancies granted before August 14, 1974, if the landlord was resident at that date.

2. The tenant shares some accommodation – such as a lounge or kitchen/living room, but not a bathroom – with the landlord.

3. The rent includes payment for genuine board or personal services.

'Board' can be as little as a daily continental breakfast. The services must be personal to the tenant – for example, room cleaning or porterage but not a common lift.

4. It is a holiday letting. *See:* HOLIDAY ACCOMMODATION

5. The accommodation is let by a college or university to a student.

Notice to quit

A landlord who wants a private tenant to leave must first send a written 'notice to quit' to the tenant. The tenant must be given at least 28 days' notice. (Some tenants will be entitled to a longer period of notice under their lease.) If these conditions are not observed, the notice is invalid. *See:* LANDLORD AND TENANT

The notice will also be invalid unless it gives the tenant information about his or her basic rights and where legal advice can be obtained.

If the tenant refuses to leave when the written notice expires, the landlord cannot lawfully evict him or her without obtaining a sheriff court order for possession. Such an order can be made only on the grounds mentioned below.

When the court may grant possession

Apart from certain situations in which a sheriff court *must* allow repossession (see below), a landlord can only get a possession order against a protected tenant if:

● He satisfies the sheriff that it is reasonable to make an order, *and*

● He can establish one of the following grounds:

1. Suitable alternative accommodation is available for the tenant and his family.

The court will be satisfied on this point if the landlord produces a certificate from the district (or islands) council, stating that they will provide suitable accommodation by a set date. If the landlord cannot produce such a certificate, he will have to satisfy the court that any alternative accommodation available:

● Will receive the same legal protection as the tenant's existing accommodation.

● Will be reasonably suitable to the tenant's income and needs – for example, the size of his or her family or the need to be within reasonable travelling distance of work.

2. The tenant is in arrears with the rent or has broken some other important term of the lease.

3. The tenant or someone living with him:

● Has caused nuisance or annoyance to neighbours, or

● Has been convicted of using the house for immoral or illegal purposes – such as prostitution, or

● Has allowed the house or furniture provided by the landlord to deteriorate through damage or neglect.

4. The tenant has given notice to quit and the landlord – relying on that notice – has either contracted to sell or let the house or will be seriously prejudiced if he cannot get possession.

5. The tenant has:

● Transferred the tenancy to someone else, or sub-let, without the landlord's permission.

● Sub-let part of the house and charged an unfair rent *See:* SUB-TENANCY

6. The tenant was employed by the landlord and the house goes with the job. The tenant's job must have ended and the landlord must reasonably require the house for another full-time employee. *See:* TIED HOME

7. The landlord reasonably requires the house as a residence for himself, for an adult son or daughter, or for parents or parents-in-law. The court must be satisfied that the landlord will suffer greater hardship than the tenant if the possession order is not made.

This ground cannot be used if the landlord bought the house after March 23, 1965 (or after May 24, 1974, if the house is let furnished).

8. Overcrowding is creating a health risk, and could be prevented by evicting a lodger or sub-tenant.

When the court must order possession

The court *must* grant a possession order to a landlord who owns the house in which the tenant lives, if:

1. The landlord once lived in the house and:

● Wishes to live there again (or a member of his family, who also lived in the house, does).

● Wishes to sell it in order to buy one more suitable for his place of work.

● Has defaulted on the MORTGAGE and the house is to be sold.

- Has died and the house is to be sold – or is needed by either a family member living with the landlord at his death or someone who has inherited it.

2. The landlord bought the house for his retirement and:

- Has retired from regular employment and wishes to live in the house.
- Wishes to sell the house and buy one more suited to his needs.
- Has defaulted on the mortgage and the house is to be sold.
- Has died and the house is to be sold – or is needed by either a family member living with him at his death or someone who has inherited it.

3. The landlord is a member of the ARMED FORCES and wishes to reside in the house.

Repossession will generally only be allowed if the owner informed the tenant (in writing) before the tenancy began that the house might be repossessed under one of these grounds. Also, the house must not have been let since 1965 (1980 where the owner is in the armed forces) on any other basis. However, the court can allow repossession even if these conditions are not satisfied, where it considers it would be fair to do so.

All landlords The court must also grant a possession order to any landlord

WHAT A NOTICE TO QUIT MUST STATE

How tenants must be informed of their legal rights under the Rent (Scotland) Act

The notice must be a clear directive to leave the whole of the premises and surrender possession to the landlord or his agent

Four weeks is the minimum notice for ending any tenancy. The period can be much longer, however, depending on the terms of the agreement

If the tenant does not leave the dwelling, the landlord must get an order for possession from the court before the tenant can be lawfully evicted. The landlord cannot apply for such an order before the notice to quit has run out

The tenant who does not know if he has any right to remain in possession after a notice to quit has run out or is otherwise unsure of his rights, can obtain advice from a solicitor. Help with all or part of the cost of legal advice and assistance may be available under the Legal Aid Scheme. He should also be able to obtain information from a Citizens Advice Bureau, housing advice centre, rent officer or rent assessment committee office

To John Donald Ross:

I the undersigned as landlord hereby give you notice to quit and remove from the premises known as 11 Bannatyne Avenue, Glasgow, G31., which you hold of me as tenant thereof on 23rd May, 1983 next or at the end of the week of your tenancy which will end next after the expiration of four weeks from the service upon you of this notice.

I hereby draw your attention to the information contained in the Schedule hereto being information prescribed for the purpose of section 131 of the Rent (Scotland) Act 1971 by the Notices to Quit (Prescribed Information) (Protected Tenancies and Part VII Contracts) (Scotland) Regulations 1980. (S1 1980/1667)

SCHEDULE

1. Even after the notice to quit has run out, before the tenant can lawfully be evicted, the landlord must get an order for possession, that is to say a decree of removing or warrant of ejection, from the court.
2. If the tenancy is a protected tenancy (other than a short tenancy) under the Rent Acts, the court can normally give the landlord such an order only on the grounds set out in those Acts.
3. If the tenancy is a short tenancy within the meaning of section 34 of the Tenants' Rights Etc (Scotland) Act 1980, and the landlord has served timeous notice of his intention to apply for an order for possession, the court must grant the order.
4. Where a Part VII contract was granted before 1st December 1980, the tenant may ask the rent assessment committee to postpone the date when the notice to quit expires for up to six months, as long as he does so before the notice runs out.
5. If the tenant does not know the nature of his tenancy or is otherwise unsure of his rights, he can obtain advice from a solicitor. Help with all or part of the cost of legal advice and assistance may be available under the Legal Aid Scheme. He can also seek information from a rent officer, rent assessment committee office, citizens' advice bureau or a housing aid centre.

Dated the 25th day of April 1983

If a landlord wishes to give a tenant notice to quit, he must do it in writing. If he does not draw up the document correctly, the tenant can safely ignore it. It is not enough to reclaim possession of the premises.

The landlord must include in the notice information about the tenant's rights under the Rent (Scotland) Act and where he can go if he is unsure about his position.

(whether or not an owner) if:

1. The house was let as a SHORT TENANCY.

2. The tenancy is an 'off-season' let – for not more than 8 months – of a house used each year for holiday lets. *See:* HOLIDAY ACCOMMODATION

3. The house is normally let to students by a college or university and has been let to the tenant during a vacation.

4. The house is needed for a minister, or an agricultural employee (provided it was previously let to such an employee).

5. The house was specially adapted or designed for a disabled person and is needed for such a person, provided there is no such person in the house already.

Except for disabled persons' housing, the landlord can only get possession in these circumstances if he gave written notice before the tenancy began that the house might be repossessed under one of these grounds. However, the court can ignore any failure to do so in the case of a SHORT TENANCY.

The sheriff can postpone possession proceedings if he thinks fit. He can also delay the date when any possession order takes effect. This can be made conditional on the tenant, for example, paying any rent arrears.

Temporary security

Some tenants who are not protected tenants under the Rent (Scotland) Act may be entitled, under Part VII of that Act, to ask a rent assessment committee or a sheriff to suspend a notice to quit. This applies to:

- Tenants with resident landlords.
- Tenants who share living accommodation with their landlord.
- Tenants whose rent includes a payment for furniture or services – for example, personal services or the supply of heat, light and hot water.

The tenant must have exclusive use of the premises (the rateable value of which must fall below certain limits). In addition, he or she must not have a holiday letting or pay a substantial amount of rent for board.

Tenancies granted before December 1, 1980 If a tenant receives a notice to quit, he or she should write to the local rent assessment committee (the address can be found in the telephone directory under 'Rent Registration Service'). The application must be made before the notice to quit expires: if not, the committee will be unable to help.

The application should not be a request for a delay in the proposed eviction; instead, as a technicality, the tenant must apply for a reasonable rent to be fixed for the property.

When the committee receives the application, the notice to quit is automatically suspended. The committee inspects the property, then holds a hearing as soon as possible – usually within 6 weeks.

The landlord can object to the application. The tenant should try to convince the committee that he or she has been a good tenant and would suffer undue hardship if forced to leave.

If the committee thinks the application is justified, it can give the tenant security against eviction for up to 6 months. It may also fix a new, higher or lower, rent.

Before the period of security expires, the tenant can apply for an extension. There is no legal limit to the number of extensions which can be granted, but a committee will rarely grant more than one.

If the application is refused, the suspended notice to quit starts to operate again. However, 7 days must elapse before the notice can expire. The landlord will still need a court order to evict the tenant.

If notice to quit is received after the tenant refers his or her rent to the committee, the notice will be suspended for up to 6 months from the committee's decision.

Tenancies granted after December 1, 1980 If the tenancy is granted after this date, the tenant cannot obtain any security from the rent assessment committee.

However, a proper notice to quit (at least 4 weeks) must still be served and a sheriff court order is always needed. The court can delay the repossession for up to 3 months and can impose conditions – for example, about payment of any rent arrears.

After the court order

The possession order will give the date after which the landlord is allowed to regain possession of the house. If the tenant still refuses to leave, he or she can be forcibly evicted by a SHERIFF OFFICER.

Inheriting a protected tenancy

It is possible to inherit a protected tenancy automatically when the tenant dies. The person wishing to inherit the tenancy must have been using the house as his or her only, or main, home at the time of the tenant's death and be:

- The deceased tenant's spouse.
- If there is no spouse, a member of the deceased tenant's family – including a cohabitee in a stable relationship. The family member must have lived with the tenant for at least 6 months immediately before the tenant's death. If family members cannot agree on who should take the tenancy, the dispute can be settled by the sheriff.

The person who inherits is called a 'statutory' tenant by succession, but can become an ordinary, 'contractual' tenant by signing a new tenancy agreement with the landlord. The tenancy, whether statutory or contractual, can be inherited once more under the same rules, but cannot be inherited again. *See also:* FLAT; LANDLORD AND TENANT; RENT PROTECTION

EVIDENCE

The courts' rules for getting at the truth

A witness in a court case – whether criminal or civil – must usually give evidence in person. Before giving evidence, the witness must swear an OATH or affirm that he or she will tell the truth. A witness who lies can be prosecuted for PERJURY. *See:* WITNESS

Written evidence from a witness is generally not admissible in court. Documents such as letters normally become evidence only when a witness tells in court how they came to be written or received. However, there are a number of exceptions – for example, the evidence in an undefended divorce action need only take the form of written statements. *See:* DIVORCE

In court a witness is first examined by the side for whom he or she is appearing; this is called the 'examination in chief'. The witness may then be cross-examined by the other side and re-examined by his or her own side. One purpose of cross-examination is to test the witness's reliability and credibility.

A number of basic rules apply to evi-

THE WIFE WHO STOLE THE FURNITURE

A husband or wife can be compelled to give evidence against each other if he or she is the victim – even if there has been no physical injury.

Mrs Harper separated from her husband after a number of serious quarrels. He had been convicted of assaulting her on three occasions.

It was alleged that Mrs Harper subsequently broke into Mr Harper's home and removed most of his furniture to a store. Mrs Harper was charged with theft. Her husband gave evidence for the prosecution and she was convicted.

She argued that her husband should not have been allowed to give evidence where the offence only involved injury to his property.

DECISION

The appeal court held that Mr Harper was a competent witness and could be compelled to testify against his wife.

dence given in court:

• Burden of proof. The party bringing the case must produce enough evidence to prove it. In criminal cases, where the standard of proof is stricter than in civil cases, the prosecution must prove the accused guilty 'beyond reasonable doubt'. In civil cases the pursuer has to prove the defender liable only 'on a balance of probabilities'.

Because of these different standards of proof, a motorist who causes a road accident may be acquitted in a criminal prosecution for careless driving, but be sued successfully for damages in a civil case arising out of the same accident.

• Corroboration of evidence. In both civil and criminal cases, the evidence of one witness concerning a crucial fact must generally be supported, or 'corroborated', by the evidence of a second witness. For example, it would not be enough for one witness to testify to the identity of a person alleged to have committed an assault; there would have to be supporting evidence from another source.

This does not mean that two eyewitnesses are always necessary. The first witness's evidence, identifying a person alleged to have committed an assault, might be corroborated by, for example, circumstantial evidence that the person's fingerprints were on a weapon used in the assault.

In some circumstances, corroboration of evidence is not needed – for example, in an action for damages for personal injuries or where a driver is prosecuted for failing to obey directions given by a policeman or traffic sign.

• Hearsay evidence. Evidence which is hearsay, or second-hand, is usually inadmissible in court. For example, you should not bring a witness, Mr Smith, to tell the court what Mr Brown told him about an assault or accident. Mr Brown should be a witness and describe what he saw himself.

• Opinion. The sole task of all except expert witnesses is to present the facts of the case as they know them and not to draw conclusions from the facts. It is for the court or jury to draw conclusions. So an opinion given by a witness will generally be inadmissible as evidence; and a question will be inadmissible if its purpose is to obtain an opinion from a witness.

For example, a witness to a road accident may tell the court that he saw a motorist driving at what he assessed to be a certain speed. But he may not add, 'I thought he was driving recklessly', or be asked what his opinion was as to the motorist's driving.

However, an expert witness – such as a doctor – can properly be asked for his opinion on matters in which he is skilled. His opinion does not need to be corroborated.

• Leading questions. A leading question is one which whittles down the witness's range of possible answers to a mere 'Yes', or 'No' and suggests the desired reply. For example, it is a leading question to ask 'Were you not frightened?' rather than 'How did you feel?'

A lawyer should not put leading questions to his own client at the initial examination of his evidence, but may do so on re-examination – although his opponents may successfully object. However, a lawyer may put leading questions when cross-examining the opposition witness.

• Child evidence. A child can give evidence in court if he or she is thought able to state and understand what he or she has seen or heard, and also understands the duty to tell the truth. It is for the judge to decide – perhaps after questioning the child – whether a child may give evidence.

• Husband or wife evidence. A husband or wife cannot generally be made to give evidence against a spouse in criminal cases. For example, a wife who sees her husband committing an assault cannot be made to give evidence by the prosecution.

However, this is not so where the husband or wife is the victim of an offence. For example, a wife who has been assaulted by her husband can be compelled by the prosecution to give evidence. So can a spouse who has only suffered damage to property.

EXAMINATION

The conditions that govern school tests

A school decides whether or not a pupil is to be allowed to sit a Scottish Certificate of Education examination.

Parents who feel that their child should be allowed to take an examination, despite a contrary decision by the school, should discuss the matter with the head teacher. Schools and education authorities try to be helpful in such cases.

If after discussion the school still refuses to enter the child, the parents have no legal power to get the decision changed.

The parents can approach their local COUNCILLOR, MEMBER OF PARLIAMENT or the local government OMBUDSMAN, but none of these has any legal power to enforce a change of attitude. They can use only their influence.

Challenging a result

There is no appeal by an examination candidate direct to the Scottish Examination Board on grounds of unfair questions or unjust marking. However, there is a system of appeal by schools on behalf of pupils and by colleges on behalf of further education candidates in their second or later year of full-time study.

Such an appeal would be on the ground that a candidate had not done

CANDIDATES WITH SPECIAL PROBLEMS

A candidate may have a particular personal problem that affects his performance – for example, a sudden attack of asthma, recent illness or family bereavement. It should be reported to the invigilator at the time of the examination and not left until the results have been published.

A medical certificate should be produced if possible.

Where it is known in advance that a candidate will be unable to sit an examination under the normal conditions, it is the responsibility of the school or college to inform the Scottish Examination Board of this.

They will be willing to make arrangements for candidates with special problems: in some circumstances they will allow the examination to be taken at home, or in hospital. They may provide a reader or a writer for the candidate, or even examination papers in Braille.

The examination supervisors – invigilators – must, as part of their job, report to the board anything which might affect the performance of the candidates during the examination. A fire alarm or similar disturbance could seriously affect candidates' concentration.

Any event of this kind should be reported to the board, who will take it into account when the papers are marked.

Arriving too late Examination timetables are published in advance. A candidate who arrives late will not normally be allowed extra time to complete the paper. Sometimes, such as for aural comprehension exams, he or she may not be allowed to enter at all.

Someone who appears at the examination centre on the wrong day, or in the afternoon for an examination which took place in the morning, will not be allowed to sit the examination.

Missing the examination Where a school pupil or a further education candidate in the second or later year of study is unavoidably absent for an examination, the school or college may appeal on his or her behalf, and a pass may be awarded on the basis of previous work.

himself or herself justice in the examination. It would have to be backed up by earlier work of the candidate – preferably work done under examination conditions.

Re-checking papers The Scottish Examination Board will always conduct a 'clerical' check – if this is requested by a school – to ensure that no examination answers have been left unmarked, or that marks have been added up correctly. They will not normally carry out any further re-checking or alter marks awarded.

Penalties for cheating

If someone is caught cheating during an examination, his or her paper will automatically be disqualified by the Scottish Examination Board. In some circumstances all papers taken by a person who has cheated will be ruled out; in others only the paper in which he or she was found cheating.

When there has been collusion or copying between two pupils during an examination, both are likely to be disqualified, on the ground that the board and invigilator cannot easily decide who copied from whom.

Impersonation It is a criminal offence for a person to be impersonated in an examination. Both the impersonator and whoever is impersonated can be charged with fraud. The court has discretion as to the penalty imposed. *See:* FRAUD

Publication of exam results

The government has made regulations which set out the information about exams that must be published by all state schools with children of 15 and over, except special schools.

Each school must publish its policy on entering pupils for exams, the exams normally taken, and the year at school when pupils usually sit an exam. They must also publish the number in that year group, and the number of grades attained at each level in each subject.

Schools do not have to publish last year's figures as a comparison, or to indicate how many took each subject and failed altogether.

EXCLUSION CLAUSE

When a contract condition is invalid even if it is accepted

A condition in a contract that seeks to limit or take away a person's basic legal rights may be void, even if the contract has been signed and accepted.

Under the UNFAIR CONTRACT Terms Act 1977, which applies to most contracts, including contracts of sale, hire-purchase and employment, some of these conditions – usually called exclusion clauses – are automatically invalid:

1. If they seek to exclude one party's right to compensation for death or injury caused by the negligence of the other party or one of his agents in the course of a business – say an employee acting in the course of his work.

2. If they try to evade or weaken a dealer's obligation to see that the goods he sells are of suitable quality and fitness for the purpose for which they are required.

That second category applies only to sales direct to consumers, however. It does not cover goods that are bought by way of trade – including goods bought by ordinary consumers at trade discount prices.

Some other exclusion clauses and conditions will be held to be valid by the courts if they can be shown to be fair and reasonable, provided they were known by the party who is penalised by them and both sides had similar bargaining strengths when the contract was made. *See:* UNFAIR CONTRACT

EXECUTOR

Winding up a dead person's estate

When you make a will, you should name one or preferably two people to be responsible for carrying out your wishes after your death. These personal representatives, called executors, will take charge of your affairs, collect everything belonging or owing to you, pay all the debts and taxes and divide what is left among the beneficiaries of your will according to your wishes.

If your executor is not one of your heirs, it is a good idea to leave him a modest sum for undertaking the responsibility. Being an executor can be a time-consuming task. Make sure that the people you have in mind are willing to act before you appoint them – they have a right to refuse.

Whom to choose

When most of an ESTATE is to be left

to one beneficiary – such as the widow or widower – he or she is usually the best choice as executor. To have someone else responsible for winding up your estate could seem an intrusion into the beneficiary's private affairs.

If the person who will benefit most under the will is not suitable – because of frailty or language difficulties, for example – appoint another relative or close friend, preferably someone with good business sense and who is on good terms with the other heirs. But do not appoint executors who are much older than you, as they may die first.

A second executor It is always safer to name more than one executor – in case one is ill or abroad at the time you die. Another advantage is that two people may find it easier to reach a decision – such as how to dispose of property – than one executor working alone. A widow or widower may well welcome the support of a sympathetic relative or friend as co-executor.

Where the will sets up a TRUST – perhaps for children – trustees are needed to administer it. It is better to have at least two trustees in case one should die, leaving the trust without anybody to administer it. The trustees are usually the same people as the executors.

If your estate is to be divided among several people or if you own a business or your affairs are complex, you should ask your solicitor or accountant to be co-executor, working with your personal executor. Whereas personal executors are unpaid, professional executors will require a fee which is deducted from the estate. The fee will be based on the amount of work which they have to do and on the value of the estate. An executor can only charge a fee if the will says so.

Another circumstance in which you might appoint an impartial professional as executor is when the beneficiaries are on bad terms with each other and would not accept a relative's decision.

Professional executors Some banks and insurance companies advertise professional executor services, offering skill and experience, easy access for you and your heirs and continuity of service – unlike individuals, the bank does not die, become ill or go on holiday. On the other hand, there is a lack of the personal touch that you can get from choosing executors yourself.

The cost of a professional service ranges from between 2 to 4% of the gross value of the estate, depending on its size, with a minimum fee of £200, plus VAT. In addition, fees are payable for legal work such as obtaining CONFIRMATION or selling the house. The fee may be reduced if the estate is unusually simple – particularly where the main asset is the house taken over by the widow or widower. Generally it is not in the interests of the beneficiaries to use professional executor services for modest estates.

Keeping your executors informed

You should tell your executors what you own and where they can find essential documents. From time to time, particularly if your situation changes radically, keep them informed about the state of your finances and property.

The duties of an executor

- Locating the will. If someone has died and appointed you his executor, you will need to obtain his WILL. It is your formal appointment – though not your legal authority – to handle his affairs. The will also directs you how to settle those affairs. Once the will has been obtained, it is a good idea to register it in case it gets lost. It may be registered either at the local sheriff court or in the Books of Council and Session at Edinburgh.
- Arranging the funeral. Your first duty as executor is to organise the FUNERAL. Look at the will to see if it contains any instructions. The widow(er) and next of kin can veto cremation or handing over the body for medical research, but normally the dead person's wishes are carried out where possible. Before handing over a body for medical research make sure that the hospital still wants it. *See:* DEATH, Registration of; DEATH GRANT; TRANSPLANT.
- Finding out what has been left. If the dead person kept his papers together and up-to-date and informed you regularly about his financial state, finding out what is left may be a simple process requiring only a rough assessment of the value of his belongings, before you can proceed to the next stage.

Normally, however, you need to examine his personal papers and consult his bank manager, accountant or solicitor.

Pass books for banks, building societies, co-operative societies and similar institutions must be sent off to be made up to the date of death. You may be asked to produce a copy of the death certificate and the will, before the dead person's bank or professional adviser agrees to disclose confidential information.

You should be able to value some of the property yourself – for example, the house and car – by comparing the items with others advertised in local newspapers. But you would have to call in an expert valuer to estimate the worth of specialist objects such as antiques.

- Finding out what debts are owed. When you have compiled an account of the value of everything the dead person has left behind, you should deduct from it the sum of his debts – including bank and building society loans, rent, rates, income and other taxes, telephone, gas and electricity bills, tradesmen's bills, hire-purchase payments and any amounts due on credit cards. The undertaker's account for the funeral is also considered a debt of the estate.

If you suspect that there are outstanding debts that you cannot trace, put advertisements in local newspapers calling on all creditors to submit their claims to you. Advertisements should also be put in trade journals if the dead person was in business. If you are a main beneficiary, you may – with the others

PAYING LEGACIES AND DEBTS

Mrs Macrae, a childless widow, leaves property and goods worth £30,000. Her will bequeaths her home worth £20,000 to her brother, a cash legacy of £5,000 to her sister, and the residue to a charity.

If the debts, taxes and expenses come to £2,000, the charity receives only £3,000 but the others receive their legacies in full.

If the debts etc. come to £7,000, the charity receives nothing, the sister gets £3,000, but the brother still gets the house.

If the debts etc. come to £17,000, neither the charity nor the sister receive anything. The house has to be sold and the brother gets £13,000.

WHEN THERE IS NO EXECUTOR

If the will does not appoint executors, or they have died, or are unavailable, the person inheriting the residue of the estate can be confirmed as executor.

Where there is no will, a relative can apply to the sheriff court to be appointed executor. Generally the relative must inherit from the estate under the rules of INTESTACY, but one of the children may be appointed if the widow(er) feels unequal to the task. An executor appointed by the court has the same powers and duties except that he cannot resign. A simplified procedure can be used for small estates. *See:* CONFIRMATION.

Where an estate appears to have no heirs, persons holding the dead person's property should inform a government official called the Queen's and Lord Treasurer's Remembrancer, 5/7 Regent Road, Edinburgh.

On being informed the Remembrancer then advertises for heirs. If none appear he pays the debts and retains the balance on behalf of the Crown.

who benefit – decide not to advertise since you would have to pay any debts that come to light after the estate is distributed.

• Applying for authority to wind up the estate. When you have worked out the extent of the property, apply for legal authority to collect it (called CONFIRMATION), sell whatever is necessary, and divide the estate according to the will or, if there is no will, according to the rules of INTESTACY.

• Assets that can be dealt with before confirmation. Some matters can be settled before confirmation, though mostly they do not involve the executors directly.

The surviving holder of a joint bank or building society account may continue to draw money out. But it may have to be paid over to the executor if another person inherits it – according to the will or the rules of intestacy – or it is required for payment of debts or 'legal rights'. *See:* INTESTACY

Where the house is jointly owned, and provided that the share of the first to die is to go to the survivor, the survivor normally acquires the deceased's share automatically – though where all the money to pay for the house came from the dead person, he can by will leave his share to someone else. But the home may have to be sold to meet debts.

Life-insurance policies that are payable to someone else can be claimed by that person simply by producing a copy of the death certificate. Such money is not taxed as part of the estate, but the existence of the policies must be disclosed so that the Capital Taxes Office can check that no tax is payable on it.

However, if the policy was an 'own life' scheme, one insuring the dead person for his own benefit, it cannot be cashed before confirmation and is taxed as part of the estate.

Friendly and provident societies may pay up to £1,500 to those entitled by the will or by the rules of intestacy or those nominated as executors but not confirmed. Anything over this sum is paid only to confirmed executors.

• Gathering the assets. When you have obtained confirmation, you must register it with all the institutions that hold the dead person's assets – such as banks, building societies, life insurance companies, stockbrokers and storage firms. Send each of these in turn the confirmation and ask them to transfer the assets and property to your name.

Alternatively, you can have specific items transferred directly to those who are to receive them under the will or the rules of intestacy. For example, if the dead person left a block of shares to someone, you can have them put straight into his name – if they are not needed to pay off debts.

• Clearing the debts. All debts must be settled before the estate can be divided out. If the debts exceed the assets, consult a solicitor.

The funeral bill takes priority over all other debts and must be paid for out of the estate. But a headstone or any other memorial must be paid for by those who wish to provide it.

Arrears of rates and taxes and the expense of obtaining confirmation take priority over the normal debts of the dead person.

Unless it is clear that there is plenty of money, you should not pay other debts until 6 months from the date of death. All creditors taking legal action within that period are equally entitled to payment. You can charge any expenses you have incurred – for example travel, postage, fees for legal or accountancy work – against the estate.

Paying all the debts may take a long time, particularly if there is an outstanding tax bill – for example, if the dead person was self-employed, his tax for several past years may need adjusting. There may also be queries from the Capital Taxes Office over the value of various items in the estate and over new assets that come to light.

When land or a house is involved, the Office insists on a valuation by the district valuer before agreeing a figure for CAPITAL TRANSFER TAX.

When the Office has been satisfied, apply for a clearance certificate showing that all tax due has been paid.

• Legal rights. After paying debts you should find out whether the widow(er) or the children are going to claim 'legal rights'. Write to each of them indicating the probable value of their legacies (if any) and their legal rights, and suggest they seek independent legal advice.

• Distributing the estate. The will is seldom read out after the funeral nowadays. However you may well decide – even before confirmation – to tell the main beneficiaries the likely size of the estate and their inheritances.

Anyone – even an unrelated member of the public – can obtain a copy of the will and the inventory of the estate from the appropriate sheriff court once confirmation has been granted.

You are not required to hand over

YOU NEED TO RAISE MONEY TO PAY DEBTS

As executor of the deceased, you must also decide whether it is necessary to sell any part of the estate to pay debts, repay any loan that has been obtained to pay capital transfer tax, cover the expenses of administering the estate or pay cash gifts specified in the will. *See:* CONFIRMATION

You have complete authority to decide what must be sold, but you may not sell items that have been specifically bequeathed unless there is not enough cash without them to meet the debts and expenses.

Remember that premium bonds qualify for draws for 12 months after the holder's death. It may be wise to keep them.

any items or money to the heirs until you have cleared all possible problems and debts of the estate. To be safe you should not make any distribution for at least 6 months or until the debts are finally settled.

However executors often decide to make quick payments of small gifts, or small amounts on account of larger legacies, as soon as they know they are not needed for paying debts. For example, if the dead person left his treasured fishing tackle to a fellow-angler, it is likely that he would have wished it to be handed over promptly.

Legacies of specific objects or investments (special legacies) must be made over unless needed for paying debts. The recipient must pay the cost of transporting and insuring any objects, unless the will says otherwise.

Legacies of money are paid only if there is enough after payment of debts, expenses and special legacies. If there is insufficient to pay all in full, each person only gets a proportion.

The residue of the estate is the last in the queue. A person who has been left the residue only gets what is left after all the debts, expenses and other legacies have been met.

A beneficiary can take a cash legacy or his share of the residue in another form – a block of shares or a car of equal worth, for example – but must pay the difference into the estate if the value of the object exceeds the amount he is entitled to. The value of such assets is assessed at the date of transfer, not at death.

- Transferring land. If the dead person left land or a house, you will have to sell it or transfer it into the name of the beneficiary.

To carry out the transfer you need to complete a document called a 'docket', which must be signed by the executors. Since the docket forms part of the title deeds to the land, it is best to have it prepared by a lawyer.

Where a house or land is bequeathed, the estate, not the beneficiary, normally has to pay the proportion of capital transfer tax due on the property, unless the will says otherwise. The beneficiary is, however, liable for all of its debts – such as a secured loan.

If the house you are transferring carries a building society loan, the building society may be prepared to continue the loan with the new owner.

- Preparing a final account and dividing the residue. Having paid all the legacies – and before you share out what is left – prepare a set of accounts listing all the assets and debts of the estate and all the payments and transfers you have made.

Take care to include any interest that has accumulated on assets, and remember to provide for taxes for which you – as executor – may be liable, such as interest on the executry bank account.

Give a copy of the accounts to each of the people who are to share in what remains of the estate – the residue – which you must divide among them when they have approved your accounts.

When the residue has been divided, you have, in all probability, completed your duty as executor. But if the will sets up a trust you may find that you have been appointed as trustee. Where a new asset comes to light years later you may be called in again to deal with it. Other executors will have to be appointed to deal with it if you are no longer alive.

EXEMPTION CLAUSE

When a trader, manufacturer or any other individual or organisation tries to take away rights that you might otherwise have, he or it usually does so by using a special clause – called an exemption clause – in a notice, contract or other document.

In many cases, the clause may be ineffective. *See:* UNFAIR CONTRACT

EXPENSES

When the Inland Revenue allows expenses to be free of income tax

Expenses can be set against income tax both by employees and by self-employed people. Claims must be made each year on the taxpayer's INCOME TAX return.

Expenses of employment

Employees can off-set against tax only expenses that they have incurred 'wholly, exclusively and necessarily' in carrying out their duties. All expenses must have been absolutely essential.

Among the expenses that are allowed against income tax are:

1. Essential tools that have to be provided by the employee himself.

Inland Revenue interprets 'essential' strictly and may not allow certain items, arguing that if they were essential, the employer would provide them. For example, an office worker might not be allowed to claim for the cost of a briefcase.

However, many trade unions agree set allowances for tools or protective clothing, or for other working materials, that members can claim without query.

2. Protective and special clothing – for example overalls, laboratory coat, footwear or helmet.

Most employees cannot claim for clothes just because they are required to look smart while at work. But some people in the entertainment industry are allowed to claim for clothing, make-up and hairdressing.

3. Business use of employee's own car, including capital allowances.

Business use does not include travelling to and from work.

Any contributions made by the employer to the running costs of the vehicle must be deducted from the amount claimed.

The AA Schedule of Estimated Running Costs for different cars is accepted by Inland Revenue.

4. Business use of the employee's own telephone.

He is entitled to charge for all business calls plus part of the rental in proportion to the amount he uses the telephone for business. He must deduct any contributions the employer makes.

5. Subscriptions and fees to professional associations relating to his employment.

Union subscriptions are covered if the union concerned is more than a mere negotiating body. But if it produces professional periodicals and concerns itself with codes of conduct, the Inland Revenue may allow part of the subscription. The amount is frequently negotiated between the union and the tax authorities.

The cost of studying for additional qualifications and the cost of obtaining professional magazines are not allowable expenses.

6. Business travel and subsistence.

The cost of getting to and from work and expenses reimbursed by the employer are not claimable.

The cost of meals at work is not allowable even if, for example, an employee is kept late in an emergency. Meal expenses while working away from home, if it is necessary to stay elsewhere overnight, can be claimed.

7. An employee's contributions to a superannuation scheme operated by the employer.

If the job does not offer a pension, an employee's private contributions to a retirement annuity policy are allowable.

8. Business entertainment.

Entertainment expenses are allowable only if they cover 'reasonable entertainment' of overseas customers. An employee cannot claim such entertainment expenses against the tax on his salary if they are reimbursed by the employer and he has already claimed expenses tax relief against trading profit. Expenses tax relief cannot be claimed twice – once by the employer and once by the employee.

An employee can claim other expenses not reimbursed by his employer.

When employees regularly incur expenses on their employer's behalf, Inland Revenue normally allows them to draw the expenses from the employer untaxed – provided that the employer guarantees that they were all genuine expenses.

If an employee then claims the same expenses against his taxable income he is technically guilty of attempted fraud and could be fined or imprisoned.

One way to show that expenses are necessary in the course of the job is to have them written into the contract of employment – for example, by having a paragraph in your letter of employment stating that you are expected to make business telephone calls from home or that you are expected to provide meals for clients at home.

WHAT YOU CAN CLAIM

The expenses that can be offset against income tax are carefully defined. Receipts are not always necessary but should be included for expenses incurred at home.

Expenses of the self-employed

Self-employed people can claim many more deductions than can people who are employees. The Inland Revenue's requirement for the self-employed is that the expenditure be 'wholly and exclusively' for the purpose of the business. The word 'necessarily' is not mentioned.

Expenses that can be offset against income tax are:

1. Cost of stock bought for resale and other business materials, including discounts allowed on sales and bad trade debts.

2. Cost of employing staff – wages, national insurance, pensions and redundancy payments.

3. Cost of maintaining, running and repairing equipment.

The capital cost of buying equipment is not allowable.

4. Costs of running premises: rent, rates, heat and light, insurance, cleaning and maintenance.

Improvements, such as extensions, are not allowed, and if any part of the rates and rent is claimed, CAPITAL GAINS TAX may have to be paid if the premises are sold.

5. Delivery, carriage and postage costs.

6. Office expenses, such as stationery, telephone and printing.

7. Professional revenue charges – for example, audit fees, the legal costs of debt collection, preparation of contracts and the settling of trade disputes.

8. Cost of business travel and hotel bills. The cost of travelling to the business address is not included.

9. Cost of entertaining overseas customers.

10. Gifts to customers – provided that the gifts are not worth more than £2 each and that each gift contains a conspicuous advertisement for the donor.

The gift must not be food, drink or tobacco unless the donor trades in, or manufactures, these items.

11. Interest payments on money borrowed for use in the business, including interest on overdrafts and hire-purchase contracts.

12. Donations to charity.

Expenses not allowed against income tax include:

- All private payments – for example, expenses connected with family or domestic activities.

The Inland Revenue always looks closely at wages paid to members of a proprietor's family. For example, if someone's wife is paid £50 a week to answer the telephone and it is found that a commercial rate for such duties would be only £10, £40 will be added to the business's taxable profit.

- A proprietor's own withdrawals from business income, regarded as taxable profit. When he withdraws cash and spends part of it privately and part on the business, only the business expenditure can be claimed.
- Capital expenditure, fines and legal costs, political donations and payments of tax – other than PAYE and national insurance contributions – on behalf of the employees.

When landlords can claim

Landlords can claim:

1. The cost of repairing and maintaining their property – including the cost of gardening if that is specified in the lease. They cannot claim the cost of property improvement.

2. Regular expenses such as rates, feu duty, lighting of common passageways and insurance.

3. The cost of managing the property, including rent collection, advertising, accountancy and legal charges.

4. Interest on the mortgage of any property let or available for letting throughout the year.

5. The cost of providing any services, and the wear and tear of any furniture, provided that the lease makes the landlord responsible for such services and for the good condition of furniture.

EXTORTION

When persuasion can be a serious crime

The crime of extortion is popularly known as blackmail. It involves obtaining money or any other benefit by improper threats.

Some threats – for example, threats of violence to persons or property – are in themselves criminal and are merely made more serious by being accompanied by a demand for money or other benefit.

Not all demands for money or benefit under threats will be criminal. For example, a person who is owed money cannot write to the debtor: "Pay me by next week or I will beat you up". But he can write: "Pay me by next week or I will sue you".

However, it is extortion for anyone to threaten to bring *criminal* proceedings in order to obtain payment of a debt. *See:* DEBT COLLECTOR.

The victim of an extortionist may well have committed some indiscretion which could harm his reputation if it became publicly known. For this reason, although the courts cannot generally forbid publication of their proceedings, the Press, at the court's request, will not publish the name of a victim in a case of extortion.

The penalty for the crime of extortion is at the discretion of the court, within its sentencing limits.

EXTRADITION

Returning a person to another country for trial

If a person who is accused of committing a serious offence in a foreign country comes to Britain, he or she may be returned to that country to face trial. This process, called extradition, operates only between countries that have special treaties.

The United Kingdom, for example, has extradition treaties with over 40 countries and special arrangements, which work in virtually the same way as extradition, with Commonwealth countries, dependencies and Eire.

Commonwealth The surrender of accused persons between the UK and Commonwealth countries or UK dependencies is governed by the Fugitive Offenders Act 1967. Though tèchnically not extradition, the procedure is similar.

Eire A warrant for arrest issued in Eire can be given effect in Britain simply by having it signed by a magistrate in the area where the accused person is believed to be. This applies to any indictable offence or one punishable by at least 6 months' imprisonment.

Asking for extradition

In Britain, a request to have a person extradited to another country (excluding the Commonwealth and Eire) must be approved by the Secretary of State – usually the Home Secretary.

A magistrate – normally the Metropolitan stipendiary magistrate at Bow Street magistrates' court in London, although it can be a Scottish JP or sheriff – will grant a warrant to detain the person if there is sufficient evidence against him. Even if first detained in Scotland, the person is usually transferred to London. He will then be committed to prison – if the magistrate thinks the evidence is sufficient to justify committal for trial in England – to await the Home Secretary's decision.

If the crime is committed at sea and the boat puts into a Scottish port, or if an accused's life or health would be endangered by being transferred to London, a sheriff can commit the accused to prison in Scotland to await the decision of the Secretary of State for Scotland.

If a person is arrested in Scotland for extradition to Eire or a Commonwealth country, all of the proceedings will also take place in Scotland.

The accused has 15 days from the date of committal to apply to the English High Court (or, if in Scotland, the High Court of Justiciary) to challenge the committal. If he does not do so, or if his application fails, he can apply for release if he is held in prison for more than 2 months after committal.

Anyone facing extradition can apply for LEGAL AID . He can also apply for BAIL, though it is seldom granted.

POLITICAL TERRORISM

Crimes – including murder, kidnapping, other serious offences against the person and hijacking – carried out by terrorists are no longer always protected because the motive for carrying them out is political.

Such terrorists cannot avoid extradition from, or punishment in, any country which has signed the European Convention on the Suppression of Terrorism (1977). The signatories include Britain.

People who cannot be extradited

A person cannot be extradited if:

1. The offence of which he is accused is political. In law that means any offence committed in connection with or as part of a political disturbance. That definition applies only in cases of extradition, however. For other purposes of criminal law, political crime does not exist.

2. He can show that, although the crime for which extradition is sought is not political, the country seeking the order really wants to punish him for a political offence.

3. The country seeking the order does not have a law preventing a person who has been extradited for one offence from being punished for some other offence until he has had the opportunity of returning to the country that surrendered him.

4. He is in his own country and it has a separate treaty prohibiting the surrender of nationals. Britain and Denmark, for example, have an arrangement that excludes the return of Britons to Denmark and Danes to Britain.

5. The accused person has diplomatic immunity or is a member of certain international organisations, such as United Nations agencies.

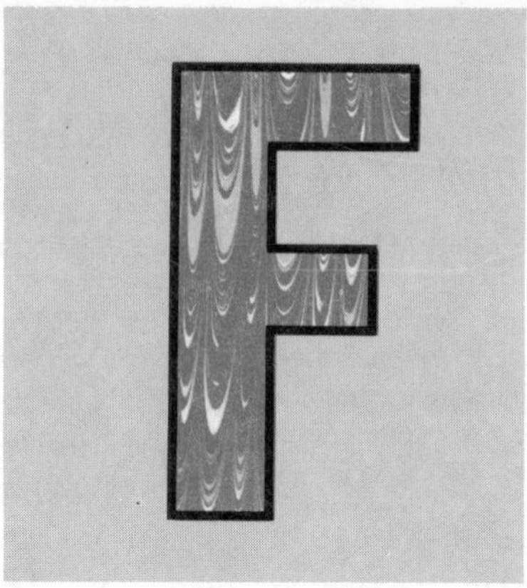

FAIR TRADING

How the state supervises sales methods

The Office of Fair Trading is a state-supported organisation set up to ensure that traders carry on business fairly. The Office, which is independent of the Government, and headed by a Director General, also controls the administration of the Consumer Credit Act 1974. *See:* CREDIT AGREEMENT

To protect the public, the Office of Fair Trading looks for anti-competitive practices and monopolies; and for company mergers that create a monopoly which might restrict competition and lead to unnecessarily high prices, or where the value of the assets taken over is more than £15 million.

Under the Fair Trading Act, a monopoly – the domination of the market in particular goods or services by one supplier or group of suppliers – exists if at least one-quarter of the goods or services being considered is supplied by, or to, one person or group of companies.

If there is any doubt about the fairness to the public of a monopoly or proposed merger, the Director General of Fair Trading may ask the Monopolies and Mergers Commission to report on whether the arrangement is against the public interest.

Restrictive practices The Office of Fair Trading is also responsible for compiling a register of agreements, made between traders, which fix prices or restrict supplies. The agreements are then referred to the Restrictive Practices Court which decides whether they are in the public interest. If they are not – or if they are not registered – they are void.

How the consumer is protected

To protect the economic interests of consumers the Office of Fair Trading constantly keeps under review the commercial activities of traders. There are three particular functions of the Office relating to consumer protection.

Codes of practice A wide range of codes of trading conduct, negotiated with trade associations, exist to protect the customer. Among them are those dealing with electrical appliances, funerals, radio, electrical and television retailers, travel agents, shoe sales and repairs, laundries, mail-order suppliers and motor traders.

New laws If the Office of Fair Trading finds some widespread trading practice that misleads, confuses or adversely affects the right of consumers, the Office may recommend that the practice should be made a criminal offence. This would be done by an order of the Secretary of State for Trade and Industry. Among the orders already made are those banning the use of certain exemption clauses and requiring information to be given in mail order advertisements. *See:* MAIL ORDER; UNFAIR CONTRACT

Action against traders If a trader persists in committing criminal offences – for example, under the Trade Descriptions Act 1968 – or breaking contracts, the Director General of Fair Trading, in addition to a prosecution, can ask for an assurance that he will trade fairly.

If he refuses – or gives an assurance and then breaks it – the Director General may ask the Restrictive Practices Court to make an order forbidding the trader to continue his unsatisfactory conduct. Breach of such an order amounts to CONTEMPT OF COURT and the trader can be imprisoned.

If you wish to complain about an unfair trading practice, write to the Office of Fair Trading, Field House, Bream's Buildings, London EC4A 1PR.

The Office of Fair Trading has already obtained assurances from restaurants and hotels that they will comply with the food hygiene regulations, and from shops and suppliers of services that they will no longer supply defective goods or carry out defective workmanship and will promptly return money to dissatisfied customers.

FAMILY ASSETS

Who owns what in the home

Each member of a family is entitled to his or her own property and has no claim on the property of any other member of the family. Even very young children can own property, but it has to be administered for them by someone of full age, such as their parents.

If one member of the family is being sued for DEBT, the property of another member of the family cannot be seized and sold to clear the amount owed.

However, a husband and in certain circumstances a wife are obliged to ALIMENT, or maintain, each other and their children. A court may order either partner to make regular payments to the other partner or for their children.

A wife who neither owns nor rents the family home usually has OCCUPANCY RIGHTS in the home. This means that she cannot be lawfully evicted by her husband, even if he is the sole owner or tenant. A woman who is living with a man in his home, but is not married to him, can ask a court for occupancy rights. *See:* COHABITATION

When a marriage breaks down

When a marriage breaks down, neither partner has any legal right to a share

WHOSE BELONGINGS?

Each member of the family is entitled to his or her own property, but either may be ordered to pay money to the other when the marriage breaks down.

in property owned by the other – including the family home.

However in an action of SEPARATION or DIVORCE (but not NULLITY) the court can order either partner to pay a regular allowance to the other. In divorce cases there can also be an order for payment of a lump sum. The children also have a legal right to be supported by one or both parents.

When deciding on the award of a lump sum in a divorce action, the court will look at all the property of each partner – for example, the home, cars, stocks and shares and bank accounts. *See:* MATRIMONIAL PROPERTY

When a family member dies

When a member of the family dies, his or her property can be transferred to a relative or, where there is a WILL, to some other person. *See:* INHERITANCE; INTESTACY

FAMILY FUND

Special help for handicapped children

The Family Fund, which is government financed, provides special help for severely handicapped children who are being cared for at home. It is independently administered by a private charity, the Joseph Rowntree Memorial Trust.

The aim of the Family Fund is to give help not normally provided by the statutory services. It can help to provide laundry equipment, holidays, transport, telephones, clothing, bedding, recreational and many other items.

There is no formal means test for applicants to the Family Fund, but help is not given to families unless they are in financial need. Apply, giving the child's full name, age, address, details of handicap and the help needed to the Family Fund, P.O. Box 50, York YO1 1UY.

FAMILY INCOME SUPPLEMENT

Extra money for low-wage households

A family living on a low wage from full-time work may be entitled to a cash benefit known as Family Income Supplement. To qualify, there must be at least one child under 16 (or under 19 if still at school) in the house; and the claimant – who can be employed or self-employed – must be working at least 30 hours a week (24 hours in the case of a single parent).

Where a couple are living together, whether married or not, Family Income Supplement can be paid if either partner is in full-time work; or if both work. But if a claimant's partner has been out of work for less than 3 months, and is receiving certain benefits – unemployment, sickness or invalidity benefit, statutory sick pay, supplementary allowance or a TOPS course allowance – the Supplement cannot be paid until the benefit ends or the 3 months are up.

The adults in the household need not be the parents of the children so long as they provide for them; but foster children do not count because foster parents are already paid for keeping them.

How to make a claim

Claims are made on leaflet FIS 1 obtainable from any post office or social security office. Normally, claims are dealt with entirely by post without a home visit or interview. If you think you are entitled, claim at once, even if you cannot give all the details asked for on the form. You can always send the details later. But if you claim late, the payments will not be backdated.

The amount To qualify for Family Income Supplement the family's normal weekly income must be below a 'prescribed amount' laid down for each size of family. The amounts from November 1983 to November 1984 are:

Number of Children	Prescribed amount (per week, gross before tax)
1	£85.50
2	£95.00
3	£104.50
4	£114.00
5	£123.50

More than 5 children, add £9.50 for each child.

Income To calculate a family's normal income, gross earnings – before tax and national insurance contributions – must be worked out. This includes the earnings of both partners.

For a wage or salary earner, 'gross earnings' means average earnings for the last 5 weeks, or 2 months if paid monthly. If earnings during that period are higher than usual, the claimant should say so on the claim form. Gross earnings may then be worked out over another, more favourable, period.

For the self-employed person, Family Income Supplement is based on net profit. This is normally the profit shown in the latest accounts, but if the figure is abnormally high, an estimate of current

WHEN YOU DO NOT WORK FOR AN EMPLOYER

A self-employed person working for at least 30 hours a week can claim Family Income Supplement.

profit should be submitted.

The following amounts are not included as income:

- A child's income, other than maintenance payments from an absent parent.
- Child benefit.
- Educational maintenance allowance.
- Housing benefits.
- Attendance allowance.
- Constant attendance allowance.
- Mobility allowance.
- The first £4 of a war disablement pension.
- Payments for foster children.

If the total income is less than the prescribed amount, the Family Income Supplement payable is half the difference. For example, the prescribed amount for a family with 3 children is £104.50. If total income is £90.50, the difference is £14 and the Family Income Supplement payment would be £7 a week.

Maximum payments There is a limit to the amount of Supplement that a family can claim, depending on the number of children. For a one-child family the maximum is £22 a week and it increases by £2 for each additional child. These figures are usually raised annually, at the same time as the income limits.

How long Family Income Supplement payments are normally awarded for 52 weeks and will continue at the same rate during that period, even if income rises or falls or the size of the family changes.

Anyone who falls sick or loses his job can go on drawing Family Income Supplement on top of any national insurance benefits until the end of the 52 week period; but Family Income Supplement will be taken into account in deciding if the family is entitled to SUPPLEMENTARY BENEFIT.

Extra benefits Any family receiving Family Income Supplement is also entitled to some other benefits – free milk and vitamins for children under 5 years 1 month and expectant mothers, free school meals, dental treatment, glasses and prescriptions, and payment of fares for hospital treatment. So it is worth claiming the Supplement even if the family's income is not much below the prescribed amount.

Appeals Anyone who disagrees with the refusal of Family Income Supplement or the amount awarded can appeal to the local social security appeal tribunal.

FATAL ACCIDENT INQUIRY

Investigating fatal accidents and sudden deaths

Public inquiries will be held where certain types of death occur:

- A public inquiry will be held into the death of a person who appears to have died in an accident in the course of his job.
- A public inquiry will be held into the death of any person who is in legal custody – for example, in prison or in a police station.
- The Lord Advocate, if he thinks it necessary in the public interest, can order a public inquiry into any sudden, suspicious or unexplained death.

The inquiry takes place before a sheriff (sitting without a jury). It need not be held in a court, although it usually is. The inquiry is conducted on the lines of a civil case.

The evidence for the inquiry is collected by the procurator fiscal. The fiscal must also give details of the time and place of the inquiry to the deceased's spouse, or nearest known relative – or to his employer if death resulted from an accident at work. The general public is informed about the holding of an inquiry by a notice in the Press.

The procurator fiscal presents the evidence at the inquiry – for example, by calling witnesses. Persons such as the deceased's relatives or employer, fellow-employees, trade union representatives and inspectors of mines and factories may appear at the inquiry and give evidence.

The examination of a witness at an inquiry will not prevent criminal proceedings being taken against that witness at a later stage. However, no witness can be made to answer any question which tends to show he is guilty of a crime or offence.

At the end of the inquiry the sheriff will make a decision, or 'determination', stating:

- The details (time, place and cause) of the death.
- Any reasonable precautions which might have prevented the death.
- Any defect in a system of working which contributed to the death.

The sheriff may also recommend the adoption of certain safety measures in future.

The sheriff's determination cannot be used in evidence or founded on in any subsequent court proceedings – civil or criminal – arising out of the death.

FATAL INJURY

The rights of relatives to claim damages.

Claims for DAMAGES can sometimes be made against someone who kills another person or causes him injuries from which he later dies. The most common example is where the death was caused by negligence.

However, claims can also be made if the killing was intentional, or – in some cases – if the person responsible was in breach of some contract. For example, a retailer can be sued if he sold dangerously DEFECTIVE GOODS that killed his customer.

Claims by the executors

If the person who died lived for a time after his fatal injuries, he may have raised an action for damages himself. *See:* PERSONAL INJURY.

His executors can proceed with this action on behalf of his estate in so far as it relates to financial loss incurred in the period up to his death – for example, the cost of any property damage and wages lost. But his claim for pain and suffering, known as solatium, dies with him.

Claims by relatives

Certain relatives can claim damages to compensate them for any loss of financial support that they suffer as a result of the death. They may have been receiving financial support at the time – as with a non-working wife – or be able to show that they would have been supported financially by the dead person at some time in the future.

The relatives who can claim if they can show such losses are:

- Husbands and wives, including divorced husbands and wives. (Cohabitees in a stable relationship can also claim.)
- Children (including illegitimate and adopted children, and other children accepted by the dead person as part of his family) and other descendants.
- Grandparents, and other direct ancestors, such as great-grandparents.

HOW DAMAGES ARE ASSESSED AFTER A FATAL INJURY

Mr Macdonald was severely injured in a car accident. The driver was liable. As a result of his injuries he died, a year later, aged 38. He was unable to work after the accident.

He is survived by his widow (aged 37), an adopted child (aged 15) and another child (aged 5). He left a will naming his brother as his EXECUTOR. The assessment was 3 years after the accident.

Damages due to his brother as executor of the estate

• Estimate what his after-tax pay would have been from the accident to his death:

Gross pay	£7,000	
Less Tax	£1,500	£5,500

• Calculate sickness and invalidity benefit paid to him:

Sickness Benefit	£840	
Invalidity Benefit	£2,100	
	£2,940	
Less 50% (mandatory reduction)	£1,470	
	£1,470	
Deduct the net benefit figure		£1,470
		£4,030

• Calculate value of any damage to his belongings in the accident:

Clothing	£70	
Watch	£30	£100
		£4,130

• Calculate cost of any medical expenses incurred:

Private physiotherapy		£100
		£4,230
Add interest at 6%		£254
		£4,484

Damages due to his widow and children

1. *For loss of financial support:*

• Estimate what annual pay he would have been earning at date of death

Gross pay	£7,700	
Less tax	£1,700	£6,000

• Deduct a figure to represent the amount of money he spent on himself (e.g. for clothes, fares, his own food, hobbies etc.) Say 30% of his after tax pay:

30% of £6,000		£1,800
		£4,200

• Calculate the loss of financial support to the family from the death to date

2 years at £4,200	£8,400	
Add interest at 6%	£504	£8,904

Continued overleaf

• Brothers, sisters, uncles, aunts, nephews, nieces and first cousins.

Any of these relatives can also recover any reasonable costs incurred in connection with the funeral or burial.

Close relatives – parents, spouses, and children – and any stable cohabitee of the dead person can also claim a sum to compensate them for the psychological and social loss suffered through being deprived of the dead person's companionship and guidance.

How the damages are assessed

The typical claim is by a wife along with her children.

Claim for loss of support The court puts a figure on the loss by assessing how much money the dead person would have spent on the claimant and for what period of time. In a typical family claim, a sum of money is worked out and then divided up among the claimants.

The sum to be divided up is arrived at by finding out, first of all, how much of the dead person's take-home pay was spent on the family. This produces a figure for the year in which he died. That is then multiplied by a figure which is related to the number of years he would have gone on providing support. Where a widow is claiming, this will usually be until he retired. Her prospects of remarriage are entirely disregarded.

The figure used to multiply take-home pay is much lower than the number of years involved. For example, if a 42 year old man died, leaving a widow of 38, the figure would probably be around 13.

Of the total sum calculated, the widow would get around three-quarters and the rest would be divided among the children. Very young children are given about four times more than children nearing school-leaving age.

If a non-working wife is killed, the husband may be able to claim for the cost of employing domestic help, particularly to look after the children.

Claim for funeral expenses This is worked out from evidence of the cost involved. If the funeral was excessively extravagant, some part of the cost could be excluded as being unreasonable.

Claim for loss of companionship and guidance of the dead person For a widow or widower, the amount partly

HOW DAMAGES ARE ASSESSED AFTER A FATAL INJURY *continued*

- Calculate the loss of financial support to the family for the future by applying the 'multiplier'.

The judge will decide that as a fit 38 year old at the time of his death, with a stable job and marriage and a happy family, Mr Macdonald would have gone on supporting his family till retirement. The judge will choose a multiplier of 13 (slightly less than the maximum of 15 for a rather younger man').

The multiplier relates to the whole period, since the death, in which loss of financial support is anticipated. As the first 2 years have already been dealt with separately, they are deducted from the multiplier.

Multiplier: 13	
Less years since death (2)=11	
£4,200×11	£46,200
Total for loss of financial support	£55,104

- Divide this between the widow and children:

Widow's share (about 75%)	£41,104
Older child's share (age 15, about 5%)	£2,800
Younger child's share (age 5, about 20%)	£11,200
	£55,104

2. For loss of society and guidance:

If the judge awarded around the maximum amount, the sum would be:

Widow	£7,000	
Add interest on part relevant to last 2 years (probably £1,400 – 20% of £7,000 – at 6%)	£84	£7,084
Older child (age 15)	£1,100	
Add interest on part relevant to last 2 years	£13	£1,113
Younger child (age 5)	£3,300	
Add interest on part relevant to last 2 years	£40	£3,340

3. Funeral expenses to widow:

Cost of cremation, flowers etc.	£500

Total amount of damages

(1) To brother as executor of the estate		£4,484
(2) To widow:		
Loss of support	£41,104	
Loss of society and guidance	£7,084	
Funeral expenses	£500	£48,688
(3) To older child:		
Loss of support	£2,800	
Loss of society and guidance	£1,113	£3,913
(4) To younger child:		
Loss of support	£11,200	
Loss of society and guidance	£3,340	£14,540
Total damages		£71,625

depends on the prospects of their continuing to live happily together. The figure is likely to be around £7,000.

Younger children will get more than older children – perhaps £3,300 for a 5 year old and £1,100 for a 15 year old.

When damages are reduced

If the dead person contributed to his own death the damages will be reduced by a percentage *See:* CONTRIBUTORY NEGLIGENCE

No deductions are made for financial advantages that arise because of the death. So anything inherited is disregarded, along with insurance payments and social security benefits.

FEU DUTY

Paying your superior

If you own a house or land, it will almost certainly be held on feudal tenure and you may have to pay a small sum of money once or twice a year to your feudal SUPERIOR. This sum is feu duty, all that remains of the medieval rule that the vassal had to pay his superior for the right to remain in possession of the land.

Originally it was common for the payment to take the form of military service. Nowadays it is always in money and, because of inflation, the sum is usually very small.

If you fail to pay feu duty for five years, the superior can raise a court action to 'irritate' the feu. This means he can evict you without compensation and occupy the house or land himself. Even after the action has been raised, it is not too late to pay off the arrears provided this is done before the court decree is recorded in the REGISTER OF SASINES.

The feudal system of landownership is gradually being dismantled in Scotland. One sign of this is that feu duty is now being phased out:

- **Existing feu duties** must be redeemed by the seller whenever land is sold. An owner is also free to redeem his feu duty at any time. Redemption means paying to the superior a sum equal to the annual feu duty multiplied by the feu duty 'factor'. This factor varies from day to day but is usually about 9. After redemption the land is perma-

PAYING FEU DUTY ON TIME

If you fail to pay feu duty in time, your superior has a number of different ways of enforcing payment

nently free from feu duty.

• **New feu duties** Since 1974 it has not been possible to create new feu duties on the rare occasions in which land is still feued rather than sold outright.

FIDELITY INSURANCE

Protection against theft by an employee

An employer whose employees regularly handle large sums of money can take out an insurance fidelity policy to cover himself against fraud or theft by any of them.

A policy can cover particular types of employee – such as wage cashiers or betting shop staff. Or it can be more limited, giving cover for one particular, named employee. This is suitable for a small business, or for sports, holiday and Christmas savings clubs, where one official handles finance.

On the proposal form, you must state the precise duties to be carried out by the person in respect of whom you wish to insure.

The insurance company must be told if he or she has any criminal convictions, unless they have become spent convictions under the Rehabilitation of Offenders Act 1974. *See:* REHABILITATION.

If you have ever lost money through anyone's dishonesty, this must also be disclosed.

The insurance company may want to know if any references were checked when the person concerned was first employed or first took up his present duties If they were not, the insurers may make their own inquiries.

All relevant facts must be declared on the proposal form, otherwise the insurers may later disclaim liability *See:* INSURANCE POLICY

If you (the employee) are refused a fidelity policy, you may be sacked. But if you have worked long enough with your employer you may be able to claim UNFAIR DISMISSAL. You have no legal right to know why the insurance company refused to issue a policy.

Taking precautions against loss

An insurance company issuing a fidelity policy may insist that the employer – or club committee – makes an effort to prevent the loss of cash by dishonesty.

For example, a regular check of cash tills, or regular inspection of club or business accounts or bank statements, may be required. Failure to take such precautions when required by the conditions of a policy would enable the insurers to avoid liability.

The insurers must also be notified of any change in the employee's duties as soon as it takes place. A cashier, for example, may be promoted to manager, or a club treasurer may resign and be replaced. If the insurers are not told of any such change, they can avoid liability for any subsequent loss.

Some insurance companies stipulate that the policy-holder must tell them at once if there is a suspicion that an employee is being dishonest. When told, they can demand that the police be informed, or – if so agreed in the policy – that the employer sue the suspected person for fraud or to recover property stolen. In such cases, the insurers usually undertake to pay the employer's legal expenses.

An employee whose suspected dishonesty is reported to an insurance company could sue his employer for defamation. But he is unlikely to win the case unless he can prove that the report was made out of spite, as the court would normally accept the employer's plea of 'qualified privilege' – that he was obliged by contract to inform his insurers of such suspicions.

When money is lost

A fidelity policy lays down a maximum sum that can be claimed in case of loss. Some policies require the employer to make all possible attempts to recover the money.

The insurers will pay only for money lost while a policy is in force. If a theft is committed before the policy is taken out, but discovered only when it is in force, no compensation is paid.

FILM CENSORSHIP

How standards in the cinema are controlled

All cinemas – indeed any premises – that show films or videos for private gain, whether to the public or not, must be licensed annually by the district or islands council. The council can attach conditions to the licence, stating the type of films that can be shown in its district and who should not be allowed to see them. A cinema that ignores these conditions may lose its licence.

In practice, the committee of councillors responsible for licensing requires cinemas to observe the guidelines laid down by the British Board of Film Censors, an independent body whose work has government approval but which has no legal powers.

The committee can vary the Board's recommendations. For example, it can rule that a film with a '15' certificate should not be shown to anyone under 18. Or it can allow the showing of a film for which the Board has refused a certificate (though this is unlikely).

A filmgoer has no legal right to appeal against the committee's decision or against a certificate issued by the Board of Film Censors.

Rules for clubs

A film or video club operated for private gain must not be run without a licence from the council.

If the licence permits, the club can show films that have been given a 'Restricted 18' (18r) certificate by the Board of Film Censors. This allows the

HOW THE CENSORSHIP BOARD WORKS

The Board of Film Censors, set up in 1913 by the film industry itself, views every film intended for public showing, and decides whether it should be cut, shown only to restricted audiences or not shown at all.

Its verdict cannot be enforced, but is intended to guide or persuade distributors and local councils. In practice, local councils usually accept the board's decisions.

The board gives a certificate (right) to every film which it approves for public showing.

Every film that is to be shown in British cinemas is submitted by its distributors for examination by the board. Each is seen by at least two examiners who are expected by the board to take into account changing public attitudes.

They may in very rare cases decide not to give a certificate at all if they consider that a film merely exploits sex or violence. Yet they may approve one that they consider approaches responsibly a serious problem of sex and morality in society. Sometimes independent experts are consulted by the examiners and even invited to see the film.

When the examiners do not agree, the film may be seen by two other examiners.

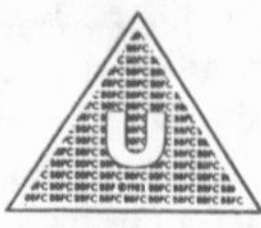

Universal. The film is approved as suitable for showing to all

Parental guidance. Some scenes may be unsuitable for young children

The film is not suitable for children under 15

The film is suitable only for adults and no person under 18 should be admitted

To be shown in segregated premises only. 18 and over

films to be shown to members aged 18 and over, but in segregated premises only. So in a multi-screen cinema, these premises would have to be totally separate from the rest of the cinema. The club, however, still risks prosecution for obscenity or indecency.

FINANCE HOUSE LOAN

A cash loan from a finance company or other money lender is subject to the same rules as other CREDIT AGREEMENTS, as long as it does not exceed £5,000 (£15,000 from May 20, 1985).

Even if the sum borrowed does exceed £5,000, however, if you believe that the interest being charged is unfairly high, you can ask a sheriff court to alter it in your favour. *See:* INTEREST CHARGE

FINE

Making an offender pay

A fine is a financial penalty imposed on an offender. It is the most common sentence passed in the criminal courts. The offender is ordered to pay a specified sum of money immediately or within a fixed period. Failure to pay may result in the offender being sent to prison.

For some offences – for example, ROAD TRAFFIC OFFENCES – there is a maximum fine that can be imposed. If no maximum is laid down, the maximum fine which can be imposed depends upon the sentencing power of the court in which the CRIMINAL PROCEEDINGS are brought.

The amount of the fine (which is not tax deductible) usually reflects the gravity of the offence, but when imposing a fine the court must also take into account the financial means of the offender.

The court is unlikely to impose a large fine on any person of inadequate means.

Time to pay

A court will only rarely order a fine to be paid immediately.

Usually the offender is given time to pay and may also be allowed to pay by instalments.

Unless a fine (or the first instalment) is paid at the time it is imposed, the court must normally allow an offender at least 7 days to pay the fine (or the first instalment).

If the court thinks the offender is incapable of managing his affairs well enough to save money for the fine, it can make a supervision order under which a social worker is appointed to assist and advise him on payment of the fine.

An offender who has been allowed time to pay can make an application to the court requesting further time for payment. The application will be granted unless the court is satisfied that the offender has deliberately failed to pay the fine or that he is unlikely to be able to pay if further time is allowed.

No time to pay

The court may refuse to allow time for payment if:

1. The offender possesses sufficient means to pay the fine immediately.

2. The offender, on being asked if he wants time to pay, does not request it.

3. The offender has no fixed address.

4. There is some other special reason why no time should be allowed – for example, the offender is about to serve a prison sentence for another offence.

If the offender fails to pay in these circumstances, the court may sentence him to prison.

TIME TO PAY

In most cases, a court will allow a convicted person time to pay any fine imposed.

THE PRISON SENTENCES FOR UNPAID FINES

As a last resort, courts can jail an offender who refuses to pay a fine. The maximum length of the sentence depends on the amount owed.

Amount due	Jail for up to
Up to £50	7 days
£51 to £100	14 days
£101 to £400	30 days
£401 to £1,000	60 days
£1,001 to £2,000	90 days
£2,001 to £5,000	6 months
£5,001 to £10,000	9 months
over £10,000	12 months

Failure to pay

When a court allows time for payment, or payment by instalments, it will not normally impose, at the same time, the period of imprisonment to which the offender will be liable if he fails to pay. If the fine is not paid, the offender will be ordered to attend a 'means inquiry' at the court to discover the reason for non-payment.

If his circumstances have changed for the worse since the fine was imposed, the fine may be reduced or even cancelled. But often he will simply be given more time to pay or the instalments will be reduced.

However the court also has various sanctions which can be used against defaulters:

Search The court can order the offender to be searched on the spot. Any money found on him can be used to pay the fine.

Prison The court may impose a period of imprisonment in proportion to the amount of the fine which remains unpaid.

Community work A person who fails or refuses to pay a fine may be given the chance of doing unpaid community work as an alternative, but that is not automatic. *See:* COMMUNITY SERVICE ORDER

Diligence The court may order recovery of the fine by the legal methods (called diligence) used to enforce a DEBT decree. This may be ordered at any time after a fine has been imposed.

If the offender has a bad criminal record, or his offence is serious, the court may, at the same time, impose not only a fine but also the period of imprisonment to which the offender will be liable if he fails to pay. If the fine is not paid in such a case, the offender will be imprisoned without any inquiry into the reason for his default.

FINGERPRINTING

When the police have a right to take your fingerprints

The police can take fingerprints from anyone who gives consent. Because of their age, PUPIL children cannot personally consent to being fingerprinted, but their parents can give the necessary consent.

Usually the police will only ask someone to consent to being fingerprinted so that innocent people can be eliminated from their inquiries – for example, they may wish to take the prints of a family whose home has been broken into. Such prints should be destroyed after the case is over.

When consent is unnecessary

The police have the right to take a person's fingerprints without his consent in two situations:

• **Detention** Where someone is suspected of committing an offence punishable by imprisonment, the police can detain him in a police station for up to 6 hours in order to carry out investigations. *See:* DETENTION

When a person has been detained in this way the police can take his fingerprints or palmprints, without his consent and without a warrant. If the suspect resists, the police can use reasonable force to obtain the prints.

If no CRIMINAL PROCEEDINGS are to be taken against the suspect, or he is not found guilty at his trial, the record of any prints taken from him during detention must be destroyed immediately.

• **Arrest** Where a person is under ARREST and is in police custody, the police can take fingerprints from him without his consent and without a warrant. If he resists, reasonable force can be used. However, if the person arrested is no longer in police custody – for example, if he has been released on BAIL or committed to prison – the police cannot obtain his fingerprints without his consent unless they have a warrant.

HOW FINGERPRINTS ARE KEPT

When someone is convicted his fingerprints will be taken and kept permanently on file.

If the arrested person is not found guilty at his trial, the record of the prints must be destroyed unless he has been previously convicted of crime.

If a person who is not in police custody after detention or arrest refuses to have his fingerprints taken, an application must be made to a sheriff to grant a warrant for this purpose.

What happens to fingerprints after a conviction

When someone is convicted, fingerprints already taken are kept permanently in police files. If prints have not already been taken, the criminal is fingerprinted after being admitted to prison. So if a convicted person is not sent to prison – for example, if he is fined, admonished or put on probation – he cannot be fingerprinted then.

Even when a convicted person's prison sentence is ended, he cannot ask for his fingerprints to be destroyed.

If there is a complaint against the police

Someone who later claimed that his fingerprints had been taken illegally could make a formal POLICE complaint, or attempt an action for DELICT. If force was used, he could also allege ASSAULT.

FIRE

When a careless person burns someone's property

Anyone who, by negligence, starts a fire that harms another person or his property, is liable for damages.

This is so even if the person did not actually light the fire, but caused it by, for example, storing petrol and highly inflammable material together. He may also be liable if the fire was started by someone authorised to be on his property – for example, a plumber using a blowlamp carelessly. In such a case, the plumber is also liable for damages.

If a person intentionally started a fire on his property and through no fault of his own it spread onto his neighbour's property, he would probably not be liable for damages.

Even when the victim of a fire has FIRE INSURANCE, the person responsible for the fire may still have to pay damages. The insurance company is entitled to sue him for recovery of the sum that it paid out to the insured.

Anyone who intentionally burns someone else's property is dealt with under a charge of FIRE-RAISING.

Bonfires It can be an offence to have a bonfire, if it causes a nuisance. *See:* AIR POLLUTION; NUISANCE

FIRE INSURANCE

How to protect yourself against loss by fire

By taking out a householder's INSURANCE POLICY, you insure your building and its contents against damage by fire – as well as against other risks. Although it is more usual to insure some properties – for example, a granary – against fire only, most dwellings are covered against fire by comprehensive policies.

Fire insurance under a household comprehensive policy covers damage or destruction by fire, lightning, earthquake and explosion. Such a policy also covers other risks. *See:* PROPERTY INSURANCE

Taking out fire insurance

When you complete the insurance proposal form – whether for a comprehensive policy or, in rare cases, for fire only – take care to set a proper value on your building and possessions. Describe them in detail (where required) and make sure that the insured value is enough to cover rebuilding of the property if it is completely destroyed.

In completing the form, you must also disclose all material facts. For example, if you have ever suffered loss by fire, you must disclose that to the insurers. You must also tell them if another company has refused to insure you or your property, or to renew any type of policy for you.

Even matters not related to fire or insurance – such as criminal convictions (unless spent) – must be disclosed, if they would be relevant to the reliability of a policyholder. *See:* REHABILITATION

If a policyholder has lied about any fact, or has withheld relevant information, the insurers are entitled to refuse any claim that he makes.

Understanding the conditions of the policy

Every policy contains conditions which, if you break them, entitle the insurance company to reject your claim: read the conditions carefully before signing the proposal. If necessary, ask for a copy of the type of policy that will be issued to you.

For fire insurance, there are usually conditions entitling the company to avoid paying compensation:

- If you have not notified the insurers of damage to, or destruction of, the property.
- If you have disposed of the property.

Making a claim

Your policy will probably require you to make any claim within a certain period, such as 30 days. The claim should give full details of the damage and how it was caused. If there is any difficulty about complying with that requirement, ask your insurer to extend the time limit.

What you can claim for after a fire

Any accidental fire damage is covered by fire insurance, whether or not there has been negligence by the insured person.

Fire insurance can in theory be claimed only if there has been ignition, although ALL RISKS INSURANCE may cover damage caused by heat alone – such as scorching. In any case, despite the wording of a comprehensive or fire-only policy, the insurer normally pays compensation for scorch damage.

Damage by smoke You can claim for smoke damage caused by a fire that breaks out in your home or near-by, but not for damage caused by smoke leaking from a faulty heating stove.

If a fire brigade causes damage while putting out a fire – if, for example,

THE WOMAN WHO HID HER MONEY IN THE FIREPLACE

Anything that is burned by accident – no matter how or where – can properly be claimed for.

Mrs Flora Harris became nervous about her valuables after burglars tried to break into her flat in Putney, London. On December 2, 1939, when she was about to go out, she wrapped up her jewellery and £128 in notes in a newspaper and hid them in her fireplace, under an unlit fire.

Next morning, she lit the fire. By the time she remembered her hoard in the grate, most of the money and jewels had been destroyed.

Mrs Harris claimed their value under her Lloyd's fire-insurance policy, but was refused. She then sued the Lloyd's underwriter, Mr Poland, who had sold her the policy.

In the English High Court, Mrs Harris maintained that, as the hoard had been ignited accidentally and had not been intended for fuel, the fire was covered by her policy. Lloyd's contended that as the fire had been in a grate and had not spread beyond, it could not be covered by fire insurance – but only under an 'all-risks' policy.

DECISION

Lloyd's were ordered to pay. The court ruled that since the property had been burned accidentally, it did not matter that it was the property – and not the fire – that was not in its proper place.

carpets and decorations are drenched in water or chemical foam – you can claim. You are also covered for any damage caused to property while it is being removed from the path of the fire.

If your house has to be demolished to prevent flames spreading from a neighbouring property to other houses, that is regarded as a loss by fire – even though the flames have not touched your house – and you can claim.

How much you can claim

When making a claim, you must prove the value of your loss. If, for example, your house is insured for £40,000 and is then totally destroyed by fire, you should receive the full sum, provided that you can prove that the property was worth that amount. You can do so by proving the purchase price and allowing for any general rise in prices that has occurred since you bought the property. The insurance company's adjuster can also be shown any similar properties in your immediate neighbourhood.

If you can prove only a value of, say, £35,000, that is the maximum sum you can recover.

A householder's policy sometimes contains a clause – known as an 'average' clause – to protect the insurers against under-insuring. If your property is under-insured, you will receive only a proportion of the cost of the damage.

If, for example, a property is worth £80,000 but is insured for only £40,000, the most you can recover from the insurer is half the value of the damage.

If the property is insured for £60,000 – three-quarters of the value – you can claim up to three-quarters of your loss.

Whether there is an average clause or not, you can expect to be asked to declare on the proposal form that you have stated the full value of the property.

If such a declaration is given, and you subsequently make a claim, the insurer may be able to show that you were under-insured. If so, the insurer may refuse to pay.

If no average clause applies, which is the usual position, and the declaration does not apply for the future, the insurer is not entitled to insist on 'averaging' or refuse to pay. You should resist any attempt to compensate you for less than the amount for which you have insured.

Loss of business If fire causes you loss of business – for example, if your shop burns down – you can claim for that loss of business only if you have taken out consequential loss insurance.

Deliberate fire-raising If someone deliberately sets fire to your property, you are still entitled to claim on your insurance.

The only bar to such a claim would arise if a policyholder knew that the fire was to be started. *See:* FIRE-RAISING

When a home is made uninhabitable

If your home burns down or is made uninhabitable by fire, then – provided that you have consequential loss insurance – you can claim the cost of alternative accommodation as well as the cost of the damage. A comprehensive policy usually includes that benefit, but a fire-only policy seldom does.

An accommodation claim is covered by a section of the policy usually called 'loss of rent', which allows an extra 10 per cent on top of the total insured value for the cost of housing you until your property has been restored.

However, the insurance company will not pay to accommodate you at a higher standard of living than you are used to. It will normally meet the bill for an enforced stay at a reasonable hotel – deducting from the bill what you would have spent if you had still been living at home. You would be entitled to stay in a luxury hotel only if there was no other accommodation available.

If you are put up by relatives or friends, the insurer will pay towards the expense of staying with them, provided that you can produce receipts.

You are normally expected to pay your hotel and rent bills and claim for them afterwards. However, the insurance company may agree to make an advance payment before the final settlement.

Landlord's loss If a tenant is forced out of his home by fire damage, his landlord can claim 'loss of rent' compensation provided that the landlord has taken out consequential loss insurance. The tenant should generally insure against loss of accommodation as well as loss of his belongings.

WHAT HAPPENS WHEN YOU ARE UNDER-INSURED

How an 'average clause' in a household contents policy can work

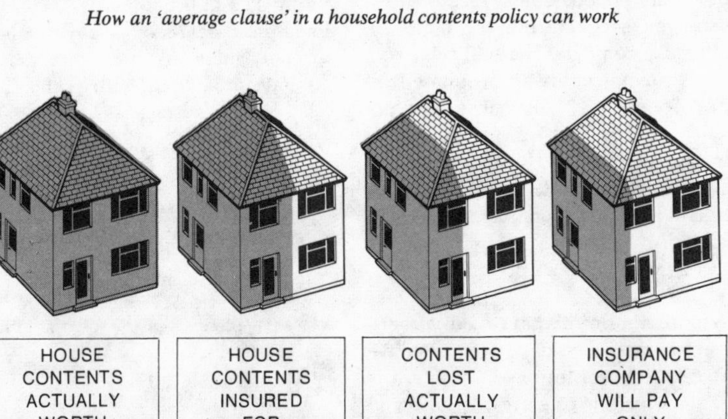

Check your policy carefully to ensure that it does not contain an average clause. Such a clause is unusual in general household comprehensive policies, but if your insurer includes one, you must be sure to declare the full value of the property and its contents each time you renew the policy. If the house contents are insured for only a proportion of their full value, the insurers will pay only that proportion of the value of any claim for loss. For example, if the full value of the contents is £10,000 but they are insured for only £5,000, and goods worth £3,000 are stolen, the insurers will pay only £1,500.

FIRE-RAISING

Criminal injury to property

Fire-raising – setting fire to someone else's property – is the most serious kind of criminal injury to property. It covers two main offences:

1. Wilful fire-raising This offence is committed when a person intentionally sets fire to:

- Buildings – for example, houses, shops, sheds and warehouses.
- Growing corn or growing wood.
- Mine-shafts.

2. Culpable and reckless fire-raising This offence is committed when a person:

- Recklessly sets fire to anything.
- Intentionally sets fire to any kind of property that is not covered by the offence of wilful fire-raising.

The property set on fire must belong to someone else. A person is not guilty of fire-raising if he sets fire to his own property.

However, it is a crime to set fire to one's own property in such a way as to endanger or alarm others. A minor case may be prosecuted as BREACH OF THE PEACE.

A fire-raiser who unintentionally causes death is guilty of CULPABLE HOMICIDE unless he has shown an utter disregard for life, in which case he is guilty of MURDER.

The penalty for fire-raising is at the discretion of the court, within its sentencing limits.

FIRE SERVICE

Calling the brigade in an emergency

It is the duty of the local fire brigade to answer all emergency calls at any time to attend a fire.

Anyone can call the brigade free of charge by dialling 999 on the telephone.

You may be asked for your address or telephone number and the fire brigade headquarters may call you back to check details.

It is a criminal offence to make a false call. The maximum punishment is 3 months' imprisonment and a £1,000 fine.

The fire brigade will also undertake rescue work, especially when life is in danger. They can be called to road, industrial or building-site accidents – for example, when a ditch caves in and buries someone – or home accidents.

Putting out a fire Firemen on duty, and the police, have a right to force their way into any property at any time of the day or night in order to put out a fire or prevent damage.

No notice need be given to the owner of the premises. Anyone who tries to stop a fireman entering a building which is on fire commits an offence and can be fined up to £400.

When you have to pay

The local fire authority can charge for any service other than putting out fires, but in practice no charge is made in any emergency when life is in danger.

A charge is also unlikely when suffering or injury has been caused. For example, parents would probably not get a bill for the rescue of a child whose head was trapped in railings.

Any charge is payable by whoever calls the brigade. The charge will cover a hire fee for any vehicle used, as well as an hourly rate for each man taking part. Whoever calls the brigade is usually told in advance what the charge is likely to be.

Pumping out floods Firemen will pump out flooded homes or factory premises, but a charge may be made. In practice, a company is usually charged, but private homes are often pumped out free of charge – especially if the occupier is old or disabled.

Fire prevention The local fire authority will advise private householders or firms in business premises on methods of fire prevention.

They will also check private fire hoses and extinguishers.

The fire authority have a duty to ensure that certain kinds of premises have effective fire precautions.

These include theatres, hotels and boarding-houses. Plans showing escape routes, fire fighting appliances and warning notices have to be submitted to the authority.

Once the authority are satisfied they issue a fire certificate. Inspections can be carried out at any reasonable time to make sure the precautions are still being taken. Instructions can also be given to factory owners to take various precautions.

FIREGUARDS

Compulsory protection for fires and heaters

All gas and electric fires and oil heaters offered for sale must be fitted with a proper fireguard when they are offered for sale. That regulation includes any fire using liquid gas or gas in a portable container. Any trader or supplier who puts a fire or heater on sale without a guard is committing an offence under the Consumer Safety Act 1978, and can be jailed for up to 3 months and fined up to £2,000. The trading standards officers of regional and island authorities are responsible for enforcing the regulations. *See:* CONSUMER SAFETY

If someone is injured or if his property is damaged because a fire or heater has been sold without a proper guard, he can claim damages under the Consumer Safety Act.

When a child is hurt

It is not an offence for a person to use a heater or a fire in the home without a proper guard. But if a child under 7 is killed or seriously injured by an open fire which is insufficiently protected, the person in charge of the child can be prosecuted under the Children and Young Persons (Scotland) Act 1937.

Exempted heaters A fire or heater specially made for industrial use does not have to be fitted with a safety guard

SAFETY RULES

A guard on a fire or a heater, to comply with the law, must pass strict tests laid down by the British Standards Institution. The guard must:

- Stand up to 11 lb. pressure for at least 1 minute and still meet all other safety requirements.
- Spring back to its original position automatically, if it is a hinged guard.
- Give at least 1¾ in. of clearance from the flame or element.
- Be far enough away from the element or flame to prevent a piece of material, placed against the guard, from bursting into flame in less than 10 seconds.
- Stand a hammer blow, if made of glass.
- Be accompanied by a warning, on the appliance, that the guard should not be removed.

if the appliance is not suitable for heating residential premises.

Other heaters exempted include electric fires designed only to fit on a ceiling, and any heater so designed that the flame or element is completely enclosed within the structure of the appliance, so that there is no danger of personal injury from contact with the flame or element.

FIREWORKS

How safety laws apply

It is a criminal offence to let off fireworks in a street or public place, even if there is no danger and no one is frightened or annoyed by them. The maximum penalty is a £1,000 fine.

Factories where fireworks are made must be licensed by the Health and Safety Executive. Anyone who makes fireworks on unlicensed premises can face a fine of up to £2,000 if tried summarily in the sheriff court, or an unlimited fine on indictment.

Fireworks and explosives must not be sold to anyone who appears to be under the age of 16, whether by a shop or an individual. The maximum penalty for that offence is a £1,000 fine.

Fireworks may not be hawked, sold or exposed for sale in a street or public place: the maximum fine is £50.

All fireworks except sparklers, jumping crackers, 'throw-downs' – which explode on hitting the ground – and fireworks weighing less than $\frac{1}{8}$ oz. or intended for export, must be marked with the name and address of the manufacturer. The maximum penalty for failing to do so is a £400 fine.

FISHERMAN

Special benefit for the self-employed

A self-employed fisherman whose income includes a share of the gross earnings or profits derived from a boat's catches pays a higher rate of Class 2 NATIONAL INSURANCE CONTRIBUTIONS than other self-employed people. In return, he qualifies – unlike other self-employed people – for unemployment benefit.

He does not get benefit for the first 3 days' unemployment, but is paid thereafter for each working day on which he is not employed. If he makes a fresh claim within 8 weeks of the first, he does not have to wait 3 days before beginning to receive benefit.

To claim unemployment benefit, the fisherman must have done no fishing on the days concerned – and must not have refused any reasonable opportunities of fishing work.

Fishermen liable for the higher Class 2 contributions also pay Class 4 contributions – a percentage of their annual profits *See:* SEASONAL WORKER

FISHING

When permission is needed to go fishing

The sea around the Scottish coast belongs to the Crown for the public use. This includes all tidal waters – sea lochs, bays and the tidal part of rivers.

Non-tidal rivers, streams and lochs are in private ownership. Whoever owns a river bank owns the river itself, up to half-way across. Lochs belong to the owner or owners of the surrounding land.

The most valuable fishing is for salmon. For this reason, the right to fish for salmon exists separately from the ownership of the water; the person entitled to fish salmon in a particular stretch of a river is not usually the owner of that stretch.

The right to other fish – brown trout, and coarse fish such as grayling, pike and perch – follows the ownership of the water. This means that everyone can go fishing in the sea or other tidal waters, but only the owners of non-tidal waters – or persons who have the owners' permission – can go fishing there.

FISHING THE WRONG WAY

It is illegal to fish by securing rods to the bank.

You will therefore need permission if you want to fish for salmon, or if you want to fish for other types of fish in non-tidal waters. For fishing locally, the simplest thing to do is to join an angling club. For fishing on holiday, permits can usually be obtained from angling clubs, tackle dealers, or hotels in the area you are visiting. The Scottish Tourist Board publishes useful booklets on fishing and sea-angling.

In Scotland, unlike in England, you do not need an official licence to go fishing.

Fishing without permission It is a criminal offence to fish for salmon without permission. The fish are confiscated, and the maximum penalty is a fine of £2,000 and imprisonment for up to 3 months.

It is not an offence to fish for other freshwater fish without permission, unless the waters are among the few covered by protection orders made by the Secretary of State for Scotland. However, the owner of the waters may go to court and obtain an INTERDICT to prevent you from trespassing on his property. *See:* POACHING; TRESPASS.

Close seasons There is no close season for sea-fishing, but periods have been set aside in which it is a criminal offence to fish inland. These coincide with spawning time and are designed to allow fish to breed in safety.

The close season for salmon varies from area to area, but usually runs from early September to early February for net fishing, and from early November to early February for rod fishing. Even during the open season, net fishing is forbidden from noon on Saturday until 6 a.m. the following Monday, and no salmon fishing of any sort is allowed on Sunday.

The close season for trout in all areas is from seventh October to fourteenth March inclusive. There is no close season for coarse fishing.

Illegal methods Explosives, poisons and electrical devices may not be used for fishing, either inland or at sea. The only legal method of angling in inland waters is with a single rod and line. The rod must be held, not fixed to the bank, or left lying on the bank. Salmon roe and lights are among the items that cannot be used as bait or lures.

FIXTURES AND FITTINGS

When an article becomes part of the house

The owner or occupier of a house often carries out improvements by adding new fixtures and fittings.

If the thing added is a fixture, it becomes a permanent part of the house. If the thing added is a fitting, it is not, in law, part of the house at all.

Why the difference matters

The difference between a fixture and a fitting is very important in two common situations:

- *If you are a tenant.* Any fixtures that you add are part of the house and so belong to the landlord. Unless you have made some special arrangement, you must leave them behind at the end of your lease. You cannot usually claim compensation. However, any fittings that you add are still yours and can be taken away with you.
- *If you are a seller.* When you sell your house, the buyer is entitled to have all the fixtures because they are part of the house. But he is not entitled to the fittings and you can take them away with you.

You are free to make some different arrangement with the buyer in the MISSIVES OF SALE. Such an arrangement is usual, partly because it is not always clear whether a particular object is a fixture or a fitting, and partly because the buyer often wants to have some of the fittings – for example, carpets and curtains. *See:* HOUSE BUYING AND SELLING

Telling the difference

Whether an article is a fixture or a fitting depends on the answer to three questions:

1. Can the article be removed without seriously damaging either it or the house? If it cannot, it is definitely a fixture. If it can, it may be a fitting. For example, a light bulb is a fitting but the socket is a fixture; a tin opener screwed

FIXTURES OR FITTINGS?

When an article is attached to a house or garden, it is not always easy to tell whether it has become part of the house or garden as a fixture, or whether it is just a fitting.

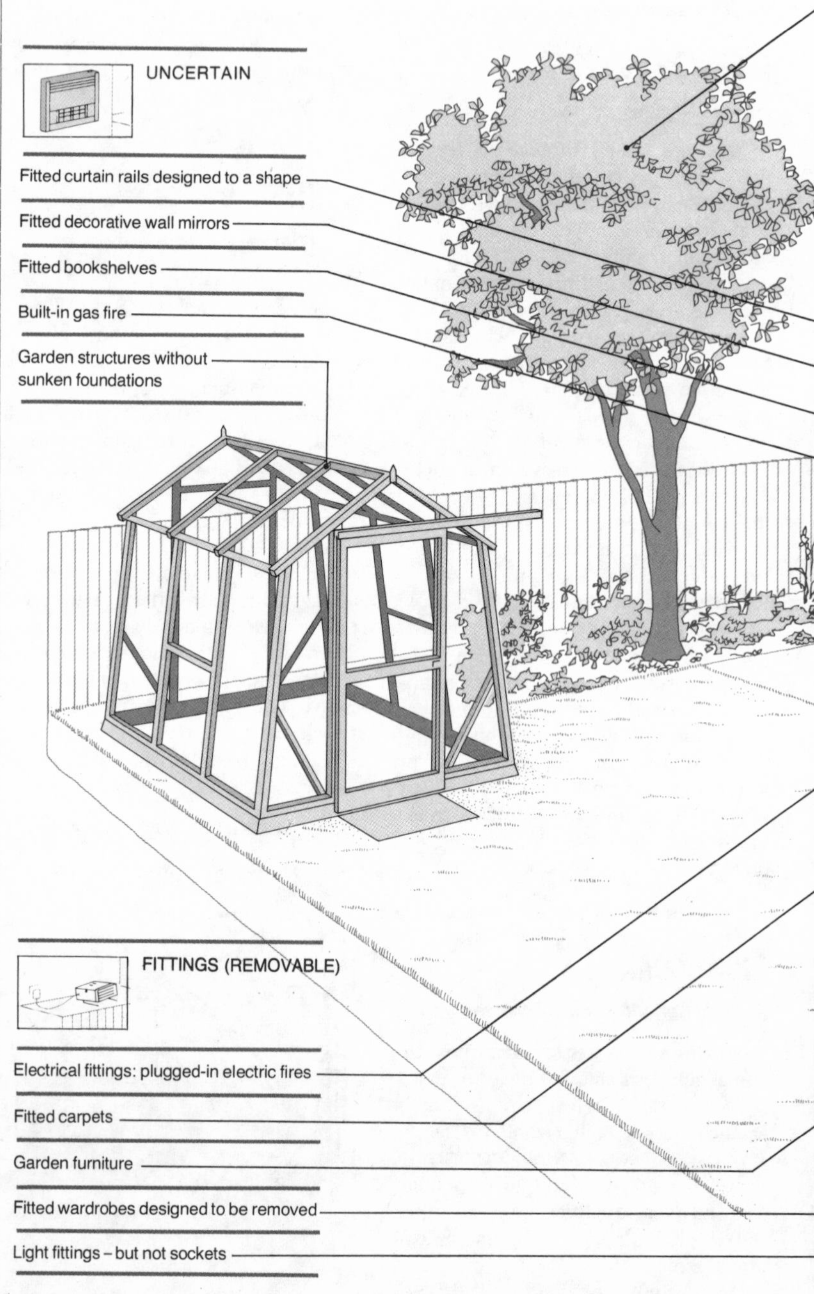

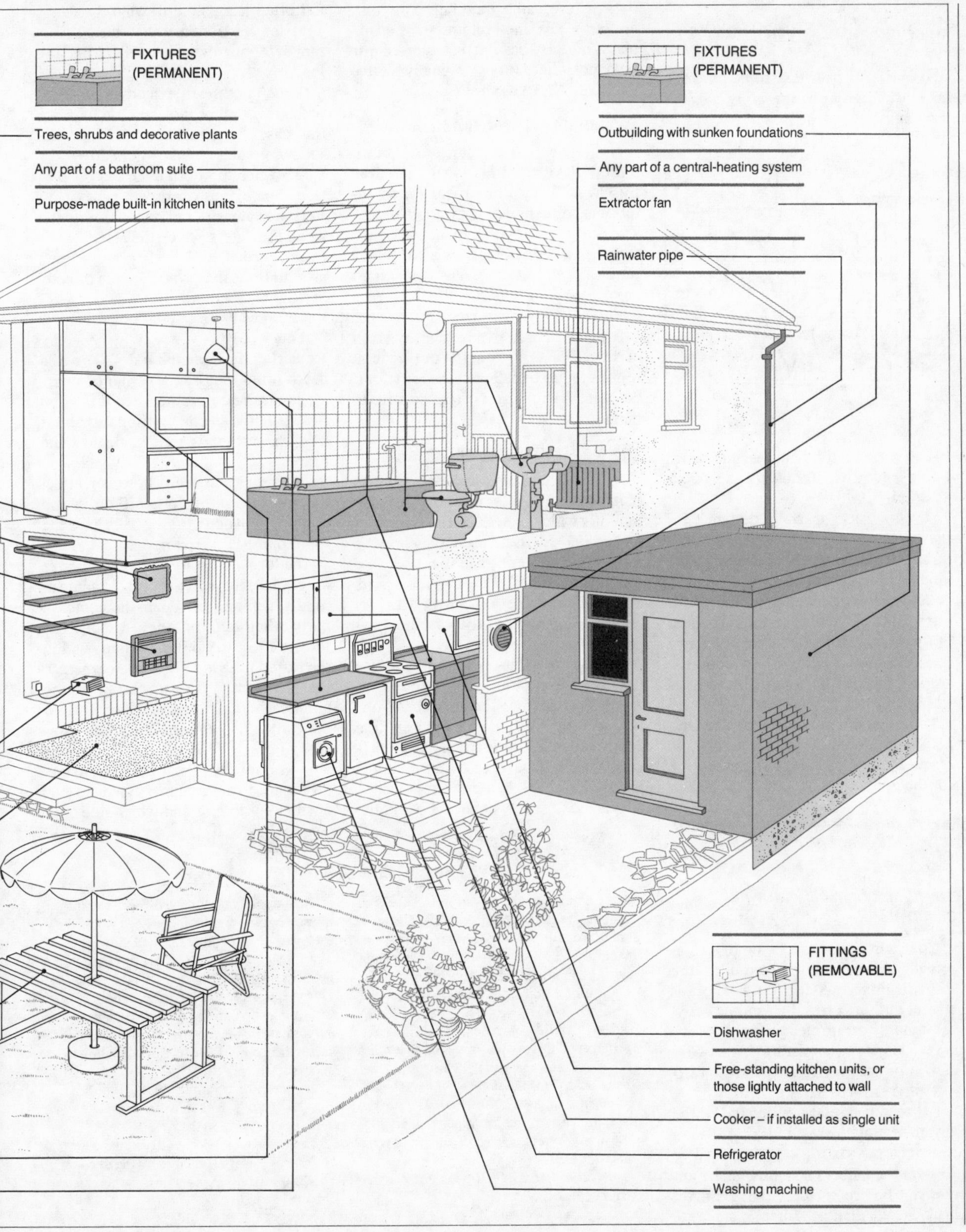
FIXTURES
(PERMANENT)
Trees, shrubs and decorative plants
Any part of a bathroom suite
Purpose-made built-in kitchen units
FIXTURES
(PERMANENT)
Outbuilding with sunken foundations
Any part of a central-heating system
Extractor fan
Rainwater pipe
FITTINGS
(REMOVABLE)
Dishwasher
Free-standing kitchen units, or those lightly attached to wall
Cooker – if installed as single unit
Refrigerator
Washing machine

YOU CAN'T TAKE IT WITH YOU WHEN YOU GO

A house seller or tenant cannot usually take away something he has installed if it is a fixture and not a fitting.

to the wall is a fitting but a sink, which would leave a gaping hole if taken out, is a fixture.

2. Is the article specially designed for the house? If it is, it is probably a fixture. For example, purpose-made kitchen units are fixtures.

3. Did the person attaching the article intend it to be for the permanent benefit of the house? If he did, it is probably a fixture. For example, a new door is a fixture but a picture hung on the wall is a fitting.

If the person in question is a tenant, he is considered no less likely than an owner to have intended the article to be for the permanent benefit of the house.

FLAT

The rights of tenants and owner occupiers

The rights of people living in flats as private tenants are protected by the Rent (Scotland) Act. If the landlord is a local authority, or other public body, the tenants are protected by the Tenants' Rights (Scotland) Act. *See:* COUNCIL TENANCY; EVICTION; HARASSMENT; RENT PROTECTION

All tenants are also protected by the law governing the relationship between LANDLORD AND TENANT.

Resident landlords A private tenant may not be protected by the Rent Act if he and his landlord live in separate flats in the same building. This only applies where the building – for example, a house – has been converted into flats, not where it was originally built as flats. *See:* EVICTION

Responsibility for repairs

If a tenement or block of flats is rented, the landlord is usually required by law to keep the structure and exterior of the building in good repair. That includes the common entrance and stairs, and the roof. He is also usually required to maintain gas and water pipes, and electrical wiring. *See:* LANDLORD AND TENANT

A private landlord may employ a firm of house factors to carry out general repairs on his behalf. If there is a factor, the tenant should report all repairs to him.

The rights of owner occupiers

In any tenement or block of flats there are always some parts of the building which benefit all the owners of the individual flats. Examples are the roof and the entrance passage and stairs. Sometimes these common parts are held in CO-OWNERSHIP by everyone, sometimes they are the property of just one person.

If you are a flat-owner and want to find out the position in your building, you will often find the answer in your title deeds. You may have the title deeds yourself, but if you have a mortgage they will be kept by the building society or other lender. The solicitor who acted for you when you bought the flat often has a note of what the deeds contain. If necessary, he can also arrange to borrow the deeds from the lender.

Sometimes the title deeds do not deal with any or all of the common parts. In that case the general law provides the following rules about ownership:

Roof Each top floor flat owns the section immediately overhead.

Entrance passage and stairs Co-owned by all the flats to which they lead.

Front garden and back green Each ground floor flat owns the area directly in front and behind.

External walls Each flat owns the part that encloses it.

Repairing the common parts The title deeds often require the owner of a particular common part to keep it in good repair. If the deeds say nothing about this, the owner is free to neglect the property.

The neglect must not, however, affect the owners of the other flats in the building. If it does, they usually have the right to insist on repairs.

The local authority always has power to require all the flat-owners in a building to maintain or repair the common parts, whether or not they own them. If they fail to carry out the repairs within the stated time, or if it is an emergency, the local authority can carry out the repairs itself, and recover the cost from the owners in proportion to their rateable values.

If, as a result, a flat-owner has to pay for repairs to a common part which does not belong to him and which he is not

OWNER OCCUPIERS IN GLASGOW

House factors are usually employed to manage rented property, but in Glasgow they are also used by the owners of tenement flats as a convenient way of dealing with common repairs. This practice goes back to the time when the flats were first sold.

The liability of tenement owners for repairs will usually be contained in a 'deed of conditions' drawn up when the flats were sold. This document, which is registered in the REGISTER OF SASINES, may set out the procedure for repairs, including the appointment of a factor and his powers and duties.

If you wish to see this document, consult your solicitor.

The factor charges each owner an annual fee – which can be increased only with the owners' agreement. He will then see to any minor repairs which are notified to him by any one of the owners.

If a major repair is required, the factor will usually do nothing until he obtains the agreement of all the owners to have the repair carried out. He has no legal duty to supervise the property.

Owners are normally billed quarterly for the factor's fees and the cost of any repairs.

The owners can decide to dismiss a factor unless this is prohibited by the deed of conditions or some other document which is binding on them.

made liable to repair in the title deeds, he can recover the cost from the neighbours who do own the common part.

FLATSHARING

How the law treats you when you live with others

When two or more people decide to share a rented house, they often arrange matters between themselves informally, and only one of them has dealings with the landlord. It is generally wiser, however, for each to ensure that he is protected under the Rent (Scotland) Act by establishing a JOINT TENANCY.

If the group does not do that, any member other than the one in whose name the accommodation is leased, may be regarded in law as a sub-tenant, or a LODGER who can be asked to leave at any time, or even a trespasser. *See:* SUB-TENANCY; TRESPASS

When a flatsharer seeks supplementary benefit

People living in shared accommodation and claiming SUPPLEMENTARY BENEFIT may find that the kind of sharing arrangement they have affects the amount of benefit they get.

The basic difference is between those classed as householders – which includes tenants – who are entitled to maximum help in paying rent, rates, mortgage interest and other items connected with housing, and those classed as non-householders, who receive proportionately less.

A person living with a close relative, but not responsible for paying the rent, is a non-householder. He is entitled to the non-householder benefit rate and, if 21 or over, to a fixed amount towards the rent – £3.10 a week in 1983–84.

If he is paying his way as a lodger and is not living with close relatives, supplementary benefit will cover board and lodgings – so long as they are not unreasonably expensive – and an allowance for personal expenses.

When two or more people – other than those living as husband and wife – are joint tenants living as a single household, they are treated as joint householders for supplementary benefit purposes.

A joint householder is entitled to the non-householder rate of supplementary benefit, *plus* the difference between that rate and the single householder rate divided by the number of people who are sharing.

He is also entitled to a rent rebate or rent allowance from the housing authority to cover his share of the rent. *See:* RENT ALLOWANCE; RENT REBATE

FLOWERS

When picking a bloom is an offence

Flowers are legally part of the land on which they grow, and therefore belong to the landowner. A person who picks and removes flowers without permission from the owner is guilty of THEFT.

If the person does not remove the flowers, but instead destroys them on the land, he is guilty of malicious mischief or VANDALISM.

Some species of wild flowers and plants are specially protected by Act of Parliament. Anyone – including the owner – who picks, uproots or destroys them is guilty of an offence. *See:* PLANTS AND FLOWERS

FOOD

How the law safeguards what you eat and drink

It is a criminal offence in Scotland to sell for human consumption any food that is not of the nature, substance or quality demanded by the buyer.

Under the Food and Drugs (Scotland) Act 1956 anyone selling food that is usually consumed by humans, but which proves unfit for human consumption, is guilty of a criminal offence, even if:

- He took precautions to avoid the offence.
- He was not negligent.
- The food sold is proved to be not injurious to health – for example a mouldy but harmless pie.

It is also a criminal offence to interfere with food or drink by adding or removing any substance so as to make it injurious to health.

The maximum penalty for all these offences is an unlimited fine, imprisonment for 1 year, or both.

If you think that the food you buy is not satisfactory, complain to the environmental health department of your district or islands council, which may decide to send a sample to the public analyst.

If you are given food that you suspect to be dirty, complain to the council's

DATE MARKING ON FOOD

The law on date marking of food changed on January 1, 1983. Until then, there was no legal requirement to mark foods with any information about their 'minimum durability' – although this was often done voluntarily by manufacturers.

Minimum durability

Under the new rules, most foods which can reasonably be expected to keep – if properly stored – for 12 months or less (18 months or less after January 1, 1985) must be marked with a date indicating their 'minimum durability'. This is the length of time for which the food can reasonably be expected to keep, provided it is properly stored.

If the food is expected to keep for 3 months or less, minimum durability must be indicated by the words 'Best before', followed by the date – for example, 'Best before 12 July'.

If the food is expected to keep for more than 3 months, only the month and year need be given, so long as the words 'Best before end' are used – for example, 'Best before end July 1984'.

If the food is only expected to keep for 6 weeks or less, it can be marked with the words 'Sell by', followed by the latest recommended date of sale and an indication of its expected keeping time – for example 'Sell by 12 July. Best before 17 July'.

Where any storage conditions need to be observed for the food to keep, this must be stated.

Exceptions

Certain foods do not need to be date marked. They include fresh fruit and vegetables (unless peeled or cut into pieces), bread and other flour confectionery normally eaten within 24 hours, deep-frozen food, edible ices, cheese intended to ripen in its packaging and drink with more than 10 per cent alcohol.

environmental health department. The procurator fiscal may decide to prosecute the seller and could apply for a closure order under the Control of Food Premises (Scotland) Act 1977 if the seller is convicted.

In both cases you, as the buyer, might gain nothing from any prosecution – though the courts now have power to award compensation for any injury or suffering that you have been caused. *See:* CRIMINAL COMPENSATION ORDER

Cleanliness where food is sold

Hygiene regulations under the Food and Drugs (Scotland) Act are administered by the district or islands council and cover all places where food is prepared or sold for human consumption. It is an offence for a shop, stall or restaurant not to comply with the regulations. The maximum penalty is an unlimited fine, 1 year's imprisonment, or both.

- Premises must be clean and sanitary and free from vermin and insects.
- Clean handbasins and lavatories must be available to staff. They must have adequate supplies of soap, nail brushes and towels (or other drying facilities).
- Staff must not smoke or spit while handling food. Hands must be clean.
- Any open injury – say, a cut finger – must be covered with a waterproof

WHEN THE FOOD YOU BUY IS UNSATISFACTORY

An environmental health officer may make a test purchase at the shop you name and send it to the public analyst.

FOOD INGREDIENTS THAT NEED NOT BE LISTED BUT MUST CONFORM TO REGULATIONS

Some prepacked foods – for example, chocolates, sweets, ice cream and bread – must be labelled with an accurate description but they do not, like many other prepacked foods, have to bear a list of ingredients in weight order.

They are, however, subject to other regulations.

If a manufacturer claims that his produce provides energy, calories, proteins, vitamins or minerals, the claims must be clear and he must be able to substantiate them with scientific evidence if he is later challenged.

Nothing can be called a 'slimming aid' unless it has been proved to help slimming.

Bread over 10 oz.	Must be sold by weight
White bread	Must have Vitamin BI, iron and chalk for calcium content
Brown or wholemeal	At least 0.6% fibre and up to 5% soya or rice flour
Wheatgerm	10% processed wheatgerm
Protein bread	At least 22% protein
Milk bread	At least 6% milk solids
Starch reduced bread	Under 50% carbohydrate
Eggs	Grade A (fresh) eggs must be sold in 7 grades: size 1 (70 g and over) to size 7 (under 45 g)

THE SAUSAGE MANUFACTURER WHO WAS LIABLE

A manufacturer as well as a retailer can be convicted of selling food not of the nature, substance or quality demanded.

A firm of sausage makers supplied a packet of sausages to a fishmonger who had a travelling shop.

The fishmonger sold the packet to a customer, who discovered that one of the sausages had a piece of metal in it.

The sausage makers were charged with selling food not of the nature, substance and quality demanded by the customer.

They argued that they were not liable, since the offence could only be committed by someone – such as the fishmonger – who sold the food directly to a customer.

DECISION

The makers were convicted.

The sheriff said that the offence related to the sale of any food which was ultimately intended for human consumption, whether sold by a manufacturer, wholesaler or retailer.

THE MINCE WHICH WAS MEANT FOR DOGS

A shopkeeper commits an offence if he sells to a customer food which is not fit for human consumption, even although he did not intend it to be sold.

The manager of a butcher's shop was charged with selling adulterated mince to a local authority sampling officer.

The manager had added some preservative to the mince, intending to sell it as dog food, but had forgotten to tell an employee, who sold it to the sampling officer.

The manager was not in the shop at the time, but telephoned the sampling officer later in the day, when the mistake was discovered.

The sheriff acquitted the manager on the ground that he had told the officer as soon as possible that the mince was not for human consumption.

DECISION

The High Court of Justiciary ordered the sheriff to convict the manager.

There was no doubt that there had been a genuine mistake, but that did not prevent the offence being committed.

The food had been left where it could be sold to customers, without any indication that it was not for human consumption.

dressing while staff are handling food.

- Premises handling food must ensure that it cannot easily be contaminated.

Restaurant rules

A caterer convicted of a hygiene offence can be imprisoned and fined. A sheriff court, on the application of the procurator fiscal, can also make a closure order that prohibits anyone from using the premises for selling food until all danger to health has been removed.

It is a criminal offence to disobey a closure order, which must be displayed prominently on the premises. The maximum penalty is a £2,000 fine.

MINIMUM FOOD STANDARDS

Under the Food and Drugs (Scotland) Act 1956, regulations have been made laying down standards for many foods. They include the following, which must contain a minimum proportion of certain ingredients, as listed here:

Sausage rolls	At least 12½% meat (10½% if uncooked)
Meat pies	At least 25% meat (21% if uncooked)
Fish cakes	At least 35% fish
Beef sausages	At least 50% beef
Pork sausages	At least 65% pork
Meat paste	At least 70% meat
Fish paste	At least 70% fish
Fish spread	At least 70% of the named fish
Suet (shredded)	At least 83% suet
Suet (block)	At least 99% suet
Jams	Varying from 25% minimum fruit content for blackcurrant, (35% if 'extra jam') to 35% for other fruits (45% if extra jam)
Marmalade	At least 20% citrus fruit
Mincemeat	At least 30% vine fruits and citrus peel
Instant coffee	Must contain at least 96% coffee
French coffee	'French coffee', a coffee-chicory mixture, must have a minimum of 51% coffee
Liquid coffee essence	Must contain between 15% and 55% coffee
Coffee-chicory essence	Must contain between 15% and 55% coffee and chicory
Milk	At least 3% milk fat and 8½% milk solids
Dried milk	Between 26% and 42% milk fat (up to 1½% if skimmed)
Condensed and evaporated milk	Between 9% (7½% for condensed milk) and 15% milk fat; and at least 31% milk solids (25% for condensed milk)
Double cream	At least 48% milk fat
Single cream	At least 18% milk fat
Whipping cream	At least 35% milk fat
Butter	At least 80% milk fat, a maximum of 2% solids, natural colouring only, and not more than 16% water may be added. If it has more than 3% salt, it must be labelled 'salted butter'
Margarine	At least 80% fat (which can include up to 10% butter), no more than 16% water. Must have added Vitamins A and D in the mixture of vegetable, animal and fish oils used

Sales of produce

Sales of cooked produce by voluntary organisations (WRI sales of home-made jams and chutney, for example) are exempt from inspection by local environmental health officers.

Following legislation in 1981, housewives and others producing cooked food for sale in such circumstances are not liable to have their kitchens inspected.

Controlling what goes into your food

A trader or shop can be prosecuted for selling food not of the nature, substance or quality demanded. Whether what was supplied was the food demanded must always be decided by the court. There are three separate offences:

- The 'substance' refers to the ingredients.
- The 'nature' refers to what is made out of the ingredients.
- The 'quality' refers to different grades.

If a restaurant sells margarine when butter is ordered, it can be convicted of selling food not of the substance demanded, unless the waiter has made clear what he is serving.

The composition of some foods is controlled by food standards orders under the Food and Drugs (Scotland) Act. In other cases, codes of practice are agreed between representatives of the trade.

Sometimes the code of practice is more specific than the legal regulations. For example, the law says that a fish 'spread' must have 70 per cent of the named fish, but fish 'paste' must have 70 per cent of fish, without specifying a minimum quantity of the named fish.

The code of practice further lays down a minimum amount of different kinds of fish paste: salmon 'spread' must, by law, contain 70 per cent of salmon. Salmon 'paste' must, by law, contain 70 per cent fish. But the code goes further and lays down that the 70 per cent of fish in the 'paste' must have 25 per cent salmon in it.

When a customer has a doubt about the content of food, the public analyst, if requested, will give a detailed analysis free of charge.

WHO THE PUBLIC ANALYST IS AND HOW HE WORKS

Every regional council appoints at least one public analyst – a chemist who has passed an examination set by the Royal Institute of Chemistry.

In addition to food, his work deals with other consumer protection and trade description matters and also public health hazards – for example, poisonous waste.

When dealing with a complaint about food, the public analyst examines one-third of a test sample obtained from the premises facing a complaint.

Of the remainder, one third is retained by the environmental health officer who is investigating the case; and one third is given to the seller of the food, who may arrange for his own independent analysis.

If someone sells you short measure

If you have been given short weight in a shop or at a market stall, keep the bag with the purchase and contact the trading standards officer, who will make a test purchase.

If the customer is prepared to give evidence in court, the shop may be prosecuted under the Weights and Measures Act 1963. The maximum penalty is a £2,000 fine.

FOOT AND MOUTH DISEASE

Official powers when animals are infected

Wide emergency powers are available to the UK Ministry of Agriculture and inspectors of regional and islands councils when an outbreak of foot and mouth disease is discovered among farm animals.

People can be banned from using fields and footpaths in a large area around the farm where an infected herd has been kept. All dogs have to be kept inside, chained up outside, or kept on a lead.

Failure to comply with the regulations is a criminal offence and police have powers of arrest. The penalty can be a fine of £2,000 or more, or imprisonment for up to 2 months in the case of a second or subsequent offence.

Farmers are entitled to compensation from the Ministry of Agriculture for any loss they suffer when they have to destroy an infected herd.

FOOTBALL POOL

How the law controls the promoters

A football pool is a form of pool betting in which all money staked and all winnings paid are part of a common pool. Football pool promoters must be registered with the local council – district or islands – for the area in which they have their headquarters.

Parliament has laid down strict requirements for the conduct of the pools. Prizes must be available to all entrants. If one entrant bets twice as much as someone else, his winnings must be twice as high. The amount won must depend on the accuracy of the forecast. The promoter must appoint a chartered accountant, approved by the local council, to verify all figures.

If there is a dispute

The entry form that you sign after filling in the coupon says: 'I agree to abide by the company's rules, which govern all entries, and agree that this transaction is binding in honour only'.

That 'honour clause' prevents you taking the company to court in case of a dispute, although members of the Pool Promoters' Association will investigate complaints and, if a mistake is proved, will pay the complainer what he should have won. In any event, the Scottish courts regard such gaming contracts as unenforceable (although they may enforce a contract which is concerned with the winnings resulting from gaming).

A WINNING ENTRY MUST ARRIVE ON TIME

The pools competitor must ensure that his entry is completely correct and legible and that it is posted in time.

It is for the pools competitor to ensure that he completes his entry correctly and legibly, and that it is sent to the pools company in plenty of time.

Entries that are in any way incorrect – for example, if the coupon is not signed – will not be accepted. Nor will those delivered to the promoter after matches have begun. They must reach the promoter by noon on Saturday, and proof of posting is not proof of delivery. Late entries are disqualified – and you cannot sue the Post Office over a delayed entry, because it is protected by law against such claims.

Dealing with collectors

As an alternative to posting the coupon yourself you can hand it to an official collector whose job it is to pass entries in bulk to the promoter. He may

THE PUNTER WHO GOT HIS SHARE

The courts will not enforce gaming contracts, but they may enforce agreements to share money arising out of a bet.

Mr C and Mr F each contributed half of the stake money on pool coupons and agreed to share any winnings equally. Mr F completed the coupons and sent them in under his name. He won £5,184.20 but refused to give Mr C his half share. When sued for this, he argued that the agreement between him and Mr C was a gaming contract and therefore unenforceable by the courts.

DECISION

The court held that the contract between Mr C and Mr F was not a gaming contract though it was incidental to one. So Mr C got half of the winnings.

do so in person, by using the railway or a road parcels delivery service, or he may post the entries.

Although a collector is paid a commission by the promoter, he is regarded as the competitor's agent, so if he fails to ensure that your entry arrives in time, you cannot sue the promoter.

There is no formal contract between the competitor and the collector. You could take him to court and, if you prove he has been negligent, you might be awarded damages. But that would be worthwhile only if his negligence deprived you of a substantial win, and if he could pay.

Locally organised pools

Pools run locally – usually to raise funds for charity – are subject to the special provisions of the Pools Competitions Act 1971. The promoter must be registered with the local council and also needs a licence from the Gaming Board. *See:* GAMBLING

The Board can attach conditions to the licence, such as the number and type of competitions to be held.

FOOTPATH

Where walkers' rights are protected

In most parts of Scotland, walkers are well served by a network of footpaths, which can be used by pedestrians alone. *See:* RIGHT OF WAY

FOREIGN DIVORCE

Divorces that are recognised in Britain

A couple married in Scotland can be divorced in certain circumstances in another country. A divorce or a legal separation is recognised in Scotland if it is effective under the law of the country in which it was granted and if one of the couple lives there habitually or is domiciled there or is a national of that country. *See:* DOMICILE

It is also valid if one of the couple is domiciled in a country which recognises the decree. A husband, for example, who is domiciled in California can get a divorce in Mexico from his wife living in Edinburgh in circumstances where it would not be directly recognised in Scotland. A Mexican divorce is recognised in California and it is valid in Scotland because the husband lives in California.

A foreign decree will not be recognised in Scotland if it is granted under conditions contrary to the British concept of justice. A husband or wife, for example, must be given a reasonable opportunity to appear in court to object to the decree.

So a husband who becomes domiciled in Nevada and obtains a quick divorce there may find the decree invalid in Scotland unless his wife was given sufficient time to get there.

FOREIGN EMBASSY

Protecting the interests of citizens abroad

An embassy is a government office set up in a foreign country to represent the government's interests in that country and to look after the interests of its citizens working or travelling there.

An embassy is headed by an ambassador – or occasionally a chargé d'affaires – who keeps diplomatic contact with the country in which he is stationed. There are also commercial staff to deal with matters of trade; registry officials to record births and deaths of their nationals living in the country; and officials to deal with passports, stranded holidaymakers and people arrested or in prison.

The embassies of Commonwealth countries in Britain are known as high commissions, but they do the same job. Most embassies are situated in the capital city of a country, but many bigger nations also have consulates – which are, in effect, branch offices – in other important ports and cities.

Only a few countries do not have embassies in London. They usually ask another country with an embassy to look after their interests.

Embassy functions The main purpose of a foreign embassy is to act as an intermediary between its own government and the government of the host country. The commercial department works to encourage trade between the two countries.

Consular functions The consular department can renew passports, and it also has the power to administer the foreign estate of any of its nationals who die in the country. It issues visas and looks after the day-to-day interests of its nationals visiting or resident in the country, advising them about health regulations or legal restrictions.

It can help, for example, with illness or with visitors who have lost their money, and it will usually see that they get back safely to their country.

For most legal purposes an embassy is in effect regarded as the territory of the country which it represents. British police, for example, have no powers to enter, say, the Soviet embassy and arrest a Soviet citizen suspected of crime, although they can ask for the person to be handed over. Foreign staff at an embassy also have protection from the laws of the host country.

Because of the inviolability of diplomatic premises, a citizen of a country might seek refuge in a foreign embassy – for example, if he feared for his life during civil disturbances. *See:* DIPLOMAT

Arrested aliens When a foreign national is arrested in Britain, the police should inform his embassy – or he should be allowed to do so himself.

The embassy has a right of access to its nationals held in custody and a right to arrange legal representation if the prisoner so wishes. If he is sent to prison, embassy officials can pay regular visits and the prisoner is allowed to contact them.

HELPING NATIONALS WHEN THEY ARE ABROAD

The embassy will normally help you if you lose your money, and see you get home safely.

Addresses of embassies, consulates and high commissions can be found in a public library.

FOREIGN INCOME

Tax owed on money earned abroad

If you are a citizen of the United Kingdom, and therefore liable to British tax, but travel abroad as part of your job, you may be entitled to tax relief on the part of your earnings that arises from your work overseas.

There are two levels of relief:

- Partial, which can be claimed by people who usually go abroad on business for at least 30 days in a tax year – that is, April 6 to April 5. No partial relief will be given from 1985–86 onwards.
- Total, which can be claimed by people who work abroad for a continuous period of 1 year or more.

Both types of relief can be claimed by employees of British or foreign-owned companies, and partial relief by the self-employed.

If you believe you qualify, you should claim when you submit your annual tax return. The return form contains a section for detailing earnings from duties performed abroad. *See:* INCOME TAX

Your tax inspector may ask for proof that you have worked overseas – an employer's declaration, or travel receipts if you are self-employed.

Claiming partial relief

If you spend 30 days or more abroad on business in 1984–85, you can obtain tax exemption on 12½ per cent of your overseas earnings for the time you are away (it was 25 per cent in 1983–84). For an employee, earnings from duties performed abroad are generally calculated according to a formula in which the salary during the tax year is divided by 365 days and then multiplied by the number of days overseas.

Example: Mr Y is a salesman earning £7,000 a year. During 1984–85 he spends 70 days abroad on business.

The proportion of his salary arising from duties performed abroad is:

$$\frac{\pounds 7{,}000}{365} \times 70 \text{ days} = \pounds 1{,}342.47$$

He does not have to pay tax on 12½ per cent of that amount – £167.81.

REDUCING YOUR TAX BILL

When you spend 30 days or more abroad in any tax year, you do not have to pay UK tax on a fraction of the earnings you make abroad.

The same rule applies to self-employed people. In either case, any capital allowances to which they are entitled are deducted from gross earnings before the exemption is applied.

How the 30 days are calculated

The 30 overseas days needed to claim tax relief on earnings from duties overseas do not have to be continuous. You can make several short trips – for example, 5 trips of 6 days each – and, provided that they are all in the same tax year, you will qualify.

The days must be 'complete' – those on which you were outside the UK at midnight. If you fly from London to Paris at 7 a.m. and return at 11 p.m. on the same day, that does not count as a day abroad. However, if the flight from Paris arrives in London after midnight you will have accrued one day.

Time spent travelling outside the UK towards your foreign destination counts as time away.

If you are outside the UK on business for 7 or more consecutive days, Saturdays and Sundays may be included in your total, even though you did not work over the weekend. If you take an occasional weekday off for local sightseeing, that counts towards the total too, provided that the main purpose of the trip was business.

Claiming extra relief

Although the basic formula for calculating earnings from duties abroad is directly related to the number of days spent overseas, the tax authorities may accept a claim for higher relief in some circumstances. The decision is left to local tax inspectors and must be negotiated with them. But if you think you are entitled to higher relief, say so on your tax return.

Extra relief might be granted if, for example, you were sent abroad for 9 months to work on a specific project, but were required to come back for a few days each month to report on progress to your employer. You should claim the full 9 months' relief.

The Inland Revenue may also grant extra relief if it can be shown that an employee's main duties are performed abroad, and that the time he spends working in the UK is only incidental. An engineer whose chief task is servicing his company's installations overseas, but who returns to the UK between assignments, might come into that category.

In such cases, it greatly helps the employee's claim for relief if he has a 'split contract', with separate sections in it to cover, respectively, his work in the UK and that overseas.

He must still declare his total earnings to the Inland Revenue, but the overseas section of the contract is evidence of the extent of his duties abroad. If a service engineer receives £3,000 – one-third of his total salary – for waiting time in the UK and £6,000 for his main duties overseas, he can argue that he is entitled to relief on the £6,000 – even though he may have spent more than one-third of the year in the UK.

The Inland Revenue accepts the principle of 'apportionment' in split contracts – higher payment for work overseas because of higher wage rates in the foreign location – provided that it appears 'reasonable'. But if there is no specific provision for that in the contract, the tax authorities are unlikely to accept a claim for extra relief based on the argument that local pay rates are higher than those in the UK.

Companies cannot avoid the tax rules by a split contract that makes a UK resident technically an employee of an associated foreign concern while he is working abroad. If there is any link between the two employers, he must pay tax on his earnings from both.

Expenses Travel and accommodation

expenses paid by an employer for an employee on business overseas are not liable to tax, provided that the employee is not saving money by having them paid.

Claiming total relief

Someone who works for a period of at least 365 days outside the UK for a British or a foreign employer pays no UK tax on his earnings abroad during that time. However, he must still pay any tax due from income arising in the UK – for example, if he has let his house, from rent.

The 365 day qualification period does not have to be continuous, but:

1. No single return visit to the UK can be longer than 62 consecutive days.

2. The total number of days spent in the UK must not exceed one-sixth of the total time of his employment abroad.

Example: An engineer working in the Middle East spends 170 days there and then comes home for a holiday of 40 days before returning to his job.

His employment abroad on the day he goes back to the Middle East has lasted (170+40)=210 days, of which the holiday in the UK represents about one-fifth.

To reduce the proportion to one-sixth and keep his tax relief, the engineer must remain in the Middle East for at least a further 30 days, because:

$$\frac{\text{40 days' holiday}}{\text{(170+40+30 days' employment)}} = \frac{40}{240} = \frac{1}{6}$$

An employee who works abroad for more than 365 days can bring all his earnings back to the UK afterwards. They are not liable to UK tax.

People who cannot claim relief

Civil servants and members of the armed forces cannot claim relief on earnings from duties overseas. Gas and oil rigs in the UK sector of the North Sea do not qualify as 'overseas'.

Paying local taxes on money earned abroad

A British resident who works abroad and who is paid there may be taxed locally on his income. Whether he is or not depends on the foreign country's tax rules.

If his earnings for duties performed abroad are taxed overseas, he can claim tax relief in the UK, so that the total amount paid in tax is not more than the amount due in the country – the UK or the one where he worked – that has the higher tax rate. That is called double taxation relief. In some cases double tax agreements will provide that he pays tax in one country only.

The UK has double taxation agreements with all major nations except the USSR, and with most smaller ones.

Example: A lecturer is promised a gross fee of £500 for speaking at a conference overseas. Under the rules of the country in which the conference is held, tax of £140 is deducted before the fee is paid – giving a net foreign income of £360.

UK tax applied at the basic rate to £500 would be £150, leaving a final net figure of £210.

However, by claiming double taxation relief, he can offset the £140 paid abroad against the £150 that is due in the UK. His UK tax liability is then (£150–£140)=£10, and the net amount he finally keeps is (£360–£10)=£350.

If the amount paid in tax abroad is higher than that payable in the UK, no further UK tax is due – but the difference between the two amounts cannot be reclaimed.

Foreign investments

Since October 1979, UK residents who have dividends accruing to them in a foreign currency can decide to keep the money abroad or bring it back to Britain in whatever form or currency they wish.

The exchange control regulations that formerly made it necessary for the dividends to be repatriated in sterling were abolished on October 23, 1979.

The payments are liable to income tax, and basic income tax may be deducted by the British bank receiving them. If tax has already been deducted in the country from which the payments come, double taxation relief can be claimed. Sometimes double tax relief is given in advance by reducing the rate of tax deducted by the British bank.

Pensions from abroad

The first 10 per cent of a foreign pension paid to a UK resident is not liable to income tax. Pensions for service in former or existing colonies that have become the responsibility of the Crown Agents also get the 10 per cent relief, provided that they became payable before April 1973.

German government pensions paid to victims of Nazi persecution are not taxed in the UK.

FOREIGN MARRIAGE

When a wedding abroad is valid in Scotland

If a British subject gets married abroad, the validity of the marriage depends on the law of the country in which the parties claim DOMICILE, unless it is conducted under Scots law.

It will be recognised in Scotland, provided it is recognised in the country of domicile of each of the parties and is conducted according to the law of the country where it took place. If you have a church wedding in France, you must have a civil ceremony as well for your marriage to be recognised in France and also in Scotland.

However, if Scots law recognises a divorce granted to one of the parties, one exception to this rule is that he or she will be free to remarry although the country of domicile does not recognise that divorce. For example, a Spaniard obtaining a divorce recognised in Scotland would be regarded by Scots law as free to marry, even though Spain did not regard the divorce as dissolving the previous marriage.

The laws of the country of domicile about who may validly marry whom must be observed. A man wishing to marry his cousin cannot do so if either of them is domiciled in a country where the marriage of cousins is illegal. However, if the prohibition is regarded as unreasonable by Scots law – for example, a ban on marriage between people of different races – the marriage will be regarded as valid in Scotland.

Provided it was legally recognised in the country of domicile, a polygamous marriage is legally recognised in Scotland for many purposes although it cannot be conducted in this country.

The Scottish courts will grant decrees concerning such marriages – for instance, for ALIMENT of wives or children, and for CUSTODY OF CHILDREN.

See: POLYGAMY

A polygamous marriage contracted by a man or woman domiciled in Scotland may not be recognised by the Scottish courts even though it is recognised in the country in which it takes place.

Under Scots law

A marriage can be conducted abroad under Scots law if one of the parties is Scots by domicile. It is legal if carried out by an 'authorised marriage officer' – for example, a British ambassador, embassy official, high commissioner or British consul.

A serviceman abroad can be legally married by a chaplain to the forces or by anyone nominated by the serviceman's commanding officer. A Service marriage can also take place on a Royal Navy ship in foreign waters, if the ceremony is conducted by a chaplain.

It is no longer possible to be married by a ship's captain while at sea.

Anyone married abroad, or under foreign law, who is in doubt about the validity of the marriage can apply to the Court of Session for a 'declarator' (a declaration) that the marriage is valid. Consult a solicitor about this.

If the court refuses a declarator, the marriage is not valid in Scotland. If it declares it to be valid, the marriage is binding in the normal way. Neither party can go through another marriage ceremony without committing bigamy.

If the marriage is declared invalid, the partners will have no claims to aliment and INHERITANCE will be affected.

Dissolving the marriage A marriage contracted in another country can be dissolved in Scotland, under Scots law, provided that at least one partner has been resident in Scotland for at least a year, or is domiciled here. *See:* FOREIGN DIVORCE

FORESHORE

The freedom to use beaches for pleasure

Most of Scotland's beaches – the foreshore between the high and low watermarks of ordinary spring tides – belong to the Crown and are administered by the district or islands council for the area in question.

Normally anyone is entitled to use a public beach for recreational purposes. However, the council can pass BYELAWS covering various matters – for example, the playing of games, or the use of the beach for ponies or vehicles.

The council also has power to regulate the activities of swimmers, water skiers and people sailing boats, but only within the first 1,000 metres out to sea from the low watermark.

A private landowner whose land runs alongside a public beach cannot keep the public off the foreshore. He can, however, prohibit people from crossing his land to reach the foreshore, unless there is a public RIGHT OF WAY. Any member of the public who persists is a trespasser and can be removed by the use of reasonable force. *See:* TRESPASS

You have a right to keep certain of the things you might find on a beach. *See:* BEACHCOMBING; WRECK

Private beaches

Some stretches of the Crown foreshore have been sold or leased for private use. But a beach that has a sign claiming it is private may in fact not be. The local council will often be able to tell you if it is genuinely private.

Even where a beach is private, the general public still have the right to use it for launching or beaching a boat, and for catching fish other than salmon. They probably cannot use a private beach for any other recreational purpose.

Beaches in government control

Some stretches of foreshore are used by government departments – for example, by the Ministry of Defence as gunnery ranges. The department sometimes has power to exclude the public entirely.

Other stretches – for example, Aberlady Bay in East Lothian – have been designated by the Nature Conservancy Council as nature reserves. The public are not usually excluded, but their activities can be controlled by byelaws made by the Council.

FORGERY

The criminal offence of issuing a false document as genuine

The most common type of forgery is imitating someone's signature. This is forgery even if the imitation bears no resemblance to the genuine signature.

However, merely forging a signature is not itself a crime: it has been said that anyone may amuse himself by counterfeiting signatures. The crime is 'uttering' a forged document – that is, using a forged document with intent to deceive.

Any document can be a forgery if it pretends to be genuine – for example, a medical prescription on which the doctor's signature has been forged. It is also forgery to write unauthorised words or figures above a genuine signature on a document, or to make unauthorised amendments to it – for example, by altering the amount of a cheque.

The document must be 'uttered' for the crime to be committed – for example, by presenting a forged prescription as genuine to a chemist or presenting a forged cheque for payment at a bank. The crime is committed immediately the forged document is uttered as genuine – either by the forger or some other person who knows it is not genuine. It is not necessary for the deceit to be successful. If it is, the crime of FRAUD has been committed.

Presenting a forged document is not a crime unless there is intent to deceive the person to whom it is presented as to its genuineness. So it is generally not a crime to present a forged document while at the same time admitting that it is a forgery – in that case there can be no deception. The only exception to this is forged banknotes: because of the risk of forged banknotes being circulated, it is a crime to utter such notes even when admitting that they are forgeries.

The penalty for uttering forged documents is at the discretion of the court, within its sentencing limits.

Currency notes and coins

Banknotes and coins are specially protected by Act of Parliament. There are a large number of offences concerning them, including the following:

- Making a counterfeit of a currency note or coin, with the intention that it be passed or tendered as genuine.

Maximum penalty 10 years' imprisonment or unlimited fine, or both.

- Making a counterfeit of a currency note or coin without lawful authority or excuse.

Maximum penalty 2 years' imprisonment or unlimited fine, or both.

FORGING BANKNOTES

It is a crime to utter a forged banknote even when it is admitted that it is a forgery

● Passing or tendering as genuine anything which is known or believed to be a counterfeit of a currency note or coin.
Maximum penalty 10 years' imprisonment or unlimited fine, or both.
● Possessing, without lawful authority or excuse, anything which is, and which is known or believed to be, a counterfeit of a currency note or coin.
Maximum penalty 2 years' imprisonment or unlimited fine, or both.
● Reproducing – on any substance whatsoever and whether or not on the correct scale – any British currency note without official written permission.
Maximum penalty An unlimited fine.

All these offences cover banknotes which are customarily used as money in the country where the note was issued, and therefore include Scottish bank notes. *See:* LEGAL TENDER

When money is counterfeit

A forged banknote is worthless and must be handed over to the police or delivered to a bank. If you discover that a banknote in your possession is forged, do not try to use it. As already stated, that would be a criminal offence.

If you were given the note in payment for something, you are entitled to claim its face value from the person who gave it to you. Even if he did not know it was forged, he is assumed in law to have represented it as worth its face value when he passed it to you.

If he knew it was forged, he can be prosecuted, and he still owes you that sum of money. If you received forged money as a gift, you have no legal claim against the person who gave it to you.

If you pay someone with a forged note unknowingly, you have committed no offence, but you must pay again.

FOSTERING

Caring for someone else's child in your own home

Couples who take other people's children to live in their own homes, and look after them as if they were their own children, are known as foster parents.

Foster parents may be selected by the social work department (of the regional or islands council) to look after children in the department's care. Or they may be private foster parents – that is, people who bring up children in their own homes through a private arrangement with the natural parents of the children. *See:* CHILDREN IN CARE.

Local authority fostering

Many children who are in the care of the social work department would benefit from being placed with a foster family. If you want to apply to become a foster parent to such children, you should write to your local social work department. Ask for information about fostering and for a visit from a social worker to discuss fostering with you.

The social worker will probably want to visit your home several times and may arrange for you to go to a meeting, along with other interested families, to get full information on what fostering involves.

Before accepting you as a foster parent, the social work department will have to be sure that you are suitable to look after other people's children. They will therefore need quite a lot of information about you – for example, about your home, your job and how your own children are cared for.

Personal references will be taken up and health checks (possibly including a medical examination) made. The department will also check with the police whether you have any criminal record. A person will not be accepted as a foster parent if convicted of an offence which makes him or her unsuitable to care for children – for instance, cruelty, neglect or assault.

After this is completed, the department will decide whether you are suitable to be a foster parent. If you are not accepted, you have no legal right of appeal against the department's decision.

Who can be foster parents?

Foster parents are usually married couples, but single women are sometimes accepted. Single men cannot act as council foster parents unless they are the grandfather, uncle or elder brother of the child who needs fostering.

Placing a child with foster parents

When a child is placed with foster parents, the social work department will usually ask them to sign an agreement to care for the child in the best possible way. They will also have to agree to arrange any necessary medical and dental care, and encourage the child to follow his or her own religion.

Foster parents must allow a social worker from the department to see the child at any time. The social worker will visit regularly to discuss the child's progress at home and school and help with any problems which arise. The social worker will also try to maintain the links between the child and the natural parents.

The social work department must review a child's case every 6 months. It can remove a child from foster parents if that is in the child's best interests – but not if the child has lived with the foster parents for 5 years or more *and* the foster parents have notified their intention to apply to adopt the child. In this case, the social worker can only remove the child with the permission of a court or justice of the peace. *See:* ADOPTION; PLACE OF SAFETY ORDER

Natural parents can remove their child from foster parents unless there is a compulsory order detaining the child in local authority care – for example, a SUPERVISION REQUIREMENT made by a children's hearing or an order taking over parent's rights – or the child has been in the department's care for 6 months or more.

If the child is under a compulsory order, the natural parents will have to apply to the children's hearing, court or local authority which made the order, asking for permission to have the child back. If the child has been in voluntary care for 6 months or more, the social work department may require the natural parents to give 28 days' written notice of their intention to remove the child. *See:* CHILDREN IN CARE

Short and long term fostering

Some foster parents will arrange with the social work department to foster children at very short notice, in an emergency. Others will agree to care for children for short periods of time – often for up to 6 months.

Children needing emergency or short-term care have usually experienced some crisis, such as the breakdown of their parents' marriage or the death or illness of a parent. Some may have been removed from their home under a place of safety order because they were in serious danger.

Where a child is being fostered for a long period of time, the natural parents may be in regular contact with the child and the foster parents. Natural parents retain their right to see their child unless the local authority has taken over parents' rights. *See:* CHILDREN IN CARE

When foster parents plan to adopt

Fostering and adoption are very different legally. A foster child who is adopted by foster parents becomes a full member of their family, as if he or she were their natural child.

If foster parents have looked after a child for 5 years or more, and they apply to adopt the child, then neither the natural parents nor the local authority can take the child away without a court order. Even where the child has lived with the applicants for less than 5 years, the natural parents cannot take the child away if they have agreed to the adoption. *See:* ADOPTION

Seeking custody It is possible for foster parents to be given CUSTODY of a child in their care. A court may order this if it considers it would be in the child's best interests.

Private fostering

Any person who looks after a child who is not related to him or her, under a private arrangement, for a period of more than one calendar month, must notify the social work department of the arrangement. This applies whether or not the person is being paid by the natural parents to foster the child.

The social work department should be notified in writing at least 2 weeks before the child is to be fostered. A social worker will then visit the prospective private foster parents at home and will also make police and health checks on the family. A person who has been convicted of offences against children, or whose own children have been compulsorily removed, will not be allowed to become a foster parent.

It is an offence not to notify the social work department that a child is to be fostered privately or to foster a child after being prohibited from doing so. The maximum penalty is a £2,000 fine or 6 months' imprisonment, or both.

When a private foster parent is registered as suitable by the department, a social worker will visit regularly to ensure that any foster children are being properly cared for. The social worker must be allowed into the house to inspect the premises: refusal is an offence.

If a child is at risk in a private foster home, the council can apply to a sheriff – or to a J.P. if the child is in immediate danger – to remove the child to a safe place. The child, even if 17, can then be taken into care.

Fostering payments

Regional and islands councils pay fostering allowances to foster parents looking after children in their care. The level of the allowance is fixed annually and varies from one council to another.

The purpose of the allowance is to meet the expenses of looking after the child. It will cover the cost of food and clothing and will increase with the child's age. Councils can make exceptional additional payments to foster parents for some items – for example, special clothing or equipment, or dietary needs.

Foster parents are not entitled to CHILD BENEFIT for looking after children in the care of a council.

The natural parents of a child who is privately fostered can make their own arrangements for paying the foster parents.

'Professional' foster parents Many councils offer increased payments, or a salary or fee, to people who are prepared to foster children with special needs – for example, severely handicapped children or adolescents with behavioural problems. These 'professional' foster parents will be assessed by a social worker but may also be asked to attend training sessions and regular group meetings with other professional foster parents.

Foster parents caring for a very severely handicapped child will receive help from the social work department with aids and adaptations. They may also be able to claim ATTENDANCE ALLOWANCE or MOBILITY ALLOWANCE for the child. *See:* DISABLEMENT

FRAUD

Dishonestly obtaining goods or money from someone

Fraud occurs when someone achieves a practical result by false pretences. For a person to be guilty of fraud, the false pretence must have been made deliberately, with the intention of producing that result.

The result must have some legal significance – for example, deceiving someone into parting with his property. Merely to deceive a person into failing to attend a party, for example, would not amount to fraud.

The law will ignore some false pretences – for example "trade puffs". Manufacturers and retailers who puff up or boast about the merits of their goods are not committing fraud so long as it does not amount to deliberate MISREPRESENTATION of the facts.

Examples of criminal fraud include:

- A person paying for goods with a cheque which he knows will not be honoured by his bank.
- A window cleaner who is paid after falsely claiming to have cleaned windows while the householder was out.
- An antique dealer selling, as genuine, antiques which he knows are copies.
- A person obtaining a bank overdraft or credit, by falsely pretending to be financially sound.
- A person obtaining services – for instance, those of a solicitor or accountant – by falsely pretending that he intends to pay for them.

An accused person can defend himself against a charge of fraud by showing

HAULED OVER THE COALS

A practical result brought about by deceit may be enough to complete the crime of fraud, even if the person deceived has not been harmed in any way.

Adcock was a coal-miner. He and the other miners had a contract which entitled them to a guaranteed weekly wage plus a bonus for producing more than a minimum number of containers of coal.

Adcock marked a container as his own, although it belonged to another miner. But during that week, neither of them exceeded the minimum number of containers needed to obtain the bonus. So Adcock's deception did not affect his wage, or the wage of the other miner, and caused no loss to his employer.

Adcock was charged and convicted of fraud. On appeal he argued that he should not have been convicted because no-one had suffered through his deceit.

DECISION

The High Court dismissed Adcock's appeal. It was enough that his deceit had made the employers do something which they would not otherwise have done, namely to credit him with another miner's coal.

that his alleged victim was not influenced by the pretence or knew that it was false.

Many special offences of fraud have been created by Act of Parliament – for example, frauds connected with bankruptcy, food and drugs, weights and measures, coinage, and social security. These statutory frauds do not usually require that a practical result has been brought about by the deception: for example, it is an offence merely to impersonate a police officer even although nothing results from the impersonation.

The penalty for fraud is at the discretion of the court, within its sentencing limits. In the case of a statutory fraud, the penalty will usually be in the relevant Act of Parliament.

FREE MILK

Help for families with low incomes

Families who are drawing SUPPLEMENTARY BENEFIT or FAMILY INCOME SUPPLEMENT, or who have a low income, are entitled to 1 pint of free milk a day for each child under school age and for an expectant mother. They are also entitled to free supplies of vitamins A, D, and C.

A parent not receiving supplementary benefit or family income supplement who believes that the family income may be low enough to qualify should obtain leaflet MV 11, which gives the income levels, from a post office or social security office. Fill in the attached claim form and post or take it to the local social security office.

How to obtain tokens for free milk

Families who qualify for free supplies receive tokens from the Department of Health and Social Security. The tokens can be exchanged with a milkman for a pint of milk a day for an expectant mother and for each child between 1 and 5 years 1 month (or older if the child is not at school). If the child is under 1 year, a mother can obtain 1 pint of milk a day for herself, if she is breast-feeding, or 2 packs of dried milk each week from a child health clinic.

Tokens can also be exchanged at the clinic for vitamin tablets (for expectant or nursing mothers) and vitamin drops (for children up to the age limit mentioned above).

Families on supplementary benefit or family income supplement receive the tokens by post when they are sent their order books by the Department of Health and Social Security.

If these are not sent, parents should write to the local social security office or, if they are receiving family income supplement, to the Department of Health and Social Security, Family Income Supplement, Poulton-le-Fylde, Blackpool FY6 8NW.

Milk for children in day care

Children attending a day nursery or play group approved by the local authority, or being looked after by an approved child minder, are entitled to one-third of a pint of free milk on each day that they attend for 2 hours or more. Day-care milk is given in addition to any free milk the family may already be getting.

Organisers of day nurseries and play groups and child minders should apply to the local social work department.

Children of 5 to 16 who are too handicapped, physically or mentally, to attend an ordinary or special school are entitled to a pint of free milk a day. To claim, obtain form FW20 from the local social security office.

School milk The duty to provide free school milk was abolished in 1980. However, an education authority can continue to supply milk if it wishes, and can make a charge for it. *See:* SCHOOL MEALS AND MILK

FREE SAMPLE

When goods are given away free

Anyone who receives a free sample of goods is not entitled to replacement or compensation for its value if the sample is faulty.

A free sample is not a sale, for no money is paid or payable. The recipient does not therefore have any of the rights of a buyer.

NO CATCH

When a free sample is given, the recipient has none of the rights of someone who buys goods.

However, if the free sample is so faulty as to cause injury or damage, anyone who suffers may be able to sue the manufacturer or supplier if they have been negligent. *See:* NEGLIGENCE

FRINGE BENEFIT

When tax must be paid on extras

Many firms give their employees fringe benefits in the form of cars, accommodation, medical insurance, luncheon vouchers and cash handouts. Tax should be paid on almost all of these benefits, though the form in which they are given can reduce the tax liability.

In general, tax liability is reduced when the benefit consists of an article or gift rather than cash.

Secretary's dress An employer buys his secretary a new dress or outfit for £50 so that she will look smart at the office. She wears it – but he remains the owner of the dress.

After 12 months the employer gives the secretary the outfit. Its value then as second-hand clothing is £30 – and that is the amount on which the secretary should pay tax.

When two levels of taxation apply

Employees are divided into two groups for the taxation of fringe benefits. Different rules apply to each.

1. Higher-paid employees – generally, anyone earning over a certain amount (£8,500 or more in the 1984–5 tax year); and any director, irrespective of his earnings, unless he works full-time for the company, has 5 per cent or less of the shares and earns under £8,500.

2. Lower-paid employees – generally anyone earning less than £8,500.

Higher-paid employees are taxed on what it costs the employer to provide the benefit. Lower-paid employees are taxed on the secondhand value, if any, of the benefit.

ON THE FRINGE

Most fringe benefits received by employees are taxable. The amount of tax payable depends on the kind of benefit received and the employee's level of earnings.

In the case of higher-paid employees, when an asset is loaned to the employee rather than given to him, the annual benefit is measured at 20 per cent of the cost of the asset to the employer. Thus, if a television costing £400 is loaned by the company to an employee, the annual taxable benefit is £80. The rules are different for the loan of a company car.

HOW TAX IS ASSESSED ON PRIVATE USE OF A COMPANY CAR

Scale rates apply to cars used for more than 2,500 miles a year for business purposes. One and a half, or half, times the scale rate applies in certain other cases

The Inland Revenue puts an annual cash value on the private use of a company car, the amount depending on how much the car is used, its age, engine capacity and original cost. This amount is then subject to tax.

The amounts shown below took effect on April 6, 1984.

CARS ORIGINALLY COSTING UP TO £16,000

	Cylinder capacity	Taxable benefit
Vehicle less than 4 years old	1300 cc or less	£375
	1301–1800 cc	£480
	Over 1800 cc	£750
Vehicle more than 4 years old	1300 cc or less	£250
	1301–1800 cc	£320
	Over 1800 cc	£500

CARS ORIGINALLY COSTING £16,000–£24,000

	Cylinder capacity	Taxable benefit
Under 4 years old	Any	£1,100
Over 4 years old	Any	£740

CARS ORIGINALLY COSTING MORE THAN £24,000

	Cylinder capacity	Taxable benefit
Under 4 years old	Any	£1,725
Over 4 years old	Any	£1,150

Having a company car

A company car that is also used privately is treated as a taxable benefit only if issued to a higher-paid employee. A lower-paid employee does not have to pay tax on a company car unless its provision is related to a cut in pay.

The basic measure of benefit is called the 'scale', which quantifies the annual benefit according to engine size or cost of the car, and its age. These benefits are usually increased annually.

If the car is used for only 2,500 miles or less of business use a year, the benefit is one and a half times the scale rate. Second and subsequent company cars are also charged at one and a half times the scale benefit, irrespective of business use. If the business use in a year is 18,000 miles or more, the scale benefit is halved.

Free petrol If a higher-paid employee is supplied with any free petrol for a company car which is also used privately, the petrol is treated as a taxable benefit. Tax is paid, not on the value of the petrol, but on a fixed amount that

HOW THE TAXMAN TREATS COMPANY 'PERKS'

Different taxation levels depending on type of benefit

If an employee receives fringe benefits from his company in addition to his wage or salary, in nearly all cases he is liable to pay income tax on all or part of their value, depending on the type of benefit being enjoyed and the employee's earnings.

Benefit	How it is taxed
Firm's car used not more than 2,500 miles a year for business, by a 'higher paid' employee	1½ times scale benefit.
Firm's car used more than 2,500 miles a year for business, by a 'higher paid' employee	Scale benefit.
Pool car	No tax payable.
Loans from employer at favourable rates of interest	Tax payable on the difference between the commercial rate and the rate charged unless it is less than £200, or if the interest is allowed as tax relief. Loans to 'higher-paid' employees are taxed unless used for certain purposes. A loan to buy a family home would not be taxed, but one to buy a boat used for leisure would.
Housing or accommodation paid for by firm	Tax payable on the gross annual value of the tenancy, plus any costs paid by the firm such as rates and heating. Tax relief if the employee has to live in the house to do his job.
Television sets, washing machines or other consumer goods	Tax is payable on the amount paid by the employer for the article if it is new, but on the value at the time if the gift is secondhand. Secondhand goods given to 'higher-paid' employees may be taxed more heavily.
Medical insurance	Tax free.
Luncheon vouchers	Taxable over 15p.
Cash or transport vouchers	Full value is taxable.
Staff canteen meals	Tax free if the canteen is open to all staff without distinction of status.
Travelling and entertaining expenses	Tax free if the whole amount is spent on the employee's behalf.
Removal expenses	Tax free.
Credit cards	Since April 6, 1982, net cost to employer of providing credit cards for employee is taxable.

depends on the car's engine capacity.

In the 1984–5 tax year, the amounts were: £375 (1300 cc or less); £480 (1301 cc to 1800 cc); and £750 (over 1800 cc). If business use of the car in the tax year is at least 18,000 miles, the amounts are halved.

When a house is provided with the job

Self-contained accommodation provided for a worker is tax free only when it is essential for the worker to occupy the house in order to do his job.

For workers such as hotel staff who live on the premises, the accommodation is tax free if it is provided free. But if a deduction is made from salary for the cost of the accommodation, the gross salary is taxed, with no allowance against the accommodation charge.

Take, for example, the head waiter of a holiday hotel who lives on the premises and is paid £6,000 a year salary. If, say, £600 a year is deducted from his salary for accommodation, he pays tax on the full £6,000.

If, however, he is paid only £5,400 a year and is given free accommodation, he will be taxed only on £5,400. It is always better to have the free accommodation and the lower salary.

When the cost of removal may be reimbursed

No tax is payable on removal expenses paid by a company to an employee who is moved to a new area.

Such tax-free expenses can include legal costs for buying and selling a house, removal services and refitting of carpets – or even new carpets if he has to fit larger rooms.

If an employee is moved to an area where housing is more expensive than where he previously lived, he can be paid a reasonable rent allowance, tax free, for about 5 years.

When free meals are provided

If an employer provides subsidised or free meals in a staff canteen, the employees are not taxed on the value of those meals – provided that the service is available to all members of the staff irrespective of rank, and there is no attempt to provide better facilities for certain groups such as directors and senior management.

If a dining-room is provided for the exclusive use of the directors, therefore, they should declare the value of the meals they receive and pay tax.

When a meal allowance is paid by the employer

When an employer reimburses an employee in cash for the cost of meals incurred by him even while on duty, the employee must pay tax on the amount received.

Thus, if a clerk is required to work overtime and is paid, say, £1.50 by his employer to defray the cost of buying an evening meal near his office, the £1.50 is taxable, and the employee cannot claim for any tax relief for the cost of the meal he has purchased.

In some cases, however, when standard payments are made to employees regularly obliged to buy meals away from home and the employer's base, Inland Revenue may agree with the appropriate trade union or professional body to allow some part of the payments tax free.

When overnight expenses are reimbursed

An employee's expenses for a stay away from home overnight are not taxable when they are reimbursed by his employer. This would cover the cost of accommodation, travel, reasonable entertainment, evening meal and breakfast. Inland Revenue does not normally allow the cost of lunches as tax free – even when the employee is away overnight.

Any vouchers other than luncheon vouchers – for example, cash vouchers or those for specific goods and services – are taxable on their full value.

FUEL BILL

What to do if a bill cannot be paid at once

Anyone who is worried about paying gas or electricity bills should contact the local gas or electricity office and ask about paying on easier terms.

The local gas or electricity office will give advice on easier-payment schemes. For example, payment can be made through a budget account, by which the probable cost for the year is divided into monthly or weekly instalments and any balance on either side is cleared at the end of the year.

Otherwise, special savings stamps, produced by the gas and electricity authorities, can be purchased and collected in a book by the customer, to be put towards a bill.

Help from your social work or social security office

Someone who cannot pay even on easier terms may be able to get help from his local social security office or social work department.

If he is not in full-time work, and receives (or is entitled to) SUPPLEMENTARY BENEFIT, he may be able to get extra money for heating (see below).

If he is in full-time work and therefore not entitled to claim supplementary benefit, and cannot pay a fuel bill, he can ask the social work department for help – but he should only do so after seeking help from the fuel board. If lack of heating or lighting will cause danger to life or health, the department may make an emergency lump-sum payment towards the bill.

This lump-sum payment is made under section 12 of the Social Work (Scotland) Act 1968. There is no right to such a payment: it is for the social work department to decide whether to make it.

Section 12 help can only be given if there are children or old people in the home, or someone who is sick or disabled. The department may consider assisting with the bill or entering into negotiations with the fuel board. If payment is made, all or part of it may have to be repaid.

Local charities, on the advice of a social worker, may make a payment to clear a fuel bill for an elderly, sick or disabled person.

Direct payment to the fuel board

If a person on supplementary benefit has been unable to budget for the cost of fuel, and owes £27 or more to the gas or electricity board, which cannot be cleared by a lump-sum payment of benefit, the social security adjudication officer may decide that part of his weekly benefit should be deducted and paid direct to the fuel board. This can be done either at the person's own request or at the discretion of the adjudication officer – but only if, in the officer's opinion, it would be in the interests of the person and his family, if any. The fuel board will then agree not to disconnect the fuel supply.

The deduction consists of a payment – usually £2.70 a week – towards the debt and payment of a further sum towards the estimated cost of current weekly consumption.

Preventing disconnection of gas and electricity

The electricity and gas industries operate a code of practice aimed at preventing disconnection of fuel supply for unpaid bills, but only in certain circumstances.

The code states that if a consumer is drawing supplementary or unemployment benefit, or if he is blind, severely sick or disabled, or if all the people in the house are old age pensioners, the gas or electricity office should be told about any difficulty in paying. The local social security office should also be contacted.

A consumer who has a child under 11, or is drawing FAMILY INCOME SUP-

INCREASES IN SUPPLEMENTARY BENEFIT PAYMENTS TO PROVIDE FOR EXTRA HEATING

Ill or elderly beneficiaries qualify for more help

If someone who is receiving supplementary benefit has to pay higher heating bills because of illness or frailty or, for example, because a house is unusually difficult to keep warm in winter, he should ask for an extra weekly payment.

Reason for extra heating	Increase
Mobility restricted because of old age or frailty	£2.05
Chronic illness – for example, arthritis or bronchitis	£2.05
Accommodation difficult to heat – for example, because it is damp	£2.05
Accommodation exceptionally difficult to heat	£5.05
Housebound, or unable to go out without help	£5.05
Serious physical illness, requiring extra warmth	£5.05
Serious physical illness that requires constant day and night room temperature	£5.05
Confined to bed, or unable to walk without help, because of physical illness, and in need of extra heating day and night	£5.05

PLEMENT, and is in difficulty with his bill, should also tell the gas or electricity office and contact the social work department.

If the social security office or social work department is asked to help, the fuel supply will not be disconnected for 14 days, or possibly longer.

Supply will not be disconnected if the consumer agrees to pay his bills regularly and to pay off arrears by instalments within a reasonable time. Nor will supply be disconnected if a prepayment meter is installed, set to collect the debt within a reasonable time.

Supply cannot be disconnected between October 1 and March 31 if all the people living in the house who have an income are old age pensioners – except where they are clearly able to pay their bills and have not done so.

If someone moves without paying the bill

If you move into a house, flat or other accommodation, and the previous occupier has left without paying a fuel bill, you are not responsible for seeing that the bill is paid. The gas or electricity board is not entitled to disconnect your supply on the ground that the previous occupier failed to pay.

When you move out, you must give the gas or electricity board at least 24 hours' notice. If you fail to do so you may have to pay for any gas or electricity used on the property until the meter is next read or your change of address has been notified by a new occupier requesting a supply. *See:* ELECTRICITY SUPPLY; GAS SUPPLY

Extra supplementary benefit

Anyone on supplementary benefit may be entitled to extra help with heating bills. This can take one of two forms:

Increase in weekly payments Weekly supplementary benefit payments are increased in cases where fuel costs are likely to be heavy. If this is because the claimant or his wife is 70 or over, or there are children under 5 in the house, or because one or more of them needs extra warmth as a result of illness or restricted mobility, the increase is usually £2.05 a week; but in the case of serious illness or disability it is £5.05.

A person receiving MOBILITY ALLOWANCE, ATTENDANCE ALLOWANCE or constant attendance allowance with DISABLEMENT BENEFIT is also entitled to an increase of £5.05.

Someone whose house is difficult to heat adequately is entitled to a heating increase of £2.05; if the house is exceptionally difficult to heat adequately, the increase is £5.05. If a heating increase for illness or restricted mobility is also payable, the total heating increase is £5.05.

Weekly increases are also given where the home is centrally heated. The amount depends on the number of rooms. If there are not more than 4 rooms, ignoring a bathroom, lavatory or hall, the increase is £2.05. For more than 4 rooms it is £4.10. But a central-heating increase will not be paid in addition to a heating increase given for other reasons – only the higher of the two increases will be given.

Lump-sum payment A person receiving supplementary benefit, whose fuel bill comes to more than the amount he has put aside to pay for it, as a result of abnormally high consumption in a period of exceptionally severe weather, is entitled to a lump-sum payment to cover the cost of the excess over normal consumption. This is reduced by the amount of any capital over £500.

A lump sum is also payable where the reason for not putting aside enough to pay the fuel bill is the cost of running an unfamiliar heating system – for example, underfloor central heating. In this case, the lump sum is half the fuel costs incurred for any period during the first 6 months' use of the system.

A lump sum will also be paid to cover a fuel bill if this is the only way to prevent serious risk or damage to health or to safety.

A person may not be getting supplementary benefit which he could have claimed – such as an increase for heating. Or he may have spent money put aside for fuel bills on some other need for which a lump sum could have been paid. If so, a lump-sum payment can be made towards a fuel bill he cannot reasonably meet.

If someone on supplementary benefit has got into difficulties with fuel bills, a payment will be made to cover the charge for installing a prepayment meter, if that is considered necessary, or for reconnecting the fuel supply after arrangements have been made for payment of the debt by either a lump-sum payment or deductions from the weekly benefit. *See:* SUPPLEMENTARY BENEFIT

FUNERAL

Making the arrangements after a death in the family

No one has a legal right to insist on how his or her body should be disposed of after death. Those who have to arrange a funeral are not bound to carry out any wish expressed, such as a preference for cremation or burial – even if the wish is set out in a will. In practice, however, such wishes are usually respected.

If you have a special request about the disposal of your body after death, put it in writing – either in your will, or in a letter to the EXECUTOR and your family – and tell them about it orally.

If you want part or all of your body to be used for medical purposes, you must say so in a declaration written separately from your will and signed by two witnesses who can be members of your family. The declaration is legally binding on your heirs and executors, and you should send a copy of it to any hospital or institution which you wish to benefit.

If you particularly do not want your body to be so used, make your wishes clear in your will. Executors or next of kin cannot give permission for the medical use of your body if you have made your objection known. *See:* TRANSPLANT; DEATH

Making the arrangements for a funeral

A body must not be disposed of until a registrar's certificate has been issued. *See:* DEATH, Registration of

If a dead person has left a will, it is the duty of his executors to arrange the funeral. If there is no will, or if the executors are not immediately available, the funeral must be arranged by the person – whether owner or tenant – who occupies the premises in which the body is lying.

If the body is in a public institution, such as a hospital, those in charge of the institution normally ask the dead person's relatives to take responsibility – and will arrange the funeral only if that request is refused.

When there are no relatives or executors, and the person did not die in a hospital or other public institution, it is the duty of the district or islands council to arrange a funeral.

The local social work authority – a regional or islands council – can arrange the funeral of someone in their care, or to whom they gave assistance.

Where a funeral can be held

A funeral, by burial or cremation, can be public or private: it can be held at sea, or by any other method of disposal that does not cause a nuisance or health hazard. It is usual to employ a funeral director, but executors or relatives can organise the funeral themselves.

Choosing a funeral director

Having decided what type of funeral is required, the executors or relatives may if they wish seek itemised cost estimates from several funeral directors and compare their charges and services. The basic minimum offered for a local funeral – a simple coffin, hearse, one following car, bearers and the services of the funeral director in arranging ceremonial details and the necessary certificates – costs from about £275 upwards. That does not include the burial or cremation fee – or the cost of more cars, flowers, obituary notices, a headstone and other extras.

If you have been unable to compare funeral directors' costs and subsequently feel that you have been overcharged – or if the funeral director has been negligent – bring your complaint to his notice. If you do not get satisfaction complain to the National Association of Funeral Directors, if he is a member. Its address is 57 Doughty Street, London WC1N 2NE.

The association's disciplinary and conciliation committee will hear your case and can recommend damages or a refund. If their recommendation does not satisfy you, ARBITRATION can be arranged through the Institute of Arbitrators.

If the funeral director is not a NAFD member, or if you are not satisfied with the decision, complain to the trading standards officer at your regional or islands council.

When embalming is required A body may be preserved for cosmetic and hygienic purposes, by replacing the blood with a chemical, formalin. The funeral director should ask the executors or relatives if they have any objection to this process.

Embalming must not be carried out until the registrar's certificate has been issued, as it may obscure the cause of death.

Paying for the funeral

The government DEATH GRANT – a maximum of £30 – covers only a small part of the cost of a funeral, but other financial help may be available to those in need. *See:* FATAL INJURY; SUPPLEMENTARY BENEFIT

The funeral director's bill has priority over all other debts of the ESTATE except tax claims and must be paid by the executors before they distribute any legacies. For tax purposes, it should be submitted as a debt of the estate, even though it was not incurred by the dead person himself.

If a funeral is arranged by a hospital or local authority – in the absence of relatives or executors – it is entitled to recover the cost from the estate, if any, and to receive the death grant.

Arranging a burial

Most cemeteries are owned and managed by district and islands councils. But some, especially in large cities, are owned by private companies or the Roman Catholic Church. Churchyards of Church of Scotland churches are now the responsibility of local authorities who maintain them and arrange burials.

Before a burial can take place a lair or grave-space must be purchased. It can, however, be used for several burials up to a maximum, usually 6, laid down by the cemetery or churchyard authorities. A lair may be bought in advance of the need for it arising. The right to burial in a certain lair is demonstrated by possession of a certificate. People arranging a burial should look for any lair certificate in the possession of the dead person.

Cemetery authorities impose various restrictions on monuments to maintain the appearance of the grounds or facilitate grass-cutting. You should therefore check with them before ordering any memorial or planting shrubs. It is usually possible to pay a sum for the upkeep of the lair in perpetuity.

Closing a burial place

A petition to the sheriff to close a churchyard or cemetery may be drawn up by 2 householders residing within a hundred yards of it or by the local authority or by 10 local ratepayers. They must claim that it is a danger to health or offensive or contrary to decency.

After the petition has been advertised, the sheriff holds a public inquiry and, if he accepts the allegations, issues a statement of his findings. The burial ground will then be closed by an Order in Council. The district council must provide a suitable alternative burial ground.

Special rules for cremation

Special safeguards must be observed before a body can be cremated, to ensure that there are no unresolved doubts about the cause of death.

When the death is not reported to the procurator fiscal When someone has died in ordinary, unsuspicious circumstances there is no need to report the

AN UNDERTAKING BY THE UNDERTAKERS

Since 1979 the public has been protected by a code of practice that the 2,200 members of the National Association of Funeral Directors (including CWS Co-operative Funeral Services) agreed in consultation with the Office of Fair Trading. Members of the association are pledged to:

- Offer a basic, simple funeral service.
- Give a written estimate of all funeral charges and an itemised invoice.
- Ensure that advertising is clear, honest and in good taste.
- Provide full and fair information about services and prices and offer guidance on certification and registration of death, social security benefits and the application of insurance policies whenever this is appropriate.
- Provide speedy and sympathetic handling of complaints.
- Provide suitable training for management in client relations.
- Display the association's symbol on the premises.

death to the PROCURATOR FISCAL. Instead, if the body is to be cremated, the funeral director will provide a copy of Form A, the application form for cremation.

It must be completed by the deceased's executor, nearest relative or by the person arranging the funeral. It has to be counter-signed by a householder to whom the applicant is known.

The doctor who treated the deceased during his last illness, or was his usual doctor – although not necessarily the one who signed the death certificate – must identify the body and complete Form B, giving information about the deceased's treatment and manner of death.

A confirmatory certificate, Form C, must be completed by another doctor who is not a partner of the first doctor, nor a relative of the deceased. He must have seen the body and made a careful external examination. The doctor who completes Form B normally arranges for another to complete Form C. The two doctors must each sign a separate declaration that they do not suspect that the deceased died a violent or unnatural death, or believe that the cause of death is unknown, or that further inquiry is desirable. If an inquiry is necessary the procurator fiscal will carry it out.

The certifying doctors are entitled to charge a fee which is paid by the funeral director, who adds it to his total funeral bill.

When the death is reported to the procurator fiscal If a death is reported by the doctor or by the registrar of deaths, the procurator fiscal makes his own inquiries or asks the police to do so. When he is fully satisfied, he issues Form E which permits cremation at a named crematorium. If he is not satisfied he may release the body for burial only or order a post-mortem.

Form F, the authority to cremate, is the final stage. This form is issued by the medical referee to the crematorium after he has seen Forms B and C or E. Each crematorium has a medical referee – a local doctor who checks all applications for cremation. If the medical referee is not satisfied with the information on the forms he can refuse permission to cremate.

If death occurs abroad and it is desired to have the body cremated in Scotland, the consent of the Scottish Home and Health Department must be obtained. The funeral director should arrange this.

Most crematoria in Scotland are owned and run by district councils. A few are privately owned. The charge for an adult cremation is between £25 and £115.

The person instructing the funeral will be asked what kind of service is desired and there may be a fee for this. He will also have to decide what is to be done with the ashes.

FURNISHED TENANCY

How the law protects tenants

Since August 14, 1974, tenants of furnished as well as unfurnished accommodation have been protected by the Rent (Scotland) Act – though there are important exceptions. Protected tenants usually have security of tenure and are entitled to apply to a rent officer to have a fair rent fixed. *See:* EVICTION; RENT PROTECTION

Unprotected tenants

A tenancy – furnished or unfurnished – will not be protected if the landlord lives in the same house, or in another flat in the same building – providing it is a building *converted* into flats – and there has been a landlord there since the tenancy began.

This rule applies to all tenancies granted after August 14, 1974; and to all furnished tenancies granted before that date, if the landlord was resident on that date. It does not apply if, immediately before the tenancy was granted, the tenant was a protected tenant of the same house, or another one in the same building.

However, the tenant may still be able to get some temporary security of tenure from a rent assessment committee or a sheriff. *See:* EVICTION

A tenant of furnished accommodation who is not protected under the Rent (Scotland) Act, and whose landlord does not live on the premises, may also be able to get temporary security if part of the rent is for the use of furniture. Where accommodation is let furnished, part of the rent will be legally considered to be in payment for the use of the furniture.

When a premium is required

Some landlords ask prospective tenants to pay a deposit, described as 'returnable', against any loss or damage to furniture during the tenancy. Provided the deposit does not exceed 2 months' rent and is *genuinely* returnable, it will not be an illegal charge. If these conditions are not met, the charge is illegal and the landlord can be fined up to £400. *See:* KEY MONEY

A tenant can refuse to pay an illegal charge, but if he does, he may not get the property. It may be best to pay the sum demanded and then claim the money back from the landlord. If he refuses to pay, the tenant should make it clear that he knows that he is protected against exploitation by the Rent (Scotland) Act 1984. He should also say that he is willing to take court action to recover the money.

Selling the furniture It is within the law for a landlord to sell the furniture to the tenant at a reasonable price – the tenancy then becomes unfurnished. However, if the furniture is sold at an excessive price, as a condition of granting or continuing the tenancy, the excess will be treated as an illegal charge.

When furniture is damaged

A tenant is not liable for any damage caused to furniture through normal wear and tear, or for repairs which are necessary as a result. He has to pay, however, for any deliberate damage or for damage caused through negligence. If necessary, the landlord can sue for compensation in the sheriff court.

An unprotected tenant can be evicted for damaging or neglecting furniture. So can a protected tenant, if the sheriff thinks it is reasonable to order eviction.

FURNITURE STORAGE

When you leave furniture in a store

If you leave furniture at a warehouse or depository for storage, you enter into a CONTRACT with the owners. Before doing so, look carefully at their conditions of storage as they may try to restrict your rights and increase theirs.

The conditions are normally printed on the quotation you receive and they may be repeated on the agreement form you eventually sign. Conditions to beware of are those that seek to exclude any liability for loss or damage.

Although the depository is bound to take reasonable care of your furniture, you should make your own arrangements for insuring it against fire and theft, and any other likely or possible risk that you may be aware of, such as flooding, while it is in store – unless the storage company agrees to arrange such cover for you.

It will not be liable to compensate you if the furniture is damaged in a fire that is not the fault of the company or its servants. Nor will it have to reimburse you if the furniture is stolen – provided that it can show that it took reasonable precautions against theft.

Even if the loss or damage is the storage company's fault, it may try to shelter behind an exemption clause in its printed conditions. That can be effective only if the clause is fair and reasonable, as required by the Unfair Contract Terms Act 1977. *See:* UNFAIR CONTRACT

GAMBLING

Where and when you can place a bet

It is legal to bet on cards, horse and greyhound racing, bingo games, dice games, a FOOTBALL POOL, prize competition or properly licensed lottery, but there are complicated laws governing how you can bet, and restricting the places where gambling can be carried on.

It is illegal, for example, for any type of betting to be carried on in unlicensed premises or in the street, and no one under the age of 18 can bet – except privately in his own home.

In general, the law aims to restrict gambling to such places as casinos, horse-race courses, dog tracks, betting shops, bingo halls and private clubs that have been licensed by the local authority and are controlled by laws aimed at protecting the gambler.

Gambling is permitted in public houses only on games of skill such as darts, shove ha'penny or chess and on games of chance such as cribbage and dominoes.

There are two ways to bet:

- Gaming – which is betting with other players in a game of chance, such as roulette or cards, or in a pool, such as a football pool, from which a fixed, or unfixed, sum will be paid to anyone who wins.
- Wagering – which is a bet struck between two people on the outcome of an event, such as a horse race or a general election, in which one of them will win and the other will lose.

Debts incurred in gaming or wagering cannot be recovered through the courts.

CONTROLLING THE PEOPLE WHO CONTROL GAMING

The Gaming Board was set up by the Government in 1968 to control all gaming in Britain's casinos and clubs.

The Board has 40 full-time inspectors who keep a thorough check on the personal and financial background of all the people involved – of the operators themselves, the financial backers, the croupiers and the dealers.

Casinos need a certificate of consent from the Gaming Board before they can apply to the local licensing board for a gaming licence. The Board issues certificates only to casinos where the operators and staff have its approval.

The Board can withdraw its consent later if it finds it was given any false information, and can order a casino to re-apply for consent if it changes hands or if any major changes are made at the club.

The Board – and anyone else – can also object when the casino makes its annual application for a renewal of its gaming licence.

A person or company applying for a certificate of consent from the Board can apply at a personal hearing and be represented by a solicitor. If the Board refuses consent it does not have to give any reasons and can keep confidential any information given to it by private individuals.

OBJECTING TO A CASINO LICENCE

Gaming licences are renewed annually by the local licensing board. Applications are usually heard in May, but the club must advertise its application in the local press in March.

Anyone who wants to object must send two copies of a statement, briefly outlining his reasons, to the board's clerk before April 15. He is then told the date of the hearing which he can attend in person or through his lawyer.

An objector has the right to organise opposition to a licence – perhaps by lobbying councillors or writing to the local press for support.

The board can reject a gaming licence application for a number of reasons, including noise, nuisance, unsuitable premises, inadequate parking facilities or the existence of other gaming clubs in the area. It can also take objections into account by granting a licence but imposing specific restrictions on it.

Someone making a frivolous objection may be ordered to pay expenses.

Gambling in a casino

Casinos are gambling clubs in which only the players taking part in games of chance can lose: the clubs can never lose. They must have a certificate from the Gaming Board and a licence from the local licensing board of the district or islands council.

Casinos operate two types of betting games:

Unequal chance Games such as roulette, blackjack and the various forms of baccarat (punto banco, chemin de fer), in which the casino, or 'house', runs the bank. This acts like a bookmaker, offering odds to the players, who bet with the bank on the outcome of the game. The odds always favour the bank.

In roulette, for example, there are 36 numbers to choose from, but there is also one zero on the wheel which a gambler can also bet on. The odds against any number's coming up are, therefore, 37 to 1. The greatest odds the house ever offers is 35 to 1. In the past some roulette wheels had two zeros on them, which put the odds more in the house's favour, but that system was outlawed by the Gaming Act 1968.

Equal chance Games such as backgammon, poker and dice games in which all the players have a mathematically equal chance of winning. If there is a bank, each player must be given an equal chance of holding it by being offered the bank.

The employees or operators of a casino offering games of equal chance are forbidden by law to take part in the games, except as banker.

Who can play Anyone wanting to play in a casino must be at least 18 and must have been a member for at least 48 hours. He must also have signed, at least 48 hours before he can play, an 'intent to gamble' declaration.

Those rules do not apply to members' guests, however, and there is no legal restriction on the number of guests a member may take into a casino. Each club usually imposes its own limits.

The permitted hours of play vary from area to area.

Casino members pay an annual subscription and may also be charged entrance and table fees.

No credit available

Casino operators and their staffs are forbidden to lend money or give any form of credit to allow someone to gamble or cover his losses. But anyone not connected with the club can lend money for such purposes.

A gambler can buy gambling chips at a casino and pay for them by cheque, but the casino must pay the cheque into its own bank account within two days. If the player wins, he must not be given back his own cheque, but must be paid in cash or given a cheque by the casino management.

Failure to observe that basic rule can lead to a casino's losing its gaming licence – and so to its closure.

Gambling in a proprietary club

Some commercial, privately owned gaming clubs specialise in just one or two games, such as backgammon and baccarat, and are not generally known as casinos. However, they need a full casino licence if they want to charge a profitable entry and participation fee.

Without a licence, they are limited to a total charge of 10p per person per day.

Betting with a bookmaker

Bookmakers are companies or individuals who take wagers from the public. They do not need a certificate from the Gaming Board, but they do need a licence from the local licensing board to open a betting shop.

Bookmakers make their own odds and offer bets on horse racing, dog racing, football matches, beauty contests, general elections – in fact almost anything where the outcome is still to be decided.

A gambler can bet with a bookmaker on credit, by telephone or by post, or at a racecourse. Or he can walk into a betting shop and place a cash bet. Neither party has any way of enforcing payment by law.

If a gambler lays a bet by credit with a bookmaker and loses, the bookmaker cannot sue him. He may, quite legitimately, send debt collectors to get the money from him, but these collectors must not make unlawful threats to the client to obtain payment. *See:* DEBT COLLECTOR

If the bookmaker defaults

If a bookmaker refuses to pay out on a win, there is nothing the punter can do legally to get the money from him. In practice, failure to pay by a bookmaker is unlikely – unless the bookmaker has gone bankrupt or disputes the validity of the bet.

One of the functions of the National Association of Bookmakers is to uphold its members' reputation. It can order a member to pay out a winning bet. If he still refuses, he can be expelled from the Association, and be blacklisted.

A blacklisted bookmaker would find it virtually impossible to get permission to take bets on a racecourse, and he would almost certainly be refused a licence to open a betting shop.

Similarly, any gambler who refused to settle his account with a bookmaker might find himself listed by the Association, making it impossible for him to lay a bet with an official bookmaker.

When there is a dispute

Any dispute over horse-race betting is adjudicated by Tattersall's Committee, a semi-official body set up about 200 years ago and consisting of mem-

THE EMPLOYEE WHO TOOK BETS

Gambling is prohibited in unlicensed places, whether indoors or outdoors. The word 'place' has been widely interpreted by the courts.

David Darrah was a shipyard worker in Greenock. During his lunch-break from 12 to 1 he regularly took bets from fellow workers in a shed used to house machinery.

When a search was made one day, Mr Darrah was found to be in possession of a number of betting slips, pay-out slips and I.O.U's, two newspapers and a sum of cash.

He admitted carrying on betting transactions in the shed, but argued that he could not be convicted of 'using a place for betting', as he had no control over the shed, but merely permission to eat his lunch there.

DECISION

When Mr Darrah was found not guilty in the sheriff court, the Crown appealed, and Mr Darrah was convicted in the High Court. The court decided that any place which is reasonably localised and defined can be a 'place' used for betting within the meaning of the Act.

THE PUNTER WHO LOST HIS WINNINGS

The courts will not order payment of any gambling debt.

Mr Charles Robertson was in the habit of placing bets with an Edinburgh bookmaker called Ernest Balfour. One morning he won £34 on a horse called 'Swift and True', and followed this up by winning £10 on 'Scottish Horse' the same afternoon.

The bookmaker acknowledged the debt, paid part of it and asked for a fortnight's grace to pay the rest. Mr Robertson agreed to this, and promised to keep quiet about the debt in the meantime. After the fortnight was up, the bookmaker refused to pay and Mr Robertson sued him for his winnings.

DECISION

The court refused to grant decree for recovery of the debt. This was a gambling transaction which the courts would not enforce.

bers of the public and people from the racing world.

Both bookmakers and gamblers can take disputes to the committee. It cannot legally enforce its decision, but it can tell the bookmaker and gambler whether the bet was valid, and it can ask the loser to pay.

Because of the committee's close connection with the authorities who run racing and because its opinion is held by them as final in any dispute, a gambler or bookmaker who failed to obey a committee ruling could be banned from all British race tracks.

A gambler or a bookmaker who takes a dispute to Tattersall's has to pay a fee of between £1 and £75, depending on the amount at stake in the disputed bet.

Most horse-race tracks where bookmakers operate have a man known as a ring inspector, who can adjudicate in any dispute, and who can have a bookmaker or a gambler expelled from the course.

Greyhound tracks also have advisory committees to settle disputes, with powers to ban bookmakers and gamblers.

Betting on the Tote

The Totalisator Board is a state-run betting agency which operates POOL BETTING on horse races, and is subject to different rules from those that apply to bookmakers. Any profits the Tote makes are reinvested in racing.

The Tote cannot lose, because it deducts a fixed percentage for running costs from the total amount of money bet on any one race, and shares out the remainder among all the winning bets placed with it.

Greyhound tracks run their own totalisator betting pool.

How betting shops are controlled

A bookmaker needs a licence from the local licensing board to open a betting shop. Applications are heard usually every 3 months, and are advertised first in the local press.

An objector has 14 days after the day of the advertisement to send two copies of a statement to the board's clerk. Otherwise he is not allowed to attend the hearing.

The board can refuse a licence on various grounds – for example, if a sufficient number of other bookmakers are already in business in the area or if there is a church or school near by.

No one under the age of 18 is allowed in a betting shop. But to secure a conviction, the prosecution must show that the bookmaker or his staff knew the youth was on the premises and knew, or ought to have known by his appearance, that he was under age.

Betting shops may be used only for betting. Refreshments, music, dancing and other entertainments are forbidden. So are radio and television unless they are in a back room and cannot be heard by the customers in the shop. The Exchange Telegraph 'blower' service, a private, subscribers' service which relays commentaries and results from the race-course, is allowed.

Restrictions on private gambling

Betting by telephone or through the post is permitted and so are wagers between members of a private club or between people who live or work on the same premises. A hospital in-patient, for example, can lay a bet with a porter, and so can a hotel resident with a waiter.

But betting in the street or in other unauthorised public places, even between private individuals, is illegal. A public place for the purpose of gambling has never been defined by law, and the term is open to interpretation in every new case that arises.

Unless you are at home, it is an offence to bet with anyone under the age of 18 or to employ anyone under that age to place or negotiate bets.

In a members' club Clubs that are run by and for the benefit of the members themselves need licences only to sell alcohol, for entertainment or for gaming machines.

However, before any club can operate gaming, it must have at least 25 members; it must not be temporary; and gaming must not be the principal reason for the club's existence.

Even within these broad definitions, the attitude of the licensing authorities varies from area to area.

In a public house Games of chance can be played for money only with the permission of the local licensing board. And even if it grants the publican a licence, it invariably sets a very small limit on the stakes – perhaps 10 or 20 pence.

Licensed lotteries, sweepstakes, raffles and gaming machines are allowed, but any other form of betting or wagering, including the passing of betting slips and the payment of any winnings due, is illegal.

Gaming is allowed in private rooms on licensed premises, provided that the public is not admitted. An organisation may hire a room for that purpose or the landlord may hold a private gambling session.

At home Domestic gambling is entirely free from legal control, but anyone running a game in his own home would be guilty of a criminal offence if he tried to make a profit, by charging an entry or table fee, for example.

In a card club Privately owned clubs which deal exclusively in bridge or whist can charge a maximum of £6 per person per day.

When a syndicate gambles

If two or more people form a partnership or syndicate to gamble, they can take legal action against each other to recover their winnings. If, however, the member of the syndicate entrusted with the job of placing the bet fails to do so, the others cannot sue him.

Gambling by machine

Coin-operated gambling machines where predetermined combinations of symbols constitute winning bets can be installed in cafes, public houses, hotels, clubs, casinos and works canteens, but the operator must have a licence from the local licensing board.

Fruit machines, as they are known, have fixed percentage pay-outs, so only players can lose. Most of them are cash machines. *See:* GAMING MACHINE

GAME

When you can shoot animals and birds for food

Two types of game are hunted in Scotland:

- Ground game, that is rabbits, hares and deer.
- Game birds, such as pheasant, partridge, grouse, snipe and woodcock.

Game is protected by the law. You cannot usually shoot game without a game licence and the permission of the owner of the land in question. Even if you have these, it is still illegal to

WHEN A GAME BIRD MUST NOT BE SHOT

The calendar that tells a hunter to hold his fire

Bird	D J F M A M J J A S O N
Black game	Dec 11 – Aug 19
Grouse	Dec 11 – Aug 11
Partridge	Feb 2 – Aug 31
Pheasant	Feb 2 – Sept. 30
Snipe	Feb 1 – Aug 11
Woodcock	Feb 1 – Aug 31
Capercaillie	Feb 1 – Sept. 30

A hunter risks a fine if he shoots one of Scotland's varieties of game birds during its close season.

shoot if it is the animal's close season.

Who can hunt

Game still in its wild state does not belong to anyone. When it is captured or killed, it becomes the property of the person carrying out the capturing or killing.

This does not, however, mean that everyone is free to hunt game. The game is public, but the land on which game is found or from which it can be shot is usually private. Only the landowner, or those who have his permission, can use the land to hunt game. Anyone else is a poacher and is committing a criminal offence which may lead to heavy fines and the confiscation of the game. *See:* POACHING

OBTAINING A GAME LICENCE

Anyone who hunts game without a licence can be fined up to £100, even if he shoots nothing.

There are three different types of game licence, all obtainable from post offices.

Red licence	Lasts for a year from July 31
Green licence	From August 1 to October 31
Blue licence	From November 1 to July 31

It is also possible to take out a licence for a specified period of 14 days.

Gamekeepers have to apply for a special licence which lasts for a year.

Anyone intending to use a gun should also have a firearms certificate. *See:* GUN

Game licences

The landowner's permission is not enough, however. In order to hunt legally you also need a game licence. The penalty for hunting without a licence is a fine of up to £100.

Even a motorist who accidentally kills game is not legally entitled to take the animal he has killed unless he has a game licence.

At any time when you are hunting game you can be required to show your licence by the owner or occupier of the land, or by anyone who has a game licence himself. If you have forgotten to bring the licence with you, you must give your name and address and the name of the place where the licence was taken out.

You can sell game if you have a licence, but only to a licensed game dealer.

In a limited number of circumstances a game licence is not needed at all. For example, the owner or occupier of enclosed land, and those authorised by him, can shoot hares, rabbits and deer on the land without a licence. Some wild birds that can be shot – such as ducks, geese and wildfowl – are not strictly speaking game and so no licence is required. *See:* BIRDS

If you are not actually hunting game yourself, but are merely helping someone else, you do not need a licence as long as your companion has one. For this reason, beaters do not need licences.

Close seasons

Most game animals are protected by a close season – a period of several months each year during which it is illegal to hunt them. This is so that they are able to breed in safety.

The close seasons for the most important game birds are listed in the adjoining table.

The different varieties of deer are also protected by close seasons. For a complete list see ANIMAL. There is no close season for the other two kinds of ground game, rabbits and hares. Hares are protected indirectly, however, because it is illegal to sell them during the months from March to July inclusive.

Even during the open season there are some restrictions on hunting. Woodcock, snipe and some birds cannot be shot on Sundays or on Christmas Day. It is also illegal to hunt rabbits and hares with firearms, or deer by any means, at night during the period from the first hour after sunset to the last hour before sunrise.

GAMING MACHINE

Controlling the robots that offer fun and profit

A gaming machine is any machine on which a game of chance, or skill and chance combined, can be played for gain or amusement by putting in a coin or token.

That definition covers pinball machines, fairground 'penny-in-the-slot' machines and the many kinds of 'one-armed bandit' or fruit machine, on which a predetermined combination of symbols – often pictures of various fruits – constitutes a winning bet.

Under the 1968 gaming laws, there are three categories: machines that pay out big cash jackpots, machines that pay small prizes in cash or in kind, and machines played only for pleasure.

When there is a jackpot

The strictest controls are on fruit machines offering large cash prizes – known in law as 'jackpot' machines.

They can be operated only in premises that already have a full casino licence, in a BINGO CLUB or in a proprietary or members' club registered with the local authority. *See:* GAMBLING

No more than two machines are allowed, a single 'play' must cost no more than 10p and prizes must be in cash, not tokens.

There is no limit on the jackpot, but in practice it is rarely more than £100. The gaming machine manufacturers – through their organisation, the British Amusement Catering Trades Association – have reached a private agreement with the Gaming Board not to exceed that amount.

The association has also agreed with the board that all jackpot machines will pay back at least 73 per cent of the money staked.

When there is no jackpot

The second and largest category of gaming machines is what the law calls amusement-with-prizes machines. Like jackpot machines, they are almost always 'one-armed bandits' or fruit machines.

These can be installed in places open to the public, such as public houses, cafes, hotels and arcades. Their operators – with the exception of people who run travelling shows and fairs – must obtain a permit from the local authority, which takes each case on its merits when deciding how many machines to allow. The permit lasts for 3 years.

HOW FRUIT MACHINES ARE CONTROLLED

You win by getting a correct combination of fruit symbols but the prize must be paid out in cash, not tokens.

HOW THE OPERATORS ARE SUPERVISED

The sale and distribution of gaming machines is supervised by the Gaming Board. Anyone who supplies machines on hire, or sells or maintains them for a living, needs a certificate from the board, which investigates his background and that of his principal associates.

The certificate lasts for 5 years, but can be revoked at any time. The board's inspectors check from time to time on the activities of those involved in the business.

Any private individual with a reasonable objection to the way a gaming-machine business is being run should complain to the board or the police.

There is a maximum stake of 10p and a maximum cash prize of 50p. If the prize is in the form of tokens or valuables, it can be worth up to £2, and a player must be able to exchange his tokens for goods or non-cash prizes.

The Gaming Board has agreed with the trade association that the pay-out on amusement-with-prizes machines should be no less than 70 per cent of the money staked.

When there is no prize

No permit or licence is needed for a machine that does not offer a prize – for example, space invaders, a pin-ball or penny-in-the-slot machine or a mechanical horse race in a fairground or amusement arcade.

The most the player can hope for is to do well enough to win a free game or his money back.

Gaming for charity

Anyone running a charity function or non-commercial entertainment such as a bazaar, fête, dinner-dance or sporting event, can provide gaming machines – including jackpot machines – without a permit, but only if none of the proceeds, after expenses, is for private gain.

The machines must be incidental to the entertainment: they must not be the main or only inducement for people to attend.

GARAGE

When servicing or repairs are badly done

Work on your car by a garage must be done with reasonable care and skill. The garage is liable for any loss or damage caused by lack of care or skill and for the cost of having faulty workmanship put right elsewhere.

It is also liable for any personal injuries that result, either to you or anyone else.

If a garage refuses to put right faulty work, and you decide to sue, always obtain an independent opinion about the work from another garage or from a qualified engineer – possibly from one of the motoring organisations.

When new parts are provided

Parts or materials supplied by a garage must be reasonably fit for their purpose – which means that the garage is liable if any part proves unsuitable or defective and results in loss or injury, even if the defect is not the garage's fault.

However, a garage's liability to pay compensation for faulty parts is limited to the car owner. Third parties cannot claim unless the garage has been negligent.

When your car is damaged

The garage has a responsibility to take reasonable care of your car while it is being repaired or serviced. If it is damaged or stolen due to the garage's negligence you can claim compensation. It is for the garage to prove that it was not negligent if it wishes to avoid paying your claim.

Garages often try to absolve themselves from liability by displaying notices on the premises or printed on order forms saying that cars are left at the owner's risk. Such notices, if part of your contract (they normally are), are invalid if they are unfair and unreasonable. *See:* UNFAIR CONTRACT

No such clause can take away your rights to compensation for death or personal injury in the case of NEGLIGENCE.

WHEN YOU RENT A GARAGE

A written agreement is not necessary when you rent a garage, unless you are renting for a period of more than one year. But it is always sensible to put matters in writing: there is less chance of argument over what was agreed.

Condition of the garage

It is an implied term of an agreement to let a garage that it is reasonably fit for the purpose. It should therefore be sufficiently wind and water tight. If it is a lock-up garage, it should have a reasonably secure lock.

If the garage is not reasonably fit for the purpose, ask the landlord to repair it. If he fails to do so within a reasonable time, he is in breach of the agreement. You can carry out the repairs yourself and sue him – or withhold rent – to recover the cost.

The landlord does not need to provide a garage that is reasonably fit for the purpose, or to maintain the garage, if that is an express condition of the agreement.

You must take reasonable care of the garage and are liable for damage caused deliberately or by neglect. You must also take reasonable care for the safety of anyone who comes into the garage.

Working in a garage

It is important to tell the landlord what the garage is to be used for. A tenant cannot, for example, carry out any business activity – such as commercial repair work – if he has rented the garage for domestic use. If he did break his agreement, he would certainly have to relinquish his lease.

If the tenant intends to carry out repairs to his own car he should tell the landlord, for such work could be noisy and a nuisance to neighbours.

Paying the rent

Although a rent book is not needed for the hire of a garage, some record of rent payment should be kept to avoid any subsequent dispute. Payment by cheque is usually enough because clearance of the cheque is evidence of payment.

Either landlord or tenant can give notice to quit in writing. The length of notice should be 40 days or, where the lease is for 4 months or less, one third of the period of the lease.

A garage owner who tries to stop a tenant using the garage without proper notice could be sued.

Code of trade practice

Some garages belong to a trade association – for example, the Scottish Motor Trade Association, the Motor Agents' Association and the Society of Motor Manufacturers and Traders – and therefore observe a code of practice approved by the Director General of Fair Trading.

GAS SUPPLY

Your right to have gas piped into your house

For most domestic users in Britain the legal duty to supply gas rests with a body called the British Gas Corporation. In Scotland the Corporation operates under the name of 'Scottish Gas'.

When you move into a house or flat that is connected to a gas main, you are entitled to obtain a supply of gas from the Gas Corporation – provided that the property and equipment is safe and that you do not owe money to the Corporation for gas previously supplied anywhere in Britain. A payment may have

GARAGE FIRE WRECKED A CUSTOMER'S CAR

A garage is liable for unexplained damage to a car while it is stored awaiting repair.

Mr Sinclair, an Edinburgh taximan, left his car at Mr Juner's garage to be repainted and for some repairs to be carried out. The work could not be started immediately but the car was stored at the garage.

Before the work was completed the car was destroyed in a fire at the garage. The cause of the fire was unexplained.

In the Outer House of the Court of Session it was decided that the garage proprietor was not liable as the storage of the car was free.

DECISION

On appeal this decision was reversed. Where a garage has a car on its premises in order to carry out work on it, it cannot be said to store it free. The total charge for repairs reflects the cost of garaging. So the garage proprietor was liable for the destruction of the car because he could not show that its loss was not his fault.

GARAGE THAT WAS SUED OVER FAULTY MATERIALS

A garage is liable for any loss or damage caused by defects in spare parts fitted while a car is being repaired or serviced.

The Brent Cross Service Company fitted six new connecting rods into the engine of a car owned by G. H. Myers and Company. The rods were supplied by the makers of the car. The following month one of the rods broke, causing damage to the engine. Myers therefore sued the garage.

DECISION

When the case went to appeal, it was ruled that there was an implied condition that the rods were reasonably fit for their purpose, even though the garage had no means of discovering the defect. The garage was ordered to pay compensation.

A PUNCTURE REPAIR THAT CAUSED AN ACCIDENT

Even a passer-by hurt in an accident which is caused by faulty workmanship can claim compensation from the garage that did the work.

Mr Hancock had a puncture on his lorry repaired by Mr Peter's garage. Later, while the lorry was being driven down the street, the flange which kept the tyre on the wheel came off. The flange mounted the pavement and hit a pedestrian, Mrs Stennett, on the leg.

Mrs Stennett sued Mr Hancock and Mr Peters for damages over her injury.

DECISION

The court dismissed the claim against Mr Hancock because it was reasonable for him to rely on the work done by Mr Peters's garage. Clearly, the flange had come off because of negligence by one of Mr Peters's workmen. As a result, Mrs Stennett was awarded damages against Mr Peters.

to be made for the supply.

Go to your local gas office or showroom and complete a standard form of application. Enquire about the various easy payment methods (budget payments and savings stamps) and maintenance contracts.

The Gas Corporation can demand a deposit from an applicant, and is especially likely to do so if he or she has been a bad payer. The Corporation must pay interest to the consumer on any deposit held for over 6 months.

Making a connection

If your property is not connected to a Gas Corporation distribution main, but is within 25 yards of one, you can insist on your property being supplied from the main. You may be asked to pay the cost of any piping required on your land, and any excess over 30 feet from any pipe of the Corporation.

A house owner whose property is more than 25 yards from the nearest main cannot insist on connection. The Corporation can refuse to link the house to the main or it can ask the house owner to pay the full cost of the connection.

Paying for your gas

Houses supplied with gas are usually provided with a credit meter which monitors the amount of gas used. Gas is measured in cubic feet but is charged to the customer at a fixed price for each therm (105.5 megajoules) provided by the gas supplied.

Most meters are read every 3 months by a Corporation employee, and a bill for the number of therms used is sent to the customer. There is also a quarterly standing charge – £9.90 in 1984. The charge is reduced to the cost of gas actually used, if that is less.

If the meter reader finds no one at home, an estimated bill will be issued, based on your bill for the equivalent quarter of the previous year.

If an estimate seems unusually high, you can read the meter yourself and complete the self-reading facility on the reverse of the gas bill. Return the bill to Scottish Gas and an amended bill, based on your readings, will be issued. The next official meter reading will adjust any under or over charge which may have taken place on the previous estimated account.

CHECKING A COIN METER

How to be sure that your money buys the right amount of gas

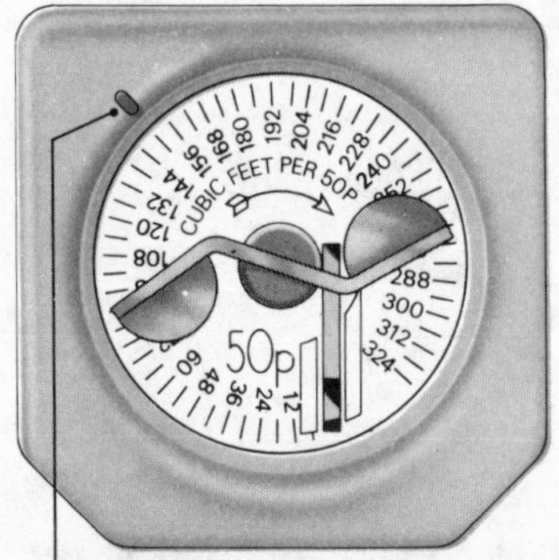

Read the figure on the dial opposite the setting mark. This shows the number of cubic feet of gas the meter gives for one coin, for example 120 cu. ft. for 50p. Check at your local gas showroom that this is the correct rate.

Every prepayment gas meter has a setting mark to show how many units a coin should buy. If the price changes, the landlord alters the setting.

A consumer can have a prepayment meter installed provided that it is safe and practical to do so. This allows him to pay for his gas with coins as he uses it.

Challenging a meter reading

A gas meter may be registering more fuel than you have actually used. If you suspect such a fault, ask your local gas office to have the meter tested.

A gas meter is considered accurate if it runs fast or slow by no more than 2 per cent. If your meter is found to be over this limit, it will be treated as having registered wrongly from the date when the first of the two immediately previous meter readings was taken. Any allowance to be made or surcharge due as a result of the fault must be paid to or by the consumer.

The same inspection and payment system operates if you have a prepayment meter in your home.

If you ask for a test, the local gas office will arrange for a new meter to be fitted, and your meter will be removed and sent to the Department of Energy for testing. A test certificate showing the degree of accuracy of the old meter will be sent to you, but the meter itself will not be refitted. The Department also has power to examine a meter in use.

If the old meter is found to be faulty, you will not be charged for the test. If it is not found to be faulty, a fee is charged to cover disconnection, reconnection and the test.

Changing your meter

A customer cannot insist on changing from one type of meter to another. Scottish Gas may agree to replace a credit meter with a prepayment meter if it is safe and practical to do so and the consumer can show genuine hardship.

Each application will be considered on its merits – but a prepayment meter will not be provided where there is a meter box or external meter.

A prepayment meter can be changed to a credit meter free of charge.

Gas offences

It is an offence to tamper with gas pipes and fittings belonging to the Gas Corporation. It is also an offence to tamper with a meter, insert foreign or counterfeit coins or attempt to alter the readings. The prosecution must prove that someone accused of one of these offences acted wilfully, fraudulently or negligently.

It is an offence to reconnect a supply which has been disconnected by the Corporation.

The maximum penalty for all these offences is a fine of £400.

The quality of your gas

The Gas Corporation must supply gas of a minimum pressure, purity and calorific value. It must also make sure that all gas supplied has a distinctive smell, so that leaks can be detected. Regular checks are made by independent examiners from the Department of Energy and the Corporation can be fined up to £2,000 for failing to maintain any one of those standards.

If you find or suspect a gas leak

If you suspect a gas leak, turn off your supply immediately at the meter and tell your local gas service department. The gas mains tap is normally near the meter. The emergency number of the nearest available service department is always listed in the telephone directory under 'Gas'.

By law, the Gas Corporation must prevent gas escaping from any pipe belonging to it within 24 hours of receiving written notice about the escape, unless there are exceptional circumstances that prevent its immediate attendance. If it fails to do so, it can be prosecuted and fined up to £400.

If your house is destroyed by a gas explosion, the district or islands council has a duty to provide you with permanent accommodation. You may also be able to claim for your loss under a household insurance policy. *See:* FIRE INSURANCE; HOMELESSNESS

Taking safety measures

Any gas user who fails to comply with safety rules laid down by law can be fined up to £2,000. You can obtain the leaflet 'Help Yourself to Gas Safety' from your local gas showroom or office.

You must not use, or let anyone use, a gas appliance on your premises if it is known or suspected to be dangerous. Only competent and qualified workmen are allowed to install or service any gas appliance. You can sue the Gas Corporation for NEGLIGENCE if one of its employees services or installs appliances incompetently.

Contractors listed by the Confederation for Registration of Gas Installers work only under strict safety conditions and are qualified to service and install appliances.

The van symbol that shows that a workman who installs or services gas appliances is qualified to do the work safely. CORGI stands for Confederation for Registration of Gas Installers.

When your home can be entered

A gas official is not entitled to enter or try to use force to enter your home without your consent, unless it is an emergency or he has obtained a warrant authorising entry from a justice of the peace.

The warrant must state why entry is required:

- To inspect apparatus.
- To check how much gas has been used.
- To disconnect apparatus thought to be dangerous.
- To disconnect the supply.

At least 24 hours' notice of intended entry must have been given before the warrant can be issued.

An official who enters your home, whether under a warrant or otherwise, must leave your home as secure as he found it. If he leaves it insecure and someone enters and steals from you, you can sue the Gas Corporation for the loss arising from the official's negligence.

If he causes any damage by entering the property, he must make it good. If he fails to do so, claim compensation from the Corporation – or sue it.

It is not an offence to refuse entry to an official without a warrant, except in an emergency. But if he has a warrant it is a criminal offence to obstruct him.

When the supply can be cut off

The Gas Corporation has the right to disconnect a supply, or refuse to connect a new supply, if:

- A consumer still owes money 28 days after a written demand has been made and after a further 7 days' notice of disconnection has been given.
- Appliances or piping on the premises are unsafe.
- A consumer has tampered with the meter or with pipes and fittings.

The supply cannot be disconnected on the ground that a consumer has failed to pay the bill for equipment bought from Scottish Gas – for instance, a gas fire or cooker.

Under a code of practice on disconnection agreed between the Gas Corporation, the Department of Energy and the National Gas Consumers' Council, the Corporation should not disconnect the supply of a consumer who is suffering genuine hardship if a firm arrangement can be made with the consumer to pay arrears and guarantee future payments. Let Scottish Gas know as soon as possible if you are in financial difficulty.

Your local social security office or social work department may be able to help you pay any arrears or make arrangements for them to be paid. *See:* FUEL BILL

If the consumer who is in arrears is a retirement pensioner, and all the people in the house with incomes are also pensioners, the supply will not be disconnected between October 1 and March

WHEN A LANDLORD SELLS GAS TO A TENANT

A landlord is legally entitled to resell gas to a tenant. He can do this through his own meter, or by fitting a special meter, or by including the cost of gas in the rent charged.

If he includes it in the rent, a special section should be set aside in the rent book stating the rate charged for gas.

If a tenant is supplied through the landlord's meter, any money due at the end of the tenancy belongs to the landlord and not to the Gas Corporation.

A tenant can ask his local gas office to be supplied direct, provided that he has not made an oral or written agreement with his landlord to pay the landlord for gas.

A tenant who is supplied by his landlord and who has difficulty in paying for gas will receive the same consideration from the local social work department or social security office as if he were supplied direct by the Gas Corporation.

What a landlord can charge

A landlord who resells gas to a tenant must not charge more than the maximum resale price fixed from time to time by the Gas Corporation.

The tenant can check the approved local maximum price from a leaflet *Gas – how much can landlords charge?* obtainable at any gas office. This contains a table of the maximum extra resale charges allowed.

Ask your landlord to provide a bill showing the amount of gas used, the dates of the readings and charges made – and check the charge against the table of permitted charges.

If a tenant discovers that his landlord is overcharging him for gas, the Corporation will not help him to recover the money, but he can sue the landlord in the sheriff court for the excess, or he can withhold the amount of the overcharge from the rent and tell the landlord he is doing so.

A landlord who refuses to provide gas to a tenant, or disconnects the supply as a means of forcing him to leave the premises, can be prosecuted for HARASSMENT. The tenant can also sue him for breach of CONTRACT.

31 – unless it is clear that they can pay, but have not done so.

Arranging to end the supply

Anyone leaving a property should give the local gas office at least 24 hours' notice in writing. Failure to do so will make him liable to pay for any gas used on the premises until the next meter reading or until a new occupier requests gas.

When something goes wrong

If you have a complaint about your gas supply or about any service, contact your local gas showroom or office. If you are still not satisfied, contact the Gas Consumers' Council for Scotland, 86 George Street, Edinburgh. The Council is an independent body set up to represent the interests of gas consumers.

GIFT

Making sure that a present does not go wrong

Someone who is 18 or older, and who understands fully what he is doing, can legally make a gift of any property – including money – to anyone he chooses, as long as the property is his to give.

For a gift to take effect:

- The ownership of the property must be transferred; and
- The giver must make it clear that this transfer was intended as a gift.

Transferring ownership

The way in which ownership is transferred depends on the type of property being gifted;

- Land and buildings are transferred by a CONVEYANCE which has to be registered in the REGISTER OF SASINES or LAND REGISTER. In practice, the help of a solicitor is needed. It is not enough just to hand over the title deeds of the property, with a note confirming the gift.
- Ordinary goods – for example, household furniture, books, television sets, motor cars – are transferred by delivering them physically to the person receiving the gift.
- Money is transferred by delivering the actual notes and coins. If the money is in an ordinary bank account it can also be transferred by writing a cheque.

If the money is in a post office, building society or other savings account, the giver completes the appropriate forms to transfer the money to the recipient's bank account and then lodges the forms with his own savings pass book. Alternatively, the recipient can collect the money in cash, provided that he can produce the giver's pass book and that the giver has sent written instructions to the post office, building society or other savings organisation.

- Shares and unit trust holdings are transferred by signing a transfer form obtained from the company or trust and handing it over to the new owner with the share or unit certificate. The transfer is not completed until the company or trust managers have registered the change of ownership.

Intending a gift

However, it is not enough just to transfer ownership. The law will not recognise this as a gift unless it is also clear that at the time of the transfer the giver intended to make a gift – and did not, for example, expect payment for it.

Challenging a gift

Most gifts are never challenged. But difficulties can arise if, shortly after making the gift, the giver changes his mind, or dies, or has his property seized by creditors.

The legal rule is that no person will be presumed to have given away his property. If the gift is challenged, it is up to the recipient to prove that it was meant as a present. If he cannot do so, he will have to return it or pay its value.

How can a recipient prove a gift? If the property in question is land or a building, the conveyance will probably make things clear.

But with other kinds of property, there will often be nothing in writing, and proof may be very difficult indeed. So if the gift is substantial and there seems a possibility that it might be challenged sometime in the future, the giver should make a written note recording what the gift is and when it was given. This note can then be given to the recipient of the gift, or lodged with a solicitor or a bank for safe-keeping.

Tax on gifts

The donor or the recipient may be liable for CAPITAL TRANSFER TAX and for CAPITAL GAINS TAX on the gift. If the gift is of land or shares, STAMP DUTY may also be payable.

Gifts from a bankrupt

A person who is insolvent is not allowed to make a gift, even although he has not been declared bankrupt. Similarly, a person cannot make a valid gift to his spouse within the period of a year and a day before he is made bankrupt.

In either case, the recipient can be made to hand the gift back so that it can be sold for the benefit of the creditors. *See:* BANKRUPTCY

Undue influence

A gift can be challenged if it was only made because the giver was subjected to undue influence. This is most common where there is some special relationship between giver and recipient. For example, a doctor may persuade a sick and elderly patient to make him a gift, or a grown-up child may put pressure on an elderly parent to give something away.

GOLDEN HANDSHAKE

Reducing the tax bill after losing a job

If you lose your job through redundancy or dismissal, and receive a 'golden handshake' lump-sum payment in compensation, you may receive the money tax-free (or at least taxed only at a specially low level).

Some lump-sum payments received by employees are wholly taxable if they have a contractual right to it (for example, a footballer receiving a percentage of his transfer fee) but, by concession, the Inland Revenue tax contractual compensation normally only if the amount is no more than would have been paid to the employee if no such contract existed.

From April 6, 1981, the first £25,000 of any normal golden handshake has been free of tax (£10,000 before that). The balance is then taxed at a specially low rate.

Statutory redundancy payment

Any compensation for REDUNDANCY under the Employment Protection (Consolidation) Act 1978 is tax-free.

A GOLDEN HANDSHAKE MAY BE TAX FREE

The first £25,000 compensation for loss of office is tax free.

But if other payments are also made the redundancy payment uses up part of the £25,000 tax-free limit.

Example: A man is made redundant and is paid a total of £28,000, described as being £4,000 statutory redundancy pay and £24,000 compensation for loss of office. Since only the first £25,000 is tax-free, he must pay tax on £3,000.

The amount left to be taxed should not however be taxed as heavily as if it were an addition to his salary in the year he left the job. Anyone made redundant is entitled to the benefit of an arrangement known as 'top-slicing relief'.

As from April 6, 1982, this means that the tax on the next £25,000 is reduced by half. Tax on the third slice of £25,000 is reduced by a quarter, and any excess (that is, of golden handshakes of more than £75,000) will be fully taxed.

When payment is made

If you are made redundant your compensation has to go through the usual PAYE tax system which automatically allows for the £25,000 tax-free payment, but possibly not for any top-slicing relief to which you may be entitled on larger sums. So your payment may be over-taxed initially.

Some large employers, faced with dismissing large numbers of workers, may make an informal arrangement with the Inland Revenue to take account, if it is relevant, of some top-slicing relief when PAYE is deducted.

However, a small company dismissing one of a few employees is unlikely to have such an arrangement. In that case you must claim any excess back from the Inland Revenue. The full details may not be settled until long after the end of the tax year in which you leave your job.

As soon as the tax year ends, on April 5, ask your Inspector of Taxes for a written assessment of your liability on the lump sum. Ask specifically for top-slicing relief to be given.

COMPENSATION THAT IS FREE OF TAX

Certain compensation payments are free of tax, no matter what the amount:

- Ex gratia payments on the termination of a job caused by death or disability of employee.
- Terminal grants to members of the armed forces.
- Ex gratia payments at the end of a job in which the employee worked abroad for 75 per cent or more of his entire service or for the whole of the last 10 years.
- Ex gratia payments when the employee has served more than 20 years, at least half of them abroad, including any 10 of the past 20 years.

When you can claim interest from Inland Revenue

If too much tax is deducted and the Inland Revenue does not repay for an exceptionally long time, you may be entitled to claim interest.

The Inland Revenue does not have to pay interest, however, until it has held your money for one clear tax year. For example, if tax is over-deducted in November one year and repaid the following November, you are entitled to interest because the tax year runs from April to April.

If the repayment is made in May, 17

HOW TOP-SLICING RELIEF WORKS

Top-slicing relief is a special method of reducing the amount of income tax that needs to be paid on redundancy or dismissal pay-offs.

The method, illustrated here, has been operative since April 6, 1982.

The relief treats the taxable part of the compensation as the last part of income, and thus suffering the highest rates. The notional tax on the compensation that has been calculated is then halved to arrive at the actual amount payable.

Example

A man is made redundant in 1984–85. He had earned £14,000 up to the date when he was made redundant, has other income of £3,000 in the same tax year and was married.

He received compensation of £59,000, a sum which included a redundancy payment of £5,000.

Income:	
Earnings	£14,000
Other income	£3,000
Total income	£17,000
Deduct:	
Married man's allowance	£3,155
Total taxable income	£13,845
Tax payable at 30%	£4,153
Compensation:	
(including redundancy pay):	£59,000
Tax exempt	£25,000
Total taxable:	£34.000

£1,555 @ 30%	£466
£2,800 @ 40%	£1,120
£4,900 @ 45%	£2,205
£7,500 @ 50%	£3,750
£7,500 @ 55%	£4,125
£745 @ 60%	£447
£25,000	Notional Tax £12,113
Take one half of the notional tax on this slice	
£12,113×50%	£6,056
Remaining £9,000 @ 60% notional tax	£5,400
Take three quarters of the notional tax on this slice	
£5,400×75%	£4,050
Tax on income	£4,153
Tax on compensation.....£6,056	
£4,050	£10,106
Total tax payable in 1983–4	£14,259

months after the over-deduction, you are entitled to interest, but it is reckoned only from the beginning of the new tax year, so on a repayment made in May you get only one month's interest.

GOODS, Carriage of

Someone who carries goods for money is legally bound to take reasonable care of them, but he is generally not liable for any loss or damage unless that is due to some negligence on the part of his employees or himself. If you have valuable goods to send somewhere, insure them. *See:* CARRIAGE OF GOODS

GOODS, Defective

A person who buys goods that do not match the way they are described in the shop or advertising material, or are unfit for the purpose for which they are intended, has rights against the seller. Sometimes he can return the goods and get his money back. Sometimes he has to keep the goods but can claim compensation if they need repairing or are worth less than he paid. *See:* DEFECTIVE GOODS

GOODS, Ownership of

A buyer's right to goods he has paid for

Ownership of goods is not always easy to prove, and a person who loses property, or has it stolen, may not be able to reclaim it.

There are no title deeds with ordinary, moveable goods. When valuable articles, such as jewellery or an expensive watch, are bought, it is wise to get and to keep a written receipt.

Buying goods

Normally, goods become the property of a person after he has made a CONTRACT with the seller and agreed to pay money for the goods.

If, however, the goods did not belong to the seller in the first place, they may not legally become the property of the buyer.

That is true even if the seller and the buyer both genuinely believed that the sale was a valid one. The goods may have been stolen and passed to the seller without his knowing.

In that case, they still belong to the person from whom they were stolen. If he can trace the goods and prove ownership, he can recover them without payment.

In England, stolen goods bought in an open market become the property of the buyer – that is the ancient, legal rule known as market overt. However, there is no such rule in Scotland.

COMPENSATION FOR RECLAIMED GOODS

Anyone who has goods reclaimed from him by an original owner after he has bought them from someone else has a right to get back the money he paid for them.

The Sale of Goods Act 1979 lays down that the seller must legally have had a right to sell the goods. If he did not, the buyer can sue him for the full amount paid – even if he has had use of the goods for some time.

Selling through an agent

Goods sold through an authorised agent become the property of the buyer even if the original owner never gets the money for them.

For example, if someone leaves a table with a secondhand furniture dealer, and it is eventually bought, there is no legal way that the original owner can reclaim the table from the buyer if the middleman – the secondhand furniture dealer – refuses to hand over the money or is unable to do so. The original owner's only legal course of action is to sue the dealer for the money he received for the table.

A recognised agent in the business of buying and selling can sell goods left with him if the owner did not ask him to sell them. In such a case, the goods become the property of the person who buys them from the dealer.

That can happen when an article, say a valuable painting, is left with an auctioneer for valuation, and the painting is sold at the next auction.

The original owner can claim against the auctioneer. *See also:* HIRE PURCHASE

GOODS, Rental of

The strict laws covering hire agreements

There is no legal difference between renting, leasing or hiring goods. All differ from HIRE PURCHASE in that the customer never becomes the owner of the goods, no matter how much he pays or how long the rental agreement lasts.

The Consumer Credit Act 1974 covers hire purchase, and gives protection to rental customers as well. The legislation applies to most rental agreements lasting 3 months or more in which the total payments do not exceed £5,000 (£15,000 after May 20,1985).

Understanding the agreement form

The legislation lays down strict rules about the way the rental contract must be set out, how it should be signed and the number of copies the hirer should receive. An agreement is probably unenforceable if these rules are broken. *See:* CREDIT AGREEMENT

Read your rental agreement carefully to see that it does not impose conditions you find unacceptable. It may, for example, insist on a minimum period of hire before you can terminate the agreement, though in most cases the law stipulates that the minimum period cannot be longer than 18 months.

A hirer may also be required to keep

WHEN NO PAYMENTS ARE MADE

A rental company is entitled to repossess its goods with a court order.

the goods at a particular place. For example, a rental agreement may insist that a television set is not moved from the hirer's address or that a hired car should be housed in a garage.

Even when there are no such explicit conditions, the hire company is entitled to ask at any time for information about where the goods are. The maximum penalty for refusing to give this information is a £400 fine.

A hirer must take reasonable care of the goods he is renting. If anything happens to them because of his negligence he must pay compensation. It is advisable, therefore, to insure the goods for their full value. Some hire agreements may insist on insurance. If you are in doubt about the actual value, ask the hiring company.

Conditions of hired goods

Goods that are hired must be adequate for the purpose for which they are known by the hire company to be wanted and they must match any description given in advertisements or in the agreement itself.

Some agreements stipulate specific arrangements for the company to maintain or service the goods and those arrangements may be subject to various conditions. None is valid, however, if it seeks to absolve a hire company from its duty to supply a consumer with goods in adequate condition.

If you fail to pay

When a hirer fails to pay the rental the hire company can sue for the sum due or seek return of the goods by a court order.

However, before attempting to repossess its property, the hire company must serve a default notice on the hirer, otherwise he can sue for damages for loss of enjoyment of the goods.

A sheriff court has wide powers to help hirers who face claims. It can allow extra time to pay debts or refuse to allow repossession.

Indeed, if a sheriff decides that the hire payments, when added to the value of the goods to be repossessed, yield an excessive profit he can order some of the money to be repaid to the hirer.

If a hirer finds it difficult to continue payments, therefore, he is well advised to allow the case to go to court and to appear himself to ask the sheriff to vary the rental agreement in his favour.

Ending an agreement

Your right to pull out of a hire agreement is restricted. You can terminate the agreement ahead of time only if it has run for at least 18 months – unless a shorter time is stated in the agreement. You must then give 3 months' notice that you wish to end the rental. If the hire charges have been paid more often than once every 3 months you need give only one rental period of notice.

A hirer whose payments exceed £300 a year cannot terminate the agreement ahead of time unless the agreement itself says he can do so. If he terminates, he must return the goods immediately.

When a rental agreement breaks the law

Any person or company hiring goods to the public must hold a licence from the Office of FAIR TRADING. If not, he or it cannot take legal proceedings against a hirer who breaks the terms of the agreement without the special permission of the Office.

Such permission is rarely given but it might be granted if, for example, a trader had applied for a licence but had not yet received it or if he had previously held a licence but failed to renew it.

An unlicensed trader can be prosecuted and, if convicted on INDICTMENT, can be imprisoned for 2 years and fined an unlimited amount.

GOODS, Sale of

The legal contract between buyer and seller

When goods are sold, the seller and the buyer enter into a CONTRACT which confers rights and imposes obligations on both parties. The contract need not be in writing.

Quality of goods

There is no law governing the quality of goods sold by a private individual, but if you buy something from a business, such as a shop or tradesman, you are entitled to goods of 'merchantable quality' – which means that they must be reasonably fit for their purpose. *See:* DEFECTIVE GOODS

Goods sold under a specific description must correspond exactly with that description. If they do not, the seller – even a private individual – can be sued under the Sale of Goods Act.

Ownership of goods

The seller must own the goods or at least have a right to dispose of them. If he does not, and the true owner later demands the return of the goods, the buyer is entitled to recover his money from the seller. *See:* GOODS, Ownership of

Collection and delivery

Unless there is a specific agreement about delivery, it is a buyer's responsibility to collect the goods. If a seller agrees to deliver he can ask the buyer to agree to pay extra.

If a specific time is fixed for the goods

THE MAN WHO BOUGHT A STOLEN CAR

A person who sells must be the owner of the goods or have the right to dispose of them. Otherwise an innocent buyer, who is later forced to hand the goods over to the true owner, is entitled to his money back from the person who sold them to him.

Mr Divall bought a car from Mr Garbett and then re-sold it to Mr Rowland for £334. Mr Rowland, a car dealer, subsequently sold it to Colonel Railsdon for £400.

Five months after the original purchase, police said that it was a stolen car and seized it. Mr Rowland refunded the £400 to Colonel Railsdon and then sued Mr Divall for the £334.

The judge in the High Court in London said that Mr Rowland was not entitled to all his money back because he and Colonel Railsdon between them had had the use of the car for 4 months. Mr Rowland appealed.

DECISION

The English Court of Appeal said that the Sale of Goods Act laid down an implied condition on the part of the seller that he had a right to sell the goods. Mr Divall had broken that condition. Mr Rowland was entitled to a full refund.

to be handed over and they are not ready by then, the buyer may have the right to cancel the agreement. When no time is fixed, the buyer is entitled to the goods within a 'reasonable' period, but he should give the seller a specific deadline – say 1 or 2 weeks – by which the goods are to be produced before he can cancel the agreement.

Paying the price

A seller can refuse to hand over the goods until the agreed price has been paid, unless the buyer and seller agreed beforehand that payment could be made later or by instalments. If the buyer fails to pay, the seller can give notice of his intention to sell them elsewhere. If he does so and gets less than the original agreed price, he can claim the difference from the buyer who let him down.

A seller can sue for the price of goods that have been delivered, but he cannot sue for the price of goods that have simply not been collected unless there is a specific agreement for payment to be made on a certain date regardless of delivery.

Return of goods

If you have reasonable cause to reject goods that have been delivered to you – for example, if they are faulty, or if the wrong quantity is delivered – you can insist that the seller collects them. You are not bound to return them, provided you tell the seller you reject them.

However, you cannot reject the goods once you have told the seller you have accepted them. Nor can you reject them if you keep the goods for longer than you need to examine them without telling the seller that you are dissatisfied, or if you treat them as your own – for instance by building some electrical parts into your house. In such cases you can sue for damages if the goods are defective.

GRADUATED PENSION

An earnings-related supplement to retirement pension

Graduated pension was an earnings-related pension scheme introduced by the government in April 1961 and wound up in April 1975. Most employed people had to pay into the scheme a weekly contribution directly related to their earnings.

The number and size of their contributions determined the amount of graduated pension they were entitled to at retirement, in addition to the normal weekly retirement pension covered by ordinary national insurance contributions (which used to be paid at a flat rate).

Calculating the amount When the graduated scheme ended, the Department of Health and Social Security issued to each contributor form GR20, which informed him of the total amount of his contributions. From that figure, he can work out the weekly amount of graduated pension to which he is entitled.

Every contribution of £7.50 for men and £9 for women bought the contributor a weekly graduated pension payment of 2½p. For example, a man who paid £177 in contributions over the years would have contributed 23⅗ units of £7.50, and with the units rounded up to 24, would have received on retirement 24 times 2½p a week – that is, 60p a week.

Increase in rate Since 1978, graduated pensions have been increased each year in line with price rises. In 1983–4, each £7.50 or £9 unit was worth 4.44p a week. So a man with 24 units will now get, not 60p, but £1.07 a week.

The maximum number of units that could have been earned during the graduated pension scheme is 86 (men) or 72 (women).

In 1983–4 the maximum weekly payments of graduated pension were £3.82 (men) and £3.20 (women).

How payment is made

Graduated pension is ordinarily paid with retirement pension. People not entitled to a retirement pension because they have not paid enough national insurance contributions – or, in the case of a married woman, because her husband has not yet retired – can obtain any graduated pension to which they are entitled as a separate payment.

A wife receives nothing from her husband's graduated pension contributions, but a retired widow of 60 or over is entitled to half the graduated pension earned by her husband in addition to any graduated pension earned on her own contributions. A retired man of 65 or over is similarly also entitled to half the graduated pension earned by his late wife.

Where graduated pension is not paid with retirement pension, it is paid by quarterly Girocheque. The earnings rule does not affect graduated pension.

See: RETIREMENT PENSION

Extra pension Any man who decides not to retire at 65 (or a woman at 60) and not to draw any pension, can earn extra graduated pension. The amount due is increased by 7½ per cent per year for each complete year that retirement is postponed.

If you need information

If you have lost form GR20, which tells you the total amount of the contributions you paid, or if you wish to challenge the amount stated, contact your local Department of Health and Social Security office.

Be prepared to provide, if possible: your national insurance number, the names and addresses of your employers between April 1961 and April 1975, the dates you worked for them and any works or staff number you had, the amounts of graduated pension contributions that you believe you paid, and details of any occupational pension schemes into which you were contracted out from the graduated pension scheme.

GRAFFITI

Sometimes amusing, but always an offence

It is an offence intentionally or recklessly to destroy or damage another's property. This is the crime of malicious mischief. Many cases of malicious mischief are now prosecuted as the crime of VANDALISM.

Anyone who paints graffiti on walls, whether the property is public or private, or inscribes on them in other ways commits the crime of malicious mischief or vandalism.

Penalties: When these crimes are tried in summary CRIMINAL PROCEEDINGS in the SHERIFF COURT, the maximum penalty is 3 months' imprisonment (or 6 months if the culprit has a previous conviction for the same crime) or a

£2,000 fine, or both. In the DISTRICT COURT the maximum penalty is 60 days' imprisonment or a £1,000 fine, or both.

The culprit may be ordered by the court to pay compensation. *See:* CRIMINAL COMPENSATION ORDER.

The owner of the property on which graffiti is inscribed can also sue the offender, claiming compensation for the damage. *See:* DAMAGES

GUARANTEE

When a manufacturer promises to compensate you

If you buy goods from a retailer, there is no direct contract of sale between you and the manufacturer. That means that your rights if the goods do not work properly are against the retailer, not against the maker. *See:* DEFECTIVE GOODS

It is only when defective goods cause foreseeable injury or damage that a manufacturer has a direct liability to pay compensation – to anyone who suffers, not only individual purchaser of the goods. *See:* MANUFACTURERS' LIABILITY

But injury or damage caused by defective goods is not as common as defective goods that need repair or replacement. Although the buyer has rights against the retailer where goods need repair or replacement, the retailer may not be as skilled in servicing the goods as the manufacturer, or have as large a stock of spare parts.

Even if he is skilled and does have the stock, it is the manufacturer's reputation which is affected by the defect. For that reason, many manufacturers do accept that they have a responsibility to deal with defects by issuing a guarantee (sometimes called a warranty) with the goods, particularly electrical equipment and cars.

UNDER GUARANTEE?

Not all goods are covered by a manufacturer's guarantee, but in certain fields – particularly electrical equipment and cars – it is customary for the makers to back up the retailer's legal duties by promising to put right any fault or replace the goods.

Your rights under a guarantee

Your rights under a guarantee depend on the precise wording of the guarantee document.

Most guarantees cover defective components and defective workmanship. There is usually a promise to repair faulty parts or faulty goods or to replace them if the manufacturer prefers.

Sometimes the guarantee says it does not cover labour costs, and there is often a statement that it is the consumer's responsibility to pack the goods properly and to pay for their carriage to the manufacturer's place of business.

A guarantee is usually for a fixed period – 6 months or 12 months, perhaps – from the date of sale, or for a certain amount of usage, such as 10,000 miles in the case of a car.

Sending back a card

A guarantee may legally set conditions that must be complied with before it operates – for example, that it depends on the customer's completing and returning a postcard to the manufacturer within 10 or 14 days of buying the goods.

That means that the manufacturer could insist on this having been done before he honours the guarantee. In practice many do not bother to check on returned cards before repairing faulty goods if it is clear that the goods are still within the guarantee period, or if the customer has a retailer's receipt. They use the cards mainly to gain statistical information about sales.

Until 1977, there was a good reason why guarantee cards should not be returned: some contained an exemption clause, stating that in return for the benefits of the guarantee the consumer would agree to give up his legal rights against the manufacturer to claim damages if personal injury or damage to property was caused by the manufacturer's negligence. The card to be returned required the consumer to sign that he accepted that clause.

Under the UNFAIR CONTRACT Terms Act 1977, however, such clauses are no longer valid. Even if there is one in your guarantee, and even if you sign a card saying that you accept the clause, it can not take away your legal right to sue the manufacturer if you suffer injury or damage because of the negligence of the manufacturer or any of his employees. *See:* NEGLIGENCE

As a result, there is no longer any disadvantage in signing and returning a guarantee card. As a manufacturer could refuse to comply with the guarantee if a card had not been returned, it is advisable to complete and return it.

How the retailer is affected when goods are defective

Under the Sale of Goods Act 1979, a buyer has legal rights to compensation from the retailer if the goods are defective, even if the defect was not the retailer's fault. *See:* DEFECTIVE GOODS

Nothing in a guarantee can take away or diminish those rights. It must not contain any wording that purports to have such an effect, and it must contain a clear statement that the buyer's rights under the Sale of Goods Act (usually described as his statutory rights) are not affected.

Even if a guarantee says that the consumer is to be responsible for labour costs or for the cost of returning the goods to the manufacturer, he is still entitled to be compensated for such expenditure by the retailer.

In many cases it is possible for a consumer to combine the enforcement of his statutory rights against the retailer and his rights against the manufacturer under the guarantee. If goods are defective he can complain to the retailer who may advise him to take advantage of the guarantee.

If the buyer agrees to do so it does not relieve the retailer of his obligations under the Sale of Goods Act, and if exercising rights under the guarantee involves the buyer in expense the retailer must compensate him.

GUARANTOR

Agreeing to accept liability for someone else's debt

Someone who agrees to stand as guarantor (the legal term is 'cautioner') for another person's debt becomes personally liable if the money is not repaid. If you sign such a guarantee you are promising that if he does not pay, you will.

Only written guarantees are enforceable. If you are asked to sign a document in connection with credit which is being given to someone else, read it carefully. Never sign a guarantee unless you are willing and able to pay up if the worst comes to the worst.

Remember that the person for whom you are standing guarantor does not have to be dishonest for the debt to fall on you. He may just have bad luck, become ill or lose his job.

If the debt is being paid by instalments the guarantor is liable not simply to keep up the regular payments but to settle the whole account in a lump sum. Even one missed payment could result in the entire debt falling on the guarantor.

The person or company that advanced the credit does not have to sue the original debtor before claiming from the guarantor.

A guarantor who does have to pay can sue the original debtor to recover the money.

Credit agreements

If you have agreed to act as guarantor in a credit transaction regulated by the Consumer Credit Act, you are relieved of all your obligations if the person for whom you are providing financial backing legally withdraws from or ends the deal. *See:* CREDIT AGREEMENT

If the Consumer Credit Act applies, you cannot ever be made to pay more than the person for whom you are standing guarantor would have had to pay. Nor can you be made to pay in a different way – for example, if the agreement stated that the amount due could be paid by cheque, you cannot be made to pay cash.

Fidelity guarantees

Where someone guarantees that another person will behave in a trustworthy fashion, that is a fidelity guarantee. This kind of guarantee may be required by an employer before he agrees to employ someone, especially when the employee may have to handle money – as, for example an insurance agent does. In such cases, the guarantor is entitled to full disclosure of all the relevant facts known to the employer, otherwise the guarantee cannot be enforced. *See:* FIDELITY INSURANCE.

LOOK BEFORE YOU LEAP

Make full inquiries before you become a guarantor.

Mr Hutchison owed about £1,400 to the bank. £300 of this was an overdraft and the rest was due for a number of debts. He asked Mr Greenshields to guarantee his account to the extent of £300. Greenshields did not know much about Hutchison's financial affairs, but he told the bank that he would be willing to guarantee £300.

However, the bank did not tell Greenshields that Hutchison owed them another £1,100. In the belief that the debt was only £300, he granted a guarantee for £500. When Hutchison could not pay, the bank asked Greenshields to pay £500 under the guarantee.

By then, however, Greenshields had found out the true position. He said he was not liable because the bank had not disclosed this to him.

DECISION

Mr Greenshields was liable to pay the whole £500. The bank was not bound to disclose the true extent of the debt, because it was entitled to assume that Greenshields had enquired fully into Hutchison's financial position.

GUARDIAN

Protecting the financial and other interests of children

A guardian is a person, normally a parent, who looks after a child's financial and other interests. The guardian of a PUPIL child – a girl under 12 or a boy under 14 – is called a TUTOR; the guardian of a MINOR child – a girl aged 12 and over or a boy aged 14 and over, but under 18 – is known as a CURATOR.

The parents of a legitimate or adopted child are automatically his or her guardians. A father and mother have equal guardianship rights and each can act without the agreement of the other. Any disputes can be resolved by a court.

Pupil children As guardians, the parents will administer, on the child's behalf, any property or money belonging to the child. They will also raise any necessary legal proceedings – for instance, an action for DAMAGES to compensate a child who has been injured through another person's negligence.

If one parent dies, the surviving parent becomes sole guardian. However either parent can name a person – either in a WILL or a deed – to act as a guardian on his or her death. If the surviving parent does not object, the named guardian then acts jointly with that parent.

A named guardian who is objected to by the surviving parent, or believes that parent to be unfit to have CUSTODY of the child, can apply to the sheriff court. The sheriff may decide that either of them will act as sole guardian or that both must act together. He can also award custody to the named guardian if this is necessary for the child's welfare.

If a child's parents are dead, and there is no named guardian, the Court of Session or the sheriff court can appoint someone called a 'factor loco tutoris' to administer the child's property. This person – who may be a relative but is usually a solicitor or accountant – can continue to act for the child until adulthood.

A court will sometimes appoint a special guardian, called a curator ad litem, to look after the interests of a child in legal proceedings. *See:* CURATOR

Minors As guardians, parents do not act on behalf of a minor: their function is to consent, or to withhold consent, to the minor's transactions.

If one parent dies, the surviving parent becomes sole guardian – although he or she may act jointly with a guardian named by the dead parent. If both parents die and there is no guardian, a minor can apply to the Court of Session or sheriff court for one to be appointed.

If a minor starts or defends a court action, his or her guardian will usually need to be involved in the proceedings. If there is no guardian, the court can appoint one for this purpose. *See:* CURATOR

Illegitimate children

The parents of an ILLEGITIMATE CHILD do not automatically become the child's guardians. Nor are they entitled to name a guardian for the child in the event of their deaths. As a result, an illegitimate child has no guardian (although some Acts of Parliament treat the mother as guardian for their purposes).

However, if a guardian is needed for legal proceedings, or to administer property, one can be specially appointed by the court.

Local authority guardianship

A child may be taken into care by a regional (or islands) council if he or she is orphaned and has no guardian; or if the guardian has abandoned the child or is unable to provide proper care.

The council can assume parent's rights – including guardianship – over a child in their care if:

- The child has no parent or guardian.
- The parent or guardian is unable or unfit to care for the child. *See:* CHILDREN IN CARE

GUARDIAN'S ALLOWANCE

Additional benefit for someone who is looking after a child

A person entitled to CHILD BENEFIT for a child in his or her care may also be entitled to a guardian's allowance (£7.60 a week in 1983–4). This is paid if any one of the following applies:

- The child's parents, natural or adoptive, are both dead; or, if there is only one adoptive parent, that parent is dead.
- The child's parents are divorced, one is dead, and the other neither maintains nor has custody of the child.
- The child is illegitimate, the mother is dead and the paternity of the father has not been established.
- One parent is dead, the applicant did not know the whereabouts of the other parent at the date of death, and still does not know despite reasonable efforts to trace that parent.
- One parent is dead and, at the date of death, the other has 5 years or more (or an indefinite period) to serve in prison.

One of the child's parents must have been born in the UK, or have lived in Britain for at least 52 weeks in any 2 year period after the age of 16.

Applicants are normally relatives. A parent cannot claim for a child, except when the child has previously been adopted by someone else. *See:* ADOPTION

How to claim

To claim the allowance, the applicant should obtain form BG 1 from a social security office. No claim can be made for FOSTERING a child in local authority care, since no child benefit is payable.

GUN

Police control over the use of firearms

Anyone who owns a gun of any sort – including a shotgun, rifle or pistol – should normally have a certificate issued by the police. Only low-powered airguns can be used without police permission.

There are two kinds of certificate:

- Shotguns – covering all smooth-bore weapons with barrels that are 24 in. or more long.
- Firearms – covering all other guns that can inflict injury – even if, like starting pistols, they were not designed to do so. A certificate is also needed for imitation guns if they can be converted to fire live ammunition, without using any special skill, tools or equipment.

A firearms certificate specifies the type of arms and the ammunition which the holder can buy and use.

Anyone hunting or shooting GAME must have a firearms certificate even if he already has a game licence.

No one under the age of 14 can be allowed a shotgun or firearms certificate, and the police may also refuse an application by anyone they consider unfit to have a gun. Anyone refused a certificate can appeal to the sheriff court. There is no appeal against that court's decision.

When a certificate is not needed

Some people do not require a firearms or shotgun certificate:

- Anyone shooting at an artificial target at a time and in a place approved by the police. That includes most members of rifle clubs on club premises.
- Anyone without a certificate who borrows a gun from a person who has a certificate, provided that he fires the gun on land owned or rented by the holder of the certificate, and in the presence of the owner of the gun.
- People who carry guns for a certificate holder under the holder's instructions. They are not, however, allowed to fire the guns.
- Collectors who keep antique guns as ornaments – even if they are in working order – and the holders of low-powered air guns.

Obtaining a certificate

Application forms for shotgun and firearms certificates are usually available at police stations. The maximum penalty for making a false statement in an application is a £2,000 fine and 6 months' imprisonment.

Temporary permit The police can issue a temporary permit for a shotgun or firearm in certain circumstances – for example, to the executors of a dead person's estate to cover possession of any guns until they are sold or handed over to their eventual new owner.

When a gun is missing Owning and using a gun of any sort can be dangerous and there are several penalties for misuse.

A gun must be kept in a safe place and the police should be told immediately if a gun is missing or stolen. They must also be told if anyone holding a certificate changes address.

A person holding a valid certificate can sell, give, lend or hire his gun only to someone who also has a valid certificate or is a registered firearms dealer.

When a gun is sold, the police who issued the certificate must be told within 48 hours. Otherwise the buyer commits an offence by having a firearm without a licence.

Police do not always need a warrant to search premises for firearms, and they can arrest anyone who is suspected of possessing a firearm without a warrant.

Sawn-off shotguns It is a criminal offence to shorten a shotgun barrel to less than 24 in. without police permission. *See also:* AGE OF MAJORITY

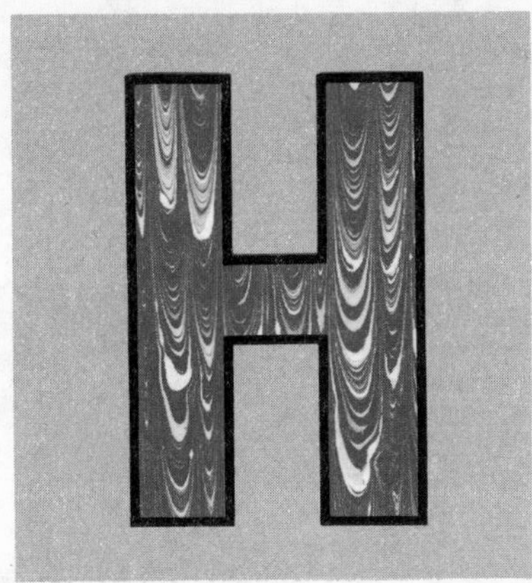

HAIRDRESSER

Legal protection against incompetent treatment

No qualification or registration is needed to set up in business as a hairdresser, but anyone who does so has a legal responsibility to show reasonable care and skill in treating his customers' hair. A customer who is caused suffering because of the hairdresser's lack of care or skill can sue for damages.

Special hours of business for hairdressers

Although other shopkeepers and traders may be restricted to opening and closing at certain times, hairdressers are not prevented from doing business by visiting clients in their homes or in their clubs or hotels outside normal opening hours. *See:* SHOPS

IF SOMETHING GOES WRONG

A customer who is caused actual suffering because of a hairdresser's negligence or lack of care can sue him for damages.

THE WAITER WHO WAS GOING GREY

A hairdresser must use care and skill not only in dressing hair but also in choosing the right materials for the job.

Mr Watson, who was a waiter in Manchester, found that his grey hairs made it harder for him to find work. From time to time, therefore, he went to Mrs Buckley, who was a hairdresser, to have his hair dyed.

On one visit she suggested that he should try a new dye. Soon after she applied it, Mr Watson developed dermatitis – a skin disease – and had to go into hospital.

It was found that the dermatitis was caused by an excessive amount of chromic acid which had got into the new dye accidently. Mr Watson sued Mrs Buckley for damages.

DECISION

The judge ordered Mrs Buckley to pay damages.

Mr Watson, he ruled, was entitled to expect that any materials used by Mrs Buckley were reasonably fit for their purpose.

HALF-BROTHER AND SISTER

When marriage is allowed and forbidden

You cannot marry your half-sister or half-brother – that is someone to whom you are related only through your mother or father. But you can marry the half-sister of a deceased wife or the half-brother of a deceased husband. *See:* MARRIAGE

HALLMARK

When 'gold' must indeed be gold

When a trader describes something as being gold, silver or platinum, examine it carefully to see whether it is hallmarked – punched with a series of special marks to prove what quantity and quality of the precious metal it contains. If there is no hallmark, the article must usually be described as rolled gold, plated gold, plated silver or plated platinum, unless it is very small or so thin that it cannot be hallmarked.

With that exception, it is a crime to give an unhallmarked article a trade or business description indicating that it is wholly or partly made of gold, silver or platinum. The maximum penalty is an unlimited fine and 2 years' imprisonment.

The only other circumstances in which a trader is entitled to use the descriptions 'gold' and 'silver' is when he is referring simply to the colour of an article. Then he must make clear that it is only colour that is being described.

Any trader who deals in articles of precious metal must display in a conspicuous part of his premises an official notice issued by the British Hallmarking Council, explaining the hallmarking system. The maximum penalty for not doing so is an unlimited fine and 2 years' imprisonment.

Altering a hallmark

It is a criminal offence for anyone, whether in the course of trade or business or not, to alter or repair a hallmarked article, or to remove, alter or deface a hallmark, without the written consent of the office that hallmarked it originally – called the assay office.

WHAT A HALLMARK TELLS YOU

Hallmarks give buyers of gold and silver a guarantee of the quality and origin of a particular article. The maker's, or sponsor's, mark indicates the name of the manufacturer; the standard mark guarantees the metal content; the assay office mark indicates where the article was tested and marked; the date letter shows when it was marked.

A MODERN SILVER HALLMARK

Maker's mark
Each individual smith or firm in the trade can register a punch at the assay office based on initials

Sterling silver
The English mark is a lion. Formerly its head was turned and crowned

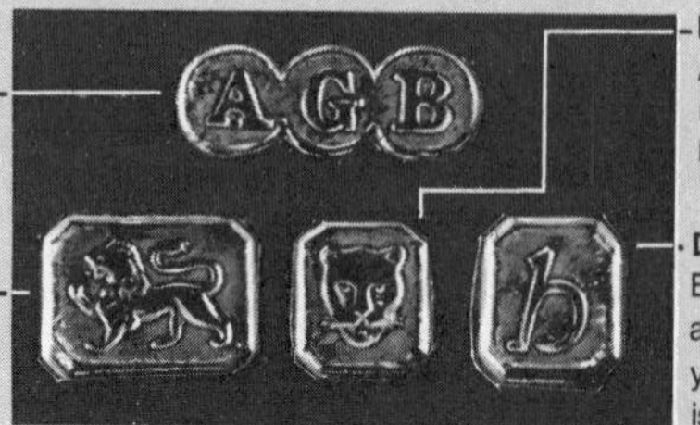

London assay
A leopard head has been used since AD 1300. Early on, it was crowned

Date letter
Each assay office designs a distinctive letter for each year. The ornate B shown is for 1957

Anyone who counterfeits or alters a hallmark, or possesses a die for doing so, can be sent to prison for up to 10 years on conviction.

MAKERS' MARKS

TS PB AB IP
MB WM

Makers punch their own mark on articles before sending them for assay. The solder, as well as the metal, must be of the required quality.

However, it is not an offence if the article is fit only for remanufacture.

The assay offices have also given certain general 'consents', and specific written consent is not required in the cases which they cover – for example, the coating of a silver article bearing an approved hallmark. Copies of the general consents can be obtained from the Assay Office, Goldsmith's Hall, 15 Queen Street, Edinburgh.

The maximum penalty for those offences is an unlimited fine and 2 years' imprisonment.

The maximum penalty for counterfeiting or forging a hallmark is 10 years' imprisonment.

When you have a complaint

If you believe that you have been defrauded over the purchase of a hallmarked article, complain to the trading standards department of your regional or islands council and ask it to refer the complaint to the assay office whose mark is stamped on the article.

To test the quality, the assay office will remove, imperceptibly, a sliver of metal, and it will report its findings to the trading standards department.

HARASSMENT

Protection for people in their homes

Every person who has a right to occupy a house or flat – whether as a tenant, as someone with permission to occupy, or as a spouse with OCCUPANCY RIGHTS – is protected by the criminal law against unlawful EVICTION or harassment by anyone.

It is unlawful to evict a tenant (or someone with Part VII protection) without a court order; or to evict a woman with occupancy rights. *See:* LICENCE TO OCCUPY.

Harassment can take many forms – for example, violence or threats of violence, cutting off electricity, gas or water supplies, changing locks, creating a constant din, sending abusive or threatening letters or putting excrement through the occupier's letter box.

To amount to the offence of harassment, the conduct complained of must be meant to cause the occupier either to:

- Give up his home, or
- Not to exercise any right – for instance, to complain to the environmental health department that the house is unfit to live in – or to seek any remedy – such as suing for breach of contract – in respect of the home.

When an occupier is harassed, there are three main steps that he or she can legally take:

Calling the police An occupier who believes that he or she is being harassed should report the matter to the police. However, harassment can be difficult to prove if it takes such forms as abusive behaviour or language, or excessive noise during the night.

The police may be reluctant to intervene in such cases unless there is clear evidence that the conduct of the harasser amounts to another crime in addition to harassment. *See:* ASSAULT; BREACH OF THE PEACE

Civil action A victim of harassment may also be able to sue the harasser in a civil court for DAMAGES. However, harassment by itself is not a legal wrong.

To get damages, the victim must be able to show that the conduct of the harasser amounts to a DELICT – for instance, that the victim has been injured, or his belongings have been damaged – or is a legal NUISANCE.

Interim interdict When the harassment is severe and the police are reluctant to intervene, the quickest and most effective remedy is to raise an action for damages against the harasser and at the same time apply to the sheriff for an interim INTERDICT – an order requiring the harasser to stop his unlawful activities.

A solicitor will usually be able to obtain an interim interdict within 24 hours. If necessary, emergency LEGAL AID can be applied for, although this will take another 1–2 days.

Penalties

The maximum penalty for the offence of harassment or unlawful eviction is a £2,000 fine and 3 months' imprisonment if the offender is convicted in summary CRIMINAL PROCEEDINGS; or an unlimited fine and 2 years' imprisonment if the offender is convicted on indictment.

The number of prosecutions for harassment is very low and the fines tend to be fairly small. But in some cases people convicted of harassment have been

QUALITY MARKS

SILVER

Britannia silver

Edinburgh
London
Birmingham
Sheffield
after 1975

Foreign silver mark after 1904

Sterling silver

London
Birmingham
Sheffield
after 1975

Edinburgh
after 1975

Edinburgh
Glasgow
before 1975

Common control mark after 1975

Foreign silver after 1904

PLATINUM

Edinburgh
London
Birmingham
Sheffield
after 1975

Common control mark

Assay offices started to hallmark platinum only in 1975. The figure 950 refers to the number of parts of pure platinum out of 1,000

22, 18, 14, 9 carat
after 1975

Common control mark (18 carat)

GOLD

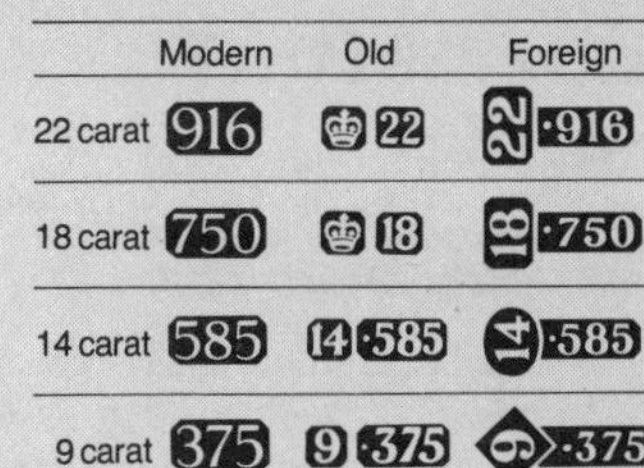

	Modern	Old	Foreign
22 carat	916	22	22 ·916
18 carat	750	18	18 ·750
14 carat	585	14 ·585	14 ·585
9 carat	375	9 ·375	9 ·375

Carat standards were first introduced in 1477. The new standards indicate the number of parts per 1,000 of pure gold

DUBLIN

22 carat

20 carat

18 carat

The main concern of hallmarks has always been the proportion of pure metal to alloy, and the maintenance of standards has long been regarded as a prerogative and duty of the state. Until 1976 it was a domestic matter in Britain, and, even then, the common control mark that was agreed internationally extended outside the country only to Austria, Finland, Sweden and Switzerland.

OFFICE MARKS

BRITISH ARTICLES

London
gold and
silver

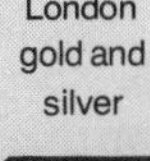

Edinburgh
gold, silver
and platinum

Birmingham
silver

Birmingham
gold before
and after 1975

Sheffield
silver
before 1975

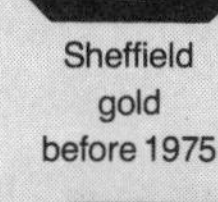

Sheffield
gold
before 1975

Sheffield
gold, silver
and platinum
after 1975

Chester
gold and silver
closed 1962

Dublin silver

Dublin gold

Glasgow
gold and silver
closed 1964

IMPORTED ARTICLES

Since 1842 there have been special hallmarks for foreign plate. Articles that can be shown to be more than 100 years old are exempt

	London	Birmingham	Chester	Dublin	Edinburgh	Glasgow	Sheffield
Gold	Ω	Δ			X		Ω
Silver	Ω	Δ			X		Ω

DATE LETTER

Since 1975, the four British assay offices still operating – Edinburgh, London, Birmingham and Sheffield – have all adopted the same date letter

Collectors of antique plate encounter marks of assay offices that have long been closed, each with its own system of date marks. Exeter and Newcastle closed in 1883, Norwich by 1701, York in 1857, Chester in 1962 and Glasgow in 1964. Dublin marks struck before April 1, 1923 are recognised as British. The Dublin harp is always accompanied by the figure of Hibernia.

sentenced to the maximum prison sentence and fined heavily.

HEALTH AND SAFETY AT WORK

Making sure your workplace is safe – your rights and responsibilities

Everyone is entitled to a safe and healthy place of work, and it is the employer's duty to provide one. If he fails to do so, he can be prosecuted and anyone who is injured can sue him for damages. *See:* ACCIDENT AT WORK

Safety at work is governed by more than 30 Acts of Parliament, but following the Health and Safety at Work Act 1974, it is the Government's intention to replace them with regulations backed by codes of practice worked out in consultation with the relevant industries.

What an employer must do

Employers have a legal duty to ensure 'so far as is reasonably practicable' the health, safety and welfare at work of all employees. In particular, they must provide and maintain:

- Safe machinery, plant, tools and equipment.
- A safe and healthy working environment.
- A safe working system, including secure handling, storage and transport.
- Safe entry and exit arrangements – a proper fire exit, for example.
- Information, training and supervision necessary to ensure the safety of employees.

In addition, an employer has a general duty for the safety of non-employees – such as visitors to his company, or neighbours and passers-by outside. This has been held by a court to include giving them safety information.

An employer may not charge his workers for any health or safety arrangements specifically required by law – they could not, for example, be asked to contribute towards the cost of protective clothing stipulated in regulations.

Self-employed people must conduct their business so as to ensure that people not in their employment are not exposed to health or safety risks.

THE LIFT THAT FAILED ONLY ONCE

Employers may have to pay when something goes wrong, even although no one can show where they were at fault.

A Factories Act stated: 'Every hoist or lift shall be of good mechanical construction ... and be properly maintained'.

A worker at a gas-works was killed when he fell with a bogie down a lift-shaft. The lift mechanism should not have allowed the lift gates to open when the lift was not level with them. The lift worked perfectly before and after the accident and nothing was found to account for the failure.

DECISION

The fact that the lift had failed once, without explanation, was enough to make the employers liable to compensate the widow. They had failed in the duty that the statute placed on them.

What employees must do about safety

Employees have a legal obligation:

- To take reasonable care to avoid injury to themselves and to others.
- Not to interfere with or misuse any safety equipment.
- To co-operate with their employer in complying with statutory regulations.

An employee (or employer) who flouts safety regulations, even if he does not cause an accident, can be prosecuted and fined up to £2,000 in a sheriff court. Very serious cases could be tried by a jury. Then the penalty would be an unlimited fine, and up to two years in prison.

For example, if a metal welder refused to wear protective goggles, stipulated in regulations, he could be:

- Disciplined by his employer.
- Refused compensation for any injuries sustained.
- Prosecuted.

However, the employer could still be liable for claims for damage from anyone else injured in such an accident because he is liable for his employees' negligence in the course of their employment.

The trade union rôle in health and safety

When a company recognises a trade union, that union is entitled to appoint safety representatives from among the company's employees.

The employer has no right to veto an appointment.

Such representatives – who may also be shop stewards – must have been employed by the company for at least 2 years, or have 2 years' experience in similar employment. Their function is to represent the staff in discussions with the employer on health and safety, to investigate any staff complaints or accidents and to carry out regular inspections of the workplace.

Safety representatives have no special legal responsibility to ensure safety, apart from their normal duties as employees.

They are entitled to time off work with pay to carry out their function and to receive relevant training. The Government recommends that safety representatives should keep themselves informed about the law on health and safety, their employer's policy and the hazards associated with their work. They are entitled to information from employers on safety performance and plans and any research into likely hazards. There is no limit to the number of safety representatives that may be appointed, but it should correspond to the size of the workforce and the dangers involved in the industry.

An employer must set up a safety committee, comprising managers, supervisors and safety representatives, if any two safety representatives ask him (in writing) to do so. Such committees are designed to promote employee involvement and management-union co-operation on safety.

As safety representatives are usually shop stewards, they can use union power to enforce their demands.

More important, however, are the powers of the factory inspectorate. When a safety representative is aware that the rules are being broken and the company has refused to put matters right, he should contact the local inspector.

How safety at work is enforced

If you think that conditions or

HEALTH AND SAFETY RULES FOR SHOPS, OFFICES AND RAILWAY PREMISES

How the law protects and imposes duties on employees

Area	What the law says
Cleanliness	Floors and steps must be cleaned at least once a week. Refuse must not be allowed to accumulate in work areas.
Overcrowding	40 sq. ft or 400 cu. ft must be allowed for each employee in every room.
Ventilation	Adequate supplies of fresh or purified air must be in circulation.
Temperature	The premises must have a reasonable temperature: not less than 60.8°F after the first hour's work. A thermometer must be displayed prominently on each floor of the premises.
Lighting	The premises must have enough suitable lights.
Toilets	There must be enough suitable and clean toilets – separate for men and women. The number depends on the size of the workforce. For example, 5 WCs for men and 5 for women would be needed for a staff of between 76 and 100 of each sex, though fewer would be needed for the men if urinals were provided.
Washing facilities	Enough suitable basins must be provided for men and women, on the same scale as toilets. Hot and cold, or warm, running water, soap and drying facilities must be available.
Drinking water	Staff must have adequate, accessible drinking water, with either a cup or fountain provided.
Clothes storage	There must be room for hanging up outdoor clothing and reasonably practical arrangements for drying them.
Seating for rest periods	There must be reasonable facilities for sitting down, where work is not disturbed. Shops must provide at least one seat for every three employees.
Seating for work	Where work can or must be done sitting down, a seat with proper support, suitable both to the worker and to the type of work he or she is doing, must be provided.
Eating facilities	Where shop or office workers eat their meals at work, suitable facilities must be available to them.
Lifts	Both the lift and its gates must be safe. They must be thoroughly examined by a competent person at least once every 6 months. The lift's maximum load – such as '6 persons or 900 lb.' – must be prominently displayed in the cabin.
Fire precautions	Most places of work must have a valid fire certificate from the local fire authority. This certificate is granted only when the fire authority's safety conditions – such as sufficient exits and extinguishing equipment – are met.
First aid	If there are more than 400 workers there should be a first aid room. For other places of work the equipment and facilities required vary according to the circumstances, but all should have at least one first aid box. Offices and shops would not normally have to have a qualified first aider present unless there were more than 150 employees. For factories or any premises with a degree of hazard there should be a first aider where there are more than 50 employees. More detailed guidance for these rules can be found in pamphlet HS(R) 11, obtainable from HMSO.

methods at your work are unsafe or unhealthy, do not wait for an accident to happen: report the matter immediately to the head of your department. If no action is taken, get in touch with the local office of the Health and Safety Executive – the address can be found in the telephone book – and ask for the inspector who deals with your branch of industry. Your name will not be given to your employer unless you agree.

If you belong to a union recognised by the company, report the hazard to your safety representative. If you do not know who that is, ask your shop steward to pursue the complaint with the management.

Inspectors are entitled to visit a workplace at any time and to enforce health and safety legislation. They can, for example, remove or destroy any article that they believe is causing imminent danger of personal injury.

If an inspector finds that a law has been broken, he can serve the employer with an improvement notice, directing him to make certain changes within a set time. Or he can issue a prohibition notice, requiring him to end a dangerous practice.

In cases of serious danger, he can order a piece of machinery, a workshop or, in theory, even a whole factory to be closed until the risk has been remedied.

An employer can appeal – within the period of the notice – to an INDUSTRIAL TRIBUNAL against an improvement or prohibition notice, which may be suspended during the course of the hearing.

The tribunal can modify the terms of the notice, as well as cancelling it or confirming it.

If the appeal fails, he can appeal against the tribunal's decision – only on a point of law – to the Court of Session. In most cases, the tribunal is likely to uphold the inspector's order, but may, exceptionally, give the employer longer in which to comply.

Anyone who fails to comply with such a notice can be prosecuted in a sheriff court and fined up to £2,000 and £200 for each day that the offence continues after the conviction. If the offence is tried by a jury, the penalty is up to 2 years' imprisonment and an unlimited fine, plus the £200 per day.

In addition, anyone who is injured because health and safety regulations were neglected can sue the employer for damages. When a company is prosecuted for contravening a health and safety provision, any director or manager who consented to the offence or who negligently allowed it to happen, may also be guilty and punished separately.

When you have a complaint

If you decide to leave your job because you feel you have been exposed to risk due to your employer's failure to maintain health and safety standards, you may be able later to obtain compensation for UNFAIR DISMISSAL.

Similarly, someone who has been dismissed can succeed in a claim of unfair dismissal if he can prove his employer's neglect of health and safety was the reason.

If you live near, or regularly pass by, a factory or building that constitutes a risk to health or safety – for example, by

HOW COMPANIES ARE OBLIGED TO PREPARE A SAFETY POLICY

General rules that should be laid down and published prominently – for everyone's protection

Anyone employing five or more people must prepare a safety policy statement, bring it to the attention of employees, and display it prominently. It must be revised as necessary, and changes notified to all employees. Some typical rules are laid out below.

Although flexibility may be possible, the policy statement should:

- State the intention to provide safe and healthy conditions.

RULE 1
NO SMOKING

YOU MAY NOT SMOKE IN ANY AREA WHERE **NO SMOKING** NOTICES ARE DISPLAYED

Although smoking is permitted in most parts of the factory there are some places where the risk of fire is so great that the practice cannot be allowed. A match or cigarette end carelessly thrown away in such places might easily cause a fire or explosion which could endanger lives and everyone's job.

RULE 2
HORSEPLAY

HORSEPLAY IS PROHIBITED

Practical joking or horseplay in a factory can be extremely dangerous. As applied to your job it means throwing things, tripping up other people, directing a compressed air jet at someone or any act which may startle or distract other employees.

RULE 3
USE OF GUARDS & SAFETY DEVICES

Employees must make use of guards and safety devices fitted to the machines they operate. Under no circumstances may a guard be made inoperative or be removed from a machine.

Guards are provided for the benefit of employees and if the guards on your machine are not in good order you must report the matter to your supervisor at once.

RULE 4
TRUCK DRIVING

Unless you are an authorised driver you must not drive a fork lift truck or other power operated factory vehicles.

Power operated trucks require specialised knowledge and training to operate them safely and unauthorised operation by untrained people could cause a serious accident.

RULE 5
PERSONAL PROTECTIVE CLOTHING

You must wear protective equipment on jobs for which it is provided.

Safety spectacles, safety footwear, gloves etc., are provided for some jobs because experience has shown the need for them. Refusal to make use of them is a breach of safety rules.

RULE 6
REPORTING INJURIES AND OBTAINING TREATMENT

You must seek immediate medical treatment for any injury you receive no matter how slight it may seem to be. On returning from the medical department you should report the incident to your supervisor.

Immediate medical treatment may be the means of avoiding complications such as infection which can easily result from an apparently trivial injury. Failure to report your injury at once may prejudice your claim to any social security benefit or compensation to which you might be entitled.

emitting foul fumes, or leaving dangerous obstacles in the public's way – contact the Health and Safety Executive, which can enforce the regulations.

If you have been injured by an organisation that has neglected health and safety, you can sue for damages. *See:* NEGLIGENCE

In certain sectors – principally non-industrial activities such as shops and offices – health and safety legislation is enforced by the LOCAL AUTHORITY. The Health and Safety Executive can refer you to the appropriate council department if you want to obtain further information.

HEALTH CENTRE

Putting many medical services under one roof

In many areas, health centres are provided by the area health board to bring various aspects of health care under one

- Describe rules and arrangements made for health and safety.
- List the names and phone numbers of those responsible for safety and of employee safety representatives.
- Give details of safety training and supervision schemes.
- Define the responsibility of the company and of individual employees for maintaining safety.

If the company recognises a trade union, the safety representatives that it nominates are usually consulted before a safety policy is formulated.

When no union is recognised by a company or individual employer, there is no legal rule that the workers must be consulted about safety, but many employers find it useful to do so.

RULE 7
PERSONAL CLOTHING

When working on or around machines do not wear loose fitting clothing or dangling neck ties. Always wear good sound shoes. Women employees should not wear high heels.

Loose clothing and long hair can be caught up in moving machinery much more easily than most people realise. Light shoes invite a serious foot injury.

RULE 8
AUTHORISED PERSONS ONLY

Unless you receive a direct instruction from your supervisor you must not:—

1) Enter an Electric Sub Station, Transformer Room or other enclosure containing electrical equipment.
2) Enter a Gas Meter House.
3) Go on to the Factory Roof.
4) Climb on any machinery or up girders.

Admission to certain parts of the factory is restricted to employees who are authorised to go there in the course of their normal duties. Generally these places present some danger which may not be readily apparent to people who have not received specialist training and instruction.

RULE 9
RUNNING

DO NOT RUN IN THE FACTORY

Running in the factory is an extremely unsafe practice and many accidents are caused through it. Because of the hazards involved it is expected that all employees will exercise good common sense and not run – even in case of fire, walk to the nearest exit.

FACTORIES ACT 1961

It is not generally realised that there are requirements in the Factories Act which apply to EVERY PERSON employed in a factory and cases of legal action by H. M. Inspector of Factories are not unknown.

roof. The size of the centres varies: the larger ones may include not only doctors but also dentists, health visitors, district nurses, social workers and physiotherapists.

Doctors who join a health centre pay rent and contribute to its running costs, but the main expenses are paid by the area health board.

If a doctor or dentist gives up his individual practice and moves to the better facilities of a health centre, his patients are not consulted in advance. They must however be given notice.

If you do not wish to attend a health centre – if, for example, it is too far away – you are entitled to change to another doctor.

If you stay with your present doctor, your rights to his services, including home visits, are not affected. But on moving to a health centre he may enter into partnership with other doctors. In this case you would normally be expected to accept treatment from whichever doctor was on duty when your own was unavailable. *See:* DOCTOR AND PATIENT; HEALTH VISITOR

HEALTH COUNCIL

Public representation in the health service

It is the duty of each area health board to establish local health councils – one or more – to enable the interests of the public to be represented in the National Health Service.

The members are either nominated by local authorities in the area or appointed by the health board after it has consulted appropriate voluntary organisations. They get expenses for travel and loss of earnings.

Their function is to advise the health boards on the health service and consider questions relating to the provision of health services in their area or district.

Health councils have the power to obtain information from health boards about the planning and operation of the health service in their area. They also have the power to visit hospitals and other health board establishments. The health board must meet with each council at least once a year.

Each local health council must submit an annual report to the health board on its own activities and on the operation of health services in its area.

HEALTH SERVICE COMMISSIONER

A channel for your grievances about health care

Complaints of maladministration in the Health Service are handled by the Health Service Commissioner and his staff. They are concerned with all action taken by or on behalf of area health boards (which run hospitals, clinics and community nursing services) and the Common Services Agency of the Scottish Health Service (which runs the ambulance and blood transfusion services, among others).

A complaint can be made that someone has suffered injustice or hardship through maladministration or failure to provide proper service. The complaint should first be brought to the attention of the organisation responsible.

If no satisfaction is obtained, then a formal complaint can be made in writing to the Health Service Commissioner for Scotland, 71 George Street, Edinburgh, EH2 3EE. Normally it should be made within 12 months of the action complained of. He will investigate and issue a report. *See:* OMBUDSMEN

HEALTH VISITOR

How they supplement the medical services

No one is forced to see a health visitor but most people – including family doctors – welcome their aid.

Health visitors are always qualified nurses and provide a wide range of advice and practical help to augment the services of doctors, specialists and hospitals.

Among their main jobs are visits to the homes of mothers-to-be, nursing mothers, elderly people and patients who have just come out of hospital.

Often the health visitor will call without a request from the patient. It may, for example, be at the suggestion of a family doctor.

A call is usually made automatically to nursing mothers after the health visitor has been notified of the birth by the area health board. The visitor will check that mother and child are progressing and give advice.

If a health visitor gave negligent advice and a patient suffered harm as a result, she and her employers could be sued for DAMAGES. The health visitor should inform the doctor in charge of the case about patients whose symptoms call for further attention. Failing to do so could also lead to a negligence action, as the patient could be denied essential treatment.

Childcare

Health visitors advise on immunisation for children and run clinics where children can have hearing, eyesight and other aspects of their development checked.

Helping the elderly and the handicapped

Home contact with elderly people enables health visitors to check that they are claiming the full range of state benefits and entitlements, and to arrange for services such as meals on wheels and attendance at day centres and clubs.

Health visitors call on handicapped people in their homes to give advice and help and arrange for supportive services.

Health education

Health visitors may run anti-smoking and obesity clinics and advise on family planning.

HERITABLE PROPERTY

Land and things attached to land

Heritable property is the technical name lawyers give to land and to things growing on or attached to land such as trees, houses and fixtures. *See:* FITTINGS AND FIXTURES. All other property is known as MOVEABLE PROPERTY. Which of the two categories a particular piece of property falls into can sometimes affect what happens to that property on the owner's death. *See:* DISINHERITANCE; INHERITANCE; INTESTACY; WILL

HIGH COMMISSION

Embassies of the Commonwealth

Britain and other Commonwealth nations do not have embassies in each other's countries. Instead, they have High Commissions, which perform the same basic functions. *See:* BRITISH EMBASSY; FOREIGN EMBASSY

HIGH COURT OF JUSTICIARY

Scotland's highest criminal court

The High Court of Justiciary is the highest criminal court in Scotland. It has existed since 1672. Its judges consist of the Lord President of the Court of Session (who presides as Lord Justice-General), the Lord Justice-Clerk, and the remaining Court of Session judges, who sit in the High Court as Lords Commissioners of Justiciary,

The High Court acts as both a trial court and a court of appeal. As a trial court, it is the only court in Scotland which can try cases of murder, rape, incest and the very rare cases of treason, deforcement of messengers at arms and breach of duty by magistrates.

The High Court also frequently tries culpable homicide and large scale frauds and sometimes allegations of corruption against local authority councillors and officials.

At trials, one judge sits with a JURY of fifteen. The High Court's powers of sentence are usually unlimited.

High Court cases are almost always tried in the sheriff court building of a town in which or near which the crime is said to have been committed, such as Inverness, Aberdeen, Dundee, Perth, Dumfries, Jedburgh, Ayr, Stirling, Airdrie and Oban. But Glasgow has a special building to accommodate the High Court and in Edinburgh it has its own court-room.

When sitting as an appeal court, the High Court always sits in Edinburgh and hears appeals from sheriff and district courts and from verdicts in its own trials. At least three judges hear appeals. The procedure differs depending on whether the procedure at the trial was summary or solemn. There is no appeal to the House of Lords. *See:* CRIMINAL PROCEEDINGS

HIGHWAY CODE

The road users' guide to safety

The Highway Code, produced by the Department of Transport, is a guide to all road users. But it is not law, and disregarding the code is not in itself an offence.

The code can however play an important part in legal proceedings. If someone charged with a driving offence can be shown to have disobeyed the code, the court can take that as evidence in assessing his guilt.

For example, a motorist who has knocked down a child who ran out from a parked ice-cream van, and who is then prosecuted for driving without due care, may plead that the child darted out without warning. But clause 54 of the code warns motorists, 'Be careful near a parked ice-cream van – children are more interested in ice-cream than in traffic,' and it emphasises the point with a photograph.

The prosecution could invoke that clause of the code as evidence that the motorist should have taken particular care when passing the van.

On the other hand, if someone charged with a driving offence can show that he was conforming to the code, the court can take that into account in his favour.

Civil actions The code has the same function in civil actions over road accidents. If you have been injured in a road accident and are claiming DAMAGES (compensation), it helps your case if you can show that the person you are suing disregarded the Highway Code.

Conversely, if you ignored the code, that may be taken to be CONTRIBUTORY NEGLIGENCE on your part. If so, the amount of compensation you may be awarded will be reduced.

THE PEDESTRIAN WHO WAS KNOCKED DOWN AT A JUNCTION

A motorist must bear the Highway Code in mind when a pedestrian is in the road.

In 1963, 73-year-old Mr Alfred Frank started to cross a street at a junction controlled by traffic lights that were in his favour. He had almost reached the central refuge when he was knocked down and seriously injured by a car that had turned right into the street when the lights changed in its favour.

The court ordered the driver of the car, Mr Peter Cox, to pay Mr Frank compensation of £3,547.

Mr Cox appealed, on the ground that Mr Frank should have looked out for his car.

DECISION

The court dismissed the appeal, invoking clause 60 of the Highway Code, which says that a motorist turning at a road junction must give way to pedestrians who are crossing the road into which the motorist is turning.

HIRE AGREEMENT

Anyone who hires goods without intending to become the outright owner is protected by the Consumer Credit Act 1974 over cancellation of hire agreements, methods of repossession by the hirer and difficulties over payment of hire fees. *See:* GOODS, Rental of

HIRE PURCHASE

The hiring that ends with a sale

A hire-purchase contract is a special form of instalment purchase. It takes the legal form of an agreement to hire goods with the intention of eventually owning them outright.

The hirer pays a deposit and regular instalments to cover the purchase price and INTEREST CHARGE on that sum. The final payment includes a nominal amount by which the hirer takes up an option to buy.

If a finance company is involved when you buy goods on hire purchase you make a direct contract with that company, not with the trader who supplies you with the goods. That is because, technically, the finance company has bought the goods from the trader and therefore owns them.

As a result, the trader who supplies the goods cannot be sued for any defect in them unless he was negligent and damage or injury was caused. You must normally sue the finance company. In any case, it is usually better to do so because the finance company has equal liability and is more likely to be able to pay if you win your case.

If a company sells you something on hire purchase, it automatically promises that:

1. It owns the goods offered to you.
2. The goods will be delivered in sound condition.
3. You will be allowed to enjoy the use of the goods without interference from the company provided that you pay the instalments promptly.

In return, you, as 'hirer' and would-be purchaser, undertake to:

1. Accept delivery of the goods ordered, unless there is something wrong with them.
2. Take care of the goods.
3. Keep the goods insured, where required by the agreement.
4. Not sell or pawn them, or deal in them in any way, without the company's permission. In most cases, anyone who buys goods that are still on hire purchase has no right to them and will lose them if the legal owners find out they have been sold.

One exception is when someone as a private individual – not a company or car dealer – buys a car, not realising that the vehicle is on hire purchase and that it still belongs to a third party. In that case, the buyer has a legal right to the car he has bought. *See:* CREDIT AGREEMENT

HOAX CALL

The penalties for mischievously raising a false alarm

A hoax telephone call or some other kind of bogus message which creates false public alarm or causes needless inconvenience or work is treated seriously by the law.

The main offences are:

• Wasting the time of the police by making a deliberately false report. The maximum penalty is at the court's discretion, within its sentencing limits.

• Placing or sending a hoax bomb or sending a warning about a hoax bomb by telephone or writing. Maximum penalty – 5 years' imprisonment.

• Deliberately making a false fire alarm to any fire brigade. Maximum penalty – 3 months' imprisonment or £1,000, or both.

• Sending a false message by telephone to cause annoyance, inconvenience or needless anxiety. Maximum penalty – £400 fine.

• Committing a BREACH OF THE PEACE through a hoax which could cause alarm to the public. The penalty is at the discretion of the court.

WHEN A HOAX IS NOT AMUSING

It is an offence to send a false message by telephone for the purpose of causing annoyance or inconvenience.

THE NON-EXISTENT BIKE

It is an offence to waste the time of the police by making a deliberately false report.

Mr Gray paid a visit to a friend. When leaving, in order to save his friend the trouble of driving him home, Mr Gray falsely stated that he had a bike with him which he had left outside.

The friend insisted on walking with Mr Gray to his bike. On discovering there was no bike, the friend assumed that it had been stolen and insisted to Mr Gray that the matter be reported to the police. Instead of admitting that he had lied, Mr Gray agreed to report the matter.

At the police station, Mr Gray accused no one of the 'theft'. He insisted that he did not want the police to take any action or make any investigation as a result of his report.

Mr Gray was charged with wasting police time by telling lies.

DECISION

Mr Gray pled guilty to the charge and was sentenced to 14 days' imprisonment. On appeal his sentence was reduced to a fine.

HOLIDAY ACCOMMODATION

When a holiday tenant can be forced to leave

If accommodation is genuinely let for the purpose of a holiday, the tenant will have no security of tenure. At the end of a valid NOTICE TO QUIT, which must be at least 4 weeks, the tenant loses his legal right to remain on the premises.

However, if the tenant fails to leave at the end of the notice period, the landlord cannot evict him from the property without first obtaining an EVICTION order from the sheriff court. Provided that it is a genuine holiday letting, the court must grant the order.

When the agreement is a sham

There is no legal definition of a holiday letting. The court decides on the facts of the individual case. If the letting is for a short period – say, 3 months or less – and is described in the lease (the tenancy agreement) as a holiday letting, the court will normally accept it as such.

But some landlords may get a tenant seeking normal accommodation to sign a lease which describes the tenancy as a holiday letting, in order to deprive the tenant of his security of tenure under the Rent (Scotland) Act 1984.

If a tenant signs such a lease – whether or not he has read it – and realises only later that he has signed away his protection under the Act, then the only way in which he can obtain security of tenure or RENT PROTECTION is by producing evidence to satisfy the court that the lease is a sham.

He would need to show, for example, that he had said nothing to the landlord which might mislead him into thinking that the tenant wanted the property as holiday accommodation – or that the landlord told him initially that the lease was merely a device to avoid the Rent

NO SECURITY OF TENURE

Although a holidaymaker has no security of tenure, he can only be evicted by a court order.

(Scotland) Act and would not be enforced.

Out-of-season lettings

A tenant who rents accommodation, out of season, which is normally let as holiday accommodation will be protected by the Act, so long as it is not a genuine holiday letting or the tenancy is not excluded from protection on other grounds. *See:* EVICTION

But there is one major exception. If the lease is for not more than 8 months, and the house was let as genuine holiday accommodation during the 12 months before the tenancy began, the landlord will be able to obtain an eviction order against the tenant. However, the court will not grant the order unless the landlord gave written notice to the tenant, on or before the date when the tenancy began, that he might seek to recover possession under Case 13 of Schedule 3 to the Rent (Scotland) Act.

HOLIDAY ENTITLEMENT

Your right to an annual vacation

Almost all full-time employees in Britain get at least 3 weeks' paid holiday a year, not counting bank holidays. More than one-third of them get 4 or more weeks' holiday. But there is no general law that gives employees the right to holidays, with or without pay, or even to a day off on bank holidays.

For most people, holiday entitlement is fixed by the EMPLOYMENT CONTRACT, the terms of which may be written or implied. In law, an employer is usually free to offer any holiday arrangements he wishes when engaging a new employee. If the employee accepts, the arrangements become legally binding upon both parties to the contract.

Custom and practice

Generally, holiday entitlement is established by collective agreement or by custom in the company or trade concerned. If entitlement is not set out in a written contract or a written statement of employment terms, it can be implied from a collective agreement or from custom. *See:* EMPLOYMENT CONTRACT

No matter how holiday arrangements are established, an employer cannot reduce them once they have become part of a written or unwritten employment contract. If he does so without the consent of the employee, he will almost invariably be in breach of the contract.

Protected groups

Farm workers and employees in trades and industries covered by WAGES COUNCILS – for example, hairdressing – have minimum holiday entitlements that are defined by law. They are laid down in Orders prepared by the Scottish Agricultural Wages Board (for farm workers), or by the appropriate Wages Council.

The only other group of workers whose holiday rights are laid down, in part, by law are women and people under the age of 18 who work in factories. The Factories Act 1961 says that they must receive 6 weekdays off per year. At least 3 must fall between March 15th and October 1st.

Qualifying periods

Most employers insist on a qualifying period before a new recruit is allowed to take a holiday with pay. They are legally entitled to do so, provided that the qualifying period is an express or implied part of the employment contract.

One common qualifying arrangement allows 1 day off for each month worked in the preceding 'holiday year' – which, in many companies, is calculated from April to April – to be taken after at least 6 months' service.

For example, an employee who starts work on September 1 will complete 7 months' service by the end of the 'holiday year' on the following March 31. He may then be permitted to take 7 working days off for that year's summer holiday.

Many employers increase holiday entitlements according to length of service – for example, by agreeing to an extra week for an employee who has completed 5 years with the company.

When holidays may be taken

The time of year when holidays can be taken is sometimes decided by custom and practice. For example, if a factory shuts down for 2 weeks every August, it is an implied condition of employment that employees should take their holidays at that time.

An employer is entitled to restrict the amount of holiday that may be taken at one time, either by writing that condition into individual contracts, or by making a company rule that becomes, by inference, part of those contracts.

A typical restriction for employees entitled to 4 weeks' holiday might be that they can take no more than 2 weeks at once, that at least 1 week must be taken outside the period June–September and that holidays not taken before a certain date cannot be carried over into the next year. In such a case, it is the employee's responsibility to ensure that he receives his full holiday.

If permission for a holiday is refused

An employer may refuse permission for a holiday at a particular time because of pressure of work or some other factor that makes it inconvenient. Whether or not he is entitled to do so depends on the contract and the circumstances.

Provided that the employer gives adequate advance warning that certain dates are unacceptable – for example, when the holiday schedules are drawn up or when the request for time off is first made – he is within his rights. If, however, he gives permission but subsequently withdraws it, he may be in breach of contract.

If an employee is dismissed for taking a holiday when permission has been given and then withdrawn, he can make an UNFAIR DISMISSAL claim to an in-

YOUR RIGHT TO CLAIM UNEMPLOYMENT BENEFIT WHILE YOU ARE ON HOLIDAY

If you take a holiday from your job, with or without pay, you cannot usually get unemployment benefit during your vacation. But you may be able to get benefit if you have to take unpaid holidays and, since the previous March 1, you have already had your current holiday entitlement – even if taken in a previous job.

Employees who are employed on a series of fixed-period contracts, with unpaid breaks in between, can claim benefit for the breaks. So a temporary teacher can claim for school holiday breaks – but not if employed under a single contract that continues to run during holidays.

Unemployed people claiming benefit who go away on holiday may lose their entitlement, because one condition for getting benefit is that the recipient must be available for work. However, benefit is not always stopped for that reason.

An unemployed person intending to go on holiday should inform his unemployment benefit office well in advance. If his destination is in Britain, Northern Ireland or the Isle of Man, he can usually continue to get benefit for up to 2 weeks. He will have to fill in a special holiday form and give his holiday address and telephone number (if any).

If an unemployed person cannot give a holiday address because he is camping or touring, he is not eligible for benefit, as he cannot easily be contacted if work becomes available for him. But he may be able to arrange for benefit to continue if he agrees to telephone the benefit office each morning or as requested, or to pick up mail at a named post office.

Benefit is not normally payable if the holiday is outside Britain, Northern Ireland or the Isle of Man. However it may be continued during a short trip to an EEC country to look for work. *See:* EUROPEAN COMMUNITIES; UNEMPLOYMENT BENEFIT

dustrial tribunal. The tribunal, when deciding whether or not the dismissal was unfair, will consider whether the employer acted reasonably in all the circumstances.

When payment is taken instead of holidays

Some employers offer employees extra pay to continue working during part of their holiday entitlement, but that practice is not approved of by the trade unions.

An employee cannot be compelled to work during the holiday to which he is otherwise entitled unless that is a specific or implied term of his employment contract.

If an employee leaves his job before taking all of his holiday entitlement, he has the right to be paid for the holidays not taken only if that is provided for in his employment contract.

It is not sufficient that holidays accrue due to him throughout the holiday year. To obtain 'accrued' holiday pay for those days, there must be an express or implied term to that effect in his employment contract.

If he takes the matter to court, it will be his responsibility to prove that he is entitled to accrued holiday pay.
See: PAY

HOLIDAY HOME

Special rules and restrictions on a second home

Anyone who has acquired a second home in the country or at the seaside for use at weekends and for holidays is faced with particular legal problems that do not affect the owner of just one home.

The first difficulty is insurance. Insurance companies do not normally cover property that is likely to stand empty for considerable periods, unless some special arrangement has been made. If you do not inform the insurance company that the property you are asking it to insure is a holiday home, the insurance company may terminate the policy and not pay out on a claim, if it discovers the true position.

The insurer should therefore be told the value of the property, the number of occasions during the year when it is likely to be occupied, its precise location and any other fact you think might be relevant. You will almost certainly be charged an additional premium.

Full cover is always expensive. The insurer normally insists that all services are turned off when the property is unoccupied, and that satisfactory arrangements are made for security checks on the property from time to time. In particular, liability for damage by water and frost is likely to be excluded.

Liability for rates You do not have to pay rates on property that is not occupied for 3 months or more in the financial year (April to April), as long as it is also completely unfurnished. After a house has been empty for 6 months, however, the local authority may, at its discretion, require you to pay rates.

Mortgage relief

If your holiday home has been bought with the help of a mortgage, you are not usually entitled to claim tax relief on the interest payments, even if you do not have a mortgage on another property. That is because tax relief is available only on mortgage payments secured on a main or principal home.

The one exception is the case of a taxpayer whose employment requires him to live elsewhere, in a house provided by his employer. In those circumstances, the employee can buy one home as his own and claim tax relief on the interest payment even if he only uses the home for holidays. *See:* MORTGAGE

When the holiday home is sold

When you sell a holiday home you may have to pay CAPITAL GAINS TAX on any profit you make. The only profit that is exempt is what you make on selling your main residence. If you own two homes, and you live in both to some extent during the year, you may choose one to be treated as your main residence for exemption. If it is likely that the sale of your holiday home will make a greater taxable gain than the sale of your second house, choose the holiday home.

A house that is always let to tenants cannot be selected for exemption, although one that is only let occasionally might still qualify.

To establish which home you wish to be considered tax-exempt, you must inform the Inland Revenue in writing within 2 years of buying the second home. Otherwise, the question will be decided for you by the Inland Revenue. If that question cannot be agreed between you and your tax inspector, it will be decided by the Appeal Commissioners. *See:* INCOME TAX

Renting a holiday home

If a holiday home is genuinely let to a tenant for the purpose of a holiday, the tenant will have no security of tenure.

The landlord can, if necessary, end the tenancy by serving a valid NOTICE TO QUIT on the tenant at the end of the holiday period. If the tenant fails to leave at the end of the notice period, the landlord cannot evict him or her without obtaining an EVICTION order from the sheriff court.

Where the holiday home is let out-of-season, for not more than 8 months, the landlord can evict the tenant if he refuses to leave – provided certain conditions are met. He must apply to court for an eviction order. *See:* HOLIDAY ACCOMMODATION

HOLOGRAPH WRITINGS

Documents in handwriting

A holograph writing is a document entirely in a person's own handwriting. It is valid as long as it is signed at the end by the writer – no witnesses are necessary.

Typed documents may be treated as holograph documents if the person writes in his own handwriting, above his signature, 'adopted as holograph'. This avoids having to write out lengthy documents.

A signed document which is partly printed or typed and partly written – for example, a will form filled up in handwriting – may be treated as holograph if all the essential parts of the document are in writing. It is best not to rely on this: add 'adopted as holograph' or have the document witnessed by two people.

It is easier to challenge a holograph document than one which has been properly signed and witnessed. If a holograph document is alleged to be a forgery, it is up to those saying it is valid to convince the court that this is so. But where the document is properly signed and witnessed, the challengers have to prove their case.

Holograph wills

A WILL or CODICIL is quite often a holograph writing. This has many advantages:

- It is easy to do, especially for people who are unable to get documents typed very easily.
- It can be prepared in secret, since no witnesses are needed.
- It is valid as long as it is signed at the end. Most people making their own wills remember to do this.

But there are disadvantages:

- A holograph writing is easier to challenge as a forgery.
- It may be difficult to prove genuine, since there are no witnesses to give evidence that they saw the person who died write and sign it. Also a person's handwriting may change in character near death, so that there is doubt about the will's authenticity.
- Before the executors named can obtain CONFIRMATION, two people who are acquainted with the deceased's handwriting must swear that the will is genuine.

A HOLOGRAPH WILL

How you can make a will without witnesses:

I, Colin McDonald, 6 Napier Avenue, Aberdeen, leave all my property to be divided equally between my wife and son.

Colin McDonald
5 January 1983.

Above is a simple example of a holograph will. It is valid so long as it is in your own handwriting and you sign it at the end. No witnesses are needed and you do not have to use a lawyer.

A holograph will does not have to be written on any special form: an ordinary piece of paper will do. Put the date on and make sure that you set out your wishes clearly.

HOME HELP

Assistance in the home for the sick and the infirm

A home help is somebody paid by the regional (or islands) council to help with the cooking, cleaning and shopping in a household where the person who normally looks after the home is unable to cope.

The reason for the inability may be illness, pregnancy, convalescence, or the fact that the person normally in charge of the home is simply too old or infirm. Help is also generally available to clean a long-neglected home.

Obtaining a home help

To apply for a home help, contact the organiser of the service at your local social work department. The organiser will visit your home and assess the amount of help needed – from a few hours a week to daily attendance. There is often a waiting list for help, but urgent requests receive priority.

In some areas the home help service is free. In others, there is a charge which may be a flat rate or be based on income. There is no charge if the applicant is receiving SUPPLEMENTARY BENEFIT.

HOME IMPROVEMENT

When you need permission to make changes in your home

Most major home improvements must be approved by the appropriate local authority. If you live in the Highland, Borders or Dumfries and Galloway regions, the appropriate authority is the regional council. If you live in any other part of Scotland, it is the district or islands council.

Two separate departments of the council are usually involved. The planning department is concerned with outward appearance and the effect on the locality of any new building work. The building control department is concerned with the safety and health of the persons who live in the building, and with energy conservation.

Planning control is mainly achieved by planning officers exercising their judgment as to the suitability of any proposed building for its locality. It is impossible to lay down hard and fast rules that would apply to every development, although there are rules describing minor work that does not require planning permission. Such work is known as 'permitted development'.

Building control is more precise and is operated by building inspectors who are responsible for ensuring that the constructional work and the installation of certain fittings complies with the building regulations.

If your house has been classified as being of special architectural or historic interest, you will also require Listed Building consent for any alteration that may affect its character. Such permission is applied for and granted together with a planning application. *See:* BUILDING PRESERVATION

IF IN DOUBT, ASK!

Not all home improvements require council permission, but if you are in doubt, ask.

You should also check your title deeds. They sometimes have conditions preventing you from carrying out certain types of improvement without the permission of your SUPERIOR or some other person.

How to get your improvement plans approved

If approval is required, you must apply separately to the planning and building control departments. In some councils, the two work closely together and application forms for both can generally be obtained from either. You can then return the forms to the one office – with enough drawings for both. The drawings that have to be prepared for building control approval will usually be suitable also for obtaining planning approval – or can easily be made so.

Approval takes the form of a building warrant from the building control department and planning permission from the planning department. If a building warrant is refused, it is normally easy to obtain approval by amending your plans. But if planning permission is refused, there may be no way of gaining approval except, perhaps, by appealing to the Secretary of State for Scotland.

If you have any reason to think that planning approval might be withheld, it would be wise to apply at first only for 'outline planning approval'. You will then know whether to go ahead, or abandon the proposal.

The planning and building control departments may suggest amendments to your scheme before the council consider it.

Obtaining planning permission

Immediate neighbours have to be given formal notification that you have applied for planning permission. As well as completing various forms you will have to pay a fee to the council.

Planning applications are heard frequently, in some councils as often as once a week. The council is legally bound to let you have its decision within 2 months of the application. Once granted, planning permission is valid for 5 years; it lapses if work has not started by then.

If planning permission is refused – and you do not wish to amend your plans – you have the right of appeal to the Secretary of State for Scotland, within 6 months of receiving notice of disapproval.

If he considers the appeal justified, he will arrange for an inquiry to be held. This may be by written representation or by public hearing. You and the council will be invited to give evidence. On the basis of the findings, the Secretary of State will grant or reject your application.

If you do not obtain the appropriate permission or do not carry out work strictly according to the plans approved, the council can serve you with an enforcement notice, ordering you to demolish the unauthorised work and to rebuild it in accordance with the approved plans or otherwise to council approval – at your own expense. If you ignore that notice, you can be prosecuted and fined. *See:* PLANNING PERMISSION

Obtaining a building warrant

As long as your application complies with the building regulations, the council must grant a warrant. It cannot reject an application without giving reasons. If your application is rejected, there are several courses open to you.

First, discuss the matter with the building inspector and find out if the council would be likely to relax any regulation contravened, on the ground that your proposal is a reasonable one. You can apply for a relaxation without the building inspector's support, but

HOME IMPROVEMENTS THAT NEED APPROVAL

Understanding when you have to notify the council of work that you wish to undertake

Many minor home improvement jobs are automatically permitted – you do not need to tell the council what you intend to do or wait for permission. But major additions and alterations, or work that could cause danger or inconvenience to others, are likely to be governed by planning permission or building approval rules. Starting without a permit could be costly.

Type of work	**Is planning permission needed?**	**Is a building warrant needed?**
Any extension that is to project in front of the house or above the rooftop	Yes	Yes
A porch	Yes	Yes
Any extension that is less than 50 m³ or one-fifth the size of the house (one-tenth for a terrace house), whichever is greater, up to a maximum of 115 m³	No	Yes
Any extension bigger than 50 m³, or one-tenth the size of the house, whichever is the greater	Yes	Yes
Any extension that is larger than 115 m³	Yes	Yes
A shed in front of the house	Yes	No if less than 5 m² floor area and 3 m high
A shed of limited size (with ridge roof up to 4 m; other roof up to 3 m) not in front of the house	No	
An oil-storage tank in front of the house	Yes	Yes
An oil-storage tank of up to 3,500 l capacity not in front of the house	No	Yes
A fence or garden wall higher than 1 m on a boundary to a road having vehicular traffic, or 2 m on any other boundary	Yes	No
A front fence lower than 1 m or a back or side fence (other than one to a road with vehicular traffic) lower than 2 m	No	No
A new or altered access from a trunk or classified road	Yes	No
Alterations to existing structural work	No – unless external	Yes
New or altered stairway	No	Yes
New or extended habitable rooms	No – unless extension is in front of house	Yes
New or extended drainage, internal or external	No	Yes
New or altered flue pipes	No	Yes
A new toilet	No – unless extension is in front of house	Yes
Replacing existing sanitary and heating appliances	No	No – if no structural work is required
Fitting new solid fuel heating appliances	No	Yes
Fitting new electric heating appliances	No	No
Fitting new gas heating appliances	No	No – if the work is done by the Gas Corporation and no structural work is required
Installing fitted furniture, such as wall cupboards	No	No
General repairs	No	No
Painting the inside or outside of the house	No	No

without it your chances of success would be much reduced.

If there is little chance of obtaining a relaxation, your best course is to amend the plans so that they comply with the regulations. The building inspector will advise you, but you do not have to adopt his suggestions if you do not like them. There may be other ways of satisfying the regulations. The professional advice of an architect or surveyor might enable you to succeed quickly.

You can appeal to the Secretary of State for Scotland against a refusal of the council to relax a regulation, or to the local sheriff court against a rejection of your plans by the council, but you would need to feel very strongly about your proposals, and to have adequate professional support, before attempting to do either.

Once a building warrant has been granted it remains valid for 3 years, and extensions can be granted.

As building work proceeds you may have to give notice that work has been done or is about to be done. You will find particulars in the building regulations, but you can more easily obtain the necessary information from the building inspector.

If you fail to keep to the terms of the building warrant, or if you have not bothered to obtain a warrant in the first place, the council can order you to demolish and rebuild at your own expense. If you refuse, the council can carry out the work for you and recover the expense. You can also be prosecuted and fined.

Once you have carried out the work you must apply to the council for a certificate of completion. It is an offence to use the new home improvement without this. *See:* BUILDING REGULATIONS

Raising money for home improvements

Most people need help to meet the cost of repairing or extending their home – often as much as several thousand pounds, even for a do-it-yourself job. You may be able to obtain an IMPROVEMENT GRANT or INSULATION GRANT from your local council to cover part of the cost, but you could also need a loan to pay the rest of the costs involved.

Interest on loans for home improvement is eligible for income tax relief. The way this is calculated was changed in April 1983.

For loans taken out after that date, interest payments are reduced by the percentage at which basic rate tax is payable. If, for example, you have taken a loan of £2,000 at 15% interest, your annual interest repayments are reduced by 30 per cent (the current basic rate), from £300 to £210.

Where to get a loan

- If you have a council mortgage, or have obtained a local authority grant for improving your property, you can ask the council for a loan to meet the outstanding expense. Such loans are given at a preferential rate and usually take the form of a second mortgage on the house.
- Building societies give home-improvement loans to clients who have a savings account or MORTGAGE with the society. The loan can be short or long term; the amount given and the rate of interest depend on the state of the society's finances, but are usually more favourable than other lending institutions.
- If you do not have a building society account, ask your bank manager. Most banks offer loans for home improvement.
- If you cannot get a loan from your bank manager, you can borrow from a finance house at a higher interest rate. Finance houses – many of whom advertise nationally – demand less security than banks, but charge more.
- Insurance companies lend money to people who have life assurance policies to offer as security. Their rates are relatively low, but the loan may affect the amount of protection offered by the policy – so read the loan agreement carefully before signing it.

The hidden cost of home improvement

By improving your home, you will have increased its value: by the same token, the improvements you make will mean that you will have increased the rateable value of your home.

When the work is completed, the council is entitled to reassess your property and raise your annual RATES bill.

HOME TEACHING

When a child is educated at home

Every child of compulsory school age – that is, 5 to 16 years – must receive efficient education, either by making him or her attend a school regularly or by other means. It is the parents' duty to see that this happens. *See:* SCHOOL

Education authorities must fix an annual 'school commencement date'. A child who has not reached the age of 5 by that date will not have to start school until the next commencement date. Education must continue until the child is approximately 16. *See:* SCHOOL AGE

Special rules when a child does not go to school

If you choose to educate your child at home, either yourself or by employing a teacher, you are entitled to do so provided you can show the local education authority that the education provided is efficient.

Some parents decide to educate their children at home because they are against schools on principle: others do so because they are dissatisfied with local schools.

Whatever the reason, if you decide on home education you must be consistent. You cannot keep a child at home in the summer and send him or her to school in the winter, or provide some lessons at home and send the child to school for others.

In certain circumstances – for example, if a child is psychologically unable to face going to school – the local education authority has the power to provide the child with free home teaching.

When a parent chooses home education

If your child is not sent to school the local education authority will want to know why. It will want proof, such as samples of work and lists of books being used, that the teaching you are providing is systematically organised – and is right for your child.

It may ask for a timetable of subjects and the qualifications of the teacher – although it is not legally necessary for the teacher to be qualified.

The authority will send an official –

possibly one of its professional advisers – to check on the child's progress, and is more likely to be satisfied with the education being provided if you have followed its advice on subject matter and methods of teaching. Careful records should be kept to show what the child has done.

If the local authority is not satisfied

If you fail to convince the local education authority that you are giving your child a satisfactory education, it will make a SCHOOL ATTENDANCE order against you, requiring you to send your child to a named school.

If you do not agree with the making of an attendance order, you have 14 days in which to appeal to the sheriff court. You can argue your case for educating your child at home and can call witnesses to support your methods. The court will decide whether to continue, amend or revoke the attendance order.

If you simply ignore the attendance order, or ignore a sheriff's decision to continue it, you can be fined up to £400, or imprisoned for up to a month, or both. If you continue to keep your child at home, you are liable to further court appearances and to the same maximum penalties.

When a child cannot go to school

If a child cannot go to school at all because of serious illness or because a place at a suitable school cannot be found – perhaps because he or she is handicapped – the local education authority may make special arrangements to provide a home teacher.

If you think your child requires home teaching, you should contact your local education authority. You can find its address under your regional (or islands) council in the telephone directory. If attempts to find a teacher fail, the authority may be prepared to pay for a correspondence course from an accredited correspondence college.

Home teaching is only used as a last resort, as local authorities like to get children back to school as soon as possible. That applies even when a child has had a serious illness or accident, or is severely handicapped.

If a child's home is a long way from a suitable school, that is not in itself a reason for the child to receive home teaching. In such a case the local authority is obliged to find and pay for board and lodging for the child near the school or arrange for him or her to attend a boarding school.

NO EASY OPTION

When a parent decides to educate his child at home, he must be able to prove to the local authority that the teaching is efficient.

HOME WORKER

How the law affects you if you work from home

If you regularly work from home either as an employee or as a self-employed person, you can claim income tax relief on the running costs of that part of your house or flat which you use for your job, provided that you pay those costs yourself and are not reimbursed for them by an employer or client.

To establish your right to claim relief, you must first satisfy the tax inspector, either in a letter or by visiting him, that a significant part of your working time is spent at home. If you are an employee who occasionally brings a file home to study in the evening, you will not qualify. On the other hand, if you have set aside facilities – a desk and filing cabinet, for example – for weekend and evening work, you may obtain a nominal allowance of £25–£30 a year for the expense involved.

Keeping records

The Inland Revenue requires all self-employed people to produce annual accounts of income and expenses, whether they work from home or from other premises. *See:* SELF-EMPLOYED

If you are an employee who works from home and you intend to claim income tax relief on expenses for which you have not been reimbursed, keep a careful record of those expenses, with bills and receipts, to submit to the tax inspector when you complete your annual tax return. There is space on the return form for an expenses claim.

What you may claim

The items that someone working from home may set against tax vary according to the circumstances. The tax inspector decides what they are, but if you disagree with his assessment you can appeal against it. *See:* INCOME TAX

In submitting your claim, you should list all expenses that can conceivably relate to business. The inspector will eliminate any that do not qualify for relief, but he may not offer to include any you have forgotten to mention.

The items for which relief may be claimed fall into three categories:

1. Raw materials – for example, wool or fabrics used in knitting or dressmaking.

2. Business equipment – for example, a typewriter, sewing machine or vehicle used for business.

3. Operating expenses – including electricity bills, telephone accounts, stationery and postal costs, local authority rates, accountant's fees, advertising costs and insurance premiums to cover business equipment. Travel expenses arising from business may also be claimed.

A home worker may seek tax relief under any or all of those heads, whether he is an employee or self-employed. However, many of the items are normally reimbursed by employers and, if they are, they do not qualify for an additional allowance.

How relief is assessed

Once the tax inspector has accepted a list of items on which he will allow relief, he determines the proportion of the cost of each that can be offset against tax. If you disagree with his decision, you can appeal against it.

Some items are obviously business expenses. If your work involves typ-

CLAIMING YOUR COSTS

Home workers are entitled to claim some of their home running costs against their income tax liability.

ing and you have to buy your own paper and carbon paper, you can normally offset most of the cost. However, the inspector needs to satisfy himself that the record of your outlay is accurate – so you should ask for, and keep, receipts – and that the amount is reasonable in the light of your job.

Household running costs are less straightforward, because the bills do not generally distinguish between domestic and business expense. In deciding the proportion of such expenses that can be set against tax, the inspector takes into account the amount of time spent working from home and the facilities set aside at home for business use.

For example, if you live in a 6-room house, work entirely from home and have set aside one room mainly for business, the inspector starts his calculations by assuming that a sixth of your household running costs qualify as business expenses.

However, he may adjust that proportion up or down according to circumstances. He might argue that you would have had to heat and light the room even if it were not used for work and reduce the allowance. On the other hand, if your work involves electrical equipment you may succeed in persuading the inspector that your electricity bill is higher than it would otherwise have been and that your allowance should therefore be increased.

If you work at home only occasionally, you will normally obtain only token relief of £25–£30.

The arrangements for offsetting the cost of business equipment against tax also vary according to the circumstances and according to the nature of the equipment itself.

For example, the full price of typewriters and calculators must be offset in the year in which they were bought. But you cannot claim more than 25 per cent of the price of a car in any single tax year.

THE HOME WORKER WHO GLUED SHOE HEELS

Whether a home worker will be treated as employed or self-employed depends on the circumstances. A home worker who consistently works regular hours for a lengthy period is likely to be treated as employed.

Mrs Cope assembled shoe heels at home for Airfix Footwear Ltd. Each afternoon the materials for assembling 12 dozen pairs of heels were brought to her house and she worked on them until midnight or the following morning.

Mrs Cope generally worked 5 days a week, with occasional breaks when demand was low. She had done so for 7 years. She was paid weekly 'wages' but had no income tax deducted. The company paid no national insurance contributions on her behalf.

Mrs Cope lost her job and made a complaint of unfair dismissal to an industrial tribunal. She could only make such a claim if she was an employee. The tribunal decided that she was, but Airfix appealed to the Employment Appeal Tribunal on the ground that she was a self-employed person, in business on her own account.

DECISION

The Tribunal decided that Mrs Cope was employed by Airfix. If the work had been sporadic or casual, it might not have been possible to classify her as an employee. But her work was regular and that was enough to indicate the existence of an EMPLOYMENT CONTRACT. The industrial tribunal, therefore, had the power to hear her complaint.

The inspector may reduce the allowance on business equipment if he thinks it fulfils a domestic function as well. If you use your car both for business and for pleasure, he will want to know the proportion of motoring time devoted to each. Typewriters, sewing machines and electric drills are presumed to have a domestic use.

Avoiding capital gains tax

If you work mainly from home and set aside part of your house or flat solely for business, the Inland Revenue may charge you CAPITAL GAINS TAX when you sell the premises. The tax would be levied on the proportion of the profit from the sale equal to the proportion of the premises used for your work.

However, the tax is payable only if there is exclusive business use of the room or rooms. You can avoid it if you can show that there was some domestic use as well. So get the children to do their homework in your office or study, or keep it as a spare bedroom for guests. If you have a workshop, store your own decorating materials and household equipment there.

If you have previously claimed that part of the house was set aside solely for business to obtain income tax relief, you will be charged capital gains tax on it. So in claiming income tax relief, always qualify the claim by saying that there is occasional private use as well.

When the rates may be affected

Valuation and rating legislation provides that only dwelling houses attract domestic RATES. Premises used for business or commerce are liable to higher rates.

The term dwelling-house is, however, interpreted broadly. You will not have to pay higher rates if, for example:

- You use a garage or outbuilding for some commercial purpose, provided that it was not built or altered for that reason. Someone who repairs cars from home and adds an inspection pit to his garage to help him does not have to pay extra rates. But if he puts in a counter and a sales window to sell spare parts to customers, his rates will be increased.
- Someone living in the house uses a room or rooms for some commercial purpose, provided that it is not set apart entirely for that reason. If you convert your front room into a shop or waiting

room, your rates will be increased, but if you and your family use it from time to time for business typing or sewing they will not be.

The rates authorities consider the nature and extent of the business, any physical alterations to the premises and the degree to which the business is publicised in determining whether additional rates must be paid.

A home worker who makes major alterations to his house – for example, the building of an extension to serve as a waiting room – requires PLANNING PERMISSION.

If you do not own the premises

Someone who rents a house or flat and works from home may be breaking the terms of his tenancy agreement. Such agreements do not normally forbid occasional light work – for example, typing or sewing – provided that it does not disturb other tenants, but the exact wording should be checked.

Insuring business assets when you work from home

If you work from home, a normal household contents insurance policy is sufficient to protect you against the loss of inexpensive business items - for example, a pocket calculator – but you may need to make special arrangements for any more valuable articles – an electric typewriter, stocks of goods for resale, large quantities of cash and business files and documents – that you think you may eventually have to keep at home. Check the terms of your household contents policy carefully and, if in doubt, ask the insurance company.

Contents policies are devised for private dwellings. If you are regularly visited by numbers of clients or customers, you may be required to pay a higher premium. The additional cost is a tax-deductible business expense. *See:* INSURANCE

Employment protection rights for home workers

A person who works at home is only entitled to EMPLOYMENT PROTECTION rights – for instance, the right to compensation for unfair dismissal or redundancy – if he is an employee. *See:*

CAUTION CAN CUT COSTS FOR THE HOME WORKER

If a home worker is obviously using his home extensively for business purposes, he may have to pay higher rates. Caution is advisable.

EMPLOYED PERSON

A home worker who is in law SELF-EMPLOYED has no such rights – although he will be entitled to a minimum wage if covered by a wages council order. *See:* WAGES COUNCILS

Whether a home worker is employed or self-employed depends on the circumstances. In one case a home worker was held to be an employee because she had worked for the same company for 7 years, generally for 5 days a week. In another case, a home worker who was able to decide on a casual basis whether or not to work was regarded as self-employed.

Full-time employees who work from home instead of from their employer's premises do not lose any of their employment protection rights and their employment contracts are governed by the same rules that apply to other full-time employees.

However, employees who work for less than 16 hours a week – or fewer than 8 hours a week if they have been with the same employer for 5 years or more – are excluded from most employment protection rights. *See:* PART-TIME WORKER

A home worker has the same liability to pay national insurance contributions and the same right to social security benefits as other employed and self-employed people.

Health and safety Most of the regulations on HEALTH AND SAFETY AT WORK do not apply to home workers. In 1979 the Health and Safety Commission made draft regulations for their protection, but these are not yet in force.

However, if a home worker uses a machine provided by his employer and is injured because of a defect in it, he can sue the employer for NEGLIGENCE, even though the real fault lay with the manufacturer of the machine.

HOMELESSNESS

A housing authority's duty to provide accommodation

Any person who is homeless or threatened with homelessness is entitled to advice and assistance from the local housing authority and, in certain circumstances, to accommodation.

Applications for help should be made to the housing department of the district (or islands) council. Most councils have a homeless persons officer to deal with such applications. Some of the larger councils – for instance, Glasgow District Council – have a special 'homeless persons unit'.

Applicants who have a 'priority need' are legally entitled to accommodation. This accommodation can be either temporary or permanent, depending on whether or not the applicant has become homeless, or threatened with homelessness, 'intentionally'.

People entitled to help

People are legally homeless if they have no accommodation that they are entitled to occupy. Examples are:

- Evicted tenants.
- People who lose their homes through fire, flood or other disaster.
- People turned out by their relatives.
- People sleeping rough.
- People squatting without permission.
- Immigrants who are allowed to enter the UK, but have nowhere to live.

Some people who have accommodation which they are entitled to occupy are treated as legally homeless:

- People who cannot gain entry to their homes – for instance, tenants who have been unlawfully evicted.
- Women who risk being assaulted by a husband or cohabitee if they continue to live in the accommodation.

• People who have a caravan or houseboat, but no site or mooring for it.

Temporary accommodation People do not stop being legally homeless merely because they are living in temporary, 'emergency' accommodation – for instance, a relative's house, night shelter or women's refuge.

Threatened homelessness People who are threatened with losing accommodation are entitled to help if they are likely to become homeless within 28 days.

What 'priority need' means

A housing authority is legally obliged to provide accommodation only for those applicants who are believed to have a 'priority need'. A priority need arises in the following circumstances:

1. Where the applicant has a dependent child. The child does not need to be living with the applicant: it is sufficient that he or she might reasonably be expected to do so. This would cover the situation where a child has been taken into local authority care because of the lack of accommodation. *See:* CHILDREN IN CARE

2. Where the application is the result of an emergency – for instance, fire, flood, storm or any other disaster.

3. Where the applicant or someone living with him (or who might reasonably be expected to live with him) is vulnerable because of old age, mental illness or handicap, physical disability or other special reason. A 'special reason' could include a woman at risk of being battered or an adolescent at risk of sexual or financial exploitation.

4. Where the applicant is pregnant. A priority need also arises if an applicant is living (or might reasonably be expected to live) with someone who is pregnant.

If a housing authority believes that an applicant may be homeless, and may have a priority need, it is legally obliged to arrange temporary accommodation while further inquiries are made. The accommodation may be a local authority reception centre, a hostel, a council house, a refuge for battered women or a guest house or hotel. Families must not be split up (unless a child's welfare requires him or her to be taken into local authority care).

Applicants with no priority need If a housing authority is satisfied that an applicant has no priority need, it is legally obliged to provide only advice and assistance. It may, for instance, provide information about welfare and housing benefits, or discuss putting the applicant's name on the council's housing waiting list. It may also supply names and addresses of accommodation agencies, hostels, lodgings and housing associations.

PROTECTING THE PROPERTY OF HOMELESS PEOPLE

A housing authority must take reasonable steps to protect the property of homeless people who are entitled to temporary or permanent accommodation – but only if there is a risk of loss or damage and no other arrangements have been made. The property will normally be stored.

The authority can charge for this service. It can also give itself the right to dispose of the property if, for example, it is later abandoned.

In other cases the authority cannot be required to protect property, but it can do so at its discretion.

When homelessness is 'intentional'

Once an applicant is considered to have a priority need, the housing authority will make inquiries to discover:

• Whether the applicant became homeless (or threatened with homelessness) 'intentionally' – that is, through his own deliberate act or omission. Examples are giving up a satisfactory home or refusing to pay rent. Someone who loses his home because he genuinely cannot meet rent or mortgage payments should not be treated as intentionally homeless.

An applicant who is considered to be intentionally homeless need only be provided with temporary accommodation for long enough to provide him with a reasonable opportunity to obtain other accommodation. There is no duty to provide permanent accommodation. But advice and assistance must also be given.

• Whether the applicant has a 'local connection', not with it, but with the area of another housing authority. A local connection exists if, for instance, the applicant lives or works in that area, or has family associations with it.

If such a connection exists, the duty to provide accommodation lies with that other authority. But if the applicant runs the risk of domestic violence in that authority's area, the duty remains with the first authority.

Permanent accommodation If the applicant has a priority need and is not considered to be intentionally homeless, the authority must arrange permanent accommodation. This will usually be a council house or flat, but the authority can also fulfil its duty by, for instance, finding private accommodation or providing a loan to buy a house.

The accommodation should be adequate for the needs of the applicant and his family, and also be fit to live in.

If the applicant is threatened with homelessness, the housing authority must take reasonable steps to prevent this – by, for example, trying to prevent an eviction taking place.

Challenging a decision

A homeless person who is unhappy about the handling of his application should contact his district (or islands) councillor, or his MP. A local advice agency, such as a Citizens Advice Bureau, may also be able to help.

If a housing authority appears to have failed to carry out its duties properly, the applicant can ask the Court of Session to order it to do so. He can also seek DAMAGES for any resulting loss. Pending its decision, the court can be asked to grant interim INTERDICT to prevent the loss of any temporary accommodation provided by the authority. *See also:* BATTERED WOMEN; OMBUDSMEN

HOMOSEXUALITY

It is an offence to commit a homosexual act in public

In general, a homosexual act in private between two males is not an offence if both parties consent to it and are 21 or over. A 'homosexual act' means sodomy (anal intercourse) or an act of gross indecency (which is something less than sodomy).

If these conditions of consent, age and privacy are not met, the homosexual act will be an offence.

Consent If a man compels another male to have homosexual relations, whether through force or threats of force, he commits the crime of indecent ASSAULT. The penalty for this is at the court's discretion, within its sentencing limits.

If a male is so mentally defective that he is incapable of leading an independent life or preventing himself being seriously exploited, he cannot give any lawful consent to a homosexual act. It is a defence for an accused person to show that he neither knew nor could be expected to know about the victim's mental condition.

Maximum penalty 2 years' imprisonment or an unlimited fine, or both.

Age Both males must be aged 21 or over. If at least one of them is under age, both are guilty of an offence.

Maximum penalty 2 years' imprisonment or an unlimited fine, or both.

Privacy Whether a homosexual act is committed 'in private' depends on the circumstances. The act will not be private if it is in a place where any member of the public *might* (without special effort) see it being committed – it is not necessary that anyone *actually* sees the act. But it is not prevented from being private merely because someone looks through a keyhole.

However, a homosexual act cannot be treated as private if:

- More than 2 persons take part or are present.
- The act is committed in a public lavatory.

Special cases

Homosexual acts in private between consenting males aged 21 or over are still criminal in the following cases:

- Where the act is committed on a UK merchant ship between crew members (whether or not members of the same ship).

Maximum penalty 2 years' imprisonment or an unlimited fine, or both.

- Where the act is committed with a mental patient, by a man on the staff of a hospital (or with responsibility for mental patients).

Maximum penalty 2 years' imprisonment.

- Where the act involves a member of the armed forces, who can be charged with an offence under the Army, Air Force and Naval Discipline Acts.

Maximum penalty 2 years' imprisonment.

Female homosexuality

A homosexual act in private between consenting female adults is not a criminal offence in Scotland.

HORSE RIDING

Laws that must be obeyed by riders

Someone who rides a horse on a public road must be able to control it in traffic. If he cannot, and an accident results through, for example, being unable to stop at traffic lights, the rider can be sued for compensation by an injured road user. *See:* NEGLIGENCE

No licence is needed to ride a horse on the highway and there is no age limit for anyone who wishes to do so, provided that the rider can control the horse.

Riders should keep to the left-hand side of the road. Anyone who is leading a horse, whether on foot or while riding another horse, should also keep to the left and keep the led animal on the left. In one-way streets riders must proceed only in the direction of the traffic and keep to the left.

It is an offence to ride or drive a horse on a pedestrian footpath or pavement by the side of the road. Obstructing the footpath with a horse is also an offence.

It is an offence to ride a horse in a reckless manner which endangers members of the public. A person who intentionally rides a horse at someone is guilty of ASSAULT (whether or not the victim is injured).

It is also an offence to be drunk in charge of a horse in a public place.

Riding schools Anyone who wishes to run a horse riding school must obtain a licence from the local district (or islands) council. If the application is rejected, the applicant can appeal to the sheriff court.

Once the licence is issued, council officers will inspect the riding-school premises, to ensure that the horses are being kept in safe and suitable conditions.

The licence-holder should have an insurance policy covering him against liability for any injury sustained by anyone who hires a horse or who, in return for payment, uses one of his horses in the course of riding lessons. The insurance policy should also cover injury or damage to any other person during the hire or use of the horse.

HOSPICE

Comfort and care for the terminally ill

Hospice care is an organised system of nursing and other help for patients who are thought to be dying.

The care is provided either in a hospice centre or in the patient's own home. Emphasis is placed on the control of symptoms and prevention of pain through the use of drugs, and on support and guidance for the family both before and after the patient's death.

There are about 40 centres in Britain specialising in the care of such patients. Some are run by the National Health Service. Others such as St. Columba's, 15 Boswall Road, Edinburgh, are run by religious or voluntary organisations.

In many areas, hospice services are free through the National Health Service. In others some payment may be necessary. Anyone seeking advice on the availability of hospice services should ask his or her family doctor or local health board.

HOSPITAL

The rights of a person receiving hospital treatment

Under the National Health Service, a doctor is legally obliged to send a patient to hospital if the patient needs treatment that only a hospital can provide.

Except in an emergency, such as an accident or sudden illness, hospitals will accept only patients sent by a doctor. No one can just walk in and demand treatment.

There is, though, no right to receive hospital treatment. The courts have held that the provision of hospital services must be subject to availability of resources. The only prospect of bringing a successful claim for refusal of treatment against a health board would be to show that staffing levels were totally inadequate, or that treatment was refused because of an incorrect diagnosis by a duty doctor.

But once in hospital and under treatment, a patient has a right to be treated with reasonable skill and care and can sue for damages if he does not get it.

If you are referred to hospital

Most patients are referred to hospital by their family doctors. The doctor writes to the hospital for an appointment, or gives the patient a letter to take to the doctor in charge of the relevant clinic, and the patient makes his own appointment.

A hospital does not have to accept a patient sent by a family doctor. A doctor or patient cannot insist that the patient should see a particular consultant.

Treatment as an outpatient A doctor at the hospital decides if a person is to be treated as an inpatient or outpatient. Outpatients are treated by a clinic doctor, who will report to the family doctor on the condition of the patient and treatment given.

Treatment as an inpatient Most hospitals have a waiting list for beds, and except in exceptional cases, such as a person whose condition suddenly worsens, referred patients wait their turn.

The hospital admissions department will inform you by letter when a bed is available, and tell you where to report. They will also send you information about visiting times and rules.

Patients are not limited to hospitals in their own area. They can ask to join the waiting list of a hospital elsewhere, even though their doctor might not agree.

FORCING A PERSON TO GO INTO HOSPITAL

No one can be forced to enter hospital unless:

- He is mentally ill and has been compulsorily admitted under the Mental Health (Scotland) Act 1984.
- He has an infectious disease, such as smallpox or tuberculosis, and has been ordered into hospital under the Public Health (Scotland) Act 1897.
- He is unable to look after himself because of chronic illness or old age and has been removed to hospital under the National Assistance Act 1948 *See:* INFECTIOUS DISEASE; MENTAL DISORDER

DECIDING TO CLOSE A HOSPITAL

When a health board plans to close a hospital – or part of it – it should consult the local HEALTH COUNCIL, whose job is to represent the interests of the public.

If you object to the closure of a hospital, contact your health council – you will find the address in the telephone directory – and make your views known.

Sometimes this can lead to speedier admission and, therefore, treatment.

When a patient's consent is needed

A patient can refuse any form of treatment, so the hospital doctor needs the patient's consent before he can do anything. The patient can tell the doctor – orally or in writing, voluntarily or in answer to the doctor's question – that he is willing to have the treatment offered.

He can also imply consent, for example by rolling up a sleeve and offering an arm for injection, or opening his mouth

THE WOMAN WHO WAS STERILISED WITHOUT HER CONSENT

If a patient signs a consent form when he or she is not in a fit state to do so, the consent is invalid.

A woman went into hospital for a caesarian section for the birth of her fifth child. Her four previous deliveries had all been by caesarian section and the doctors believed that, in view of her gynaecological condition, further pregnancies could endanger her life. They tried to persuade her to be sterilised, but she refused.

Just before the operation, when she was under the effects of the first anaesthetic, the woman was asked to sign a form authorising sterilisation. Believing the form authorised only the caesarian section, she signed.

She later discovered that she had been sterilised. She sued the doctors and the area health authority. She maintained that her consent was invalid as she was given the form when she was not in a state to comprehend fully what she was signing.

DECISION

The judge found that the woman had signed a consent form when she was not in a state to understand it. Consent to the sterilisation was invalid. She was awarded damages of £3,000.

THE OPERATION THAT WENT WRONG

Consent to an operation can be valid when a doctor has held back facts which could cause distress and jeopardise the success of the operation.

Mrs Hatcher was a lady who occasionally broadcast for the BBC. She went into St Bartholomew's Hospital in London suffering from a toxic thyroid gland and an operation was advised.

She asked if there was any risk to her voice. She was reassured by the doctors.

In the course of the operation, the nerve was so badly damaged that she could not speak properly. She could not broadcast again.

She sued Dr Black, the physician, and Mr Tuckwell, the surgeon, for advising the operation, and Mr Tuckwell for damaging the nerve.

At the hearing, Lord Denning told the jury that Mr Tuckwell had admitted that on the evening before the operation he told Mrs Hatcher that there was no risk to her voice, when he knew that there was some slight risk. He had done so for her own good because it was of vital importance that she should not worry.

'In short, he told a lie, but he did it because he thought in the circumstances it was justifiable.

'You should find him guilty of negligence only when he falls short of the standard of a reasonably skilful medical man, in short, when he is deserving of censure – for negligence in a medical man is deserving of censure.'

DECISION

The jury found against Mrs Hatcher and she was ordered to pay the doctors' legal expenses.

YES – BY IMPLICATION

A doctor is entitled to assume that a patient has given his consent to treatment if he behaves as if he had no objections – for example, by opening his mouth for examination.

for the doctor to examine his throat. A patient treated without his consent or against his wishes can sue the doctor or health board for assault.

If a patient refuses a particular treatment he can be asked to leave the hospital, unless that would clearly jeopardise his health.

When written consent is needed

Doctors usually ask for written consent before any surgery, or hazardous treatment such as radiation therapy or electro-convulsive therapy.

The patient, or the parent or guardian in the case of a child, is asked to sign a form which gives details of the intended operation or treatment. This says that the person has been told what treatment is to be carried out and fully understands it.

When a patient is unable to sign his own form – he may be unconscious, confused or mentally retarded – it can be signed on his behalf by his next-of-kin or guardian.

Signing the form Do not sign the form until the doctor has explained clearly what he intends to do. Any dangers or side-effects should be explained.

A doctor will be justified in not telling a patient everything if skilled and experienced doctors rightly accept this as the proper practice.

When the risks of an operation are too high – such as a 50–50 chance organ transplant – a doctor would not be justified in holding anything back.

It is unwise to sign a consent form that gives the doctor permission to carry out any surgery or treatment he considers necessary.

Patients are sometimes asked to do this when they are undergoing an exploratory operation. If the surgeon finds diseased organs, he can then remove them without further consent. If you have not signed, the surgeon must get your permission to perform anything other than the exploratory operation. That means more than one operation, but you have the right to choose.

If there is anything to which you would never give your consent, you can write this on the form.

When consent is not given

A patient who refuses consent cannot be treated, even in an emergency, no matter how serious the consequences are likely to be.

If the patient is unconscious – after an accident for example – and his life or future health is in jeopardy, a doctor can treat him even if he knows that the patient would have refused.

Next-of-kin or relatives should be asked to consent – but even if they refuse, the doctor is legally entitled to do whatever is necessary to save the

OBJECTING ON RELIGIOUS GROUNDS

The wishes of a patient who objects on religious grounds to any particular treatment must be respected by the doctor. However, if a patient needing an operation refuses a blood transfusion the surgeon may refuse to operate – or he may refuse to promise that a transfusion will not be given.

WHEN CHILDREN UNDER 16 GO INTO HOSPITAL

Special problems may arise when a child needs hospital treatment

Consenting to treatment

Hospitals usually require parents to give consent, orally or in writing, before treating a child under 16 – though consent is probably not legally necessary if the child is a MINOR.

If the child has been taken into care, consent to treatment can be given by the local authority or whoever has custody of the child.

If both parents refuse consent, no treatment will be given, even though the child may want it. But if the child's life is in danger, emergency treatment will be given without consent of a parent.

If the parents refuse consent to treatment essential to the child's health, they can be prosecuted for wilful neglect. A CHILDREN'S HEARING can also place the child under supervision and ask the parents to co-operate with the hospital – but it cannot force them to do so.

If the child refuses

If the parents give their consent, but the child refuses treatment, the doctor is probably not legally entitled to go ahead if the child is a MINOR – unless the treatment is necessary to save life.

In an emergency

If a child needs emergency treatment and the parents cannot be contacted, a doctor can treat the child without their consent.

Religious objections

Even if the parents refuse consent on religious grounds, a doctor may still carry out any treatment that is necessary to save the child's life.

If the child suffers because of the lack of treatment, the parents can be charged with wilful neglect. The child can also be placed under supervision by a children's hearing.

Visiting children

Hospitals are recommended to allow unrestricted visiting in children's wards and to provide accommodation for mothers, particularly of young children.

If accommodation is not provided and you are determined to stay with your child at night, you should be firm and tactful about your intention. If the night sister is unhelpful, ask to see the hospital administrator.

The National Association for the Welfare of Children in Hospital will also help. It has 9 branches in Scotland.

Providing education

The local education authority is responsible for the education of children even when they are in hospital. If they are well enough to be taught, teachers may visit them there. Arrangements may also be made for children to sit examinations in hospital. Schools are provided in hospitals which cater for children with physical or mental handicaps.

patient's life and prevent permanent harm. He is not entitled to do more than that.

When treatment such as the amputation of a limb is necessary, the doctor should wait for the patient's consent. But if he believes delay would cause, or probably cause, the patient's death he is legally justified in going ahead and giving whatever treatment he thinks is necessary.

Consent of spouses There is no legal obligation on a husband or wife to obtain the other's consent for sterilisation, abortion or the fitting of a contraceptive device although some doctors are reluctant to proceed in such cases without the agreement of the other spouse.

Mental patients If a patient has been detained under the Mental Health (Scotland) Act, his consent is needed for hazardous or irreversible treatment, but not for other forms of treatment. *See:* MENTAL DISORDER

Examination by students

Patients should be warned if medical students are likely to be present when they are examined or treated. Everyone has a right to refuse to have students around their bed, without prejudice to treatment. A patient who agrees to be treated or examined by or in the presence of students, can later change his mind.

If a patient is led to believe that he is being examined or treated by a qualified doctor, when in fact he is not, any consent will be invalid.

Dental hospitals In a dental hospital most types of routine treatment are carried out by students. Anyone has a right to refuse to be treated by a student, but this may mean a delay before he can be seen by a qualified dentist.

Seeing your case notes

A patient's hospital record is the property of the health board. If it is a manual record, the patient has no legal right to see it. If it is a COMPUTER RECORD, he does – though there may be exceptions. A doctor does not have to tell a patient what is wrong with him or to reveal the results of tests or X-rays.

If a patient sues, or has decided to sue a doctor or hospital, for negligence for example, he can ask a court to order the hospital to make available all relevant documents.

WHEN SOMEONE NEEDS TREATMENT IN A HOSPITAL AT SHORT NOTICE

If your doctor decides you need urgent hospital treatment, he can call an ambulance to take you there.

A doctor at the emergency department will decide what treatment you need and whether to admit you as an in-patient. If there is no bed available, he should inquire whether there is one at another hospital.

If you are taken by ambulance or make your own way to a hospital that does not have an emergency department, the hospital is entitled to refuse you even if it means a long delay in your being treated.

If you have been injured in an accident or suddenly taken seriously ill, you are entitled to go to a hospital emergency department without an ambulance or referral by your doctor.

Paying for peace and quiet

Some hospitals provide pay beds – beds in a small room rather than in a large ward – for National Health Service patients who prefer privacy. (There are around 95 pay beds in Scottish hospitals.) A charge is made for the beds, and this varies according to the hospital and the facilities provided.

Allocating the beds There is no legal obligation for a hospital to supply such beds, but if it does, it allocates them when patients are admitted – they cannot be booked in advance.

If a patient needs privacy for medical reasons, his doctor may try to get a pay bed. In such cases there is no charge.

Accommodation may also be provided in health service hospitals for private patients, but this is uncommon in Scotland.

Discharging a patient

Any patient, except one compulsorily detained under the Mental Health (Scotland) Act 1984, the Public Health (Scotland) Act 1897 or the National Assistance Act 1948, can discharge himself from hospital at any time. However, a hospital will not discharge a patient until his treatment is completed and the doctor in charge of his case considers it is safe for him to go.

Self discharge If a patient leaves hospital against the advice of a doctor, he will be asked to sign a form stating that he is doing so. However, if he refuses to sign he cannot be prevented from leaving. The signed form relieves the hospital of liability should the patient suffer harm from his discharge. If he refuses to sign, it will be harder for the hospital to deny liability.

Discharge by doctor A doctor will discharge a patient only when treatment is complete, and when he believes the patient is well enough to go. The patient should check that he has a supply of any drugs needed; whether he has to return to the outpatient department; and if any sickness certificates are needed for his employer and social security office.

A person who does not feel fit enough to be discharged, or feels that he should remain in hospital for any other reason – perhaps there is no one at home to look after him – should ask the doctor if he can stay longer.

Early discharge If a patient is discharged before it is medically safe, and he suffers injury as a result, he may be able to sue the doctor for negligence. It is also negligent for a doctor to discharge a patient being treated after a suicide attempt, if there is a likelihood that he will make another attempt unless given further treatment.

Visiting patients in hospital

Many hospitals have open visiting –

WHAT A SISTER SAYS GOES

Visitors are allowed into the hospital at the discretion of the doctors and nursing authorities. They must observe any rules laid down.

that is, usually any time between limits fixed by the hospital, for example, 2 p.m. and 8 p.m. But visitors may be asked to leave at meal times.

If a patient is very ill, or in need of rest and quiet, visiting may be restricted at the discretion of the ward sister.

A visitor asked to leave a ward should do so. No one has a right to stay on hospital premises without permission.

You should not take food or drink to a patient without first asking the ward sister if you may do so.

THE PATIENT WHO JUMPED THROUGH A WINDOW

A health board is bound to take simple and reasonable precautions against even unlikely behaviour by patients in its care.

A patient was admitted to Gartnavel Mental Hospital, Glasgow, after trying to commit suicide at home. On her second night in hospital she was placed in a single room forming part of a first-floor ward.

During the night she climbed on to a radiator and opened the window. It was a kind which swings open on central pivots at each side. She fell 16 feet to the ground, breaking her back, and was left paraplegic for life.

The patient sued the Greater Glasgow Health Board for damages. The judge heard evidence that a device could easily and cheaply have been fitted to the windows to reduce the distance they would swing open. This had been done at other hospitals.

DECISION

The judge held that although a hospital cannot be held liable for every mishap to patients in its care, it must take precautions against all known risks which can easily be averted. The patient got £8,300.

Your social security rights

If you are receiving a social security benefit, it may be reduced while you are in hospital. The reason is that social security benefits are intended to help with ordinary needs at home, or with special needs arising from disablement. While in hospital some of these needs are met by the National Health Service. Benefits are therefore reduced or withdrawn altogether.

If you are in hospital privately, and are meeting the entire cost of your upkeep, *no* reduction is made in any social security benefit you may get, except INVALID CARE ALLOWANCE.

If you get:

- Retirement pension (including the pension for the over-80s);
- Widow's benefits;
- Sickness benefit, invalidity pension, non-contributory invalidity pension/ severe disablement allowance, or unemployability supplement (payable with disablement benefit);

your benefit will usually be reduced after 8 weeks in hospital by £6.80 (in 1983–4) if it includes an allowance for a dependant (£13.60, if not). If you are normally cared for in a local authority home, your benefit may be cut at once.

After a year in hospital, you can get only £6.80 for yourself. But if you have a dependant, you can:

- Have your benefit paid to a dependant.
- Receive £6.80 and have the rest – or only the dependant's part – paid to a dependant.

If you have no dependant, or have only the dependant's part paid over, a weekly sum – in 1983/4, your personal benefit rates less £20.40 – can be set aside during a second year in hospital only. This will be used to provide 'resettlement' benefit, a weekly payment to help you out when you leave hospital.

After 2 years in hospital, benefit will probably be further reduced

Other benefits affected are:

Attendance allowance (including constant attendance allowance payable with disablement benefit). These payments stop after 4 weeks in hospital.

Invalid care allowance That usually stops 12 weeks after you, or the person you look after, goes into hospital.

Supplementary benefit If you are a single person without children, benefit is reduced (to £6.80 plus an allowance for any mortgage interest) as soon as you go into hospital. If you have a partner, and either of you is in hospital, benefit is reduced by £6.80 after 8 weeks – except when another benefit you get is reduced.

If you are a single parent, your personal benefit is reduced to £6.80 after 8 weeks, but the amount payable for your eldest child increases to £26.80. If your children go into care, you are treated as a single person without children.

Additional payments for special diets or for extra heating on health grounds stop when your personal benefit is reduced. Other additional paypments may be reduced immediately or after a number of weeks.

The amount payable for a child who is in hospital is reduced to £6.80 after 12 weeks.

If you are still in hospital after 2

WHAT TO DO IF YOU WANT TO MAKE A COMPLAINT

Every area health board has its own method of dealing with complaints. This is usually shown in the hospital handbook given to patients before they enter hospital.

Minor complaints

Complaints about routine matters can be dealt with by the ward sister, or outpatient clinic sister.

Serious complaints

If you have a serious complaint, say, about treatment, you can take it up with the consultant in charge of your case. If you are not satisfied with his response, you can write to the hospital administrator or the district administrator. If you are still not satisfied write to the secretary of the area health board. You can get the addresses from the telephone directory.

Very serious complaints, such as those alleging injury or deprivation of medical care, can be dealt with at area level from the start.

On major issues of complaint, the Secretary of State may arrange for an inquiry to be held.

Complaints of bad administration, which do not relate to diagnosis or treatment, should be made to the HEALTH SERVICE COMMISSIONER.

Help with complaints

If you need advice on making a complaint, contact your local HEALTH COUNCIL or the Patients' Association, 11 Dartmouth Street, London, SW1.

years, or if you are unlikely to be discharged, benefit will be paid separately for your partner and children.

Housing costs If you are in hospital, HOUSING BENEFITS can continue for up to a year. After that, a partner or a dependant can claim. If you have neither, benefit stops.

Help with hospital fares

If you have to travel to hospital for treatment as either an out-patient or an in-patient, or if you are leaving hospital for good, you may be able to get help with your fares, and, if you qualify, the fares of an escort – provided the hospital agrees that one is needed.

If you get FAMILY INCOME SUPPLEMENT or SUPPLEMENTARY BENEFIT, show your order book at the hospital. If you do not get one of these benefits but have a low income, claim on the form attached to DHSS leaflet H11, which you can get at the hospital or a DHSS office. Your bus or train fares, or petrol costs, can then be paid

If you live in the Highlands and Islands and have to travel more than 30 miles (or 5 miles by water), and your fares are over £1, you may also qualify. Ask at a social security office.

If you are visiting a close relative or household member in hospital, and you get supplementary benefit, you can claim extra benefit to help with fares.

Going home

If you occasionally go home from hospital during a spell of in-patient treatment when your benefit has been reduced, you may be able to get it increased again on being allowed home for a few days. Tell your local DHSS office of any time you are at home.

When you are ready to leave hospital for good, tell the local DHSS office in good time so that your full benefit can be restored. Ask at the hospital if you need money for the journey home.

HOW A HOTEL LIMITS ITS LIABILITY TO GUESTS

If you have anything valuable, ask for it to be put in the safe

NOTICE

LOSS OF OR DAMAGE TO GUESTS' PROPERTY

Under the Hotel Proprietors Act 1956, an hotel proprietor may in certain circumstances be liable to make good any loss of or damage to a guest's property even though it was not due to any fault of the proprietor or staff of the hotel.

This liability however—

(*a*) extends only to the property of guests who have engaged sleeping accommodation at the hotel;

(*b*) is limited to £50 for any one article and a total of £100 in the case of any one guest, except in the case of property which has been deposited, or offered for deposit, for safe custody;

(*c*) does not cover motor-cars or other vehicles of any kind or any property left in them, or horses or other live animals.

This notice does not constitute an admission either that the Act applies to this hotel or that liability thereunder attaches to the proprietor of this hotel in any particular case.

A hotel is protected against guests' claims only if it displays this special notice – printed in plain type and positioned conspicuously near the reception area or entrance. If it does not do so, it can face claims for the whole amount of a guest's loss.

HOTEL

When a traveller must be given food and shelter

Any establishment that is defined in law as a hotel has a duty to provide food, drink and accommodation for any customer who is in a fit state and who appears to be able and willing to pay.

The proprietor is relieved of that legal obligation only if he has no food or drink available or if all rooms have been taken, or if the would-be customer has previously shown himself to be an undesirable guest. A hotel-keeper who disregards these duties is liable in an action of damages.

If the hotel has a licence, a complaint might also be made to the local licensing board. If the refusal shows discrimination on grounds of race or sex, damages may be awarded by a sheriff court. *See:* RACIAL DISCRIMINATION; SEX DISCRIMINATION

The law, however, distinguishes between a hotel (or inn) and private or residential hotels, boarding houses or public houses without accommodation. To qualify for the legal status of a hotel, the establishment must be willing, in the words of the Hotel Proprietors Act 1956, to give service to travellers 'without special contract'.

The owners or staff of the other kinds of premises mentioned can – within the limits of the Race Relations Act and the Sex Discrimination Act – refuse to serve anyone without giving a reason.

If the bill is not paid

Anyone who dishonestly leaves any category of hotel without paying the bill and with intent to avoid payment is committing a criminal offence.

The proprietor of an inn or hotel has extra rights, however. He can exercise

NO FIT STATE

A hotelier must provide food, drink and accommodation only for customers who appear to him to be in a fit state, able and willing to pay, and not proven undesirables.

what is called a LIEN, by holding any luggage brought to the hotel by the guest – even if it does not belong to the guest – until the bill is paid.

If the bill is not paid after 6 weeks, the proprietor can sell the luggage by public auction. The only condition is that he must advertise the auction in both a national and local newspaper at least a month before it is held.

If the sale raises more money than is needed to pay for the bill and auction expenses, the excess belongs to the guest.

The law does not allow a hotel proprietor to seize or sell any vehicle or property left in a vehicle, or any live animal.

Looking after a guest's property

When a guest takes sleeping accommodation at an inn or hotel, the proprietor is normally fully liable for any loss or damage to his property – even if that loss or damage is not caused by the hotel staff's NEGLIGENCE.

An exception is made for an 'Act of God' – some natural cause, which human precautions could not have prevented. But since steps can be taken to stop thieves, whether employees or outsiders, the proprietor would be liable for a guest's losses by theft.

The hotel can, however, reduce its liability by displaying a special notice under the Hotel Proprietors Act 1956. Then it is liable for loss or damage only up to a total of £100 with a maximum of £50 for any one article. But it is still fully liable, without any limit, if the property was stolen, lost or damaged through the negligence or wilful act of its staff, or if it was deposited – or offered for deposit – for safe custody.

A hotel proprietor can also avoid liability if he can show that the loss or damage did not take place during the period beginning at midnight before the guest arrived and ending at midnight after he left.

Hotels that do not display the special notice under the Hotel Proprietors Act, but instead still display a notice under the Innkeepers Liability Act 1863, are not protected from legal claims if property is lost or damaged. The 1863 Act was repealed in 1956.

Displaying the prices of rooms

Every hotel or inn – if it has 4 or more bedrooms or 8 or more beds – must display a price notice. The maximum penalty for not doing so is a £1,000 fine. Bedrooms and beds normally occupied by the same person for more than 21 nights do not count towards these qualifying totals.

The notice must be displayed in a prominent position in the reception area or at the entrance, where it can be read easily by anyone seeking sleeping accommodation at the hotel. It must be legible and state the current prices payable per night for:

- A bedroom for occupation by one adult.
- A bedroom for occupation by two adults.
- A bed other than in a room for one or two persons; and this must state whether it is in a dormitory or a room to be shared with other guests.

If different rooms have different prices, it is enough to state the lowest and highest price in each category.

If a service charge is made, the price list must give details. It must also state whether the prices include VAT. If they do not, the amount of VAT payable must be stated as a sum of money.

If the price of meals is included – whether or not they are taken – the tariff must say so. The meals affected must be identified – for example, 'including breakfast' or 'including breakfast, lunch and evening meal'.

The notice may include additional information – such as whether morning tea is provided, or whether there is a laundry service – but that extra detail must not detract from the prominence to be given to the compulsory information.

If you feel that a hotel is not displaying an adequate notice, complain to the trading standards department of the regional (or islands) council, which is responsible for seeing that hotels comply with the rules.

HOUSE BUYING AND SELLING

How ownership of a property is transferred

The sale of a house is conducted in two distinct stages:

1. The seller fixes a date, known as the closing date, by which time all the people interested in buying must make a *written* offer. The seller decides which offer to accept, and his written acceptance creates a CONTRACT, known as MISSIVES OF SALE, binding both parties. Neither party can then change his mind.

2. On an agreed date, known as the date of entry, the buyer pays the purchase price and the seller hands over the CONVEYANCE, the other title deeds and

HAVING A HOUSE SURVEYED

Is it necessary?

Yes. A house is probably the biggest investment you will ever make. Do not take a risk. Only a surveyor has the expertise necessary to spot defects. If you buy a house which turns out to have structural defects, you may be unable to resell it.

When?

Before your solicitor makes a written offer. The surveyor's report may cause you to offer less, or not to offer at all.

What kind of survey?

If you are borrowing money, the building society or other lender will instruct its own *valuation survey*, which you will have to pay for. If you are not borrowing money, you can instruct your own valuation survey.

A valuation survey is of limited use because:

- It is not a full *structural survey*. Its purpose is simply to put a value on the house.
- Not all building societies give details of the report – although if they remain willing to lend, you can assume that it is reasonably favourable.
- If the surveyor is negligent you will probably not be able to sue him unless you ordered the survey yourself.

To be absolutely safe you would have to instruct your own structural survey. This is almost never done, partly because of the expense of such a survey (several hundred pounds), and partly because you may finish up paying for several surveys if you are not successful in buying the first house you offer for.

Some surveyors offer a *house-buyer's report and valuation*. This is much cheaper than a structural survey but more thorough than a valuation survey. You may be able to persuade your building society to accept this instead of its usual valuation survey.

A STEP-BY-STEP GUIDE TO BUYING AND SELLING A HOUSE

IF YOU ARE A BUYER

Finding a house See as many houses as possible to get an idea of prices. It may be possible to agree a price privately with the seller, but if there are other people interested you will usually have to make a blind offer, on or before the closing date. The seller will have fixed an upset price and your solicitor will guide you on how much more than this you should offer.

Making an offer Your solicitor prepares and signs an offer on your behalf. Remember that he does not normally visit the house. It is your responsibility to inspect the property and then to raise any questions with him – for example, about the state of the fences or where the drains run.

Also make sure that the solicitor is clear about what is and is not included in the sale – for example FIXTURES AND FITTINGS or a removable garden shed – so that everything is included in the offer.

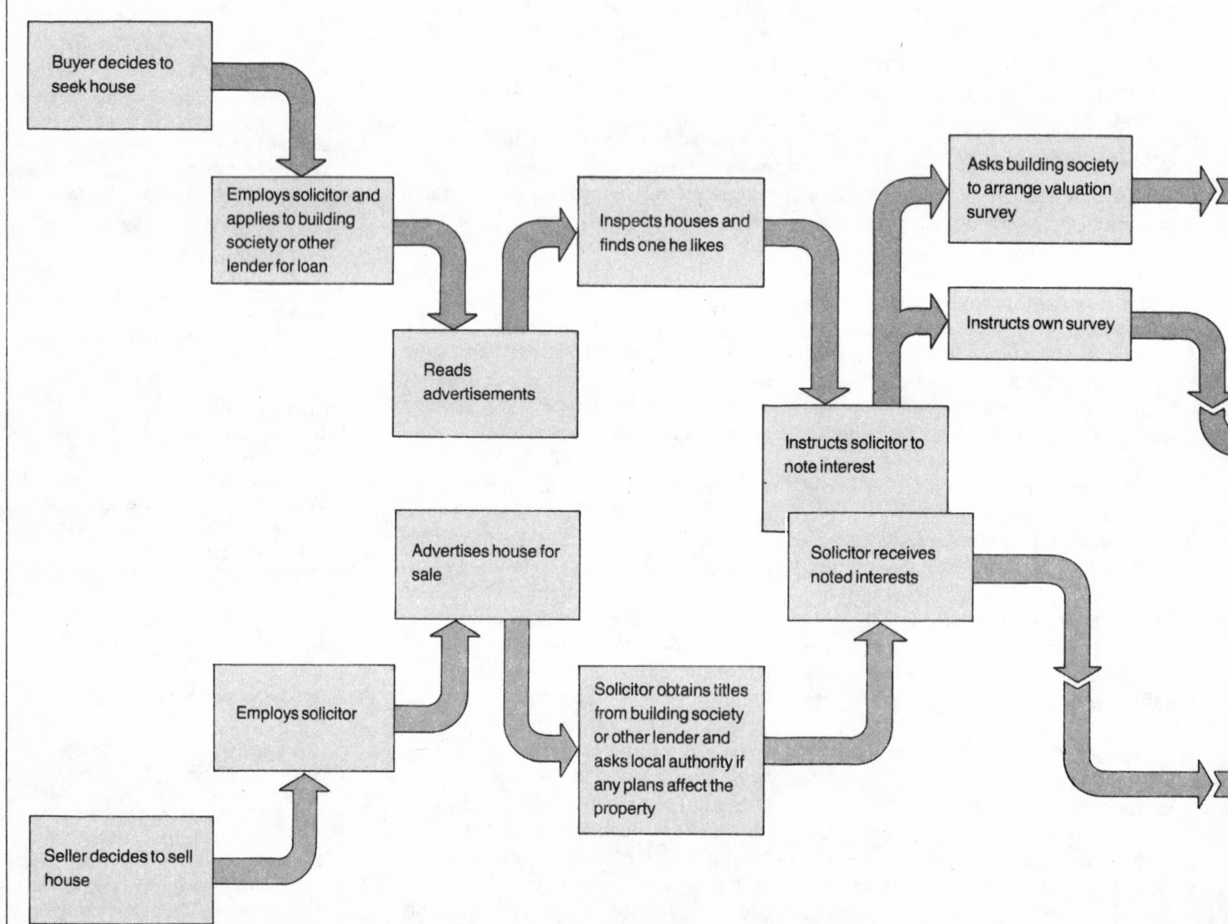

IF YOU ARE A SELLER

Finding a buyer You can advertise and conduct verbal negotiations with potential buyers without professional help, but most people instruct a solicitor or ESTATE AGENT to do this for them.

You will in any case have to employ a solicitor once you have received an offer and it makes some sense to employ him from the very start.

A solicitor will advise on the upset price (the price in excess of which offers are invited) and on the amount of advertising. If your town has a solicitors' property centre, he will be able to use this as a cheap and effective alternative – or addition – to newspaper advertisements.

Not all solicitors charge for this preliminary service, and those who do charge different amounts. You should therefore ask about this before agreeing to hire any particular person.

If your offer is accepted, you will be legally bound to buy the house. So do not make the offer unless you are sure that you can really afford it, bearing in mind that you will have to meet a number of other expenses such as solicitors' fees and, sometimes, STAMP DUTY.

If, like most buyers, you are borrowing money, the building society or other lender will not make the loan unless the house satisfies its surveyor. You cannot make an offer until the survey is carried out. You may also wish to have a more extensive survey arranged privately.

Legal paperwork There is usually a period of several weeks between the acceptance of the offer and the date of entry. During this time your solicitor will be busy examining the title deeds to make sure the seller really owns the property and that there are no important conditions and restrictions on use.

He prepares a draft CONVEYANCE and sends it to the seller's solicitor for approv-

Continued overleaf

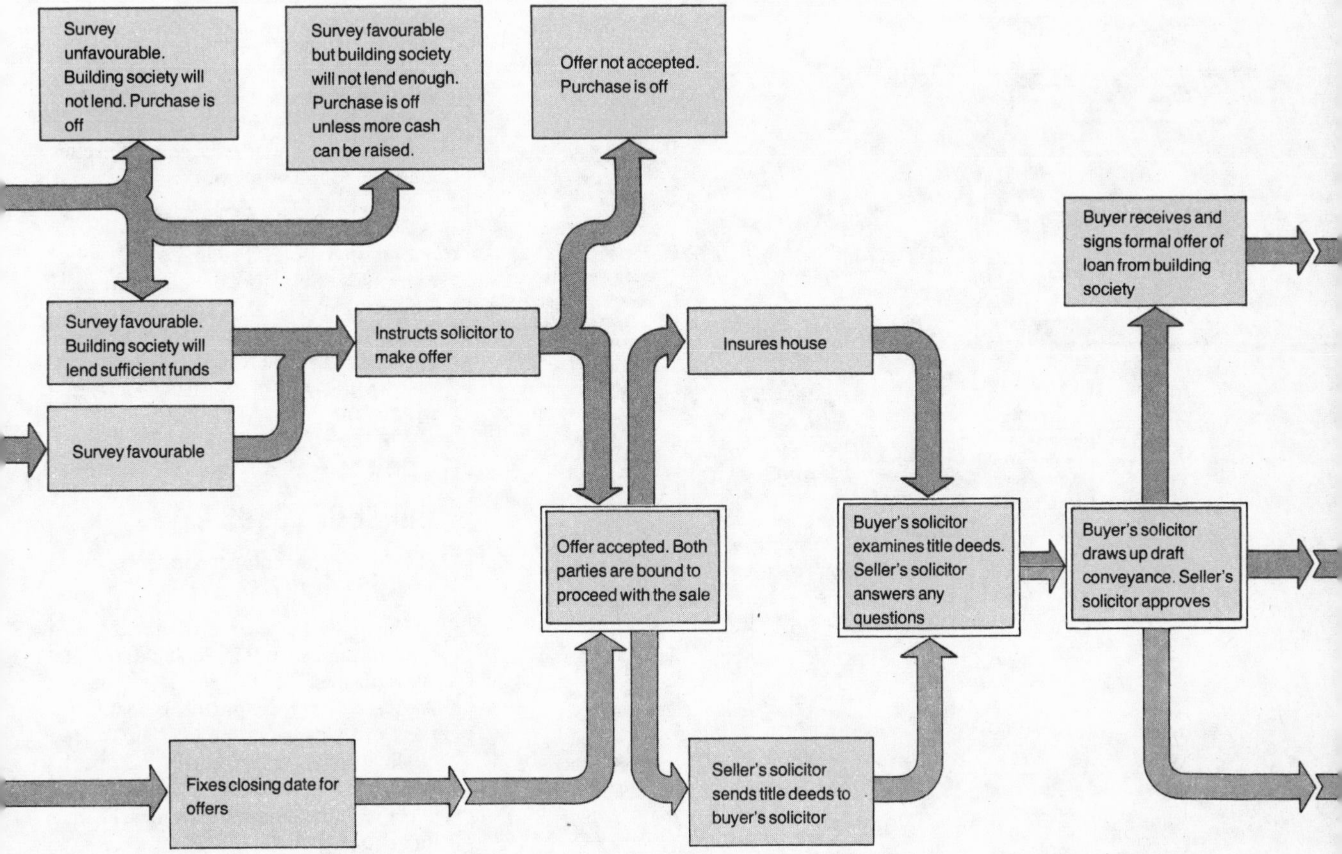

Survey unfavourable. Building society will not lend. Purchase is off

Survey favourable but building society will not lend enough. Purchase is off unless more cash can be raised.

Offer not accepted. Purchase is off

Buyer receives and signs formal offer of loan from building society

Survey favourable. Building society will lend sufficient funds

Instructs solicitor to make offer

Insures house

Survey favourable

Offer accepted. Both parties are bound to proceed with the sale

Buyer's solicitor examines title deeds. Seller's solicitor answers any questions

Buyer's solicitor draws up draft conveyance. Seller's solicitor approves

Fixes closing date for offers

Seller's solicitor sends title deeds to buyer's solicitor

Houses are also sold by estate agents – much more common in Scotland than they once were – and you may prefer to use their services. Estate agents charge a fee – often 1½ per cent of the sale price plus the cost of advertising plus VAT – but may be able to get a higher price which would absorb the extra expense.

Estate agents cannot undertake conveyancing and so you will still have to use a solicitor later on.

Receiving offers When someone intends offering for your house he may try to agree on a price with you privately. Unless you expect the house to be difficult to sell, or the amount offered is very large, you should refuse to negotiate and ask him to wait until a closing date is fixed. His solicitor will then formally 'note interest' by telephone with your solicitor.

Once several people have noted interest in this way a closing date can be set, by which all offers must be received. You can then decide which offer to accept – usually

Continued overleaf

A STEP-BY-STEP GUIDE TO BUYING AND SELLING A HOUSE (*continued*)

continued from previous page

al. He also prepares the mortgage documentation.

Moving in You have the intervening period to make arrangements for moving. Besides hiring removal contractors to transport your furniture, see that you will be supplied with services such as gas, electricity and telephone. Ask several removal companies for estimates: their charges vary considerably. When the date of entry arrives you will have to pay the purchase price in full before you can collect the keys. Quite often the mortgage cheque does not reach your solicitor in time and it is necessary to take out a BRIDGING LOAN.

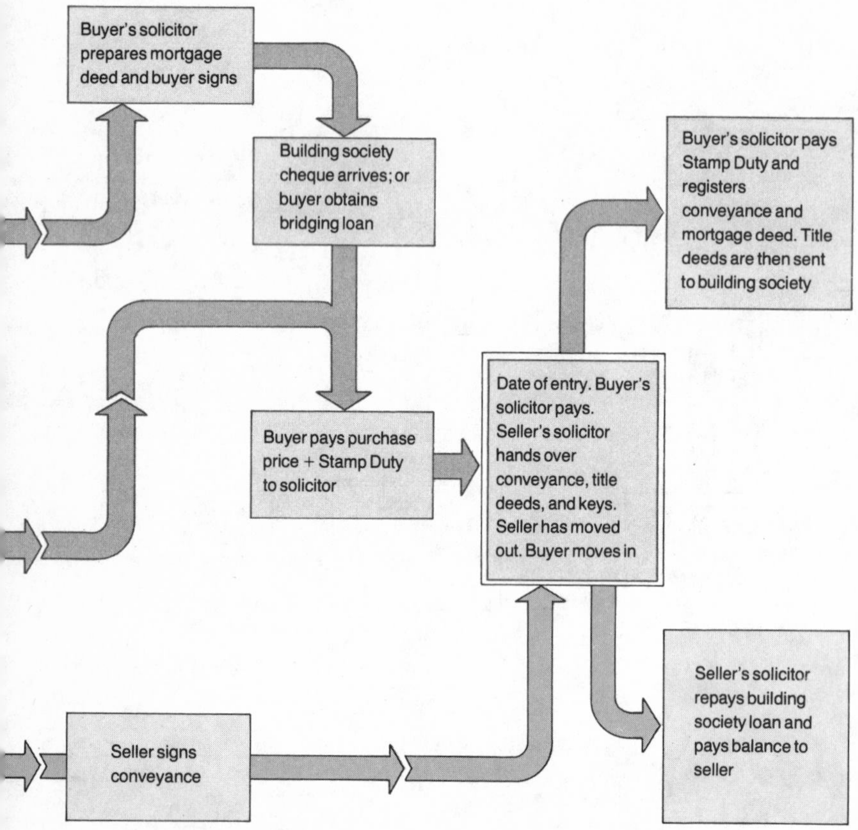

Buyer's solicitor prepares mortgage deed and buyer signs

Building society cheque arrives; or buyer obtains bridging loan

Buyer's solicitor pays Stamp Duty and registers conveyance and mortgage deed. Title deeds are then sent to building society

Buyer pays purchase price + Stamp Duty to solicitor

Date of entry. Buyer's solicitor pays. Seller's solicitor hands over conveyance, title deeds, and keys. Seller has moved out. Buyer moves in

Seller signs conveyance

Seller's solicitor repays building society loan and pays balance to seller

continued from previous page

the highest – and your solicitor will sign and send a written acceptance on your behalf. This creates a contract which is binding on both you and the buyer.

Legal paperwork During the weeks between acceptance of the offer and the date of entry your solicitor sends the title deeds to the buyer's solicitor and answers any queries he may have. He approves the conveyance, asks you to sign it, and keeps it until the date of entry.

Moving out You must move out not later than the date of entry. Don't forget to notify the electricity, gas and telephone authorities so that a final account can be prepared.

the keys. The buyer can now move into the house. Strictly speaking, he is not the owner until he has recorded the conveyance either in the REGISTER OF SASINES or, if the house is within one of the areas where the new system of REGISTRATION OF TITLE operates, the LAND REGISTER.

In theory there is nothing to stop either party from conducting the legal formalities himself. But in practice they are usually too complicated for this to be wise, and it is normal to employ a SOLICITOR.

From January 1, 1985, solicitors will abandon the existing system of charging standard fees on a scale fixed by the Law Society of Scotland. Different solicitors will then charge different amounts for the same work.

You will save yourself money by asking several solicitors' firms for a quotation before deciding which one to employ. Solicitors are listed in the Yellow Pages and a quotation can easily be obtained by telephone. *See:* FEU DUTY; MORTGAGE; PROPERTY INSURANCE; REGISTRATION OF TITLE; SUPERIOR

HOUSE OF LORDS

Scotland's final court of appeal in civil cases

The highest civil court of the Scottish legal system sits not in Scotland, but at Westminster. It is the House of Lords. Appeals, however, are heard only by the Lord Chancellor and certain other qualified peers called Lords of Appeal in Ordinary (Law Lords), and by other peers who happen to be, or have been, judges of high rank.

The majority of the judges are English, as the House of Lords is also the highest court of England and Wales (and Northern Ireland) in both civil and criminal matters. But it is usual for two of the Law Lords to be Scottish.

An appeal lies to the House of Lords from most decisions of the Inner House of the COURT OF SESSION. Appeals from Scotland usually number less than a dozen a year. The Law Lords sit informally, without wigs or gowns, in a Committee Room (or sometimes the Chamber) of the House and listen to arguments presented by advocates and barristers. Appeals are usually heard by five Law Lords, which means that the Scottish Law Lords are in a minority.

There is no appeal to the House of Lords in Scottish criminal cases. *See:* CRIMINAL PROCEEDINGS

HOUSEBREAKING

Breaching the security of a building

There is no crime called 'housebreaking': the crime is THEFT by housebreaking. This is an aggravated theft, meaning that it will be punished more severely than theft alone. If nothing is actually stolen, the crime is housebreaking with intent to steal, or attempted housebreaking with intent to steal.

The penalty for these offences is at the court's discretion, within its sentencing limits.

House The crime is committed not only by breaking into people's homes but also by breaking into any roofed building – for instance, a shop or factory.

Breaking Entry need not involve any damage to the building. 'Breaking in' can be carried out in the following ways:

- Forcing or breaking down outside doors, walls or roofs.
- Using a pick-lock, skeleton-key or stolen or found key.
- Raising or opening a window.
- Entering by unusual and unauthorised means – for example, by a chimney or sewer.
- Entering by trickery.

It is not housebreaking to gain entry by opening an unlocked door or turning a key left in the lock, because in these circumstances the building is not secure.

The housebreaking must be prior to and for the purpose of the theft. The crime is not committed by someone who steals and then has to break out of the premises. In this case the crimes committed are theft and malicious mischief (or VANDALISM).

Opening lockfast places

If a housebreaker forces open locked rooms, cupboards, drawers, desks, cash-boxes or any other locked receptacle, and steals some of the contents, he is guilty of the crime of 'theft by opening lockfast places'. The penalty is at the court's discretion.

This crime frequently occurs in combination with housebreaking. If the purpose of the break-in is to gain access to any locked place or receptacle, and some of the contents are stolen, the crime is theft by housebreaking and opening lockfast places.

It is also a crime to open a lockfast place with the intention to steal.

Some connected offences

If a person is found in or on a building, and it is reasonable to suppose that he intended to commit a theft, he is guilty of an offence.

Maximum penalty 3 months' imprisonment or a £1,000 fine, or both.

If a person has been convicted of theft at least twice, and is found in possession of any tool or equipment usually used in theft – for example, a screwdriver – he is guilty of an offence if it is reasonable to suppose that he intended to commit theft.

Maximum penalty 3 months' imprisonment or a £1,000 fine, or both. The court can also order confiscation of the equipment.

HOUSEKEEPING MONEY

Sharing the proceeds equally

If a wife saves money from a housekeeping allowance provided by her husband and buys something with it, that purchase is treated in law as belonging equally to both. Similarly, if a wife wins the pools with an investment from the allowance, the husband is entitled to half the winnings.

If money saved out of the housekeeping is put into a bank or other savings account, the couple have an equal right to share it.

However, the couple are entitled to make an agreement not to share equally any money or property derived from a housekeeping allowance. Ownership will then depend on the terms of that agreement.

THE WIFE WHO WON THE POOLS

Money derived from a housekeeping allowance made by a husband to his wife belongs to both equally. This is so even if the wife is alone responsible for the money coming into the household.

Mr Pyatt paid his wife a regular amount of housekeeping money. Mrs Pyatt used a little of this money on the football pools and won £14,000.

Mr Pyatt claimed that half of his wife's winnings belonged to him. He based his case on the Married Women's Property Act, 1964, which says that money derived from a housekeeping allowance made by a husband to his wife belongs to both spouses in equal shares.

DECISION

The court agreed with Mr Pyatt. The fact that the amount of the winnings had been due to skill or luck on Mrs Pyatt's part did not prevent her husband being entitled to an equal share.

HOUSING ACTION AREA

Demolishing and improving substandard houses

District and islands councils have wide powers to demolish or improve houses which fall below the 'tolerable standard'.

A house falls below the tolerable standard unless it:

- Is structurally stable.
- Is substantially free from rising or penetrating damp.
- Has satisfactory provision for natural and artificial lighting, for ventilation and for heating.
- Has an adequate piped supply of wholesome water available within the house.
- Has a sink provided with a satisfactory supply of both hot and cold water within the house.
- Has a water closet available for the exclusive use of the occupants of the house and suitably located within the house.
- Has an effective system for the drainage and disposal of foul and surface water.
- Has satisfactory facilities for the cooking of food within the house.
- Has satisfactory access to all external

doors and outbuildings.

The council may deal with sub-standard houses either individually or by declaring an area of sub-standard housing to be a 'Housing Action Area'.

Individual houses

If a council considers that a house does not meet the tolerable standard, and should be demolished, it will make a 'demolition order'. This requires the house to be vacated within a set time – which must be at least 28 days from the date of the order – and to be demolished within 6 weeks of being vacated.

If the house is, for example, a tenement flat, and other flats in the tenement meet the tolerable standard, the council will make a 'closing order' instead. This prohibits the house from being used as living accommodation.

Where the house is capable of improvement, the council can make an 'improvement order', requiring the owner to bring the house up to the tolerable standard and put it into a good state of repair.

Declaring a Housing Action Area

If the council is satisfied that most of the houses in a particular area fall below the tolerable standard, it can deal with them collectively by declaring the area to be a Housing Action Area for Demolition or Improvement, or both.

The council must first pass a 'draft resolution' declaring an area to be scheduled for demolition, improvement or both. The resolution must then be sent to the Secretary of State for Scotland for his approval. He has 28 days from acknowledging receipt of the resolution to annul it, state that he does not oppose it or notify the council that he wishes more time to consider it.

If the Secretary of State agrees to the resolution, or fails to reply within 28 days, the council can go ahead. It must then publish its intentions in at least 2 local newspapers. All affected owners, tenants and occupiers must be personally informed and told that they have 2 months in which to make representations about the resolution.

The council must consider any representations which are made before deciding to continue with its plans. If it decides to go ahead, it will pass a final resolution and submit it to the Secretary of State. This must also be published and all affected persons must be informed.

Demolition If a council is satisfied that most of the houses in an area do not meet the tolerable standard, and that the most effective way of dealing with the area is to demolish all such houses, it can declare the area to be a Housing Action Area for Demolition.

Improvement If the council is satisfied that most of the houses in an area do not meet the tolerable standard, or lack one or more of the 'standard amenities', but are worth improving, it can declare the area to be a Housing Action Area for Improvement. The standard amenities are: a fixed bath or shower, wash-hand basin, sink (all with hot and cold water) and a w.c.

Demolition and Improvement If the council considers that some of the houses in an area should be demolished, but that others are worth improving, it can declare the area to be a Housing Action Area for Demolition and Improvement. The council must first be satisfied that most of the houses are below the tolerable standard, or lack one or more of the standard amenities.

Improvement grants

Owners and tenants in Housing Action Areas may be entitled to improvement grants to help pay the cost of providing standard amenities or bringing the house up to the tolerable standard.

If a house is not in a Housing Action Area, but the council has made an improvement order requiring the house to be brought up to the tolerable standard, the owner is entitled to an improvement grant towards the cost. *See:* IMPROVEMENT GRANT

Compensation for losing your home

An owner or tenant whose home is closed or demolished, or who is permanently displaced because of improvement works, may be able to obtain:

- A 'home loss' payment – to compensate for the personal upset and distress caused through being compulsorily displaced. The applicant must have occupied the house for at least 5 years.
- A 'disturbance' payment – to compensate for the reasonable expenses involved in moving home.
- A 'well-maintained' payment – which may be paid where a closing or demolition order or a compulsory purchase order has been made in respect of a house which falls below the tolerable standard, but which has been satisfactorily maintained.

For more information about these payments, contact your district or islands council.

HOUSING ASSOCIATION

An alternative to private landlords and councils

Housing associations are non-profit-making organisations that exist to provide accommodation either through CO-OWNERSHIP or by renting.

Most of those that provide rented homes are registered with a government body, the Housing Corporation, and receive financial help from it. Some cater for specific social groups, such as the elderly, the disabled or single-parent families. There is usually a selection process from a waiting list similar to that for council housing. The associations' estates are normally administered by professional housing managers.

The associations tend to be more flexible in their attitudes than local authorities, however, and set out to meet the needs of people who cannot find what they want in the rest of the private and public housing sectors.

How to apply

The address of the nearest housing association can be obtained from any Citizens Advice Bureau or the Scottish Federation of Housing Associations, 42 York Place, Edinburgh. Write to the association's letting officer, who will explain the procedure for his association and send an application form. The associations have no legal duty to house anyone, however, and it is entirely for them to decide whether to offer a tenancy to an applicant.

Assessing a fair rent

A housing association registered with the Housing Corporation is not legally obliged to charge a tenant a fair rent fixed by the local rent officer. However, it is a condition of receiving housing association grant – a payment from the government towards the capital cost of providing housing – that an association must register fair rents.

The 'fair rent' register can be inspected at the offices of the rent officer: there is a separate section of the register that covers housing association rents. *See:* RENT PROTECTION

If a tenant finds he is paying more than the fair rent, he can tell the association that he intends to deduct the excess that he has already paid from future rent.

If he finds that no fair rent has been registered, he can ask the rent officer to register one.

Security of tenure

Tenants of registered housing associations are entitled to a written lease (the tenancy agreement), and have security of tenure under the Tenants' Rights (Scotland) Act 1980.

The grounds on which such tenants can be evicted are the same as for council tenants. So are the legal procedures which must be followed, and the powers which are available to the sheriff court. *See:* COUNCIL TENANCY

However, the tenants of a registered housing association will not have security of tenure if the association is also a registered society under the Industrial and Provident Societies Act 1965 and its rules restrict membership to tenants or prospective tenants and prevent non-members becoming tenants.

Inheriting a tenancy

It is possible to inherit a housing association tenancy automatically when the tenant dies. The rules are the same as those which apply to council tenants. *See:* COUNCIL TENANCY

Buying the house

The tenants of housing associations do not have the right to buy their homes (although the tenants of certain housing co-operatives do). But housing associations can sell if they wish.

Scottish Special Housing Association

The Scottish Special Housing Association, which is government-financed, was originally set up in 1937 to build homes and alleviate unemployment in depressed areas. Since then it has expanded into Scotland's second biggest public landlord. The Association, in co-operation with local housing authorities, has built and now lets over 90,000 homes throughout Scotland.

SSHA tenants have the same security of tenure as council tenants. Unlike tenants of other housing associations, they are not entitled to have a fair rent fixed by the rent officer. *See:* COUNCIL TENANCY

SSHA tenants also have the same right as council tenants to buy their homes. *See:* COUNCIL HOUSE SALE

Complaints

If a tenant feels he has been treated unfairly by a registered housing association, he should write to the Housing Corporation, 19 Coates Crescent, Edinburgh EH3 7AF. *See:* LANDLORD AND TENANT

HOUSING BENEFITS

Your right to help with rent and rates

A person who is responsible for paying rent or rates may be entitled to one or more housing benefits to help with the cost of these payments. The amount of benefit payable depends on the person's income, age, how many children and non-dependants he has and whether he (or a partner) is handicapped.

Housing benefits are administered by local housing authorities and by the Scottish Special Housing Association. Before April, 1983 (November, 1982, in the case of most council tenants) SUPPLEMENTARY BENEFIT claimants were entitled to extra benefit to cover rent and rates. Since then, housing benefits have been paid instead. But boarders and crofters on benefit still receive help with housing costs from the DHSS.

The benefits that you may be entitled to

The benefits that are available are:

- **Rent rebate** Granted to tenants of district and islands councils, new town corporations and the Scottish Special Housing Association. The rebate is made to the person responsible for paying rent (who need not be the tenant), and takes the form of a reduction in the amount of rent payable.
- **Rent allowance** Granted to most other tenants. The allowance is made to the person responsible for paying rent and takes the form of regular payments direct to that person.
- **Rate rebate** Granted to tenants and owner-occupiers. The rebate is made to the person responsible for paying rates (who need not be the tenant or owner) and takes the form of a reduction in the amount of rates payable. However a private tenant who is paying rates direct to his landlord will receive the rebate in the form of regular payments.

If you are refused benefit

You have no automatic right of appeal to a court or tribunal if the housing authority refuses to pay you a housing benefit, or pays you less than you expect. However, you can ask for the decision to be reviewed by the authority and, if you are still not satisfied, by a committee of councillors (or of new town corporation or SSHA Council members). If you are unhappy about their decision, you should seek advice about the possibility of legal action.

Getting more information

If you want to find out more about these benefits, or to make an application, contact the housing department of your district or islands council, or the SSHA. All councils must provide written information free of charge.

If you claim supplementary benefit, you do not have to apply to the housing department for housing benefits. The Department of Health and Social Security will send the housing authority a certificate confirming that you are on benefit and you should then receive the housing benefits to which you are entitled. *See:* RATES; RENT ALLOWANCE; RENT REBATE; SUPPLEMENTARY BENEFIT

HUMAN RIGHTS

When an individual can resort to international law

Britain does not have a written constitution or any single law that lays down the citizen's rights, overriding all other legislation. But Britons can, in certain circumstances, seek to enforce the European Convention on Human Rights and Fundamental Freedoms.

The convention is not directly enforceable through British courts because Parliament has not enacted it into British law. But it is binding on signatory countries, including Britain.

The convention confers on the citizens and residents of the signatory countries the general right to:
- Life, liberty and security of person.
- Fair administration of justice.
- Respect for private and family life, home and correspondence.
- Marriage and founding a family.
- Education.
- Enjoyment of possessions.
- Free elections at reasonable intervals.

The convention also generally guarantees freedom of:
- Thought, conscience and religion.
- Expression and opinion.
- Assembly and association with others.

and freedom from:
- Torture, inhuman and degrading treatment and punishment.
- Slavery, servitude and forced labour.
- Retrospective criminal legislation.

In guaranteeing all those rights, governments are expected not to discriminate on grounds of race, colour, origin, sex, language, religion, opinion, birth, ownership of property or other status.

Anyone who feels his own rights or those of someone else have been violated can complain to the European Commission of Human Rights, 67006, Strasbourg, France.

The right to life

It is not a violation of the right to life to kill someone in order to:
- Defend yourself or someone else from unlawful violence.
- Make a lawful arrest.
- Prevent a lawfully detained person escaping.
- Act lawfully to quell a riot or insurrection.
- Carry out a death sentence passed by a court.

The right to liberty

The convention does not guarantee the right to liberty to:
- Convicted criminals.
- Persons detained so that they can be brought before a court on reasonable suspicion of having committed an offence, or prevented from escaping after committing an offence.
- Children whose education needs to be supervised (for example in a detention centre or remand school).
- People who need to be isolated to prevent the spread of infectious diseases.
- Alcoholics, drug addicts, vagrants and people of unsound mind.
- Illegal immigrants or people subject to deportation or extradition.

Freedom from slavery

The right to freedom from slavery, servitude and forced labour does not apply to:
- People required to work during detention (a prison sentence, for example), during conditional release from detention or as an alternative to detention (for example, work carried out under a COMMUNITY SERVICE ORDER).
- Members of the armed forces or conscientious objectors.
- Citizens required to perform compulsory service during an emergency threatening the community – for example, war, a natural disaster, or other state emergency.
- Anyone obliged to perform normal civic duties – such as jury service.

The right to justice

The right to fair administration of justice, liberty and security of person entitles a detained person to be told promptly, in detail and in a language he understands, the reasons for his detention and what charges he faces.

He must be promptly brought before a magistrate or someone else with judicial power and is entitled to trial within a reasonable time or to release pending trial, subject to guarantees being provided that he will appear for trial.

Everyone is entitled to take court proceedings to establish speedily whether his detention is lawful and to be released – with a right to compensation – if it is not.

Everyone is entitled to a fair hearing, within a reasonable time and by an independent and lawful tribunal, of any criminal charge against him, or to determine his civil rights and duties.

Generally, trials must take place, and judgment be pronounced, publicly. But the Press and public may be excluded from all or part of a trial:
- In the interest of morals, public order or national security.
- When the interests of juveniles or the protection of the private lives of the parties requires (for example in divorce or custody cases).
- When, in the court's opinion, publicity would prejudice the interests of justice.

The convention says that everyone charged with a criminal offence has the right:
- To be presumed innocent until lawfully proven guilty.
- To have adequate time and facilities to prepare his defence (including access to a lawyer).
- To defend himself in person, through a lawyer of his own choice or through free legal assistance.
- To call and examine witnesses on his own behalf under the same conditions as witnesses against him.
- To have a free interpreter if he cannot understand or speak the language used in court.

One article bans retrospective legislation, but it does not rule out conviction for any act or omission which, when it occurred, was only criminal according to the general principles of law recognised by civilised nations – for example, terrorism, piracy, hijacking, genocide and war crimes.

The right to privacy and family life

Men and women of marriageable age have the right to marry and found a family according to national laws governing these rights.

Everyone has the right to respect for his private and family life, his home and his correspondence. No public authority may interfere with that right, unless it is lawful and necessary to do so in the interests of:
- National security – for example, telephone tapping to detect a spy.
- Public safety and the prevention of crime or disorder – for example, opening of letters in some cases.
- National economic well-being – to prevent tax evasion or flouting of exchange controls, for example.
- Health – as when a child is taken into official care, and parental rights are de-

nied, for the sake of the child's psychological well-being.

- Morals.
- The rights of others.

Freedom of thought

The freedom of thought, religion and conscience includes the right to change one's belief and the right of religious practice, worship and teaching, in private or in public, alone or with others.

That right is subject to the same limitations as the right to respect for private and family life, except that it cannot be limited on grounds of national security.

Freedom of expression

The right to freedom of expression and of opinion also gives people the right to receive and impart information and ideas without official interference and regardless of frontiers.

But governments are not prevented from requiring broadcasting or cinemas to be licensed.

Like several other rights, it can be limited on grounds such as public safety, health and morals, and also to protect the rights of others.

The right of assembly and association

The right of peaceful assembly and freedom of association includes the right to form and join – and, perhaps, not to join – a trade union. But it does not prevent lawful restrictions barring members of the police, the armed forces and people in state employment from belonging to unions.

This right too is subject to limitation in the interests of national security, public safety, prevention of crime or disorder, and protection of health, morals and the rights of others.

The rights of freedom of expression, freedom of assembly and association, and freedom from discrimination are guaranteed even to aliens living in a signatory country.

The right to enjoyment of possessions

The convention states that individuals and organisations shall not be deprived of their possessions, except as the law prescribes – for example, through compulsory purchase of land.

The right to education

No one shall be denied the right to education and the state must respect the right of parents to ensure that their children are educated in conformity with parents' religious and philosophical convictions.

However, this right is not violated by the provision of sex education in schools against parents' wishes.

Emergencies

Signatory states are permitted to repeal most of their obligations under the convention during war or other emergency – such as terrorism.

A state cannot repeal its obligations to protect the right to life – except during warfare declared under the Geneva Convention – or its obligations concerning the use of torture and retrospective legislation.

Any measures repealing a state's obligations must be notified to the Secretary General of the Council of Europe, and he must be told when they cease to operate.

Conditions that must be met when making a complaint

Before a complaint about an alleged violation of one or more of these rights can be considered by the European Commission of Human Rights, the commission must be satisfied that it meets several conditions.

The complainer must first have exhausted all available remedies within the country where the violation of rights is alleged to have taken place.

A complaint against the prison system in Scotland for example, would need to have been finally rejected by the Secretary of State for Scotland before it could be submitted to the commission.

The Commission must receive a complaint within 6 months of the final decision within the country concerned.

Conditions for individuals

Five further conditions apply to any complaint made by an individual, but not if it is made by one government against another government. The complaint must not be:

- Anonymous – although the commission may decide to keep a complainer's name secret.
- Substantially the same as a matter already dealt with by the commission, or already submitted to another system of settling international disputes – for example, arbitration.
- Incompatible with the provisions of the convention – for example, by using the convention to prevent another person from obtaining something to which he is entitled under national law.
- Manifestly ill-founded – for example, if a complainer's interpretation of his rights is obviously not reasonable.

HOW TO MAKE A HUMAN RIGHTS COMPLAINT

If you feel that your rights under the European Convention have been violated by any member government which accepts the right of individual petition – including Britain – you can complain directly to the European Commission of Human Rights in Strasbourg.

A complaint – called an application – can be made by any individual, group or organisation.

Any complaint should set out the facts of the case, reasons for thinking there has been a violation of rights and details of the steps taken to get the matter put right. This information is needed to prove that you have exhausted all means of redress available in the country concerned – one of the conditions of admissibility laid down by the convention.

You would need, for example, to give details of letters, phone calls or meetings with officials, and of decisions by courts or government ministers.

There are no fees to pay for making a complaint. No costs will be awarded against you if your complaint is not upheld or if it is ruled inadmissible.

If the complaint raises legal complexities or involved, factual questions, or you are uncertain whether it is admissible, it may be useful to be represented by a lawyer who is familiar with the convention and its machinery. But you do not have to have legal representation.

Free legal aid is available to complainers whose limited financial means would otherwise prevent them from pursuing a complaint. However, the Commission has not yet published details of how this scheme operates.

- An abuse of the right to petition the commission – for example, as part of an election campaign.

A decision on whether a complaint is admissible may first require written or oral arguments by all the parties concerned.

How complaints are dealt with by the commission

When it receives a complaint, the Commission of Human Rights first decides whether the complaint is relevant to the convention. It then invites written observations from the government against which the complaint has been made. The complainer has the right of reply to these comments.

The Commission then decides whether the complaint is admissible and gives the reasons for its decision, which is final.

Once a complaint has been ruled admissible, the Commission starts its full investigation of the facts of the case. It can interview the complainer, witnesses and officials involved, and visit places concerned in the case.

Having established the facts, the Commission must try to achieve a settlement it approves of between the government involved and the complainer. If an acceptable settlement is reached, the Commission draws up a report, briefly recording the facts of the case and the solution achieved, and the case is closed.

If no acceptable settlement is reached, the Commission gives a longer factual report to the Council of Europe's Committee of Ministers, together with an opinion on whether the convention has been breached.

Governments concerned in a case also receive this information, but the complainer does not. It is for the Committee of Ministers to decide whether the report and opinion should be published. They are automatically published if the case is brought before the European Court of Human Rights.

Sometimes a complainer withdraws his complaint after it has been ruled admissible but before the Commission has issued an opinion. The Commission can – if it feels that the case raises issues on which an opinion would clarify the meaning of the convention – continue to consider the case and give a report and opinion in due course. The Commission itself can decide to publish this information in such cases.

After it has given an opinion on a complaint still outstanding, the Commission asks either the Committee of Ministers or the European Court of Human Rights to decide whether there has been a breach of the convention.

How a government can be punished

The European Convention was agreed in 1950 by members of the Council of Europe – a political,

THE TAWSE CASE

An education authority cannot insist that parents allow their child to suffer corporal punishment.

Mr and Mrs Cosans objected strongly to corporal punishment in schools. One day their son broke a school rule, but, as his parents wished, refused to be belted. He was suspended from school until he accepted the punishment. The suspension continued until he reached the school leaving age.

Mrs Cosans applied to the European Commission of Human Rights, saying her rights to have her children educated in accordance with her philosophical convictions had been denied. She also alleged that the suspension violated her son's right to be educated.

The Commission agreed with Mrs Cosans' first allegation and referred the case to the Court of Human Rights.

DECISION

The Court agreed with the Commission, and also accepted Mrs Cosans' second argument. Parents' 'philosophical convictions' included seriously held views on punishment – the state education system could not impose its own views on such matters as a condition of providing education.

As a result of this decision, Scottish law will have to be changed so that parents' views on discipline, not those of teachers or education authorities, are enforced.

THE EUROPEAN COURT OF HUMAN RIGHTS

The Court of Human Rights – which is also based in Strasbourg – consists of judges from each member state of the Council of Europe. They act independently of the state which nominates them for election by the council's Constituent Assembly.

Usually, only seven judges sit at one time. Cases are generally heard in public, but the court may decide to go into closed session. The court's decisions and the reasons for them, are published. They are referred to the Committee of Ministers to be carried out.

How jurisdiction is limited

There are two important restrictions on the court: it can only accept a case if the state or states involved accept the jurisdiction of the court. Most Council of Europe members – Britain among them – do so. Secondly, each case is referred to the court as a dispute between states arising out of the alleged breach of an agreement between them – that is, the convention.

For this reason, an individual complainer does not take part in the proceedings, unless called as a witness. Nor is his case argued by a lawyer. But his lawyer may be asked to 'assist the court' and is often invited to join the team which presents the commission's report to the court.

Proceedings, based on the report, at first take place by means of written submissions and replies between the parties. The case is then examined at a hearing.

If the court decides that the convention has not been breached, the case is closed. There is no appeal.

When damages can be awarded

When the court rules that there has been a violation of rights, it can award damages or expenses. The court can require parties to the case to 'take such action as is necessary to give effect' to its judgments. This may mean that reparation must be made to the injured party under the terms of national law or, as in the case of Committee of Ministers' rulings, it can lead to a change of practice by the offending government.

When a government against which a complaint has been made takes remedial action before the court has made judgment, the court can strike a case off its list. The same can happen when a settlement is reached during its deliberations.

THE COMMITTEE OF MINISTERS

The Committee of Ministers is a political body consisting of one representative from each member state of the Council of Europe. Its decisions on complaints under the convention require a two-thirds majority. They are reached in private, there is no appeal against them, and they are binding.

The Commission can decide to refer a case to the court for judgment instead of itself considering it. Any government involved in a case can also bring it before the court. But the Committee of Ministers must consider a case if it has not been referred to the court within 3 months of an opinion being given by the Commission.

If, after considering a case, the Committee of Ministers decides that there has been no breach of the convention, the parties involved in the complaint are informed. No further action is taken.

When a violation is proved

When the Committee decides that there has been a violation of rights, it sets a time limit for the offending state to change its law or policies so that there can be no similar breach of the convention in the future.

If the state does not do so, the Committee decides how to give effect to its call for remedial action. The convention does not specify how this can be done. But signatories to the convention undertake to carry out the Committee's decisions, and if they do not, they can be suspended from membership of the Council of Europe.

Political pressure to conform to the convention is the ministerial committee's strongest sanction: often a member state brings its practices into line with the convention before it has been required to do so.

economic and social forum to which any democratic state in Europe can belong.

The convention is legally binding on the 21 governments that have signed it. Not all signatories, however, recognise the right of individuals to complain to the Commission about alleged contraventions. Some only accept complaints by other signatories.

Some states do not accept the jurisdiction of the European Court of Human Rights over complaints. In that case, complaints can be judged only by the Committee of Ministers, the Council of Europe's main political body.

Any government that does not comply with a decision of the committee or of the court can be suspended from membership of the Council of Europe. For the same reason, the convention is enforceable only against a government that has undertaken to be bound by it, and not against other bodies or individuals.

Which countries individuals can complain against

Although 21 countries have accepted the European Convention, not all of them accept all of its provisions.

The right of individuals, groups and organisations to complain to the Commission of Human Rights, as well as the jurisdiction of the Court, is recognised by Austria, Belgium, Britain, Denmark, the Federal Republic of Germany (West Germany and West Berlin), France, Iceland, Ireland, Italy, Liechtenstein, Luxembourg, Netherlands, Norway, Portugal, Sweden and Switzerland, but not by Cyprus, Greece, Malta, Spain and Turkey.

Britain has extended its acceptance of the European Convention on Human Rights to Bermuda, the Cayman Islands, Channel Islands, Falkland Islands, Isle of Man, St Helena, Brunei, the Turks and Caicos Islands, British Virgin Islands, Antigua, Montserrat and St Christopher.

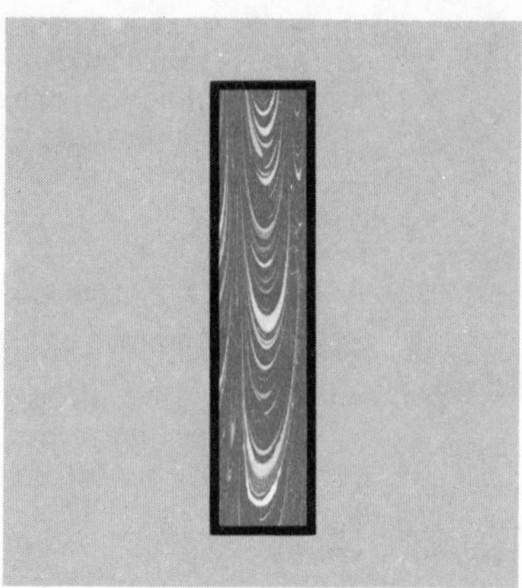

IDENTIFICATION PARADE

Safeguarding a suspect against false identification

If the police suspect a person of a crime and have a witness to the incident, they may ask the suspect to take part in an identification parade.

If the suspect is not under ARREST, he is not obliged to attend an identification parade. But if he is under arrest, he cannot refuse to take part in such a parade.

If the suspect is being temporarily detained (for up to 6 hours) by the police, an identification parade can only be held if he consents. *See:* DETENTION

The decision to hold an identification parade usually rests with the police officer in charge of the case, or with a superior officer. But in some cases the PROCURATOR FISCAL may order the police to hold a parade, if he thinks it necessary.

In addition, a person who is charged with an offence can apply to the sheriff court at any time for an order directing the procurator fiscal to hold an identification parade. The sheriff will grant the application provided that the following conditions are all met:

- A parade has not already been held by the fiscal.
- The fiscal has refused to hold – or has unreasonably delayed in holding – a parade after being asked to do so by the suspect.
- The sheriff considers the application to be reasonable.

Whenever an identification parade is held, the suspect is entitled to have his solicitor present to observe the parade – so long as the solicitor can attend within a reasonable time.

A parade is usually held in a police station or, occasionally, in a prison. If necessary, it can be held in other premises, such as a village hall or school.

Composition of the parade

An identification parade consists of at least 5 people in addition to the suspect. If there are 2 or more suspects, the parade will be increased by one additional person for each additional suspect. Alternatively, separate parades will be held for each suspect.

Members of an identification parade are usually drawn from members of the public who happen to be passing the police station. Such people can refuse to take part in a parade.

So far as possible, the parade members must be of similar age, height, dress and general appearance to the suspect.

If the suspect has a physical disability – for instance, if he has only one leg – this should be concealed. This can be done by the whole parade standing behind a counter. If the suspect has some other identifying characteristic, such as wearing glasses, this should also be concealed – for example, the whole parade may be asked to wear glasses.

The suspect has the right to object to the composition of the parade – on the ground, for instance, that the appearance of a member of the line-up is not similar to his own.

The people taking part in the parade will be lined up, usually with their backs to a wall, and numbered consecutively from left to right. The suspect can take up any position in the parade and can change his position after each witness.

When you are a witness

If a person is called as a witness, he must not be allowed to see a suspect or members of the parade before the identification parade takes place, nor be told anything about the suspect by the police.

Only one witness at a time will be admitted to view the parade. If the witness is a child, he or she can be accompanied by a parent or guardian, but must not be influenced in any way in arriving at a decision.

Any witness is entitled to request a member of the parade to put on a hat or spectacles, walk, or say a particular phrase. If a witness cannot identify – or wrongly identifies – anyone in the line-up, the police will record that no positive identification has been made.

If the witness recognises someone in the parade, he will be asked to state the number given to that person. The police officer in charge of the parade will then take down the name of the identified person. The officer will then repeat the name to the witness within the hearing of that person.

A witness who has inspected a parade must not be allowed to mix with other witnesses who have still to do so.

Other ways to identify a suspected person

If a suspect has not been arrested, and refuses to take part in an identification parade, the police can arrange for informal identification without telling him. For example, if a suspect is known to frequent a particular place, the police may take the witness there and wait – perhaps in a car – until the suspect passes by.

When the police do not know the identity of the person they are seeking, they may ask a witness to look through books of photographs of people who have been convicted of similar crimes in the past. A witness must not be helped to identify any person.

If a witness makes a positive identification from photographs, other witnesses should not be shown photographs but should be asked to attend an identification parade.

ILLEGITIMATE CHILD

Rights of someone whose parents are unmarried

A child born to parents who are not married to each other at the time of the birth is illegitimate. However, if the parents later marry each other the child automatically becomes legitimate from the date of the marriage.

If the marriage is void, the child will be illegitimate unless at least one parent did not know the facts – for instance, about the existence of a previous marriage – and believed they were legally married. *See:* NULLITY

If one of the parents marries someone else – not the other parent – the child remains illegitimate, even if the marriage takes place before the birth. However, if the child is adopted by the married couple, he or she immediately becomes their legitimate child.

Rights of an illegitimate child

For most practical purposes, illegitimate children have equal rights in law with those who are legitimate.

An illegitimate child is entitled to be maintained by both parents. If, for instance, the father fails to maintain his child, he can be ordered to do so by a court. *See:* ALIMENT; AFFILIATION AND ALIMENT

If a parent makes a WILL or executes a deed giving property to his or her 'children', the term 'children' includes any illegitimate children unless there is evidence to the contrary – for instance, a reference to 'lawful children'. Instead of accepting a legacy in a will (or if no legacy at all is left), an illegitimate child has the same right as a legitimate child to claim 'legal rights' from the parent's estate. *See:* DISINHERITANCE

An illegitimate child also has the same rights as a legitimate child to share in the estate of a parent who has died without making a will. *See:* INTESTACY

An illegitimate child can claim DAMAGES for a relative's death (and vice versa) in the same way as a legitimate child can. *See:* FATAL INJURY

However, an illegitimate child has no right, as a legitimate child does, to share in the estate of any relative other than a parent – for instance, the estate of a brother, sister or grandparent – unless named in a will. If the relative dies intestate (that is, without making a will) and there are no other claimants, the estate will then fall to the Crown.

Nevertheless, an application can be made to the Crown by an illegitimate relative for a gift from the relative's estate. Contact the Queen's and Lord Treasurer's Remembrancer, 5/7 Regent Road, Edinburgh.

An illegitimate child cannot inherit any honour or title.

Rights of the parents

The father of an illegitimate child has fewer rights than the father of a legitimate child.

The parents of a legitimate child have equal custody rights, but only the mother of an illegitimate child has an automatic right to custody. However, the father can apply to a court to be given custody or access. When considering the application, the court must bear in mind the child's welfare. *See:* CUSTODY OF CHILDREN

The consent of both parties is usually necessary before a legitimate child can be adopted. But if the child is illegitimate, the father's consent is not necessary unless a court has awarded custody of the child to him. He can still apply for custody even if adoption proceedings have started.

Either parent can apply to adopt their illegitimate child, either alone or with a marriage partner. The child is then treated for virtually all purposes as a legitimate child. *See:* ADOPTION

The DOMICILE of a legitimate child is normally that of the child's father. But the domicile of an illegitimate child is that of the mother.

The parents of a legitimate child automatically become his or her guardians at birth, and are then entitled to look after the child's financial and other interests. But the parents of an illegitimate child do not automatically become his or her guardians, and the child therefore has none.

If an illegitimate child needs a guardian for a particular purpose – for instance, to administer property or raise a court action – an application can be made to a court to appoint one. It is possible for either parent to be appointed. *See:* GUARDIAN

Social security benefits are payable for a dependent child, whether the child is legitimate or illegitimate. *See:* DEPENDANT

A person who is looking after an illegitimate child whose mother has died may be entitled to a GUARDIAN'S ALLOWANCE. The allowance cannot be paid to the child's father.

A single parent bringing up a child can claim an additional personal INCOME TAX allowance, whether the child is legitimate or illegitimate.

Registering the birth

Of the parents, only the mother can register the birth of an illegitimate child. The registrar cannot register the birth on information supplied by the father alone.

The father's name cannot be recorded in the register of births unless he signs the register along with the mother or both make statutory declarations that he is the father.

However, even if the father's name is not recorded at birth, it can be added later if:

- Both parents make declarations that he is the father (the father must do so within 12 months of the birth).
- His paternity is established by a court in affiliation and aliment proceedings.
- The child's mother dies and the father applies to the sheriff, within 12 months of the birth, for an order requiring his paternity to be registered.

The child can then be re-registered with the father's name. *See:* BIRTH REGISTRATION

Children of a foreign marriage

A child may be regarded as legitimate even if his or her parents' foreign marriage is not valid in this country – provided that the child is considered to be legitimate by the laws of the country where both parents are domiciled.

Where the parents have different domiciles, the child's legitimacy under the laws of either country may be enough to make him or her legitimate in the UK.

Acquiring British Citizenship An illegitimate child who is born to a British father and a foreign mother cannot automatically obtain British citizenship through his or her father (as a legitimate child can). However, any child –

whether illegitimate or not – can acquire British citizenship in a number of other ways. *See:* CITIZENSHIP

If an illegitimate child cannot obtain British citizenship in these other ways, the Secretary of State can be asked to register the child as a citizen. He may do so at his discretion.

An illegitimate child with a British mother and a foreign father can acquire British citizenship through the mother.

IMMIGRATION

When permission is needed to enter Britain

Under the Immigration Act 1971, the right to enter the UK at any time and stay without restriction depends on CITIZENSHIP.

Under the British Nationality Act 1981, British Citizens are entitled to enter and remain. So also are COMMONWEALTH CITIZENS who before the 1981 Act came into force had a right of entry because of a UK born parent, or a husband with a right of entry. British Dependent Territories Citizens and British Overseas Citizens have no right to enter the UK (except under the Special Voucher Scheme – see below).

British Citizens and others who are entitled to admission cannot be refused entry to the UK and are not liable to deportation. But they may require a 'certificate of entitlement' if not UK born, naturalised or registered.

Anyone else needs official permission to enter Britain and official approval to remain.

An EEC citizen is entitled to come for up to 6 months to look for work and to stay on if he or she finds a job. For others seeking work, see WORK PERMIT.

How permission varies

The terms on which other travellers, their spouses and children are allowed to enter Britain vary according to their origin, purpose and financial situation. Permission can be given for:

- A short temporary stay.
- A limited period, but on the understanding that if things go well they will be permitted to settle here.
- An indefinite stay.

Settlement means a person has his home in Britain, without restriction on the length of his stay or on his right to work. But settled people do not have a right of abode until they gain citizenship. They remain liable to DEPORTATION, and if they leave Britain for more than 2 years, they can be refused re-entry.

The officials who control immigration

Government immigration policy is applied by entry clearance officers, immigration officers and Home Office staff.

Entry clearance officers check the applications that most immigrants have to make before setting out. They work in British embassies, high commissions and consulates abroad, as employees of the Foreign and Commonwealth Office.

Immigration officers are stationed at airports and docks to decide whether and on what terms travellers can be admitted. They are employed by the Home Office and advised by Health Department medical officers.

If a person breaks any conditions of his stay he can normally be prosecuted or, alternatively, the Home Office may decide to deport him.

Preliminary clearance

Anyone subject to immigration controls who wants to enter Britain can apply for clearance in his own country. In some situations he will not be admitted to the UK unless he has done so, and as a result airlines and shipping companies will not accept bookings for him.

For example, a person coming to settle here on the basis of relationship to a person already settled here must have an entry clearance. So must a person coming to engage in business here, or a person of independent means.

The only people who do not need entry clearances nowadays are visitors (including people coming for medical treatment) and other people who are essentially coming only for a very limited period, such as au pairs and working holidaymakers who are Commonwealth Citizens. Anyone who is coming with the intention of later getting permission to live here permanently must have an entry clearance.

Entry clearances are not compulsory

THE MAN WHO STAYED AWAY TOO LONG

A settled immigrant has a right to leave Britain and return – but not if he is away for more than 2 years. The limit is extended only if the immigrant's closest ties are in Britain and he has spent most of his life in the country.

Dharam Bir Taneja, an Indian accountant born in 1934, came to Britain in 1962 and stayed until May 1970, when he left to study in the United States. He returned in April 1972 – within the time limit for admission as a returning resident – but after a week went back to the United States.

In March 1974 Mr Taneja again applied for readmission and was granted an entry certificate by the clearance officer at the British consulate-general in Chicago. But he did not use it.

When Mr Taneja applied once more in November 1974 – 7 months after his latest time limit had expired – he was refused entry clearance.

In an appeal to an immigration adjudicator, a lawyer argued on Mr Taneja's behalf that the rules gave the officer power to relax the time limit. He should have done so in Mr Taneja's case because illness had prevented him from using the first entry clearance, and because his life was in Britain – he had gone to study in America only so that he could further his career in Britain, not to set up permanent residence.

The entry officer forwarded a report by Mr Taneja's own doctor that apart from bouts of depression there was no evidence of real illness. He argued that Mr Taneja had lived in Britain for only 8 of his 42 years, and had no close relatives in Britain. The appeal was dismissed.

When the case was taken to the Immigration Appeal Tribunal, it had to decide whether the adjudicator could have been wrong in law to rule that the circumstances did not allow the use of a discretionary power.

DECISION

The appeal was dismissed. Mr Taneja was obliged to return to India as soon as he had finished his course of study.

for students, but most students would find it very difficult to gain admission without one.

Forms of application vary with the country of departure and the traveller's purpose. The applicant must prove his or her identity and may be asked for proof of family relationships, occupation or financial situation.

The entry clearance officer must be satisfied that the facts in the application are correct – a requirement that can take years to meet if it depends on proving a family relationship in India, Pakistan or Bangladesh. If the officer considers that the immigration rules allow entry for the stated purpose, he stamps the applicant's passport with either an entry certificate (for people from British Commonwealth countries), or a visa (for aliens).

Entry clearance officers abroad can also issue certificates of entitlement to the right of abode to those who, through having a right of entry, need them.

When the traveller arrives in Britain

An immigration officer must admit a person holding an entry clearance, unless:

- He believes it was obtained by misstatement or concealment of facts. However, the burden of proof lies upon the immigration officer.
- Changed circumstances disqualify the application – for example, if a woman already in Britain rejects a man who says he is coming to marry her.
- He finds grounds for refusal for medical reasons or because a traveller's presence is considered likely to harm the community.

Unless there is a deportation order against them, the wife or children under 16 of any Commonwealth citizen settled in the UK before 1973 cannot be refused admission.

No one whose usual home is in Britain and who returns after an absence can be refused admission on medical grounds alone. However, he may be refused admission if he has been away for over 2 years.

A medical officer's role

Anyone who wants to stay in Britain for more than 6 months can be referred by the immigration officer to a medical inspector. So can anyone, even if coming for a shorter period, who seems to need medical treatment or who mentions that he has a medical problem.

If the medical inspector reports that a traveller's admission is not desirable – for example, because he or she has an INFECTIOUS DISEASE – or that an immigrant may not be able to support himself or his dependants because of his condition, the immigration officer normally refuses admission.

If the person needing treatment is a returning resident who cannot be refused entry on medical grounds, he or she can be ordered by the immigration officer to report to a medical officer of health so that treatment can be arranged.

SPECIAL GROUNDS FOR REFUSING ENTRY

A traveller who would otherwise qualify at least for temporary admission can be refused entry if:

- A medical inspector advises that he should be excluded.
- He refuses to be medically examined.
- He is under a current deportation order.
- He has been convicted of an extraditable crime in any country.
- His exclusion is considered 'conducive to the public good' because of his character, conduct or associations – a provision used mainly to prevent criminal, subversive or terrorist activities.
- He cannot convince the immigration officer that he will be admitted to another country after staying in Britain.

If entry is refused

If an immigration officer refuses entry, he must give the traveller a printed notice, carrying the authority of a chief immigration officer or immigration inspector and showing the reason for refusal. The notice must state the time limit for appealing, and an appeal form must be supplied with it.

The right to appeal can usually be exercised only after a traveller has left the country – unless he arrived with a valid entry clearance. Then he is entitled to remain in Britain until an appeal is heard.

An immigration officer has the power to order the detention of a person who is refused admission, while outward travel is arranged. A passenger can also be held in custody while his or her claim to admission is investigated or an appeal is heard. Special detention accommodation is provided at or near Heathrow Airport, London, but a detained traveller may be sent to PRISON if other secure accommodation is not available.

After 7 days' detention a person must be told of his or her right to apply for BAIL. Applications are decided by government-appointed appeals adjudicators at hearings that are open to the public.

Instead of detaining a traveller whose claim to admission is being investigated,

OFFENCES AGAINST THE IMMIGRATION LAWS

An immigrant breaks the law if he:

1. Knowingly enters Britain without permission or in breach of a DEPORTATION order.

2. Obstructs or misrepresents facts to an official executing the Immigration Act, or refuses to answer questions or produce a required document.

3 Alters or falsifies a passport or entry certificate, or possesses a forged document with the intention of using it to gain entry.

4. Knowingly remains beyond the time limit of his permission to enter, or breaches any other condition of that permission – usually a prohibition against taking employment.

Maximum penalty: £1,000 fine and 6 months' imprisonment, with a recommendation for deportation if the court thinks fit. But in many cases offenders are detained and expelled by the Home Office without prosecution.

It is an offence for any person to give shelter to an immigrant who he knows or has reasonable cause to believe is an illegal entrant or has broken a condition of his stay.

If an overstayer marries, his wife can be convicted of harbouring him, although prosecution is unlikely. The maximum penalty is a £2,000 fine and 6 months' imprisonment.

The most serious immigration offence is to be concerned knowingly in arrangements to bring an illegal entrant into Britain. The maximum penalty is 7 years' imprisonment.

an immigration officer can allow temporary entry on condition that the person hands over his or her passport and reports back by a specified time. Restrictions can be imposed on the traveller's movements – for example, residence at a certain address.

When a stay is limited

A person with a work permit is usually permitted to enter for 12 months. A person who is not a worker and who does not qualify for immediate settlement can be admitted for a limited time. Immigration officers have wide powers of choice when granting temporary stays, and the time allowed could be anything from a day to 12 months, provided that the traveller can support himself without working for the period that he wants to stay. The maximum period is normally 6 months.

Someone who qualifies only as a visitor and is given a limited stay will be forbidden to take employment – paid or unpaid – without obtaining the consent of the Department of Employment, or to engage in a business or profession without the Home Office's consent.

Extending a limited stay

A person who wants to stay longer than the time limit stamped in his or her passport, or wants to have a ban on work removed, should send the passport to the Home Office immigration department with a letter explaining the claim. A personal approach is likely to involve hours of waiting.

Application for an extension must be made before the time limit expires – even if only 1 day before. It automatically gives the applicant the right to remain for 28 days after a decision is made, or until the end of any extension granted, which could be for a period shorter than 28 days.

The length of extension is normally similar to the period allowed on entry.

Anyone who applies for extension before a time limit has expired is entitled to appeal against a refusal.

If someone on a limited stay fails to apply for an extension before the time is up, he is likely to be refused the extension – even if it would have been allowed otherwise – and has no right to appeal against refusal. He can be prosecuted and jailed for up to 6 months for overstaying his time limit, or the Home Office could decide to deport him for some breach of his conditions. He then would have a right of appeal.

When a limited stay can be made permanent

A traveller seeking permanent settlement can be admitted for a limited period at first, on the understanding that if he meets certain conditions he will be given extensions of time and will eventually qualify by length of residence. He must, however, have an entry clearance for admission.

Extendible entry on that basis can be granted to:

- Workers (see WORK PERMIT).
- Businessmen and the self-employed.
- Self-employed artists and writers.
- People of independent means (who must have at least £150,000 capital or an income of at least £15,000 a year, and also meet certain other conditions.
- Those intending to marry a person in the UK.

The Home Office seldom allows extension of a stay for a purpose that was not stated when a traveller arrived. Someone who comes as a visitor but could qualify to settle – for example, a man who sees an opportunity to start a business – will have to leave when his time is up, and make a new application.

Businessmen, artists and writers

People who can support themselves by self-employment or by business activities can be admitted initially for 12 months. Permission to stay can be renewed year by year until they qualify for permanent residence after 4–5 years.

Anyone who wants to enter to start a business must prove to the entry clearance officer that he has enough money or other assets (at least £150,000) to meet expenses and potential liabilities, and that his profits will maintain him and any dependants with him.

A man who intends to earn his living by investing in an existing business must show that it needs his money and services. His investment must be in proportion to the return he will gain – not simply a disguise for paid employment.

A self-employed artist or writer must satisfy the entry clearance office – and the Home Office when he applies for extensions of his stay – that his work is genuinely freelance and is enough to maintain him and any dependants.

Independent means

Someone with enough capital or stable income to support himself and his family without working can be granted an entry clearance as a person of inde-

TRAVELLERS WHO MUST GO HOME

People with no prospect of qualifying for permanent residence can be admitted to Britain for a limited time. They have the right to ask for extensions, but must leave the country eventually or risk expulsion, prosecution or both.

Temporary admission is granted to:

- Visitors with enough money to meet all expenses, including the cost of outward travel. A visitor will be forbidden to take employment or to set up a business or profession, but may negotiate individual business deals. Persons entering for medical treatment must have funds to pay for it. Otherwise they will be refused medical care except in genuine emergencies. Reciprocal agreements for free emergency care exist with all EEC countries, Austria, Bulgaria, Czechoslovakia, Finland, German Democratic Republic, Hungary, Israel, Malta, New Zealand, Norway, Poland, Portugal, Rumania, Russia, Sweden and Yugoslavia. Visitors are normally admitted for 6 months extendible to 12 months. They may have some difficulty in entry if the immigration officer thinks they are really seeking work, or settlement.
- Students enrolled for full-time courses at institutions recognised by the Home Office. They can be admitted for periods of 12 months at a time. A person hoping to enrol can be given a shorter time limit, extendible if he or she succeeds. The maximum total period is 4 years. Students are normally forbidden to take employment but consent may be given if they apply to take part-time or vacation work. A student must have funds to support himself and dependants – he can bring a wife and children under 18.
- AU PAIR girls.
- Working Commonwealth citizen holidaymakers between the ages of 17 and 27 who may take incidental jobs – but not make a career – while in Britain.

In practice this provision is available almost exclusively to young Canadians, Australians and New Zealanders, who are given 6 or 12 month stays, extendible for up to 2 years.

pendent means; but he will have to show that he has at least £150,000 in capital or income of not less than £15,000 under his control in the UK, and also that his admission is in the 'general interests' of the UK or that he has close connections with the country (for example, that he has relatives here or has lived here for a long time in the past).

Intention to marry

A woman who convinces an immigration officer that she intends to marry a man settled in the UK is given permission to stay for 3 months. She must also convince the officer that adequate maintenance and accommodation are available for her (for she is not allowed to work).

As soon as the marriage has taken place, the woman will be given indefinite leave to remain in the UK.

A man who wants to marry a woman settled here will not be allowed to live here unless the woman he plans to marry is a British Citizen. Even then, he will not be able to come if he has not met his prospective wife, or unless he proves that he is not marrying primarily to get into the UK, or if adequate funds and accommodation are not available (for he is not allowed to work). The same applies to a man who is already married to a UK woman.

PROVING HER INTENTION IS HONOURABLE

A fiancée may be admitted without an entry certificate if she can convince the immigration officer that she is definitely to marry.

Unless the man shows that the couple intend to live together permanently, entry will be refused. A man who is admitted or allowed by the Home Office to remain here on marriage will only be given 12 months' leave to stay initially (though he will be allowed to take work). He will be allowed to settle here after that time, if the marriage still exists and the couple are living together.

An indefinite stay

Two classes of people are admitted to Britain for indefinite periods – no limit is stamped in their passports – although they are not British Citizens or entitled to admission to the UK:

- Diplomats and their official staff, who are exempt from immigration control as long as the British Government continues to recognise their diplomatic status.
- Commonwealth citizens with any grandparent born in Britain. They are officially admissible if they intend to seek or take up employment, and in practice they can remain even if they do not find it, and can settle permanently. They remain liable to deportation unless they qualify for citizenship.

The relatives who can follow

A person settled in Britain without restriction on his or her stay has the right to be joined by relatives, but only by:

- A wife.
- A husband.
- Children under 18.
- Unmarried dependent daughters between 18 and 21.
- Dependent parents and grandparents (in exceptional circumstances).
- Elderly or disabled near relatives living alone (in exceptional circumstances).

In each case, the person already settled, officially called the sponsor, must be able to show that he or she can and will support and accommodate the relatives without the help of public funds.

The only exception to that requirement is made when the sponsor was settled in Britain on January 1, 1973, and is being joined by a wife or children under 16.

Any relative wanting to join a settled immigrant must have an entry clearance before setting out for Britain.

Wives joining husbands A wife who applies to join her husband after he has settled in Britain must show proof of the marriage and that he can maintain her. If it took place in an area without an adequate system of registration she must produce extensive supporting evidence and may have to undergo medical examination to help establish her identity. The difficulty of proving a marriage on the Indian subcontinent, for example, can lead to a delay of years before an entry clearance is issued. A woman 'in permanent association' with a man may be regarded as a wife.

Husbands joining wives It is now impossible for a husband to join a wife who has settled in the UK, unless she is a British Citizen and the immigration officer is convinced that it is not a bogus marriage.

Children under 18 A child under the age of 18 is entitled to enter only if both parents are already settled in Britain or are being admitted for settlement at the same time. 'Parents' can mean step-parents, adoptive parents or the parents of an illegitimate child, but all relationships have to be proved.

A parent who is alone in Britain can sponsor a child only if the other parent has had no responsibility for the child's upbringing, or if it can be shown that exclusion will be harmful – for example, because living conditions with the parent in the home country are undesirable.

When an application is made for a child to enter Britain from a country with no adequate system of birth registration, the child is questioned by an entry clearance officer and may be required to undergo medical examinations, including X-rays, to confirm age and parentage.

If a child's answers to questions about family relationships differ from those of the mother or other children, the officer can refuse all the entry clearances on the ground that he is not satisfied they are related.

Children over 18 A son of 18 years or older cannot normally be admitted to join parents settled here, but must qualify in his own right. A daughter over 18, but under 21, may perhaps be admitted if she is unmarried and fully dependent, was living with the family overseas, and has no other close relatives in the country of origin to turn to.

Parents and grandparents Elderly parents (at least one must be over 65), or widowed mothers of any age may be able to qualify to join children settled here if they can prove that they are dependent on these children and that they have no other close relatives in their own country to turn to.

A sponsoring child must show that he or she can accommodate and maintain not only the parents or grandparents, but also any further people who might be admissible later as dependants of them. An entry clearance officer will want evidence that the sponsor has been sending money regularly to cover most of the upkeep of parents or grandparents. In practice very few parents or grandparents are admitted.

Other near relatives Brothers, sisters, aunts or uncles of settled immigrants are admitted only in a narrow category of 'distress'.

Children born in the UK A child born in the UK may not be a British Citizen (see CITIZENSHIP), but will usually be allowed to remain for the same period as his or her parents. If they settle, or become British Citizens, the child has the right to register as a British Citizen. But a child who leaves the UK for 2 years or more loses the right to re-enter and therefore to become a Citizen.

THE IMMIGRANT WHO DECEIVED THE AUTHORITIES

An immigrant can be deported if he obtains entry by deception, but not if he merely fails to disclose material facts.

Salamatullah Khawaja was a Pakistani who wanted to live in Britain. He applied for a visa to come to study. Before a decision was taken on his application, he arrived at an airport and said that he wanted to enter as a visitor for a short time.

He was given leave to enter for one month. During that time he married a woman settled here, and applied to stay permanently. In fact he had previously married the same woman abroad. She had flown to Britain with him, but presented herself to a different immigration officer. He always intended to stay permanently. He was detained as an illegal entrant, pending deportation.

DECISION

The House of Lords decided that his deception made him an illegal immigrant, just as if he had landed on a beach late at night. But the Home Office must usually prove that such a person has told lies. Mere failure to disclose material facts is not enough – though silence, when coupled with other factors, can sometimes amount to deception.

THE LITTLE GIRL WHO HAD TO SHARE HER BED

For a child to be allowed to leave one parent and join the other, undesirable conditions at home must also be proved to be unavoidable.

Monica was 12 when an application was made on her behalf to the British High Commission in Kingston, Jamaica, for clearance to join her father in Britain. He had left Jamaica when she was 6 months old.

The entry clearance officer refused because immigration rules say that both parents should be in Britain. Exceptions are made only when the sponsoring parent has had sole responsibility for the child's upbringing, or if 'family and other considerations' make the child's exclusion undesirable.

In an appeal to an immigration appeals adjudicator, a lawyer argued on Monica's behalf that overcrowding in her home, where she shared a bedroom and apparently a bed with a sister and two older half-brothers, was a danger to her welfare.

It was also alleged that her stepfather, who had little income, resented her being in his house when her father could well afford to take her.

The entry clearance officer, defending his decision, argued that Monica was better off in a familiar environment than with a 'virtual stranger' who had been back to Jamaica for only 4 weeks, when she was 11.

The adjudicator noted that Monica had a grandmother in the same neighbourhood. She had lived with her until she was 9, and still visited her. He concluded that Monica's situation could be remedied in Jamaica, and dismissed the appeal.

The Immigration Appeal Tribunal consented to a further appeal on behalf of Monica – by then 14. It had to decide whether the adjudicator was right to rule that undesirable circumstances must also be unavoidable.

DECISION

The Tribunal agreed with the adjudicator. Monica's appeal was dismissed and she had to stay in Jamaica.

How the special voucher scheme works

A restricted number of British Overseas Citizens are admitted into Britain every year for 'settlement' (see CITIZENSHIP). These are the 'East-African Asian' refugees. Some come direct from East Africa, others via India.

All such people have the right to settle in Britain but they must wait in their present country of residence for entry clearance before they travel. Their flow from the Indian subcontinent and East Africa is regulated by an annual quota of entry clearances, which is usually referred to as the 'Special Voucher Scheme'.

Quota clearances are issued only to heads of households, so in families where husband and wife have different citizenship, the passport of the husband usually decides their right to settle. If he has given up his UK citizenship and only his wife holds a UK passport, the whole family is excluded.

Widows, divorced women and wives who are family breadwinners because their husbands are disabled can qualify as heads of households in their own right. If they hold UK passports they and their children are admitted, along with a disabled husband. Single people over 18 of either sex are treated as heads of households if they hold UK passports.

Refugees Entry for permanent settlement is also allowed occasionally to a REFUGEE or to people who arrive seeking POLITICAL ASYLUM.

When an immigrant can appeal

Almost any ruling under the Immigration Act can be challenged by the person it affects. However, there is no right of appeal for people who are:

- Refused a work permit.
- Refused extension of their stay in

THE TIME LIMITS FOR IMMIGRATION APPEALS

Immigration decisions against which there is a right of appeal, and the time limits in each case, are shown below:

Decision	Time limit
Refusal of entry clearance abroad	3 months
Refusal of entry on arrival – no clearance issued abroad	28 days after leaving UK
Refusal of entry on arrival – clearance issued abroad	Lodged immediately by passenger claiming right to wait in Britain
Refusal of certificate of entitlement abroad	3 months
Refusal of certificate of entitlement by Home Office	14 days
Refusal to extend time limit on stay or to cancel other conditions such as work ban	14 days
Refusal of stay for person previously exempt, such as a diplomat who resigns his post	14 days
Deportation	14 days from notification of intention to make order. No appeal against order itself
Removal – when legality of expulsion is challenged	28 days after leaving
Removal – when appellant objects to country to which he is being sent	14 days. Destination is normally country of nationality, but Home Secretary can direct removal to any country he thinks likely to admit person removed
Refusal to allow re-entry by cancelling an earlier deportation order	28 days

Late appeals An immigration appeals adjudicator may accept an appeal lodged after the time limit if he thinks there are special circumstances. But once an adjudicator has given his decision on an appeal and stated a time limit on any further right of appeal, a late claim is not permitted in any circumstances.

Britain after disobeying a time limit.

● Refused entry by order of the Home Secretary on grounds of public good or the like.

● Deported on grounds of public good, if the Home Secretary certifies that the decision was made for political reasons or in the interests of national security. In that case the Home Secretary can appoint a committee to hear arguments before the deportation order is carried out, but it cannot be legally challenged.

Anyone else can have a decision on his or her case reviewed by an immigration appeals adjudicator. Adjudicators sit at various centres in Britain, but not abroad, so appeals by people who are refused entry or who are expelled have to be heard in their absence. However, someone who arrives with a valid entry clearance and is then refused entry on special grounds has the right to remain in the country – usually in detention – until the appeal is heard.

An appeal against an adjudicator's decision can be made to the Immigration Appeal Tribunal in London, but usually only on arguable points of law or if a person being expelled claims to be a political refugee who should not be returned to his own country.

A few cases involving deportation on grounds of public good, or deportation of the family of a person being deported, go directly to the tribunal.

In any immigration appeal the only issues are whether the ruling appealed against was made within the law, or whether an official's power of discretion – for example, in deciding whether a family relationship is satisfactorily proved – was properly exercised. No appeal authority has the power to say that someone should be allowed into Britain or be allowed to stay if the case falls outside those limits.

Although there is no direct right of appeal to the courts, the Court of Session probably has the power of judicial review. That means that if judges find that a decision by an official authority such as the Immigration Appeal Tribunal is clearly wrong in law, they could make an order quashing the decision – declaring it invalid.

How the appeal system works

Any official who refuses an application under the Immigration Act must issue a notice stating his reasons, and telling the applicant of his or her right of appeal and the time limit for lodging an appeal.

Whenever there is a right of appeal, a 'notice of appeal' form with directions on how to complete it must also be issued.

The completed form must be returned within the time limit to the official who made the decision. It is his duty to forward it as quickly as possible, with a statement of the facts and his reasons for the decision, to an appeals office which arranges hearings.

An appellant – the person making the appeal – has the right to be represented by a lawyer, or he may be represented by someone else with the appeals adjudicator's permission.

The time taken for a case to be heard depends on the type of appeal and the area where it arises. Entry clearance appeals lodged on the Indian subcontinent can take up to 18 months – but the appeal of someone who is refused entry after arriving with an entry clearance is likely to be heard within a week. Such a person has the right to wait – in detention – until his case is decided.

The appeals office notifies the appellant or his representative of the time and place of the hearing, giving usually 4–6 weeks' notice. It also sends copies of the official's explanatory statement and any other documents – for example, medical reports – which make up his case.

If the appellant wants to submit documentary evidence of his own, he should send it to the appeals office at least a week before the hearing.

Hearings are public and can be reported – though it is rare for the Press or any people not involved in the case to be present. An adjudicator can exclude the public from hearing certain evidence, or prohibit its being reported, if he believes that it is in the interests of one of the parties.

The immigration official's evidence is contained entirely in his statement and supporting documents, but the appellant is free to give spoken evidence – interpreters can be provided at government expense – and to call any witnesses.

The decision is normally given in writing, usually within 1 month, and posted to the appellant. He is informed of his limited right to appeal further to the tribunal, and of the time limit on that.

No costs are awarded to either side for appeals to the adjudicator or to the tribunal.

Immigrants' tax and national insurance obligations

Immigrants have similar obligations to other British residents. They must pay INCOME TAX on any taxable income, and must pay NATIONAL INSURANCE CONTRIBUTIONS out of any earned income.

On income from British sources, an immigrant can claim a whole year's personal tax allowance even if he or she starts work partway through the tax year.

Income from overseas sources is fully taxed if the immigrant makes his home in Britain – even if he has not been granted permanent residence. But if his stay is temporary he is taxed only on income sent into the country. A lump sum payment from a former employer overseas is not taxed in Britain.

Immigrants must pay CAPITAL GAINS TAX on any profit from the sale of overseas assets if they become permanent UK residents.

Those assets are also liable to CAPITAL TRANSFER TAX if they are given or bequeathed to others.

Interest on British Government securities, which is tax-free if held by overseas residents, becomes liable to income tax when an immigrant makes his home in Britain.

Social security benefits

The qualification rules for most social security benefits make no distinction between British Citizens and other people living here.

A non-citizen can apply for supplementary benefit, but if he was admitted to the UK on the condition that he maintained himself (for example, as a visitor) or on the basis that some other person would maintain him, he may be refused benefit. But in some cases he may be given money for day-to-day living requirements.

Obtaining help and advice

Two organisations provide help and advice on immigration matters. They are:

- The United Kingdom Immigrant Advisory Service, 115 Wellington Street (2nd Floor), Glasgow (041 227 6051) and Brettenham House (7th Floor), Savoy Street, London WC2E 7EN (01 240 5176). The Service is a government-funded but independent organisation which provides, amongst other things, free legal advice and representation.
- The Joint Council for the Welfare of Immigrants, 44 Theobalds Road, London WC1X1 8SP (01 905 5527/8).

IMMUNISATION

Society's first line of defence against the 'killer' viruses

Immunisation, which includes inoculation and vaccination, is the most successful method yet devised to protect whole communities against the spread of serious contagious and infectious diseases.

Large numbers of people can be made immune quickly and effectively by inoculating or vaccinating. Strictly, inoculation means introducing an infective substance into the body by breaking the skin. Vaccination is injecting with cowpox to combat smallpox. 'Vaccination', however, is generally used to describe inoculation.

Immunisation is voluntary and is generally available free under the National Health Service, especially for children and whenever an epidemic breaks out.

Adults may sometimes have to pay – for example, if you plan to visit a foreign country where certain diseases are always found. You will usually get free immunisation if the foreign country requires it because of an outbreak of disease in Britain, but not if it is merely a routine requirement.

When an adult is required to pay for immunisation for foreign travel, any children must also be paid for.

Many foreign countries ask for proof that you have been immunised against any disease that is prevalent there (for example, cholera), or that may have recently broken out in Britain.

The necessary form can be obtained from your GP or from a travel agent or local health board office. The vaccination will usually be administered by the GP, who will then enter the details on the certificate, and stamp it.

There are also private clinics where you can be vaccinated for a fee. There is one at Heathrow Airport, for instance. If you want to find one ask your travel agent for details when you make your initial booking arrangements.

Once stamped, the certificate will not be valid for a few days. You must wait 10 days in the case of yellow fever, and 6 days with cholera. But they are then valid for 10 years and 6 months respectively.

Protecting the young

Babies, infants and children are particularly susceptible to some diseases,

NOT TO BE OVERLOOKED

The Scottish Home and Health Department frequently runs campaigns to remind parents of when children should be immunised.

TAKING ADVANTAGE OF THE FREE PROGRAMME OF IMMUNISATION AGAINST DISEASE

Children – and in some cases adults – can receive free immunisation against certain diseases. The health authorities recommend specific age periods for the different vaccines and intervals of time between each inoculation.

Age	Vaccine	Interval
First year	Three doses of polio vaccine *and* three doses of triple vaccine (whooping cough, diphtheria and tetanus) sometimes without the whooping cough	6–8 weeks between the first and second dose; 4–6 months between the second and third
Second year	Measles	At least 3 weeks after the last polio and triple vaccine
4–5 years	'Booster' dose of polio and double vaccine (tetanus and diphtheria)	About 3 years after previous dose of polio and triple vaccine
11–13 years	Tuberculosis and, for girls, German measles vaccine	The German measles vaccine should be at least 3 weeks after that for tuberculosis
Adulthood	Polio and tetanus vaccine	No recommended interval

such as tuberculosis. Other diseases, such as German measles, are more dangerous in adults. To meet both needs, the health authority provide immunisation from an early age, free of charge.

From time to time, the Scottish Home and Health Department and the area health boards run poster campaigns to remind parents of the vaccinations required by children and of the procedure for obtaining them under the National Health Service.

Usually, parents are told of a suitable age at which their children should be taken to the family doctor. If they are at school, a day is set aside for vaccination by a medical officer.

The course recommended by the Scottish Home and Health Department is to be immunised first against polio, diphtheria, whooping cough and tetanus. Inoculations against measles, tuberculosis and, for girls, German measles, are given later.

Parents are entitled to refuse to allow their children to be inoculated.

Immunisation for adults

Adults who were not vaccinated as children against polio and tetanus can receive the treatment free under the National Health Service.

Women of child-bearing age can receive a free inoculation against German measles. Otherwise, adults are normally required to pay for immunisation unless a disease of epidemic proportions has broken out in Britain or in a country they are intending to visit.

There is no entitlement to free treatment before an epidemic starts, even if it is known to be imminent.

Dangers of immunisation

Because immunisation involves infecting the body with weakened strains of a disease, there is always a slight risk in agreeing to be vaccinated or inoculated.

In certain circumstances, which a doctor should foresee, whooping cough vaccine may be dangerous to a child and German measles vaccine to an unborn child. No pregnant woman therefore should be vaccinated against German measles.

A doctor who fails to consider a child's health before vaccinating against whooping cough, or who fails to check a woman for pregnancy before immunising her against German measles, can be liable for DAMAGES for negligence if the child is damaged or if the woman gives birth to a handicapped child. *See also:* VACCINE DAMAGE

IMPOTENCE

When a husband or wife cannot consummate a marriage

Impotence – the inability of one marriage partner to have sexual intercourse with the other – can be a ground for a decree of NULLITY, ending a marriage. That applies, however, only if the incapacity has been present from the beginning of the marriage and only if it cannot be cured by some reasonable treatment.

In a man, impotence is usually an inability to have or sustain an erection. In a woman, it is usually either a physical defect or a nervous condition of vaginal spasms preventing intercourse. But impotence is not necessarily caused by a particular physical defect: frigidity or extreme dislike of intercourse can be sufficient.

A husband or wife who is impotent with his or her marriage partner may be able to have full intercourse with another partner. That, however, does not effect the granting of a nullity decree.

See: CONSUMMATION OF MARRIAGE

IMPROVEMENT GRANT

Financial help for people in sub-standard houses

Anyone – whether an owner or a private or council tenant – can apply to his district or islands council for a grant towards the cost of improving his home to a minimum standard.

However, if the applicant is not the owner of the property, he must first obtain the owner's written consent, both to the application and to the grant conditions which will be imposed.

Grants can be made to help pay the cost of:

- Providing a house with the 'standard amenities' – that is, a fixed bath or shower, wash-hand basin and sink (all with hot and cold water) and a lavatory.
- Improving a house to a basic standard.
- Converting an existing house or building to provide new housing.
- Carrying out certain essential repairs.
- Adapting a house for a disabled person.

When a grant cannot be made

A grant cannot be made in the following circumstances:

1. If the house was built, or provided by conversion, after June 15, 1964. However, a council can ask the Secretary of State for Scotland to waive this requirement – he may do so if, for instance, the house is to be adapted for a disabled person.

2. If the application is made by the owner or a member of his family; the house is to be occupied by such a person; and the rateable value is above a specified limit.

This limit varies from area to area – from £225 in Orkney to £465 in Bearsden and Milngavie. It is doubled where a house is being converted into 2 or more houses. Ask your council about the limit in your area.

However, this rateable value restriction does *not* apply to:

- A house in a HOUSING ACTION AREA for improvement.
- A house which is subject to an improvement order because it does not meet the tolerable standard or lacks a fixed bath or shower.
- A house to be occupied by a disabled person.
- Creating a self-contained flat in a large house, so long as the owner or a member of his family will not occupy the flat.
- Conversion of a building which is not a house.
- Grants for standard amenities.

3. If improvement works have already begun – unless the council is satisfied that there was good reason to begin before the grant application was approved.

THE TOLERABLE STANDARD

An improvement grant may be payable to help bring a sub-standard house up to a minimum, or 'tolerable' standard.

A house will meet this standard if it:

- Is structurally stable.
- Is substantially free from rising or penetrating damp.
- Has satisfactory provision for natural and artificial lighting, for ventilation and for heating.
- Has an adequate piped supply of wholesome water available within the house.
- Has a sink provided with a satisfactory supply of both hot and cold water within the house.
- Has a w.c. available for the exclusive use of the occupants of the house and suitably located within the house.
- Has an effective system for the drainage and disposal of foul and surface water.
- Has satisfactory facilities for the cooking of food within the house.
- Has satisfactory access to all external doors and outbuildings.

Conditions which will be imposed

It is a condition of all improvement grants (including repairs grants) that for 5 years after completion of the improvements, the house:

- Must be used as a private home (this condition is not broken if part of the house is used as a shop, or for business purposes).
- Must not be occupied by the owner or a member of his family except as a main residence.
- Must be kept in a good state of repair.

These conditions attach to the house, not to the applicant. A new owner must observe them unless he voluntarily repays the grant.

If any conditions are broken, the council can order them to be kept or demand repayment of the grant, with interest.

Grants for standard amenities

An applicant is *entitled* to a grant to help pay the cost of installing one or more of the standard amenities (see above), so long as the council is satisfied that the house will then be provided with all the standard amenities and meet the 'tolerable standard' (see the table on the left).

If the house is unlikely to have a habitable life of 10 years or more, the condition that the house should be provided with all the standard amenities does not apply.

The amount of the grant is 50 per cent of the expense approved by the council. The amount of approved expense depends on the number of amenities provided, but will not usually be more than £2,275, plus up to £3,000 (£1,200 if the house is likely to have a habitable life of less than 10 years) for any associated repairs.

STANDARD AMENITIES GRANTS

Grants are available for the following standard amenities. The amount is 50 per cent of the approved expense, up to the limits set out below.

Amenity	**Limit of approved expense**
A fixed bath or shower	£340
A hot and cold water supply at a fixed bath or shower	£430
A wash-hand basin	£130
A hot and cold water supply at a wash-hand basin	£230
A sink	£340
A hot and cold water supply at a sink	£290
A w.c.	£515
Total	£2,275

Grants for general improvements

A person who wishes to improve his home to a basic standard may be able to obtain a grant towards the cost. The financial assistance available depends on whether or not the house is in a Housing Action Area.

Housing Action Areas If your house comes within a Housing Action Area and is below the 'tolerable standard', you will be entitled to a grant if improvement works will:

- Bring your house up to the tolerable standard; and
- Result in your house being in a good state of repair.

If the council thinks that the house has a life of at least 10 years, it may also require all the standard amenities to be provided.

The grant payable is 75 per cent of the approved expense up to the maximum approved expense of £10,200. Where the house is in a pre-1914 tenement, this may be increased to £11,400. If you are the owner of the house and in financial hardship, a grant of up to 90 per cent may be paid.

Other areas In all other areas the grant is paid at the council's discretion and is usually 50 per cent of the approved expense, up to the maximum approved expense of £10,200. However, if the house is below the tolerable standard, or lacks a fixed bath or shower, the grant will be increased to 75 per cent.

Before making a grant, the council must be satisfied that the house will:

- Last for at least 30 years – or, if the council thinks fit, for between 10 and 30 years.
- Comply with building regulations.
- Be free of basic construction defects.
- Have the standard amenities,
- Have proper lighting and ventilation.

Grants are not given for houses which are already adequate. So you cannot, for example, generally get an improvement grant to install central heating or to rewire, except as part of a comprehensive scheme of improvement. However, you may be able to get an INSULATION GRANT towards the cost of insulating your loft.

House conversion Discretionary grants are also available for converting a house into 2 or more flats or for converting a building – such as a barn or warehouse – into one or more houses. The same conditions apply.

Improvement orders Even if a house is not in a Housing Action Area, an owner is entitled to a grant if his house is below the tolerable standard, or has no fixed bath or shower, and the council has made an improvement order requiring him to bring the house up to that standard. The grant is 75 per cent of the approved expense (up to 90 per cent in cases of financial hardship), up to the maximum approved expense of £10,200.

Grants for repairs

The council may provide a grant towards the cost of essential repairs which, if left undone, would threaten the useful life of a house. Grants cannot normally be made for routine maintenance, such as electrical rewiring. Consult your council if you are not sure whether to apply for a repairs grant or a general improvement grant.

A repairs grant can only be made where the owner of the house would suffer financial hardship if he had to meet the full cost of the repairs. However, this rule does not apply if the grant is made for the replacement of lead plumbing or if the repair work to be carried out is of a substantial and structural character.

The grant is paid at the council's discretion. The amount is up to 50 per cent of the approved expense, up to a maximum approved expense of £4,800.

However, if the house is in a Housing Action Area, an applicant will be *entitled* to a grant – so long as the council is satisfied that the house will then reach a tolerable standard and be in a good state of repair. The grant is 75 per cent of the approved expense – 90 per cent if an owner would suffer financial hardship – up to the maximum of £4,800.

Repairs notices If a house is in a state of serious disrepair, the council may serve the owner with a repairs notice. The owner will then be entitled to a repairs grant of up to 50 per cent, up to the £4,800 maximum.

Lead plumbing Since 1982, repairs grants have been available to replace lead plumbing – particularly lead-lined tanks. A grant of up to 75 per cent may be made, up to the £4,800 maximum. There is no financial hardship test, the rateable value limits do not apply and houses built or converted after June 15, 1964, are also eligible.

Assistance for disabled people

Improvement grants can be paid, at the council's discretion, to adapt a house to meet the needs (including employment needs) of a disabled person. A grant of up to 75 per cent of the approved expense can be made, up to the maximum approved expense of £10,200.

If the house has a standard amenity – for instance, a bath or lavatory – which is not accessible to the disabled person, a grant can be paid to provide one which is accessible.

The social work department of the regional (or islands) council *may* be prepared to make 100 per cent grants available to certain disabled people.

When a grant is paid

An improvement grant must usually be paid within a month of the date when the works are completed. The council may be willing to pay the grant in instalments while the works are being carried out, but it cannot pay more than 50 per cent (75 per cent in Housing Action Areas) until the works are completed.

However, in either case no grant will be paid until any works are completed to the council's satisfaction.

When a grant is refused

If a council refuses to pay a grant, it must give its reasons in writing. If you believe that you are entitled to a grant, you may wish to consider taking legal action against the council.

If the council refuses a discretionary grant, there is no right of appeal. However, your district councillor may be able to help you to have the decision changed in your favour. *See also:* OMBUDSMEN

Environmental improvement grants

Grants may also be available to owners and tenants to help them improve the amenities in their area – for instance, to provide a play-area for children or to renovate a back-court.

Improvements by council tenants

If a council tenant is allowed to undertake home improvements which add to the value of the house, he may be able to recover some or all of the cost from the council when he leaves. *See:* COUNCIL TENANCY

INCEST

When sexual intercourse is prohibited

Incest is the crime of sexual intercourse between people related to each other within the forbidden degrees of marriage. The forbidden degrees include blood relatives and relatives by marriage.

Blood relatives

Incest is committed by a male or female person who has intercourse with persons known to be related to him or her as follows:

Relatives of male	Relatives of female
Mother	Father
Daughter	Son
Grandmother	Grandfather
Granddaughter	Grandson
Great grandmother	Great grandfather
Great granddaughter	Great grandson
Sister	Brother
Aunt	Uncle
Niece	Nephew

These relationships extend to relatives of the 'half-blood'. They therefore include relationships such as half-brothers or half-sisters, half-brothers or half-sisters of a parent, and children of a half-brother or half-sister.

Relatives by marriage

Incest is also committed by a male or female person who has intercourse with persons known to be related to him or her as follows:

Relatives of male	Relatives of female
Mother-in-law	Father-in-law
Daughter-in-law	Son-in-law
Grandmother-in-law	Grandfather-in-law
Granddaughter-in-law	Grandson-in-law
Step-mother	Step-father
Step-daughter	Step-son
Step-grandmother	Step-grandfather
Step-granddaughter	Step-grandson

These relationships remain within the forbidden degrees even after the marriage which created the relationship has ceased to exist, for example, by divorce.

If both parties to the intercourse know of the blood or marriage relationship, both are guilty of incest.

Maximum penalty Incest is prosecuted in the High Court of Justiciary. The maximum penalty is life-imprisonment.

A child who is involved in an incestuous relationship is very unlikely to be prosecuted, but may be referred to a CHILDREN'S HEARING which will consider whether compulsory measures of care are necessary. Before this happens, the child may first be removed from home under a PLACE OF SAFETY ORDER.

Help and advice on incest is available from Incest Survivors' Group, c/o Strathclyde Rape Crisis Centre, P.O. Box 53, Glasgow G2 1YR (041 221 8448).

Other offences

If a female is related to a male person within any of the forbidden degrees, and he has intercourse with her against her will, he can be charged with RAPE as well as incest. It is also rape to have intercourse with a girl under the age of 12 years, whether or not she consents.

Maximum penalty Life-imprisonment.

Other offences include:

- Having intercourse with a girl under the age of 13, whether or not she consents.

Maximum penalty Life-imprisonment.

- Having intercourse with a consenting girl aged 13 or above and below 16 years of age.

Maximum penalty 2 years' imprisonment.

INCITEMENT

The offence of encouraging others to commit a crime

It is a criminal offence to incite someone else, by threats, persuasion or other pressure, to commit a crime – even if the crime is never carried out.

Maximum penalty The penalty for incitement is at the discretion of the court.

Some special offences of incitement have been created by Act of Parliament. These include:

- Incitement to racial hatred by using words at a public meeting or in any public place, or publishing or distributing written materials, which threaten, abuse, or insult any racial group in Great Britain.

Maximum penalty 2 years' imprisonment or an unlimited fine, or both.

- Incitement to disaffection by attempting to seduce any member of the armed forces from his duty or allegiance to the Queen.

Maximum penalty 2 years' imprisonment or an unlimited fine, or both.

THE MAN WHO REFUSED TO BREAK THE LAW

It is a criminal offence to incite anyone to break the law. It is not necessary that the incitement be successful.

Kay and Strain worked out a scheme to defraud an insurance company.

They approached a man and suggested to him that they would enter his house and steal his wife's fur coat. The man was then to get his wife to make a claim on the insurance company for the loss of the coat. Kay and Strain would then take a share of the insurance money.

The man pretended to go along with the scheme but, in fact, told the police. Kay and Strain were caught removing the fur coat from the house. They were charged with inciting the man to defraud the insurance company.

The defence argued that the two should not have been charged with incitement because the man had not been persuaded to commit the crime.

DECISION

The High Court said that the charge was a proper one because incitement to commit a crime, even though the incitement is unsuccessful, is itself a crime.

INCOME TAX

How personal circumstances and occupation decide your tax liability

In principle, the more income you receive for work done in the UK, the greater the proportion the tax man can claim. But tax liability differs from person to person because:

- Income from some sources is exempt from taxation.
- Some income is not taxed because of the way it is spent.
- Personal allowances are made for individual needs before tax is charged.

People whose whole income is exempt from taxation – for example, diplomats – or whose taxable income is less than the tax relief and personal allowances available, pay no tax at all.

Tax is calculated on the amount of income left after exemptions and allowances in each tax year, which runs from April 6 to April 5. It is charged at percentage rates that depend on income. In 1984–5 the rates were as follows:

Income	Rate of tax
• Up to £15,400	30%
• £15,401–£18,200	40%
• £18,201–£23,100	45%
• £23,101–£30,600	50%
• £30,601–£38,100	55%
• Over £38,100	60%

The sources of taxed income

The law does not define 'income'. Instead it lists the sources of payments that may be liable to be taxed. The sources of your income decide how you are taxed – by PAY AS YOU EARN deductions, by half-yearly instalments, or on demand after the tax year is over.

Taxable income sources are grouped in the following schedules:

- Schedule A – profits from land and buildings.

INCOME THAT IS NOT TAXED OR FULLY TAXED

You do not have to pay income tax on:
- Pools dividends, lottery and competition prizes, racing and other betting wins.
- Premium bond wins.
- Interest on national savings certificates, bonuses on SAYE contracts, and maturity bonuses on British savings bonds.
- Defence bonds and national development bonds on redemption.
- Voluntary payments from relatives – including from husband to wife and children after DIVORCE or SEPARATION.
- Educational grants.
- Housing improvement grants.
- Gifts from employers to mark special occasions – unless an amount is so large that the Inland Revenue sees it as a disguise for wages.
- Bonuses – but not wage or salary increases – from employers for gaining educational or professional qualifications.
- Part of retirement or REDUNDANCY lump-sum payments.
- National Savings Bank interest up to a set limit – £70 in 1984–85.
- The capital part of purchased annuities.
- Certain allowances and gratuities in the reserve or auxiliary armed forces.
- Compensation to victims of Nazi persecution, if exempt from German tax.
- Sickness benefit.
- Invalidity pension and allowance.
- Maternity allowance and grant.
- Family income supplement.
- Child benefit.
- Supplementary benefit paid to pensioners, or those not required to register for work.
- War-widow's pension.
- Death grant.
- Child's special allowance.
- Guardian's allowance.
- Wounds and disability pensions paid to the armed forces.
- Disablement benefit (including supplements).
- Attendance allowance.
- Mobility allowance.
- Severe disablement allowance/non-contributory invalidity pension.
- Social security benefit increases payable for child dependants.

But some social security payments are taxed:
- Retirement pension (including any invalidity addition).
- Widow's allowance or pension.
- Widowed mother's allowance.
- Industrial death benefit.
- Invalid care allowance.
- Unemployment benefit.
- Supplementary benefit paid to people who are unemployed or involved in trade disputes.

- Schedule B – commercial woodlands.
- Schedule C – interest on government securities.
- Schedule D: Case I – trading profits; Case II – professional or vocational profit; Case III – interest and other annual payments (not covered in Schedule C): Case IV – interest on foreign securities; Case V – foreign assets or trading profits; Case VI – any other profits, including furnished letting.
- Schedule E – employment earnings, including wages, salaries, bonuses, fees and the value of benefits not paid in cash and pensions.
- Schedule F – dividends and other company distributions.

Building society interest and income received from trusts and settlements are taxable, although not in any schedule.

Most personal income is earned from employment – Schedule E – and is taxed as it is paid, under the PAYE (pay as you earn) system.

Tax is also deducted from many annual payments before they are made – particularly those under Schedule F – but only at the basic tax rate, so people on higher incomes may have to pay more when their total income for the year is known.

People who earn business, trading or professional income under Schedule D are responsible for paying their own tax.

How PAYE works

Most tax on income earned through employment is deducted before the employee gets his or her money, under the PAYE system.

The employee's estimated tax liability for the year is divided into approximately equal instalments corresponding with each pay period, and the employer is responsible for deducting and passing these to the Inland Revenue.

A wage or salary earner taxed under PAYE should not have to pay extra to complete his liability at the end of a year unless he has other income, or unless his employer has failed to deduct enough. But an employee who stops work or whose family responsibilities increase during a tax year is likely to be owed a refund of overpaid tax.

Tax on some annual payments – for example, ALIMENT or periodical allowance paid under a court order – and on some INVESTMENT INCOME such as company dividends, is also deducted in advance. But only the basic rate of tax is applied at this stage, so someone with a high taxable income may have to pay more when the year ends.

A person whose only income is a wage or salary taxed under PAYE need not make an income tax return each year, but may be required to make one every 3 years or so to confirm that his or her circumstances have not changed.

Anyone who is taxed under PAYE has the right to ask his Inspector of Taxes to make a check on the tax paid if it seems too high.

Being taxed without PAYE

Tax on the earnings or personal profits of SELF-EMPLOYED people, on FOREIGN INCOME, and on any other income which is not already taxed, is calculated by the Inland Revenue after the taxpayer sends in an income tax return.

Under that method of charging, known as assessment, it is the taxpayer's duty to pay the sum demanded within certain time limits. He does, however, have a right of appeal against an assessment.

How to complete your tax return

A taxpayer uses an income tax return to declare all amounts and sources of income and make all claims to tax relief and allowances. That information enables Inland Revenue to calculate how much should be paid in any tax year.

If you receive business or professional income, bank or loan interest, maintenance or trust payments, or other investment or foreign income in any tax year, you must make an income tax return for that year. People who receive such payments regularly can expect to be sent a return form each year.

If your income requires you to make a return and you do not receive a form by the end of the tax year, it is an offence not to notify the Inland Revenue that you are liable for tax. You are subject to a penalty of up to £100.

If your only income is from employment, and all of it has been taxed under PAYE, you may be sent a return form

RETURN IT – OR BE PENALISED

You are subject to a penalty if you do not complete and send back an income tax return form within 30 days of issue.

only once every 3 years or so, to confirm that your source of income and personal circumstances have not changed.

Anyone who is sent a return form is required to send it back completed within 30 days of the issue date shown on it. Failure to do so may result in a penalty of up to £50 plus tax unpaid.

In practice the Inland Revenue takes no action unless a return is not received by mid-June. After that a reminder notice is sent. If it is ignored, a tax inspector can obtain an order for payment of tax and fines from an appeal commissioner. The defaulter is then liable to be proceeded against for recovery of a legal DEBT.

A PAYE taxpayer who does not receive a form should ask for one if he or she is likely to be entitled to a new allowance in the coming year.

A husband is responsible for declaring his wife's income details in his own return if they live together, unless one of them has arranged with the tax office for separate assessment.

If an unmarried child under 18 is living at home and has taxable income, a parent or guardian is responsible for his or her returns.

Working out your personal allowances

Everyone is entitled to earn some money without paying tax on it. The amount allowed varies because the law accepts that your personal responsibilities affect your ability to pay. So a married man can claim more than a single person.

The cash value of each type of allowance is set each year, along with tax rates. When tax is deducted through PAYE, the employer is told how much to take from the taxpayer's wages through a coding system. The code number allocated depends entirely on the information submitted to the tax office by the taxpayer. When he wants to claim further allowances – or stop claiming those to which he is no longer entitled – he must do as the self-employed taxpayer does each year: submit an income tax return, giving details of his earnings and circumstances, or write to his tax office – for instance when he is getting married.

Anyone who is liable to pay income tax – even a baby – qualifies for a basic personal allowance. Widowed, divorced or separated people are classed as single. So are married couples if husband and wife are both working and choose to be taxed separately on their earned incomes; each is entitled to a single allowance.

Married allowance

A man's personal allowance (£2,005 in 1984–5) is increased (to £3,155 in 1984–5) if he is married and his wife lives with him.

It does not matter whether or not she works, unless they choose to be taxed separately on earned income and retain a single allowance each. But the allowance cannot be claimed in full in the year in which he is married.

When a husband first claims the increased allowance he must send his MARRIAGE CERTIFICATE to the tax office, if it is asked for. A man who lives with a woman but is not legally married to her cannot claim.

A man who is separated can claim the increased allowance if he is wholly and voluntarily supporting his wife. He cannot claim if she has any other form of income. And if he pays her under any formal, legally enforceable arrangement – for example, a court order for aliment or periodical allowance – he does not qualify for a married allowance. Instead he can gain tax relief by claiming his payments as an allowable expense on his tax return.

When a man marries A newly married man is granted one-twelfth of the increased allowance for each month or part-month of marriage in the first tax year.

The only men who gain no immediate tax advantage from marriage are those who already have charge of children – for example, widowers. Claiming the

THE BEST TIME TO MARRY AND SAVE INCOME TAX

How even a day's difference can lose or save a great deal of money

A tax year always starts on April 6, so tax months start on the 6th of each calendar month.

Because every married man is entitled to a higher tax allowance than a single man, a man who marries partway through the tax year qualifies for part of the increase.

His share is calculated in monthly portions – one-twelfth of the annual increase is allowed for each month he has been married.

A wedding on, say, September 6 is no different from one on October 5 – both dates fall in the same tax month. But a bridegroom who marries one day earlier, on September 5, gains an extra part of the increased allowance because he qualifies in the previous tax month.

Say the marriage allowance is £1,200 higher than the single person's allowance, and the rate of income tax is 30 per cent. This would give him an extra tax allowance of £100 a month, and a saving of tax of £30.

If he applies immediately for a change of PAYE tax code the saving is made through lower deductions from his pay packet.

Otherwise he qualifies for a refund when the tax year is over.

Time of year The best time to marry is towards the end of the first month of the tax year – on or just before May 5 – so that the husband receives the full year's married allowance.

If either husband or wife does not use up all their allowances in the tax year of marriage, the balance can be transferred to the other spouse. But this cannot be done if they marry on the first day of the tax year, April 6.

TWO WAYS A COUPLE CAN BE TREATED SINGLY BY THE TAXMAN

Deciding between separate assessment and separate taxation

There are two ways in which a wife's tax affairs can be handled individually: by separate assessment or separate taxation.

Separate assessment does not change the amount of tax a couple have to pay. The wife is responsible for making her own return and paying her own tax, and she is entitled to any refund of tax she overpays.

An application for separate assessment is generally made when a husband wishes to avoid liability for tax on his wife's income.

Separate assessment can be arranged by applying in writing at any time up to 3 months before or 3 months after the start of the tax year on April 6. Either partner can apply – the consent of the other is not needed.

Arranging separate taxation

Working couples on higher incomes may benefit by claiming separate taxation of the wife's earnings. The husband remains responsible for their joint tax return and liability, but the wife is treated as a separate individual on her earned income.

The wife receives a single tax allowance, and her earnings above that amount are taxed at their own rate rather than being added to her husband's. So in effect her income starts at the bottom of the tax scale instead of being taxed at her husband's higher rate. Unearned income – for example, interest on savings – is still taxed at the husband's rate.

The husband loses his married allowance and his wife's earned income relief, so the claim only becomes worth while when a certain level of income is reached. The level can vary from year to year.

A claim for separate taxation – which must be signed by both partners – may be made at any time from 6 months before the tax year starts to 12 months after it ends.

The effect on tax

The point at which a couple will start to save money by having their earnings taxed separately depends on the tax scales and allowances set by the Government.

Example: A husband earns £16,000 from employment and his wife £10,000. His unearned income from investments is £400, her bank interest is £600. The marriage allowance is £3,155 and the single person's allowance and wife's earned income relief are £2,005.

A joint tax return would show:

Husband – all income		£16,400
Wife – all income		£10,600
Total income		£27,000
Less		
Marriage allowance	£3,155	
Wife's earned income allowance	£2,005	£5,160
Net taxable income		£21,840
Tax levied on £21,840:		
£15,400 @ 30%		£4,620
£2,800 @ 40%		£1,120
£3,640 @ 45%		£1,638
Total tax		£7,378

But under separate taxation the same couple's return would show:

Husband

Earned income	£16,000
Unearned – self and wife	£1,000
Total income	£17,000
less single person's allowance	£2,005
Net taxable income	£14,995

Wife

Earned income	£10,000
less single person's allowance	£2,005
Net taxable income	£7,995

By this method the tax levied on each is:

Husband

£14,995 @ 30%	£4,498.50

Wife

£7,795 @ 30%	£2,398.50
Total tax levied on	£4,498.50
husband and wife	+ £2,398.50
	£6,897.00
Saving	
Normal calculation	£7,378
Separate taxation	−£6,897
	£481

But if either of them had earned £5,000 less, a claim for separate taxation would have been foolish.

Their combined tax bill would have been £5,196, while the total of their separate bills, because of the loss of the husband's married allowance, would have been £5,397 minimum.

On the figures used for tax rates and allowances in this example, separate taxation is an advantage only when the couple's total earned income is approximately £24,000 or more.

In practice this cut-off point varies from year to year because of changing tax scales introduced in each Budget.

When a husband stops earning

If a working couple are both taxed by PAYE, the husband's code takes into account most allowances and other forms of tax relief.

The wife's code includes only her earned income relief, if they are taxed jointly, or her single allowance if they are taxed separately.

If a husband is no longer employed, a working wife may apply to have the family's allowances transferred on to her code so that her PAYE deductions are reduced immediately.

Otherwise, when the tax year ends, the allowances are automatically offset against the wife's earnings on a joint income tax return.

married allowance disqualifies such a man from receiving a special child-care allowance that is granted for the whole year. Rather than give up a full allowance in exchange for a part-year one, he should delay his claim until the following tax year.

When a woman marries The Inland Revenue regard a woman as single until the end of the tax year in which she marries. She remains responsible for her own tax liabilities.

Unlike her husband she does not qualify for any new tax allowance – although if she gives up her employment she will receive a refund of part of the year's PAYE deductions.

The next year Unless a couple arrange to be assessed separately, a husband is held responsible for his wife's tax liability from the start of the first full tax year after marriage. The rate at which she is taxed depends on the size of their two incomes added together.

Wife's earned income relief

When a wife's earnings are taxed with her husband's, he gains a tax relief equal to an extra single allowance – in addition to the married allowance he can already claim – except in the year in which they get married.

That extra tax relief applies only to EARNED INCOME. If the wife's earnings are less than the amount of the allowance, the difference cannot be offset against any other income she has, or against her husband's income.

Additional personal allowance

An extra personal allowance may be available to a taxpayer who is bringing up a child alone. This allowance is equal to the increase a married man is granted on the single allowance. It is usually claimed by people who are widowed, divorced or separated, or by unmarried mothers. But a married man can receive the extra allowance – in addition to his married allowance – if his wife's physical or mental condition makes her completely unable to care for their child. A medical certificate is needed in such a case.

Claiming the extra allowance – which equals the difference between the married and single allowances – disqualifies a taxpayer from claiming an allowance for the employment of a housekeeper or someone else to care for children.

Housekeeper allowance

A widowed person who has a resident relative or employee as a housekeeper is entitled to a small allowance – £100 in 1984–5. If the housekeeper is a married female relative, the claim must certify that her husband is not receiving a marriage allowance for her.

The same allowance is granted to a single taxpayer who has a relative living in the house to care for a brother or sister, provided that the claimant already qualifies for the child allowance.

Age allowance

An increased personal allowance is granted to a taxpayer aged 65 or over, subject to an income limit – £8,100 in 1984–5. The allowance rates are about 25 per cent higher than the normal single or married allowances. In 1983–4 they were £2,490 for a single person and £3,955 for a married man.

The age allowance is given to single taxpayers – including widowed, separated or divorced people – as soon as they are 65, and to married men when either they or their wives become 65. It is payable for the full year and can be claimed on the income tax return form at the beginning of the tax year. The tax office will then adjust the tax-payer's code, and he will be awarded a refund.

Income limit When a taxpayer is earning more than the limit set for the present tax year his age allowance is cut by two-thirds of the excess.

For example if a couple's income is £9,300 and the limit is £8,100 – an excess of £1,200 – the allowance is reduced by £800. On high incomes, this method of reduction can remove the age allowance altogether. But it cannot remove a taxpayer's right to a basic single or married allowance, granted regardless of income. Qualification for the age allowance does not stop a taxpayer claiming other allowances.

A wife's earned income relief still applies to married couples after the wife has retired, if she gets a pension on her own national insurance contributions.

Retirement pensions

Pensions, whether State or private, are taxable income and must be declared to the Inland Revenue. There are a handful of exceptions – for example, pensions paid to victims of Nazi persecution are tax-free.

The only circumstance in which you are entitled not to pay the tax is when it is not paid because of a fault by the Inland Revenue, the failure to pay is discovered more than a year after the end of the tax year in which it was due and your income is less than £9,500 (in 1984) a year. However, if a retirement pensioner is presented with a large bill for unpaid tax, he is unlikely to have to pay interest.

A woman who receives a retirement pension in her own name – as a result of having paid her own national insurance contributions – is entitled to wife's earned income relief. The allowance is claimed by stipulating the separate contributions on the tax return form.

Lump-sum payments Tax is not due on lump-sum payments from an OCCUPATIONAL PENSION scheme approved by the Inland Revenue. Ex-gratia payments from an employer are treated in exactly the same way as compensation for loss of office in that up to £25,000 is free of tax.

Investment income A retired person whose income is below the tax threshold can obtain a rebate of tax deducted at source on certain investment income – for example, company dividends and interest on some government securities. But tax deducted from building society interest can only be offset against tax due and cannot be repaid. Building societies are not good investments for people who do not pay income tax.

Child's services allowance

A taxpayer forced by age or ill health to depend on the services of a daughter or son can claim a small allowance – £55 in 1984–5. The child must live with and be maintained by the claimant. A widowed person can benefit by claiming instead a housekeeper allowance, which is usually worth about twice as much.

Dependent relative allowance

Taxpayers can claim a special allowance for any dependent relatives – including in-laws – that they support, whether or not they live with them. The relative can be a widowed, divorced or separated mother; or any relative unable to look after himself or herself because of old age (65 or more in the tax year) or infirmity. In 1984–5 the allowance was £145 for a single, divorced, widowed or separated woman; and £100 for others.

If the relative's taxable income is more than the basic single rate of old age pension, the claimant's tax allowance is reduced. It goes down £1 for every £1 of excess income, and can be removed entirely. A taxpayer can often gain more benefit by paying a covenanted sum to the relative instead of seeking the dependent relative allowance. *See:* COVENANT

Blind allowance

A blind person registered with the local social work department can claim an additional allowance (£360 in 1984–5). A married man can claim the allowance if his wife is a blind person. If both are blind they can claim a double allowance. *See:* DISABLEMENT

Widow's bereavement allowance

When a man entitled to the married

man's allowance dies, his widow will be entitled (for that tax year and the next one) to an allowance equal to the difference between the married and single allowances. *See:* WIDOW'S TAX

Assessment of tax liability

If tax on some or all of your income was not deducted before you were paid, it is charged against you by assessment. That means that Inland Revenue works out how much is owed and sends a demand for payment.

An assessment is also used to confirm the accuracy of deductions under PAYE or to check the claims of people who believe that they have paid too much tax.

Calculations are based on the income tax return completed by the taxpayer, plus any other information the Inland Revenue might receive from people who have paid income to the taxpayer.

If no return is made, or an inspector of taxes thinks that a return is incomplete, he is entitled to guess what the taxpayer owes. His guess is likely to favour the Government, and the taxpayer may also be prosecuted for tax evasion.

Whenever an assessment shows that tax has been underpaid or overpaid, a notice of assessment is sent to the taxpayer. It is a form intended to explain how the taxable income was calculated after taking allowances into account, the rates at which tax is levied, and how the tax figure compares with the amount already paid for the year.

If an inspector of taxes finds that PAYE coding was accurate and the amount deducted is right, no notice of assessment is sent. But the taxpayer has the right to ask for one.

When assessment shows that tax has been overpaid, a refund is sent with the notice of assessment.

If an employee whose main income is taxed by PAYE is found to have underpaid, and the amount owed is not large, the tax office usually arranges for the employer to recover it by adjusting PAYE deductions in the following year.

When an assessment shows that tax is owed which cannot be recovered by PAYE adjustments – usually because the taxpayer is self employed or retired – the notice of assessment serves as a demand for payment.

The taxpayer has 30 days in which to appeal against the assessment, or else must pay the amount demanded directly to the tax office. Time limits for payment vary according to the type of income, and interest charges are added – at 8 per cent a year from December 1, 1982 – for later payment.

Tax inspectors have the additional power to make revised assessments if they discover that not enough tax was paid in an earlier year. Reassessments cannot normally go back more than 6 years, but if a tax inspector believes that the underpayment was intentional, he can seek an appeal commissioner's consent to go back as far as 1936–7.

Reassessment of an earlier year is most commonly called for because a tax inspector has underestimated the profits of a self-employed person. Estimates are often needed when annual accounts are not ready by the time of the original assessment.

Another likely reason for reassessment is a reconsideration of the way of treating certain income. This happens, for example, when a profit treated as a private capital gain, not large enough to be taxed, is later seen to be a taxable business trading profit. Such reconsideration is not likely to arise under PAYE unless an undisclosed source of other income is discovered, or unless, through some mistake, the taxpayer's allowances were too high.

THE TIME LIMITS FOR MEETING A TAX DEMAND

When tax is demanded in a notice of assessment, and has to be paid directly rather than by an adjustment of future PAYE deductions, the inspector of taxes also sends a notice stating the time limit for payment. In many cases the amount owing is split up, and the different time limits are applied in the following way:

Type of income	Payment due
Self-employed profits (during previous tax year)	Half by January 1 in tax year. Half by following July 1
Investment income received without deduction	All by January 1
Investment income received net, with basic rate tax already deducted	All by following December 1

Example: A taxpayer meets his tax liability for the 1984–5 tax year – from April 6, 1984 to April 5, 1985 – by making payments in the following order:

1. Employment earnings – deducted under PAYE.

2. Self-employed profits – half by January 1, 1985.

3. Self-employed profits – second half by July 1, 1985.

4. Bank interest received without deduction – by January 1, 1985.

5. Company dividends and public loan interest, basic rate tax deducted at source – by December 1, 1985.

If an assessment is not raised in time for the normal payment dates to be met, then tax is payable 30 days after the date the assessment is issued.

Interest is charged on late payments.

When you can appeal

If you disagree with the amount of tax demanded in the assessment, you can lodge an objection within 30 days of the date on it. An appeal form may be sent with the notice. If not, ask for form 64-7 from any tax office.

On this form you can give notice of your intention to appeal against the amount of income assessed and against the amount of tax demanded. You are required to say how much tax you believe is being overcharged, and any postponement of payment applies only to that amount. Any amount that is not being challenged must be paid within the normal time limit.

Most appeals are made because an inspector of taxes has based his assessment on estimated figures – for example, when a self-employed person's annual accounts are not ready. As soon as the actual figures are supplied, there is automatically a reassessment. In these cases, therefore, giving notice of an appeal is simply a way of gaining more time in order to get the figures ready.

If a tax demand is disputed after final figures have been taken into account, it is usually because of a disagreement over the allowance for some item of expenditure, or over whether certain income is taxable. The inspector who assessed the tax must try to settle the dispute informally, by letter or in a personal discussion with the taxpayer.

Going for a hearing

The inspector has an obligation to try to settle the appeal informally. If this cannot be done, he must bring it for hearing before a tribunal of commissioners.

Generally the taxpayer has the right to choose between the special commissioners (a panel of full-time tax experts) or the general commissioners appointed in local areas. The latter are chosen from the business and professional community and are paid only their expenses.

Certain technical appeals must go to the special commissioners.

A hearing before commissioners is conducted along the lines of court proceedings, but is not open to the public and cannot be reported. The taxpayer, who can be represented by an accountant or a lawyer, is responsible for his own expenses even if the appeal succeeds.

Either side can make a further appeal on a point of law to the Court of Session and finally to the House of Lords. The successful side can claim expenses from the other if a tax appeal reaches a court.

WHEN YOU DO NOT HAVE TO WAIT

People who are regularly entitled to a tax refund are often paid quarterly automatically.

Obtaining a tax refund

If too much tax is taken from your income by deductions during the year, you are entitled to a refund.

Under PAYE, most overpayments occur when employees die, stop work or qualify for new allowances part way through a tax year. In other cases, taxpayers discover that allowances that should have been claimed in some previous year were overlooked. Refunds can be claimed up to 6 years later.

Where the person or company responsible for paying some part of someone's income also deducts tax – for example, company dividends, public loan interest, trust income and maintenance payments – the recipient may have been overtaxed, particularly if he or she has little or no other income.

A self-employed person can offset a business loss against other income, reclaiming tax already paid. But although a reduction of United Kingdom tax liability may be claimed on foreign income if tax has already been paid abroad, it can never be the basis of a repayment.

How to claim a refund

If changed circumstances entitle you to an extra personal allowance and you are taxed by PAYE, notify the tax office which handles your deductions. Your employer will give you the address if you do not have it. Be prepared to prove your claim – for example, with a marriage certificate.

As well as changing your tax code so that deductions will be lower in future, your employer will be authorised by the Inland Revenue to return overpaid tax to you, either in a lump sum or by offsetting it against your tax instalments for the rest of the year.

If you have been out of work for 4 weeks or more, if you retire permanently, or if you are a married woman giving up work for the rest of the tax year, ask the tax office for a refund claim form. Your refund will be sent by post.

If you receive payments that are already taxed, other than by PAYE, give the details in your income tax return and attach evidence – the warrants that come with company dividend or public loan interest cheques, or the certificate (form R185) that the payer of trust income or aliment or periodical allowance under a court order is obliged to give you. Any overpayment of tax will show up in your assessment, and a refund follows automatically.

The tax that is deducted from interest payments to building society investors is never refunded.

People who regularly qualify for refunds – for example, pensioners, divorced mothers, and children with investment income – may not need to wait until the end of the tax year. In many cases their tax office will make refunds in quarterly instalments.

If you are seeking a refund of tax paid in an earlier year, rather than the current year or the year just ended, start your claim by telephoning or writing to the inspector of taxes at your tax office.

Interest on refunds If a tax refund is delayed for more than 12 months after the end of the tax year in which tax was overpaid, the Inland Revenue are obliged to pay interest on any amount over £25. The annual interest rate was set at 8 per cent from December 6, 1982.

When a taxpayer goes on strike

Any significant loss of income during a strike will probably mean that an employee's PAYE deductions before the strike will prove to have been too high.

However, no tax refund can be made while an employee is on strike, or laid off because of a strike in which he has a direct interest – such as his wages being increased as a result of it. Any refund will be paid when the employee returns to work.

Since July 5, 1982, UNEMPLOYMENT BENEFIT and SUPPLEMENTARY BENEFIT paid to the unemployed, and supplementary benefit claimed by strikers in respect of adult dependants, have been taxable.

INDECENCY

Sexual conduct which the law forbids

Indecent behaviour by itself is not criminal, but it may become so in certain circumstances.

Assault An ASSAULT is more heavily punished if it is accompanied by indecent behaviour – for example, touching the private parts of someone's body, without consent. The penalty is at the court's discretion, within its sentencing limits.

Indecency towards children It is a crime for someone to indulge in 'lewd, indecent and libidinous' practices towards children of either sex under the age of puberty. This would cover, for instance, committing sexual acts, such as intercourse in the presence of a child. The child's consent is irrelevant. The maximum penalty is life imprisonment.

It is also an offence for a man or woman to indulge in such practices towards a girl between the ages of puberty and 16. The punishment is up to 2 years' imprisonment.

It is an offence for a man to have sexual intercourse with a girl under 13. The maximum penalty is life imprisonment.

It is also an offence to have intercourse with a girl between 13 and 16, and the maximum penalty is 2 years' imprisonment. However, if the accused is under 24 years of age, and has never been charged with a similar offence, it is a defence for him to show that he reasonably believed that the girl was 16.

Any person – for instance, a parent – who has custody of a girl under 16, and causes or encourages her to be seduced or indecently assaulted, commits an offence and is liable to up to 2 years' imprisonment.

Indecent exposure It is not a crime for a person merely to expose his or her sexual organs. However, it is an offence if it occurs in a situation which is calculated to outrage public decency – for example, where a man exposes himself to passing women. The penalty is at the court's discretion, within its sentencing limits.

Exposure of the sexual organs can also be punished as a BREACH OF THE PEACE, if it takes place in public.

Gross indecency It is an offence for a male to commit an act of gross indecency in public with another male. The maximum penalty is 2 years' imprisonment.

Gross indecency in private, involving more than 2 males or a man under 21 years of age, is also punishable. Gross indecency is not defined, but commonly consists of handling of the genitals. *See:* HOMOSEXUALITY

Shameless indecency All shamelessly indecent conduct is criminal. This offence has been much developed by the courts in recent years.

It is not clear exactly what conduct is prohibited as being shamelessly indecent. However, it does cover the selling or public display of 'soft-porn' magazines, as well as the showing of 'blue' movies. It also prohibits sexual intercourse in public and may even extend to strip-teases in pubs.

INDEPENDENT AND GRANT-AIDED SCHOOLS

Educating a child outside the state system

In Scotland the vast majority of children attend schools within the state system. Schools outside that system are either grant-aided schools, which are partly supported by money from the tax-payer, or independent schools.

Parents who send their children to an independent or grant-aided school have a contract with the school owners and are considered to have accepted the conditions of entry and the school rules.

Such rules often include a condition that parents must give a term's notice of withdrawal or pay a term's fees in lieu of notice. But if you can show that the school has failed to keep its side of the contract – for example, by not giving a service it had promised to provide – you may be able to ignore such a condition.

Independent and grant-aided schools have the same duty as state schools to look after their pupils.

The local authority can, if it chooses, provide milk, meals and clothing for an independent or grant-aided school as it does for its own schools, and it may decide to allow the school to use library, swimming pools and other facilities. The school health service may provide medical and dental treatment.

Independent and grant-aided schools have more freedom to expel pupils because, unlike a local education authority, they do not have to provide an alternative place at another school. However, the power of expulsion must be exercised reasonably.

Registering and running an independent school

Any independent school providing full-time education for five or more pupils of compulsory school age must be registered with the Registrar of Independent Schools in Scotland. The registration is provisional until the school has been inspected and the Secretary of State for Scotland advises the proprietor that the registration is final.

You can start a new school and run it for a month so long as you apply for registration within that month. But after that you are committing an offence if the school is not registered.

The maximum penalty for continuing to run an unregistered school is a fine of £1,000.

When there is a complaint

If the Secretary of State for Scotland believes that an independent school is unsatisfactory on any of four grounds, a notice of complaint can be served on the school stating full details of the complaint, any measures needed to remedy the deficiencies and a time limit for carrying these out. The four grounds are that:

- All or part of the school premises are unsuitable for use as a school.
- The accommodation provided on the premises is unsuitable, taking into account the number, ages and sex of the pupils.
- Deficient and unsuitable instruction is being given.
- The proprietor or any teacher employed there is not a fit person to be the proprietor of an independent school or a teacher at any school.

The school is given 1 month to appeal against the complaint. If it does so, the appeal is heard by the Independent Schools Tribunal.

After hearing the evidence, the Tribunal can make an order to;

- Annul the notice of complaint.
- Strike the school off the register.
- Strike the school off unless measures recommended by the Secretary of State are carried out.
- Disqualify the premises or part of them as unsuitable, or limit the number of pupils.
- Disqualify the proprietor from being a proprietor of a school or a teacher from teaching in any school.

If the school does not appeal, the Secretary of State can make any of the orders the tribunal might have made.

People who fail to obey the terms of an order can be prosecuted. The Secretary of State can remove a disqualification if circumstances change.

Assisted places scheme

Under the Education (Scotland) Act 1981 the Scottish Education Department subsidises some places at independent and grant-aided schools for children whose parents could not otherwise afford the cost. *See:* SCHOOL GRANT

In session 1983/84, 42 Scottish schools took part in the scheme. If you are interested you should apply first of all to the school which you would like your child to attend. If he or she is accepted, help will be given with the cost of fees and incidental expenses – but not with lodgings.

The schools are responsible for selecting pupils for an assisted place, and the amount of money allowed depends on the parents' income.

INDICTMENT

Detailing the criminal charges against a person

An indictment is the document which sets out the criminal charge brought against a person who is to be prosecuted before a judge and jury in the High Court of Justiciary or sheriff court, under solemn CRIMINAL PROCEEDINGS. It also orders the accused person to appear in court and answer the charge.

Only serious crimes are prosecuted on indictment. Less serious crimes are prosecuted on SUMMARY COMPLAINT.

The prosecutor must serve the indictment on the accused person at least 29 clear days before the trial date. Attached to the indictment will be a list of the witnesses, documents (such as medical reports) and articles (for example, weapons) which the prosecutor intends to produce at the trial.

A list of any previous convictions which the prosecutor intends to put before the court in the event of a guilty verdict will also be served along with the indictment.

At the time the indictment is served, the accused will either have been released on BAIL or be in prison awaiting trial. If he is in prison, the indictment will be delivered to him by a prison officer. If he is on bail, it will be delivered by a law officer – for example, a SHERIFF OFFICER or police constable.

The indictment will be served on the accused personally. But if he cannot be found, it can be left at his home with a member of his family. If there is no one at home, the indictment will be fastened to the outside door.

If an accused person fails to appear in court to answer an indictment, a warrant will be issued for his arrest. It is an offence for a person on bail to fail to appear.

If having to appear in court at the time stated on the indictment would cause serious difficulties, the court can be asked to adjourn the trial to a later date. This may be necessary where, for example, more time is needed to prepare the defence case or defence witnesses are unable to appear. The application should be made as soon as possible after service of the indictment.

INDUSTRIAL DEATH BENEFIT

Who is entitled to payment – and in what circumstances

Industrial death benefit is payable when someone dies as a result of an ACCIDENT AT WORK or an INDUSTRIAL DISEASE. Most claimants are widows, but it may also be paid to widowers, children, parents and other dependent relatives.

Widows may be better off claiming industrial death benefit rather than

WHAT AN INDICTMENT CONTAINS

The indictment sets out the criminal charges brought against a person to be prosecuted before a judge and jury. The trial may take place in the High Court of Justiciary or sheriff court. But with certain crimes – for example murder or rape – the trial must be in the High Court.

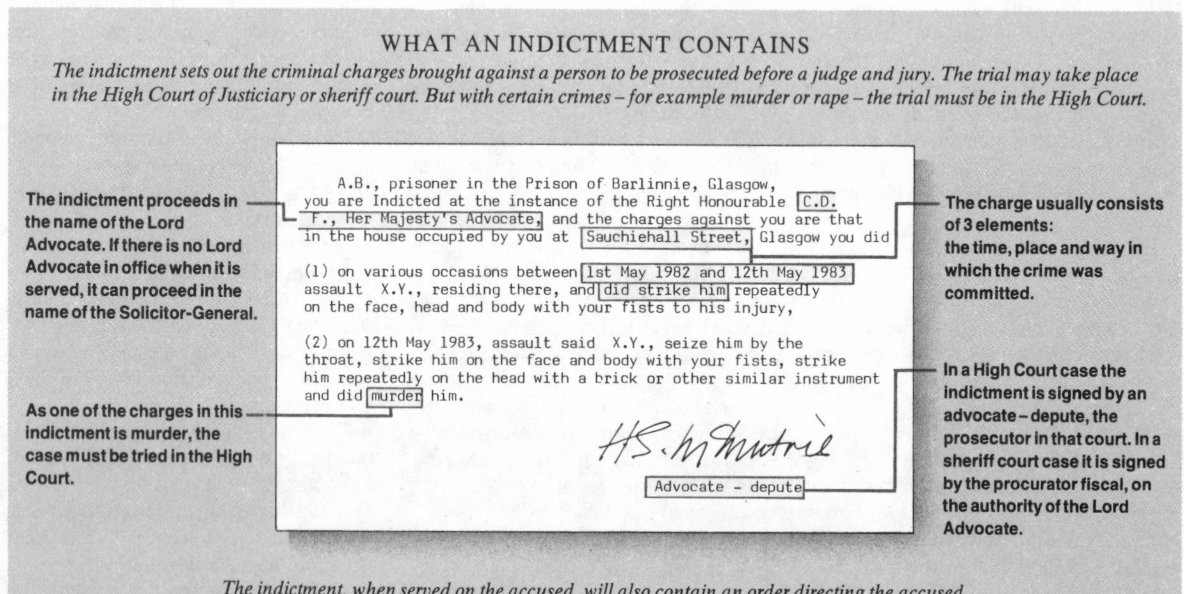

A.B., prisoner in the Prison of Barlinnie, Glasgow, you are Indicted at the instance of the Right Honourable C.D. F., Her Majesty's Advocate, and the charges against you are that in the house occupied by you at Sauchiehall Street, Glasgow you did

(1) on various occasions between 1st May 1982 and 12th May 1983 assault X.Y., residing there, and did strike him repeatedly on the face, head and body with your fists to his injury,

(2) on 12th May 1983, assault said X.Y., seize him by the throat, strike him on the face and body with your fists, strike him repeatedly on the head with a brick or other similar instrument and did murder him.

H.S. McMurtrie

Advocate - depute

The indictment, when served on the accused, will also contain an order directing the accused to appear in court at a particular time to answer the criminal charges.

widow's benefit – the long-term rate is slightly higher. However, the government plan to abolish industrial death benefit soon, and to replace it with payment of widow's benefit. Existing rights to death benefit will be safeguarded.

When a widow can claim

The amount of industrial death benefit varies. The highest rate – £47.65 a week in 1983/4 – is paid during the first 26 weeks after the death. After 26 weeks the benefit is paid at either a high or a low permanent rate.

The high rate – £34.60 a week in 1983/4 – is paid to the widow if at least one of the following applies:

- She is also entitled to an allowance for a child.
- She lives with a child under 19 for whom the deceased was entitled at his death to draw CHILD BENEFIT.
- She is over 40 when she no longer satisfies either of the above conditions.
- She was over 50 at the date of death.
- She was permanently incapable of supporting herself on his death.
- She is pregnant by her late husband.

In all other cases the low permanent rate – £10.22 in 1983/4 – is paid.

If the deceased had been drawing constant attendance allowance (payable with DISABLEMENT BENEFIT), there is no need to prove that an industrial accident or disease caused the death.

When a marriage breaks down

A woman permanently separated from her husband at the time of his death can claim only if she was receiving, or was entitled to receive (and actively seeking to enforce payment of), regular sums of money from him.

Death benefit ceases when a widow remarries. Instead, she receives a gratuity equal to 1 year's benefit. Benefit also ceases if she lives with a man as his wife.

When there are children

An extra allowance is paid for the deceased's children if he was entitled – or treated as entitled – to child benefit for them, and so is the person claiming the allowance.

A widow receives a higher allowance – £7.60 for each child in 1983/4. If she remarries, she receives a lower allowance – 15p for each child. Other claimants – who must contribute to the child's upkeep – normally receive the lower allowance. The lower allowance will be abolished in November, 1984.

When others can claim

A husband can claim benefit if his wife dies as a result of industrial injury or disease – provided he was permanently incapable of supporting himself at the time of her death and his wife had been contributing more than half the cost of his maintenance.

The rate awarded to a widower is the higher permanent one. It is paid for life, regardless of whether the widower cohabits or remarries.

Parents may claim benefit – but only 75p a week each, or £1 for a single parent – if the deceased paid more than half the cost of their maintenance. If he paid less, a small sum – up to £78, or £52 for a single parent – may be paid.

Other relatives who may be entitled to benefit are grandparents and great-grandparents, children, step-children, grandchildren, and great-grandchildren, brothers, sisters, half-brothers, half-sisters, step-brothers, step-sisters and even parents-in-law. Anyone who is such a relative by ADOPTION is also included.

The relative can claim benefit – £1 a week – if the deceased contributed more than half the cost of his maintenance and he (or, if a married woman, her husband) is permanently incapable of supporting himself. Otherwise a temporary allowance of £1.80 for 13 weeks only may be claimed.

If the deceased's contribution was less than half, and the relative (or her husband) is permanently incapable of supporting himself, a small sum – up to £52 – may be paid.

A woman looking after the deceased's children and living with him at the date of the accident or onset of the disease may claim benefit of £1 a week. But she must continue to look after the children after his death, and not remarry or live with a man as his wife.

How to claim

Claims for industrial death benefit for widows and children should be made on form BW1, obtainable from your local social security office. Other claimants should use form BI 200, also obtainable from the social security office.

All claimants must be able to produce a death certificate in respect of the deceased; widows also need a MARRIAGE CERTIFICATE and a BIRTH CERTIFICATE for any children. Others will have to produce evidence of their relationship with the deceased. But do not wait until you have collected all the evidence you need. Delay can affect your rights, so put in the claim and follow up with the evidence as soon as possible.

INDUSTRIAL DISEASE

Compensation for illness contracted at work

If you are incapacitated by a disease contracted at work, you can usually claim sick pay from your employer for up to 8 weeks of SICKNESS. Thereafter, or if you cannot get sick pay, you can usually receive SICKNESS BENEFIT and, if you remain off work, INVALIDITY PENSION.

If the disease is 'prescribed', you can get sickness benefit or invalidity pension even if you have not paid enough contributions. DISABLEMENT BENEFIT OR INDUSTRIAL DEATH BENEFIT can also be claimed. Leaflet NI 2, available from your social security office, has a list of the 51 prescribed diseases.

INDUSTRIAL INJURY BENEFIT

Compensation for injury at work

Until 1983, if you suffered injury in an ACCIDENT AT WORK or from an INDUSTRIAL DISEASE, you were entitled to industrial injury benefit, payable at a higher rate than SICKNESS BENEFIT. However, industrial injury benefit was abolished in April, 1983.

Now, if you suffer such injury or disease, and you cannot work, you can usually claim sick pay from your employer for the first 8 weeks of SICKNESS. Thereafter, or if you cannot get sick pay, you can usually get SICKNESS BENEFIT and, if you remain off work, INVALIDITY PENSION. These can be paid even if you have not paid enough contributions, so long as any disease you have is 'prescribed' (see above).

If you suffer a permanent disability as

a result of an industrial accident or disease, you will also be entitled to DISABLEMENT BENEFIT The amount of benefit depends on your degree of disability. Those assessed at less than 20 per cent disabled are entitled to a lump sum; those assessed at 20 per cent or more are entitled to a weekly allowance.

INDUSTRIAL TRIBUNAL

The 'courts' that hear most employment cases

Industrial tribunals are statutory bodies, similar to courts, which decide many cases arising under employment law.

They deal mainly with legal disputes between employers and employees and sometimes with those between employers and other bodies – for example, industrial training boards. But most of the cases involve REDUNDANCY or UNFAIR DISMISSAL.

Some employment matters are outside the tribunals' scope and are dealt with in the ordinary courts. They include:

- Claims for breach of CONTRACT, including arrears of wages.
- WRONGFUL DISMISSAL claims.
- Prosecutions under the HEALTH AND SAFETY AT WORK rules.
- Claims for personal injury.
- Claims concerning social security benefits (which are dealt with by social security tribunals).

Getting legal representation

Either party involved in a hearing can choose to be represented by a lawyer. But LEGAL AID is not available to meet lawyers' fees for appearing at a hearing and, whatever the outcome of the case, each party usually has to pay his own expenses. As a result, many people plead their own cases, sometimes with the help of their employers' association or trade union.

In cases involving equal PAY or SEX DISCRIMINATION, the EQUAL OPPORTUNITIES Commission may assist with the presentation and the expenses. In hearings arising from RACIAL DISCRIMINATION, the Commission for Racial Equality sometimes gives similar help. To obtain the assistance of either Commission, write to it with details of the case.

HOW TRIBUNAL MEMBERS ARE APPOINTED

Each tribunal has three members – a legally qualified chairman, appointed by the Lord President of the Court of Session, and two other people, who do not have to be legally qualified, but who are chosen for their 'knowledge or experience of employment in industry or commerce'.

One, representing employers, is chosen from a list of people appointed by the Secretary of State for Employment after consultation with the Confederation of British Industry (Scottish Council). The other, representing employees, is chosen from a list of people appointed after consultation with the Scottish Trades Union Congress.

Industrial tribunals sit in the major cities and in large towns. Their hearings are normally open to the public, but a tribunal can hear a case in private at the request of one of the parties. Such requests are rarely granted and never without good reason – for example, if the evidence might contravene the Official Secrets Act or reveal business secrets to rivals.

Tribunal proceedings are less formal than those of ordinary courts, but their decisions are just as binding. Like courts, they can order witnesses to attend and can also order the production of documents as evidence. Failure to comply with such orders without reasonable excuse carries a penalty of up to £400 and, if the person concerned is a party to the case, the claim or defence may be struck out.

How to apply to a tribunal

The procedures for applying to an industrial tribunal are the same whether the applicant is an employer or an employee.

1. Before making the application, check that:

- You are entitled to do so. A full-time employee who has been in his job for less than a year cannot normally claim unfair dismissal. Two years' service is necessary to claim redundancy. Part-timers who work less than 16 hours a week may have fewer employment-protection rights than full-time staff. *See:* EMPLOYMENT PROTECTION
- An industrial tribunal is the correct place to take your case, and that it is not one – for example, a claim for wages arrears – that is outside the tribunal's scope.

Employers' associations or trade unions can give general advice on whether a claim to a tribunal might be justified. Your local job centre, employment office or unemployment benefit office can supply a series of free booklets containing information to help you decide whether to make an application and how to do so.

Booklet, *ITL1 – Industrial Tribunals Procedure* – is a broad guide to the way in which tribunals work.

Other booklets offer more specific information on claims for unfair dismissal and redundancy and on other applications under the rules on job protection, as well as claims involving sex discrimination, race relations and trade union rights.

2. Check the time limit within which your application must reach the tribunal.

Claims for unfair dismissal must be submitted within 3 months of the date on which you left the job. If the application is not submitted within that time, it is unlikely to be heard.

3. Ask your job centre, employment office or unemployment benefit office for form IT1 (Scot) on which to submit your claim. On it, you must include your name and address, the name and address of the person, company or organisation whose action you are disputing and the grounds on which you are seeking a tribunal decision. If someone else is to represent you at the tribunal hearing, you must give his name and address on the form.

If you belong to a trade union or a trade or professional organisation, it may be able to advise you on how to complete the form. Alternatively, the local CITIZENS ADVICE BUREAU can give general guidance, or you can seek the help of a solicitor. You may be entitled to financial assistance to meet the solicitor's fees for helping you complete the form, though not for his attendance at the hearing. *See:* LEGAL ADVICE

4. When the claim form has been completed, make a copy and send the original to the Central Office of the Industrial Tribunals for Scotland.

THE CASES AN INDUSTRIAL TRIBUNAL CAN HEAR

Tribunals can order many different payments to be made to employees

Industrial tribunals decide many cases involving employment law. They have power to determine an applicant's legal rights and often to make financial awards up to maximum limits fixed by law. These limits are increased from time to time.

Type of case	Power/Maximum financial award
Appeals against health and safety improvement and prohibition notices	May cancel or uphold notice. *See:* HEALTH AND SAFETY AT WORK
Appeals against levies under the Industrial Training Act	May order levy to be cancelled or varied
Employees' financial rights when employer is insolvent	Declaration of entitlement to payment by Department of Employment. *See:* PAY
Employer's claim for redundancy rebate	May order rebate to be paid. *See:* REDUNDANCY
Equal pay claims	Back-dated earnings entitlement for up to 2 years. *See:* PAY
Failure to provide itemised pay statement	Compensation equal to unnotified deductions for up to 13 weeks. *See:* PAY
Failure to provide written particulars of employment	Declaration of terms of employment. *See:* EMPLOYMENT CONTRACT
Failure to provide written reasons for dismissal	2 weeks' pay. *See:* DISMISSAL
Guarantee payments	£50 in any 3 months. *See:* LAY OFF
Maternity pay	90 per cent of wages for up to 6 weeks. *See:* MATERNITY
Protective award if employer does not observe redundancy procedures	If fewer than 10 employees, 28 days' pay. 10–99 employees, 30 days' pay. 100 or more employees, 90 days' pay. *See:* REDUNDANCY
Racial discrimination	£7,500. *See:* RACIAL DISCRIMINATION
Redundancy	£4,350. *See:* REDUNDANCY
Sex discrimination	£7,500. *See:* SEX DISCRIMINATION
Time off for trade union duties and activities	Compensation at discretion of tribunal. *See:* TIME OFF WORK
Time off for public duties	Compensation at discretion of tribunal. *See:* TIME OFF WORK
Time off for ante-natal care	Lost earnings. *See:* TIME OFF WORK
Time off, if made redundant, to look for alternative work or arrange training	Two fifths of week's pay. *See:* TIME OFF WORK
Trade union membership: discrimination short of dismissal by employer	Compensation at discretion of tribunal. *See:* TRADE UNION
Unfair dismissal	Basic compensation: £4,350. Compensatory payment: £7,500. Failure to comply with order for reinstatement or re-engagement: £7,540. Special award: £20,000. *See:* UNFAIR DISMISSAL
Unreasonable exclusion or expulsion from a trade union	£11,850. *See:* TRADE UNION

When the claim has been submitted

When the Central Office receives an application for a hearing, it allocates the case to a tribunal in the applicant's area.

The tribunal sends a copy of the application form IT1 to the other party in the case – called the respondent – with form IT3 (Scot), called a notice of appearance. The respondent must complete form IT3, stating whether he intends to contest the application and, if so, on what grounds, and return it to the address shown on it within 14 days.

If the respondent intends to fight the case, it is in his interests to keep his declaration of the grounds for doing so as simple as possible, to avoid giving the claimant information that he may use in evidence in the hearing

A respondent should return form IT3 whether or not he disputes the claim. If he does not send it back, he may lose his right to take part in the tribunal proceedings and therefore to have any influence on the amount of any award made against him

If it is not possible to return the form within 14 days, it should be sent as soon as possible with a note explaining the reason for the delay. The tribunal can extend the time allowed. A copy of the completed form IT3 is sent to the applicant.

Obtaining more details

If the details of one party's case are vague, the other party can request the tribunal to issue an order requiring more information to be given to him. To obtain the order, he should write to the tribunal specifying the information that he requires.

Fixing the date of the hearing

When the tribunal has fixed a time and place for the hearing, it notifies both parties at least 14 days in advance.

If either party has nominated someone else to represent him at the hearing, the notice of the hearing is sent to that representative.

Each party is responsible for informing any witnesses that he may be calling of the time and place of the hearing.

If you cannot attend

If for any reason you cannot attend a hearing on the date fixed, tell the tribunal immediately. It may then decide to rearrange the hearing on a new date. Alternatively, you can, with the tribunal's permission, submit your side of the case in writing But if you do so, you will not have the opportunity to question witnesses.

Holding a pre-hearing assessment

The tribunal, at either party's request or on its own initiative, may arrange a 'pre-hearing assessment' on the ground that one party's case is unlikely to succeed. The tribunal considers the case, after notifying both parties, but does not hear evidence or reach a final decision.

If the tribunal decides that success is unlikely, it may warn the party concerned that if he insists on a full hearing, and loses, he may be ordered to pay the other party's expenses. But it cannot stop him going ahead. If he does, the full hearing is before different tribunal members.

Settlements and conciliation procedure

In most cases involving industrial tribunals – though not those arising from redundancy payments – copies of the application and the respondent's reply are sent by the tribunal to the ADVISORY, CONCILIATION AND ARBITRATION SERVICE (ACAS) well before the hearing. An ACAS officer may then contact the parties to try to help them reach a private settlement.

Neither is obliged to accept an ACAS offer of help. To refuse it does not prejudice the outcome of the hearing.

If the offer is accepted, information given to the ACAS officer cannot be admitted as evidence at a later hearing without the permission of the person who provided it.

Because of the volume of work involved, ACAS cannot take up all the cases of which it is informed. If you believe that the service can help, contact it at Franborough House, 123 Bothwell Street, Glasgow G2 7JR (telephone 041-204 2677).

If the parties to a dispute reach a private settlement, with or without the assistance of ACAS, before the hearing, they must immediately inform the industrial tribunal in writing.

The settlement should be approved by an ACAS conciliation officer, otherwise it will not be binding and the employee will be free to proceed with a complaint to the industrial tribunal.

Before an employer makes a voluntary settlement in a dispute arising from a redundancy payment, he should consult the Department of Employment. If he is not legally obliged to pay, he may lose his right to a rebate. *See:* REDUNDANCY

Calling witnesses

Either party to a dispute can call witnesses to appear on his behalf at the hearing. They may be required to give their evidence on oath or solemn affirmation.

The person summoning a witness is responsible for informing him of the date and place of the hearing. The witness can be paid an allowance for expenses and loss of earnings in connection with attendance at the tribunal.

If a witness is reluctant to appear – perhaps because he fears to do so might prejudice his own job – the person wanting to call him can ask the tribunal for a witness order compelling him to attend.

To obtain a witness order, write to the tribunal giving the case reference number, the name and address of the witness and a brief summary of the type of evidence he would be called upon to give. If an order is issued the secretary of the tribunal serves it by recorded delivery.

The penalty for defying a witness order is £400.

The rules of evidence in an industrial tribunal are broader than those in other courts. Hearsay, for example, may be admitted, although it is given less weight than direct evidence. Someone knowingly giving false evidence on oath or affirmation is subject to the law on PERJURY.

Documentary evidence

Once a case is raised before an industrial tribunal, the tribunal is required to consider all matters arising from it that come within its scope, whether or not they are specifically mentioned in the original application.

A claim involving a redundancy payment may, for example, raise the circumstances surrounding the applicant's dismissal, and the tribunal will examine whether or not it was fair.

Because of this, both parties to a dispute should take with them to the hearing all documents relating to the employment.

If documents are not released

In preparing his case, an employee in dispute with his employer may want to study company documents of which he does not have a copy – for example, written rules or a personal file. If the employer refuses to make them available, the employee can apply to the tribunal for an order requiring their production at the hearing or for an opportunity to allow him to study or copy them beforehand.

To obtain the order, he should write to the tribunal stating which documents are required.

If the tribunal agrees that the request is reasonable, it serves notice on the employer, giving a date by which he must comply. If he fails to do so, he may be fined up to £400.

Attending the hearing

Most industrial tribunal hearings are scheduled for 10 a.m. However, if a 10 a.m. hearing is expected to last only a short time, another case may be scheduled for 11.30 a.m. All those involved in a hearing – including any witnesses – should ensure that they arrive well beforehand.

The tribunal clerk normally explains the procedure before the hearing. The tribunal itself decides the order in which evidence is to be heard and witnesses are to be called.

The parties – or their nominated representatives – may give their own evidence, question their own witnesses and those of the other party, and address the tribunal. The tribunal members can question the parties and witnesses to elicit relevant facts.

The tribunal may announce its decision, with reasons, at the end of the hearing or it may decide to postpone a ruling until a later date. In both cases, the parties eventually receive a written summary of the decision and the reasons for it.

If the tribunal decides that further witnesses must be called or additional documents produced, it can decide upon an adjournment until a specified later date.

When an award is made

If the tribunal awards financial compensation, the person or organisation against whom the award is made should pay it directly to the applicant.

If an applicant has difficulty in obtaining payment of a financial award, he should write to the Secretary of the Tribunals. He can issue a certificate of the decision which allows enforcement of the award by a SHERIFF OFFICER. A certificate will not be issued until the period for appeal (42 days) has expired.

Tribunals do not normally award expenses against the loser of a case: each party has to meet his own. However, a tribunal may award expenses if it decides one party has acted frivolously, vexatiously, or unreasonably, or if a hearing is adjourned or postponed because of some action or failure by one party and the delay causes financial loss to the other.

In cases involving unfair dismissal an applicant may inform his employer that he wishes to be reinstated or re-engaged. If he does so at least 7 days before the hearing, and an adjournment or postponement is necessary because the employer fails, without good reason, to say whether the applicant's job is available, the employer must pay the expenses arising from the adjournment.

How to appeal

Either party can appeal against a decision by an industrial tribunal on an issue of law, but not usually one of fact. They must do so in writing to the EMPLOYMENT APPEAL TRIBUNAL in Glasgow within 42 days from the issue of the written summary of the tribunal decision. Information on how to appeal is sent with the written decision.

In certain circumstances, an industrial tribunal can review its own decision and, if necessary, amend it. It will do so if:

- There has been an error by the tribunal staff.
- Notice of the hearing has not been sent to one of the parties.
- One of the parties or a witness who was entitled to be present was not there.
- There is new evidence, the existence of which could not reasonably have been foreseen when the hearing began.
- The interests of justice have not been served.

A request for a review may be made orally to the tribunal at the end of a hearing, or in writing within 14 days from the issue of the written decision.

Travel and other expenses

Part of the costs of attending a tribunal hearing can be met from public funds, provided that the tribunal chairman is satisfied that the attendance of the person making the claim was justified.

Both parties in the case and all witnesses, on whichever side, can claim certain out-of-pocket expenses. So can representatives of the parties involved, provided that they are not full-time officials of a trade union or an employers' association, advocates or solicitors.

Expenses should be claimed from the clerk of the tribunal immediately after the hearing.

Travel Second-class rail fare, if the place of the hearing is more than 6 miles from home or place of work in the United Kingdom, or more than 6 miles from the point of arrival in the UK. If a motor vehicle over 500 cc is used, a mileage allowance of 13.2p per mile (in 1984) may be claimed.

An additional allowance of 2p per mile is granted for the first passenger and 1p for other passengers in the vehicle who are eligible for expenses for attending the hearing.

Subsistence If the period of absence from home to attend the hearing is less than 2½ hours, no subsistence allowance can be claimed. Other rates are:

2½–5 hours' absence 98p
5–10 hours' absence £1.95
More than 10 hours' absence £4.70

If absence from home overnight is unavoidable for any of the parties or witnesses, there is an allowance of £27.20 per night.

Loss of earnings Employees and self-employed people who actually lose earnings as a result of attending a hearing may claim the amount lost, up to a maximum of £21 per day.

No extra allowance can be paid, however, if the work concerned is advanced or deferred and the earnings are therefore made up.

Unemployed people who lose their benefit through attending a hearing may also claim up to £21 to compensate for the benefit they have lost.

Records of tribunal cases

Details of applications to any Scottish industrial tribunal, including the names and addresses of the parties, are entered in a register open to public inspection. It is kept at the Central Office of the Industrial Tribunals in Glasgow. There is no fee for consulting it.

The tribunal decision, or the withdrawal of an application, is also recorded in each case.

THE DOCUMENTS YOU SHOULD TAKE TO A HEARING

Any documentary evidence that may be of assistance to the industrial tribunal in deciding a case should be taken to the hearing.

The documents should include:

1. The written contract of employment (if any) or written statement of its terms, and any other documents relating to it – for example, the company rule book.

2. Details of pay in the employment – wage slips or the company paysheets.

3. Details of pay in any new employment.

4. Documents relating to other benefits received from the employer and from any new employer – for example, travelling expenses, vehicle allowances and subsidised housing.

5. Any booklets or memoranda giving details of pension and superannuation schemes.

6. Details of any expenses incurred in taking up a new job – for example, bills for removals.

7. Documents relating to income tax paid or refunded and to unemployment and other social security benefits that have been received.

If the case involves a dismissal or redundancy, both parties should take their copies of the notice of dismissal and other relevant correspondence – for example, a written warning for misbehaviour if one has been given, previous commendations for good work and any references given on leaving.

If the company issues written job descriptions and standards of performance –the criteria by which an employee's ability is assessed, for example – those should be taken, too.

INFECTIOUS DISEASE

Controlling the natural spread of disease

Any doctor who treats a patient suffering from one of the infectious diseases must notify the chief administrative medical officer of the area health board, so that the patient can, if necessary, be isolated and all likely contacts traced.

The infectious diseases are:

acute poliomyelitis
(paralytic and non-paralytic)
acute polioencephalitis
anthrax
cholera
continued fever
diphtheria
dysentery
(including amoebic and bacillary dysentery)
enteric fever
(including typhoid and paratyphoid fevers)
erysipelas
lassa fever
leprosy
leptospiral jaundice
malaria
Marburg disease
measles
membranous croup
meningococcal infection
ophthalmia neonatorum
plague
puerperal fever
rabies
relapsing fever
scarlet fever
smallpox
tuberculosis
typhoid
typhus
viral haemorrhagic fever
viral hepatitis
whooping cough
yellow fever

If there is reason to believe that a person is or has been suffering from – or carrying – an infectious disease, and that person refuses to be medically examined, a medical officer can obtain an order from a sheriff or justice of the peace for a compulsory examination.

There is similar power to examine a group of people where one of them is suspected of being a carrier of an infectious disease.

The patient can be required to provide blood or urine specimens and to submit to any tests necessary for the diagnosis of his condition – including bacteriological and radiological tests.

If a medical officer is refused admission to premises, he can obtain a warrant from a sheriff or justice of the peace to enter – by force if necessary. It is an offence wilfully to obstruct a medical officer who has a warrant. The maximum penalty is a fine of £400 and 6 months' imprisonment.

If a person with an infectious disease has no proper accommodation, or his accommodation is such that it is not possible to take proper precautions to prevent the spread of disease, a sheriff or justice of the peace can order him to be detained in hospital. The detention is for as long as it is necessary to prevent the spread of the disease and he can be restrained from leaving – by force, if necessary.

There is no right of appeal against any of these orders. However, if someone believes that he has been wrongfully detained on such an order, he can sue the medical officer and his employer, the area health board, in the sheriff court or Court of Session. Alternatively he can complain to the HEALTH SERVICE COMMISSIONER if his detention is due to maladministration by the medical officer.

Acting on the advice of the medical officer, district and islands councils have power to disinfect premises occupied by someone suffering from an infectious disease and to destroy articles – for example, clothing or bedding – if this is necessary to prevent the spread of disease. (Compensation is payable for articles destroyed.) If refused entry, they are entitled to break in.

If the council need to remove people from the premises because of the infectious disease, or because they wish to disinfect, they can apply to a sheriff or justice of the peace for a warrant to allow them to so so. Someone who is displaced must be provided by the council with temporary accommodation, free of charge.

Penalties for offences

It is a criminal offence for someone who knows that he is suffering from a notifiable disease to go to work, to travel on public transport or to appear in any public place where he might spread the disease, without taking proper precautions. The maximum penalty is a £50 fine.

It is also an offence for a person suffering from an infectious disease, or living in an infected house, to carry on any trade or business without taking proper precautions to prevent the spread of the disease. The maximum penalty is a £50 fine.

Parents who send a child to school when told by the medical officer not to do so, because the child has (or has had) an infectious disease, can be fined up to £50.

Compensation for employees

Anyone ordered to stop work by the medical officer because of a notifiable disease (or because of food poisoning) is entitled to compensation for loss of earnings from the district or islands council. Any dispute about the amount of the compensation can be referred to arbitration.

Examination of travellers

Anyone arriving from abroad on board a ship or aircraft can be examined by a medical officer if he has reason to believe the person is suffering from a notifiable disease. The person can also be removed to an isolation hospital or be required to have his person and clothes disinfected.

A person who intends to travel abroad can be prevented from embarking on a ship or aircraft if the medical officer believes he is suffering from a disease covered by the International Health Regulations.

In the case of smallpox, the person will be allowed to embark if he satisfies the medical officer that he is protected by vaccination or through a previous smallpox attack.

Surveillance The medical officer may put a person arriving from abroad under surveillance for a period, even although he is showing no symptoms of any infectious disease, if he has come from an area notified as infected by the World Health Organisation – for example, an area infected with cholera, smallpox or yellow fever.

A person who is put under surveillance can be required to give his name and address and intended destination, and must notify any change of address. He may also be required to report at regular intervals to the medical officer for the area which he is visiting, and to submit to medical examination.

INHERITANCE

Receiving something from a dead person's estate

There are many ways in which a person can receive money or property from a dead person's ESTATE (after payment, of course, of any taxes and debts which are due from it).

- By will. Anyone can direct who is to inherit his money and other property (after payment of taxes and debts) by making a WILL. These directions are followed unless they do not make sense or the person who was to inherit died first.

Other deeds – such as nominations, special destinations or entails – may also direct who is to inherit.

- By legal rights. The widow(er) and the children (including illegitimate and adopted children) can claim 'legal rights' – a sum of money – if they have been left nothing, or are not satisfied with what they have been left. *See:* DISINHERITANCE
- By the rules of intestacy. If there is no will, the dead person's estate is divided among the widow(er), children, parents or other relatives, according to legal rules. Children include adopted and illegitimate children. These rules also apply to property which is not disposed of under the terms of a will. *See:* INTESTACY
- From the Crown. The Crown takes over the property of a dead person where there is no will and no relatives can be found to inherit by the rules of intestacy. The property is administered by the Queen's and Lord Treasurer's Remembrancer.

Gifts can be made out of the property to applicants who have a moral but not a legal, claim – for example, to a close friend who looked after the deceased for a long time without payment, or an illegitimate brother.

- By maintenance. An ex-wife or ex-husband of the deceased may have been awarded a periodical allowance on DIVORCE. The deceased's estate has to keep up these payments, but the executors may go back to the court to get them reduced or ended.

Any ALIMENT payable to a spouse or children normally ceases on death. But if they are unable to support themselves, they have a right to continued payment out of the deceased's estate.

How tenancies are inherited

The widow(er) of a tenant can take over the tenancy of the house which is rented from a local authority or housing association. To do this, he or she must have been living there when the tenant died. Alternatively, a member of the tenant's family (over 16) can take over the tenancy as long as he or she lived in the house throughout the year before the tenant's death.

These rights are not available if the tenancy has been inherited once already, but a new tenancy may be granted in such a case.

Even if the widow(er) or other member of the family does not wish to take over the tenancy, they can stay there for up to 3 months after the tenant's death. *See:* COUNCIL TENANCY

Similar rights apply in respect of houses rented from private landlords. The tenancy, however, can be inherited twice before it comes to an end. *See:* EVICTION

If the tenancy is not to be taken over, the tenant's family is usually allowed a reasonable period in which to find alternative accommodation.

Service tenancies and tied accommodation cannot be inherited – they come to an end on the tenant's death.

Tenancies of farms and crofts can be bequeathed by will unless this right is excluded in the lease. Where there is no will, the tenancy can be transferred to a member of the tenant's family. In either case the landlord may object if he thinks the proposed new tenant will not be able to cultivate the holding properly.

How titles are inherited

The way in which a hereditary peerage or baronetcy is inherited depends on the terms of the original grant of the title. Only a minority of pre-1707 Scottish peerages were limited to male descendants. Some had special terms which might be varied subsequently; others – for example, the Earldom of Errol – could pass to or through daughters as well as sons.

Titles granted since 1707 can usually be inherited by males only, but even here there are exceptions – the Earldom of Mountbatten of Burma, for example, can pass to females.

A title is normally inherited by one of the direct descendants of the original title-holder. But if there are no descendants, some titles can pass to other relatives – such as the descendants of the original title-holder's brother.

The older a title, the more extensive are the number of descendent relatives of the original title-holder. It is therefore more likely that a remote relative may inherit. Sir Winston Churchill, for example, would have succeeded to the Dukedom of Marlborough if the 9th Duke had had no son. But John Maxwell Erskine's title of (1st) Baron Erskine of Rerrick can only pass to his son because, so far, no-one else can be a direct descendant.

No adopted or illegitimate person can inherit a title, nor can a title be claimed through such a person. But an illegitimate person who has been legitimated by the marriage of his parents can inherit or pass on a Scottish title.

INITIAL WRIT

Starting a sheriff court case

An initial writ is the document which is generally used to start a civil action in the sheriff court – for example, an action for damages, divorce or custody of a child. (Some debt, eviction and other actions are started by a separate document, called a SUMMONS.) Court rules lay down the form which the initial writ must take.

The initial writ should be signed by the party raising the action (the pursuer), or by his solicitor. It should then be lodged at the sheriff court. A copy will then be served on the person who is being sued (the defender), usually by recorded delivery post, but sometimes by a SHERIFF OFFICER.

The initial writ should state the sheriffdom and sheriff court district in which the action is being raised, and should contain the names and addresses of all the parties. There should then be a 'crave', setting out the remedy which the pursuer seeks from the court. For instance, the pursuer may seek payment from the defender of, say, £3,000, interest and the expenses of the action.

The 'condescendence', which follows the crave, contains short statements setting out all the relevant facts on which the pursuer is relying. For instance, in an action for breach of CONTRACT the condescendence may detail the contract, delivery of goods by the pursuer and failure by the defender to pay the price.

At the end of the initial writ there must be 'pleas-in-law', which summarise the legal reasons why the court should grant the remedy which the pursuer seeks.

An initial writ should be read carefully by a defender. He should consider whether he wishes to dispute the pursuer's claim in any way. If he does, he should seek legal advice concerning any possible defences. The initial writ should explain where and when defences should be lodged. (The time limits for doing so are fairly short.)

If a defender does nothing after he receives an initial writ, the pursuer may obtain a court decree against him in his absence.

INSANITY AS A DEFENCE

When a person cannot be held responsible for a crime

A person facing a criminal charge can plead insanity as a defence if, at the time of the offence, he was suffering from a 'complete alienation of reason' in relation to the crime charged. The 'alienation' must be due to a disease of the mind which is lasting or permanent.

If an accused person intends to rely on a defence of insanity in solemn CRIMINAL PROCEEDINGS (the procedure used in serious cases), written notice to that effect must be lodged in court 10 clear days before the trial. If this is not done, the court has power to allow the notice to be lodged at any time until the oath is administered to the jury on the day of the trial.

There is no time limit for a notice in summary criminal proceedings. However, the accused should give notice to the prosecutor as soon as possible before the trial – and not later than the time when the first prosecution witness is called.

If the prosecutor believes that the accused was insane at the time of the offence, he can competently raise the 'defence' of insanity himself – regardless of the wishes of the accused.

When a defence of insanity succeeds, the accused is found not guilty by reason of insanity. He is then detained in a mental hospital – usually the State Mental Hospital at Carstairs – for an indefinite period.

The test of insanity

The test of insanity is a general one. For the defence to succeed, there must be proof of a total 'alienation of reason' in relation to the crime charged, and this must be the result of mental disease.

The courts have not created a list of diseases, but assess the medical evidence given in each case. However, the disease must be lasting or permanent: a temporary malfunction of the mind due to deliberately taking drink or drugs would not be sufficient.

If there is not enough evidence of insanity, the accused may instead be found to be of DIMINISHED RESPONSIBILITY. This is a state of mind bordering on insanity, and caused by mental disease. Again, a temporary malfunction caused by deliberately taking drink or drugs would not amount to diminished responsibility.

Unfit for trial An accused person may be insane at the time of his trial (whether or not he was insane at the time of the offence). Where the accused is suffering from a mental disease, he cannot be tried if he is:

- Incapable of understanding the nature of the charge against him.
- Incapable of understanding the court proceedings.
- Unable to instruct his defence.

The plea of 'insanity in bar of trial' can be raised by the prosecutor, the defence or the judge.

The matter is usually decided by the judge after hearing medical evidence. If the plea is successful, the accused person will be committed to a mental hospital. If he later returns to sanity, the case can be re-opened.

INSECTS

Protecting endangered species

Some insects and other kinds of invertebrate animals are protected by law because there is a danger of their becoming extinct.

It is an offence deliberately to kill, injure or take any such insect or animal; or to disturb it in its refuge or damage or destroy the refuge – unless it is in a private house. It is also an offence to possess such an insect or animal, whether alive or dead. The maximum penalty is a fine of £2,000.

The protected species are:

Beetles	Rainbow leaf
Butterflies	Chequered Skipper Heath Fritillary Large Blue Swallowtail
Crickets	Field Cricket Mole Cricket
Dragonflies	Norfolk Aeshna
Grasshoppers	Wart-biter
Molluscs	Carthusian Snail Glutinous Snail Sandbowl Snail
Moths	Barberry Carpet Black-veined Essex Emerald New Forest Burnet Reddish Buff
Spiders	Fen Raft Spider Ladybird Spider

INSULATION GRANT

Help to pay for the cost of saving heat

Grants are available from your local district or islands council to insulate your loft. To qualify you must have no loft insulation at all at present.

The amount of help available changes from time to time. At the moment you can claim 66% of the cost or £69, whichever is the lower.

If you are an old age pensioner, or if you (or one of your dependants) are severely disabled, you are entitled to claim a higher amount – at present 90%, or £95, whichever is the lower. To qualify for this higher amount you must also be receiving a supplementary pension, or a rent rebate or allowance, or a rate rebate.

You must apply to the council and obtain approval before any work is

CHECKING THE WORK

When a grant is made, the local council is entitled to send an inspector to check the insulation work.

started. If you have an uninsulated cold water tank or pipes in the loft, or an uninsulated hot water tank anywhere in the house, these must be insulated at the same time. You can carry out the work yourself or employ a contractor. When the work is completed you apply to the council for payment.

INSURANCE

Buying protection against the hazards of life

Almost everyone requires insurance at some time. In every case there is a risk of something happening that would impose a financial burden, so people make a contract to pay a premium to an insurance company and in return the company agrees to pay a lump sum or periodical payments should the risk materialise.

Insurance may sometimes be compulsory. For example, it is illegal to drive a car on the road without MOTOR INSURANCE, and a building society will not advance a loan on a property unless PROPERTY INSURANCE has been taken out.

Most forms of insurance are not compulsory but are often advisable. If holidaymakers fear the possibility of being ill abroad, having to cancel the booking or having their luggage stolen, they can take out travel insurance. Everyone runs the risk of causing loss to others by a DELICT: a tile from the roof of a house might fall on a passer-by or a dog may cause a road accident. To meet these risks LIABILITY INSURANCE is available.

Breadwinners in families have financial commitments which they meet out of earnings. If they die early these commitments can still be met if LIFE ASSURANCE has been taken out. Anyone accident-prone may want to take out PERSONAL ACCIDENT INSURANCE.

People are free to insure against any conceivable risk if they find an insurer willing to provide for it. But insurance is not a form of gambling, so the insured must have an insurable interest in the subject of the insurance. If you own the favourite for next year's Ayr Gold Cup you can insure against the risk that he might be unfit to run. However, if you are not the owner and merely place an ante-post bet on the horse, you cannot hedge your bet by asking an insurance company for cover similar to that they would give to the owner.

On the other hand, if you are organising a summer fete you can insure against the risk of a wet day.

Using a broker

Anyone planning to take out insurance can either deal directly with an insurance company or go to an insurance broker who will know the terms offered by the rival companies and who can advise on which is best suited to individual needs. A broker's services are free. He gets his income as commission from the company whose policy the client eventually chooses. Despite that commission, he has a duty to act in the best interests of the client.

The proposal form

Taking out any kind of insurance involves filling in a proposal form. The questions you have to answer enable the insurance company to assess the risk and decide on what terms it will offer you cover.

You have a duty to supply all relevant information. If someone seeking PROPERTY INSURANCE, for example, has had a fire in the past, he must say so on the form.

The consequences of misrepresentation or failing to disclose relevant information can be very serious indeed. The company could refuse to pay out on a future claim if relevant information is not given correctly on the proposal form. *See:* INSURANCE CLAIM

You also have a duty to tell the insurance company if your circumstances change after you have completed the form. For example, someone who took out FIRE INSURANCE on his house would have to tell the company if he subsequently replaced his tiled roof with thatch. If he failed to notify the company and the house was burned down, the company would be unlikely to pay out.

The small print

After receiving a completed proposal form, the insurance company issues an INSURANCE POLICY, which constitutes the terms of the CONTRACT. Before that stage is reached, you should ask to see a draft or copy of the policy and read the fine print carefully. If you have a broker, consult him and ask his advice. The document will contain many conditions which define the circumstances in which liability will be accepted and the extent of that liability.

Make sure that the risks you want to be covered against are specified and that the amounts you can claim are adequate. For example, a person who insures against the theft of valuable jewellery should make sure that the small print does not exclude items above a certain value. He should also decide whether to accept any excess clauses that might, for example, prevent him

YOU MUST HAVE AN INTEREST

To insure something legally, you must have what the law calls an 'insurable interest' in it.

from claiming the first £50 of any loss.

Paying the premium

Most forms of insurance are kept in force by the payment to the company of regular premiums, usually once a year. It is the responsibility of the insured to pay each premium when it is due, although most companies send out reminder notices and allow a few days' grace for the premium to be paid before cancelling the cover.

If the event you have insured against should occur, you must make an INSURANCE CLAIM in writing. If you cannot agree with the company on the sum to be paid in settling the claim, the dispute can ultimately be resolved by court proceedings or ARBITRATION.

INSURANCE AGENT

The person who is paid to sell insurance

An insurance agent, unlike an INSURANCE BROKER, works for only one company, or at most for a small number of companies. Insurance companies employ agents as salesmen to promote their policies over those of rival companies.

An agent will normally represent no more than say three companies. You may not get impartial advice from him, but an agent for a company in the British Insurance Association or Life Offices' Association should reveal that he is an agent and deal fairly with you. Go to a broker if you are in doubt.

Many insurance agents are part-time and it is not uncommon to find solicitors, accountants, travel agents, garages and others acting as agents.

INSURANCE BROKER

Free help available when you choose an insurance policy

When you are seeking insurance you can choose a company and policy yourself, but the range is so vast that it is usually better to obtain the advice of an insurance broker. He has knowledge of several or many companies and should be able to recommend the one best suited to your individual needs.

THE GUITARIST WHO WAS A BAD RISK

An insurance broker must exercise professional care in helping a customer to complete a proposal form.

Mr McNealy was a property repairer by trade but also played guitar in a part-time group. He went to an insurance broker to insure his car and, on his advice, filled in a proposal form for an insurance company, giving his occupation as property repairer. There was no question on the form about part-time jobs.

After an accident in the car Mr McNealy was sued successfully for damages by a passenger who was injured through his negligence. A court upheld the insurance company's refusal to pay out on the policy on the ground that Mr McNealy's failure to disclose that he was a part-time musician rendered the policy void.

DECISION

The court held that the broker was negligent in not asking Mr McNealy about part-time jobs when he knew the policy would not be available to someone like a part-time musician. The broker was therefore liable to compensate Mr McNealy in full for all the damage to his car, the damages awarded to the passenger and all legal costs.

Under the Insurance Brokers (Registration) Act 1977, no one is allowed to call himself an insurance broker unless he is registered with the Insurance Brokers' Registration Council.

Among the registration requirements is the need to have professional indemnity insurance.

Not even a broker gives impartial advice over the entire range of insurance companies. He earns his livelihood mainly from commission paid by companies whose policies he sells, as agent.

Most of a broker's services are free to the customer, including help to complete the proposal form. Ask about any fee before you engage him.

An insurance broker charging someone who is taking out insurance must, under the Insurance Brokers' Registration Council code of conduct, disclose that charge to his client in advance.

If a broker is to recover uninsured losses for a client, he must disclose in advance the basis or scale of his eventual charges.

Like other professional advisers, an insurance broker can be sued for PROFESSIONAL NEGLIGENCE if he gives you negligent advice which results in your suffering damage or loss. *See:* INSURANCE AGENT; MOTOR INSURANCE

INSURANCE CLAIM

Obtaining compensation as smoothly as possible

If you suffer a loss against which you think you are insured, inform your insurance broker or company as soon as possible. Your policy may require you to report the loss within a given time, and some policies require you to notify the police or fire brigade.

If you have any doubt about whether your insurance policy covers you for a particular loss, claim. But remember that making a deliberately fraudulent claim is an offence and may also cancel any rights you have under a policy.

When you inform your insurance company, you are sent a claim form, asking for details of how the loss occurred, with dates and times, who was to blame, and a detailed account of the items lost or damaged and their value.

Assessing your claim

In settling a claim, the insurance company applies the principle that you are not entitled to profit from misfortune. If, for example, you insure a new bicycle for £50 and it is later stolen you can claim only its current value – possibly well below £50. So while it is foolish to be under-insured it is pointless to insure something for more than its true value.

If the sum you are claiming is small – less than £20, say – the insurance company normally sends you a cheque within a few days. With larger claims, the company may ask an independent assessor – called a loss adjuster – to inspect the damage or consider the loss and decide what amount should be paid.

If you disagree with an assessment you too can seek the advice of a loss adjuster. You do, however, have to pay for his services, so unless you feel the company's assessment is grossly short of the true value it may not be worthwhile.

When a claim is settled

When an insurance company settles a claim it usually asks you to sign a form of discharge absolving the company from further responsibility in the claim. If you later discover that you could have claimed more, you can still try to pursue the extra claim even if you have signed the form of discharge. Most companies accept any reasonable claim – no matter how much later.

When there is a dispute

Most insurance claims are satisfactorily settled at branch level. If not, you should write to the chief executive of your company at its head office.

If you finally fail to agree, you may be able to take your claim to the Insurance Ombudsman Bureau, to which over 100 insurance companies belong. The Ombudsman is an independent solicitor whose job is to try to settle your dispute. Write to him at 31 Southampton Row, London WC1B 5HJ.

The Ombudsman deals with non-life claims and certain aspects of life policies, but not with third party claims. He will only look at your complaint if your company is in the scheme and if you complain within 6 months of your final failure to agree with it.

If the Ombudsman decides in your favour, and you accept his ruling, the company must pay you any award up to a maximum of £100,000 (£10,000 a year if a life claim). If you reject his ruling, your legal rights are not affected.

More than 60 other companies have set up the Personal Insurance Arbitration Service. Cases are decided by an independent arbitrator, but only if the company agrees to the referral. His decision is binding on *both* parties.

INSURANCE POLICY

Why it is important to read the policy document carefully

An insurance policy is a CONTRACT made between you and your insurance company.

As soon as you receive it you should read every line carefully. If it contains anything you object to or omits anything you want to have included, write to the company immediately.

Most policies have five parts:

- Preamble – a generalised introduction stating that an agreement has been reached between the company (the insurer), and you (the insured).
- What is insured – describing exactly what is insured against what eventualities.
- Exceptions relieving the insurance company from liability. These vary according to the class of insurance. For instance, an exception for loss or damage by earthquake is normally found in a FIRE INSURANCE policy but not in a MOTOR INSURANCE policy.
- Conditions – the really vital terms of the policy. If you do not comply with them, the insurance company can avoid liability. Conditions vary according to the type of insurance. A burglary policy may stipulate that a burglar alarm should be set; an employer's liability policy may require certain precautions to prevent accidents; a motor insurance policy may insist on proper maintenance of the car.

The burden of proving a breach of a vital term lies with the insurance company.

- Schedule – which includes the basic details that apply only to your policy: the policy number, your name and address and other personal information, what is insured for how much, when the premiums are payable, the date the policy begins and the period of insurance.

Once a policy has been issued no material alteration can be made without the consent of both parties. Changes and additions are made by a new document, known as an endorsement, being attached to the existing policy.

Assigning an insurance policy

Most insurance policies include a clause determining whether the policy and its benefits can be passed – that is, assigned – to someone else.

In most cases you must have the insurance company's written agreement if you want to assign a policy – and you must also hand over the goods or property insured to the person who is to benefit. So if you wanted to give your household fire insurance policy to someone else you would have to give them the house as well.

Assignation happens automatically when an insured person dies (except in the case of policies personal to the insured person, such as life and health insurance). The policy passes to his representatives or next of kin. Similarly, in bankruptcy the policy usually passes to the debtor's trustees.

UNDERSTANDING THE SMALL PRINT OF THE POLICY

Make sure that you understand your insurance policy. As soon as you receive the document, go through it line by line. If there are any sections that disturb or surprise you, consult the company at once.

Cancelling a policy

A policy may include a condition allowing the insurance company to cancel the policy at any time, and setting out how this may be done and what premium will be returned. The company may do this, for instance, because of the number of claims being made under the policy. As a policy holder, you can cancel only if the policy authorises you to do so, except that certain rights to cancel are given by law in respect of LIFE ASSURANCE.

When a policy lapses

Motor insurance policies have to be renewed before the existing policy expires. Other types of policy often allow a period after the premium is due (days of grace), for payment and renewal of the policy. But failure to renew makes the policy lapse; and no claim in respect of an event occurring after the lapse will be successful. Normally the insurance broker or agent will remind you that your next premium is due. But if no such reminder reaches you and you fail to renew, the policy still lapses. *See:* INSURANCE; INSURANCE CLAIM; LIFE ASSURANCE; PROPERTY INSURANCE

INSURANCE PREMIUM

Paying to protect yourself against possible risks

The premium is the amount paid by an insured person to the insurers in return for their willingness to accept the risk being insured against – for example, the risk of a house being destroyed by fire or of injury to the insured person.

The amount to be paid varies greatly according to the market rates. For example, car-insurance premiums are higher if a vehicle is to be driven in Glasgow rather than in the country. Similarly, higher premiums are generally charged each year to take account of inflation.

The premium is usually payable either when the proposal form is sent to the insurers or when the proposal is accepted. If a premium is not paid on time, on the renewal date of a policy, the insurance lapses. But most insurance companies will allow a few days' grace.

In certain cases you may be able to claim back part of the premium you have paid – for example, when there has been double insurance.

INSURANCE PROPOSAL FORM

The vital first step in arranging cover

The first step in taking out any kind of insurance is to fill in a proposal form. The form is supplied either by the insurance company direct, or by a broker. It contains questions that enable the insurer to assess the risk and decide how much premium the person seeking insurance will be charged.

An insurance proposal form, however, is not merely an application for cover. It forms part of the eventual insurance contract and should not be signed until a copy of the policy has been carefully read.

Anyone who makes untrue or misleading statements on a proposal form, or who conceals any relevant information in completing it, risks the rejection of any claim he may make later under his insurance policy. The person seeking insurance must volunteer any fact that could affect the company's judgment, even if the form does not include a question on that point.

For example, a FIRE INSURANCE proposal form may not ask whether the applicant has a criminal record of any kind.

But if he has served a prison sentence for any type of crime, he ought to mention it on the form. Otherwise, if his house later burns down, the insurance company may refuse to pay.

In practice, British Insurance Association companies and Lloyd's, as well as the Life Offices Association and Associated Scottish Life Offices, have agreed not to deny liability over a private – as opposed to business – policy, provided that any defect in the information is innocent and that the correct information, if known, would not have materially influenced the insurer's judgment.

INTERDICT

A court remedy to prohibit a legal wrong

An interdict is an order of a civil court – either the COURT OF SESSION or a SHERIFF COURT – which prohibits a person from carrying out or repeating a legal wrong (an unlawful act). It is similar to the 'injunction' which is granted by the English courts.

An interdict may be sought in many different situations – for example:

- Where a homeless person is to be evicted from temporary accommodation, but claims he has a legal right to be permanently rehoused. *See:* HOMELESSNESS
- Where a factory creates a NUISANCE through fumes or noise.
- Where a landowner threatens to block a public RIGHT OF WAY.
- Where a trade union halts an employer's business by unlawfully bringing its members out on STRIKE.
- Where a publisher distributes (or intends to distribute) a book which is alleged to be defamatory.
- Where a father threatens to remove his children from the legal custody of their mother.

If a person who is affected by an alleged legal wrong (whether actual or threatened) applies to court for an interdict, it is up to the judge to decide whether or not to grant the order: he need not do so even if satisfied that a wrong exists or is threatened.

For instance, the judge may decide that granting an interdict would not be appropriate in the circumstances, and leave the complainer to claim damages instead.

An interdict may be sought in a court action along with other orders. For instance, in a divorce action a wife may seek not only a decree of divorce and an order giving her custody of the children: she may also seek:

- An interdict to prevent her husband from assaulting or molesting her.
- An interdict to prevent her husband removing the children from her care.
- An interdict to prevent her husband disposing of his capital in order to defeat her financial claims.

In these situations, it will be necessary to satisfy the court that there is a threatened wrong – for instance, that the husband has recently assaulted his wife and has threatened to do so again; or that the husband has been making plans to remove the children from Scotland; or that the husband has been transferring his capital from Scotland to a foreign country.

Getting interim interdict

An interdict should be sought without delay, otherwise it may be too late. The order will not be granted if, for example, a father has already removed his child from Scotland.

There are special procedures to enable a person to obtain an 'interim' (temporary) interdict urgently. This can sometimes be done on the same day as the court action is raised – even before the other party has been given notice. Emergency legal aid may be available. *See:* LEGAL AID

Application for interim interdict is usually made to a judge sitting in chambers (his private rooms). The interdict can be granted, without proof, on the basis of the allegations made by the applicant.

When deciding whether to grant interim interdict, the judge will consider whether the 'balance of convenience' lies in favour of granting interdict – that is, whether the party seeking the interdict is likely to suffer greater hardship than the other party if interdict is not granted.

DICKIE DIRTS AND DIRTY DICKS

A court may grant an interim (temporary) interdict to prevent a legal wrong. When deciding whether to grant interdict, the court will consider whether or not the 'balance of convenience' lies in favour of granting it.

Flaxcell Ltd., a company which sold cut-price jeans, traded under the name 'Dickie Dirts' and, to a lesser extent, under the name 'Dirty Dicks'. They also advertised under both names and alleged that they had established a considerable market, reputation and goodwill in Scotland.

In September, 1981, Mr Freedman opened a shop called 'Dirty Dicks' in Glasgow, also selling cut-price jeans. Flaxcell Ltd. applied to the Court of Session for an interim interdict to stop Mr Freedman trading as 'Dirty Dicks', on the ground that it was likely to confuse customers and harm their business.

DECISION

Flaxcell Ltd. obtained an interim interdict against Mr Freedman. The judge said that he was satisfied that the name was likely to confuse customers and potential customers and that Flaxcell Ltd. was likely to suffer loss of business if Mr Freedman continued to trade under the name.

The judge also considered whether the balance of convenience lay in favour of granting the interdict. Flaxcell Ltd. had traded as 'Dirty Dicks' since 1976. Mr Freedman, on the other hand, had only traded as 'Dirty Dicks' for a month and also traded under a different name at another address. The judge therefore decided that the balance lay in favour of granting the interdict.

The penalty for ignoring an interdict

Once an interdict or interim interdict is granted, it must be served, usually by a court officer, on the person who has been interdicted. If that person ignores the interdict and carries out or repeats the prohibited wrong, he will be in CONTEMPT OF COURT. He can then be brought before the court which granted the interdict and perhaps fined or, in serious cases, imprisoned.

INTEREST CHARGE

A trader must state the real cost of buying on credit

Anyone who borrows money or buys goods or services on credit is entitled to know the full cost of the arrangement.

A CREDIT AGREEMENT must show the true annual rate of interest – not merely the flat rate that is charged. An advertisement that quotes an interest rate must include the true rate. For example, a couple buy a £100 refrigerator on credit. They agree to pay £110 – a flat rate of interest of 10 per cent – in 11 monthly instalments of £10. Their debt is reduced by each monthly payment, but the interest charge is not. The couple are paying 10 per cent on money they no longer owe.

A true interest rate is based on a calculation of the average time a borrower has the use of money on credit. In that example, the couple pay a true annual rate of over 21 per cent.

True interest rates vary not only according to the cash amount charged, but also according to the repayment arrangement. The rate on a debt repaid in weekly instalments would be even higher, because the borrower has less use of the full amount of the loan.

A credit customer who believes that he has been misled should ask his local authority TRADING STANDARDS office to check the agreement.

Traders who mislead the public on interest rates may be prosecuted. The maximum penalty is an unlimited fine and/or up to 2 years' imprisonment. A sheriff court has the power to order a reduction of interest if it is found to be excessive.

When a trader or lender quotes the total charge or cost of the credit taken, he must include not only the true annual rate of interest, but also the other charges the debtor must pay under the agreement, even if they are not payable for the use of the credit as such – for example, insurance premiums, service charges, or the lender's surveying charges on a mortgage.

MAKE SURE YOU ARE NOT BEING OVERCHARGED

In law, you must be told the true rate at which you are paying interest on any credit transaction.

INTERNATIONAL PRIVATE LAW

Disputes across legal boundaries

As more and more people travel, work or take holidays abroad, their rights after an accident, loss of property or a dispute may involve the laws of both Scotland and a foreign country.

Equally, the validity of a marriage or divorce in another country may have to be considered here if the husband or wife lives in Scotland, and so may a foreign will if the beneficiaries or property are here.

The Scottish legal system is separate from that of England and Wales. So when you have a legal problem, England often has to be treated, for legal purposes, as a foreign country.

A set of rules, known as international private law (or private international law), has been developed to determine which country's laws operate in different situations.

In some cases you can enforce your rights in a Scottish court, even though foreign laws may decide what your rights are. In other cases you would have to seek a legal remedy in a foreign court.

None of these rules relate to crime. Normally crime is dealt with by the laws of the country where it is committed. However, some countries apply sections of their criminal law to their citizens abroad. *See:* CITIZENSHIP; EXTRADITION

The court in which a dispute with a foreign element can be settled

Where your claim arises out of a foreign contract, or an accident occurring abroad, you will generally have to bring your case in the courts of the country where the other party lives. The foreigner involved could sue you in your own country or also, probably, in the country where the contract is to be performed or the accident occurred.

Where the other party is a company, it can be sued here if it is a United Kingdom company which has certain specific links with Scotland.

If a question arises about the validity of a marriage, Scottish courts will normally be prepared to hear the case provided either party has a Scottish DOMICILE or has been resident in Scotland for one year. If a contract is to be carried out in Scotland, Scottish courts will normally hear the case, provided the defender is properly given notice of the proceedings. In a dispute about a house, or similar property, the Scottish courts will hear the case if the property is situated in Scotland.

Occasionally, the Scottish courts will decline to hear a case which they are able to deal with, because they consider the courts of another country to be more appropriate.

Which country's laws apply?

There is another equally important question: which country's laws will apply? A Scottish court may hear a case but apply another country's rules to decide the question before it.

This 'choice of law' question depends on the area of law concerned.

A dispute concerning the validity of a foreign marriage, for instance, will sometimes depend upon the law of the country where the marriage took place, and sometimes upon the domicile of the parties, even though a Scottish court hears the case. In the case of disputes over goods carried between countries, and other international transactions, there are special rules adopted by international agreement.

In the case of an accident in which someone is injured, the law to be applied is usually that of the country in which the accident occurred. But if the case is being pursued in a Scottish court, the claim would have to be good under Scots law, as well as being so under the law of the place where it occurred.

The validity of a foreign will is an even more complicated question. Whether someone has the legal power to make a will depends, in the case of moveable property, on his or her domicile; and, in the case of immoveable property, on where it is situated. The formalities with which a will has to comply (for instance, how many witnesses there must be) is a matter for the law of the testator's domicile, *or* his usual residence *or* his country of nationality.

Recognising and enforcing foreign judgments

Judgments made by foreign courts will normally be recognised by the Scottish courts – at least if the decision is final and the rules applied are not wholly at odds with Scots law.

For instance, a divorce pronounced in a foreign country will generally be recognised here as long as:

- It was obtained from a court or in other proceedings – even though the particular ground for divorce may not be found in Scots law, and
- At least one of the parties to the marriage was domiciled in that country, or was normally resident there, or is a citizen of that country.

Divorces granted by religious bodies will in some circumstances be recognised. If a divorce is not recognised, then any purported remarriage will not be recognised either.

Divorces in England and Wales are automatically recognised in Scotland, and vice versa.

Foreign judgments for debt are generally recognised in Scotland and many of them may be enforced in Scotland by special statutory procedures. English and Welsh judgments are enforceable on the strength of a certificate from the original court.

GETTING INTO TROUBLE ABROAD

If you get involved in an alleged offence abroad, you have to submit to the criminal law of the country where it happened.

INTERNATIONAL WATERS

Offshore legal limits

British law extends only to the limit of United Kingdom territorial waters – at present 3 nautical miles (3.456 land miles) off shore. Beyond that lie international waters where limited British law applies only on British ships and oilrigs. *See:* SEA

INTESTACY

When someone dies without leaving a valid will

If you do not make a WILL, your property must be distributed after your death according to the rules of intestacy laid down in the Succession (Scotland) Act 1964. These rules are adjusted from time to time to allow for inflation.

Although the rules may produce the result you wish, it is better to make a will – especially if you have a lot of property. Only by making a will can you:

- Leave money to charities or persons outwith your family.
- Leave different amounts to each child.
- Leave small gifts to friends.
- Reduce CAPITAL TRANSFER TAX.
- Avoid extra legal fees in having an EXECUTOR appointed by the court.

Appointing an executor

If you die intestate – that is, without leaving a valid will – your nearest relatives have to apply to the local sheriff court to be appointed as executors to administer your property.

Where the prior rights (see below) of a surviving husband or wife will swallow up the whole estate, he or she is entitled to be appointed sole executor. Even if the children inherit too, the surviving spouse is usually made an executor – although the children can apply as well.

The surviving spouse may not want to apply – perhaps because of poor health or inexperience in business matters. Practice varies between sheriff courts as to whether a surviving spouse who inherits the whole estate can renounce his or her right to apply for appointment as executor, so that a son or daughter can apply to be appointed instead.

If the person who has died leaves no spouse or descendants, the right to apply passes in turn to the dead person's parents, brothers and sisters (or their children), half-brothers and sisters (or their children), uncles and aunts (or their children) and grandparents.

Where several relatives are of equal standing – for example, if a widow dies leaving several children – they have equal priority, but usually agree between themselves who shall apply. However they all have a right to apply and if they do, all will be appointed. There is no limit to the number of executors who may be appointed, but usually one or two is quite sufficient.

What the executor does

After the executor has been appointed by the court, his tasks are very similar to those of an executor appointed by a will. But he cannot resign without the court's consent. He must get a guarantee (a bond of caution) from an insurance company that he will administer the estate properly – though not if he is a surviving spouse who inherits the whole estate. He must:

- Calculate the total value of everything left by the dead person.
- Subtract all the dead person's debts.
- Fill up the appropriate Inland Revenue forms and pay any CAPITAL TRANSFER TAX due.
- Apply for CONFIRMATION.
- Gather in the ESTATE, pay taxes and debts, and distribute what is left according to the rules of intestacy.

If the deceased's affairs are complicated, the executor may need to consult a solicitor or an accountant.

How an estate is divided

The distribution of the estate depends on whether there is a surviving widow or widower and which other relatives are alive.

The surviving spouse's rights are cal-

THE RULES OF INTESTACY

How the law divides an estate when there is no will

Surviving relatives	Division of property
1. Widow/er only – no children, grandchildren, parents, brothers, sisters or their children.	Widow/er takes the whole estate.
2. Widow/er and children.	Widow/er takes house (or £50,000, if worth more), furniture and plenishings up to £10,000, cash up to £15,000 and one-third of the remaining moveable estate. The remainder of the estate is divided equally among the children, or their descendants if any have died. A child's share will be affected if he was given money by the deceased while alive, either on marriage or to set him up in business.
3. No widow/er but children alive.	The estate is divided equally among the children. Illegitimate and adopted children have the same rights as legitimate children in their parents' estates. Step-children cannot benefit. If any of the children have died, their legitimate or adopted descendants are entitled to their parent's share.
4. No widow/er, or descendants, but parents, brothers or sisters alive.	The estate is divided into two. One half goes to the parents, in equal shares if they are both alive. The other half is divided equally among the brothers and sisters or their descendants if any have died. Half brothers and sisters can share only if there are no full brothers or sisters. If only parents – or only brothers, sisters or their descendants – survive, the whole estate is divided among that group.
5. No widow/er, descendants, parents, brothers, sisters or their descendants, but other relatives alive.	The estate is divided equally among the nearest relatives. The order of priority is: ● Full uncles and aunts or their descendants. ● Half uncles and aunts or their descendants. ● Grandparents. ● Full great uncles and aunts or their descendants. ● Half great uncles and aunts or their descendants. ● Great grandparents, and so on.
6. No relative traceable.	The estate passes to the Crown. It is administered by the Queen's and Lord Treasurer's Remembrancer, who may make gifts to those with moral but no legal claims (e.g. an illegitimate brother) or people who looked after the deceased for a long time.

led 'prior rights', because they have priority over other claims. He or she is entitled to the house owned by the deceased, or £50,000 if it is worth more. If the deceased was a tenant, he or she is entitled to inherit the tenancy. But in both cases the widow(er) must have been living in the house at the date of death.

Next the widow(er) is entitled to the furniture and other effects (but not a car) up to £10,000 in value. Finally he or she is entitled to a maximum of £25,000 in cash unless there are children or other descendants alive, in which case only £15,000 can be claimed.

If there is anything left after prior rights – and often there is not – the surviving spouse and the children take their 'legal rights'. Illegitimate and adopted children have the same rights as other children, but step-children cannot benefit.

The surviving spouse has the legal right to one third of the remaining MOVEABLE PROPERTY and the children share another third between them. Where there are no children, the widow(er)'s share is one-half. Where there is no widow(er), the children's share is also increased to one-half.

The remaining one-third (or one-half) of the moveable property, together with any HERITABLE PROPERTY (other than the house taken by the widow(er) under prior rights) is then divided amongst the nearest relatives. The order of priority is:

- Children (including illegitimate and adopted children).
- Grandchildren.
- Great grandchildren (and remoter descendants, generation by generation).
- Brothers, sisters and parents.
- The widow(er).
- Uncles and aunts.
- Grandparents.
- Great uncles and aunts.
- Great grandparents, and so on.

If no relatives, however remote, can be traced, the estate passes to the Crown and is administered by an official called the Queen's and Lord Treasurer's Remembrancer.

Members of an equal group of relatives – such as the children – share equally in the estate. If one has died beforehand, his descendants are entitled to his share.

DIVIDING UP AN INTESTATE ESTATE

Below is an example of how a simple estate is divided up among the relatives of a dead person who has left no will.

Example

Hugh — Mary

Andrew   [Robert]

Fiona   Jean

Hugh dies without a will, leaving a house (£25,000), furniture and plenishings (£8,000), and life policies, savings and a car totalling £21,000. Robert, one of his sons, died before him.

Mary – his widow – takes the house, contents and £15,000 as prior rights. The balance (all moveable) amounts to £6,000. Mary takes £2,000 (⅓) as legal rights.

Andrew and Robert, their sons, would have shared £2,000 as legal rights between them had Robert survived his father. Andrew gets £1,000, while Robert's daughters, Fiona and Jean, divide their father's share (£1,000) between them.

The remainder of the estate (£2,000) is divided among Andrew and Robert's children in the same way as the legal rights – Andrew £1,000, Fiona and Jean £500 each.

Partial intestacy

When a will does not deal with all the deceased's property, the executors named in the will divide up the unwilled property according to the rules of intestacy. So if the house is unwilled, the widow(er) will get it. But the widow(er) must deduct from the prior right to cash – that is, the sum of £25,000 or £15,000 – any sum left to him or her by the will.

INVALID CARE ALLOWANCE

A benefit for persons caring for severely disabled people

If you are caring for a severely disabled person, you may be entitled to an invalid care allowance (£20.45 a week in 1983–4). To qualify you must:

- Be between the ages of 16 and 65 (60 if you are a woman).
- Spend at least 35 hours a week looking after the disabled person.
- Not be earning more than £12 a week.
- Not be attending full-time school or college or university.
- Normally live in the United Kingdom.
- Be in the United Kingdom and have been present there for at least 26 weeks out of the 12 months before receiving benefit.

To qualify, the disabled person must be receiving:

- ATTENDANCE ALLOWANCE; or
- A constant attendance allowance payable with industrial DISABLEMENT BENEFIT, with WAR PENSIONS, with workmen's compensation (payable to people injured before July 5, 1948) or with an allowance under the Pneumoconiosis, Byssinosis and Miscellaneous Diseases Benefit Scheme.

Until June 1981, invalid care allowance was paid only to people looking after severely disabled relatives. But since then it has been possible for people caring for persons other than relatives to qualify as well.

When the allowance is not paid

The allowance is not payable to a married woman who is living with her husband, or is separated from him but is receiving maintenance from him equal to at least the amount of the allowance. Nor is it paid to a woman living with a man as his wife.

You will not be eligible for the allowance if you are receiving another social security benefit that is as much as, or more than, the allowance. If the other benefit is less than the allowance, you can claim the difference.

Even if you are already receiving SUPPLEMENTARY BENEFIT, you can claim the allowance – but it will reduce your benefit pound for pound.

Increases for dependants

You can claim an increase in your allowance for:

- Any children for whom CHILD BENEFIT is payable (£7.60 for each child in 1983–4).
- Your wife, if she is living with you and

is not earning more than the increase (£12.25 a week in 1983–84). The increase will be reduced by any social security benefit the wife is receiving (except for mobility allowance, attendance allowance or industrial disablement benefit).

If you cannot claim for a wife, you can obtain an increase (£12.25 a week in 1983–4) for a woman if:

- She lives with you.
- She has care of children for whom you claim an increase.
- She does not earn more than £12.25 a week – apart from what you pay her.

Calculating earnings

When you calculate what you or your dependants earn for the purpose of claiming this allowance, you should deduct reasonable expenses connected with the employment. For instance – fares, overalls, tools, trade union subscriptions and luncheon vouchers up to a maximum of 15p a day.

When you retire

The allowance ceases to be payable when you reach the age of 65 – 60 if you are a woman – and draw a higher amount in retirement pension.

If you do not claim your pension, or the amount is less than the allowance, you can continue to draw the allowance after you reach pensionable age, provided you still satisfy the qualifying conditions.

After 70 (65 for a woman) you can continue to draw the allowance even if you are no longer caring for the disabled person.

How to claim the allowance

If you think you qualify for the invalid care allowance, get leaflet NI 212 from your local social security office and complete the claim form – DS 700 – which is attached to it. Send this form back to the social security office without delay.

Claims cannot be backdated for more than 3 months unless there is good cause for the delay, and in no circumstances for more than 12 months.

If you are refused an allowance, you can appeal to a social security appeal tribunal against the decision. The reason for refusal and details of how and where to appeal will be explained in the notification sent to you by the social security office.

How other benefits are affected

You are not liable to pay NATIONAL INSURANCE CONTRIBUTIONS while you are not working. But to protect your right to other social security benefits, you are normally credited with a Class 1 national insurance contribution for each week in which you receive invalid care allowance.

These credits count towards other benefits, such as sickness benefit, unemployment benefit, widow's benefit and retirement pension.

Home responsibilities protection

If you are receiving invalid care allowance, your contribution credit will protect your entitlement to a full RETIREMENT PENSION or your wife's entitlement to a full WIDOW'S PENSION or WIDOWED MOTHER'S ALLOWANCE.

However, if you give up work to look after a severely disabled person, but are *not* entitled to invalid care allowance, you will not be credited with contributions to protect your pension rights or those of your widow. In that situation, you can apply for 'home responsibilities protection' (HRP) – a scheme which reduces the number of qualifying years of contributions normally needed for full retirement pension, widow's pension or widowed mother's allowance to be payable.

When your retirement pension is being worked out, the number of years for which you get HRP is deducted from the number of qualifying years of contributions you would normally need for a full pension. You will get a full pension as long as the reduced number of qualifying years does not fall below 20.

The same rule applies to widow's pension and widowed mother's allowance, except that the number of qualifying years required for a full pension or allowance can be reduced to less than 20 provided that it is at least half of the years which are normally required.

You qualify for HRP for any tax year in which you:

- Look after someone who is receiving attendance allowance or a constant attendance allowance, for at least 35 hours a week; or
- Receive supplementary benefit so that you can stay off work to look after an elderly or sick person at home.

If you are looking after someone who is getting an attendance allowance or a constant attendance allowance, you must apply for HRP at the end of each tax year, on a form obtainable from the local social security office. If you have been receiving supplementary benefit for the whole tax year to look after someone at home, there is no need to apply: protection is granted automatically.

A leaflet (NP 27) explaining HRP and containing an application form is available from your local social security office.

Dependent relative allowance

If you pay INCOME TAX, and any relative of yours is incapable of looking after himself or herself and is living with you, you can claim a special dependent relative tax allowance.

INVALIDITY PENSION

Benefit paid to disabled people who cannot work

Anybody of working age who is unable to work because he or she is disabled may be entitled to an invalidity pension, whether or not he or she has paid NATIONAL INSURANCE CONTRIBUTIONS.

Two kinds of pension

There are two kinds of pension:

- Contributory – payable in place of SICKNESS BENEFIT and MATERNITY allowance to men and women who have paid enough national insurance contributions, or have suffered an industrial accident or disease.
- Non-contributory – for men and women who are incapable of work and have not paid enough contributions to receive the contributory pension. It is only paid to married women if they are also unable to do normal household duties.

From November, 1984, the non-contributory pension is to be gradually replaced by a new benefit – severe disablement allowance.

Contributory pension

The contributory pension is paid in place of and at a higher rate than sickness benefit.

To qualify you must have been incapable of work – and eligible for sickness benefit or maternity allowance – for a total of 168 days, not counting Sundays. That can be one continuous spell, or several periods of 4 or more days provided you do not work for more than 8 weeks between each period.

The qualifying period is reduced from 168 to 120 days if you get the maximum 8 weeks' statutory sick pay from your employer, and then (or within the next 8 weeks) receive sickness benefit or maternity allowance. *See:* SICKNESS

Widows and widowers can sometimes qualify for the pension even if they do not qualify for sickness benefit. Ask at your local social security office.

How to claim

Claim in the same way as for sickness benefit – that is, by completing a sick note and sending it to your local social security office. If you are already receiving sickness benefit, invalidity pension will be substituted after the qualifying 168 (or 120) days, and will be sent to you together with any invalidity allowance (see below) payable.

You must continue to send sick notes regularly to ensure that your pension is not delayed or forfeited.

If you are refused an invalidity pension or are dissatisfied with the amount, you can appeal to a social security appeal tribunal.

What you must not do

While you are receiving benefit you must not:

- In any way delay your recovery.
- Leave your present address without saying where you can be found.
- Do any work unless it is part of your treatment, or you have good reason to do it. You cannot earn more than £22.50 a week (in 1983–4).
- Refuse to be medically examined by a regional medical service doctor.

If you break any of those rules without good cause, you can be disqualified from receiving invalidity benefit for up to 6 weeks.

How much you may receive

If you have no dependants, you will get invalidity pension of £32.60 a week (in 1983–4), plus any invalidity allowance to which you are entitled.

You can get an increase of £19.55 a week for a wife or for a female cohabitee caring for your children. This will be reduced if she earns more than £45 a week. You can get the same increase for a husband provided he earns no more than £19.55 a week.

If you do not claim for a partner, you can get £19.55 for a dependent adult relative who lives with you.

You can normally get an increase for a dependent child – £7.60 a week in 1983/4. If you live with your husband, you can only get the increase provided he earns no more than £19.55 a week.

From November, 1984, no increase will be paid for a child if your partner or cohabitee earns £80 or more a week (after certain deductions). The limit is increased by £10 for each extra child.

You may also be entitled to an additional pension based on national insurance contributions paid as an employed person since April 6, 1978. See leaflet NI 16A, available from your local social security office.

Invalidity allowance

If you are receiving an invalidity pension and were under 60 – 55 if you are a woman – on the first day of the 168 (or 120) days you needed to qualify for a pension, you are entitled to an invalidity allowance. The allowance should be paid automatically. If it is not, write to your local social security office.

How much you get The amount of allowance depends upon how old you were when your incapacity began.

In 1983–4 the weekly rate of invalidity allowance payable with invalidity pension was:

For incapacity beginning:

Under age 40 or before July 5, 1948	£7.15
Age 40–49	£4.60
Age 50–59 (men) Age 50–54 (women)	£2.30

Once you have been granted an allowance, you continue to draw it at the same rate throughout your period of incapacity even though you may enter a different age group.

For example, if you were aged 38 when you first received your allowance, and were still incapacitated and unable to work at 42, you would continue to receive the under-40 allowance.

Non-contributory pension

The non-contributory invalidity pension is for men and women who are of working age but are unable to work and are not entitled to sickness or invalidity benefit because they do not have enough national insurance contributions. The weekly rate is £20.45 (1983–4). You can claim another £12.25 for a partner, and £7.60 for each child.

A married woman is not eligible unless she is living apart from her husband and receiving maintenance worth less than the pension. She may, though, be entitled to the non-contributory invalidity pension for married women if she is unable to perform normal household duties (see below).

To qualify, you must:

- Be at least 16 – or 19 if still at school or full-time college (unless you are receiving education or training especially arranged for disabled people).
- Be under 65–60 if you are a woman.
- Have been incapable of work for at least 28 weeks immediately before the date you claim.
- Have been present in the UK for a total of at least 10 years in the last 20, and for at least 26 weeks during the 12 months before payment begins.

To apply, complete the claim form attached to leaflet NI 210 – available from the local social security office.

The pension can still be paid after you reach 65 – 60 if you are a woman – so long as you were entitled to it immediately before reaching that age.

Young disabled people aged 16 and 17 can count time on NCIP towards qualifying for the higher long-term rate of SUPPLEMENTARY BENEFIT.

Married women A non-contributory invalidity pension (£19.70 in 1982–3) is available to:

- A married woman who is living with her husband.
- A married woman who is living apart from her husband and who is receiving maintenance payments equal to or more than the amount of the pension.
- A single woman living with a man as his wife.

To qualify, you must not only satisfy the conditions for ordinary non-contributory invalidity pension; you must *also* have been continuously incapable of performing your normal

WHAT HAPPENS WHEN YOU RETIRE?

If you retire at 65 (60 if a woman) and draw a RETIREMENT PENSION, your contributory invalidity pension ceases. But if your retirement pension is based on your own insurance contributions, any invalidity allowance you received will be added to it.

The same rule applies when you reach the age of 70 – (65 if a woman) – if you continue to work until that age. Invalidity pension is not payable after 70 (or 65).

When you choose late retirement

If you do not retire at 65 or 60 but will be entitled to a retirement pension on your own contributions when you eventually do retire, you are entitled to draw an invalidity pension – up to the age of 70 or 65 if you are a woman – when you are incapable of work.

If you are drawing a retirement pension and then cancel your retirement between the ages of 65 and 70 – 60 and 65 if you are a woman – you can draw an invalidity pension if you subsequently become incapable of work.

In both cases, invalidity pension will be paid at a correspondingly reduced rate if retirement pension would not have been payable at the full rate.

Increases for dependants

You can claim an increase for a dependent wife and children in the same way as if you were drawing a retirement pension. If no increase is payable for a wife you may be able to claim for a woman caring for any children.

Widows and widowers

If you are a widow or widower who is entitled to a basic retirement pension on both your own and your late partner's contributions, you may be able to receive an invalidity pension at the rate of the two pensions added together. If you want to find out more about this, contact your local social security office.

What happens about income tax

Invalidity pensions and allowances are not taxable. But if you are receiving a retirement pension which has been increased by the amount of invalidity allowance you were receiving before you retired, that increase is taxable.

household duties for at least 28 weeks.

You do not qualify merely because there are some normal household jobs which you can no longer do. You must be unable to do normal household duties to a *substantial* extent.

If you think that you are entitled to the non-contributory pension, ask for leaflet NI 214 at your local social security office and complete the claim form – BF 450 – which is attached to it.

Severe disablement allowance From November, 1984, a new benefit – severe disablement allowance – will gradually replace the non-contributory pension. It will be paid at the same rate. To get it, you must be incapable of work for at least 28 weeks immediately before claiming.

People already receiving non-contributory pension will automatically get the new allowance instead. Others can claim if they are not entitled to contributory pension. The rules about age limits and residence remain the same. There are *no* special rules for married women.

You must satisfy new disablement rules if you do not qualify for the allowance automatically. You will only get the allowance if:

- Your incapacity began not later than the age of 20; or
- You are at least 80 per cent disabled.

The test is the same as the one that applies to DISABLEMENT BENEFIT.

Appealing If you are refused a non-contributory pension or severe disablement allowance, you will be told the reason for the refusal. You can then appeal to a social security tribunal.

INVENTIONS BY EMPLOYEES

When an employee invents something as part of his job

If an employee invents something as part of his job there are two sets of circumstances in each of which the employer is entitled to claim ownership of the invention:

1. If the employee makes his invention 'in the course of his normal duties', it belongs to his employer – provided those duties make it reasonable to expect that such inventions will be made. The Patents Act 1977 does not define 'normal duties' and there is as yet little case law. But, for example, a research worker who invents something related to a project that he has been asked to undertake by his employer would not be able to claim the invention for himself, although he might be entitled to a 'fair share' of any proceeds.

2. If, because of the employee's work and responsibilities, he has a 'special obligation' to further his employer's interests, anything he invents as the result of his job belongs to his employer. That rule is aimed particularly at senior staff – for example, a director of research and development might not be actively engaged in research, but he would be expected to put his full skill and knowledge at his employer's service.

In all other circumstances the invention belongs to the employee and he is entitled to patent it and to receive any royalties arising from it.

If the employer patents an invention made by one of his employees but which belongs in law to the employer, the employee-inventor is entitled to be named as the inventor on the patent.

Your employment contract

Many companies put rules about employees' inventions into their employment contracts. However, the employer cannot use the rules to secure the right to an invention that has nothing to do with the employee's job.

Any rule which seeks to deprive the employee of his rights in inventions belonging to him is void and unenforceable. Nor does the employer have the automatic right to an invention that, while partly related to the employee's job, does not arise directly from it and was worked upon by the employee in his own time, using his own materials and off his employer's premises.

Claiming a fair share

If an employee invents something that, by law, becomes his employer's property, he may be entitled to a 'fair share' of any profits, as compensation.

To succeed in his claim, the employee must show that his employer has derived 'outstanding benefit' from patenting the invention. The size and nature of the employer's business are taken into account when deciding if the benefit has been 'outstanding'.

If the employer and the employee cannot agree on what is a 'fair share', the employee has a legal right to apply to the Comptroller-General of Patents, Designs and Trade Marks at the Patent Office, 25 Southampton Buildings, London W.C.2, or to the Court of Session, for an order requiring his employer to pay him compensation. The Comptroller or Court can order the payment of a fair share if they think this would be just.

The employee can lodge a claim for compensation at any time during the life of the patent on the invention concerned – 20 years – or within 1 year of the date on which the patent expired.

Collective agreements Some collective agreements deal with employees' rights to patent inventions and to collect royalties from them. If an agreement provides for the payment of compensation, an employee who is a *member* of the union that signed the agreement loses his legal right to apply to the Comptroller-General or the Court of Session for compensation.

INVESTMENT INCOME

'Unearned' money that carries an extra tax liability

Investment income is not clearly defined in tax law, but is taken generally to mean anything other than EARNED INCOME.

Most investment income was, until April 5, 1984, liable to an additional rate of tax known as the investment income surcharge, levied over and above normal income tax.

Although investment income surcharge has been abolished with effect from the 1984–5 tax year, it remains payable in respect of income taxable in earlier years. *See:* INCOME TAX.

In practice, investment or 'unearned' income falls into one of six main categories:

- Company dividends.
- Interest from government and local authority securities and loans.
- Bank interest.
- Building society interest.
- Rents from property.
- Income from trusts and settlements.

The surcharge rates varied from year to year. For 1983–4, they were:

First £7,100 of investment income .. Nil
Over £7,100 .... 15%

How the surcharge is worked out

With some types of investment income – mainly company dividends, interest from building societies, and certain government or local authority securities and loan stock – the taxpayer actually receives a *net* amount.

The basic rate of income tax has already been deducted at source.

To assess any investment surcharge that is still to be paid, the net amount is 'grossed up' – converted back to what it was before the deduction of the basic income tax.

The surcharge is then worked out on the full, untaxed sum.

Allowances Personal tax allowances cannot reduce a person's liability to pay the investment income surcharge unless he has little or no earned income. His personal allowances would have to exceed the total of his earned income and the part of his investment income that is free of surcharge.

However, the taxpayer may be able to reduce his liability to surcharge by deducting some 'annual charges' from the investment income. These include mortgage interest, interest on money borrowed to buy commercial property or for use in a family business, and maintenance payments.

IRISH CITIZEN

When a person holding an Irish passport comes to Britain

Since the partition of Ireland in 1921, inhabitants of the six Counties of Northern Ireland – that is, Antrim, Armagh, Down, Fermanagh, Londonderry and Tyrone – are normally British Citizens (see CITIZENSHIP), but are eligible also to obtain a passport issued by the Republic of Ireland.

Entry to the United Kingdom

A citizen of the Republic of Ireland does not need a passport or any kind of permission to enter any part of the United Kingdom, including Northern Ireland. He has the right to live and work permanently in the United Kingdom and to vote in all British elections. He is entitled to stand as a candidate in British and European elections.

When he can be sent home

An Irish citizen, who is not also a British citizen, can be excluded from the United Kingdom and sent to the Republic of Ireland if:

- He is convicted of an offence involving imprisonment within 5 years of his taking up residence in the United Kingdom, and a court recommends his exclusion. He cannot be excluded if he had lived in the United Kingdom for 5 years or more when he was convicted.
- He took up residence after January 1, 1973, and the Home Secretary considers his exclusion to be conducive to the public good. He cannot be sent away for the public good if he was normally resident in the United Kingdom before January 1, 1973.
- The Home Secretary or Secretary of State for Northern Ireland decides that he has been involved in the 'commission, preparation or instigation of acts of terrorism'.

Someone born in Northern Ireland can be excluded from Great Britain and sent back there unless he has lived in Great Britain for the past 20 years.

Becoming a British citizen

If an Irish citizen who has been ordinarily resident in the United Kingdom for 5 years wishes to become a British citizen, he can apply for NATURALISATION to the Home Office.

Obtaining an Irish passport

Under Irish law, an Irish citizen – or someone whose father, grandfather or grandmother was an Irish citizen – is entitled to apply for a passport issued by the Republic of Ireland.

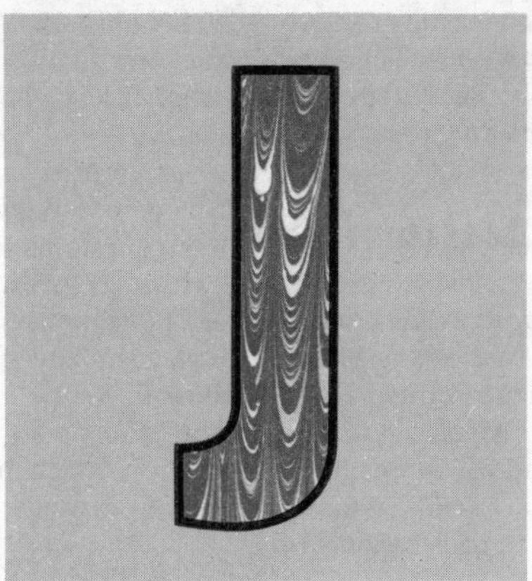

JOINT TENANCY

Protection against eviction for people sharing accommodation

Anyone sharing a rented house, flat or other living accommodation will only be able to obtain full security of tenure – that is, protection against eviction – if he can show that he is either a tenant or a joint tenant.

A joint tenancy exists where two or more people share the use of rooms in a flat or house and have equal responsibility for the rent and for observing the other conditions of the tenancy. A joint tenancy is often entered into by a husband and wife, or by a group of friends or students.

Joint tenants in the private sector have the same rights as sole tenants to security of tenure and rent protection under the Rent (Scotland) Act. *See:* EVICTION; RENT PROTECTION.

Joint tenants in the public sector – that is, tenants of district and islands councils, New Town Development Corporations, the Scottish Special Housing Association and registered housing associations – have the same rights as sole tenants to security of tenure under the Tenants' Rights (Scotland) Act 1980. *See:* COUNCIL TENANCY

Where a tenancy is joint, each tenant is legally responsible for ensuring that the rent is paid. So if one tenant is in practice responsible for paying the rent to the landlord, and disappears after failing to do so, the other tenants are legally obliged to pay the arrears. They are then entitled to sue the tenant who has disappeared for his share of the rent and any other bills.

Where a joint tenancy is disputed

A tenancy will clearly be joint if all the occupants of the house are named in the lease, or have signed it. Even if only one of them is named in the lease, or has signed it, the others may still be joint tenants if there is sufficient evidence that the landlord treated them as being responsible for the rent and for the other obligations under the lease.

An occupant who is not a joint tenant may instead be a sub-tenant of another person in the house who has rented the premises from the landlord. So long as that person is allowed to sub-let, the occupant will have a valid tenancy. But if sub-letting is forbidden, and the occupant is in the house without the landlord's permission, he is in the same position as a squatter and has no legal right to remain. *See:* SUB-TENANCY; SQUATTER

Alternatively, an occupant who is neither a joint tenant nor a sub-tenant may have a permission, or licence, to occupy his accommodation. *See:* LICENCE TO OCCUPY

Separate leases If each occupant in a house signs a separate lease with the landlord, there will not be a joint tenancy. Each occupant will have a separate tenancy and will be responsible only for the rent which he or she agreed to pay.

Notice by joint tenants

If one joint tenant gives notice to the landlord that he intends to give up the tenancy, that is sufficient to terminate the tenancy of the other joint tenant(s). The landlord may then enter into a new lease with any tenant who wishes to remain.

If the landlord does nothing, and any remaining tenant continues to live in the house and to pay rent, a new lease will be created by implication.

Joint tenants and supplementary benefit

Joint tenants are treated as joint householders for SUPPLEMENTARY BENEFIT purposes. Each is entitled to the non-householder rate of benefit, plus the difference between that and the single householder rate divided by the number of joint tenants.

Joint tenants are also eligible to claim HOUSING BENEFITS.

JUDGE

Complaining about judges

Scottish judges, whether in the High Court of Justiciary, the Court of Session, sheriff or district courts, frequently give reasons for their decisions. These decisions are usually based on Acts of Parliament or previous decisions of the courts (called 'precedents'), though occasionally the matter may be within the judges' discretion.

For reasons of public policy, judges cannot be sued for any words spoken or acts done whilst performing their judicial functions – providing they have not exceeded their powers. Even where a judge has acted in excess of his powers, his conduct may not be actionable unless it was caused by malice.

Abusive or intemperate criticism of a judge can amount to CONTEMPT OF COURT. However, that offence is intended to safeguard the administration of justice, not the dignity of judges. It follows that no criticism of a judge's decision or behaviour, however vigorous, can amount to contempt of court providing it keeps within the limits of reasonable courtesy and good faith. Fair comment, honestly made, which is in the public interest is neither DEFAMATION nor contempt.

The borderline between criticism and abuse is a fine one. It is not defamation to allege that a judge is incompetent, or that he has acted unjudicially – for example, by talking too much or falling asleep on the bench – so long as you can prove it. Nor, if you have the evidence, is it defamation to say that a judge has displayed racial, sexual or political bias in his remarks in a case – though it might be contempt to attribute his decision to bias.

However, it is clear that it would be contempt to describe a judge (as someone once did) as a 'microcosm of conceit and empty-headedness who would have made an excellent bus conductor', or to suggest that a judge was corrupt. Indeed, it might be contempt to attribute a decision to judicial corruption or bias even if the allegation can be shown to be true.

JUDICIAL EXAMINATION

Questioning in private by the prosecutor

After his arrest, a person who is to be prosecuted before a judge and jury under solemn CRIMINAL PROCEEDINGS – used for serious cases – will be brought before a sheriff for 'judicial examination'. This will usually take place on the day after the arrest (excluding weekends).

Before his appearance for judicial examination, the accused person will have received a copy of the petition detailing the criminal charge against him.

An accused person has the right to a private interview with a solicitor before he is judicially examined. He also has the right to have a solicitor present at the examination.

If the accused does not have a solicitor of his own, or if he is unavailable, the LEGAL AID duty solicitor in attendance at the sheriff court can assist. The sheriff has the power to delay a judicial examination for up to 48 hours from the time of the accused's arrest in order to allow time for the solicitor to attend.

The judicial examination is held in chambers (private rooms) in the sheriff court. The sheriff, sheriff-clerk, PROCURATOR FISCAL, the accused and his solicitor, and police escorts will be present. Where the prosecutor – who for this purpose is always the procurator fiscal – intends to question the accused, a tape recording is made of the proceedings and a shorthand writer will also be present to keep a verbatim record of the questions and answers. Members of the public and press are excluded.

What happens at the examination

At the examination the accused is given the opportunity to make a declaration, or statement, explaining his involvement in the alleged crime. However, he is under no obligation to make such a declaration and will rarely do so. More usually, the accused's solicitor will state that no plea or declaration is to be made.

The accused may then be questioned by the prosecutor. This will not happen in every case: the decision whether to ask questions is at the discretion of the prosecutor. The accused is not put on oath and he can take the advice of his solicitor before answering or can refuse to answer any question.

However, the refusal of an accused person to answer may be commented on by the judge, prosecutor or a co-accused at the subsequent trial. This may happen where the accused person states in evidence at the trial something which could have been stated in answer to a question asked by the prosecutor during the judicial examination.

Any questions asked by the prosecutor must be for the purpose of obtaining 'any denial, explanation, justification or comment' which the accused may have concerning:

- The criminal charge – for instance, the nature and details of any defence, such as alibi, incrimination or the victim's consent.
- Any confession allegedly made by him to, or in the hearing of, a police officer. But in this case the accused cannot be questioned unless the prosecutor provides both him and the sheriff with a written record of the alleged confession.
- The content of any statement made by the accused at the examination.

When framing his questions, the prosecutor cannot challenge the truth of anything said by the accused, or repeat a question which the accused has refused to answer, or put leading questions. *See:* EVIDENCE

The sheriff must make sure that all questions are fairly put to, and understood by, the accused person. The sheriff must tell the accused that he can consult with his solicitor (present at the examination) before answering any question.

The accused's solicitor is not allowed to intervene directly during the course of the questioning.

However, with the sheriff's permission he can question his client in order to clear up any ambiguity in an answer given to the prosecutor, or to give his client the opportunity to answer any question which he has previously refused to answer.

Committal to prison

At the end of the judicial examination (including one where the accused is not questioned), the prosecutor will ask the sheriff to commit the accused to prison, either for further examination or to await trial. A committal for further examination is for not more than 8 days, after which the accused must be committed for trial.

The sheriff will grant the prosecutor's request unless the accused has applied for and been granted BAIL at the judicial examination.

Within 14 days of the examination, the prosecutor must provide the accused and his solicitor with a written copy of the record of the questions asked and answers given at the examination.

The accused can object if he thinks that the record is inaccurate or incomplete. The sheriff will then hold a private hearing and may authorise corrections to be made.

The record of the proceedings at the judicial examination can be lodged in court and used as evidence at the accused's trial.

A further examination

An accused person may be brought back before the sheriff for further examination. This will usually only happen if some new matter comes to the attention of the prosecutor after the first judicial examination.

The procedure at a further examination is the same as at the first examination, but the prosecutor cannot ask questions on matters previously examined. The sheriff may delay any further examination for up to 24 hours in order to allow time for the accused's solicitor to attend.

JUDICIAL FACTOR

An administrator appointed by a court

Where property is not being properly administered or is in dispute, a court may appoint a person – called a judicial factor – to look after it. For example, a court may appoint a factor to manage an insane or senile person's property or to administer an estate where the deceased's debts exceed his assets.

The factor is usually a solicitor or an accountant. He is supervised by the court and has to make up an inventory of the property under his control and submit accounts of his administration. *See:* CURATOR

JURY

When a citizen must help to administer justice

Anyone who denies a charge of serious crime will be tried by a jury of fellow citizens in the HIGH COURT OF JUSTICIARY or SHERIFF COURT. The law imposes on most adults the duty to serve as jurors, when required.

It is an offence to ignore a jury citation or to fail to attend court when required. The maximum penalty is a £400 fine, but it can be remitted later by the judge.

In general, any man or woman aged 18 or over, and under 65, is qualified and can be called for jury service, unless they are not on an electoral roll or have not resided in the UK, Channel Islands or Isle of Man for at least 5 years after the age of 13.

People who are not eligible

A citizen is ineligible for jury service if he or she falls into one of two categories:

- Professional – judges, justices of the peace, chairmen of tribunals, advocates, solicitors, procurators fiscal, prison officers, social workers involved in probation, police officers (including special constables), members of children's panels and reporters.

Any such person who has taken part in the occupation or activity in the 5 years before the question of jury service arises (or 10 years in the case of judges, justices of the peace and chairmen of tribunals) remains ineligible.

- Medical – anyone who because of a mental disorder is receiving treatment as an in-patient or as an out-patient for more than one day a week or has had his affairs taken over from him.

If, by mistake, someone who is not eligible is called to serve on a jury, he should inform the clerk of court immediately. Anyone called for jury service is sent a list of categories of people not allowed to serve.

To accept a citation and sit on a jury when ineligible or not qualified can lead to a maximum fine of £400.

THE ROLE OF A JURY IN A CRIMINAL COURT CASE

How a jury is chosen to hear evidence and reach a verdict in a case.

1. A jury of 15 jurors is selected by ballot. The clerk of court draws names from a jar. Each juror called may be challenged. If he is not, he takes his place in the jury box.
2. The jurors raise their hands as they are put on oath by the judge to deliver a true verdict.
3. The jurors, without any explanation of what it is hoped to prove, listen to the unfolding of the prosecution's case through the questions put to witnesses, and their answers. They will be given the opportunity to look at any vital piece of evidence such as a weapon or damaged clothing. They may be asked to examine photographs of the scene of the crime. They are allowed to take notes. In the same way they listen to the defence case, unless it is simply that the prosecution has produced no case requiring an answer. After the prosecution and defence lawyers have gone over the evidence in their closing speeches, the judge sums up, giving the jury directions on the law and drawing their attention to significant features of the evidence. The jury then retire to consider their verdict.
4. In the jury room the jurors choose a foreman to chair their discussions and act as spokesman. They discuss the evidence and must stay together until they have managed to reach a verdict in the case.
5. The jury returns to the court where its foreman tells the judge what verdict it has reached on each of the charges.

People who are disqualified

Anyone who has been sentenced to imprisonment for life or for 5 years or more is disqualified, whether or not he served the sentence. So is anyone who has been in prison on a sentence of 3 months or more, unless his conviction has been wiped out. *See:* REHABILITATION

Someone who serves on a jury knowing he is disqualified is liable to a fine of up to £2,000.

When someone can be excused

Some people may be excused jury service if they wish – for example, peers, Members of Parliament, practising doctors, vets, dentists, nurses, midwives, full-time members of the armed forces and clergymen.

Anyone who has attended for jury service within the previous 5 years is also entitled to ask to be excused. So may anyone excused by a judge from jury service for a certain number of years. Anyone who wishes to use an excuse should write immediately to the clerk of court.

Apart from all these excuses, you may wish to be excused because of some personal circumstance. It might be pregnancy, having to go into hospital, being deaf or blind, having made holiday arrangements, having special commitments at work, which if disrupted would cause great inconvenience to yourself or others. But ordinary inconvenience to yourself is often an unavoidable part of being a juror and is not an excuse.

If you think you have a good excuse, get in touch with the clerk of court as soon as possible.

How jurors are chosen

Jury lists based on local electoral registers are kept by sheriff clerks. At intervals jury revisal notices are sent out to batches of electors. People then have a first opportunity to mention any reason why they may not be liable for jury service.

Fourteen days before a trial or series of trials is due to take place, citations are sent out to up to 45 jurors believed to be qualified.

The citation gives the date on which jury service is to begin, but not the date when it is to end – because it is impossible to know when a trial may finish.

Calling a jury

Substantially more than the 15 people needed for any given case are called, on the assumption that some will have good reason for not attending and others will be rejected, or successfully challenged, by the defence or prosecution. They are called in prescribed proportions from the local government areas adjacent to the court.

The final jury of 15 is chosen on the first day of the trial, by ballot. All names are put in a jar: the first 15 drawn by the clerk of the court form the jury – but they may be rejected if there are objections or challenges from defence or prosecution.

As each name is read out, the juror takes a seat in the jury box. When all 15 are seated they take the oath together.

Peremptory challenges Each accused through his lawyer can challenge up to three jurors without giving a reason. So can the prosecutor. That is called a peremptory challenge. The defence lawyer simply says 'object' – and the judge tells the person that he or she will not be needed for that trial.

A peremptory challenge may be made for many reasons: do not take it as a personal affront. It is part of a defence lawyer's role to try to select a jury that he thinks will give his client the best chance of acquittal.

A juror who has been rejected should remain in court until allowed to leave. He might be needed for another case.

Challenge for cause Both defence and prosecution can challenge any number of jurors 'for cause' if they think that the fairness of a trial could be jeopardised by the presence of any of those jurors.

A challenge for cause can be made, for example, if it is thought that a juror knows someone involved in the case, or has heard or read something about it that might influence him.

It is for the judge to decide whether such a challenge is valid. Once the challenge has been made, he may question the juror himself – or allow the defence or prosecution to do so, though this is not usually encouraged. Questions on political or religious opinions are not allowed.

Taking the oath After any challenge the jurors stand as a group and take an OATH. Anyone who rejects oaths may make an affirmation instead.

During a trial

When the jurors have been sworn, the clerk of the court reads out the charge against the accused, a copy is given to each juror and the trial begins.

The jury must listen to everything that is said, the evidence and cross-examination of witnesses, the closing speeches of prosecution and defence and the judge's summing up, or charge, in which he directs the jury on points of evidence and law.

The judge may send the jury out of court to the jury room if there are matters that they ought not to hear – for example, if the prosecution or defence lawyers want to ask the judge whether it is in order to refer to a previous conviction of the accused or a witness, or to a statement which the accused is alleged to have made to the police.

Coping with the evidence

Jurors are entitled to take notes during the case, to help them to assess the evidence. It is particularly advisable to do so during a long and complicated trial.

If no writing materials have been supplied, you may ask the court officer for some. If that does not produce results, ask him to ask the judge. If he refuses to do so, you may raise your hand in the jury box and put the request to the judge himself.

Asking questions Jurors are not allowed to ask witnesses questions, for fear that they may put inadmissible questions and produce inadmissible replies that could make it necessary to begin the trial again.

But a question from a juror can be conveyed by passing a note to the judge, who will either answer the question himself or put it directly to the witness, on the juror's behalf, or to one of the lawyers concerned in the case. Alternatively, he may say that the question cannot be asked.

If the witness has already left the witness box, the judge may recall him to deal with the juror's question.

Leaving the courtroom If a juror wishes to leave the courtroom other than during an adjournment – for example, to go to the lavatory – he should speak to the court officer or pass a note to him, or through him to the judge. The judge can then order a short adjournment.

However, repeated interruptions are a source of irritation, and jurors are well advised not to drink a lot of liquid before the hearing starts or resumes.

At the end of each day's hearing, jurors go home unless they have had to travel a long way from home. If they have, a special overnight allowance is paid to each.

If for any reason a juror is unable to continue with a trial, it does not have to be abandoned, provided that at least 12 of the 15 jurors remain.

A judge can discharge a juror for various reasons, including sickness, or the making of threats to him or her.

THE JUROR WHO WAS GOT AT

If someone tries to put pressure on a juror, it will not necessarily lead to the trial being abandoned or the conviction quashed. The jury can continue to act after any of their number up to three have left for any reason.

One day, near the end of a lengthy trial of three men in the High Court, a woman juror told the judge during the lunch break that she had been approached by a man. She said that he had tried to bribe her to acquit one of the accused and that she had told her fellow-jurors about it. The judge released her from the jury without telling the others why, and the trial continued.

The accused were convicted. They all appealed, claiming that they had been prejudiced by the judge allowing the trial to go on with one juror less, for reasons that the jury might have been able to piece together.

DECISION

The Court of Criminal Appeal held that any impression in the minds of the remaining jurors was wiped out by the judge's direction to them to ignore the discharge of one of their number.

The Court also pointed out that if any approach to a juror could form a good ground of appeal, it would be an easy way for the friends of an accused person to get a conviction quashed.

HOW A JUROR IS REIMBURSED

Jurors receive no wage or fee for their service, but they can claim certain cash allowances.

The allowances are not large and most jurors who are in business or who lose pay can expect to suffer a financial loss during their jury service.

Subsistence

The amount of the daily subsistence allowance, covering meals and other expenses, depends on the length of time, each day, that the juror is away from home. The maximum allowance, in 1984, was £4.60 for a 10-hour day. For absence overnight a special allowance is paid.

Travel

A juror who travels to and from court by public transport may claim the second-class rail or bus fare. Taxi fares are paid only if there is no alternative transport.

Jurors who use their own cars or motorcycles may claim a mileage allowance. For cars, the 1984 rates were 13.2p per mile.

Financial loss

Jurors may claim allowance for loss of earnings. In 1984 the maximum was £21 a day for the first 10 days and £42 for each subsequent day.

An employer is not obliged to pay a juror's wages or salary while he is absent on jury service.

But if an employer dismisses someone because of that jury service absence, it would be treated as an UNFAIR DISMISSAL.

Reaching a verdict

After the evidence and closing speeches by prosecution and defence, the judge sums up the evidence and arguments to the jury. The court officer then leads the jurors into their jury room. He and a female officer wait outside so that no one can interfere with their discussions.

Choosing a foreman The first duty of the jury on retiring is to choose one of their number to act as foreman. The foreman, who can be a woman, becomes the jury chairman and spokesman until the end of the case, and announces its verdict to the court.

There is no set procedure for choosing a foreman: it is for the jurors themselves to decide how they will choose, and whom they will select.

Nor are there any rules about how a jury should arrive at its verdict. Their discussions, however, are confidential.

Queries and delays If jurors are in doubt about a point of law or evidence, they should ask the court officer to take a message to the judge. He can recall the jury and give the question and answer in open court in the presence of lawyers for the prosecution and defence.

Although jurors usually go home at the end of each day's hearing during evidence, argument or summing up, once they have begun to consider their verdict, they must stay together until the verdict is reached.

If they cannot reach a decision by the end of the first day, they are given overnight accommodation, usually in a hotel.

No one may go into the jury room while they are considering their verdict, except, with the approval of the judge, to bring meals or refreshments, a personal or business message, or medical aid.

The jury can return a verdict of guilty, not guilty or not proven. They can do so unanimously or by a majority. At least 8 jurors must support a verdict of guilty, even if during the trial the number of jurors has fallen below 15. A separate verdict must be given for each charge. Sometimes the judge will direct them that it is open to them to return a verdict of guilty of a lesser crime than one charged.

Jury secrets

It is CONTEMPT OF COURT for a juror to divulge to anyone what went on in the jury room. To publish such information is also contempt of court.

Juries in non-criminal cases

In some types of civil actions in the Court of Session, evidence may be taken before a jury if it is requested by one or both of the parties and the judge agrees. This procedure is used in only about a dozen cases a year, usually cases of damages for personal injuries.

The jury consists of 12 people qualified in the same way as members of criminal juries. It can return a verdict by a majority. It can still return a verdict by a majority if its members are reduced, provided they do not fall below 10.

In civil jury trials, if the jury finds in favour of the pursuer it also decides how much damages to award.

JUSTICE OF THE PEACE

Judges who sit in the district courts

Justices of the peace are people of some distinction in local communities who are appointed partly as an honour and partly to carry out some minor functions within the legal system.

The Secretary of State for Scotland appoints justices in the name of the Queen, on the recommendation of a local advisory committee which exists in the area of every district or islands council. Those chosen must live in or within 15 miles of that area.

Besides these justices, district and islands councils can nominate up to one quarter of their members to serve as justices in their areas. But they serve as justices only while they continue as members of the council and retain its nomination.

People who were magistrates or police judges in the burghs which were dissolved on 15 May 1975 also continue to hold office as justices of the peace. They can do so indefinitely.

Justices set up Committees in every area. They organise the running of the DISTRICT COURT and draw up a duty rota of justices to staff it. Justices receive loss of earnings, travelling and subsistence allowances, but are otherwise unpaid.

Justices also have duties in signing and approving many legal documents – for example, warrants enabling the police to search and arrest or giving officials power to enter homes. *See:* ENTRY, Right of

On reaching the age of 70 or becoming infirm, justices are put on to a supplemental list. They then become ineligible to sit on the bench but may still sign certain documents, such as a divorce AFFIDAVIT.

KEY MONEY

Illegal payments in addition to rent

'Key money' is the popular term for a payment known in law as a 'premium'. A premium is usually a cash payment required by a landlord in addition to rent due, as a condition of granting or continuing a tenancy. But anything which can be expressed in money terms may be a premium – for instance, a condition that a prospective tenant should sell an article or property to the landlord at less than its market value.

WHEN KEY MONEY IS ILLEGAL

If an illegal premium is charged by a landlord, the tenant should inform the police. He is entitled to recover the amount – for example, by deducting it from future rent payments.

It is a criminal offence for any person – for instance, a landlord, his agent or an outgoing tenant – to demand or receive a premium as a condition of granting, continuing or renewing a tenancy protected by the Rent (Scotland) Act. If the tenancy attracts only temporary security of tenure under the Act, and a fair rent has been registered, it is an offence to demand – but not to receive – such a premium. *See* EVICTION

The penalty is a fine of up to £400. If a person is convicted of demanding or receiving an illegal premium, the court can order him to repay the sum to the tenant. Alternatively the tenant can recover the amount by deducting it from his future rent payments.

Loans Where the tenancy is protected, the landlord cannot evade the law by requiring a tenant or prospective tenant to make a loan to him instead. That is also an offence, punishable by a fine of up to £400.

Payments which are illegal

A premium includes the following:

- A payment demanded in addition to rent – for example, a deposit required as security for rent arrears.
- Certain payments demanded by an outgoing tenant as a condition of assigning (transferring) his tenancy to someone else – for example, a price charged by the outgoing tenant for agreeing to assign the tenancy.
- Any excess over a reasonable price charged for furniture or fittings that a tenant or prospective tenant is required to buy from the landlord.

Even if the price is not excessive, it is an offence for a landlord not to provide a written inventory of any furniture or fittings, with the price of each item stated.

- Rent (of protected tenancies only) which is demanded before the beginning of the rental period for which it is due. If the rental period is more than 6 months, any requirement to pay rent for that period more than 6 months before it ends will be illegal.

Returnable deposits

A deposit which is returnable to a tenant or prospective tenant at the end of the tenancy is not an illegal premium, so long as it:

- Is paid as security for payment of electricity, gas and telephone bills, or for any other domestic supplies.
- Is paid as security for damage to the house or its contents.

However, such a deposit will be an illegal premium if it amounts to more than 2 months' rent. *See:* LANDLORD AND TENANT

KIDNAPPING

It is a serious offence to carry off a person against his will

Kidnapping is the popular name for the crime of abduction. It involves carrying off a person by force, or detaining someone against his or her will, without lawful authority. *See:* ABDUCTION

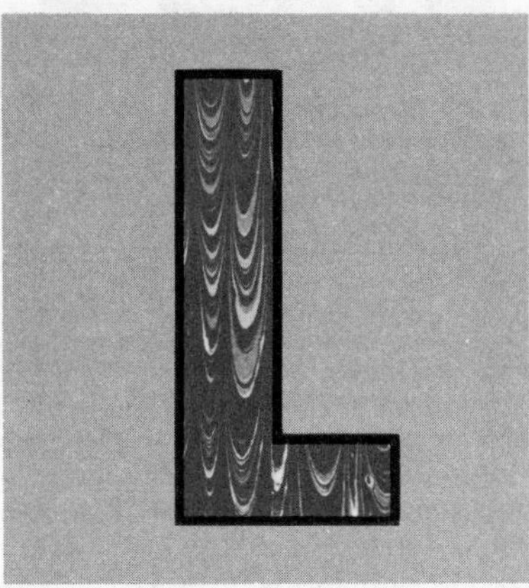

LABELLING

It is against the law to sell some goods without description

Pre-packed foods, proprietary medicines and some potentially dangerous domestic equipment must carry a label when they are offered for sale. If they do not, the person selling them is committing an offence.

Many other goods can be sold without a label, but if a manufacturer or trader decides to attach a label to them voluntarily, the information given must be accurate.

Anyone who sells goods with a label that gives false or misleading information about them commits a criminal offence and can be fined or imprisoned. *See:* TRADE DESCRIPTIONS

A shopper who buys goods that do not comply with a description on the label, on which he relied, has a legal right to reject the goods and demand his MONEY BACK.

Special, even more stringent rules apply to food and drugs. Anyone who sells or displays any food or drug that is wrongly labelled can be prosecuted under the Food and Drugs (Scotland) Act 1956. The maximum penalty under summary procedure is 6 months' imprisonment and a fine of £400. Under solemn procedure it is 1 year's imprisonment and a fine of £1,000.

A trader prosecuted under the Trade Descriptions Act for a false description can be imprisoned for up to 2 years and face a fine of any amount, if convicted under solemn procedure. *See:* CRIMINAL PROCEEDINGS

SPECIAL RULES FOR FOOD LABELLING

Pre-packed food must be marked or labelled with the usual name of the food, or carry an accurate description of it.

Some foods have a name laid down by law: for example, fish, and varieties of potato and melon.

There must be a list of ingredients, including added water, listed in descending order of weight.

Pre-packed food must also be marked or labelled with an indication of minimum durability (see FOOD), any special storage conditions or conditions of use, the name and address of the manufacturer, packer or seller, the place of origin, and instructions for use if necessary.

Foods which need not carry a list of ingredients include: cheese, butter and fermented dairy products consisting of milk products and salt only; flavourings; and food consisting of one ingredient.

Goods that can be dangerous

Certain goods such as electrical equipment to be used in the home, or paraffin heaters, must carry accurate information telling the buyer how to use them safely.

For example, refrigerators, toasters and electric fires must carry the colour code for wiring and instructions on how to fit a plug correctly; paraffin heaters must give an explanation of the safe way to operate them; and nightdresses that are flammable must have a label saying 'Warning – keep away from fire'.

The maximum penalty for failing to display a safety label on goods for sale is 3 months' imprisonment and a fine of £2,000.

LAND COURT

The court which deals with farming and crofting matters

The scandal of the Highland Clearances in the last century led to the passing of the Crofters Holding Act, 1886, the first of a number of Acts of Parliament designed to protect and regulate agricultural tenancies in the Highlands and Islands. At the same time the first Crofters Commission was set up to carry out both judicial and administrative functions under the Act.

In 1912, the protection given to small tenants in the Highlands area was extended to the rest of Scotland, and the Scottish Land Court was established in place of the original Crofters Commission. (The Commission was recreated and given new functions in 1955.) More recent Acts of Parliament have added to the Land Court's powers concerning both crofting and agricultural holdings generally.

The Land Court consists of a chairman and four members of court. The chairman is legally qualified and has the rank of a COURT OF SESSION judge. The

JUDGING 'ALFRESCO'

The Scottish Land Court will sometimes sit in the open air.

members are not lawyers, but are appointed for their agricultural expertise. One of them must be a Gaelic speaker. Each member is assisted by a legal assessor.

Some cases are decided by a member sitting alone. Others are heard by the chairman and two members. There is an appeal from the decision of the Court to the Court of Session, but only on a matter of law.

Much of the Land Court's work is still concerned with crofting matters, such as fixing a fair rent, settling a boundary dispute or determining the price to be paid when a crofter acquires the ownership of his croft.

However, the Court also has important non-crofting powers. For example, a dispute over an agricultural notice to quit will often come before the Land Court. The Court can also be asked to act as an arbiter in agricultural matters if both parties agree to this.

Deciding a case usually involves inspecting the ground concerned, and the Land Court therefore travels widely throughout Scotland, including the most remote parts. Cases may be heard in Edinburgh, but more frequently the Court will sit in a local sheriff court, a village hall, a crofter's sitting room, or even in the open air. *See:* CROFTING

LAND REGISTER

Scotland's new register of titles to land

The Land Register of Scotland was set up in 1981. It replaces the existing register, the REGISTER OF SASINES, in the areas affected by REGISTRATION OF TITLE – the new system of land registration.

The first three areas to operate registration of title are Renfrewshire, Dunbartonshire and Lanarkshire. Over the next ten years or so the new system will be extended to the rest of Scotland.

In the areas in which registration of title applies, the details of all important legal deeds concerning land must be registered in the Land Register. The deeds that this most commonly applies to are conveyances, mortgages and certain leases. *See:* CONVEYANCE; MORTGAGE

Until details are registered, the deed is not properly effective. For example, if you buy a house but do not register the conveyance, the house continues to belong to the seller. This means that he could re-sell to someone else.

Unless it is being registered for the first time, the property will already have its own title sheet in the Register. The registry staff alter the title sheet in the light of the new deed. For example, if the deed is a conveyance, they score out the name of the seller and enter the buyer's name as the new owner. The buyer then obtains an updated copy of the title sheet, called a land certificate.

A charge is made for registration. The amount depends on the value of the land or, in the case of a mortgage, the amount of the loan.

Like the Register of Sasines, the Land Register is a public register. Members of the general public can inspect the title sheet of a particular property on payment of a fee. The Register is at Meadowbank House, 153 London Road, Edinburgh and office hours are 10 a.m. to 4 p.m., Monday to Friday.

LANDLORD AND TENANT

The rules that apply when you rent your home

Some private houses and flats are rented out directly by landlords; others are let by agents who manage the property on the landlord's behalf.

If you register with an ACCOMMODATION AGENCY in order to obtain accommodation, you can be charged a fee only when you agree to take one of the properties on its list. It is illegal for an agency to demand payment for registering your name or giving you access to its list of vacant properties.

It is a criminal offence for a landlord or his agent to charge a premium, or KEY MONEY in addition to normal rent as a condition of granting a tenancy. A premium includes certain deposits, rent payments sought too far in advance and excessive prices charged for furniture and fittings to be purchased by a prospective tenant. If you have to pay any such sum, you can sue for its return in the sheriff court or, if it has already been paid to the landlord, you can deduct it from your rent payments.

Council houses Most rented homes in Scotland are let by 'public' landlords – district and islands councils, new town corporations and the Scottish Special Housing Association. They allocate houses on a priority basis to people on their waiting lists. The rules about waiting lists and allocation must be made available to the public. *See:* COUNCIL TENANCY

Signing an agreement

If you agree to rent privately for more than a year, you should enter into a *written* lease, or contract, with the landlord – failure to do so may prevent you having any rights against third parties, such as a new landlord who buys the property. If the tenancy is for a year or less, a written lease is not necessary – but it is advisable to have one so that you know what your rights and obligations are.

If you rent from a district or islands council, a new town corporation, the Scottish Special Housing Association, a registered HOUSING ASSOCIATION or a housing co-operative, you are legally entitled to a written lease. *See:* COUNCIL TENANCY

Always read a written lease *carefully* before signing it. Pay particular attention to any conditions concerning maintenance and repairs, deposits, payment of rates, permission to sub-let and the landlord's right to repossess. If you are renting privately, check to see whether the landlord has the right to introduce another tenant into the house without your consent. You should also check that the document clearly creates a tenancy and does not give you merely a

READ CAREFULLY BEFORE SIGNING

If you are asked to sign an agreement, read what it says about the period of the lease, rates, repairs and sub-letting.

permission, or licence, to occupy. *See:* LICENCE TO OCCUPY

If you have any doubts that you cannot resolve by talking to the landlord, go to a CITIZENS ADVICE BUREAU or advice centre, or to a solicitor. Once you sign the agreement, you will be bound by it. If you break any conditions – for example, a ban on sub-letting – the landlord can sue you for damages and may also be able to obtain an order for your EVICTION from the sheriff court.

The landlord may reserve the right in the written agreement to enter the premises at reasonable times to satisfy himself that you are keeping them in good condition, or to carry out repairs.

If the tenancy is protected by the Rent (Scotland) Act, 1984, the landlord has an implied right to enter at reasonable times to carry out repairs. It is also a condition of the 'implied repairs provision' (see below), which is part of most leases, that the landlord or his agent will be given access at reasonable times, on giving 24 hours' notice, to view the state of the house.

If a landlord's visits (or those of his agent) are unnecessarily frequent, or take place at unreasonable times, he may be guilty of HARASSMENT.

The lease will usually state the amount of rent and the date on which payment is due. If you are renting from a private landlord, you may wish to check with your local rent registration office (the address is in the telephone directory) whether a fair rent has been registered for the house under the Rent (Scotland) Act.

If no fair rent has been registered, you can check the register of rents to see whether you are being asked to pay an excessive amount compared to other local rents. If you are, you can ask the rent officer to fix a fair rent. *See:* RENT PROTECTION

Paying rent

Private tenants who have security of tenure under the Rent (Scotland) Act – including those with temporary security only – are entitled to a rent book or other similar document, but only if rent is payable weekly. It is an offence for the landlord not to provide this and he can be fined up to £1,000.

Other private tenants are not entitled to a rent book. If they do not get one, and are paying rent in cash, they should ask for receipts. If there is no written agreement, these receipts – or the bank's record of cheques made out to the landlord – may be important evidence that a tenancy exists.

Tenants in the public sector are not entitled to a rent book, but in practice one is often provided.

Rent should be paid promptly. Failure to pay is one of the main grounds on which a landlord – public or private – can obtain an EVICTION order. If you are having difficulty in paying – for instance, because of sickness or unemployment – consider discussing the matter with your landlord as soon as possible. You should also seek advice on whether you are receiving all the HOUSING BENEFITS to which you may be entitled.

Maintenance and repairs

One frequent cause of dispute between landlord and tenant is the responsibility for repairs to the premises.

Under common law, every lease contains an implied condition that the landlord must keep the premises in a reasonably tenantable condition. That includes keeping them wind and watertight. He need only repair any relevant defects if he is told about them – unless he should have known about them.

If the landlord fails to repair defects that he knew or ought to have known about, he will usually be in breach of the lease. The tenant can claim damages for any loss suffered as a result.

The common law does not require the landlord to make good any defect caused by the tenant's own negligence, the actions of a third party, or an exceptional and unexpected occurrence – such as an extremely severe storm.

The 'implied repairs provision' Parliament has added to the protection given by the common law. Under section 8 of the Housing (Scotland) Act 1966, every lease of a house – private or public – automatically contains an 'implied repairs provision', so long as the lease was granted after July 3, 1962 and is for a period of less than 7 years (most leases are).

Under the implied repairs provision, the landlord must maintain:

1. The structure and exterior of the house – including windows, doors, drains, gutters and external pipes.

2. Water, gas and electricity installations – for example, pipes and wiring. Burst water pipes are therefore the landlord's responsibility (unless caused through the fault of the tenant).

3. Sanitary installations – for instance, basins, sinks, baths and toilets.

4. Installations for space heating or for heating water.

WHEN THE LIGHTS GO OUT

The tenant should report major defects to the landlord, who is usually responsible for dealing with them. But minor repairs are normally the tenant's own responsibility.

The landlord is not liable for defects that he does not know about. Nor is he responsible – except under the terms of the lease – for any fittings or fixtures for making use of the supply of water, gas or electricity. This would include, for example, taps, tap washers, electrical switches, and gas and electricity appliances.

The implied repairs provision does not apply where repairs are necessary because of the tenant's failure to use the premises in a proper manner. Nor does it require a landlord to repair or rebuild property destroyed or damaged by fire, storm, flood or other 'inevitable accident'. However, unlike the common law (above) it does apply where repairs are necessary because of damage caused by third parties – for example, where windows are broken by vandals.

The implied repairs provision cannot be excluded or altered by any term in the lease – except on application to the sheriff court. Any term in a lease which requires the tenant to carry out or pay for the repairs covered by the provision is invalid.

A landlord's duty of care Under the

Occupiers' Liability (Scotland) Act 1960, a landlord who is responsible for maintaining a house must take reasonable care to ensure that *anyone* on the premises does not suffer injury or damage through his failure to maintain them. If the landlord does not take reasonable care, and injury or damage results, he can be sued for compensation.

Making improvements

If your tenancy is protected by the Rent (Scotland) Act, you cannot carry out improvements (except interior decoration) without your landlord's written consent, unless your lease allows you to do so.

If your landlord is a district or islands council, the Scottish Special Housing Association, a new town corporation, a registered housing association or a housing co-operative, you are never entitled to carry out any improvements (except interior decoration) unless you have your landlord's written consent.

In both cases, the landlord must not withhold consent unreasonably. If you are refused consent, you have the right to apply to the sheriff for an order requiring the landlord to consent. If consent is given, but the landlord imposes conditions which you think are unreasonable, you can ask the sheriff to strike them out.

Increasing the rent If the landlord of a house for which a fair rent is registered carries out any improvements to the house, he can apply to the rent officer to have a new rent registered, even although 3 years have not expired since the original rent was registered. Improvements, or replacements of fittings and fixtures, carried out by the tenant cannot usually be taken into account by a rent officer when deciding what the fair rent should be.

A public sector landlord cannot increase the rent because of improvements made by a tenant. When the tenancy ends, the landlord can pay compensation to the tenant to take account of the amount by which the value of the house has been increased because of the improvements. But there is no *right* to compensation.

Sub-letting rented property

Under common law, a tenant who has rented an unfurnished house or flat has the right to sub-let all or part of it to someone else. The tenant of furnished accommodation has no such right. However, the common law right to sub-let can be removed by a ban on sub-letting contained in the lease itself – most leases contain such a prohibition.

A tenant who lawfully sub-lets becomes the landlord to the sub-tenant – but he remains the tenant of the original landlord. The law treats a sub-tenant like any other tenant. If he rents privately, he may be entitled to security of tenure and to a fair rent. *See:* EVICTION; RENT PROTECTION

Public sector sub-tenants Tenants of district and islands councils, the Scottish Special Housing Association, New Town Development Corporations, registered housing associations and housing co-operatives cannot sub-let – or take in lodgers – unless they obtain their landlord's consent. This must not be unreasonably withheld.

If your landlord refuses to consent to sub-letting or lodgers, you can apply to the sheriff for an order requiring it to consent. You cannot apply to the sheriff if the landlord refuses consent because it considers that you intend to charge an unreasonable rent or to ask for an illegal payment in addition to the rent. *See:* KEY MONEY

A sub-tenant in the public sector has no security of tenure and no right to have a fair rent registered. However the tenant must inform the landlord of any proposed increase in the rent payable by a sub-tenant. No increase can be made if the landlord objects.

Illegal sub-letting If a tenant sub-lets when he has no legal right to do so, his landlord may apply to the sheriff court for an EVICTION order against the tenant. The sheriff will grant the order if he thinks it would be reasonable to do so.

If a sub-let is illegal, the sub-tenant has no right to remain in the house if the landlord wishes him to leave. He is in the same position as a SQUATTER and could be charged with criminal TRESPASS if he refused to go.

The landlord is entitled to use reasonable force to evict an illegal sub-tenant, but the safest method may be to obtain a court order requiring him to leave. *See:* SUB-TENANCY

Ending a tenancy

A tenant who wishes to leave must give the landlord at least 28 days' written notice of removal, to end on the day the lease expires. His lease may require him to give a longer period of notice than this. Notice that is verbal or of less than 28 days is invalid and will not end the tenancy.

If a private landlord wants to remove a tenant, he must serve on the tenant a written NOTICE TO QUIT giving at least 28 days' notice. The lease may require him to give a longer period of notice.

A notice to quit is invalid and cannot end the tenancy if:

- It is not in writing.
- It gives the tenant less than 28 days'

THE TENANT'S WIFE WHO WAS BURNED

A landlord must take reasonable care to keep rented premises in good repair. If he does not do so, and someone is injured as a result, he may have to pay substantial damages.

Mrs Lamb was the wife of a tenant of Glasgow District Council. She suffered from epilepsy.

One day, during an epileptic fit, she fell and hit the front of a 'sofono' coal fire. The fire, which was not properly attached to the grate, tipped forward and spilled burning coal on to her. She was severely burned.

Mrs Lamb sued Glasgow District Council for damages. She claimed that the council was in breach of its duty under the Occupiers' Liability (Scotland) Act 1960 to take reasonable care so that persons like herself did not suffer injury. The council argued that they had no duty to inspect Mrs Lamb's flat or to repair defects unless they knew about them. In their view they had taken all reasonable steps to prevent injury.

DECISION

The court decided that the council was liable.

It had a duty to inspect the premises before Mr and Mrs Lamb took occupation, but no inspection had taken place. The judge considered that any reasonable inspection would have revealed the defective fire.

Mrs Lamb was awarded almost £11,000 in damages.

notice to quit the premises.

- It does not expire on the day the lease expires.
- It does not give the tenant certain information about his legal rights. *See:* EVICTION

A landlord cannot obtain an eviction order unless he has given the tenant a valid notice to quit.

If nothing is said about notice in the lease, and the tenancy is for 4 months or less, the notice required is at least one third of that period or 28 days, whichever is longer; if it is for between 4 months and a year, at least 40 days' notice must be given. If the lease is for a year or more, and ends on Whitsunday (May 28) or Martinmas (November 28), notice must be given at least 40 days before May 15 (if Whitsunday) or November 11 (if Martinmas).

Public sector tenancies A different procedure applies where the landlord who wishes to evict is a district or islands council, the Scottish Special Housing Association, a New Town Development Corporation, a registered housing association or a housing co-operative. The landlord serves, not a notice to quit, but a notice of possession.

This notice does not bring the tenancy to an end, but tells the tenant the date after which the landlord may start eviction proceedings. (The procedure which applies to council tenancies applies to all these landlords. *See:* COUNCIL TENANCY)

Evicting a tenant

No tenant can be evicted without a court order, even although a notice to quit has expired. A landlord who evicts a tenant without such an order, or harasses a tenant to force him to leave, is guilty of an offence. *See:* HARASSMENT

A private tenant who has security of tenure under the Rent (Scotland) Act may be entitled to remain in his home. But if he has no security of tenure, the sheriff must grant the landlord an eviction order if he applies for one – although he can delay the date when it is to take effect. *See:* EVICTION

Council and other public sector tenants who have security of tenure under the Tenants' Rights (Scotland) Act 1980 may also be entitled to remain in their homes. But if such a tenant has no security of tenure, the sheriff must grant the landlord an eviction order – though again he can delay the date when it takes effect. *See:* COUNCIL TENANCY

LAUNDRY

The code that guarantees care of your belongings

You are entitled to expect a commercial laundry or dry-cleaner to take reasonable care of articles that it accepts, and to use skill in cleaning and pressing them. A laundry is not liable for loss or damage if it can show that it took reasonable precautions. A legal claim for compensation can succeed only if it was negligent.

But the Association of British Launderers and Cleaners, to which more than 75 per cent of launderers and dry cleaners belong offers further safeguards that should make legal action unnecessary. Its code of practice, drawn up in consultation with the Office of Fair Trading, requires members:

- Not to use any EXEMPTION CLAUSE to avoid legal liability.
- To reprocess on request, free of charge, any article that is unsatisfactorily processed due to the laundry's fault.
- To pay fair compensation for loss or damage caused by negligence, fire or housebreaking.
- To display prices for processing standard articles.
- To complete orders by the time stated, unless prevented by exceptional circumstances.

High-value items Although the code forbids exemption clauses, Association members may ask a customer to state the value of an expensive or unusual item, and quote a special price.

Owner's risk If a launderer or cleaner expects damage to an article no matter how much care is taken, he can warn the customer that it is accepted only at the owner's risk. That stipulation should be printed or written on the customer's receipt. It does not relieve the laundry from liability if it is negligent.

Fire and housebreaking A laundry is not liable to pay compensation for loss or damage from fire or housebreaking, if it was not itself negligent. But under the Association's code, members pay compensation to any customer who is not covered by his own insurance.

When there is a dispute

The Association's Customer Advisory Service helps to settle disputes between customers and its members. Its address is Lancaster Gate House, 319 Pinner Road, Harrow, Middlesex HA1 4HX. Independent laboratory tests to resolve technical questions are arranged without charge, provided that customers agree to abide by the findings.

Faulty goods Provided that it is not negligent, a laundry is not liable for damage caused by faulty manufacture – for example, colours that run – unless it could reasonably have been aware of it before starting work. Nor is it liable if goods are labelled with the wrong cleaning instructions, or easily damaged through misuse by the customer.

Assessing compensation If an article is lost, or damaged beyond repair, you do not have a right to the full cost of replacement. Previous wear and tear is taken into account – so if an article is lost halfway through its assumed useful life, a customer is entitled to only half the cost of replacing it.

Dealing with launderettes

Launderette companies and other operators of self-service washing or dry-cleaning machines are legally responsible for the safety and efficiency of their equipment, and for the reliability of their staff.

They must conduct their business with reasonable care – with the degree of supervision, maintenance and skill that a reasonable person could expect.

A customer who can show that a launderette proprietor failed in that duty, and that his negligence caused personal injury or damage to clothing, is entitled to compensation. If a claim is rejected, the proprietor can be sued.

Contract terms saying that the proprietor accepts no liability protect the proprietor only if they are fair and reasonable. They can never protect him if his negligence caused personal injury.

'Service' washing If a customer pays a special charge and leaves clothing to be attended to by staff, he or she is entitled to expect a reasonable standard of cleaning as well as reasonable care.

Compensation can be claimed for loss or damage if the attendant is negligent – but not if the customer fails to warn that an article needs special care.

LAW SOCIETY OF SCOTLAND

The body which controls solicitors

The Law Society of Scotland was set up by Parliament in 1949. Its main objects are to promote the interests of the solicitors' profession in Scotland and the interests of the public in relation to that profession. So it is both a professional association and a watch-dog over its members.

All solicitors practising law in Scotland must be members and must hold a current practising certificate issued annually by the Society. Before admission they must satisfy educational and other standards set by the Society.

The Society lays down rules for its members affecting such matters as the keeping of accounts. The money of clients, for example, must be kept in a separate account (or accounts) from those of the firm. Solicitors are not allowed to form partnerships or share fees with anyone except other solicitors.

The Law Society has a Complaints Department at its offices at 26 Drumsheugh Gardens, Edinburgh. If you have a complaint against a solicitor, you should address it in writing to the Complaints Department. They will first send a copy of your letter to the solicitor and ask for his comments. If the complaint seems to be of a kind which the Society can deal with, and is not trivial, it may be passed on to one of two Complaints Committees, one for court matters and the other for non-court matters.

Complaints may be about such matters as delay, not answering letters or excessive fees. The Committee will try to bring about an acceptable resolution of the client's grievance. But if the complaint involves evidence of something more than minor professional misconduct, other courses of action may be taken:

- Where there is evidence of professional negligence. This may give rise to a claim for DAMAGES against the solicitor (who will be insured against such claims). The Law Society keeps a list of solicitors who are prepared to take proceedings against other solicitors.
- Where there is evidence of dishonesty. The evidence will then be referred by the Society or the complainer to the police or procurator-fiscal. Members of the Society subscribe to a Guarantee Fund, which reimburses those who have suffered by a solicitor's dishonesty.
- Where there is evidence of serious or persistent professional misconduct. Then the Society will prosecute its member before the Scottish Solicitors' Discipline Tribunal. After inquiry it has power to strike the solicitor's name off the roll, suspend him from practice for a period, fine him up to £2,500 or censure him. The solicitor can appeal to the Court of Session.

There is a Lay Observer who will look into any grievance which a member of the public may have over the Law Society's handling of his complaint. Her address is 20 Walker Street, Edinburgh.

The Law Society of Scotland also administers the system of LEGAL AID and LEGAL ADVICE in Scotland.

LAY-OFF

When an employee's job is temporarily cut back

An employer facing a temporary decline in business – for example, because a strike has interrupted the supply of essential materials – may not be able to provide the usual amount of work for his employees. If he cannot afford to pay full wages while work is slack, he may decide to lay off, or suspend, some or all of his employees. Usually that means that he tells them not to report for duty until asked to do so and he reduces or stops their pay during their enforced absence.

Alternatively, he may introduce short-time, cutting the number of hours that employees are required to work each week and therefore the amount he must pay them.

When lay-offs and short-time are unlawful

An employer is not entitled to lay off an employee, or put him on short-time, unless the arrangement is provided for in the EMPLOYMENT CONTRACT. If it is not, an employee who is laid off or put on short-time can leave his job, claim 'constructive' dismissal and make an UNFAIR DISMISSAL claim to an industrial tribunal.

If the claim is upheld, the tribunal will normally make an award of compensation either for UNFAIR DISMISSAL or for REDUNDANCY, depending on the circumstances. Compensation for unfair dismissal, which can normally be claimed by full-time employees after they have completed 1 year's service with their employer, tends to be higher than that for redundancy, which can be claimed only after 2 years' service. However, unfair dismissal compensation can be reduced because of conduct – for example, leaving a job too hastily. Redundancy pay cannot be.

An employee who is laid off or put on short-time and who is eligible for both types of award should mention both on his tribunal application. The tribunal will then decide which is appropriate.

A PART-TIME WORKER may not be able to claim unfair dismissal or redundancy. However, if he is paid off or put on short-time in breach of his contract he can leave and sue his employer for WRONGFUL DISMISSAL to recover any earnings to which he is entitled.

When a claim is too hasty

An employee who leaves when he is told he is to be laid off or put on short-time for only a day or two may be unable to obtain compensation for unfair dismissal, even though the arrangement is not provided for in his contract of employment.

Tribunals consider whether the person making a claim has acted reasonably in the circumstances. Someone who leaves because of the loss of a few hours' earnings might well be held to have left without sufficient justification.

However, if the lay-off or short-time working lasts, or is likely to last, for several weeks, or if the employer persistently introduces 1 or 2-day lay-offs or short-time, the employee would probably succeed in his claim.

When the contract is not clear

An employment contract need not usually be in writing. If it is not, or if some details are missing, the terms can be agreed orally between employer and employee, or be derived from a relevant collective agreement or from custom and practice in the company or industry.

However, an employer will find it difficult to prove his right to lay employees off or to put them on short-time unless there is a clear written provision on the subject, either in a written state-

WHEN LAY-OFFS AND SHORT-TIME ARE PROVIDED FOR IN THE CONTRACT

Even if an employee's contract requires him to accept being laid off or put on short-time, he may still have the right to apply for a redundancy payment, though not to claim unfair dismissal.

He may do so if, because of a shortage of work:

- He has been laid off for at least 4 consecutive weeks or for at least 6 weeks during the previous 13 and has not been paid anything other than the statutory guaranteed payments.
- He has been on short-time for a least 4 consecutive weeks or for at least 6 weeks during the previous 13, and his weekly earnings have been less than half the normal amount.

Before making an application, the employee must tell his employer in writing, no later than 4 weeks after the end of the period of short-time or lay-off, that he intends to do so. He must also give at least 1 week's NOTICE – or longer if that is required by the contract – that he intends to leave.

Once an employee has done this, he can make a written application to his employer for a redundancy payment. However, the employer can contest the claim if he believes that normal working is likely to be resumed soon.

To do so, he must give written notice to the employee, within 7 days of receiving notice of his intended redundancy claim, that there is a reasonable expectation that, within the next 4 weeks, the employee would start a period of at least 13 weeks' full employment.

The claim can then be decided only by an industrial tribunal.

ment containing the terms of the employment contract given to all workers or in a collective agreement covering his company. *See:* EMPLOYMENT CONTRACT

In some occupations there is an accepted custom of not paying workers who cannot do their jobs because of bad weather. But in many others the procedure, though common, is not sufficiently established to count as custom.

Accepting a voluntary cut in earnings

Many employees accept being laid off or put on short-time when there is no requirement in their contract to do so, in the hope that business will soon pick up and their full earnings will be restored.

They do not necessarily forfeit their right to make a claim against their employer if the lay-off or short-time is extended beyond the period originally agreed.

For example, an employee may accept that he is to be laid off for 3 or 4 weeks. If he is then told that there will be no work for him for 3 or 4 weeks more, he can still succeed in a claim for redundancy or unfair dismissal.

An employee may agree to be laid off or put on short-time on one occasion, but refuse on another, without losing his right to make a claim. However, if he accepts more than once or twice, his employer may argue that the arrangement has thereby become an implied condition of the contract.

To safeguard his rights, an employee who agrees to a lay-off or short-time should write to his employer (keeping a copy of the letter) stating that, while he accepts the decision for a specified period, he does so reluctantly and it is not a condition of his contract.

Guaranteed work agreements

More than half of Britain's manual workers and many employees in white-collar jobs are covered by guaranteed work agreements, known as GWAs, negotiated between trade unions and employers.

GWAs define the circumstances in which employees may be laid off or put on short-time and stipulate the minimum weekly wages that must be paid until full earnings are restored.

Once a GWA has been negotiated through collective bargaining, it normally becomes part of the individual employment contract of workers in the company or sector concerned.

Most GWAs specify a minimum qualifying period – for example, 4 weeks' employment – before a worker becomes covered by its provisions. Most also allow the employer to insist that workers must carry out alternative jobs if they are available.

Being paid during lay-offs

A worker who has been in his job for at least 4 weeks may be entitled to payment from his employer if he is laid off, even though there is no guaranteed work agreement.

Under the Employment Protection (Consolidation) Act 1978, employers must normally make guarantee payments to employees who lose at least 1 full day's work through being laid off.

To qualify, the employee must have been laid off either:

- Because of a reduction in the employer's demand for the type of work the employee normally does; or
- Because some other occurrence – for example, a strike at a supplier – has affected the business.

Employees laid off because of an industrial dispute involving other mem-

WHEN NO RIGHT TO LAY OFF WAS ESTABLISHED

A court or tribunal will not be prepared to hold that an employer has the right to lay off an employee without pay unless there is sufficient evidence that this is part of the employment contract.

Mr McCarthy worked in Burroughs Machines' assembly factory at Strathleven. Because of industrial action at another factory owned by Burroughs, Mr McCarthy was laid off without pay.

After 4 weeks he wrote to Burroughs and claimed a redundancy payment. The firm rejected his claim on the ground that they had not dismissed him but had lawfully laid him off.

Mr McCarthy applied to an industrial tribunal for a redundancy payment.

DECISION

The tribunal decided that Mr McCarthy had been dismissed and that the dismissal was due to redundancy. There was nothing in Mr McCarthy's contract which gave Burroughs the right to lay him off without pay.

There had been three occasions in the previous 6 years when lay-offs had occurred but that was not sufficient evidence of a right to lay off.

bers of their employer's staff, or staff in an associated company, are not eligible for the payment. Nor are employees who unreasonably refuse suitable alternative work.

Also ineligible to receive a guarantee payment are part-time workers, those who normally work outside Great Britain, members of the police and armed forces, dock workers and share fishermen. *See:* EMPLOYMENT PROTECTION

How much can you get?

An eligible employee is entitled to a guarantee payment for up to 5 days in any period of 3 months.

The basic entitlement is normally daily pay up to a maximum of £10 a day (in 1984), to a total of 20 × £10 a year, or £200.

There are complicated rules for calculating hourly and daily pay rates from the basic working week and customary overtime.

Example: Ann Evans is a machinist. She earns £1.50 an hour for a basic 42 hour week worked over 5 days. She also works 5 hours' overtime each week, at £2.50 per hour.

Basic and overtime hours and payments are added together to obtain the hourly rate used to establish guarantee pay:

$$\frac{(£1.50 \times 42 \text{ hours}) + (£2.50 \times 5 \text{ hours})}{42 \text{ hours} + 5 \text{ hours}}$$
$$= \frac{£63 + £12.50}{47} = £1.61 \text{ hourly rate}$$

To establish the length of Ann's working day, her basic and overtime hours are added together and divided by the number of days she works per week:

$$\frac{42+5}{5} = 9.4 \text{ hours per day}$$

Her daily rate, for the purpose of the scheme, is therefore the hourly rate multiplied by the length of the working day:

$$£1.61 \times 9.4 = £15.13 \text{ per day}$$

However, as the scheme has a ceiling of £10 per day, that is the amount to which she is entitled.

THE WORKER WHO REFUSED TO DO HIS OLD JOB

An employee who is laid off is not entitled to a guarantee payment under the Employment Protection (Consolidation) Act 1978 if he unreasonably refuses an offer of suitable alternative work from his employer.

Mr Purdy was a coach trimmer. Business was slack, and as an alternative to being laid off he was offered work in the finishing shop, where he had previously been given a job for 5 months because other employment was not available.

He refused and claimed a guarantee payment from his employer through an industrial tribunal.

DECISION

Mr Purdy was not entitled to the payment, because his refusal to do another job was unreasonable. Although the job offered was outside his normal trade, it was suitable in the circumstances.

THE FOREMAN WHO FOUND ANOTHER JOB

If an employee is laid off for several weeks and finds another job in that time, he does not forfeit his right to claim compensation from his former employer.

Mr Smith was a foreman. Because of a shortage of work, his employers told him he was to be laid off, initially for 2 or 3 weeks and perhaps for up to 7 weeks. He left the job, found another within a fortnight and then sought a redundancy payment from his former employers.

DECISION

Mr Smith was entitled to a redundancy payment. His employment contract did not provide for him to be laid off and, as he had not agreed to the arrangement, he was within his rights to regard himself as having been dismissed.

Claiming guarantee pay

Under the employment protection rules, an employer is responsible for making guarantee payments to eligible workers. He cannot recover the cost from the state.

If the employer does not make a payment, eligible employees can complain to an industrial tribunal up to 3 months after the date on which the money should have been received. The tribunal can order the employer to pay, though it cannot fine him for not having done so.

Claiming social security benefits

Someone who is laid off or put on short-time may be entitled to claim UNEMPLOYMENT BENEFIT, provided that he meets the qualifying conditions. If he is laid off, he becomes entitled to benefit after he has been unemployed for 3 days. If he is on short-time, he must suffer at least 2 days of unemployment in a period of 6 consecutive days (excluding Sundays and holidays). He becomes entitled to benefit after 3 days of unemployment.

Unemployment benefit is not payable for any days for which guarantee payments are received, nor if the lay-off is the result of a STRIKE in which the employee is involved.

Few workers on short-time are eligible for SUPPLEMENTARY BENEFIT, but those who are laid off may meet the qualifying conditions.

LEARNER DRIVER

Restrictions on motorists who have no full licence

A learner driver who has not passed the Department of Transport driving test holds only a provisional driving licence and must display an L-plate on the front and back of any car he drives. He must be accompanied, when he drives, by a qualified driver who holds a licence valid for the type of vehicle being driven. He cannot drive on a motorway until he has a full licence.

A learner motor cyclist does not have to carry a qualified person, but he must have L-plates. If a learner motor cyclist does carry a passenger, the passenger must have a full licence and be qualified to ride a motor cycle. A learner must not ride a motor cycle of more than 125 cc.

L-plates can be bought at most motor accessory shops or they can be home-made, provided that they conform to the regulations – a red letter 'L' measuring 4 × 3½ × 1½in. on a white background 7 in. square.

Always remove or cover L-plates when a qualified driver is at the wheel, as recommended in the Highway Code. It is not, however, an offence to fail to do this.

What a supervisor must do

If you are a qualified driver overseeing a learner you must try to prevent him from 'acting unskilfully or carelessly'. If your driver commits an offence you may be guilty of AIDING AND ABETTING if you are encouraging him in unsafe manoeuvring.

You may be prosecuted for careless driving yourself if you are in control, or partly in control – for example, if the vehicle has dual controls – and you fail to take proper precautions and preventive action.

The same standard of care applies to a learner driver as to a qualified driver. *See:* CARELESS DRIVING

Taking the driving test

All applicants for provisional licences are sent a copy of *Your driving test – and how to pass it.* It is sent free when you apply for a provisional licence.

If you pass the test, you are given a certificate of competence and you can drive immediately without L-plates. You are not obliged to apply for a full licence until your provisional licence expires, but you must carry your certificate with your licence.

If you fail the test, you must wait at least a month before taking another test. You can, however, apply for a firm date at once.

LOOK, NO L-PLATES

If you pass your test you can drive immediately without L-plates; you do not need to obtain a full licence first.

LEGAL ADVICE

Sources of advice and help

Britain has no single national policy on the provision of legal services. As a result there are many different official and voluntary agencies which offer legal advice and help. Many provide their services free of charge.

Citizens Advice Bureaux (there are 60 in Scotland) can give advice on practically any legal problem. If their trained advisers cannot answer your problem, the bureaux will either obtain the necessary information from their national office in Edinburgh or fix an appointment for you to see a local solicitor (often at the weekly legal session which is held at most bureaux).

Legal advice centres are staffed by practising or academic lawyers. They provide advice and help and (like Citizens' Advice Bureaux) occasionally represent claimants before tribunals. It is rare for them to be able to undertake court representation.

Trade unions often provide legal services for their members, but usually by referring them to a firm of lawyers retained on a consultancy basis. A union usually provides help with employment problems – for example, accident claims, redundancy claims and entitlement to injury benefits.

Housing advice centres, operated by some local authorities and by independent bodies such as Shelter, specialise in housing matters, such as tenants' rights, eviction, homelessness and housing grants.

Consumer advice centres, run by some local authorities, provide advice on consumer law and tell shoppers their rights.

Many other organisations provide legal advice and occasionally representation on cases which fall within their own field of interest – for example, the Commission for Racial Equality, the Equal Opportunities Commission, Planning Aid, Citizens' Rights Office (welfare problems), Gingerbread (single parent problems), Scottish Women's Aid (battered women), Disablement Income Group and the Scottish Council for Civil Liberties. The AA and the RAC provide legal advice on motoring problems, to their members.

Agencies providing legal advice can be of assistance in three main ways. First, they can advise you whether your problem is one to which there is a legal answer and whether that answer is worth pursuing. Secondly, they can tell you whether there are any lawyers in the local area who are able and willing to handle your kind of problem. Thirdly, they can usually give you an idea whether you are likely to be eligible for the statutory Legal Advice and Assistance and LEGAL AID schemes.

Another way to locate a solicitor in your area who handles your type of case is to look at the Directory of General Services provided by Solicitors, or the Solicitors' Referral List. These are available in public libraries, police stations, Citizens Advice Bureaux, information centres, sheriff courts, social work department offices and some sub-post offices.

These publications indicate the areas of law (for example, matrimonial, employment, consumer or social security) with which each solicitor claims to be familiar. They also reveal whether the solicitor is available outside normal office hours, speaks a foreign language and operates the various legal aid schemes or the £5 scheme.

The £5 scheme

Many of the solicitors who appear in the General Directory or the Referral List have agreed to operate this scheme. Under it they will provide an initial interview to help identify a person's problem and possible answers to it, for a fixed fee of £5. Subsequent interviews are likely to be charged at the normal, higher rate. If you wish to take advantage of this scheme, make this clear when you arrange the interview.

Legal advice and assistance

The Legal Advice and Assistance Scheme, sometimes called the 'pink form' scheme because of the colour of the form that has to be completed, covers the first £50 of a solicitor's fee for legal advice. The scheme permits a solicitor to give immediate advice and assistance, oral or written, on any matter involving Scots law.

Applicants must not be under 16 years of age (though an application can be made on behalf of PUPIL children or a MINOR under the age of 16) and must fall within the financial limits of the scheme. Representation in court proceedings is normally excluded under the scheme, but your solicitor may use it to sit with you in the court or tribunal and advise you what to say.

The financial limits of the Scheme To qualify financially for the scheme an applicant's disposable income and disposable capital must fall within certain limits. These limits are adjusted from time to time to take account of rises in the cost of living.

Disposable capital is the total value of an applicant's assets, excluding the value of his or her home, furniture, clothing, car and tools of trade. If, after deducting the allowances for dependants (in 1984, £200 for the first, £120 for the second and £60 for each other dependant), the applicant's disposable capital exceeds £730, then he or she is ineligible for the scheme.

Disposable income is assessed on an applicant's earnings in the seven days prior to the application. It is the figure left after deducting tax, national insurance and allowances for dependants. In 1984 allowances were:

- £13.73 for each child up to 10 years of age.
- £20.55 for each child of 11–15 years of age.
- £24.75 for each dependant (or child) of 16–17 years of age.
- £32.17 for each dependant of 18 or over.
- £30.68 for a husband or wife.

If your disposable capital is below £730 and you are in receipt of Supplementary Benefit or Family Income Supplement, or your disposable income is less than £49, then you qualify for assistance under the scheme, free of charge.

If your disposable income exceeds £49 but not £55, you will have a contribution of £5 to pay. Thereafter for every £4 by which your disposable income exceeds £55 you will have an extra £4 or £5 contribution to pay. Thus if your disposable income exceeds £75 but not £79 in that week, you will have a contribution of £30 to pay. If your disposable income exceeds £103 then you are ineligible for the scheme.

In assessing disposable capital and disposable income the resources of husband and wife (and of cohabitees in a stable relationship) are added together. This does not apply if the individuals concerned have opposed interests in relation to the problem on which advice is being sought.

How the Scheme operates If you think you may be eligible, you should find a solicitor who operates the scheme. Such solicitors are identified in the Directory of General Services or the Solicitors' Referral List.

Usually the solicitor will advise you in his or her office, but the advice may be given elsewhere, for example at an applicant's home (if he or she is disabled or infirm), at a hospital bedside, in a police station or in the precincts of a court. Alternatively, if you have good reason you may authorise an adult to attend the solicitor's office and apply for assistance on your behalf.

The solicitor will complete the pink form for you. If you are eligible, he or she will ask you to sign the form and pay any contribution that may be due. (Contributions can be paid by instalment if the solicitor agrees.)

Once the solicitor has given you £50 worth of advice, he or she will usually apply for an extension in order to be permitted to give you further advice. If the application is successful you will not have to pay another contribution. If it is not, you will have to pay for any additional fees incurred.

If you recover money or property as a result of assistance received under the scheme, this may have to be used to cover all or part of your solicitor's fees. This provision is sometimes known as the 'statutory charge'. It means that your solicitor's fees (including VAT) are met in the first place from any expenses paid by your opponent, secondly from your contributions (if any), thirdly from any sums recovered and only lastly from the legal aid fund.

The 'statutory charge' does not apply to payments of ALIMENT, pensions or most welfare benefits. Moreover, if your solicitor considers that payment of his or her fees out of any property recovered would be impracticable, or would cause grave hardship or distress, he or she may apply for authority not to operate the statutory charge. Many applications of this sort are granted – but not if you have received LEGAL AID as well as Legal Advice and Assistance in relation to your problem.

LEGAL AID

How you can get help to meet the expense of going to court

People involved in civil or criminal cases can often get financial assistance to help pay court expenses and legal fees under the legal aid scheme. Assistance in non-court cases is known as LEGAL ADVICE.

Who qualifies for aid Anyone involved in a court case who believes he or she has insufficient money to pay the LEGAL EXPENSES can apply for legal aid. The rules used for working out whether or not a person qualifies differ depending on whether the case is a civil or a criminal one. (A civil case is a dispute between parties who are seeking to obtain a benefit for themselves. Criminal cases are brought by the state – the Crown – against individuals or bodies who are alleged to have broken the criminal law.)

Legal aid in civil cases

Applicants who wish to obtain legal aid in civil cases must qualify both on financial and on legal grounds.

Making the application To apply for civil legal aid you must find a solicitor who undertakes legal aid work. (Most solicitors' firms operate the civil scheme.) Such solicitors are identified in the Directory of General Services or the Solicitors Referral List. *See:* LEGAL ADVICE

The solicitor will use the £5 scheme or the 'pink form' scheme (see LEGAL ADVICE) to advise you whether it would be worth while to make a legal aid application. If you decide to go ahead, the solicitor will fill out the form on your behalf.

The first part of the form concerns your personal circumstances and your general eligibility for the scheme. The second part is a statement of the financial circumstances of the applicant. Your solicitor will ask you for details of your job, salary, savings, assets and rent

MEETING YOUR LEGAL BILLS

Anyone involved in a court action may be able to receive financial help through the legal aid system for any court expenses or legal fees incurred.

or mortgage payments. If you are married, details of your spouse's financial circumstances will also be required unless you are separated or your spouse has a contrary interest.

Your solicitor will send both parts of the form and a memorandum setting out the details of your case to the appropriate legal aid committee – the local committee (in sheriff court cases) or the Supreme Court committee (in Court of Session cases). That committee will consider whether you qualify for legal aid on legal grounds.

The legal tests

The first requirement is that legal aid must be available for your type of case. Legal aid is not available for proceedings before tribunals – for instance, an INDUSTRIAL TRIBUNAL or social security appeal tribunal. Thus most employment or social security cases are excluded. Nor is it available in actions of DEFAMATION, for election petitions or for a do it yourself DIVORCE.

If legal aid is available for your type of case the committee must still be convinced that the case has a reasonable prospect of success. It must also decide whether it is reasonable that you should be granted legal aid.

Lastly, legal aid is not available to people who could have their legal expenses paid for by someone else. So if you are a member of a trade union which will pay for your case as one of the benefits of membership, you may be refused legal aid.

If your application is turned down on legal grounds, your solicitor can appeal this decision to the Legal Aid Central Committee. There is no further appeal from that Committee's decisions.

The financial tests

Even if you qualify on legal grounds, you must also satisfy certain financial tests.

The income and the capital assets of applicants must fall within certain limits. The assessment of your income and capital is made by the Department of Health and Social Security. You will either receive a form to be returned by post or be asked to attend for interview, so that the financial statement contained in the second part of your application form can be checked. If you have pay slips, bank statements or passbooks to support your original statement, this can be helpful.

If an applicant fails to attend for interview or fails in other ways to assist the DHSS in making its assessment, his or her application may be treated as abandoned.

Disposable income The DHSS firstly assesses how much 'disposable income' the applicant has – that is, the amount of spare cash left over after certain living expenses have been paid. The Department's starting point is the applicant's likely income in the twelve months from the date of the application. (If you are granted legal aid and your means or commitments change substantially during the year, you must tell your solicitor. Your income may then be redetermined by the DHSS.) If you are married your spouse's likely income is added on, unless you are separated or in legal dispute with him or her.

From this overall total are deducted tax, national insurance contributions, reasonable work expenses, rent or mortgage repayments, rates and fixed rate allowances for any dependants. What is left is your disposable income.

If your disposable income exceeds £4,925 (1984 figures) in a year, you will have to pay your own legal expenses. If it is less than £2,050 in a year, or if you are in receipt of Supplementary Benefit or Family Income Supplement, you are eligible (on income grounds) for legal aid to cover the full expense of your action, without having to make a contribution from your income.

If your income is between the two figures you are eligible for legal aid (on income grounds) but you will have to make a contribution yourself – usually a quarter of the amount by which your disposable income exceeds £2,050 a year.

Disposable capital If your income is below £4,925, your capital will also have to fall within certain limits before you are entitled (on financial grounds) to legal aid.

If you are eligible for legal aid on income grounds, the DHSS will then assess your 'disposable capital'. It will first assess the total value of your assets – including savings, investments, valuable jewellery – and the amount you could borrow against an insurance policy. The assets of your spouse are included unless you are separated or have conflicting interests in relation to the matter under dispute.

The value of your house, furniture, clothes, tools or trade equipment and, usually, your car is excluded. So too is the value of any item which is the subject of the dispute.

From this total certain capital allowances may be deducted. These include any debt likely to be repaid from capital in the next 12 months, such as rent arrears. The figure which is left is your disposable capital.

If your disposable capital exceeds £4,500 (1984 figures) you will normally not be eligible for legal aid. However, if your income is very low or the action is likely to be very expensive, the legal aid committee may still grant you legal aid. If your disposable capital is less than £3,000 you are eligible (on capital grounds) for legal aid without a contribution from capital. If it is between £3,000 and £4,500 you will have to pay some part of your legal expenses – probably the amount by which your capital exceeds £3,000.

When you have to make a contribution

The DHSS adds together your contributions (if any) from capital and income. This total is known as your 'maximum contribution'. Unless your circumstances change substantially, leading to a redetermination of your means, you will never have to pay more than your maximum contribution towards the cost of your own legal expenses, even if your case goes to appeal.

If you are offered legal aid with a contribution, this may be below the maximum contribution. The legal aid committee estimates what it considers your case is likely to cost. If this esti-

HOW TO WORK OUT WHETHER YOU ARE ELIGIBLE FOR LEGAL AID IN A CIVIL ACTION

A step-by-step guide to assess means against possible needs within the state scheme

Start here with **CHART NO. 1.** Only if you are eligible under Chart No.1 need you go on to Chart No.2

Income			
Enter your weekly gross income, including that of your spouse (unless you are in dispute with the spouse – e.g. divorce), and any child benefit you receive			£216.88 (**A**)
But you are allowed certain deductions:			
Weekly NI and tax payments		£65.00	
Reasonable work expenses (e.g. cost of travel, tools, trade union dues, childminding)		£6.50	
If you live with your husband or wife and also maintain him or her, you can also deduct an extra £30.68		£30.68	
For each dependent child you can also deduct an amount equal to the current supplementary benefit allowance plus 50%	**Age** / **£** 0–10: 13.73 11–15: 20.55 16–17: 24.75 over 18: 32.17	£13.73	
Weekly rent or mortgage payments + rates		£45.00	
Add up all these deductions			£160.91 (**B**)
This is your **'weekly disposable income'** (Deduct **'B'** from **'A'**)			£55.97 (**C**)
Now multiply **'C'** *by 52*			× 52
This is your **'annual disposable income'**			£2,910.44 (**D**)

If **'D'** exceeds £4,925, you are not eligible for legal aid

If **'D'** is less than £2,050 then you are eligible for legal aid. You will not have to make any contributions towards your legal costs, unless you have more than a certain amount of capital. Turn to Chart 2 to see how much capital you must have before you might be asked to make a contribution

If, **'D'** is between £2,050 and £4,925 you are eligible for legal aid, but you will have to pay a contribution towards the cost. This contribution could be as much as ¼ of the amount by which **'D'** exceeds £2,050. In addition, you may have to pay an extra contribution, depending on the amount of capital you have: turn on to Chart 2, to see how much that could be

Income contribution in the example above is:
£2,910 *minus* £2,050 .... £860.44
Divide £860.44 by 4 .... £215.11

Maximum income contribution **£215.11**

mate – known as your 'actual contribution' – is less than your maximum contribution, you will only be asked to pay the lower figure in the first place.

At the end of the case you may be asked to pay more (but still only up to the level of your maximum contribution). Alternatively, you may even get a refund if the expenses incurred are less

This is **CHART NO. 2.** You should only refer to this chart if you have already been through Chart No. 1

Capital

List the value of all your assets. But you need not include your house, furniture, clothes, tools, trade equipment, or any item which is the subject of the dispute. Unless your car is of exceptional value, it too can be excluded.

Cash savings, bank accounts, national savings certificates, shares, etc	£2,640	
The amount you could borrow on the security of an insurance policy you have	nil	
The fair, realisable, value of your assets (e.g. boat, caravan, antiques).	£770	
If you have a business, write down the amount that you could reasonably take out of it, without impairing its profitability or commercial credit.	nil	
Add up all your assets. This is your **'disposable capital'**		£3,410 **(E)**

If **'E'** exceeds £4,500 the Law Society has a discretionary power to refuse you legal aid

If **'E'** is less than £3,000, then you cannot be expected to use any of your capital to contribute towards your legal fees. Whether or not you will be eligible for legal aid, and whether or not you will have to make a contribution to your legal expenses will depend entirely on the amount of your income. Refer to Chart 1

If **'E'** is between £3,000 and £4,500, the Law Society has a discretionary power to ask you to make a contribution towards your legal fees. This contribution will be the amount by which **'E'** exceeds £3,000

Capital contribution in this example is:

£3,410 *minus* £3,000 .... £410

So maximum contribution is:
Maximum income contribution £215.11
plus
Capital contribution £410.00

Maximum contribution **£625.11**

Two factors are involved in deciding whether the state is prepared to give you financial help in a civil action. A legal aid committee must be satisfied that you have a good case that is worth pursuing. If it does not think so, you can appeal to the legal aid central committee. But you must also qualify financially for legal aid. Such qualification depends both on your income and on any capital assets you have built up, other than your home, furniture, clothes, car (usually) and tools and equipment that are essential to you earning your living.

than the sum which you have already paid.

If the legal aid committee offers you legal aid subject to a high maximum contribution, or turns down your application on financial grounds, in theory it is not possible to appeal. However, in practice the DHSS will supply your solicitor with a breakdown showing its assessment of your means if you ask for one.

If you feel that the DHSS has made a mistake, you can ask for your means to be reassessed by the DHSS. If you are still not happy, you can always refuse to pay the contributions demanded of you. If you do so, you will not be granted legal aid.

If you have accepted an offer of legal aid which is subject to a contribution from capital and income, your capital contribution will normally have to be paid in one sum when legal aid is granted. Contributions from income can usually be paid by instalments at regular intervals over one year, starting from the date of the legal aid award. Once you have paid the first instalment your solicitor will receive a legal aid certificate to cover the work involved in your case.

If you have difficulty in keeping up payment of the instalments for a good reason, such as being off work due to illness, then you may be given more time. But you must ask the legal aid committee for this, otherwise legal aid may be withdrawn.

Even if you have been successful in your action and expenses have been awarded against the other side, you must continue paying the outstanding contributions until the legal aid committee authorises you to stop. (The legal aid regulations require this so that there is no loss to the legal aid fund should the other party fail to pay the expenses awarded against him or her.)

When a limited certificate is granted

Sometimes the aid granted in civil cases will be a 'limited certificate', which means that the solicitor is authorised to go only to a certain stage in the action – to obtain a medical report or counsel's advice, for example.

When that stage is reached, the legal aid committee looks again at the case to see if the provision of more legal aid is justified.

Emergency legal aid

Normally it will take up to two months, and sometimes longer, for your legal aid application to be processed. But where there is a real emergency – for instance, a wife is being threatened with assault or the removal of her child by her husband – it is possible to apply for emergency legal aid. If the legal grounds of your case are sufficient, you can be granted emergency legal aid in 48 hours or less.

There is no means test in such applications. However, a full legal aid application must accompany the emergency application and if you are eventually refused legal aid on financial grounds, you will be required to pay for any expense incurred under the emergency legal aid certificate.

The withdrawal of legal aid

If you fail to maintain your instalment payments without good reason, your legal aid certificate may be suspended or discharged. Legal aid may also be withdrawn if the legal aid committee considers that it is unreasonable that you should continue to receive it. This usually occurs where a client has failed to respond to communications from his or her solicitor or from the DHSS.

When a civil legal aid case comes to an end

The general rule in civil cases is that the loser pays the winner's expenses, as well as his or her own lawyer's fees and expenses. *See:* LEGAL EXPENSES

However, the amount paid by a legally aided loser towards his or her own legal expenses is limited to his or her 'maximum contribution'. But he or she may still have to pay something towards the winner's expenses. On application to the court this liability to pay the winner's expenses may be modified to the level of the loser's maximum contribution and in some cases is reduced to nothing.

If the legally aided person wins, but the losing party does not pay the winner's expenses, then the winner's contributions and any assets recovered in the action may be retained by the legal aid authorities.

Legal expenses insurance

If you are likely to be ineligible for legal aid, it is possible to take out a legal expenses insurance policy to guard against the risk of being involved in certain types of legal action. Ask your solicitor about this.

Legal aid in criminal cases

Legal aid in criminal cases takes three forms. Advice under the 'pink form' scheme (see LEGAL ADVICE), the duty solicitor scheme, and criminal legal aid.

The duty solicitor scheme The duty scheme is designed to ensure that those most urgently in need of legal help – that is, those people held in custody on a criminal charge – receive that help. At every district and sheriff court there are duty solicitors available to such people on a rota basis.

Under the scheme, every person who has been taken into custody charged with murder, attempted murder or culpable homicide is entitled to be visited and advised by the duty solicitor until the time of his or her JUDICIAL EXAMINATION in the sheriff court. In addition, in all cases where the accused is charged with a serious offence which will be tried by judge and jury under solemn procedure, the duty solicitor can be asked to advise and represent the accused at his or her judicial examination. *See:* CRIMINAL PROCEEDINGS

In less serious cases (summary cases), the duty solicitor will visit and advise accused persons in custody and represent them (if they so wish) at their first appearance in court.

Criminal legal aid If an accused person wishes to plead not guilty and would like to have financial assistance to help pay for the expense of a lawyer, he or she can apply for legal aid. The appropriate form is available from the clerk of the court or from a solicitor who undertakes criminal cases. It is the court, not a legal aid committee, which decides who shall be awarded legal aid.

The tests for granting criminal legal aid The judge has to consider whether the applicant has other rights to (or facilities for) representation – for example, because of membership of a motoring organisation which offers legal representation in such cases to its members.

Secondly, the judge has to consider

whether the financial circumstances of the applicant are such that he or she can afford to meet the expenses of his or her defence without undue hardship. There are considerable variations in the application of this test since its meaning is unclear and judges differ in the thoroughness of their investigation of the applicant's means. (There is no time for an investigation of the applicant's means by the DHSS.)

If the case is a summary case, there is an additional test: the judge must be satisfied that in the circumstances it is in the interests of justice that legal aid should be awarded. The test ensures that legal aid is not available in very minor cases.

Awards of criminal legal aid Over 99% of applications in solemn cases and over 60% of applications in summary cases are granted. If an application is refused there is no appeal against the decision. However, if there is a material change in the applicant's circumstances (financial or otherwise), which affects his or her eligibility, it is possible to make a further application.

If the court grants an application, then the accused person is entitled to the services of a solicitor of his or her choice and, if necessary (and if the legal aid committee approves in sheriff court cases), those of counsel. They will represent the accused person until the conclusion of the case and the accused person will have to pay nothing. Even if the accused person is convicted, there can be no award of expenses against him or her.

Appeals

You can apply for legal aid to appeal in both civil and criminal cases. In civil cases the same rules apply as in the original case. In criminal cases you must be unable to pay for your own appeal and you must satisfy the legal aid committee that you have substantial grounds for raising the appeal and that it is reasonable that you should receive legal aid.

LEGAL EXPENSES

The cost of going to law

Normally, a bill or account from a solicitor for legal services is made up of two elements – outlays and fees.

Outlays are expenses incurred on the client's behalf. For example, if you are buying a house your solicitor has to pay for a Search in the property registers (the LAND REGISTER and the REGISTER OF SASINES), for the costs of recording your new title deed in the property register, and stamp duty, as well as for stationery, postage and telephone calls. He will charge all these outlays to your account.

Fees are the solicitor's charges for handling the case. You will be required to pay VAT at the current rate on these fees, but not on the outlays.

Seeking an estimate

A distinction must be drawn between litigation (court) work and non-court work. Court work done by solicitors (but not advocates) is charged at rates laid down by the courts (and by the Secretary of State in legal aid cases). However, because the duration and outcome of litigation is difficult to predict, so too is its cost. It is generally easier to predict the approximate expense of non-court work, which is usually charged in accordance with the recommended table of fees, or charges, issued by the LAW SOCIETY OF SCOTLAND.

It may be possible to find a solicitor who is willing to offer a binding quotation for what your case will cost, though this is more common where litigation is not involved. Although none of them may be able to give you a precise figure at the outset, it is still worth while telephoning firms for a rough estimate before you decide to engage a solicitor.

However, check that you are comparing like with like. For example, one firm may include VAT in its estimate, while another may itemise those amounts separately later. Even more importantly, one firm may include outlays while the other may not.

It is often useful, particularly if your problem may lead to litigation, to give your solicitor a spending limit and to instruct him that if the expenses of the action look like exceeding this figure, then he should come back to you for authority to continue.

TIMING YOUR BILL

Many solicitors have some means of calculating how much time is spent by themselves and their staff on every client's case.

Payment for non-court work

Non-court work includes buying and selling houses and businesses, drawing up leases and contracts, drafting wills and administering estates. The charges for such work must be fair and reasonable, taking into account the circumstances of the case. What is 'fair and reasonable' depends on:

- The importance of the matter to the client.
- The amount of money or value of property involved.
- How complex or novel the case turns out to be.
- The degree of skill involved.
- How much time it takes.
- The number and importance of any documents involved.
- Where and how the work is done.

In practice, most solicitors use the Law Society's table of fees as a guide to maximum charges. These may be reduced or modified in certain circumstances.

Where property is being transferred, solicitors have hitherto charged for their services in accordance with scale fees approved by the Law Society. However, from January 1, 1985, scale fees on property transfers will be abolished. Different solicitors will then charge different amounts for the same work.

You will save yourself money by asking several solicitors' firms for quotations before deciding which firm to employ. Solicitors are listed in the Yellow Pages and a quotation can easily be obtained by telephone.

Many solicitors have some form of

timekeeping system whereby they record daily the actual time spent on each case they are handling. So where there is no scale fee for the matter in question, solicitors will often charge according to the time spent. The time will be charged for at an hourly rate – in most cases the rate recommended by the Law Society (£40 per hour in 1984).

You may be charged more for a senior partner's time than if your work has been done by an assistant solicitor. Again, if your case involves special difficulties your solicitor can exceed the recommended rates. A solicitor can also come to special arrangements with his client concerning the rates to be charged, provided he does so before doing the work.

When court work is involved

In any civil court case – where one person or company is suing another – the loser is normally ordered to pay the winner's legal expenses as well as his or her own. However, if the winner has turned down a formal offer to settle (called a tender) which was made earlier in the case, and the award made by the court is less than the rejected offer, then the losing party will only have to pay the winner's expenses up to the date of the offer to settle. Moreover, the winner will have to pay the loser's expenses from that date.

There are special rules in divorce cases. The husband is normally required to pay his wife's expenses. But where the ground of the divorce is 2 years' separation with consent, or 5 years' separation, and the case is undefended, couples commonly agree to share the cost of the divorce or to be responsible for their own expenses.

In 'do it yourself' divorce cases it is not necessary to consult a solicitor. The overall expenses normally amount only to around £50. A pursuer receiving legal advice and assistance, supplementary benefit or family income supplement need pay nothing. *See:* DIVORCE

Even when the loser pays, however, he does not have to compensate the winner for all his expenses – known as 'solicitor and client' expenses.

He must pay only those that were 'reasonable for conducting the case in a proper manner' – called 'party and party expenses'.

Any other expenses incurred by the winner's lawyers that were not strictly necessary must be paid by the winner himself. For example, if a Queen's Counsel has been briefed when a less senior advocate would have been enough, or unnecessary diagrams and plans for the scene of a road accident have been prepared, the expenses involved would have to be paid by the winner of the case as 'solicitor and client' expenses.

When a case has been decided and the court orders the loser to pay the winner's expenses, the winner's solicitor sends the loser's solicitor a detailed account of the expenses to be paid. If they cannot agree a figure, the account is then lodged with the Court Auditor) for 'taxation' (scrutiny).

The Auditor will fix a date for a hearing, at which the loser's solicitor makes objections to particular items in the account. The Auditor then decides whether or not these items were reasonably required for the proper conduct of the case and whether they have been charged at the appropriate rate. If either party is dissatisfied with the Auditor's decision, he can appeal.

Rates for court work As with non-court work, the solicitor can make a special charging arrangement with his client before any litigation, allowing him to be paid at more than the normal rate.

The normal rates for solicitors are higher if an action is raised in the Court of Session rather than in the sheriff court. In addition, if the action is raised in the Court of Session, fees to counsel will inevitably be incurred. In the sheriff court this is not necessarily so, and the court must agree that the case justifies the employment of counsel before the fees can be charged to the losing party. If the sheriff decides that counsel is not necessary, the client whose solicitor chose to employ counsel will nevertheless remain responsible for his fees.

If you sue successfully for less than £1,000, you will be awarded your expenses against the loser at a reduced scale. There are further reductions where the sum awarded is less than £250 and even more when it is less than £50.

Legal aid expenses

Pursuers who are legally aided in the action will have been assigned a 'maximum contribution' (the most they can be called on to pay for their own legal expenses) and an 'actual contribution' (what they will be required to pay for the time being). Both figures may be nil. If they are not, the contribution can usually be paid by instalments. *See:* LEGAL AID.

Once a case is completed, the legally aided party's solicitor will submit his account to the Law Society for 'taxation', or scrutiny. The solicitor (and any advocate who has been briefed) will receive only 90 per cent of his taxed fees from the legal aid fund, because it is a legal aid case.

If the pursuer is successful in the action, he will be expected to continue with his 'actual contribution' instalment payments (if any). This is to prevent any loss to the legal aid fund.

A loss to the legal aid fund can arise for the following reasons:

- There is no award of expenses against the defender.
- Even though expenses are awarded against the defender, the defender does not pay them or only pays them by instalments.
- Any award of expenses against the defender will only be for 'party and party' expenses and this may be less than 90 per cent of the 'solicitor and client' expenses of the winner.

Under the legal aid regulations, the Law Society is entitled to make good any loss to the legal aid fund out of:

1. The expenses (if any) paid by the other side;
2. The pursuer's legal aid contribution; and
3. Any assets or damages recovered in the action.

For this reason, any damages or assets recovered by a legally aided pursuer must first be paid to the Law Society.

If the total contributions paid by the pursuer exceed the loss to the fund, then the excess will be repaid to the pursuer. However, if they do not cover the loss to the fund, then the pursuer may be required to pay additional contributions up to the level of his maximum contribution. If this additional sum is still insufficient to meet the loss to the fund, the Law Society can deduct the balance from any damages or assets recovered in the action. (This is sometimes known as the 'statutory charge'.)

If you receive legal aid for a court action which is unsuccessful, the most you can be called on to pay for your own legal expenses is your maximum contribution. If the winner's expenses have been awarded against you then the court can be asked to modify your liability to pay these to such a sum as, in the opinion of the court, it is reasonable for you to pay. In practice this sum will rarely exceed the size of your original maximum contribution and often it is reduced to nothing at all.

This possibility of modification is one of the greatest benefits of legal aid as it makes certain that even if a legally aided party loses he will not be faced with intolerable expenses.

Expenses in criminal cases

In Scotland, unlike England, there is never an award of expenses in criminal cases. Thus, even if an individual is found 'not guilty' he does not recover the expenses of his defence from the prosecution. Equally, if he is found 'guilty' the prosecution cannot recover the expenses of the case from him.

Paying an advocate

Advocates' fees are not fixed, but in legal aid cases there is an 'approved' scale. Usually they are negotiated by the advocates' clerks with the instructing solicitors after the work has been done.

An advocate can sue neither his client nor the solicitor (unless the solicitor has received money to pay the advocate) for non-payment of his fee. But he can make a complaint against the solicitor to the Law Society. In practice, solicitors regard themselves as personally liable for advocates' fees and so (unless the client is legally aided) will ask clients to make payment in advance before instructing an advocate.

Paying a solicitor

Unless you are eligible for legal aid or legal advice and assistance or a solicitor knows you very well, it is likely he will ask you for an advance payment, called money on account, before he agrees to take your case.

When a solicitor's final bill is submitted, it is payable immediately. If you want to pay by instalments, arrange that with the solicitor at the outset. If you do not settle his bill, the solicitor is entitled to retain all the papers relating to your case – which means, for example, that you cannot change solicitors and continue your action. *See:* LIEN

Interest on funds held for clients

Solicitors often hold funds on behalf of their clients – for example, an executry estate, the proceeds of the sale of a client's house or damages which have been recovered in an action. A solicitor will be required to earn interest on those funds if – bearing in mind the sum involved and the length of time for which it will be held – this is reasonable.

As a guideline, the Law Society has stated that if the sum involved is not less than £500 and it is likely to be held for at least 2 months, then it is reasonable that interest should be earned for the client.

If a client is aggrieved that interest has not been paid to him on funds which have been held by his solicitor on his behalf, he is entitled to require the solicitor to contact the Law Society. The Law Society will provide a certificate stating whether or not interest ought to have been earned for the client and, if so, the amount of the interest.

Questioning your bill

A solicitor is not entitled to deduct his fees from money held on his client's behalf unless he has received prior authority from the client to do so. If you think your solicitor has not been 'fair and reasonable' in charging for his work, you should ask him for an explanation of the bill.

If the discussion with your solicitor fails to resolve your doubts, and the bill relates to non-court work, you can ask the Law Society for an informal scrutiny of the bill. This will cost you nothing. However, the Society will only tell you whether the recommended rates have been charged, where such rates exist. If there is no set fee under the Table of Fees for the work in question, the Society will not state whether the fee charged is reasonable.

If you are still not satisfied, or if the bill relates to court work, you can ask for the account to be 'taxed' by the Court Auditor. Since such a taxation will be at your expense it is always worth trying to negotiate an agreed figure with your solicitor in an attempt to avoid the necessity of a taxation. If this fails you can ask a solicitor at a legal advice centre or a Citizens Advice Bureau whether it would be worthwhile to request that the account be taxed.

When a solicitor can sue

In any case, whether it involves court work or not, a solicitor is entitled to sue a client for unpaid fees. However, he cannot obtain a court decree to recover the fees unless he has first had the account taxed by the Court Auditor.

The Auditor will fix a date for the taxation and the client may attend to state his or her position. Once the Auditor has fixed a figure to which the solicitor is entitled, the court will grant judgment for this amount, unless the client has a defence to the action. The usual defence is that the solicitor has not done the work for which he is charging.

LEGAL TENDER

When money must be accepted

Debts and purchases must be paid for in cash of legal tender unless the creditor or seller is willing to accept payment in another form, such as a cheque or postal order.

Bank of England £1 notes (but no other notes) are legal tender in Scotland. Scottish bank notes are not legal tender anywhere, even in Scotland, but none the less they are accepted without question in Scotland and even in parts of England.

Apart from the £1 coin and gold coins, which are legal tender for any amount, the following are legal tender:

- 50p, 25p (crowns) and 20p coins, for payment of amounts up to £10.
- 10p and 5p coins, for payment of amounts up to £5.
- 2p, 1p and ½p coins, for payment of amounts up to 20p.

LEVEL CROSSING

Where a railway line crosses the road

There are three kinds of level crossing in Britain:

- Crossings with gates or barriers which go right across the road, usually operated either by an attendant or by remote control.

● Crossings with half-barriers across the left side of the road, which drop automatically when a train approaches.
● Open level crossings with no gates, barriers or attendant, at which a motorist must look and listen for the approach of a train before proceeding.

There are warning signs before all level crossings, often accompanied by double white lines to prevent overtaking. Motorists should approach a level crossing at moderate speed, keeping a good distance from the car ahead, and cross with care only if there is no train approaching and the road on the other side is clear. Some crossings have flashing red lights, or amber lights and bells, to warn that a train is near. You must stop at these lights, but, if you are already on the crossing when they begin to flash, keep going ahead.

To cross on a red light, or when the gates begin to close or the barriers to descend, is an offence. You could be prosecuted for failure to observe a traffic sign and be disqualified from driving and fined. *See:* RECKLESS DRIVING

LIABILITY INSURANCE

How you can insure against having a claim against you

Businessmen, traders and other employers can take out liability insurance to safeguard themselves against claims for DAMAGES in respect of accidents involving employees or the public:

1. Employer's liability Virtually all private employers are legally obliged to take out insurance to provide at least £2 million cover against claims arising for their legal liability for the death or injury of any employee. The only circumstance in which such cover is not compulsory is when the employee is a close relative or domestic servant. *See:* EMPLOYER'S LIABILITY

Every employer is required to display copies of his insurance certificate in a prominent position at each place of business. The maximum penalty for not doing so is a fine of £500.

2. Public liability A businessman or trader can if he wishes insure against the risk of claims from members of the public – for example, from a customer who slips and injures herself in a shop. *See:* PUBLIC LIABILITY INSURANCE

Many householders' policies also contain a liability cover.

LIBEL AND SLANDER

When writing or speaking too freely can be dangerous

Anyone who accuses or criticises another person to the damage of his character, credit or reputation risks being sued for defamation.

Scots law, unlike English law, does not draw any particular distinction between defamation by the written word – called libel – and defamation by the spoken word – called slander. *See:* DEFAMATION

LICENCE TO OCCUPY

When an occupier does not have tenants' rights

If a person has a right to occupy premises – whether a room or a whole house – to the exclusion of others, and pays rent, he may be treated by the law as a tenant. *See:* LANDLORD AND TENANT

However, a person who has the exclusive use of premises will not be treated as a tenant if a court thinks that the parties did not intend to create a tenancy. Instead, that person will be treated as having entered into a contract which confers only a permission, or licence, to occupy the premises. A LODGER, for instance, will not usually be treated as a tenant for this reason.

The parties' intention may not be what it seems. For instance, a person may sign a document describing itself as a 'licence' and making it clear that no tenancy is being granted – only a permission to occupy. But a court, looking at all the circumstances, including the nature of the occupation, may decide that the document is a sham and that in law a tenancy has been granted.

Sharing accommodation If a person has no exclusive right to occupy any accommodation – because it is all shared – and the owner reserves the right to introduce somebody else, he is likely to have merely a permission to occupy. Where the accommodation is all shared, but the owner cannot introduce others, it may be possible to show that there is a JOINT TENANCY

The legal protection available

If a person only has a permission to occupy premises, he is not a protected tenant under the Rent (Scotland) Act. But if he has Part VII protection, he cannot be lawfully evicted without a court order. Unlawful eviction is an offence. *See:* HARASSMENT

Part VII protection A person with a permission to occupy will normally be entitled to limited protection under Part VII of the Rent (Scotland) Act 1984, if the following conditions are met:

1. His rent includes payment for furniture or services – for example, room-cleaning or the supply of heat, light and hot water.

2. He has exclusive use of some accommodation.

3. He does not pay a substantial proportion of his rent for board.

4. He is not occupying the premises for a holiday.

If these conditions are met, the person concerned will have a Part VII contract. He will then be entitled to ask the local rent assessment committee to fix a fair rent if he thinks that his rent is too high. Before doing so, he should check the register of Part VII rents at the local rent registration office (the address is in the telephone directory). *See:* RENT PROTECTION

A person who entered into a Part VII contract before December 1, 1980, may be able to obtain up to 6 months' security of tenure if he is served with a NOTICE TO QUIT. To obtain this, he must first apply to the rent assessment committee for a fair rent to be fixed.

This cannot be done if the contract was entered into after December 1, 1980. But in that case the sheriff can be asked to delay any eviction for up to 3 months. *See:* EVICTION

LICENSED PREMISES

Obtaining permission to sell alcohol

The sale of alcoholic liquor can only be carried on in premises which have been licensed for that purpose by a local licensing board.

Licensing boards A licensing board exists in each district and islands area in

Scotland. Some areas have been divided by their councils into licensing divisions, each with its own licensing board.

A board consists of at least one quarter of the members of the district or islands council, elected by the council. In a licensing division at least one third of the board's members must be councillors – including regional councillors – within the division. This is to ensure local representation.

Boards meet quarterly in January, March, June and October of each year to consider licensing applications.

Liquor licences

A licensing board can grant the following kinds of liquor licence:

Public house licence This authorises the sale of alcoholic liquor in a public house for consumption on or off the premises.

Off-sale licence This authorises the sale of liquor for consumption off the premises for which the licence has been granted.

Hotel licence This gives the same authorisation as a public house licence, except that it applies to hotels.

Restricted hotel licence This authorises the sale of liquor to persons taking table meals in a hotel, and to hotel residents.

Restaurant licence This authorises the sale of liquor to persons taking table meals in the premises.

Refreshment licence This authorises the sale of liquor for consumption on the premises when food and non-alcoholic drink are also on sale.

Entertainment licence This authorises the sale of liquor for consumption in cinemas, theatres, dance halls and clubs.

Off-sales are not allowed on premises with a restricted hotel, restaurant, refreshment or entertainment licence.

A licence can be refused – or not renewed – if the applicant or premises are unsuitable, or if it is likely to cause undue nuisance or a threat to public order or safety. It can also be refused if there are already enough licensed premises in the area. The board must hear any objections from local residents and organisations, or from the chief constable.

A licence lasts for 3 years, but can be suspended during that time. *See:* LIQUOR OFFENCES

Permitted opening hours

If premises have a public house or refreshment licence, the permitted opening hours on weekdays are 11 a.m. to 2.30 p.m. and 5 p.m. to 11 p.m. The opening hours for Sundays are 12.30 p.m. to 2.30 p.m. and 6.30 p.m. to 11 p.m. A separate application must be made for Sunday opening.

If the premises have a hotel, restricted hotel, restaurant or entertainment licence, the permitted opening hours are the same as above. However, no application is required for Sunday opening.

The holder of a public house, hotel, restricted hotel, restaurant or entertainment licence can apply to the local licensing board for an occasional or regular extension of the permitted opening hours. An occasional extension may, for instance, be granted for a public entertainment such as a local festival.

A regular extension can be granted if the licensing boards think it desirable, bearing in mind the social circumstances of the area in which the licensed premises are situated, or the activities taking place in the area. Many public houses in large towns have been granted a regular extension of the permitted hours and are authorised to sell liquor on weekdays (but not Sundays) between 11 a.m. and 11 p.m. *See:* HOTEL; LIQUOR OFFENCES; OFF-SALE LICENCE; PUBLIC HOUSE

LIEN

When goods are held until a customer pays his bill

Lien is the legal term given to the right to retain another person's property until he has paid a debt – such as a HOTEL bill – or performed some other legal obligation. The right often arises when a tradesman has been given another person's property to work on and the work is not paid for.

For example, a watch repairer need not let a customer have his watch back until the repair charge is paid – even though the watch is worth much more than the charge. If no price was agreed beforehand, the repairer can hold the watch until a reasonable price is paid. If there is a dispute over what price is reasonable, a customer should seek legal advice from a solicitor or from a citizens advice bureau.

The lien of a tradesman, or of a company offering a service such as laundry or dry-cleaning, extends only to the item of goods on which money is owed. For example, a garage cannot hold a lien on a car because the owner has not paid for repairs to a motor mower that he has already collected.

The holder of a lien must take reasonable care of the property and is liable if the goods are damaged through his negligence.

Professional lien

Lawyers, accountants, bankers and some other professional men have wider powers of lien. If they are owed money by a client they can hold documents or securities even though they do not relate to services for which the money is due.

LIFE ASSURANCE

How a tax concession cuts premiums

Certain life assurance policies issued prior to March 13, 1984 qualify for tax relief on premiums paid. No tax relief is given in respect of policies issued after that date.

Since 1979 relief has been given by a flat 15 per cent being deducted from the premiums before they are paid over. The person paying must be resident in the United Kingdom, other than in the Channel Islands or in the Isle of Man. Relief is given even if the person paying does not pay any income tax.

Example If your premiums total £500 a year, you are entitled to £75 relief, so you pay only £425.

If you use the endowment method of repaying your house loan, you get tax relief on the life-assurance premiums as well as on the loan interest. *See:* MORTGAGE

Premiums qualify for relief if:

- The policy was issued before March 13, 1984.
- The policy is on the life of the person paying the premiums or of that person's husband or wife.
- The premiums do not total more than a sixth of your income or £1,500 a year,

whichever is the greater. Any excess does not qualify.

- A capital sum is payable at death.
- The sum assured is at least 75 per cent of the total premiums, if death occurred at age 75.
- The paying term is at least 10 years.
- Premiums are payable at intervals of a year or less.

In the case of some small policies, when premiums are paid weekly or monthly, payments are not reduced. Instead, the sum assured is increased.

Example If you take out a policy with premiums based on an assured sum of £1,000, the value of the policy is increased to £1,176.

LIFE SUPPORT

A doctor's duty to try to save a seriously ill person

A seriously ill person can sometimes be saved from death by the use of an artificial respirator, or life-support machine. The decision whether to use one rests entirely with the doctor.

It is also legally his decision alone when a life-support machine is to be switched off. He must, however, be sure that the patient is clinically dead – which means that his brain is no longer functioning. When organs are to be removed for transplant, he may keep the machine operating after death to prevent deterioration.

The doctor normally discusses the decision in advance with the next of kin, but is not legally obliged to do so.

A doctor who switches off a life-support machine while a patient is still alive could face a charge of MURDER. If he fails to carry out the proper tests to establish if life is extinct, or seriously misjudges the results, he could be charged with CULPABLE HOMICIDE. The machine can be switched off only if the tests show beyond doubt that the patient is dead.

When a patient can choose

Most patients ill enough to be placed on a life-support machine are not likely to be conscious. Those who are have an absolute right to refuse treatment by a life-support machine even if this means their certain death.

In some cases, however, a doctor would be entitled to decide that illness has seriously damaged the patient's mental faculties and that the patient shows no sign of being able to understand the situation. In that case, the doctor can couple the patient to a life-support machine, even though the patient has refused.

No right to insist A patient, however ill, has no right to insist on treatment by a life-support machine even if one is available. He can merely ask; the decision whether to use it rests with the doctor.

Where a doctor refuses to use a life-support machine when one is available, and a reasonable doctor would use it, the doctor and his employers can be sued for NEGLIGENCE if the patient subsequently dies.

When relatives are involved

Relatives of a seriously ill person have no more right than the patient to insist that a life-support machine should be used. Nor have they any right to insist that the machine be turned off.

Although relatives cannot prevent a doctor from switching off a life-support machine, he usually informs the next-of-kin when tests indicate that the patient is dead and the life support is to be withdrawn.

If the relatives have good reason to disagree, their only course is to apply to a court for an INTERDICT restraining the doctor from switching off the machine.

In practice, however, after discussion with the relatives, the doctor should normally allow them to get a further opinion, from a doctor of their own choosing.

LIFERENT

Use of property for life only

A person who has the 'liferent' of property – called a liferenter – is entitled to use it for his or her lifetime only. But he or she cannot sell it or leave it by will. When the liferenter dies, the property passes to the person – called the fiar – entitled to it under the will or other deed setting up the liferent.

Where money or investments are liferented, the liferenter only receives the interest or dividends, but cannot touch any of the capital.

A liferenter of a house is usually entitled to live in it or let it, but cannot sell it. Normal repairs, running expenses and rates are paid for by the liferenter. Major repairs – for example, underpinning defective foundations – are borne by the fiar.

If the furniture and other effects in the house are also liferented, they can only be used in that house – they cannot be sold or removed for use elsewhere.

Creating a liferent The commonest method of creating liferents is by will. The will appoints trustees to hold the property. The trustees allow the liferenter to use the property or to receive the income from it during his or her lifetime. On the liferenter's death, the trustees hand it over to the fiar named in the will.

Liferents are useful to provide for a widow(er) and yet make sure that the property eventually passes to the children. A straightforward bequest of the property, rather than a liferent, might allow the widow(er) to fritter it away or leave it to his or her own family. Liferents also prevent children squandering their inheritance or provide for children who are incapable of looking after themselves.

Generally speaking, liferents are not worthwhile unless the property is valuable. Professional trustees charge fees and there are always administrative expenses. Another drawback is that the liferenter may find it difficult to make ends meet on the annual income when the cost of living increases. But the trustees may lend or give some of the capital if the will allows this.

The liferenter and the fiar can agree to bring the liferent to an end. This arrangement usually involves the liferenter receiving a lump sum in return for giving up his or her life interest in the property.

LIQUOR OFFENCES

The penalties for breaking the licensing laws

Alcoholic liquor can be sold only in premises which are licensed for that purpose by a licensing board. There is a licensing board for each district and islands area in Scotland. Some areas, though, are divided into licensing divisions, each of which has a separate licensing board. *See:* LICENSED PREMISES

Boards have the power to make byelaws governing licensed premises – for example, for the purpose of improving the standards of such premises.

Offences by customers Among the offences which can be committed by customers on licensed premises are:

- Drinking after hours – that is, still being in possession of your glass, with drink in it, more than 15 minutes after the last bell. *Maximum penalty* £400 fine.
- Buying alcoholic drink when under 18, or buying it for someone under 18. *Maximum penalty* £400 fine.
- Being in licensed premises while drunk. *Maximum penalty* £50 fine.
- Aiding a drunken person to obtain drink. *Maximum penalty* £400 fine.
- Behaving while drunk in a riotous or disorderly manner in a public house. *Maximum penalty* £400 fine or 60 days' imprisonment, or both.
- Being riotous, quarrelsome or disorderly and refusing to leave a public house when asked to do so. *Maximum penalty* £50 fine.

Offences by publicans Offences that can be committed by publicans include the following:

- Selling alcoholic drink without a licence. *Maximum penalty* £2,000 fine.
- Selling alcoholic drink to, or allowing consumption by, persons under the age of 18. It is a defence that the publican had no reason to suspect that the person was under 18. *Maximum penalty* £400 fine and loss of licence.
- Allowing drinking after hours. *Maximum penalty* £400 fine and loss of licence.
- Supplying alcoholic drink on credit. This does not include accepting payment by credit card for a meal and drink or for liquor sold in premises which have a hotel, restaurant or entertainment licence. *Maximum penalty* £400 fine and loss of licence.
- Selling liquor to someone who is already drunk. *Maximum penalty* £400 fine and loss of licence.
- Allowing illegal gaming in a public house. *Maximum penalty* £400 fine and loss of licence.
- Allowing known thieves or prostitutes to meet or remain in a public house, or allowing stolen goods to be deposited there. *Maximum penalty* £400 fine and loss of licence.
- Permitting a BREACH OF THE PEACE, drunkenness, or riotous or disorderly conduct. *Maximum penalty* £400 fine and loss of licence.
- Employing someone under 18 to work behind the bar. *Maximum penalty* £400 fine and loss of licence.

Certain people – the chief constable, a community council, anyone occupying property in the neighbourhood of licensed premises, any organised church representing residents in the neighbourhood – have the right to complain to a licensing board, requesting that a licence be suspended 'in the public interest'.

The board can order suspension if it considers that the licence-holder is no longer a fit and proper person to hold a licence or that the use of the licensed premises has caused undue public nuisance or a threat to public order or safety.

In considering any complaint, the board will pay attention to any misconduct on the part of the licence-holder – for example, if he breaks a byelaw made by the board – and to any misconduct on the part of customers, either in the premises or the immediate vicinity. *See:* LICENSED PREMISES; OFF-SALE LICENCE; PUBLIC HOUSE

LIST D SCHOOLS

Homes for children in trouble

List D schools are homes where children who are considered to need compulsory care are sent by children's hearings, for an unspecified length of time. Some may be offenders, some school truants and some may have had offences committed against them. Courts may also sentence children found guilty of more serious offences to a fixed period of detention in a List D school. *See:* CHILDREN'S HEARING

While in the school the children receive a normal education, and are involved in activities designed to develop their characters and personalities in acceptable ways. As a reward for good behaviour they are usually allowed to spend some weekends at home, and parents are encouraged to visit the school. A few schools maintain hostels for the over-16s to help them adjust to an unrestricted life.

List D schools are owned and administered by local authorities, the Church of Scotland and the Roman Catholic Church, and by voluntary organisations. But they receive grants for capital expenditure from the government; and local authorities and the government together pay a weekly charge for each child sent by a hearing.

There are about 20 schools. They are classified by age, religion and sex. Children are seldom admitted below the age of 11 and usually are released at or before reaching the age of 16. But the order of a children's hearing, and therefore the detention, may occasionally continue till the child is 18.

If it seems necessary to keep a child in secure conditions in a List D school, a children's hearing must give its approval.

LITTER

When it is unlawful to dispose of rubbish

Whether or not there is a warning notice, it is an offence to throw down, drop or deposit general litter, such as cigarette packets, sweet wrappers, beer cans or bottles, in an open-air public place, such as a street or park. It is not an offence under the Litter Act 1958 to drop litter in a shop or theatre. However, some local authorities have their own byelaws which may make it an offence to litter places other than those covered by the Act.

The maximum penalty for dropping general litter is a fine of £400.

When large items are dumped

It is an offence to dump furniture, mattresses, television sets and dismantled parts of cars or whole cars. *See:* ABANDONED VEHICLE

It does not matter whether the dumping place is public or private property, provided that it is in the open air, and it is not an authorised dump. The maximum penalty is a fine of £1,000 or 3 months' imprisonment, or both.

When someone is prosecuted

A litter prosecution can be started

KEEPING BRITAIN TIDY

It is always an offence to drop litter in any open-air public place – even when no suitable rubbish bins are provided.

under summary CRIMINAL PROCEEDINGS in the sheriff or district court up to 6 months after the offence is committed.

In deciding on a penalty, the court takes into consideration the type and amount of litter deposited, the risk of injury to other people and the need to deter others from dropping litter. For example, a person who drops jagged metal or broken glass will usually have to pay a larger fine than someone who drops a cigarette packet – and someone who drops broken glass in a children's playground will be punished more severely than someone who does so on unused land.

Special rules about poisonous substances

Special laws apply to the dumping of poisonous substances. Under the Control of Pollution Act 1974, for example, it is an offence to dump substances such as cyanide or asbestos except at specially designated dumping places. The maximum penalty is an unlimited fine or 2 years' imprisonment, or both.

LIVING APART

When a married couple have separate homes

A man and woman who are married to each other have a duty to live together. However, this duty is not enforceable by law and there is nothing to prevent them deciding to live separately. Nevertheless, they are still bound by the rights and duties of marriage, particularly that of ALIMENT for each other and for their children.

When a couple decide to live apart, they should make arrangements for CUSTODY OF CHILDREN, aliment and dividing up their property. If they can agree, they should have a written agreement drawn up. They can do this themselves – or even have a verbal agreement – but it is better to have a formal agreement drawn up by a solicitor.

Once the solicitor has done this, the agreement can be registered in the Books of Council and Session (an official register). If this is done, payments of aliment under the agreement can be enforced and are also eligible for tax relief.

The fact that a couple have a registered separation agreement does not prevent either of them going to the court later to ask for different arrangements to be made.

Living apart, whether by agreement or not, is one of the principal grounds for DIVORCE.

The marriage can be ended after 2 years' separation if both partners want a divorce, or after 5 years if one of them opposes it.

A husband or wife who has custody of children and is living apart from his or her partner can claim extra CHILD BENEFIT for a first or only child (£4.05 in 1983–4), provided he or she is not living with another person as husband and wife. *See:* SEPARATION

Dividing the home Where the couple are joint owners of the family home, they can make their own arrangements for dividing it – for example, they may agree to sell the home and split the proceeds equally.

If they cannot agree, either of them can apply to the Court of Session or sheriff court for an order requiring the house to be sold and the proceeds to be shared. This is known as an action for division and sale.

The court can refuse to order division and sale if it would be unreasonable. In reaching its decision, the court looks at all the surrounding circumstances, including the couple's behaviour, their needs and resources, the needs of any children and what alternative accommodation is available.

LOCAL AUTHORITY

How local services are administered

Local authorities – the regional, district and islands councils – are responsible for providing most of the government services which need to be administered locally. They are the successors to a long tradition of local self-government in our cities, towns and rural areas.

Local authorities provide an enormous range of services – from running schools, colleges and libraries, caring for children and the elderly, providing housing and public transport, and maintaining roads, to collecting refuse, controlling building operations, preventing air pollution, and maintaining food standards in shops and restaurants. They are not, however, responsible for such services as social security – administered locally by the Department of Health and Social Security – or health care – the responsibility of area health boards.

The structure of local government

In May, 1975, the structure of Scottish local government was dismantled and the old familiar structure of counties, districts, large and small burghs and counties of cities (Aberdeen, Dundee, Edinburgh and Glasgow) gave way to a new pattern.

In mainland Scotland there are now 9 regions – Borders, Central, Dumfries and Galloway, Fife, Grampian, Highland, Lothian, Strathclyde, and Tayside – and these regions are further divided into 53 districts. Strathclyde, the largest region in population terms, is divided into 19 districts whilst Borders, the smallest, contains 4 districts.

In the islands there are 3 separate local government areas – Orkney, Shetland and the Western Isles – which are not sub-divided into districts.

Each of the regional, district and islands areas has an elected council with certain statutory responsibilities for that area. Although parish councils and community councils have limited functions in England and Wales, there have been no 'grassroots' local authorities at the parish level in Scotland since 1929. Scottish community councils are not local authorities proper and are discussed separately (see below).

Local authority responsibilities

As the islands areas are not subdivided into districts, the islands councils have to provide the full range of local government functions – apart from the fire and police services, which are administered jointly by boards covering the whole of the Highland Region and the 3 islands areas. Otherwise the islands councils perform all the functions which, on the mainland, are divided between the regional and district councils.

Regional councils are responsible for those services which, for the sake of efficiency, usually require a large area or population or large financial resources – for example, education, social work, roads and structure planning. District councils are responsible for important functions such as housing, cleansing and local planning and building control. A full list of local authority responsibilities is set out separately.

Unlike in England, where the pattern changes in the metropolitan areas, there is an almost uniform distribution of functions between regions and districts in Scotland. The only exception is that the libraries, local planning, development control and building control functions (which in most of Scotland are handled by district councils) are regional responsibilities in the Borders, Dumfries and Galloway, and Highland Regions. Following changes made in 1982 there are very few functions which can be performed in the same area by both the regional and district council.

Practically all the important functions of local authorities are conferred on them by general Acts of Parliament, which apply equally to all authorities in Scotland of the same type. Thus the general powers and duties of one regional council are practically identical to those of another.

It is possible, however, for any authority to seek to add to its general powers by asking the Secretary of State for Scotland to issue a Provisional Order containing new powers. Such an Order has to be publicised and, if there are objections, made the subject of a public inquiry. If it is approved by the Secretary of State, the Order passes through Parliament, usually in a formal way, and becomes law.

This procedure has often been used to give an authority the power to deal with a local problem. Although many such powers have recently been extended by the Civic Government (Scotland) Act 1982 to cover the whole of Scotland, it is still available for that purpose. *See:* PARLIAMENTARY BILL

The internal organisation of local authorities

The services which a local authority has to provide are, in law, the responsibility of the full council, consisting of the elected chairman (sometimes called a 'provost' or 'convener') and COUNCILLORS.

Whilst the council itself will make the final decision on matters of great significance (such as the determination of the level of the RATES) it is normally much too large and unwieldy a body and meets too infrequently to run all its services on a day-to-day basis. Instead, all councils take advantage of the powers they have to delegate responsibilities to committees and subcommittees. These make most decisions on behalf of a council.

To a large extent, a council is free to decide the number of committees it has and their composition and responsibilities. Certain committees, however, are required by law.

Regional and islands councils must have an education committee and a social work committee, to which their education and social work functions are

THE GRASS-ROOTS COMMUNITY COUNCILS

Along with the completely new structure of local authorities introduced in 1975, there came another novelty – the creation of community councils.

Some may have seen community councils as a revival of the old parish councils which disappeared in Scotland in 1929, but their function is very different.

Unlike those parish councils, and unlike modern English parish councils and Welsh community councils, Scottish community councils are *not* a third tier of local government; they do not have specific statutory responsibilities; and they do not have the power to levy RATES.

Instead they are intended to act as a 'sounding-board' rather than to have any executive role.

The general purpose of a community council is 'to ascertain, co-ordinate and express to local authorities and other public authorities the view of the community it represents'.

A council also has power, in the interests of the community, to take whatever action appears to it to be expedient and practicable.

Community councils are left very much to their own devices within that remit and no special rules of law apply. They have to find their own resources, although their district or islands council may help them by giving financial assistance, or through the provision of accommodation and other services.

Unlike local authorities proper, community councils were not directly created, nor were their areas of responsibility and powers laid down, by any Act of Parliament. Instead, all district and islands councils were required to draw up for their own areas a scheme providing for the establishment of community councils in due course.

Such schemes, which were prepared subject to periods of public consultation and to eventual approval by the Secretary of State, had to set out the boundaries of community council areas and the rules by which they would be run – for example, those governing elections to and meetings of the councils.

This method of setting up community councils has produced great diversity. Some councils cover large areas and populations; some small. Some are entirely directly elected (in a variety of ways); some have members representing other local organisations. Some are relatively well financed; others are poorer. Some are very active in their communities; some are virtually moribund.

In some parts of the country, community councils have not even got off the ground because of the failure of the prescribed minimum of 20 local electors to apply to have a community council established.

In theory, schemes throughout Scotland provide for a total of over 1,300 councils. Of these, about 1,100 had been set up by 1984.

If you wish to find out whether a community council has been established in your area and, if so, how to get in touch with it, you should contact the office of the Director of Administration of your district or islands council.

normally delegated. The membership of the education committee is partially prescribed, in that it must include people who are not members of the council – at least two teachers from the authority's own schools and three individuals representing the churches. *See:* EDUCATION AUTHORITY

Otherwise, committees are established to undertake responsibility for a particular service (district councils, for example, will normally have a housing committee) or for two or three services combined (many regional councils have a 'protective services' committee for the fire and police functions).

Most committees and sub-committees are made up entirely of councillors. However, with the exception of the finance committee (which must consist of councillors alone), out-

THE SERVICES PROVIDED BY LOCAL AUTHORITIES

How regional and district councils share the burden of providing local services

Each of the three islands areas – Orkney, Shetland and the Western Isles – has a single local authority and there is therefore no difficulty in identifying the council responsible for each service to be provided. With the exception of the fire and police services, which are administered by two joint committees covering all three islands areas as well as the Highland Region, all local authority services are administered by the relevant islands council.

The table below indicates how, on the mainland, the provision of the main services is shared between the regional and district councils.

Service	Provided by	What the service entails
Courts	District council	Providing for administration of district courts.
Education	Regional council	Securing adequate and efficient provision of school and further education.
		Providing associated facilities for social, cultural and recreational activities and for physical education.
		Providing school meals and transport.
		Ensuring school attendance.
		Providing careers advisory service.
Elections	Regional council	Maintaining electoral register.
Environmental Services	Regional council	Providing and maintaining water and sewerage services.
		Controlling animal disease.
		Maintaining consumer protection services (including weights and measures).
	District council	Protecting environmental health by smoke, noise and pest control.
		Collecting refuse.
		Maintaining food standards, hygiene and labelling.
		Maintaining slaughterhouses.
		Enforcing building control.[1]
		Providing and maintaining burial grounds and crematoria.
		Providing public conveniences.
		Providing allotments.
Fire and Police	Regional council[2]	Providing an equipped and trained fire brigade and advising on fire prevention.
		Providing for the equipment of the police force and appointing its senior officers.
		Arranging for civil defence.

Housing	District council	Providing, maintaining and selling council houses.
		Managing council houses and determining rents.
		Administering housing benefits (rent rebates and allowances and rate rebates).
		Securing the improvement, repair or demolition of substandard housing.
		Providing grants and loans for the purchase, improvement and repair of houses.
		Providing housing for the homeless.
Industrial Promotion	Regional and district council	Taking measures to establish and develop industry.
Leisure Services	District council	Providing and maintaining public libraries.[1]
		Providing and maintaining museums and art galleries.
		Providing and supporting sporting, cultural and social facilities, including theatres and other places of entertainment.
		Providing and maintaining public parks.
		Providing community centres.
		Promoting tourism.
Licensing	District council	Issuing licences for the sale of liquor, gaming, cinemas, theatres, taxis, dogs, etc.
Planning	Regional council[1]	Undertaking strategic planning by the preparation of regional reports and structure plans.
	District council[1]	Preparing local plans.
		Deciding upon applications for planning permission.
		Maintaining conservation areas.
	Shared by regional and district councils[1]	Enforcing development control.
		Providing caravan sites.
Rating and Valuation	Regional council	Levying rates on all property in the area and, by appointment of an assessor, providing for its valuation.
Social Work	Regional council	Arranging for the provision of personal social services, especially for children, disabled and elderly people, the sick and the mentally handicapped.
Transportation	Regional council	Constructing and maintaining roads (with the exception of motorways and trunk roads), footpaths, bridges and street lighting.
		Providing and/or subsidising public transport services (in Strathclyde, through the Passenger Transport Executive).
		Constructing and maintaining airports.
		Operating ferries and harbours.

Notes

1. In the Borders, Dumfries and Galloway and Highland Regions, the building control, library and planning functions (discharged by district councils elsewhere) are performed by the regional councils.

2. For the purposes of providing fire and police services, the Borders Region is combined with Lothian and the Highland Region is combined with the three islands areas.

siders may be appointed to a committee provided that no fewer than two thirds of all its members are councillors. The principal consideration for councils organised along party lines (as most are) is to ensure that committees reflect the political balance of the council.

A councillor has no absolute right to membership of any committee at all. But in practice all councillors are members of at least one.

In most authorities the work of the individual service committees, together with that of any 'resource' committees (dealing, for instance, with finance or manpower) is co-ordinated by a committee frequently called a 'policy and resources' committee.

Even with this network of committees, no modern council could expect to carry out all its statutory functions without the assistance of its full-time staff. In some cases, decision-making is formally delegated to individual officials, but the usual pattern is for officials to act as advisers to committees and the council as they make decisions, and then to implement them.

A council can appoint as many employees as it thinks fit, although the statutory and administrative requirements of some services may leave it little freedom – for example, as to numbers of teachers or policemen. There are few specific named posts which have to be filled (a council is not legally obliged, for instance, to appoint a chief executive or a director of finance) but relevant authorities must appoint directors of education and social work, chief constables and chief fire officers.

Just as the work of committees may be co-ordinated by a policy and resources committee, the work of a council's senior officials who head the administrative departments is often co-ordinated by forming them into a management team led by the chief executive.

Local authority finance

The way in which local authorities are financed is closely regulated by the law. They may only raise and spend money in ways which are statutorily approved.

For both practical and legal purposes, the expenditure of local authorities is best seen as divided between revenue and capital expenditure.

Revenue expenditure Revenue spending principally covers recurrent items such as salaries and wages, rents and repairs on council property, maintenance of equipment and machinery, maintenance of roads and 'administrative' costs. Each year a council draws up its budget of revenue expenditure based upon the estimated cost of services to be provided by each department.

A very small part of this total will be paid for by charges made for the provision of some services. A housing authority, for instance, will derive substantial income from rents; and other sources of income may include bus fares and payments for home-help services or school meals.

For the most part, however, local authority revenue expenditure has to be financed by taxation. In the past, this meant principally the local property tax – the RATES.

Although rates remain an important annual source of income, it has been accepted for many years that income from rates has to be supplemented by national taxation supplied each year by the Secretary of State for Scotland, in the shape of a 'rate support' grant. On average, authorities receive rather more than twice as much by way of grant as they raise for themselves in rates.

The rules governing the rate support grant are complex. In essence, they involve an annual procedure in which the Secretary of State, in consultation with representatives of the local authorities in the Convention of Scottish Local Authorities (COSLA), decides the total amount of grant which will be made to councils as a whole, and then the formula according to which that total is to be distributed among them. The details of this formula vary from year to year, which means that the size of grant to individual councils changes.

The main purposes of rate support grant can be discovered by looking at the three parts, or 'elements', into which both the national aggregate grant and the individual grants are divided.

The 'needs element' is designed to compensate those authorities upon whom the demands for services are greatest. The 'resources element' supplements the income of those authorities with lower than average income from rates. The 'domestic element' does not really assist authorities directly at all, but is a subsidy which they must pass on by lowering the level of rates charged on domestic (as opposed to industrial or commercial) property.

In addition to the rate support grant, which supplements income from rates for local authority services generally, the Secretary of State makes a separate 'housing support' grant to (in 1984–5) 26 of the 56 housing authorities. This supplements rent and rate contributions to housing accounts. He also makes specific grants in support of certain other services – most importantly, a 50 per cent grant for police services.

So the Secretary of State, through his power to determine the level at which authorities collectively or singly receive grant, is able to exert considerable influence over their spending. This influence has been extended by the Local Government (Miscellaneous Provisions) (Scotland) Act 1981. This gives the Secretary of State power to reduce the level of rate support grant to an authority which, in his opinion, is planning excessive or unreasonable spending.

The Local Government and Planning (Scotland) Act 1982 gives the Secretary of State extra powers to deal with what he considers excessive spending. Instead of – or in addition to – cutting the level of grant, he can order the authority to cut its own rate poundage to an amount producing an overall level of expenditure (including that financed from grant) acceptable to the Secretary of State. For the first time, the Secretary of State has aquired power to limit the revenue expenditure of local authorities.

In 1984 this power was further extended to allow the Secretary of State to fix the rate levels of local authorities as a whole – popularly known as 'rate-capping'.

Capital expenditure Financial control over capital spending on projects such as buildings and roads is, however, quite familiar to local authorities. To finance these projects, authorities are entitled to raise money by borrowing from statutorily approved sources, by mortgage or by the issue of bills or bonds.

It is for authorities themselves to decide which sources of capital to use, and to what extent, but they can do so only in relation to capital projects approved in advance by the Secretary of State. Nowadays it is usual for approval to be given by reference to 'blocks' of spending on groups of projects, rather than to individual schemes.

Keeping accounts Local authorities are required to keep accounts of their income and expenditure, and abstracts of these accounts are open to public inspection. They are also examined by auditors acting under the Controller of Audit, on behalf of the Commission for Local Authority Accounts.

Apart from good accounting practice, these auditors are also looking for signs of illegal expenditure. If this is discovered then (following an inquiry and, if necessary, a reference on matters of law to the Court of Session) the Commission may recommend to the Secretary of State that those responsible – whether councillors or officials – must make good the loss to the authority. The Secretary of State has discretion in this matter but he cannot order an individual to make good such a loss if he is satisfied that the person acted in good faith.

Central government controls

The financial controls available to the Secretary of State are certainly the most important he has, but they do not stand alone. Whilst local authorities are separate legal entities, with powers of their own, many of their functions can be carried out only under the supervision or with the consent of the Secretary of State.

The Secretary of State, for instance, must approve the structure plans of regional and islands councils; he may veto HOUSING ACTION AREA resolutions; and he must give his approval to compulsory purchase orders. Local authority byelaws must also be confirmed by him. And, very importantly, he has the power to lay down in delegated legislation many of the detailed rules according to which local authority functions are carried out. *See:* STATUTORY INSTRUMENT

In the rare case of a local authority's total failure or refusal to carry out a statutory function, the Secretary of State has the power to hold an inquiry and to order that the function be performed. Such an order may, if necessary, be further enforced by the Court of Session.

Challenging local authority actions

Although local authorities have wide powers to affect people's lives, this does not mean that they are free from normal legal controls. If an authority enters into a contract, it is usually subject to the normal contractual obligations which arise as a result. If its employees act negligently and cause injury or loss, the local authority will be liable. This might happen if, for instance, a council vehicle is driven carelessly or a school teacher is negligent when supervising children, or an official negligently offers misleading advice.

Apart from breach of contract and negligence, some local authority actions and decisions can be legally challenged by a statutory right of appeal for affected persons to the SHERIFF COURT. One of the most common appeals is by parents against whom school attendance orders have been made, because they have failed to ensure that their children attend school or receive a proper education. Another is appeals against house demolition and closing orders.

In such cases, the sheriff has wide powers to substitute a different decision if he thinks fit. However, it must be stressed that an appeal to the sheriff can take place only in those circumstances where it is specifically provided for by an Act of Parliament.

In addition, however, local authorities (along with other public bodies which were created and given powers by statute) are strictly limited to the functions authorised by Act of Parliament. If they adopt unauthorised procedures or exceed or abuse their powers or fail to discharge their functions, then their actions may be challenged in court.

But a council does not exceed its powers if it simply does something which, while not specifically authorised, is incidental to its statutory functions. Furthermore, all councils are given the power, subject to very strict financial limits, to undertake functions which they believe to be in the interests of their area or its inhabitants, over and above the specific statutory functions authorised by individual Acts of Parliament.

One special challenge to the legality of a local authority's actions can occur when the Accounts Commission discovers illegal expenditure. It should be added that it is open to any individual to complain to an auditor about any aspect of an authority's abstract of accounts. The auditor will then begin an investigation.

In some cases (perhaps the best example is the refusal of planning permission), a special appeal against a local authority's decision can be made to the Secretary of State, who may substitute a different decision if he thinks fit. But there is no general right of administrative appeal to the Secretary of State – although, in the case of a council's alleged failure to perform a duty, he may be persuaded to use his default powers to intervene. A recent example of the use of this power was the Secretary of State's attempt to enforce the 'right to purchase' provisions in the Tenants' Rights, Etc. (Scotland) Act 1980 against councils reluctant to sell houses to their tenants.

Another form of challenge available to a person upset by a local authority act or decision, where maladministration is alleged, is to complain to the Commissioner for Local Administration. *See:* OMBUDSMEN.

Short of complaint to the ombudsman, court or minister, a person dissatisfied with some aspect of a local authority's service can always complain direct to the authority itself by writing to the chief officer responsible for that service (or to the chief executive) or to his local councillor.

LODGER

When you live in someone else's house

The term 'lodger' is popularly used to refer to a person who has the use of a room, or rooms, in someone else's house. In law that person may be a tenant, or someone who merely has a permission, or licence, to occupy the accommodation – meaning that he has no tenants' rights. *See:* LICENCE TO OCCUPY

Lodgers who are tenants Whether or not a lodger is a tenant depends on the nature of the CONTRACT, or agreement, between the parties.

If the parties enter into a written

lease, the lodger will be a tenant. This, however, is rare: usually there is nothing at all in writing. In such cases, the courts will normally take the view that there was no intention to create a tenancy, only an intention to enter into a contract conferring a permission to occupy – even though the lodger has the exclusive use of his accommodation.

Even if a lodger is a tenant, he may still be unable to obtain full security of tenure and rent protection under the Rent (Scotland) Act if, for example:

- The rent includes payment for board – that is, meals.
- The rent includes payment for personal services – for example, room-cleaning or the provision of clean sheets.
- The landlord resides in the house.
- He is a sub-tenant and the house is rented from a district or islands council, a New Town Development Corporation, the Scottish Special Housing Association, a registered housing association or a housing co-operative.

Nevertheless, a lodger who is excluded from protection under these rules may still be entitled to rent protection and to temporary security of tenure under Part VII of the Rent (Scotland) Act. *See:* EVICTION; RENT PROTECTION; SUB-TENANCY

A lodger who is a tenant – whether protected or not – cannot be evicted without a court order. It is an offence for anyone to evict such a person unlawfully or harass him with the intention of forcing him to leave. *See:* HARASSMENT

Lodgers who are not tenants Most lodgers fall into this category and are treated as having a permission, or licence, to occupy their accommodation. If they have Part VII protection, they cannot be evicted without a court order. They can apply to a rent assessment committee to have a fair rent fixed and may also be able to obtain temporary security of tenure if they are served with a NOTICE TO QUIT. *See:* LICENCE TO OCCUPY

Taking in lodgers

If you are a tenant, and you wish to take in lodgers, you should first of all check your lease. It may forbid you to take in lodgers without your landlord's permission.

If you are the tenant of a district or islands council, a New Town Development Corporation, the Scottish Special Housing Association, a registered housing association or a housing co-operative, you cannot take in lodgers without your landlord's written permission, which must not be unreasonably withheld.

If you think permission has been unreasonably withheld, you can ask the sheriff to order the landlord to give permission. However, you cannot make such an application if permission has been withheld because the landlord thinks that you intend to charge an unreasonable rent or to demand an illegal deposit. *See:* KEY MONEY

If a person receiving SUPPLEMENTARY BENEFIT has accommodation available for 3 or more lodgers, one third of their payments – less any deductions made from his housing benefit because he has lodgers in the house – will be treated as earnings for the purpose of calculating his benefit rate.

See: LANDLORD AND TENANT

LORD ADVOCATE

The government's chief lawyer in Scotland

The Lord Advocate is the government's chief law officer in Scotland and is also a member of the government. He is appointed by the Prime Minister from among senior advocates who are members of the ruling party or sympathetic to it. Usually, but not always, he is an M.P. or a member of the House of Lords.

As chief law officer, he has a number of important duties. He is the government's chief adviser on questions concerning the application of Scots law and the effect on Scots law of new United Kingdom legislation. His office in London – the Lord Advocate's Department – is responsible for drafting all Scottish Bills. He raises and defends civil actions to which a government department in Scotland is a party.

The Lord Advocate is also the head of the system of public prosecution in Scotland. He will prosecute personally in major cases of public significance, and indictments are drawn up in his name. In addition, he appoints the advocates-depute who conduct most prosecutions in the High Court of Justiciary. *See:* CRIMINAL PROCEEDINGS; CROWN OFFICE; INDICTMENT

The Lord Advocate is also responsible for advising the Queen, through the Secretary of State for Scotland, on filling many official appointments, including those of sheriff, and judge of the Court of Session and High Court.

LOST PROPERTY

What the finder must do

Finders are not keepers. If you find lost property, you are not obliged to pick it up. But if you do, you must hand it over to the police or tell them that you have it – unless you can trace the owner yourself.

However, articles found in places like shops or cinemas may instead be handed to the manager, who must then inform the police. The police may require the manager to hand the property to them or allow him to retain it to see if the owner comes back.

Property found in a TAXI should be handed to the driver, or to the police.

A person who is in possession of lost property, and fails to deliver or report it to the police, is guilty of an offence. The maximum penalty is a fine of £100.

What the police must do

The police must keep lost items for at least 2 months (unless they are perishable) and try to trace the owner. If the owner does reclaim his property, he may have to pay a charge (including any police expenses) and may also be ordered to pay a reward to the finder.

After 2 months, unclaimed property can be disposed of by the police. Valuable items will be sold and a reward may be paid to the finder. Other items will usually be given to the finder if he wishes them.

If the police sell property for £100 or more, and the owner is later traced, he is entitled to receive compensation for up to a year after the sale. The amount of the compensation is the sale price less any police charges or expenses and any finder's reward.

Special rules for public transport

When you find something on a bus, you must hand it to the conductor or driver, or to the operator's lost property office. The rightful owner is entitled to have his property back – but only if he pays the bus company a fee.

If the lost property is worth more than 50p, the company must keep it for at least 3 months (except where it is perishable). If it is not claimed by then, the company can dispose of the property as it thinks fit.

There are similar rules for trains and aircraft.

Rubbish

Ordinary household rubbish, once collected, belongs to the district or islands council. It is, strictly speaking, an offence to remove anything from a dustbin or skip without permission from the council or the owner.

LOTTERIES

Running a fund-raising draw for a club or society

A lottery is a prize draw in which no skill is involved. It is illegal to operate one for private gain. People taking part in a lottery each buy tickets of a fixed price, and amounts of money or a number of prizes are distributed among winners chosen by lots or by pure chance. A raffle is a form of lottery.

Any sports or social club, charity, local authority or non-profit-making body can operate a lottery providing all the proceeds are used solely for the organising body and providing it meets all the conditions laid down by the Lotteries and Amusements Act 1976.

Rules for lotteries A lottery is legal only if the following rules are applied:

1. No skill is involved; prizes must be awarded by chance alone.
2. No ticket costs more than 50p.
3. The price is printed on each ticket, along with the name and address of the organisers and the date on which the lottery, or draw, is to take place.
4. The amount of money collected by the sale of tickets is not more than £10,000 – more can be raised only if the lottery is registered with the Gaming Board.
5. No more than 25 per cent of the total money raised is used for expenses – the figure is only 15 per cent for registered lotteries collecting more than £10,000.
6. Only half or less of the total amount raised is given away in prizes, and no single prize is worth more than £2,000, but this figure can be increased in lotteries controlled by the Gaming Board.
7. The person organising the lottery is a member of the club or society and is authorised by the committee.
8. Tickets are not sold to anyone under the age of 16.
9. Details of the money raised, the expenses deducted and the way in which the profits are to be spent are sent to the district or islands council.

Any society or organiser who runs a lottery and breaks any of these regulations commits an offence. The maximum penalty is 2 years' imprisonment or an unlimited fine.

Planning a lottery A club or society which wishes to run a lottery or a series of lotteries must first write to the district or islands council to be registered as a lottery operator. The registration fee is £20 and there is a renewal fee of £10 to be paid on January 1 each year.

The council can refuse registration only on the grounds that one of the officials or organisers has been convicted of fraud or an offence under the Lotteries and Amusements Act, or because the club or society is not a non-profit-making body run for the benefit of its members, or is not a charity. A club or society can appeal against refusal to the sheriff court.

Selling the tickets Tickets for a registered and properly organised lottery can be sold at the club or society's premises or in private houses.

But they cannot be sold in a gaming club, at a bingo hall, from a vending machine, in a licensed betting office, or in an amusement arcade, and they must not be sent through the post.

No club, society or local authority can hold more than 52 lotteries in a year, and at least 7 days must elapse between each lottery.

Local council lotteries All local authorities are permitted under the Lotteries and Amusements Act 1976 to operate local lotteries to raise money, but before they can do so they must register with the Gaming Board.

They cannot run more than 52 lotteries in any one year and many of the same rules apply as those for clubs and societies. Tickets can, however, be sold in street kiosks and in shops.

Local society lotteries Once a club or society has registered with the local authority, it can run up to 52 raffles or lotteries a year.

LADY LUCK CHOOSES THE WINNERS

A lottery is a prize draw that involves no skill. It must not be operated for private gain.

Small lotteries Lotteries or raffles can be run at social events such as sports meetings, fêtes, socials and dances, providing any profits go to the organising body and are not for private gain.

The organisers do not need to be registered with the district or islands council, providing:

- The lottery is not the main purpose of the event.
- Tickets are sold only at the event.
- No cash prizes are given.
- Not more than £50 is deducted from the proceeds for prizes.
- The result of the lottery is declared during the event. Prizes totalling more than £50 in value can be given only if some of them are donated.

Private lotteries These are legal if they are organised exclusively among a group of people who work together, live on the same premises, or all belong to the same club or society.

Expenses can be deducted only for printing and stationery and the rest of the proceeds must be used up in prizes or for the mutual benefit of the group.

Tickets must not go on general sale, must not be sent through the post, and the purpose of the lottery must be advertised on the tickets.

Claiming the prize No one taking part in a lawful raffle or lottery who fails to receive his prize can sue the organisers for it. Even if a lottery is lawful, no winner can sue for his prize.

LOWER EARNINGS LIMIT

When paying national insurance contributions is compulsory

Every employed person whose earnings from one employment in any tax year reach a certain level – called the lower earnings limit – must pay Class 1 NATIONAL INSURANCE CONTRIBUTIONS on the whole of his earnings – and so must his employer. If, however, his earnings are below that limit, neither he nor his employer pays Class 1 contributions.

The lower earnings limit changes in April of each year. In the tax year 1984–5 the limit was:

- £34 a week for those paid weekly.
- £147.33 a month for those paid monthly.
- £1,767.96 for those paid annually.

You can check the up-to-date limit by asking for leaflet NI 208 at your local social security office.

Separate employments

When someone works for two or more employers who do not carry on business in association with each other, each employment is treated separately. If no single employment provides earnings above the lower earnings limit, then neither the employee nor his employer pays Class 1 contributions – even if the total earnings are above the lower earnings limit.

If, for example, you employ a part-time cleaner, neither she nor you have to pay Class 1 contributions unless you pay her more than the lower earnings limit. The fact that she earns more than that limit by also working for someone else is irrelevant. *See:* UPPER EARNINGS LIMIT

LUNCHEON VOUCHER

When tax must be paid

The first 15p of luncheon vouchers provided by an employer for his employees is not taxed. For any vouchers over that daily limit, however, the employee must be taxed, whatever his earnings.

MAGISTRATE

A judge in the district court

In its widest sense, the word 'magistrate' refers to any person who exercises judicial authority. It therefore covers all Scottish judges, including High Court judges and sheriffs.

However, the word is popularly used to describe a judge who sits in the DISTRICT COURT – that is, a JUSTICE OF THE PEACE or a stipendiary magistrate.

Stipendiary magistrate A stipendiary magistrate, unlike a justice of the peace, is a full-time, salaried judge who sits in the district court. He must have been legally qualified for at least 5 years.

Any district (or islands) council can appoint a stipendiary magistrate, so long as the Secretary of State for Scotland has approved the establishment of the office in the district court concerned, and also the appointment. So far, the power has only been used in Glasgow, where 3 stipendiary magistrates sit in the Central District Court.

When a stipendiary magistrate sits in a district court, that court has the same summary criminal jurisdiction and powers as a sheriff.

See: CRIMINAL PROCEEDINGS

MAIL ORDER

The rules that control buying and selling through the post

Mail order customers are protected partly by law and partly by codes of practice drawn up by advertising agents and publishers.

By law, advertisements or catalogues inviting people to order goods by post must include the supplier's name and operating address – a post office box number is not enough.

If money is sent with an order, it must be returned as soon as possible if the order is not accepted. A customer can sue if there is an unreasonable delay.

No CONTRACT exists until the supplier accepts an order. So the customer has no right to demand goods if a supplier chooses to reject his order, and no right to compensation if he then has to pay more to buy the goods elsewhere.

But once goods are sent, there is a binding contract. The customer is entitled to his or her money back if the goods do not correspond with their description. If their quality proves unsuitable for their normal purpose, the customer has the right to demand their replacement, or else a refund. *See also:* DEFECTIVE GOODS

Advertiser's code of practice

In addition to any legal requirements, the Advertising Standards Authority administers a code of practice which should be adhered to by advertising agencies and publishers. This code requires mail order suppliers who ask for any money in advance to:

- Provide samples of their goods at the address shown in an advertisement, so that callers can examine them.
- Refund payment in full if goods are returned undamaged within 7 days of receipt. It is not necessary for the customer to give any reason for this. The customer is entitled to try the goods during that period, unless the supplier has previously made it clear that a trial is not permitted – for example, when any use of the goods would make them unfit for sale to anyone else.
- Send goods within 28 days of receiving an order – or failing that, notify the customer within 28 days, with a reply-paid postcard and the offer of a refund. If the customer prefers to wait for the goods he should be sent progress reports every 14 days.

The Mail Order Traders Association

THE EVIDENCE YOU NEED TO CLAIM A REFUND

If a mail order advertiser fails to meet your order and your money is not refunded within 28 days, the newspaper or magazine that ran the advertisement will investigate.

If it was a 'display' advertisement – not merely a small ad in a classified column – the publisher should be able to arrange a refund, through a customer-protection scheme, even if the trader's business has gone into liquidation.

But you need proof: a record of the payment, including details of when it was made, to whom and for what goods.

When ordering from an advertisement, keep it in a safe place afterwards with a note of the publication it appeared in and the date of publication. If you are required to clip anything from the advertisement, make sure you have a note of any important details – particularly the full name and address of the advertiser.

If you pay by cheque, cross it, endorse it 'Account payee only', and fill in all the details on the counterfoil or payment list in your cheque book.

If you send a postal order, cross it, fill in the counterfoil and keep it with your record of the advertisement.

If you have to pay by cash – it is better not to, because there is no way of tracing it later – you should do so only in a special post office envelope for registered mail. Keep the receipt with your record of the advertisement.

After 28 days, if nothing is heard from the supplier, contact the advertisement manager of the newspaper or magazine.

also administer their own code.

Citizens advice bureaux should hold copies of the codes of practice approved by the Director General of Fair Trading. A suspected breach of a code may be checked with them and a complaint under the code made to the code administrator.

If an advertiser defaults

Most established newspapers and magazines take part in a scheme that guarantees a mail order customer his money back if an advertiser's business collapses and orders are not met. It applies only to what they call 'display' advertisements – not to small ads in their classified columns.

Publishers can refuse to print advertisements that do not conform to the Advertising Standards Authority code.

If a customer hears nothing from an advertiser within 28 days of sending money, he should notify the advertisement manager of the newspaper or magazine concerned. Refund claims should be lodged within 3 months of the date of the advertisement in a daily or weekly newspaper, or in the case of other publications, within 2 months of placing the order.

When books are sent by post

Leading publishers who supply books or records by post are subject to the code of practice of the Mail Order Publishers' Authority which requires that:

- Goods may not be sent unless requested.
- Advertisements must state postage and packing charges or quote an inclusive price.
- Advertisers must supply a clearly displayed and simple summary of the essential points of an offer, for the customer to keep.
- If a customer is invited to undertake a continuing commitment – for example to a book or record club – he or she must have the right to cancel it at any time, or after a stated period which must not exceed 1 year.

When credit is offered

Mail order companies offering delayed payment are bound by the laws covering any CREDIT AGREEMENT. They must state the full cost, including any extra charges, and if there is an INTEREST CHARGE, the true annual rate of interest must be given.

Even a mail order company must offer its goods for cash as well as on credit terms – 'credit only' selling is illegal.

If you order goods on credit after choosing from a catalogue or samples left at your home by a representative, your right to cancel the agreement during a 'cooling-off' period depends on whether your decision followed sales talk. *See:* DOORSTEP CREDIT

If there is no oral negotiation and your decision is based only on what you read, you have no right to a 'cooling-off' period and cannot cancel.

MAINTENANCE

Providing for your spouse and children

'Maintenance' is an English legal term, but it is popularly used in Scotland to refer to aliment – that is, regular payments made by someone for the support of his or her spouse or children. *See:* ALIMENT; AFFILIATION AND ALIMENT

The word 'maintenance' is also sometimes used to refer to a periodical allowance – the regular payments which a person may be ordered to pay to his or her former spouse following a divorce. *See:* DIVORCE

MALICIOUS PROSECUTION

Claiming damages for a wrongful criminal prosecution

Prosecutions in Scotland are carried on under either 'solemn' (for serious cases) or 'summary' (for other cases) procedure and are almost entirely in the hands of the public prosecutors. Anyone who is charged with an offence, but who is subsequently cleared by a court, may be able to claim DAMAGES in certain limited circumstances. *See:* CRIMINAL PROCEEDINGS

Solemn procedure

Under solemn procedure the prosecution takes place before a judge and jury, either in the High Court of Justiciary or the sheriff court.

In the High Court, prosecutions take place in the name of the LORD ADVOCATE, and the prosecutor can be either the Lord Advocate or the Solicitor General. More usually, however, the prosecution is undertaken by an advocate-depute.

In the sheriff court the prosecutor is the procurator fiscal, who acts on the authority and instructions of the Lord Advocate.

All public prosecutors have absolute privilege in taking solemn criminal proceedings and cannot be sued for damages in any circumstances – even where it is alleged that there was no good reason for the prosecution and that it was motivated by malice. The only possible remedy is to raise the matter in Parliament.

Summary procedure

Under summary procedure the prosecution takes place before a judge sitting alone, either in the sheriff court or district court.

The prosecutor is the procurator fiscal. He acts on his own authority, and in his own name, and can be found liable in damages.

However, a procurator fiscal will only be liable for taking summary proceedings if:

1. The person claiming damages has suffered imprisonment as a result of the prosecution.

2. The criminal proceedings have been quashed by the High Court.

3. The person suing proves that the procurator fiscal acted out of malice and had no good reason for bringing the prosecution.

An action for damages must be started within 2 months of the proceedings which are being complained about.

False information

If a person gives information in good faith to the police or a procurator fiscal, and a prosecution is started as a result, then he is not liable if the information turns out to be incorrect.

However, if the person acted out of malice and without good reason, he can be sued for damages by whoever is prosecuted.

Private prosecution

Anyone bringing a PRIVATE PROSECUTION will be liable in damages if it can be proved that he acted maliciously and without good reason.

MANUFACTURERS' LIABILITY

When you can claim compensation from the maker

If you are sold DEFECTIVE GOODS you can claim compensation from the shop for breach of contract. That compensation can include PERSONAL INJURY compensation – for example, if you are scalded when a hot-water bottle bursts.

However, if the hot-water bottle bursts and scalds someone else, he cannot sue the shopkeeper for breach of contract because he made no contract with the shop. His best course is to sue the manufacturer of the hot-water bottle for NEGLIGENCE.

Points that have to be proved when a claim is made

For a negligence claim to succeed, it must be shown that the maker had a duty of reasonable care to the person claiming damages and that he failed in his duty by not taking reasonable care. It must also be shown that the damage done, which the manufacturer should have reasonably foreseen, was caused by his failure to take reasonable care. For example, a pedestrian injured by a car defectively made so that it has inadequate brakes can claim compensation from the manufacturer. A repairer can also be sued for his negligence.

It is no defence for a manufacturer to say that the defect might have been discovered by someone else between the time when the car left his factory and the time when it caused harm. He must show that he could reasonably have expected some intermediary to have checked the product and found any defect of the kind that caused the harm.

The law recognises how difficult it might be for the consumer to prove the manufacturer careless. It eases his task by holding that negligence can be inferred from the existence of the defect in the circumstances.

When foreign-manufactured goods are involved

When you are injured by defects in a product that has been manufactured abroad – for example, a faulty brake in a foreign car – you can usually sue the manufacturing company in the normal way if the company has a place of business in Scotland.

Even if the foreign company does not have a place of business in Scotland, you may still be able to sue it in a Scottish court if the DELICT took place in Scotland, or if the breach of contract took place here. *See:* INTERNATIONAL PRIVATE LAW

MARRIAGE

Only a recognised ceremony can ensure a couple's rights

The law gives special rights and protection to the partners in a marriage – but only if the marriage is legally valid. Living together confers some, but by no means all, of such rights or protection. *See:* COHABITATION

In a legally valid marriage, a man and a woman unite as husband and wife. They accept the duty to live together, behave reasonably towards each other and support each other. Each has the right to be alimented (maintained) by the other and to have sexual relations – to the exclusion of anyone else.

Marriage must be entered into voluntarily, but it cannot be ended merely by agreement. Unlike most other legal contracts it lasts for life unless it is dissolved by a court decree. *See:* DIVORCE

Who can marry

Partners to a valid marriage must be:

- At least 16 years of age.
- Not already married.
- Not so closely related that their marriage is forbidden by law.
- Of the opposite sex. A man who has a 'sex-change' operation and lives as a woman cannot validly marry another man – the law still treats him as male.

If any of those conditions is not met, the arrangement is not a valid marriage. It is legally 'void', meaning that it is treated as if it had never taken place.

In addition, a couple must be married in accordance with certain legal procedures. These vary, depending on whether there is a religious element to the ceremony. Certain errors in procedure will not affect the validity of a marriage, provided it has been properly registered.

A marriage can be challenged on other grounds – for example, by showing that one partner's participation was not truly voluntary – but in that case it remains in existence unless it is declared void by a court. *See:* NULLITY

Parental consent

When a Scottish couple decide to marry, neither of them requires the consent of their parents for the marriage to go ahead.

Who gives official permission

Although others can perform the ceremony, only a district registrar can give legal approval for a marriage to go ahead. The district registrar represents the state registry of births, deaths and marriages in each district.

THE SNAIL IN A BOTTLE OF GINGER BEER

A manufacturer must take care to see that a consumer does not suffer injury to health from a product.

A friend treated Mrs M'Alister to a bottle of ginger beer in a cafe in Paisley. It was served from an opaque brown bottle covered with the maker's label and there was a cap on the bottle. Mrs M'Alister drank some. Then her friend poured the rest out of the bottle and 'a snail, which was in a state of decomposition, floated out of the bottle'.

Mrs M'Alister claimed that as a result of the nauseating sight of the snail and the ginger beer which she had already consumed, she suffered shock and gastroenteritis. She claimed damages from the makers.

DECISION

The House of Lords held that any manufacturer of an article of food or medicine sold in a manner which prevented the distributor or purchaser from seeing or discovering any defect had a legal duty to take reasonable care that the article was free from anything that could cause injury to health. The manufacturer could be liable for negligence and the case was sent back to the Court of Session for proof.

When a couple intend to marry, *each* of them must complete a 'marriage notice' (an official form available from the district registrar's office). Each marriage notice should be submitted to the registrar of the district in which the marriage is to take place, along with:

- A fee of £3.25.
- The person's BIRTH CERTIFICATE.
- If the person has been divorced or has had a previous marriage annulled, a copy of the divorce or nullity decree.
- If the person is widowed, a copy of the previous partner's death certificate.

THE MARRIAGE SCHEDULE

This is the document, issued by the district registrar, which gives permission for the marriage to go ahead.

The schedule must be signed by both contracting parties. If one of them is unable to write, he or she must insert a cross (X) or other mark. The person celebrating the marriage or someone else present should insert the words 'His (or Her) mark'. The mark must be attested by two witnesses of at least 14 years of age.

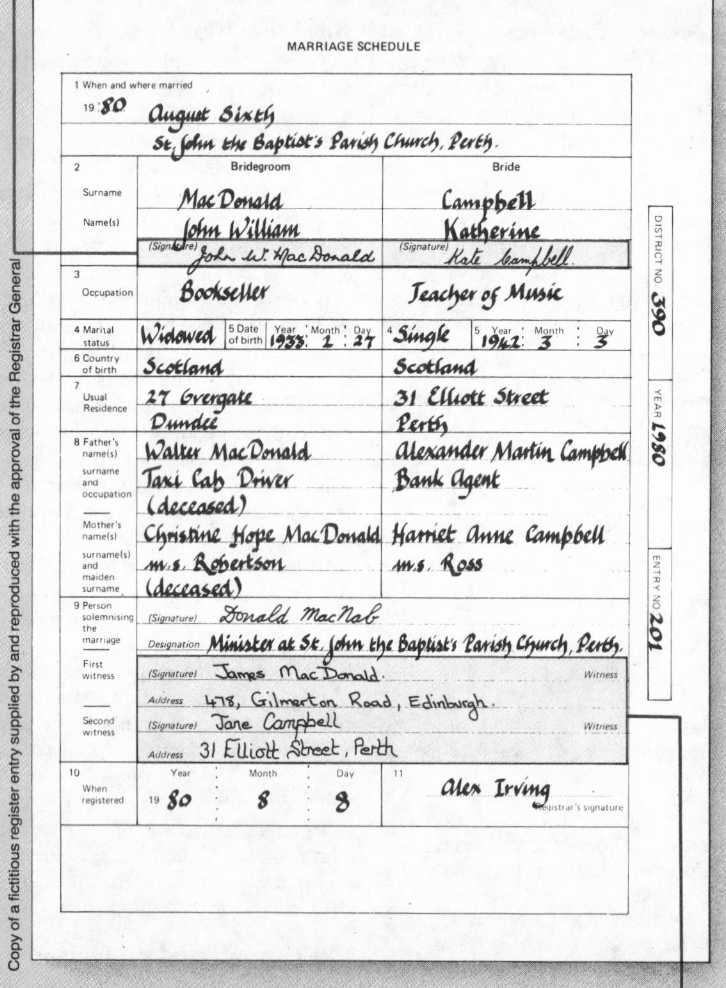

MARRIAGE SCHEDULE

	Bridegroom	Bride
1 When and where married	19 80 August Sixth St. John the Baptist's Parish Church, Perth.	
2 Surname	MacDonald	Campbell
Name(s)	John William	Katherine
(Signature)	John W. MacDonald	Kate Campbell
3 Occupation	Bookseller	Teacher of Music
4 Marital status	Widowed	Single
5 Date of birth (Year, Month, Day)	1933 : 2 : 27	1942 : 3 : 3
6 Country of birth	Scotland	Scotland
7 Usual Residence	27 Overgate Dundee	31 Elliott Street Perth
8 Father's name(s) surname and occupation	Walter MacDonald Taxi Cab Driver (deceased)	Alexander Martin Campbell Bank Agent
Mother's name(s) surname(s) and maiden surname	Christine Hope MacDonald m.s. Robertson (deceased)	Harriet Anne Campbell m.s. Ross
9 Person solemnising the marriage	(Signature) Donald MacNab Designation Minister at St. John the Baptist's Parish Church, Perth.	
First witness	(Signature) James MacDonald. Witness Address 478, Gilmerton Road, Edinburgh.	
Second witness	(Signature) Jane Campbell Witness Address 31 Elliott Street, Perth	
10 When registered (Year, Month, Day)	19 80 : 8 : 8	11 Alex Irving Registrar's signature

DISTRICT NO. 390 · YEAR 1980 · ENTRY NO. 201

Copy of a fictitious register entry supplied by and reproduced with the approval of the Registrar General

Two witnesses must sign the marriage schedule. Both must be at least 16.

The marriage schedule should be available to the registrar or an approved celebrant before he solemnises the marriage. Even if it is not, the marriage is valid once it has been entered in the marriage register.

A person who is not permanently resident in the UK will be asked to produce a 'certificate of no impediment', issued by the relevant authority in his or her own country, stating that there is no impediment to his or her marrying. Most European countries issue such certificates but other countries may not do so.

If a person cannot produce such a certificate, he or she must state the reason. However, if the person has lived in the UK for at least 2 years, no such certificate is required.

The marriage notice and the other documents can be sent to the district registrar by post, or can be delivered by either party to the marriage or by anyone else.

A couple cannot normally marry until at least 15 days after the marriage notices have been received. In special cases, however, such as where a soldier is posted overseas at short notice, permission may be given for the wedding to take place sooner.

It is best to complete the marriage notices several weeks before the wedding is to take place.

Once the district registrar has received the marriage notices, the couple's names and the date on which they intend to marry are displayed in a prominent place at the registrar's office – normally in the window. This is so that anyone who knows of a legal impediment to the marriage can object to the district registrar.

Once the 14-day 'waiting period' has passed – and there have been no objections – the district registrar issues the 'Marriage Schedule'. This document gives the couple permission to marry and states where and when the marriage is to take place. If it has been more than 3 months since the couple submitted marriage notices, the registrar can refuse to issue the marriage schedule. The parties will then have to submit fresh marriage notices and wait for another 2 weeks.

The marriage schedule must be collected by one or other of the couple who are to marry.

What happens next depends on whether the couple intend to marry in a civil ceremony (at the registrar's office) or in a religious ceremony (before a minister, priest or official of a recognised religion).

APPROVED CELEBRANTS

Ministers, priests or authorised officials of the following religious bodies are allowed to conduct marriage ceremonies without being individually registered as approved celebrants by the Registrar General for Scotland:

- Church of Scotland
- Baptist Union of Scotland
- Congregational Union of Scotland
- Episcopal Church in Scotland and other Churches of the Anglican Communion
- Free Church of Scotland
- Free Presbyterian Church of Scotland
- Hebrew Congregation
- Methodist Church in Scotland
- Religious Society of Friends (Quakers)
- Roman Catholic Church
- Salvation Army
- Scottish Unitarian Association
- United Free Church of Scotland

Arranging a registrar's office wedding

If a couple decide to be married in a civil ceremony, the ceremony will be performed at the registrar's office by the district registrar or an assistant registrar. Only in exceptional circumstances – for example, serious illness making it impossible for one party to attend at the office – will the ceremony be performed anywhere else.

The ceremony can take place at any time, on any day of the week, but it is usually performed during normal office hours.

The registrar cannot perform the marriage ceremony unless:

- He has the marriage schedule, properly completed.
- The marriage fee has been paid.
- Both parties to the marriage are present.
- Two people, aged 16 or over, are present as witnesses.

Each of the parties to the marriage must declare that there is no legal reason why they cannot marry and that she or he accepts the other as husband or wife. The registrar then declares them to be husband and wife.

The marriage schedule is signed by the registrar, the couple and the two witnesses. The registrar then registers the marriage.

The marriage fee for a civil ceremony is £10. The MARRIAGE CERTIFICATE – a copy of the entry in the marriage register – which the couple are given costs £2.

Arranging a religious wedding

All ministers, priests or officials of some religious organisations are authorised to conduct marriage ceremonies and do not have to be individually registered – for example, ministers of the Church of Scotland and priests of the Roman Catholic Church. In addition, certain ministers, priests or officials of other religious bodies are individually registered and therefore able to conduct marriages. If you are in doubt, contact your local district registrar, who has a list of the persons (called celebrants) who are authorised to conduct marriages.

In a religious wedding, the celebrant must conduct the ceremony according to the form recognised by the religious body to which he belongs. However, he cannot perform the marriage ceremony unless:

- The couple produce the marriage schedule for him.
- Both parties to the marriage are present.
- Two people, aged 16 or over, are present as witnesses.

There is no legal rule that a religious marriage must take place in a church.

Each of the parties to the marriage must declare that there is no legal reason why they cannot marry and each must accept the other as husband or wife. The celebrant must declare them to be husband and wife.

So long as both parties to the marriage are present, any failure to comply with the other procedural requirements will not invalidate the marriage once it has been registered. If both parties are not present, the marriage will be void and the celebrant will be guilty of an offence.

After the celebrant has performed the ceremony, the marriage schedule is completed in the same way as for a civil ceremony. It should then be delivered or posted to the district registrar within 3 days.

If the marriage schedule is not returned within 21 days, the registrar can issue a written request for it to be sent or delivered within 8 days. If the schedule is still not returned, he can order one of the couple to deliver the schedule personally to his office within 8 days. The maximum penalty for failing to do so is a fine of £400.

The cost, if any, of a religious marriage will vary with the religious body concerned. Additional charges may be made for 'extras' – for example, the presence of an organist.

Marriage with a person from abroad

A person who does not normally live in Scotland can marry here only if the marriage is allowed by the law of his or her DOMICILE as well as by the law of Scotland.

If you live in England or Wales (but not Northern Ireland) you can submit to the Registrar a certificate for marriage issued in England or Wales – a 'Superintendent Registrar's certificate' – as an alternative to giving marriage notice. This can only apply when the other party lives in Scotland, or both parties live in England or Wales but one has a parent living in Scotland.

THE RELATIVES WHO CANNOT MARRY

A man cannot marry his:

Mother (including adoptive mother or former adoptive mother), daughter (including illegitimate, adopted or former adopted daughter), grandmother, grand-daughter, sister, half-sister, aunt, niece, great-grandmother, great grand-daughter, former wife's mother, former wife's daughter, father's former wife, son's former wife, grandfather's former wife, former wife's grandmother, former wife's grand-daughter, grandson's former wife.

A woman cannot marry her:

Father (including adoptive father or former adoptive father), son (including illegitimate, adopted or former adopted son), grandfather, grandson, brother, half-brother, uncle, nephew, great-grandfather, great-grandson, former husband's father, former husband's son, mother's former husband, daughter's former husband, grandmother's former husband, former husband's grandfather, former husband's grandson, grand-daughter's former husband.

Scots law will ignore the fact that a marriage is prohibited by the law of a person's domicile if the prohibition would not make the marriage void from the outset in that domicile.

MARRIAGE CERTIFICATE

Providing proof that you are married

Every married couple is entitled to be given a certificate which proves that they are married.

The certificate is a copy of the entry of the wedding in the marriage register kept at the registrar's office where the marriage was registered. It shows the names of the husband and wife, their marital status – single, widowed or divorced – their occupation and address and those of their parents, and the names and addresses of the witnesses.

If the couple were married in a religious ceremony, the certificate must give the name and position of the person who officiated.

A marriage certificate issued at the time of the marriage costs £2. It is usually given to the couple when the marriage is registered, but may sometimes be sent to them by post. The certificate belongs equally to a husband and wife: neither has a special right to keep it.

You are not required by law to hold a marriage certificate, but, as it must be produced for certain official purposes – such as applying for a visa to visit certain countries – it is advisable to take the one offered at your wedding. If you decline and need a copy more than one month after registration, you will have to pay £5 for it.

How to obtain extra copies

If you lose your marriage certificate or need an extra copy, apply to the registrar's office where the marriage was registered.

If more than a year has passed since the marriage, you can apply to that registrar's office or to the General Register Office (Scotland), Registration Branch, New Register House, Edinburgh.

The extra copy will cost £5 and can be applied for in person or by post. You must supply the names of the marriage partners. If you cannot give the date and place of the marriage, there may be an additional fee.

How to check marital status

If you want to know whether someone is or has been married, you are entitled to search the indexes at the General Register Office. The fee for this is £5.25 per day.

Anyone – not only the parties to a marriage – can obtain a certificate of any entry contained in the registers on

HOW A MARRIAGE IS REGISTERED BY THE STATE

The official document that certifies a couple have been legally married

The marital status of the man and woman prior to the marriage must be entered on the certificate – for example, single, widowed or divorced

The certificate is a copy of the official entry made in the marriage register of the district in which the marriage took place

Extract of an entry in a REGISTER of MARRIAGES MF 112375

Registration of Births, Deaths and Marriages (Scotland) Act 1965

District No 390	Year 1980	Entry No 201
Marriage in the district of Perth		
1. When and where married* 19 80 August Sixth, St John the Baptist's Parish Church, Perth.		

	Bridegroom	Bride
2. Surname	MacDonald	Campbell.
Name(s)	John William	Katherine
(Signed)	John W. MacDonald	Kate Campbell
3. Occupation	Bookseller	Teacher of Music
4. Marital Status	Widowed	Single
5. Date of birth (Year / Month / Day)	1933 2 27	1962 3 3
6. Birthplace	Scotland	Scotland
7. Usual Residence	27 Overgate, Dundee	31 Elliott Street, Perth
8. Father's name(s), surname and occupation	Walter MacDonald, Taxi Cab Driver (deceased)	Alexander Martin Campbell, Bank agent
Mother's name(s), surname(s) and maiden surname	Christine Hope MacDonald m.s. Robertson (deceased)	Harriet Anne Campbell m.s. Ross

9. Person solemnising the marriage: (Signed) Donald MacNab, Designation: Minister at St. John the Baptist's Parish Church, Perth

Witnesses with addresses: (Signed) James MacDonald, Witness, 478 Gilmerton Road, Edinburgh; (Signed) Jane Campbell, Witness, 31 Elliott Street, Perth

10. When registered: Year 19 80, Month 8, Day 8 — 11. (Signed) Alex Irving, Registrar

12.

Extracted from the Register of Marriages for the District of Perth on Eleventh August 1980 Alex Irving Registrar

The above particulars incorporate any subsequent corrections or amendments to the original entry made with the authority of the Registrar General.

Warning

It is an offence under section 53(3) of the Registration of Births, Deaths and Marriages (Scotland) Act 1965 for any person to pass as genuine any copy or reproduction of this extract which has not been made by a district registrar or assistant registrar and authenticated by his signature.

Any person who falsifies or forges any of the particulars on this extract or knowingly uses, gives or sends as genuine any false or forged extract is liable to prosecution under section 53(1) of the said Act.

XM4(R)

Copy of a fictitious register entry supplied by and reproduced with the authority of the Registrar General

After the district registrar has registered a marriage, a copy, or 'extract', is provided as a certificate of marriage. A certificate is not required by law. However, there are certain circumstances when a certificate is needed for official purposes – for example, certain countries require a marriage certificate when someone is applying for a visa to emigrate to the country.

WHEN A MARRIAGE CERTIFICATE MUST BE SHOWN

- A copy of the marriage certificate must be lodged in court when an action of DIVORCE or judicial SEPARATION is raised.
- If a husband and wife want to share a joint passport, they must send a copy of the marriage certificate.
- A husband and wife may be asked to prove that they are married, by producing a marriage certificate, when applying at a foreign embassy for a visa to travel abroad, or to emigrate.
- A foreigner who married a British citizen and wants to remain in Britain would have to show his or her marriage certificate to the Home Office in order to obtain the permit.
- Any married person making or changing claims for certain social security benefits, or wanting to retain the right to pay married women's reduced-rate contributions, will have to produce a marriage certificate to the Department of Health and Social Security.

For example, a widow paying reduced rate contributions is entitled to continue to do so after she remarries. When she applies for a 'certificate of election' confirming her right to pay such contributions, she must enclose her marriage certificate. The certificate will be returned without delay.

A woman applying for widow's benefits need show only her husband's death certificate to qualify.

payment of a fee of £5.

When a marriage is declared a NULLITY or is dissolved by DIVORCE, the General Register Office is informed of this.

In the case of nullity, no more copies of the certificate will be issued. In the case of divorce, the certificate will show that this has taken place.

The entry in the register remains unchanged if one of the parties dies, so anyone can still obtain a copy of the marriage certificate as if the party were still alive.

Anyone who uses a marriage certificate for the purposes of FRAUD can be prosecuted. So can anyone who presents as genuine a certificate which has not been made by a district registrar or assistant registrar and signed by him – the penalty is a fine of up to £50 on summary conviction.

MARRIAGE GUIDANCE

When help is available to maintain a relationship

When a marriage is in danger of breaking up, either or both partners can voluntarily seek advice and counselling through the Scottish Marriage Guidance Council, 58 Palmerston Place, Edinburgh. The Council can give you the address of your local marriage counselling service. Neither party has to heed any advice or counselling which is given.

When one partner in a domestic dispute goes to see a solicitor, the solicitor may suggest marriage guidance. Neither partner is obliged to comply with this suggestion.

SETTLING A COUPLE'S DIFFERENCES

Marriage guidance counsellors are available to advise any couple whose marriage is in danger of breaking up.

All marriage guidance counsellors maintain complete confidentiality in respect of information they are given. In theory, a counsellor could be called upon to give evidence in a divorce action in court, but in practice this does not happen.

MARRIED WOMAN

How marriage affects her social security rights

Until April 5, 1977, married women at work could choose whether to pay full or reduced-rate NATIONAL INSURANCE CONTRIBUTIONS. Since then, the only married women who can still pay at a reduced rate are those who:

- Were married before April 6, 1977, and
- Chose before May 11, 1977 to continue at the reduced rate, and
- Since April 5, 1978 have not had two consecutive tax years during which they have not been liable to pay Class 1 contributions and have not been self-employed.

All other married women at work must pay the same contributions as men and single women.

The reduced rate of contribution in 1984–5 was 3.85 per cent of earnings up to £250 a week.

Women who are paying at the reduced rate can elect to pay full contribution by applying to their local social security office on Form CF. 9 – attached to leaflet NI 1, available from the office. The full rate becomes payable from the April following their choice. Once a woman has chosen full liability she cannot change back to the reduced rate.

Women who are resuming work after two complete tax years away from it must pay at the full rate.

Reduced-rate contributions do not count for benefit purposes. So you have no right to unemployment benefit or to sickness and invalidity benefit – unless your sickness is due to an injury at work. A retirement pension may be payable on your husband's contributions, but it will be much less than a pension based on your own insurance contributions. *See:* RETIREMENT PENSION

How supplementary benefit is affected

If a married woman lives with her husband, either can claim supplementary benefit for both of them.

The partner who claims must show that during the 6 months immediately before the claim (excluding breaks totalling up to 3 weeks) he or she satisfied certain conditions – such as working at least 8 hours a week or being unable to find full-time work. Where the partner who claims is a pensioner, different conditions apply. *See:* SUPPLEMENTARY BENEFIT

If a husband who is receiving supplementary benefit fails to support his family adequately, the benefit can be paid to his wife to protect her interests

SOCIAL SECURITY BENEFITS FOR MARRIED WOMEN

Circumstances in which national insurance contributions are required, in order that a married woman can make her claim

Benefit	Type of national insurance contributions needed to qualify
Maternity Allowance	Full rate
Unemployment Benefit	Full rate
Sickness Benefit	Full rate (none if industrial injury)
Invalidity Benefit	Full rate (none if industrial injury)
Retirement Pension	Full rate for maximum pension; reduced pension may be paid on husband's contributions
Death Grant	Full rate; or may be paid on husband's contributions
Widow's Benefit	Husband's contributions
Child's Special Allowance	Full rate (former husband's contributions)
Maternity Grant	None
Guardian's Allowance	None
Attendance Allowance	None
Industrial Injuries Benefits	None
Mobility Allowance	None
Non-Contributory Invalidity Pension/ Severe Disablement Allowance	None
Child Benefit	None
Family Income Supplement	None
Supplementary Benefit	None

or those of her children.

A wife whose husband is living with her, but refuses to support her, can also claim supplementary benefit in her own right on the ground of urgent need, but she may have to repay it later if she is in a position to do so.

MATERNITY

The rights of a mother-to-be

Expectant mothers are entitled to a comprehensive range of maternity services covering treatment, care and advice, and usually to some financial help from the state.

There are also extra rights and cash benefits for working women who become pregnant.

Obtaining medical care

Pregnancy tests can be arranged through your family doctor. If a test is positive, the next step is to decide what kind of ante-natal care you want.

Some family doctors provide ante-natal care themselves. Their names are on a list of medical practitioners published by area health boards and available at main post offices and public libraries. You have the right to consult a doctor on the list purely for maternity care while continuing to use your own doctor for other medical matters.

Many women choose to have their ante-natal check-ups in the outpatients department of the nearest hospital – even if the baby is to be born at home. Your family doctor will arrange the first visit to the hospital.

Time off work

A pregnant employee must be given reasonable time off by her employer during working hours to receive ante-natal care advised by a doctor, midwife or health visitor. She must produce at her employer's request a certificate that she is pregnant and an appointment card, except when it is the first appointment during her pregnancy. The amount of pay to which she is entitled is her normal pay as though she had not been absent.

If the employer refuses time off, or refuses to pay wages, she can complain to an industrial tribunal. This should be done within 3 months of the date of her ante-natal appointment.

Having the baby at home

You are entitled to insist on having your baby at home. In practice few women do, and most doctors advise against it, particularly if it is a first child. If you do insist on having the baby at home against your doctor's advice, he may suggest you find another doctor. *See:* DOCTOR AND PATIENT

A midwife – who can now be a man – is allocated to every home delivery. She visits the mother-to-be before the birth to check that everything is ready, and is present at the birth. Your doctor will also try to be present.

It is an offence for anyone other than a registered midwife or registered medical practitioner to attend a woman in childbirth, unless:

- The case is one of sudden or urgent necessity.
- The woman is attended by a trainee midwife or doctor as part of his or her training.

The maximum penalty is a £1,000 fine.

When the baby is born

Most births, whether at home or in hospital, take place naturally. But if a birth is exceptionally late, or if the mother has been in labour for a long time, the doctor may suggest that birth be induced by the use of drugs. The mother's consent must be obtained.

In difficult births the doctor may suggest using forceps. Again, the mother's permission will be sought.

If a normal birth is not possible, the doctor may decide to deliver the baby by a caesarian section operation, in which he cuts into the abdomen to remove the child.

The mother will be asked to sign a consent form. If she is not fully conscious the operation can proceed without her consent, but an attempt would probably be made, if there was time, to obtain the consent of the next of kin – for example, the husband – although this is not legally essential.

If mother or baby is harmed because of negligence by nursing or medical staff, damages can be claimed in the courts. For example, delay in deciding on the method of delivery, causing brain damage to the baby, might amount to negligence.

Help that is available after birth

Mother and baby will receive regular home visits by a HEALTH VISITOR to help and advise on baby care and feeding. There is no obligation to see a health visitor if you do not want her services.

Non-contributory maternity grant

Almost all expectant mothers are entitled to a maternity grant – a lump-sum social security payment – to help with the general expense of having a baby.

The grant, which in 1983–84 was £25, can be claimed from the 14th week before the baby is due to 3 months after the baby is born. If you claim between 3 to 12 months after the baby is born, you will only get the grant if you had a good reason for not claiming earlier.

If more than one child is born, the mother can claim the maternity grant for each child who lives at least 12 hours. If all the babies were to die within 12 hours, the grant would still be paid for one birth.

In a single birth where the baby is stillborn, the grant is paid only if the pregnancy lasted at least 28 weeks.

Until July, 1982, a minimum amount of NATIONAL INSURANCE CONTRIBUTIONS had to be paid before a woman could get maternity grant. But since July 4, 1982, the grant has been non-contributory. Instead of contribution conditions having to be met, the woman must satisfy the test of having been in the United Kingdom for 26 out of the 52 weeks before confinement.

Mothers on supplementary benefit

An expectant mother receiving supplementary benefit (or whose husband is receiving it) is entitled to a lump-sum payment to enable her to buy essential items for the baby. So is a woman who is receiving supplementary benefit and who has recently given birth.

The payment cannot be made until 6 weeks before the baby is due. The maternity grant of £25 and any savings over £500 are taken into account in deciding how much she will get. The grant will be ignored if the woman can show she spent it on non-maternity items for which an extra lump-sum payment could have been made. *See:* SUPPLEMENTARY BENEFIT

Items that can be provided include baby clothes and nappies, a cot mattress, sheets and blankets, feeding bottles, and a second-hand cot, pram (or carrycot) and baby bath.

A lump-sum payment can also be made for maternity clothing needed at any time while the family is on supplementary benefit.

An expectant mother or young child in a family getting supplementary benefit or FAMILY INCOME SUPPLEMENT is entitled to FREE MILK – a pint a day. Other families with low incomes also qualify.

Special provisions for working women

Pregnant women who have been working may be entitled to other payments as well as the maternity grant, and they have special rights if they want to resume their employment after having the baby.

There are two payments to which they may be entitled – maternity allowance from the state and maternity pay from their employer.

Maternity allowance Maternity allowance is a weekly contributory benefit (£25.95 in 1983–84) payable to a pregnant woman to allow her to give up work in good time before the baby is born. It is payable for 18 weeks, starting 11 weeks before the baby is due. The allowance is increased by 15p for each child – this stops in November, 1984 – and by £16 for a husband who does not earn more than that amount.

Maternity allowance is payable only if the expectant mother herself has paid a minimum amount of full-rate national insurance contributions. Reduced-rate contributions paid by some married women and widows do not count.

To obtain the allowance, the woman must have paid Class 1 (employee's) contributions on earnings of at least 25 times the LOWER EARNINGS LIMIT, or equivalent Class 2 (self-employed) contributions, in any one tax year. Contributions credited during sickness or unemployment do not count. She must

HOW A WORKING WOMAN'S MATERNITY BENEFITS ARE CALCULATED

A working woman may be entitled to three separate maternity payments – maternity grant, maternity allowance and maternity pay.

In the case of a woman earning £100 a week and paying full-rate national insurance contributions the amount (1983–4) will total:

Maternity pay at 90% of weekly salary	£90.00
Less flat-rate maternity allowance	£25.95
Net maternity pay per week	£64.05
Maternity pay is paid for 6 weeks – 6 × £64.05	£384.30
Plus maternity allowance of £25.95 per week for 18 weeks	£467.10
Plus maternity grant of £25.00	£25.00
Total maternity payments	£876.40

also have paid or been credited with contributions on earnings of at least 50 times the lower earnings limit in the relevant tax year.

The 'relevant tax year' is not the same as the calendar year in which you are claiming. For example, if your baby was expected between March 20, 1983 and March 17, 1984, the relevant tax year was 6 April, 1981 to 5 April, 1982. If the baby is expected between March 18, 1984 and March 23, 1985, the relevant tax year is 6 April, 1982 to 5 April, 1983.

Even if you do not have contributions or credits on earnings of 50 times the lower limit, you may be able to get a reduced allowance. Special credits can be given to school leavers, students, apprentices, divorced women and widows to enable them to meet the requirements.

Maternity allowance is not payable while you continue to do any paid work, nor if you are getting an equal or higher rate of unemployment, sickness, invalidity or industrial death benefit.

To claim maternity allowance, complete form BM4 – on which you also claim maternity grant – as soon as possible after the 14th week before the baby is due. If you claim later than the 11th week you may lose benefit. The allowance is paid by means of a book of orders which can be cashed at a post office.

Maternity pay In addition to maternity allowance, you can claim 6 weeks' maternity pay from your employer when you leave to have a baby if:

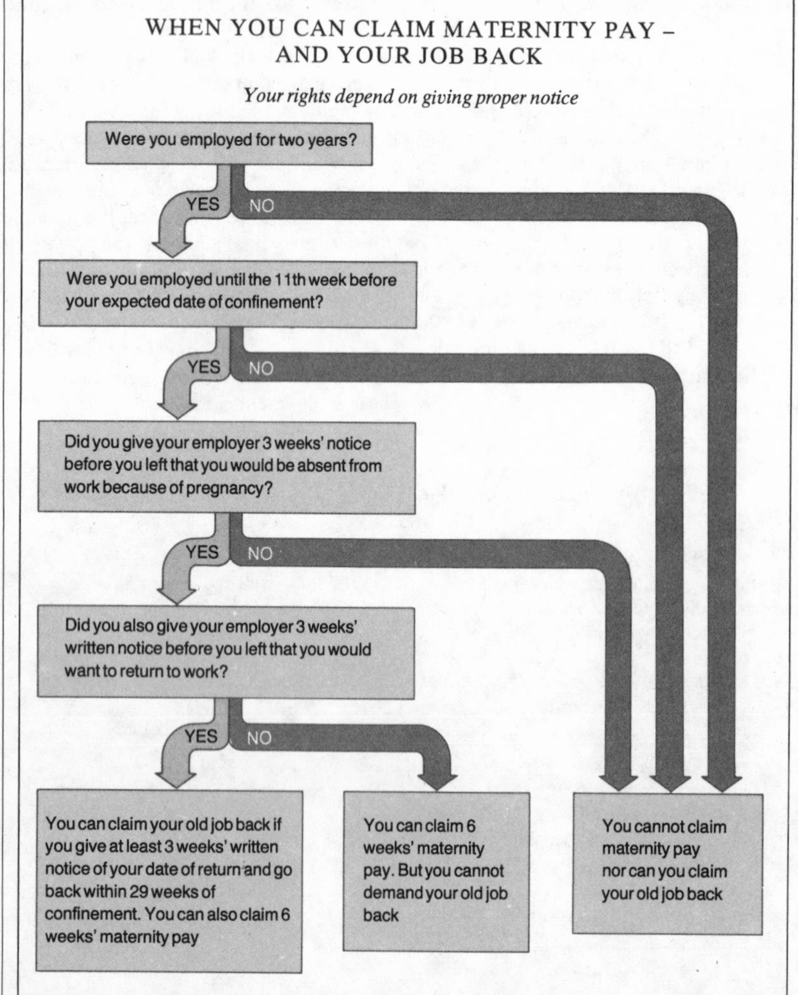

● You have been continuously employed by your employer for at least 2 years by the beginning of the 11th week before the baby is due. Normally, only weeks in which you usually work at least 16 hours are counted towards the 2 year period. However, if you have been employed by your employer for 5 years, weeks in which you usually work at least 8 hours can count. *See:* CONTINUOUS EMPLOYMENT

● You continue to be employed until at least the beginning of the 11th week before the baby is due. You need not actually be at work until the 11th week so long as you continue to be an employee – for example, you may be on holiday or on sick leave.

If you are dismissed before the beginning of the 11th week because your pregnancy makes you incapable of doing your job (or it would be illegal for you to do it) you are still entitled to maternity pay provided you would have had 2 years' employment by the 11th week if you had not been dismissed. It is important to wait until your employer dismisses you for incapacity; if you resign before the 11th week because the job is too much for you, you will lose your right to maternity pay.

You can work beyond the 11th week if you want without affecting your right to maternity pay or maternity leave.

You must give your employer at least 3 weeks' notice that you will be absent because of pregnancy, otherwise you will not be entitled to maternity pay. If you have to leave earlier than expected, and are unable to give 3 weeks' notice, you must inform your employer as soon as possible. The notice need not be in writing unless the employer requests, though it is advisable to put it in writing so there can be no dispute.

Your employer can refuse to pay you if you do not produce a medical certificate showing when the baby is due.

You are entitled to 6 weeks' maternity pay at the rate of 90 per cent of your usual pay. But flat-rate maternity allowance is deducted from that, even if you are not entitled to claim it – for example, if you have been paying a married woman's reduced-rate national insurance contribution. Maternity pay is also taxable.

Your employer can pay either weekly, or in a lump sum when you leave. He reclaims the money in full from the

Maternity Pay Fund administered by the Department of Employment.

If your employer fails to pay, you can complain to an industrial tribunal within 3 months. It can order payment to be made. If your employer does not comply – or if he is insolvent – contact the Department of Employment. It can pay you out of the Maternity Pay Fund if satisfied that your claim is well-founded.

Getting your job back

You are entitled to your job back after having a baby if:

- You have been continuously employed by your employer for at least 2 years by the beginning of the 11th week before the baby is due. (Normally, only weeks in which you usually work at least 16 hours are counted towards the 2 year period. However, if you have been employed by your employer for 5 years, weeks in which you usually work at least 8 hours can count.)
- You continue to be employed until the beginning of the 11th week before the baby is due, although you need not actually be at work.
- You give your employer at least 3 weeks' *written* notice – you can give him less if this is not reasonably practicable – telling him that you will be absent because of pregnancy and that you intend to return to work. You must also tell him your expected date of confinement – and, if he requests, provide a medical certificate to confirm it.
- You return to work within 29 weeks beginning with the week in which the confinement falls. You have the right to postpone your return once, for up to 4 weeks, if you give your employer a medical certificate stating that you are not well enough to return to work.
- You give your employer at least 21 days' written notice of your proposed date of return.

Your employer is entitled to ask you (in writing) not earlier than 49 days after the expected date of confinement whether you still intend to return. If he does so, you must confirm in writing to him within 14 days – or longer if that is not reasonably practicable – that you intend to return. If you do not, you will lose your right to return.

The 29 week period can be extended if there is a strike, holiday or some other interruption beyond your control.

Your employer is entitled to delay your return by up to 4 weeks if he gives you a reason before your proposed date of return.

Alternative work If, because of redundancy, your old job is not available when you return, you are entitled to be offered any suitable available vacancy. You must be offered employment terms which are not substantially less favourable than those of your original job.

If you are not offered a suitable vacancy which is available, you are entitled to treat yourself as unfairly dismissed (see below).

If you cannot get your job back because of redundancy, and no suitable vacancy exists, you may be entitled to a redundancy payment. *See:* REDUNDANCY

Refusal to allow return to work If a woman is entitled to return to work, but her employer refuses to take her back, she will be treated as continuously employed until the date she would have returned, and as dismissed with effect from that date. She can then make a complaint of unfair dismissal to an industrial tribunal. When deciding whether or not such a dismissal was fair, the tribunal will consider whether the employer's reason for refusing to take her back would have been sufficient to justify dismissal had she been at work.

However, a woman who is not allowed to return will *not* be treated as dismissed – and therefore will have no right to make a complaint of unfair dismissal – if:

- Immediately before she left work, her employer (and any associated employer) employed no more than 5 people; and
- It is not 'reasonably practicable' for her employer to give her back her job, or to offer her a suitable alternative vacancy.

Nor will she be treated as dismissed – no matter how many are employed – if:

- It is not reasonably practicable, for a reason other than redundancy, for the employer to give her back her job; and
- She unreasonably refuses alternative work on terms not substantially less favourable than those of her original job.

Getting advice The rules on maternity pay and getting your job back are complex and are strictly applied. Seek advice on your case from a trade union official, local Citizens Advice Bureau or other advice agency.

Dismissal because of pregnancy

The dismissal of a woman simply because she is pregnant is unfair in law, unless the employer can show that the pregnancy prevents her doing her job adequately or that the law forbids the employment of a pregnant woman (as it does, for example, with jobs involving exposure to radiation).

However, the employer must offer any suitable vacancy to a pregnant employee who cannot continue with her job for either of those reasons. If he does not do so, the dismissal will be unfair.

Certain part-time employees cannot claim unfair dismissal if they are sacked because they are pregnant. *See:* PART-TIME WORKER

WHEN A MISCARRIAGE LOST AN EMPLOYEE HER JOB

It is usually unfair to dismiss a female employee for reasons connected with her pregnancy.

Miss B, aged 18, was employed in a bottling factory. Her medical record was not good, and she had a high rate of absenteeism. Between January and March 1976 she had been given oral and written warnings that her attendance must improve or she would be dismissed.

In June 1976 she told her manager that she was pregnant but said she would work normally until the birth. She had a miscarriage and was admitted to hospital on July 18.

Miss B was given notice by her employer when she returned to work on July 27. She took her case to an industrial tribunal.

DECISION

The industrial tribunal held that Miss B's dismissal was unfair. Despite her poor medical record she had been sacked for absences arising from her pregnancy. When her company refused to reinstate her she was awarded compensation.

A woman is protected against dismissal for pregnancy only after she has been working for her employer for 1 year (2 years if no more than 20 have been employed during those 2 years). *See:* UNFAIR DISMISSAL

MATRIMONIAL PROPERTY

Who owns what in a marriage

Each partner in a marriage is entitled to keep his or her property, whether it was acquired before or after marriage. The other partner has no legal right to it. However, a couple can hold property in their joint names if they wish – the matrimonial home, for example, is often jointly owned.

If the marriage breaks down, the parties keep their own property and can agree to share out the jointly owned matrimonial property between them according to their needs and the contribution each has made. Each partner is entitled to half of any property which is jointly owned, regardless of what they contributed towards it.

If the parties cannot agree about who should take what, each is entitled to keep his or her own property and to have joint property sold, if necessary, to obtain the half-share of its value.

WHO OWNS THE WEDDING PRESENTS?

When wedding presents are given to a couple there may be a dispute as to which partner owns them. The courts decide such disputes by looking, amongst other things, for evidence of the intention of the person who gave the present.

Paul and Susan married in 1946 and Paul's mother gave a wedding present of £20. They used it to buy a bed, a mattress and four pillows.

Three years later, Paul and Susan separated. Paul raised a court action for delivery of these items. He claimed that since the money to buy them had come from his mother, they belonged to him.

In her evidence, Paul's mother said that she had intended to give the money to both of them.

DECISION

The court refused to order delivery of the items to Paul. The judge said that the intention of the donor (Paul's mother) determined who owned wedding presents. In this case, therefore, the bed, mattress and pillows, having been bought with money intended for both of them, belonged jointly to both.

Where there is a dispute over ownership of property

When a couple disagree over who owns a particular item of MOVEABLE PROPERTY – that is, nearly everything except land and buildings – either one can apply to the sheriff court or the Court of Session for an order deciding the dispute. The court will decide who is the rightful owner and order the property to be handed over to that person. For example, if a wife has possession of a motor car and her husband proves that he paid for it and never gave it to her, the court will order the wife to hand it over.

The court can also decide a dispute over HERITABLE PROPERTY – that is, land or buildings, including houses, flats and shops. The court will look first of all at the documents of ownership (known as 'title deeds'). If you claim part or full ownership of the property and your name is not mentioned in the documents, you must comply with a special procedure in order to succeed.

This requires that your partner – whose name appears in the title deeds – must admit (either in writing or on oath in court) that the property in dispute is really owned wholly or partly by you. You will need to consult a solicitor about this.

The matrimonial home

If there is a dispute about ownership of the matrimonial home, the ordinary rules apply. The spouse whose name is on the title deeds is legally the owner. However, each spouse will normally have OCCUPANCY RIGHTS in the home and will therefore be legally entitled to live there.

Where one spouse commits or threatens violence against the other, or against children, the innocent spouse who has occupancy rights can ask the Court of Session or sheriff court to order the violent spouse to leave the home, even although he or she owns it. *See:* BATTERED WOMAN

If the matrimonial home is rented by one spouse only, the other spouse will normally have occupancy rights and will therefore be legally entitled to live there. Again, the court can order the spouse who is the tenant to leave if he or she has been violent.

If you are not a tenant but your partner is, you can apply to the court to have the tenancy transferred to you. In deciding whether to order the transfer, the court must consider all the circumstances, including the conduct of you and your partner, your means and needs, and the needs of any children.

Wedding presents

The ownership of wedding presents depends on the intention of the person who gave them. Even if this intention is not expressly stated, the kind of present given may provide sufficient indication of whom it was meant for.

For instance, if a husband is a keen gardener and his wife has no interest in gardening, a gift of hedgeclippers would probably be seen as a present to the husband alone.

In the absence of any evidence as to intention, the presents are presumed to belong to husband and wife equally.

When the courts intervene in the marriage

When there is a judicial separation, each spouse is entitled to keep his or her own property. However, the court can order one spouse to pay ALIMENT to the other. Aliment continues until divorce or until the partner receiving it dies, unless the partner who is paying applies successfully to the court for cancellation of the payment. Either partner can ask the court to vary the amount payable if there has been a change of circumstances. *See:* SEPARATION

When a court grants decree of divorce, each party again keeps his or her own property. But the court can order one partner to pay the other a fixed sum of money at regular intervals – called a 'periodical allowance'. This allowance continues until the partner receiving payment dies or remarries, or the partner who is paying successfully applies to the court for cancellation of the allow-

PROPERTY RIGHTS IN THE FAMILY HOME

Many family homes are owned jointly by the husband and wife. This means that both of them have a legal right to live in the house and neither can sell it without the consent of the other.

If one partner wishes to sell the house, but the other partner refuses consent, the partner who wishes to sell can raise a court action for the 'division and sale' of the house.

When considering whether to allow the sale, the court must consider all the circumstances, including:

- Whether the partner bringing the action offers – or has offered – the other partner suitable alternative accommodation.
- The conduct of the partners.
- Their needs and financial resources.
- The needs of any children.

The court can refuse to allow the sale or can postpone making an order – perhaps to allow a partner to find other accommodation. If it allows the sale, it can attach conditions to its order.

If the house is in the husband's sole name, his wife will have legal OCCUPANCY RIGHTS – unless she has signed these away. If she has these rights, and the house is sold, the buyer generally cannot move in unless she has given formal, written consent to the sale.

However, if she does not consent the husband can apply to the court for an order dispensing with her consent. The court can make the order if:

- Her consent is unreasonably withheld.
- Consent cannot be given because of physical or mental disability.
- She cannot be found.
- She is under 18.

A wife who has no rights of ownership in the family home may be able to apply to the Court of Session or sheriff court for help if she is turned out by her husband. If she has occupancy rights, the court can order her husband to allow her back into the house. If he does not comply, he will be in CONTEMPT OF COURT.

Where the husband has committed or threatened violence against his wife or children, his wife may also be able to obtain a court order excluding him from the house. *See:* BATTERED WOMAN

All these rights apply equally to a husband if the ownership of his home is in his wife's name alone.

ance. Either partner can ask the court to vary the amount payable if there has been a change of circumstances.

In addition, the court can order one partner to pay the other a capital (lump) sum. This is a 'once only' payment and cannot be varied later. *See:* DIVORCE

Although the Scottish courts have no power – as the courts have in England and Wales – to transfer property from one partner to another on divorce, the possibility of obtaining a capital sum may result, in practice, in a transfer or loss of property.

For example, a home is owned by a husband and is worth £40,000. His wife, who has custody of the children and needs money to provide a new home, successfully asks the court to award her a capital sum of £20,000. If the husband has insufficient savings, he may be forced to sell the house to raise the money. Alternatively, he may decide to transfer the whole house to his wife – in which case she will have to pay him £20,000. She may be able to raise this amount by obtaining a MORTGAGE.

If there is a decree of nullity, the court cannot order either party to pay anything to the other. *See:* NULLITY

MEALS ON WHEELS

When hot meals are taken to people who are unable to cook for themselves

Most regional and islands councils provide a mobile service to deliver hot meals to elderly or handicapped people who are unable to cook for themselves. Special diets are often catered for.

Some councils run the service themselves; others work in conjunction with the Women's Royal Voluntary Service.

The meals are cooked at a central kitchen and delivered in heated containers by vans or private cars. Meals may be provided daily or only on certain days of the week.

Applying for meals

Anyone who is unable to cook for himself or herself – such as the bedridden, housebound, mentally and physically handicapped, or frail or confused elderly people – and has no-one who is able to cook for him or her may be provided with meals on wheels. However, there is no legal right to receive meals.

Ask your doctor, district nurse, health visitor or social worker to apply to the council offices on your behalf.

Cost A charge is made for each meal. It will usually be paid to the person who delivers the meal.

MEDICAL CARD

Your passport to free health treatment

Every person registered for free Health Service treatment with a family doctor has a medical card issued by the area health board. Anyone who does not have a card could find it difficult to get free treatment from a doctor, dentist or optician, because they are entitled to ask to see it if they have doubts about a patient's identity.

How to get a medical card

Every child whose birth is registered is allocated a National Health Service number by the registrar. The number is on form EC 58, handed to the person who registers the birth. It should be taken to the family doctor, who will sign it and send it to the health board for the area. The board then issues a medical card, which has the child's NHS number on it.

Changing doctors

Anyone who changes doctors should take his medical card to the new doctor

YOUR RIGHT TO TREATMENT

A National Health Service doctor is entitled to see a patient's medical card if he has doubts about his identity. But he cannot refuse any necessary treatment.

who, if he accepts him, will send it to the area health board. The board will issue a new card.

A new card must also be issued if a person is changing address, but intends to stay with his family doctor. *See:* DOCTOR AND PATIENT

When a card is lost

A free medical card will be issued by the area health board to anyone who loses his medical card.

Tell the board your full name, address, the name of your doctor and your NHS number if you have it. If you have not kept a note of the number, or cannot remember it, there may be a delay while the board checks the NHS central register.

A patient without a medical card may be refused free NHS treatment by a doctor who doubts the patient's identity, but that is very unlikely. The doctor is still legally required to give the patient any necessary treatment. If a charge is made for the treatment, the patient can apply to the board within 14 days. If it is satisfied that he was on the doctor's list, it can make the doctor withdraw his account or refund to the patient any fee paid.

A temporary resident can apply to a local doctor to accept him as a patient for up to 3 months. After that he will have to make arrangements for a change of doctor.

Special rules for foreigners

Overseas visitors will generally be charged for any NHS hospital treatment that they receive. But there are exceptions. Visitors who will not be charged include:

- Those who receive emergency outpatient treatment in hospital.
- Those who have come to settle.
- Those who have lived in the UK for at least one year.
- Those who are in the UK because of their work.
- Those who have been accepted as refugees. *See:* REFUGEE
- Those who come from countries with whom the UK has reciprocal arrangements – that is, EEC countries and some others such as Norway and Sweden.

If an overseas visitor is wrongly charged, he can reclaim his money by presenting his receipt to the local health board.

MEDICAL CERTIFICATE

A doctor's confirmation of a medical condition

General practitioners are required by the terms of service in their contract with the area health board to issue certain medical certificates free of charge to patients who need them to prove a medical condition.

The principal reasons for which certificates are issued are:

- To confirm pregnancy so that an expectant mother can obtain welfare foods and maternity benefits.
- To register a death – necessary under the Registration of Births, Deaths and Marriages (Scotland) Act 1965. *See:* DEATH, Registration of
- To register a still-birth – necessary under the same Act.
- To help claimants to obtain social security and housing benefits, when evidence of disability or incapacity is needed.
- To confirm that a person entitled to any payment out of public funds, such as a pension or supplementary benefit, is incapable through MENTAL DISORDER of managing his property – necessary under the Mental Health Act 1983. This allows payment to be made to someone else.
- To establish medical unfitness for JURY service.
- To enable someone to be registered as an absent voter because of physical incapacity. *See:* ELECTION; ELECTORAL REGISTRATION

Claiming social security benefits

Before October 1976 a doctor issued a medical certificate to a patient needing evidence of incapacity for the purpose of claiming sickness or invalidity benefit. This has since been replaced by a certificate in the form of a doctor's statement.

The statement, which is issued free, records a doctor's advice that the patient should refrain from work, rather than certifying that the patient is suffering from a certain disease and unable to work. The statement also contains a diagnosis of the disorder causing absence from work.

Refusing a patient

If a doctor refuses to issue one of the above certificates when a patient's condition entitles him to it – or if he charges for it – he will be in breach of his terms of service and can be reported to the area health board, which will investigate the matter. The complaint must be in writing and lodged within 6 weeks of the doctor refusing the certificate. *See:* DOCTOR AND PATIENT

Giving false information

A doctor who issues a certificate, although he knows there are no valid grounds for it, to enable a patient to obtain social security benefit commits an offence under the Social Security Act 1975. He is liable to a maximum penalty of £2,000 and 3 months' imprisonment, as well as disciplinary action by the General Medical Council.

Anyone who gives a doctor false information to obtain a certificate, or knowingly uses a certificate containing false information, for the purpose of obtaining benefit is liable to the same maximum penalty.

Someone who obtains benefit by knowingly using false information can be prosecuted for FRAUD.

How to obtain a certificate

If you need a certificate you should go to your doctor and explain why you need it. If you are ill and cannot get to the surgery, you can ask the doctor to visit you.

Examination Before issuing a certificate, a doctor must examine you – either physically or orally. If you refuse to be examined he will not issue the certificate.

Collecting Usually the doctor will give you the certificate when he has examined you. But if there is a delay – perhaps he needs more evidence, or the certificates are not immediately available – he will ask you to collect it later. If you have sent someone else to collect it the person should be known to the doctor or receptionist, or carry a letter of authority from you. The contents of a certificate are confidential and a doctor is entitled to refuse to release it to anyone other than the person for whom he issued it.

If an employer wants proof

If you are off work through sickness or injury, your employer must usually provide you with sick PAY for the first 8 weeks of absence. SICKNESS BENEFIT is not available during that period.

Your employer may insist that you provide medical evidence of your illness, in the form of a doctor's statement, after a certain number of days' illness. Your contract of employment may require you to do so.

If you need a private certificate

If you need a certificate for private purposes – rather than to establish your right to a state benefit – your doctor is entitled to charge any fee he chooses.

The amount he charges will depend upon the amount of work he has to do.

Types of certificate Some of the reasons for which a doctor is asked for a private certificate are:

- To confirm sickness – for school or employer, for instance.
- To establish fitness for a particular purpose, such as taking up a new job, playing rugby or other sport at school, or driving a vehicle.
- For vaccination or inoculation.
- For insurance purposes.

Medical report If an employer or insurance company requires more detailed evidence than a certificate and you are asked to have a medical examination, this will usually be paid for by whoever asks for the medical report. But the doctor must have your permission before he can pass on the information.

MEDICAL NEGLIGENCE

When a patient can take action for negligent medical care

A doctor can be sued for NEGLIGENCE if he harms a patient by failing to exercise the standard of care and skill expected from a competent medical practitioner in his position. The standard of care and skill expected from a doctor is the same whether he is treating a patient under the National Health Service or privately.

A doctor is not automatically negligent on each occasion when he makes a mistake. The position which he holds will be relevant in deciding whether there has been negligence. For example, a general practitioner is only expected to act as a reasonably competent general practitioner: he is not required to have the skills of a specialist. He will not be considered to be negligent if he has done something which an ordinary skilled doctor, acting with ordinary care, would have done. Nor is he necessarily negligent if he does not act in the way most doctors in his position would have done.

However, no allowance is made for a doctor's inexperience. Except in an emergency, a doctor should not undertake treatment unless he is qualified and competent to give it. If he is not, he should take appropriate steps to refer the patient to someone who is.

Proving that a doctor was negligent

If you are attempting to prove in court that a doctor has been negligent, expert evidence from other doctors – particularly those with wide experience of the aspect of medical practice involved – will be of very great importance. Usually, the crucial question is: what is the normal practice in the medical profession for dealing with your medical condition?

Sometimes the basic facts of a case will suggest that a doctor must have been negligent. For example, in one case a patient went into hospital for a kidney operation, but was mistaken for another patient and was circumcised instead. However, even in a case where a layman would conclude that a doctor must have been negligent, a court may accept that there is a perfectly good explanation for his actions and that they do not amount to negligence. In these cases, therefore, expert evidence will still be important.

Proving the negligence caused harm

If you are suing a doctor (or his employers) it is not enough to prove that the doctor was negligent. You must also prove, on 'the balance of probabilities' (the standard of evidence required in civil cases), that the doctor's negligent acts caused the harm about which you are complaining.

HOW TO SUE

Anyone who thinks that he has been harmed as a result of medical negligence should consult a solicitor. If there is sufficient evidence, the patient can sue the person or authority responsible for the negligence.

Suing a GP

A patient can sue his general practitioner for negligence committed by the practitioner or by anyone in his employment – for instance, a nurse who works in the practice. If the nurse harms a patient, the patient can sue the nurse, and the doctor as her employer.

If a general practitioner is in partnership with other doctors, each is responsible for the negligence of the others. So if a negligent doctor is unable to meet a claim for damages against him, the other doctors can be required to pay. In practice, doctors are invariably insured against medical negligence; indeed those who work in the National Health Service are required to be insured.

Suing a hospital doctor

If a National Health Service hospital doctor is negligent, the patient can sue the doctor and the area health board which employs him. Sometimes it is difficult to establish who was negligent, as treatment might have been given by more than one doctor and might have involved other hospital employees, such as nurses. But since they are all employed by the health board, the board will be liable so long as the patient can prove that someone was negligent, even if he cannot prove whom.

If negligence occurs because the board fails to provide suitable qualified and experienced staff, or to take reasonable care to ensure that equipment is in proper working order, the board will be liable as a result of these shortcomings.

Private treatment

If a doctor treats a patient privately in a National Health Service Hospital, the health board is not responsible for any negligence on the doctor's part. The patient can sue only the doctor. However, if the board supplies equipment and back-up facilities such as x-rays, it will be liable if a patient is harmed because of its failure to keep these in a reasonable condition.

If the hospital allocates staff to look after the private patient, they will be acting in their capacity as hospital employees, and they and the health board will be liable for any negligence occurring through their fault.

Establishing the connection between the doctor's negligence and the harm suffered usually requires the court to assess complicated scientific evidence. This is particularly so in cases where the patient already suffers from some illness or injury, perhaps in a dormant state.

In one case a doctor turned a man away from a hospital casualty department without examining him. As it was early in the morning on New Year's Day, the doctor simply assumed that the man was drunk. But the man had been poisoned with arsenic and he subsequently died. Nevertheless, scientific evidence showed that the amount of arsenic in his body was so great that nothing could have been done to save him. Although the doctor had been negligent in turning him away, this had not caused his death.

When a doctor fails to explain the risks

All medical treatment involves some degree of risk. If the patient has consented to a particular treatment or course of treatment, the doctor need not tell that patient all the possible risks. He need only say what a reasonable doctor would be expected to say in the circumstances.

If a patient is not warned, and is harmed as a result of the treatment, it will then be a question of expert evidence as to whether he should have been told.

If a doctor carries out treatment without obtaining a patient's consent, he can be sued for any harm which results – unless the treatment was carried out in an emergency and it was not possible to obtain the patient's consent.

For example, if a woman goes into hospital for a routine operation, such as for removal of her appendix, but is sterilised without her consent, the doctor will be liable.

When a diagnosis is wrong

If a doctor makes an incorrect diagnosis which results in no treatment (or the wrong treatment) being given, he may be guilty of negligence. For instance, he may fail to notice obvious symptoms, or to carry out tests which are normally conducted when certain symptoms are apparent. But he will not be blamed if he is unable to diagnose correctly a condition that is very rare or difficult to detect.

If a doctor prescribes carelessly

A doctor must take reasonable care to ensure that any drugs which he prescribes or administers to a patient are suitable for the patient's condition and that the patient is not seriously allergic to them. Some people, for example, are allergic to antibiotics such as penicillin, and suffer if they take them.

A doctor will be negligent if he writes out an incorrect prescription. If the patient is then harmed through taking either the wrong drug or an incorrect dosage, he can sue the doctor.

Side effects Many drugs have all sorts of side effects. Sometimes these are so severe that they make it dangerous for the patient to do certain things. In that situation the doctor should warn the patient against such activities, if it seems reasonably likely that he would otherwise continue with them.

For example, a drug may cause drowsiness in some patients. If it is likely that the patient will drive, or operate machinery, the doctor should warn him against doing so.

If it is dangerous for the patient to eat or drink certain foods while taking a drug, this must be pointed out.

Certain antidepressant drugs – for example, monoamine-oxidase inhibitors (MAOI) – are incompatible with many other drugs, with foods such as cheese, yeast and meat-extracts, hydrolysed vegetable protein, and with alcohol. To mix them can be fatal.

Injections If the drug is to be injected, the doctor must take care that the correct dosage is used, that the needle is strong enough for the type of injection and not liable to snap, and that he injects into the correct part of the patient's body. For instance, to inject into an artery instead of a vein could cause death.

German measles Before a woman is inoculated against German measles (rubella), a doctor must make sure that she is not pregnant, as the vaccine could damage the foetus.

When a surgeon is negligent

If an operation is not successful, or causes damage to the patient, the surgeon will be liable only if it can be shown that he was negligent. It is not enough to show that he made an error of clinical judgment if any reasonable surgeon, acting with due care and skill, could have made a similar error.

If a surgeon operates on the wrong patient, or performs the wrong operation, the patient can sue him for negligence. It is the surgeon's duty to satisfy himself that he has the right patient before him, that the details of the operation are correct and that the patient has been correctly marked out for surgery.

THE HYPODERMIC NEEDLE WHICH BROKE

A doctor will be liable for negligence if he falls below the standard of skill and care to be expected of a reasonably competent doctor.

Mrs Jemima Hunter suffered from a chest complaint and her treatment was a course of penicillin injections into one of her muscles.

She had eleven such injections, all without incident, but on the twelfth occasion the needle broke. She had to be taken to hospital to have the remainder of the needle removed from just above her pelvis.

Mrs Hunter sued the doctor who gave her the injection. She alleged that he had been negligent because he had failed to use a needle which was sufficiently strong to inject into a muscle.

Her case was heard by a judge sitting with a civil jury. She lost, and appealed.

DECISION

The appeal court allowed Mrs Hunter's appeal. In their view the judge had given wrong directions to the jury as to the test which they were to apply when deciding whether the doctor was liable.

The judge had told the jury, wrongly, that the doctor could only be liable if he had been grossly negligent. But the appeal court said that what they should have been told to consider was whether the course which the doctor adopted was one which no professional man of ordinary skill would have taken if he had been acting with ordinary care.

The court ordered the case to be heard again before another jury.

A surgeon may also be guilty of negligence if he causes a patient's condition to worsen, or injures him, during the course of an operation, except in the case of an unavoidable accident – such as a scalpel slipping due to the patient having a muscle spasm.

If a swab or instrument is left inside a patient after an operation, the surgeon can be sued for negligence if harm has resulted. But he will not be guilty of negligence if the operation had to be abandoned urgently because of a sudden deterioration in the patient's condition and there was no time to check that all swabs had been removed.

MEDICAL RECORD

Access to medical information

Doctors, whether in general practice or in hospital, must keep records of the illnesses and treatment of their patients. In the National Health Service the records are the property of the Secretary of State for Scotland. In private practice they belong to the doctor. Patients are not entitled to see records held manually except in the case of actions for DAMAGES, where details of treatment are relevant.

In these circumstances there are procedures open to the patient whereby the records can be made available. This will involve an application to the Court of Session or sheriff court. It would almost certainly be necessary to obtain the advice of a solicitor.

Although the records are the property of the Secretary of State, any court action to have them made available would be taken against the area health board, as custodians of the records.

Different rules apply to medical records held on computer. Patients may have a right of access to these. *See:* COMPUTER RECORD.

Medical records must be made available, on request, to the area health board and to medical officers appointed by the Secretary of State. However, they must not be disclosed to anyone else, other than the patient, without the patient's consent, and even then only at the discretion of his doctor. In practice, they are disclosed only to other doctors, and perhaps nurses, who are sharing or assuming responsibility for treatment.

NOT FOR YOUR EYES

Patients are not entitled to see their medical records except in the case of an action for damages.

Similarly, the disclosure of the results of medical examinations – for insurance companies and prospective employers, for example – can be made only with the consent of the patient, who will be asked to agree this in writing.

If a doctor discloses confidential information without a patient's consent, he can be sued or reported to the General Medical Council. *See:* DOCTOR AND PATIENT

Doctors may not break the law or their code of ethics if they disclose a patient's record to police who are seeking someone who may have had to have treatment as a result of being involved in a serious crime. In any case, the police may seize documents using a search warrant.

When a doctor makes a mistake in his records – for example, if he gives incorrect details about treatment – and the patient later receives the wrong treatment because of that error, the doctor will be liable for his mistake. A doctor may also be liable to DEFAMATION proceedings if he makes defamatory comments in a patient's records which are then disclosed to a third party.

MEMBER OF PARLIAMENT

The role of your parliamentary representative

Anyone aged 21 or over is entitled to take his seat in the House of Commons when he has been elected to represent a constituency – unless he is disqualified by law.

A candidate's return to Parliament can be challenged only by an election petition. If a voter or defeated candidate believes that a disqualified person has been elected he can lodge a petition within 21 days in the Court of Session – but he must also provide a guarantee or security for the sum of £1,000.

The petition is heard publicly by two Court of Session judges who form an Election Petition Court. The court's judgment is reported to the Speaker of the House who is bound to accept its findings.

The duty of an MP

It is every MP's duty to represent all his constituents in the House of Commons, at party discussions and to government ministers and their departments – whether or not they voted for him.

If an MP is not a member of the Government he can take any other job he likes, but all MPs must declare all their financial interests to the Speaker. A comprehensive register of those interests is kept in the House of Commons library and is open for public inspection.

An MP is not above the law and can be arrested or prosecuted in the same way as anybody else.

Contacting your MP

If you want to contact your MP, go to one of his regular constituency 'surgeries' – most MPs hold them. You can find out about these from his local party headquarters.

You can also write to him at the House of Commons, London SW1A 0AA. If Parliament is in recess your letter will be forwarded to him.

You may also write to any other MP. It is a House of Commons convention that MPs always inform the constituent's own MP of any contact that is made.

Lobbying an MP at the House of Commons

If you wish to see your MP at the House of Commons you can, by custom, lobby him – which means literally to see him in the central lobby of the Houses of Parliament. But you have no legal

WHEN YOU CANNOT BECOME AN MP

You cannot be a member of the House of Commons, even if elected, if you are:

- An alien. Citizens of Ireland and of Commonwealth countries are not aliens.
- Under 21.
- Detained in hospital because of MENTAL DISORDER.
- A peer or peeress in your own right, other than a peer of Ireland, unless you disclaim the title.
- Imprisoned or detained under a sentence of more than 1 year.
- Bankrupt. You remain disqualified until you obtain your discharge.
- Convicted of corrupt and illegal practices at elections.
- A minister of the Church of Scotland.
- A minister of the Church of England or the Episcopalian Church of Scotland, or any other Protestant clergyman ordained by a Bishop – except a minister of the disestablished Church of Wales.
- A Roman Catholic priest.

Other Christian ministers and clergymen of non-Christian denominations are not disqualified.

- The holder of a public office – such as a judge; civil servant; member of the regular armed forces; full-time member of a police force; member of certain boards and commissions or certain administrative tribunals. A full list of the disqualifications is set out in the House of Commons Disqualification Act 1975.
- Expelled by resolution of the House of Commons.

right to do this. You should write in advance to arrange an appointment, but even without one you can tell the messengers that you wish to talk to him. You will be asked to fill in a green card stating whom you wish to see and why. The messengers will then try to deliver it to the member.

Pressure groups Pressure groups sometimes organise mass lobbies so that their members can meet MPs to make their opinions known on as wide a basis as possible. However, as no procession or demonstration is allowed within a mile of the Houses of Parliament, mass lobbies take place through small groups and individual members meeting their own constituency MPs.

Often that means queueing for admission to the House, so anyone intending to lead a mass lobby would be advised – though not obliged – to inform the police so that necessary arrangements for controlling and protecting a crowd can be made. It would also be advisable for him to inform sympathetic MPs so that they can be in the House to accept the lobby.

Petitioning Parliament with a grievance

The right of any citizen to petition Parliament with a grievance is a fundamental principle that has been exercised for many centuries. There is no special petition form, but certain formal wording must be used. The top copy must be handwritten and every sheet must have the prayer written or printed at the top. There must be no attachments and no words added between the lines.

Delivering a petition A petition can either be sent to the Clerk of the House of Commons or handed in to an MP, who will then pass it on to the office concerned.

Very rarely – perhaps if the petition is a nationwide one – an MP may present it publicly in the House. It would not be debated, but would be referred to the committee for public petitions, and the Government may, after consideration, issue a reply.

Parliament's watchdog committees

One way in which MPs seek to check Government actions is through Select Committees, specialist committees of a few MPs. The powerful Public Accounts Committee, which scrutinises the accounts produced by all Government departments, is long-established; but in 1979 the House of Commons set up 14 new committees, each with about 10 MPs, to examine home affairs, foreign affairs, defence, trade and industry, environment, education and science, health and social services, Treasury and Civil Service, agriculture, energy, employment, transport, Scottish affairs and Welsh affairs.

These committees can take evidence from any member of the public. They have power to demand the attendance of any witness or the production of any document. In practice, they interview (in open session) ministers, senior civil servants, and representatives of organisations or individuals who have views on the subject they are investigating. Their reports can be influential.

The spending watchdog The National Audit Act 1983 set up a National Audit Office responsible to MPs, not the government, for auditing all public funds to ensure economy, efficiency and effectiveness in implementing policies.

The Office, which is headed by the Comptroller and Auditor General, can check the accounts of government departments and bodies receiving more than half their income from public funds. Its work is supervised by a Public Accounts Commission, composed of MPs.

How an MP's seat can become vacant

A Member of Parliament cannot legally resign his seat. However, he can be disqualified from sitting in the House if he becomes bankrupt and remains so for 6 months, or if he is expelled by the House, or if he accepts an office of profit under the Crown.

If an MP wants to give up his seat, however, he can apply for the Stewardship of the Chiltern Hundreds or of the Manor of Northstead – both Crown properties. If it is granted he is ineligible to sit in the Commons and his seat becomes vacant. His seat also becomes vacant if he dies. *See:* ELECTION

MENTAL DISORDER

How the law tries to balance welfare and personal freedom

Part of the legal responsibility for the care of mentally ill and mentally handicapped people rests with regional and islands councils – which in practice means their social work departments. Councils are responsible for:

- Appointing mental health officers from among the social workers in their area.
- Providing residential accommodation in the community.
- Exercising guardianship functions.
- Supervising people who are mentally handicapped.

● Providing after-care and other necessary services.

In practice, however, a great deal of the day-to-day care of people who are mentally disordered is provided by the health services. Area health boards are responsible for the provision and administration of mental hospitals in their area. Community psychiatric nurses, who are employed by health boards and work under the direct control and supervision of consultant psychiatrists, give nursing care to psychiatric outpatients – including patients who have been discharged from hospital.

There are a few private mental hospitals in Scotland – all run by religious organisations – that provide treatment for mentally disordered people. These hospitals must be registered with the Secretary of State for Scotland.

The Secretary of State is under a duty to provide special hospitals – called State hospitals – for people who are compulsorily detained and who need special security because of their dangerous, violent or criminal tendencies. There is only one such hospital in Scotland – the State Mental Hospital at Carstairs. This is under the control of the Secretary of State but is run by a management committee on his behalf.

The Mental Welfare Commission

Since 1962 an independent body called the Mental Welfare Commission has existed to protect the interests of mentally ill and mentally handicapped people in Scotland. The Commission has a number of powers, including the power to:

● Enquire into any allegation of ill-treatment or improper detention.
● Enquire into cases involving loss of or damage to the property of someone who is mentally disordered.
● Make regular visits to patients who are detained in hospital or subject to guardianship.
● Discharge patients who are detained in hospital or subject to guardianship.

See: MENTAL WELFARE COMMISSION

THE RIGHTS OF A PATIENT'S RELATIVES

One relative – called the 'nearest relative' – has the right to apply to the sheriff for an order committing a mentally disordered person to hospital or guardianship. He can also order the patient's discharge (subject to the doctor's agreement).

The nearest relative is the first person in the following list who normally lives in the UK and is either caring for the patient or was caring for him before his committal:

● Husband or wife.
● Child aged 18 or over.
● Father or mother.
● Brother or sister aged 18 or over.
● Grandparent.
● Grandchild aged 18 or over.
● Uncle or aunt aged 18 or over.
● Nephew or niece aged 18 or over.
● Someone aged 18 or over who has lived with the patient for at least 5 years – but only if the patient's spouse (if any) does not live with them.

If there are two or more people in the same category, the elder or eldest one is the nearest relative, regardless of sex.

A husband or wife who is separated from the patient, either under a separation agreement or a court order, cannot be the nearest relative. Nor can a spouse who has (or has been) deserted. But a cohabitee will be treated as a husband or wife if the couple have lived together for at least 6 months and the patient's spouse – if any – does not live with them.

A mother and her illegitimate child can be the nearest relative of each other, but a father and his illegitimate child cannot be.

Adoptive relationships are included in the list. So are half-blood relationships, although full-blood ones have priority.

If a local authority has taken over parents' rights in respect of a child, the authority is the nearest relative – but not if the child is married or one parent still has parents' rights. *See:* CHILDREN IN CARE.

If a child has a legally-appointed guardian, that person is treated as the nearest relative. So is any person who has been given custody of a child by a court or under a separation agreement.

Appointment by the sheriff

A sheriff can be asked to appoint a suitable person to be a patient's nearest relative if:

● The patient has no nearest relative, or none can be found.
● The nearest relative is unable to act because of illness or mental disorder.

The application can be made by any relative, or by someone living with the patient. That person can ask to be appointed as the nearest relative or can name someone else. A mental health officer can also apply for the regional or islands council, or some named person, to be appointed.

The nearest relative can also make the application if he or she does not want to act as such.

Compulsory detention of the mentally disordered

So far as possible, the treatment and control of mental illness and mental handicap is done on a voluntary basis. Most people in mental hospitals are there of their own free will, as 'informal' patients. Like patients in general hospitals, they are free to refuse treatment and to leave when they choose.

However, in a number of cases – perhaps around 2,500 a year – it is considered necessary to admit a mentally disordered person to hospital compulsorily under the Mental Health (Scotland) Act 1984. And very occasionally someone who is mentally disordered is placed under compulsory guardianship in the community in order to protect his welfare.

A person can only be detained in hospital if the following conditions are met:

1. He must be suffering from 'mental disorder' – that is, mental illness or mental handicap of any kind. Someone who is merely promiscuous, immoral, sexually deviant or addicted to drugs or alcohol cannot be treated as mentally disordered.

The disorder must be of a nature or degree that makes it appropriate for him to receive hospital treatment.

2. Treatment must be necessary for his health or safety or to protect others, and only be possible if he is detained.

Someone who is psychopathic can only be detained in hospital if these conditions are met *and* treatment is likely to help his condition or prevent it worsening.

A mentally handicapped person can only be detained if these conditions are met *and*:

● He is so handicapped that his intellect and social functioning are severely impaired.

If he is not, but the impairment is 'significant', he can be detained if treatment is likely to help his condition or prevent it worsening.

● His handicap is associated with unusually aggressive or seriously irresponsible conduct.

A person can only be taken into guardianship if the following conditions are satisfied:

- His disorder is of a nature or degree that justifies guardianship.
- Guardianship is necessary in the interests of his welfare.

Children Children of any age can be detained in hospital under the 1984 Act. But only children aged 16 or over can be taken into guardianship.

A mentally disordered child may come before a CHILDREN'S HEARING. If they think that the child should be detained in hospital, they must report this to a mental health officer. The officer will then decide what to do.

Patients' rights Patients who are detained in hospital or taken into guardianship must be given written and verbal information about their rights.

Detention in hospital

The Mental Health (Scotland) Act 1984 provides three different procedures for detaining mentally disordered people in hospital:

- An emergency procedure – used to detain someone in hospital urgently. Emergency detention is carried out on the recommendation of one doctor and lasts for up to 72 hours.
- A short term procedure – used to detain someone beyond the emergency period of 72 hours. If a psychiatrist states that continued detention is necessary, the patient can be detained for a further 28 days.
- A formal procedure – used if a longer period of detention is thought necessary. This requires an application for compulsory admission to be made to a sheriff, either by a mental health officer or the patient's 'nearest relative'.

The formal procedure was originally meant to be the main way of initially detaining mentally disordered people. But in practice most compulsory admissions are carried out under the emergency procedure. The formal procedure is normally used to detain people who are already in hospital.

The role of the mental health officer

Each regional and islands council has a duty to appoint enough social workers to act as mental health officers in its area. Those appointed must have sufficient qualifications, experience and competence in dealing with mentally disordered people. The Scottish Office is to issue instructions on what is required.

It is the job of a mental health officer to make applications to the sheriff for hospital detention or guardianship under the Mental Health (Scotland) Act. Although an application can be made by a patient's nearest relative, an officer has a duty in certain circumstances to make it himself – for instance, if he thinks an application is necessary but the nearest relative is unwilling to make it.

A mental health officer must consider making an application for compulsory detention if this is requested by a person's nearest relative.

Apart from making applications, a mental health officer can advise a patient's family on what detention involves, the likely treatment, the procedures for discharge and the right to appeal.

However, much of the work of mental health officers involves helping to arrange emergency admissions and providing care and aftercare for all mentally disordered people in the community. They may also occasionally be involved in removing mentally disordered people to a place of safety, or in returning escaped patients.

Emergency admissions

A doctor may consider that a person is so mentally disordered that it is urgently necessary to detain him in hospital for his own health or safety, or the protection of others.

If he feels that using the formal procedure would involve too much delay, he can use the emergency procedure instead. This requires him to complete a form recommending that the person be removed to hospital immediately.

The doctor must examine the patient personally on the day that he signs the recommendation. If possible, he must also obtain the consent of a relative or a mental health officer to the making of the recommendation – even if the patient is already in hospital voluntarily.

If he obtains such consent, he must say so in the emergency recommendation form. If he does not, he must state why it has not been possible to obtain it.

Once signed, the emergency recommendation is sufficient authority for the compulsory removal of the patient to hospital. This must be done within 3 days of the recommendation being made. The patient can then be detained for a maximum period of 72 hours.

Once the patient has been admitted, the hospital must, if possible, inform the patient's nearest relative, the Mental Welfare Commission and (unless the patient was already in hospital when the recommendation was made) a responsible person living with him.

The emergency procedure can be used to detain a patient who is in hospital voluntarily, if it is feared that he might otherwise discharge himself and be a danger to himself or others. For instance, it might be used to detain a patient who was thought likely to attempt suicide or to attack a member of his family.

Sometimes a voluntary patient may try to discharge himself before a doctor can be found to complete an emergency recommendation. If this happens, a registered mental nurse has power to detain him until a doctor arrives, but only for up to 2 hours.

Continuing detention Once the 72-hour period expires, the patient is legally free to leave hospital or to stay on as a voluntary patient. He cannot be detained again under the emergency detention procedure.

However, if detention is still considered necessary he can be detained for a further period under the 'short term' procedure.

Short term detention

If detention is still considered necessary after the 72-hour emergency period expires, the patient can be held for a further period of 28 days.

Before this can be done, the hospital must obtain a report on the patient's condition. This must contain a statement from a psychiatrist that the patient's disorder justifies detention for at least a limited period, and that detention is necessary for the patient's health or safety, or to protect others.

Where possible, the consent of the patient's nearest relative or a mental health officer must be obtained.

Once the patient is detained, the hospital must inform the Mental Welfare Commission within 7 days. It must also inform the local social work department and, if possible, the nearest relative – unless either consented to the detention.

If the social work department is informed, a mental health officer must then interview the patient within 21 days and provide a report to the responsible doctor and the Commission on the patient's social circumstances.

The patient must be told that he is entitled to appeal to a sheriff against his detention. His rights are the same as those of a patient held under the formal procedure – see below.

SOCIAL SECURITY BENEFITS FOR PEOPLE SUFFERING FROM MENTAL DISORDER

A person who is mentally disordered is entitled to the same social security benefits as the victim of physical illness or disability.

The type and amount of benefit depends on whether the patient is in hospital or residential care, or is receiving treatment while still in the community.

A person who is off work because of a mental disorder can usually claim sick PAY from his employer for the first 8 weeks of his illness. Thereafter he can claim SICKNESS BENEFIT provided he has paid sufficient NATIONAL INSURANCE CONTRIBUTIONS. After 20 weeks, if he has not been admitted to hospital, that benefit is replaced by INVALIDITY PENSION (which may include an additional invalidity allowance).

A patient who has not been able to work, and so pay the required national insurance contributions, can qualify for a non-contributory invalidity pension if he is in private care. If he is at home or in a private institution, he may also qualify for ATTENDANCE ALLOWANCE.

A mental patient in hospital can receive sickness benefit at the normal rate for 8 weeks, then at a reduced rate because he is maintained free of charge. After 1 year in hospital he normally receives only pocket money and the balance of his entitlement during the second year is saved for him. It is paid out to help his resettlement if he is discharged to rejoin the community.

Pocket money continues throughout a patient's stay in hospital or residential care, but the resettlement account is not added to after the second year. If a patient is not capable of understanding the use of money, it can be used on items for his personal comfort and enjoyment.

A patient receiving SUPPLEMENTARY BENEFIT will have his benefit reduced immediately he goes into hospital, if he has no dependants. If he is one of a married couple, or living with someone as husband and wife, benefit will be reduced after 8 weeks in hospital. Additional payments for such things as heating, diet and wear and tear on clothing may be stopped immediately.

If a patient qualifies for a RETIREMENT PENSION, this is paid instead of sickness benefit. However, the pension is reduced after 8 weeks, again after 1 year and again after 2 years. There is a maximum amount that can be deducted. The remainder must be given to the patient if he is capable of managing it, or be held in an account for him if he is not. *See:* HOSPITAL

If an accident at work causes mental disorder, the victim has the same right to DISABLEMENT BENEFIT as the victim of physical injury. Victims of crime who suffer mental disorder as a result may be able to obtain CRIMINAL INJURIES COMPENSATION.

Formal admissions

The short term procedure can only be used once. If a patient requires to be detained for a longer period, the formal procedure must be used. An application must be made to a sheriff, either by a mental health officer or the patient's 'nearest relative' (see page 427).

Generally, a mental health officer need only make an application if *he* thinks that he ought to. But if two doctors recommend detention (see below) and one of them asks him to make an application, he must do so – even if he disagrees with it. He must tell the sheriff about any objection he has.

Once a mental health officer decides to make an application, he must, if possible, inform the patient's nearest relative and tell him of his right to object to the application. If the relative objects, this will be recorded on the application form.

The officer must then interview the patient in the 14 days before making the application. He must satisfy himself that detention is the most appropriate way to provide the care and treatment that the patient needs.

If the nearest relative makes the application, he must have seen the patient in the previous 14 days.

An application for admission must be supported by two 'medical recommendations'. One recommendation must be from a psychiatrist. The other, if possible, must be from the patient's own doctor, or another doctor who knows him. Both doctors must have examined the patient personally, either together – unless the patient or his nearest relative objects – or within 5 days of each other.

Normally, if the patient is to be admitted to a NHS hospital, only one of the doctors can be on its staff. Where the hospital is private, neither can be. But if the case is very urgent and there would be a delay in obtaining an outside doctor, both recommendations can come from doctors on the hospital staff. One must work at the hospital for less than half the time that he is contractually bound to spend on NHS work; and if one is a consultant, the other must not work under him.

Each medical recommendation must contain:

- A statement that the patient is suffering from mental illness or mental handicap, or both.
- A statement as to which of the conditions for hospital detention (see page 427) apply.

Each recommendation should include a full clinical description of the patient's condition and (if possible) a statement of the circumstances giving rise to the application. It should also state why treatment as an out-patient or voluntary patient is not appropriate.

The application will be valid so long as both recommendations state that the patient is mentally ill, mentally handicapped, or both. If one doctor says only that the patient is mentally ill, but the other says only that he is mentally handicapped, the application will be invalid.

Approval by the sheriff The application form (which includes both medical recommendations) must be submitted to the sheriff within 7 days of the last medical examination. The sheriff is entitled to consider the application in private and must do so if the patient or applicant requests it.

The sheriff can hear anyone he wants. The patient, however, has a right to be heard, either personally – unless there is a good reason for not allowing this – or through a representative. If the sheriff thinks that the patient's health or treatment would be affected by being present, he can exclude him from all or part of the proceedings. He cannot, however, exclude a representative.

The sheriff cannot refuse an application without giving the applicant – the nearest relative or a mental health officer – the opportunity to give evidence and call witnesses. He must also give the same opportunity to the nearest relative, if he or she objects to the application.

If the sheriff approves the application, the patient can be compulsorily admitted to hospital within 7 days – or compulsorily detained if in hospital already. The Mental Welfare Commission must be told within 7 days of the admission, and sent a copy of the application. So must the regional or islands council – but not if the application was made by a mental health officer.

If the council is told, a mental health officer must interview the patient within 3 weeks and provide a report on his social circumstances for the Commission and the doctor responsible for his treatment. This is unnecessary if the patient has already been interviewed in the previous 4 weeks, while under short term detention.

Compulsory detention is initially for a period of up to 6 months. But most patients are not detained for that length of time. Each one must be medically examined during the fourth week of detention. Many are then discharged from detention because one or both of the detention conditions no longer apply. They may, however, remain in hospital as voluntary patients.

If a patient is not discharged at this stage, the nearest relative, the regional or islands council and the Mental Welfare Commission must be told.

Renewing detention A patient can be detained in hospital for much longer than 6 months if the doctor responsible for him considers that the legal conditions for detention still exist.

The doctor must first examine the patient himself – or obtain a medical report on him from another doctor – within the 2 months before the 6-month period expires. He must also consult those principally concerned with the patient's treatment.

If he is then satisfied that detention can legally continue, he must report this to the hospital management and the Mental Welfare Commission. That is sufficient authority to detain the patient for another 6 months – there is no need to apply to the sheriff.

Detention can then be renewed for further periods of 1 year, so long as the same procedure is followed. The patient and his nearest relative must be told about each renewal.

How a patient can regain his freedom

The doctor responsible for a compulsory patient must discharge him at any time if he is satisfied that one or both of the legal conditions for detention (see page 427) no longer exist.

A patient can ask to be discharged at any time. If this is refused, he can ask the Mental Welfare Commission to discharge him. The Commission has the same powers and duties as the hospital doctor so far as discharge is concerned. It can interview the patient privately and give him an independent medical examination.

Every detained patient has a right of appeal to a sheriff against any renewal of his detention. The hospital has a duty to tell patients about this right.

A patient has the right to be examined in private, by a doctor of his own choosing, to obtain medical evidence for his appeal.

In an appeal, the patient and any representative of his have the same right to be heard as they have when the sheriff is considering an application for hospital admission.

If the sheriff is satisfied that one or both of the legal conditions for detention no longer exist, he must order the patient's discharge.

Discharge by the nearest relative A patient's nearest relative can order his discharge (unless he is in the State Hospital). To help him decide whether to do so, he can have the patient examined in private by a doctor of his own choosing.

But the fact that the nearest relative orders a patient's discharge does not mean that he will be released. The relative must first give the health board at least 7 days' notice of his intention to order discharge. If during that period the patient's doctor reports to the board that legal grounds for detention still exist, any discharge order made by the relative will have no effect. However, if no such report is made, the patient can be discharged.

If discharge is refused, the nearest relative can appeal to the sheriff within 28 days. The sheriff is bound by the same rules that apply to appeals by patients.

If the nearest relative decides not to appeal, or appeals unsuccessfully, he must wait for 6 months before he can again order the patient's discharge.

Refusing consent to treatment

A patient who is compulsorily detained can usually be treated without his consent. For certain forms of treatment, however, his consent is required. The rules are:

1. Some forms of treatment that are dangerous, irreversible or not fully established – a leucotomy (a type of psychosurgery) or a hormone transplant to reduce male sexual drives – will not be possible without the patient's consent *and* the agreement of an independent doctor appointed by the Mental Welfare Commission.

In addition, the independent doctor and 2 laypeople appointed by the Commission must certify that the patient has consented and is capable of understanding what the treatment involves.

2. Some other forms of treatment – electro-convulsive therapy (ECT) and drugs administered for more than 3 months – can be given with or without consent.

If the patient consents, his doctor – or an independent doctor appointed by the Commission – must first certify that he has consented and is capable of understanding what is involved. If he does not consent, or is incapable of understanding what is going on, the treatment can still be given – provided the independent doctor agrees.

3. Urgent treatment – to prevent death, serious deterioration or suffering, or violent behaviour – can be given without the patient's consent. The treatment must not be irreversible, unless necessary to save the patient's life. Nor must it be dangerous, unless necessary to save the patient's life or prevent serious deterioration.

4. The patient can withdraw his consent at any time – but he may still be treated against his will under these rules.

5. If treatment is to be given under these rules, the Mental Welfare Commission must be told within 7 days. It

HOW MENTAL DISORDER AFFECTS A PATIENT'S OTHER RIGHTS

People suffering from mental disorder may lose some of their rights or be subject to special rules.

Voting Mentally disordered people are not expressly prohibited from voting at elections. But a person who is clearly of unsound mind can be prevented from casting his vote even if his name is on the ELECTORAL REGISTER

A voluntary patient in a mental hospital can vote in person if his name is on the register. If his illness prevents him doing so, he may be able to get a postal vote on the ground of physical incapacity. *See:* ELECTION.

If a voluntary patient is in a mental hospital when a new register is being drawn up, he cannot use the hospital as his registered address. But he can complete a declaration form allowing him to be registered at his home address – or at another address where he has lived. He can then obtain a postal vote.

A compulsory patient whose name is already on the electoral register may be able to obtain a postal vote on the ground of physical incapacity. But he cannot register at an outside address, or at the hospital address, when a new register is being drawn up. He will therefore be unable to vote.

Driving Someone who is suffering from severe mental handicap can have a driving licence refused or revoked by the Department of Transport.

Firearms It is an offence for someone to sell firearms or ammunition to a person whom he knows – or ought to know – is mentally disordered. A licence to own a firearm can be refused or cancelled if the applicant or holder is considered to be mentally disordered.

Marriage A marriage can be annulled if one partner was so mentally disordered at the time of the marriage that he or she was incapable of giving valid consent to the marriage. *See:* NULLITY

Incurable insanity is no longer a ground of DIVORCE. But the symptoms of mental disorder could amount to unreasonable behaviour, which is a ground of divorce.

Living apart for 2 years is a ground of divorce, provided both partners consent. A period spent in hospital will count towards the 2 year period. A mental patient may have sufficient understanding to consent; if not, the partner seeking the divorce will have to wait for a further 3 years, since living apart for 5 years is a ground of divorce even though there is no consent.

In all divorce cases the court will appoint a guardian, or CURATOR ad litem, to protect the interests of a mentally disordered defender.

Wills A WILL made by a mentally disordered person is valid if it can be proved that the person knew what he was doing when he made it. It is sensible to obtain two medical statements confirming that the person is mentally fit at the time he makes the will.

Jury service A mentally disordered person is ineligible for JURY service if he is receiving treatment as an in-patient or outpatient for more than 1 day a week, or has had his affairs taken over.

Civil proceedings If a mentally disordered person is incapable of acting for himself in court proceedings, he can be represented by a curator bonis – a guardian appointed by the court – who can act on his behalf. A curator bonis can, for example, pursue a claim for DAMAGES on the disordered person's behalf.

Contracts A contract – for example, a hire purchase agreement – will be void (meaning that it is invalid and has no legal effect) if one of the parties to it was so mentally disordered at the time of making it that he was unable to understand what he was doing.

can review non-urgent treatment – except for treatment in '2', above, to which a patient has been able to consent. If it thinks fit, it can stop the treatment.

6. All other forms of treatment can be administered without the patient's consent, if given by or under the direction of the doctor responsible for his case.

Emergency cases These rules do not apply to people detained under the emergency procedure. But the official view is that they can be lawfully treated without their consent, if the treatment is recognised and necessary for their disorder.

Guardianship in the community

In Scotland there is a tradition of 'boarding-out' mentally handicapped, and occasionally mentally ill, adults with specially appointed guardians in the community. The practice has recently fallen into disuse – numbers fell from 2,440 in 1960 to around 300 in 1984. However the government has recently made changes to encourage the practice.

A guardianship application is made to a sheriff in the same way as a hospital application. But there are important differences:

- Only patients aged 16 or over can be taken into guardianship.
- Guardianship can only be imposed on the grounds that the patient's disorder justifies it and his welfare requires it.
- The application requires an additional recommendation from a mental health officer, saying why guardianship is necessary for the patient's welfare.

The application is addressed to the regional or islands council. It must name the guardian, who has to be someone chosen or accepted by the council, or the council itself. The applicant – for example, the nearest relative – can be appointed guardian.

A guardian has certain legal powers over a patient. These include:

- Deciding where the patient lives.
- Making the patient attend places for treatment, work, education or training.

He cannot, however, consent to treatment on the patient's behalf.

Guardianship initially lasts for up to 6 months. It is reviewed by a doctor and mental health officer before that period expires and will be continued if legal grounds for guardianship are still thought to exist. There will be another review after 6 months, and at yearly intervals thereafter.

The patient can ask the Mental Welfare Commission to discharge him from guardianship. He also has the same right as a hospital patient to appeal to the sheriff against any renewal.

The nearest relative can also order discharge, subject to the same rules that apply to hospital patients (except that 14 days' notice must be given).

A patient under guardianship must be visited by a social worker at least every 3 months. A doctor must visit at least once a year. The Commission must also make regular visits.

Removal to a safe place

A mental health officer – or a medical member of the Mental Welfare Commission – can demand entry to the home of a mentally disordered person who is suspected of being ill-treated, neglected or unable to care for himself. If entry is refused – or is likely to be – a J.P. can issue a warrant authorising a police constable to enter and remove the person to a safe place – usually a hospital. The constable must be accompanied by a doctor (except when the police have themselves obtained the warrant).

A constable can also remove to a safe place any mentally disordered person found in a public place. No warrant or medical examination is required. The person must appear to need immediate care or control.

Detention in a safe place can last for up to 72 hours. The patient may then be discharged, treated voluntarily or compulsorily detained.

THE NURSE WHO WAS CHARGED WITH ASSAULT

Someone – such as a doctor or nurse – who uses reasonable force to control or restrain mental patients cannot be convicted of any criminal offence arising out of his actions, unless he acts in bad faith and without reasonable care.

A male charge nurse in an Inverness mental hospital was charged with assaulting a number of mentally handicapped children. He was accused of throwing water over two patients and hitting others on the face, sometimes with his knuckles.

The accused had been a nurse for 22 years and had an unblemished record. His defence was that the children were often aggressive and difficult to control. He had merely used a limited amount of force to control them.

He had thrown water over one child to calm him down – and had succeeded. He had also struck a child on the face because he was attacking another child and that was the only way to break his grip. There was no evidence that the child had been caused pain or distress.

DECISION

The sheriff acquitted the nurse of all the charges against him. The Mental Health (Scotland) Act gave immunity against conviction provided someone such as the accused acted in good faith and took reasonable care. Excessive force would not be justified, but the force used by the nurse was the minimum necessary to control the patients.

Nevertheless, the nurse was dismissed and he also lost his claim for UNFAIR DISMISSAL.

When an accused person is mentally disordered

The criminal courts – the district court, sheriff court and High Court of Justiciary – have special powers to deal with accused persons who are, or appear to be, mentally disordered.

Before trial When a court commits an accused person for trial, it can order him to be detained in hospital during the committal period so that a psychiatric report can be obtained. This can only be done on the evidence of a doctor. The accused cannot be detained in hospital if the doctor in charge of his case does not think his condition is serious enough to justify detention under the Mental Health (Scotland) Act. *See:* REMAND

Where a trial is to take place in the sheriff court or High Court, the court may decide, after hearing medical evidence, that the accused is so mentally disordered that he is unable to defend himself properly or to instruct lawyers to defend him. If so, it must make a finding of 'insanity in bar of trial' – meaning that the trial is abandoned.

In cases tried without a jury (under summary proceedings) the court must then make either a hospital or a guardianship order, committing the accused to hospital or guardianship under the Mental Health (Scotland) Act. In cases tried before a jury (under solemn proceedings) the accused must normally be committed to the State Hospital at Carstairs.

After trial If a mentally disordered person is convicted in the sheriff court or High Court of an offence (other than murder) punishable by imprisonment, the court can order him to be detained in hospital or received into guardianship. Two doctors – one of whom should have psychiatric experience – must first testify that the accused's condition justifies detention under the Mental Health (Scotland) Act.

In cases tried before a jury, the court can order the offender to be detained in the State Hospital if he needs special security because of his dangerous, violent or criminal tendencies.

In rare cases an accused person tried before a jury may be acquitted on the ground of insanity at the time when the offence was committed. If this occurs, the court must order him to be detained - normally in the State Hospital. *See:* INSANITY AS A DEFENCE.

A district court cannot order an offender to be detained in hospital or received into guardianship. But if it thinks that he is mentally disordered, it can send the case to the sheriff court. The sheriff can then decide whether to order detention or guardianship.

Restricting release When a court orders an offender to be detained in hospital, it can also order his release to be restricted indefinitely, or for a fixed period. A restriction order can only be imposed if it is necessary to protect the public from serious harm.

When a restriction order is made, detention continues indefinitely (or until the end of the period stated in the order) without the need for renewal. The offender, however, can be released by the Secretary of State for Scotland. He also has a right of appeal to a sheriff between 6 and 12 months after detention, and during each subsequent year.

An offender whose release is not restricted has the same rights as other detained patients, except that his nearest relative cannot order his discharge.

Probation A court can make it a condition of a PROBATION order that an offender undergoes psychiatric treatment for up to 12 months, either in hospital or as an out-patient.

The court must first be satisfied that the offender's mental condition does not justify compulsory admission and that it can be treated. The offender must agree to the order and to undergo the treatment.

Protecting mental patients

It is an offence for any manager, officer or employee of a hospital or nursing home to ill-treat or wilfully neglect any mental patient, whether an in-patient or out-patient. It is also an offence for anyone to ill-treat or wilfully neglect a patient under his guardianship or care. The maximum penalty is 2 years' imprisonment or an unlimited fine, or both.

Any male manager, officer or employee of a hospital or nursing home commits an offence if he has sexual intercourse with a female mental patient (including intercourse on the premises with a female out-patient). So does any man who has intercourse with a female mental patient in his guardianship or care, or in the care of the regional or islands council. It is a defence for the man to prove he did not know that the woman was suffering from mental disorder. The maximum penalty is 2 years' imprisonment or an unlimited fine.

The same rules apply to a homosexual act committed against a male mental patient.

It is an offence for any man to have sexual intercourse with a female who is so mentally handicapped that her intelligence and social functioning are significantly impaired. It is a defence for the man to prove that he did not know the woman was suffering from that degree of handicap. The maximum penalty is 2 years' imprisonment or an unlimited fine.

A male who suffers from a similar degree of mental handicap cannot consent to a homosexual act. It is an offence to commit a homosexual act with such a person, even if he is 21 or over and the act takes place in private. It is a defence for the accused to prove that he did not know that the person was suffering from that degree of handicap. *See:* HOMOSEXUALITY

Complaints of ill-treatment or offences against mentally disordered people should be made to the hospital authorities, the police or the Mental Welfare Commission. The Commission has a duty to investigate complaints and will conduct its own inquiry where necessary.

Protecting the affairs of the mentally disordered

If a mentally disordered person cannot manage his property or affairs, a court can be asked to appoint a *curator bonis*, or guardian. If no one else applies, the regional (or islands) council or the Mental Welfare Commission can do so. *See:* CURATOR.

Hospital authorities can receive and hold money and valuables on behalf of a mentally disordered patient who is unable to manage his own affairs. The authorities can spend the money or dispose of the valuables for the patient's benefit. If their value exceeds £500, they must first obtain the consent of the Mental Welfare Commission. This will normally be given for sums up to £4,000; for larger amounts, however, the Commission will usually recommend the appointment of a guardian.

The Mental Welfare Commission has a legal duty to investigate any case where the property of a mentally disordered person is in danger of being lost or damaged, or where his money is not being properly used. *See:* MENTAL WELFARE COMMISSION

HOW A PATIENT'S MAIL CAN BE INTERCEPTED

There are no restrictions on the mail of voluntary patients. Nor any on the incoming mail of compulsory patients.

However, mail sent by a compulsory patient can be intercepted and withheld if the person to whom it is addressed has given written notice that he does not want to receive mail from the patient.

Special rules apply to patients detained in the State Hospital.

Mail sent by them can be intercepted and withheld if addressed to someone who has given notice that he does not want it. But it can also be withheld if it is likely to endanger anyone; or to cause distress to the person to whom it is addressed or to any other person – except for someone on the hospital staff.

However, mail sent by State patients – other than mail addressed to someone who does not want it – can never be withheld if it is addressed to any one of the following:

- A patient's legal adviser.
- The Mental Welfare Commission (including a Commissioner or someone appointed by the Commission).
- An Ombudsman.
- A Minister, MP or member of the House of Lords.
- The European Commission or Court of Human Rights.
- A health board or health council.
- A local authority.
- A judge or court clerk.

The incoming mail of State patients can also be withheld if this is necessary for their safety or to protect others.

If mail is withheld from any patient, the Mental Welfare Commission must be told. If it is withheld under the special rules applying to State patients, the patient – or the person who sent the mail – can ask the Commission to review the decision. It has power, if it thinks fit, to order the hospital to release the mail to the patient.

Providing care outside hospital

Regional and islands councils have a legal duty to provide after-care services for all mentally disordered people – whether or not they have been hospital patients. In discharging this duty they must co-operate with health boards and voluntary bodies.

Residential care For people recovering from mental illness, hostels can be a useful bridge between hospital care and living independently. There are around 1,000 hostel places in Scotland. Most hostels offer individual counselling and group discussions to help the residents settle back into the community.

Some social work departments make arrangements to provide accommodation in private households for people leaving psychiatric hospitals. The cost of board and lodging is paid by the patient himself. Patients receiving SUPPLEMENTARY BENEFIT will be given an allowance to meet the board and lodging charge.

Social workers based in a hospital or area team will arrange hostel or private accommodation when a patient is considered fit to leave hospital.

Increasingly, residential care is being provided through other forms of supported accommodation – for instance, 'cluster flats', which are groups of bedsits, and 'group homes', which are council houses in which a number of former patients live together with support from the community psychiatric services. Some of this supported accommodation is provided by housing associations. *See:* HOUSING ASSOCIATION

Day care Health boards run special day hospitals which people can attend on a daily basis. These hospitals provide therapy, including occupational therapy, and social activities. In Strathclyde there is a day centre, run by local authority staff, that provides a similar service, although with more emphasis on social interaction and social skills.

Voluntary help Many voluntary organisations offer help and support to people suffering or recovering from mental disorder. Some provide supported accommodation and day centres; others offer a visiting service to people in hospital or in their own homes.

There are also 'self-help' groups that offer mutual aid for fellow sufferers, particularly in the areas of phobias, depression and schizophrenia – the Phobics Society and the National Schizophrenia Fellowship are two examples. If you would like more information about the organisations operating in your area and how to get in touch with them, contact the Scottish Association for Mental Health, 67 York Place, Edinburgh, EH1 3JB.

WHEN PARENTS OBJECT TO SPECIAL SCHOOLING

Mentally handicapped children who require special education will have a file called a 'Record of Needs' kept on them by the local education authority. The authority must keep such a record for all such children who are of school age, and review their cases regularly.

Before recording a child, the education authority must assess his or her needs. The child must undergo a medical and psychological examination and a report must be obtained from the child's teacher.

If parents disagree with the decision of the education authority to record their child as having special educational needs, they have the right to apply to an appeal committee set up by the education authority. The committee will then refer the matter to the Secretary of State for Scotland for a final decision. If he agrees that the child should not be recorded, he must order the education authority to destroy the child's record.

Parents of a mentally handicapped child have the right to request that their child be placed in a school chosen by them. If the education authority refuses to grant their request, they have a right of appeal to the local appeal committee.

The committee can confirm or reject the education authority's decision. If the committee confirms the authority's decision, there is a further right of appeal to the sheriff court.

MENTAL HANDICAP

The services that aim to keep mentally handicapped people in the community

The Mental Health (Scotland) Act 1984 defines mental disorder as including all forms of mental handicap. By including mental handicap within the Act, compulsory powers can sometimes be used to detain seriously mentally handicapped people in hospital, or place them under guardianship. *See:* MENTAL DISORDER

However, most mentally handicapped people need care and assistance rather than compulsory measures. The law therefore requires regional and islands councils to provide services within the community for the care and education of people who have a mental handicap. Others services are provided by central government.

These services include:

- Prevention and early detection of mental handicap through family planning, advice in cases where there is a history of handicap and preventive immunisation against rubella (German measles).
- Assessment facilities for mentally handicapped people.
- Social work support for the families of mentally handicapped people.
- Education provided by specialist teachers.
- Residential accommodation – necessary, for instance, where both the parents of a mentally handicapped person are dead and there is no one to care for him or her.
- Sheltered housing.
- Medical and nursing care.
- Sheltered employment facilities.
- Continued training facilities in adult training centres.

When a child is handicapped

Parents who suspect that their young child is not developing normally should seek advice from their health visitor or family doctor. Arrangements can then be made for specialist examination and assessment.

If a serious mental handicap is confirmed, parents should be told about the advice, counselling and support services offered by the regional or islands council's social work department and by voluntary agencies. These services can help the parents to care for their child in the best possible way and also to understand what they may expect as their child grows up.

Many regional and islands councils allocate some children's centre places to handicapped children (see DAY NURSERIES). There are also schemes to make available relief care for parents of handicapped children by providing residential units, accommodation with other families or specialised hospital units. Practical assistance from community nursing services and home helps may also be available.

Regional and islands councils can help with adaptations to a house, as well as practical aids, if a child's mental handicap causes physical disabilities. It may also be possible to obtain an IMPROVEMENT GRANT from the district or islands council to help pay for the cost of adapting a house.

If a severely mentally handicapped child needs constant care and attention – whether by day or by night, or both – and is at least 2 years old, he or she is entitled to an ATTENDANCE ALLOWANCE. A parent can make a claim to the Department of Health and Social Security on behalf of the child.

Arranging special education and training

Local education authorities provide special schools for the mentally handicapped, as well as special classes in normal schools. The majority of handicapped children will live at home and attend school on a daily basis, with transport being provided by the education authority.

Regional and islands councils provide adult training centres for mentally handicapped people over school-leaving age. Adult training centres aim to provide people who have left school and are unable to cope with normal employment with:

- Continued practical education.
- Art and craft work.
- Training in social skills – for instance, the use of money, the use of transport, and cooking.

Some regional and islands councils provide sheltered employment facilities. There a mentally handicapped person can undertake simple tasks for which a small wage is paid.

Regional and islands councils also provide residential facilities for mentally handicapped people who cannot continue to live with their families but are unable to look after themselves on their own. Social workers will provide support for the family as well as the handicapped person. In addition, councils can arrange with voluntary organisations to provide residential and training facilities.

When less severely handicapped people reach working age, careers, youth employment and disablement resettlement officers will work together to find suitable work in the community.

Voluntary organisations often run social clubs and activity groups for the mentally handicapped. Your local social work department will be able to advise you about the clubs in your area.

Some education authorities are developing special further education opportunities for mentally handicapped people. Ask about this at your education authority office.

MENTAL WELFARE COMMISSION

The body which provides protection for the mentally disordered

The Mental Welfare Commission is an independent body first set up under the Mental Health (Scotland) Act 1960. Its job is to protect the welfare and interests of all mentally disordered people in Scotland, whether in hospital (as voluntary or compulsory patients) or in the community.

The Commission consists of at least 10 members. Of these, at least 3 must be doctors and at least 3 must be women. One member must be an advocate or solicitor of at least 5 years' standing. The Commission has a majority of non-medical members so that patients who are detained can be assured that decisions concerning their freedom are not entirely in the hands of doctors.

The Commission also has the services of medical officers, who visit and examine patients on its behalf.

The functions of the Commission

The Commission has a number of functions under the Mental Health (Scotland) Act 1984. These include:

• **Discharging patients** The Commission must enquire into any case where it appears that a mentally disordered person may have been improperly detained in hospital.

It has a duty to discharge a compulsorily detained patient if it is satisfied that his mental condition does not justify detention for treatment, or that detention is not necessary for his own protection or that of others.

The Commission must also discharge a patient who has been received into guardianship if it is satisfied that his mental condition no longer justifies guardianship, or that his welfare no longer requires it.

The proper statutory procedures must be followed when a patient is detained in hospital or received into guardianship. The Commission must be told about each case. When it involves hospital detention under the formal procedure, or guardianship, the Commission must also be given a copy of the application and recommendations.

If the procedures have not been properly followed, the Commission must point this out to the hospital or local authority. Since the detention is invalid, the patient must either be discharged or detained properly. If necessary, the Commission can order his discharge.

In order to carry out these functions, the Commission is entitled to be informed about all patients who are detained in hospital or taken into guardianship.

• **Inquiring into complaints of improper treatment** The Commission must investigate allegations of ill-treatment, or lack of proper care or treatment of any mentally disordered person. Most complaints concern ASSAULT, which is a criminal offence. Others allege deliberate neglect or sexual offences. *See:* MENTAL DISORDER

The Commission receives complaints from many different sources – including patients, relatives, friends and hospital staff. If a complaint against a staff member is justified, the Commission may recommend that the person concerned be disciplined, or even dismissed. In cases involving alleged criminal offences, the matter will be reported to the police.

• **Supervising certain forms of treatment** The Commission is responsible for appointing independent doctors who must agree to the giving of certain types of treatment to detained hospital patients – particularly those types of treatment that are dangerous, irreversible or not fully established. The Commission may be able to review the treatment, and can order it to stop. *See:* MENTAL DISORDER.

• **Protecting property** The Commission has a duty to investigate any case where a mentally disordered person's property (including money) may have been lost, damaged or misused because of his inability to manage his affairs. It may recommend the appointment of a guardian – called a *curator bonis* – where a person has substantial funds. If necessary, it can apply to court for such an appointment to be made. *See:* CURATOR

Where smaller amounts are involved, the hospital authorities are entitled to administer the funds or property for the patient's benefit. (In some cases, the consent of the Commission must first be obtained.) The Commission will investigate complaints that the authorities are not using the money properly. *See:* MENTAL DISORDER

• **Visiting detained patients** The Commission must make regular visits to patients who are detained in hospital or under guardianship in the community. The visitors must include a medical Commissioner or medical officer.

The Commission must visit a hospital patient during a third year of detention – unless he has already been visited, or he appealed to the sheriff during the previous renewal of his detention. (Patients whose detention was renewed for 2 years under the old rules that applied until 1984 need not be visited until their fifth year of detention.)

When visited, a patient is entitled to a private interview if he asks for one. The medical Commissioner or medical officer is also entitled to examine the patient in private and to inspect his medical records.

• **Taking someone to a place of safety** A medical member of the Commission has the same power as a mental health officer to seek entry to premises where a mentally disordered person is suspected of being ill-treated or neglected, or unable to care for himself. *See:* MENTAL DISORDER

Holding a formal inquiry

In 1972 the Commission was given power to hold a formal inquiry into any complaint of ill-treatment, lack of proper care or treatment, or unlawful detention. When holding such an inquiry, the Commission acts very much as a court of law.

It can require witnesses to attend and give evidence under oath; and there is the same protection from actions for defamation as is given to statements made in court.

The commission has no power to punish or discipline hospital staff, or to order changes in procedures. However, the findings of an inquiry are sent to the Secretary of State for Scotland as well as to the hospital authorities concerned, and they will usually be acted upon.

The Commission's other work

As part of its duty to look after the interests of people who are mentally disordered, the Commission also:

- Gives advice and makes recommendations to the Secretary of State, to health boards and to local authorities.
- Gives advice to hospitals on precautions which should be taken to reduce the risk of accidents to patients.
- Gives advice on protecting legal rights – for example, the right of a person to claim DAMAGES for injuries caused by someone else's negligence.
- Inspects hostel accommodation to ensure that it is of a sufficiently high standard.

If you want to get in touch with the Commission, write to it at 22 Melville Street, Edinburgh. From 1985, it will have to produce annual reports.

See: MENTAL DISORDER

MINIBUS

Using a vehicle to transport members of groups

Anyone who wants to operate a minibus – a vehicle that can carry more than 8 but not more than 16 passengers – must have a road service licence. If the vehicle is a public service vehicle a PSV licence is also needed.

The only exceptions are people who drive such vehicles on behalf of educational, social welfare, religious or other community groups. They need only a special permit, which is obtainable (for a fee) from the traffic commissioner of the area in which the vehicle is normally kept, or from the local education or social work authority.

Scotland is treated as one traffic area, and its traffic commissioners operate from 24 Torphichen Street, Edinburgh. In England and Wales, traffic commissioners operate in London, Birmingham, Bristol, Cambridge, Eastbourne, Leeds, Manchester, Newcastle and Cardiff.

A minibus for which such a permit has been granted must not be used for the general public and it must be operated only by the body to whom the permit is issued. Any special conditions imposed must be obeyed, and the vehicle must carry a disc showing that it is permitted to operate as a minibus. The organisation in whose name the minibus is operated can charge fares, but it must not make a profit from doing so.

A minibus driver must be over 21 and hold a full DRIVING LICENCE.

MINICAB

When you are driven in a hired car other than a taxi

Only licensed taxis are allowed to ply for hire at stances or in the street. Members of the public, however, can order private hire cars, sometimes known as minicabs, to pick them up at one address and take them to another. The hire is usually done by telephone, but it can also be done in person at a minicab office.

Under the Civic Government (Scotland) Act 1982, every district and islands council has the right to operate a licensing scheme for private hire cars and their drivers, in the same way that taxis are licensed. But whereas the council fixes the fare for taxis, the operators of hire cars are free to decide their own charges.

Under such a licensing scheme, every hire car must have a hire car licence issued by the council. Before issuing the licence, the council must be satisfied that the car is suitable for hire and that it is properly insured.

The council has the right to inspect a car which has been licensed, to ensure that it is safe. If it is not, the council can suspend the licence until any defects have been put right.

Under a licensing scheme, every driver of a hire car must obtain a hire car driver's licence from the council. A licence will be issued only to someone who has held a full driving licence for at least a year. The council can require an applicant to undergo a medical examination, and can refuse to grant a licence if it is not satisfied that he is physically fit to drive.

If a licensing scheme is in operation, it is an offence for someone to operate or drive a hire car without a hire car or hire car driver's licence. The maximum penalty is a fine of £1,000.

It will usually be a condition of a licence that a licence plate or disc should be fixed to the vehicle.

It is an offence for a hire car to carry a sign suggesting that it is a taxi. The maximum penalty is a fine of £400.

Finding out if a car is licensed

If you are in doubt whether a car you intend to hire is licensed to carry paying passengers, ask the proprietor of the car service or find out from the administration department of your district or islands council.

MINOR

Protecting and restraining under-18's

In law, a minor is anyone aged at least 12 (if a girl) or 14 (if a boy), but under 18. Someone of that age cannot vote, serve on a jury, or buy drink in a bar. He can, however, make legally binding contracts and be held responsible for civil or criminal wrongs. *See:* AGE OF MAJORITY

Although 18 is the age at which young people gain full legal status in most matters, the law sets minimum ages below that for a wide variety of lesser rights and responsibilities. *See:* AGE OF MAJORITY

Suing a young person

A minor is legally responsible for his actions. So a 16 year old who knocks someone down while cycling on the footpath is liable. But usually there is no point in suing a minor for damages when he is unlikely to be able to pay.

Parents can be sued for the wrongdoings of their child only if the child acted as their agent or if they failed to exercise reasonable supervision over the child's activities. For example, a father who allows his 14-year-old son to drive the family car for him can be sued if there is an accident. But if a boy kicks a football through a neighbour's window his parents are unlikely to be liable.

Can a young person sue?

A child who is a victim of someone else's negligence can sue. He can even sue his parents – for instance, if he is negligently injured while he is a passenger in a car driven by his father, he can obtain compensation from his father's insurance company.

Handling money

Most cash transactions made by minors are fully binding. For example, a youngster who spends all his pocket-money on a new toy and then, once outside the shop, changes his mind will probably have no more legal rights to his money back than anyone else. But there are special laws designed to discourage traders, banks and others from taking advantage of minors.

A minor can claim that any contract of importance to which his father, mother or other CURATOR has not given consent is void. So traders are well advised to get the signature of a parent or guardian when dealing with someone under 18.

Moreover, during the 4 years after reaching 18 a minor can claim that he has suffered serious loss because of an unwise transaction, and ask for it to be cancelled. But this does not apply if he pretended to be over 18, or had set up in a trade or business and was contracting in the course of it.

Buying on credit It is a criminal offence, punishable by 1 year's imprisonment and/or a fine of up to £2,000, to send advertising material to a minor inviting him to borrow money or obtain goods or services on credit or encouraging him to send off for further information about credit facilities.

When criminal charges are involved

No child under 8 can be charged with a crime. Most offences by children under 16 are dealt with by children's hearings. But serious offences, or those where a child under 16 is involved with someone over 16, will be dealt with in court. *See:* CHILDREN'S HEARING

From the age of 16 a child can be held in a detention centre or young offenders' institution.

THE BOY WHOSE CLAIM FOR DAMAGES WAS TOO LOW

A minor can get out of any transaction which, owing to his inexperience, turns out to be seriously to his disadvantage

In 1972 a boy of 15 was injured at work. His employers' insurance company offered him damages of £125.

After consulting his mother and an elderly friend of the family (the boy had lost touch with his father, who had divorced his mother many years before), he accepted this offer.

His mother countersigned a document in which he acknowledged payment of £125 and gave up any legal claims arising from the accident.

Much later, in 1976, he sued his employers, claiming that the agreed settlement undervalued the claim and that his youthful inexperience had been taken advantage of.

DECISION

The judge agreed that the sum was inadequate and acceptance of it amounted to grave and serious loss. He treated the settlement as invalid and awarded the boy £600, a figure which took account of the decline in the value of money since the accident.

Employing minors

There are strict controls on the kind of work minors can do and on the number of hours they can put in. The controls are aimed mainly at under-16's, to safeguard their health and welfare, prevent interference in their education and protect them from exploitation.

No one under 13 can be employed. Someone under 16 cannot be employed before 7 a.m., or after 7 p.m., or for more than 2 hours on any school day. Nor can such a person be employed in any factory, mine or quarry. Work in shops, however, is permitted.

Being employed or taking part in street trading – for example, selling newspapers – is forbidden below the age of 17. There are also restrictions on performances by children under 16 at public entertainments. *See:* PUPIL

MISREPRESENTATION

When a false statement causes someone to enter into a contract

If someone is induced to enter into any CONTRACT by a false statement of fact – called a misrepresentation – made by the other party to the contract, he can ask a court to set the contract aside. He may also be able to claim DAMAGES for any resulting loss.

A misrepresentation can be one of three kinds, depending on the state of mind of the person making it:

- **A fraudulent misrepresentation** A misrepresentation is fraudulent if the person making the statement knows or believes that it is false, or does not believe that it is true, and makes it to induce someone to contract with him.

For instance, a car salesman may tell a potential customer that a car has done only 30,000 miles when he knows that it has actually done 100,000 miles. If the customer then buys the car, having been strongly influenced by the salesman's statement, he has been induced to enter into a contract by a fraudulent misrepresentation.

- **A negligent misrepresentation** A misrepresentation is negligent if the person making it is under a special duty to take care in the advice and information he gives, and fails to do so. A professional man – for instance, a banker, accountant or architect – has such a duty.

So if a bank manager advises a client, without checking thoroughly, that the repayment terms of a loan are more favourable than they in fact are, and as a result the client agrees to the loan, he has been induced to enter into a contract by negligent misrepresentation. The bank *may* then be held liable – there is still some doubt in the Scottish courts on this point.

- **An innocent misrepresentation** A misrepresentation is innocent if the person making it is not aware that his statement is false and has taken all due care in making it.

For instance, a car salesman may state his genuine belief, based on the mileometer reading and the condition of the engine, that a car has done only 30,000 miles when it has in fact done 100,000 miles. If the statement induces a customer to buy the car, it will amount to an innocent misrepresentation.

Statements which are not misrepresentations

Some statements which turn out to be wrong do not amount to misrepresentations in law. For example, a statement of opinion or intention, honestly made, is not a misrepresentation, even if it induces someone to enter into a contract. But it will be a misrepresentation if it is dishonestly made, with the intention of deceiving.

False or misleading statements in advertisements will not be treated as misrepresentations if they would not normally be taken seriously. For instance, it would not be misrepresentation for a firm of car manufacturers to induce people to buy their cars through an advertisement stating that the cars were 'noiseless as birds in flight'. No reasonable person would take such a statement seriously.

However, false statements contained in advertisements may be misrepresentations if a reasonable person could be expected to take them seriously. For example, it would be a misrepresentation to induce a customer to buy a car through a false statement in an advertisement that its petrol consumption at 30mph was 50 miles to the gallon.

When the law will ignore a misrepresentation

A misrepresentation is only relevant if it induces another person to enter into a contract, or is an important factor in persuading him to do so. Also, it must relate to something substantial: a person cannot get out of a contract by arguing that he was influenced by a false statement to which a reasonable person would have given little or no weight. For instance, a person who buys a car cannot ask a court to set aside the contract because the salesman falsely stated that the boot had an automatic light.

When silence can amount to misrepresentation

It is not usually misrepresentation to fail to disclose any relevant facts – unless, for instance, a potential customer has asked for the information and it has been deliberately withheld. However, certain contracts – for example, insurance contracts – require complete honesty and in such cases silence can amount to misrepresentation.

THE ENGINEER WHO JOINED AN AILING COMPANY

If a person is induced to enter a contract by a misrepresentation, he may be able to get out of the contract

Mr Wilson, who ran an engineering business in Aberdeen, advertised for a partner to join him in what he described as an 'established' business. Mr Ferguson, an engineer, expressed interest and during negotiations Mr Wilson was very optimistic about future prospects.

He claimed that the business was 'booming and bursting to get out', and that the current year would be the best so far. He explained that a reduction in profits in the previous year was a consequence of exceptional costs incurred in closing down a branch.

Encouraged by Mr Wilson's optimism, Mr Ferguson became his partner. He soon discovered that Mr Wilson's optimism was completely misplaced. That year, far from being profitable for the company, showed a substantial loss, a fact which Mr Wilson could easily have ascertained at the time he was negotiating with Mr Ferguson.

Mr Ferguson took legal action in the Court of Session to dissolve the partnership agreement.

DECISION

The court accepted that Mr Wilson had not acted fraudulently in making the inaccurate profit forecast, but agreed that this information was so important that it justified allowing Mr Ferguson to withdraw from the partnership.

For instance, if you have taken out life insurance, but have failed to disclose information about your health, or dangerous activities that you engage in, which the insurance company ought to have been told about and which would have caused them to refuse to insure you, you are guilty of a misrepresentation – even though you were not asked for the information.

What you can do if there has been misrepresentation

If you have entered into a contract because of a fraudulent or negligent statement, you can ask a court to set aside the contract, and can claim damages for any loss which you have suffered. If the false statement was made by an employee in the course of his employment – for instance, a salesman in a shop or garage – you can sue that person's employers instead. In addition, you are entitled to have returned to you any money or property transferred as a result of the contract.

If someone has entered into a contract because of a false statement, innocently made, he can ask the court to set the contract aside and can demand the return of any money or property transferred. But he cannot claim damages for any loss which he has suffered.

When misrepresentation is a criminal offence

Some misrepresentations made by traders are also criminal offences under the Trade Descriptions Act 1968. They include false statements – whether deliberately, negligently or innocently made – about such matters as:

- Quantity (including size, area and weight).
- Method of manufacture.
- Fitness for purpose.
- Place and date of manufacture.
- Previous ownership or use.
- Price – that the sale price is less than a recommended or previous price.

For the offence to be committed, the description must be false to a material degree. It need not result in a person entering into a contract as a result.

It is a defence for a trader to show that the false statement was mistakenly made, or was based on information supplied by someone else; or that he had taken reasonable care to avoid making a false statement. *See:* TRADE DESCRIPTIONS

When misrepresentation is a breach of contract

Sometimes, making a false statement can amount to breach of a term in a contract.

For instance, under the Sale of Goods Act 1979 there is an implied term in every contract for the sale of goods that they are reasonably fit for any particular purpose mentioned by a customer. So if a customer asks a shop assistant for a pair of waterproof shoes, and selects a pair on the false assurance of the assistant that they are waterproof, he or she has been induced to enter into a contract by a misrepresentation. However, the shop is also in breach of the contractual term that the shoes must be fit for the particular purpose – walking in the wet – mentioned by the customer. This entitles the customer to reject the shoes and to claim a refund of the price.

MISSING PERSON

Your right to 'disappear' without trace

People over the age of 16 can go where they like without letting anyone know their whereabouts, unless specifically ordered by a court to live in a certain place. *See:* BAIL; PROBATION

The police search for missing persons only if they are suspected of a criminal offence, if there are fears for their safety (perhaps because of old age or poor health), or if they are under 16. They do not help to trace a person against whom someone wants to bring a civil action – for instance, a husband who has deserted his wife and family.

If young people under 16 are traced, they are returned to their families. But if such a person is beyond parental control, or is suffering a lack of parental care, he or she may be referred to a CHILDREN'S HEARING for compulsory measures of care and protection.

The International Investigation Department of the Salvation Army, 110–112 Middlesex Street, London E1 7HZ, offers a voluntary service to relatives who are anxious to trace a member of the family who is over 17.

The aim of this service is reconciliation. If a missing husband or wife is traced, counsellors try to reconcile the missing partner with the family, but they will keep his or her new address secret. They do not disclose an address to enable a deserted partner to take legal proceedings. They will, however, act as a 'post-box' to enable the two parties to correspond if the missing person so wishes.

Private detectives undertake to try to trace missing persons, but their fees and expenses can be high if the time taken is lengthy or much travel is involved.

The fact that a person has chosen to move to an area where he is unknown in no way lessens his legal obligations – for instance, his duty to maintain his family. A court can compel his attendance to hear any claims against him, unless he has left the country.

If the whereabouts of a person are unknown and he is thought to be outside Scotland, there is a procedure by which he can be effectively cited in court actions by sending a copy of the documents to the Extractor of the Court of Session, Edinburgh. A solicitor's help will be needed.

Presumption of death If a missing person is thought to have died, or has not been known to be alive for at least 7 years, any person with an interest can seek a declaration from the Court of Session or sheriff court that the missing person has died. *See:* DEATH, Presumption of

MISSIVES OF SALE

When the sale must go on

When someone wants to buy a house or other building, or a piece of land, that is up for sale, his solicitor writes a formal letter to the seller's solicitor making a written offer for the property. If the seller agrees to the offer, his solicitor writes back a formal letter accepting it. Sometimes several letters have to be exchanged before the parties reach full agreement.

Once agreement is reached, there is a completed CONTRACT. Neither the seller nor the buyer can then change his mind. Because the offer and acceptance take the form of letters, the completed contract is known as 'missives of sale'.

There is usually a gap of several weeks between completion of the missives and the date when the buyer gets entry to the property. On the date of entry the buyer pays the purchase price and is given, in exchange, the keys and the CONVEYANCE transferring ownership of the property. *See:* HOUSE BUYING AND SELLING

MOBILE HOME

The rights of people living in mobile homes

People who live in mobile homes on sites that are licensed by the district or islands council are entitled to legal protection under the Mobile Homes Act 1983 and the Caravan Sites Act 1968. There is no protection when the licence is granted for holiday use only.

You can check with your council whether your site is protected.

Your right to a written agreement

The Mobile Homes Act 1983 gives protection to mobile home *owners* who agree to rent pitches on protected sites – including local authority sites. They must occupy the mobile home as their only or main residence.

The site owner must give each resident a written statement within 3 months of the date of the agreement between them. The statement must be in a form prescribed by law. It must:

- Give the names and addresses of the parties and the date on which the agreement commenced.
- Give details of the pitch.
- Set out the terms of the agreement that are implied by law.
- Set out the express terms of the agreement.

The implied terms

The implied terms are those that are automatically included in the agreement by law. They cannot be overridden by an express term in the agreement.

The implied terms cover:

Duration The agreement will normally last until it is terminated by:

- The resident giving at least 4 weeks' notice; or
- The site owner making a successful application for termination to a court. A

'court' means either a sheriff or an arbiter agreed by the parties.

The court will allow the agreement to be terminated if it is satisfied that one of the following applies:

1. The resident has breached a term of the agreement and has failed to comply, within a reasonable time, with a notice asking him to remedy the breach. The court must be satisfied that it is reasonable to allow the agreement to be terminated.

2. The resident is not occupying the mobile home as his only or main residence.

The site owner can also terminate the agreement every 5 years if he can satisfy the court that the mobile home is of such an age or in such a condition that it is having a detrimental effect on the amenity of the site – or is likely to have such an effect within the next 5 years.

If the resident fails to leave after the owner terminates the agreement, he can only be evicted by order of a sheriff (not an arbiter). The order can be applied for along with the application to terminate the agreement.

The resident can delay the eviction by asking the sheriff to suspend the order for up to 12 months – except when the site is owned by a local authority. If the court does so, after considering all the circumstances, it can impose whatever conditions it thinks fit. It is possible to apply for further 12-month extensions.

It is an offence for the site owner to evict a resident without a court order, or to harass him to force him to leave.

Overpayments Where an agreement is terminated, the resident is entitled to recover any payment made for a period following the termination.

Sale of mobile home The resident is entitled to sell the mobile home and to assign (transfer) the agreement to a person approved by the site owner. If the owner's consent is unreasonably withheld, the court can be asked to order him to consent.

If the resident does sell and assign his agreement, the site owner is entitled to a maximum of 10 per cent commission on the sale.

Gift of mobile home The resident is entitled to give the mobile home, and assign the agreement, to a member of his family approved by the site owner. If approval is unreasonably withheld, the matter can be decided by the court.

Re-siting of mobile home If the site owner can require a resident to move to another pitch on the site, that pitch must be broadly similar to the original one. All costs and expenses must be paid by the site owner. Any dispute can be referred to the court.

The express terms

The written statement must set out the express terms of the agreement – that is, the terms agreed between the site owner and resident in addition to the implied terms.

The express terms will usually include details of pitch fees and other charges – such as charges for services. The services provided – such as electricity or gas – will also usually be set out. If the owner sells gas or electricity to a resident, he cannot charge more than a maximum amount. *See*: ELECTRICITY SUPPLY; GAS SUPPLY

If a dispute arises about the express terms, either party can refer the matter to the court. This can only be done within 6 months of the written statement being given. The court can alter or delete express terms. It can also add new terms on:

- The resident's right to undisturbed possession.
- Sums payable by the resident, when they are to be paid, and their review at yearly intervals.
- The provision of services, or their use by the resident.
- Preserving the amenity of the site.
- Maintenance and repair of the site and mobile home.
- Access to the pitch by the site owner.

Inheriting the agreement

If the resident dies, his widow (or her widower) can inherit the written agreement and all the rights that go with it.

If there is no widow(er), a member of the resident's family living with him at the time of his death can inherit the agreement. Relations by marriage and of the half-blood are included. So are stepchildren, adopted and illegitimate children, and cohabitees.

If you rent your home

If you rent your mobile home on site, you are not protected by the 1983 Act. But you may be protected under the Rent (Scotland) Act if your home is immobilised and connected to services. *See:* EVICTION; RENT PROTECTION

Even if the Rent Act does not apply, you must be given at least 4 weeks' notice to quit and you can only be evicted by order of a sheriff. It is an offence to evict you without an order, or to harass you to force you to leave. The sheriff cannot refuse an eviction order, but you can ask him to suspend its operation for up to 12 months. Further 12-month extensions can be applied for.

If you are homeless

If you are evicted, or have no site for your home, you may be entitled to accommodation from the local housing department. *See:* HOMELESSNESS

MOBILITY ALLOWANCE

Cash help to enable a disabled person to get out and about

Anyone aged 5 or over who is unable or virtually unable to walk can apply for a social security payment called mobility allowance. To qualify he or she must:

1. Be under 66. Claimants aged 65 must be able to show that they qualified for the allowance before reaching 65.

2. Normally live in Britain, be there when claiming and have been present there for a total of at least 52 weeks out of the previous 18 months.

3. Be unable or virtually unable to walk. A person will be treated as virtually unable to walk if his ability to walk out of doors is limited, given the distance, speed, length of time or manner in which he can walk without experiencing severe discomfort.

A person will also be treated as unable or virtually unable to walk if the exertion needed to walk would threaten his life or lead to a serious deterioration in his health.

If someone can (or could) walk satisfactorily by using artificial aids, such as a stick, he will not be treated as unable or virtually unable to walk.

The difficulty in walking must be due to a physical condition. Someone suffering from agoraphobia, for example, cannot get the allowance.

4. Be likely to remain unable or virtually unable to walk for at least 12 months from the date of his claim.

5. Be able to make use of the allowance – that is, be able to get out of doors and benefit from increasing mobility. So a person in a coma, or who cannot be moved for medical reasons, is ineligible.

How to claim the allowance

If you think you are eligible, obtain leaflet NI 211 from your social security office and complete the attached form. If you cannot sign the form yourself, someone else can sign it for you.

Disabled child If you are the parent of a disabled child under 16 who is living with you, you can claim on his or her behalf. If the child lives elsewhere, or is in local authority care, the person in whose household he or she lives, or the responsible local authority official, should claim.

What medical evidence is needed If the DHSS does not have enough medical evidence in its own records to grant your claim, it will ask you to attend a medical examination – usually near your home. Your travelling expenses will be paid, as will those of any escort needed to accompany you. If you cannot travel, you will be examined at home.

If you qualify for the allowance, you will receive it until the age of 75 (provided that you continue to satisfy the conditions), or for a fixed period of at least a year. If the latter, you will be able to make another application at the end of that period.

Making an appeal

If you are refused an allowance on medical grounds, you can appeal against the decision to an independent medical appeal tribunal. The reason for refusal and details of how and where to appeal will be explained to you in the notification sent to you by the local social security office

How the allowance is paid

The allowance is paid weekly and is increased in November of each year. The current rate is always given in leaflet NI 196, which you can get from your local social security office. In 1983–4 it was £19 a week.

How other benefits are affected

If you are receiving any other social security benefits – such as INVALIDITY BENEFIT or ATTENDANCE ALLOWANCE – you are still entitled to receive a mobility allowance. The allowance is not counted as income when calculating any entitlement you may have to SUPPLEMENTARY BENEFIT.

You cannot receive a mobility allowance if you are already receiving a vehicle or private car allowance under the NHS or the war pensioners' vehicle service. But you can choose to have a mobility allowance instead of these. If you wish to change, you should get leaflet NI 225 from your local social security office and complete the form.

Income tax Mobility allowance was made tax free from April 1982.

Hiring or buying a car

If you are receiving mobility allowance, you may be able to buy or lease a car through MOTABILITY.

Car licence If you receive mobility allowance, you may be able to get exemption from VEHICLE EXCISE LICENCE.

MONEY BACK

What you can do when goods are defective

A buyer is entitled to get his money back if goods are defective – provided that he acts in time.

The law regards the goods as sufficiently defective to allow the purchaser to reject them if they are:

- Not as described. For example, someone who buys a handbag or briefcase labelled 'Real leather' and later finds a label saying it is made of plastic can take it back to the shop and get a refund.
- Not of merchantable quality. Goods sold by a shopkeeper must be reasonably fit for the usual purpose for which people buy goods of that kind. For example, a man who finds a hole in a new shirt can get his money back.
- Not fit for the purpose. For example, if someone is sold a colour TV set after telling the dealer that he wants one that will get good reception in a 'fringe' area, the set should get that kind of reception. If not the buyer can return it and get a refund.

Goods can also be rejected if they were bought in reliance on a false statement about them by the shopkeeper.

When time is important

Purchases should be examined thoroughly as soon as they have been taken home, for the buyer's right to reject defective goods does not last for long. You must do so within a 'reasonable time'.

What is a reasonable time cannot be laid down in advance. It depends on all the circumstances, including the type and quantity of the goods. It is usually based on the time a reasonable buyer would take to examine them to find out if they are satisfactory or not.

Once the goods are found defective, they should not be used. Using goods may imply acceptance and may lose the buyer his right to reject them. Moreover it might lead to dispute over whether the goods were really defective when they were sold or whether they have been damaged by the buyer.

Your right to a cash refund

Anyone entitled to have his money refunded has the right to insist on cash. A credit note can be spent only in the same shop, and once it is accepted the buyer may have lost his right to exchange it for cash.

Goods must be returnable

It is not possible to reject goods if they have been used up. If food has been eaten and it is found defective only when it makes you ill, you cannot legally reject it. There is no longer anything to reject. You do, however, have the right

REFUNDS WITH A SMILE

Anyone can demand his money back if the goods are defective, not as described or not fit for their purpose – if he acts in time.

to claim damages to compensate for any loss suffered.

If the goods were completely worthless, the damages will amount to the same thing as getting your money back. If the defective goods caused illness or damage, the damages could be more than the purchase price.

Even if the goods were not worthless and did not cause injury or damage, the buyer would be entitled to the difference between what he had paid and what they were worth.

To claim in all of these circumstances however, might involve you having to take legal action. As a first step, without incurring costs, consult your local trading standards office. *See:* DEFECTIVE GOODS

MORTGAGE

The loan that enables a purchaser to buy a home

Most people who want to buy a house or flat need to borrow most of the purchase price by way of a mortgage loan.

The loan is made on the security of the property being bought and you will have to sign a mortgage deed, called a standard security. This means that if you stop repaying the loan the lender has the power, ultimately, to sell the house and recover the money.

Most mortgages are obtained from building societies, but banks, life insurance companies, and local authorities also give loans. The amount depends on your financial standing and the sort of home you want to buy. You repay the loan, and interest on it, over an agreed period – generally 20 or 25 years.

It is sometimes difficult to get a mortgage, but it may be easier if you have had money invested with a building society for some months before the mortgage is needed. Even if you have only a small amount of money to invest, it is better to save with more than one building society.

Where to get the money

Different sources of mortgage give loans on different types of property. Interest rates may also differ.

Building society In deciding how much it will be prepared to lend, a building society is mainly concerned to ensure that the borrower is not overcommitting himself.

Generally, a society will be prepared to lend up to 2½ times an applicant's gross annual earnings, although societies do differ to a limited extent in the income multiple they use. If there is to be a joint loan to two people, the multiple may be up to 2½ times the gross annual income of the higher earner plus the amount of the other income.

Additional payments such as commission and overtime may be taken into account, depending on their permanency and regularity.

A borrower is expected to be able to raise part of the house price himself – normally from 10 to 30 per cent of the value put on the house by the society (a figure which comes from the valuation survey that it has carried out). The value will usually be less than the price you actually have to pay to buy the house.

In certain circumstances you may be able to arrange a mortgage of 95 per cent or 100 per cent of the value. You will have to convince the society that you are able to meet higher monthly repayments of the loan without undue strain on your budget.

If the advance exceeds 80 per cent (sometimes 75 per cent or 70 per cent) of valuation, the society will require some form of additional security. This usually takes the form of an indemnity by an insurance company for which a single premium is paid at the time the loan is taken out. The building society makes all the necessary arrangements.

Local authority A district or islands council will sometimes lend as much as 100 per cent of its valuation of a property in its area. The valuation, like that of a building society, may be lower than the selling price of the property. However, council mortgages are not always available: a yearly allocation is set aside, but demand often exceeds supply.

A local authority is more likely than a building society to offer a mortgage on older properties.

A local authority mortgage may run over a longer period than a building society loan, but the interest rate may also be slightly higher. To apply for a local authority mortgage, write to the housing department at your district or islands council offices.

If you are buying a council house from a local authority, and cannot obtain a sufficient loan from a building society, the authority must give you a loan. *See:* COUNCIL HOUSE SALE

Life-insurance company Sometimes it is possible to arrange a mortgage with an insurance company – paying regular interest and relying on an endowment policy to repay the capital sum when it matures.

Having a policy with a particular company will not entitle you to a loan – but it may help.

The interest rate for an insurance-linked mortgage is usually slightly higher than for a building society loan.

Bank Banks have recently become much more willing to make mortgage loans. They have their own rules about minimum loans, repayment periods and interest rates – so ask your bank for details to compare with the building society terms.

A bank may be willing to lend a higher sum than a building society would be prepared to consider. It may also make loans to well-established customers for property purchase over a short period, something which a building society would not normally do.

WHERE TO GO FOR ADVICE

Delays in buying a house usually arise from difficulties in arranging a mortgage. If you intend buying a property, seek advice as soon as possible – and certainly before making an offer for a house.

If you are a building society investor, contact the manager of your local branch and find out if he is willing to lend as much money as you need.

If you do not save with a building society, the simplest way to arrange a loan is probably to ask your solicitor for help.

Sometimes the solicitor or estate agent selling a particular house has arranged that a loan will be available for the person buying it.

A home buyer should be frank about his financial position. Overstating your income will only delay a mortgage being arranged, because if the figures do not tally when your application is checked – for example, when a building society consults your employer – the application will be referred back to you – or even rejected.

ADVANTAGES AND DISADVANTAGES TO CONSIDER WHEN CHOOSING A MORTGAGE

Working out what the difference between capital-repayment and endowment loans means to you

When you take out a loan, you have to decide between two different kinds of mortgage: the capital-repayment and the endowment.

Capital-repayment

The simplest and most common mortgage is the capital-repayment mortgage, where a borrower repays the loan and the interest on it at regular monthly intervals over a period of, usually, 20 or 25 years.

Interest is calculated on the balance of the debt outstanding at the beginning of a building society's financial year. For example, if you originally borrowed £20,000 and at a particular time have paid off £4,000, you will then be paying interest on the remaining £16,000 and not the full £20,000.

At the start of the mortgage, the interest accounts for the majority of the monthly payment and the actual loan is reduced quite slowly.

Endowment

In an endowment policy the borrower only pays interest. The capital is repaid at the end of the loan in one go by the maturing of a life INSURANCE POLICY. The borrower pays for the policy by monthly premiums.

An endowment mortgage can be arranged with a building society and an agreed insurance company, or can sometimes be arranged direct with an insurance company only.

In either case the size of the monthly insurance premium is fixed when the policy is taken out and does not change thereafter. It is calculated on the size of the loan and the borrower's age, occupation and state of health.

The amount of interest payable varies only if the mortgage rate changes. It is based on the full amount of the loan, for the full period of the contract and not – as with a capital-repayment mortgage – on a gradually decreasing loan.

'With profits' By paying higher premiums, you can take out a 'with profits' endowment policy which will eventually be worth much more than an ordinary policy giving similar insurance cover.

The home-buyer's loan is paid off in the same way when the policy matures, but he receives any profits from his invested money as well. If he dies before the policy matures, his wife or family receive any profits accrued.

Which one?

The first question you have to decide is whether or not you want your life insured. The purpose of life insurance is to pay off the whole loan if you die before the mortgage ends. If you are married you will probably want life insurance, but if you are single you may not.

Endowment mortgages are tied to a life insurance policy. Capital-repayment mortgages are not. This means that if you do not want life insurance you must go for a capital-repayment mortgage. But if you want life insurance, you can make a choice between the two kinds of mortgage.

Endowment mortgages cost more than capital-repayment mortgages, allowing for the fact that under the capital-repayment method a separate life insurance policy is also required. But endowment mortgages receive greater tax relief. The reason for this is that tax relief only covers the interest part of mortgage repayments. With an endowment policy all mortgage repayments are repayments of interest. With a capital-repayment mortgage, part of the repayments are repayments of capital.

Even when tax relief is taken into account, however, a capital-repayment mortgage plus a separate life insurance policy is probably cheaper for most people than an endowment mortgage. This was not always so. Endowment mortgages taken out before March 14, 1984 attracted additional tax relief on the life insurance premiums, thus reducing their total cost.

For borrowers who pay tax at rates greater than the basic rate, the extra tax relief produced by the endowment mortgage may still make it more attractive.

Cost is not, however, the only matter to consider. Each type of mortgage has one advantage not shared by the other:

- Most endowment mortgages are 'with profits' so that a tax-free capital sum is paid to the borrower at the end of the loan. The real value of this sum depends on the rate of inflation over the loan period and cannot be accurately assessed.
- Under capital-repayment mortgages the size of the loan is gradually reduced as repayments are made. A borrower selling his house before the end of the mortgage term thus has more money available.

Even if your loan is from someone else, you may well use a bank for a BRIDGING LOAN, to cover the period between buying a new house and selling the old one.

Staff mortgages Some employers arrange private mortgages for certain staff. In the case of banks and insurance companies especially, they are likely to be at a very low rate of interest. If the employee leaves the job, he normally has to negotiate a new loan with another lender.

Applying for a mortgage

When you apply for a mortgage you have to fill in an application form which usually includes questions on your age, family, occupation, income and nationality, and authorises a request for references from your bank and employer. If you are self-employed, the lender will require an accountant's certificate of your earnings, or figures approved by the Inland Revenue.

You will have to pay a survey fee for the valuation of the property you want to buy, and the lender's legal fees for drawing up the mortgage deed.

The valuation is carried out on behalf of the lender so that it can judge the suitability of the property for mortgage purposes and decide how much can be lent. Not all lenders give details of the surveyor's report – although if they are willing to lend you can assume that it is reasonably favourable. The valuation is not a structural survey, however, and if you have any doubts about the house you may want to arrange a second survey yourself. *See:* HOUSE BUYING AND SELLING

If the lender decides that you are a suitable borrower, you will receive an 'offer of advance', usually on a standard form, giving details of the size of the offer, the current rate of interest (with the right to vary this at any time) and the period of the loan. This document also lists any restrictions on the offer – for example, some money may be retained from the loan until you have carried out certain work to the house.

Accepting an offer

If you agree to the terms, you sign the acceptance form and return it to the lender. But if there are restrictions that you do not agree with, contact the lender or your solicitor to see if the details can be changed before you sign. If you are buying a home that is still being built and for which payment has to be made in instalments, your solicitor can make sure that the money is made available at various stages of the work.

If you do not wish to accept an offer, it is advisable always to write informing the lender. There is no reason to assume that he will not deal with you again because you have turned down his offer.

After you have accepted the offer, the lender's solicitor will check the ownership of the property and draw up the standard security – the legal document recording the transaction and setting out the size and terms of the loan. You will have to pay the solicitor's fees.

The lender, especially if it is a building society, usually employs your solicitor to do this. This reduces the cost because your solicitor will have to check the ownership in any case in the course of buying the house.

You can generally choose to make the monthly payments on the loan and the interest charged, either directly to the lender, by standing order from a bank or through the national girobank system.

Insuring a capital-repayment mortgage

When you arrange an endowment mortgage, it is linked to a life-insurance policy and gives you the security of knowing that, if you die, the policy will immediately pay off your mortgage debt.

But if you arrange a capital-repayment mortgage you have no such protection unless you specifically arrange a mortgage-protection policy.

A mortgage-protection policy can be paid for by a single premium when the policy is first taken out, or premiums can be paid over a period of years. Tax relief is not available for policies taken out after March 13, 1984.

If the insurer dies, the policy produces a lump sum to pay off the loan or a large part of it.

If a borrower sells his home and pays off his mortgage to buy another, the policy can be kept up to protect the second mortgage. A further policy will be needed if the amount borrowed is higher.

If the period of the mortgage is extended because the interest rate rises, you may also be able to have the policy extended.

When your mortgage is paid off at the end of its term, the insurance company's obligation on a mortgage-protection policy normally ends. It does not have anything to pay out either to you or to the lender.

You can, however, take out a mortgage-protection policy with 'survival benefit' by paying a higher premium. A cash sum is paid to you at the end of the policy term, in the same way as any endowment policy.

The obligation to insure a mortgaged home

Building societies and other lenders insist that your mortgaged home is insured against fire and other risks – for example, flood or storm. A society usually states, in its mortgage offer, how much insurance must be taken out. In most cases the society takes charge of the insurance premium payments, by paying the insurance company and charging the borrower, either directly or through his account.

The policy usually covers the full reinstatement value of the property. The value alters with rising building costs and it is necessary to increase the insurance cover regularly. The policy may do this automatically. If it does not, it is up to you to arrange it.

How changing interest rates may affect you

The rate of interest on mortgage loans has to be variable because the rate which societies pay their investors is dependent on movements in the general level of interest rates. Rates for local authorities, banks and insurance companies also rise or fall with the national trend.

A rise of as little as 1 per cent in the interest rate can have a substantial effect on a borrower.

For example, if a borrower has an endowment mortgage of £20,000, his monthly repayments at an interest rate of 12 per cent are £140 for the loan and, say, £35 for the insurance policy: a total of £175. But if the rate went up to 13 per cent his monthly repayments would rise to £186.67, an increase of £11.67. The difference over 20 years would be around £2,800.

An increased interest rate does not alter the insurance premiums.

When interest rates rise, a borrower may be able to avoid the increased re-

SPECIAL HELP FOR FIRST-TIME BUYERS

Many people are put off buying their own home because of the difficulties of finding enough money for the first purchase. To help first-time buyers there is a special Government scheme called the Homeloan Scheme.

The main benefit under the Homeloan Scheme is a tax-free bonus of up to £110. To qualify for this you must be a first-time buyer, *and*:

1. Save with a recognised savings institution for at least two years. Recognised institutions include building societies, banks, trustee savings banks and the National Savings Bank.

2. Keep at least £300 in your savings account throughout the year before you buy the house. The amount of the bonus depends on the balance in your account during this period. The bonus ranges from £40 where the balance is between £300 and £400, to a maximum of £110 where the balance is over £1,000.

3. Buy a house for not more than the price limit fixed by the Government. This limit rises periodically with inflation. In 1984 it was £23,400.

4. Take out a mortgage which is at least £1,600 and not less than 25 per cent of the purchase price.

If you think you will be able to satisfy these conditions, you can take advantage of the scheme by asking your savings institution for the application form. This form gives notice of your intention to save under the scheme. The two year savings period does not begin until the savings institution accepts your notice.

Additional loan

If at any time when you apply for the Homeloan bonus the balance in your savings account is at least £600, you are also entitled to an additional loan of £600. This is on top of the loan arranged with your building society or other lender. The additional loan is interest-free for the first five years.

payments by having the length of his mortgage agreement extended.

If you have an endowment mortgage, however, you do not have that choice. You must keep to the agreed purchase period and pay higher interest instalments. That is because if you continued to pay at the previous, lower rate, the additional interest would mount up, the debt would increase and the endowment policy would no longer cover the total debt.

In rare cases – usually staff mortgages from banks or insurance companies – the mortgage deed may state that the loan has a fixed rate of interest.

Mortgage repayment difficulties

Building societies will make loans only to people who they believe are able to keep up the necessary repayments. However, circumstances do change, and inevitably some people will face financial difficulties. For example, illness may be responsible for lowering a home-buyer's income, or he may be made redundant.

Building societies are generally sympathetic to borrowers whose circumstances have changed, but it is important for the home-buyer to contact the building society as soon as he believes he is going to have difficulty in making his regular payments.

The worst thing to do is to let arrears mount up without explanation, because the building society may then be unable to offer any help at all.

If there is only a temporary short-fall of income, the society may be able to put a capital-repayment mortgage on to an interest-only basis for a time. However, if the mortgage is a relatively new one, this is not likely to have a significant effect on the repayments.

SUPPLEMENTARY BENEFIT may be available to a home-buyer who is not in employment, so he should contact his nearest office of the Department of Health and Social Security. If he obtains benefit, he can receive an additional amount to cover payments of mortgage interest (but not capital).

If repayment problems seem likely to be permanent, it may be best for a home-buyer to sell the existing property and buy or rent a property that is more appropriate to his means.

When a borrower fails to make his repayments

If a borrower fails to make the repayments required under the mortgage deed, the lender can call up the loan, bringing it to an end.

If the borrower still refuses to pay, the lender can use various methods of recovering the amount he has lent (plus any arrears of interest and other expenses). These include evicting the borrower or anyone else in the property, and then selling it.

The lender must sell for the best price that he can reasonably get and he must hand over any surplus to the borrower unless there is a second mortgage over

HOW TAX RELIEF AFFECTS THE COST OF A MORTGAGE

If you borrow money to buy a house as your main home, and it is not used for business, you are entitled to tax relief on the mortgage interest payments. Relief is limited to a loan ceiling which is increased from time to time. In 1984 the ceiling was £30,000. Interest on any more than that does not qualify for relief.

If you have an endowment mortgage that was taken out before March 14, 1984, you also gain tax relief on the life insurance premiums.

The method of giving tax relief was altered in April 1983. Until that date, borrowers paid mortgage interest to the lender in full, and were then given a tax allowance reduced their tax bill.

Since April 1983 a new method, known as MIRAS, has been in operation. Borrowers no longer pay the full amount of interest to the lender. Instead, their monthly payments of interest are reduced by the basic rate of tax, currently 30%. No tax allowance is now given, except to borrowers whose income takes them into the higher tax brackets.

The reason for the change was purely administrative. The overall effect of both methods is exactly the same. Under the old method, borrowers paid more to the lender by way of interest, but less to the Inland Revenue by way of income tax. The new method reverses this. Less is now paid to the lender, but correspondingly more to the Inland Revenue.

Relief for life insurance premiums, where available, works in the same way except that the permitted deduction is only half the basic rate of tax.

Example: A couple buy a house with a capital-repayment mortgage of £20,000. At an interest rate of 10 per cent they owe £2,000 in the first year. In addition, they will have to repay a certain amount of capital, say £300.

If the basic rate of income tax is 30 per cent, and the couple only pay tax at the basic rate, they are entitled to £600 (30 per cent of £2,000) as tax relief on the *interest* repayments. No tax relief is available on the *capital* repayments.

The amount payable to the lender under MIRAS is therefore not the full £2,300, but only £1,700.

The couple's life insurance policy will not attract tax relief.

Option mortgage

Until April 1983, borrowers could choose to join the option mortgage scheme instead of claiming tax relief. Repayments to the lender were reduced by a subsidy paid directly by the government. The subsidy scale was broadly equivalent to tax relief at the basic rate of tax.

The purpose of the scheme was to benefit borrowers whose income was not sufficiently high to take full advantage of the mortgage tax allowance.

The recent change in the system of making tax allowances has meant that low income is no longer the bar to tax relief which it was before. As a result, the option mortgage scheme was discontinued in April 1983.

Borrowers who formerly used the scheme will have noticed little difference in their new monthly payments.

WHEN HOUSE VALUES RISE

Borrowers who have a mortgage may be able to obtain a further loan to pay for home improvements or business development.

ARRANGING A FURTHER ADVANCE

After a few years, because of inflation, it is likely that your home will be worth more than you paid for it. That increase in value can often be the basis of a further loan – if, for example, you want to make improvements.

You can arrange a second mortgage with your existing lender, usually at the same rate of interest that you pay for your initial loan.

For example, if you borrowed £10,000 for a £14,000 house 10 years ago and the house in now worth £35,000, £27,000 of the present value may be available as security for a second loan. That is because you have probably paid off around £2,000 of the original loan, leaving a debt of £8,000 to set against the £35,000 new value.

Once you have been given the second loan, the lender will either increase your monthly payments or extend the period of the first mortgage.

To apply for a further advance, contact the manager at your building society or bank. If the loan is for home improvements, he will be able to advise you on whether you may be able to qualify for a local authority IMPROVEMENT GRANT instead.

GETTING AN OUTSIDE LOAN

A borrower may alternatively obtain a second mortgage from a finance company. You can expect to pay high interest on such a loan – in some cases as high as 25 per cent.

If a borrower defaults on payment to a second lender, he can call up the mortgage and sell the house – but only if he first pays off the debt to the main lender.

If the proceeds from selling the house do not cover both debts, the second lender then has to sue the borrower for debt, or if necessary start proceedings to make him bankrupt.

Before signing a loan agreement with a finance company, you should ask a solicitor or Citizens Advice Bureau adviser to check it.

The hidden cost Whatever the source, or amount, of the further advance, a considerable amount of legal documentation is required. This costs money.

the same property.

Recovering a debt in this way is costly and unpleasant, and for that reason most lenders go to considerable lengths to settle the matter amicably.

How the law protects a borrower

The Consumer Credit Act 1974 contains a number of important provisions designed to protect borrowers. The Act does not, however, apply to three of the main suppliers of mortgages: building societies, local authorities and most insurance companies. It does apply to banks and finance companies.

It is an offence under the Act to publish an advertisement that gives a false and misleading impression of mortgage facilities – for example, of their true cost or true rate of interest.

Where a loan is for less than £5,000 (£15,000 after May 20, 1985), a prospective borrower has a breathing space before agreeing to the terms of the loan.

He must first be given a copy of the agreement that he will be asked to sign. He must then be allowed 7 days in which to consider it, after which he can be sent a copy of the formal contract. He then has a further 7 days to consider the terms.

During this legal breathing space the lender must not communicate with the borrower in any way unless the borrower asks him to. At the end of this period the prospective borrower can be asked to sign and return the formal contract if he wants the loan.

The borrower can pull out at any time before signing. After signing, he is bound to the terms of the contract.

If the lender does not follow the correct procedure and you refuse to repay the loan, he cannot sue you for the money, or repossess or sell your house or land, without a court order. The court is unlikely to make an order unless the lender can prove there was a genuine, reasonable and honest mistake that caused the breach in procedure. *See:* CONSUMER CREDIT; CONSUMER PROTECTION; CREDIT AGREEMENT

Selling a mortgaged home

A mortgage on your home does not prevent you from selling it. Unless the mortgage deed says otherwise, you are legally entitled to pay off the debt after giving two month's notice of your intention to do so. The notice has to follow a particular form and you would need your solicitor's help.

In practice, most lenders do not insist on formal notice, and do not expect two months' warning.

Some lenders make a charge if a borrower redeems his mortgage within 5 years of raising it. The fee can be 3 months' interest on the loan remaining at the time of the sale.

The sale of the property and the redemption of the mortgage are completed at the same time, so that the money from the buyer can be used to pay off the mortgage.

You may also be able to pay off your mortgage more quickly by increasing your payments. But the building society or other lender will want to be sure you can afford the increased payments before agreeing to that.

MOT TEST

Car safety – by order

On their third birthday – 3 years after first registration – vehicles become due for the statutory annual vehicle test, commonly known as the MOT test.

The test covers lighting equipment, steering, suspension, brakes, tyres and roadwheels, seat belts and general items such as windscreen wipers, washers, exhaust system and horn. The condition of the vehicle structure is examined for any fractures, damage or corrosion which could effect the correct functioning of the braking system or the steering mechanism.

Tests are conducted by authorised examiners at approved testing stations displaying the triple triangle sign.

If the car passes the test, the examiner signs and issues a test certificate. If the car fails, he issues a notification of refusal, specifying the defects. In all cases, the examiner issues a list showing what has been checked and its condition.

In 1984 the fee for a vehicle test was £9 for a car and £5.40 for a motor cycle.

If the car is left at the testing station to be repaired, only one fee is payable. If it is removed, but within fourteen days taken to the same or another testing station for repair and re-testing, only half the normal fee is payable.

A car can be tested up to 1 month before its current test certificate is due for renewal. The new certificate will run from the expiry date of the old.

Generally, it is illegal to use or permit to be used on a public road any 3-year-old vehicle without a current test certificate. The maximum penalty is a fine of up to £400, but there is no risk of endorsement or disqualification. A police constable can require production of a test certificate on demand or within 5 days at a nominated police station.

It is a defence to a charge of not having an MOT certificate that the driver has made an appointment with a testing station and was in fact on his way directly there at the time that he was stopped. If, however, the vehicle is actually defective, the driver can be prosecuted.

A road vehicle licence will not be issued without production of a current test certificate.

Failure to have a current MOT certificate could affect an insurance claim.

MOTABILITY

A government-backed scheme to provide cars for disabled people

Disabled people may be able to use their MOBILITY ALLOWANCE to lease or buy a car through Motability, a registered charity which operates with government support.

The Motability scheme covers all recipients of mobility allowance, whether they can drive or not, and includes the parents of disabled children.

Motability will lease cars to applicants, or make new or used cars available on hire purchase. A car is paid for by the applicant agreeing to have his or her mobility allowance paid over to Motability Finance Ltd., a finance company which purchases the cars and then leases or sells them to applicants.

Buying or leasing?

The type of arrangement which you can make with Motability depends on the length of time for which mobility allowance has been awarded.

- If you have an award of mobility allowance for more than the next two years, you can make arrangements to buy a used car on hire purchase.

You can select the car you wish to purchase. But it must be under 4 years old and have done no more than 40,000 miles. The supplier must be a dealer who holds a franchise from a car manufacturer and who is willing to have the car inspected by the Automobile Association.

If the car is satisfactory, Motability Finance Ltd will pay a sum of money to the dealer. The amount depends on the length of the agreement – which can be 2 or 3 years – and whether you are willing to hand over the whole of your allowance. If the amount paid is less than the purchase price, you will have to pay the balance yourself.

Although your mobility allowance will be paid direct to Motability Finance Ltd., you will receive any increase in the rate of allowance which takes effect during the course of the agreement.

- If you have an award of mobility allowance for more than the next three years, you can lease a car from Motability. You can lease British Leyland or Talbot cars for 4 years, and Ford or Vauxhall cars for 3 years. At the end of that period, you can apply to lease another car.

If you lease a car, you do not own it when the lease ends. Also, the whole of your mobility allowance (including any increases) must be paid over to Motability Finance Ltd. However, unlike hire purchase, maintenance and servicing are paid for.

- If you have an award of mobility allowance for more than the next four and a half years, you may be able to purchase a new car through Motability. You will have to pay a deposit, which is the difference between the purchase price of the car and the amount of money made available by Motability Finance Ltd.

Other help

In certain circumstances Motability may be able to help if you cannot afford to pay for any necessary adaptations to your car, or for driving lessons.

People receiving mobility allowance may be eligible for exemption from vehicle licence tax. Ask for details at your local social security office. *See:* VEHICLE EXCISE LICENCE

Electric wheelchairs You can also use your mobility allowance to buy an electric wheelchair on hire purchase over 2 years. Motability will give you details of the wheelchairs available.

Leaflets and application forms for all these schemes are available from Motability, Boundary House, 91–93 Charterhouse Street, London EC1M 6BT. *See:* MOBILITY ALLOWANCE

MOTOR CYCLE

A rider must be sure his machine is not dangerous

The rider of a motor cycle is responsible for the safety of his machine when it is on the road. He must see that the tyres are in good condition and that the brakes and lights are in proper working order.

Tyres For motor cycles of 50 cc or less there is no minimum depth of tread, as there is for car tyres, but the tread must be visible for at least three-quarters of the breadth of the tyre around the circumference. Over 50 cc the minimum depth is the same as for car tyres. All motor-cycle tyres are cross-ply.

Brakes There must be two independently operated brakes, one for each wheel, or one braking system with two means of operation. No parking brake is required.

Noise The maximum noise level for motor cycles over 125 cc is 90 decibels, and for those under 125 cc it is 80 decibels. This compares with 87 decibels for cars. It is an offence to alter a motor-cycle's silencer to increase the noise.

Lights Motor cycles without a sidecar need only one front white light, one red rear light and one red reflector. No parking light is needed, but a stop light is compulsory.

Traffic indicators are not compulsory, but if they are fitted they must comply with the same rules as those for cars.

Mirror At least one rear-view mirror is compulsory on machines first used after October 1, 1978.

Speedometer Only motor cycles of more than 100 cc are required to have a speedometer in working order. It must be accurate to within 10 per cent.

Passengers It is an offence for the rider of a motor cycle without a sidecar to carry more than one passenger. The passenger must sit astride a fixed pillion

PENALTIES FOR MOTOR-CYCLING OFFENCES

The charges that affect only motor cyclists and their pillion passengers

	Offence	Maximum penalty
Brakes	Riding or permitting use with defective brakes	£1,000 and endorsement. Disqualification is at the court's discretion
Helmet	Riding with no helmet – even as a pillion passenger	£100
Lights	Riding or permitting use with defective lights	£1,000
Mirror	Riding or permitting use of cycle first used after Oct 1, 1978, without rear-view mirror	£1,000
Noise	Adapting silencer to increase noise level	£1,000
Passenger	Carrying a pillion passenger without footrests	£1,000
	Carrying an unqualified pillion passenger when only a provisional-licence holder	£1,000 and endorsement. Disqualification is at the court's discretion
Speedometer	Riding or permitting use of motor cycle with no, or defective, speedometer	£1,000
Trailer	Towing a trailer by solo motor cycle	£1,000
Tyres	Riding or permitting use with defective tyre	£1,000 and endorsement. Disqualification is at the court's discretion

seat, and the cycle must have suitable footrests.

A learner rider of a solo motor cycle cannot carry a passenger unless that passenger holds a current, valid, full licence to ride a motor cycle.

Crash helmets Both the motor cyclist and his pillion rider must usually wear a CRASH HELMET.

Trailer Solo motor cycles must not be used to draw a trailer – except to tow another motor cycle that has broken down.

MOTOR INSURANCE

Compulsory and voluntary cover for drivers and vehicles

Whenever a motor vehicle is on a public road – whether it is driven, towed, pushed or parked – the owner and the person in charge of it must be insured against the risk of injury to other people. *See:* INSURANCE

The law requires every vehicle owner to buy at least that minimum amount of insurance before the vehicle goes on the road. It holds him responsible for seeing that anyone else who drives it with his permission is also covered.

Any owner with a valid driving licence should be able to obtain the legal minimum cover from a motor insurance company.

Insurers are not bound to provide cover but do not normally refuse. They are entitled, however, to charge more of someone they regard as a high risk, and to impose their own limits on who else can drive a vehicle.

Instead of taking out an insurance policy, the Road Traffic Act 1972 permits a driver to deposit, in court, the sum of £15,000. This will only remove the legal requirement of insurance when the car is driven under the control of the person making the deposit. You should only consider this alternative if your driving record is so bad that no insurance company would want to take the risk of insuring you.

Voluntary cover

Most vehicle owners can buy wider insurance cover on a voluntary basis. What it includes depends on an insurance company's willingness to accept the risk, and the owner's willingness to pay the premium asked.

Charges to cover the same risk will vary between companies, and one company's charges may vary according to its view of the owner's experience and reliability.

Four types of insurance policy are usually available for a private car:

- Road Traffic Act – the minimum laid down by law.
- Third party only.
- Third party, fire and theft.
- Comprehensive – the widest cover under a standard policy.

When you arrange insurance, make sure that you know exactly what is included in a policy.

If a policy document is not available, or its wording is confusing, ask for a leaflet or brochure that summarises the risks covered, and states the main limits or exclusions.

Choosing a policy

If a motorist or his car are considered an unreasonably high risk, an insurance company is entitled to refuse to give him full insurance.

In other cases a driver may be required to take out comprehensive insurance by the person from whom he borrows or hires a car.

Otherwise it is up to a motorist to decide what insurance, beyond the legal minimum, he needs and can afford.

Road Traffic Act only

A policy that is limited to the requirements of the Road Traffic Act 1972 covers you only for personal injury caused to someone else by your vehicle. Such a policy includes cover for claims by any passengers in your car and it provides payment for emergency hospital charges. Costs incurred with the insurer's consent in dealing with any claim covered by the policy are also included.

A 'Road Traffic Act-only' policy does not cover injury to yourself, or damage to other people's property or to your own.

For that reason, a motorist should never settle just for Road Traffic Act insurance if he can obtain more extensive cover.

Third party only

A third party policy includes the protection provided by a Road Traffic Act policy, and covers liability for damage to someone else's vehicle or other property. It also provides cover for any legal expenses that may be incurred in defending yourself or another permitted driver against a claim for damages after an accident.

The cover includes the expenses of any appeal, and the sum insured for that purpose is unlimited.

However, it is for the insurance company to decide how far an appeal may be taken when it is paying your legal expenses.

If the motorist is subsequently charged with culpable homicide or causing death by reckless driving, the policy normally covers his defence expenses up to, say, £1,000.

A 'third party only' policyholder is usually insured for driving other cars or motor cycles that do not belong to him, provided that he has the owner's permission and is not hiring the vehicle or buying it under a hire purchase agreement. If he is covered for business use, the policy will cover use of such other vehicles on business.

That extra cover may not be available to a driver under the age of 25, or if he already owns an exceptionally high-powered vehicle. The policy states any such limitations.

Third party, fire and theft

If you take out a third party, fire and theft policy you have third party cover plus insurance against the theft of your own vehicle, any damage to it caused by a thief, and any loss or damage caused by fire.

Damage when someone steals or attempts to steal something in your car – for example, a radio – is covered. Damage to your car in a collision is not, unless it has been stolen.

The amount that insurers will pay on a claim for fire or theft is normally limited to the sale value of the vehicle at the time of the loss, as shown in motor trade guides or newspaper advertisements offering similar vehicles.

The amount for which the car is insured is usually the maximum the insurer will pay. However, if that estimated value is lower than the 'book' price, the insurers may decide to pay more than the 'insured' value.

Some insurers charge an extra premium when the vehicle is to be kept in the open, instead of in a locked garage – especially in a big town. Alternatively, they may require you to fit an approved anti-theft device.

If a higher premium or anti-theft lock is required, you will be told so when you are given the quotation. But you should also read your policy carefully

THREE WAYS TO ARRANGE MOTOR INSURANCE

When you need to insure a vehicle, you have a choice of dealing:

- Direct with a company.
- Through an INSURANCE BROKER.
- Through an INSURANCE AGENT.

A registered broker should be able to obtain the policy best suited to your needs, at the lowest possible price. You pay no extra for his services.

Dealing direct

Most insurance companies have public offices in main towns and are prepared to take motor insurance proposals.

You may well get the quickest decision that way. But you may not get the best policy or lowest premium available – and unless you have an expert knowledge of motor insurance law, you may be at a disadvantage when it comes to making a claim that is disputed by the company or another party.

There is no reduction in premiums for dealing direct. The company simply saves the commission it would have paid to a broker or agent.

Dealing with a broker

A registered broker can deal on your behalf with most insurance companies. He can offer a wide range of policies with different types of cover, and he can obtain a range of premium quotations for the same type of cover,

A broker usually has special contacts with a few companies. That may be because they pay him a higher commission, but he is just as likely to favour them because he can deal with them more simply.

That may mean that he overlooks a cheaper premium, and so you lose money by dealing through him. But a strong connection between broker and insurer can help you if there is difficulty over a claim later. It is also a major advantage to someone whose accident record makes it hard to get full insurance.

You are entitled to ask a broker for several alternative premium quotations, or for details of any special features of policies offered by various companies. Essentially, however, you are relying on his knowledge and judgment.

At different stages of an insurance transaction a broker acts on behalf of both sides – you and the insurance company. He has a legal duty to provide proper professional services. If he fails through negligence and either side loses by it, he can be sued for damages.

If a broker thinks your proposal is acceptable to a company and you agree to the premium quotation, you normally pay the premium to him immediately. He issues a temporary cover note to show that your insurance is effective immediately – although the company can still reject your proposal – and you are entitled to put your car on the road.

Your payment is acknowledged and your insurance cover is valid even if a broker becomes insolvent before he has passed your premium on to the company. Later, if a broker becomes insolvent while he is holding money intended for you – for example, a refund or a claim settlement – you would have the right to 'rank' as a creditor. But insurance companies would normally settle directly with you.

Dealing with an agent

An insurance agent's services may be helpful if you live in a remote area where companies or brokers cannot be contacted.

An agent – typically an accountant, bank officer, solicitor or motor trader – can work in much the same way as a broker, but he does not have access to the same range of contacts and information. Nor does he usually have the same degree of authority to act for either side.

He is still obliged to exercise proper care, however, and can be sued for negligence.

to check on anti-theft requirements.

Comprehensive

About two-thirds of all car policies issued in Britain give comprehensive insurance. It is advisable for any car that has a reasonable cash value.

In addition to third party, fire and theft cover, a comprehensive policy insures against collision damage to your own car and various other risks.

It does not matter if the damage to your car is your own fault – or even if you break the law – provided that you are licensed to drive at the time.

Companies offer varying ranges of cover, but a good comprehensive policy would include;

• *Damage to your car* The company pays the cost of moving your car – usually to the nearest competent repairer – the cost of repairs based on an agreed estimate, and the cost of returning the car to you.

If estimated repair costs exceed the market value of the car at the time, the claim is treated as a total loss and you are paid the market value. The damaged vehicle then becomes the property of the insurers, who can dispose of it as scrap or for spare parts.

If the car is less than 12 months old, and the cost of repair is likely to exceed 50 or 60 per cent of its list price when new, the insurers normally agree to replace it with a similar make and model.

You do not have to accept a replacement. If you do not wish to do so, or if the appropriate car is not available, the claim will be dealt with on a normal repair basis. They will pay the full repair costs even if they exceed 60 per cent of the list price.

Claims for broken windscreen or windows, without loss of no-claim discount, may be limited by the insurers to, say, £75 or £50 per claim.

• *Damage excess* When cover for damage to your vehicle is restricted under the policy, with the insurers expecting you to pay the first part of any repair costs, that payment is known as damage excess.

Compulsory damage excess of £50 or more is normally required if the insured driver is under 25, or has not held a full United Kingdom driving licence for 12 months.

If the driver has a bad record of accidents or motoring convictions, or his car has proved to be a high insurance risk, he too may be required to pay a damage excess of as much as £150 – or perhaps more.

The excess may be required on more than one ground – for example, if the driver is under 25 and his car is considered a high risk. In that case, the two excess figures may be added together.

Even if no excess is required by the insurers, you can volunteer, when taking out the insurance, to pay part of any damage repair costs. A voluntary excess arrangement reduces your premium but one imposed at the company's insistence does not.

• *Personal accident benefits* Insurance companies offer many variations of personal injury cover in their comprehensive policies. Some policies restrict injury cover to the policyholder only. Most, however, cover the policyholder and spouse.

Some policies give cover to anyone who is injured while in the vehicle, provided that the driver is someone allowed to drive under the policy. Cover may not always be restricted to people travelling in the insured vehicle: it may apply to any private car in which the insured persons are travelling. Some insurers will not, however, offer personal accident benefit if the policyholder is under 21 or the car is a high-powered type.

Under any personal accident policy, the injury must arise directly from normal use of the car. The cover would not, for example, apply to a child who was accidentally injured by another child while they were playing with something sharp inside the car.

If the policyholder dies because of an accident, anyone else insured under his personal accident policy can still claim on it.

Sums insured can vary from £1,000 to £6,000 for death, total blindness or permanent disablement, with lesser amounts to compensate for specified injuries such as the loss of a limb or the sight of one eye.

If someone is temporarily disabled – confined to bed or a wheelchair – by an injury, the company may pay a lump sum to provide benefit for a limited period. A typical cover provides £20 a week for up to 26 weeks.

Some companies offer to double the rates of death or injury compensation if an accident victim is wearing an approved seat belt at the time.

An age limit of 70 or 75 is usually set on personal accident benefits.

• *Medical expenses* Cover for the medical expenses of anyone injured in an accident involving the insured car usually provides a lump-sum payment of up to £100 for each injured person. The cover includes dental fees.

Insurers may choose not to offer medical expenses cover for a high-powered car.

• *Personal possessions* Clothing and personal property carried by anyone in the insured car are covered against any loss or damage arising from normal use of the vehicle. The cover is usually limited to £100 and does not include cash or trade goods.

SPECIAL COVER FOR AN ALMOST-NEW CAR

Special insurance – called extended warranty or car component insurance – can be taken out to cover the cost of repairs when the manufacturer's normal warranty on a new car expires.

Second-hand cars can also be covered by extended warranty insurance, though not if the car is over a certain age or has done a high mileage – 4 years or 40,000 miles are typical limits.

Most extended warranty policies are arranged by the car dealer when the vehicle is bought. The policy normally covers major components such as engine, gearbox, transmission, steering, brakes and electrical equipment up to a specified limit, which decreases as the car gets older.

A typical extended warranty policy would cover a used 1600cc car, with a mileage of 30,000, up to £500 per claim, reducing to £250 after a mileage of 70,000, with a maximum policy payment of £1,400. The premium would be £97, and the policyholder would have to pay the first £15 of each claim.

An extended warranty policy usually stipulates regular servicing according to the manufacturer's requirements. If do-it-yourself servicing is allowed, invoices for materials must be produced when you claim against your policy.

Some extended warranty policies include part of the cost of hiring a car while the repair is being carried out.

If you intend to carry a large quantity of property in your car – for example, when going on holiday - arrange separate cover for it. Remember to lock your car whenever you leave it. Payment of theft claims may depend on the circumstances.

Personal effects cover may not be offered for an open sports car, but it is normally given for a vehicle with a movable sunshine roof.

● *Additional cover* Some insurers provide additional benefits, for no extra premium:

1. Fire damage to a garage, up to a specified amount – say, £500.

2. Loss of any part of the vehicle licence fee that cannot otherwise be recovered, if the vehicle is lost or totally destroyed.

3. Additional travel or overnight accommodation costs arising from an accident. The benefit is payable for all those who were in the car.

4. Part of the cost of hiring a car if your own is stolen or is immobilised after an accident. The cover is for a limited period – usually 14 or 28 days – and may exclude the first three days after the theft or accident.

Some companies may be willing to provide wider cover for car-hire costs, but require an extra premium payment or even a separate policy.

WHAT TO LOOK FOR IN MOTOR INSURANCE

How the cover offered by a 'comprehensive' policy can vary

Any comprehensive car insurance policy covers you for third-party risk, and the loss of your car or damage to it through accident, fire or theft.

Other protection and particular combinations of benefits vary according to the company and how much you are prepared to pay in premiums.

Type of cover	Often available	Sometimes available
Medical expenses – each person	£100	£150
Personal accident benefit	Whole family	Any passenger
Double benefit if seat belt worn	No	Yes
Right to buy a new car	In first 12 months if over 50% damage	In first 15 months
No-claim discount on premium	Up to 60%	Up to 65%
Discount 'step back' after a claim	3 years	Only 2 years
Windscreen or window replacement without affecting discount	First claim	Every claim
Fire damage to garage		£500
Personal property in car	£100	£125
Driving other vehicles	Private cars	Any car or motor cycle
Loss or damage abroad	Normal UK cover	Free bail bond, plus cover for risk of forfeiture
Loss or damage in transit abroad	Sea only	Sea and air
Legal expenses to defend charge of culpable homicide or causing death by reckless driving	£1,000	Unlimited
Car hire after theft	£50	£60
Hotel or fares after accident	£5 each	£10 each
Suspension rebate – when car is off road	25%	50%
Automatic insurance cover if you change cars		14 days
Right of appeal in dispute over claims	Amount of payment	Any dispute

No car policy offers all of these benefits. An owner has to decide which is best suited to his needs and his budget. In doing so, he also has to take into account that insurance companies impose varying 'excess' figures – the amount an owner might have to pay himself before a claim is met. That applies particularly to young drivers, those with a poor driving record or inexperienced drivers of any age.

Completing the proposal form

Legally, an insurance company does not offer to sell you a policy. You offer to buy one, and your offer is called a proposal.

A proposal does not bind either side to a contract unless it is accepted and you accept the premium charge, but the proposal form is still the most important document in an insurance transaction.

On it you agree to comply with the conditions of a policy from the time your insurance cover starts – although it may be up to 60 days before you receive the policy document.

In completing the proposal form you must also tell the company all that it needs to know in order to decide whether to insure you and, if so, what premium to charge.

The company may ask for more information after receiving your proposal and before reaching its decision. Until then you are likely to be protected by the temporary insurance described in a cover note, but if you are in any doubt, check with the broker or company before you take your car on the road.

Disclosure of facts The proposal form includes a declaration that to the best of your knowledge you have answered all questions truthfully and have not withheld any material fact – that is one which might influence the company's decision, such as an earlier driving disqualification.

If a motorist later makes an insurance claim, or a claim is made against him, and the company discovers that he misstated or withheld a material fact in his proposal, it may be entitled to refuse payment.

What you will be asked

When you complete your proposal form you must give all essential details about yourself, the vehicle and anyone else who is expected to drive it.

Yourself Give your full name, address, age and occupation. If you have a secondary job, you must mention it – even if you are not specifically asked to do so.

Your vehicle You will be asked for precise details of the vehicle being insured – including your arrangements for garaging the car. You may be asked to estimate the yearly mileage that the vehicle will travel.

Other drivers You may wish your policy to be restricted to covering one or two other people. If so, you need give only their personal details, including driving records.

If, however, your policy is to cover any driver who takes the vehicle on the road with your permission, the matter becomes more complicated – and the premium could be higher.

You should name any person who, to your knowledge, is likely to drive the vehicle. That normally includes any member of your immediate family who holds a driving licence and lives with you.

There is no need to name a representative of the motor trade – such as a garage employee taking your car on a test run. But note that your cover does not extend to others, such as car-park attendants, unless you have explicitly given permission.

If a family member is likely to become a qualified driver during the first policy period, normally 12 months, you should include details now.

It is not necessary, however, to mention a relative or friend who might possibly, on an odd occasion, drive your vehicle.

You must always tell the insurance broker or company in advance if a driver not previously named is to use the vehicle regularly. But if only a single journey is involved, and you know the driver to be mature and experienced, with no record of accidents or convictions, there is normally no need to inform the company.

If you know that a proposed driver has a poor driving record – or if you are in doubt – you should not allow him to drive your vehicle. An 'any driver' policy covers only any driver who, if you disclosed all that you knew about him, would have been covered by your insurers for no extra cost when you took out the policy.

TELLING ABOUT YOUR DRIVING RECORD

The insurance proposal form asks you for details of any accident or other loss connected with the use of any vehicle in which you have been involved in the previous 3 to 5 years, and any motoring conviction. The same questions apply to any other driver or potential driver whom you name on the form.

Even if an accident or loss was not the subject of an insurance claim – by you or anyone else – mention it on the form.

If you have been involved in an accident within the time stated on the form, you must mention it, whether or not you consider you were to blame. Even if you cannot remember precise details of an accident or other loss, be as accurate as possible.

Apart from accidents and other losses, you must also disclose:

- Any physical disability or illness that is likely to affect the driving ability of anyone named on the proposal form.
- The name of any insurer who has refused insurance, cancelled a policy or required special terms or premiums.
- Whether the car is to be used for business as well as private purposes – and the nature of that business.

If you have previously been insured as a motorist and are entitled to a no-claim discount, mention the fact on the proposal form *See:* MOTOR INSURANCE PREMIUM

Getting a quotation

As soon as you have completed the proposal form – and sometimes before – the insurance company, broker or agent normally gives you a written quotation of the premium that you will be expected to pay. *See:* MOTOR INSURANCE PREMIUM

That quotation does not bind you or the insurer. Once the insurer has considered the information supplied on the proposal form, he may decide that the premium should be higher. If he does so, you are entitled to reject the quotation and try a different insurer.

Normally, if you wish to have temporary cover while your application is being considered you must pay at least part of the suggested premium. If you do not you are unlikely to be given a MOTOR INSURANCE COVER NOTE, which you legally must have before you take the car on the road.

If you or the insurer subsequently withdraw from the contract, you cannot insist on having all your money returned: the insurer will charge you for the time during which you have used the temporary cover and so have been a risk to him. That charge – known as a 'time on risk' payment – is usually a percentage of the premium originally quoted. It costs very much more proportionately than a full year's cover.

Time on risk continues until the insurer, agent or broker receives the cover note back from you.

MOTOR INSURANCE CLAIM

When you have to report damage or injury

As soon as you know you have a reason to make a claim against your MOTOR INSURANCE policy, inform your insurer, broker or agent.

If you deal with a broker or agent you will be given an accident report and claim form. If you deal direct with the company, a form will be sent to you.

You must give full details of the incident, including, if possible, names and addresses of witnesses, victims and anyone else involved; say how the accident happened; give estimates of speed and weather conditions; state whether the police were called and if prosecutions are pending; and add full descriptions of any damage and/or injuries.

It is a condition of all insurance policies that every incident that could give rise to a claim either by or against the policyholder must be reported.

Some accidents that appear trivial at the time can result in sizeable claims – for example, over an injury that does not show up until some time later.

Insurers are reluctant to take over from policyholders who try to handle matters themselves and then find them too complicated.

A company can refuse to negotiate or settle a claim at all if the accident report form was not completed at the right time. Someone who drives a car that is owned and insured by his employer must of course report an accident to the employer.

Most policies make clear that a claim will be rejected if the policyholder admits liability to other people involved in an accident, but the way in which the rule is implemented may depend on the circumstances of the admission.

Completing the form does not automatically mean that you are making a claim, and so risking the loss of your no-claim discount. You can, if you wish, mark the form 'For Information Only', and make it quite clear in a covering letter that you do not wish the insurance company to take any action.

What to do after a motor accident

If you are claiming against your insurance after an accident:

- Contact your insurer or broker as soon as possible after the accident and give brief details of: the location, date and time of the accident; the vehicles involved and the names of the other drivers and, if possible, their insurance companies; whether anyone was injured and, if so, brief details of their names and the extent of their injuries; a description of the extent of the damage to vehicles or property; whether the police attended the accident; details of any witnesses and the present location of your vehicle.

Report the accident to the police within 24 hours, if there was damage to someone else's property or someone was injured and the police did not attend. Reporting to the police, however, is not necessary if you give your name and address, those of the owner of the vehicle and its registration mark to anyone who at the time of the accident has reason to ask for them.

- Obtain an estimate from a garage for repairs to your vehicle.
- Complete the accident form that your insurers will send to you as soon as you have notified them of the accident. The form includes a request for a sketch map of the accident area, and you may have to re-visit the area to provide details.
- Send any correspondence that you receive from any other parties involved to your insurers. Do not acknowledge such letters, but if you disagree with anything that has been said in the letters, tell your insurers.
- Advise your insurers immediately if you receive any notice of intended prosecution.
- If you claim for any personal effects that were damaged, or for medical expenses, provide evidence of the value of the effects or the amount of the expenses when you claim.
- Once your insurers have authorised the repairs to be made to your vehicle, the garage may start work on the vehicle. The bill is sent to your insurers, but you will have to pay any excess due under your policy. The garage asks you to sign a 'satisfaction note' stating that the repairs have been completed satisfactorily. If you then find the repairs are not satisfactory, get in touch with your insurers who will contact the garage.

Claiming against someone else

If you are claiming from another party after an accident:

- Inform your own insurers as soon as possible and give brief details of what took place.
- Write to the other party involved as soon as possible. Send your letter by recorded delivery and state that you hold him responsible for the accident. Tell him that you will submit your claim in due course. Always mark your correspondence 'without prejudice', and keep a copy.
- If the other party does not respond, send a second letter by recorded delivery reiterating your claim, and suggest that failing to respond could lead to legal action being taken on your part.

Usually, the other party or his insurers will reply. When you receive a reply, send the other party details of your claim and copies of any supporting documents – for example, an estimate for repairs to your vehicle from a garage. In certain cases, his insurers will want to inspect your vehicle before it is repaired.

- Once his insurers have inspected the vehicle, or agreed to the estimate, in-

HOW ANOTHER DRIVER'S MISTAKE CAN COST YOU MONEY

If your motor insurance company has to pay out on your policy, it will affect your no-claim discount when you renew your insurance – even if the payment is for damage that was not your fault.

To reduce the time and expense it takes to settle claims if the blame has to be apportioned between two drivers in a collision, insurance companies have agreements with each other to accept liability on what they call a 'knock for knock' basis.

That means that each company pays for repairs to its own policyholder's vehicle provided they have both issued comprehensive policies. They will then decide whether or not their own client was entirely blameless and adjust his no-claim discount accordingly.

If the same company insures both drivers, and one is clearly to blame for the accident, the other driver can expect the claim not to be recorded against him.

But if two companies are involved, the innocent driver can best save his no-claim discount by producing absolute proof that he did not contribute to the accident.

An insurance company should accept:

- The evidence of independent witnesses to the collision and to what happened before it. Such witnesses must be prepared to be interviewed by an insurance inspector and if necessary to be cross-examined in a court.

Passengers in the motorist's car are not regarded as independent witnesses.

- Unchallenged evidence given in a court prosecution of the other driver. His conviction for a driving offence is not enough in itself: the other driver's failure to take precautions against his bad driving might have contributed to the collision.

The unchallenged evidence must make clear that the innocent driver was entirely blameless.

- Proof that the other driver admits liability. An oral apology at the scene of the accident is not enough, even if witnesses heard it, because it does not prove that the allegedly innocent driver was not at least partly to blame.

A written apology entirely excusing the innocent driver is needed.

The innocent driver is, however, unlikely to get a satisfactory admission of liability until his no-claim discount is already threatened. The other driver is likely to be aware that his own policy conditions include a provision that he must not admit liability to another party.

Suing the other driver

If you lose your no-claim bonus as a result of the accident you may be able to recover this item of loss in a successful claim against the other motorist for NEGLIGENCE.

struct your garage to go ahead with the repairs. You must pay the bill for repairs in full and seek reimbursement from his insurers. You are not entitled by law to claim a reimbursement of an expense until it has been incurred.

• The other party's insurers will either agree to reimburse you or they may hold you partially or totally to blame for the accident and refuse to pay all of the bill. In that case, it is up to you to continue negotiating with them until you reach what you feel is a fair settlement. Any statement from an independent witness to the accident will help your claim.

If you are unable to reach a settlement, seek advice on how to pursue your claim from a solicitor, an insurance broker or a motoring organisation.

• If your claim involves damages for any personal injury involved, seek advice as soon as possible from a solicitor or motoring organisation on how to claim.

Getting the car repaired

Usually a motorist with comprehensive insurance can ask any garage to carry out repairs, but the insurers may prefer the work to be done by a garage they have approved.

If the damage is substantial, the insurers appoint an engineer to inspect the car, agree the repair costs and authorise the work to begin. For smaller amounts, the motorist can tell the garage to start the work as soon as he has sent an estimate to the insurers and it has been approved.

If the motorist tells the garage to go ahead, he is responsible for paying the bill himself and has to recover the money from his insurers.

On the other hand, when the repairs are authorised directly by the insurance company, the bill will be sent to it by the garage and the motorist can normally collect his car without any payment other than any excess due under his policy.

Betterment payments In some cases the motorist may have to make an extra payment after his car has been repaired if the work done has made the vehicle markedly better than it was before the accident. For example, if it is impossible to match the paint on a damaged area without respraying the whole car the insurers may ask the motorist to pay for part of the cost. In such cases the insurance company still pays the full garage bill and then claims a share from the motorist.

WHO PAYS IF THERE IS NO INSURANCE

All motor-insurance companies are members of the Motor Insurers Bureau, whose chief function is to provide an insurance 'safety net' for road victims. Its address is Aldermary House, 10–15 Queen Street, London, E.C.4.

The bureau pays damages for third party personal injuries caused by a motorist who is either not insured adequately or who cannot be traced. It does not pay for damage to vehicles or other property.

The bureau can refuse to pay out until the motorist has been sued and damages fixed by a court. If the motorist cannot be traced the bureau will consider paying damages if it decides he could have been successfully sued.

The bureau itself can be sued if its decision or award in such cases seems unsatisfactory.

If the car is a write-off

If the insurance company's engineer decides that the car cannot be economically repaired it is 'written off' as a total loss. If the policy includes provision of a replacement car of similar make and value, the insurance company can choose between buying the motorist a car, or having the original car repaired. If the damaged car was less than 12 months old, however, the insured driver can choose.

Most insurers limit the amount to the car's estimated sale value as stated by the motorist when he took out the policy. In times of inflation the estimated value may be considerably below the current market value, but the insurers are within their rights to insist on the lower figure.

Vintage or other very unusual cars may be valued according to a figure agreed between the owner and the insurance company when the policy is taken out and in subsequent years, and this is the amount paid in the event of a total loss.

If the car is being bought on hire purchase, the hire-purchase company has first right to any total-loss payment and the motorist gets only the balance.

A few policies give the insurance company the right to cancel the policy immediately after a total-loss payment, so that it can negotiate new terms with a higher premium. That loss of premium is a recoverable item of damage if you are claiming against the other motorist for NEGLIGENCE.

If the car is stolen

Most stolen cars are recovered within a few days, so a motorist who is a victim of a car theft cannot expect an immediate total-loss payment under a comprehensive insurance policy. Many insurers are prepared to pay up if the car is not found within 28 days.

A car theft must be reported to the police to substantiate the claim, as well as to the insurance company. If the car is found after payment has been made it becomes the property of the company.

Damaged cars A stolen car which is found to be damaged after it is recovered can be repaired under both a comprehensive or a third party fire and theft policy – just as if it had been damaged in a collision. The only difference is that the owner does not generally have to pay any accidental damage excess following a theft.

If a comprehensive policy includes an extra benefit allowing a motorist to hire a car when his own is unavailable because of damage, he can claim for hire of the car if he was to blame for the damage.

There are no general rules for such cover, but the motorist is usually entitled to make arrangements immediately, pay the bill later and pass it to the insurance company for reimbursement. It may be up to the motorist to prove that the costs incurred were reasonable and necessary. *See:* INSURANCE CLAIM

MOTOR INSURANCE COVER NOTE

Obtaining temporary cover

An insurance cover note is a temporary certificate of motor insurance. It is issued by the insurance company or agent, usually for 30 days (sometimes for as long as 60 days), to cover the period between agreeing to insure a

WHEN A COVER NOTE TAKES EFFECT

Once your motor insurance cover note has been put in the post to you, it is legally in your possession, and you are protected by it.

driver and sending him the policy and the permanent certificate. If the note is issued by an insurance company, they may send it to the broker to be passed to you.

The note sets out the essential points of the insurance cover, such as whether it is comprehensive or third-party, who may drive the vehicle and what it may be used for.

Your insurance technically comes into force only if the cover note is either in your possession or has been put in the post to you. The post office is legally your agent, and once the note is put in a post box, it is considered to have been delivered to you.

It is a criminal offence to use an uninsured vehicle. Never take a vehicle on the road unless you know, with absolute certainty, that you are covered by insurance. Even if the broker tells you that he is putting a cover note in the post, it is not safe to drive until you are sure that he has done so. He is acting as the insurance company's agent, not yours, and while the cover note is in his possession it is not regarded as having been delivered to you.

MOTOR INSURANCE POLICY

The document that explains what cover you have

Your insurance policy sets out the details of your cover in formal terms. Although you may not receive the policy for some time after the cover started, you are bound by its terms and condi-

TEMPORARY INSURANCE COVER FOR YOUR CAR

The document that shows you are properly insured

POLICY NUMBER MVK 1234567/09/10.

DATE OF ISSUE 1st SEPTEMBER '82.

MOTOR DEPARTMENT COVER NOTE No. X 0953096

General Accident GENERAL ACCIDENT FIRE AND LIFE ASSURANCE CORPORATION LIMITED

PROPOSER'S NAME AND ADDRESS MUST BE KEPT WITHIN THIS BOX

A B SMITH
5 St JOHN'S PLACE,
PERTH.

COVER NOTE

Having proposed for the insurance of the motor vehicle in accordance with the details described in the Schedule and having paid the amount stated below the risk is hereby covered in terms of the Insurer's usual form of policy applicable thereto and to the Special Conditions or Restrictions (if any) indicated below for the period and time stated unless the cover be terminated by written notice to the Proposer at the above address in which case the insurance shall thereupon cease and a proportionate part of the annual premium will be charged for the time this insurance has been in force.

PERIOD OF COVER: 60DAYS from 10.0 a.m. on 1st SEPTEMBER, 1982 AMOUNT PAID £ 50.
until the same time on the sixtieth day thereafter.

SCHEDULE

MAKE, MODEL AND TYPE OF BODY	Year of Manufacture	Cubic Capacity	Plated Weight	Carrying Capacity (if not plated)	No. of Seats	ESTIMATED VALUE VEHICLE	ESTIMATED VALUE TRAILER	Registration Mark or Engine or Body Number
FORD FIESTA L	1982	957	–	–	4	£ 4011	£ –	ABC.123X

COVER Please insert figure 1, 2 or 3 in box
1 Comprehensive
2 Third Party Fire/Theft
3 Third Party Only
[1.]

USE Please insert figure(s) 1, 2 or 3 in box
1 Social Domestic and Pleasure
2 Business by Policyholder in person
3 Business of Policyholder
[1]

REASON Please insert figure 1, 2 or 3 in box
1 New Business
2 Substitution (see below)
3 Addition
[2]
If 2 insert Registration Mark of vehicle replaced DEF 456.T.

SPECIAL CONDITIONS OR RESTRICTIONS AS PER POLICY

AGENT
For and on behalf of the General Accident Fire and Life Assurance Corporation Limited

CERTIFICATE OF MOTOR INSURANCE

I hereby certify that this cover note satisfies the requirements of the relevant Law applicable in Great Britain, Northern Ireland, the Isle of Man, the Island of Guernsey, the Island of Jersey and the Island of Alderney.

MV 45

GENERAL ACCIDENT FIRE AND LIFE ASSURANCE CORPORATION LIMITED
Head Office: General Buildings, Perth, Scotland PH1 5TP
AUTHORISED INSURERS

Chief General Manager

The hour can be as vital as the date if the driver is stopped by the police and asked to produce evidence of insurance

This tells you the type of cover which is being provided. Comprehensive insurance covers possible loss to yourself, as well as to third parties

A policy for social, domestic and pleasure use of the car can be held to be invalid if the driver uses the car for business

The purpose of an insurance cover note is to provide the driver with insurance while the policy is being prepared by the insurance company. A driver may be taking a considerable risk if he takes someone's word that a note has been posted to him and drives his car on the road before he has received the note and checked the period for which it is valid.

tions from the beginning – unless you can show that it is not what you were led to expect.

The policy may appear difficult to understand, but try nevertheless to read it carefully, to ensure that you have the cover you asked for. If you think the document is incorrect, or if you cannot fully understand it, consult the company, or the broker or agent who arranged the insurance.

If there is an error in the policy, the insurer must put it right, no matter how much time passes before you discover it. If anything in the policy is capable of more than one meaning, a court would tend to interpret it in your favour.

The policy document, usually a booklet, sets out full details of your cover and any conditions or restrictions.

The restrictions

The details include a list of certain general restrictions on your cover:

- *Who can drive* If your cover is restricted to use of the vehicle by certain drivers, they are usually referred to as 'those named in the certificate of insurance'. Despite any such restriction, however, a comprehensively insured vehicle is normally covered against damage while it is in the hands of a motor tradesman for maintenance or repair. A car park attendant would not normally be covered.
- *Limit on use* Your policy may state that the cover is limited to social, domestic or pleasure use of the car. In that case it cannot be used in the course of work or business – but simply driving to or from work is normally considered as a domestic use. Most policies exclude use of the car for racing or rallying.
- *Outside liabilities* The policy excludes any risk that has not been agreed in advance by the insurer. For example, if you have an accident under a comprehensive policy, you are covered for injury and vehicle damage. But if the accident prevents you from delivering business goods, and you lose money, you cannot claim on your policy for that loss unless such a claim is specifically provided for. That would usually require a separate policy.
- *Nuclear risk* The policy will exclude all losses arising from any atomic source, such as a nuclear power station. That is because such losses, by law, are the responsibility of the user of atomic material.
- *War risk* A loss arising from war between nations is not normally covered.
- *Losses abroad* Losses arising from riot, civil commotion or earthquake are normally excluded, except for third party liability.

If you expect to take your vehicle to an area where such risks might arise, you can try to arrange additional insurance to cover personal injury or damage to your own vehicle and other property. In any case, you are likely to need special insurance to meet the requirements of a foreign country.

The conditions

The following are the conditions normally set out in the policy document:

- *Making a claim* You must notify the insurer of any possible claim by or against you as quickly as possible. You must also, when necessary, co-operate fully with your insurer in reaching a settlement of any dispute with a third party.
- *Cancelling a policy* The company sets out the terms on which, if it chooses, it can cancel your policy before it expires.

That is likely to happen only if the company finds that it has taken an unexpected risk, or suspects that it has been defrauded but cannot prove it.

The cancellation clause sets out how the policy may be cancelled, and what proportion of your year's premium would be returned. It usually includes your right to cancel the arrangement – for example, if you decide to sell your car and as a result no longer need insurance.

Rules may vary according to whether it is the insurer or you cancelling. If the insurer cancels, he will repay an amount in proportion to the unexpired period of the policy. For example, if your year's policy has run 5 months, you may be repaid 7/12ths of the year's premium.

But if you cancel the insurance, you are likely to be charged the 'short period' rate, which is high. The insurer may repay only 40 per cent of a year's premium even though the policy has been in force for only 5 months.

If it has been in force for, say, 6 months, the repayment may drop to 30 per cent of the year's premium.

If your policy has been in force for more than a year before you cancel, your insurer may be prepared to make a pro rata repayment of premium. He is not, however, obliged to do so.

If any claim has been met on the policy – to you or to someone else – the insurer will not repay any of the premium.

- *Dual insurance* A loss connected with your car may sometimes be covered by more than one insurance policy. For example, if something is stolen from the vehicle, the theft may be covered by both your motor insurance and a household policy.

If that happens, you may be entitled to claim on both policies, but remember that a 'motor' claim will affect your no-claim discount. Whichever insurer deals with the claim, they will not ask the other insurer to contribute.

- *Care of the vehicle* You are required to maintain your car in an efficient and roadworthy condition. A motorist who blatantly fails to repair a defect, and who is then involved in an accident caused by the defect, could find that his insurer rejects any claim.

For example, if after the accident the insurer's inspecting engineer finds that the insured vehicle has one tyre in a condition that does not comply with the law, the fact may be overlooked. But if 3 or 4 tyres are in an illegal condition, the insurer could well reject liability. *See also:* MOTOR VEHICLE

You must also take reasonable steps to protect yourself from loss by theft. For example, if you leave your ignition key in an unlocked car, and the vehicle or its contents are then stolen, you may be considered not to have taken reasonable steps and may find that your insurer refuses to pay compensation.

- *Policy endorsements* The standard wording of a policy can be changed by the insurer adding a clause, known as an endorsement. That can be done either when the policy is first issued, or at any time afterwards, if you agree.

An endorsement may restrict your cover or may increase it – for example, it may provide additional insurance covering personal effects for a small extra premium.

Some policies are issued with a full list of possible endorsements and a key to show which, if any, apply to your particular insurance. Other policies have endorsements stuck inside the

PROOF THAT YOU ARE MEETING THE ROAD TRAFFIC ACT REQUIREMENTS

Once your insurance contract is completed, you are sent your policy and a certificate of insurance which shows that you are complying with the minimum requirements of the Road Traffic Act.

The certificate is a vital document: you must always produce it at the request of the police – for example, if you are involved in an accident in which someone is injured. It must also be produced to the vehicle licensing authority when you renew your vehicle licence.

The certificate mentions your name, your insurance policy number, the period for which you are insured, who may drive on your insurance and whether you can drive other vehicles on the same insurance.

It also says for what specific purposes the vehicle can be used under the insurance – for example, for domestic and pleasure purposes but not for business use.

Some certificates give the registration number of the vehicle. Most, however, do not specify the vehicle insured, but use some 'blanket' form of wording such as: 'Any motor car owned by the policyholder or hired to him under a hire purchase agreement.'

If a particular vehicle is specified on the certificate, you will need a new certificate each time you change your car. If the 'blanket' wording is used, you do not need a new certificate – but you must give the insurer full details of any new vehicle as soon as you buy it.

The certificate may not give all the details of your cover or its limitations. For example, your policy may exclude anyone under 25 from driving your car, but there is no provision for any such restriction to appear on a certificate of insurance.

It is your policy, not your certificate, that spells out your insurance rights.

main document. You should make sure that you know which endorsements affect your cover.

When there is a dispute

If a motorist is not happy with a decision by his insurance company – for instance over the amount they are prepared to pay on a claim – the policy document may provide for ARBITRATION. But only the policyholder has this means of settlement, not a third party who may have a claim against the policyholder. *See:* INSURANCE CLAIM

MOTOR INSURANCE PREMIUM

How the insurer decides how much you should pay

The way in which insurance premiums are decided by insurance companies can vary greatly from one company to another.

Specially low premiums may be charged for a particular class of car, or for a driver in a particular occupation, or for the employees of a particular company – even on their private cars.

Specially high premiums are charged for certain types of car or driver, and for anything else that the insurer considers an extra accident risk.

If your premium is subject to an extra charge – known as a 'loading' – you are entitled to know, at the quotation or renewal stage, how much extra you are being asked to pay over and above the basic premium, and why.

If you agree to pay a higher premium, you are entitled later to ask the insurer to reconsider – either when the policy is due to be renewed, or if there is a change in the circumstances that led him to impose the extra charge.

The following are the main factors that an insurer takes into account when working out your premium:

- *The vehicle* All modern cars are given an insurance group rating, usually recommended by either the Motor Conference (for insurance companies) or the Lloyd's Motor Underwriters' Association (for Lloyd's underwriters).

There can be variations between the two sets of ratings, but they are largely similar.

The most important factors that contribute to a rating are the power of the car and the potential cost of repairs. Other considerations include an assessment of the type of driver that a particular kind of car may attract.

- *Where the car is kept* The cost of your insurance also depends partly on where your car is based. Insurers divide the country into areas and grade them according to the local traffic density, accident and theft rates.

A mainly rural area such as Caithness or Argyll has a low rating. Central Glasgow, on the other hand, will have one of the highest rates in Scotland.

Some companies charge extra to insure a car kept in a major city if it is not kept in a garage.

- *How much you drive* From the use to which you say that the vehicle will be put, your insurer will estimate whether you are likely to have a high or low yearly mileage. It is assumed that the higher the mileage, the greater the exposure to risk of accidents.

Someone who uses his own car for business and travels extensively may not be able to obtain the normal 'private and business use' cover without paying much more.

On the other hand, if you volunteer to be restricted to social, domestic and pleasure use only, some insurers charge a reduced premium.

- *Value of the vehicle* If you are insuring your car comprehensively, the insurer is unlikely to be much influenced by the value of the vehicle unless it is one of the more expensive models – costing, say, more than £10,000.

Repair costs for lower valued cars vary little, so premiums are similar. Specialist and high-value cars are charged extra.

For a third party, fire and theft policy, however, the value of the vehicle is taken more into account because it represents a greater proportion of the total risk.

- *Your job* A motorist's occupation, or the occupation of a named 'other driver', may also mean a higher premium because the company considers that certain occupational classes carry a higher than normal risk of accident. That may be because they have unusually active social lives, or because they frequently have to drive quickly in unfamiliar places. Professional sportsmen and entertainers are typical high-risk categories.

However, insurers have widely varying attitudes to such professions, and if you are in such a job, seek professional advice from a broker when arranging your insurance.

- *Age and experience* If a driver is under the age of 25, he is likely to be charged a higher premium than someone in the older, experienced group.

There are many variations in the treatment of drivers according to age and experience. Some insurers continue charging a higher premium until the driver is 34.

At the other end of the scale, premiums may be reduced for an experienced driver at the age of, say, 51. The more usual qualifying age, however, is 60 or 65.

'Experience', to an insurer, is a combination of age and the length of time a driver has held a full United Kingdom licence. Provided that you are over 25 and have held such a licence for 12 consecutive months, you will not normally be charged an extra premium on the ground of inexperience.

If, however, you cannot meet those requirements, you will probably be charged a higher premium. If you take out comprehensive cover, you may also have to accept a damage excess.

Some insurers do not impose the excess on a driver who has held a foreign licence for more than 2 years.

When considering a foreign driver's application for insurance, an insurer takes into account three factors: whether he has a sufficient grasp of the English language, whether he is familiar with British traffic conditions – including the need to drive on the left – and how much driving he has done outside Britain.

There is no formal English language test, either written or oral, so the insurer, broker or agent must assess the applicant's grasp of the language as best he can – by, for example, the way in which the proposal form is completed.

A foreign driver who has been permanently living and driving in Britain for 3 years or more should normally have no difficulty in obtaining insurance without special restrictions.

● *Accidents and convictions* In most instances, insurers will ignore a single accident that is disclosed on a proposal form – whether or not the driver seeking insurance was to blame. But a driver with a record of two or more accidents may be asked to pay a higher premium.

Many insurers are more interested in the circumstances of an accident than in the cost of the resulting damage or injury.

A driver who, for example, makes a slight misjudgment of speed or distance, and has a crash that results in expensive damage to two vehicles, will not normally be penalised as heavily by his next insurer as will someone who causes an accident by reckless or drunken driving but who is lucky enough to cause relatively slight damage.

Most motoring convictions are considered seriously by insurers. Although minor offences, such as illegal parking or an isolated speeding conviction, are not likely to affect your insurance, a motorist who has more serious convictions – for example, a conviction for reckless driving – is likely to be charged a higher premium.

Someone who has a record of both accidents and convictions will almost certainly have to pay more for his insurance, and is also likely to be given only restricted cover.

Once a loading has been imposed for convictions or past accident claims, the insurer will not usually alter the terms for at least 2 years – and even then may not remove the loading altogether.

A loading imposed for a very serious driving offence, such as causing death by reckless driving, may not be removed

WHEN YOU QUALIFY FOR A NO-CLAIM DISCOUNT

A driver whose insurance is not claimed against for a whole year is entitled to a percentage reduction in his premium for the following year – although that individual reduction is likely to be outweighed by regular overall increases in motor insurance premiums.

The discount, generally known as 'no-claim bonus', depends on an absence of any claim on the policy whether by the insured driver or by someone else. It does not matter whether or not he was to blame for the incident that led to the claim. The discount increases in size over a series of claim-free years, to a maximum of 60 or 65 per cent.

If you change your insurer, you are entitled to take your discount with you. You are credited with the same number of claim-free years – but the discount rate is not necessarily the same.

In considering a change of insurance company, a motorist has to take into account the basic premium as well as the no-claim discount rate.

Example: Your company gives a 3rd-year discount of 40 per cent of your premium of £200. You pay £120. Another company offers a better discount – 50 per cent. But if your basic premium is going to be more than £240, you lose money by changing over.

Proving a no-claim record If you change your insurer, and wish to transfer your no-claim discount, you must produce proof of your no-claim record with the previous insurer.

You need to show the new insurer the renewal notice from the previous insurer – which indicates the amount of no-claim discount – or a letter from that insurer confirming that a discount has been allowed, and for how long.

Some insurers allow you a discount that you have earned while driving abroad. Other insurers may offer only a reduced discount for foreign driving, and some may not allow it at all.

Few insurers allow a motor-cyclist who has earned discount to transfer it to another type of vehicle, or allow a discount to a motorist whose accident-free record was achieved in cars he did not insure – for example, someone who drove his company's cars. However, a record of safe driving could be a bargaining point in negotiating the basic premium, if necessary.

Nor can the discount normally be transferred from one driver to another. No-claim discount is earned by a motorist rather than his vehicle, and someone else using the vehicle may not be as reliable as the original policyholder.

An exception is when one policy is issued to cover two or more cars, and the policyholder is the main user of only one of them.

If any other vehicle covered by the policy is mainly used by someone else – for example, the policyholder's son or daughter – and the insurers are aware of this, that person can usually take out his or her own insurance and benefit by the vehicle's no-claim record.

If a claim is still outstanding when the policy is due for renewal, the no-claim discount will be lost or reduced, though if the matter is subsequently settled without the insurance company having to make a payment the discount will be reinstated.

Some insurers allow the policyholder to repay a claim made in the previous year if it proves to be less than the no-claim discount that would otherwise be lost.

entirely for 5 years or more. Such a loading is normally decreased in yearly stages, starting after 2 years.

If a motorist filling in a claim form mentions a conviction that is covered by the REHABILITATION of Offenders Act, the insurer must disregard it.

- *Physical disability* A driver who has a physical disability, such as loss of an eye or limb, is not normally required to pay a higher premium because of that disability, unless it has happened so recently that he may not have had time to learn to cope with it.

If the disability is recent, a higher premium may be charged for 2 or 3 years, until the motorist has shown that he is still able to drive safely. However, a disability is generally more likely to result in a restriction on the insurance cover than an increase in premium.

For example, if the insured car has to be specially adapted to allow the disabled person to drive, his policy will almost certainly not allow him third party cover for driving other, non-adapted cars.

If a driver suffers a chronic illness, such as diabetes, heart disease or epilepsy, he is likely to have to pay a higher premium and to accept restrictions on his insurance cover. That is because it is usually uncertain when and where the illness may suddenly affect the motorist.

Paying by instalments

Many insurance companies and brokers allow premiums to be paid by instalments rather than in an annual lump sum, though there is a small surcharge. A typical charge is £4.50 extra for paying by five instalments. Paying by instalments does not usually affect the insurance, but if it does this fact must be mentioned in the policy. The most likely effect is a condition that a total loss claim is met only if the total premium is paid.

MOTOR VEHICLE

The driver's responsibility for the safety of his car

Anyone who drives or owns a vehicle has a legal duty to see that it is safe to be on the road.

The steering, brakes and lights must work efficiently, the tyres must have a proper tread and the windscreen wipers must work.

Anyone using, or allowing to be used, a car that fails to comply with all or any of the safety regulations commits an offence and can be fined a maximum of £1,000; and after endorsements totalling 12 points or more, he will be disqualified from driving. Only the most important items are dealt with here.

Steering It is an offence to drive a vehicle on the road with steering that is inefficient or not properly adjusted. Excessive play on the steering wheel is the most common fault.

A steering wheel that can be turned up to 30 degrees without moving the wheels is unsafe and can lead to prosecution. Of course, excessive play under 30 degrees may still be unsafe.

Tyres The grooves of a tread pattern must be at least 1 mm deep for at least three-quarters of the breadth of the tyre all the way around its circumference. That is the part of the tyre which normally touches the road. Tyres must be properly inflated.

Superficial cuts on the walls or on the shoulders of a tyre are not illegal, but a cut more than 25 mm deep is. Tyres are legally considered defective if the ply or cord is showing through the wall of the tyre or if there are bulges or lumps in it.

It is an offence to put one radial and one cross-ply tyre on the same axle.

Number plates Every vehicle must have number-plates, with the vehicle's registration number displayed, at the front and the rear. It is an offence to drive without them, or to drive when the plates are so covered by mud or dirt that they are impossible to read.

Front number-plates can be black on a white background, or white on black, but all rear number-plates must be black on a yellow background. They must be clearly visible from 75 ft in daylight. The rear number-plate must be illuminated at night and must be visible from 60 ft. The maximum penalty is a fine of £400.

Speedometer Most vehicles first registered since 1937 must be fitted with a working speedometer. The only exceptions are slow-moving vehicles, such as trucks, moving at less than 25 mph, motor-cycles of less than 100 cc, and invalid carriages.

It is an offence to drive a vehicle if the speedometer is not accurate within a margin of 10 per cent at speeds over 10 mph.

Mirrors Most cars built after 1978 must have at least two rear-view mirrors one of which must be on the offside exterior. On cars first used since April 1, 1969, internal rear view mirrors must have protective edges to prevent injury in an accident.

Goods vehicles and large passenger vehicles must be fitted with two mirrors so that both sides of the vehicle can be seen as well as the rear.

Windscreen wipers An automatic windscreen wiper must be fitted to every vehicle unless the driver can see clearly to the front without looking through the windscreen, either by opening it or looking over it. Washers that can clean the area swept by the wipers are compulsory.

Horn Only works trucks and pedestrian-controlled vehicles do not need to be fitted with a horn that can give an easily heard warning of approach.

Gongs, sirens, two-tone horns and bells are banned from all vehicles except police or fire service vehicles, ambulances and vehicles used by salvage corps.

All vehicles first used since August 1973 must have a horn that gives a uniform, continuous sound and it must not be strident.

A motorist must not sound a horn while his vehicle is stationary, except in traffic, and not at all between 11.30 p.m. and 7 a.m. in areas where there is a 30 mph speed limit.

Brakes Every driver must be sure that the brakes in his vehicle can stop the vehicle in a reasonable distance in the most adverse conditions. The hand brake and the brakes on each of the four wheels must all be effective.

The Highway Code says that the shortest stopping distance of the average family car, including thinking distance, on a dry road with good brakes is: 75 ft at 30 mph; 175 ft at 50 mph; 315 ft at 70 mph.

Lights a vehicle must have

A driver must be able to see a safe distance ahead at night and his car must be easily visible to others. To ensure this, the law requires that all vehicles carry white lights at the front (there is no provision in the Regulations for yellow headlamps) and red lights at the rear. New cars used after April 1, 1981, must have high-intensity rear foglamps.

The lights must be positioned to show the width of the vehicle and used in a way that does not dazzle or confuse others.

Lights and reflectors should be kept clean and must always be in good working order – you can be stopped and reported for breaking lighting regulations even during daytime.

When lights must be on The lights on a motor vehicle must be switched on during the hours of darkness – that is from half-an-hour after sunset to half-an-hour before sunrise. Outside built-up areas, where street lamps are more than 200 yds apart, full or dipped headlamps must be used, and it is an offence to drive only on sidelights. Full or dipped headlamps must also be used when visibility is poor, such as in fog, heavy sleet or rain, even if it is daytime.

When a motor vehicle is parked in a road the sidelights must be left on except when the vehicle is in a road with a speed limit of 30 mph or less, off a main bus route and in the light of a street lamp. Unlit vehicles must be parked:

- At least 15 yards away from a junction.
- Close and parallel to the kerb.
- Facing in the direction of the traffic flow.

Trailers and vehicles with projecting loads must not be left without lights on a road at night.

Front lights There must be two white lights on either side of the front of the vehicle. They must be at the same height from the ground and not more than 400 mm from the outermost side of the vehicle.

It is an offence to drive a car, night or day, with only one working white light at the front. Front lights must by law have a dipped beam and a main beam which can be switched on or off on both lamps simultaneously. Sidelights do not need to dip.

Rear lights Two matching red lights must be fitted to the rear of all motor vehicles. They must be the same height from the ground and not more than 400 mm from the outermost edge of the vehicle.

Rear lamps must be wired so that if one fails the other continues to operate.

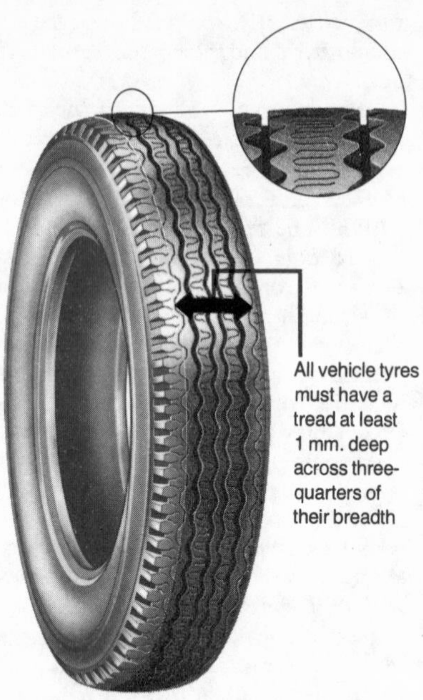

The grooves of the tread pattern on vehicle tyres must cover three-quarters of the breadth all round the circumference and must be at least 1 mm deep.

Two red reflectors must also be fitted, one each side of the vehicle. If an unlit rear lamp also acts as a reflector, then it will qualify within the law as a reflector, whether it is lit or unlit.

Illegal lights It is an offence for any car to show a red light to the front, or to show a white light to the rear – except while reversing.

Stop lamps Cars in use since 1971 must be fitted with two red stop lamps at the rear. These lights must be operated by applying the brakes, show a steady light and be wired so that one will stay alight if the other's bulb fails. Stop lamps must be at the same height on either side of the vehicle, at least 2 ft apart.

Direction indicators It is compulsory for all cars to have direction indicators, either one pair at each side, or one pair at the front and one pair at the rear, or one rear pair and one pair of shoulder indicators. They must show amber to both front and rear. Pre-1965 cars may still have arm indicators which can show white and red to front and rear and be fitted at a height of 17–90 in.

All indicators must work from the same switch and there must be a device inside the car to show when they are operating. If your vehicle has broken down on the road and is causing an obstruction, you may use the indicators as a hazard warning.

Non-obligatory lamps All obligatory lights must be fitted by manufacturers to strict regulations. Some non-obligatory lights can be fitted, but these, too, must meet strict requirements. You can fit reversing lamps and fog or spot lamps. Reversing lamps must not exceed 24 watts, show a white light to the rear and deflect downwards to minimise dazzle. Not more than two may be carried.

A single spot lamp may be used only in addition to a car's headlights when driving where there is no street lighting. It must be white or yellow and fixed 24–42 in from the ground.

Silencer An efficient silencer must be fitted to all cars and it must not be altered so that noise is increased. It is an offence to use a car that creates an excessive noise and the driver can be fined up to £1,000.

Smoke A car must not give off vapour, smoke or sparks which could cause damage to property or injury to a person. The maximum penalty is £1,000.

Selling a car

If you dispose (by sale or otherwise)

A PARKED CAR WITH FAULTY TYRES

It is an offence to have on the road a car with faulty tyres, even if it is not being driven.

In 1972, Mr Mitchell parked his car outside his home. The front and rear tyres on the near side were defective.

A policeman questioned Mr Mitchell who said that he knew the tyres were defective, but that he had been ill and had no intention to use the car. He was prosecuted, but the case was dismissed on the ground that Mr Mitchell did not intend to use the car. The prosecutor appealed.

VERDICT

The appeal court ruled that the car was capable of being used, and so an offence had been committed. They sent the case back to the lower court for conviction.

of a vehicle of which you are the registered keeper, you should, as seller, immediately complete the relevant part of the vehicle registration document and send it to the DVLC at Swansea. The address is on the form. You should give the rest of the registration document to the buyer, who must also complete the appropriate part of it and send it to the DVLC. If the buyer is a dealer, he has other obligations.

MOTORWAY DRIVING

The special rules that apply to motorways

Motorways are specially designed dual-carriageway roads for swift-moving traffic, and special regulations apply to them. Drivers can be fined and disqualified from driving for breaking these regulations.

People who are not allowed to use a motorway

It is an offence for pedestrians, learner drivers, cyclists or moped riders to use a motorway. Tractors, other agricultural vehicles and some invalid carriages are also banned.

It is an offence for a driver to pick up or to set down a passenger or hitch-hiker on any part of a motorway, including any slip roads to and from the motorway.

The verges, or hard shoulders, alongside a motorway can be used by drivers only in an emergency, such as breakdown, an accident or illness.

Any vehicle that has been driven on to a motorway verge must not stay there longer than necessary, whatever the emergency.

Special motorway signals

It is an offence to ignore flashing light signals which operate on motorways in dangerous or unusual conditions such as fog.

In normal conditions the signal panels are blank, but when there are dangerous conditions ahead, amber lights flash and the signal shows a temporary maximum speed that must not be exceeded, or indicates that certain lanes are closed ahead. Ignoring these warnings may result in prosecution.

DROWSY DRIVER STOPPED TO REST

A motorist who feels sleepy must not park on the verge of a motorway, because the situation is not an emergency. He would be expected to have used his common sense and not started or continued his journey in such a condition.

Driver Arthur Bernard began to feel drowsy as he drove towards a motorway. He had reached the slip road before he saw somewhere suitable to park. The next intersection he knew was 10 miles away, so Mr Bernard stopped on the hard shoulder of the slip road.

He was sitting awake at the wheel when police arrived. Mr Bernard explained that he was sleepy, but he was prosecuted. The court held that he had stopped in an emergency and dismissed the case. The prosecution appealed.

DECISION

The appeal court held that Mr Bernard was fully aware of his condition before reaching the motorway, so there could be no emergency and an offence had been committed.

The penalty for stopping unlawfully on the hard shoulder is a fine of up to £1,000. This is, however, the only offence on a motorway for which a driver's licence may not be endorsed.

If the signal shows a red, flashing light, drivers must not pass the signal in the lane it controls. When the restriction has been passed, the signal indicates by a lighted, diagonal bar that normal rules apply.

Observing lane discipline

Drivers who wander from lane to lane or who doggedly remain in an overtaking lane can be prosecuted for driving without reasonable consideration.

On a two-lane carriageway, the left-hand lane must be used, except for overtaking.

This 'keep left' rule also applies to three-lane motorways, but drivers can stay in the middle lane when there are slow-moving vehicles ahead in the left-hand lane and similarly if the middle lane is full of traffic they will soon be overtaking, vehicles are permitted to remain in the third carriageway.

The right-hand lane on a three-lane motorway is barred to vehicles over 3 tons – except coaches – and to any vehicle drawing a trailer.

It is always an offence for such vehicles to use the right-hand lane, even for overtaking.

Any vehicle that is permitted to use the right-hand lane should do so only if it is reasonable and safe to overtake another vehicle.

Overall speed limit The maximum speed limit on any motorway is 70 mph (60 mph for heavy lorries) and a driver who exceeds that speed can be disqualified and ordered to pay a fine of up to £1,000.

Special penalties for motorway offences

The maximum penalty for breaking motorway regulations is a £1,000 fine.

A driver who reverses, makes a U-turn or drives in the wrong direction on a motorway can be fined up to £1,000 and disqualified from driving. *See:* DRIVING DISQUALIFICATION

MOVEABLE PROPERTY

Property that can be moved

Moveable property is the technical name that lawyers give to property which can be physically moved, such as furniture, books and motor cars. Most kinds of intangible property – for example, shares in a company, or bank accounts – are also regarded as moveable.

All other property is known as HERITABLE PROPERTY.

Which of the two categories a particular piece of property falls into can sometimes affect what happens to that property on the owner's death. *See:* DISINHERITANCE; INHERITANCE; INTESTACY; WILL

MUGGING

The offence with a new name but a long history

No offence of mugging as such is recognised by the law. Many different crimes may be involved.

To use violence while committing a theft is ROBBERY. If the violent attempt to steal fails, a charge of ASSAULT with intent to rob can be brought. The penalty in either case is at the discretion of the court, within its sentencing limits.

If no theft was attempted, a charge of assault may be brought.

The culprit may also be ordered by the court to pay CRIMINAL INJURIES COMPENSATION.

MURDER

The wilful killing of another person

Murder is the unlawful killing of another person, either:

- Intentionally – where an accused person has inflicted injury with the deliberate intention of killing his victim; or
- Unintentionally – where an accused person has inflicted injury without any intention of killing, but in circumstances which show that he had a reckless disregard for his victim's life, not caring whether he lived or died.

Intentional murder

For murder to be intentional, the accused person must have intended to kill someone – but it need not be the person who was killed. For instance, if a man deliberately fires a gun at his wife, but misses her and unintentionally kills his son, he is guilty of murder, even although he did not intend to kill his son. It is enough that he intended to kill his wife.

Unintentional murder

Unintentional murder occurs where an accused person had no intention to kill, but did intend to cause personal injury to his victim, and acted recklessly, with complete disregard for any fatal consequences.

This type of murder can be committed only where the killing is the result of another crime, such as assault, rape or robbery, which itself involves an intention to injure the victim.

However, an unintentional killing caused by a violent crime will not automatically be murder. It will only be murder if the accused person inflicted the injuries with a reckless indifference for the consequences of his actions. If such 'wicked recklessness' is absent, the killing is not murder but the lesser crime of CULPABLE HOMICIDE.

For instance, if a person dies as a result of an assault, where death was neither intended nor probable, the crime is culpable homicide.

But if an assailant uses a lethal weapon – such as a knife or axe – to assault his victim, the use of that weapon shows that he did not care whether the victim lived or died, and any resulting death is murder.

Lawful killings

A hangman who carries out a death sentence (which is still possible for treason), or a soldier who kills in the line of duty, is not guilty of murder; the killing in these cases is lawful.

A person who intentionally kills in self-defence will not be guilty of murder if he can show that he used violence only as a last resort and that he used no more force than was necessary.

An accused person can defend himself against a murder charge by alleging that he was provoked by the victim. But even if his defence succeeds, he will still be guilty of voluntary culpable homicide.

The sentence for murder

Murder is always tried before a jury in the HIGH COURT OF JUSTICIARY.

If a person under 18 is convicted of murder, he will be ordered to be detained in a place, and under conditions, determined by the Secretary of State for Scotland.

If the offender is aged 18 to 20, he will be sentenced to detention in a young offenders' institution, and is liable to be detained for life. He will be transferred to prison at any time between the ages of 21 and 23.

If the offender is 21 or over, he will be sentenced to life imprisonment.

When passing sentence, the judge may recommend that a minimum number of years should be served. The judge must state his reasons for making such a recommendation, which can be appealed against.

A person sentenced to life imprisonment, or to detention in a young offenders' institution, may be released on licence by the Secretary of State. However, the Secretary of State must first receive a recommendation to that effect from the Parole Board, and must consult the Lord Justice-General (the senior criminal judge in Scotland) and, if he is available, the trial judge who imposed the sentence.

Anyone who is released on licence is subject to the conditions of his licence for the rest of his life and can be recalled to prison. *See:* DIMINISHED RESPONSIBILITY; DRUNKENNESS AS A DEFENCE; INSANITY AS A DEFENCE; PAROLE

NAME, Change of

Getting official recognition for a change of identity

Anyone can call himself by any name he chooses, unless his reason for doing so is fraudulent. But simply changing names can lead to many complications unless the change is officially recorded.

The Registration of Births, Deaths and Marriages (Scotland) Act 1965 provides an official system for recording a change of first name and surname (including simply changing spelling, or adding or removing hyphens). The procedure varies according to the age of the person concerned:

Up to the age of 2 A parent or other qualified person can apply to the Registrar General to record any change of name occurring within the first 12 months of a child's life – for example, during a baptism ceremony. Only one such change may be made.

Up to the age of 16 A parent or other qualified person can apply to the Registrar General to record a change of name. The Registrar General must be satisfied that the new name has been used by the child for at least two years before the application. If he is not, he can insist on being shown a newspaper notice advertising the intention to apply for a change of name and stating that this name has been used by the child for the previous two years.

Only one change of first name and one of surname is allowed. A child whose name was already changed before the age of 2 cannot have it changed again until over 16.

Over the age of 16 The person wishing to change his or her name may apply to the Registrar General to have it changed, on the same conditions about using it for two years and the possibility of being required to advertise. The consent of a parent or guardian is needed if the applicant is under 18.

Only one change of first name and three changes of surname can be recorded in this way. There must be a gap of 5 years between any such changes of name.

If the change of name is required under a WILL, or occurs when a male person marries, the rules about using the name and about the number of changes do not apply.

The Registrar General keeps a special register, called the Register of Corrections, to record all these changes. Copies of entries in it can be supplied. There are fees to be paid for applications and copies. Although changes have to be made by the Registrar General in Edinburgh, you should first make inquiries of your local registrar if you live in Scotland.

When a child is adopted, special arrangements are made for recording a change of name in the Adopted Children Register. *See:* ADOPTION

Anyone may notify the general public of a change in his or her name through advertising the fact in the newspapers. This might be in addition to, or instead of, registration of the change.

However the change of name is done, it is wise to notify the tax, social security and health authorities of the new name, to avoid confusion.

To give a false name to the police when accused of certain ROAD TRAFFIC OFFENCES is in itself an offence. To give somebody else's name may amount to the offence of attempting to pervert the course of justice. *See:* PERVERTING THE COURSE OF JUSTICE

A suspect or potential witness is obliged to give his correct name and address to a constable at the scene of an apparent offence. Not to do so is an offence.

Marriage and divorce

A married woman can continue to use her maiden name if she wishes. She may use both – in different situations. For instance, she may continue to use professionally the name she has established, while being known by her married name in private life.

If she is divorced, she can still use her married name – or any of her married names if she has been divorced more than once – or revert to her maiden name. But a divorced woman who uses her former husband's name must not do

THE MAN WHO USED TWO NAMES

It may be an offence to use a name other than your own on an official application.

Mr Chalmers applied for a certificate of motor insurance. He gave his name on the proposal form as John Barnetson McKay.

He was prosecuted under the Road Traffic Act for making a false statement for the purpose of obtaining insurance. The sheriff acquitted him on the ground that anyone was free to use any name he chose, and the charge was therefore irrelevant.

The procurator fiscal appealed.

DECISION

The appeal court over-ruled the sheriff and sent the case back to him.

The court said that it was not possible to have two genuine names at the same time. If a man knew his name was A, and stated his name was B, that was a false statement and, in some circumstances, an offence.

so in a way that implies that she is still married to him. If she does, her former husband can seek a court INTERDICT to stop her.

The woman could also be sued for DEFAMATION if, by representing herself still to be his wife, she implies that a woman he has later married is not his legal wife.

A widow may revert to her maiden name after her husband's death.

Living together

A woman who lives with a man to whom she is not married can change her name to his by simply using his name.

If she does so, she should write to the social security, tax and health authorities and to anyone else with whom she is likely to have business, so that official documents and records can be altered. She may also wish to advertise the change in a newspaper.

NATIONAL HEALTH SERVICE

Free and available to all residents

The National Health Service is generally free (apart from, for example, PRESCRIPTION charges) and is available to everyone resident in the United Kingdom. It is not necessary to be a British Citizen or to have paid national insurance contributions.

People using the NHS have to be resident to qualify. British people permanently living abroad are not entitled to come back and use the NHS free (British women married to foreigners returning to have their babies have to pay). But servicemen and women, and people working overseas on contract from here, would normally be eligible for treatment.

Foreign visitors and holidaymakers are given emergency treatment free of charge if they fall ill or are injured, or an existing medical condition suddenly flares up, and they have to receive outpatient treatment in hospital. In other circumstances, they may be charged. *See:* MEDICAL CARD

Health care abroad

Most EEC countries run insurance-based health services. Until July 1982, people from the UK wishing to use these services had to prove that they had paid sufficient social security contributions. Since then, however, self-employed and non-employed people have also been able to qualify.

Britons visiting the EEC normally need to obtain form E111 from their local social security office. This form – called a 'health passport' – gives the names of those (including dependants) who are entitled to treatment. Some EEC countries (Ireland and Denmark) require only an ordinary passport.

Since patients in some EEC countries have to pay part of the cost of treatment, it is advisable to take out private insurance to top up the free treatment available. For a list of these countries see leaflet SA30, available from social security offices.

The same leaflet provides a table of medical services in non-EEC countries. From it you can judge whether you should take out private medical insurance. Some of these countries have agreements with the UK by which each will treat the other's nationals.

People going from the UK to work in another EEC country are usually entitled to use the health and social security services of that country. But they need a 'certificate of entitlement', obtainable from the DHSS Overseas Branch, Newcastle upon Tyne NE98 1YX. Leaflet SA 29 gives more details.

NATIONAL INSURANCE CONTRIBUTIONS

How you pay for certain benefits

Most employees and self-employed people have to pay national insurance contributions. But other people can pay them voluntarily in order to qualify for certain benefits.

There are 4 different kinds of contributions:

- Class 1 contributions – paid by employed people and their employers. These contributions are earnings-related and the employee's share is deducted by the employer. If you have two or more jobs, you must pay contributions for each job in which you earn more than £34 (in 1984–5) a week. If you pay more than the maximum amount of contributions for the year, you can get a refund (see below).
- Class 2 contributions – paid by self-employed people. These contributions are paid at a flat rate.
- Class 3 contributions – paid voluntarily in order to qualify for certain benefits – retirement pension, widow's benefit, child's special allowance and death grant. The contributions are paid at a flat rate.
- Class 4 contributions – paid by self-employed people. These are income-related and are paid on a fixed band of income (which is varied upwards each year). Class 4 contributions are paid in addition to Class 2 contributions.

All these contributions are paid into the National Insurance Fund. The Treasury then adds to the Fund a 'top-up' of 11 per cent of total contributions (not counting the sums that are allocated to funding the NHS and the Redundancy and Maternity Pay Funds).

The Fund pays for the following benefits: unemployment, sickness, invalidity and widow's benefits, maternity allowance, retirement pension, child's special allowance, death grant and non-contributory industrial injuries benefits. Other social security benefits are financed out of general taxation.

How you qualify for benefits

Your right to a contributory benefit (or, in some cases, to the full rate of benefit) depends on your meeting the appropriate contribution conditions for that benefit. The rules are complicated but you will find them set out in leaflet NI 40 (for employed people) and NI 41 (for self-employed people), available from your local social security office.

For instance, to qualify for UNEMPLOYMENT BENEFIT you must satisfy *both* the following conditions:

1. You must have actually paid Class 1 contributions on earnings of at least 25 times the weekly LOWER EARNINGS LIMIT (£34 in 1984–5) in any one tax year since 1975. (You will satisfy this condition if you paid 26 flat rate contributions in any tax year before 1975.)

2. You must have paid *or been credited with* Class 1 contributions on earnings of at least 50 times the weekly lower earnings limit. These must have been paid in the income tax year which ended in the calendar year before that in which you claim benefit. For instance, if you claim in July 1984, your right to benefit

PAYING NATIONAL INSURANCE CONTRIBUTIONS

There are four classes of national insurance contributions:

• Class 1. All employees aged between 16 and 65 (60 for women) whose earnings reach the LOWER EARNINGS LIMIT (£34 a week or £147.33 a month in 1984–5) pay Class 1 contributions on the whole of their earnings up to the UPPER EARNINGS LIMIT (£250 a week or £1,083.33 a month in 1984–5). Class 1 contributions are also paid by office holders, such as company directors, paying Schedule E income tax.

Class 1 contributions consist of a 'primary' contribution, payable by the employee, and a 'secondary' contribution, payable by his employer. Primary contributions are deducted at source by the employer, along with income tax.

The amount of the contributions depends on an employee's earnings and on whether he is contracted out of the state pension scheme. *See:* RETIREMENT PENSION

In 1984–5, employees who were not contracted out of the scheme paid 9 per cent of their gross earnings up to the upper earnings limit. Their employer paid secondary contributions equal to 10.45 per cent of those earnings, plus a 1 per cent 'surcharge'. The surcharge is to be abolished from October, 1984.

Contracted-out employees paid 9 per cent of their gross earnings up to the lower earnings limit and 6.85 per cent of the remainder up to the upper earnings limit. Their employer paid 10.45 and 6.35 per cent, plus the surcharge, over the same earnings range.

Since April 1978, men and women have had to pay the same contributions. However, married women and widows who were entitled to pay a reduced rate of contribution at that date still have the right to do so. In 1984–5 the reduced rate for Class 1 contributions was 3.85 per cent. (The employer still pays his normal contributions.) A woman loses this right if she is neither employed nor self-employed for two consecutive years after April 1978.

If you are over retirement age (65 for a man, 60 for a woman), you do not have to pay contributions – although your employer does. Get a certificate of age exemption from your social security office and give it to your employer. You can get a refund if contributions are deducted by mistake.

• Class 2. If you are self-employed, between 16 and 65 (60 for women) and are earning more than the small earnings exception (total net earnings, after certain deductions, of less than £1,850 in the tax year 1984–5), you have to pay the flat-rate Class 2 contribution – £4.60 a week in 1984–5.

Women pay at the same rate as men, except for those married women and widows who have opted for reduced liability to pay contributions. They do not have to pay any Class 2 contributions. Nor do self-employed people over retirement age even although they have not retired.

A self-employed person who expects his or her earnings to be below the small earnings exception, and who wishes not to pay Class 2 contributions, must apply for a certificate of exception. However, he or she should think carefully before doing so, as it means losing the right to benefits such as sickness benefit, affecting the right to retirement pension and affecting a widow's right to widow's benefit. Get leaflet NI 27A from your local social security office – it contains an application form.

If you are both employed and self-employed, you are liable for Class 1 and Class 2 contributions up to a specified amount.

You must pay Class 2 contributions as you earn, either by direct debit of your bank or National Girobank account, or by stamping a contribution card obtained from your social security office with National Insurance Stamps bought weekly from a post office. Failure to do so can mean a fine of up to £200.

• Class 3. You can choose to pay Class 3 contributions if you do not pay Class 1 or Class 2 contributions, or if your contribution record in any tax year is insufficient to qualify for benefit, or if you have been excepted from paying Class 2 contributions.

Class 3 contributions are payable at a flat rate – £4.50 a week in 1984–5. They can be paid by direct debit of a bank or National Girobank account, by cash or cheque, or by stamping a contribution card.

Class 3 contributions will help you qualify for certain social security benefits – retirement pension, widow's benefit, death grant and child's special allowance. If you are within 5 years of retirement, you should check whether Class 3 contributions will be of any value to you. For more information, see leaflet NI 42, available from your local social security office.

• Class 4. If you are self-employed, you may have to pay an earnings-related contribution on top of your Class 2 contribution. It is payable on profits and gains chargeable to income tax under Cases I and II of Schedule D, and is collected by the Inland Revenue along with Schedule D tax.

In 1984–5, the Class 4 contribution was 6.3 per cent of profits or gains between £3,950 and £13,000. The maximum annual contribution was £570.15.

A man or woman over retirement age (65 for a man, 60 for a woman), and anyone not resident for tax purposes in Britain, does not have to pay Class 4 contributions.

For more information about Class 4 contributions, get leaflet NP 18 from your local social security office.

depends on your contributions during the tax year April 6, 1982 to April 5, 1983. If you have paid or been credited with contributions on earnings of less than 50 times the required amount, but at least 25 times, unemployment benefit is still payable, but at a reduced rate.

Credits Contributions may sometimes be credited to you even though you have not actually paid them. Credits may be given:

• When you are unemployed or sick (Class 1 credits only).

• To someone aged at least 16 who has not yet started work (Class 1 credits – but only Class 3 credits to help qualify for retirement pension and widow's benefits).

• To someone aged 60–64 who has stopped working (Class 1 and Class 2 credits).

• When you are on an approved course of full-time training; or finish an apprenticeship or full-time education (Class 1 credits only).

• To someone receiving maternity allowance, invalid care allowance, or unemployability supplement payable with disablement benefit (Class 1 credits only).

• To a woman whose marriage ends through death or divorce (Class 1 credits only).

These credits help you to start or maintain your contribution record for contributory benefits – except for widow's allowance, child's special allowance and death grant (although credits paid before 1975 count for the death grant). But you (or your husband) must also have *paid* contributions at some time to obtain these benefits.

When you can pay too much

If, as an employee, you pay Class 1

contributions in more than one job, you may be paying more than the maximum amount of contributions payable in any one tax year (£1,192.50 in 1984–5).

If you have paid too much, you can apply for a refund as soon as the tax year ends. You can do this on form CF 28F, obtainable from your local social security office.

You can avoid paying too much and having to wait for a refund by:

- Deferring payment of contributions for one or more of your jobs.
- Paying in advance the maximum amount of contributions due for the year.

For information about deferment or payment in advance, see leaflet NP 28, obtainable from your local social security office. An application form is attached to the leaflet.

NATIONAL INSURANCE LOCAL TRIBUNAL

How to appeal if your claim for social security benefit is rejected

If your claim to a social security benefit is turned down, or you disagree with the amount awarded, you can usually appeal to an independent national insurance local tribunal.

In 1984 local tribunals are to be merged with supplementary benefit appeal tribunals. They will then be known as social security appeal tribunals. *See:* SOCIAL SECURITY APPEALS; SUPPLEMENTARY BENEFIT

Local tribunals hear appeals on all contributory benefits, and on child benefit, invalid care allowance and maternity grant. Occasionally they also hear appeals on non-medical matters concerning entitlement to disablement benefit, mobility allowance, attendance allowance and severe disablement allowance.

Most appeals on these last four benefits concern medical matters. They are not heard by local tribunals. Those involving attendance allowance are dealt with by the Attendance Allowance Board. Those involving disablement benefit, mobility allowance and severe disablement allowance are heard by medical appeal tribunals, and are appeals against an initial decision by one or more specially appointed adjudicating doctors. *See:* SOCIAL SECURITY APPEALS

A few matters are dealt with, not by local tribunals, but by the Secretary of State for Social Services. These include matters relating to national insurance contributions, whether a claimant is an employed earner and which of two people is entitled to child benefit.

Local tribunals do not deal with appeals about SUPPLEMENTARY BENEFIT or FAMILY INCOME SUPPLEMENT. These are heard by supplementary benefit appeal tribunals.

How you can appeal

Benefit claims are decided in the first instance by insurance officers – to be renamed adjudication officers in 1984 – at social security and unemployment benefit offices.

If an insurance officer turns down your claim, he must send you, as soon as reasonably possible, a notice that tells you of your right to appeal to a local tribunal within 28 days of the notice being sent.

If you decide to appeal, you can obtain an appeal form from your local social security or unemployment benefit office. But you do not need to do so; a written appeal letter is sufficient.

On the form (or in your letter) you should say that you wish to appeal and then state, briefly, why you want to do so. If you are going to be represented – for example, by a welfare rights officer, trade union official or Citizens Advice Bureau adviser – give that person's name and address and ask for the case papers to be sent to him or her.

Even if you do not appeal until after the 28 day limit has expired, you should still send in the form or letter, saying why you did not send it earlier. The tribunal chairman may give permission for a late appeal if he thinks there was a good reason for the delay.

Preparing for a hearing

A few weeks after lodging your appeal, you will receive case papers from the clerk to the tribunal in your area, and be told where and when your appeal is to be heard. If you, or a witness, cannot attend, telephone the clerk. An adjournment is granted for any good reason.

The case papers sent to you are exactly the same as those which the members of the tribunal see before they hear your appeal. They include the insurance officer's submission to the tribunal, justifying his decision against you.

The insurance officer's submission gives references to relevant Acts of Parliament and regulations, and to decisions reached by the SOCIAL SECURITY COMMISSIONERS in similar cases. You have the right to see any of this material at your local social security office. If you contact the tribunal clerk, he will arrange for you to do so.

Appearing at the tribunal

Your hearing is held informally – usually in a room provided by the DHSS.

The chairman, always a lawyer, sits at a table flanked by the two other members of the tribunal. One is chosen from a panel representing employers and the self-employed, the other from a panel representing employees – usually trade union nominees.

You sit at the table opposite the tribunal. There is space beside you for any witness you wish to call, or simply for someone to accompany or represent you. The tribunal clerk and the insurance officer will also be present.

Anyone can act as your representative, but if he is a solicitor you will have to pay his fee – LEGAL AID is not available for tribunals. However, a solicitor may be willing to represent you under the Legal Advice and Assistance Scheme. *See:* LEGAL ADVICE

The chairman should first of all explain the proceedings to you. He will then usually ask you to put your case. It is up to you to prove your case, so be sure that you produce all the evidence – including documents and witnesses – that you need. Neither you nor your witnesses take an oath.

The chairman or members may question you. The insurance officer is invited to do the same and may also make points of his own. You are entitled to put questions to him.

After all the evidence is heard, you wait in another room while the tribunal comes to its decision. The insurance officer also goes out. You will usually be told what that decision is immediately.

A few days later you will be sent full details of the tribunal's findings and the reasons for its decision. If you are not satisfied with it, you have 3 months in which to appeal to a Social Security

Commissioner. You should take expert advice before deciding to do so.

If the tribunal's decision is unanimous, you will need permission from the tribunal chairman to appeal to a Commissioner. You can apply for this when you are told the decision at the hearing, or you can make a written application within 28 days of receiving the written decision. If your application is refused, you can ask the Commissioner for leave to appeal. *See:* SOCIAL SECURITY COMMISSIONERS

Expenses If you or your witnesses lose wages or incur travelling expenses by attending your appeal hearing, tell the tribunal clerk. You will be reimbursed for travelling expenses and also receive money (up to a fixed limit) to cover loss of earnings. Representatives from voluntary organisations can also claim travelling expenses.

NATIONALISED INDUSTRY

When the state controls a business

Many important industries and services – called nationalised industries – are controlled by the government on behalf of the public. Special public corporations have been established by Acts of Parliament to run these industries.

The major public corporations are British Gas, the South of Scotland Electricity Board, the North of Scotland Hydro-Electric Board, British Rail, the Post Office, British Telecom, British Airways, the Scottish Transport Group (which consists of the Scottish Bus Group and the ferry operators, Caledonian MacBrayne) and National Bus Company (which provides bus services in England and Wales), the National Coal Board and the British Steel Corporation.

The detailed running of the nationalised industries is in the hands of chairmen and directors who are appointed by the government. They are responsible to various government departments, whose ministers have authority over major financial decisions but no power to intervene in day-to-day commercial operations.

Consumer representation

Members of the public have no direct control over the way nationalised industries are run. Nor do Members of Parliament, except that they can take part in decisions on general policy – for instance, when a government wishes to take legal powers to nationalise an industry, or a political argument develops over financial losses.

However, consumers are directly represented in the service industries. There are over 40 nationalised industry consultative and consumer councils or committees (often referred to as NICCs) covering the electricity, gas, coal, rail and ferry, posts and telecommunications industries. NICCs are almost all statutory bodies, whose members are appointed by the government.

In Scotland, the important consumer bodies are: the Electricity Consultative Councils for the North and South of Scotland, the Gas Consumers' Council for Scotland, the Domestic Coal Consumers' Council, the Transport Users' Consultative Committee for Scotland (trains and ferries, but not buses) and the Post Office Users' Council for Scotland (the Post Office and British Telecom).

These bodies can take up complaints and representations from consumers, and may also make recommendations on policy matters. But they have no power to direct the running of the nationalised industries. *See:* ELECTRICITY SUPPLY; GAS SUPPLY; POST OFFICE; RAIL TRAVEL; TELEPHONE

NATIONALITY

The relationship of people to the country where they belong

Nationality is, in law, a legal link between a person and a state, usually acquired by birth, but sometimes through parentage or long residence.

Nationality has no exact definition in Britain – in law it generally has the same meaning as CITIZENSHIP. Confusion sometimes arises because the word is used to describe membership of a nation which does not constitute a state. There is, for example, no such thing in law as Scottish or English nationality, although people often refer to both.

The concept of nationality is, however, important in international law. Treaties may give rights to nationals of states which are signatories to them; and, in general, a state may represent its nationals at diplomatic level against other states. A state may also be obliged to receive any of its nationals who are expelled from another country.

In treaties, the word 'national' may be defined, and the definition may not coincide with citizenship. There is, for example, a special definition of 'UK national' for European Community purposes which is not closely related to existing citizenship law.

In other cases, so far as the UK is concerned, the word 'national' probably includes British Citizens, British Dependent Territories Citizens, British Overseas Citizens, British Subjects (as defined by the British Nationality Act 1981) and British Protected Persons (at least if they hold no other citizenship).

What to put as your nationality

Asking for someone's nationality – for example, in a job application form – can cause confusion and produce the wrong answer. A carefully designed form should provide for people to state separately their:

- Country of birth.
- Country of citizenship.
- Country of usual residence.
- Country of present residence.

All four may be different – and might give a person a claim to nationality.

Example: A New Zealand-born nurse lives in Edinburgh during a working holiday. She was brought up in Sydney and carries an Australian passport. Her permanent home is in Fiji, where her parents have taken citizenship. So in various senses she 'belongs' in New Zealand, Australia and Fiji. And if either of her parents was born in Britain, she is a British Citizen: the law says that she 'belongs' in this country too, and cannot be deported from here.

If you are asked to state your nationality, give your country of citizenship. If you are not a British Citizen, but have a UK work permit or have been accepted for settlement, that should be stated.

NATURAL JUSTICE

Basic rules that ensure you get a fair hearing

Courts, arbiters, tribunals, inquiries and many other bodies with powers to

THE FOOTBALL CLUB THAT WAS TRIED IN ITS ABSENCE

Everyone is entitled to due notice of any charge against him and an opportunity to answer it.

St. Johnstone Football Club in Perth decided to hold a benefit match for one of its players. It allowed its supporters' club to make most of the arrangements for the match.

After the game was played, the Scottish Football Association, to which St. Johnstone F.C. belonged, got to hear of it. The secretary of the Association wrote pointing out that to let a supporters' club arrange games was against Association rules and St. Johnstone F.C. had already been warned about this. The letter ended: 'It has been decided that your club be severely censured and fined £25. Please let me have your remittance'.

St. Johnstone complained to the Court of Session that it had been tried and punished in its absence and that this was against natural justice. It asked the Court to declare the fine invalid.

DECISION

The judge agreed and declared the fine to be of no effect. By the rules of the Association, members promised not to use the courts in their disputes, but the judge decided that this made no difference: the courts could not be shut out in this way.

THE BOARD THAT DISCUSSED MATTERS BEHIND CLOSED DOORS

In proceedings before courts, tribunals and boards, everyone must have a chance to answer all the points raised.

Nazir Ahmed applied to Stirling licensing board for a new off-sale licence in the village of Fallin. At a private meeting of board members, held before the public hearing, a representative from Fallin said that there were already too many licences in the village. This man was a member of Fallin Miners' Welfare Club, which already had off-sales facilities.

At the public hearing the matter of over-provision of licences was never raised. But it was discussed again in private when the board adjourned to consider the application. The licence was refused.

Mr Ahmed appealed to the sheriff court, claiming that he had been given no chance to answer the point about there being too many licences in Fallin.

DECISION

The sheriff agreed that the board's proceedings were contrary to natural justice. After hearing evidence on the number of licences in Fallin, he granted Mr Ahmed a new licence.

The sheriff also commented that members of boards should not appear to be judges in their own cause, for this would also be against natural justice.

make decisions affecting individuals must abide by certain basic rules of fair play, known as rules of natural justice.

The main rules are:

1. The members of the deciding body must not be biased. Nor should they appear likely to be biased – by, for example, having a financial or other interest in the case which they are deciding.

So if a company sacks an employee, and he makes a complaint of unfair dismissal to an industrial tribunal, no director of the company should sit as a member of the tribunal.

2. You must be given a fair hearing. Evidence must not be given behind your back and you must be allowed to put your side of the case in your own way – within reason – and in your own time.

The remedies that are available

If you suspect bias in a body (other than a court) deciding your case, mention it to the chairman. He may decide to adjourn the hearing so that a differently constituted body can hear the case. If a court decides a case against you and you think that the rules of natural justice have not been complied with, consult a solicitor about the possibility of lodging an appeal.

If you discover that there may have been some bias only after your case in a tribunal is over, you can apply to the Court of Session (or sometimes the sheriff court) to have the decision quashed. In some cases, however, you may have a special, statutory right of appeal – for instance, you can appeal to the Employment Appeal Tribunal against a decision of an industrial tribunal, or to a Social Security Commissioner against a decision of a social security tribunal, if you suspect there has been bias. All these remedies are also available if you suspect that you were not given a fair hearing.

NATURALISATION

How an alien can become a British citizen

A person can apply to become a British Citizen by naturalisation. The process can take up to 2 years and will cost £160 – payable when the application is made. Several conditions – about residence and good character, for example – must first be fulfilled.

An application form can be obtained from H. M. Immigration Office, 16 Princes Square, 48 Buchanan Street, Glasgow G1 3JG, or the Home Office Immigration and Nationality Department, Lunar House, Wellesley Road, Croydon CR9 2BY. The form requires two referees, who must be British Citizens over 25 — unrelated to the applicant — who have known him for 3 years or more.

The form is sent to the Home Office Immigration and Nationality Department. The applicant may then be interviewed by a policeman. If the application is approved, the Home Office sends the applicant an oath of allegiance that must be sworn before a sheriff, solicitor or J.P. The applicant is then issued with a certificate of naturalisation.

The Home Secretary can refuse an application, and often does so. He does not need to state his reasons and there is no appeal.

Some people have the right to register as British citizens, including the wives of British citizens (though this is to be phased out). The fee is £55.

See: CITIZENSHIP

NEGLECTED LAND

How to force an owner to clean up eyesores

The LOCAL AUTHORITY responsible for planning control in a particular area may consider that the amenity of the areá is seriously damaged by the neglected condition of any land. If so, it can issue a 'waste land notice', which instructs the owner and the occupier of the land to tidy it up.

A waste land notice might be issued where land has been allowed to become overgrown with weeds, or where rubbish has piled up on a site. Waste land notices can also be issued where a building has been allowed to become ruinous or dilapidated; the owner and the occupier can be ordered to do whatever is necessary to stop it spoiling the amenity of the neighbourhood.

There is a right of appeal to the Secretary of State for Scotland against a waste land notice.

If a notice is ignored, the planning authority can carry out the necessary work and then claim the cost from the owner of the land. Sometimes, however, the owner cannot be found and the authority may have to decide whether to clean up the site at its own expense.

If an owner allows what are called 'injurious weeds' to grow unchecked on his land, he can be reported to the Secretary of State for Scotland, who can order him to prevent the weeds from spreading. Injurious weeds are those – such as spear thistle or ragwort – which spread quickly and can stifle and kill farmers' crops.

If the owner ignores the order, he can be prosecuted and fined.

Apart from injurious weeds, a person can grow any weeds he likes. But if they spread from his land to your land, you may be able to take a civil action against him for NUISANCE.

CLEANING UP UNTIDY LAND

An owner who neglects his land can be ordered by the local council to tidy the site.

NEGLIGENCE

Damages can be claimed for injuries caused by carelessness

Anyone who injures another person or harms his property through an act of carelessness can be required to pay DAMAGES for negligence.

The law expects a person to take reasonable care in whatever he is doing. Motorists, for example, are expected to drive with sufficient care that they do not mount the pavement and run down pedestrians. And employers are expected to see that their goods and equipment are stored safely and do not fall down on top of employees. *See:* EMPLOYER'S LIABILITY

Householders are expected to take reasonable care of their property and to see that there are, for instance, no broken floorboards or windows which might cause injury to someone coming to the house. *See:* OCCUPIERS' LIABILITY.

Similarly, professional men such as doctors or dentists are expected to show sufficient skill and care not to cause injury to their patients. *See:* MEDICAL NEGLIGENCE

Three points must be proved in any court action for negligence:

- The defender owed a duty to the pursuer to take care.
- The defender was in breach of that duty.
- The breach of duty caused harm to the pursuer.

When there is a duty of care

Carelessness alone does not make a person liable for negligence. The pursuer has to prove that the defender should have foreseen that his actions could result in injury to someone and that he had a responsibility towards the person whom he harmed.

A building contractor, for instance, has a duty to take care that no one is harmed on his building site. A nursery school has a duty to take care not to let the children run into the road. A man who makes or repairs goods has a duty to take care that they do not harm people who use them.

In certain other situations, however, there is no duty of care. For instance, a person who watches a blind man walk over a cliff to his death has no duty of care to the man, even though he could foresee the harm and prevent it without difficulty. Similarly, someone who sees a badly injured person lying at the roadside, but does not stop to help, cannot be sued for negligence even if the person dies.

A motor-cyclist who knocks down a child has a duty of care to the child – but he probably cannot be sued for negligence by a woman 30 yards away who faints on seeing the accident and breaks an arm. *See:* NERVOUS SHOCK

The law draws no fixed lines on where a duty to avoid foreseeable harm begins or ends. But in most cases of physical injury or damage to property caused by a defender's positive acts – as distinct from his omission or failure to act – a duty of care is already recognised. And new cases in the courts constantly lead to the creation of new areas of duty.

How much care must you take?

In deciding whether a person has failed in his duty to take care, the courts apply an imaginary yardstick: did the defender take the care that would be taken by a reasonable man?

That standard of care cannot be defined; it depends on the circumstances of each case and the attitude of the court hearing it. The question to be answered

WHEN YOU ARE SUED FOR NEGLIGENCE

Damages awarded for negligence can be high, but you can take out insurance to protect yourself in the event of a claim.

All motorists have to be insured by law against the risk of negligently injuring other people in accidents.

Employers must insure against injury to workmen caused by negligence. *See:* ACCIDENT AT WORK; EMPLOYER'S LIABILITY

Householders face risks too. A tree in the garden could fall on to a roadway, injuring a passer-by. Or a dog could dash into the road, causing a driver to crash his car. Comprehensive policies can cover such claims. *See:* PROPERTY INSURANCE

THE TEENAGER WHO SHOULD NOT HAVE BEEN ON THE RAILWAY LINE

Occupiers of dangerous property need only take reasonable steps to secure the safety of the public. People who willingly run risks by entering such property are barred from getting damages.

One Saturday night in 1974, 15 year old Anne McGinlay and her boyfriend were hit by a train about a quarter of a mile from Shettleston station in Glasgow. Anne's boyfriend was killed and her own injuries destroyed her memory of the accident.

It was proved that they had got onto the railway line through a gap in the fencing, either on their way to or from a nearby disused brickworks which was a popular spot for courting couples.

Anne sued the British Railways Board for damages, alleging that they had been negligent in failing to fence the line adequately to keep people off.

DECISION

The House of Lords decided that the Board had not been negligent. The fencing, although broken, was sufficient to indicate to people of the couple's age that they should keep off. In any event, Anne had taken the risk of injury upon herself. She had experience of crossing the line to go up to the disused brickworks and she admitted that she was aware of the risk of being hit by a train.

is: were the actions of the defender those of a person of reasonable intelligence and behaviour?

It is no defence for a defender to say that he acted to the best of his ability, if that ability falls below the level that the court would expect from its imaginary reasonable man. A person whose reactions are slower than average is not excused from liability for negligence.

Knowledge that a situation is dangerous increases a defender's duty to take care. For example, a motorist who regularly uses a hazardous stretch of road is expected to show a higher degree of care than someone who is a stranger to the road. So is a tradesman, such as a decorator, who is left alone in a house: if he fails to lock the door when he leaves, and the house is broken into, he can be sued for negligence.

CAN YOU GET YOUR DAMAGES?

The first question in all cases where you have suffered damage because of someone's behaviour is – should you sue?

In many cases there is no precedent to guide you on whether a claim for negligence will succeed. Ask your solicitor to write first to the other person, claiming damages.

If he refuses to accept liability, you and your solicitor must decide if the claim is worth pursuing in the courts.

Try to find out if the other person is insured. If not, he may have no means of paying damages even if they are awarded to you.

Failing to use your skills

Anyone who is given a task because he claims to have a particular skill is negligent if he causes loss or injury by failing to use it. For instance, a doctor who fails to diagnose an illness cannot claim that he acted to the best of his ability if a doctor of reasonable skill would have diagnosed it.

However, a person is only expected to show the skill of his particular profession. For instance, people who have their ears pierced by a jeweller cannot claim damages merely because their ears become infected – the jeweller has to show only the skill of a jeweller, not that of a doctor.

When the extent of injury cannot be foreseen

A person who has failed to take reasonable care is liable for negligence even if the extent of any injury which he causes could not have been foreseen.

For instance, a man who strikes someone a gentle blow on the head, and causes a fractured skull because the bone is only egg-shell thick, cannot defend himself by claiming that he had no idea that his gentle blow would cause such damage.

When contributory negligence is involved

A person's injuries are sometimes partly his own fault, even when he is the victim of someone's negligence. This is called contributory negligence. In such cases any damages awarded are reduced, usually in proportion to the amount of blame that is attached to him.

For example, a moped rider who is not wearing a crash helmet, and who suffers head injuries in an accident caused by the negligence of another person, is partly to blame for his injuries. So is a car passenger who is injured because he fails to wear a seat belt.

Sometimes a person who sues may be entirely to blame for injuries received through someone else's negligence.

For example, a photographer who goes too near the jumps at a horse show has no claim if a horse falls on him and injures him, even though the rider is careless. Similarly, a spectator who is dozing on the boundary line at a cricket match cannot complain if he is hit by the ball.

It is no defence to an action for negligence for a motorist to put a notice in his car that all passengers travel at their own risk. If his careless driving causes injury to passengers, he is liable for negligence.

NEIGHBOUR

Settling disputes with the people next door

Most disputes with neighbours can be settled tactfully between the people involved, but when an irritation such as noise or fumes is persistent, a householder may be able to sue for NUISANCE.

The nuisance may be caused by excessive bonfire smoke, noisy radios, dangerous boundary walls or noisy work at night.

It may be a defence for a neighbour to show that the activity has been going on for years without complaint.

The complainer can go to court for an INTERDICT stopping the nuisance, and can also claim damages if he has suffered any loss. *See:* AIR POLLUTION; BOUNDARIES, WALLS AND FENCES; NOISE OFFENCES

If branches from a neighbour's tree overhang your property, you are entitled to cut them off. You should return the branches. *See:* TREE

NERVOUS SHOCK

Claiming damages for injuries that are not physical

If a person suffers nervous shock as a result of an accident, whether or not he was actually involved, he can sometimes claim damages for NEGLIGENCE. He must be able to prove that the defender was careless, that the accident and its effect on him was reasonably foreseeable and that the shock which he suffered was a medically recognised condition.

For such a claim to succeed, the shock must result from actually seeing or hearing the accident or its immediate aftermath.

If the person who suffers shock is a close relative or fellow employee of someone injured in the accident, the court is more likely to decide that the nervous shock was foreseeable and to award damages even if the person came upon the accident some time after it occurred – particularly if the injuries that he sees are especially horrifying.

If a person suffers nervous shock because of witnessing an accident to a stranger, he is unlikely to be able to obtain damages.

THE FISHWIFE WHO HEARD THE MOTORCYCLE CRASH

A person who suffers nervous shock as a result of seeing an accident to a stranger is unlikely to get damages.

Mrs Euphemia Bourhill was a fishwife who sold fish in the Colinton district of Edinburgh. She was 8 months pregnant.

One day she was alighting from a tram in Colinton Road and the driver was helping her to put her creel of fish on her back. Just then, a motorcycle sped past the tram and collided with a car. The motorcyclist was killed only 40 feet from Mrs Bourhill, but out of sight behind the tram.

Mrs Bourhill heard the noise of the crash and, as she said in her evidence, 'got in a pack of nerves. I did not know whether I was going to get it or not'. She sued the executors of the estate of the dead motorcyclist for damages, on the ground that his negligent riding had caused her nervous shock. She was able to prove that the shock had prevented her from carrying on her business for some time.

DECISION

The court said that Mrs Bourhill was not entitled to recover damages. Although each case has to be looked at according to the circumstances, it was clear that nervous shock to a mere bystander was not something which might have been reasonably foreseen by the motorcyclist.

THE MOTHER WHOSE CHILD LOOKED LIKE A BLACK BUNDLE

A mother may be able to recover damages for nervous shock if she sees her child with serious injuries shortly after an accident caused by someone's negligence.

Mrs Bain raised an action for damages against Kings & Co. Ltd. on the ground that she had suffered nervous shock from seeing injuries caused to her son by the company's negligence.

She alleged that the company's workmen had carelessly left a 25 gallon drum of bitumen in a temporary depot in Dalkeith where children were allowed. Her son, along with other children, had been playing with the drum when it was punctured and set alight by one of the children. They pushed the drum into the River Esk but it exploded, injuring the children.

Mrs Bain heard the explosion at the gate of her house 150 yards away.

Shortly afterwards her son was brought up to the house, suffering from horrifying injuries.

Mrs Bain said that he resembled a 'black bundle', was covered in tar, had his hair singed and also skin hanging off his legs.

She claimed that she had suffered nervous shock at the sight of these injuries but Kings & Co. argued that they were not liable.

DECISION

The court held that it was possible for damages to be recovered by a mother in such circumstances.

The judge stressed the fact that she was the victim's mother, the horrifying nature of the injuries and the short space of time between the accident and her witnessing the injuries.

The court allowed her to present evidence of what happened to support her case.

NEW HOUSE

A 10 year safeguard against bad building and subsidence

Almost all new houses are covered by the registration scheme run by the National House-Building Council. The purpose of the scheme is to protect house-buyers against defects caused by bad building and subsidence for a period of 10 years.

If you are buying a new house, or one that is less than 10 years old, check that it is registered under the scheme. Building societies will not usually give a mortgage if it has not been registered.

Even when a house is more than 10 years old and no longer covered, it is of interest to a buyer to know that it was built to the standards laid down by the scheme.

Protection under the scheme

The National House-Building Council lays down detailed requirements for the design and construction of houses registered under the scheme. The purchaser is protected where these requirements have not been followed by the builder.

The protection given to a purchaser depends on the age of the house:

- For the first *two* years after the house is completed the builder must put right *any defect* caused by not following the Council's requirements. You will find this obligation set out in clause 6 of the Scottish House Purchaser's Agreement which the original buyer and the builder both sign.

There are some restrictions, however. For example, normal wear and tear and normal shrinkage are excluded. You must notify the builder of the defect in writing as soon as possible, and within the two year period.

If the defect is one covered by the Agreement, but the builder nonetheless refuses to put it right – for example, because he has gone out of business – you are covered by the Council Insurance Policy. Write to the Council at 5 Manor Place, Edinburgh.

- Most minor defects should have shown themselves within the first two years. After this period ends, the scheme covers you for *structural defects* which appear during the next *eight* years. If such defects appear it is the Council, not the builder, which has to pay for repairs.

The defect must be caused by the builder's failure to follow the Council's requirements. Examples are collapse of the joists, or dry rot. The Council cannot be asked to pay more than the purchase price of the house as adjusted for subsequent inflation.

Protecting second buyers

It is not just the original buyer who is protected by the scheme. Subsequent buyers are also protected during the first 10 years of the house's life.

If you are a second buyer, you cannot claim for defects that were apparent before you bought the house. For this reason you should make sure that your surveyor draws any defects to your attention so that they can be put right by the seller.

Other legal safeguards

A defect in your house might not qualify for the scheme – for example, a minor defect discovered after the two year period.

In such a case the builder may still be liable under clause 3 of the Scottish House Purchaser's Agreement. This requires him to build the house 'in an efficient and workmanlike manner and of proper materials and so as to be fit for habitation'.

Any claim must be made within 20 years of the date the Agreement was signed.

NEXT OF KIN

How the law distinguishes between relations and spouses

Legally, a person's closest relatives are his next of kin – excluding his mother and those related to him through her.

Since 1964, being a person's next of kin has lost its significance as far as INHERITANCE is concerned: other relatives apart from next of kin can now inherit when that person dies leaving no spouse and no valid will. *See:* INTESTACY

The estate now goes, in order, to

1. Any children, who share everything equally.
2. Remoter descendants.
3. Parents, brothers and sisters and their descendants.
4. Uncles, aunts or their descendants.
5. Grandparents.
6. Great uncles, great aunts or their descendants.
7. Greatgrandparents, and so on.

Married people frequently give the name of their spouse as next of kin, on forms such as those signed on entry to hospital. That has no legal meaning since spouses are not blood relatives and therefore not next of kin, but it identifies the person to be contacted in an emergency.

NOISE OFFENCES

Using the law to stop a nuisance caused by noise

A householder can take action through his local district (or islands) council or through the courts to stop someone – a company or an individual – from making a noise that is causing a NUISANCE.

The noise may be from factory works, from lorries or even from a neighbour's stereo record player consistently played too loudly. Generally, you should be able to show that the noise causes disturbance or material inconvenience, such as regular loss of sleep, excessive vibration or damage to property.

When the council can act to stop the nuisance

The simplest course of action is to complain to the police, who will visit the source of complaint and ask those concerned to stop the nuisance. A prosecution will not normally result, however.

If the problem continues, go to the environmental health department of your district or islands council and ask it to serve a noise-abatement notice on the offending premises.

If the council agrees that the noise is a nuisance and issues an abatement notice, whoever occupies the premises named in the notice will be forbidden from continuing to make the noise or will be restricted to making it only during certain times of the day.

If the noise continues, the occupant of the premises can be prosecuted. Unless it can be shown that the occupant has taken the best practicable steps to reduce the noise, he can be fined up to

SOURCES OF NOISE NUISANCE

Building sites If building work is causing you annoyance, complain to your local council. They may issue an abatement notice and make specific regulations – for example, to use a pile driver only within certain hours.

Musical instruments It is an offence for someone to play a musical instrument or sing in a public place to the annoyance of someone else. The maximum penalty is a £100 fine.

Radios and record players Anyone who operates a radio, television, tape-recorder or other sound equipment, such as a record player, in or adjacent to a public place, to the annoyance of another person commits an offence and can be fined up to £100.

Loudspeakers and chimes The Control of Pollution Act 1974 lays down national regulations about the use of loudspeakers and chimes in the streets.

It is an offence to use a loudspeaker or chimes in a public place between the hours of 9 p.m. and 8 a.m. Loudspeakers and chimes can be used on vehicles selling food and drink, but only between noon and 7 p.m., and only if the noise does not cause unreasonable annoyance to local residents.

A short burst on the chimes of an ice-cream van is allowed; a long tune is not.

The maximum penalty is a fine of £2,000, plus £200 for every day the noise continues.

Car horns Anyone who sounds the horn of a motor vehicle at any time while the vehicle is stationary is committing an offence, unless there is danger to another, moving vehicle.

It is also an offence to sound a horn of a moving vehicle between 11.30 p.m. and 7 a.m. without reasonable cause. The maximum penalty for both offences is £100.

Noisy public-house customers A neighbour continually annoyed by noisy customers leaving a public house at night can oppose the publican's application for a renewal of licence or even ask for the licence to be suspended. *See:* LICENSED PREMISES; LIQUOR OFFENCES

£2,000, plus up to £200 for every day the noise continues.

When a noise is considered to be a very serious nuisance, the council may take proceedings in the sheriff court or Court of Session for an INTERDICT to stop the noise. If the noise then continues, the person responsible can be fined or imprisoned.

Taking action yourself

If the district or islands council refuses to issue a noise-abatement notice, or delays in doing so, anyone suffering from a noise nuisance can apply to the local sheriff court for a noise abatement order. If you wish to do this, you should consult a solicitor.

The sheriff can issue a noise-abatement notice with the same requirements as one issued by the council. The same penalties can be imposed on someone who fails to comply with it.

An alternative course of action is to seek an interdict on the ground that the noise is a common law nuisance. *See:* NUISANCE

Rates reduction A householder who fails to get a noise nuisance stopped can apply to the regional (or islands) council for a reduction in the rateable value of his property.

NOTARY PUBLIC

Making documents genuine

A notary public is an official who by his signature and stamp declares formal documents to be authentic. For example, affidavits in bankruptcy and divorce are drawn up by a notary public and are sworn to before him by the person making the statement.

If a person is blind or unable to write – because of illness, for instance – certain legal documents, such as wills, can be signed on his behalf by a notary public.

Documents required under many foreign law systems often have to be authenticated by a notary. A Scottish notary will usually be qualified to do this.

All enrolled solicitors – and only solicitors – can be made notaries. They are appointed by the Court of Session and are entitled to charge fees for their services. *See:* AFFIDAVIT; DIVORCE

NOTICE

When employment comes to an end

The relationship between an employer and an employee is defined by the EMPLOYMENT CONTRACT. That may be a comprehensive written agreement or simply an oral understanding, the conditions of which are drawn from custom and practice.

If either party wants to end the agreement, he must normally inform the other by giving notice of his intention. If he does not do so, he is in breach of contract and can be sued.

How notice is given

Notice need not be in writing to be valid unless that is specifically provided for in the employment contract. However, it is in the interests of the party serving notice to do so in a letter and to keep a copy, in case of future dispute. Anyone – employer or employee – who believes he has been given oral notice should immediately ask for written confirmation.

Determining how long the notice period should be

Many employment contracts specify notice arrangements, including the length of the notice period before the employment relationship is finally severed. In addition, minimum notice periods (see above) are fixed by law for most types of employee, though not for those who work mainly abroad, or for part-time employees normally working less than 16 hours a week – unless they work at least 8 hours a week and have been continuously employed for 5 years. *See:* EMPLOYMENT PROTECTION

The minimum statutory notice entitlements cannot be reduced by an employment contract. So an employee dismissed after 13 years' service is entitled to 12 weeks' notice, even though his contract says he should get less. On the other hand, if the contract provision is more generous than the legal minimum, the contract applies.

A 'reasonable' notice period

If the contract does not specify a notice period and the length of notice becomes a matter of legal dispute – for example, in a claim for UNFAIR DISMISSAL – courts and tribunals consider not only the statutory minimum provisions, but also what would be 'reasonable' under the circumstances. The factors they take into account include length of service, the nature and seniority of the job and the notice customarily given to others in equivalent positions.

Thus a monthly paid employee who, by statute, is entitled to only 1 week's notice, may be able to argue successfully that he should receive a 'reasonable' period of 1 month, particularly if his colleagues are awarded that amount of notice.

There is no firm rule to determine what is 'reasonable' notice if there is no contract provision. But the more senior the job, the longer the notice period is likely to be – 6 months or more in the case of highly placed executives.

Dismissal without notice

Some offences by employees – particularly those which endanger the lives of others or involve a grave breach of the employer's trust – are so serious that they call for summary dismissal – that is, dismissal without notice. However, if the dismissed employee takes his case to a court or an industrial tribunal, the court or tribunal has to be satisfied that dismissal without notice was justified. *See:* DISCIPLINE AT WORK

Giving the reasons for notice

An employee who hands in his notice is not obliged to give his reasons. Nor is

THE LAW ON MINIMUM NOTICE PERIODS

The minimum period of notice that must be given to most full-time employees who work in Britain is linked to *continuous* length of service.

Length of service with employer	Notice period
Less than 1 month	None
1 month to under 2 years	1 week
2 years to under 12 years	1 week for each complete year
12 years or more	12 weeks

an employer who dismisses an employee under any duty to give reasons.

However, dismissed employees – apart from those who have been in the job for less than 6 months, certain part-timers and those who normally work abroad – are entitled to demand the reasons for their dismissal in writing.

An employee who wants to know why he has been given notice, or summarily dismissed, should write a formal letter to his employer asking for the information, keeping a copy of his request. If the employer has not replied within 14 days, or if his reply is inadequate or untrue, the employee can complain to an industrial tribunal. If the complaint is successful, the employer can be required to pay compensation of 2 weeks' wages to the employee. The tribunal can also state what it finds to be the reasons for the dismissal. *See:* DISMISSAL

If an employee leaves without notice

An employee must give at least 1 week's notice if he has been employed for a month or more. So if he simply walks out of his job, without giving notice, and for no good reason, he is in breach of contract and can be sued for damages.

In practice, whether or not the employer is likely to sue depends on the nature of the employee's job. If he is a workman who can easily be replaced, the employer is unlikely to sue him because he would be unable to show much financial loss. But if he is a valued research chemist, the cost to his employer of his departure may be high and a court might award substantial damages.

An employer who does not want to go to court has another sanction which he can use against an employee who leaves without giving notice. He can refuse to supply a REFERENCE, which he is not obliged to give even if the employee has given notice.

An employer who arbitrarily refuses to pay wages, or unjustifiably changes an employee's job, usually commits a serious breach of contract. If he does, the employee can leave at once without being in breach of his contract, and can complain of UNFAIR DISMISSAL to an industrial tribunal on the ground that he has been constructively dismissed. *See:* CONSTRUCTIVE DISMISSAL

Alternatively, he can leave and raise an action for damages in the sheriff court to obtain payment for what would have been his notice period.

Payment in lieu of notice

An employee who has been dismissed cannot insist on working out his period of notice if his employer does not want him to do so. All he is entitled to is any accrued earnings plus his wages for the notice period – called payment in lieu of notice.

If he does not receive such payment, he can attempt to recover it by raising a sheriff court action for debt. But he will not succeed if the court decides that his conduct justified instant dismissal.

An employee who leaves with payment in lieu of notice is still entitled to claim a REDUNDANCY payment, or to make a complaint of unfair dismissal to an industrial tribunal.

If an employee does not complete his notice period

An employee who is given notice is not obliged to work out his full notice period if, for example, he finds another job. However, if he leaves before his notice period expires, he may forfeit his pay for the remainder of the period.

An employee who leaves before his notice period expires can still claim unfair dismissal. The rules about redundancy payments are more complex and legal advice should be obtained before leaving. *See:* REDUNDANCY

NOTICE OF INTENDED PROSECUTION

When the prosecution must warn a motorist

Within 14 days of certain alleged motoring offences the prosecutor must send the driver or the registered owner of the vehicle a written notice that a prosecution may be brought, unless he was warned of this at the time when the offence was committed.

The offences are:

- Reckless, careless or inconsiderate driving.
- Failure to obey a traffic sign or a police direction.
- Leaving a vehicle in a dangerous position.
- Speeding.

There is no need to send a warning if an accident occurs at the time of the offence or immediately after it is committed, provided that the accident is due to the presence on the road of the vehicle involved in the offence.

It is not easy for a driver to have his case dismissed because no written notice of the intended prosecution has been received. The burden is on him to prove that no notice was sent.

If the prosecutor has evidence that a notice was sent by registered post or recorded delivery to the driver's or owner's last known address, the courts will accept that it was served. That applies even if the notice was returned as undelivered or never reached the person for whom it was intended.

The courts will also allow a case to proceed if the prosecutor is unable to serve 14 days' notice because he cannot find the driver's name and address or the name and address of the registered owner.

The prosecutor does not have to go ahead with the case after giving notice of intended prosecution to a driver or vehicle owner. He does not have to tell that person if he decides that there will be no prosecution.

The only time limit imposed upon the prosecutor is that legal proceedings must start within 6 months of the alleged offence.

As an alternative to serving a notice of intended prosecution the prosecutor may, within 14 days of the alleged offence, serve a SUMMARY COMPLAINT on the accused.

NOTICE OF POSSESSION

When a local authority wants a tenant to leave

If you rent your house from a district or islands council, a new town corporation, the Scottish Special Housing Association or a housing association, your landlord must serve you with a written notice of possession before it can take legal proceedings to evict you.

The notice – called a 'Notice of Proceedings for Recovery of Possession' – will be sent by recorded delivery, or delivered by a SHERIFF OFFICER. It tells you that after a set date (which must be at least 4 weeks after the date on which the notice was served) the landlord may start sheriff court proceedings to evict you. The ground on which eviction may be sought – for example, that rent has not been paid – will also be stated.

The notice will contain information about your legal rights.

A notice of possession is valid for 6 months from the date when the landlord can start eviction proceedings. You must be served with a new notice of possession if your landlord wants to evict you after that period has expired.

A notice of possession does not bring your lease to an end. It is a document which your landlord must serve on you before he can start court proceedings to evict you. If the notice is wrong – for instance, if it gives you less than 4 weeks' notice – it is invalid. Court proceedings cannot be started until a valid notice is served.

You do not have to leave your home when you receive a notice of possession – you can only be lawfully evicted by order of the sheriff court. If you are a secure tenant, your landlord may not be able to obtain such an order. *See:* COUNCIL TENANCY

NOTICE TO QUIT

When a private landlord wants a tenant to leave

When a tenant rents a house from a private landlord, he must be given a proper notice to quit before he can be made to give up the premises.

The notice to quit must be in writing. In it, the landlord must give a clear direction to the tenant to leave the whole of the premises and to deliver up possession. The length of the notice period must be stated, as well as the day on which the premises are to be vacated.

The notice period must be at least 4 weeks. Sometimes the tenant's lease will require a longer period of notice to be given. *See:* LANDLORD AND TENANT

The notice period must also expire exactly on the day when the current period of renting (usually a week, a month or a quarter) ends.

The notice to quit must give the tenant written information about his legal rights. The exact information which must be given is set out in statutory regulations. *See:* EVICTION

A notice to quit is invalid if it is not in writing; or the notice period is shorter than the law (or the lease) requires; or it does not expire on the day the current period of renting expires; or the tenant is not given information about his rights. A landlord can only take court proceedings to evict a tenant after he has served a *valid* notice.

When a valid notice to quit expires, your lease comes to an end. However, you do not have to leave your house – your landlord must obtain a court order before he can take steps to evict you. If you are a protected tenant, he may not be able to do so. *See:* EVICTION

Local authority tenants You will not be served with a notice to quit if your landlord is a district or islands council, a new town corporation, the Scottish Special Housing Association or a housing association. Instead you will be served with a NOTICE OF POSSESSION, telling you that eviction proceedings may be taken against you.

NUISANCE

How the law protects your right to a quiet life

You are entitled to live in and enjoy the use of your property without having to suffer excessive disturbances coming from other people's property. The law of nuisance exists to protect these rights.

Many activities which cause disturbance are controlled or prohibited by Act of Parliament because they damage the environment. These are sometimes called 'statutory nuisances' (see below). Other methods of controlling possible disturbances also exist: for example, a local authority may refuse PLANNING PERMISSION for a development which it considers will create a nuisance.

Generally, however, these laws do not give individual members of the public any right to sue – they are enforced by local authorities and the police. But under the general law of nuisance, occupiers of property – usually owners or tenants – are entitled to seek a court order, or INTERDICT, banning or limiting any excessive disturbance. Failing to obey such an order is CONTEMPT OF COURT, and the person concerned can be fined or even imprisoned.

If injury or damage is caused to you or to your property – for instance, if your health suffers because of excessive noise, or the foundations of your house are weakened because of excessive vibrations – you can ask the court for DAMAGES as well as an order banning or limiting the disturbance. *See:* PERSONAL INJURY

The basis of your right to sue

You may have the right to sue either because the activity to which you object amounts to a common law nuisance or because there is a clause in the title deed of your property which allows you to sue for certain specified disturbances. It may be that you have the right to sue on both these grounds.

Common law nuisances Whether you own property or rent it, you are entitled to be protected against nuisances coming from other people's property. This includes not only nuisances coming from the property of your immediate neighbours but also those from further off – including public road works.

Any type of activity that causes substantial annoyance can be a nuisance. That includes activities which cause physical damage – for instance, washing which is ruined because of smoke from a neighbour's bonfire, or walls which are damaged because of vibrations caused by the operation of heavy machinery.

But it is not necessary for there to be physical damage. Excessive noise, for instance, can amount to a nuisance. So a pop group which rehearses in the middle of the night can be stopped if the amount of noise created is unreasonable. Offensive smells – for example, from the cooking of a neighbouring restaurant – can also be a nuisance.

Certain activities can amount to nuisances if they affect the nature of the area. Brothels can be prohibited for this reason; so can sex shops – at least in residential areas.

How serious must the trouble be?

For the trouble about which you are complaining to amount to a nuisance, a court must consider it to be more than is reasonably tolerable. Whether it is depends on the circumstances.

THE ADVOCATE WHO SAID THE SOLICITOR NEXT DOOR WAS A NUISANCE

A normal human activity may be a nuisance if it is not tolerable in the circumstances.

Mr Francis Watt Q.C., an advocate, of 3 Moray Place, Edinburgh, sued Mr Harvey Jamieson W.S., a solicitor, of 4 Moray Place, Edinburgh. He alleged that Mr Jamieson's gas hot water heater had discharged gallons of sulphur-impregnated water into the walls of his home, causing them to disintegrate and dry rot to set in.

Mr Jamieson argued that even if this had happened, it was not in law a nuisance.

DECISION

The court decided that if the facts were proved, the disturbance caused by the gas hot water heater could amount to a nuisance.

Even if it was not unusual to have a gas hot water heater, it could be intolerable to other property owners in the circumstances.

THE NOISY KENNELS THAT AFFECTED THE NEIGHBOURS

An activity may amount to a nuisance if it becomes excessive.

Mr and Mrs Shanlin lived in Birdston Road, Milton of Campsie, about 170 feet away from the boundary of Mrs Collins' boarding and breeding kennels.

In 1968, Mr and Mrs Shanlin applied to the sheriff court for a permanent order to control the noise made by the dogs at the kennel, but were unsuccessful. In 1971 they tried again.

By this time there were 50 to 60 dogs boarding at the kennels and up to 40 dogs kept there for breeding and showing. The noise was so bad that the Shanlins had taken to going on holiday at the busiest periods. Their health, particularly that of Mrs Shanlin, was badly affected.

DECISION

The sheriff decided that the noise was sufficient to seriously disturb any normal person. The dogs barked, whined and howled at all times of the day and night. In his view the level of noise amounted to a nuisance.

Mr Shanlin was awarded £100 damages and Mrs Shanlin was awarded £750. In addition the sheriff granted an order forbidding Mrs Collins to carry on her business in a way which caused substantial disturbance and inconvenience to the Shanlins.

People are expected to put up with a normal amount of disturbance. If they are hypersensitive, they will not be able to establish that the disturbance is a nuisance unless it would not be tolerated by a normal person.

If you live in a noisy industrial area, you will not be able to get a court order prohibiting normal factory noise. But you may well be able to get an order prohibiting the same level of noise if you live in a quiet, leafy suburb.

Where a disturbance is considered to be a nuisance, the person carrying it on cannot argue that you knew it was going on before you moved into the area. However, you may fail to get the nuisance banned if it can be proved that you expressly or impliedly agreed to it – for instance, if you allowed a neighbour to go ahead and invest a substantial sum of money in a project which was clearly going to cause a disturbance.

Even where you do not acquiesce in a nuisance, you may lose your right to challenge it in court if you tolerate it for 20 years or more.

An Act of Parliament may authorise an activity which would otherwise amount to a nuisance – for instance, the operation of an oil-refinery in a previously non-industrial area. In that case, you will not be able to prevent the activity on the ground that it is a common law nuisance. However, only activities covered by the precise words of the Act will be included – disturbances which are not normally associated with the operation of a refinery, for example, would be unlikely to be covered, and could be banned.

Nuisances in title deeds It is common to find in the title deeds to property that certain activities are prohibited. For instance, a CONVEYANCE may ban the carrying on of business on certain land. If that land has houses built on it – for example, a tenement or even a whole housing estate – the ban will apply to each one.

Often the activities prohibited by title deeds are also nuisances at common law. But a wider range of activities can be prohibited by the deeds. For example, the keeping of pets may be banned and this condition can be enforced even though the pets are properly looked after and are not a nuisance to anyone.

If someone is causing you annoyance, and you wish to find out whether his activities are prohibited by his title deeds, consult a solicitor. If they are, you may be able to enforce the condition in his title deeds yourself or persuade the SUPERIOR to do it for you.

Statutory nuisances

Parliament has passed many laws dealing with environmental pollution and public health. Some of these laws only control or prohibit an activity if it amounts to a substantial disturbance or inconvenience to the public. Nowadays, however, most anti-pollution laws are quite precise about what is permitted and their enforcement depends only on whether the rules have been broken. This, applies, for example, to smoke and noise pollution. *See:* AIR POLLUTION; NOISE OFFENCES

The most important enforcement agencies are district and islands councils. In addition to many specific anti-pollution powers, they also have wide-ranging powers under the Public Health (Scotland) Act 1897 to control a variety of general nuisances – for example, premises that are dangerous or create a health risk, polluted streams and other watercourses, lavatories, animals kept in insanitary conditions, decaying cemeteries and businesses that are potential health hazards.

If a nuisance does exist, the council can obtain a sheriff court order requiring it to cease. Before seeking such an order, the council can serve an order on the person responsible, requiring him to take steps to end the nuisance. If the person responsible cannot be found, the council can serve the notice on the owner or any occupier (such as a tenant) of the premises concerned.

If a council refuses, or fails, to deal with a public health nuisance – even one that exists in its own houses – within 14 days of being told about it, 10 ratepayers can apply to the sheriff for an order requiring the nuisance to be dealt with. *See:* COUNCIL TENANCY.

If you suspect that someone is contravening the anti-pollution laws, you should contact the environmental health department of your district or islands council.

NULLITY

How legal defects can invalidate a marriage

Nullity is the legal term for something that does not exist. When a court declares a marriage to be a nullity, or 'null and void', it is then treated as if it had never existed.

Court actions for nullity of a marriage are much rarer than DIVORCE actions – there are only a handful of cases each year – because the grounds on which a marriage can be annulled are much more limited.

Some marriages – called 'void' marriages – do not legally exist because the basic legal requirements were not met when they were performed. Anyone with an interest – and not just the marriage partners – can take legal proceedings to have such a marriage annulled. A court decree, declaring there to be no marriage, may not always be strictly essential, but it is advisable to obtain one to make the position clear.

Other marriages – called 'voidable' marriages – are legally valid, but can be annulled by a court. In Scotland a marriage is voidable, and can therefore be annulled, only if one of the partners is impotent, and has been throughout the marriage. Unlike void marriages, a voidable marriage can be challenged only by one of the partners.

When a marriage is void

A marriage is void if:

- Either partner is under the age of 16.
- Either partner is already married.
- The partners are the same sex. A man who has a sex-change operation cannot validly marry another man, as the law still treats him as male.
- The partners are prohibited from marrying because they are too closely related. *See:* MARRIAGE
- Either partner did not genuinely consent to the marriage. A marriage will also be void if any consent given was not voluntary or was not validly obtained – for example, because consent was given through fear, or obtained by deception – or if unsoundness of mind (including extreme drunkenness) made either partner incapable of giving proper consent. Misleading someone into marrying you by lying about wealth, occupation or social position is not enough to make your partner's consent invalid.

The fact that the marriage formalities were not properly complied with – for instance, the person who conducted the ceremony was not authorised to do so – will not result in a marriage being void, once it has been registered. *See:* MARRIAGE

When a marriage is voidable

Either partner can seek a decree of nullity on the ground of his or her own impotence, or the impotence of the other partner. The impotence must be permanent and incurable, and must have existed at the time of the marriage.

The impotence need not have a physical cause – it can be due to, for example, frigidity or extreme dislike of the sexual act. However, in such cases it may be difficult to distinguish impotence from wilful refusal to consummate the marriage – which is *not* a ground for annulment, although it may be ground for divorce. If there is any doubt, annulment and divorce can be sought in the same court action. *See:* CONSUMMATION OF MARRIAGE; IMPOTENCE

The partner who is alleged to be impotent can successfully oppose annulment of the marriage on the ground that the other partner has behaved in such a way as to accept the marriage. Adopting a child, for instance, might be sufficient to indicate acceptance.

Obtaining annulment of a marriage

Only the Court of Session in Edinburgh can annul a marriage – a sheriff court cannot do so. The procedure is similar to that in a contested divorce case, with evidence being given in court.

THE MARRIAGE THAT WAS NEVER CONSUMMATED

A partner who is impotent can take action to annul his or her own marriage, so long as the impotence is permanent.

George and Mary married in 1950. Although George did not suffer from any physical disability, he did suffer from a psychological inability to have sexual intercourse. This existed at the time of the marriage.

In 1952 George sought medical advice and received hormone treatment. His doctor thought that the treatment might cure him, but by then Mary was unwilling to co-operate with him. As a result, the marriage was never consummated.

In 1966 George raised an action of nullity on the ground of his own impotence. This was opposed by Mary.

DECISION

The court granted decree of nullity, on the ground that George had shown that he had been impotent throughout the marriage.

In reaching this decision, the court considered whether the impotence was permanent, since Mary had prevented him from finding out whether the treatment had actually worked. It was decided that in the circumstances of the marriage his condition was permanent.

THE MARRIAGE THAT LACKED TRUE CONSENT

If both partners do not genuinely consent to a marriage, it is void.

A and B went through a marriage ceremony in a Glasgow registrar's office in 1975. Both partners were of Pakistani origin and of the Moslem religion.

After the wedding, neither partner saw or spoke to the other again. Neither considered that they were validly married, since their religion required all marriages to be conducted according to Moslem custom.

The woman raised an action of nullity on the ground that there had been no genuine consent to the marriage, and it was therefore void.

DECISION

The court granted decree of nullity, as it accepted that neither partner had given any real consent to the marriage.

LEGAL AID may be available.

When a court is considering an application for annulment of a marriage, it has the same powers in relation to access to, and custody of, children as it has in actions for judicial separation or divorce. *See:* ACCESS TO CHILDREN; CUSTODY OF CHILDREN

When granting a decree of nullity, the court has no power (as it has when granting decree of divorce) to order one partner to pay a periodical allowance or lump sum to the other. However, the court can make an award of ALIMENT for the support of any children.

Foreign marriage It may be difficult to have a marriage annulled if it took place abroad. The court will have to consider whether the formalities required in that country were complied with. *See:* FOREIGN MARRIAGE

The effect of annulment

A marriage which is void has no legal effect. So when it is annulled the partners are treated, for income tax and social security purposes, as if they had not married. If the man was receiving the married man's tax allowance, he may be reassessed for income tax and have to pay additional tax (but only in respect of the previous 6 years). The woman will not be able to obtain widow's benefit if he dies.

The child of a void marriage is illegitimate unless, at the time of the marriage and of the child's conception, one or both partners did not know the fact – such as a prohibited relationship or a pre-existing marriage – which made their marriage void.

When a voidable marriage is annulled, the man will probably not be reassessed for income tax. For social security purposes, the marriage is treated as a valid marriage which has been ended by divorce.

The child of a voidable marriage is treated as legitimate.

NUMBER-PLATE

Transferring a 'cherished' number

The law lays down strict rules for showing the registration number of a vehicle. *See:* MOTOR VEHICLE

It also makes provision for transferring a sought-after, or 'cherished', number – for example, one spelling the owner's initials – to another car.

BUYING A SPECIAL NUMBER-PLATE FOR THE CAR

You can buy the vehicle to which the plate is attached; or buy the plate only and then have it transferred.

There are several ways of obtaining the number-plate you want:

- You can buy and use the vehicle to which the number-plate is attached.
- If you buy – or already own – the vehicle to which the number-plate is attached, you can arrange for its transfer to another vehicle you own – for example, a new car that you have just purchased.
- You can buy the number-plate from someone who has it on his own vehicle and arrange for its transfer.
- The Department of Transport is compiling a list of unclaimed or out-of-use number-plates. They plan to sell these to the public for registration on purchasers' vehicles.

Arranging transfer

To transfer a number-plate, apply to your local vehicle licensing office. You need to fill in form V317 – 'Application for Transfer of Vehicle Registration Mark'.

Make an appointment with the local licensing office for the car bearing the cherished number to be inspected – to make sure that its details agree with the registration document (log book).

The cherished number is then transferred to your car, and the other vehicle is issued with a new number corresponding with its year of manufacture. Each vehicle is given a new registration document showing its new licence number. The old number on your car disappears from use.

What it costs The fee for transferring a cherished number is £80.

NURSERY SCHOOL

Education for children under 5 years old

Nursery schools and classes, where children between the ages of 3 and 5 can learn through play and social contact, are available in many areas but education authorities (regional and islands councils) are not required by the Education (Scotland) Act 1980 to provide them. They are given the *power* to provide them if they choose to do so.

Nursery schools run by the education authority are free. They must be held in safe and adequate buildings and have qualified teachers and staff.

When nursery schools are open

Nursery schools are part of the education system and their hours and holidays approximate to those of primary schools.

Many nursery schools take children for only half the day – one group attending in the mornings and another in the afternoons. The children have books, music and play games indoors and outdoors.

Some nursery classes are attached to local authority schools, sharing the same building, and the children move into the infants department when they reach 5 years of age.

Who can go to nursery school

Although there has been a steady increase in recent years in the number of pupils in nursery schools in Scotland, there are still insufficient places for all the under-5s who could attend.

The level of provision varies greatly over the country, with the majority of children attending on a part-time basis. Many others attend DAY NURSERIES run by local authorities, or privately run nurseries and playgroups.

State nursery schools usually give priority to children with special needs, such as those with language difficulties or other handicaps, children from a

ONE-PARENT FAMILY, or children living in deprived conditions.

If there are not enough nursery school places in your area, you can get together with other parents and write to the Director of Education to try to persuade the education authority to open more. You can also seek support from your local councillors.

Private nursery schools Privately run nursery schools have to register with the local social work department, which lays down regulations about buildings and staffing and has the power to supervise them. The regulations vary from area to area.

How parents can participate

The legal position of a child in a nursery school is exactly the same as that of an older child in a more senior school, except that, as education is not compulsory under 5 years of age, it is easier to take the child away. The school takes over the parents' authority and responsibility during school hours. It is up to the teachers how far they consult parents about their children.

Closing nursery schools

Since the passing of the Education (Scotland) Act 1981, education authorities cannot close their nursery schools without following the standard procedure for school closures. This requires consultation with parents and school councils.

Nursery classes attached to a primary school are subject to the same procedure when the education authority wants to close all such classes. *See:* SCHOOL

OATH

Making a binding promise to tell the truth

Anyone who gives evidence in court, or in some tribunal and most arbitration hearings, must first make a formal promise to tell the truth. The person can usually choose whether to make the promise in the form of a religious oath or a non-religious affirmation. Both are legally binding and breaking either can result in prosecution for PERJURY.

Taking an oath

In Scotland persons are put on oath by raising the ungloved right hand while standing, and repeating after the judge: 'I swear by almighty God' ('and as I shall answer to God at the great day of judgement' is sometimes added here) 'that I will tell the truth, the whole truth and nothing but the truth'. The Bible is not used.

However, members of non-Christian religious faiths may take the oath in a manner appropriate to their beliefs. Moslems, for example, may be allowed to swear on a copy of the Koran, if one is available.

If a procedure for taking the oath is inconvenient or impractical, the court can insist that the person affirms instead. This is what usually happens in the case of witnesses who are neither Christians nor Jews.

Making an affirmation

A person who chooses to make a non-religious affirmation promises to tell the truth by saying: 'I, John Smith, do solemnly, sincerely and truly declare and affirm . . .' followed by the words of the oath.

How oaths are valid

Oaths and affirmations are binding even if a mistake is made in the formal words of procedure. Someone who takes an oath cannot later claim that it was not binding because he does not believe in God.

OBSCENE PUBLICATIONS

Curbs on the portrayal of sex

A publication is obscene if it is likely to deprave and corrupt those who may see it by its depiction of sex.

It is not an offence to buy or read an obscene publication. However, it is an offence to publish obscene material in any form, including books, magazines, pictures and films. Publication usually means selling the material or exposing it for sale.

The selling, or exposing for sale, of obscene material can also be charged as the crime of shamelessly indecent conduct. Shameless indecency is a wide and vague offence which can also be used to prosecute the showing of obscene films or plays and even 'go-go' dancers in public houses. *See:* INDECENCY

The penalty for these offences is at the discretion of the court.

There are a number of other laws concerned with obscene or indecent material. Material is indecent when it shocks the average and reasonable person.

It is an offence to:

- Make, print, publish, sell or offer for sale obscene material.
- Distribute or offer to distribute obscene material for gain.
- Possess obscene material for gain.
- Display indecent material in any public place, or in any place which the public can enter without seeing a notice warning them of indecency.

Maximum penalty The penalty for any of these offences is up to 2 years' imprisonment and an unlimited fine.

- Send indecent or obscene material through the post.

Maximum penalty 12 months' imprisonment and an unlimited fine.

- Send a book, magazine, leaflet or advertisement which is unsolicited and which describes or illustrates human sexual techniques.

Maximum penalty A £2,000 fine.

OBSTRUCTION

Interfering with the execution of police duties

It is an offence to assault, resist, hinder or obstruct a police officer who is carrying out his duties. For example, if a police officer is in the process of arresting someone, and he is acting within his powers, it is an offence to try to stop him or try to rescue someone in his custody.

The maximum penalty is 3 months' imprisonment and a £1,000 fine. Where the accused has a previous conviction for the same offence within the past 2 years, the maximum penalty is 9 months' imprisonment and a £2,000 fine.

The fact that the person arrested is later acquitted will not excuse the behaviour of anyone who interferes at the time of the arrest.

The obstruction, however, must involve some physical force, such as an assault. It is not obstruction to give false information to the police – although this may be the crime of attempting to pervert the course of justice. *See:* PERVERTING THE COURSE OF JUSTICE

The police officer must also be entitled to do whatever he is doing. For example, he must not arrest anyone

TELLING LIES IS NOT OBSTRUCTION

An accused person can only be guilty of obstructing the police if he has used physical force. It is not obstruction simply to give false information.

Hugh Curlett, the holder of a provisional driving licence, was driving a lorry in Saltcoats, Ayrshire. He was accompanied by his father, who did not have a driving licence. The lorry collided with another vehicle.

During the police investigation of the accident, Hugh attempted to avoid prosecution for driving without adequate supervision by falsely stating to the police that his brother, James, who held a full licence, was also a passenger in the lorry. James and his father supported this story.

On being found out, Hugh, James and their father were prosecuted for deliberately obstructing the police in the execution of their duty. They were convicted, and appealed.

DECISION

The appeal court acquitted them. It said that obstruction had to have some physical aspect in order to be criminal.

without reasonable cause. If he does, the arrest is not legal and resistance does not amount to obstruction of a police officer.

Similarly, if the police want to search your home without a search warrant, and you refuse to let them do so, you are not necessarily guilty of obstruction. But they may have a right to enter to execute an arrest warrant. In such cases they may also have the right to search. If you physically resist them, you will be guilty of obstruction.

OCCUPANCY RIGHTS

Protecting your right to live in the family home

If one marriage partner is the sole owner or tenant of the family home, the other partner will usually have statutory 'occupancy rights' in the home. These rights, which are to be found in the Matrimonial Homes (Family Protection) (Scotland) Act 1981, arise automatically on marriage – you do not need to apply to a court for them.

If a married couple own or rent their home *jointly*, neither has any statutory rights of occupancy – but only because such rights are unnecessary. In this case each partner has a legal right to occupy the home as a result of being a joint owner or tenant.

You can only have statutory occupancy rights in a home situated in Scotland. However the 'home' does not need to be a house, or even your main residence: it can be a mobile home, a caravan, a houseboat – in fact, any accommodation used as a family residence, even if only occasionally. 'Home' includes a garden and other buildings that go with the accommodation.

The rights that are given

Since it is usually the husband who is the sole owner or tenant of the family home, it is the wife who normally has statutory occupancy rights. What follows, therefore, is based on that state of affairs. However it should be remembered that the rules apply *equally* to a husband whose wife is the sole owner or tenant.

A wife with statutory occupancy rights has:

1. A right not to be excluded from the family home, or any part of it, by her husband.

2. A right to return to the home if she has been excluded from it.

In addition, she can do the following even if she does not have her husband's consent:

- Pay any rent, rates, mortgage or other loan instalments due by him.
- Pay any bill which he has incurred in respect of the home – for instance, a bill for work carried out on the home.
- Carry out essential repairs. She can also carry out any non-essential repairs which have been authorised by a court.
- Force a landlord to carry out his duty to maintain the home.
- Protect her right to live in the home by taking steps which her husband is entitled to take. For instance, she can defend EVICTION proceedings taken against her husband by the landlord, if he fails to do so himself.
- Make any payments due by her husband for furniture and household effects (but not vehicles) which he owns, rents or is in the course of buying. She can also carry out any essential repairs to such items. This provision allows her, for example, to pay HP instalments on furniture, have the cooker mended or pay the television rental.

Recovering the cost If a wife makes payments which are her husband's responsibility, she can apply to the sheriff for an order determining how the cost should be divided between them, given their respective finances. For instance, if a wife is faced with paying her husband's mortgage instalments, she can apply to the sheriff for an order requiring her husband to pay all future instalments.

If the wife has actually paid out money, the sheriff can order her husband to repay her.

When occupancy rights are threatened

A wife with statutory occupancy rights cannot be lawfully prevented from exercising them, except:

- Where she gives up her rights.
- Where her husband loses his right to the home – for example, through BANKRUPTCY or an eviction.
- Where a marriage ends through death, divorce or annulment.
- By order of a court.

It is an offence for anyone to evict her without a court order, or to harass her in order to force her to leave. *See:* HARASSMENT

If a wife is unlawfully evicted by her husband, she can enforce her right to live in the home only by applying to court – either the sheriff court or Court of Session. If the court orders her husband to allow her to return, but he refuses, he will be in CONTEMPT OF COURT and may be fined or even imprisoned.

A wife can also ask the court for an order:

- Restricting her husband's occupancy rights – for instance, by prohibiting him from living in part of the home.
- Regulating the occupancy rights of both partners – for instance, by allowing them the exclusive use of separate parts of the home, or the same parts but at different times.

• Protecting occupancy rights – for instance, by granting an INTERDICT to prevent her being evicted by her husband.
• Giving her the right to possess and use furniture and other household effects (but not vehicles) belonging to her husband.

What the court must do When considering whether to make any of these orders, or an order enforcing a wife's occupancy rights, the court must look at all the circumstances, including:

1. The conduct of both partners.
2. Their needs and financial resources.
3. The needs of any children.
4. Whether the home, or items in the home, are used for business purposes.
5. Whether the husband has offered the wife suitable alternative accommodation.

None of these orders can be made if the effect would be to exclude the husband from the home entirely.

In an emergency the court can make an interim (temporary) order – so long as the husband is given an opportunity to put his case, either personally or through his lawyer.

WHEN CONTROL IS JOINT

If a couple own or rent their home jointly, each partner has a legal right to live there and neither can evict the other. Nor can either of them prejudice the rights of the other by entering into any transaction affecting the home – for instance, the sale by one of them of his or her half-share in the home. A third party who as a result acquires a right to the home cannot move in.

If either partner is violent, the other can apply to a court for an order excluding that partner from the home. *See:* BATTERED WOMAN

Either partner can carry out non-essential repairs or improvements without the other partner's consent, so long as these have been authorised by a court. And if either of them spends money on the home, with or without the consent of the other, the court can be asked to divide the cost fairly between them.

Selling the home

When a home is jointly owned, either partner can raise a court action – called an action of division and sale – to have the house sold. The court must look at all the circumstances, including the couple's conduct and needs, and may refuse to allow the sale, or postpone it.

Giving up occupancy rights

A wife is free to give up her occupancy rights in the family home. But she can only do so by signing a written, witnessed statement (a 'renunciation') to that effect. This must be done in the presence of a solicitor who is a NOTARY PUBLIC, before whom she must swear an oath that she is giving up her rights of her own free will, without coercion of any kind. If she does not do this, her renunciation will have no effect.

The renunciation of occupancy rights is only in respect of a named family home. If the couple move to a new home, the wife's occupancy rights will automatically revive – unless she renounces them again.

A wife could be asked to give up her occupancy rights as a condition of her husband obtaining a home. A building society, for example, could ask her to do this as a condition of granting her husband a MORTGAGE – though normally they do not do so. So could a landlord who offers a tenancy to her husband.

A wife should think very carefully before she gives up her statutory occupancy rights. If she does give them up, she will have no legal right to live in her own home. Nor will she be able to evict her husband if he is violent (see below). Legal advice should be obtained.

Protecting occupancy rights against third parties

A wife's occupancy rights would be of little use if her husband could prevent her living in the home by selling it or, if it is rented, transferring the tenancy. The law therefore allows her to continue in occupation even if he does sell or transfer the home to another person. That person has no right to live in the home as long as the wife continues to occupy it.

This rule also applies to any other kind of transaction by the husband that results in a threat to his wife's occupancy rights – including taking out a mortgage or granting a trust deed on behalf of creditors.

When there is no protection The rule will not apply if a wife has already given up her occupancy rights; or the transaction was binding on her husband before they married or before September 1, 1982. Nor will it apply if she gives her formal, written consent to the transaction. In these cases a third party can require her to move from the home.

LIVING TOGETHER

If an unmarried couple are living together, and the man owns or rents the home, the woman has no automatic occupancy rights. He can evict her when he wishes, without a court order.

However, she is entitled to apply to a court to be granted statutory occupancy rights. The court, when deciding whether to grant these rights, must look at all the circumstances, including the length of time the couple have lived together and whether they have any children.

Occupancy rights can be granted for an initial period of up to 3 months. The court can grant further extensions for up to 6 months at a time.

If an unmarried woman has occupancy rights, she is entitled to protect these rights by making payments – such as rent – which the man is required to make. She can also take action – such as defending eviction proceedings – when he fails to. However, unlike a married woman she can lose her occupancy rights if the man sells or transfers the home to someone else.

What is said above applies equally to a man who is living with a woman in a house owned or rented by her.

Building societies usually require a wife's formal consent to a mortgage taken out by her husband (instead of asking her to give up her occupancy rights). They can then remove her and sell the house if he later defaults.

It is sometimes possible to dispense with the need for a wife's consent. Her husband – or anyone with an interest, such as a building society – can ask a sheriff to dispense with consent on the ground that she is withholding it unreasonably; or is incapable of giving it; or cannot be found; or is under 18.

Buying in good faith A wife will lose her occupancy rights if someone buys the home from her husband on the strength of a sworn statement by him that there is no one with occupancy rights living there – or on the strength of a document stating that she has given up her rights or consented to the sale. But the buyer must act in good faith. If he knows that the husband is lying, or fails to make reasonable enquiries, the wife will not lose her rights.

Bankruptcy If the husband's property is sequestrated, and the home has to be sold, his wife will lose her occupancy rights. She can ask the court to end the sequestration and protect her occupancy rights – but it can only do so if satisfied that the purpose of the sequestration was mainly to defeat her rights.

Evicting a violent husband

If a wife has occupancy rights, she can apply to the sheriff for an order requiring her husband to leave the home. The sheriff can only grant the order if the husband's removal is necessary to protect his wife or children against injury, whether physical or mental. *See:* BATTERED WOMAN

OCCUPATIONAL PENSION

Providing for retirement through your job

The state provides a RETIREMENT PENSION in two parts – a basic flat rate paid to national insurance contributors and an additional earnings-related pension. The additional pension can, alternatively, be provided by a private, occupational scheme operated by employers and employees.

About half of Britain's working population are members of occupational pension schemes. In some, both employers and employees make contributions. In others, the employer pays it all. Many companies make membership of an occupational pension scheme a condition of employment.

Most schemes pay a pension based either on the final year's salary before retirement or on the average salary over a number of years. A typical scheme pays 1/60th of the salary for each year of membership in the scheme up to a maximum of 40/60ths – a pension amounting to two-thirds of the salary.

An alternative scheme might pay a lower fraction of the salary – say half – but with the addition of a lump sum equal to, perhaps, $1\frac{1}{2}$ times the salary.

Contracting out

When the earnings-related part of the pension is paid by an occupational scheme, it is known as the guaranteed minimum pension. That means it is equal to the amount that would be paid by the state, though many pension schemes pay considerably more.

A scheme that undertakes to pay the guaranteed minimum pension and fulfils certain other conditions allows the employer and employee to contract out of that part of the state scheme, with a consequent reduction in both their national insurance contributions.

An employer who wants to start a contracted-out scheme must give 3 months' notice to all employees and trade unions concerned. They can raise objections either to the employer or direct to the Occupational Pensions Board. If the objection is over-ruled, however, there is no provision for appeals, though if the Board appeared to have acted beyond their legal powers, the matter could be raised in the courts.

All occupational pension schemes must be approved by the Board before they can be contracted out.

When there are tax advantages

Schemes which fulfil certain conditions qualify for income tax advantages:

- The scheme must be established under a trust that cannot be wound up.
- The scheme's only purpose must be to pay pensions or similar benefits at death or on retirement.
- Employees' contributions must not be more than 15 per cent of their pay.
- Employees must not get contributions refunded except in very limited circumstances.

If an employee leaves and cannot transfer his rights to his new employment, his pension is usually 'frozen' until he reaches retirement age.

- Pensions must not be more than two-thirds of basic pay for 1 year out of the last 5 years at work or, alternatively, of average total pay for 3 or more consecutive years out of the last 10 years at work. The pension can, however, be linked to the cost of living index.

If the scheme meets the conditions, no income tax is paid on either employer's or employee's contributions.

If you change jobs

There are special safeguards covering the pension rights of someone who leaves a job in which he was a member of an occupational pension scheme.

The safeguards apply from April 6, 1975, to pension rights for those who, at the time of leaving, are 26 or over and have been contributing to the scheme for 5 years or more.

If the scheme is not contracted out of the state scheme, the pension rights will normally be preserved by the employer, to be paid when the leaver eventually retires.

As an alternative the pension rights may be transferred to a new employer's scheme.

If the scheme is contracted out, the rights must either be preserved by the employer or transferred to another contracted-out scheme.

An early leaver in a contracted-out scheme who does not meet the age and length of service qualifications for a preserved pension must have his guaranteed minimum pension rights transferred to the state scheme, and his employer has to pay a special premium to the state.

Refund of contributions

Normally, the rules covering the preservation and transfer of occupational pension rights prevent repayment of contributions.

But refunds can be made in certain circumstances, providing the employee is leaving the job and not just the scheme and providing the rules of the scheme do not forbid refunds.

The main circumstances under which refunds or part refunds can be made are:

- If the period of service covers any period of occupational pension scheme membership prior to April 6, 1975.
- If the employee leaves his job after less than 5 years. But if the scheme is contracted out, only after the guaranteed minimum pension has been transferred to the state scheme by the payment of a special premium.

Refunds of contributions are taxable.

If a scheme is wound up

An employer who wants to end a contracted-out occupational pension scheme must either preserve the employee's pension rights, to be paid on retirement; or transfer them to another scheme; or pay a special premium for the state to take over responsibility for the guaranteed minimum pension.

Providing pensions for widows

Contracted-out schemes must pay at least half the guaranteed minimum pension to the widow of a member.

Under the state scheme, a widow who qualifies for WIDOW'S PENSION or a WIDOWED MOTHER'S ALLOWANCE normally gets all of the additional pension built up by her husband's national insurance contributions on top of her basic flat-rate pension. So, in order that the widow of someone contracted out of the state scheme is not worse off, the state makes up the guaranteed minimum pension to a full pension.

The widow's guaranteed minimum pension must be paid to her and not to anyone else. But any benefit above the guaranteed minimum can, without her permission, be paid to another dependant; be reduced if she is more than 10 years younger than her husband; or not paid at all if the marriage took place after the husband's contracted-out employment ended and within 6 months of his death.

Claiming a pension

Four months before you reach the official state retirement age – 65 for men, 60 for women – the Department of Health and Social Security will ask you to make a claim for your state pension.

At the same time you will be told the amount of guaranteed minimum pension due to you under any contracted-out occupational pension scheme of which you have been a member. You will also be given the name and address of the administrators of the scheme.

Once you have this information, however, the responsibility for claiming the pension – including anything preserved under schemes you left in the past – is yours. Keep all documents relating to former schemes, and let the administrators of the schemes know if you change your address.

Benefits should be claimed when they become due. If you do not claim within 6 years you may lose money.

The earnings rule by which a retirement pension is reduced in respect of earnings over a certain level does not apply to the earnings related portion of a pension, but only to the basic flat rate part.

The guaranteed minimum pension cannot be arrested or seized if the person receiving it goes bankrupt.

The Department of Health and Social Security operates a tracing service for occupational pension schemes. The address is: Department of Health and Social Security Records Division, Special Section A (101B), Newcastle upon Tyne, NE98 IYX.

How an occupational pension affects unemployment benefit

Many people retire before the normal state retirement age of 65 (men) or 60 (women) with an occupational pension scheme.

By registering as unemployed, they get national insurance contribution credits, which in turn helps them keep a full national insurance record and get an eventual full RETIREMENT PENSION. During the first year they registered as unemployed, they can also qualify for UNEMPLOYMENT BENEFIT – £27.05 a week during 1983–4 for a single person.

The Government decided that from April 1981 occupational pensions over a certain level would reduce the amount of unemployment benefit payable to men aged 60–64. This level was set at £35 in 1981 and means, in effect, that occupational pensions over £35 will reduce any unemployment benefit you may be entitled to on a 10p for 10p basis. So, if your occupational pension is £62.10 or more a week for a single man, and £78.80 for a married man, you will not be able to get unemployment benefit. This does not stop you being credited with national insurance contributions. These are given to you automatically.

OCCUPIER'S LIABILITY

Taking care for other people's safety on your property

Anyone who occupies land or buildings (including houses) must take reasonable care to see that he does not cause injury or loss to people who are on his property. He must make sure that the property is in a reasonable state of repair and take all reasonable steps to secure the safety of people entering onto it.

If an occupier fails to take sufficient care, and as a result someone is injured or suffers loss, he can be sued for NEGLIGENCE.

Who is an occupier?

The occupier is the person who has possession and control of the property. Often this will be the owner. So if you own your home and live in it, you are the legal occupier.

However, it is possible to be an occupier even though you are not an owner. For example, if you are a tenant – whether you rent from a local authority or a private landlord – you are the legal occupier of your home. And if you are buying a new home, but take up residence before the conveyancing (that is, the process of transferring ownership) is completed, you automatically become the legal occupier even though you are not yet the owner.

The law applies to land as well as buildings. A contractor on a building site, for example, is usually the legal occupier of the site and must therefore take care to ensure that the site is reasonably safe for anyone entering it.

When is an occupier at fault?

There are many situations in which an occupier can be at fault, and be liable to be sued for injury or loss caused to someone else.

For instance, if a chunk of plaster falls from your bedroom ceiling onto a guest, and he is injured, you will be liable if you knew or ought to have known that the ceiling was not in good repair. You will also be liable if someone falls down the stairs in your house because the stair carpet is insecure, or injures himself through tripping over a loose floorboard, and you were aware of the danger, or ought to have been.

Businesses can also be liable if they fail to take sufficient care for the safety of customers and passers-by. For example, a customer who slips on a patch of black ice on a walkway leading from the pavement up to a shop may be able to sue if no reasonable steps were taken to clear it. And a passer-by who is injured by a slate falling from the roof of a shop or office may be able to obtain damages if he can show that the roof was inadequately maintained.

Some properties involve very obvious dangers – for instance, railway property, with its fast-moving trains and overhead power lines; or electricity generating stations, with their potentially lethal transformers. Occupiers of this sort of property must take reasonable steps to inform people that they should not go onto the property and expose themselves to danger. What steps are reasonable will depend on the age of the injured person and whether his entering the property should have been anticipated.

The fact that an injured person is a trespasser does not prevent the occupier of the property being liable if he has been negligent. However, in deciding whether the occupier was at fault, a court will consider whether the presence of such a trespasser should have been anticipated.

For instance, if there are young children around who can reasonably be expected to tamper with dangerous machinery, a court may consider that a reasonable occupier would have erected an impenetrable barrier to keep them out. But if there are older children, the court may consider that it would be sufficient to erect a barrier which they would have to take some trouble to overcome.

Where adults are concerned, the occupier of dangerous property would not be expected to take as much care. Even a broken fence might be treated as sufficient indication to such a person that he should not go through it – onto a railway line, for example.

If the dangers are not obvious, an occupier may be expected to put up a warning notice. However, that will not necessarily be sufficient on its own – particularly if it is a highly technical notice which is difficult to understand.

When people other than the occupier are responsible

Sometimes the responsibility for making sure that premises are reasonably safe lies with someone other than the occupier. For instance, where the occupier is a tenant, the *landlord* may be liable if an accident occurs through lack of maintenance or repair for which he, the landlord, is responsible. Most landlords of publicly and privately rented housing are legally responsible for maintenance and repairs. *See:* LANDLORD AND TENANT

A tradesman may also be liable if he leaves premises in an unsafe condition. For instance, an electrician will be liable if he negligently connects electrical wiring and someone is electrocuted as a result.

A professional man can also be liable if he is negligent. An architect, for example, may be negligent in designing a building, choosing its site or supervising its construction. If someone is injured as a result, the architect will be liable. *See:* PROFESSIONAL NEGLIGENCE

THE BUILDING THAT WAS AN ADVENTURE PLAYGROUND

Occupiers of derelict buildings must take reasonable steps to prevent children who are in the area being injured in them.

In March 1970, 10 year old Graham Telfer was injured when he fell through the roof of a derelict building in Kinning Park, Glasgow. The legal occupier was the Co-op, which was negotiating the sale of the building to Glasgow Corporation.

It was easy for children to get into the building and many of them did so. It offered every possible allurement for them – sliding doors that had come off their runners and could be pushed in, inspection pits full of water and rubbish, glass partitions to be broken, a roof with pigeons and pigeons' eggs, 'wee round spiral stairs' and even, for a time, a derelict van. The building had in effect become a glorified adventure playground for the children of the neighbourhood.

Graham Telfer sued the Co-op for damages for the injuries which he had received.

DECISION

The court decided that the Co-op was liable to pay damages for the boy's injuries.

Occupiers of derelict buildings in areas frequented by children were required to take reasonable steps to keep them out of such buildings. The Co-op had not taken such steps.

However, Graham's damages were reduced by half because he knew that he should not have been there and was therefore partly responsible for his own injuries.

OFFENSIVE WEAPON

From guns and knives to bottles and lethal potatoes

Anything capable of causing injury can be classed as an offensive weapon, but whether it is illegal to possess such an object depends on the circumstances.

Offensive weapons fall into three categories:

- Objects which are deliberately made to cause personal injury, such as guns (except airguns and guns used for killing game), swords, bayonets, daggers, truncheons or knuckledusters. It is an offence to have such an object in a public place without lawful authority or reasonable excuse.
- Objects which have been adapted to cause personal injury – for instance, a broken bottle, a potato with a razor blade stuck in it, a severed bicycle chain or a sharpened piece of cutlery. It is an offence to have such an object in a public place without lawful authority or reasonable excuse.
- All other objects which have not been specially designed to cause personal injury – for example, a shotgun, air-rifle, sheath-knife, pen-knife, hammer or steel-capped boots.

It is an offence to have such an object in a public place if the prosecution can prove that the accused person intended to use it to cause personal injury. So a pair of steel-capped boots may be classed as an offensive weapon if they are worn by a football supporter, although they would not be considered offensive if worn by someone simply to go to work.

If a case involving an offensive weapon is tried summarily (before a judge without a jury) the maximum penalty is 3 months' imprisonment or a £2,000 fine, or both. In cases dealt with under solemn procedure (before a judge and jury), the maximum penalty is 2 years' imprisonment or an unlimited fine, or both. *See:* CRIMINAL PROCEEDINGS

Flick-knives There are special laws forbidding the manufacture, sale or possession of flick-knives – knives with a concealed blade that springs out. The maximum penalty for breaking these laws is 6 months' imprisonment and a £1,000 fine.

THE THIEF WHO OWNED A SHEATH-KNIFE

Possession of an object which is not designed as a weapon, but may be used as one, is an offence only if there was an intention to use it to cause personal injury.

David Rennicks was arrested after breaking into premises in Airdrie owned by the Co-operative Society Ltd. He was found to have a sheath-knife in his possession.

He was charged with housebreaking with intent to steal, and with having an offensive weapon in his possession. He pleaded guilty to the housebreaking charge but denied the offensive weapon charge.

In his evidence to the sheriff he explained that he had the knife in his possession for use as a housebreaking tool, not to cause personal injury.

DECISION

Rennicks was acquitted of the offensive weapon charge after the sheriff decided that he did not have the knife for the purpose of causing personal injury.

THE TAXI–DRIVER'S COSH

The courts will rarely accept self-defence as an excuse for possessing an offensive weapon.

William Grieve was a taxi-driver in Edinburgh. At 11 o'clock one night he picked up a Mr and Mrs Luck and took them to their destination in Pilrig, Edinburgh.

Mr Luck then began to argue over the extra charge made by Mr Grieve because there was more than one passenger. During the argument blows were struck and Mr Grieve produced from his driver's compartment a 2 foot length of rubber hose with a piece of metal at the end.

The quarrel ended and both men separately reported the matter to the police. On investigation, the police found the rubber hose in the taxi and Mr Grieve was charged with possession of an offensive weapon.

Mr Grieve's defence was that Edinburgh taxi-drivers were at risk of attack at night and that it was usual to carry some object for self-defence. The trial judge rejected this defence and convicted Mr Grieve. He appealed.

DECISION

The appeal court upheld Mr Grieve's conviction. It said that one of the purposes of prohibiting offensive weapons was to stop citizens taking the law into their own hands. Taxi-drivers were no more entitled to carry an offensive weapon in case of attack than any other member of the public.

Lawful authority or reasonable excuse

The people who have 'lawful authority' to carry weapons are soldiers or policemen who carry rifles or truncheons in public as a matter of duty.

It may be a 'reasonable excuse' for carrying an offensive weapon that you need it for self-defence, but the courts will only rarely accept this as a justification. Such a situation might arise if you are carrying a large sum of money and have a weapon to protect yourself against robbery.

Searching for weapons

A police constable can stop and search any person he reasonably suspects of carrying an offensive weapon in public. It is an offence to obstruct the constable in the execution of his duty – for example, by refusing to wait to be searched. Anyone who does so can be arrested and fined up to £1,000.

OFFICIAL SECRETS

Preventing the disclosure of official information

Anyone who comes into possession of information from a government source may be committing a criminal offence under the Official Secrets Acts if he passes it on to an unauthorised person.

The Acts cover only information obtained from central government, not local government. But that includes much more than military or other matters obviously affecting state security.

A civil servant, for example, who discloses what goes on in the Department of Health and Social Security or the Scottish Office commits an offence under the Official Secrets Acts. A local government official, on the other hand, who reveals information about his council's social work department would not be guilty of such an offence – although he might be disciplined by the council if disclosure was forbidden, either expressly or by implication, under the terms of his employment contract.

The penalty for passing on or receiving information contrary to the Official Secrets Acts is 2 years' imprisonment and an unlimited fine. *See:* ESPIONAGE; TREASON

People engaged on government work are often asked to sign an Official Secrets Acts declaration. Such a declaration has no legal effect and it is not an offence to refuse to sign. However, refusal is likely to prejudice the chances of employment in some cases.

Access to information

The Official Secrets Acts are only one aspect of government secrecy. Cabinet proceedings, for example, are secret – indeed, the existence of many (though not all) of the various Cabinet Committees is not even publicly acknowledged. There is no legal right of access to government documents. When documents are 30 years old, some are made available in the Public Records Office, but the government decides which to release and the citizen has no right to see those which are withheld.

In addition, official agencies operate secret rules and guidelines in countless day to day matters, such as deciding priority for the installation of telephones, or deciding whether to prosecute alleged offenders.

Individuals have no right to information on such matters and an MP has no right to investigate them. Many such matters are also outside the jurisdiction of the ombudsman.

OFF-SALE LICENCE

Regulations for shops that sell alcohol

Any shop that sells alcohol, as the whole or part of its business, needs an off-sale licence – a licence stipulating that the drink purchased can only be consumed off the premises.

Off-sale licences are granted by the licensing board of the district (or islands) council and have to be renewed every three years.

An off-sale licence allows alcohol to be sold from 8.00 a.m. until 10 p.m. On Sundays there are no permitted off-sales.

It is generally illegal to sell alcohol to anyone under 18. The maximum penalty is a £400 fine and loss of licence.

It is also illegal to allow alcohol to be drunk on the premises. The maximum penalty is a £400 fine and the risk of disqualification from holding a licence.

See: LICENSED PREMISES; LIQUOR OFFENCES

OMBUDSMEN

The officials who keep watch on other officials

The job of an ombudsman is to guard members of the public against injustice or unfair treatment by government officials. Although appointed by the government, he has the same independence from it as a judge.

The ombudsman's role is largely that of watchdog. He cannot punish erring officials or reverse their decisions; he can only expose bad administration and criticise those responsible. But his judgment usually leads to prompt action by the official bodies he criticises. If they fail to make amends, his opinions can be used as a weapon against them in Parliament, in local councils or in the media.

When a complaint is made

When a complaint is made, an ombudsman will listen to both sides in private. He has the same power as the courts to order people to give evidence and documents to be produced for inspection. Any attempt to obstruct him or his officials can be punished by the Court of Session as CONTEMPT OF COURT.

At the end of his inquiry, the ombudsman gives an opinion on whether there has been bad administration or injustice. He can recommend changes in the system of administration and suggest that the authority concerned should recompense a person he considers to have been badly treated. But his decisions *cannot* be legally enforced.

Three categories of ombudsman

There are three sorts of ombudsman, each with his own investigating staff:

- The parliamentary ombudsman, officially known as the Parliamentary Commissioner for Administration. He deals with complaints against central government departments – for instance, the Department of Health and Social Security or the Scottish Office.
- The health ombudsman, officially known as the Health Service Commissioner for Scotland. He has the task of investigating complaints about the Scottish health service. In practice the Parliamentary Commissioner for Administration acts as the Scottish health ombudsman – and also as health ombudsman for England and Wales. In Northern Ireland complaints are dealt with by a Commissioner for Complaints.
- The local government ombudsman, officially known as the Commissioner for Local Administration in Scotland. He is responsible for investigating complaints against Scottish local authorities. There are three Commissioners in England and one in Wales. Complaints in Northern Ireland are dealt with by a Commissioner for Complaints.

Grounds for complaining

In considering a complaint, an ombudsman has no power to question the law or a government decision. He can look only for evidence of 'maladministration' by public officials. There is no legal definition of 'maladministration', but the following paragraphs give an idea of what can be considered reasonable grounds for complaint.

- Delay. Delay caused by inefficiency – for instance, in processing a social security claim – is maladministration. Delay caused by industrial action is not, provided the department takes reasonable steps to limit its effects.

A council was reprimanded for taking 7 days to inform a mother that her daughter had been placed in care.

- Rules. Internal departmental rules should normally always be followed. But in some cases ombudsmen have decided that the rules themselves amount to maladministration and ought to be changed.
- Discrimination. Government and local authority departments are expected to treat everyone in the same way, without discriminating on grounds of race, sex, religion, social status or anything else. An ombudsman can look at departmental files to reassure himself on this point.
- Procedure. Failing to follow statutory procedures can amount to maladministration.
- Concealing facts. Failure to keep people informed of decisions that affect them – for example in planning matters – is considered to be maladministration. Ombudsmen have wide powers to obtain information about concealment.
- Misbehaviour. Officials have been reproved for rudeness or inconsiderate behaviour.
- Faulty advice. It is maladministration for an official to give incorrect or misleading advice, either in printed form or in person, to a member of the public.
- Inefficiency. Loss of a file or letter, failure to keep an appointment and bad arithmetic on a tax demand are examples of inefficiency which have been criticised by ombudsmen.

If a department applies the law correctly, it cannot be found guilty of maladministration, however unfair or ridiculous the result may appear. But the ombudsman may report to Parliament any injustice caused by a law.

How a complaint is pursued

When an ombudsman receives a complaint which he decides he can consider, he makes a request for the relevant facts or documents from government ministers, councillors or officials involved. In practice these are almost always made available, as failure to do so may lead to proceedings for contempt of court.

An ombudsman's inquiry is not restricted by the Official Secrets Act, and his findings are protected from the laws of DEFAMATION.

The person who has complained is usually interviewed at his home, where he can have a Member of Parliament, a local councillor, a friend or a lawyer to help him. The procedure is private. At no time does the complainer have to meet the officials against whom he has made his complaint. There is no opportunity for cross-examination, as there is in the courts.

Staff at the department involved are

questioned by the ombudsman's investigators, and their files will be scrutinised. The department is given the opportunity to check the facts in any statement to be included in the ombudsman's report; but it cannot comment on any conclusion he draws.

What does it cost?

It costs nothing to complain to an ombudsman – even if your complaint is not upheld. If you choose to consult a solicitor before making a complaint, you may be able to get legal advice free, or at a reduced cost. *See:* LEGAL ADVICE

Making a complaint to the parliamentary ombudsman

The Parliamentary Commissioner for Administration deals with all complaints made against government departments and official Crown bodies.

He can investigate any action that has been ordered or carried out by any minister or official of a government department, or anyone acting as agent for the department.

Who can complain? Anyone, or any organisation – except for a national or local government committee or department, or an organisation wholly or mainly financed by public funds. However, individual members of such bodies can complain if they consider themselves personally to be victims of maladministration.

The ombudsman cannot investigate a case in which the complainer has (or had) a right of appeal to a tribunal – for instance, a social security tribunal or industrial tribunal – or a right to take legal proceedings in respect of the matter complained of – unless he thinks it is unreasonable to expect the complainer to take action of this kind.

All complaints must normally be made within 12 months of the time when the action complained of first came to the attention of the complainer.

How to complain All complaints to the parliamentary ombudsman must be made through a member of the House of Commons – but not necessarily through the Member of Parliament who represents the complainer's constituency.

Usually the first step is to give your own MP full details of your complaint and all the circumstances. He is not obliged to pass your case to the ombudsman: he may be able to deal with it successfully himself, or he may think that the matter should not be pursued.

If that happens, and you still want to press your complaint, you must contact another MP and ask for his help.

It is possible for you to write directly

HOW THE OMBUDSMEN'S POWERS ARE LIMITED

An ombudsman has no power to question the law or a decision by Government. He is limited to investigating 'maladministration' of laws and government decisions.

He has no power to interfere with a nationalised industry, a private body such as a trade union or a professional organisation. He cannot question the findings of a court or tribunal.

When there is some other way

An ombudsman cannot normally investigate a complaint when the complainer has the right of appeal to some other body or person.

You cannot, for example, complain to him that you are being charged too much tax or that you are not getting enough social security benefit, because in both cases you can appeal to an independent tribunal.

That applies also to decisions by local planning committees, because persons affected can appeal to a government minister.

When a policy decision is involved

When a decision is made by a government official – say a social security or tax official – and there is no evidence of bad administration, the ombudsman cannot accept a complaint from the person affected.

If, for example, you wish to complain about a ruling on supplementary benefits, you can complain only about any administrative failings which may have led to the decision.

There is one exception to that rule – where a decision is so unjust that the ombudsman rules that the decision itself amounts to maladministration.

When legal issues are in dispute

Legal disputes, which would normally come before the courts, can be settled only by the courts, and the ombudsman cannot interfere.

When professional skill is criticised

A decision taken by a person using his professional judgment cannot be questioned by an ombudsman. The health ombudsman, for example, cannot criticise a clinical decision taken by a doctor.

If a doctor decides that a patient should wait for an operation because other cases are more urgent, the ombudsman cannot intervene.

A complaint can be considered only if it is shown that the hospital handled the waiting list in an inefficient manner.

Specific restrictions in each category

In addition to those general limitations on the ombudsman's powers of inquiry, there are particular restrictions in each of the three categories:

The parliamentary ombudsman cannot deal with:

- Complaints of individual pay and conditions of employment made by any publicly paid employee.
- Government contracts, commercial deals or tenders, or government securities.
- Any matter involving national security or any investigation of crime ordered by the Home Secretary.
- Honours.
- Extradition.
- Any action taken by British officials (except consuls) outside the United Kingdom.
- Matters in the Channel Islands or the Isle of Man.
- Foreign affairs, if the Foreign Secretary rules that the action complained of could affect international relations.

The health ombudsman cannot deal with:

- Pay and conditions in the Health Service.
- Contracts for the supply of drugs.

The local ombudsman cannot deal with:

- Individual working conditions or dismissal of local government staff.
- Local contracts involving bus services, docks, markets, entertainment, or the running of industrial estates – but he can deal with complaints about the buying and selling of land and the provision of local services such as housing.
- General policy or spending decisions of the local council.
- Police action in the investigation or prevention of crime.
- Internal school matters relating to curriculum, discipline and management – but he can investigate complaints against the general administration of education and the procedures for changing schools or allocating children to certain schools.

WATCHDOGS THAT HAVE MORE THAN JUST A BARK

Much of the power of the ombudsmen derives from their ability to expose bad administration and to suggest improvements. They may even recommend compensation for the victims.

to the ombudsman at Church House, Great Smith Street, London SW1P 3BW or 71 George Street, Edinburgh EH2 3EE. But if you do so, the ombudsman will then ask your MP if he would like to have the matter investigated. Unless the MP – or another Member – agrees, the ombudsman cannot take your complaint any further.

A complaint need not be made directly by the person involved. It can be made on his behalf by an agent, such as a lawyer, or by an organisation, such as a trade union.

A complaint can be made on behalf of a person who is dead – for instance, by a widow who believes her husband was unfairly dealt with – or on behalf of a person who is mentally or physically unable to complain himself. The complaint can be made by a member of the family, or even by a friend.

When the ombudsman reports When the ombudsman's investigation is complete, he issues a report, setting out his conclusions and any criticism he may have of the department or individuals involved. His report is sent to the MP who handled the complaint and to the department and any individual named in the complaint.

If the ombudsman is convinced that injustice has been caused, he may also lay his report before each House of Parliament.

The ombudsman is barred by law from saying anything more about the case. But the MP or the complainer can pursue it further if they wish, either by taking the matter up with the Minister concerned, raising it in the House of Commons or by seeking further press publicity.

The ombudsman's report is protected against any action for defamation, but subsequent publicity about the complaint is not. Nor is it certain that the OFFICIAL SECRETS Acts do not apply to such publicity.

In most cases the department concerned puts the matter right if the ombudsman upholds a complaint. If it fails or refuses to do so, the MP involved may decide to take further action, or the House of Commons Select Committee which scrutinises the ombudsman's work may ask the department to explain why no action has been taken.

Complaining to the health ombudsman

The Health Commissioner for Scotland and his staff handle complaints of maladministration in hospitals or elsewhere in the Scottish Health Service. They examine allegations of injustice or hardship caused by maladministration, failure in a service, or failure to provide a service which is supposed to be provided.

The health ombudsman can investigate the area health boards – which administer hospitals – and the Common Services Agency for the Scottish Health Service, which administers certain central services such as the ambulance and blood transfusion services.

He cannot investigate any complaint that can be (or has been) dealt with by the MENTAL WELFARE COMMISSION.

General health policy in Scotland is directed by the Scottish Home and Health Department of the Scottish Office. Any complaint of maladministration there should be made to the Parliamentary ombudsman.

Who can complain? Anyone, or any organisation – except for a national or local government committee or department or an organization wholly or mainly financed by public funds. All complaints must normally be made within 12 months of the time when the action complained of first came to the attention of the complainer.

HOW THE OMBUDSMAN GOT HIS NAME

The first ombudsman (which is a Swedish word meaning agent or representative) was appointed in 1809 by the Swedish Government. The idea has since been copied by several other countries.

In Britain the ombudsmen do not have such strong powers as in Sweden. The jobs are usually given to lawyers or senior civil or public servants.

The ombudsman cannot investigate a case in which the complainer has (or had) the right to take legal proceedings in respect of the matter complained about, unless he thinks it is unreasonable to expect the complainer to take such action.

If someone has died, or is unable to make a complaint himself, a relative or friend can make the complaint on his behalf.

How to complain Complaints should normally be made first to the area health board involved (or to the Common Services Agency). It should be given a reasonable time to investigate the complaint and reply to it. If the result of this is unsatisfactory, write direct to the Health Service Commissioner for Scotland, 71 George Street, Edinburgh EH2 3EE.

When the ombudsman reports The ombudsman's report is published in the same way as that of the parliamentary ombudsman. The authorities concerned usually react in the same way as government departments do to the parliamentary ombudsman's report.

Complaining to a local government ombudsman

The Commissioner for Local Administration in Scotland deals with complaints against local authorities, their committees and employees. That covers regional, district and islands councils (but not new town development corporations or community councils), water development boards, river purification boards; and also committees such as the education, fire service, police and social work committees. Also covered are Children's Panel Advisory Committees. *See:* CHILDREN'S

PANEL; LOCAL AUTHORITY

The Commissioner cannot investigate the actions of individual police officers. *See:* POLICE

The Commissioner can investigate any allegation that injustice has been caused by maladministration.

Who can complain Anyone, or any organisation – except for a national or local government committee or department or an organisation wholly or mainly financed by public funds. All complaints must normally be made within 12 months of the time when the action complained of first came to the attention of the complainer.

The ombudsman cannot investigate a case in which the complainer has (or had) the right to take legal proceedings in respect of the matter complained about, unless he thinks it is unreasonable to expect the complainer to take such action.

How to complain Complaints should be made first of all to the authority involved. It should be given a reasonable time to investigate the complaint and to reply. If the reply is unsatisfactory, you should then make your complaint, in writing, to a councillor who is a member of the authority. He can then pass the complaint on to the Commissioner.

If the councillor fails to do so, you can complain directly to the commissioner. Write to him at 5 Shandwick Place, Edinburgh EH2 4RG.

When the ombudsman reports When an investigation is completed, the Commissioner sends a copy of his report to the complainer, any councillor who referred the complaint to him and the authority to which the complaint relates.

The authority must make the report available for public inspection for 3 weeks and must advertise that fact in the local press – unless the Commissioner rules that the matter should be kept private in the public interest.

If the complaint has been upheld, the Commissioner's report will recommend what action should be taken – for instance, an apology, a change in council procedures or compensation.

The local authority must consider the report and tell the Commissioner what action it proposes to take. If no satisfactory action is taken within a reasonable time, the Commissioner will issue another report, drawing attention to the matter. He cannot, however, force the authority to take any action.

ONE-PARENT FAMILIES

The extra help that can be obtained

Single parents of either sex, whether divorced, separated, deserted or unmarried, can claim extra 'one-parent' benefit of £4.05 a week (in 1983–4) for the first child in the family who qualifies for CHILD BENEFIT.

A single parent who is not working can also claim SUPPLEMENTARY BENEFIT to provide the family with a minimum income. The amount of benefit payable depends on the parent's other income, the number of children and whether anyone in the family has any special needs. A single parent – father or mother – is not required to be available for work to qualify for benefit so long as at least one dependent child is under 16.

When calculating the amount of supplementary benefit payable, most other social security benefits, including child benefit and the one-parent benefit are taken into account in full. So a single parent on supplementary benefit gains no advantage from the one-parent increase because it reduces the amount of supplementary benefit payable.

A single parent who has a low-paid job may be able to qualify for FAMILY INCOME SUPPLEMENT. He or she need only work at least 24 hours a week, instead of the 30 hours required of other claimants.

How aliment affects benefit

Most sources of income, including any ALIMENT (maintenance) paid by the other parent, or periodical allowance (following a DIVORCE) paid by a former partner, are taken into account in full when calculating a single parent's entitlement to supplementary benefit.

If no aliment is being paid, the Department of Health and Social Security may urge a single parent claiming benefit (who will usually be a woman) to press for payment, and to take legal action if necessary. They may also approach her husband or the father of her child themselves, and invite him to make voluntary payments. However, if she will not press for payment, or the man refuses to pay, the Department will pay benefit. It is then entitled to take court action itself against the man in order to recover some of the cost of paying benefit. *See:* ALIMENT

A woman who is receiving aliment or periodical allowance under a court order may be able to get the man to agree to pay the money direct to the Department of Health and Social Security. Her supplementary benefit can then be paid in full without deducting the aliment or periodical allowance, and she will not have to worry about payments not being paid on time, or being made only irregularly.

The earnings limit

A single parent can earn up to £4 a week without affecting the amount of supplementary benefit payable. In addition, he or she can keep half of any earnings between £4 and £20 a week, again without affecting benefit.

Any remaining earnings (net) are taken into account when calculating the amount of benefit payable. However, certain expenses, such as fares to work or the cost of employing a CHILD MINDER, can be deducted from the net earnings figure when the calculation is being made.

A woman receiving supplementary benefit as a single parent may have it stopped if she lives with a man as his wife. *See:* COHABITATION

How tax is reduced

If a single parent pays INCOME TAX, his or her liability may be reduced by an additional personal allowance – even though the child allowance itself has not been granted since April 1979.

The additional personal allowance – £1,150 in the 1984–5 tax year – is claimed in advance of an income tax return. Taxable income is reduced by the amount of the allowance. *See:* INCOME TAX

Other kinds of assistance

You may be able to obtain help from your local social work department if you decide to take a job. Local authority day nurseries give priority to the children of single parents. Alternatively, the social work department should be able to provide you with a list of people who are registered child minders. *See:* CHILD

MINDER; DAY NURSERIES

Help is also available from many voluntary organisations. For information, contact the Scottish Council for Single Parents, 44 Albany Street, Edinburgh EH1 3QR. The Council is a co-ordinating body consisting of all those organisations that are concerned with one-parent families.

Gingerbread (Association for One-Parent Families) is a self-help organisation which provides social contacts and support through regular meetings. For more information, write to Gingerbread, 38 Hope Street, Glasgow G2 6AE (or 4A Lauriston Gardens, Edinburgh, EH3 9HH).

OPTICIAN

What to do if your eyes need testing

Free sight-testing is available for everyone under the National Health Service, but most people have to pay something towards the cost of any spectacles that they may need.

If you would like your sight tested, make an appointment with an optician after making sure that he accepts work under the National Health Service – most opticians do.

Ophthalmic opticians are qualified to test sight and supply glasses. Ophthalmic medical practitioners are doctors who are qualified to test sight. Dispensing opticians are qualified only to supply glasses.

Lists of approved ophthalmic medical practitioners, ophthalmic opticians and dispensing opticians are kept by your local health board.

If you are housebound, an optician may be prepared to test your eyes at your home. The test will still be free but you may have to pay for the visit. Alternatively, ask your doctor to arrange a sight test for you in hospital.

Your choice of glasses

The optician will tell you if you need glasses. You then have four choices:

- You can have NHS lenses fitted to a NHS frame.
- You can have NHS lenses fitted to a private frame (if it is the right shape and otherwise suitable).
- You can have private lenses in a private frame.

WHEN IN DOUBT, ASK AN OPTICIAN FOR A FREE TEST

Ophthalmic opticians who accept work under the National Health Service do not charge for sight testing unless they have to travel to the patient's home.

- If you already have spectacles, you can ask the optician if the frame is in fit condition and otherwise suitable to take new NHS or private lenses.

When glasses can be obtained at no cost

Statutory charges are payable for NHS lenses and NHS frames, but some people are entitled to receive NHS spectacles without any charge:

- Children under 16 years of age or young persons under 19 receiving full-time education in a school, college or university.
- Persons who receive (or whose partners receive) supplementary benefit or family income supplement, or who get free milk and vitamins or free prescriptions because of low income.

People with a low income who do not fall into the above categories are entitled to free glasses or a reduction in NHS charges. They should ask the optician for form F1, fill in details of their financial circumstances and send it to the local social security office. If the charge has already been paid, a refund can be claimed on form F6, obtainable from the local social security office.

For more information about NHS glasses and what counts as low income, ask for leaflet G11 at your post office or local social security office.

How to complain about an optician

Anyone who is dissatisfied about a sight test or spectacles provided under the NHS should complain in writing within 6 weeks to the local health board secretary. *See:* DOCTOR AND PATIENT

If the spectacles are unsatisfactory, first discuss it with the optician.

Complaints about the standard of service, such as missed appointments or long delays, should also be made to the health board.

If injury or loss is suffered, for example through an accident caused by wrongly prescribed or dispensed glasses, it may be possible to raise a legal action for NEGLIGENCE.

Patients cannot complain to the health board about private lenses or frames or the prices charged for them. All frames and lenses supplied privately are sold under the same rules and laws as any other consumer goods.

Any complaints about private treatment can be made to the Association of Optical Practitioners or, in the case of dispensing opticians, to the Association of Dispensing Opticians, 22 Nottingham Place, London, W1.

Complaints about improper behaviour by an optician can be made to the General Optical Council, 41 Harley Street, London, W1.

Ending the opticians' monopoly on selling glasses

In 1984 legislation was before Parliament to end the opticians' monopoly on the sale of spectacles. Ordinary retailers are to be allowed to sell them – but only on a prescription issued in the previous 2 years, following a sight test by a qualified optician or doctor.

Retailers will not be able to sell spectacles for children under 16. Nor will they be able to sell contact lenses.

NHS spectacles will cease to be generally available, but they will still be provided free of charge to the present exempt groups – children under 16 and people on supplementary benefit, family income supplement or low incomes.

The present restrictions on advertising will be relaxed to allow opticians the freedom to advertise.

Free sight-testing will remain available to everyone.

OVERCROWDING

When too many people stay in one house

There are legal limits to the number of people who are allowed to live in any one house.

A house which is so overcrowded that it is dangerous to the health of those who live in it can be dealt with as a statutory NUISANCE. The district (or islands) council can order the overcrowding to cease.

Evicting tenants

Overcrowding can sometimes result in the EVICTION of tenants and their families. For these purposes, a house is considered to be overcrowded if:

- Two people of opposite sex and over the age of 10 (except husband and wife) have to sleep in the same room.
- There are insufficient rooms for the people who live in the house.
- The rooms are too small for the number of people.

If a house is rented from a private landlord and has been overcrowded for at least 6 months, the tenant loses any security of tenure he may have under the Rent (Scotland) Acts. However, the sheriff can only make an eviction order if he thinks it is reasonable to do so and if suitable alternative accommodation is available. *See:* EVICTION

Overcrowding is also a ground for evicting tenants of public authorities and housing associations. Before granting an eviction order, the sheriff must be satisfied that suitable alternative accommodation is available. *See:* COUNCIL TENANCY

Obtaining a home

The overcrowding standards mentioned above are used by many housing authorities in the allocation of council houses to people on their waiting lists. Some authorities set higher standards, however. If you are living in overcrowded conditions, you are likely to get a home more quickly than someone who is not.

If you lose your home because you have been living in overcrowded conditions, you may be able to obtain accommodation from the housing authority. *See:* HOMELESSNESS

HOW TO TELL IF A HOUSE IS OVERCROWDED

A house will be treated as overcrowded if any one of the following conditions applies:

1. If two people of opposite sex, who are at least ten years old and are not living as husband and wife, have to sleep in the same room.

2. If the number of people per room (meaning a bedroom or living room) sleeping in the house is more than the following:

Rooms in the house	Number of people
1	2
2	3
3	5
4	7½
5	10
Each extra room	2 more

A child under 1 is not counted and a child between 1 and 10 counts as a half. A room with a floor area less than 50 sq. ft. is not counted.

3. If the number of people sleeping in the house, given the floor area of each room, is more than the following:

Floor area of room	Number of people
Under 50 sq. ft.	nil
50 to 69 sq. ft.	½
70 to 89 sq. ft.	1
90 to 109 sq. ft.	1½
110 sq. ft. or more	2

When floor area is being calculated, no account is taken of parts of a room which are less than 5 feet in height, nor of parts of the floor covered by a fixed bed or other fixture, or a sink.

OVERLAPPING BENEFITS

How the state avoids paying out twice

A person who finds himself in a position to claim more than one state benefit for the same risk is normally prevented from actually being paid twice by what are known as the overlapping benefits regulations.

For example, the overlapping rules allow a widow over 60 to draw only the larger of RETIREMENT PENSION or WIDOW'S PENSION. In the same way, a man receiving a maintenance allowance while training for a new job cannot get full UNEMPLOYMENT BENEFIT.

Some benefits are not affected by the overlapping benefits rules and can be paid in addition to other state payments. These are MATERNITY GRANT, DEATH GRANT, ATTENDANCE ALLOWANCE and MOBILITY ALLOWANCE.

Graduated retirement benefit under the existing regulations is not adjusted unless the recipient also gets a Category D RETIREMENT PENSION (payable to people over 80 who do not get any other retirement pension), a non-contributory INVALIDITY PENSION or an INVALID CARE ALLOWANCE.

All social security benefits except MOBILITY ALLOWANCE and ATTENDANCE ALLOWANCE are taken into account in assessing entitlement to SUPPLEMENTARY BENEFIT.

PAINTINGS

When you buy a painting 'by a named artist'

Leading auctioneers (who are usually members of the Society of Fine Art Auctioneers) have three ways of giving the name of an artist said to have produced a particular painting.

For example, a painting may be described as being by John Constable, J. Constable, or Constable.

The full name – John Constable – means that the auctioneer is satisfied that the painting is the authentic work of the named artist.

The surname with initials – J. Constable – means that the auctioneer is not absolutely sure that the painting is by the artist named, but that it is the work of the period during which he painted and may be wholly or in part his work.

The surname alone – Constable – indicates that the auctioneer is not willing to say that the painting is by the named artist, but that it is a work of the school of the named artist or one of his followers, or in his style.

What to do if you are misled

If you buy a painting in the belief that it is by a particular artist, but it proves later not to be genuine, your rights depend on whether the painting has been sold by description under that artist's name.

If it has been, it is a term of the contract of sale, under the Sale of Goods Act 1979, that it should correspond with the description. If that term is broken you have the right to reject the painting and get your money back, and to claim damages if the value of a genuine painting would have been greater than the price you paid.

Even if you do not reject the painting, you can claim damages to the value of the difference between the values of the true painting and the painting you bought. *See:* DEFECTIVE GOODS

When there is an exemption clause

If you bought the painting from an art dealer at an art gallery – privately and not in the course of a business – your rights are not affected by any exemption clause in the sale details.

If you bought it at an auction, the exemption clause would be invalid unless it was fair and reasonable. *See:* UNFAIR CONTRACT

If the painting was not sold by description, you might nevertheless be able to claim you were induced into buying the painting by the seller's MISREPRESENTATION.

PARENTAL OBLIGATIONS

The duties of parents towards their children

The most important legal duty that parents have is to house, feed, clothe and properly provide for their children. This is known as the duty to ALIMENT. In theory, this duty continues even when the children are adults, if they are not able to provide for themselves.

The father has the primary responsibility to maintain legitimate children. If he cannot do so adequately, a mother with sufficient income of her own is expected to contribute. Where the father is dead or unable to support the children, the mother becomes primarily responsible.

If the father leaves home and fails to maintain his children, the mother can take legal proceedings to force him to pay something towards their support. Once the children reach the age of 16, any legal proceedings have to be in their name and not the mother's.

If it is the mother who has primary responsibility, and she fails to support the children adequately, they can take legal proceedings against her through a legal guardian, or curator, specially appointed to represent them in court. *See:* ALIMENT; CURATOR

In the case of illegitimate children, both parents are equally responsible for supporting them. If the father fails to contribute voluntarily, the mother can take legal proceedings against him. *See:* AFFILIATION AND ALIMENT; ILLEGITIMATE CHILD

Treating children properly Parents are also under a legal obligation to treat their children properly. It is a criminal offence for a parent to deliberately assault, ill-treat, neglect or abandon a child under 16. The offence can be committed by, for instance, failing to feed and clothe a child properly, or leaving a young child alone in the house.

Parents must make sure that children receive proper care and attention – including medical treatment – when they are ill. A parent may be guilty of criminal neglect if he fails to call a doctor when one is needed, or ignores a doctor's advice, or refuses to allow a blood transfusion or operation on religious grounds.

If a parent mistreats a child in this way, the child may be referred to a CHILDREN'S HEARING. In serious cases the child may first be removed from home under a PLACE OF SAFETY ORDER. *See:* CHILD ABUSE

Children must be educated

A parent has a duty to ensure that every child of school age is given an 'efficient' education – either at school or by other means. It is an offence to fail to do so. *See:* HOME TEACHING; SCHOOL

Parents must not be careless

A parent has a duty not to harm his child through carelessness. If he does – by, for instance, driving a car negligently – the child can sue him for compensation. *See:* NEGLIGENCE

When parents are liable

Parents have a duty to exercise reasonable supervision over their PUPIL children – that is, girls under 12 and boys under 14. If they fail to do so and the child injures someone or damages property as a result, they can be sued for compensation by the person who has suffered.

So if a parent leaves the ignition key in his car and his 11 year old son drives the car out of the driveway and collides with another car, the parent may be liable for failing to take reasonable care.

A parent may also be held legally liable if injury or damage is caused by failing to ensure supervision over a MINOR – a girl aged 12, or a boy aged 14, but under 18. However, the older the child the less likely it is that a court would say that the parent's supervision had been inadequate.

PARKING

Where and when you can leave your car

No one can leave a vehicle parked indefinitely at the roadside without committing an offence, even where there are no clear restrictions. A motorist is not allowed to make a garage of the road.

A person who leaves a car, lorry or van stationary at the kerbside for a long period in an unrestricted area may be prosecuted for causing an unnecessary obstruction of the road. A vehicle parked anywhere on the public highway is obstructing that part of the road on which it is parked, but it will only be an offence if the parking is unreasonable – for example, if the vehicle might obstruct the flow of traffic.

As a general rule, a person has no more legal right to park his car in the road outside his own home than anyone else has. However, some streets are designated for residents' parking only. It is an offence to park in such a street without displaying a permit. In the hours of darkness, the car must be parked with its nearside to the kerb.

Urban restrictions

In towns and city centres, parking is governed by strict controls with yellow lines, 'No Parking' signs and parking meters all limiting a motorist's right to stop and stay.

In such a restricted area, parking at the roadside is legitimate only for certain loading or unloading and fetching or delivering. It depends on what you are fetching or carrying.

Stopping in order to get fish and chips or takeaway food is not loading for these purposes. The exemption applies for loading or unloading goods which a person could not reasonably be expected to carry by hand. Unloading frozen fish from a vehicle for the fish and chip shop would be within the exemption.

Necessary as distinct from convenient loading or unloading is allowed. Picking up passengers and luggage without delay would probably be allowed; but it would not usually be considered necessary for you to park your car outside your bank to cash a £10 cheque.

Another factor taken into consideration is time. A van driver might be allowed 20 minutes to unload his goods, but would probably be booked after an hour or more on a yellow line.

When there are yellow lines

A single yellow line painted at the kerbside means all parking is banned except for loading and unloading, fetching and delivering, for at least 8 hours between 7 a.m. and 7 p.m. on the working days of the week.

This can sometimes be extended to Saturday afternoons and Sundays. You may, however, park at night (or on Sundays, if not included in the restriction period).

Small plates are erected on posts at the roadside, usually at 200 ft intervals, stating the time between which the restriction applies.

For example, the plate may state that the restriction period is 'Mon–Sat: 8 a.m.–6.30 p.m.'

The ban covers every part of the roadway, not just the kerbside, and includes the footpath and any verges.

Double yellow lines mean there is a total ban on parking at any time of the night or day. Do not park without checking the time plate. It is an offence to park on a yellow line during a restricted period and, where there are no fixed penalties, a driver who does so can be fined up to £400.

Where you must never park

In addition to areas that are marked, there are other places where the Highway Code says you should not park your car:

- Where it causes danger to other vehicles or pedestrians – for example, near a school entrance or crossing, where it hides a traffic sign, on a footpath, pavement or cycle path, on or near a bus stop, on or near a level crossing.
- Where it obscures another driver's view of the road, for example, within 15 yds of a junction, on a bend, on a brow of a hill, on a humpback bridge, near a zebra crossing.
- Where it leaves too narrow a passage for other vehicles, for example, opposite a traffic island, beside another stationary vehicle, opposite another stationary vehicle on a narrow road.
- Where it interferes with traffic, for example, on flyovers, in tunnels and underpasses, on fast main roads (except in a lay-by), on a single-track road, blocking a vehicle entrance to properties, or where it would prevent the use of properly parked vehicles.
- Where there is an entrance or exit for emergency vehicles, for instance, at hospitals and fire and police stations.

When a car breaks down

A driver is generally not held to be guilty of a parking offence if he is prevented from proceeding by reasons beyond his control. A car left for a long time with a sign 'broken down' may still be booked – and to be acquitted the owner will need evidence that the car really was out of commission.

Running out of petrol probably does not constitute a breakdown because running out of petrol is avoidable. Wardens will therefore book anyone who does so and parks in a restricted area.

Parking in a meter zone

In some areas parking is allowed only

at kerbside meters and the driver puts coins into the meter for a fixed period of parking. When the time is up he must move his vehicle or incur an excess charge. A driver who does not pay within 7 days can be fined up to £50.

When a driver's time is up he must move his vehicle from the parking bay, and cannot return to the same meter for at least an hour. It is legal to drive out of one parking bay and pull into another across the road. If a driver goes round the block and back into the bay he has just vacated, he can be fined £50.

Payment for use of a parking meter bay must be made when the vehicle is parked. No time is allowed for going to get change. It is an offence to 'feed' a meter, that is, to return later and put more coins into the meter to buy more time. The penalty is a fine of up to £50.

When a motorist leaves his car in a parking space for longer than the time he has paid for and the yellow card is showing on the meter, he is liable to an excess charge. If he leaves it there until the red card is showing, he will incur a fixed penalty of £10 and the car can be towed away. He can, however, use up any surplus time shown on the meter when he arrives at the parking space, even without putting in a coin.

When a meter is out of order

It is not an offence to park without paying at a meter which is out of order. But if the meter has a hood over it saying that its use is suspended, anyone parking there commits an offence.

CAUSING AN UNREASONABLE OBSTRUCTION

It is an offence to cause an unreasonable obstruction on a public road.

Parking elsewhere in a meter zone

Roadside notices warn motorists when they are entering a zone where street parking is restricted to meters only. The hours during which meter parking operates vary and are clearly stated on the signs and at the meters.

It is an offence to park anywhere else in a meter zone, even where there are no yellow lines.

When penalties are fixed

In most areas there is a fixed penalty of £10 for breaking parking regulations. If this penalty is paid within 21 days, there is no conviction against the driver. Failure to pay can lead to a prosecution and a fine of up to £50.

Towing away parked cars

Cars causing an obstruction or left in contravention of parking restrictions can be removed by the police and kept in a car pound until removal and storage charges, as well as any parking penalties, are paid.

PARLIAMENTARY BILL

How laws are made by Parliament

Any Act, before being passed by Parliament, starts life in draft form as a Bill. It becomes law only when it comes into effect as an Act of Parliament, after passing through all its stages in the House of Commons and House of Lords and receiving the Royal Assent.

A Bill may be either 'public' or 'private'. A public Bill is one that is introduced by the government or by a member of either the House of Commons or House of Lords. A Bill introduced by such a member is known as a 'private member's Bill', but is nonetheless a public Bill.

Parliament considers between 60 to 70 government Bills, and many private members' Bills, during each parliamentary session. The session usually runs for a 12 month period from October or November. Any public Bill which has not received the Royal Assent by the end of the session in which it is introduced is automatically dropped. The same thing happens when a general election is called.

A private Bill (or, in Scotland, a Provisional Order) is presented by a body or company or individual to bring about an alteration or increase in powers – as, for instance, where a local authority or harbour authority wants to extend its jurisdiction or to provide a new service which is not among its existing permitted functions.

A Bill may be introduced into the House of Commons or the House of Lords, but all finance Bills must originate in the House of Commons.

Public Bills

Once a Bill has been drafted, it is presented by its sponsor – the minister or individual member in whose name it is being proposed – to the Public Bill Office of the House in which it is to be introduced.

Finance Bills and (usually) politically sensitive Bills start in the House of Commons.

Others – such as consolidating Bills, which merely bring together existing legislation on a particular subject – normally start off in the Lords.

In either case, the Bill must pass through a lengthy process in each House, consisting of three 'readings' study in detail in committee and a report stage when the committee reports to the full House. The Bill then receives the Royal Assent and becomes an Act of Parliament.

However, if a Bill is amended in the House of Lords, after it has been through the Commons, it is returned to the Commons so that the amendments can be considered.

If the Commons disagrees with any of the amendments made in the House of Lords, it alters them and sends the Bill back to the Lords. In most cases, the Lords accept that later decision of the Commons.

If there is no agreement between the Houses before the end of the session, the Bill is lost unless the Parliament Acts are invoked by the Commons. The House of Lords may refuse to pass a Bill, but it nevertheless becomes law if the Commons have passed the Bill in two successive sessions and one year has elapsed between the Second Reading of the Bill in the first session and its Third Reading in the second session.

The Lords are not entitled to amend any part of a finance Bill.

THE STAGES OF A PUBLIC BILL

How a Bill becomes an Act of Parliament

First reading The Bill is formally introduced to the Commons or Lords. Its title is read out and it is ordered to be printed. There is no discussion.

Second reading Members of the full House debate the general principles of the Bill and vote on whether it should be studied by a committee.

If the House decides it is not in favour of what the Bill purports to do, it votes against the Bill – and the Bill is abandoned at once.

A Bill which exclusively concerns Scotland may be debated and voted upon by the Scottish Grand Committee.

Committee stage The Bill is discussed in detail, clause by clause, and any amendments are made to it. In the Lords, the committee is the full membership of the House. In the Commons, all finance Bills and some Bills of major importance are referred to the Committee of the Whole House for detailed discussion by all members.

Otherwise, a public Bill in the Commons is discussed by a committee known as a Standing Committee, which must have at least 16 and not more than 50 members, chosen by the Commons Committee of Selection. The membership reflects the political balance of the House, although the chairman of a standing committee does not always belong to the majority party.

When particular members have an interest in a Bill, they are generally selected to sit on the committee. A Bill exclusively concerning Scotland will be discussed by one of the two Scottish Standing Committees. Each committee consists of around 18 members.

It is at the committee stage that the opposition party can voice its objections to a Bill, but any member of the House is entitled to table an amendment at the Public Bill Office. Opponents may make amendments to try to delay a Bill or simply to embarrass the Government. The Government may also put down amendments.

Report stage The committee reports its suggested amendments back to the full House. The House may decide to accept the amendments or it may decide to make further amendments or refer the bill to another committee.

Third reading When the amendments are agreed by the House, the Bill receives its third reading. It is then sent to the other House where it has to pass through the same procedural stages. Any amendments made by the other House then have to be accepted or rejected by the first House.

Royal Assent When a public or a private Bill has passed through all its stages in both Houses, it receives the Royal Assent.

Once Parliament has been informed of this, the Bill becomes an Act of Parliament – but it may not become law immediately. The date of coming into force of the Act may be set out in the Act or may be left to be fixed later by the Secretary of State by means of an order.

The Royal Assent is no longer given by the sovereign in person in Parliament – Queen Victoria was the last to do so in 1854. The Speakers in each House now simply inform members that the Royal Assent has been given.

In theory, it is still possible for the Queen to refuse to give her consent to a Bill. However, that has not happened since 1708, when Queen Anne vetoed a Scottish Militia Bill.

Scottish private legislation procedure

When a public authority, or any other person, wishes to obtain parliamentary powers affecting public or private interests only in Scotland, it almost always uses the 'Provisional Order procedure' set out in the Private Legislation Procedure (Scotland) Act 1936 and in related General Orders. This is instead of the private Bill procedure used for Bills affecting England and Wales.

The promoters of the new law start by depositing 50 copies of a draft order embodying the law with the Secretary of State for Scotland at the Scottish Office in London, on March 27 or November 27. They must also deposit 50 copies of a petition asking him to issue the Provisional Order. Advertisements have to be inserted in newspapers and in the Edinburgh Gazette, and the draft order must be scrutinised by 'examiners' to make sure that it complies with General Orders.

Copies of the order must be made available for inspection and sale at certain offices. Objectors to the order can petition against it by depositing at the Scottish Office, London, 30 copies of their petition 'praying' to be heard, addressed to the Secretary of State.

The draft order is referred to the Chairman of Committees, representing the Lords, and the Chairman of Ways and Means, representing the Commons. If they report that the order, or part of it, relates to matters outside Scotland, or raises questions of novelty and importance, the normal private Bill procedure must be used for the part of the order in question.

Any remaining part will continue to be dealt with under Provisional Order procedure.

If the Chairmen report that the order may proceed, the Secretary of State, if the order is opposed or if he thinks it necessary, directs an inquiry to be held by Commissioners, who are normally two peers and two MPs. The inquiry is held in public at a suitable place in Scotland.

Each party is normally liable for his own expenses (regardless of the outcome of the inquiry), for a share of the shorthand writers' fees and transcription costs and for certain fees under the Act.

The Commissioners take evidence on oath from supporters of and objectors to the order, who can be legally represented. They can also summon witnesses and require documents to be produced.

They then report to the Secretary of State with a recommendation that the order should be made, or made with amendments, or refused.

If the order is unopposed and no inquiry is to be held, the promoters have to appear before Counsel to the Secretary of State, for the purpose of giving evidence on oath about the statements in the order.

If the Secretary of State makes the order, with or without modification, a Confirmation Bill is presented to Parliament as soon as practicable. It proceeds through Parliament, using a simplified and usually formal procedure, and becomes a public Act after receiving the Royal Assent. If the objectors maintain their opposition in Parliament, however, after an inquiry has been held by Commissioners, they may be heard by a Joint Committee of both Houses, which will then report to both Houses.

PARLIAMENTARY PRIVILEGE

MPs can say what they like in the House

MPs and members of the House of Lords are immune in respect of all statements made during parliamentary proceedings. This is known as parliamentary privilege.

This means that an MP or peer can say what he likes – even if it is a damaging lie – during parliamentary proceedings, whether in the debating Chamber or in committees, without risk of being sued for DEFAMATION or prosecuted under the OFFICIAL SECRETS Acts.

Parliamentary papers, including reports of parliamentary proceedings in *Hansard*, are also privileged, and no action for defamation can be taken for anything written in them.

The limited privilege of press and broadcasting

Reports, either in newspapers or in broadcasts, of speeches delivered during debates are also protected, but only provided the reports are without malice and are published in good faith.

There is no privilege for anything said or written by MPs or peers which is not in the course of parliamentary proceedings. For example, an MP who says something defamatory in the bar of the House of Commons or writes something defamatory in his constituency newsletter can be sued.

Breaches of parliamentary privilege are investigated by the Committee of Privileges, which is made up of MPs or peers from all parties. Its report and recommendation is made to the House, which decides what is to be done. *See:* CONTEMPT OF PARLIAMENT

THE LETTER THAT TESTED AN MP'S LEGAL IMMUNITY

An MP who writes to a Minister is not taking part in parliamentary proceedings – so he can be sued for what his letter says.

A Member of Parliament, Mr G. R. Strauss, in 1957 alleged a 'public scandal' in the disposal of scrap materials by the London Electricity Board.

He made his allegation in a letter to the Paymaster-General, who represented the Minister of Power in the House of Commons.

His letter was referred to the electricity board chairman, who demanded that the statement be withdrawn. When Mr Strauss refused, the board's solicitors threatened to sue for libel.

The MP complained to the Commons that the threat amounted to a breach of parliamentary privilege. The House of Commons committee of privileges ruled that Mr Strauss had been engaged in 'a proceeding in Parliament' when he wrote the letter to the Paymaster-General. So the electricity board, in threatening to sue, had breached privilege.

But a committee ruling has no effect unless it is confirmed by a majority of the whole House of Commons. In the debate that followed, supporters of the ruling argued that 'proceedings in Parliament' must include everything said or done by a member in the exercise of his function, as well as in the formal parliamentary business of debating in the chamber.

Opponents of the ruling said that the privilege afforded to MPs was meant to protect only the open, published business of Parliament – not correspondence. An MP could discharge all his responsibilities openly, without claiming further protection.

DECISION

The Commons passed a resolution that Mr Strauss' letter was not part of parliamentary proceedings. So the board – which had dropped its legal threat anyway – had committed no breach of privilege.

PAROLE

When a prisoner may be granted conditional release

No prisoner has a right to be freed on parole – which means on his word of honour – but all have a right to be considered for it after a certain length of time in prison.

The point when a prisoner becomes eligible for parole depends on whether he is serving a fixed term or an indefinite sentence.

Fixed-term prisoners

A prisoner sentenced to a fixed term of more than 18 months can be considered for parole after serving one-third of his sentence or 12 months, whichever is the longer period.

Unless they decline the right, prisoners are automatically considered for parole by a local review committee at the prison, which is composed of the prison governor, a local authority social worker and at least one 'independent' member. They take into account the prisoner's background, his behaviour in prison, the likely circumstances after his release, the offence he committed and whether it is in the public interest to recommend parole.

The committee's recommendations are passed to the Secretary of State for Scotland, who forwards the names of those he considers fit for release to the Parole Board for Scotland – a body that includes judges, psychiatrists and experts in prison affairs. The Board reports back to the Secretary of State, who then acts on its decisions.

In 1982, out of 772 prisoners on fixed sentences entitled to consideration for parole, 94 declined. Of the 386 considered by the Board, 261 were recommended for parole.

Indefinite sentences

Prisoners serving life sentences or young offenders detained indefinitely are also eligible to be released on licence, but the minimum time they must serve before being considered is not specified. A preliminary review is held after 3 years, but it is rare for release to be considered before 7 years.

Even if the board recommends parole in such cases, the Secretary of State must consult the Lord Justice-General (Scotland's senior criminal judge) and (if he is still available) the judge who conducted the original trial, before making a decision.

In 1982, out of 33 prisoners on life sentences considered by the Board, 31 were recommended for release.

When parole is refused

No reason need be given for refusing parole and a prisoner cannot appeal against the decision. However, his case will be reconsidered at regular intervals.

Conditions of parole

A prisoner released on parole is subject to strict conditions. He must remain under the supervision of a social worker and follow the social worker's instructions. He must also 'be of good behaviour and lead an industrious life'. The parole licence continues until the normal date of release in the case of an adult fixed-term prisoner, until the end of the total sentence for an offender under 21 when sentenced, and for life for those serving indefinite sentences.

Parole may be ended, and the prisoner recalled to prison at any time, either by the Parole Board, the Secretary of State or by a court if the offender is convicted of an indictable offence punishable by imprisonment. Reasons must be given for ending parole.

PART-TIME WORKER

The legal rights of certain part-time employees

For the purposes of EMPLOYMENT PROTECTION law, a part-time worker is defined as someone who normally works for an employer for less than 16 hours a week.

Most employment protection rights depend on an employee having a particular period of CONTINUOUS EMPLOYMENT. Normally, a working week counts as part of a period of continuous employment only if the employee is employed for 16 hours (or more) in that week; or, if he is not, his EMPLOYMENT CONTRACT normally involves working for 16 hours (or more) each week.

Because of this, a part-time worker cannot achieve a period of continuous employment and is therefore denied many of the employment rights which are available to most other employees.

However, there are two exceptions:

1. Where a part-time employee has worked for an employer for a continuous period of 5 years. If the employee normally works at least 8 hours a week, every week then counts as part of a period of continuous employment.

2. Where an employee's contract of employment, which normally requires 16 hours' (or more) work each week, is altered to require between 8 and 16 hours' work each week. An employee can then count any week during which he works 8 hours (or more) as part of a period of continuous employment. But no more than 26 of such short-time weeks can be counted.

In these two situations, a part-time employee *can* qualify for employment protection rights.

A part-timer's legal rights

Part-time employees, like other employees, always have an employment contract, even although there may be nothing in writing. The contract obliges the employer, amongst other things, to pay the agreed wages, provide a safe work place and co-operate with his employee. But apart from their contracts, part-timers not included in the exceptions mentioned above have few other legal rights.

Written statements Part-timers have no right to a written statement of the terms of their employment contracts. If the employer refuses to put details of the job in writing, there is nothing they can do. *See:* EMPLOYMENT CONTRACT

Notice Minimum NOTICE periods laid down by law for most employees do not apply to part-timers. However, they are still entitled to some notice. If the period of notice is not stated in the employment contract, it must be a 'reasonable' period – that is, normally at least a week for weekly paid employees.

Dismissals Part-timers cannot claim UNFAIR DISMISSAL, no matter how unjust their sacking may be. Nor can they claim a REDUNDANCY payment if work is no longer available for them. Furthermore, unlike most full-time employees they cannot insist on being provided with written reasons for their DISMISSAL.

Maternity Female part-timers are not entitled to MATERNITY pay from their employers. And if they give up work, they are not entitled to return to their old jobs after the birth of their children.

Pay Part-timers cannot claim any statutory guaranteed pay if they are laid off or put on short-time. Nor are they entitled to demand an itemised statement of their pay. They are, however, entitled to statutory sick pay. *See:* LAY-OFF; PAY; SICKNESS

Time off Part-timers do not have the rights which most other employees have to take time off work for public and trade union duties, to take part in trade union activities or to look for another job following notice of redundancy.

However, female part-timers do have the right to take time off to keep ante-natal appointments. *See:* MATERNITY; TIME OFF WORK

Additional work

The hours that a part-timer is required to work are stated or implied in his employment contract. If he occasionally works for longer than the contract requires, he remains a part-timer, whether the extra hours are paid at overtime or normal rates.

However, if an employer regularly asks a part-timer to work extra hours, taking the weekly total to 16 hours or more, it can be argued that he is full-time.

Reducing hours

An employer cannot reduce a full-time employee's hours to reclassify him as a part-timer, without the employee's consent. If he does so, the employee can leave and claim unfair dismissal.

However, if the employee does not protest, and accepts the change, he may be held to have accepted the alteration in his employment contract. If he then resigns, he will not be able to succeed in a claim for unfair dismissal.

Paying tax

An employer must deduct income tax from a part-timer's wages under the PAYE system, as he does for full-time workers.

However, many part-timers' wages, with tax allowances taken into account, fall below the tax threshold, so no deduction needs to be made.

A part-time worker who is SELF-EMPLOYED is responsible for paying his own tax under Schedule D.

National insurance

Part-time workers are subject to the same national insurance rules as those who work full-time.

If a part-timer is an employee, he and his employer must pay Class 1 national insurance contributions, provided that he earns more than the LOWER EARNINGS LIMIT (which was £34 in 1984–5). *See:* NATIONAL INSURANCE CONTRIBUTIONS

PASSPORT

The document you must have to travel abroad

No one needs a passport to leave Britain. But other countries may not admit anyone who has no passport – and an airline or shipping company may refuse to issue a ticket.

People may be allowed into Britain without a passport if they can produce some other identity document or if they are refugees, stateless or from a country with no passport system.

Your passport establishes your identity, and calls on foreign governments and people to respect your freedom as a British Citizen. If a serious problem arises, it proves your right to the help and protection of British diplomatic representatives.

A passport is a state document that remains government property. No citizen is normally refused one, but an application may be declined, or a passport withdrawn, from anyone, although normally only from:

- A child under the age of 18 who wants to leave Britain against the wishes of his parents or guardian.
- Someone for whom an arrest warrant has been issued.
- Someone who is granted BAIL.
- Someone who has not repaid the cost of government help to return to Britain.
- In rare cases, a person whose activities cause the Government to rule that granting him a passport is not in the public interest – for example, someone suspected of seeking foreign aid for terrorism in Britain.

There is no appeal against refusal of a passport.

The two types of passport

Britain issues a standard passport that is valid worldwide, and a visitor's passport that is simpler and cheaper, but limited in use. Both are available to British Citizens, British Dependent Territories Citizens and British Overseas Citizens. The standard passport can also be issued to British Protected Persons.

Standard passport A standard United Kingdom passport of 30 pages costs £15, or £30 if the 94 page version is required. It is valid for 10 years (5 years, renewable for a further 5 years, if issued to a child under 16).

Visitor's passport A British Visitor's Passport is intended only for holiday visits to certain countries that recognise it. It costs £7.50 and is valid for 1 year.

Families On either type of passport, the holder's wife, husband, children under 16 or even the children of relatives can be included at the time of issue. A standard passport including a wife or husband costs £22.50 (£45 for the 94 page version); a visitor's passport costs £11.25.

Someone included in that way can travel only in the company of the passport holder. Children aged 16 and over need separate passports.

Separate standard passports for children over 5 can be issued if requested, but are not issued to younger children except in rare circumstances – for example, when an infant travels with someone who is not a parent or relative. A visitor's passport is not issued separately to children under 8.

How to obtain a passport

Application forms for both types of passport are available at all main post offices. With the completed form, countersigned by someone of professional standing – for example, a clergyman or doctor – who has known you for at least two years, you must supply:

- Proof of British Citizenship.
- A marriage certificate or other proof of change of name, where appropriate.
- Two identical, recent photographs taken full-face, without a hat, and measuring no more than $2\frac{1}{2} \times 2$ in. or less than $2 \times 1\frac{1}{2}$ in. One photograph must be endorsed on the back by the person who countersigns the application.

Waiting time If all the application requirements are met, a visitor's passport is issued immediately at any main post office.

Applications for a standard passport must be posted to the correct regional office as shown on the form. The passport will be posted back to you. You should submit your application at least 4 weeks before you want your passport – from April to August, the delay may be even greater.

When a woman marries

A woman who marries and already has a passport can choose to:

- Use it until it expires and continue to travel under her maiden name.
- Have the name in it altered for a fee of £3.

A woman who has no passport when she marries can:

- Apply for one of her own.
- Apply with her husband for a joint passport.

If a couple intend to go abroad immediately after their wedding, a bride-to-be can apply in advance for a standard passport in her married name. It is post-dated so that it becomes valid only on their wedding day.

A visitor's passport cannot be issued in a woman's married name until after her wedding.

Special rules for Europe

British passports issued since the be-

WHERE A SIMPLIFIED PASSPORT IS ACCEPTED

A low-cost British Visitor's Passport, valid for 1 year, is recognised for holidays of up to 3 months in the following countries:

Andorra
Austria
Belgium
Bermuda
Canada
France
–including
Corsica
Gibraltar
Greece
Italy
–including
Sicily
Sardinia
Elba
Liechtenstein
Luxembourg
Malta
Monaco
Netherlands
Portugal
–including
Madeira
Azores
San Marino
Spain
–including
Balearic and Canary Islands
Switzerland
Tunisia
Turkey
West Germany
–including
West Berlin *(only if going by air)*

The following countries form a common travel area. Visits on a Visitor's Passport to these countries as a whole must not exceed 3 months in any 9 month period:

Denmark
–including
Greenland
Faroe Islands
Finland
Iceland
Norway
Sweden

If you have to travel through any other country to reach your destination, you will need to apply for an ordinary passport.

ginning of 1973 include a declaration that the holder has the right of abode in the United Kingdom. That entitles a British Citizen to seek or take up work in other European Economic Community countries, and to claim a residence permit if he continues in business or employment.

Anyone whose passport was issued before 1973 is entitled to have the declaration of his right of abode added to it. He should send the passport to the Home Office nationality department in London.

As a result of the British Nationality Act 1981, new passports will now indicate which class of citizenship a person holds. Those with a right of abode become British Citizens. *See:* CITIZENSHIP

Other countries' requirements

The various visas or permits that may be required for admission to other countries are stamped or stapled into a passport. It is a traveller's own responsibility to make sure that he has whatever permission is needed to enter another country. Airlines, shipping companies and major travel agencies can give accurate information.

Some foreign embassies require visa applicants to hand over their passports while applications are checked – a process that can take weeks. For that reason, someone who needs visas for several countries should apply well in advance.

If you lose your passport

The loss of a passport in Britain should be reported to the police. Application should then be made for a new one in the usual way. If time is short, a restricted passport lasting a year can be issued quickly.

If you lose your passport when you are abroad, report it to the local police then go to the British consul where you can obtain a temporary passport. The replacement fee can be paid when you return home.

If your original passport contained a visa which you require to continue your travels, you must go to the consul of the appropriate country to obtain a new visa. That could be a slow process and there is usually no way of speeding things up.

Passport offences Using a false passport or giving false information to obtain a passport are offences carrying a maximum penalty of £2,000 and 3 months' imprisonment.

PATENT

How to prevent anyone from copying a new invention

Anyone who invents a new device or process can prevent others from copying it by taking out a patent, giving him the sole right for 20 years to manufacture, use or commercially exploit his invention.

No one else – not even someone who genuinely invents the same device independently – can use it if a patent is in force.

Almost anything can be patented so long as it is new and not an obvious development of something else, and it is capable of use in industry or agriculture.

However, a patent cannot be obtained for discoveries, scientific theories or mathematical methods. The theory of gravity, if discovered today, could not be patented, though a new machine based on the theory could be.

Literary, musical and artistic works cannot be patented, but they are protected by COPYRIGHT. Nor can you get a patent for a particular method of doing business – a new accounting process, for example – nor for computer programmes, new rules for playing a game or the mere presentation of information, such as a new layout for a form.

Medical treatments for people and animals are not patentable, nor are animal varieties – for example, new breeds of cattle or sheep. New plants and seeds have a different protection under the Plant and Seed Varieties Act 1964.

APPLYING FOR A PATENT IN GOOD TIME

If you are developing an idea in a field where there is likely to be competition from rivals, make sure that you apply for a patent as early as possible.

Applying for a patent

A patent is obtained by filing an application at the Patent Office, 25 Southampton Buildings, London, WC2A 1AY. Special forms must be obtained.

The application must contain a description of the invention, including drawings if necessary.

The claims – the most important part of the patent – are a precise statement of what the inventor is claiming as his own invention. The patent will be infringed by anyone who makes something that

AN ATTEMPT AT INTERDICT WHICH WAS BELOW THE BELT

If the claims in a patent application are not carefully worded, they may allow a rival to copy an idea.

The 'Y-front' design for men's underwear was patented by Lyle and Scott in 1935. Some years later, they tried to interdict Wolsey from manufacturing a design of underpants called 'X-fronts', alleging an infringement of their patent.

Wolsey argued that the specialty of Lyle and Scott's 'Y-fronts' was that they included a separate piece of material called the 'crotch portion'. Since their 'X-fronts' contained no such separate piece of material, they argued that the patent had not been infringed.

DECISION

The court held that Lyle and Scott's claims only related to underpants with this separate piece of material. There was no infringement of the patent by Wolsey, and interdict was refused.

falls within the claims.

If a claim is badly drawn up, it may be possible for someone else to copy the invention without infringing the patent. For that reason, applicants should seek advice on drawing up the application from a member of the Institute of Patent Agents, Staple Inn Buildings, London WC1V 7PZ.

The Patent Office may grant a patent immediately or may require amendments to be made to the claims. If amendments are required, the revised application must be made acceptable within 4½ years from the date it was first filed, or the application lapses.

A patent will only be granted if the invention is new.

In patent law, an invention is not new if it has been shown in public, or a description of it has been published, before the application is filed. Inventors must therefore take care not to publicise their work before filing their application.

However, an invention can be shown to a potential manufacturer without affecting a patent application – provided it is done in confidence. *See:* TRADE SECRET

Cost The patenting process costs £165 – £10 application fee, £70 for a Patent Office search and £85 for the Patent Office examination of the application. These are government fees only. Help from a Patent Agent can cost considerably more than that. And further government fees of about £2,300 over 20 years are needed to keep the patent in force.

Enforcing patent rights

If a patented invention is used by someone else, the holder of the patent can seek a court INTERDICT to restrain the infringement. He can also sue for damages.

PATERNITY

When the father of an illegitimate child denies responsibility

An unmarried mother who wishes to claim maintenance for her child can raise an action for affiliation and aliment against the man she alleges to be the father. *See:* AFFILIATION AND ALIMENT

PAWNBROKER

Pledging goods as security for a loan

New laws on pawnbroking, contained in the Consumer Credit Act 1974, come into force in May, 1985. What follows is based on those new laws.

Money can be borrowed from a pawnbroker by leaving goods with him as a 'pledge' – security for the loan – on agreed interest terms. No maximum limit is set on the interest that can be charged, although a sheriff court can reduce any interest rate that, in its view, is excessive. The loan is unlikely to represent the full value of the goods.

Goods can be redeemed – recovered by paying back the loan and interest – within 6 months, or any longer period fixed by the agreement. The pawnbroker cannot make an extra charge for giving them back.

The borrower can usually redeem the goods after the time limit expires. But the pawnbroker can make a charge for their safekeeping – which must be no higher than the rate he was charging as interest – or sell them.

If he decides to sell them, and the credit (or credit limit) is more than £50, he must give the borrower 14 days' written notice. The borrower can ask the sheriff for more time to pay. If he does not – or his application fails – the pawnbroker can sell the goods.

If the pawnbroker makes more money by selling the goods than he is owed, he must hand over the balance to the borrower. If he makes less, he is not entitled to recover the shortfall from the borrower unless he can prove that he exercised all reasonable care to get the true market value.

The pawnbroker is liable for any damage to pledged items. If the item is lost, the owner can sue him.

HOW PAWNBROKERS ARE REGULATED

A pawnbroker must be licensed by the Office of Fair Trading, and his credit arrangements are subject to the same controls as any other CREDIT AGREEMENT. His licence might be withdrawn if a pattern of complaints from a number of people is established.

The rules about signing an agreement and supplying copies of it apply in the same way as for other forms of credit, such as hire purchase or bank loans, and a borrower can ask a sheriff court to alter the agreement if he feels that the interest is extortionate. *See:* INTEREST CHARGE

Giving a receipt Anyone who pawns an article must be given a receipt at the time. The form of the receipt is laid down by law. It must give the borrower information about the agreement and about his legal rights. If he loses the receipt, he can still recover the goods by making a formal declaration or statement that they are his, and paying back the loan and interest.

A pawnbroker who fails to supply a pledge agreement or a receipt in the form laid down by law, or refuses to return goods without reasonable cause, can be fined up to £1,000.

Under-age customers It is illegal for a pawnbroker to take a pledge from anyone under the age of 18. If he does so, he can be fined up to £2,000 under summary CRIMINAL PROCEEDINGS, or be fined an unlimited amount or imprisoned (or both) under solemn criminal proceedings.

WHEN A PAWNBROKER MUST REFUSE A PLEDGE

It is an offence for a pawnbroker to accept an article in pawn from someone who is under 18.

PAY

Your right to wages or salary from work

When an employer and employee enter into an EMPLOYMENT CONTRACT – which may be in writing or simply an oral agreement – the employer is under a legal duty to pay wages. The rate and frequency of payment is usually expressly stipulated, or implied from the terms of a relevant collective agreement.

If no mention is made of money, an obligation on the part of the employer to pay a reasonable wage will be implied as part of the contract. If there is a dispute about the amount, the employee can ask a court to order the employer to pay him *quantum meruit* – the Latin term meaning 'as much as he has deserved'. That amount can be established by determining how long the employee has worked, the skills involved and the wages paid to other people doing comparable jobs.

How wages are fixed

In Britain there is no statutory minimum wage – as there is in many other countries. Most people's pay is fixed either by direct negotiation with the employer, or through COLLECTIVE BARGAINING by trade unions and employers.

However, in some parts of industry where trade unions have traditionally been weak – for instance, the retail trades and hairdressing – minimum rates of pay (including rates of pay for holidays or lay-offs) are established through WAGES COUNCILS and are legally enforceable.

Equal pay Every woman has an 'equality clause' in her employment contract. This entitles her to the same pay and conditions as a man in the same employment – or a male predecessor – if:

- Her work is the same as his; or
- Her work is broadly similar to his; or
- A job evaluation study has rated her work as equivalent to his; or
- Her work is of equal value to his, given the demands made on her.

A woman has no right to equal treatment if her employer proves that there is a genuine and material difference – other than one of sex – between her case and the man she is comparing herself with.

So an employer can pay a man more than a woman if he has superior skills, or is genuinely in a higher grade or more senior. But he cannot pay the man more merely because he is a man or he asks for a higher wage.

A woman doing work of equal value to a man will also lose her right to equal treatment if her employer proves that differences in pay and conditions are genuinely due to factors *other* than personal differences – for instance, economic circumstances. But these factors cannot be based on sex. This defence is also possible if the comparison is with a male predecessor.

If a woman thinks that she is being paid less than she is entitled to, she should seek advice and assistance from her trade union or from the Equal Opportunities Commission, 249 West George Street, Glasgow.

She is entitled to apply to an industrial tribunal for an order declaring her entitlement to equal pay. It can award her arrears of pay for up to 2 years. Even if her employer decides to provide her with equal pay, she can still apply to the tribunal to recover unpaid arrears for that period.

A woman whose job terminates can still make a claim for equal pay and for arrears – but she must do so within 6 months of the date of termination.

Low pay An employee whose wages are low and who has at least one child to support may be able to obtain a social security benefit called FAMILY INCOME SUPPLEMENT.

How wages must be paid

Under the Truck Acts of 1831 to 1940 – which apply, very broadly, to employees engaged in manual labour – an employee must be paid wages in cash. It is an offence for an employer to pay benefits in kind instead – such as luncheon vouchers, food or petrol.

However, under the Payment of Wages Act 1960, employees covered by the Truck Acts can be paid wages by cheque or directly into a bank account, so long as they request this in writing. The employer is not obliged to accept the request. If he does, either party can cancel the arrangement by giving 4 weeks' written notice.

Employees who are not covered by the Truck Acts can be provided with benefits in kind as part of their wages.

In 1983 the government announced its intention to repeal the Truck Acts.

Obtaining a pay statement

Most employees are entitled, under the Employment Protection (Consolidation) Act 1978, to receive an itemised pay statement from their employer each time they are paid their wages or salary. Those who are not are certain part-time employees, merchant seamen and employees who work mainly abroad. *See:* EMPLOYMENT PROTECTION; PART-TIME WORKER

There is no standard form, but the statement must show:

Gross pay The total amount earned by the employee during the period covered by the statement, including overtime and bonus payments (although these do not have to be detailed separately).

Deductions All deductions – including INCOME TAX, NATIONAL INSURANCE CONTRIBUTIONS, and trade union dues – must be itemised, stating what they are and the amount deducted in each category. However, if some deductions are the same each pay day, they can be added together under the heading 'fixed deductions', if the employee has previously received written notification of what they are for, the amounts in each case and the frequency with which they are made.

Net pay The amount the employee receives after all deductions have been made from gross pay.

Payment method Sometimes an employee is paid partly in cash and partly by cheque or credit transfer. In such cases, the methods used, and the amounts paid in each way, must be shown on the statement.

If an employer fails to supply an itemised pay statement which meets the legal requirements, the employee can complain to an industrial tribunal. The tribunal can declare that the statement should be provided and outline the form it should take.

It can also punish the employer by ordering him to pay any unnotified deductions made in the 13 weeks before the tribunal application. So if the employer failed to tell the employee, in a proper statement, that he was deducting tax and national insurance contributions, he could be ordered to pay the employee up to 13 weeks' tax and contributions.

When an employer fails to pay

If an employer fails to pay wages in full and on time, and the employee has carried out his side of the contract, the employee can recover the amount due by raising an action for DEBT in the sheriff court.

GETTING THE RATE FOR THE JOB

If nothing is said to you about payment, you are entitled to get quantum meruit – meaning the rate which your work deserves.

If an employee decides to leave his job because he has not been paid his full wages on time, he may be treated as 'constructively' dismissed and be able to obtain compensation for UNFAIR DISMISSAL from an industrial tribunal. However, a tribunal is not likely to decide that the employer's conduct amounts to constructive dismissal if he is only a day or two late in paying – unless he has been late persistently, without good reason.

If an employee is protected by the Truck Acts, it is an offence for his employer not to pay him his full wages. So it would be an offence for the employer to attempt to recover an overpayment of wages by deducting it from the employee's next payment of wages. The employee is entitled to recover the sum deducted.

Complaints about infringements of the Truck Acts should be made to the Wages Inspectorate at the Department of Employment.

When an employer is insolvent If an employer becomes bankrupt, or goes into liquidation, and owes wages to an employee, that employee becomes a preferential creditor. His claim, up to a maximum of £800, for wages payable during the four months before the employer became insolvent is given priority over the claims of ordinary creditors. Any other amounts owed to employees are treated as ordinary debts.

Apart from this right, most employees can recover from public funds money owed to them by an insolvent employer. A written application for payment must first be made to the Department of Employment.

The Department can pay the employee out of the Redundancy Fund for the following debts owed by an employer (subject to a maximum of £145 a week for pay debts):

- A maximum of 8 weeks' pay.
- Any pay due in respect of the statutory minimum period of NOTICE.
- A maximum of 6 weeks' holiday pay to which the employee became entitled in the previous year.
- A basic award of compensation for UNFAIR DISMISSAL.
- Fees paid by apprentices and articled clerks.

The Department will normally make a payment only when the debt is confirmed by the trustee in bankruptcy or the liquidator. But it may be prepared to pay the employee after 6 months, even although the debt has not been officially confirmed, if it thinks that this may take some time.

If the Department refuses to make a payment, or pays less than the employee thinks he is entitled to, he can complain within 3 months to an industrial tribunal. The tribunal can declare that the money should be paid, or that a different amount should be offered.

Once payment is made, the Secretary of State for Employment takes over the employee's right to rank as a preferential creditor for his unpaid wages.

Payment while you are off work

Whether or not you are entitled to be paid when you are away from work depends on the reason for your absence, the terms of your contract, or both.

Holidays There is no statutory right to paid holidays and your entitlement will depend on the terms of your contract. *See:* HOLIDAY ENTITLEMENT

Pregnancy If you leave work to have a baby, you may be entitled to statutory maternity pay and also to maternity allowance. *See:* MATERNITY

Lay-off If you are laid off work, or put on short-time, you may be entitled to guaranteed wages under the terms of your contract. If not, you may be able to obtain statutory guaranteed pay or unemployment benefit. *See:* LAY-OFF

Sickness If you are off work through SICKNESS, you may be entitled to full or partial payment of wages under the terms of your contract. If you are not, you are normally entitled to a minimum amount of statutory sick pay from your employer for the first 8 weeks of sickness. No SICKNESS BENEFIT is payable for that period.

An employee who is not entitled to statutory sick pay can claim sickness benefit instead. *See:* NOTICE

PAY AS YOU EARN

The system of deducting tax from wages

All employees have their income tax deducted automatically from their pay by their employer under the system known as Pay As You Earn – PAYE.

Each year, every employee receives a coding notice from the Inland Revenue listing the personal allowances and expenses to which he is entitled and on which he pays no tax.

The notice also allocates a code number based on those allowances. For example, an employee with allowances of £2,000 gets a code number of 200; if the allowances are £1,200, the code is 120. A letter is added to the code to show allowances:

- L – single person's allowance or wife's earned income allowance.
- H – married man's allowance; single person's allowance with additional personal allowance.
- D – liability to higher-rate tax.
- P – age allowance for single person.
- V – age allowance for married couple.
- T – all others: if you don't wish other letters to be used.

Using the code number and tax tables, the employer must deduct the appropriate amount of tax from each person's pay and pass it to the Inland Revenue each month.

Checking your code

Always check your coding notice to see that you are getting all your allowances. If you think it is wrong, inform the tax office, otherwise too much tax may be deducted.

Tax refunds

If you are temporarily off work – through sickness, being on strike or some other reason – and you do not receive any wages for that period, an adjustment will be made to the tax deduction from your next wage.

If you lose your job permanently, you may be entitled to a tax refund if you have unused personal allowances. However, if you are receiving UNEMPLOYMENT BENEFIT, that counts (since July 1982) as taxable income and so reduces the refund to which you might otherwise be entitled.

Additional income

People with sources of income apart from their wages – for example, working widows and pensioners, or those with more than one job – may have all the tax collected from one source. This will depend on the source of the other income. It would not, for example, be collected from a retirement pension, but it might be from a second job.

A second source of income should be mentioned on your tax return form. The Inland Revenue will also be notified by the employer.

Those with more than one source of income do not normally qualify for refunds. *See:* INCOME TAX

PEDESTRIAN ACCIDENTS

How a victim of negligent driving can sue

A pedestrian injured because of a motorist's NEGLIGENCE can claim damages in the courts. But the amount he receives may be reduced if he was to some extent to blame for the accident.

The court might consider him guilty of such CONTRIBUTORY NEGLIGENCE if he had been:

- Walking on the road instead of the footpath.
- Walking on the left side of the road instead of facing the oncoming traffic.
- Stepping off the kerb without looking.
- Crossing at a junction when the lights were in favour of the vehicle involved.
- Using a Pelican PEDESTRIAN CROSSING when the lights were red.

A motorist can sue a negligent pedestrian for damages – for example, if the pedestrian caused an accident by carelessly stepping into the road.

THE PENALTY FOR IGNORING A PEDESTRIAN CROSSING

A driver who does not stop to give precedence to a pedestrian on a zebra crossing can be fined – and have his licence endorsed.

THE WALKER WHO CAUSED A ROAD DEATH

Someone who steps on to a road without looking and causes a traffic accident can be liable for damages.

Mr M, one of a theatre crowd going home on a summer night, was walking on a wide grass verge beside a main road. A scooter rider, Mr B, was driving in the same direction, close to the left side of the road.

M, intending to cross, stepped on to the road. The scooter collided with him and B was thrown off. As a result of the accident he died of his injuries.

B's widow sued for damages, alleging that M was negligent in failing to ensure that it was safe to step on to the road. M in his defence claimed that B should not have been driving so close to the verge.

The court had to decide which of the two was responsible for the accident, or whether the blame should be shared.

DECISION

The exact distance between the scooter and the verge could not be discovered. But the court held that this did not matter: M's negligence in not looking to his right was the sole cause of the accident. B's widow was awarded damages.

PEDESTRIAN CROSSING

When a driver must give way

There are two types of pedestrian crossing in the United Kingdom – zebra crossings and pelican crossings. Zebra crossings are gradually being phased out in favour of pelican crossings.

Zebra crossings

A zebra crossing is indicated by black and white stripes across the width of the road and flashing amber Belisha beacons mounted on posts or brackets at each end of the crossing.

Vehicles must give way as soon as a pedestrian is within the limits of the crossing. But they are not obliged to give precedence if the pedestrian is still on the kerb, nor if the vehicle reaches the broken white line immediately in front of the crossing before the pedestrian.

A pram and the person pushing it are treated as a single unit. So a motorist must give precedence if a pram is on the crossing, even although the person pushing it is still on the pavement.

If there is a central reservation halfway across, the parts on each side are treated as separate crossings (although there need not be beacons on a central reservation). A motorist approaching the crossing on one side does not have to give way to a pedestrian already walking on the crossing on the other side.

A pedestrian who joins a zebra crossing other than from the kerb still has precedence over vehicles once he has actually reached the striped area.

The pedestrian should not remain on any crossing longer than necessary and can be fined up to £400 for so doing.

Parking within the zigzag area It is an offence to park so that any part of a vehicle is within the zigzag area leading up to and away from a zebra crossing. It is also an offence to overtake a vehicle on the approach to a crossing within the zigzag lines.

A motorist is regarded as having overtaken once any part of his vehicle passes the front of the other vehicle, even if he subsequently drops back again.

The maximum penalty for parking within the zigzag area, failing to give precedence or overtaking at a zebra

MOTORIST WHO THOUGHT HE HAD THE RIGHT OF WAY

Motorists must give way as soon as a pedestrian steps on to a zebra crossing.

Mr Charles Neville, a motorist, was prosecuted for failing to give precedence to a pedestrian.

He argued that he had reached the zigzag area before the pedestrian stepped out and, as this was part of the controlled area, he had precedence. Mr Neville was cleared by the trial court but the prosecution appealed.

DECISION

The appeal court ruled that the zigzag area was only a warning of a crossing ahead. The pedestrian reached the striped area before the vehicle and therefore had precedence. Mr Neville was convicted.

POLITE PEDESTRIAN HURT ON A CROSSING

A motorist is still guilty of failing to give precedence on a zebra crossing even if a pedestrian, out of politeness, allows him to proceed first.

Two men using a crossing halted halfway over to let a car pass. A second car, driven by Mr Gordon Bedford, followed the first one over the crossing and hit one of the men.

Mr Bedford was charged with failing to give precedence. He argued that he thought the pedestrians had waived their precedence.

DECISION

The trial court cleared Mr Bedford but the prosecution appealed. The appeal court ruled that a belief that a pedestrian has waived his precedence is no defence. Mr Bedford was found guilty.

crossing is a fine of £400, and an endorsement or possible disqualification.

Pelican crossings

A pelican crossing is one at which the traffic is controlled by traffic lights and there is a light signal to tell pedestrians when to cross.

A driver must halt at a red light and at the amber light when it is first shown, unless he cannot safely do so. At the flashing amber light after the red light he must respect pedestrians already on the crossing. He must not move forward until it is safe to do so.

A driver must not cause his vehicle to stop on the carriageway between the studs of the crossing unless he is obliged to do so.

The maximum penalty for a driver misusing a crossing in any of the above ways is a £400 fine and endorsement or possible disqualification.

An illuminated 'red man' signal tells the pedestrian that he should wait on the kerb, and a steady 'green man' signal that he may use the crossing. At some pelicans there is also a bleeping sound to tell blind people when the steady 'green man' signal is showing. At the flashing 'green man' signal the pedestrian may continue across the carriageway but he should not start to do so.

It is not an offence for a pedestrian to ignore the pedestrian signals, but he would be held guilty of CONTRIBUTORY NEGLIGENCE if he was involved in an accident. He can, however, be fined up to £400 for loitering on a crossing, and is obliged to cross with reasonable despatch.

School crossings

School crossings do not need to be established on existing zebra or pelican crossings. The motorist is advised by a road sign, sometimes with a flashing light, when such a crossing is in use.

The lollipop man or woman, who must be dressed in the official clothing and display the lollipop sign, has no authority to stop traffic except to allow children walking to or from school to cross the road.

Driving through a lollipop 'stop' sign is an offence. The penalties are a £400 fine and a licence endorsement or possible disqualification.

PERFORMING RIGHT

When you need permission to perform plays, songs and music

Song-writers, composers and playwrights have the right to control and benefit from the public performance of their work. That right, known as the 'performing right', is part of COPYRIGHT and lasts for the author's lifetime plus 50 years.

In that time, any unauthorised public performance of a song, play or piece of music is an infringement of the performing right.

Putting on a show

If you want to stage a play or an opera in public you must seek permission beforehand, unless the author or composer has been dead for more than 50 years.

There is usually a notice inside the front cover of a script or score stating how to get permission.

The British Theatre Association has an information service for its members giving details of the rights and royalties attached to plays, the names and addresses of authors' agents, and useful information on other aspects of staging a performance.

Membership costs £12.50 a year, and is open to amateur or professional directors and stage managers, drama societies, clubs, schools and universities. The association's address is 9 Fitzroy Square, London W1P 6AE.

When a performance is public

Any performances that are not private or domestic are considered public – including those in private clubs, public houses, hotel lounges and restaurants.

If a radio or television plays in, say, a cafe or student common room, any music or play that is broadcast counts as a public performance.

But teachers and pupils performing in school are not affected provided the audience is limited to fellow teachers and pupils.

Protecting composers

It is impossible for song-writers and composers to keep track of all public performances of their work, but the Performing Right Society Ltd, known as the PRS, acts on their behalf.

Membership, which is free, is open to composers, lyric writers – and their heirs – and music publishers.

Members assign their performing rights to the Society, which then grants licenses to broadcasting organisations and to the owners or occupiers of places where music is played to the public. It also protects these rights by taking legal proceedings if necessary.

The Society charges royalties for licences. After deducting its costs, the Society distributes these to members, and to similar societies abroad for distribution to their members.

Normally the royalties are divided between writers and publishers – two-thirds to the writer and one-third to the publisher. That may be varied by agreement but it is a rule that the writer's share must never be less than half.

The society has more than 40 standard tariffs – mainly for bingo halls, discotheques, cinemas, hotels and restaurants, public houses, village halls, clubs, factories, juke boxes and shops.

If you run any of these and play music to your clients or employees, you should apply for a licence to the Society at 29 Berners Street, London W1P 4AA.

Records and tapes

Recording companies also have performing rights in their discs and cassettes and can charge a fee if they are played in public.

These charges are collected by the companies' own rights organisation, Phonographic Performance Ltd – PPL.

So wherever music is played in public from a tape or record two licences are needed – one from the PRS and the other from PPL.

The PPL licence can be obtained by writing to its offices at Ganton House, 14 Ganton Street, London W1V 1LB.

Although you need both licences to play taped background music in a cafe, only a PRS licence is needed to play background music from the radio or television.

Recording at home

If you make a tape recording of an existing record, even for private use only, you are infringing someone's copyright. Although you can videotape a live television broadcast free of charge for private use, you cannot videotape a film broadcast on television without infringing copyright.

The maximum penalties for making, selling or by way of trade possessing a pirate film are £400 or 2 months' imprisonment.

If a charge is unfair

If you think you are being over charged for a licence or that the terms for it are unfair you can appeal to the Performing Right Tribunal – PRT – which will investigate the case.

The PRT was set up in 1957 to resolve disputes between bodies like the PRS and PPL and people needing licences. The tribunal consists of a chairman – a barrister or solicitor – and up to four other members.

A complaint to the tribunal can be made in writing to: The Secretary to the Performing Right Tribunal, Room 105, The Patent Office, 25 Southampton Buildings, London WC2A 1AY.

Where either the PRS or PPL has negotiated a tariff with a representative organisation, such as a restaurant or cafe owner's association, the PRT is unlikely to rule that the rate is unfair – even though an individual cafe owner may think it too much in his case.

PERJURY

The perils of lying in court

Anyone who takes an OATH or makes an affirmation in a court or tribunal must tell the truth. If he does not, and it can be shown that what he said was relevant or important, he can be prosecuted for perjury.

An accused person who gives false evidence at his trial may be guilty of perjury in the same way as any other witness.

Before someone can be convicted of perjury, the prosecution must prove that he deliberately lied. It is a defence for an accused person to prove that his false evidence was unimportant or irrelevant to the case.

Penalty The penalty for perjury is at the discretion of the court, within its sentencing limits.

Anyone who induces someone else to commit perjury, by persuasion, bribery or threats, is guilty of 'subornation of perjury'. The penalty is the same as for perjury.

Apart from perjury before courts and tribunals, it is an offence to give false information:

- To obtain a marriage, birth or death certificate.
- In any company accounts.

Maximum penalty The penalty for either of these offences is up to 2 years' imprisonment and an unlimited fine.

- To gain admittance to a professional register – for example, by lying about a medical degree.

Maximum penalty 12 months' imprisonment and an unlimited fine.

- To obtain the grant of a driving licence.

Maximum penalty A £400 fine.

A CHARGE OF PERJURY

A person accused of a crime who gives false evidence at his trial may be guilty of perjury. In practice, however, such a person is rarely prosecuted.

Cairns stood trial in Glasgow High Court for the murder of a man, Malcolmson, inside Barlinnie Prison in Glasgow.

During his trial, he gave evidence in which he denied murdering Malcolmson and assaulting and stabbing him. He was acquitted.

However the prosecutor later charged Cairns with perjury, alleging that he had lied at his trial when he had denied assaulting and stabbing Malcolmson.

The defence argued that if an accused person gave evidence on oath denying the crime charged, and he was acquitted, it was incompetent to charge him later with perjury in respect of his evidence. That would mean that he would be standing trial twice for the same offence.

DECISION

The High Court rejected the defence argument and approved the perjury charge.

The Court said that the perjury charge was wholly different in nature from the original charge of murder. It took place at a different place and on a different date.

As it happened, Cairns died before the date of his trial for perjury.

PERSONAL ACCIDENT INSURANCE

Providing compensation for death or injury

Financial provision for you if you are injured in an accident – and for your family if you are killed in one – can be provided through a personal accident insurance policy.

The proposal form for this type of insurance includes questions designed to assess the risk involved – about your age, sight, hearing, state of health, drinking habits, and about any circumstances that might make you particularly liable to accidents.

Anyone completing an application form must disclose all material facts and make no deliberately misleading statement. *See:* INSURANCE

The exact wording varies from policy to policy, but most relate to 'bodily injury caused by violent accidental, external and visible means, which, independently of any other cause, causes death or disablement'.

The injury can include broken bones, sprains, ruptures or almost any kind of physical disablement, but shock alone is not classed as an injury. Medical evidence of the injury must be provided in support of any INSURANCE CLAIM.

The word 'accident' means something unexpected and fortuitous, but it may cover not only such things as train crashes or falls but also injuries sustained while, for example, playing tennis or cricket.

A person deliberately injured by someone else may still be able to claim it as an 'accident' – for example, if he were stabbed while walking home at night. If he had provoked the attack, however, by taunting his assailant, he would not succeed in his claim.

When you can claim

Different policies may lay down different conditions about how serious the effect of an injury must be before your claim will be allowed.

Common phrases such as 'unable to perform his usual business or occupation' or 'inability to resume his normal calling', mean the company will pay out if the person is unable to carry out a substantial part of his usual working routine.

But if the policy stipulates 'inability to attend to business of any kind', nothing will be paid unless you are completely incapacitated.

When you cannot claim

Most personal accident insurance policies list specific exceptions to the company's liability – for example, accidents while the insured person is engaged in a hazardous pursuit, such as mountaineering, is under the influence of drink or is exposing himself to obvious risk.

So if someone is injured while trespassing on a railway line, for example, the company can refuse to pay.

You can arrange cover for any extra risk – for example, if skiing is your hobby – by paying an extra premium.

Most policies exclude death or injury by poisoning, even if it is taken accidentally, or by 'anything inhaled' – which is designed to rule out death caused by gas left on in a room by mistake.

How claims are settled

Most personal accident policies provide for a lump sum to be paid for death or injury and weekly payments for a fixed period in the case of disablement.

A typical policy might offer, for example:

- Death after an accident: £2,000.
- Loss of two limbs or two eyes: £2,000.
- Loss of one limb and one eye: £2,000.
- Loss of one limb or one eye: £1,000.
- Permanent disablement: £2,000.
- Temporary disablement: £10 a week for up to 104 weeks.
- Temporary partial disablement: £4 a week for up to 104 weeks.

You can insure for any multiple of these amounts for a corresponding increase in premium.

PERSONAL INJURY

How damages are awarded for losses suffered in an accident

If you are injured in an accident, you may be able to obtain DAMAGES – that is, financial compensation – for any loss which you suffer as a result. Usually, but not always, you will have to prove that someone else was guilty of NEGLIGENCE. But whatever the grounds for your being entitled to damages, the rules for working out the sum of money that you are entitled to are the same.

Only a small minority of accident compensation claims are actually decided by the courts. In most cases the parties concerned reach a compromise settlement either without legal proceedings having to be raised at all, or by negotiation after the action has been brought but before the court hearing.

As a result, there is always a great deal of uncertainty about the precise amount of compensation that you may get. For instance, the possibility of your claim not being upheld at all if a court hearing did take place, and the possibility of your being found partly to blame and having your damages reduced because of your CONTRIBUTORY NEGLIGENCE, are complicating factors which may have to be taken into account when deciding what the level of compensation should be.

Even when your compensation claim is heard before a court, it can be difficult to assess the level of damages because of uncertainty about how your injuries might develop in the future and therefore about how your enjoyment of life and employment prospects might be affected. There are legal rules for working out the damages payable, but these are often difficult to apply. As one judge has said, the rules can be as effective as a broad axe with a blunt edge.

What you get, therefore, may depend greatly on the negotiating skills of your solicitor or advocate, and on his ability to assess correctly the value of your claim. Accordingly, you should always seek expert advice when you decide to make a claim for damages for personal injury.

How damages are assessed

The purpose of an award of damages is to put you in the position that you would have been in had the accident not occurred. In many cases, of course, it will not be possible for money to achieve this. However, an award of damages (or an out-of-court settlement) can effectively compensate you for specific, financial losses that can be traced to your accident.

For instance, an award of damages can compensate you for:

- Earnings that you have lost through being unable to work.
- Earnings that you may lose in the future through being unable to work at your previous job or having your working life cut short.
- Expenses that you have incurred as a result of the accident – such as the cost of medical treatment.
- Replacing or repairing property and possessions damaged in the accident –

such as a car, clothing or a watch.

But quite apart from these, an award of damages can also compensate you for any pain and suffering, loss or impairment of bodily functions and loss of amenities – by which lawyers mean the things that you will not be able to do in the future because of your injury, such as sport or playing a musical instrument – caused by the accident. The technical name for this part of the compensation award is 'solatium' (pronounced 'sol-ayshium').

Your claim for damages can therefore be broken down into two main parts:

- Your claim for financial loss.
- Your claim for solatium.

Your claim for financial loss

Loss of earnings – including future earnings – is usually a very important part of any award of damages.

If you have to stop work because of the accident, you can claim for the money you have lost. To work out the sum which should be claimed, it is first necessary to calculate what you would have earned up to the time your claim is settled, or decided by a court. A figure will then have to be calculated to cover any earnings which you are likely to lose in the future.

Loss of actual earnings To calculate your loss of earnings in the period up to the settlement, or court hearing, the total amount that you would have earned during that period must first be worked out. If you were employed (rather than self-employed), this means the gross wages or salary that you would have received. Income tax and sick pay – but not national insurance contributions – must then be deducted.

If you can show that your pay would have risen during the period in question – because, for instance, a new pay award has been successfully negotiated by your union – you are entitled to assume that your earnings would have been paid on the basis of the new figures. On the other hand, if it can be shown that you would have become unemployed in any event during that period – for instance, because your factory has closed down – you will not be able to recover earnings for the period in which you would have been unemployed.

Self-employed people are entitled to recover the net profit that they have lost

WORKING OUT WHAT YOU ARE ENTITLED TO

The following is an example of how a typical claim for damages following an accident is worked out.

Mr S, who is 58, had an accident when he was 55. He was a pedestrian injured by a car. The car driver was to blame but Mr S was 20 per cent to blame himself.

In the accident his left leg was crushed, his trousers were ripped open and his glasses were smashed. His leg had to be amputated half way down the thigh and he spent three months in hospital.

For two months after the accident, his head injuries gave him double vision. He now has an artificial limb, which he cannot bend, and requires two sticks to walk. He is still in pain. He has changed from being a very vigorous and active man to being completely depressed.

His medical condition is not expected to improve. In addition, he has had to leave his job and will never be able to go back to work.

His claim

1. *Loss of Earnings*		
(a) From the date of the accident to the present:		
First year expected gross earnings	£4,160	
Less 4 weeks sick pay	322	
	3,838	
Less Income tax	780	
		3,058
Second year expected gross earnings	4,576	
Less income tax	860	
		3,716
Third year expected gross earnings	5,034	
Less Income tax	946	
		4,088
		10,862
Less ½ Sickness Benefit (of £500)	250	
½ Invalidity Benefit (of £2,200)	1,100	
Supplementary Benefit	105	
		1,455
		9,407
Add interest at 6% a year (3 years)		1,593
		11,000
(b) Loss of earnings in the future		
Net present yearly loss after tax: £4,088 × 4	£16,352	
Less ½ 2 years expected Invalidity Benefit £3,120	1,560	
		14,792
2. *Solatium*		
Amount awarded	15,000	
Add interest at 5½% a year on £7,500 as attributed to the past (3 years)	1,350	
		16,350
3. *Expenses*		
		222

[continued over]

4. *Property Damage*		
New pair of trousers	18	
New spectacles	57	
Add interest at 12% a year from the date of payment of the bills	9	
		84
Total value of the claim		
Loss of earnings to the present	11.000	
Loss of earnings in the future	14,792	
Solatium	16,350	
Expenses	222	
Property Damage	84	
	42,448	
Less 20% for Contributory Negligence	8,489	
TOTAL		£33,959

from their business. This normally has to be worked out by an accountant.

If you work for your own company, you can only recover the loss of your net salary, like any other employee. You cannot recover any loss of company profits which have arisen because you were unable to give your expertise and effort to the business.

Loss of future earnings The first rule to be borne in mind, when working out a figure to represent the loss of future earnings, is that the future, by its nature, is never certain.

The figure will depend on the length of time for which you are expected to be off work. If your injuries are severe and permanent, that may well be for the rest of your expected working life – that is, until what would have been the normal retiring age for you.

However, the figure is not calculated merely by taking your annual loss of earnings and multiplying it by the number of years involved. There are two reasons why this is not done:

1. Your working life might not have lasted until your retirement. Events might well have turned out differently – for instance, you might have ceased work or even died before the end of your working life through natural causes or some other accident.

2. By investing the money you receive as damages, you can earn interest on it which will increase the total amount of money obtained. To award you your annual loss of earnings multiplied by the total number of years that you expect to be off work would mean that you would be over-compensated – at the end of the day you might have more money than you had lost.

To avoid this happening, a rather artificial method is used to calculate your future loss of earnings. Your present yearly loss of earnings (after tax) up to the present time is multiplied by a figure which is smaller than the number of years during which you expect to be unable to earn. This figure, though related to that number of years, is not a fixed proportion of them. This is because the courts do not use figures which are higher than 16 or 17.

Multipliers of 16 or 17 would be appropriate in the case of someone who expected to work full-time until the age of 65 and who became permanently disabled at the age of 30 or less. For a man aged, say, 47, with similar injuries, the appropriate multiplier might be 9 or 10. There is some flexibility – a multiplier may be smaller than that normally used if, for example, there is evidence which shows that you would not have gone on working regularly anyway.

If you are able to work after your accident, but your earning power is reduced because you have to take a lower paid job as a result of your accident, you can be compensated for the difference between your after-tax earnings before and after the accident.

If you have been able to return to work and to earn the same amount as before, you may still be able to get compensation to take account of the possibility that your accident may make it difficult for you to continue being employed in such a position in the future.

For instance, your employers may take you back because they value your services and are prepared to disregard your disability. But if you had to apply for a comparable position in another firm in the future, you could find yourself at a disadvantage compared to people with no disability. The courts will award around £1,000 for this sort of disadvantage.

Reduction in life expectation One result of a serious accident may be that your expectation of life is reduced by some years. In some cases it may be so reduced that your likely date of death is within what was previously the span of your normal, expected working life. If this is so, damages are awarded to cover your loss of earnings in these 'lost years' of life.

However, the amount of damages is reduced by what you would be expected to have spent on living expenses, which it is now assumed you will not live to incur.

Inflation In calculating the amount representing your expected future loss of earnings, no account is taken of inflation. This means that the sum awarded may well be inadequate in the long term to maintain your standard of living at the level it would have been had you continued to earn. This may happen even if the money is sensibly invested.

Expenses

Your accident may have resulted in your having to pay out money on, for instance, medical treatment or adaptations to help you cope with your disability. So long as they are reasonable, you can recover the cost of these and other relevant expenses as part of your damages.

You do not have to use the National Health Service for medical treatment – you can claim for any medically justifiable, private treatment that you have as a result of your accident, whether or not it is also available on the NHS. You may have private physiotherapy, for instance, or spend a period of convalescence in a private nursing home.

However, you are unlikely to know whether you will be able to recover any damages until some time after your accident. Because of the possibility that they might not be able to recover the cost, few accident victims incur private medical expenses.

SOLATIUM FOR PAIN, SUFFERING AND GENERAL DISADVANTAGE

The following awards of solatium were made in 1981. They give an indication of how much the courts are likely to award, in addition to damages for financial loss, to compensate for pain and suffering.

- A 28 year old man's left foot and right leg were crushed. The leg required an operation. He continued to have permanent stiffness in his foot and pain on walking. It was thought that he might need another operation in the future. £5,000 was awarded.
- A 67 year old woman broke her shoulder and had minor knee injuries. The shoulder had to be pinned. Afterwards she could not raise her arm more than ninety degrees. The evidence was that her condition would not get better. She could still do most of her housework. £3,000 was awarded.
- A 55 year old miner had his right knee crushed and suffered a minor fracture of one of the bones in his leg. He was left with some permanent pain. £3,600 was awarded.
- A man in his late forties suffered a slipped disc. £1,200 was awarded.
- A man in his late forties broke his left wrist. The judge found that he had completely recovered by the time of the court hearing. £1,000 was awarded.
- A man aged 46 got dermatitis. This gave one of his hands a dry and leathery appearance. There was a small amount of inconvenience. £750 was awarded.

If you are able to recover the cost of long-term, institutional nursing care, and you are entitled to damages for loss of earnings in the period during which you were (or will be) receiving such care, a deduction will be made from your compensation for loss of earnings. This is to take account of the amount that you have saved through not having to spend money on housekeeping during that time.

After your accident, you may have been looked after by a married (or unmarried) partner or by certain other close relatives. If so, you can recover for that person, in your damages action, a sum representing reasonable payment – including reasonable expenses – for his or her services.

You can obtain this sum even if the relative had no thought of being paid – unless he or she knew that you were suing (or intended to) and agreed to look after you for nothing.

Damage to property

Some of your property may have been damaged or destroyed at the same time as you were injured. For instance, your car may have been badly damaged, or your clothing or watch ruined. If this is so, part of your damages can include a figure representing the *lower* of the following two figures:

1. The market value of the damaged article – after making an allowance for any scrap or second hand value which it may have.

2. The cost of repairing the article.

However, if the article is unique or unusual, you may be able to recover the cost of repair even if that is *more* than the market value.

In addition, you can recover the cost of hiring a replacement for the property which has been damaged or destroyed – a car, for instance – until the repairs have been carried out or you are able to obtain a new article.

Obtaining solatium

You are entitled to compensation over and above your financial losses, to compensate you for the fact that your life has been changed by the accident. The award, known as solatium, is meant to compensate you for pain and suffering, loss of faculties (for instance, limbs or eyesight) and loss of amenities (not being able to do things, such as swimming or diving or watching television, because of the injuries suffered in the accident).

Solatium is payable for the loss of some faculty, such as a limb, even although you may not be aware of the loss – because you are, for example, permanently unconscious.

The level of payment will depend partly on the severity of your injuries and partly on the effect that they have on you as an individual. It will also depend to some extent on your age – the younger you are, the longer you will be disadvantaged.

If one result of the accident is that your life expectancy is reduced, and you know this, the amount of solatium will be increased since this will obviously affect your enjoyment of life.

When the amount of solatium payable is being assessed, evidence about the effect of your injuries on you is crucial. What is relatively trivial to one person may be extremely serious to another. For instance, if you are a keen sports player, an apparently minor hand injury may affect your enjoyment of life much more than it would other people.

For the same sort of reason, the courts take the view that scarring is less upsetting as you get older. Because of this, young people have more account taken of scarring in the assessment of their claim than do older people.

Since the amount of solatium awarded is related to the circumstances of each victim, it is not possible to lay down exact figures for particular types of injury. Lawyers will make a rough assessment of claims by making comparisons with previous court awards in similar cases.

The amounts awarded by the courts range from a couple of hundred pounds for a minor injury to £30,000 for a catastrophic injury. The relative levels of payment have risen gradually in recent years – though not quite as fast as the rate of inflation. This is something which should be borne in mind when making comparisons with awards in previous years.

Deductions from damages

To arrive at a final figure for the damages to be awarded for personal injury (but not for any property damage), certain deductions are made to take account of some social security benefits that are payable (or are expected to be payable) to an injured person. However, the majority of payments that are received from other sources are not deducted.

Some social security benefits are deducted in full; one half of certain others, received (or expected to be received) for 5 years after the accident, is deducted:

- **Payments which are not deducted** Payments from a charity, such as a disaster fund. Payments from any insurance that you had taken out against accident or disability. Redundancy payments. Retirement pensions. Mobility allowance, attendance allowance and constant attendance allowance.

• **Benefits deducted in full** Unemployment benefit. Family income supplement and supplementary benefit paid *before* the award of damages.

• **Benefits deducted at rate of one half** Sickness benefit. Invalidity benefit. Non-contributory invalidity pension. Disablement benefit.

Interest on damages

Because your right to be paid damages arises at the time you are injured, you are entitled to interest on the sum awarded. The rate of interest varies – at present it is 12 per cent a year for expenses and property damage, running from the time that you incur the cost.

Interest on past loss of earnings is usually awarded at half this figure (6 per cent a year) on the whole sum due from the date of the accident. This rule avoids the need to calculate the interest separately on each week of earnings lost.

The solatium payment is divided into two parts: one part to represent the disadvantage that you have already suffered and the other to represent the disadvantage that you are expected to suffer in the future. Interest of 6 per cent a year is awarded on the first of these sums from the date of the accident. *See also:* FATAL INJURY

PERVERTING THE COURSE OF JUSTICE

Interfering with the process of the law

At one time, 'perverting the course of justice' was a general term covering a number of crimes – such as PERJURY and prison breaking – which involved an attempt to defeat or pervert the course of justice.

In recent years, however, an attempt to pervert the course of justice has come to be treated as a specific offence itself. Broadly speaking, the offence penalises conduct which interferes with the bringing, progress and result of judicial proceedings. Prosecutions arise from interfering with witnesses, failing to attend court as a witness, and fabricating false evidence.

For example, if a motorist and his passenger concoct a story that leads to the wrong person being suspected of an offence following an accident, both are guilty of attempting to pervert the course of justice.

Some conduct which falls within the broad offence of attempting to pervert the course of justice may also amount to some other crime. Interfering with witnesses, for example, is also punishable as CONTEMPT OF COURT. In such circumstances, an offender will be prosecuted for one offence.

Penalty The penalty is at the court's discretion, within its sentencing limits.

THE FRIENDS WHO TOLD LIES

Making a false statement to the police for the purpose of avoiding prosecution can be charged as an attempt to pervert the course of justice.

James Peek was involved in a road accident when the vehicle he was driving collided with a parked car. He failed to stop after the accident.

During the subsequent investigation, Peek and another man, Michael Dean, told the police that Dean, and not Peek, had been the driver of the vehicle.

Peek and Dean were charged with attempting to pervert the course of justice. Dean appealed against his conviction on the ground that no court proceedings were pending when the lies were told to the police. In other words, he was claiming that there could be no attempt to pervert the course of justice when no 'course of justice' had begun.

DECISION

The Appeal Court dismissed Dean's appeal. It stated that the course of justice had already begun, as the police were investigating an incident which almost certainly would lead to the criminal prosecution of the driver for road traffic offences.

In giving false information, Dean had tried to prevent this prosecution, and justice being done, by diverting police attention towards himself and away from the real culprit.

PEST CONTROL

What to do if your home is overrun by pests.

If your home is plagued by pests of any kind, you can seek advice from the Environmental Health Department of your district or islands council.

Councils vary in the service which they provide. All will give advice on how to deal with a great variety of pests, including rats and mice, parasites, wasps, bees, ants and birds. Some may be prepared to get rid of certain pests for you free of charge, or for a small charge.

No council, however, is legally obliged to get rid of pests for you. Generally, you will have to take action yourself. You will find lists of firms in your area which specialise in pest control under 'Pest and Vermin Control Services' in the 'Yellow Pages' section of the telephone directory.

Rats and mice A district or islands council has a legal duty to make sure that its area is, as far as possible, kept free from rats and mice. But it is not obliged to get rid of rats or mice for you. Some councils do offer such a service; others are prepared only to inspect your home and to give you advice on poisons and how to use them.

If any householder or trader fails to take action to rid his premises of rats or mice, the council can serve a notice on him ordering him to do so and detailing the steps to be taken.

Anyone who fails to obey such a notice commits an offence and can be fined up to £400.

If the council has to take action to destroy the vermin, it can recover its expenses from the householder or trader concerned.

Parasitic insects If your house becomes infested with insects such as lice, bedbugs, fleas or cockroaches, the council will usually be prepared to treat your home with a suitable insecticide, free of charge. It may also offer a free disinfestation service for bedding and clothing.

Wasps and bees Your council may be prepared to give you assistance to clear out a wasps' nest.

If you are troubled by a swarm of bees, the council may have a list of beekeepers in the area who are pre-

GETTING RID OF RATS AND MICE

The environmental health department of your district or islands council will give you advice on how to kill rats or mice. It may also be prepared to get rid of them for you.

pared to deal with the swarm.

Serious pests If you find serious pests – such as the colorado beetle – you should immediately contact the police or the Department of Agriculture and Fisheries for Scotland, Chesser House, Gorgie Road, Edinburgh.

PETROL STORAGE

Restrictions to avoid dangers

In general, a petroleum-spirit licence is needed to store petrol. Private individuals, and commercial users such as garages, have to apply to the regional or islands council for such a licence and observe the restrictions attached to it.

However, if the quantity stored – whether for sale or private use – is kept in separate, sealed containers, holding no more than one pint each, and the total amount so stored is no more than 3 gallons, no licence is needed.

Private users of larger quantities of petrol (but not those who sell it) may also store it without a licence, but they have to observe stringent conditions, under threat of criminal penalties:

- The petrol must be for use only in an internal combustion engine, such as that for a vehicle, lawn mower or generator.
- If it is stored in metal cans, they must be sealed and be clearly marked 'Petroleum Spirit – Highly Inflammable'.
- If it is stored in plastic containers (which has been permitted since June, 1982), they must be of up to 5 litres capacity, of an approved design, and marked or labelled with the following information:

1. The manufacturer's name.
2. The month and year of manufacture.
3. The nominal capacity of the container in litres and half litres rounded down to the nearest half litre below.
4. The words and figures 'Complies with S.I. 1982/630'.
5. The words 'PETROL' and 'HIGHLY FLAMMABLE'.
6. An appropriate hazard warning sign.
7. An appropriate phrase or phrases in English indicating the precautions to be taken.

Metal containers If petrol is stored in metal containers, the storage place must:

- Be in the open air, or well-ventilated.
- Have fire-fighting equipment to hand.
- Be separated from any house by a non-inflammable partition.

No more than 60 gallons can be kept in any one storage place. (Storage places less than 20 feet apart count as one.)

In addition, the petrol cannot be kept in containers of more than 2 gallons unless the storage place is more than 20 feet from a building or road, precautions are taken to prevent spillage and the council is informed.

If the petrol is stored within 20 feet of a building, the petrol can only be kept in the fuel tank of a vehicle, boat or aircraft, and in no more than two other 2 gallon containers, unless the council is notified otherwise.

Plastic containers Up to two plastic containers of petrol can be kept in a vehicle, boat or aircraft. And up to two such containers can be kept in a safe place in a house, and in any other safe places more than 6 metres apart.

Penalties Offences against these regulations carry a penalty of up to £2,000. But anyone charged with breaking the rules can plead that he took all reasonable precautions and care.

PHOTOCOPYING

When you may have to pay a fee

Students, and people who are engaged in private study, are generally allowed to photocopy portions of books and documents for personal use – provided that they do not later publish them. But it is never permissible to make any commercial use of such photocopies. *See:* COPYRIGHT

PICKETING

When peaceful persuasion is within the law

When there is an industrial dispute between an employer and his workers – it may be a STRIKE, a go-slow or a work-to-rule – the workers may try to persuade other employees not to work, or to persuade workers in other firms not to deliver or collect goods.

The usual way of doing this is to gather outside the employer's premises and try to persuade others not to enter. This is known as picketing.

There is no legal right to picket – but there is no law which expressly forbids it either. However, depending on the circumstances, picketing may result in civil or criminal liability, or both.

When a picket breaks the law

If there is a trade dispute – a dispute between workers and their employer that is wholly or mainly about employment matters – it may be lawful for someone to picket at or near the employer's premises to further the dispute.

For the picketing to be lawful, the premises must be his place of work (unless he is a trade union official, who can picket at the workplace of a member of that union), he must put his case peacefully and he must commit no offence. He cannot then be prevented from picketing, sued for damages or prosecuted.

If a picket breaks any of these rules, action may be taken against him in the civil or criminal courts.

When a union breaks the law

Picketing may be 'official', meaning that it is authorised by a trade union. If it is, and it is unlawful, the employer affected can take legal proceedings in the civil courts against the union as well as the employees who are picketing. Indeed, it is likely that the employer will proceed only against the union.

The union will not be liable for any unlawful picketing by its members that it does not authorise. *See:* STRIKE

Breaking the criminal law

Peaceful picketing (see below) is not itself an offence – but a number of offences may be committed in the course of it. Picketing that is not peaceful may well amount to an offence.

The offences that may be charged are:

Obstruction A picket commits a criminal offence if he obstructs the passage of pedestrians or vehicles along a pavement or street.

For instance, a picket can attempt to stop a lorry at the factory gates in order to persuade the driver to turn back. But it is for the driver to decide whether he wants to stop. If he does not wish to be persuaded, the picket commits an offence if he blocks the driver's way.

A driver should exercise due care when approaching or driving past a picket line. Although he does not have to stop, he will be liable for NEGLIGENCE if he carelessly injures a picket – though the picket may be held to have contributed to his injuries if he deliberately stood in the middle of the road. *See:* CONTRIBUTORY NEGLIGENCE

Sit-ins If pickets occupy their employer's premises – instead of picketing outside them – without his consent, they may be prosecuted for criminal TRESPASS or for wrongfully 'besetting' a place of business (see below).

Breach of the peace A picket who creates a public disturbance, or who puts other people in a state of alarm, commits a BREACH OF THE PEACE and may be prosecuted. The offence is also committed if the picket's behaviour is considered *likely* to cause a breach of the peace.

Obstructing the police It is an offence to obstruct the police in the execution of their duty.

For instance, if the police think that continued picketing will lead to a breach of the peace – perhaps because there is a risk of violence or there are too many pickets – they may order the picketing to stop or the numbers to be reduced. Anyone who physically resists such an order may be prosecuted for obstruction (or breach of the peace).

Intimidation It is an offence for a picket to use or threaten violence, or damage property, to intimidate others. *See:* ASSAULT; VANDALISM

It is also an offence for a picket to attempt to stop someone going about his lawful business by seriously intimidating him or his family; watching or besetting (that includes occupying) his home, place of work or business; persistently following him about (including by car); or hiding or interfering with his property.

To commit this offence, the picket's actions must amount to at least a DELICT. The maximum penalty is a fine of £400 or imprisonment for 3 months.

Other offences Depending on the circumstances, a picket can be charged with a variety of other offences. For example: using threatening, abusive or insulting language; distributing or displaying material containing threatening, abusive or insulting words; or carrying an OFFENSIVE WEAPON.

Agreement on numbers

The government's Code of Practice on Picketing (see below) recommends that the number of pickets at any entrance to a workplace should not normally exceed six. The police may come to an agreement with the organisers of the picketing to limit the pickets to that number at each workplace entrance.

If more than that number turn up, this may lead to a fear by the police that a breach of the peace may occur. They may then order the extra pickets to leave. Failing to obey may be prosecuted as a breach of the peace.

Breaking the civil law

A picket is immune from civil liability for 'peaceful picketing' – that is, where:

1. His picketing is 'in contemplation or furtherance of a trade dispute'.

2. He pickets at or near his *own* place of work or, if he is a union official, at the place of work of one of his members.

3. His purpose is only to peacefully obtain or communicate information, or peacefully persuade someone to work or not to work.

A picket who breaks any one of these rules loses his immunity. So if, for instance, his picketing causes breaches of employment contracts, or interference with contracts with suppliers or customers, the employer affected can apply to court for an INTERDICT to stop it. If the picketing has union authorisation, the employer will probably seek interdict against the union instead.

Failing to obey an interdict amounts to CONTEMPT OF COURT and may lead to a fine or even imprisonment.

The employer can also sue for damages for any loss caused to him. He can sue the picket – though this is rare – or the union if it authorised the picketing. There are statutory limits on the amount of damages payable by unions. *See:* STRIKE

Furthering a trade dispute

As we have seen, pickets lose their immunity against civil liability if they are not furthering a trade dispute – that is, a dispute between workers and their employer which is wholly or mainly about terms and conditions of employment or other workplace matters.

So a dispute that is purely political – such as a dispute about an employer allegedly supporting policies of apartheid in South Africa – will not be a trade dispute.

ORGANISING A PICKET LINE

Anyone involved in a trade dispute who wants to organise a picket line outside the employer's factory, should ensure that he is acting within the law. To do so, he should:

- Seek advice from his union head office.
- See the local police and find out the number of pickets they will allow outside the premises and where they should stand so as not to obstruct the street or pavement.
- Ensure that all official pickets wear badges and know exactly how they must behave within the law, and turn away anyone who tries to join the picket who is not an official picket.
- Ensure that the wording on any placards or banners is lawful and not likely to cause a breach of the peace because it is insulting or likely to incite racial hatred.
- Obey any police instruction that is reasonable – for example, if a person is asked to move.
- Ensure that the protest remains peaceful.
- Ensure that workers from other places of work do not join the picket lines.

THE PICKET WHO BROKE A POLICE CORDON

The police can prevent picketing if public order is threatened.

When electricians went on strike at the St. Thomas' Hospital building site at Lambeth Palace Road, London, in 1973, non-union labour was employed to do their work.

On March 28, a crowd of 30 to 40 demonstrators, including four official pickets wearing armbands, met outside the site. They intended to approach the coach carrying the replacement workers and try to dissuade them from working during the strike and the driver from carrying them to work.

Fearing that a breach of the peace might be caused, a police superintendent ordered his men to cordon off the path of the coach. He refused to allow even the official pickets to pass through the cordon. When the coach left the site, Peter Roger Kavanagh, a former TGWU official, tried to push through to speak to the driver. When blocked by the police, he punched Constable Hiscock.

Kavanagh was arrested and charged with assault and obstructing the police in the execution of their duty. At the hearing before Lambeth magistrates Kavanagh claimed in his defence that the police had acted unlawfully in preventing the official pickets – who had a right to peacefully persuade – from approaching the coach. The magistrates found that the police were justified in preventing disorder and Kavanagh was found guilty, fined £10 for assault, £10 for obstruction and made to pay £10 costs. He appealed to the High Court.

DECISION

The High Court upheld the conviction. It ruled that picketing may not impinge on the duty of the police to prevent a breach of the peace.

Nor will a dispute be a trade dispute if it is only partly about job-related matters and mainly about something else – such as a political or ideological issue. For example, in a recent case it was decided that British Telecom employees who took industrial action mainly to preserve BT's monopoly rather than to protect jobs were most unlikely to be treated as carrying on a trade dispute.

Even if there is a trade dispute, a court may decide that pickets are not 'furthering' it – that, for example, their actions are motivated purely by spite or revenge. If this is so, immunity will again be lost.

The 'place of work'

An employee (except for a trade union official) can lawfully picket only at or near the entrance to the factory, office or other place at which *he* works.

If he pickets at someone else's place of work, whether in support of a dispute with his employer or a dispute involving that other person's employer, he has no immunity against civil liability – even if he is furthering a trade dispute.

A mobile worker – such as a lorry driver – or someone who works at a place where picketing would be impracticable, can picket at any premises of his employer from which he works or from which his work is administered.

Secondary picketing

The phrase 'secondary picketing' is used to describe picketing at your own place of work, but in support of a dispute between *another* employer and his workers.

If you engage in secondary picketing to further a trade dispute, you may lose your immunity from civil liability. Whether you do depends on the purpose of your picketing, its likely effect and the relationship between your employer and the employer in dispute.

If you only interfere with employment contracts – that is, you prevent people from working normally – you will get immunity. But if, by doing so, you also interfere with commercial contracts – contracts that the employer has with suppliers and customers – you will only get immunity if:

- Your employer is a supplier or customer of the employer in dispute.
- Your main purpose is to *directly* prevent or disrupt the supply of goods or services between the two of them.
- Your picketing is likely to achieve that purpose.

So if your employer is not a supplier or customer of the employer who is in dispute, you will get no immunity. Nor will you get it if you act *indirectly* – by deliberately interfering with your employer's contracts with someone else – or your main purpose is, for instance, merely to settle a grudge.

Furthermore, if a court thinks that your picketing is unlikely to achieve its purpose, you will have no immunity.

The Code of Practice

In 1980 the government issued a Code of Practice on picketing which explains the law and the role of the police and gives practical guidance on how picketing should be organised and conducted.

Failure to observe the Code does not of itself render anyone liable to court proceedings. But a court can take account of the Code whenever it appears relevant in any case.

Copies of the Code of Practice can be obtained from the Department of Employment, Pentland House, Robb's Loan, Edinburgh EH14 1UE.

PLACE OF SAFETY ORDER

Immediate protection for a child at risk

A child under 16 who is seriously at risk can be compulsorily removed from home to a place of safety – for instance, a foster home, a children's home or the home of a relative.

A police officer or any other person – in practice it is usually a social worker – can apply to a court or a JUSTICE OF THE PEACE for a warrant authorising the removal of a child to a place of safety. This can be done on any one of the following grounds:

- The child is likely to be caused unnecessary suffering or serious injury to health because of lack of parental care. *See:* CHILD ABUSE
- An offence under the Children and Young Persons (Scotland) Act 1937 is thought to have been committed against the child – that is, wilful ill-treatment or neglect; allowing a child under 16 to beg; exposing a child under 7 to the risk of burning; allowing a child under 16 to endanger himself or herself through taking part in public performances.
- A sexual offence has been committed against the child, or against another child in the same household. This covers offences such as INCEST, unlawful sexual intercourse, indecent behaviour

and involving a girl in prostitution.

- The child has joined, or is likely to join, a household containing someone who has committed a sexual offence.
- An offence involving bodily injury has been committed against the child.
- The person in charge of the child is moving around and preventing the child from getting a proper education.

Gaining entry The warrant does not entitle a social worker to enter the child's home if entry is refused. In that situation, a justice of the peace can issue a warrant authorising a named policeman (but no one else) to enter the home and remove the child to a place of safety.

Referring the child to a children's hearing

A child can be detained for 7 days under a place of safety order. However, a REPORTER to the local Children's Panel must arrange for the child to be brought before a children's hearing – on the very next day (if possible) or within the 7 days – if compulsory care is thought to be necessary.

The children's hearing can deal with the child in the same way as any other child who comes before it. *See:* CHILDREN'S HEARING.

If the hearing is unable to dispose of the case immediately, it can continue the order for a further 21 days. If necessary, the order can be continued for three further periods of 21 days, but no longer.

The child, or the child's parents, have three weeks in which to appeal to the sheriff against a hearing's decision to continue the order.

PLANNING BLIGHT

Where planning proposals or decisions affect the value of your property

There are several situations in which you may have a remedy if a planning decision or planning proposals lower the value of your property.

Planning blight

Planning blight arises when you cannot sell your home, or can only get a reduced price for it, because it is likely to be acquired by COMPULSORY PURCHASE at some future date. This can happen where, for example, your property is on the line of a proposed new road or is in a HOUSING ACTION AREA.

Where the house you own and occupy is 'blighted' in this way, and you have tried to sell it on the open market but cannot find a buyer except at a reduced price, you can send a 'blight notice' to the authority responsible for the proposals – that is, the authority which would eventually acquire the property if the proposals were carried out.

A BLIGHT NOTICE THAT FAILED

To succeed in forcing a public authority to purchase a 'blighted' property, the property owner must show that he has been unable to sell the property in the open market at a reasonable price because of the authority's proposals.

In 1972 the owners of a shop, who wished to force the highway authority, Glasgow Corporation, to purchase it, served a blight notice on the Corporation. The shop was affected by proposed road improvements, due to be carried out at some indefinite future date, and the owners claimed that when they had put the shop on the market they had been unable to obtain any offers for it.

Glasgow Corporation refused to accept the blight notice, saying that the inability to sell the shop was due to various circumstances for which the Corporation was not responsible – including a recently-opened shopping centre in the vicinity, an excess of older shops left vacant, and parking restrictions on roads in the area. It was for these reasons, claimed the Corporation, and not because of the road proposals, that the shop was not attractive to purchasers.

The shop owners referred the dispute to the Lands Tribunal for Scotland.

DECISION

The Tribunal decided it was for the shop owners to prove that their inability to sell the shop was due to the local authority's road proposals rather than the shop's other disadvantages. The owners had failed to do this. The Tribunal therefore upheld the Corporation's objections to the blight notice.

The effect of a successful blight notice is to compel the authority to buy the house immediately for the full market price – that is, what it would be worth if no development was planned. However, the law on planning blight is complex and it may be wise to ask a solicitor or surveyor to act for you.

If the authority wishes to contest a blight notice, it must issue a counter-notice within two months. If you object to the counter-notice, you can refer the dispute to the Lands Tribunal for Scotland for a decision. If the authority does not send out a counter-notice within the two-month period, the blight notice takes effect automatically.

Compensation for the house is calculated in the same way as if the authority was acquiring the property by compulsory purchase. The effect of the 'blighting' proposals is ignored in making the valuation. Where your house is bought by an authority as a result of a blight notice, you cannot claim a home loss payment but you are entitled to claim for professional advice, removal expenses, etc. *See:* COMPULSORY PURCHASE

If the compensation cannot be agreed, you can appeal to the Lands Tribunal for Scotland.

Construction and use of public works

Where your home is affected by, for example, noise, dirt and fumes resulting from the construction or use of new public developments – such as a new motorway – you cannot normally take civil action for NUISANCE. However, there may be some steps you can take.

If disturbance from *construction* work becomes very serious, you can request the public authority responsible for the development to pay the cost of temporary alternative accommodation for you and your family. In the case of noise from *major road works,* you may be able to benefit from a sound insulation scheme.

Where the value of your house has gone down because of noise, fumes, dirt and the like, resulting from the *use* of new public works – for example, noise caused by traffic on a new road, or

DEPRECIATION DUE TO AIRCRAFT NOISE

When the value of a house has gone down because of physical factors – for example, noise, smell, fumes or dirt – caused by the use of new or altered public works, the owner can claim compensation for the loss of value.

Mrs Barbara Inglis owned a house in a village near Edinburgh Airport. In 1976 a new runway came into operation at the airport. Mrs Inglis' house was directly in line with the new runway and most of the aircraft taking off from the airport flew over the house.

She claimed that the value of her house had been reduced by £2,000 because of the increased noise, vibration and fumes from aircraft taking off and landing on the new runway.

The operators of the airport, the British Airports Authority, refused to accept that the house had depreciated in value. Mrs Inglis therefore took her claim to the Lands Tribunal for Scotland.

DECISION

Mrs Inglis succeeded in her claim, though she did not receive as much compensation as she had asked for. The Lands Tribunal was satisfied that the increased aircraft noise was likely to cause any prospective purchaser of the house to make a lower offer than he would otherwise have made.

As to the calculation of the amount of compensation, the tribunal said that they had to consider, first of all, the value the house would have fetched in the open market if there had been no new runway in operation. They decided on a figure of £13,000. The tribunal then compared this sum – the value on a 'no runway' basis – with the actual value of the property, which was assessed at £11,700. The resultant depreciation in value, £1,300, was the amount to be awarded to Mrs Inglis.

aircraft approaching a new airport runway – you can in some circumstances claim compensation for the lost value.

To be eligible for compensation you must be able to show that the value of your home has been reduced by at least £50. There is a time limit for claims. You would be well advised to seek professional advice in making your claim.

If your claim is successful, the authority will pay reasonable expenses in addition to compensation. Disputes over the amount of compensation are settled by the Lands Tribunal for Scotland.

If your house is affected by noise from traffic on a new highway, or one which has had an extra carriageway added, you are entitled to sound insulation if the noise exceeds a certain level. Even if the noise does not reach that level, the highway authority may be prepared to make a grant for sound insulation. *See:* AIRCRAFT NOISE

If your home is affected by, for example, increased noise from public works, you can seek a reduction in rent or rateable value.

Purchase notice

If you have been refused PLANNING PERMISSION to develop your property, it is only very rarely that you will be entitled to compensation. However, if the property, in its existing state, is virtually useless, you may be able to compel the planning authority to purchase it.

For example, if you have a small allotment garden on which you are refused permission to build a cottage, you may be able to force the authority to buy the land. A 'purchase notice' has to be served on the authority. Although you might only be paid a small amount, you would be relieved of the expense of useless property.

PLANNING OBJECTION

Your rights to oppose development proposals

You have an opportunity to make your views known to the planning authority on most proposals for new development.

Development plan

The local authorities responsible for planning control in an area must prepare a development plan and must update it periodically. A development plan consists of a structure plan – which sets out in very broad terms the policy framework for future development in the area – and one or more local plans, containing detailed planning policies and proposals. A local plan will, for example, show the line of proposed new roads.

Before an authority finalises its ideas about proposals to be included in a plan (or in an amendment to a plan), the public must be given an opportunity to express their views on the plan's content. Once the authority has finalised the draft plan, the proposals must be advertised and there is an opportunity for formal objection. Objections to a local plan are considered at a public inquiry, at which an objector can argue his case.

The development plan is used as a guide in the making of day to day planning decisions by the planning authority and it is therefore important to object to proposals you dislike before the plan is finally approved.

Planning applications

All applications for PLANNING PERMISSION – that is, permission to carry out a particular development – are entered in a register kept by the planning authority. The register contains full details of each application and is open to public inspection.

Every application receives some form of publicity before it is considered by the planning authority. This means you have an opportunity to make your views known to the authority at a time when they may influence its decision. But you have *no* right of appeal against a grant of planning permission.

Publicity for planning applications

An applicant for planning permission need not own the land for which he is making application, but he must notify the landowner. The owner has 21 days to make his views on the application known to the planning authority. The tenant of agricultural land must also be notified.

Where a developer applies to carry out 'bad neighbour' development – that is, development falling within one of 15 specified categories – he must advertise the application in a local newspaper and display a notice on the site. Anyone who cares to make representations to the planning authority has 21 days in which to do so.

'Bad neighbour' development includes proposals for licensed premises, hot food shops, bingo halls, cinemas, funfairs, buildings over 20 metres in height, and any development which will alter the character of an area of established amenity or which will cause disturbance at night.

All applications, other than those for 'bad neighbour' development, must be individually notified to immediate neighbours. Neighbours (and others) are allowed 14 days to make their views known to the authority.

You might, for example, wish to object to proposals for an extension to a neighbour's house on the ground that it will overshadow your home.

If a planning application is refused by a planning authority, the applicant can appeal to the Secretary of State. In such a case an objector will be able to make his views known – either at a public inquiry or, if the appeal is dealt with by written submissions, in writing. *See:* LOCAL AUTHORITY

PLANNING PERMISSION

How a council can control the development of your property

LOCAL AUTHORITY planning permission is needed for most building or engineering work that changes the outside appearance of a property and for any 'material' (that is, substantial) change in the use of property.

If, for example, you wish to build a large extension to your house, or to convert it into two separate dwellings, or to start running a guest house, you will have to obtain permission from the local authority responsible for planning control in your area.

Some minor alterations or additions, such as the construction of a garage, do not require the planning authority's permission so long as certain conditions are observed. However, special rules apply to listed buildings and in some conservation areas. *See:* BUILDING PRESERVATION: CONSERVATION AREA

You should always check with the planning authority as to whether or not planning permission is necessary. Even if it is not required, consent under the BUILDING REGULATIONS may well be necessary.

Use of land as a CARAVAN site may need not only planning permission but also a site licence.

If a development or change of use needs planning permission, but you go ahead without it, you can be ordered to stop. If you ignore the order you can be fined and any building work may have to be pulled down at your expense.

ADVERTISING ON YOUR LAND

Hoardings, permanent signs and most other advertising displays on private land require local authority consent. Permission is not required, however, for temporary election notices and 'for sale' signs. *See:* BILL-POSTING

Obtaining permission

An application for planning permission must be made on a form obtained from the planning authority. You must also submit a plan identifying the land together with such drawings as are necessary to describe your proposals. A fee is payable on the making of an application, the amount depending on the cost of the work and the size of the development.

Certain types of planning application must be advertised; in other cases you must notify your immediate neighbours that you are making an application. *See:* PLANNING OBJECTION

The planning authority may take up to 2 months to decide whether to grant planning permission. If you do not get a decision within 2 months, you can appeal to the Secretary of State for Scotland as if your application had been refused (see below).

The authority's decision will often be guided by the development plan for the area. You are entitled to see a copy of the plan at the planning authority's office. *See:* PLANNING OBJECTION

What you can do if permission is refused

If the planning authority turns down your application for planning permission, you have 6 months within which you can appeal to the Secretary of State for Scotland. You can obtain an appeal form from the Scottish Development Department, New St. Andrew's House, Edinburgh EH1 3SZ.

You have the right to demand that a public inquiry should be arranged for the hearing of your appeal. At the inquiry you have the right to put your case – either personally or through a lawyer (at your own expense) – to call witnesses, and to cross-examine anyone giving evidence for the planning authority.

Alternatively, and provided both you and the planning authority agree, your appeal can be dealt with by means of written statements submitted by you and the authority. This may be cheaper and quicker than a public inquiry.

At best it will be several months before an appeal is decided. For this reason it may be worthwhile to continue discussion of your application with the planning authority to see if some acceptable compromise can be reached.

NATIONAL SCENIC AREAS

In order to ensure a high standard of development in Scotland's 'National Scenic Areas' – parts of the country in which the scenery is of a very high quality – new development in such areas is regulated by specially restrictive planning controls. In these areas certain types of development which would not require planning permission elsewhere need the consent of the planning authority. Before granting permission the planning authority must consult the Countryside Commission for Scotland.

PLANTS AND FLOWERS

How the law protects plants in the wild

Plants, including flowers, are legally part of the land on which they grow and therefore belong to the landowner. Anyone who picks or removes them without the owner's permission is guilty of THEFT; and anyone who damages or destroys them is guilty of VANDALISM, or malicious mischief.

The owner can also sue the culprit for DAMAGES if he causes him any loss.

Special conservation laws

Parliament has passed special laws to protect wild plants. Because of these, even a landowner may be prohibited

WILD PLANTS THAT MUST NOT BE DISTURBED

Because they are in danger of extinction, 61 species of wild plant are specially protected by law. It is generally an offence for anyone to pick, uproot or destroy them:

Adder's tongue spearwort	Norwegian sandwort
Alpine catchfly	Oblong woodsia
Alpine gentian	Oxtongue broomrape
Alpine sow-thistle	Perennial knawel
Alpine woodsia	Plymouth pear
Bedstraw broomrape	Purple spurge
Blue heath	Red helleborine
Brown galingale	Ribbon water-plantain
Cheddar pink	Rock cinquefoil
Childling pink	Rough marsh-mallow
Diapensia	Round-headed leek
Dickie's bladder fern	Sea knotgrass
Downy woundwort	Sea lavender
Drooping saxifrage	Sickle-leaved hare's-ear
Early spider orchid	Small alison
Fen orchid	Small hare's-ear
Fen violet	Snowdon lily
Field cow-wheat	Spiked speedwell
Field eryngo	Spring gentian
Field wormwood	Starfruit
Ghost orchid	Starved wood-sedge
Greater yellow-rattle	Teesdale sandwort
Jersey cudweed	Thistle broomrape
Killarney fern	Triangular club-rush
Lady's-slipper	Tufted saxifrage
Late spider orchid	Water germander
Least lettuce	Whorled solomon's-seal
Limestone woundwort	Wild cotoneaster
Lizard orchid	Wild gladiolus
Military orchid	Wood calamint
Monkey orchid	

from picking or uprooting certain wild plants on his own land.

Any wild plants Under the Wildlife and Countryside Act 1981, it is an offence to uproot – that is, to dig up or otherwise remove – any plant which usually grows wild in Britain, unless:

- The plant is on land which you own or occupy; or
- You have been authorised by the owner or occupier of the land; or
- You have been authorised by the LOCAL AUTHORITY or the Nature Conservancy Council.

The maximum penalty is a fine of £1,000 for each plant uprooted.

However, it is not an offence under the Act merely to *pick* part of any wild plant, such as a leaf or flower, unless it is specially protected (see below).

Specially protected plants Some wild plants (see the accompanying list) are specially protected by law because they are in danger of extinction. No one – not even the owner of the land on which they are growing – can pick, uproot or destroy them intentionally without a licence from the Nature Conservancy Council. Licences are issued only for scientific, educational (including photographic) and conservation purposes.

In addition, no one can sell such a plant, or advertise it for sale, without a licence from the Secretary of State for Scotland.

The maximum penalty for these offences is a fine of £1,000 for each plant affected.

You do not commit an offence under the 1981 Act if you uproot or destroy a wild plant as a result of some lawful operation – such as properly conducted farming or forestry – so long as you could not reasonably avoid doing so.

Nature reserves

Special restrictions on damaging wild plants apply in national nature reserves (some 167 have been designated by the Nature Conservancy Council) and in areas of special scientific interest (of which there are around 3,700).

In general, it is an offence for the owner or occupier of the land in these areas to carry out any operations which are likely to damage wild plants, except with the written permission of the Nature Conservancy Council.

For more information, contact the Council at 12 Hope Terrace, Edinburgh.

Wild plants that are a threat

Certain wild plants are a nuisance and it is therefore an offence to plant them in the wild, or otherwise cause them to grow there. The plants are: giant hogweed, giant kelp, Japanese knotweed and Japanese seaweed.

PLAYGROUND

How safety standards can be checked

The safety of a playground is the responsibility of the local council that controls it.

Under the Health and Safety at Work Act, which also covers recreation areas, local authorities are required to take reasonable measures to make and keep playgrounds safe.

A local authority can be prosecuted if it fails in that duty, and does not comply with an inspector's directions to improve safety.

Even without a prosecution, an inspector can issue a prohibition notice to whoever controls a playground. That could ban the use of certain equipment, or even close the playground.

An inspector also has the power to seize playground equipment if he thinks there is an immediate danger of injury.

When you see a danger

If you doubt the safety of a public playground, notify the parks or recreation department of your district or islands council. If it is a school playground, notify the headmaster.

If no action is taken and you are convinced that children are in danger, contact the local office of the Health and Safety Executive, which is listed in most local telephone directories.

An inspector will visit the playground and advise the responsible authority of any changes or improvements that are needed, and whether it should close the area in the meantime.

It is unlikely that any more formal action would be necessary. But if the authority were to disregard the inspector's advice, he could issue an improvement notice compelling it to comply, or a prohibition notice forbidding the use of the playground or some of the equipment.

When you can sue

If a child is injured in a playground it may be possible to recover PERSONAL INJURY compensation from the responsible authority – but only if NEGLIGENCE is proved.

The claim would have to establish that the authority failed in its duty to take reasonable care – for example, by neglecting normal inspection and maintenance, or not providing a reasonable degree of supervision.

Noise If noise or other disturbance from a playground has a damaging effect on the lives of residents near by, they may be able to obtain a court INTERDICT restricting activities in the area – for example, by limiting the hours it is open, or the age of the children who can use it.

POACHING

Hunting game without permission on someone else's land

Game animals are ownerless when wild and belong to the first person who kills or captures them. This is so even where the person who kills or captures them is a poacher – that is, someone who enters another person's land without permission to hunt game.

A poacher is entitled to keep the game unless he is convicted under a game law which authorises the court to order him to forfeit it.

The right to kill game

A landowner has the right to kill or capture game on his land (although until he does so he does not own the game). He also has the power to permit other persons to kill game on his land. Game licences are necessary in many cases. *See:* GAME

The meaning of 'game' varies with the different game laws – for example, one law may include rabbits and another may exclude them. But 'game' usually includes deer, hares, grouse, pheasants, partridges and black or moor game.

The game laws can be divided broadly into two groups: those that protect the right to kill game and those that protect game.

Protecting the right to kill

There are laws covering poaching at night and poaching during the day.

• **Night poaching** It is an offence for any person to enter land without the owner's permission, between sunset and sunrise, carrying a gun, net or other instrument to be used in taking or killing game. The offence is committed by being on the land for this purpose – no game need be taken or killed.

It is also poaching to take or kill any game or rabbits, after dark, on any land, public roads and paths.

Maximum penalty £1,000 fine.

If 3 or more persons, acting together, unlawfully enter any land at night for the purpose of killing game or rabbits, and any one of them is armed with a gun, crossbow, bludgeon or other offensive weapon, they are all guilty of an offence. This is so even if only one of the group is armed.

Maximum penalty £2,000 fine and 6 months' imprisonment.

• **Day-time poaching** Any person who unlawfully enters any land in the daytime in search or pursuit of game is guilty of an offence and can be fined up to £100. If the offender has blackened his face or disguised it in some other way, the maximum penalty is increased to a £400 fine.

If 5 or more persons, acting together, unlawfully enter land in the day-time in search or pursuit of game, they can each be fined up to £400.

The landowner, his employee (for instance, a gamekeeper) or anyone to whom he has given the right to take game can ask someone who is unlawfully on the land to give his name and address if he is suspected of poaching. Failure to give this information can be punished by a fine of up to £100.

The landowner or any other authorised person, such as a gamekeeper, can also seize any game found in the possession of a suspected poacher.

It is not poaching to enter land to recover game lawfully shot by you. For instance, if you shoot a grouse over your own land and it falls onto your neighbour's land, you commit no criminal offence if you enter his land to retrieve it. However, if you damage his property when doing so, he can sue you for DAMAGES.

Police powers

A police officer can arrest anyone he reasonably suspects of poaching and can enter land to make an arrest. He can also stop and search anyone in a public place whom he suspects of poaching.

Vehicles can also be stopped and searched. Any game or poaching implement can be seized.

Deer poaching

Someone who unlawfully takes or kills deer on any land is guilty of an offence and is liable to a fine of up to £1,000 (for each deer) or 3 months' imprisonment, or both. The court can also order forfeiture of the deer.

If the offence is committed by 2 or more people acting together, the maximum penalty is an unlimited fine or 2 years' imprisonment, or both. Forfeiture of the deer can also be ordered.

However, no offence is committed by someone who kills any injured or diseased deer to prevent it from suffering any further.

Illegal fishing

It is illegal for anyone (including the owner of the water) to fish for salmon without the permission of the owner of the salmon fishing rights. The penalty is a fine of up to £400. Any salmon caught can be confiscated.

Other fish – such as trout and eels – that are in enclosed ponds belong to the pond owner. It is THEFT to take these fish without permission.

Fish (excluding salmon) in other types of water apart from ponds do not belong to anyone until they are caught. Anyone fishing there commits no offence unless the waters are covered by a protection order made by the Secretary of State for Scotland. The power to make protection orders has existed only since 1976 and few have been made so far.

Protecting game

The laws that protect game – as distinct from protecting the right to kill game – do two things. They establish close seasons during which killing or dealing in various types of game is prohibited, and they also prohibit certain methods of killing or capturing game.

These game laws apply to anyone who is entitled to kill game, as well as to poachers.

Close seasons It is, for example, generally forbidden for anyone to kill a red deer stag between October 21 and June 30. The maximum penalty for doing so is a £1,000 fine per deer or 3 months' imprisonment, or both. The deer can also be forfeited.

Other close seasons cover game birds and certain types of fishing.

Illegal methods of killing Anyone who uses illegal methods to kill or capture game can be prosecuted.

For example, it is illegal to shoot a deer from an aircraft, or to use a spring trap for killing or capturing hares. Offenders can be fined or sent to prison. *See:* ANIMALS; BIRDS; FISHING; GAME

POINDING AND SALE

Selling a debtor's possessions

A court may order a debtor to pay over to a creditor money that he owes.

If the debtor fails to do so, the creditor has the right to sell certain of the debtor's belongings to recover some or all of the money that he is owed.

This procedure, which is carried out on behalf of the creditor by a sheriff officer, is called 'poinding (pronounced pinnding) and sale'. *See:* DEBT; SHERIFF OFFICER

POLICE

The guardians of law and order

The police have a duty to enforce public order and to prevent and detect crime. To do so, they are aided by specific powers granted by law – for example, to arrest or temporarily detain a person who is suspected of committing a crime. *See:* ARREST; DETENTION

But they have no general power to interfere in a citizen's life, and for much of the time they rely on the co-operation of members of the public to be as helpful as possible by providing information and answering questions.

Questioning and searching

The police are entitled to stop and question anyone they suspect of having committed a crime or who might be able to provide information about a crime that has been committed. In such circumstances you are obliged to give your name and address, but usually no other information.

If a person refuses to give his name and address in such instances, the police may arrest him without a warrant.

When dealing with motoring cases, the police have further powers to demand names and addresses and to order a motorist to stop or move his vehicle.

In certain circumstances the police are entitled to stop and SEARCH a person in the street – for example, if they suspect that he is carrying DRUGS or stolen goods.

The police may also enter a person's home in certain circumstances. They are:

- If the police have obtained a warrant to search the premises.
- To arrest a person for whom they have an arrest warrant.
- If the police are entitled to arrest a person on the premises without a warrant.
- To prevent a BREACH OF THE PEACE or injury to someone.

When the police wish to enter property for one of those reasons, they are entitled to use reasonable force to gain entry should this be refused. For example, if there was no way of gaining entry, a policeman would be entitled to break a window to get into a property. If someone tried to stop a policeman from entering he could be charged with OBSTRUCTION.

If the police do not have a search warrant and are not entitled to enter without one, they may not enter your home without your consent. If you do agree to their being in your home, they must leave as soon as you ask them to do so. You should give them reasonable time to leave.

When a warrant is issued

If the police have obtained a search warrant from a magistrate, the warrant must state the exact address and premises where a search is authorised. An occupier would be entitled to refuse the police entry to premises not specified – for example, if there is a separately let flat or outbuildings.

The warrant must also specify the law under which the search is authorised and it must give details of any articles it empowers the police to search for or take away. For example, a warrant issued under the Firearms Act 1968 empowers the police to search for and take away any firearms used in connection with an offence under the Act.

Some warrants can be used only once and then expire; others may be used several times. For example, a warrant issued under the Misuse of Drugs Act 1971 authorises as many searches as the police require to be made within a month of the date of issue. If the police use such a warrant in a public house, they are entitled to search everyone on the premises, whether or not there are reasonable grounds for suspecting them of possessing drugs.

Before allowing the police to enter, ask to see the search warrant. If the police refuse to show a search warrant, you are entitled to refuse them entry. If the warrant does not specify the exact address of the premises or the law under which the search is to be made, entry can also be refused.

Searching without a warrant

In certain cases, a senior police officer – who must be a superintendent or above – is entitled to give his officers written authorisation to search premises. He may do so, for example, if:

- He believes there are explosives on the premises and the delay in obtaining a warrant would be likely to endanger life.
- He believes immediate action is necessary to look for evidence of TERRORISM.
- He believes an offence under the OFFICIAL SECRETS Act 1911 has been or is about to be committed.

When you are legally obliged to help the police

The public have no general duty to help the police, provided that a policeman does not specifically ask for assistance. If you see a policeman who is obviously in need of help but does not ask for it, you may assist him, but you are not guilty of any offence if you do not do so.

However, if he does ask you for help, it is an offence not to give it. For example, if a policeman is being obstructed in making a lawful arrest and you refuse his request for help, you could be fined or imprisoned.

If you have a good reason for not helping – for instance, you were not fit to do so as a result of disability or illness – that would be a sufficient excuse for not assisting the policeman.

If you agree to a policeman's request for help, or volunteer to help him, and you are injured or your property is damaged, you may be entitled to compensation. *See:* CRIMINAL INJURIES COMPENSATION

There is no general legal obligation on a person to provide the police with information other than his name and address.

So if a person witnesses an offence and does not inform the police, he is not committing an offence, provided that he does not help the lawbreaker to avoid arrest or prosecution. If he does, he may be guilty of attempting to pervert the course of justice. The penalty for that is at the discretion of the court. *See:* PERVERTING THE COURSE OF JUSTICE

In certain cases, a private citizen is entitled to arrest a person he sees committing a crime. However, he needs to be sure he is acting within the law when doing so. *See:* CITIZEN'S ARREST

THE STRUCTURE OF THE SCOTTISH POLICE

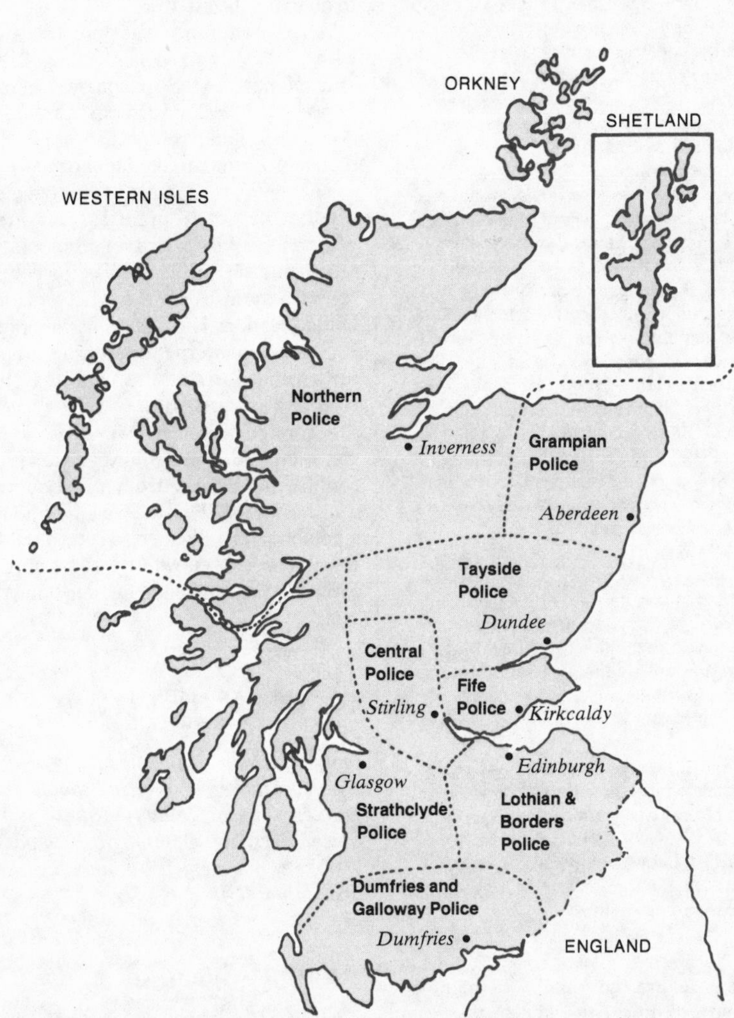

There are about 13,200 policemen and women in Scotland. They are either uniformed officers or plain-clothes police.

It is the duty of all police officers to 'guard, patrol and watch' so as to prevent crime, preserve order and protect life and property. When a crime has been committed, it is their duty to take all lawful measures, including making reports to the procurator fiscal, that are necessary to bring offenders to justice without delay.

The uniformed police maintain a public presence by patrolling streets on foot or in police vehicles, by directing traffic, or by controlling crowds or demonstrations. The plain-clothes officers are involved in detecting crime.

There are 8 police forces in Scotland:

- Central police, with headquarters in Stirling.
- Dumfries and Galloway police, with headquarters in Dumfries.
- Fife police, with headquarters in Kirkcaldy.
- Grampian police, with headquarters in Aberdeen.
- Lothian and Borders police, with headquarters in Edinburgh.
- Northern police, with headquarters in Inverness.
- Strathclyde police, with headquarters in Glasgow.
- Tayside police, with headquarters in Dundee.

Strathclyde police, which has about 6,800 officers, is the largest force in Scotland. Dumfries and Galloway, with about 300 officers, is the smallest.

Six of the police forces (but not the Northern, and Lothian and Borders forces) cover areas governed by a single regional council and it is the regional councillors who comprise the local police authority. *See:* LOCAL AUTHORITY

The Northern police force (which covers the Highland region, the Western Isles, Orkney and Shetland) and the Lothian and Borders police force cover more than the area of one regional council and the police authority is made up from several councils.

The Northern police authority consists of 16 councillors from Highland Regional Council and 2 each from the three islands councils. The Lothian and Borders police authority consists of 14 Lothian regional councillors and 4 Borders regional councillors.

The police authority appoints a chief constable to lead the force, but he must be approved by the Secretary of State for Scotland. The police authority's main responsibilities are the payment of police officers, fixing the local police strength (subject to approval by the Secretary of State) and the provision of buildings and equipment. An authority exercises little control over what the police actually do.

The chief constable makes an annual report to the police authority on the state of its police force. The authority has the power to request further reports on any matter connected with the policing of its area.

The chief constable is also responsible to the Secretary of State, who may ask him to report on any matter concerning the policing of the area.

The Secretary of State may order an independent inquiry, headed by any person appointed by him, into any matter concerning the policing of any part of Scotland.

COMPLAINING ABOUT THE POLICE

If you are dissatisfied with a police officer's behaviour towards you, complain in person to the duty officer at the local police station or write to the chief constable of the force involved. The complaint should be made without delay.

Any complaint made must be recorded and investigated. It will be passed to the deputy chief constable, who will appoint a senior officer – of the rank of inspector or above – to investigate it. In the most serious cases, a senior officer may be appointed from another force.

Giving evidence

The complainer and any other witnesses of the incident will be interviewed. They are entitled to have their solicitors present.

The investigating officer will report the facts to the deputy chief constable. If he has reason to believe that the law may have been broken by the police, he must send the evidence collected during the investigation to the PROCURATOR FISCAL.

The procurator fiscal must decide whether or not the matter should be brought before a criminal court. He will usually consult with the CROWN OFFICE in Edinburgh (the headquarters of the public prosecution system) before bringing any criminal charges against a police officer. It may be that he will require further inquiries to be made before deciding what to do.

If a prosecution is brought, the complainer and any other witnesses may be required to give evidence in court.

Offences against police discipline

The procurator fiscal may decide not to prosecute a police officer, or the officer may be tried and acquitted, or the deputy chief constable may decide that no law has been breached. However, the deputy chief constable then has to decide whether the officer has committed an offence against the police discipline code.

This code contains disciplinary offences, including incivility, drinking on duty, taking bribes, using unnecessary force, and suppression or falsification of complaints by a police officer.

If the code has been breached, a disciplinary hearing may be held. In the case of a minor breach, however, the police officer may simply receive a warning from a senior officer without the matter coming before a hearing.

Where a hearing is held, it is conducted by the chief constable, and the police officer named in the complaint appears before it. If the officer denies the disciplinary charge, the complainer and any other witnesses will be called to give evidence.

If the police officer admits the disciplinary offence, or is found guilty, the chief constable will decide whether he is to be cautioned, fined or reprimanded, to have his pay or rank reduced or, in a serious case, to be dismissed or required to resign.

A police officer found guilty of a disciplinary offence can appeal to the Secretary of State for Scotland.

If there is no hearing

After receiving the investigating officer's report, the deputy chief constable may decide that the complaint has not been substantiated and no action is to be taken against the police officer concerned. The complainer will be informed of this by letter.

There is no appeal against this decision and the complainer is not entitled to see a copy of the investigating officer's report.

Where police discipline has not been breached, but the complaint has been substantiated, the chief constable may send a written apology to the complainer.

POLITICAL ASYLUM

How a persecuted person can seek refuge in Britain

Certain people who have no right to enter the United Kingdom are sometimes allowed to do so if oppression and persecution in their homeland threaten their lives or their liberty. *See:* IMMIGRATION

The Home Office decides whether a particular person can stay. Its rules state that the persecution must be because of race, religion, nationality or membership of a political or social group.

It is not enough for a person to be trying to flee his country because he faces criminal charges, objects to doing military service, or simply cannot get a job because of his race. Such a person would be refused political asylum.

A person already in Britain who faces DEPORTATION can claim political asylum for the same reasons. And in EXTRADITION proceedings a person may be allowed to remain in Britain if he would be persecuted for his political actions or beliefs were he to be sent back to his own country.

How to seek asylum

Many people seeking political asylum do so after they have arrived at a dock or airport in the United Kingdom. Their best course is to tell the immigration officer on duty as soon as they land, or to go to a police station.

All applications for asylum are dealt with by the Home Office Immigration and Nationality Department, Lunar House, Wellesley Road, Croydon. Anyone seeking refuge can apply directly, in writing, to the Department.

The Home Office finally decides whether or not to grant asylum after getting advice from Britain's diplomatic representative in the applicant's country. It may also ask the advice of the United Nations High Commissioner for Refugees, an international organisation responsible for deciding who may be regarded as a REFUGEE.

A foreign person given permission to stay temporarily in Britain can seek free confidential advice from the London office of the UNHCR. This is helpful to a person who may have to return to his country, where knowledge of his application for asylum could be damaging to him.

WHEN AN ALIEN MAY STAY IN BRITAIN

Only the Home Office has the power to decide whether an alien should be granted political asylum – usually after much investigation through diplomatic channels in the country from which the applicant is fleeing.

POLYGAMY

When a man or woman can have more than one spouse at the same time

A polygamous marriage is one that allows the man or woman to have more than one spouse at the same time – even if he or she does not do so. A monogamous marriage is one that allows only one spouse.

A polygamous marriage cannot take place in Scotland. If a man or woman marries again while still married to the first partner, then the offence of BIGAMY has been committed.

It makes no difference if the bigamist comes from a country where polygamy is allowed.

When polygamy is recognised

A polygamous marriage is recognised in Scotland, however, if it took place in a country where polygamy is legal and if the partners, at the time of the marriage, had their DOMICILE in a country where the marriage is valid.

For example, if two Muslims domiciled in Saudi Arabia married polygamously in Morocco, the marriage would be recognised in Scotland. But if the husband married again in this country, without divorcing his other wife, the second marriage would be bigamous. *See:* FOREIGN MARRIAGE

If a polygamous marriage is recognised in Scotland, a Scottish court can grant either party a DIVORCE, NULLITY or SEPARATION decree. It can also decide on CUSTODY OF CHILDREN.

The husband has the same duty to ALIMENT all his wives and children as he would in a monogamous marriage.

Anyone who is in doubt about the validity of his or her marriage can apply to the Court of Session for a declaration that the marriage is valid. Consult a solicitor.

PORNOGRAPHY

Controlling obscene material

It is not an offence for anyone to have, or to read, pornographic material. However, such material may be made the subject of a criminal prosecution in certain circumstances. *See:* INDECENCY; OBSCENE PUBLICATIONS

POST MORTEM

Investigating the circumstances of death

A post mortem is a detailed medical examination of a dead body. It is known technically as an autopsy.

A post mortem usually requires the body to be opened up. The detailed examination which follows may involve scientific tests on the tissues and blood to find out how death occurred and what the circumstances were that brought it about.

Most post mortems are carried out at the request of the PROCURATOR FISCAL, who is obliged in the public interest to investigate the circumstances of certain deaths. But post mortems are sometimes carried out in hospital simply for the purpose of helping to further medical knowledge.

Post mortems are normally carried out soon after death, to avoid the body deteriorating and evidence of the circumstances of death disappearing.

When a post mortem is requested by the fiscal

The procurator fiscal is obliged to investigate deaths that have occurred suddenly or accidentally, or in circumstances that may call for explanation.

Anyone may report a death to the procurator fiscal. In practice, many of them are reported by the police. Registrars of Births, Deaths and Marriages have a duty to report deaths notified to them that call for investigation – there are detailed guidelines on the situations that require such reports to be made.

The purpose of the procurator fiscal's investigation is not merely to establish, with scientific accuracy, the exact cause of death. However, he may require to know this in order to achieve his main purpose, which is to ascertain the circumstances that led to a particular death.

A post mortem is not in fact required in most cases. But if the procurator fiscal thinks one should be carried out, he will present a petition to the local sheriff court. The sheriff will then issue a warrant which enables a pathologist – a doctor who specialises in carrying out post mortems – to undertake the medical examination.

In cases where there is serious suspicion about the circumstances of death, a warrant will be obtained for two pathologists to carry out the examination. They will both sign the report of their investigations; but if a prosecution should follow, only one of them need appear as a witness in court – unless the defence objects.

If there is a prosecution, pathologists acting on behalf of the accused person are given the opportunity to conduct their own examination of the body after the pathologists acting for the procurator fiscal have completed their work.

It is doubtful whether any relatives of a dead person can prevent a sheriff granting a warrant to a procurator fiscal authorising a post mortem. They might be able to do so if a procurator fiscal were shown to be acting maliciously.

THE UNAUTHORISED POST MORTEM

The widow and children of a dead person can sue if a post mortem is carried out without legal justification.

Mrs Conway's husband, Stephen, was injured at his work on a building site. He later died. The building firm that employed him expected a claim for compensation from his family.

Mrs Conway and her children alleged that the firm and their solicitors had requested two doctors to carry out a post mortem on her husband, without his family's permission. She claimed that the doctors had removed his liver and gall bladder and had not returned them.

Mrs Conway and her children sued the building firm, the doctors and the solicitors for damages for the distress caused to them.

DECISION

The court decided that if the family's allegations were proved, they would be entitled to damages. It was also decided that if the doctors were responsible for permanently removing certain organs, any damages awarded against them could be increased to take account of their actions.

When a post mortem is carried out for medical reasons

Doctors may wish to carry out a post mortem in hospital for several reasons.

A programme of medical research may depend on comparing the results obtained from post mortem examinations carried out on a number of patients who have died. The researchers may, for example, wish to find out whether certain mental conditions have any organic effect on brain tissue.

Alternatively a hospital doctor may wish a post mortem to be carried out on a patient so that he can discover the effect of any treatment given to him.

Such post mortems can only be carried out by a registered medical practitioner.

Before they are done, a designated doctor at the hospital must have made reasonable inquiries to establish that the dead person had not expressed any objection to a post mortem. He must also make reasonable inquiries of relatives, to find out whether or not they object. If there is an objection, no post mortem can be carried out.

The relatives who require to be asked are those who are available and have an obvious interest – the dead person's widow or widower and any adult children. If they are abroad, or are difficult to contact, they will not be asked.

In the case of a single person, the doctor might seek the views of a relative who was directly involved with the dead person – for instance, a brother or sister, nephew or niece.

POST OFFICE

Your rights to an efficient postal service

The Post Office is a state-owned corporation responsible for the postal services and for the National Girobank service.

Responsibility for the telephone and telecommunications services has been transferred from the Post Office to another state-owned corporation, British Telecommunications. *See:* NATIONALISED INDUSTRY; TELEPHONE

The Post Office also acts as agent for government departments, dealing with such matters as vehicle licences and the payment of social security benefits.

COMPLAINING ABOUT THE POSTAL SERVICE

Local postal complaints are usually handled by independent advisory committees attached to each head Post Office. Central or national complaints should be taken up with the Post Office Users' Council for Scotland.

Using the postal services

The postal services cover four main categories – letters, parcels, newspapers and a special service for articles for the blind.

It is an offence, with a maximum penalty of 12 months' imprisonment or a fine of £400, to send through the post:

- Anything likely to harm anyone handling it during the process of delivery.
- Anything that could damage other post.
- Anything indecent or obscene.

The Post Office can refuse to handle dangerous items – for example, sharp objects or inflammable film – which are not properly wrapped. Overseas post is also subject to customs regulations. *See:* OBSCENE PUBLICATIONS

Letters Letters can be sent first or second class according to the amount of postage paid, but neither implies any guaranteed speed of delivery.

Any lawful item except perishable goods can be sent by letter post if it comes within certain size limits – a minimum of 100 mm by 70 mm and a maximum of 610 mm by 460 mm by 460 mm. There is no maximum weight limit, but anything over 750 g must be sent first class.

Until 1981 the Post Office had the exclusive right to collect, carry and deliver letters. This was (and still is) subject to a number of exceptions, such as a letter delivered personally by the sender or by a friend of his, or by a messenger or international courier. Also excepted are court documents, letters delivered along with the goods to which they relate, bank cheques and forms connected with competitions (such as football pools).

However, in November 1981 the Post Office's exclusive right – known as 'the postal privilege' – was suspended until the end of the year 2006, but only to the extent of allowing anyone to carry letters provided a minimum charge of £1 is made for each letter.

When letters are lost

The Post Office is not legally liable for loss, damage or delay to things in the post, unless they are registered.

However, under the Code of Practice for Postal Services first issued in 1979 in consultation with the Office of Fair Trading, up to £17 compensation for loss of or damage to the contents of a letter is payable if it can be shown that the letter was posted, but was lost or damaged in the post. Proof of posting can be obtained at any post office.

For loss of, or damage to, a recorded delivery letter, compensation up to £18 is payable.

Registered post If a letter is sent by registered post (and a fee of £1 to £1.20 paid) up to £1,750 compensation is payable if it is lost or damaged, unless the Post Office shows it was not negligent. The recipient has to sign for the letter, proving delivery. The Post Office will compulsorily register, and charge a fee, if they find a letter or parcel unregistered containing any of the following worth £18 or more:

- Uncrossed postal order with payee's name not inserted.
- Cheque or dividend warrant uncrossed and payable to bearer.
- Bearer security.
- Bank or currency note.
- Postage, holiday, trading or National Savings stamps.
- Coupons, vouchers, tokens, coins, jewellery.

Redirecting letters

If a letter for someone else is delivered to you by mistake, you should forward it to the correct person or return it to the Post Office, clearly marked with the reason. You do not have to pay postage for redirecting a letter. It is an offence to keep a letter not addressed to you.

Using parcel post

The Post Office does not have a monopoly over parcels delivery. The maximum weight for Post Office parcels is 22½ kg.

No postman should ever leave a parcel on a doorstep or in a shed. It is an offence for him to do so and the Post Office is liable if it is stolen.

The Post Office is not legally liable for lost or damaged parcels but may pay up to £17 compensation under the Code of Practice. If a parcel is sent under the Compensation Fee Parcel Service, a small payment (27p to 70p) entitles the sender to up to £350 if loss or damage occurs.

Articles for the blind

Braille or talking books and other articles can be posted free so long as no personal message is included. The weight limit is 7 kg and there are also size limits.

Articles must state clearly 'for the blind'. They must arrive at the Post Office unwrapped or in an easily removable wrapper.

WIDE RANGE OF SERVICES

The Post Office, besides being the state-owned corporation responsible for postal services and the National Girobank, also provides facilities for the public to make all sorts of other official payments – for example, driving, motor vehicle, television and dog licences.

Rules about payment

Postage must be paid in advance, in stamps or by using special franking machines, for all postal services unless the recipient contributes to a Freepost or business reply service.

The only letters that are exempt from postage are those addressed to the Queen, either directly or through a member of either House of Parliament.

All unstamped or not fully stamped letters (excluding Business Reply and Freepost letters) will be sent second class. The receiver is charged the amount of the deficit (rounded down to the nearest whole penny) plus a fee of 10p per letter.

The same rule applies to parcels that are unstamped or not fully stamped.

Spoiled stamps The Post Office will refund the cost of stamps spoiled before they are used.

Complaining about the service

If a letter or parcel is lost or damaged, ask a post office for form P58, *Enquiry about a missing or damaged letter or parcel,* and send it when completed to the local head postmaster as soon as possible.

If his reply is unsatisfactory, refer it to the postal regional director. Ultimately a dispute on compensation may be referred to arbitration under the Code of Practice.

If your complaint is of delay or some other failure in delivery, refer it to the local head postmaster, along with the envelope or cover if available.

A complaint can also be raised with the local Post Office Advisory Committee (address at the start of the telephone directory) or, if it is a general complaint, with the independent Post Office Users' Council for Scotland, Alhambra House, 45 Waterloo Street, Glasgow, G2 6AT.

PREMIUM

Payment in addition to rent

A premium is a sum of money, or something regarded as the equivalent of money, which is required by a landlord from a tenant in addition to the rent due. In many circumstances it is a criminal offence to demand or receive a premium. *See:* KEY MONEY; LANDLORD AND TENANT

PRESCRIPTION

Obtaining drugs cheaply for your illness

The law divides medicines into three categories–those that are obtainable only on a doctor's prescription; those that can be bought from a pharmacist without a prescription; and those that can be bought anywhere. A doctor may, however, prescribe pills that could be bought without a prescription – aspirin or paracetamol, for example – to enable the patient to buy them more cheaply, or to make sure that he knows what the patient is taking

The details that a prescription must show

When your doctor decides you need medicine, he prescribes the appropriate drug and dosage. If you are a National Health Service patient, the prescription is written on form GP10—form HBP (Scotland) if obtained from a hospital doctor. It shows the patient's name and address, his age if under 12, the names of the drugs and the prescribed dosage. At the bottom is the doctor's signature and stamp – without which the prescription is not valid.

Patients who are exempt from charges should complete the form on the back of the prescription. The prescription should be taken to a pharmacist who will make up the drugs as directed and charge those not exempt £1.60 per item.

If the pharmacist does not have the drugs in stock he has to supply them with 'reasonable promptness' and will normally do so within 24 hours. He is obliged under the terms of the NHS contract to supply the drugs required. If he refuses to serve you during normal shop hours, complain to the area health board whose address is on your MEDICAL CARD. It can request a tribunal to remove his name from the pharmaceutical list.

Private prescriptions If you are receiving private medical treatment, you cannot be issued with an NHS prescription by your private doctor – even if he also has an NHS practice. Private prescriptions are written on the doctor's own forms, usually his headed notepaper, and entitle you to buy the prescribed drugs from a pharmacist at their full retail price, which, together with his dispensing fee, may amount to several pounds.

There are some treatments that your doctor cannot provide under the NHS. As your NHS doctor is not allowed to treat you privately, he would have to send you to another doctor to obtain a private prescription.

Where to have your prescription made up

Every dispensing chemist has to be or employ a registered pharmacist, who must be a member of the Pharmaceutical Society of Great Britain. He will have his qualifications on display. The dispensing of medicines must be done by him or under his direct supervision. If you suspect that an unsupervised and unqualified person is handling prescriptions you should report the shop to the area health board.

A list of all local pharmacists can be obtained from your doctor, hospital, police station and post office. If you need the prescribed drugs after shops are closed or during a public holiday, look in the local newspaper or in the window of a chemist's for a list showing which pharmacist is on the rota for that day. If all the chemists are closed and your doctor believes you are in need of urgent medication that he cannot provide, he would have to send you to hospital for treatment.

When drugs can be given without prescription

Some doctors, particularly in rural areas, dispense their own drugs – saving the patient the need to find a chemist. In such cases, they do not write prescriptions but must charge £1.60 for each drug.

There is no prescription or charge for medicine given to hospital in-patients. But drugs supplied to out-patients by the hospital pharmacy require both a prescription and charge. So do medicines provided at a health centre.

PAYING PRESCRIPTION CHARGES IN ADVANCE

Anyone who needs a lot of medicine, for example, someone suffering from a number of ailments at the same time, but who is not exempt from prescription charges, can buy a pre-payment certificate (or 'season ticket') entitling him to medicine without further charge for a limited period.

You can apply for the certificate on form EC 95 – obtainable at the post office and social security office. It costs £8.50 for one lasting 4 months and £24 for a year. This is of benefit if you need more than 5 items in 4 months or 15 items in a year.

When you are entitled to free prescriptions

Some patients are exempt from prescription charges. All they need to do to have their prescriptions dispensed without charge is to complete the appropriate box on the back of the prescription form. Those exempt are:

- All children under 16, men aged 65 and over and women aged 60 and over.
- People, and their dependants, receiving supplementary benefit or family income supplement.
- Others aged 16 or over on incomes only a little above this level, whether or not in work.
- Expectant mothers and mothers who have had a child in the last 12 months.
- People suffering from certain medical conditions, including the housebound, epileptics and diabetics.
- War and Service disablement pensioners (for prescriptions required for their disablement only).

A pharmacist cannot require a patient to prove that he or she is exempt, but the health board checks all prescriptions.

To claim exemption falsely is an offence and may result in prosecution. Any debt arising may be recovered.

Men over the age of 65, women over 60 and children under 16 are entitled to free medicine simply by ticking the box on the back of the prescription.

They do not have to apply for a certificate of exemption or prove their age.

Expectant mothers can receive free drugs by filling in form FW8 – obtainable from a doctor, midwife or health visitor – and sending it to the area health board. They send back a certificate, which entitles the woman to exemption until her child is 12 months old.

Mothers with a baby of less than 12 months, who did not apply for exemption while they were pregnant, can do so by filling in form A on leaflet P11 – obtainable from the post office and social security office – and sending it to the health board.

People suffering from certain chronic illnesses – including epilepsy requiring control by drugs, and diabetes – who are housebound can apply for exemption on form C in leaflet P11. Your doctor can advise you if you are eligible.

War pensioners and anyone receiving supplementary benefit are issued with an exemption certificate by the Department of Health and Social Security.

People with low incomes, who do not qualify for supplementary benefit or family income supplement, can apply for exemption by filling in form B on leaflet P11 and sending it to the local social security office. If they qualify, they are sent a certificate exempting them from prescription charges for 12 months. They may re-apply annually.

How to claim a refund of prescription charges

If you have qualified recently for exemption – if, for example, you are newly pregnant – but have not yet received an exemption certificate, you must pay the prescription fee. You can, however, claim a refund on form EC57, obtainable from the pharmacist, which you must send to the local social security office within 3 months of paying the charge.

PRESERVATION ORDER

Historic buildings – or even a single tree – can be protected

The LOCAL AUTHORITY responsible for planning control in a particular area has various legal powers to preserve the environment.

It can, for example, decide that a particularly attractive part of its area should be designated a CONSERVATION AREA. Designation should help to ensure that the area is protected against any unsuitable development.

The planning authority can issue a BUILDING PRESERVATION notice in respect of any individual building which is not already protected, but which the authority considers to be of special architectural or historic merit.

Trees can be protected by means of TREE preservation orders. An order can apply to a wood, copse or single tree.

Preserving buildings

A building preservation notice is effective for a maximum of 6 months. During this period the Secretary of State for Scotland considers whether or not the building should be permanently safe-guarded by being included in the list of buildings of special architectural or historic interest. *See:* BUILDING PRESERVATION

Anyone wishing to alter, extend or demolish a listed building, or a building subject to a building preservation notice, must first ask the planning authority for consent. If it is refused, he can appeal to the Secretary of State for Scotland.

The owner of a listed building or a building subject to a preservation notice is not legally bound to keep it in repair. The planning authority can, however, issue a repairs notice ordering him to make specified repairs within a given time. If he fails to comply, a COMPULSORY PURCHASE order for the property can be made.

The owner of a protected building may be able to get a grant or a loan from the authority or from the Secretary of State to help keep up the property.

If the Secretary of State does not list a building in respect of which a building preservation notice was issued, the planning authority cannot issue another one on that building for 12 months, and must compensate the owner for any loss the notice has caused him.

Preserving trees and woods

A tree preservation order made by a planning authority does not need the approval of the Secretary of State.

Once a tree preservation order has been made, the tree cannot be felled, lopped or seriously damaged unless:

- It is dead, diseased or dangerous; or
- Consent has first been obtained from the planning authority (after a written application).

HOW TO OBTAIN A PRESERVATION ORDER

If you want to stop someone knocking down or redeveloping one of your favourite buildings, or chopping down trees in your area, you can ask your local planning authority to issue a preservation order protecting them.

You may stand a better chance of succeeding if you apply as part of a neighbourhood group rather than as an individual. It may pay, for example, to organise a petition to the council.

Ultimately it is the duty of the Secretary of State for Scotland to preserve historic buildings, and he can order a building to be listed without reference to the local authority.

Buildings most likely to be preserved are:

- Any that were built before 1700 and survive in something like their original condition.
- Most buildings built between 1700 and 1840.
- Buildings associated with well-known characters or events – such as the home of a famous writer.
- Buildings that represent aspects of social and economic history – such as railway stations, factories or theatres of different periods.
- Buildings that have a special group value, standing perhaps in a handsome terrace or crescent.

If consent is refused, you can appeal to the Secretary of State for Scotland.

If a tree obstructs the view of drivers of vehicles using a road, the highway authority can order the owner or the occupier of the land on which the tree stands to fell it or cut it back.

Penalties for damaging preserved trees and buildings

There are heavy penalties for altering, demolishing or damaging a building that is listed or is subject to a building preservation notice, or for damaging a tree that is protected by a preservation order.

PRESS COUNCIL

How to make a complaint against a newspaper

The Press Council is an independent body set up by the newspaper industry in 1953 to deal with complaints about ethical and professional standards in British newspapers and periodicals. Half its members are drawn from the press and half are laypeople. Its chairman is usually a judge or lawyer.

The council does not make legal judgments when considering allegations such as defamation or obscenity. Those are dealt with by the courts. Nor does it have powers to make awards or to prevent publication. It investigates complaints of breaches in acceptable standards of journalism and, if it considers there is a case to answer, will order a hearing and publish its findings. It cannot, however, oblige the offender to publish these findings.

If you have a complaint against an item in a newspaper or magazine, write first to the editor. If you are not satisfied with his response, write to the Press Council, enclosing a copy of the item. Its address is 1, Salisbury Square, London, EC4. You must lodge your complaint within 3 months of publication.

The council may ask you to attend a hearing at which you and staff of the newspaper may be invited to give evidence.

PRICE REDUCTION

How the law restricts 'bargain' claims

Any shop or trader making false, misleading or meaningless claims that its, or his, goods or services are sold for less than their normal price risks prosecution.

It is an offence to state on a label or poster, or in an advertisement, that something is simply worth a higher price, or worth a certain amount more. The penalty is a fine of up to £2,000.

However, a trader is in most cases allowed to advertise his price in comparison with a manufacturer's recommended retail price – sometimes abbreviated to MRP or RRP – provided that the information is correct. Such comparisons are not allowed for beds or mattresses, electric or gas domestic appliances, carpets and furniture, radios, TV's, record and video players, because manufacturers' price recommendations often bear no relation to anyone's charges.

BARGAIN PRICE THAT STAYED THE SAME

To prove that a price-reduction claim is false, a prosecution must show that no higher price was charged in any continuous period of 28 days during the previous 6 months.

On five Sundays in June and July 1969, House of Holland offered a sunchair bed for 45 shillings. Each advertisement said: 'All prices further reduced.'

The weights and measures inspector for the London Borough of Brent prosecuted on the basis of evidence that the same price had been charged for 2 months. Therefore the 'further reduced' claim must be false, he argued. Harrow magistrates agreed, and convicted the company.

On appeal, the English High Court had to decide whether the prosecution had proved the offence.

DECISION

The judges observed that although the prosecution had called evidence of the company's pricing for 2 months, the court was told nothing about the preceding 4 months. If a higher price had been charged for any 28 day period during these 4 months, no offence would have been committed.

The High Court found that no offence had been established, and quashed the conviction.

Quoting a rival's prices

A claim that one company's price is lower than another's is illegal unless the rival supplier is identified.

The advertiser must also be able to show that he had good reason to believe that the higher price was the one his rival normally charged, and was still charging when the claim was made.

The penalty for breaking this regulation is a fine of up to £2,000.

Quoting an earlier price

A claim that goods (not services) are being sold for less than the trader's previous price is permitted only if the goods were previously being sold by the same trader or by others who are named. Moreover, unless the trader states otherwise, the earlier price mentioned for goods must have been constant for at least 28 days within the preceding 6 months.

Anyone who breaks these laws risks a fine of £2,000 under summary procedure, and up to 2 years' imprisonment or an unlimited fine if convicted on indictment.

Where to complain If you believe that a pricing law has been broken, inform the trading standards office of your regional or islands council. It will investigate your complaint.

PRISON

A place of detention for law breakers

Scottish penal establishments are administered by the Scottish Home and Health Department. There are various types of establishments, including detention centres, young offenders institutions and prisons. The kind of establishment a person is sent to depends on sex, age, sentence and whether or not the person has been convicted.

A person has no choice over which institution he or she is kept in, but representations can be made to the Scottish Home and Health Department if it is felt that the allocation is wrong. In addition, those detained in establishments far from home may be able to save up their visits and have a temporary transfer nearer home to receive them.

Remand prisoners

Persons awaiting trial, sentence or the hearing of an appeal who have been refused BAIL are held in prison. Those awaiting trial or sentence are normally kept in the institution nearest to the court at which they are to appear.

During this time remand prisoners may be given various privileges in relation to letters, visits, food, clothing and work. Prisoners who are appealing against their sentence do not receive these privileges but have full and free access to legal advisers.

Restrictions on sentencing

Courts are encouraged to look on custodial sentences as a last resort, to be used only for serious or persistent offenders.

For offenders aged between 16–21 the court must be convinced that no other sentence is appropriate and give reasons for that conclusion. It must also call for a social enquiry report before passing a custodial sentence. The same rules apply in the sentencing of those over 21 who have not previously served a sentence of imprisonment or detention.

Social enquiry reports are prepared by social workers employed by the regional council. They will visit the offender and his home before writing the

ALLOCATING PRISONERS

Male and female inmates are kept in different institutions. Those under 21 are kept in institutions separate from those over 21, except on remand.

All females who receive custodial sentences in Scotland go to Cornton Vale in Bridge of Allan. This institution has a separate prison for those over 21, and a and a young offenders institution for those under 21.

Males under 21 who are sentenced to a period of less than 28 days or more than four months serve their sentence in a young offenders institution. Those with sentences of between 28 days and four months go to a detention centre.

Males over 21 are allocated to a prison in accordance with the sentence they are serving, the place of conviction or – if the sentence is one of more than 18 months – the nature of their offence, their previous criminal history, their attitude towards rehabilitation and aptitude for trade training. Those serving less than 18 months generally spend the time in their local prison – Barlinnie or Low Moss for Glasgow, Saughton for Edinburgh, Perth for Tayside, Inverness for Highland Region and Aberdeen for Grampian.

Those serving over 18 months undergo an allocation procedure at the National Classification Centre at Edinburgh prison. First offenders are normally kept in Edinburgh or transferred to open prison. Ordinary prisoners who have a positive attitude and some ability are sent to Perth. Other ordinary prisoners go to Peterhead or Aberdeen, depending on their age; the younger ones go to Peterhead.

Transfers between prisons are common, depending on the inmate's response to treatment.

SECURITY CATEGORIES

All inmates are placed in a security category on admission and this category determines to a great extent the amount of freedom the prisoner is allowed within the institution. The four categories and the rules applying to them are as follows:

Category A The highest security category is for those inmates who must in no circumstances be allowed to get out, either because of national security or because their violent behaviour would pose a danger to the lives of the public or police.

Such prisoners are subject to constant supervision, frequent searches and changes of cell. A light remains on in their cell all night and all their clothes, except pyjamas, are removed at night. The night officer must observe them at least every hour. They are specially allocated to, and closely supervised at, work and are searched each day on return from work.

Category B Inmates who ought to be kept in very secure conditions but do not require maximum security. These prisoners are not allowed outside the prison and are under supervision at all times within the prison during the day.

All untried inmates are either category A or B. Those sentenced to more than 3 years or who have committed an offence involving serious violence or sexual assault or who have previously attempted to escape will also be either A or B.

Category C Those who do not require very secure conditions but need some barrier to their escape. These inmates are allowed considerable freedom of movement within institutions without supervision and can be employed or attend functions outside the prison with supervision.

Category D Those who can reasonably be trusted to serve their sentence in open conditions are in the lowest security category. In open prisons there is a minimum of supervision and few physical barriers to escape. Inmates are allowed access to telephones, uncensored correspondence, regular short leaves and open visiting.

report. Medical reports from a psychiatrist or doctor may also be called for.

Concurrent and consecutive sentences

If a person is found guilty of more than one offence, he can receive a separate custodial sentence for each one, to run concurrently or consecutively.

Concurrently Running concurrently means running together. So if a person is sentenced to two years on each of two charges and six months on a third charge, to run concurrently, he serves two years (subject to remission).

Consecutively Consecutive sentences run one after another. So if the three sentences, two of two years and one of six months, were to run consecutively, the person would serve four years six months (subject to remission).

When a person enters prison

When a prisoner arrives at a prison he is closely searched and all cash and personal belongings to which he is not entitled in prison are taken from him. The prisoner must be given a receipt for all property taken from him. Any money is paid into an account under prison control.

All convicted prisoners are required to wear prison clothes and must have a bath on arrival. A medical examination must be carried out within 24 hours of admission. Haircuts are only ordered when there is a medical reason.

All other prisoners are entitled to wear their own clothes, if suitable, and to keep certain possessions. They may also have full meals sent in for them instead of prison food, and have specially furnished cells at their own expense.

How a prisoner must behave

Conduct of both staff and inmates within prison is governed by the Prison Rules and Standing Orders. Prisoners have few rights under these rules.

An extract from the rules is available in each cell. In the case of a prisoner who cannot read, they will be explained to him. In brief, the rules require that the prisoner should behave well, be respectful and obedient to staff and diligent in the performance of work allocated to him.

If a prisoner commits a criminal offence in prison, this may be reported to the police and dealt with in the normal way. Lesser offences against prison rules are normally dealt with internally by the governor or visiting committee. The governor receives a report on the incident on the following day (unless that is a Sunday or public holiday) and considers whether it is a matter he can deal with or whether he should submit it to the visiting committee.

If dealing with the matter himself, the governor investigates the case, hearing evidence from both sides and from any witnesses, and decides whether the prisoner is guilty or not. Sentences imposed by the governor can include loss of remission for up to 14 days, solitary confinement, deprivation of smoking and other privileges and deprivation of mattress (for male prisoners under 60 only).

The visiting committee, which hears more serious internal cases, has much greater powers. There is no limit to the remission it can take away and its other penalties are double the maximum which can be imposed by the governor. The prisoner is entitled to speak in his own defence and may call witnesses and question the witnesses of the other side.

Prisoners are not entitled to legal representation before either the governor or the visiting committee. Nor do they have any appeal unless the rules of NATURAL JUSTICE have been breached, when appeal to the Court of Session may be possible. Prisoners can, however, petition for remission to be restored if their subsequent behaviour has been good.

Visits and letters

Untried prisoners are allowed a daily visit of 15 minutes, and may send a daily letter paid for from public funds.

Civil prisoners, such as people sentenced for CONTEMPT OF COURT, can

IMPRISONMENT FOR NON-PAYMENT OF FINES

The ultimate sanction for non-payment of a fine imposed by a criminal court is imprisonment. In imposing a fine the court may immediately impose an alternative period of imprisonment, or this may be ordered by a subsequent means court.

A person imprisoned in these circumstances can obtain his immediate release by paying the unpaid balance of the fine or can buy days off his sentence by paying a proportion of the fine. The rate per day is determined by dividing the balance of the fine outstanding by the number of days in the sentence.

Any person outside the prison can make the payments and secure the release of the prisoner.

HOW A PRISONER CAN COMPLAIN

There are several channels open to a prisoner who wishes to make a complaint, and he should use them all before raising the complaint elsewhere.

The issue may be raised directly with the prison governor – or medical officer or chaplain if more appropriate. Alternatively, the prisoner may notify the governor through an officer that he wishes to see a member of the visiting committee or a prison department official (or a sheriff or justice of the peace) on his next visit to the prison. He need not disclose to the officer why he wishes to do so.

If those approaches fail to satisfy the prisoner, he can ask an officer for a form on which to make a formal complaint or 'petition' to be forwarded to the prison department for consideration.

If none of these internal channels is successful, the prisoner is entitled to write to his MP for help. If the prisoner alleges maladministration – for example, in the handling of a request for a transfer – his MP may ask the ombudsman for an investigation. *See:* OMBUDSMEN

As a last resort, the prisoner may write to the European Commission of HUMAN RIGHTS if he alleges that any of his rights have been infringed.

Getting advice from a solicitor

Any prisoner involved in legal proceedings of any kind is entitled to be visited by a solicitor and to apply for LEGAL AID. He may also write to, and conduct interviews with, the solicitor without interference from the prison authorities.

If legal proceedings have not begun, a prisoner can apply to the governor for permission to write to a solicitor about a civil, but not a criminal, matter. His application will be granted unless the matter refers to a complaint against prison authorities which has not been referred to the internal channels.

receive one 30 minute visit per week and one letter per week.

Convicted criminal prisoners are allowed to receive one letter per week, two visits of 20 minutes in the first two months of sentence and three visits of 20 minutes per two months thereafter. Additional letters can be purchased by prisoners.

Outgoing and incoming mail is subject to censorship.

Visits must normally take place within sight and hearing of a prison officer. Only those who have received a visiting pass from the prison are allowed to visit. Visitors are not normally allowed to give the inmate anything during the visit.

Visits by legal advisers, and correspondence in connection with any legal action, are freely permitted in addition to normal letters and visits.

Accommodation and work in penal institutions

Accommodation varies between institutions. Most inmates are accommodated in cells on their own but some are required to share with one or two other prisoners and some institutions use dormitories. Every inmate is entitled to one hour's exercise outside his cell each day – though in most cases work and recreation will also take place outside the cell.

Work is compulsory for all convicted prisoners, and it is an offence to refuse to work, or to be idle, careless or negligent at work. The work varies, and inmates normally work an 8-hour day, 5 days per week.

Wages are paid, the rate depending on the job and the stage of sentence for long-term inmates. The maximum wage is around £2.50 per week, but overtime pay can sometimes be earned. This money can be spent on items in the prison shop, saved for use on release or sent out to relations.

Welfare in prison

All institutions have social workers, appointed by the regional council, and chaplains for the various denominations (often including non-Christian religions). Prisoners can ask to see a social worker or chaplain at any time and arrangements can be made for special visits – for example, to deal with any domestic crisis.

Solitary confinement

There are various forms of solitary confinement. A prisoner who requests such confinement for his own protection is normally moved to a protection unit, though he will not be moved if he fears for his safety only as a result of the crime he has committed. Such prisoners are usually kept separately in their ordinary prison for a time and then reintegrated with other prisoners.

Prisoners who are violent and dangerous to themselves or to others can be confined in special cells but must not be kept there longer than necessary. Prisoners who are undergoing punishments can be confined in special cells for the duration of the punishment.

PRIVILEGES AVAILABLE

Most prisoners are entitled to general privileges – such as receiving books from friends or using the prison library.

Release from prison

All convicted prisoners who are serving more than 5 days in prison are now entitled to receive one-third remission of their sentence, provided that their

SPECIAL UNITS FOR DIFFICULT PRISONERS

A unit is maintained at Porterfield Prison, Inverness, for the accommodation of prisoners whose behaviour is causing serious problems in their normal prison.

While in this unit prisoners receive a minimum of privileges. It is not, however, a punishment unit and prisoners are kept only for the minimum period necessary until they are able to be returned to their normal prison.

The special unit at Barlinnie Prison, Glasgow, caters for selected long-term prisoners for a part of their sentence. The regime here is much more liberal than in normal prisons and many of the restrictions required elsewhere because of buildings and resource shortages are not applied in the unit.

VISITING COMMITTEES

Each penal establishment has an independent committee appointed to it whose function is to make sure that the establishment is run in conformity with the Rules. Members are appointed to the visiting committee by regional and district councils in the case of adult institutions and by the Secretary of State for young offenders institutions. The regulations require a specified minimum number of female members.

The visiting committee meets regularly at the institution to deal with requests from prisoners and disciplinary charges against prisoners.

In addition, members of the committee can have access to the institution at any time and are entitled to examine any part of the prison.

Prisoners have the right to request an interview with any member of the visiting committee while in the prison.

TRAINING FOR FREEDOM

Prisoners serving sentences of over 3 years and those with indeterminate sentences will be considered for the training for freedom scheme towards the end of their sentence.

If accepted for the scheme, they are accommodated in hostels beside the prison but go out to work each day in normal outside employment. They receive an enhanced weekly allowance and part of their wages is saved for their use on release.

While on the scheme, prisoners may be allowed three 4-hour leaves each week in addition to their working time, and they can also qualify for one 48-hour leave every six weeks.

CIVIL PRISONERS

Persons sent to prison for contempt of court or failing to maintain their families are civil prisoners and are subject to a different regime. They should be kept separately from sentenced prisoners.

Civil prisoners may at the governor's discretion be allowed to wear their own clothes, to have full meals sent in, and to use their private cash to have their cell cleaned for them or to buy such things as tobacco, books or newspapers.

Civil prisoners do not receive any remission on their sentences. They cannot be forced to work. Each week a visit of 30 minutes is allowed and the prisoner can send one letter paid for from public funds.

GRANTING PRIVILEGES TO PRISONERS

In practice, privileges are granted to most prisoners, but no prisoner has a legal right to them, and they can be withdrawn for misbehaviour.

The usual general privileges include freedom to earn and spend money, use of the prison library, receipt of suitable personal books and periodicals from friends outside, buying and smoking tobacco, and having a personal radio.

In addition to these, television, films and other recreational pursuits may be available, depending on the facilities in the institution and the length of sentence and behaviour of the inmate.

Prison governors also have power to grant special privileges – such as having a typewriter or other more personal possession in a cell, or being permitted to attend evening classes in prison.

behaviour has been good.

Prisoners due for release on a Sunday are generally released on the previous Friday or Saturday.

Parole Prisoners serving more than 18 months may be released on PAROLE but they are subject to recall to prison if they break the conditions of parole.

Temporary release A prisoner may be granted temporary release from prison, with or without escort, to visit close relations who are dangerously ill, to attend a funeral, to get married or to attend an interview for employment. Long-term prisoners may also be eligible for temporary release towards the end of their sentence.

On release a prisoner is entitled to have his possessions returned to him, to have clothing provided if he needs it and to receive his fare home. Those who have served over 14 days are also entitled to a discharge grant, calculated to meet their needs for the first week after release.

Compulsory after-care is provided for some categories of ex-inmates by social work departments. Social work assistance is also available to others who request it.

Supplementary benefit

A person in custody cannot claim SUPPLEMENTARY BENEFIT. (This includes someone awaiting trial.)

On release, a prisoner can claim benefit under the usual conditions. A grant is paid to meet his expenses for the first week.

Lump sum payments of benefit may also be payable at that stage to clear any arrears of rent, rates or furniture storage charges incurred while in prison. These payments can only be made if the person was in prison for less than a year, is now in danger of losing the accommodation or furniture and is either chronically sick, disabled or over pension age, or requires the accommodation for use by his wife or children.

If the partner of a prisoner is left without support, she can make a claim for supplementary benefit. She may also be entitled to help with costs incurred in visiting her husband.

PRIVACY

Your right to be left alone

There is no law that specifically states that the ordinary citizen has a right to privacy. But there are various legal remedies available to someone who claims that his privacy has been unjustifiably infringed.

A right to privacy usually means:

- The right to prevent others from entering your home or property.
- The right to be protected against harassment, annoyance or upset in your own home.
- The right to have personal or private information kept confidential.
- The right not to be subjected to the glare of publicity when you have done nothing to warrant it.

The 'actio iniuriarum'

Although there is no specific law protecting the right to privacy, someone whose privacy has been seriously infringed could raise a court action – called an *'actio iniuriarum'*, or action for insult.

The court *might* be prepared to grant an INTERDICT – an order requiring the infringement of privacy to cease – and also to award compensation, but only if there was intent to injure.

This remedy could be used where your telephone was being unlawfully tapped, or private detectives were persistently following you around, or a newspaper was continually ringing your home to obtain information about you or published photographs of you without your consent – in all cases with the intention of discrediting you or causing you harm or upset.

However, there is some doubt as to whether a Scottish court would grant such a remedy. In 1957 a senior Scottish judge declared that mere invasion of privacy, however hurtful, was not itself actionable. This view has been challenged but there has not yet been a court case on the matter.

Protecting the right to privacy

Apart from the *actio iniuriarum* there are laws that protect some aspects of your privacy:

Trespass You cannot sue a person, such as a squatter, merely because he enters your home or property against your wishes. But you can sue him for compensation if he inflicts damage on your property, or causes you severe upset.

Under the Trespass (Scotland) Act 1865, it is a criminal offence for anyone to occupy private property, including land, without the consent of the owner or legal occupier. You should report any infringement of the Act to the police.

Many officials of public authorities have the right to enter your home provided they observe the detailed restrictions laid down by Act of Parliament. A warrant from a sheriff or justice of the peace is usually necessary. *See:* ENTRY, Right of

Harassment In some situations, harassment of an individual can amount to an offence.

For instance, if your house is besieged by press and television reporters, the police can order them to leave if they think that a BREACH OF THE PEACE is likely. Similarly, the police may arrest a peeping Tom if they think that he is causing, or is likely to cause, a breach of the peace.

If you are a tenant, your landlord has no automatic right to enter your home. He may be guilty of HARASSMENT if he persistently attempts to gain entry or interferes with your peace and comfort.

Telephone offences Telephone tapping, whether done by the police, security services, or any other body or person may be unlawful, even if done under a warrant issued by the Secretary of State for Scotland or the Home Secretary. A person whose telephone is tapped may be able to succeed in an *actio iniuriarum* (above). *See:* TELEPHONE TAPPING

However, you have a right to be protected against upsetting phone calls. It is an offence for someone to make a telephone call that is grossly offensive or false, or is of an indecent, obscene or menacing character. You should report such a call to the police. The maximum penalty is a fine of £400.

Postal offences It is an offence for someone other than a Post Office official to open a letter addressed to you, provided his intention is to harm you. Maximum penalty is a £1,000 fine or 6 months' imprisonment, or both.

It is also an offence for any Post Office employee to open correspondence that is addressed to you, except in the course of his duties. These duties may include opening correspondence in obedience to a warrant issued by the Secretary of State – issued, for instance, when criminal investigations are being carried out.

You are entitled to protection against offensive material being sent to your home. It is an offence to send indecent or obscene publications through the post. The maximum penalty is a fine of £400 (or 12 months' imprisonment in serious cases).

It is also an offence to send someone unsolicited publications which describe or illustrate human sexual techniques. The maximum penalty for doing so is a fine of £2,000.

Confidentiality Your professional advisers – doctors, lawyers, bankers and accountants, for example – are under a legal duty to respect your privacy and not to disclose any information about your personal affairs.

So too ministers, priests, social workers, marriage guidance counsellors and other similar people have a duty not to disclose to unauthorised persons what you have told them in confidence.

If any such person does disclose confidential information, you may be able to obtain damages.

NO RIGHT TO PRIVACY

A senior Scottish judge has stated that there is no general right to privacy. But others have challenged this view.

A Border sheriff was convicted of a motoring offence. About a year later, he wrote a letter to the *Glasgow Herald* advocating stiffer penalties for other motoring offenders.

This letter aroused the interest of a reporter for another paper, who telephoned the sheriff to discuss the matter. The sheriff warned him not to refer to his own conviction but the reporter ignored the warning and wrote an ironical article. The sheriff sued the newspaper for damages.

DECISION

The Court of Session dismissed the case. The Lord Justice-Clerk said: 'I know of no authority to the effect that mere invasion of privacy, however hurtful and whatever its purpose and however repugnant to good taste, is itself actionable'.

There is no law which prohibits the press from publishing information about your private life. But if a newspaper, for example, publishes details of your private life which are untrue, you can sue it for DEFAMATION.

Even if the information is true, you may be able to obtain an interdict to prevent further publication, and also compensation, if you can show that the newspaper acted maliciously, with the intention of holding you up to public ridicule and contempt, and you have suffered loss or damage as a result.

Proceedings in courts and tribunals are usually public and you cannot normally prevent any newspaper from publishing a full and fair account of the evidence given. In divorce, separation and nullity proceedings, however, the account of the evidence must be limited to a short summary.

But certain legal proceedings are private – for instance, ADOPTION proceedings, JUDICIAL EXAMINATION before the sheriff, and the proceedings of a CHILDREN'S HEARING. This means that information given there cannot be disclosed.

Anyone, except a lawyer, can be compelled by a court to divulge confidential information. Refusal to do so will be CONTEMPT OF COURT.

Many officials are specifically forbidden to pass confidential information to others except in the course of their duties.

The police, for instance, are not allowed to disclose criminal records to outsiders. And it is an offence for British Telecommunication employees to divulge to outsiders information obtained in the course of providing data processing services, except with the consent of the person concerned.

It is an offence to disclose information about spent convictions from official records except in the course of official duties. *See:* REHABILITATION

International protection for privacy

The United Kingdom is a party to the United Nations Universal Declaration of Human Rights, and to the European Convention of Human Rights – both of which attempt to safeguard the right to privacy.

Under Article 8 of the European Convention: 'Everyone has the right to respect for his private and family life, his home and his correspondence'. A public authority must not interfere with this right except for reasons of national security, public safety, economic well-being, to prevent disorder or crime, to protect health or morals, or to protect the rights and freedoms of others.

If you believe that your right to privacy under the Convention has been breached, you can complain to the European Commission of Human Rights, 67006, Strasbourg, France. But you must first have exhausted all legal remedies that are open to you in Scotland (such as suing the person who has infringed your privacy). *See:* HUMAN RIGHTS

PRIVATE DETECTIVE

What you can expect of a reputable investigator

A private detective has no greater powers or rights than any other citizen when conducting an investigation. He can be prosecuted if he breaks the criminal law, or be sued in a civil court if his actions infringe someone else's rights.

No private detective can enter your house without permission, take anything of yours or intercept any correspondence. Nor can he remain on your property if you have ordered him to leave.

You do not have to give a private investigator any information about yourself or any other person, whatever the purpose of his inquiry and whatever credentials he may produce.

There is no official system of licensing private detectives, or of requiring them to have particular qualifications. The law simply does not recognise them.

Hiring a detective

Someone who wants to conduct a private investigation – for example, to pursue a criminal allegation when the authorities say they have insufficient grounds to prosecute – usually has no way of knowing whether a particular detective is competent and whether his charges are reasonable.

If the proposed investigation is connected with any legal proceedings, it is usually advisable to discuss it with a lawyer first. He should be able to judge whether it is worth while and whether it involves any legal risks. He may also be able to recommend an investigator.

If a detective is hired through a law firm, the firm takes responsibility for checking and paying his charges. They are passed on to the client.

Someone who wants to deal directly with a private detective is most likely to find a suitable one by contacting the Association of British Investigators (ABI), which has a nationwide membership of people who have established their competence in the field and are subject to the association's own discipline. In Scotland it has members in Aberdeen, Dundee, Edinburgh, Glasgow and Wishaw.

ABI headquarters are at ABI House, 10 Bonner Hill Road, Kingston-upon-Thames, Surrey KT1 3EP.

ABI members are bound to a code of conduct which among other things obliges them to:

- Protect the privacy and confidences of their clients.
- Ensure that a client has 'lawful and moral' reasons for asking for an investigation.
- Conduct investigations 'within the bounds of legality, morality and professional ethics'.

When there is a dispute

A detective is entitled to refuse any work that he cannot or does not want to carry out. But once he accepts an assignment, and his client agrees to his fees and conditions, a CONTRACT has been made and the normal laws governing contracts apply.

A client is entitled to refuse to pay if the agreed work is not done, and either party can sue for money owed – provided that the assignment was lawful.

How to complain The Association of British Investigators can deal with complaints of negligence or failure of duty by its members. ABI discipline is usually effective, because loss of membership could severely damage a detective's livelihood.

PRIVATE HEALTH INSURANCE

How an insurance policy can pay for your medical treatment

Patients who want to have their medical treatment privately instead of through the National Health Service can take out an insurance policy to pay for the costs. So can those who intend to use the NHS, but who wish to be covered against the extra cost of illness.

There are various all-in schemes which are offered by a number of insurance companies, covering payment of any medical bills up to a fixed ceiling, including bills for hospital treatment and nursing.

There are also fixed-benefit schemes which will provide a set payment for each day the insured person spends in hospital. The money can be spent in any way you choose.

There are also loss-of-earnings schemes which simply compensate for income lost while the sick person is away from work. These schemes are particularly valuable to self-employed people and apply whether the patient is in a private or NHS hospital.

Which scheme to choose

The choice of scheme depends on a person's individual needs and how

HOW BENEFITS VARY

Not all private health insurance schemes offer the same range of benefits. Check carefully before you decide to make a proposal.

much he can afford to set aside for private medical insurance.

The all-in scheme is the most comprehensive, but it is also likely to be the most expensive.

The fixed-benefit scheme provides cover only while the patient is in hospital – it is not suitable for a person who needs a long convalescence. The hospital bills are likely to be higher than the cash entitlement.

Loss-of-earnings schemes can be geared to a person's normal income and even increased each year to account for inflation or rising income. Benefits are paid at a fixed rate, normally for a fixed period of time, and are often related to the insured person's age.

If you earn £8,500 a year or more, and your employer pays your medical insurance premiums, they count as taxable income.

What insurance schemes covers

Do not expect even a comprehensive policy to pay for every single cost you incur in hospital or medical treatment. Almost every scheme has a maximum payment. The patient will have to pay for any expense above that figure.

Apart from nursing and treatment in hospital there are many extras to be paid for – X-rays, surgical dressings, anaesthetists, therapy, drugs. Not every scheme will cover all of those. Check when you take out a policy.

Most insurance schemes cover treatment for the cure or relief of illness or for injuries received in an accident, or dental care which requires hospital treatment. Treatment of acute psychiatric illness may be included, but there is likely to be a time-limit clause, such as a maximum number of days during which treatment will be paid for. This is because, by its nature, psychiatric treatment is often long-term.

A person already suffering from an illness or injury can sometimes insure against the cost of future treatment. Full details of the complaint, its symptoms and duration must be disclosed on the proposal form.

Few schemes cover the cost of pregnancy or childbirth, though it is possible to insure for private treatment for any complications in pregnancy, or when there is some abnormal condition. It is usually necessary for the woman to insure before she becomes pregnant.

Making a health insurance claim

In most schemes, the cost of treatment is paid directly to the insured person by the insurance company after all bills have been submitted to them.

In the event of a dispute over a bill, it is usual for the company to appoint an independent doctor to arbitrate.

Other forms of financial help available

Other forms of financial help during illness are provided by contributory insurance schemes. The British Hospitals Contributory Schemes Association, 30 Lancaster Gate, London W2 3LT, can provide information on the schemes available, including what they cost and what they provide. Some, for example, help with national health charges for dentures, with home helps and with private specialists.

Self-employed people who wish to insure against loss of earnings during illness also have a choice of policies. Usually it is best to go to an insurance broker for guidance. The amount of the premium depends not only on the sum insured for, but also on the number of weeks or months of illness which it is agreed must elapse before you qualify for payment.

Obtaining help from clubs and societies

Trade unions, employers and other groups sometimes organise sick clubs or friendly societies that, in return for a small weekly contribution, provide some financial help during sickness. Membership is normally open to only a limited number of people, however, and the scale of operation is usually small.

PRIVATE MEDICINE

How and where a patient can opt out of the National Health Service

No one requiring medical treatment is obliged to use the National Health Service. Instead he can obtain treatment on a private, fee-paying basis in a few National Health Service hospitals or in private hospitals.

Some doctors, consultants and hospitals accept both private and National Health Service patients. Some treat one or the other, but not both.

However, someone seeking treatment does not have to commit himself at the outset either to private or Health Service medicine. He can decide on a combination of the two.

For example, he may be registered with a general practitioner under the National Health Service, but he can still choose to pay for private consultancy if specialist treatment is required for a particular ailment.

Similarly, a patient registered privately with a family doctor can obtain specialist or hospital treatment under the Health Service.

No single doctor is allowed, however, to offer a patient both types of treatment – private for some purposes, non-private for others.

Hospitals Some National Health Service hospitals accept fee-paying patients. In an area where they do not, a patient seeking private treatment would have to enter an exclusively private hospital.

In both cases, it is normally the general practitioner who arranges for the admission.

What it may cost

No recommended fees are laid down by the British Medical Association for private consultations with specialists or general practitioners.

You may therefore wish to discuss the likely charge before commencing any private health care.

Some guidelines as to the 'going rate' can be obtained from the fees which the various private health insurance societies, such as the British United Provident Association, are willing to provide.

How to complain about treatment

A private medical patient has the same rights as a National Health Service patient to take action over what he considers to be MEDICAL NEGLIGENCE.

In addition, a private patient may also be entitled to withhold any fees that are payable if he has been treated negligently or inadequately. This may result in legal action being taken against him by the doctor or hospital concerned. Professional convention, however, forbids consultants to sue in court for their fees.

When the complaint is against a private hospital, it is the owners as well as the medical staff who may be liable.

If the complaint is about treatment in a National Health hospital, the action to be taken depends on who was at fault. If it was a private consultant or surgeon brought in from outside, it is he who should be sued. If any of the hospital staff were responsible, legal action should be directed against the health board and the staff member. *See:* HOSPITAL; MEDICAL NEGLIGENCE

PRIVATE PROSECUTION

The alternatives to public prosecution

Criminal prosecutions in Scotland are usually undertaken by the public prosecutor – the LORD ADVOCATE in the High Court of Justiciary and the PROCURATOR FISCAL in the sheriff and district courts. *See:* CRIMINAL PROCEEDINGS

However, there are three exceptions:

1. Prosecutions by public bodies Some public bodies and officials, such as education authorities and customs officers, have a special right to prosecute for certain offences.

For example, the parents of a child who persistently plays truant from school may be prosecuted by the local education authority for failing to ensure the child's attendance at school.

Prosecutions by authorised public bodies or officials are conducted under summary procedure (before a judge without a jury), usually in the sheriff court. They are prosecutions in the public interest and do not require the consent of the procurator fiscal.

2. Prosecutions by landowners In certain circumstances, members of the public are given the right to prosecute by Act of Parliament. For example, under the GAME laws the owner or occupier of land is given the power to prosecute any person who trespasses on his land during daytime in pursuit of game.

Such a prosecution is private and proceeds under summary procedure before a judge sitting alone. If the offence being prosecuted can be punished by imprisonment without the option of a fine, the private prosecutor must usually obtain the consent of the procurator fiscal before the prosecution can go ahead.

3. Prosecutions by victims of crime Because there is general satisfaction with the system of public prosecution in Scotland, private prosecution by the victim of a crime is practically unknown. In recent times only *two* such prosecutions have been authorised by the High Court of Justiciary – one in 1909 (for fraud) and another in 1982 (for rape).

Private prosecutions by victims can take place under solemn procedure (for serious crime) or summary procedure (for less serious crime). *See:* CRIMINAL PROCEEDINGS

Solemn procedure A private prosecution under solemn procedure is begun by serving a document called 'Criminal Letters' on the accused person. This document takes the same form as the INDICTMENT served on an accused person in a public prosecution.

A prosecution by criminal letters is possible only in the High Court of Justiciary – it cannot take place in the sheriff court.

A citizen who wishes to bring a private prosecution in the High Court must show that the alleged crime is a personal wrong against himself. He must also have applied to the Lord Advocate for his consent to the prosecution.

If the Lord Advocate refuses his consent, the citizen can complain to the High Court. The Court can order the Lord Advocate to give his consent or can authorise the citizen to go ahead without such consent.

A private prosecution by criminal letters is conducted in the same way as a public prosecution on indictment.

Summary procedure A private prosecution under summary procedure is begun by serving on the accused the same document as is used in a public prosecution – a SUMMARY COMPLAINT.

The person bringing the prosecution must show that the alleged crime is a personal wrong against himself. He must also apply to the procurator fiscal for his consent to the prosecution.

It is not clear what remedy the person bringing the prosecution has if the procurator fiscal should refuse his consent. There appears to be no right to apply to the High Court requesting it to allow the prosecution to go ahead without the fiscal's consent.

Summary private prosecutions by the victims of crime are virtually unknown.

PRIVATE STREET

What it may cost you to live in a private street

A private street is one that is not maintained out of rates or taxes.

People with houses or properties in private streets are called 'frontagers' – meaning that their properties have frontages on the street.

They are responsible jointly for the upkeep of the roadway. However, difficulties in organising repairs and getting everyone to pay his share can mean that in practice the road may fall into disrepair.

In these circumstances the householders may ask the regional (or islands) council, as the highway authority, to take over the street.

If the authority agrees, it then becomes responsible for maintaining the road. But an authority will only take over roads that are up to its standards – which means that the frontagers have first to pay for that work to be done. Alternatively, the authority may agree to have the road 'made up' by its own workmen, then ask the householders to meet the cost.

Making up a private street

The highway authority can also order the owners of property fronting on a private street to have the street

THE COST OF A 'TAKE-OVER'

When a council is to take over a private street, it will require the residents to pay to bring it up to normal standards.

made up to the authority's standards. A householder might object to such an order on the ground, for example, that the amount of traffic using the street is small.

Alternatively, the highway authority may carry out the work required to bring the road up to standard and recover the cost from the frontagers. The cost is borne by the frontagers in proportion to the lengths of their frontages. The highway authority can, however, contribute to the cost of the works.

Once a private street has been made up, any frontager may ask the highway authority to take it over as a public street. If the authority agrees to such a request, the street is thereafter to be maintained at public expense.

The authority need not, however, agree to take over the street unless the owners of at least half of the frontage of the street request it to do so.

Pavements

The highway authority can call on the frontagers of any street to make pavements. If an owner fails to do so, the authority may carry out the work at the frontager's expense. Once the pavements have been made up to standard, the authority becomes responsible for their future maintenance.

PROBATION

When a court orders a period of guidance and supervision

Any offender can be put on probation, with his consent, if the court that finds him guilty thinks this is appropriate.

Probation is a voluntary order and not a sentence. In summary cases there is no conviction, while in solemn cases there is a conviction but it only counts if the person subsequently appears in court again.

When a court orders probation

The aim of probation is rehabilitation of an offender. If a court orders probation, the offender must agree to be supervised by a social worker for the period of the order – which can be between 1 and 3 years. If he does not consent, the court must impose a sentence.

When an offender agrees to probation

Many of the people placed on probation are first offenders or young people. A social worker must supervise them in whatever way he thinks necessary.

Probation orders impose conditions on the offender. The usual conditions are that he shall behave well, do as he is told by his supervisor and tell the supervisor if he changes his residence or place of employment.

Most people on probation are allowed to live in their own homes, but an offender may be required to live in a home or hostel – especially if he is a young person with a disturbed home life.

Other conditions may also be imposed. For example, an offender may be required to undergo psychiatric treatment, or stop taking alcohol or drugs, or keep away from bad company.

When a probation order is broken

If someone on probation breaks the terms of his order, he can be brought before the court again and sentenced for his original offence. If the breach is not serious, the court will usually allow the probation order to continue, and may impose a fine of up to £400, make a COMMUNITY SERVICE ORDER or vary the requirements of the probation order.

If a person commits another offence while on probation, this is automatically a breach of probation. Unless the court which deals with the new offence is the same court which imposed probation, the new court can only deal with the new offence. Once this has been done, the original court will be notified and can then deal with the offender for the original offence. If the court is the original one, both offences can be dealt with together.

A court can end a probation order at any time on the application of the probationer or the supervisor. In both cases the supervisor must submit a report and the court must be convinced that probation is no longer necessary. Cancellation of the probation order completes the disposal of that offence.

PROBATIONARY EMPLOYEE

Working for a trial period

An employee who is initially employed for a trial, or probationary, period has exactly the same rights and duties as an employee who is not so employed. However, if he is dismissed at the end of the trial period he may forfeit a number of EMPLOYMENT PROTECTION rights which depend on working for a minimum length of time.

Like any other employee, a probationary employee has an EMPLOYMENT CONTRACT – which may be written or oral. If the contract is oral, the details of its terms – for instance, rate of pay, hours of work and holiday entitlement – will be inferred from any relevant collective agreement, from custom and practice, or simply from the stated intention of the parties.

Employment protection rights

Many employment protection rights depend on an employee – whether a probationer or not – working for a minimum period, called a period of CONTINUOUS EMPLOYMENT.

For instance, an employee must be continuously employed for 1 month to be entitled to statutory minimum NOTICE; for 2 years to be able to claim a REDUNDANCY payment; and normally for 1 year (2 years if the employer employs 20 or fewer) to be entitled to claim compensation for UNFAIR DISMISSAL.

Like any other employee, a probationary employee can count his *whole* period of service, from the day he starts work, towards his period of continuous employment. His employer cannot use the trial period to try to defeat these rights.

However, a trial period may be fixed so as to prevent a probationary employee obtaining certain employment protection rights – in particular, the right to make a complaint of unfair dismissal to an industrial tribunal. That is perfectly lawful.

So an employee who is taken on for a trial period of, say, 6 months, and is dismissed at the end of that period, has no right to make a complaint of unfair dismissal – unless dismissed because of trade union membership, or because of sex or race. *See:* UNFAIR DISMISSAL

If a probationary employee normally works less than 16 hours a week, he cannot qualify for employment protection rights which require a period of continuous employment. *See:* PART-TIME WORKER

Your right to notice

The rules about NOTICE are the same for all employees, including probationers.

If the trial period is to be less than 1 month, and the employer decides to dismiss the probationer at the end of the period, he is obliged to give only 'reasonable' notice. In practice, notice of a day, or even a few hours in some cases, might well be sufficient.

If the trial period is between 1 month and 2 years, and the employer dismisses the employee at the end of the period, he is obliged to give at least the statutory minimum notice – which is 1 week – unless the employee has been guilty of misconduct justifying instant dismissal. *See:* DISCIPLINE AT WORK; DISMISSAL; NOTICE

PROCESSION

Organising a march through the streets

Anyone who wants to organise a march, demonstration or other procession may have to inform the local district or islands council. Such councils have the power to make byelaws regulating processions.

Local laws may vary between one town and another. In Aberdeen, for example, at least 48 hours' notice of the time and route of the procession must be given to the district council. In Edinburgh, at least 7 days' notice is required. It is an offence to fail to give any required notice.

It is advisable to consult with the district or islands council or the local police to discover what local laws may apply.

In some towns, advance notice or formal permission from the district or islands council is not required. However, it is still advisable to consult with it because in all towns these councils have a general power of control and can forbid processions or order changes of route.

When the Civic Government Act 1982 comes into force on July 1, 1984, anyone organising a procession anywhere will have to give 7 days' notice to the regional or islands council. The council may forbid the procession or impose conditions, though there will be an appeal to the sheriff.

Holding a procession without giving notice will be punishable by up to 3 months' imprisonment. Taking part in one after being told to stop doing so by a policeman will be punishable by a fine of up to £400.

You should always consult the local police. Any application you make to the district or islands council will be sent by it to the police for comment.

Although individuals have the right to use the highway, the police can regulate the route of processions and redirect traffic and pedestrians where necessary.

These powers apply to all processions and not just to demonstrations and protest marches. They apply, for example, to scout marches, student rag processions and religious 'walks'.

The police have no right to ban a procession, though they can ask for a ban in certain circumstances (see below).

If a chief constable believes that a particular procession may cause serious disorder, he can impose whatever conditions and directions he thinks necessary to keep the peace.

He can, for example, specify the route to be followed. He can also restrict the use of flags and banners if he thinks their use will provoke disorder. Anyone who wilfully disobeys any such condition or direction can be fined up to £1,000 or imprisoned for 3 months.

When the police seek a ban

If the chief constable thinks that his forces are inadequate to prevent serious public disorder, he can ask the regional council to make an order, with the consent of the Secretary of State for Scotland, banning some or all processions for up to 3 months.

Anyone who defies such an order can be fined up to £1,000 or imprisoned for 3 months.

Organisers of a procession cannot appeal against police directions but may appeal against a banning order.

How to apply for permission

Before making any public announcement about a procession, get in touch

BANNING ORDERS IN GLASGOW

A chief constable who reasonably thinks he has insufficient powers to prevent serious public disorder being caused by a procession can apply to the regional council for an order banning all or some processions for up to 3 months. The regional council must obtain the consent of the Secretary of State for Scotland before making such an order.

During 1981 some IRA prisoners in the Maze prison in Northern Ireland went on hunger-strike and some died. This provoked riots in Belfast.

Supporters of the Protestant and Catholic Irish points of view organised marches in Glasgow which became very violent. As a result, Strathclyde Regional Council, with the consent of the Secretary of State, made three banning orders during the year.

These orders banned 'within the area of Strathclyde Region the holding of the following class of public processions, that is to say all public processions (other than those customarily held in the area of Strathclyde Region since before 1st January 1971) which are concerned or connected, directly or indirectly, with Northern Irish affairs or any aspect thereof or which are organised by, or with the assistance of, any person or body known or reputed to be so concerned or connected.'

As a result peace was maintained.

with your district or islands council, or the local police. They will advise you what permissions are necessary and how to obtain them.

You will have to provide details of the purpose of the march, its date, time and route, and how many people are likely to take part.

The police may suggest an alternative time or route, so that they can provide enough officers for the march or for keeping the marchers away from main traffic thoroughfares.

You would not, for example, be given permission to march down Sauchiehall Street in Glasgow on a Saturday afternoon when it is packed with shoppers – but you might be allowed to do so on a Sunday morning.

The permission for the procession will usually, but not always, be given by the district or islands council. In Edinburgh, for example, this task has been taken over by the regional council because it is the highway authority, and in this capacity would issue any street closure (from traffic) orders considered necessary to accommodate the procession.

Staging a procession

It is not an offence to stage a procession without permission. But the police can arrest marchers for obstructing the street – a power they would use only if the participants behaved unreasonably in an unapproved procession.

Anyone refusing to move on when ordered to do so can be arrested and charged with obstructing the police. *See:* DEMONSTRATION; OBSTRUCTION; PUBLIC MEETING

PROCURATOR FISCAL

The Crown's local law officer

Procurators fiscal are locally-based prosecutors appointed by the LORD ADVOCATE in the name of the Crown. They are advocates or solicitors and hold salaried, full-time appointments. Many fiscals make this their whole career.

Procurators fiscal operate from local offices throughout the country. The number of fiscals in each office ranges from one in rural areas to 40 in Glasgow. Regional procurators fiscal, 6 in number, co-ordinate and oversee the work of the fiscals in their area.

Undertaking prosecutions

If a criminal charge is not serious, and is to be prosecuted summarily in the SHERIFF COURT or the DISTRICT COURT, the decision whether or not to prosecute, the preparation of the prosecution case, and the conduct of the prosecution in court are all carried out by the procurator fiscal.

If a criminal charge is serious, the procurator fiscal makes a provisional decision that trial before a JURY in the sheriff court or HIGH COURT OF JUSTICIARY may be appropriate. He then refers the case to the CROWN OFFICE for a final decision by advocates called Crown Counsel on whether to prosecute and if so, by what procedure. *See:* CRIMINAL PROCEEDINGS

It is the procurator fiscal's task to prepare the case for the prosecution. If it is brought in the High Court, the prosecution case is conducted by an advocate depute from the Crown Office, with the assistance of the procurator fiscal.

The fiscal's other tasks

The procurator fiscal has other duties in connection with criminal procedure. He can give directions to the police on the investigation of crime. He looks into complaints against the police which involve allegations of criminal conduct. And he has to investigate all sudden, unexpected or suspicious deaths, or fires and explosions occurring in suspicious circumstances – for these may lead to a criminal case.

The fiscal also gives legal advice to local branches of other government departments – such as the Post Office, Health and Safety inspectors and Customs and Excise – on matters of criminal law and procedure, because he may have to prosecute cases arising in the course of their work.

Under civil law, it is the procurator fiscal who gathers together and presents the evidence at a FATAL ACCIDENT INQUIRY.

He also makes inquiries where a person dies without making a will and leaves no known heirs. The results of his inquiries are reported to the Crown Office. *See:* INHERITANCE

The procurator fiscal has the responsibility for dealing with any TREASURE TROVE found in his area.

Contacting the fiscal

Although most information regarding criminal conduct reaches the procurator fiscal from the police, anyone is entitled to write to the local fiscal drawing to his notice an apparent breach of the criminal law.

PROFESSIONAL NEGLIGENCE

When an expert's professional skill is in question

When you engage a professional – for example, a solicitor or accountant – to do something for you, you generally enter into a CONTRACT with him.

If he then fails to perform satisfactorily the task he has undertaken, you are entitled to sue him for breach of contract and to recover damages to compensate you for the loss you have incurred.

If, however, you have no contract with the professional involved – for example, you have no direct contract with your National Health Service doctor – you cannot sue him for breach of contract. Instead you must sue him for negligence, and be able to show that he has in some way fallen short of what could reasonably be expected of him. *See:* MEDICAL NEGLIGENCE

Even when you contract with a professional for his services, there will probably be no agreement on the degree of skill which he is expected to exercise. If there is none, the degree of skill required will be that of a reasonable professional man in the position of the professional acting for you.

In every profession there are generally accepted standards of skill. If you think that someone working on your behalf has fallen below the standard expected, try to find another person who is qualified and working in the same field and who would be willing to testify that your expert has failed in his duty to you.

Proving such failure normally requires you to show what the normal professional practice is. For example, if you allege that a doctor has failed to perform an operation properly, you will need the evidence of an experienced doctor in the field as to whether the procedures carried out were correct.

It is usually desirable to consult more than one independent witness. Finding one is a specialist task and you should consult a solicitor who is experienced in such matters.

If you feel that a solicitor whom you have engaged has failed in his duty to use a reasonable degree of skill, you can consult another solicitor about whether or not you should sue. The central office of the LAW SOCIETY OF SCOTLAND will give advice on this.

When someone else is involved

Even if you have had no direct dealings with a professional person, you may be able to sue him for loss which you have incurred as a result of his work.

To sue successfully, you will have to prove not only that the person was negligent but also that he should have had in mind that someone such as yourself might be affected by his work.

The courts are becoming increasingly willing to accept that professionals should bear in mind others who might be injured as a result of their negligent work.

So if a wall falls down and injures a passer-by, and the collapse is the result of negligence by the architect, the passer-by will usually be able to convince a court that the architect had a duty to ensure that the wall did not collapse and injure someone passing by.

When you might have a claim

Many claims for professional negligence never come to court because the expert involved prefers to settle the claim out of court for an agreed sum.

But in other cases action is not taken because the client does not realise that he might have a winnable claim. For example, you might well be able to obtain damages if:

- A solicitor gives wrong advice because he was not aware of a legal rule that he should have known about.
- An insurance broker recommends an insurance policy simply because it earns him higher commission, when he should have offered one that gave you better terms.
- A doctor prescribes the wrong drug dosage, with serious results.
- A bank manager or financial adviser suggests you should buy shares, when a more careful market analysis would have told him that they were very risky as an investment.
- An accountant fails to tell you of expenses which you could have set against your liability for income tax.

When a professional tries to escape liability

It is not often that a professional can effectively limit or exclude his liability for failing in his duty.

If you sustain PERSONAL INJURY as a result of his negligence, he can never do so. Apart from that, if he is advising you as a member of the public – rather than in the course of any business you run – he can only exclude his liability if he makes clear to you when you engage him what the limits of his liability are.

So if you engage a surveyor to report fully on a property, and his report states that it does not cover dry rot, a court would not uphold that exclusion unless it could be shown that you should reasonably have expected such an exclusion when you had the report done.

You should always seek legal advice if a professional tries to hide behind such a clause. *See:* EXCLUSION CLAUSE

PROPERTY INSURANCE

Protecting your home and its contents against damage or loss

Home-owners need two kinds of INSURANCE to protect their property – one to safeguard the premises, including outbuildings, and the other to cover the contents.

The two are often combined in a single INSURANCE POLICY, called a 'dwelling and contents' scheme, but they can be taken out separately. However, separate arrangements may complicate the process of making an INSURANCE CLAIM, if the policies are with different insurers.

There is no legal obligation to insure either your home or its contents. But if the property is mortgaged, the building society or other organisation helping with the finance will insist that the building is covered. *See:* MORTGAGE

Household contents insurance usually covers not only the items in the house and outbuildings, but also third-party claims for damages by accident – for example, if you unwittingly cause an injury to someone else – up to a maximum of £250,000. (Household buildings policies also cover third-party liability.)

Basic insurance for any building

All insurance policies for buildings give protection against damage by fire and the related hazards of lightning and explosion. *See:* FIRE INSURANCE

Five other perils can be added to the basic fire cover.

- Civil disturbances – for example, a RIOT or labour dispute.
- Damage by aircraft or items dropped from them, although damage by sonic boom cannot be claimed.
- Storm and floods.
- Leaks from tanks, pipes and other water apparatus – for example, a washing machine.
- Earthquakes.

'Storm' does not include persistent or heavy rain unless accompanied by high winds. 'Storms and floods' do not include damage by frost, subsidence or landslip or damage to fences, gates and hoardings.

Most insurance companies meet the full amount of claims for earthquake, or aircraft damage, but may require the policyholder to pay part of the cost of damage in the other categories – for example, the first £15.

The cover for water leaks does not include the cost of repairing the leak itself except, usually, in the case of pipes burst by frost.

Extra protection for houses and other dwellings

Insurance policies for houses and other dwellings include a further series of risks, in addition to those in a basic fire and additional perils policy. However, the precise arrangements vary, so check before taking out a policy.

The extra perils most commonly featured in a dwelling policy are:

- Damage to the building caused by theft or attempted theft.
- Impact by a road vehicle or animal, although the compensation may be limited or excluded if the vehicle or animal belongs to the house-owner or his family.

- Leakage from oil-fired heating apparatus, provided that it is an installation and not, for example, a movable paraffin stove.
- Frost damage to, or the bursting of, any plumbing installation in the home. Damage to other parts of the home is sometimes also covered. The policyholder usually has to pay the first £15 of each claim.
- Landslip and subsidence when the cost of the damage is more than a certain figure – say £500. There are usually special exceptions applicable to these perils.
- Accidental breakage of glass in windows and doors, and of sanitary fittings.
- Accidental damage to underground gas, water, oil and sewer pipes, drains and underground electricity and telephone cables.
- Damage caused to the building by the collapse or breakage of radio and television aerials, fittings and masts. The cost of replacing the aerial is often excluded, although most insurance companies will pay if it is brought down by a storm.

Some dwellings policies exclude damage caused by falling trees or branches. Others include that risk, and the collapse of telegraph poles and lighting standards as well.

Safeguarding the contents

Household contents policies cover the items within a home against theft, fire, flooding and the other listed perils included in most dwelling (buildings) policies, with one possible exception. Some insurance companies do not reimburse the cost of damage to household goods caused by the collapse of a radio or TV aerial.

Some articles are subject to restrictions unless you make special arrangements with the insurance company and pay a higher premium. They are works of art, stamp collections, furs, jewellery, and articles of gold, silver and other precious metals. Most policies limit the compensation payable for any one item in those categories to 5 per cent of the total sum insured, and also stipulate that the total value of all items in those categories must not exceed one-third of the overall value of the entire contents of the home. Some insurers do not include works of art and stamp collections in this latter limitation.

For example, if the contents of your home are insured for £10,000 and include a valuable painting, you will not receive more than 5 per cent of £10,000 – that is, £500 – if the painting is stolen. If you have several furs, and some valuable jewellery as well, the most you will get is one-third of £10,000 – that is, £3,333.

There is also a limit – usually £50 or £100 – on the compensation for loose cash in the house.

Items kept in the open – for example, garden furniture – are excluded.

Household contents policies do not cover articles accidentally lost or mislaid – for example, an engagement ring dropped down a sink.

The accidental breakage of mirrors, glass tops and fixed glass in furniture is included in most policies.

Losses outside the home

Household contents – including the clothes you are wearing – are covered against the perils listed in the policy if they are temporarily removed from your home and are in another building – for example, an office, hotel, laundry or cleaners. They are also protected if they are in a bank or safe deposit, although the insurance company may limit the compensation it pays in all such cases.

To protect valuable items in transit, you should take out ALL-RISKS INSURANCE.

If you work from home

Household contents policies are intended for private dwellings. If you frequently work from home, you should check that a normal contents policy is adequate to suit your needs, – particularly if the business involves the use of expensive equipment not usually found in a house or if clients or customers regularly visit the premises. *See:* HOME WORKER

Most insurance companies offer special policies for people whose home and business premises are combined – for example, shopkeepers.

TAKING IN LODGERS

If part of a house is let, the insurance company may impose extra restrictions on the owner's dwelling and contents policy. The company must be informed of the letting arrangements. In particular, to claim for theft the owner may need to show that the thief entered by forcible or violent means.

Which policy to choose?

Insurance companies offer three types of comprehensive dwelling and contents policies.

Indemnity policies An indemnity policy limits compensation to the amount needed to restore buildings or household contents to the state they were in before the damage occurred. The insured person may therefore have to pay part of the cost of rebuilding or replacement, because of previous wear and tear. Indemnity policies are the cheapest of the three.

New-for-old policies Under a new-for-old policy, the insurance company does not make a deduction for wear and tear, but agrees to provide the cost of a new replacement. However, the holder may forfeit part of his compensation if he fails to keep the building in good condition. If a damaged item is capable of being repaired, the company may pay only the repair cost.

Depending on the policy, some items may not be included in the new-for-old arrangement but be covered only by an indemnity scheme. Household linen and clothing are usually excluded. Some companies impose an age limit, and apply the new-for-old rules only to articles that are less than 2, 3 or 5 years old.

All-risk policies An all-risk policy is the most expensive of the three, but covers the widest range of perils, including accidental damage. It incorporates a new-for-old replacement scheme, but holders may have to pay the first £10 or £15 of claims for damage to a building.

Ensuring that the cover is adequate

The sum insured under any dwelling and contents policy should be adequate to cover the full value of the property at risk, or the insurance company may 'average' the claim and pay only a proportion of the cost. *See:* FIRE INSURANCE

Most companies now offer index-linked schemes, in which the value of the building is automatically adjusted according to a housing cost scale prepared by the Royal Institute of Chartered Surveyors, and the value of the contents is tied to the official retail price index.

> **THE MOVING EARTH**
>
> Insurance policies that give protection against landslip and subsidence do not automatically cover a third common type of earth movement called 'heave'
>
> Heave is caused by excessive moisture in the ground, which buckles upwards, but does not shift sideways or downwards, as it does in landslip or subsidence.
>
> Until recently, insurance companies did not accept claims for damage caused by heave. Check your policy to see that it is specifically mentioned.

That arrangement takes account of the effects of inflation, and premiums are automatically increased at each renewal date to reflect the rise in the amount of cover.

PROSECUTION

When a suspect is taken to court

In Scotland, a prosecution for a criminal offence may be either public or private.

Public prosecution Most prosecutions are brought by the public prosecutor – the LORD ADVOCATE in the High Court of Justiciary and the PROCURATOR FISCAL in the sheriff and district courts. *See:* CRIMINAL PROCEEDINGS

Private prosecution Private individuals, landowners and some public bodies may bring a private criminal prosecution in certain circumstances. *See:* PRIVATE PROSECUTION

PROSTITUTION

Offering sex for money

It is not unlawful for a woman over 16 to accept payment in return for sexual services. Nor does a man commit an offence when he pays to have sex. But prostitutes and their protectors can be prosecuted for several offences – though their clients are almost always within the law.

It is an offence to drive a woman into prostitution. Anyone who uses threats, intimidation or false pretences to procure her to have sexual intercourse can be punished by up to 2 years' imprisonment and an unlimited fine.

A man who knowingly lives off the earnings of a prostitute – it makes no difference if she is his wife – is guilty of an offence and can be punished by up to 2 years' imprisonment and an unlimited fine.

A newsagent who allows prostitutes to advertise in his window can face the same charge.

It is an offence to keep a brothel – a place where two or more prostitutes receive clients. If two prostitutes share a flat, for example, they can be charged with keeping a brothel if clients visit them there, even though their sexual activities are entirely legal. The penalty is 6 months' imprisonment and/or a fine of £1,000.

Although prostitutes can make appointments by telephone or letter, they can be prosecuted for SOLICITING if they tout for custom in a public place. A male prostitute who solicits is liable to the same penalty.

A man who seeks clients on behalf of a female prostitute is guilty of importuning. He can face an unlimited fine and 2 years' imprisonment.

A man who pesters women for prostitution in a public place can be prosecuted for a BREACH OF THE PEACE.

When a prostitute is under age

There are particularly severe penalties for using a child prostitute – even if the client believed the child to be of age.

- Anyone who has sexual intercourse with a girl under 13 – even if she solicited him – can be sentenced to life imprisonment.
- Anyone who has intercourse with a girl aged between 13 and 16 can be sentenced to 2 years' imprisonment, unless he had reasonable grounds to believe she was of age, he was himself under 24 and he had never previously been charged with such an offence.
- Homosexual relations with a male aged under 21 can be punishable by up to 2 years' imprisonment. *See:* HOMOSEXUALITY
- Indecent behaviour with a girl aged between 12 and 16 carries a maximum penalty of 2 years' imprisonment.
- A parent or guardian who procures or allows a child in his or her care to become a prostitute can be sentenced to 2 years' imprisonment.

A child prostitute who is found by police is rarely prosecuted for soliciting but is generally taken into care. *See:* CHILDREN IN CARE

> WHEN ALLOWING ADVERTISING IS ILLEGAL
>
> *Anyone who charges for allowing a prostitute to advertise her services can be prosecuted for 'living off her immoral earnings'.*

PROVOCATION

A defence against a murder charge

A person who is accused of MURDER can plead provocation as a defence.

If he can show that he lost his self-control after being provoked by his victim beyond the point at which a reasonable person would have lost control, the murder charge against him will be reduced to CULPABLE HOMICIDE.

The plea of provocation will fail if there is a substantial lapse of time between the provocation and the killing. This is because the accused person has had time to think things over and regain his self-control.

As a general rule, provocation must be physical – for instance, an assault. But in some circumstances provocation by words may be sufficient.

For example, a husband who loses control and kills his wife after she has confessed to adultery is guilty only of culpable homicide. The same rule applies to a wife who kills her husband in similar circumstances.

Other charges

Provocation is not a defence in less

serious charges, such as ASSAULT. But it can be pleaded by an accused person in order to reduce the sentence which the court may impose.

PUBLIC HOUSE

A place to drink – under certain conditions

In law, a public house is a private house and the public can be barred from it or asked to leave at the discretion of the landlord.

Unlike a HOTEL, there is no automatic right to enter a public house, unless it offers accommodation and food to travellers – becoming, therefore, an inn or hotel.

If the only reason for a landlord's refusal to serve a customer is race or sex, he is guilty of an offence. *See:* LIQUOR OFFENCES; RACIAL DISCRIMINATION; SEX DISCRIMINATION

How opening times are extended

A publican can apply to the local licensing board for an extension of opening hours by asking for:

- An extension in respect of some 'occasion' which the board considers 'appropriate'.
- An extension which allows drinks to be sold for two extra hours in the evening and one and a half extra hours in the afternoon.
- An extension allowing a permanent alteration of normal opening hours, having regard to the 'social circumstances' of the area.

When children may and may not be in a public house

Children under 14 must not enter a bar, or anywhere else in a public house mainly used for the sale and consumption of liquor, except to pass through on their way to some other part of the premises.

A child between 14 and 18 is allowed into a bar but cannot buy or drink liquor there. Children over 16 can, however, buy beer, wine, cider or perry to drink with a meal in a pub restaurant. They cannot even drink shandy at the bar.

The right measure

A public house must serve whisky, gin, rum or vodka in measures of one-sixth, one-fifth or one-quarter of a gill. A gill is a quarter-pint. In Scotland the usual measure is one-fifth of a gill.

A notice must be displayed saying which measure is being served in the pub, but those regulations do not apply to any other spirits, including liqueurs.

Most public houses sell draught beer in pints or half-pints. Regulations say it must be served in measures of one-third, one-half or multiples of one-half of a pint.

Glasses or mugs used for draught beer or cider must have the same capacity as the drink ordered, except when the glass has an engraved line to show the correct measure, or automatic measuring pumps are installed.

The licensing of public houses

The licence needed to run a pub is called a 'public house licence'. It allows the licensee or his staff to sell intoxicating liquor to be drunk on the premises or taken away.

A licence that allows the sale of liquor for taking away and drinking elsewhere is called an 'off-sale licence'.

To obtain a licence, the publican must apply to the local licensing board at one of its meetings – held at least four times a year and sometimes more frequently.

Conditions may be attached to the granting of a licence – in a holiday town, for example, the licence might operate only during the tourist season.

Objecting to a licence

The grant of a licence may be objected to by the neighbours, the police, the local community council and any local church body. These objectors may attend the hearings, the dates of which are advertised in the local press. You can also telephone the clerk to the licensing board to find these out.

When you are objecting to the granting of a licence, you should give the licensee written notice at least 7 days before the hearing, and lodge a formal notice of objection with the clerk.

The board may refuse an application for a licence where the applicant, or his premises, are not suitable, or the grant of the licence would be prejudicial to public order and safety, or would lead to the existence of too many public houses in the area. *See:* LICENSED PREMISES; LIQUOR OFFENCES

ON THE SLATE

A customer should never ask a landlord for a drink 'on the slate', meaning that he will pay at some time in the future.

It is illegal to sell liquor in a public house on credit. The licensee and the customer can be fined up to £100.

Complaining about drinks

If you think you have been given a short or watered measure of beer or spirits in a public house, complain to the regional or islands council trading standards department.

After a complaint, an officer from the department usually visits the public house and makes a test purchase without revealing his identity. He measures the drink and – in the case of spirits – may also test for inaccuracy the optic measure from which it was poured.

The officer will make at least two or three test purchases – perhaps on different occasions – to establish whether

WHEN PUBLIC HOUSES ARE OPEN

Monday – Saturday	11a.m.–2.30p.m. 5p.m.–11p.m.
Sunday	12.30p.m.–2.30p.m. 6.30p.m.–11p.m.

No public house in Scotland may open on a Sunday unless the publican has applied for, and been granted, permission for Sunday opening from the local licensing board.

These are *maximum* hours of opening: a licensee can open for shorter hours if he wishes, but he may find his licence renewal application opposed by someone who thinks he is not providing a 'reasonable service to the public'.

Drinking-up time An extra 15 minutes is allowed after closing time for customers to finish their drinks – 30 minutes if the drink was supplied to be consumed with a meal on the premises.

No drinks may be bought in that extra time, and any drink unfinished when the time expires must be left.

It is an offence to take the unfinished drink out of the public house after the drinking-up time.

PUBLICAN'S POWER

In law, a public house is a private house from which the public can be barred or where they can be refused service (except on race or sex grounds) entirely at the landlord's discretion.

there is a pattern of short-measure drinks.

If the officer's tests show that short measure has been given, he will tell the landlord, who may be prosecuted under the Weights and Measures Acts for selling spirits or beer in short measure or not in the prescribed quantity. The maximum penalty is a fine of £2,000.

Anyone who has made a complaint may be asked to give evidence in court.

Beer is classified as food, so if you complain about watered-down beer, any test sample may be examined by the public analyst. *See:* FOOD

PUBLIC LIABILITY INSURANCE

Insuring against claims from other people

The purpose of a public liability insurance policy is to protect the person insured against liability for the accidental death of or accidental injury to someone other than his employee while at work. It may also include damage to the property of others, including employees.

A public liability insurance policy may be a separate policy or it may be part of another one – for example, a house-holder's policy.

Instead of using the word 'accidental', some insurers make an exception of 'inevitable' injury or damage.

The policy can be general, covering any kind of accident to anyone other than employees covered by an EMPLOYER'S LIABILITY policy. It can also be limited by a maximum sum that can be claimed in 1 year or in a single accident.

If the accident results in the person insured being sued and the insurance company thinks the claim should be resisted in court, the company pays the legal expenses.

PUBLIC MEETING

Where and when you may hold a rally

Everyone is entitled to express his views in public and to canvass support for them, provided he does so lawfully. It is an offence, for example, to incite racial hatred or provoke violence in a public speech, or to obstruct the police in exercising their right to maintain PUBLIC ORDER.

Holding a meeting on private premises

If you want to hold a meeting on private land or in a hall, you must first obtain the consent – preferably in writing – of the owner. Make sure that he knows the purpose of the meeting and its likely size, so that he cannot later withdraw permission by claiming that he was not given all the necessary information.

The owner is entitled to refuse consent without giving a reason, but may not discriminate against you on grounds of race or sex. He may impose conditions – such as restricting the size of the meeting, or the time at which it must end – and demand a fee for the use of his property and a deposit against possible damage by your meeting.

If, for example, you want to hold a meeting in the town hall or public library, you require permission from its lawful owner, the LOCAL AUTHORITY. Like a private landlord, a local authority can impose conditions or refuse permission, except during an election – general or local – when all candidates have a right to use schools and certain other meeting places, upon payment of a reasonable fee.

If the authority refuses permission unreasonably for a non-election meeting – if, for example, it allows a hunt association to use a school hall one week, but turns down a request from an anti-hunt group for the following week – you can try to persuade individual councillors that the decision was unfair and should be reversed. Legally, however, you have no right to appeal.

If you use private property for a meeting without the owner's consent, and cause loss to the owner, he can sue you for DAMAGES

It is an offence under the Trespass (Scotland) Act 1865 for anyone to occupy private property without the consent of the owner or legal occupier. The maximum penalty is a fine of £50. *See:* TRESPASS.

If the owner sees notices of the meeting, he can seek a court INTERDICT to prevent you from using his property. To disobey an interdict is CONTEMPT OF COURT.

Even when a meeting is to be held on private premises, it is advisable to warn the police if the audience is to be large. They may wish to regulate traffic around the site, or to police the meeting if there is a possibility of violent clashes. Although the police are not entitled to attend meetings on private premises, they may enter if they reasonably suspect that a BREACH OF THE PEACE is likely to occur.

Often, when uninvited, the police attend meetings in plain clothes. As such, they have the same rights as other members of the public and you can refuse them admission if you so wish, provided that they do not reasonably fear a breach of the peace.

When a public meeting is held on private land, the organisers have the right to restrict admission to those whom they choose. They can also charge an admission fee and use reasonable force to eject anyone who enters without paying or without their consent. A reasonable number of stewards, issued with badges or armbands, may be used to keep the peace and remove trouble-makers.

Holding a meeting in public

Nobody has the right to hold a public

meeting in the street: the only right you have there is to 'pass and repass'. Nor is there any automatic right to hold meetings in public places such as parks. If you want to stage a meeting there, you need permission of the body that owns and controls the land – usually the local authority.

Local authorities have power to make byelaws for the use of their parks. They may also have byelaws regulating public meetings – allowing them only in certain places and under specific conditions – which may require the organisers of a meeting to give notice both to the town hall and to the police. Find out what byelaws are in force before organising the meeting.

It is always advisable to discuss a meeting in advance with the officer in charge of the local police station, particularly if it is a mass gathering, even if it is not required by the byelaws. The police can suggest a change of time or venue for the meeting, with the object of minimising public disturbance.

You do not have to accept their suggestions, but by not doing so you increase the risk that the police will have to disperse the meeting for causing an obstruction. *See:* PROCESSION

Keeping order at meetings

Anyone has the right to heckle at a public meeting, provided he does not seriously disrupt the proceedings. If he does, he can be arrested and charged with trying to break up a lawful public meeting, for which the penalty is 6 months' imprisonment and a fine of up to £2,000.

Alternatively, he can be charged with BREACH OF THE PEACE.

In public places, the organisers may not use stewards to keep order, but the police are entitled to attend.

PUBLIC ORDER

When someone causes a public disturbance

Anyone who behaves in a manner which the police consider is (or is likely to cause) a BREACH OF THE PEACE can be arrested.

His behaviour does not have to include an act of physical violence. If he uses threatening, abusive or insulting words that are considered likely to cause a breach of the peace, he can be charged with that offence.

A person who threatens to use serious violence can be charged with assault, even if he does not strike a blow. *See:* ASSAULT

If he acts recklessly and damages property, he could face a charge of malicious mischief or VANDALISM.

Helping someone to break the law

Anyone who is helping others to carry out a crime or encouraging others to commit a crime can be arrested.

If he makes an agreement with one or more people to carry out a crime, even though the plan is not executed, he can be charged with CONSPIRACY.

Inciting another person to carry out a crime, whether or not the crime is committed or the other person is influenced by the incitement, is also an offence. *See:* INCITEMENT

Other charges that may be brought

A person who does something in an attempt to prevent the police from carrying out their duties – for example, stopping the police attending a meeting they have a right to attend – can be charged with obstructing the police in the execution of their duty. *See:* OBSTRUCTION

Carrying an OFFENSIVE WEAPON in a public place is also an offence. Any item that is capable of causing injury may be considered an offensive weapon – for example, a spanner or a screwdriver. A steward at a public meeting is not entitled to carry a truncheon.

In many areas local authorities have introduced BYELAWS to supplement the general law – for example, they may provide that it is to be a criminal offence to act in a disorderly manner in a museum, library or PUBLIC PARK.

Certain NOISE OFFENCES are also controlled by byelaws, and a person may find that he has contravened one by playing his transistor too loudly on, for example, a public beach.

Controlling the behaviour of a group

Anyone attending a meeting or taking part in a protest march may unintentionally cause a breach of the peace by his behaviour and find himself arrested.

For example, the members of a group that assemble or demonstrate in a manner that could endanger the public peace can be arrested and charged with breach of the peace.

A group of people who assemble with a common purpose and carry out their objective with force or with the threat of using force may be charged with mobbing and rioting. *See:* RIOT

Members of a procession or a protest march may be arrested for obstructing the street if the march blocks a public street or the members are distributing leaflets.

If a procession or demonstration is considered to be interfering with the public's enjoyment of its rights, it may be stopped. For example, if a sit-in blocks what is usually a public thoroughfare, it may be dispersed by the police.

Special rules for political groups

The activities of political groups are controlled by the Public Order Act 1936.

It is, for example, a criminal offence to organise or train members of an association so that they can use force to promote a political aim. The maximum penalty is an unlimited fine or 2 years' imprisonment, or both.

It is also illegal to wear uniforms, in public, that signify an association with a political organisation or the promotion of a political objective.

For example, someone wearing a Sinn Fein black beret at a Sinn Fein rally in public could be charged under the Act.

The maximum penalty is 3 months' imprisonment or a £1,000 fine, or both.

The Prevention of Terrorism Act 1976 gave the police widespread powers to control public order. They can, for example, arrest and detain for up to 48 hours a person suspected of having committed an act of terrorism. *See:* DETENTION

It is illegal for a person to belong to or finance any forbidden organisation or to address its meetings. Wearing uniforms or insignia associated with a banned organisation is also illegal. *See:* TERRORISM

PUBLIC PARK

Places for leisure and recreation

Local authorities are entitled to provide and maintain parks, walks and recreation areas for use by the general public. But they are not obliged to do so.

Regional, district and islands councils may all provide these amenities. However, in mainland Scotland the responsibility is usually taken by the district rather than the region.

The right of the public to use these leisure and recreation areas will usually be subject to a number of conditions:

Charges If the council provides facilities such as tennis courts, bowling greens or football pitches, it can charge for the use of them.

Byelaws A council can make byelaws regulating the use of a public park. These should be displayed at the park entrance.

Byelaws will usually give opening hours (if any), require animals to be kept under control and prohibit activities which would be a nuisance to others. Failure to observe them can result in a fine of up to £25.

A council can make new byelaws changing or restricting the use that the public is entitled to make of its parks, but these must have the approval of the Secretary of State for Scotland.

Management rules In addition to byelaws, councils have power under the Civic Government (Scotland) Act 1982 to make 'management rules' governing the use by the public of land which they control or manage. Like byelaws, these management rules have to be displayed at the entrance to the park or recreation area.

Management rules do not need the approval of the Secretary of State for Scotland. But a council has to advertise its intention to make them, and objections from the public have to be taken into account before they come into force.

If someone breaks a management rule, the council has the power to exclude him from the land or premises concerned. If he refuses to leave, or returns after being excluded, he can be fined up to £100.

PUPIL

The rights of young children

'Pupil' is the Scottish legal term for a girl under 12 years or a boy under 14 years. An older child is called a MINOR.

A pupil has no legal powers, but others can act on his or her behalf. The child's financial and other interests are looked after by a guardian or guardians – who are called, in law, tutors. A child's tutors are normally his or her parents. *See:* GUARDIAN; TUTOR

A pupil cannot make a legally binding CONTRACT, but a tutor can make contracts on his or her behalf. Nor can he or she make a valid WILL. But a child, however young, can have a bank account, can own property and can also inherit property and titles.

A pupil under 8 years cannot be charged with a criminal offence.

Except where an offence or truancy is alleged, a pupil can be referred to a CHILDREN'S HEARING at any age. Babies, for example, may be referred to a hearing if they are thought to be in need of care and protection.

A pupil who has a tutor cannot take legal proceedings – for example, an action for DAMAGES to compensate him or her for injuries caused by someone else's negligence. But the tutor can take legal proceedings on the pupil's behalf.

If a pupil has no tutor, or the tutor refuses to act, he or she can start legal proceedings and then ask the court to appoint someone – called a curator ad litem – to act on his or her behalf. The court can also appoint such a person if the child is suing a tutor – for instance, a parent who has negligently caused injury to the child in a car accident. *See:* CHILDREN'S RIGHTS; CURATOR

A pupil who negligently causes injury to someone else can be sued, along with his or her tutor.

Aliment A pupil has a legal right to be maintained by his or her parents. Where parents are living together, the father has the primary responsibility. If he fails to provide adequate support, the mother must do so.

So if a child's father leaves home, the mother must continue to provide support. She can raise an action for ALIMENT on the child's behalf, to obtain financial support from the father.

Illegitimacy A pupil who is illegitimate has no legal guardian, but a court can appoint one if necessary.

The child's mother is primarily responsible for his or her maintenance, although she can take legal action against the alleged father to obtain payment from him towards the child's support. *See:* GUARDIAN; ILLEGITIMATE CHILD

ENFORCED SEPARATION

A special agent must be engaged to take an animal to quarantine premises. The animal owner is not allowed to accompany it beyond the port or airport of entry.

QUALITY OF GOODS

What a buyer is entitled to expect

Goods sold by a shop, or by anyone who is in business as a dealer, must be of 'merchantable quality'. That means they must be reasonably fit for the use to which they are commonly put. If the dealer is told by the buyer of a particular purpose for which the goods are being bought, they must also be reasonably fit for that purpose.

In deciding what is reasonable you have to take into account the description under which goods are sold. The price and other circumstances of the sale may also be relevant.

If you buy goods that turn out not to be of merchantable quality, you may have a claim for:

- A refund of the purchase price.
- A reduction of the price, if the goods are not worth what you paid but you want to keep them.
- Compensation for the cost of repairing faulty goods.

But you cannot complain later about a defect that was specifically pointed out to you before you bought the goods. Nor can you complain if you examined the goods before buying them, and should have noticed the defect yourself.

See: DEFECTIVE GOODS; MONEY BACK; TRADE DESCRIPTIONS

THE CAR THAT WAS 'HARDLY RUN IN'

Goods must be reasonably fit for their purpose – so a car must be fit for driving.

When Mr C bought an 8-year-old Jaguar, the dealers told him that at 82,000 miles, a car of that type was 'hardly run in'.

After 3 weeks and a further 2,354 miles, the engine seized and had to be scrapped. C sued the dealers for the cost of a replacement engine.

The previous owner of the Jaguar told the court that when he sold it to the dealers, he considered the engine to be clapped out, and not fit for use on a road.

C was awarded damages, but the dealers appealed. The Court of Appeal in England had to decide whether, at the price – £390 in 1972 – and in all the circumstances, the car was fit for its purpose.

DECISION

The judges ruled that the car's purpose was to be driven, and that it was not reasonably fit for that purpose. The dealers had to pay C's damages and costs.

QUARANTINE

Safety rules for bringing animals into Britain

To prevent the spread of rabies and other diseases, dogs, cats and most mammals must spend 6 months quarantined in special premises or quarters when they are brought into Britain.

There are special regulations for plants, captive birds, farm livestock and horses.

The rules apply not only to animals brought into the country for the first time, but also to those returning after a visit abroad, however brief. The fact that an animal has been immunised makes no difference.

To bring an animal into Britain you must have a licence – which will not be granted until you have made the quarantine arrangements. The three main steps are:

1. You must book accommodation at quarantine premises selected from an official list which can be obtained from the Animal Health Division 1B, Ministry of Agriculture, Fisheries and Food, Hook Rise South, Tolworth, Surbiton, Surrey KT6 7DX.

2. You must employ a carrying agent – usually a representative of the quarantine premises – to collect the animal on landing as you are not permitted to take it to the premises yourself.

3. Apply for a licence on form ID1, obtained from the Animal Health Division, along with the list of quarantine premises.

On the form you will be asked to state the port of entry. You must choose a port that has facilities for keeping animals for up to 48 hours until they can be taken to the quarantine premises.

There are such facilities at Dover, Folkestone, Harwich, Hull, Liverpool, London, Tilbury and Southampton seaports; Ramsgate hoverport; and Birmingham, Edinburgh, Gatwick, Glasgow, Heathrow, Leeds, Manchester and Prestwick airports.

The application form must be returned at least 4 weeks before the journey begins. The Ministry will issue a boarding document to be presented at the despatching point before the animal is allowed on the ship or plane.

Animals travelling by sea must be landed in a crate. Those going by air must travel the whole way in a crate.

Quarantine comfort and cost

The Ministry's approval of the quarantine premises implies veterinary supervision and minimum standards of sleeping and exercise space according to weight. Animals other than cats and dogs usually spend their quarantine in private zoos. There are special regulations for plants, birds, farm livestock and horses.

The person who brings the animal in must pay the quarantine costs. Charges vary, but a typical bill might be £2.50 a day for a medium-size dog and £1.50 a day for a cat. In addition, charges for travel and vaccinations might amount to £70 per animal.

On arrival at the premises the animal is given an anti-rabies vaccine. For that reason, and to allow it to settle, it is usually recommended that the owner does not visit for 14 days. Rules vary in different premises.

The penalties for evading quarantine regulations are: an unlimited fine and up to a year's imprisonment.

As a further protection against rabies, the imported animal may also be destroyed.

QUOTATION

When a price for work is binding on both sides

If a quotation for work to be done is given, and a firm price is specified, that price is binding as soon as the quotation is accepted by the customer.

Unless a quotation says that the price may be varied, the contractor cannot charge more even if costs go up before the work is finished.

But if extra work is asked for, or if the work described in the quotation is changed in some way, the price may be adjusted.

Estimate A quotation is different from an estimate, which is merely an indication of the probable cost of the work. An estimate is not binding on the contractor and he is entitled to charge more if the work turns out to be more expensive than he expected.

However, if a contractor is engaged to do work on the basis of an unreasonably or misleadingly low estimate made by him, he may be liable for MISREPRESENTATION.

Before you have any work done, make sure that you know whether you have accepted a quotation or an estimate.

RACIAL DISCRIMINATION

When it is unlawful to treat people unfairly

People who think they have been treated unfairly because of their colour, race, nationality or ethnic or national origins can complain that they are victims of racial discrimination, and take legal action.

There are two forms of racial discrimination:

- Direct discrimination – this occurs when someone treats a person less favourably than others because of his colour, race, nationality or ethnic or national origins.

An example would be when two people – one black, the other white – apply for a job, and the employer gives the job to the white applicant, because he prefers to take a person who is white even though he is no better qualified.

- Indirect discrimination – this occurs when a condition or requirement is applied equally to everyone, regardless of race, colour, nationality and the like, but some racial groups find it difficult or impossible to comply with that condition or requirement and there is no proper justification for it.

An example would be a requirement that all employees must be able to read and write English. Members of some racial groups might not be able to do this, and the requirement would therefore be unlawful unless the employer could show that it was necessary in order to do the job.

How to complain

There are two ways in which people who believe themselves to be the victims of racial discrimination can take legal action to seek redress:

- If they feel themselves discriminated against in applying for a job, or at work, they can complain to an INDUSTRIAL TRIBUNAL.
- In other cases they can take action in a sheriff court (except in public sector education cases, which must go first to the Secretary of State for Scotland).

But before taking legal action, they should seek advice from the Commission for Racial Equality at Elliot House, 10–12 Allington Street, London SW1E 5EH.

In addition to giving advice and assistance, the Commission may be prepared to offer conciliation, or legal assistance and representation.

It can also provide a questionnaire that can be sent to a person against whom a complaint is being made – say, a landlord or employer. This questionnaire may help decide whether legal action is justified and likely to succeed.

The questionnaire can also be obtained from a local community relations council.

Anyone who is sent a questionnaire is not obliged to complete it, but failure to do so may be taken into account by a court or tribunal. A completed questionnaire is admissible as evidence.

Powers of court and tribunal

Both a sheriff court and an industrial tribunal can declare that there has been unlawful discrimination. If they do so, they can award compensation for financial loss and injured feelings (though the sums that they award are usually fairly low).

Industrial tribunals can recommend an offending person or company to take action to reduce the effect of the discrimination on the victim. A racially motivated dismissal will normally also be an UNFAIR DISMISSAL, so compensation may be awarded for that. A tribunal can recommend re-engagement of an unfairly dismissed employee.

A sheriff court can grant an order forbidding an act of discrimination.

Where you can get legal aid

Anyone deciding to take a case of discrimination to a sheriff court may be eligible for LEGAL AID and for LEGAL ADVICE. The legal aid scheme is not available for representation at an industrial tribunal, though the legal advice scheme can be used for preliminary advice. However, the Commission for Racial Equality has power to help in *all* cases.

POWERS OF THE COMMISSION FOR RACIAL EQUALITY

The 15 government-appointed members of the Commission for Racial Equality include men and women experienced in politics, business, insurance, trade unionism, education and race relations.

The Commission's main tasks are to:

- Make sure that people of different racial groups are given the same opportunities as everyone else.
- Work towards the eventual elimination of all discrimination.
- Keep a watch on the way the Race Relations Act is working.
- Conduct formal investigations into alleged discrimination.

In the course of an investigation the Commission has the power to make a witness give oral or written evidence, but it can only enforce this power by obtaining a sheriff court order.

If it is satisfied that discrimination has taken place, the Commission can issue a notice calling on the offender to cease discriminating. If he does not do so, the Commission can ask the sheriff court for an order compelling him to stop discriminating.

Unlawful discrimination at work

There are three areas in which it is unlawful for an employer to discriminate against someone applying for a job:

- Methods used to determine who is offered the job.
- Terms of employment.
- Refusing, or deliberately failing, to offer the job.

Similarly, there are three areas in which unlawful discrimination can occur against someone who has a job:

- Terms of employment.
- Access to training, transfer or promotion opportunities, or to other benefits, facilities or services.
- Dismissal, or being treated in any other detrimental way.

But there are exceptions where race or colour is a genuine occupational qualification for the job. For instance, an employer can choose people for acting or modelling work on the basis of their race or colour if it is important to ensure authenticity. And a local authority can use only social workers of Asian origin to work with Asian families.

Discrimination in education

In education, it is unlawful for schools and colleges – whether state-supported or private – to discriminate racially by:

- Setting unacceptable terms of entry for students or pupils from particular groups, or by refusing or failing to offer them entry without good reason.
- Refusing such students or pupils benefits, facilities and services open to others.
- Taking any other action that might have a harmful effect on them.

Local education authorities must not discriminate in the travel arrangements they make to enable children to get to school. For example, it is unlawful to share children of a racial minority group evenly among schools in an area if that means that some have to travel long distances from home.

Discrimination in housing

In housing, it is unlawful to discriminate racially by:

- Fixing different terms for any premises offered – for example, asking a higher rent from a coloured person.
- Refusing on the ground of race to sell or rent a property to someone who applies first and is ready and able to pay.
- Treating a coloured person less favourably than others in any list of people needing homes. A local authority allocating homes must not, for example, discriminate, directly or indirectly, against coloured people in the way it awards points in its priority list.

Exceptions to the general rule against discrimination in housing are people renting rooms in their homes and an owner-occupier selling his home without using an estate agent or advertising his wish to sell.

Advertising and services

In advertising, it is generally unlawful to indicate an intention to discriminate racially, and anyone who publishes such an advertisement or has it published also breaks the law.

Other fields in which discrimination can be unlawful are those involving the sale and supply of goods, services and facilities. The law ensures for everyone the freedom to:

- Enter and use the facilities of any place open to the general public.
- Enter and book rooms in any hotel or guest house that has rooms vacant.
- Use facilities offered by banks, insurance, credit, loan, finance and travel companies and by places of entertainment, refreshment and recreation.
- Use the services offered by any trade or profession.

The licensee of a PUBLIC HOUSE who refuses to serve a black customer because of his colour commits unlawful discrimination.

A CLUB or association must not discriminate against people wanting to join unless it has fewer than 25 members or is established for the benefit of a particular group of people.

If the club or association did not stop discriminating, an order could then be granted against it restraining repetition of the discriminatory act. This would have the practical effect of compelling it to offer membership to the complainer.

When discrimination is allowed

It is within the law to offer services and facilities for education and training to meet the special needs of a particular racial group or – in some circumstances – to provide training for employment.

A local authority could, for example, start a youth club for Asian youngsters in an area where there was serious unemployment among them.

Clubs and associations whose main object is to benefit a particular group of people for reasons that might be racial, but do not involve colour, are also legal.

In sporting events it is not unlawful to choose someone to represent his country or other area because of his nationality – otherwise the Race Relations Act would have a disastrous effect on international competition.

RACIAL HATRED

The penalties for stirring up racist feelings

It is a criminal offence under the Public Order Act 1936 to use threatening, abusive or insulting words in a public place when racist hatred is likely to be stirred up.

It is also an offence to publish or distribute similarly offensive written material to the public if it is likely to stir up racial hatred. No offence is committed by someone who is a member of an organisation and who distributes such material exclusively to other members.

It is a defence for an accused person to show that he was not aware of the content of any written material that he published or distributed, and that he had no reason to suspect it was threatening, abusive or insulting.

To obtain a conviction, the prosecution does not have to prove that any disorder resulted or that the accused intended to incite hatred.

The maximum penalty under summary procedure is 3 months' imprisonment and a fine of £2,000. Under solemn procedure it is 2 years' imprisonment and an unlimited fine.

RAFFLE LICENCE

The registration required to run a raffle or lottery

Any social club or charitable organisation is entitled to run a raffle or LOTTERY provided that it is registered with the local district or islands council.

The law considers that any group of people who join together to form a club, organisation or association constitute a society, even if it has no offices of its own. A society is granted a raffle licence when it registers with its local council, provided that the lottery or raffle is being run for the benefit of its own members or for charity and not for any profit or private gain.

Once a society is registered, it may run up to 52 lotteries or raffles in a year, provided that it does not contravene the Lotteries and Amusements Act 1976.

If an organiser contravenes the regulations, he commits an offence. The maximum penalty is 2 years' imprisonment or an unlimited fine.

Registering a society

If your society wants to run a raffle or lottery, write to the chief executive of your local district or islands council.

Give the name of your society and the purpose for which it was established, and ask for the society to be registered as a lottery operator.

Your society will have to pay a £20 registration fee to the council, which issues an official notification form stating that the society is registered. A society is entitled to renew its registration each year. The renewal fee, payable on January 1 each year, is £10.

A council only turns down an application if the applicant has ceased to be a proper society or has contravened the Lotteries and Amusements Act – for example, by running raffles for profit – and is no longer entitled to promote a lottery.

It will also turn down an application if someone connected with the proposed lottery has been convicted of FRAUD or of contravening the lottery regulations.

If you consider that your society has been turned down unreasonably, you can appeal against the decision to your local sheriff court.

A FAIR DRAW

The rules governing even small private lotteries are designed to ensure fairness to all participants and to prevent the organisers from making private gains.

What the law requires of a raffle promoter

Anyone who promotes a raffle or lottery and registers his society with the local council must conform to certain regulations under the Lotteries and Amusements Act concerning the amount of money involved, the distribution of proceeds and the issuing of tickets.

If the turnover of a lottery is more than £10,000, it must be registered with the Gaming Board for Great Britain as well as with the local council. Application forms may be obtained from the Gaming Board, Africa House, 64–78 Kingsway, London WC2B 6BW.

To register with the Board, a society must pay a registration fee of £240 and a further £36 for every lottery run when the turnover is between £10,000 and £20,000. If the turnover is more than £20,000, a fee of £48 must be paid.

The maximum permitted turnover for a society lottery is £80,000 and no individual prize may cost more than £4,000 in amount or value.

However, if a lottery takes place less than 1 month after the previous lottery it is known as a 'short-term lottery', and its turnover must not exceed £20,000 and no prize may cost or be valued at more than £2,000.

If a lottery takes place less than 3 months but more than 1 month after the previous lottery, it is known as a 'medium-term lottery' and its turnover must not exceed £40,000 and no prize may cost or be valued at more than £3,000.

The law also requires that:

- The organiser must be a member of the society who is authorised by its committee to run the raffle or lottery.
- The organiser must make a return to the local council after the lottery, giving the date of the lottery, how much money was raised, how much went on expenses and prizes and the purpose for which the profits were used. If the lottery is registered with the Gaming Board, a similar return must be made to the Board.
- Tickets must be printed with the name and address of the organisation and the date of the raffle. They must all be priced the same and cost no more than 50p.
- Tickets may not be sold on the street, in licensed bingo or gaming clubs, licensed betting offices, amusement or prize bingo arcades or from vending machines. A ticket must not be sold to a person under 16.
- No more than half the proceeds of a raffle totalling up to £10,000 can be used for prizes, and no prize may cost or be valued at more than £2,000.
- Expenses must not be more than 25 per cent of the proceeds – except in the case of a raffle totalling more than £10,000, which is registered with the Gaming Board, when expenses must generally be no more than 15 per cent.

When a raffle need not be registered

If a raffle or lottery is run only for people who live or work in the same premises or belong to a society that is not established or conducted for gaming or betting, it is known as a 'private lottery' and need not be registered with the local council or Gaming Board.

However, the organisers must:

- Deduct only the cost of stationery and printing of tickets as expenses.
- Spend the rest of the money on prizes or for the purposes of the society.
- Ensure that each ticket costs the same and is printed with the name and address of the organisers.
- Ensure that no tickets are sent through the post.
- Ensure that the raffle or lottery is not advertised.

If the organisers fail to do so, they commit an offence. The maximum penalty is again 2 years' imprisonment or an unlimited fine.

Running a small lottery

A 'small' lottery – for example, one that is run in conjunction with another event such as a fête, sale of work, dance or sports event – is also not required to be registered with a local council or with the Gaming Board.

However, organisers face similar penalties if they do not comply with the special rules involved. They are:

- The raffle must not be the major attraction of the event.
- Proceeds must not be for private gain.
- No more than £100 may be spent on prizes, and money prizes are not allowed.
- The sale of tickets and the draw must take place during the event or entertainment.

RAIL TRAVEL

Your rights and responsibilities when travelling by rail

When you travel by train in Scotland, you have a CONTRACT with the British Railways Board. That means that the conditions they lay down for carrying passengers and luggage, and the maximum limits they set for compensation, are legally enforceable – unless a court considers that a condition is not fair and reasonable. *See:* UNFAIR CONTRACT

When there is an accident

A passenger can claim compensation for injury in an accident only if British Rail are to blame – not, for example, if vandals cause a crash which BR could not reasonably be expected to prevent. Accidents on railway property, such as stations, are covered by the laws that govern any premises to which the public has lawful access. They must be kept reasonably safe. *See:* OCCUPIER'S LIABILITY

When luggage is lost or damaged

British Rail is liable for loss or damage to luggage if it is caused by an employee's negligence. If the luggage is lost or damaged in the guard's van, the railway management has to prove that it is not to blame. The situation is reversed if the luggage is carried in a passenger compartment – then the passenger must prove the rail staff's negligence. Liability is limited to £500 but that condition might be held to be unreasonable in a court.

Rail travel abroad

The rights of a passenger who buys a ticket in Britain to a foreign destination are governed by international conventions. If there is an accident, the railway in the country where it happens is liable for compensation. Claims must be made, through British Rail, within 3 months of your becoming aware of any injury or damage. That applies only to foreign travel – in Britain the time limit for starting legal proceedings for personal injuries is normally 3 years.

If there are no seats

Buying a ticket does not entitle you to a seat. If you have a second-class ticket and all the seats are occupied, you are not entitled to sit in a first-class seat, or even to stand in a first-class corridor, without permission from a guard or inspector. Passengers with first-class tickets are not entitled to a refund if second-class passengers are given permission to sit in their carriage.

Reservations You are entitled to a seat or a sleeper berth if you make a reservation. If you find that, due to a mistake, someone else with a reservation is in your seat or sleeping compartment and there is no alternative accommodation, you can claim a refund at the station of departure. The conditions say you are not entitled to any compensation for the inconvenience caused in such cases, but that may be considered an unreasonable condition and a claim for compensation might succeed.

It is an offence against railway byelaws to use a reserved seat or compartment and keep out someone entitled to it. The maximum fine is £50.

Cancellations and delays

Under British Rail's Conditions of Carriage, which form part of the contract with each passenger, time-tables are subject to alterations without notice and there is no guarantee that trains will run on time or at all. But someone whose last train is cancelled at short notice, and cannot find alternative public transport, might succeed in a claim to BR for the cost of an overnight stay or a taxi home.

Strikes A passenger has no right to alternative transport if his train service is suspended because of an industrial dispute. But a season-ticket holder can obtain a partial refund, minus an administration charge, if he claims within 7 days of a stoppage.

Lack of facilities A passenger cannot claim a refund simply because the expected facilities are not provided on his journey – for example, if the heating system does not work, or an advertised buffet car is not available. He has every right, however, to make a complaint.

When a line has to close

British Rail may propose to stop passenger services from a particular station or on a particular line. If they do, a notice must be published six weeks before closure in two local newspapers for 2 consecutive weeks. It must also be displayed at all stations affected by the closure.

Anyone can raise objections by writing to the Transport Users' Consultative Committee for Scotland, 249 West George Street, Glasgow G2 4QE. Objections must be lodged within the 6 week period before closure. The Committee may decide to hold a public meeting to hear them.

Making an objection delays the closure until it has been considered.

The consent of the Secretary of State for Transport is needed to close a line. That cannot be given until the Committee's report on any hardship that would be caused by the closure has been considered.

When a passenger does not pay

Someone who travels on a train without a ticket, or travels beyond the distance allowed by his ticket, commits an offence. In theory he could be ordered off the train.

In practice, no passenger is put off a train even if he refuses to pay when his offence is detected. His name and address are taken if he refuses to pay or fails to produce a ticket, and he is allowed to continue his journey. It is an offence to fail to give one's name and address, or to give a false name and address.

Prosecution for fare evasion depends on whether it can be proved that a passenger intended to avoid payment. Someone who does not have time to buy a ticket, or loses his ticket, will not be prosecuted if he pays readily when asked to during his journey.

However, if you lose your ticket you can be required to pay the appropriate fare for your journey.

First-class carriage Someone who rides in a first-class carriage on a second-class ticket can be prosecuted only if he refuses to pay the difference in fares. If he is travelling on a second-class season ticket, he must pay the full first-class fare for his journey.

When other passengers offend

Most railway laws and byelaws are intended for the safety and comfort of passengers. You are entitled to ask railway staff to enforce them.

It is an offence, punishable by a fine of up to £100, to:

- Board a train while others are trying to get off.
- Smoke in a non-smoking compartment.
- Sing, use a radio, tape-recorder or record player or play a musical instrument to the annoyance of other passengers.
- Be on a train or in railway premises in a drunken state.
- Spit or throw down litter in a carriage or railway station.

Damaging or defacing railway property carries a fine of up to £400 under the railway byelaws. But serious damage can be prosecuted as malicious mischief or VANDALISM and punished by a fine or imprisonment. In either case, the cost of the damage may also have to be made good.

Using abusive or obscene language, behaving in a disorderly or offensive manner and deliberately interfering with the comfort of railway passengers also carry a fine of up to £400.

Endangering safety Any action intended to endanger the safety of passengers or obstruct a train – for example, placing something on a rail or tampering with signals – is prosecuted under the common law as reckless conduct, or – in less serious cases – as malicious mischief or vandalism. Someone who endangers safety without intending to cause injury or damage – typically a youth who throws a stone at a train – can be fined up to £400 under the railway byelaws.

Complaining about the railways

Complaints about rail services should be made first to the station manager or the Area Manager, or to the General Manager for Scotland. The addresses should be on display at every station, usually near the booking office.

If you do not get satisfaction, contact the Transport Users' Consultative Committee for Scotland, 249 West George Street, Glasgow G2 4QE. If the matter is of national importance, they will refer it to the Central Transport Users' Consultative Committee.

These committees are appointed by the government to deal with issues such as staff rudeness, train cancellations, line closures or requests for trains to make extra stops at stations where there are potential passengers.

If you wish to see a copy of British Rail's Conditions of Carriage or byelaws, contact your area manager or write to the General Manager, British Rail, 58 Port Dundas Road, Glasgow G4 0HG.

OFFICIAL WATCHDOG

The Transport Users' Consultative Committee for Scotland was set up by Parliament to deal with complaints about train services.

RAPE

Forcing a woman to have sex

The crime of rape is defined as the carnal knowledge of a female person by a male person, obtained by overcoming her will.

Rape is always prosecuted before a judge and jury in the HIGH COURT OF JUSTICIARY. The penalty is at the discretion of the court and will almost always result in a sentence of imprisonment.

Carnal knowledge

Carnal knowledge is sexual intercourse. Full intercourse does not have to take place for rape to be proved. Any degree of penetration of the vagina by the penis is sufficient.

No emission of semen is necessary, nor need the female's hymen, if still intact, be ruptured. The offence consists in the violation of the female, not the satisfaction of the male.

Any other form of sexual assault is the crime of indecent assault, the penalty for which is at the discretion of the court.

Female person

Rape may be committed on any female, irrespective of her age. A prostitute is entitled to the same protection from the law as any other female: the fact that she has sex with many males does not mean she loses her right to choose her partners.

Male person

Any male from 8 years of age (the age of criminal responsibility) can in theory be guilty of rape. In one case a boy of 13 years and 10 months was convicted of rape.

It is legally impossible for a female to rape another female or a male, although she may be guilty of indecent assault. However, a female who helps a male rape another female is art and part guilty of rape. *See:* AIDING AND ABETTING

Husband and wife

A husband can be found guilty of raping his wife.

There are no special rules that apply to the crime of rape between spouses. Provided there is sufficient evidence of lack of consent to sexual intercourse by his wife, a husband can be found guilty of the crime, even if the rape occurred while the couple were living together as husband and wife. Marital rape may, however, be difficult to prove if the spouses were living together at the time of the alleged incident.

Proof of rape will be easier if the couple are divorced or separated or if the wife has obtained a court order (INTERDICT) against her husband, ordering him not to molest her. A husband who helps another male to rape his wife is art and part guilty of rape.

Overcoming her will

To prove rape, it must be shown that

MARITAL RAPE

A husband can be prosecuted and convicted for the crime of rape committed by him against his wife.

In the High Court at Glasgow on April 5 1982, for the first time in Scotland, a husband appeared in court accused of raping his wife. They were separated.

The defence challenged the competency of this charge. They argued that it was not legally possible for a husband to rape his wife.

As authority for this view, they referred to a 19th-century textbook, which stated that by the act of marriage a wife's body was given over to the sexual command of her husband and that, as a result, there was no crime committed if the husband forced her to have sexual intercourse.

DECISION

The judge rejected this argument. He said that the old textbook relied upon by the defence was written at least 150 years ago, when the position of marriage and the status of women were quite different from what they are today.

The judge said that in modern times it was illogical and unreasonable to treat the question of rape as if it was in some way different from assault. Since a husband could be convicted of assaulting his wife, a husband could therefore be convicted of raping his wife.

The trial was allowed to proceed.

the female's will was overcome. In the ordinary case the male will have used force to achieve his end, but personal violence is not necessary. Any method of overpowering her will – for example, using threats or drugs – is sufficient provided it has the effect of overcoming the female's will to resist.

Drink or drugs

If a male gives a female drink or drugs – whose nature is concealed from her – with the object of overcoming her resistance, and if he then has sexual intercourse with her while she is insensible, he will be guilty of rape.

It is essential that the female must be made drunk by the accused for the purpose of having intercourse with her. It is not rape for a male to have intercourse with a drunk female, or with a female drugged by herself or someone else: in that case, the male has done nothing to overcome the female's will. However, this may be the crime of 'clandestine injury to woman'.

Clandestine injury

A male may have sexual intercourse with a female without her consent, but without actually overcoming her will. For example, he may have intercourse with a sleeping woman, a woman rendered insensible by a faint or fit, or a drunk woman (not made so by the accused).

In these cases the crime is not rape but 'clandestine injury to woman'. Alternatively, this can be charged as indecent assault.

Constructive rape

There are three cases where rape is committed without overcoming the female's will. It is rape for a male to have intercourse with:

- A female below the age of puberty (12), whether or not she consents.
- A mentally ill female who is incapable of giving valid consent.
- A female, by impersonating her husband.

When someone is raped

Someone who has been raped may or may not feel able to endure a police investigation. But even if not, she should visit her own doctor or local hospital to check for venereal disease, the possibility of physical damage, or pregnancy. *See:* ABORTION

If she decides to go to the police, she should:

- Go as soon as possible after the rape; the longer she leaves it, the less likely she is to be believed.
- Not wash herself or re-arrange her clothing – that is all part of her evidence. The police may need to keep her clothes, so she should take others.
- Remember the details of the incident and any words exchanged, so far as possible.

In the police station she will often be questioned by the police for some time to establish whether or not force was used. A policewoman need not be present. She has no right to have a solicitor or friend with her, but some police officers will allow this.

The police will need the evidence that an internal medical examination can provide. The examination will usually be conducted by the police doctor, but she has the right to be examined by her own doctor instead. The police may ask her to look at photographs of suspects, visit the scene of the crime or assist at an identification parade.

Rape crisis centres

A female who has been raped or sexually assaulted can contact a Rape Crisis Centre for support and advice on any medical and legal steps that should be taken. At present (1984) there are 5 Centres in Scotland:

- Aberdeen: telephone 0224–575560.
- Edinburgh: telephone 031–556 9437.
- Strathclyde (Glasgow): telephone 041–221 8448.
- Highland (Inverness): telephone 0463–220719.
- Central (Falkirk): telephone 0324 38433.

In court

The consent of the female is a complete defence to a charge of rape. An honest belief that she consented is also a defence.

The accused male can lead evidence of previous intercourse between him and the female as being relevant to the issue of consent. However, evidence of specific acts of intercourse between the female and other males will not usually be allowed.

The accused will also be allowed to introduce evidence that the female is reputedly of bad moral character, if this is considered to be relevant to her credibility as a witness.

Protecting the victim The female can ask that her address not be read out in court, and the press have agreed not to publish the names of rape victims.

RATES

Paying for local services

Anyone who occupies a property (whether or not he is the owner of it) has to pay rates to the local council. Many council and private tenants pay their rates as part of their total payment.

The amount payable depends upon the rateable value of the property and the rate in the pound charged by the council or councils in the area.

Assessing rateable value

The rateable value of property is calculated by the local assessor. He is appointed by the regional or islands council (or sometimes by councils jointly) but he acts independently in making a periodic – usually 5-yearly – valuation of all the properties in his area.

The assessor asks for information about each property's facilities. From the answers, and other information obtained from a random survey and from measurement of the building, he calculates the yearly rent at which the property might be let in current market conditions. That amount is the gross value.

From the gross value, the assessor makes certain prescribed statutory deductions and the amount left after these deductions is called the rateable value.

A list of the rateable values of every property in the area – known as the valuation roll – is available for inspection at the assessor's office.

Fixing the rate in the pound

Each council fixes its own rates by calculating its estimated total expenditure for the coming financial year (from April 1) and deducting any amount expected in central government grant. The balance is levied as a proportion of the rateable value of property in its area – known as the rate in the pound.

The rateable value of properties can vary greatly, even in the same street, but the rate in the pound is the same for all of them. So if the rate in the pound is fixed at 75p, the occupier of a house valued at £200 will pay £150 (200 × 75p) in rates whilst the occupier of a larger house valued at £400 will pay £300 (400 × 75p).

The amount of domestic water rate is separately charged, but is also calculated by reference to the rateable value of the property.

In areas with both a regional council and district councils, each council determines its own rate. The regional council, however, collects the rates on behalf of all the councils in its area.

Once fixed, the level of rate for the year cannot be raised. But under instructions from central government, a local authority can now be obliged to *reduce* its rate in some circumstances. In 1984 the Secretary of State also took powers to fix in advance maximum rate levels for all councils. *See:* LOCAL AUTHORITY

How rates are collected

When rates are due, the regional or islands council sends each ratepayer a written demand note, setting out how much he must pay. Information is also given on how the money is to be spent.

Rates are then normally payable in 10 monthly instalments, from May to the following February. Arrangements can be made for lump sum payment instead.

When rates are not paid

It is possible to appeal to the local assessor on the ground that the rates demanded have not been properly charged. But apart from that, if someone does not pay his rates when they are due, the council is entitled to give notice requiring payment within 14 days. If payment is not made, it can apply to the sheriff for a warrant for recovery of the unpaid rates *plus* a 10 per cent surcharge.

The warrant authorises sheriff officers to enter the ratepayer's home and select some of his goods for sale. After four days the goods can be auctioned and the proceeds paid to the council. After the deduction of unpaid rates and any expenses, the balance goes to the ratepayer. *See:* DEBT; SHERIFF OFFICER

Asking for a reduction

There are two ways in which a ratepayer may be able to pay lower rates – by a rate reduction or by a rate rebate.

Rate reduction A rate reduction means that the rateable value of a property is reduced, and that in turn reduces the amount of rates payable.

If at the time you purchase your house, or it is revalued, you think that the assessor has placed too high a value on it, you can appeal, even if your neighbour's house has been similarly assessed. It may be that his house is larger than yours, or that he has a garage and you do not.

The first stage is to apply to the assessor himself, stating the grounds for your complaint. If he accepts your argument, he will reduce the valuation.

If he does not, you can appeal in writing to the local valuation appeal committee. This consists of between 3 and 6 persons drawn from a panel appointed by the sheriff. Committee hearings are in public and you will be given an opportunity to state your case – as will the assessor. You may be represented by a lawyer if you wish.

The committee will give its decision in writing, and also the reasons for it. If you are not satisfied with the decision, you can appeal to the Lands Valuation Appeal Court in Edinburgh. The Court's decision is final.

Obtaining a rate rebate

If you pay rates in respect of your home, you may be entitled to a housing benefit called rate rebate from your district or islands council. Application forms are available from the council's housing department.

You do not have to be legally obliged to pay the rates yourself. It is enough if you *actually* pay them and you are:

- The husband, wife or cohabitee of the person legally responsible for paying them; or
- Some other person whom the council thinks it reasonable to treat as eligible for a rate rebate.

Your rebate entitlement depends on:

1. Your weekly needs. These are calculated according to a scale of allowances fixed by law. For information on the needs allowances, see RENT REBATE.

2. Your weekly income (after certain deductions). For the rules used to calculate your income, see RENT REBATE.

3. The rates that you are required to pay, calculated on a weekly basis. If the council thinks that your house is too large, or your rates are too high because of the house's location, it can treat you as paying less rates than you actually do. Your rebate will then be based on that lower figure. The council cannot do this if, given your family circumstances and the availability of accommodation, it is unreasonable to expect you to seek cheaper housing.

4. Whether or not you have non-dependants – for instance, a parent or adult child – living in your household.

Calculating rebate The following example shows how a rebate is worked out, except for those on supplementary benefit. (Deductions are for 1984).

- Assume annual rates of, say, £312. The weekly rates figure is therefore £6.
- Take 60 per cent of the weekly rates – that is, £3.60.
- Deduct the following sums for any non-dependants in the household (excluding children under 18, students supported by you and those receiving training allowances under the Youth Training Scheme). A married or unmarried couple are treated as one person for this purpose. (From November, 1984, a deduction will be made for 16–17 year-olds in full-time work.)

Aged 18 to 64 (59 if a woman)................................ £2.05
Aged 65 or over (60 or over if a woman)..................... £0.90
Aged 21 or over and receiving supplementary benefit £0.90

Assume a deduction of 90p. The rates figure is therefore reduced to £2.70.

- If your weekly net income is the same as your needs allowance, your weekly rebate is £2.70.
- If your weekly net income is more than the needs allowance, your rebate is £2.70 *minus* 9 per cent of the difference between income and allowance.
- If your weekly net income is less than the needs allowance, and either you or your partner (who can be a cohabitee) is of pensionable age, your weekly rebate is £2.70 *plus* 20 per cent of the difference between income and allowance. If you are below that age, your rebate is £2.70 *plus* 8 per cent of the difference between income and allowance.

If the rebate amounts to less than 10p a week (50p from November, 1984, except for those whose income is below their needs allowance), it will not be paid.)

Receiving supplementary benefit If you are entitled to SUPPLEMENTARY BENEFIT, you get a 100 per cent rate rebate, less any deductions (see above) for non-dependants.

When the Department of Health and Social Security is satisfied that you are entitled to supplementary benefit, it will send a certificate to your local housing department stating when benefit became payable. The housing department will then notify you of the amount of rate rebate awarded.

If you are a boarder or a crofter on supplementary benefit, your rates will be met by the DHSS.

How rebate is paid

A rate rebate normally takes the form of a reduction in the gross amount of rates due. Your monthly instalments will be reduced appropriately.

If you are a tenant of a private landlord and pay your rates direct to him along with your rent, your rate rebate will be paid to you monthly. It can be paid direct to your landlord if you owe more than 13 weeks' rent arrears.

If you are a council tenant, your combined rent and rates charge will be reduced.

If a rebate is refused

If you are refused a rebate, or you think that the rebate you are granted is too low, you can ask for the decision to be reviewed. The procedure is the same as for a RENT REBATE or allowance.

RECKLESS DRIVING

Severe penalties for risking other people's safety

A driver who drives in such a manner as to create an obvious and serious risk of causing physical injury to some other person on the road, or of doing substantial damage to property, is guilty of reckless driving.

The test applied by the court is whether the driving in question falls *far below* the standard expected of the competent and careful driver. This can be contrasted with the test for CARELESS DRIVING, which is that the driving must fall *below* that expected of the competent and careful driver.

If a charge of reckless driving is not proved, the court can convict of careless driving instead.

Reckless driving may take many forms. But if the driving occurred in the face of obvious dangers which were (or should have been) appreciated, or if the driver showed a complete disregard for any potential dangers that might have arisen from the way the vehicle was being driven, the offence of reckless driving has been committed.

The following situations, if they happened deliberately or recklessly, would constitute reckless driving:

- The driver had been drinking heavily.
- He crossed continuous double white lines.
- He was racing another vehicle.
- He was 'retaliating' as the real or imagined victim of bad driving by somebody else.
- He emerged from a side road, ignoring the road sign, and not looking out.
- He struck a pedestrian on a pedestrian crossing.
- He ignored a red traffic light.
- He ignored the road signs at a road junction.
- He ignored a policeman's signal.
- He overtook on the brow of a hill.
- He overtook on the inside.
- He was driving in the wrong direction in a one-way street.
- He was driving in the wrong direction on a motorway.
- He fell asleep at the wheel.
- He overtook two or more vehicles at once.
- He was driving much too fast.
- He was involved in a very bad collision, head on, he being on the wrong side of the road.
- He was driving on the wrong side of the road.
- He was involved in two or more accidents within a matter of minutes.

Defences Some defences against a charge of reckless driving are acceptable in the courts:

- An unforeseen mechanical defect – provided that the vehicle has been kept in good condition and was checked before the beginning of the journey.
- The driver was, for example, hit heavily on the head by a stone, or was suffering from an epileptic fit – provided that he had no warning and took whatever preventative measures were available.

Unacceptable defences include:

- The driver swerved to avoid a child, dog or other animal. The courts take the view that all drivers should be prepared for well-known hazards.
- The driver did not see a traffic sign. (The only case in which this defence may be accepted is if the sign was obscured and there was nothing else to warn the driver.)
- The driver was ill or tired. (Illness would be a defence only if the driver had taken every proper precaution against it.)

Maximum penalties

A reckless driving charge tried before a judge alone under summary procedure carries a maximum penalty of a £2,000 fine and imprisonment for 6 months. If prosecuted before a judge and jury under solemn procedure, the penalty is an unlimited fine and up to 2 years in prison. *See:* CRIMINAL PROCEEDINGS

Disqualification is at the discretion of the court on a first offence. If a second offence is committed within 3 years, there is an automatic disqualification of at least 12 months.

If a driver causes death by reckless driving, the maximum penalty is increased to 5 years' imprisonment and disqualification for at least 12 months is automatic.

RECONCILIATION

Trying to mend a broken marriage

A couple whose marriage has run into serious trouble are encouraged by the divorce laws to try to reconcile their differences – even though DIVORCE proceedings have already started.

When a solicitor is first consulted about raising a divorce action, he or she may mention the possibility of a reconciliation. The client may be advised to seek help from a MARRIAGE GUIDANCE counsellor, doctor or social worker.

A judge must delay the hearing of a divorce case if he thinks that there is a reasonable chance of saving the marriage. If this happens, and the couple subsequently live together, no account will be taken of the period of cohabitation for the purpose of the divorce proceedings.

Before a divorce

If a husband and wife attempt a reconciliation by continuing or resuming living together, their prospects of obtaining a divorce are not jeopardised, so long as they do not exceed the time permitted by law. The time – and the way it is calculated – depends on the basis of the divorce.

Divorce based on adultery If one partner commits ADULTERY, the couple can live together for up to three months after the other partner finds out about it without this affecting his or her right to a divorce. The three-month period starts to run as soon as the couple continue or resume living together after the adultery has been discovered – even if this only lasts for a few days.

Divorce based on desertion If one partner deserts the other for two years or more, the couple can resume living together for up to three months without this affecting the other partner's right to a divorce. Again the three-month period starts to run from the date they resume living together.

When calculating the two-year period for desertion, periods of living together totalling no more than six months are ignored. So if there has been a trial reconciliation which lasted only four months, that period does not count towards the two years. Provided that the reconciliation lasts no more than six months, you do not have to start again from the beginning – the period of desertion before the reconciliation continues to count. *See:* DESERTION

Divorce based on separation If a couple have lived apart for two years, either partner can seek a divorce so long as the other consents. If there is no consent, one partner can seek a divorce after they have lived apart for five years. When calculating the two or five-year period, periods of living together totalling no more than 6 months are not counted, but do not break the continuity of the separation. *See:* LIVING APART

Divorce based on behaviour If one partner behaves unreasonably, but the couple continue or resume living together, the other partner's right to seek a divorce is not affected. There is no limit on the length of time they can live together.

REDUNDANCY

A payment for losing your job

An employee who is made redundant – that is, dismissed because there is no longer suitable work for him – may be entitled to compensation from his employer. The minimum amount is defined by the Employment Protection (Consolidation) Act 1978, according to a formula that takes into account the employee's age, his length of service (up to a maximum of 20 years) and his rate of pay.

A redundant employee should receive his award automatically from his employer when he leaves. But if the employer does not pay – for example, because he does not accept that redundancy was the reason for dismissal – the employee can claim the money by applying to an INDUSTRIAL TRIBUNAL.

If the employer fails to pay because he is insolvent, the employee can claim a redundancy payment by making a direct application to the Department of Employment.

Employees who are not entitled

Some employees are not entitled to a statutory redundancy payment, even although they have been made redundant. They include: certain part-time workers; male employees aged 65 or over and female employees aged 60 or over; civil servants and National Health Service employees (who have their own schemes); certain registered dock workers; share fishermen; employees who normally work outside Great Britain (except in certain cases); domestic servants who are close rela-

THE FOREMAN WHO LEFT TOO SOON

An employee who believes that he is to be made redundant and who resigns without waiting to be dismissed may lose his redundancy award.

Mr Shaw was a foreman in the velvets department of a fabric company.

His employers told him that the department would eventually be closed, but without specifying a date.

Mr Shaw found another job and handed in his notice. Then he claimed a redundancy payment from his former employers.

DECISION

Mr Shaw was not entitled to an award. He had not been dismissed, merely given warning of possible dismissal. However, had a definite date been given for closure of the department, that would have been dismissal.

tives of their employers. *See:* EMPLOYMENT PROTECTION; PART-TIME WORKER

An employee cannot sign away his right to payment if he is made redundant. The only exception to that rule is if he is on a fixed-term contract of 2 years or more and he has agreed in writing – before the fixed-term expires – to waive his right to a redundancy payment.

How eligible employees qualify

An employee who is otherwise eligible for a redundancy payment must meet three additional conditions. He must:

- Have worked for his employer continuously for at least 2 years.
- Have been 'dismissed' (see below).
- Be redundant, as defined by law.

If he refuses an offer of suitable alternative employment from his employer, he will lose his right to a redundancy payment, although technically he may still be redundant. It does not affect an employee's right to a redundancy payment that he has a job with another employer to go to, or that he soon finds another job.

The 2-year service period

An employee must complete 2 years of CONTINUOUS EMPLOYMENT with his employer before he becomes eligible for a redundancy payment. Employment before his 18th birthday does not count towards the 2-year period.

Employment ends only when the employer's NOTICE of dismissal expires, or, if proper notice is not given, when it would have ended had it been given. So an employee who, for example, starts work on January 1, 1981, and receives 1 week's notice on December 30, 1982, has 2 years' continuous employment.

HOW TO MAKE A REDUNDANCY CLAIM

If you have been dismissed and believe you are entitled to a redundancy payment, you can claim it either directly from your former employer or through an application to an INDUSTRIAL TRIBUNAL.

If you decide to apply initially to your former employer, rather than to a tribunal, you must do so in a letter, stating clearly that you are seeking compensation for redundancy.

Send your letter by recorded delivery and keep a copy. The letter must not be sent before your job has ended. A claim for a redundancy payment is not valid if it is made before that date.

If you decide to apply to an industrial tribunal, either initially or because your employer has refused you payment, obtain form IT1 (Scot) from a job centre, unemployment benefit office or local industrial tribunal office.

Send it, when completed, to the Central Office of the Industrial Tribunals (Scotland), 141 West Nile Street, Glasgow G1 2RU. Your case is then allocated to a local tribunal, which will inform you when it is to be heard.

Time limits You must claim the payment from your employer or submit your application to the tribunal within 6 months of leaving your job, otherwise you may lose your right to it.

If you do so between 6 and 12 months after leaving, a tribunal will only award you a payment if it thinks it would be 'just and equitable', having regard to all the circumstances. If you claim or apply to a tribunal later than 12 months after leaving, you will not be entitled to any payment.

If you are claiming UNFAIR DISMISSAL as well as redundancy, you should make your tribunal application within 3 months of leaving your job.

How the rules define 'dismissal'

An employee is entitled to a redundancy payment if he is dismissed, or he is forced to resign because of his employer's conduct – this is called 'constructive' dismissal. He is also treated as dismissed if he works under a fixed-term contract that is not renewed.

He does not qualify if he resigns of his own accord – even though he may think redundancies are in the offing – nor if he ends his job by agreement with his employer.

Constructive dismissal If an employee resigns because of his employer's behaviour, he may be treated as constructively dismissed. For this to be so, the employer's behaviour must be a serious breach of the employment contract – for instance, a refusal to pay wages.

An employee who has been constructively dismissed has the same right to a redundancy payment as an employee dismissed in the ordinary way by his employer.

When a contract is not renewed If an employee has entered a fixed-term con-

TOLD TO LEAVE

A redundancy payment is available only to an ex-employee who has left his job against his own wishes. If he resigns, he must be able to prove that he did so only because of his employer's unreasonable behaviour.

THE EMPLOYEE WHO GOT THE NOTICE RULES WRONG

An employee who wants to leave while under notice must inform his employer in writing during the notice period laid down by law. Otherwise, he may be held to have resigned and lose his redundancy payment.

Under the employment protection rules and his contract, Mr Armit was entitled to 4 weeks' notice. On January 20 his employer told him that he was to be made redundant on March 12. On February 4 Mr Armit, who had found another job, gave oral notice that he would leave on February 12. His employer accepted this.

DECISION

Mr Armit was not entitled to a redundancy payment. In giving notice he had made two mistakes. First, he did not do so in writing. Second, he did not do so within the notice period imposed by law on his employer, in his case the 4 weeks ending on March 12.

tract – that is, a contract for a fixed period of time – which is not renewed when it expires, he may be entitled to a redundancy payment. He cannot get one if his contract was for 2 years or more and he has waived his right to a payment (see above).

Further complications

Dismissals because of redundancy may be further complicated if:

- The employer is asking for volunteers to leave.
- An employee asks to go before his notice period expires.
- An employee is facing disciplinary proceedings.
- An employee is on strike.

Voluntary redundancy An employer planning redundancies sometimes asks for volunteers. Anyone accepting voluntary redundancy should insist beforehand on a written promise from the employer that he will be dismissed for redundancy. Otherwise, if there is a later dispute, a tribunal may hold that he resigned and is therefore not entitled to a payment.

Leaving before notice expires An employee who is under notice of dismissal for redundancy can leave before the notice expires – for example, to start a new job – without losing his right to a redundancy payment.

However, he must give *written* notice – which must normally be at least one week – that he is leaving early. Furthermore, he *must* give the employer notice within the statutory minimum period of notice that the employer is legally required to give, or the contractual period of notice if that is longer. *See:* NOTICE

WHEN THE BOSS TOOK OVER

The owner of a business is not legally an employee. So if he takes on the job of an employee and dismisses him, that employee has not been replaced.

The owner of a grocery shop decided he wanted to work in it himself. He dismissed one of his assistants to make room for himself. The assistant claimed redundancy.

DECISION

The dismissed assistant was redundant. The same work was being done by fewer employees.

THE NUCLEAR WORKER WHO REFUSED A TRANSFER

An employee whose contract contains a 'mobility' clause will not be entitled to a redundancy payment if he is asked to move.

Mr Claydon worked as a draughtsman for the Atomic Energy Authority at Orford Ness, in Suffolk. In 1971 that establishment was closed and Mr Claydon was told he would be transferred to the Authority's research centre at Aldermaston, Berkshire. He refused to go and claimed a redundancy payment. His employers argued he was not redundant, because his employment contract stated: 'The employers reserve the right to require any member of the staff to work at any of our establishments in G.B. or in posts overseas.'

DECISION

The contract was clear. Mr Claydon had been offered a transfer in accordance with the terms specified in the contract and therefore he had not been made redundant.

WHEN THREE MEN COULD DO THE WORK OF FOUR

Even though the volume of work may remain the same, but reorganisation enables it to be done by fewer people, an employee who is dismissed because there is no longer a job for him is redundant.

Mr Sutton was sacked from his job as a chief accountant. His duties were shared out among his three assistants and he was not replaced. Mr Sutton claimed redundancy. His employers argued he was not redundant, because the amount of work had not changed.

DECISION

Mr Sutton was redundant. Although the work had not changed, fewer people were needed to do it.

THE OLD-FASHIONED BARMAID

In deciding whether an employee dismissed because of business changes is redundant, industrial tribunals consider what he was doing before the changes – and his employer's requirements after them. If the same work remains and the employer still needs someone to do it, the dismissed employee is not redundant.

The management of the Star and Garter public house decided to modernise the premises and to hire young, attractive barmaids. A barmaid who had been employed there for 18 years was dismissed, because it was felt she did not fit in with the pub's new image. She claimed a redundancy payment.

DECISION

The barmaid was not redundant. Her employers needed barmaids and the job she had been doing therefore still existed.

Nowadays she could probably claim UNFAIR DISMISSAL.

An employer can try to stop a redundant employee from leaving early by serving a counter-notice demanding that he should stay on until the full notice period has run out. He might do this if he wants to keep specialist staff until the last minute to maintain his business, or he hopes to find the employee a suitable alternative job which would avoid the need to make a redundancy payment.

The counter-notice must be in writing and reach the employee before the end of the notice period given by the employee. It must also state that the employer will contest any claim for a redundancy payment if the employee fails to withdraw his notice.

If the employee does not withdraw his notice, and the employer refuses to make a redundancy payment, the employee can apply for one to an industrial tribunal. The tribunal will examine the reasonableness of the employer's and employee's behaviour and can order the payment of all or part of the redundancy payment to which the employee is entitled.

Misconduct leading to dismissal An employee who is dismissed for redundancy may lose all or part of his redundancy payment if he is guilty of serious misconduct that justifies summary (instant) dismissal. If he is, his employer can avoid making a payment by:

- Dismissing him without notice; or
- Giving him shorter notice than the contract requires; or
- Giving the notice required by the contract, along with a written statement that the employer is entitled to dismiss him without notice.

This rule also applies to a dismissal

DECLARING REDUNDANCIES: STEPS THAT EMPLOYERS FOLLOW

Every employer who intends to make employees redundant should warn them as far in advance as possible.

The other steps he must follow depend upon whether:

- The employer recognises an independent TRADE UNION for the purposes of COLLECTIVE BARGAINING.
- The employee is legally entitled to a redundancy payment.
- The employer intends to claim back part of any redundancy payment from the state-run Redundancy Fund.

Warning the employee

The Code of Practice issued under the Industrial Relations Act 1971 provides that employers faced with making redundancies should:

- Give as much warning as practicable to the employees concerned.
- Consider introducing schemes for voluntary redundancy, retirement, transfer and a phased rundown of employment.
- Establish which employees are to be made redundant, and in what order.
- Offer help to employees in finding other work.
- Make no announcement about redundancies until employees and trade unions have been informed.

The Code of Practice is not legally binding, but industrial tribunals can take a breach of it into account in any proceedings that take place before them.

Consulting the union

An employer who recognises an independent trade union for bargaining purposes must consult it if he is planning to make any of its members redundant, or if he is planning redundancies among non-union members in job categories for which the union is recognised. That rule applies even if the employees concerned are not legally entitled to a redundancy payment – for example, because they have not been in their jobs for two years.

If fewer than 10 employees are to be dismissed, the consultation must take place 'at the earliest opportunity' – in practice, as soon as the employer is reasonably certain of the need for redundancies.

If the number of employees involved at any one establishment is between 10 and 99, and the employer intends to make them all redundant within a period of 30 days or less, he must consult with the union at least 30 days before the first dismissal takes effect.

If the number of employees involved is 100 or more, and the employer intends to make them all redundant within a period of 90 days or less, he must consult with the union at least 90 days before the first dismissal takes effect.

The employer must give trade union representatives written notice of:

- The reasons for the proposed redundancies.
- The number of employees to be dismissed and their job categories.
- The total number of employees, including those to be dismissed, in those job categories at the affected establishment.
- The way in which employees are to be chosen for redundancy.
- How the dismissals are to be carried out and the period over which they will be spread.

If an employer fails to observe these consultation rules, the union – but not individual employees – can make a complaint to an industrial tribunal. Unless the employer can show that there were 'special circumstances' – such as bankruptcy or a disaster – and that he took reasonable steps to follow the procedures, the tribunal can order him to pay extra compensation, called a 'protective award', to each redundant employee.

Under a protective award, an employer must pay each employee wages for a protected period fixed by the tribunal. When fewer than 10 employees are being made redundant, the protected period can be up to 28 days. If the number of employees is between 10 and 99, it can be up to 30 days. And if the number of employees is 100 or more, it can be up to 90 days.

If an employer does not pay wages under a protective award, an individual employee can complain to an industrial tribunal, which may order the money to be paid.

Notifying the government

If an employer proposes to dismiss 100 or more employees at one workplace within a period of 90 days or less, he must give written notice to the Department of Employment at least 90 days before the first dismissal takes effect.

If he proposes to dismiss 10 or more employees within a period of 30 days or less, he must give written notice at least 30 days before the first dismissal takes effect.

An employer must notify the Department even though there is no recognised union with which he has to consult.

When a redundancy payment is made

An employer who makes any redundancy payment to a dismissed employee must also supply him with a written statement of the amount and an explanation of how it has been calculated. If this is not issued, the employer can be fined up to £50.

If the employer fails to provide a statement, the employee can serve a written notice on him, asking for it to be provided. He must give the employer at least one week in which to provide it. If the employer fails to do so, he can be fined up to £400.

Claiming a redundancy rebate An employer who is obliged by law to make a redundancy payment can reclaim 41 per cent of it from the state-administered Redundancy Fund, which is financed from NATIONAL INSURANCE CONTRIBUTIONS.

He cannot normally reclaim any part of a redundancy payment that he makes voluntarily to an employee who is not legally entitled to it.

However, if an employee claims a payment more than 6 months after he leaves his job, and the employer makes a payment even although he is not legally obliged to, the Department of Employment can pay him the 41 per cent rebate if this would be 'just and equitable'.

To obtain a refund, the employer must:

- Complete form RP1 at his local employment office at least 14 days before the employee's notice period expires. If 10 or more employees are to be made redundant together, the form must be completed at least 21 days before the end of their notice period. The Department of Employment can then check on whether any payment is due.
- Claim the money within 6 months of making the payment, by completing form RP2 at the employment office and attaching to it a portion of form RP3 – the redundancy pay statement – signed by the employee. The Department of Employment has a discretion to accept late claims.

If the employer fails to give prior notice to the Department, his rebate can be reduced by up to 10 per cent. The employer can appeal to an industrial tribunal against this reduction, as well as against a refusal by the Department to pay any rebate.

REDUNDANCY OR UNFAIR DISMISSAL?

Under the UNFAIR DISMISSAL rules, redundancy is a 'fair' reason for dismissing someone. So an employee who is redundant is not normally entitled to extra compensation – in addition to his redundancy payment – for UNFAIR DISMISSAL.

However, if an employer acts unreasonably in the way he makes an employee redundant – for example, he fails to consult the employee about his impending dismissal – the tribunal may decide that the employee *was* unfairly dismissed and order compensation to be paid.

A redundancy dismissal will also be unfair if other employees doing similar jobs are not dismissed and the employee is selected for redundancy because of his trade union activities or in contravention of a customary arrangement or an agreed procedure – such as 'last in, first out'.

Because the dividing line between unfair dismissal and redundancy is often blurred, many applicants to industrial tribunals submit their claims for 'unfair dismissal or redundancy or both' – leaving the tribunal to decide the most appropriate award in the circumstances.

for misconduct *following* a normal redundancy dismissal. That may happen if the misconduct is only discovered later.

However, the employee does not necessarily forfeit his redundancy payment. He has the right to apply to an industrial tribunal for the payment – but only if a dismissal for misconduct follows a dismissal for redundancy, and occurs during the statutory minimum period of notice of redundancy (or the contractual period if longer). The tribunal can award what it considers 'just and equitable' – which may be the whole payment, part of it, or nothing.

Redundancy claims by strikers An employee who is on strike when he is made redundant will not be entitled to a redundancy payment if his employer follows the dismissal procedure outlined above. This is because strike action usually justifies summary dismissal. In this case, the employee cannot apply to a tribunal for payment.

However, if an employee goes on strike *after* receiving notice of dismissal for redundancy, he will remain entitled to a redundancy payment even though he is summarily dismissed for striking. But he must be on strike during the statutory minimum period of notice (or the contractual period of notice, if longer). His employer can request in writing that he work extra days to make up for those lost as a result of the stoppage. If the employee refuses to do so, he may lose the entire redundancy payment.

How the law defines 'redundancy'

Once it has been established that an employee has been dismissed by his employer, the law assumes that he has been dismissed because of redundancy, unless the contrary is proved.

The burden of proof is on the employer to show that the dismissal was

HOW REDUNDANCY PAYMENTS ARE CALCULATED

This ready-reckoner shows how much redundancy pay an employee is entitled to receive by law. First, find the employee's length of employment, in complete years, at the top of the table. Then read down that column until you come to the figure opposite his age last birthday, given beside the table on the left. That is the number of weeks' current pay he should get.

In working out length of service, employment before the employee's 18th birthday is disregarded. The maximum length of service that can be taken into account is 20 years (the most recent 20 years are used for the calculation).

A redundant employee is entitled to:

- Half a week's pay for each year of employment completed between the 18th birthday and the eve of the 22nd birthday.
- A week's pay for each year of employment completed between the 22nd birthday and the eve of the 41st birthday.
- $1\frac{1}{2}$ weeks' pay for each year of employment completed between the 41st birthday and the 65th birthday (60th birthday if a woman).

There is a limit of £145 (in 1984) on the amount of a weeks' pay. So the maximum amount payable by law is $£145 \times 20 \times 1\frac{1}{2} = £4{,}350$.

If the employee has reached his 64th (or her 59th) birthday, the redundancy payment he or she would have been entitled to is reduced by $\frac{1}{12}$ for each complete month of employment after that birthday. So by the time the 65th (or 60th) birthday arrives, no redundancy payment is payable.

Example: Jim McLeod joined his employers at the age of 16. He is now 35 and is being made redundant. His current earnings are £160 a week. If the weekly pay limit is £145, his entitlement is:

Service before 18 (2 years)	Nothing
Service between 18th and 22nd birthdays (4 complete years)	$4 \times \frac{1}{2}$ week's pay
Service between 22nd birthday and present (13 complete years)	13×1 week's pay
Total	15 weeks
Jim therefore receives £145 × 15 weeks *equals*	£2,175

WORKING THE SAME MACHINE – BUT REDUNDANT

If an employer takes over the premises and assets of a business, but changes the purposes for which they are used, any employees he keeps on may not be able to claim service with the previous owner as part of their total service record.

Mr Woodhouse spent 14 years as a machine operative with a Nottingham company making diesel engines. Then his employers decided to transfer to Manchester. They sold their assets in Nottingham, but not the goodwill of the business, which they were continuing.

Mr Woodhouse stayed in Nottingham, working the same machine, but now producing different products for another company. After 6 years, he was made redundant. He said he was entitled to a redundancy payment based on 20 years' service. His employers said the amount should be assessed only on 6 years – the length of time he had worked for them.

DECISION

The new owners had not bought the business, only its physical assets. So Mr Woodhouse was entitled only to a payment calculated on 6 years' service. He should have claimed a payment based on 14 years' service from the previous owners at the time they sold the business.

AGE	NUMBER OF YEARS' SERVICE																		
	2	**3**	**4**	**5**	**6**	**7**	**8**	**9**	**10**	**11**	**12**	**13**	**14**	**15**	**16**	**17**	**18**	**19**	**20**
20	1	1	1	1	–														
21	1	1½	1½	1½	1½	–													
22	1	1½	2	2	2	2	–												
23	1½	2	2½	3	3	3	3	–											
24	2	2½	3	3½	4	4	4	4	–										
25	2	3	3½	4	4½	5	5	5	5	–									
26	2	3	4	4½	5	5½	6	6	6	6	–								
27	2	3	4	5	5½	6	6½	7	7	7	7	–							
28	2	3	4	5	6	6½	7	7½	8	8	8	8	–						
29	2	3	4	5	6	7	7½	8	8½	9	9	9	9	–					
30	2	3	4	5	6	7	8	8½	9	9½	10	10	10	10	–				
31	2	3	4	5	6	7	8	9	9½	10	10½	11	11	11	11	–			
32	2	3	4	5	6	7	8	9	10	10½	11	11½	12	12	12	12	–		
33	2	3	4	5	6	7	8	9	10	11	11½	12	12½	13	13	13	13	–	
34	2	3	4	5	6	7	8	9	10	11	12	12½	13	13½	14	14	14	14	–
35	2	3	4	5	6	7	8	9	10	11	12	13	13½	14	14½	15	15	15	15
36	2	3	4	5	6	7	8	9	10	11	12	13	14	14½	15	15½	16	16	16
37	2	3	4	5	6	7	8	9	10	11	12	13	14	15	15½	16	16½	17	17
38	2	3	4	5	6	7	8	9	10	11	12	13	14	15	16	16½	17	17½	18
39	2	3	4	5	6	7	8	9	10	11	12	13	14	15	16	17	17½	18	18½
40	2	3	4	5	6	7	8	9	10	11	12	13	14	15	16	17	18	18½	19
41	2	3	4	5	6	7	8	9	10	11	12	13	14	15	16	17	18	19	19½
42	2½	3½	4½	5½	6½	7½	8½	9½	10½	11½	12½	13½	14½	15½	16½	17½	18½	19½	20½
43	3	4	5	6	7	8	9	10	11	12	13	14	15	16	17	18	19	20	21
44	3	4½	5½	6½	7½	8½	9½	10½	11½	12½	13½	14½	15½	16½	17½	18½	19½	20½	21½
45	3	4½	6	7	8	9	10	11	12	13	14	15	16	17	18	19	20	21	22
46	3	4½	6	7½	8½	9½	10½	11½	12½	13½	14½	15½	16½	17½	18½	19½	20½	21½	22½
47	3	4½	6	7½	9	10	11	12	13	14	15	16	17	18	19	20	21	22	23
48	3	4½	6	7½	9	10½	11½	12½	13½	14½	15½	16½	17½	18½	19½	20½	21½	22½	23½
49	3	4½	6	7½	9	10½	12	13	14	15	16	17	18	19	20	21	22	23	24
50	3	4½	6	7½	9	10½	12	13½	14½	15½	16½	17½	18½	19½	20½	21½	22½	23½	24½
51	3	4½	6	7½	9	10½	12	13½	15	16	17	18	19	20	21	22	23	24	25
52	3	4½	6	7½	9	10½	12	13½	15	16½	17½	18½	19½	20½	21½	22½	23½	24½	25½
53	3	4½	6	7½	9	10½	12	13½	15	16½	18	19	20	21	22	23	24	25	26
54	3	4½	6	7½	9	10½	12	13½	15	16½	18	19½	20½	21½	22½	23½	24½	25½	26½
55	3	4½	6	7½	9	10½	12	13½	15	16½	18	19½	21	22	23	24	25	26	27
56	3	4½	6	7½	9	10½	12	13½	15	16½	18	19½	21	22½	23½	24½	25½	26½	27½
57	3	4½	6	7½	9	10½	12	13½	15	16½	18	19½	21	22½	24	25	26	27	28
58	3	4½	6	7½	9	10½	12	13½	15	16½	18	19½	21	22½	24	25½	26½	27½	28½
59*	3	4½	6	7½	9	10½	12	13½	15	16½	18	19½	21	22½	24	25½	27	28	29
60	3	4½	6	7½	9	10½	12	13½	15	16½	18	19½	21	22½	24	25½	27	28½	29½
61	3	4½	6	7½	9	10½	12	13½	15	16½	18	19½	21	22½	24	25½	27	28½	30
62	3	4½	6	7½	9	10½	12	13½	15	16½	18	19½	21	22½	24	25½	27	28½	30
63	3	4½	6	7½	9	10½	12	13½	15	16½	18	19½	21	22½	24	25½	27	28½	30
64*	3	4½	6	7½	9	10½	12	13½	15	16½	18	19½	21	22½	24	25½	27	28½	30

* For women aged between 59 and 60, and men aged between 64 and 65, the cash amount due is to be reduced by $\frac{1}{12}$ for every complete month by which the age exceeds 59 or 64 respectively.

not because of redundancy. If he cannot do so, the employee will be entitled to a redundancy payment.

Often, the question of whether an employee is redundant or not can be answered simply by examining whether the employer replaced him with another employee. If he did not, the employee is almost certainly redundant. If he did, the employee is probably not redundant, although he may still be entitled to compensation for UNFAIR DISMISSAL.

There are five sets of circumstances in which a dismissed employee is, in law, redundant. If:

- All or part of the employer's business closes, whether temporarily or permanently.
- The employer's business moves.
- The employer's business is sold.
- Work is reduced or stopped, whether temporarily or permanently.
- The employee is laid off or put on short-time.

If all or part of a business closes The closure may be for financial reasons, because of the death of the employer, or as the result of other circumstances – for instance, a serious fire or flood. If no work is available for employees, and the employer cannot afford to keep them on, they become redundant.

If part of a business – for example, one factory – is shut down, the employees become redundant if suitable alternative employment cannot be found for them elsewhere in the business.

If the business moves An employee is redundant if his employer moves his business to a new site and does not offer him a job. But the situation may become complicated if the employee is offered a job at the new site and refuses to move.

If that happens, and the employee claims a redundancy payment from an industrial tribunal, the tribunal will examine the EMPLOYMENT CONTRACT to see if it contains a 'mobility' clause requiring the employee to transfer to a new location at the employer's request. If it does, the employee will not be entitled to a redundancy payment.

If there is no written requirement, tribunals examine the nature of the job itself, custom and practice in the trade or industry and the employee's previous attitude towards being moved, to see whether those imply that mobility was a condition of his contract. Some jobs – for example, project engineer or site manager – are clearly mobile. And some industries – for example, construction – require mobility from many of their employees.

When the business is sold An employer who sells up his business and dismisses his staff must make redundancy payments to them. However, if he sells the business as a going concern, the contracts of employment of his workforce are automatically transferred to the new employer. The employees cannot claim redundancy payments if they stay in their jobs.

If the new owner offers an existing employee a job different from the one he was doing before, the employee can accept it for a trial period of up to 4 weeks (or longer, by agreement with his employer). If the job proves unsuitable, and he gives it up before the trial period expires, he will not lose his right to claim a redundancy payment.

Sometimes a business does not change hands as a going concern. The new owner buys only the assets and the premises and uses them for his own business. If that happens, an employee who is dismissed by the old owner can claim a redundancy payment even though he is immediately offered a similar job by the new owner.

If work is reduced or stopped Changes in the organisation of a business – for instance, the installation of new machinery or a re-allocation of duties among the staff that allows the work to be done by fewer people – may mean that an employer no longer needs the services or skills of a particular employee. If the employee is dismissed as a result, and he is not replaced, he is redundant.

If, after a reorganisation, there is still a need for the sort of work an employee was previously doing, but he is dismissed because his employer feels that the changes have made him unsuitable to do it, he may not be able to succeed in a redundancy claim. But he can make a claim of unfair dismissal to an industrial tribunal.

If an employee is laid off If, because of shortage of work, an employee is laid off without pay or put on short-time working, he may be entitled to a redundancy payment. He must have been laid off or kept on short-time for at least 4 weeks, or for at least 6 weeks in the previous 13. If he is on short-time, he must be earning less than half his weekly pay. *See:* LAY-OFF

When another job is offered

An employer may avoid having to make a redundancy payment if he can offer a redundant employee another job on the same terms as before, or a suitable job on different terms. If the employee unreasonably refuses such an offer, he will not be able to claim a redundancy payment.

The job offer must be made before the date on which the employee's old employment ends. The job itself must start within four weeks of that date. If

THE JOB OFFERED WAS OF LOWER STATUS

If an employer offers a job which is of lower standing than the old one, it may not be suitable, even if the pay is the same.

Mr Harris was an instructor of apprentices in a joinery business. Because of changes in the organisation, he was offered alternative work as a bench hand, but at the same pay.

DECISION

The alternative job was not suitable. His previous work as an instructor gave him a status not equalled in the post of bench hand.

WHEN OVERTIME IS REDUCED

An employer who reduces the opportunities for his employees to work overtime has not made them redundant.

Lesney Products, who made toys, laid off their night shift and reorganised the hours worked by their daytime machine setters, who lost the chance to do extra overtime, worth about £14 a week. Six daytime machine setters refused to accept the change and claimed to have been made redundant.

DECISION

The six were not redundant. They were doing the same work as before.

THE EMPLOYER WHO ALTERED THE SHIFTS

If an employer changes working hours, but needs the same number of employees to do the same jobs as before, an employee who leaves or is dismissed may not succeed in a claim for a redundancy payment.

Noreen Johnson was a clerk employed by the Nottinghamshire Combined Police Authority. She and another clerk worked a 5 day week, from 9.30 until 5.30 each day.

The Police Authority changed the hours, requiring the clerks to work two daily shifts, six days a week, in alternate weeks. Noreen refused and was dismissed. She claimed redundancy.

DECISION

Noreen Johnson's redundancy claim was turned down on appeal. Her employers still required her to do the same work as before.

these conditions are not met, the job offer is not valid.

The job must be with the employer, an associated company or with new owners who have taken over the business as a going concern. An employer cannot avoid a redundancy payment by finding a redundant employee employment with another, unrelated business.

If the employee accepts such an offer, he is not regarded as dismissed by his employer.

What is unreasonable? An employee who is offered another job – whether it is a job on the same terms as before or suitable work on different terms – can refuse it without losing his right to a redundancy payment, so long as his refusal is not 'unreasonable'.

Industrial tribunals decide whether an employee's refusal is unreasonable by looking at all the circumstances, including the employee's personal situation. So they can take into account factors such as family commitments, health, distance from home and whether local employment is available.

An offer of work on different terms If a redundant employee is offered another job on different terms from his old job, it must be suitable for him.

If it is not, he can refuse it without jeopardising his redundancy payment.

In deciding whether the job offer is suitable, an industrial tribunal will look at all the facts, including the personal circumstances of the employee. It will examine not only the nature of the work offered, and the terms and conditions, but also whether it suits the employee's skills, experience, status, temperament and state of health.

Trial periods A redundant employee who is offered another job on different terms is entitled to try the job for up to 4 weeks – or longer, by agreement with the employer – without jeopardising his right to claim a redundancy payment. (If he is offered a job on the same terms as those of his previous job, he has no right to such a trial period. Once he accepts the job, he loses his right to a payment.)

If the employee works beyond the trial period, he loses his right to claim a redundancy payment. If he leaves during the trial period, he can still claim a payment, but his employer may refuse it on the ground that he has acted unreasonably in leaving the job. The employee can then claim the payment by applying to an industrial tribunal. If the tribunal considers that the job was suitable and that the employee acted unreasonably, it will refuse the payment.

An employee does not have to accept a trial period. He can refuse to try the new job, leave when the old one ends and claim a redundancy payment. However, industrial tribunals are more likely to decide that an employee has acted unreasonably, and therefore forfeited his right to claim redundancy, if he refuses to try a suitable job.

How redundancy payments affect tax and social security

Statutory redundancy payments are tax-free. But if a redundant employee receives extra money – for example, because his employer operates a redundancy scheme that is more generous than the legal minimum, or because he is compensated for loss of office – which brings his total payment to more than £25,000, he is liable for tax on the amount above £25,000. *See:* GOLDEN HANDSHAKE

An employee who receives a redundancy payment does not lose his right to UNEMPLOYMENT BENEFIT. But if he also receives payment in lieu of working his notice, he will not be entitled to unemployment benefit until the notice period represented by that payment has expired.

A lump-sum redundancy payment will be treated as capital for the purpose of calculating any entitlement to SUPPLEMENTARY BENEFIT. If the payment is more than £3,000, the employee will not be entitled to benefit until he reduces his capital (including any other savings) to £3,000 or less.

Time off during notice of redundancy

If an employee is given notice of dismissal for redundancy and has been in CONTINUOUS EMPLOYMENT for at least two years, he is entitled to reasonable time off during working hours to look for a new job or to make arrangements for re-training. *See:* TIME OFF WORK

REFERENCE

Your right to give an honest opinion of someone's character

If you are asked to give a written reference for someone, you need fear no legal consequences provided that you tell the truth, without malice, to the best of your knowledge and belief.

If for some reason you do not want to tell the truth in a reference, it is better not to give one. No one has a right to demand that you do so.

When a reference can lead to an action for damages

The person who is the subject of a bad reference can sue successfully for DEFAMATION only if he can show that the person giving the reference knew that what he wrote was untrue and wanted to harm the person he was reporting on. However, the malicious disclosure of a spent conviction may give rise to an action for defamation. *See:* REHABILITATION

Even if it can be proved that you were wrong in a reference you gave and that you thereby damaged the subject's reputation, he still cannot sue you successfully for defamation provided that your opinion was an honest one.

When a reference is too good

The person to whom you are writing the reference is entitled to expect you to tell the truth to the best of your knowledge and belief. If you dismiss a dishonest employee, but give him a reference saying he is trustworthy, his new employee can sue you for any loss he suffers if the employee steals from him.

A new employer might even succeed in an action for NEGLIGENCE if you said mistakenly that the subject of the reference was trustworthy without bothering to check within your own organisation that this was true. The risk of an action for negligence may be avoided, however, by stating in the reference that you accept no responsibility for its accuracy.

REFUGEE

When a foreigner flees his homeland

Someone with a claim for POLITICAL ASYLUM may be allowed to stay in Britain although he or she does not otherwise qualify for entry under the IMMIGRATION rules.

Britain is a signatory to a series of United Nations agreements which protect people whose life or freedom in their homeland is threatened because of their race, religion, nationality or politics. The main point of those agreements is that such people must not be forced to return home.

There is no provision, however, to admit people as refugees simply because they cannot make a living in their native land – because of a natural disaster or any other reason. They must have a well-founded fear of persecution.

REFUSE COLLECTION

Local councils have a duty to collect household waste

District and islands councils have a duty to collect all household waste. But they are not obliged to collect waste which is left in such an inaccessible or isolated place that the cost of collection would be unreasonable – so long as they are satisfied that the householder can reasonably dispose of it himself.

Councils make their own arrangements for refuse collection. They can insist that household waste is left in a proper receptacle or in a dustbin or plastic sack provided by them.

Councils provide a special collection service for items of rubbish, such as unwanted furniture or garden refuse, which cannot be disposed of in the normal manner. They can make a reasonable charge for this service.

Councils must provide tips where local householders can dispose of domestic refuse free of charge. Your local council will advise you of your nearest tip and its opening hours.

Industrial or commercial waste

Councils must collect waste from businesses, such as shops, if this is requested. They are not required to collect industrial waste – for instance, from factories – but may agree to do so. Alternatively, they can permit commercial and industrial waste to be disposed of at local refuse tips.

If a council collects commercial and industrial waste, it must normally impose a reasonable charge.

Litter

District and islands councils have a duty to keep streets and roads free of litter and rubbish, in order to protect public health and maintain the environment.

Regional and islands councils, as highway authorities, can provide litter bins in roadside lay-bys but they have no duty to do so.

District and islands councils are normally obliged to dispose of vehicles that have been abandoned on public roads or in the open on other land. *See:* ABANDONED VEHICLE; LITTER

REGISTER OF SASINES

Scotland's register of land deeds

The Register of Sasines is Scotland's national land register. The whole country is covered apart from the few areas affected by REGISTRATION OF TITLE, the new system of land registration that is being introduced. For these areas the appropriate register is called the LAND REGISTER.

The Register of Sasines dates from 1617. Since that year the law has required all important legal deeds concerning land to be registered there. The deeds most commonly registered are conveyances, mortgages, and certain leases. *See:* CONVEYANCE; MORTGAGE

Until the deed is registered it is not properly effective. For example, if you buy a house but do not register your conveyance, the house continues to belong to the seller. This means that he could re-sell it to someone else.

A charge is made for registration. The amount depends on the value of the land or, in the case of a mortgage, the amount of the loan. The deed is copied and then returned. At one time all copies were made by hand. Nowadays the deed is simply photocopied. Something like 300,000 deeds are registered every year.

Once a deed has been registered you can get a copy of it from the Register at any time. This is very useful if you have lost the original.

> **A PUBLIC REGISTER**
>
> The Register of Sasines is open to the general public. For a relatively small fee it is possible to find out quite a lot about a particular property you are interested in.
>
> The Register is divided between two different buildings, both in Edinburgh. An initial enquiry should be taken to Meadowbank House, 153 London Road (office hours 10 a.m. to 4 p.m.). By using the indexes kept there you will be able to find out whether a particular person owns property in a particular county. You will also be able to obtain a list of all the legal deeds that have been registered for a given property.
>
> You can obtain a summary of any registered deed at Meadowbank House. If, however, you want to see the complete deed or order a copy, you will have to go to the other building, Register House, which is situated at the east end of Princes Street (office hours 9 a.m. to 4.30 p.m.).

REGISTRATION OF TITLE

Simplifying property transfers

A new system of registering ownership of land is being introduced to Scotland. This system, which began in 1981, is called registration of title.

Purpose of the system

The existing system of registration dates from 1617. Registration of title, which replaces it, is designed to cure two of its worst defects:

- At the moment, when you buy a house or piece of land the CONVEYANCE is registered in the REGISTER OF SASINES. Registration is not, however, a guarantee of ownership of the property. You only own it if the person selling to you owned it before you. To check this involves your solicitor in a complicated and time-consuming examination of the old title deeds.

Under the new system of registration, the LAND REGISTER replaces the Register of Sasines. Once details of the conveyance are registered there, your title as owner is in most cases guaranteed by the state.

- At the moment it can be very difficult to tell from the vague description contained in the title deeds what the exact boundaries of a property are. Under the new system, all properties will be plotted on an Ordnance Survey map of appropriate scale.

Introducing the system

By 1984 registration of title had been introduced into Renfrewshire, Dunbartonshire and Lanarkshire. Over the next ten years or so it will gradually be extended to the rest of the country.

The first time a property is sold in an area in which the new system operates, the purchaser's solicitor applies to the Land Register for the title to be registered. The application will be accepted if the registry staff are satisfied that the person selling really owns the property.

The staff then make up a 'title sheet' summarising the title deeds. This shows the location of the property on an Ordnance Survey map, and gives details of any mortgages and conditions of use. Each property is given a number. Finally, the name of the buyer is entered as the new owner.

The buyer is given a copy of the title sheet called a 'land certificate'. If there is a mortgage over the property, the certificate is kept by the building society or other lender.

Using the system

Once the property has been registered, subsequent transfers are very easy. The buyer can check that the person selling is really the owner by making sure that it is his name that is entered in the title sheet. A simple conveyance is signed by the seller and registered in the Land Register. The registry staff then alter the title sheet by striking out the name of the seller and entering the buyer's name as the new owner.

Registration of title simplifies property transfers and removes many of the risks. One result is that the fees charged by solicitors for conveying registered property may be less than presently charged for unregistered property. The new system may even be simple enough for you to think about doing your own conveyancing.

REHABILITATION

A person's criminal record can sometimes be kept secret

After certain periods of time, some convicted offenders are allowed to 'wipe the slate clean' under the Rehabilitation of Offenders Act 1974.

The Act provides that after a set period – called 'the rehabilitation period' – certain convictions must be treated as 'spent' and the convicted person treated as a 'rehabilitated person'. It is as if the offender had not committed or been convicted of the offence.

Convictions before a foreign court also come within the Act's provisions.

When a child has been referred to a CHILDREN'S HEARING on the ground that he has committed an offence, and that ground is accepted by the child and his parents or established by the sheriff, that will be treated as a conviction for the purposes of the Act. The disposal of the case by the hearing will be treated as a sentence.

The Act is based on the principle that if a person has made a sincere and successful attempt to live down a conviction and be a law-abiding citizen, he should not have to live in fear of being prejudiced by the unwarranted disclosure of that old conviction.

Rehabilitated persons need not mention their convictions when applying for a job, a mortgage, insurance, hire-purchase, or to join a club or trade union.

For example, after expiry of the relevant rehabilitation period, a convicted thief who was sent to prison need not tell a prospective employer that he has been in prison; and a motorist fined for driving with excess alcohol in his body need not reveal his conviction to an insurance company.

Convictions become spent under the Act at the end of a fixed period from the date of the conviction. A fine, for example, becomes spent after 5 years, a 6 months' prison sentence after 7 years. A sentence of 2½ years or more can never become spent.

When the Act does not apply

There are certain cases when an ex-offender must reveal his criminal record even though, under the provisions of the Act, it is spent.

1. Spent convictions cannot be concealed when applying for a job as a lawyer, doctor, dentist, accountant, vet, nurse, chemist, clerk of court, police or prison officer, traffic warden, probation officer, social worker, teacher, or for any position that entails looking after children. In any of these cases, an ex-offender must reveal any conviction if he is asked to do so.

Details of spent convictions can also be asked about when application is made for certain certificates and licences – for example, a shotgun certificate or gaming licence.

2. Spent convictions can be revealed to the court by the prosecution in the fol-

SPENT BUT NOT FORGOTTEN

Even when a conviction is spent, it can be presented to a court by the prosecutor in any later criminal proceedings against the offender.

lowing instances:

- Criminal proceedings.
- Proceedings before a children's hearing, or on appeal from a hearing's decision.
- Applications for custody, adoption and guardianship of, or access to, children.

But apart from that, spent convictions cannot usually be revealed in other court cases.

A witness's past convictions will be revealed only in exceptional circumstances.

3. A conviction can never be spent if the sentence is more than 2½ years, even if the prisoner is released early on parole or is given remission. For example, a sentence of life imprisonment for murder remains permanently on an offender's record.

When an offender commits a new offence

A conviction that is spent remains spent, even if the offender is convicted of a new offence.

For example, a man sentenced to 6 months' imprisonment will have the sentence spent after 7 years. If he is imprisoned for another 6 months after his 7-year rehabilitation period is up, his first sentence remains spent and need never be revealed. His second sentence will become spent after a further 7 years, after which that sentence, too, need not be revealed.

HOW LONG IT TAKES FOR A CONVICTON TO BE SPENT

Different time limits based on the severity of the sentence imposed

Sentence	Rehabilitation period (from date of conviction)
Prison for over 6 months – 2½ years	10 years*
Prison for up to 6 months	7 years*
Fine	5 years*
Community service order	5 years*
Probation	1 year or the length of the order, whichever is the longer.
Absolute discharge	6 months
Disqualification	When disqualification ends
Offences in the Services	
Cashiering, discharge with ignominy or dismissal with disgrace	10 years*
Dismissal	7 years*
Detention for disciplinary offence	5 years*
Disposals of children and young people	
Detention for over 6 months – 2½ years	5 years
Detention for up to 6 months	3 years
Borstal	7 years
Detention centre	3 years
Discharge of referral by a children's hearing	6 months
Supervision requirement of a children's hearing	1 year or length of the order, whichever is longer
Residential training	

* *These periods are reduced by half if the offender was under 17 at the time of the conviction.*

A second conviction before the first one is spent will extend the rehabilitation period.

For example, a thief imprisoned for 2 years has to wait 10 years before his conviction will be spent. If after only 5 years he gets another 2-year sentence, then neither of his convictions will be spent until 10 years from the date of his second conviction.

If, during a rehabilitation period, a person is convicted of an offence for which there is no rehabilitation period, neither conviction can become spent.

When someone is dismissed

It may happen that an employer takes on a new employee and later discovers that he has a spent conviction. If he then dismisses him, the employee can claim UNFAIR DISMISSAL before an INDUSTRIAL TRIBUNAL and will almost certainly win his case.

When a conviction is disclosed

A person in an official position who wrongly discloses a spent conviction can be prosecuted and may be fined up to £1,000.

Anyone who learns of a person's spent conviction from official records – for example, court, police or government records – by fraud or dishonesty can be imprisoned for up to 6 months and fined up to £2,000.

An ex-offender whose spent conviction is publicly revealed by another person can sue for DEFAMATION, but he will have to show that the other person acted maliciously.

RELIGION

The freedom to choose your beliefs

The people of Britain are free to follow whichever religion they choose, or not to follow any religion at all. The law does not discriminate against anyone on religious grounds. *See:* RELIGIOUS EDUCATION

But the law does not make special allowances for religious beliefs, either. If, for example, a parent refused to give medicine to his child on religious grounds, he could be found guilty of wilful neglect. *See:* CHILD ABUSE

The law imposes some very limited restrictions based on religion:

• The sovereign must be a member of the Church of England and must swear an oath to uphold presbyterian church government in Scotland.
• A person who marries a Roman Catholic cannot succeed to the throne.
• Clergy of the Church of Scotland, the Roman Catholic Church, the Episcopalian Church in Scotland and the Church of England, and certain other Protestant clergy, cannot become members of the House of Commons. *See:* MEMBER OF PARLIAMENT

RELIGIOUS EDUCATION

Providing religious instruction in state schools

Under the Education (Scotland) Act, 1980, an EDUCATION AUTHORITY has the right to continue any custom of having religious observance and providing religious instruction in its schools.

If such a custom exists, the authority is not entitled to put an end to religious observance or instruction in its schools without first putting the question to a poll of local government electors in its area. It can only go ahead if it gets the support of a majority of those voting.

Discrimination is not allowed

By law, every local authority and grant-aided school must be open to pupils of all religious denominations.

Parents are entitled to withdraw their child from religious observance or instruction at such a school. They do not have to give any reason for doing so.

Pupils must not be put at any disadvantage in regard to their other studies because of their religion or because they have been withdrawn from religious observance or instruction.

Safeguards for boarders

If a child is a boarder at a local authority school and his parents want him to attend the religious services of a particular denomination, the child must be given reasonable opportunities to do so.

The same applies if the child's parents want him to have religious instruction outside school hours. The education authority can arrange for this to be given in the school, so long as it does not involve the authority in any expenditure.

Teaching religion

The way in which religious education is taught in schools varies from area to area. The government-sponsored Consultative Committee on the Curriculum has responsibility for advising on the provision of moral and religious education.

Except in denominational schools – for example, Roman Catholic schools – the religion in which the pupils are instructed is Christian but non-denominational.

Some school authorities mix religious education with other social studies such as health education, community affairs and sex education.

Can a teacher opt out?

A teacher may be appointed to teach religious education as one of his subjects. But apart from that, a teacher cannot be ordered to give religious instruction if he does not wish to.

A teacher can now obtain a teaching qualification in religious education. This is one of the changes which have been made to put religious education on the same footing as other subjects.

Another change will make it possible for a pupil to take an examination in Religious Studies for the Scottish Certificate of Education.

REMAND

When a criminal case is delayed

If there is a delay in dealing with an accused person at any stage after he first appears in court charged with a criminal offence, he stays under the court's control by a process known as remanding.

Remands occur in the following situations:

• **Accused persons waiting for trial** For example, when an accused who is to be prosecuted under solemn CRIMINAL PROCEEDINGS is remanded or committed for trial after JUDICIAL EXAMINATION.

In summary criminal proceedings a court, without calling upon the accused to plead guilty or not guilty to any charge, can remand him in custody or on BAIL for up to 7 days (or 21 days in exceptional cases) after his arrest, to allow time for inquiry into the case.

Where a court remands or commits an accused person for trial, and it appears that he is suffering from MENTAL DISORDER, the court can remand him to hospital for examination pending his trial (if it is satisfied that a suitable hospital place is available).

An accused person may also be remanded if the trial is adjourned – that is, postponed – beyond the set date (for example, because one side or the other needs more time to prepare its case) or if the trial lasts more than 1 day.

• **Remand after conviction** A court has the general power to remand a convicted person in custody or on bail, before he is sentenced, for the purpose of making inquiries about the most suitable method of dealing with him. For example, a judge may order a social enquiry report on an offender.

In addition, where the crime for which the offender has been convicted is punishable by imprisonment, and the court considers that an inquiry ought to be made into the offender's physical or mental state before deciding how to deal with him, it can remand him in custody or on bail to enable a medical examination and report to be made.

If the offender is remanded on bail, it will be a condition that he attends for any medical examination required.

An offender can also be remanded after conviction if a sheriff remits the case to the High Court for sentence.

Remanding in custody

Most accused persons who are remanded are freed on BAIL. Those who are detained in custody in a remand centre, in the remand section of a prison or in a prison hospital are subject to prison discipline. *See:* PRISON

But if they have not been convicted, they have privileges that are not accorded to other prisoners. They can:

• Receive visitors every day except Sunday.
• Consult with their lawyers as often as necessary, during reasonable hours, out of the hearing of prison staff.
• Wear their own clothing and have clothing sent in if it is suitable. At most remand establishments, however, the privilege of wearing own clothing is either not practical or discouraged.
• Have meals sent in – including a half-bottle of wine or a pint of beer.
• Receive books and papers – though

PRIVILEGED PRISONER

When an unconvicted prisoner is held on remand, he may be permitted to wear his own clothes, have visitors every day (except Sunday) and have meals sent in. He can consult his own lawyer, doctor or dentist – but always at his own expense.

these are subject to censorship.

- Send or receive an unlimited number of letters, subject to censorship (with the exception of communications to a legal adviser).
- Be treated – at their own expense – by outside doctors or dentists.
- Have a specially furnished cell, and have it cleaned at their own expense.

They cannot be made to perform any work. The majority of remand establishments find it impossible to allocate work to remand inmates because of overcrowding or security considerations. But if they do work, they will receive a prison wage.

They cannot be ordered to shave or have a haircut, unless there is a health risk. But they are not allowed to change their appearance without permission.

Time limit on remand in custody

If an untried prisoner is committed for trial under solemn criminal proceedings and is remanded in custody, he must receive the INDICTMENT within 80 days of his committal. If he does not, he must be released, but he can still be prosecuted for the offence.

If the indictment is served within the 80-day period, the trial must begin within 110 days of the date of committal. Failure to observe this time will result in the immediate release of the accused. No further proceedings can be taken against him for that offence.

Where the prosecution is under summary criminal proceedings and the accused person has been remanded in custody, his trial must begin within 40 days after the bringing of the SUMMARY COMPLAINT in court. If it does not, the accused will be released from custody and no further proceedings can be taken against him for that offence.

These time-limits can be extended in exceptional circumstances – for example, if delay is caused through industrial action by court staff.

REMARRIAGE

When someone is free to remarry

A previously married man or woman can marry again only if:

1 The previous marriage has been ended by DIVORCE.

2 The previous marriage has been declared to be a NULLITY.

3 The previous partner is dead.

A second marriage ceremony while the other spouse is alive and the first marriage still legally binding is bigamous. *See:* BIGAMY

If there has been a divorce, an ex-partner wanting to remarry can do so only after the time limit for appealing the divorce decree (14 days in the sheriff court, 21 days in the Court of Session) has expired and no appeal has been lodged. Only then can a copy of the decree be obtained.

A divorced couple can remarry each other. Each is also free to marry certain relatives of the other. *See:* MARRIAGE

A woman's remarriage automatically brings to an end any court decree for regular payments to her by her ex-husband. But a decree ordering ALIMENT to be paid for children is unaffected by the remarriage of a parent. It can only be varied or cancelled on application to a court.

Once someone who is divorced has remarried, he or she cannot start any action against the former spouse for a periodical allowance. *See:* DIVORCE

RENT ALLOWANCE

Financial help for private tenants

If you rent your home from a landlord *other* than a district or islands council, a new town corporation or the Scottish Special Housing Association, you may be entitled to a housing benefit called rent allowance to help you pay your rent. *See:* HOUSING BENEFITS

Rent allowance is paid by your district or islands council. Application forms can be obtained from the council's housing department.

The rules for calculating the rent in respect of which allowance is payable, and the amount of the allowance, are the same as those that apply to rent rebate – the equivalent benefit paid to council, new town and SSHA tenants. *See:* RENT REBATE

If a rent officer has registered a fair rent for your home, your allowance will be based on that figure.

If you are not a tenant, but merely have a permission, or licence, to occupy your home, you can still claim a rent allowance to help meet the cost of the payments that you make.

If you are buying your home under a rental purchase agreement, you can also claim a rent allowance to help towards your instalments.

Paying rent allowance An allowance is normally paid direct to you at monthly intervals. But weekly payments must often be made if you request this. Your landlord is not told about the allowance.

Claiming supplementary benefit

If you are entitled to SUPPLEMENTARY BENEFIT, you will get an allowance equal to your full rent – less if your rent is considered too high or sums are deducted from it – minus any deductions for non-dependants. *See:* RENT REBATE

When the Department of Health and Social Security is satisfied that you are entitled to supplementary benefit, it will send a certificate to your local housing department stating when benefit became payable. You will then receive your allowance from the housing department without having to make a separate application.

If you are a boarder or a crofter, you will not receive an allowance. Your supplementary benefit will be increased to cover your boarding charge or rent.

If an allowance is refused

If you are refused an allowance, or you think that the allowance you are granted is too low, you can ask for the decision to be reviewed. The procedure is the same as for a rent or rate rebate.

RENT PROTECTION

Having a fair rent registered

Private tenants who are protected against eviction by the Rent (Scotland) Act 1984 are entitled to have a 'fair rent' fixed by a rent officer for the house that they are renting. (To find out which tenants are protected under the Acts, turn to the entry on EVICTION.)

If the landlord does not apply for a fair rent to be registered, the tenant can do so himself. Alternatively, the landlord and tenant can make a joint application.

Tenants of a registered HOUSING ASSOCIATION can also apply to a rent officer to have a fair rent fixed. Normally this will not be necessary, since housing associations are required to register fair rents for their houses as a condition of receiving financial assistance (in the form of housing association grant) from the government.

Tenants of local authorities, new town corporations and the Scottish Special Housing Association are not entitled to apply for a fair rent to be fixed.

The Rent Registration Service

Scotland is split into a number of rent registration areas. In each area there are rent officers – who are full-time officials appointed by the Secretary of State for Scotland – to fix fair rents and to maintain a public register detailing the rent fixed for a particular property. The register can be inspected by members of the public during office hours.

A landlord or tenant can appeal to a local Rent Assessment Committee against a fair rent fixed by a rent officer. The Committee consists of a chairman – who is normally legally qualified – and two other members, drawn from a panel of people appointed by the Secretary of State for Scotland.

Apart from hearing appeals against decisions of rent officers, Rent Assessment Committees fix fair rents for tenants who are entitled to only temporary security under Part VII of the Rent (Scotland) Act – for instance, tenants with resident landlords. A public register of these rents is kept at the Committee's offices.

Applying for a fair rent

An application to a rent officer to fix a fair rent can be made by either the landlord or the tenant, or by both jointly. In practice, over 90 per cent of applications are made by landlords.

An application form (Form RO1) can be obtained from the rent officer. If the house is furnished, ask for Form RO1F, which contains a section requesting information on any furniture or services provided by the landlord.

You must state on your application the rent which you propose should be registered as a fair rent for the house. If you do not do so, your application will be invalid.

If you are not sure about what figure to put down, ask to see the register of fair rents to obtain some idea of the rents which have been fixed for similar properties. Alternatively, you could ask an estate agent for information on local rents. But do not worry that you have put down the wrong figure; it is the job of the rent officer to decide what the fair rent should be and your application will not be prejudiced because your figure is much higher or lower than his.

The figure that you put down should not include any sum for rates payable by the landlord. But an amount payable by the tenant for furniture should be included.

When you have completed and signed the form, send it to the rent officer. If you wish, your solicitor can do this on your behalf.

Fixing a fair rent

Although an application can be made by either the landlord or the tenant, or by both jointly, what follows assumes that the application is made by the landlord.

When the rent officer receives the application, he will write to the tenant. He will enclose a copy of the application, state when he intends to inspect the house – the inspection usually takes place a week after the letter is sent – and ask the tenant to make any representations to him about the application within 14 days.

If the tenant wishes to make representations about the application – he may, for instance, want to object to the rent proposed by the landlord – he should do so on the form provided and return it within the 14 days. He can give his reasons for objecting, but does not have to.

If the tenant does make representations within the 14 days, the rent officer must arrange a meeting between himself, the landlord and the tenant. If no representations are made, the rent officer must still arrange a meeting if he is not satisfied that the rent proposed in the application is a fair rent.

Where no representations are made and the rent officer considers that the proposed rent is fair, he can register that rent without further proceedings. This may happen after the rent officer inspects the house and decides that it is comparable with another house in the street for which he has already registered a similar rent.

Face to face Rent officers arrange meetings between landlords and tenants in about 75 per cent of cases. The purpose of the meeting is to enable the rent officer to listen to the arguments put by the landlord and the tenant and then decide what the fair rent ought to be.

The parties must be given at least 7 days' notice of a meeting, which will take place at the rent registration offices. Each can be represented by anyone he chooses, including a lawyer.

What the rent officer must consider

When deciding what the fair rent should be, the rent officer must consider all the circumstances, *except* the personal circumstances of the landlord or tenant. So he is not concerned with, for example, their financial circumstances – with whether the tenant is on a pension or the landlord is making a loss on the house – or their state of health.

The law requires rent officers to consider in particular:

- Current rents of comparable property in the area – which in practice means registered rents.
- The age and character of the house, and its state of repair.
- Where the house is situated.
- The quantity, quality and condition of any furniture provided. The rent officer will also consider the value of the furniture to the tenant. An antique

table, for example, may be valuable to the landlord, but be no more valuable than an ordinary table to the tenant.

Rent officers usually take into account the capital, or market, value of a house in fixing a fair rent. If the market value is increased because of a housing scarcity in the area, it will be reduced – perhaps by as much as a third or a half – to cancel out that scarcity element.

However, when fixing a rent the rent officer cannot take into account:

1. Any disrepair or defect caused by the failure of the tenant – or a previous tenant – to observe the terms of the lease.

2. Improvements carried out by the tenant – or a previous tenant – otherwise than under the terms of the lease.

3. Any deterioration in furniture caused through ill-treatment by the tenant or someone living in the house.

The rent officer will weigh up all these factors by using his knowledge of property values and comparable rents, by inspecting the property and by listening to representations made by the landlord and the tenant at the meeting that he may arrange.

At this meeting the tenant may tell him about lack of repairs, or dry rot, or a leaking roof, or the noise that comes from a nearby factory. The landlord may counter these statements and introduce information of his own. It is the job of the rent officer to decide what information is relevant and to use it in coming to his decision.

The rent officer does not usually announce at the end of the meeting what the fair rent will be. One tenement block, for example, may have six or eight tenants, each of whom is given the opportunity to have a separate meeting with the landlord. The rent officer will want to listen to them all before forming a total picture of the circumstances that he will have to consider.

When the rent officer decides what the fair rent should be, he will register it as the rent for the house. The figure registered must include any sums payable by the tenant for furniture or services. Any such sum must be noted separately on the register if it amounts to at least 5 per cent of the registered rent. (Furniture may be noted separately even if the sum payable amounts to less than 5 per cent.)

If the landlord pays the rates, this must also be noted in the register.

The rent officer will then inform the landlord and the tenant of his decision. If either objects to it in writing within 28 days, the rent officer must refer the matter to a Rent Assessment Committee. If written objections are received after the 28-day period expires, he may refer the matter to the Committee or first ask the Committee whether it wishes to deal with it.

A certificate of fair rent

If someone intends to build, convert or improve a house and then let it, he can apply to a rent officer for a 'certificate of fair rent' – a document issued by the rent officer stating what the fair rent for the house ought to be.

An application for a certificate can also be made by someone who intends to let a house which is not subject to a tenancy, and which either has no registered rent or a rent which was registered at least three years before.

The application form can be obtained from the rent officer. In it the applicant must state a proposed rent.

A certificate of fair rent will be issued if the rent officer is satisfied that he has sufficient information – for example, about the nature of the improvements that are to be carried out – and that the proposed rent is a fair one.

If he is not satisfied with the rent, he will call a meeting with the applicant to discuss it. He will then serve a letter of intent on the applicant stating the rent he proposes to put in the certificate. The applicant has 14 days to appeal against the rent to a Rent Assessment Committee.

Letting the house If someone obtains a certificate of fair rent and applies to have a fair rent registered for the house within three years of the date on the certificate, the usual procedure does not apply.

If the rent officer is satisfied that the proposed works have been carried out, or that the condition of the house has not changed, he will register the rent set out in the certificate. If he is not satisfied, he will inform the applicant of his right to have the matter referred to a Rent Assessment Committee.

However, any rent that is registered is provisional only. If the rent officer is not notified within a month that a tenancy has been granted, he can cancel the registration. Alternatively, he can extend the time allowed – by, for example, allowing another month for a tenant to be found – before cancelling. The notification must be done on a form obtainable from the rent officer.

The job of the Rent Assessment Committee

The procedure for referrals to a Rent Assessment Committee depends on whether or not the application to fix a fair rent is supported by a certificate of fair rent.

No certificate of fair rent Once the rent officer has referred the disputed rent to the Committee, or it has agreed to consider it, the Committee will give both parties 14 days in which to make written representations or request a hearing. It will also make whatever inquiries it thinks fit, including carrying out an inspection of the house.

If a hearing is requested by either the landlord or the tenant, the Committee will give him the opportunity to put his case. He may do so in person or through a representative – who can be a lawyer.

The Committee will then either confirm the rent fixed by the rent officer or fix a different figure – which may be *higher* or lower than that fixed by the rent officer.

If the rent is confirmed, the rent officer will note that in the register. If it is changed, he will register the new figure as the fair rent.

Certificate of fair rent Once the rent officer has referred the dispute to the Committee, or it has agreed to deal with it, the Committee will give the applicant the opportunity to make written representations or to request a hearing. The applicant can appear in person to put his case or can do so through a representative.

If the Committee agrees with the rent officer that the proposed works have not been carried out, or that the condition of the house is not the same as it was when the certificate was granted, it will order the rent officer to refuse the application for registration. But if the Committee decides that the necessary works have been carried out, or that the house is in the same condition, it will order the rent officer to register the rent contained in the certificate.

HOW MUCH YOU CAN BE ASKED TO PAY

If a fair rent is registered for your house and it is higher than the rent you are paying, you may not have to pay the whole increase at once.

The maximum increase that a landlord can charge in each 12-month period following registration is £104 (£2 a week) or 25 per cent of your *present* rent, whichever is higher. You cannot be charged more than the fair rent if the maximum permitted increase would result in your paying more than that.

Example 1
You rent a 3-apartment, top-floor flat in a tenement block in central Edinburgh. It has a kitchen/livingroom, 2 bedrooms and a bathroom. Although it has not been improved, it is in reasonable condition.

You have been paying rent of £500 p.a. The rent officer registers a fair rent of £625 p.a.

In the 12 months following registration you can be asked to pay only an extra £104, or 25 per cent of your present rent (£500), whichever is higher. Since 25 per cent of £500 equals £125, you must pay that – taking your rent in the first year to £625, the fair rent limit. You cannot therefore be asked to pay any more during the next two years unless the rent officer fixes a higher rent because of a change of circumstances.

Example 2
The landlord improves your flat and asks for a fair rent to be registered for the first time. You have been paying a rent of £500 p.a. but the rent officer registers a rent of £800.

In the first 12-month period you will have to pay an increase of £125 (25 per cent of your present rent of £500). Your rent will then be £625.

In the second 12-month period you will again have to pay an increase of £104 or 25 per cent of your present rent, whichever is higher. Your present rent is now £625 and 25 per cent of that is £156.25. You will therefore have to pay an additional £156.25 – taking your annual rent to £781.25.

In the third 12-month period you could in theory again be asked to pay an extra £104 or 25 per cent of your present rent, whichever would be higher. Your present rent is £781.25 and 25 per cent of that would be £195.31. But since the fair rent is £800, you can only be asked to pay an increase of £18.75, to take your rent up to that level.

If a higher fair rent is registered at the end of the three years, the whole process will begin again.

Example 3
The landlord asks for a fair rent to be fixed for your flat.

The rent officer registers a rent of £625 per annum. You pay the first 12 months' increase of £125, taking your rent to the fair rent limit.

Six months later the landlord has carried out improvements to your flat and asks the rent officer to register a higher rent because of the change of circumstances. The rent officer registers a rent of £800 per annum.

Since you have already paid the maximum increase permitted in that 12-month period, you cannot be asked to pay any part of the new increase for another 6 months. You will then have to pay the extra rent – subject, of course, to the maximum increase permitted for the following 12 months.

The effect of registration

Once a fair rent has been registered, an application to fix a new rent will not normally be considered during the 3 years following the date of registration by the rent officer (or, where a Rent Assessment Committee has confirmed the rent fixed by the rent officer, the date on which the confirmation is noted in the register).

There are three situations in which a rent officer will consider an application to fix a new rent before the 3-year period has expired:

1. Circumstances have changed since the rent was fixed – for instance, there has been a change in the condition of the house, the terms of the tenancy or the quantity or condition of any furniture (deterioration due to wear and tear is excluded).

If there has been such a change, the landlord or the tenant can apply for a new rent to be registered. Where the tenancy has ended and the landlord intends to carry out improvements or other works, he can also apply for a certificate of fair rent.

New rents are usually requested by landlords after they have carried out improvement or upgrading work. But tenants may also ask for a new, lower rent to be fixed if, for instance, part of the house has become uninhabitable through fire or some other disaster.

An application is dealt with in the same way as the original one. The rent officer can confirm the original rent or register a new one. A new, 3-year period starts to run from the date specified by the rent officer.

2. The landlord and tenant can make a joint application within the 3-year period for a new rent to be fixed. But it is unlikely that a rent officer would fix a different rent unless there had been a change of circumstances.

3. The landlord can apply for a new rent to be fixed in the 3 months before the 3-year period expires. But if the rent officer fixes a new rent, it cannot take effect until that period expires.

Cancelling a fair rent

A landlord and tenant can enter into a written agreement to increase the rent payable. They can then make a joint application to the rent officer to have any existing registered rent cancelled. The rent officer cannot consider the application until the existing 3-year period has expired.

If the rent officer is satisfied that the amount agreed on by the landlord and tenant is a fair rent, he will cancel the registration. Cancellation does not prevent another fair rent being fixed in the future.

When letting ends If the landlord stops letting the house, he can apply to the rent officer for the registered rent to be cancelled. The 3-year period must first have expired.

Phasing in rent increases

Once a fair rent is registered, the full amount of any increase over the previous rent may not have to be paid at once. The maximum increase that the landlord can charge in each 12-month period from the date of registration is, in 1984, £104 (£2 a week), or 25 per cent of the rent – excluding rates and service charges – payable immediately before the start of each 12-month period, whichever is higher.

If the maximum increase allowed in a 12-month period would result in the rent being more than the fair rent, then only the fair rent can be charged.

Because of the limit on annual increases, it may take a number of years for the rent paid to reach the fair rent level – perhaps more than the 3 years after which the landlord can apply for a new rent to be fixed. But even if a new rent is fixed after 3 years, the limit on the amount of increase in a 12-month period still applies.

Notice of increase The landlord must serve a notice of increase on the tenant. In it he must state what the increase in rent is to be and the date from which it is payable (this cannot be more than 4 weeks before the notice is served).

The notice can detail what the increases are to be in subsequent years to bring the rent up to the fair rent. If it does not, a new notice of increase must be served at the beginning of each 12-month period.

Service charges If the fair rent includes a charge for services that amounts to at least 5 per cent of the fair rent (see above), the landlord can recover that amount *in addition to* the permitted maximum increase.

If the tenancy agreement allows the landlord to vary the service charge – for example, to pay for the increased cost of gas or electricity – the landlord can increase the service charge and still recover it in addition to the permitted maximum increase.

THE RENT REGISTRATION AREAS

You can contact a rent officer who deals with your area at the following addresses.

If you live in the Western Isles or in the Central, Dumfries and Galloway or Strathclyde Regions, the address is: St Andrew House, 141 West Nile Street, GLASGOW G12RN (telephone 041-332 6981-9).

If you live in the Borders or Lothian Regions, the address is: 2 St Andrew Square, EDINBURGH EH22BD (telephone 031-557 0555).

If you live in the Fife or Tayside Regions, the address is: 132 Seagate, DUNDEE DD12HB (telephone 0382 28111).

If you live in Orkney or Shetland, or in the Grampian or Highland Regions, the address is: 9 Thistle Street, ABERDEEN AB1 1XJ (telephone 0224 25288).

For more information about rent increases, see page 571.

Part VII rents

Someone who is entitled to seek temporary security of tenure under Part VII of the Rent (Scotland) Act – for instance, a tenant with a resident landlord – can ask a Rent Assessment Committee to fix a fair rent for the house. (For information on who is entitled to seek temporary security, see EVICTION.)

The Committee will give both parties the opportunity to present their case, either in person or in writing. It will then decide whether to approve, reduce or increase the existing rent, or to dismiss the application. If it fixes a rent, this will be noted in a public register kept at the Committee's offices. There is no phasing of the increase.

Once a fair rent is registered, an application to increase it cannot be made for at least 3 years unless there has been a change of circumstances. But the tenant may be evicted before the 3-year period expires. *See:* EVICTION

When a new tenant moves in

A fair rent is related to the house, not the tenant, and cannot normally be altered for 3 years unless there has been a change of circumstances. So if a new tenant moves in during that period, the landlord must charge him the same rent as the old tenant would have paid had he remained. A new tenant is not a relevant change of circumstance which would allow the landlord to apply for a new fair rent.

Paying more than the fair rent

If a tenant is charged more than the fair rent, he is legally entitled to recover the excess from the landlord. He is also entitled to recover any amount charged above the maximum permitted increase for a 12-month period.

The tenant has 2 years from the date of payment in which to recover the excess. He can do so by deducting it from his rent or by taking legal proceedings.

Tenants who have had fair rents fixed under Part VII of the Rent (Scotland) Act are also entitled to recover any excess rent charged. In this case the landlord commits an offence and can be fined up to £400 or imprisoned for up to 6 months, or both. *See:* RENT ALLOWANCE; RENT REBATE

RENT REBATE

Financial help for council tenants

If you rent your home from a district or islands council, a new town corporation or the Scottish Special Housing Association, you may be entitled to a housing benefit called rent rebate to reduce the rent that you pay. *See:* HOUSING BENEFITS

Rent rebates are administered by these housing authorities. You can obtain an application form by getting in touch with the one you rent from.

To obtain a rebate, you do not have to be legally obliged to pay the rent yourself. It is enough if you *actually* pay the rent and are either:

- The husband, wife or cohabitee of the person responsible for paying it; or
- Some other person – for instance, a grown-up child – whom the authority considers it reasonable to treat as eligible for a rent rebate.

Your right to a rebate

Your entitlement to a rebate, and its amount, depend on a number of factors:

1. The weekly needs of yourself and your family. These are worked out according to a scale fixed by law. The amount depends on age, marital status, number of dependent children and whether or not you are handicapped.

In 1984 the needs allowances were as follows:

Single person £43.05
Single person with dependent child £63.50
Single handicapped person £48.00
Single handicapped person with dependent child £68.45
Married or unmarried couple £63.50
Married or unmarried couple, one of whom is handicapped £68.45
Married or unmarried couple, both of whom are handicapped £70.80
Each dependent child £11.90
Age addition if applicant or partner 65 or over (60 if a woman) 75p

2. The weekly income of yourself and your partner (including a cohabitee). This is normally worked out by estimating your average weekly earnings in the five weeks before you claim rebate (two months if you are paid monthly).

If you are receiving social security benefits – for instance, unemployment benefit, child benefit or invalidity pension – these will normally be taken into account in full, as income.

Any ALIMENT paid for a dependent child – for example, payments made by a former spouse – is counted as part of your income.

However, certain payments will be disregarded when your income is being calculated. They include:

- The first £17.45 of your earnings and the first £5 of your partner's earnings – or vice versa if your partner's earnings are greater than yours.
- ATTENDANCE ALLOWANCE, and constant attendance allowance payable with DISABLEMENT BENEFIT, with WORKMEN'S COMPENSATION and also with a war disablement pension.
- MOBILITY ALLOWANCE.
- Any SUPPLEMENTARY BENEFIT received.
- Any payments made by dependent children.
- Any payments made by non-dependants living in your household – for instance, an adult child or lodger.
- The first £4 of any industrial disablement pension, industrial death benefit, war disablement pension, war widow's pension, workmen's compensation or disability payment.

If you receive more than one of these payments, a total of £4 only will be disregarded.

- Aliment or periodical allowance paid by either partner to a child or former spouse. *See:* DIVORCE
- A FOSTERING allowance – to the extent that it exceeds £11.90.
- Interest on National Savings Certificates.

3. The amount of rent you pay. For the purpose of calculating a rebate, 'rent' includes:

- Payments made by people who are not tenants but have a permission or LICENCE TO OCCUPY their home – for example, homeless people who are given temporary accommodation. *See:* HOMELESSNESS
- Payments for services and other facilities provided – including furniture.

But it does not include sums paid for rates or board. Deductions are also made for fuel and service charges. If the applicant is a grant-aided student, the rent on which rebate is calculated is reduced by £14.70.

4. Whether or not you have non-dependants – for instance, a parent or adult child – living in your household.

Calculating a rent rebate

A rent rebate is calculated in the following way (except for supplementary benefit claimants):

- Assume you pay your landlord, say, £18 a week. Make any necessary deductions – such as weekly rates of, say, £6. That leaves a figure of £12.
- Calculate 60 per cent of £12 – £7.20.
- Deduct the following sums for any non-dependants in the household (excluding children under 18, students supported by you and those receiving training allowances under the Youth Training Scheme). A married or unmarried couple are treated as one person for this purpose. (From November, 1984, a deduction will be made for 16–17 year-olds in full-time work.)

Aged 18 to 64 (59 if a woman)................................ £6.15
Aged 65 or over (60 or over if a woman) £2.20
Aged 21 or over and receiving supplementary benefit............ £2.20

Assume that, for example, a parent over pensionable age lives with you. You then deduct £2.20 from £7.20 – £5.

- If your weekly net income (see above) is the same as your needs allowance, your weekly rebate is £5.
- If your weekly net income is more than the needs allowance, your weekly rebate is £5 *minus* 26 per cent (29 per cent from November, 1984) of the difference between income and allowance.
- If your weekly net income is less than the needs allowance, and either you or your partner is of pensionable age, your weekly rebate is £5 *plus* 50 per cent of the difference between income and allowance.

If both you and your partner are below pensionable age, your weekly rebate is £5 plus 25 per cent of the difference between income and allowance.

If the rebate amounts to less than 20p (50p from November, 1984, except for those whose income is below their needs allowance), it will not be paid.

How rebate is paid Your rebate will take the form of a reduction in your weekly rent.

Receiving supplementary benefit

If you are entitled to SUPPLEMENTARY BENEFIT, you will get a rebate equal to the full cost of your rent (excluding rates and charges for fuel or services), less any deductions made for non-dependants who are living in the house.

When the Department of Health and Social Security is satisfied that you are entitled to supplementary benefit, it will send a certificate to your local housing department stating when benefit became payable. You will then be notified about your rebate by the housing department without having to make a separate application.

If you are a boarder and you are receiving supplementary benefit, your rent will be met by the DHSS.

If a rebate is refused

If you are refused a rebate, or you think that the rebate you are granted is too low, you can ask for the decision to be reviewed by the housing authority. But you have no right to appeal to a court or tribunal.

You are entitled to receive on request a written statement showing how your entitlement or lack of entitlement to benefit has been calculated. This should normally be sent within 14 days of your request.

If you disagree with the authority's decision, write to it within 6 weeks of the decision (or, if you ask for one, the receipt of a written statement). The authority must then review its decision.

If the authority refuses to change its decision, you can make a written request for a further review by a board of at least 3 housing authority members (or at least 2, if you agree). You should make your request within 28 days of receiving the authority's decision on your original request for a review. Late requests may be heard at the authority's discretion.

The board must, if possible, hold a hearing within 6 weeks of receiving your request. You are entitled to be present, to be heard and to be represented by anyone you choose. Alternatively, you can make written representations to the committee. *See:* COUNCIL TENANCY; OMBUDSMEN; RATES; RENT ALLOWANCE

REPAIRS

Your right to have a repair done properly

If you take something to be repaired, or if a repairer calls to mend something in your home, you are entitled to expect that professional care and skill will be used in doing so. The repairer must also use only materials that are fit for the purpose. If he fails in either respect, you can sue him (or his employer) for breach of contract and claim:

- The loss in value of the goods caused by the defects for which he is responsible.
- The cost of having the defects put right by someone else.
- Compensation for your loss of use of the goods while the defects are being put right.
- The cost of any damage done to other property by the defects.
- Compensation for any injury caused.

When a repairer makes a promise

Unless the repairer commits himself to a definite time for completing the repair, the law says only that he must do so within a 'reasonable' time. But if you persuade him to give you a definite time, he must keep his word. If he does not, he is in breach of his contract and you may be able to obtain DAMAGES.

That applies also to any other promise he makes about what he will do and what materials he will use. If he misleads you deliberately or recklessly – either personally, by notices, or in an advertisement – he can be prosecuted under the TRADE DESCRIPTIONS Act.

Repairers sometimes seek to limit their liability through exemption clauses printed in receipts, quotations or notices on their premises. These are not necessarily effective in law. *See:* UNFAIR CONTRACT

Asking for a quotation

When leaving goods for repair, ask about the cost if no price list is displayed. Similarly, if you are asking a repairer to call at your home, find out how much he will charge. There may be a high minimum price, however small the repair.

TV repairers, for example, often make a minimum charge for a call, regardless of whether any repairs need to be done. If the charge to be made for the repair is likely to be substantial, you should ask for an estimate in writing. *See:* QUOTATION

If no price has been agreed at the outset, the repairer is entitled to charge a 'reasonable' price. If you do not pay what he asks, he is legally entitled to keep hold of your property, if it is in his workshop or premises, until you do. *See:* LIEN

Even when you think you are being overcharged, you must pay his price if you want your property back. Tell him, however, that you are paying 'under protest' to keep open your right to dispute the bill.

As soon as you get home, write to the repairer confirming that you paid under protest to get your property back and asking him to refund the amount of overcharge. Keep a copy of your letter.

Safe custody

You can sue a repairer for the loss of, or damage to, any of your property entrusted to him. But unless you can prove that he was negligent, he is not liable. For example, if your property is stolen from his premises in spite of normal security precautions, he does not have to pay you compensation – unless it can be proved that it was stolen by one of his employees.

If you leave for repair anything of high value, it is always advisable to arrange your own temporary insurance.

SETTLING, FOR THE TIME BEING

Even when you disagree with a repairer's charge, you must pay if you want your property back. Make sure he knows you disagree.

REPORTER

An official who deals with children in trouble

Every regional and islands council appoints an officer called the Reporter to the Children's Panel. The Reporter will have a variable number of depute and assistant reporters, depending on the workload. Most of them are qualified in law or in social work. *See:* CHILDREN'S PANEL

Although the Reporter is appointed by the council, he can only be dismissed, or be required to resign, with the consent of the Secretary of State for Scotland.

What a reporter does

The main function of a reporter is to receive information from anyone – but mostly from the police and social workers – about children who have committed offences or are otherwise in some kind of trouble. He considers the information and may make further inquiries – for example, at the child's school. Then he makes up his mind whether the child is likely to be in need of 'compulsory measures of care'. If so, he arranges for a CHILDREN'S HEARING to meet.

The child and parents are called before the hearing and an informal discussion takes place. The members of the hearing then decide what measures, if any, should be applied to the child. The reporter has the task of making notes of the discussion and recording the decision.

If there is a dispute as to whether the facts alleged about the child are really true, it is up to the reporter to present the information he has to the sheriff. He will decide the matter, normally after hearing both sides.

If the child or parents appeal to the sheriff against the decision of the hearing, it is the reporter who defends the decision in court.

In minor cases, particularly those in which a child is alleged to have committed an offence, some reporters will by letter or at an interview point out to the parents and child the consequences of such behaviour, if the allegation is true. The child will not be referred to a hearing. Sometimes, with the agreement of the family, reporters will arrange for a social worker to keep in touch with the child, and advise or arrange for him or her to take up some supervised activities.

RESET

Receiving dishonestly obtained goods

Anyone who receives goods obtained by theft, robbery, fraud or embezzlement – with the intention of keeping them from their true owner – is guilty of the crime of reset.

Reset can only be committed by someone who was not a party to the original obtaining of the goods. For example, a thief and anyone who aids and abets him cannot be found guilty of resetting the goods they have stolen. They can only be prosecuted for the crime of theft. *See:* AIDING AND ABETTING

To obtain a conviction for reset, the prosecution must prove that the accused person knew the goods had been obtained dishonestly. It is not enough that the accused merely suspected this to be so.

However, the prosecution need not prove that the accused had been directly informed that the goods were, for instance, stolen. Guilty knowledge can be inferred by the court from the circumstances in which the goods were received. A man who buys a £50 watch for £5 from a stranger in a public house should realise that the goods were probably stolen. He will be convicted of reset unless he can give a satisfactory explanation for the cheapness of the watch.

The prosecution must also prove that the accused person received the goods with the intention of keeping them from the true owner. It is not reset to receive dishonestly obtained goods with the intention of returning them to their owner. But if the receiver later decides to keep them, he is guilty of reset.

Similarly, if someone receives goods in good faith and later keeps them after learning they were dishonestly obtained, he is guilty of reset.

An accused person need not have had physical possession of the goods. Someone who arranges for a thief to sell stolen goods to someone else is guilty of reset even if he never laid a finger on the goods in question. This is because by arranging the deal he has connived at the stolen goods being kept from their true owner.

If the accused has had physical possession of the goods, he need not have retained them for any length of time. Any period of retention – even if only for an instant – is enough. The mere act of receiving the goods completes the crime. *See:* FRAUD; ROBBERY; THEFT

The husband and wife rule

A wife who receives or conceals goods dishonestly obtained by her husband is in certain circumstances exempt from the law of reset.

If the goods were brought home by the husband, and were concealed by the wife in order to protect him from detection or punishment, she will not be guilty of reset. The law takes the view that it would be unfair to expect a wife to betray her husband.

However, if she takes an active part in disposing of the goods – for example, by helping her husband to sell them – she cannot claim the privilege of exemption.

The privilege of exemption is not available to a husband.

RESIGNATION

When an employee decides to leave his job

An employee may resign from his job when he chooses, for any reason and no matter how inconvenient his departure may be to his employer. The employer is obliged to accept the resignation, although he is entitled to try to persuade the employee to withdraw it by any legal means – for example, by offering more money.

If the employee has been in the job for 1 month or more, he must give at least 1 week's NOTICE of his intention to leave. This does not apply to certain part-time workers or to those who normally work abroad. However, any employee may be required to give notice – perhaps more than a week – under the terms of his EMPLOYMENT CONTRACT. *See:* PART-TIME WORKER

An employee who resigns may be required to work through his notice period. But if his present employer chooses instead to give him payment in lieu of notice, the employee cannot insist upon continuing work.

An employee who fails to observe the notice period laid down by law or by his contract can be sued for breach of contract. But in cases of dispute his employer is more likely to refuse to supply him with a REFERENCE and may also hold back any wages or holiday pay owed, challenging the employee to sue. (Refusal to pay wages due is a breach of contract by the employer.)

Notice of resignation does not have to be in writing to be valid unless that is required by the contract. But it is in the employee's interests to write a letter and keep a copy, to avoid confusion.

An employee who resigns cannot normally claim a REDUNDANCY payment or compensation for UNFAIR DISMISSAL from an industrial tribunal. But if an employee leaves because his employer has committed a serious breach of the contract – for example, by failing to pay wages or by radically altering the employee's job without his agreement – he may be treated as constructively dismissed and be able to claim compensation. *See:* DISMISSAL

An employee who leaves because his employer commits a serious breach of contract does not have to give any

NO ARGUMENT

An employer is not entitled to refuse to accept an employee's resignation under any circumstances – although he can try to persuade him to stay in his employment. If the employee insists, however, the employer must let him go without further delay or inconvenience.

notice. But whether or not he does, he should write his employer a letter, listing the actions of the employer that he regards as breaking the contract. The letter should state clearly that he is leaving because of his employer's behaviour.

An employee who resigns without having another job to go to may lose UNEMPLOYMENT BENEFIT for up to 6 weeks.

RESTAURANT

How the law protects you when you eat out

Anyone who runs a restaurant, café, staff canteen, private club or public house serving meals is bound by the same rules of hygiene and fitness for consumption as a shopkeeper who sells FOOD. The meal, and any drinks served with it, must be of the nature, substance and quality demanded by the customer.

In addition, there are detailed legal rules about displaying prices in eating places that are open to the public at large. There must be an easily read menu with prices that a customer can see before entering. In self-service or take-away restaurants, the prices must be displayed so that they can be seen from the place where the customer chooses his food.

In licensed restaurants it is not necessary to show the full wine list in the same way. But the proprietor is required to provide an abridged wine list giving prices for the wines that are supplied, up to a maximum of six.

All prices must include value added tax. If there is a minimum price, a cover charge or a service charge, they must be mentioned at least as prominently as the price of food.

Failure to display prices properly is a criminal offence. The maximum penalty is a fine of £2,000 if prosecuted under summary proceedings or an unlimited fine if prosecuted under solemn proceedings.

Is there enough?

No minimum quantities are laid down by law for portions of food served. But if the menu states, for example, that steaks weigh 6 oz. or 8 oz., you are entitled to expect one that was of that weight before being cooked. Beer or lager must be sold in the quantity stated – usually a bottle, half pint or a pint.

Any wine served in a container must be served in a sealed bottle or in an open carafe of 25cl., 50cl., 75cl., or 1 litre. If you ask, you must be told which, either by reference to the wine list or a notice in the restaurant or by a mark on the carafe. It is an offence not to provide the information.

However, wine can also be sold by the glass, which is an unspecified amount.

Sending back a meal

If you think that what is served is inedible, undrinkable, not what you ordered or obviously inadequate, complain to the manager. Most restaurants will try to put the matter right.

But if you obtain no satisfaction, you are entitled to reject the meal and refuse to pay for it.

If you eat the meal, you can still complain about its quality, but you must pay for what you have had.

A firm booking for a table creates a contract between you and the restaurant. If the table you book is not available when you turn up, you can claim for breach of contract. Similarly, if you fail to turn up, the restaurant can sue you for any loss it incurs.

Food poisoning

If you pay for a meal that gives you food poisoning, you can claim DAMAGES from the restaurant for breach of contract. But if you entertained guests and they were also poisoned, they would have to show NEGLIGENCE on the part of the restaurant to be entitled to damages.

If you report the food poisoning to the local environmental health department, and the restaurant is successfully prosecuted under the Food and Drugs (Scotland) Act, the court can order it to pay you compensation. *See:* CRIMINAL COMPENSATION ORDER

RESTRAINT ON EMPLOYMENT

When your freedom to choose a job is restricted

As a general rule, everyone is free to take up whatever employment is available to him. But employers are entitled to protect themselves against unfair competition – and some may attempt to do so by placing legally binding restrictions on the future employment of their staff.

An employer may decide to include a clause in your EMPLOYMENT CONTRACT, or ask you to sign a separate agreement, obliging you not to go to work for a rival company, nor to do similar work in a certain locality.

Enforcing a restraint

If an employee accepts a contractual condition that restricts his future employment, but ignores it after he leaves, his former employer can apply to court for an INTERDICT ordering him not to break the contract or to cease breaking it. Failing to obey an interdict is CONTEMPT OF COURT and any employee who does so risks being fined or even imprisoned.

However, the courts do not uphold restraints on employment unless they consider them reasonable and in the public interest. It is therefore up to the employer to prove that a restraint is:

- Necessary to protect legitimate business interests.
- Not an unfair limitation on the employee's chances of making a living.
- Not against the public interest – for example, the restraint should not stop the employee from making a better product or providing a better service than his employer is willing to offer.

An employee's seniority and business knowledge – especially his access to private information that could be valuable to a competing company – are taken into account in judging whether a restraint is fair. For example, a court may consider it unreasonable to expect a salesman not to join a competing company for 2 years after leaving his old employment – but reasonable to put the same ban on a managing director.

Refusing to sign

Someone who cannot get the job he wants without agreeing to a restraint clause must decide for himself whether the limitation is fair. If he refuses to sign, and the job goes to someone else who does, he has no legal remedy.

But if someone who is already in employment loses his job because he refuses to agree to a restraint on future employment, he may well succeed in a

THE TRAINEE WHO WANTED TO WORK FOR A RIVAL

Even a world-wide restriction can sometimes be reasonable.

Mr Dickinson worked as a trainee manager for Bluebell Apparel Ltd., who made jeans. He agreed not to make any unauthorised disclosure of any trade secrets and, for 2 years after the end of his employment, not to work for any company in competition with Bluebell Apparel.

Mr Dickinson told his employers that he was going to leave to take up a job with Levi Strauss and Co., who were trade rivals of Bluebell Apparel.

Bluebell Apparel sought an interdict to restrain him from taking up a job with Levi Strauss either in the UK or elsewhere in the world, and from disclosing trade secrets he had learned from Bluebell Apparel.

The Court of Session had to decide whether the agreement was necessary to protect Bluebell Apparel's interests and whether it was reasonable.

DECISION

The Court of Session held that since the activities of Bluebell Apparel were world-wide, the restriction was not unreasonable.

Nor was it unreasonable to prevent Mr Dickinson from doing any work for Levi Strauss for the short period of the restriction.

The interdict was granted and Mr Dickinson was forbidden to work for the rival company for 2 years.

THE SALESMAN WHO REFUSED WHEN 86 OTHERS AGREED

When an employer can prove that a restraint on future employment is vital – and nearly all his staff agree – sacking a man who refuses to sign a restrictive clause is justified.

Mr Irwin, a salesman for an electrical components company, refused to sign a covenant restricting him from operating in competition with the company for 1 year after leaving it.

Ex-employees had already 'poached' some business and the sales force was losing commission earnings. For that reason only 4 of the 90-strong sales force refused to sign.

Mr Irwin was dismissed, but an industrial tribunal ruled that he had been unfairly dismissed. The company appealed.

The National Industrial Relations Court (the appeal body at the time) had to decide whether the restraint covenant was necessary and fair, and whether refusal to sign it was sufficient ground for dismissal.

DECISION

The Court found that the covenant was fair, and that the potential effect on the company of Mr Irwin's refusal to sign it was sufficiently substantial to make his dismissal fair.

claim of UNFAIR DISMISSAL before an industrial tribunal.

In those circumstances, a tribunal would judge the necessity and fairness of a restraint in the same way as a court.

RETAILER'S LIABILITY

The liability of people who sell to the public

When DEFECTIVE GOODS are sold, the retailer will be liable for any loss or damage that the purchaser suffers as a result. This is so where the goods were not of the appropriate quality, even though the retailer gave no express guarantee about their state.

The purchaser may be able to get his MONEY BACK or have the goods repaired. But that will not cover all his losses if he has been injured by the goods. He will be able to claim DAMAGES for that. *See:* PERSONAL INJURY

The retailer will be liable even though he was not at fault. He cannot, for example, escape liability by showing that the defect was a hidden flaw inside a piece of metal and that he could not have found out what was wrong. Nor is it possible for him to escape liability by showing that the manufacturer was at fault.

The retailer may be able to recover from his supplier what he had to pay in damages to someone who purchased from him. The extent of his right to do so will depend on the nature of the agreement with the supplier.

RETIREMENT PENSION

Benefit paid to people when they reach pensionable age

If you have paid the correct amount of NATIONAL INSURANCE CONTRIBUTIONS, you are entitled to a retirement pension from the state when you reach retirement age – that is, 65 for a man and 60 for a woman.

For a retirement pension to be paid to you, you must have retired, or be treated as having retired, from regular employment. This does not apply once you reach 70 (65 if a woman).

You do not have to give up work completely to be treated as having retired. You can carry on with part-time paid work provided that your weekly earnings, after deducting allowable expenses, are not more than the 'earnings rule' limit (£65 in 1983–4).

You will still be treated as retired if you earn more than that limit only occasionally. If not, you can also be treated as retired if you work only occasionally or for not more than 12 hours a week, or your work is consistent with retirement.

If you are retired, or treated as retired, the earnings rule operates until you are 70 (65 if a woman). Your basic pension will be reduced if your weekly earnings are more than £65 a week.

How a pension is worked out

The pension you receive may be made up of:

- Flat-rate basic pension.
- Earnings-related additional pension or occupational pension, or both.
- Increase for a wife who is not entitled to a pension herself.
- Increase for any children – payable if you get, or are entitled to, CHILD BENEFIT for them.
- An invalidity addition – payable if you were entitled to an invalidity allowance just before reaching 65 (60 if a woman).
- GRADUATED PENSION.
- Extra pension earned by deferring or cancelling retirement.

- An age addition (25p), payable when you reach the age of 80.

The basic pension is provided by the state. The additional pension is also provided by the state for people who are not contracted out of the state scheme. People who are contracted out because they are members of a private OCCUPATIONAL PENSION scheme must receive a minimum amount of pension from that scheme.

Basic pension

The full basic retirement pension – £34.05 for a single person and £54.50 for a married couple (in 1983–4) – is only payable to someone who satisfies the contribution conditions. To qualify, you must have:

- Paid enough contributions of any class (Classes 1, 2 or 3) in any one tax year since April 6, 1975, for that to be a 'qualifying year'. Alternatively, you must have paid 50 flat-rate contributions at any time *before* April 6, 1975.
- Completed the necessary number of qualifying years – about 9/10ths of the years of your working life.

Qualifying years A qualifying year is one in which you have paid, or been credited with, Class 1 contributions on earnings of at least 52 times the weekly LOWER EARNINGS LIMIT (£34 in 1984–5) or 52 Class 2 (self-employed) or Class 3 (voluntary) contributions.

Your working life is normally the period from the start of the tax year in which you become 16 to the end of the tax year in which you become 64 (59 if a woman).

But if you were already paying contributions towards a pension when the national insurance scheme started on July 5, 1948, the period of your working life starts from the beginning of the tax year in which you last entered insurance, or from April 6, 1936, whichever is later. If you were over 16 at July 5, 1948, but did not start to pay contributions until later, your working life starts from April 6, 1948.

Calculating your qualifying years To obtain the full basic pension, you must have completed the necessary number of qualifying years. The following table shows how this is worked out.

Length of working life	Qualifying years needed
41 years or more	Length of working life minus 5 years
31–40 years	Length of working life minus 4 years
21–30 years	Length of working life minus 3 years
11–20 years	Length of working life minus 2 years

For example, if your working life is 47 years, you deduct 5 years, which means you need 42 years' contributions (paid or credited) to qualify for a basic pension at the full rate.

Reduced pension If you do not have enough qualifying years to obtain the full basic pension, you can get a proportionately reduced pension. A table telling you how much you get is contained in leaflet NP 32, available from your local social security office. But if you have less than a quarter of the number of qualifying years needed for the full pension, you will get no pension at all.

For example, if your working life is 47 years, you deduct 5 years, which means that you need 42 qualifying years for the full pension. To get any pension at all, you need at least 11 qualifying years.

Additional retirement pension

The additional retirement pension is earnings-related. This means that the more you earned when you were working, the higher your pension will be. It is paid in addition to the flat-rate pension, and you can receive it even if you are not entitled to full basic pension, or are entitled to only a reduced one.

To qualify, you must have paid Class 1 (employed person's) national insurance contributions since April, 1978. If you have *also* been self-employed in any year, your Class 2 contributions will count.

If you are a member of an occupational pension scheme that is contracted out of the additional part of the state scheme, you do not receive the additional pension. Instead you are entitled to a guaranteed minimum pension from your scheme, approximately equal to

HOW THE EARNINGS RULE AFFECTS A PENSION

If you receive your basic rate pension when you reach 65 – 60 for a woman – but continue to work, it will be reduced if you earn more than £65 (in 1983–4). This is known as the 'earnings rule'.

Under the rule, your basic pension (including dependants' increases and invalidity addition) will be reduced by 5p for every 10p of the first £4 you earn over £65, then by 5p for every 5p earned until it is forfeited. That reduction does not apply to your earnings-related pension – that is, your additional, guaranteed minimum or graduated pension – including any extra paid for delaying your retirement.

If you are earning more than £65 gross – either as an employee or a self-employed person – you must tell your local social security office. Earnings include wages or salary, overtime, fees, commission, regular tips, bonuses – except Christmas bonuses of up to £10 – and attendance allowances if you are a councillor.

You need not include as earnings meals provided by your employer at your place of work, accommodation provided by your employer in which you have to live as a condition of employment, food or produce provided for your personal needs, or luncheon vouchers up to 15p a day.

In calculating your income you can also deduct reasonable expenses, such as trade union subscriptions, fares, cost of overalls and materials; 15p for each meal taken at work if no luncheon voucher is provided; and the reasonable cost of providing for the care of a member of your household because you are at work.

If you are self-employed and make a tax return to the Inland Revenue, your profits for the year will be calculated to a weekly amount and treated as net weekly earnings for the earnings rule. If you do not make a tax return, you may be asked to produce accounts.

If you are a man, your pension is not affected by your wife's earnings unless you are receiving a dependant's increase for her.

If you are, and her earnings go above her earnings rule limit (£45 in 1983–4), your dependant's increase will be reduced. If your wife does not live with you, but you are maintaining her and collecting the increase on her behalf, that will not be paid at all if her earnings equal or exceed the amount of that increase.

When you reach 70 – 65 for a woman – your pension will be paid in full regardless of how much you earn.

the additional pension you would have received. *See:* OCCUPATIONAL PENSION

Calculating additional pension Your additional pension builds up at the rate of 1/80th–1¼ per cent – of each year's qualifying earnings, up to a maximum of 20 years. If you contribute towards additional pension for more than 20 years, your pension will be worked out on the 20 years in which your earnings were highest.

As the first additional pensions were not paid until April, 1979, the full rate – 25 per cent (20 × 1¼ per cent) of annual qualifying earnings – will not be paid until April, 1998.

Your qualifying earnings are worked out by calculating the earnings on which you have paid Class 1 contributions in each tax year since April, 1978. Each year's earnings are revalued to take account of any increase in national average earnings during that year, and an amount equal to 52 times the weekly LOWER EARNINGS LIMIT is then deducted. Your annual additional pension is 1/80th of the total earnings for the tax years; this is divided by 52 to give your weekly pension.

If a husband and wife are contributors in their own right, they will each receive an additional pension.

If you defer or cancel retirement

If neither you nor your employer wishes you to retire at 65 – 60 for a woman – you need not do so. You can continue to work and thereby gain extra pension. If you retire and then decide that you want to work again, you can also gain extra pension by cancelling your retirement – but you cannot gain extra pension by cancelling more than once.

If you defer or cancel your retirement, your pension – that is your full pension, including additional and graduated pension but excluding increases for dependants – will be increased by 1p per £1 for every 7 weeks of postponement – about 7½ per cent increase per year.

If your wife is getting a pension on your contributions, she will usually have to agree to your cancelling your retirement. This can be done on the application form attached to leaflet NI 92, available from your local social security office.

You can claim your pension again any time after deferring or cancelling retirement. When you reach 70 – 65 for a woman – you will receive the full pension, with increases, even although you continue to work.

Invalidity addition

Your basic pension will be permanently increased by an invalidity addition if you were receiving invalidity allowance – payable with INVALIDITY PENSION – within the period of 8 weeks and 1 day before reaching 65 (60 if a woman). The addition will be the amount of allowance you were receiving.

Exemption from insurance

When you reach 65 (60 if a woman) you do not have to pay national insurance contributions.

If you continue working, you will need a 'certificate of age exception' to give to your employer. Your local social security office should send this to you automatically; but if it does not, write and ask for it.

If your employer deducts contributions, ask him for a refund. If the tax year in which the contributions were paid has ended, apply to your local social security office for the refund.

If you are self-employed and continue working, you must complete the stamping of your current contributions card. When you send it to your local social security office, tell them you have reached retirement age and ask for a refund.

Home responsibilities protection

If you cannot work regularly because you have to stay at home to look after someone, and your contribution record is not being maintained at the required level – or at all – your right to basic retirement pension can be protected under the 'home responsibilities protection' (HRP) scheme.

Under this scheme, the number of qualifying years needed for the full basic pension is reduced. When your pension is being worked out, the number of years for which you get HRP is deducted from the number of qualifying years of contributions you would normally need for a full pension. You will get a full pension so long as the reduced number of qualifying years does not fall below 20. If it does, you may still be entitled to a reduced pension.

You can get HRP for any tax year in which you:

- Get CHILD BENEFIT for a child under 16.
- Look after someone who is receiving ATTENDANCE ALLOWANCE, or a constant attendance allowance (payable with various benefits), for at least 35 hours a week. You will not be entitled to HRP if you receive INVALID CARE ALLOWANCE.
- Get SUPPLEMENTARY BENEFIT to look after a sick or elderly person at home.

You cannot qualify for HRP if you are a married woman or widow paying reduced national insurance contributions.

How to apply If you are looking after someone who is getting attendance or constant attendance allowance, you must apply at the end of each tax year. A claim form is attached to leaflet NP 27, available from your local social security office.

If you are getting child benefit or supplementary benefit to look after someone at home, there is no need to apply – HRP is granted automatically.

If you are a husband whose wife is claiming child benefit, you can have your pension protected if you have the benefit paid to you instead of your wife. To do this your wife must sign a statement telling the social security office that she does not wish to claim.

Pension for married women

A married woman who works can get a basic retirement pension on her own contributions when she reaches 60 and either retires from work or is treated as having retired.

If she is not entitled to a pension in her own right – because, for instance, she has been paying reduced contributions – she may be entitled to a basic pension on her husband's contributions. This pension is about 60 per cent of the normal basic pension – £20.45 in 1983–4. To qualify:

- She must be 60 or over and have retired or be treated as having retired;

RETIRING EARLY UNDER THE JOB RELEASE SCHEME

Employees approaching retirement can retire early under the Job Release Schemes. They receive a state allowance until they reach 65 (60 for women). They must be full-time (at least 30 hours a week) and have worked for their employer for at least the previous 12 months.

There are two schemes. Scheme 1 is for men aged 64 and women aged 59. Scheme 2 is for disabled men aged 60 to 63.

The purpose of the schemes is to provide more jobs for the unemployed. They will run until at least March 31, 1985. Applications will be received until 8 weeks before then.

As an employee you must agree to retire and not take another job or draw any state benefits until you reach 65 (or 60). Your employer must agree to replace you with an unemployed person.

As the schemes are intended to give steady full-time work to such a person, your application will not be considered if you are on short-time working, in a short-term job or threatened with redundancy or compulsory retirement.

What you get The allowance is paid at two rates. The higher rate is for those who are married and whose partner's income from all sources, after deducting tax and work expenses, is not more than £13 a week. The lower rate is paid to all others.

The rates for 1984–5 are:

	Scheme 1	Scheme 2
Higher Rate	£60.65 a week	£70.55 a week
Lower Rate	£48.00 a week	£57.35 a week

If you do take a job, and earn more than £4 in any week (after deducting work expenses), you will lose the allowance for that week. You should tell the Department of Employment about any work you do.

Tax and contributions Allowances under Scheme 1 are tax free; those under Scheme 2 are taxable. National insurance contributions are paid for you, so your basic retirement pension will not be affected. But you will not be making earnings which would count towards additional state pension.

If you are due to get an occupational pension, it too may be adversely affected.

Part-time job release Until March 31, 1985, you can receive an allowance if you and your employer agree to share your job equally with an unemployed person. This scheme also applies to men aged 62 and 63. The allowance rates are slightly less than half those payable under the full-time schemes. Men aged 62 and 63 are paid the same as disabled men.

or

- Be 65 or over.
- Her husband must have qualified for a basic pension and have retired or be treated as having retired. If he is entitled to a reduced basic pension, her pension will also be reduced.

A wife who obtains a basic pension on her husband's contributions is entitled to any graduated or additional pension for which she qualifies because of her own contributions. She can also obtain extra pension by deferring her retirement.

If a married woman is entitled to a basic pension on her own *and* her husband's contributions, she can choose the pension that is more favourable. So if the basic pension payable on her own contributions is less than that payable on her husband's contributions – because she has insufficient qualifying years – it can be raised to that level (£20.45 in 1983–4). But both pensions cannot be paid together.

If a married woman does not qualify for a pension on her own or her husband's contributions because she is under 60, he may be able to obtain a dependant's increase for her. Her earnings (if any) will affect the amount payable – the increase will be proportionately reduced for earnings over £45.

Widows If you were widowed before the age of 60, your WIDOW'S PENSION becomes your retirement pension when you reach 60 and retire.

If you are widowed after you reach 60, and are receiving a basic pension on your husband's contributions, that pension will be increased to the rate of his basic pension if he dies.

For more information on retirement pension for married women and widows, get leaflets NP 32A and NP 32B from your local social security office.

Income tax

Retirement pensions, including increases for dependants and additional and guaranteed minimum pensions, are treated as part of your income for INCOME TAX purposes. They should be included on any tax returns you have to make.

Supplementing a pension

If you are receiving retirement pension and are not working full-time, you may be entitled to a supplementary pension. If you qualify, both pensions will be paid together. *See:* SUPPLEMENTARY BENEFIT

How to claim retirement pension

About 4 months before you are due to retire, the Department of Health and Social Security will send you a claim form on which to apply for a pension. If you do not receive it by 3 months before you retire, ask your local social security office to send one.

Deferred pension If you have deferred or cancelled your retirement (see above), you must apply for your pension when you wish to retire. You must also apply if you reach 70 – 65 for a woman – and continue working. You can get an application form from your local social security office. This should be completed and returned up to 4 months before you retire or reach the age of 70 (65 if a woman).

Married women If you are a woman and want to claim a basic pension on your husband's contributions, you must make a separate application.

Delaying your claim

If you delay claiming your pension or telling the social security office about your retirement, you may lose money. Unless you have a good reason for the delay, you cannot get a pension back-dated more than 3 months before the date on which you give notice of your retirement, or 3 months before the date of your claim if you are over 70 (65 if a woman).

Even if you have a good reason, you cannot get a pension back-dated to more than 12 months before the date you notify retirement or claim the pension.

How pensions are paid

Retirement pension is usually paid

each week through an order book. You can cash the orders at a post office named by you on your claim form. You cannot normally cash them at any other post office.

Each order is valid for 3 months from the date shown on it. If you do not cash it within 3 months, you must apply to the social security office for a new one. You must cash this within 12 months, or you may lose the money altogether.

If you cannot get out to cash your own orders, you can arrange for someone else to do this for you. In this case you sign the back of the pension order, and the person collecting the pension for you signs on the line marked 'agent's signature'.

Paying into a bank If you prefer, you can have your pension paid every 4 or 13 weeks directly into a bank or National Girobank account, or into an investment account with a building society or the National Savings Bank.

Providing pensions for overseas residents

Retirement pension can be paid anywhere in the world, but generally only at the rate that was in force when you left the United Kingdom (or retired if you were abroad at the time).

Annual increases in pension (which occur each November) are not paid overseas except in countries with which Britain has reciprocal agreements – that is, in all the EEC countries, Austria, Bermuda, Cyprus, Gibraltar, Guernsey, Israel, Jamaica, Jersey, Malta, Mauritius, Portugal, Sark, Spain, Switzerland, Turkey, USA and Yugoslavia.

Pension for the over-80s

People aged 80 or over may be eligible for a special, non-contributory retirement pension. This pension is payable if you do not get a contributory retirement pension, or if your contributory pension is less than the non-contributory pension.

To qualify, you must:

- Be 80 or over and normally live in Scotland, England or Wales. You must also have lived in the UK for at least 10 years in the last 20 years before your 80th birthday; or
- Have been aged 92 or over (87 or over if a woman) on July 5, 1975 and lived in the UK for at least 10 years between July 1948 and November 1970.

In 1983–4 the non-contributory pension was £20.45 a week for a single person and £32.70 a week for a married couple. Recipients also get the 25p addition paid to all over-80s.

If you think you qualify, ask for leaflet NI 184 from your local social security office. This contains a claim form.

RIGHT OF WAY

Where you can go without trespassing

Every square inch of Scotland, including the FORESHORE, has a legal owner – an individual, a commercial concern, a statutory body such as a local authority, or the Crown. Consequently, it is a TRESPASS for you to walk anywhere other than on your own property, unless you have the owner's permission or there is some sort of right of way.

Apart from public roads, for which there are special rules, a public right of way over someone's property can only arise in two ways:

- Where the public have used a particular route continuously for twenty years, a public right to the route is established. The use must be without the permission of the owner of the land. The route must lead from one public place, for example a public road or a church, to another.
- Since 1967, local planning authorities have had power to make agreements with landowners for public rights of way to be created. All regional councils, and all district and islands councils other than those in the Highland, Borders, and Dumfries and Galloway regions, are local planning authorities for this purpose.

If there is felt to be a need for a right of way, but the landowner will not agree to one, the planning authority and the Secretary of State for Scotland both have power to impose a right of way. The landowner is then entitled to compensation for any loss.

The most spectacular example of a right of way created by planning authorities is the West Highland Way, which runs the 95 miles from Milngavie to Fort William.

Sometimes it is permissible to ride a bicycle or horse, or even drive a motor car, on a public right of way. Usually, however, it can only be used for walking.

If you would like more information about public rights of way, contact the Honorary Secretary of Scottish Rights of Way Society, 52 Plewlands Gardens, Edinburgh.

MEETING NEW FRIENDS

It is an offence to allow a bull to be at large in any field that is crossed by a public right of way.

Maintenance

When a local planning authority creates a new public right of way, it has a duty to put it into a fit condition for use by the public, and maintain it at that level. Although it also has power to maintain a right of way created by twenty years' use, it is under no duty to do so.

Members of the general public are also allowed to take steps to maintain a right of way. With the permission of the planning authority, they can put up

WHO MAY USE A PAVEMENT

Pavements are provided for the general public to walk on. They may not be used for riding, driving or cycling. It is an offence to park commercial vehicles of more than three tons on a pavement without police permission, unless there is no other way they can be loaded or unloaded.

Regional and islands councils are under a duty to provide pavements wherever they consider them necessary for the safety or convenience of pedestrians.

guide posts and direction notices.

Obstructions

The person through whose land a public right of way runs is not obliged to keep the way in a good state of repair. This does not mean that he is allowed to create an obstruction by, for example, building a large fence across it. If he does, you should report this to the local planning authority, which has a duty to assert, protect, and keep free from obstruction all ways within its area. It will then take any action, including legal action, that might be necessary.

If the landowner is engaged in agriculture or forestry, he can obtain permission from the local planning authority to put up stiles, gates and other devices to contain animals, such as fences and cattle grids. He will usually have to maintain them.

He is also allowed to plough up the path, provided he tells the local planning authority not more than seven days later, and restores the surface as soon as possible. You are still allowed to walk on a ploughed path, but you must take care not to damage the crops.

Closure

If a public right of way lies completely unused for twenty years, it ceases to be a right of way. In addition, the local planning authority (with the consent of the Secretary of State for Scotland) can close any path originally created by it which is not now needed by the public. If requested by the landowner, it can also alter the present line of a path to a different line. The alteration must not seriously inconvenience the public.

Access to open country

Strictly speaking, the public are only allowed to use a right of way for passing through. If they stop and use it for recreation of some sort,they are trespassers. In practice most landowners, certainly in the wilder parts of Scotland, do not mind walkers making use of their land in this way.

The Countryside Commission for Scotland has a duty to consult with local planning authorities to make sure that the public are in practice able to obtain access to open country for recreation. Open country is land consisting of mountain, moor, heath, woodland, cliff or foreshore.

If difficulties are discovered, the planning authority can enter into an access agreement with the owner of the land in question. The authority and the Secretary of State for Scotland both have power to impose an access order if an agreement cannot be reached.

Anyone who uses land covered by an access agreement or access order for recreation is not a trespasser and so cannot be stopped by the owner. The owner is not allowed to use the land in any way that seriously reduces the area to which the public have access, unless this is agricultural. If he does, he can be stopped by the planning authority.

If you want to find out which parts of the open country are covered by access agreements or orders, consult the relevant local planning authority, which is under a duty to keep an up-to-date map.

Private rights of way

An owner of a house or land sometimes has a private right of way over property belonging to his neighbour. This often appears in his title deeds, but it can also be established by use of the way for twenty years.

RIGHT TO LIGHT

Protecting the view from a window

In most cases there is no right to light in Scotland. You cannot stop your neighbour from building a house or growing a tree that blocks out the light to one of your windows. The neighbour is usually free to do what he likes on his own land as long as he does not trespass on yours.

In a small number of cases the neighbour – or one of his predecessors – will have entered into a legally binding agreement not to block your light. Such an agreement will probably be among the title deeds to your house. The easiest way to find out about this is to ask the solicitor who bought the house for you. If there is such an agreement, he can advise you on what action to take.

If a neighbour is about to build on his ground in a way that affects your light, the best way to protect yourself is often to object to his application for PLANNING PERMISSION.

RIOT

When it is an offence to be part of a mob

If a person forms part of a mob that is causing alarm or violence to others, he may be charged with a number of offences.

If he commits a BREACH OF THE PEACE, or seems likely to, he can be arrested by the police. He can also be arrested if he commits any other offence, such as ASSAULT, or OBSTRUCTION of the police or street.

Mobbing and rioting

Groups of people can be charged with the offence of 'mobbing and rioting'. This charge is usually used against people who are involved in gang fights or hooliganism. But it has also occasionally been used against workers involved in

THE MINERS WHO WERE CHARGED WITH MOBBING AND RIOTING

Workers who take part in a mass picket may run the risk of being charged with mobbing and rioting.

During the miners' strike of 1972 the National Union of Mineworkers organised a mass picket of Longannet Power Station in Fife. Their purpose was to stop staff coming to work and to close down the power station, which was still operating despite the coal shortage.

2,000 pickets turned up at the power station and 400 police were brought in to keep the peace. There was some disorder and 13 pickets were arrested. They were charged in Dunfermline Sheriff Court with mobbing and rioting.

The charge alleged that they: 'formed part of a riotous mob of evil disposed persons which, acting with a common purpose, did conduct itself in a violent, riotous and tumultuous manner to the great terror and alarm of the lieges, and in breach of the peace did curse, swear and utter threats of violence'.

DECISION

The jury acquitted all 13 pickets. They did not accept that the pickets formed part of a 'riotous mob'.

industrial disputes – such as the miners who picketed Longannet Power Station in Fife during the miners' strike of 1972.

The offence is committed if someone forms part of a riotous mob. The mob must:

- Contain sufficient people. There is no rule about the exact number of people needed for a group to constitute a mob. The number depends on what the members of the group do, the violence they show and the threats they use.
- Act with a common purpose. The immediate purpose must be unlawful – for example, to threaten or cause violence or stop people going about their lawful business. It does not matter that there is an ultimate purpose that is lawful – for instance, persuading an employer to increase wages.
- Cause public alarm by frightening or intimidating others or intending to do so. Actual violence is not necessary: a mob will be riotous if it assembles for the purpose of intimidating people carrying on their lawful business.

The penalty for mobbing and rioting is at the discretion of the court, within its sentencing limits.

Riot damage

Local POLICE authorities – usually the regional and islands councils – are responsible for providing an effective police service in their area. If they fail to control any unlawful, riotous or tumultuous assembly, householders or shopkeepers who suffer damage as a result can sue their council for compensation. *See:* PUBLIC ORDER

ROAD

Using – and maintaining – the public highway

A public road is any highway maintained by a regional or islands council or the Scottish Development Department (SDD). Motorways and trunk roads are the responsibility of the SDD; all other public roads, and adjacent pavements, are the responsibility of the appropriate council.

Using the roads

Although the way in which roads can be used is limited in the Road Traffic Acts, there are normally no restrictions on the type of vehicle that can use them. They are open to all traffic, vehicular and pedestrian, unless otherwise indicated by the SDD or police signs.

Pavements running alongside roads are for pedestrians only. It is illegal to park or cycle on them.

Motorway restrictions

A special set of rules applies to motorways. Certain classes of vehicle – indicated on signs at each entrance – are barred from using them.

It is an offence to drive on the hard shoulder of a motorway – which runs the entire length of each side of most motorways – except in order to stop there in a breakdown or some other genuine emergency. *See:* MOTORWAY DRIVING.

Pedestrians are not permitted anywhere on a motorway, although in practice drivers having to stop in an emergency are allowed to walk along the hard shoulder to the nearest motorway telephone.

Private roads

The owner of the land across which there is a private road – that is one which is not open to the public and not maintained by the local council or SDD – has the right to restrict its use in any way – for example by gates or cattle grids.

THE BLIND MAN WHO TRIPPED

Anyone who excavates a public road or pavement owes a duty of care to those people whom he can foresee will be put at risk by the works. That includes the blind.

In 1956 the London Electricity Board was excavating the pavement of a street in Woolwich. To protect one end of the trench it had used a punner – a heavy weight with a long handle.

The weight was on the pavement and the end of the handle was wedged 2 ft up in some railings.

A blind man walking along the road to a bus stop failed to detect the punner handle and tripped over it – even though he was using his white stick correctly. He injured himself and sued for negligence.

DECISION

The House of Lords held the Electricity Board totally liable, because it was the board's duty to erect a fence that was safe for blind people as well as for those who could see.

Who is responsible for repairs?

The highway authority responsible for maintaining a road is usually the one that should be sued in the event of an accident due to its condition. The authority must maintain it in a reasonable state of repair, bearing in mind the cost to public expenditure as well as the use that is likely to be made of it.

An exception is when a road is unadopted – for example, a newly built one on a modern housing estate. Until the council agrees or decides eventually to take it over, any repairs must be paid for by the developer or the people living on each side of the road. *See:* PRIVATE STREET

Compensation for loss or injury

If you injure yourself by stumbling over an uneven paving stone in the dark, you may be entitled to compensation from the highway authority.

Even if a court accepts that a road or pavement was unsafe, the highway authority can avoid paying compensation if it can show that it has not been negligent. For example, if the authority can show that it inspects its roads and pavements regularly, looking out for hidden

DAMAGE CLAIMS MUST SHOW NEGLIGENCE

A highway authority that regularly checks pavements is not negligent. If a minor fault appears between inspections and causes injury, no damages will be awarded.

defects such as insecure gratings, it will not be found negligent.

The same principles apply if a vehicle is damaged as a consequence of the condition of the road. For example, if a driver damages the back axle by going over a broken piece of road, he may be able to sue the highway authority successfully provided that:

- It cannot be shown that his own carelessness was the real cause of the incident – because, for instance, he was driving too fast.
- The authority has been negligent.

The courts have said that unevennesses in a road or pavement of up to an inch in depth have to be expected by pedestrians and do not usually amount to negligence on the part of the highway authority. 'Cat's eyes' and cobble stones are also normal hazards.

If a body such as a gas or electricity board is allowed to dig up a road or pavement, it will be liable along with the highway authority for any damage resulting from negligence during the period when the surface is only temporarily restored, while settling takes place.

If the damage occurs in a private street, the driver would be able to sue only the owners of the building or buildings next to the site of the accident.

ROAD TRAFFIC ACCIDENT

When a motorist must stop after an accident

A driver who is involved in an accident must stop at the scene if:

- Any person apart from himself has been injured.
- Any vehicle other than the one he is driving has been damaged.
- A horse, cow, ass, mule, sheep, pig, dog or goat – but not a cat – has been injured outside his vehicle.
- Any damage has been caused to property.

It is not necessary that the driver was himself involved in the accident. It is sufficient that the accident occurred because of his vehicle's presence – for example, if some other driver swerved to miss him, and hit a tree.

The driver must stay at the scene long enough to enable any other people involved to take his name and address, details of the vehicle's ownership if it does not belong to him, and the registration mark.

If it is not possible to comply with the law's requirements immediately – for example, when a motorist has hit and damaged an unattended parked car or knocked down a straying farm animal on a lonely road – the driver must report the accident to the police as soon as reasonably practicable, and certainly within 24 hours.

After an accident in which someone has been injured, the driver must produce his insurance certificate immediately or present proof of his insurance cover within 5 days at any police station of his choice.

Failing to stop

If a motorist who is prosecuted can satisfy the court that he was unaware of the accident, he has not committed an offence by failing to stop.

The courts, however, do not readily accept the defence of ignorance – especially when someone has been injured or a vehicle has been damaged. It does not sound very plausible that a motorist involved in an accident did not see, or hear, or feel anything.

The maximum penalty for failing to stop is a £1,000 fine, an endorsement and possible disqualification.

Calling the police

There is no obligation to report an accident to the police if names and addresses have been exchanged and insurance certificates produced when someone is hurt. A driver need not wait for the police to arrive, but it is usually in his own interests to do so if he is not to blame for the accident.

ROAD TRAFFIC OFFENCES

How motoring offenders are punished

Anyone convicted of a road traffic offence may be fined and, in certain cases, disqualified from driving. In the most serious cases – for example, causing death by reckless driving – a driver may be sent to prison.

Most motoring offences are prosecuted under summary procedure, before a judge sitting alone. The exception is causing death by reckless driving, which must be prosecuted under solemn procedure before a judge and jury. *See:* CRIMINAL PROCEEDINGS

THE PRINCIPAL OFFENCES WITH WHICH MOTORISTS CAN BE CHARGED

How the law can deal with breaches of road traffic law

Offence	Maximum penalty	Must your licence be endorsed?	Can you be disqualified?
Accident offences			
Failing to stop after an accident	£2,000 fine	Yes	At the court's discretion
Failing to report an accident within 24 hours	£2,000 fine	Yes	At the court's discretion
Failing to give name and address after an accident	£2,000 fine	Yes	At the court's discretion

Offence	Maximum penalty	Must your licence be endorsed?	Can you be disqualified?
Careless driving offences			
Driving without due care and attention	£1,000 fine	Yes	At the court's discretion
Inconsiderate driving	£1,000 fine	Yes	At the court's discretion
Leaving vehicle without stopping engine or setting handbrake	£1,000 fine	No	No

Offence	Maximum penalty	Must your licence be endorsed?	Can you be disqualified?
Careless driving offences *continued*			
Driver not in control of the vehicle	£1,000 fine	No	No
Reversing vehicle for an unreasonable distance	£1,000 fine	No	No
Opening vehicle door causing injury or danger	£1,000 fine	No	No
Driving on a footway	£400 fine	No	No
Driving in a street designated as a play street	£1,000 fine	Yes	At the court's discretion
Drink and drugs			
Unfit to drive through drink or drugs	£2,000 fine/6 months' jail	Yes	Yes Minimum 12 months
Driving with alcohol in the body above the prescribed limit–35 mg. of alcohol in 100 ml. of breath, or 80 mg. of alcohol in 100 ml. of blood, or 107 mg. of alcohol in 100 ml. of urine	£2,000 fine/6 months' jail	Yes	Yes Minimum 12 months
Failing to provide a specimen of breath for analysis or blood or urine for a laboratory test	£2,000 fine/6 months' jail	Yes	Yes Minimum 12 months
In charge of a vehicle while unfit through drink or drugs	£1,000 fine/ 3 months' jail	Yes	At the court's discretion
In charge of a vehicle while having alcohol in the body above limit	£1,000 fine/ 3 months' jail	Yes	At the court's discretion
In charge of a vehicle and failing to provide a specimen of breath for analysis or blood or urine for a laboratory test	£1,000 fine/ 3 months' jail	Yes	At the court's discretion
Failing to provide a specimen for a preliminary breath test	£1,000 fine	Yes	At the court's discretion
Driving licence offences			
Driving while disqualified	Unlimited fine/12 months' jail	Yes	At the court's discretion
Driving without a licence when no licence could have been granted	£400 fine	Yes	At the court's discretion

Offence	Maximum penalty	Must your licence be endorsed?	Can you be disqualified?
Driving licence offences *continued*			
Causing or permitting a person to drive without a licence	£400 fine	No	No
Driving with uncorrected eyesight	£400 fine	Yes	At the court's discretion
Refusing to submit to an eyesight test	£400 fine	Yes	At the court's discretion
Failing to produce driving licence to police	£400 fine	No	No
Obtaining licence while disqualified	£400 fine	No	No
Failing to produce licence to court for endorsement	£400 fine	No	No
Making false statement to obtain licence	£1,000 fine	No	No
Failure to sign licence	£400 fine	No	No
Failure to state date of birth or sex when required	£400 fine	No	No
Insurance offences			
Using vehicle uninsured against third-party risks	£1,000 fine	Yes	At the court's discretion
Forging insurance document	Unlimited fine/2 years' jail	No	No
Lighting offences			
When parked	£400 fine	No	No
When moving	£400 fine	No	No
Load offences			
Causing danger by carrying too many passengers	Car: £400 fine. Goods vehicle: £2,000 fine	Yes Yes	At the court's discretion
Causing danger by having an insecure load	Car: £400 fine. Goods vehicle: £2,000 fine	Yes Yes	At the court's discretion
Long and projecting loads	£400 fine	No	No
Exceeding the maximum gross weight or axle weight	Car: £400 fine. Goods vehicle: £2,000 fine	No	No

Continued overleaf

Offence	Maximum penalty	Must your licence be endorsed?	Can you be disqualified?
Motor-cycle offences			
Unlawful pillion riding	£1,000 fine	Yes	At the court's discretion
Driving or riding on a motor cycle without protective headgear	£400 fine	No	No
Motorway offences			
Excluded traffic using a motorway	£1,000 fine	Yes	At the court's discretion
Parking on hard shoulder	£1,000 fine	No	No
Reversing vehicle, making U-turns or driving in the wrong direction on main motorway	£1,000 fine	Yes	At the court's discretion
Reversing vehicle, making U-turns or driving in the wrong direction on slip roads	£1,000 fine	Yes	At the court's discretion
Vehicles over 3 tons using third lane	£1,000 fine	Yes	At the court's discretion
Walking on motorway or slip-road	£1,000 fine	No	No
Walking on hard shoulder or verge	£1,000 fine	No	No
Noise offences			
Sounding horn in a built-up area between 11.30 p.m. and 7 a.m.	£400 fine	No	No
Sounding horn when stationary	£400 fine	No	No
Noise caused by faulty silencer	£400 fine	No	No
Use of vehicle or trailer which causes excessive noise	£400 fine	No	No
Parking offences			
Leaving vehicle in a dangerous position	£400 fine	Yes	At the court's discretion
Wilful or unnecessary obstruction	£400 fine	No	No
Failing to park on the nearside after dark	£400 fine	No	No
Stopping on a footway	£400 fine	No	No
Offences against waiting restrictions	£400 fine	No	No

Offence	Maximum penalty	Must your licence be endorsed?	Can you be disqualified?
Parking offences *continued*			
Failure, without reasonable excuse, to make a statutory statement of ownership	£400 fine	No	No
Making a false statement of ownership	£2,000 fine	No	No
Failure to pay initial parking meter charge	£100 fine	No	No
Exceeding excess period	£100 fine	No	No
Returning to a parking meter bay within one hour	£200 fine	No	No
Parking on a suspended meter	£400 fine	No	No
Improperly parked	£400 fine	No	No
'Feeding' a parking meter by putting in more coins	£400 fine	No	No
Failure to pay excess charge	£100 fine	No	No
Tampering with a meter	£400 fine	No	No
Pedestrian crossing offences			
Breach of zebra regulations by a stationary vehicle	£400 fine	Yes	At the court's discretion
Breach of zebra regulations by a moving vehicle	£400 fine	Yes	At the court's discretion
Provisional licence offences			
Provisional licence holder not accompanied by a qualified driver	£400 fine	Yes	At the court's discretion
Provisional motor cycle-licence holder carrying a passenger who is not qualified	£400 fine	Yes	At the court's discretion
Driving without L plates	£400 fine	Yes	At the court's discretion
Provisional licence holder towing unauthorised trailer	£400 fine	Yes	At the court's discretion
Reckless driving offences			
Reckless driving	Unlimited fine/2 years' jail	Yes	Yes

Offence	Maximum penalty	Must your licence be endorsed?	Can you be disqualified?
Reckless driving offences *continued*			
Causing death by reckless driving	5 years' jail	Yes	Yes
Speed limit offences			
Exceeding speed limit on a motorway	£1,000 fine	Yes	At the court's discretion
Exceeding speed limit on other roads	£400 fine	Yes	At the court's discretion
Exceeding goods vehicle speed limit	£400 fine	Yes	At the court's discretion
Passenger-carrying vehicles limited to 50 mph	£400 fine	Yes	At the court's discretion
Traffic directions			
Disobeying a constable directing traffic	£400 fine	Yes	At the court's discretion
Disregarding a school crossing patrol sign	£400 fine	Yes	At the court's discretion
Disregarding traffic signals	£400 fine	Yes	At the court's discretion
Disregarding a stop sign	£400 fine	Yes	At the court's discretion
Disregarding double white lines	£400 fine	Yes	At the court's discretion
Disregarding other road signs – for example, signs saying 'Give Way' and 'No Entry'	£400 fine	No	No
Vehicle condition offences			
Defective brakes	£400 fine	Yes	At the court's discretion

Offence	Maximum penalty	Must your licence be endorsed?	Can you be disqualified?
Vehicle condition offences *continued*			
Defective steering	£400 fine	Yes	At the court's discretion
Defective tyres	£400 fine per tyre	Yes	At the court's discretion
Tyres of different types fitted to the same axle	£400 fine	Yes	At the court's discretion
Other vehicle parts in dangerous condition	£400 fine	Yes	At the court's discretion
Windscreen not maintained so that driver's vision is obscured	£400 fine	No	No
No seat belts or anchorage points	£400 fine	No	No
Unladen weight not marked on goods vehicle	£2,000 fine	No	No
Vehicle registration offences			
Failure to pay motor vehicle licence duty	£400 fine or five times the annual duty (whichever is greater)	No	No
Registration mark obscured or missing	£400 fine	No	No
Failure to register change of ownership	£400 fine	No	No
Forging of licence	Unlimited fine/2 years' jail	No	No
No MoT certificate	£400 fine	No	No

Automatic disqualification

Certain offences carry an automatic DRIVING DISQUALIFICATION if a person is convicted – for example, driving with excess alcohol in the body. Many offences also carry an automatic endorsement on a driver's licence. If an offence carries an automatic endorsement but no automatic disqualification, the court can decide whether to disqualify a driver.

If a driver collects endorsements worth 12 points or more on his licence within a 3-year period, he is disqualified automatically for 6 months. There may, however, be mitigating circumstances that induce the court not to disqualify or to disqualify for less than 6 months.

ROBBERY

When theft involves violence or the threat of it

Robbery is a more serious form of THEFT. It is committed only when a thief uses personal violence or intimidation to help him steal. Any personal violence used to effect a theft converts that theft into robbery. The physical force used may be trivial and no injury need be sustained by the victim. But the force used must be great enough to take the crime out of the category of a theft by surprise – such as pickpocketing.

The violence used must take place before the theft and must also be used with intent to rob. It is not robbery to assault someone and then form the intention to steal from him. Similarly it is not robbery for a thief to use force to escape after, for example, a successful pickpocketing. In both these cases the thief would be charged with the two separate offences of theft and assault.

A violent *attempt* to steal would be charged as assault with intent to rob.

Robbery by intimidation

Actual violence is not necessary for robbery. Threats of immediate personal harm by the thief may be enough. But the threatened harm must be immediate. If it is not, the crime is EXTORTION.

Penalty The penalty for robbery is at the discretion of the court.

THE PICKPOCKETS WHO PUSHED THEIR VICTIM

Even a small amount of force turns theft into robbery.

Three pickpockets worked as a team. One of them pushed their victim to make him lose his balance, while the other stole his wallet and the third kept a look-out. They were charged, not with theft, but with robbery.

The pickpockets argued that the mere pushing of their victim did not involve sufficient force for them to be guilty of robbery.

DECISION

The appeal court held that pushing was a sufficient act of force to justify a robbery conviction. They were found guilty.

SALE OF GOODS

The rights of a purchaser

Even when nothing is said, a seller in the course of a business – such as a shopkeeper or dealer – must supply goods that are of merchantable quality and fit for their purpose. In a consumer contract it is not possible to exclude or vary these obligations by an exemption clause. *See:* GOODS, Sale of

If you are sold goods that are defective, faulty or otherwise unsatisfactory, you may be entitled to a full refund. *See:* DEFECTIVE GOODS

SALES

Buying goods at 'sale' time

Goods sold by a seller in the course of a business must be of merchantable quality and fit for the particular purpose for which the seller knows they are to be used. If 'sale' goods are defective, your rights are exactly the same as if you had paid the full price. *See:* DEFECTIVE GOODS

The fact that they are 'sale' goods may be relevant, however, in the following ways:

- Merchantable quality. The term 'merchantable quality' means that the goods are as fit for the purpose or purposes for which goods of that kind are commonly bought as it is reasonable to expect in the circumstances.

In deciding what it is reasonable to expect, the price may be relevant. For example, a fur coat with a small bare patch might not be regarded as merchantable if the price is £2,500, but it might be if the same coat is reduced to £25. Goods sold in 'sales' are sometimes described as 'seconds' or 'rejects'. That might have the effect that they are to be regarded as fit for their usual purposes despite a defect – if it is reasonable to infer from the description given that there is such a defect.

If a defect is drawn to a buyer's attention before he decides to buy, he cannot later complain about that defect.

- Fitness for purpose. It may be possible for a seller to say that it was unreasonable for the buyer to rely on the seller's skill or judgment about the goods' fitness for a particular purpose if they are sold in a 'sale'.

When a bargain is illusory

Not all goods sold at sale time are reduced. Sometimes shops buy in special lines which they sell at lower prices than their regular stock. That may be because they are of lower quality, but it may simply be that they are someone else's old stock bought in cheaply – and therefore of good value.

If prices are shown as reduced, the law on price marking must be obeyed – even in a sale. *See:* PRICE REDUCTION

Members of the Retail Trading-Standards Association are encouraged to display the Association's statement of sales policy at sales time. This explains why the shop is holding a sale and states that goods specially purchased for the sale are so described.

SCHOOL

The rights and responsibilities of parents

The Education (Scotland) Act 1980 places a duty on parents to provide 'efficient' education for their children. This can be done by sending the children to the schools run by the local EDUCATION AUTHORITY – the regional or islands council – or, as the Act says, 'by other means'.

The 'other means' can be sending your child to one of the independent or grant-aided schools, or educating your child at home – in which case you would have to satisfy the education authority that your child was getting a proper education. *See:* HOME TEACHING; INDEPENDENT AND GRANT-AIDED SCHOOL

Choosing a school

If you want to send your child to an education authority school, but not the one that the education authority proposes, you can make a written request to the authority naming the school that you want your child to attend. But remember that if you do this and the authority agrees, it will be under no obligation to provide transport to and from the school of your choice.

The education authority can refuse to admit your child to the school of your choice only if one or more of the following apply:

- The authority would have to employ an additional teacher.
- It would involve significant expenditure in extending or altering the school that you have chosen.
- It would seriously affect the continuity of your child's education.
- It would seriously affect order and discipline in the school chosen, or the educational welfare of the pupils there.
- The education provided at the school is not suited to the age, ability or aptitude of your child.
- The education authority have already required the child to leave the school.
- The school chosen is a special school and the child does not require SPECIAL EDUCATION.
- The school chosen is for children of the opposite sex from your child.

You do not have to give reasons to the education authority for your request. But the authority has to give you reasons if it refuses your request.

Appealing against refusal

Education authorities have set up appeal committees to consider appeals by parents whose requests for their children to be placed at the school of their choice have been refused.

An appeal committee consists partly of people who are parents of school children, or have experience in education, or are acquainted with educational conditions in the area. It also includes people who are members of the education authority or the education committee of the authority, but they must not outnumber the other members of the committee by more than one.

The director of education, any educational adviser employed by the education authority and members of the director's or adviser's staff cannot be members of the committee. Nor can a member of the education committee act as chairman of the appeal committee.

Anyone who was involved in the education authority's decision about your request, or who was present when it was made, cannot be on the appeal committee considering your case. Neither can anyone who is a teacher, pupil or parent of a pupil at the school you want your child to go to, or the school that the education committee proposed the child should go to.

The procedure at the appeal committee hearing will be informal. You can choose whether to go and argue the case before the committee, or be represented by someone, or simply put your case in writing. If you go, you can be accompanied by three friends, including a representative.

Before the committee can confirm the education authority's decision, it must be satisfied that it is appropriate to do so and that one of the grounds for refusal given above exists.

You will be given the committee's decision, and the reasons for it, in writing. If it rejects your arguments, you have 28 days to appeal to the sheriff. The appeal will be heard in the sheriff's chambers, not in open court. His decision is final.

If the sheriff dismisses your appeal, you must accept the alternative school and hope that your child can change later.

Refusal to send your child to school at all would result in the education authority bringing a prosecution against you under the SCHOOL ATTENDANCE rules. You could face fines and ultimately imprisonment.

VISITING THE CLASSROOM

Parents do not have an automatic legal right to visit their child's school. The head teacher can ask them to leave.

When you can visit a school

Although schools generally encourage co-operation between home and school and welcome parents on many occasions, parents do not have any legal rights of access to their child's school. Nor does being a ratepayer provide any right of entry.

Anyone visiting a school is there by permission of the head teacher, who can withdraw that permission at any time, merely by asking him to leave. The police could be called to remove him and he could face a charge of BREACH OF THE PEACE if he refused to go.

Parents have a right to expect consultation with teachers about their children's welfare and progress. If you are not given information about your child's schooling, write to the head teacher and ask for it, or arrange to visit the school.

Always write or phone and ask for an appointment if you want to discuss something with the school, otherwise no one may be free to speak to you.

However angry you feel, try not to lose your temper. You will do your case no good and you may be told to leave without having the chance to put a perfectly legitimate complaint.

Parents' days

Most schools arrange parents' days, at which parents can see something of the work being done and can discuss their children's progress with teachers.

If you are not happy about the arrangements for consultation at your children's school, take it up with the head teacher and, if you are still not satisfied, with the director of education or divisional education officer.

Access to children

Parents should get the head teacher's permission if they want to contact children in school, although that would probably not be required at break or dinner-hour. It is up to the head teacher to decide whether parents may stay with their children in the classroom.

Difficulties can arise for a school if the parents of a pupil are estranged and the custody of the child is disputed. Legally, both parents have the right to custody. A school cannot be expected to take sides unless a court has awarded custody to one parent and the school has been told about this. *See:* CUSTODY OF CHILDREN

Size of classes and number of teachers

The Schools (Scotland) Code of 1956 fixed 45 as the normal maximum size of a class in a primary school or department. Classes are further restricted to 25 in a one-teacher department, 30 in a two-teacher department, 35 in a three or four-teacher department, 25 in a class for backward or retarded children and 20 in a nursery class.

In secondary schools or departments the normal maximum is 40. Classes are further restricted to 30 at secondary stages 4, 5 and 6, to 30 in a class that includes pupils at more than one yearly stage and to 20 in a class for practical instruction.

The conditions of contract negotiated nationally between teachers and the education authorities have imposed further limits on class sizes. These make 33 pupils the normal maximum for a primary class and for secondary stages 1 and 2; and 30 pupils the normal in other secondary classes.

The ratio of teachers to pupils has improved over the years. By 1980 the

ENFORCING SCHOOL DISCIPLINE

Without some order in the classroom, the process of education cannot succeed. For that reason the common law has always recognised the right of teachers to use reasonable means to enforce discipline.

The development of responsible social attitudes in pupils is also recognised as a part of education. The Schools General (Scotland) Regulations 1975 lay down that in the day-to-day running of every school the education authority must ensure that care is taken to encourage in pupils:

- Reasonable and responsible social attitudes and relationships.
- Consideration for others, and good manners and attitudes to work.
- Initiative and self-reliance, and habits of personal hygiene and cleanliness.

Pupils are expected to obey the rules drawn up by the school. But parents also have duties in respect of these rules. The failure of a parent to comply (or to allow his or her child to comply) with the rules would justify the child's exclusion from school. If your child was suspended on these grounds, you could be prosecuted for failing to ensure the attendance of your child at school without reasonable excuse.

Corporal punishment The right of a teacher to inflict corporal punishment was described in a case in 1882 as 'the power of giving his pupils moderate and reasonable corporal punishment'. But the sheriff in that case went on to say that the law would not protect the teacher 'when his chastisement is unnatural, improper or excessive'.

If a teacher was charged with ASSAULT, a court would have to decide whether the punishment that he administered was unnatural, improper or excessive by looking at all the circumstances.

Since 1968 it has been official policy in Scotland to move towards the eventual abolition of corporal punishment in schools.

In February 1982, following a ruling of the European Court of Human Rights (below), the Secretary of State for Scotland suggested that education authorities should start consultations with teachers, parents and school councils and set themselves target dates for the complete elimination of corporal punishment.

By 1984, all education authorities except the Borders regional council had either phased out corporal punishment or had agreed to do so.

Human rights in school In 1982 the European Court of Human Rights ruled that two Scottish education authorities – Strathclyde and Fife – had violated the European Convention on Human Rights. Each had refused to give the mother of a boy at one of their schools a promise that the belt would not be used to punish him. Neither boy was actually belted at school, but the court ruled that the 'philosophical convictions' of the parents should have been respected.

These cases, and the possible refusal of some authorities to ban corporal punishment, may force the government to legislate to abolish it in all British schools. *See:* HUMAN RIGHTS

Detention Your child may be kept in class during a break or lunch time, or detained after school hours as a punishment. The legal basis for detaining a child beyond the school day is sometimes questioned and is under investigation.

Schools should give you adequate warning if your child is to be kept late at school. This kind of punishment should not be used if it means that a child will miss the school bus that normally takes him home.

Suspension from school The ultimate form of action against a child who misbehaves is exclusion from school. The right of an education authority to do this is recognised in the Education (Scotland) Act 1980.

If a decision is taken to exclude your child because his behaviour is seriously affecting order and discipline in the school, or the well-being of other pupils, you must be given the opportunity to discuss the decision with someone from the school.

If you still object to the decision, you (or your child, if 16 or over) can refer the case to an appeal committee.

pupil/teacher ratio in Scotland was 20.3 pupils per teacher in primary schools and 14.4 in secondary schools.

Advice on staffing standards is issued to education authorities by central government. If it considers that authorities are staffing schools too generously, it can limit the number of posts for which it will pay rate support grant.

If you are concerned about the number of pupils in your child's class, discuss it with the head teacher or get in touch with the director of education.

When a school is to close

Education authorities no longer have to get the consent of the Secretary of State for Scotland before closing a school – unless the closure would mean, in the case of a primary school, that the pupils would have to go to another school 5 or more miles away, or in the case of a secondary school, 10 or more miles away.

Before an education authority can close any school, it must consult the parents and the SCHOOL COUNCIL. Letters must be sent to the parents, telling them what the authority wants to do and where they can get more information.

The parents and the school council have 28 days in which to comment on the proposal. Alternatively, they can make representations at a public meeting called by the authority to discuss the closure.

If you want to oppose the closing of your school, make sure that you use these opportunities to make your views known. You can can also contact your local regional (or islands) council and seek publicity through the press. Remember that you have no right of appeal against the eventual decision of the authority.

The procedure for consulting parents also applies in other circumstances – for instance, when the site of a school is to be changed. If the school is denominational, the church authorities must be consulted too. *See:* EDUCATION AUTHORITY

Information for parents

The government has made regulations under the Education (Scotland) Act 1981 making it compulsory for education authorities to give certain information to parents on request. You must be told about:

- The arrangements that can be made for a child who, due to the remoteness of his home or other exceptional circumstances, cannot get the full benefit of school education.
- The arrangements that can be made where the age, ability and aptitude of a pupil would be best catered for at one particular school.
- The arrangements that the authority makes for transporting pupils to and from school.
- The residential area from which pupils of a particular school are normally drawn.
- The secondary school to which pupils of a particular primary school would normally transfer, and the primary

schools which would normally supply pupils to a particular secondary school.

- The secondary school at which a child would normally finish his education, if he is attending a school that does not provide all the secondary stages.
- The special schools serving the area.
- The guidelines drawn up by the authority on priorities for school admissions.
- The rules about 'placing' requests, and the arrangements for appeals.

Regulations which came into force in January 1983 extend the list of topics on which information must be given. This includes information about particular schools, their educational aims, their curriculum and leisure activities, school policy on dress or uniforms and on school discipline, arrangements for school transport, school meals and milk, school policy on entering pupils for public examinations and the school's recent record in examinations.

Curriculum

A school will normally provide education in most of the subjects that are examined for the Scottish Certificate of Education. In addition, education authorities are legally obliged to continue religious observance and instruction at their schools. *See:* RELIGIOUS EDUCATION

Under the SEX DISCRIMINATION Act 1975, it is unlawful for a school to discriminate between boys and girls in the education it provides.

Parents' wishes

The Education (Scotland) Act 1980 lays down the general principle that pupils are to be educated in accordance with the wishes of their parents. But there are limitations on this:

- The wishes of the parents must be compatible with the provision of suitable instruction and training.

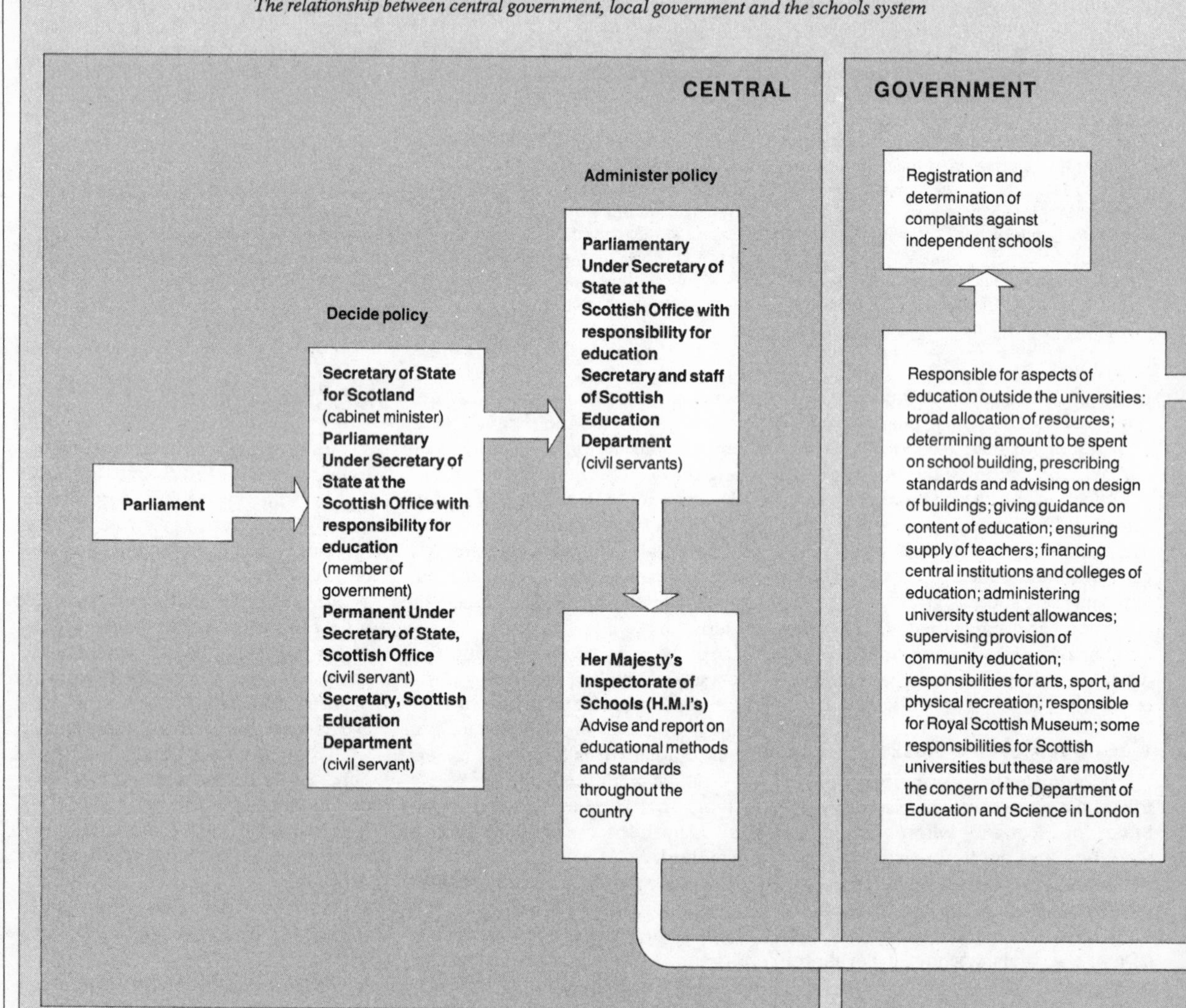

● These wishes must not cause unreasonable public expenditure.
● The parents cannot insist on their child taking a course of secondary education which the education authority thinks the child cannot reasonably be expected to profit from.

For example, you might want your child to study Latin because he or she hopes to become an archaeologist. But the school could refuse this if it meant employing an extra teacher for one pupil – under the rules this could be regarded as unreasonable public expenditure.

In practice, education authorities will do their best to solve such problems. You should consult the head teacher or the director of education. But if the authority refuses your request, you can ask for the matter to be decided by the Secretary of State for Scotland. Write to the Scottish Education Department in Edinburgh.

SCHOOL AGE

When school attendance is compulsory

Broadly speaking, school attendance is compulsory between the ages of 5 and 16. But the law lays down precise rules about when your child must start school and when he or she can leave.

An education authority must fix a 'school commencement date' for each primary school in its area. If your child's fifth birthday falls on or before the commencement date, he or she must start school on that date. But if your child's fifth birthday is after the commencement date, he or she may have to wait until the commencement date following that birthday.

However, the law obliges an education authority to accept a child who is

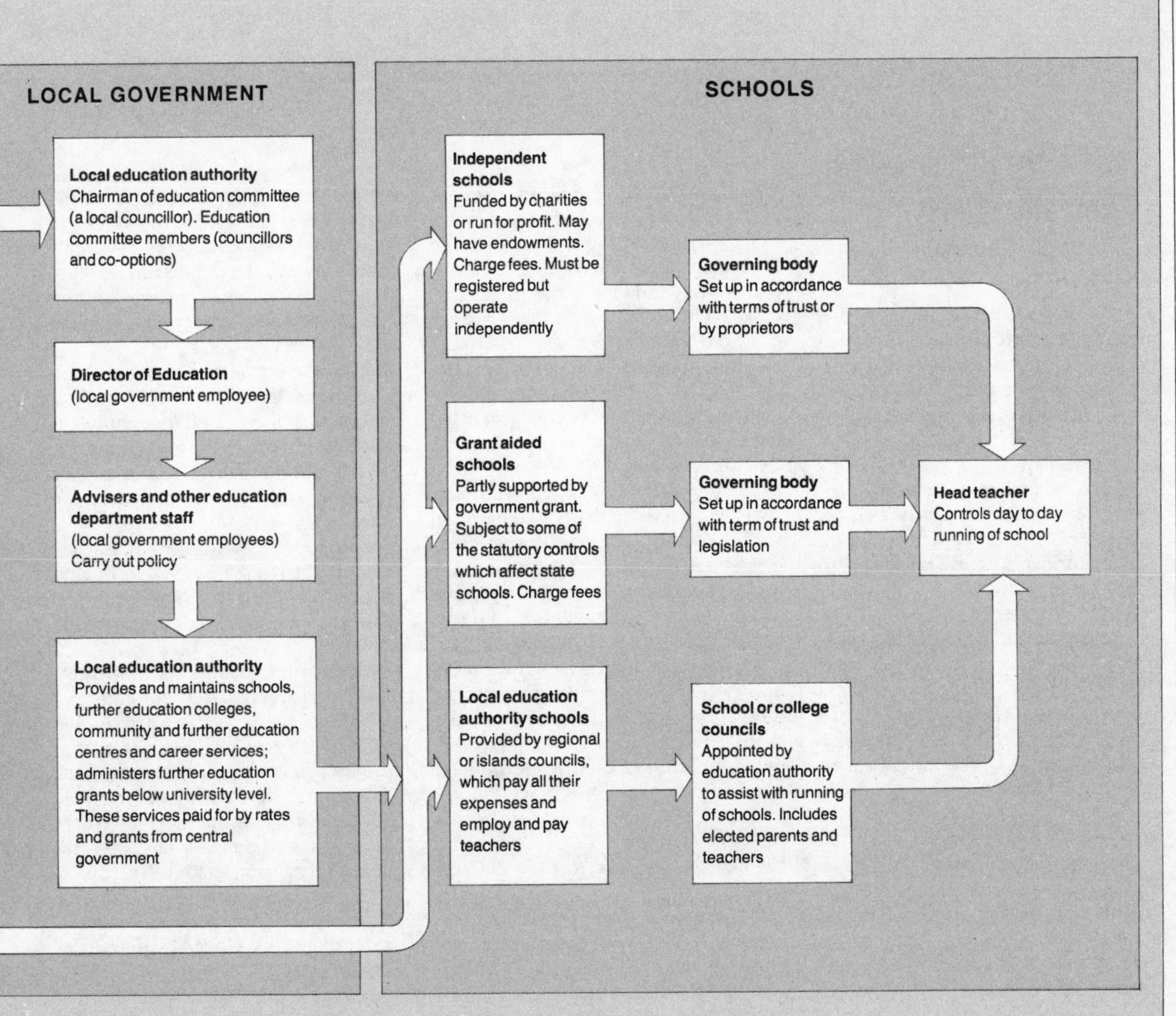

not yet 5, but will reach that age by a later date fixed by the authority. This means that many parents will have a choice of sending their child to school from the school commencement date before his fifth birthday or the one a year later.

Leaving school

For pupils of around 16, there are 2 leaving dates in each year – May 31 and a date in December (the beginning of the Christmas holidays).

If your child reaches the age of 16 between March 1 and September 30, he or she will be allowed to leave school at the end of May in that year. A child who reaches 16 later in the year, between October 1 and the end of February, can leave school in December.

There is no upper age limit for school attendance and a pupil will not be asked to leave simply because he or she is too old.

WHEN AN EXCUSE IS REASONABLE

There are only a limited number of acceptable excuses for not sending your child to school regularly. If one of these excuses can be shown to exist, you cannot be convicted of an offence under the school attendance laws.

The acceptable excuses are:

- Sickness. You do not need a medical certificate but should inform the school about any chronic condition or lengthy illness. The authority is entitled to have your child medically examined. It is an offence to refuse to permit this.
- There is no school within walking distance – that is, within 3 miles of the child's home (2 miles if the child is under 8) – and no transport has been arranged by the authority. Even if transport is arranged, it is an acceptable excuse that your child still has to walk more than 3 miles (2 miles if under 8).

This excuse does not apply where a child is placed in a school more than 3 (or 2) miles away as a result of a placing request made by you, and no school transport is available.

- Any other reason that is acceptable to the authority – for instance, an infectious disease, infestation by parasites, family holidays, religious observance, snow-blocked roads or a transport strike. It is not an acceptable excuse that your request to have your child placed in a different school has been refused.

The authority may accept an excuse that your child is beyond your control and will not attend school. In that case the child can be referred to the reporter to the children's panel.

Exemption for 15 year olds In certain circumstances, an education authority can allow a 15 year old child to stay off school to provide assistance at home.

This can be allowed only if exceptional hardship would otherwise be caused – for instance, where a widowed mother is seriously ill and would have no other assistance.

SCHOOL ATTENDANCE

Parents' duty to ensure that children attend school

The Education (Scotland) Act 1980 requires parents to provide efficient and suitable education for their child. They can do this by sending him or her to school regularly, or by other means – for instance, teaching the child at home. *See:* HOME TEACHING; SCHOOL

If parents fail to ensure that their child attends school regularly, they will be guilty of an offence – unless they can give a reasonable excuse for the child's non-attendance.

Parents will also be guilty of failing to ensure regular attendance if their child is refused admission to school because they have failed to comply with the school's rules and regulations – for instance, rules requiring the wearing of SCHOOL UNIFORM or forbidding certain forms of dress.

Dealing with truancy

All schools must keep an attendance register. If a child is failing to attend school regularly, the school will usually attempt to find out why – perhaps by sending a member of staff to the child's home. Some education authorities employ education welfare officers, part of whose job is to visit families whose children are not attending school. They will usually try at first to persuade the child to return voluntarily.

If social workers or the police discover a child who is truanting, they can refer the child to the REPORTER to the children's panel. The reporter may decide that the child needs compulsory care and arrange for the child and his or her parents to appear before a CHILDREN'S HEARING.

Prosecution If the education authority considers that parents are committing an offence in failing to ensure their child's attendance at school, it must serve a notice on one or both parents giving them up to 7 days to appear before the authority to explain the child's absence. If no reasonable excuse is given, the authority can either order the parent(s) to be prosecuted in the sheriff court or give a warning and postpone for six weeks the decision on whether to prosecute.

Whether or not it decides to prosecute, the authority can also refer the child to the reporter to the children's panel.

If the parent(s) are prosecuted and convicted, the sheriff can make an attendance order requiring them to ensure that the child attends school. Failure to observe the order is an offence.

As an alternative to making an attendance order, the sheriff can refer the child to the reporter to the children's panel – indeed, he can do this whether or not the parents are convicted, so long as he is satisfied that the child has failed to attend school regularly.

Making an attendance order If the education authority warns parents and postpones a decision on prosecution, it can make an attendance order requiring them to ensure that their child attends school. It is an offence to ignore the order.

If parents object to the order, they can appeal to the sheriff within 14 days of the order being served on them. The sheriff can confirm, vary or cancel the order.

When an attendance order is in force, the child's parents can ask the authority to change the school named in the order, or to revoke the order on the ground that arrangements have been made to provide the child with suitable education, either at another school or at home. If the authority refuses the request, they can appeal to the sheriff.

An attendance order remains in force until the child is 16, unless it is cancelled by the sheriff or revoked by the education authority.

Penalties A parent who is convicted of any of the offences mentioned above

> *THE ROAD THAT HAD NO PAVEMENTS*
>
> *Even though a child lives within walking distance of school, the parent may be justified in keeping him from school.*
>
> Mr Tunnah lived in Berwickshire, about 1½ miles from the village school. In 1969 he was prosecuted for failing to send two of his children to the school.
>
> The road to the school was a main road without pavements. Mr Tunnah could take the children (aged 8 and 5) to school in the morning by car but could not collect them in the evening. His wife would have had to take their youngest child (aged 3½) with her if she had walked to the school to collect the two children.
>
> DECISION
>
> The Sheriff considered that it would have been most imprudent to allow the children to walk home from school unaccompanied and that the mother could not reasonably have been expected to retrieve the children. He ruled that Mr Tunnah therefore had a reasonable excuse for keeping the two children from school and found him not guilty.

can be fined up to £100. If he continues to break the law, he also runs the risk of being imprisoned for up to a month.

SCHOOL COUNCIL

Involving local people in education

Under the Local Government (Scotland) Act 1973, local education authorities have to appoint school and college councils to help them run their schools and colleges.

These councils were set up to keep local involvement in education at a time when, in many cases, the administrative headquarters for education were being moved to more distant regional centres.

It is up to each education authority to decide what powers to give its school and college councils. They may be little more than advisory bodies or they may be given executive power to deal with – for example – the letting of premises, certain staff appointments, the work of the authority relating to truancy, and school placing requests.

The name 'school council' is used where the body has responsibility for schools only. In all other cases – for example, where the council is concerned with a further education college or a community centre – the name 'college council' is used.

Representation on the councils

There may be one council for a single school or for a group such as a secondary school and its 'feeder' primary schools. The parents of pupils at the school or schools must be represented on the council. The head teacher will be able to tell you who the parent representatives are.

There also has to be at least one representative of the teaching or other educational staff, and one member 'interested in the promotion of religious education'.

A college council responsible for a further education college has to have representation from the teaching or other educational staff and from crafts, industry and other employments in the locality.

If a college council is responsible for a community centre or other establishment set up by the education authority to provide social, cultural and recreational activities, it must have representation from local residents.

Getting involved

If you want to get involved in the work of a school or college council, ask for information at the school or other establishment you are interested in, or write to the director of education.

You may also find it helpful to seek the support of the school or college council if you want to influence the local education authority on a question that concerns you or your children.

SCHOOL GRANT

When financial help is available to parents

An education authority has the power, under the Education (Scotland) Act 1980, to make payments in respect of pupils whose parents are on low incomes. Payments can be made:

- To provide a child with adequate clothing and footwear.
- To enable a child to take advantage of the educational facilities that are available.

> ASSISTED PLACES SCHEME
>
> The Education (Scotland) Act 1981 set up a scheme to help parents who want their children to go to independent or grant-aided schools but cannot afford the fees. Under the scheme, the government will pay certain of these fees.
>
> The scheme covers only tuition and examination fees and certain incidental expenses. However, participating schools may be prepared to give help with boarding and other expenses.
>
> The amount of the tuition fee subsidy will depend on the family's 'relevant' income – all income before tax, including any investment income belonging to the children, less an allowance of £850 for each dependant apart from the pupil concerned.
>
> In 1983–4, a family with a relevant income of under £5,622 paid nothing towards the fees.
>
> To be eligible, a child has to be at least 10 years old at the beginning of his first session in the assisted place (assuming the session starts in August or later).
>
> Full details of the scheme, including participating schools, can be obtained from the Scottish Education Department, New St. Andrew's House, Edinburgh.

Clothing payments

If a child is unable to take full advantage of the education provided because his clothing is inadequate or unsuitable, this should be brought to the attention of the education authority.

It may be, for example, that the child has no decent school uniform or shoes, or that he has no sports gear.

It is the duty of the education authority to make sure that such a child is 'sufficiently and suitably clad'. It can fulfil this duty by making payments to the child's parent(s) to cover all or part of the cost of clothing and footwear. Whether a payment is made, and if so how much, will depend on the parents' means.

An education authority has the power to provide free clothing and footwear to boarders and to nursery pupils.

There is no right of appeal to an independent body against an authority's refusal to pay a clothing grant.

Educational maintenance allowances

An education authority has the power to make an allowance to enable a child to take advantage of the education facilities that are available. It can be paid where the pupil or the pupil's parents would suffer hardship if they had to meet the cost themselves.

An allowance can cover all or part of the cost of:

- Maintaining a child who stays on at school after the age of 16.
- Enabling a child to take a full part in school activities.

How to claim

If you want to apply for one of these payments or to obtain further information, get in touch with your school or local education office (the address is in the telephone directory).

SCHOOL MEALS AND MILK

The minimum service that must be provided

An EDUCATION AUTHORITY is no longer obliged to provide milk and a midday meal for all school pupils, although it can still choose to do so.

School milk The duty to provide school milk was largely restricted to the under-7s in 1971 and was abolished entirely by the Education Act 1980. But authorities can continue to supply milk if they choose, and are entitled to make a charge for it.

School meals The general duty to provide a midday meal for pupils was also abolished in 1980. But authorities are obliged to provide a free midday meal for pupils whose parents are receiving SUPPLEMENTARY BENEFIT or FAMILY INCOME SUPPLEMENT.

Authorities can continue to supply a midday meal for other pupils if they choose, and may make a charge for it. The meal can be provided free of charge to children whose parents are on low incomes but are not entitled to supplementary benefit or family income supplement.

Education authorities are free to decide the type of meal that should be provided for all pupils.

Schools must provide suitable accommodation for children to eat their own packed lunches. No charge can be made.

SCHOOL OUTING

Taking children on a school trip

There is no legal rule about who pays for school outings, even if they are an essential part of the curriculum. Schools are therefore quite entitled to ask for a contribution from parents towards the cost.

However, an education authority can make grants to help children whose parents cannot afford to pay. So ask your school what help is available if you have difficulty finding the money.

Ensuring the safety of children

Education authorities make their own regulations about school trips – dealing with, for instance, the ratio of adults to children, the insurance cover required and the financial and medical arrangements. There are no national regulations.

A teacher who is in charge of a school outing must take reasonable care for the children's safety during the whole time that the outing lasts. If he fails to do so, and a child is injured as a result, the teacher and his employers – the education authority – can be sued for DAMAGES.

SIGNING LETTERS OF INDEMNITY

Parents may sometimes be asked to sign a letter of indemnity, absolving teachers or the education authority from any legal liability for any accident or illness caused as a result of a school outing.

Such letters may warn parents about the risks involved, but they have no legal significance. Neither the teacher nor the authority can exclude liability for failing to take reasonable care of the children in their charge.

SCHOOL RECORDS

Information on progress at school

Every school run by a local EDUCATION AUTHORITY must keep a progress record for each pupil. The record covers such matters as educational progress, health and factors affecting the pupil's educational ability and includes any relevant information about his or her emotional and social development. It must also contain parent's names, addresses and occupations.

The information in the progress record must only be used to supervise the pupil's educational development and to give adequate advice to (or in respect of) that pupil. The contents can be shown only to authorised persons, such as careers officers, social workers and educational psychologists.

There is no legal reason why parents should not see their child's progress report. However, they have no legal right to demand to be shown manually-held records. *See:* COMPUTER RECORD.

If it is discovered that a child's progress report contains statements that are damaging and untrue, he or she may be able to sue for DEFAMATION. But it would be necessary to prove that whoever compiled the report had acted out of malice or spite.

SCHOOL TRANSPORT

Providing free transport for pupils

A local EDUCATION AUTHORITY must provide free transport – such as a bus or taxi – to take children all or part of the way to school if they live more than 'walking distance' away. Alternatively, the authority can pay their reasonable travelling expenses.

For children under 8, walking distance means 2 miles; for children aged 8 and over, it means 3 miles. In each case the distance is measured by the shortest route.

If children live more than 2 (or 3) miles from school because of their parents' request for them to be placed in a different school from the one chosen by the authority, there is no obligation to provide free transport (although the authority can do so if it wishes). *See:* SCHOOL

An education authority has discretion to provide other children with free transport – for instance, children who are disabled, or who live within walking distance but on a dangerous road.

If there are spare seats on a school bus, the education authority must allow other selected children to travel free.

SCHOOL UNIFORM

When certain clothes must be worn

If a head teacher decides that school uniform is necessary, he or she can provide for this in the school rules and refuse to admit children who fail to wear it.

If a child goes regularly to school, but is sent home each time because he is not wearing the proper uniform, his parents can be prosecuted for failing to ensure his regular attendance. *See:* SCHOOL

Generally, however, local authority schools in Scotland do not insist on the wearing of school uniform. Difficulties are more likely to arise when pupils indulge in eccentric fashions, contrary to school rules.

Clothing payments Parents who are unable to afford school uniform or proper clothing and footwear for their child can seek financial assistance from the education authority. *See:* SCHOOL GRANT

SCOTTISH CONSUMER COUNCIL

The body that represents consumers' interests

The Scottish Consumer Council was set up by the government in 1975. Its job is to watch over consumers' interests – particularly the interests of those who are disadvantaged – and to speak up for the consumer to government, industry and the public and private services. It works closely with the National Consumer Council – of which it is a committee – and with the Consumer Councils for Wales and Northern Ireland.

The Council is financed by the government, but is independent of it. The members are appointed by the Secretary of State for Trade after considering nominations by voluntary organisations and public bodies.

The Council has no statutory powers and does not handle individual complaints from consumers. Much of its work involves research into particular needs and problems – for example the problems faced by tenants, or by consumers in rural areas – and making representations to government departments, local authorities, nationalised industries and other organisations (including the EEC) whose policies affect consumers.

The work of the Council has included:

- A major research project on the problems faced by consumers in rural areas.
- Extensive work on competition policy and Scottish air travel.
- Reports on tenants' groups and tenancy agreements; and publication of a manual dealing with council house repairs.
- A report on the facilities in Scottish sheriff courts.
- A report recommending group actions in the Scottish courts.
- A report on access to social security tribunals in Scotland.
- A guide to patients' rights in the National Health Service.

If you want to find out more about the Council's work, write to it at 314 St. Vincent Street, Glasgow G3 8XW.

SEA

Laws that apply to the waters round our coasts

In law, the seas around Britain and the land beneath them are divided into five sectors:

- Internal waters.
- Territorial waters.
- Fishing zones.
- International waters.
- The continental shelf.

Internal waters include rivers, ports and harbours, the sea between the mainland and the Scottish islands and inlets that are less than 24 nautical miles (27.63 land or statute miles) wide – for example, the Tay and Clyde estuaries.

The same laws as on the mainland apply in internal waters. No foreign ship has any right to enter our internal waters – nor can British ships enter foreign waters – without consent.

Territorial waters extend for 3 nautical miles – 3.45 statute miles – from low-water mark round the coast and islands of Britain. It is a belt that generally follows the contours of the coastline and skirts around any islands. But where there are estuary indentations, the 3 miles start from the mouth of the estuary.

Foreign ships have the right to pass through territorial waters provided that they do not threaten Britain's peace or security. That does not give them fishing rights, however.

The criminal laws of Scotland and England apply in internal and territorial waters adjacent to each country, and also to platforms within and beyond these waters.

Fishing zones stretch 200 nautical miles (230.3 statute miles) round the coasts of Britain and most other maritime states. But under the Common Fisheries Policy of the EUROPEAN COMMUNITIES the waters of EEC countries are mostly open to fishing by EEC vessels.

Otherwise Britain has full control over all fishing activity in its own zone. No vessel other than a rowing boat can fish without a licence.

The skipper of a foreign fishing boat

FORFEITING THE CATCH

A foreign skipper found fishing illegally within UK territorial waters may forfeit his whole catch and face a large fine.

found fishing without authority in the British zone risks the seizure of his whole catch and gear, and an unlimited fine.

International waters are the high seas outside the territorial waters of any country. Apart from fishing-zone regulations, they are governed by a combination of international conventions and national laws.

British ships on the high seas are subject to British laws. For example, crimes committed on British ships on the high seas can be tried in the Scottish criminal courts.

The crime of piracy can be tried by Scottish courts, irrespective of the place where the offence occurred or the nationality of the ship or offender.

The continental shelf is the sea-bed off the coast, but forming part of the land mass of the adjoining country. In the case of the North Sea, the shelf links Britain with the European continent and is divided among all the shoreline countries.

Other countries throughout the world claim territorial waters, fishing zones and continental shelves, but the widths of the sectors vary.

Oil and gas rigs

Oil and gas rigs are usually subject to the laws of the country on whose continental shelf they operate. Most North Sea rigs, for example, are governed by Scots law. It is an offence carrying an unlimited fine and/or 1 year's imprisonment for any unauthorised vessel or aircraft to approach within 500 metres of any platform.

Rules of the sea

Anyone who has a vessel other than a rowing boat at sea must comply with the international Safety Of Life At Sea convention, which lays down rules about equipment and handling. Copies can be obtained from the International Maritime Organisation, 101 Piccadilly, London W1V 0AE.

Shipping lanes In busy stretches of water, such as the English Channel, vessels may have to stay in set shipping lanes, but otherwise there are no fixed routes that must be followed in international or territorial waters.

Distress calls It is the duty of every vessel to offer assistance to another vessel in distress at sea.

SEA TRAVEL

When a company can limit liability

A sea-passenger's ticket may show conditions that attempt to exclude or limit the shipping line's liability for accidents to passengers, and for lost or damaged property.

In a contract made in Britain, or where the voyage is to or from Britain, any clause seeking to exclude liability to passengers will be ineffective. However, financial limits are set by law to the amount of compensation.

Amounts of compensation are related to the price of gold, so their sterling equivalent varies. The approved limits in 1984 were approximately as follows:

Death or personal injury	£33,000 for each passenger
Lost or damaged cabin baggage	£590 for each passenger
Lost or damaged vehicle, including possessions inside	£2,360 for each vehicle
Other baggage lost or damaged	£850 for each passenger

Those figures are not guarantees of what will be paid. They are ceilings to what might be recoverable in a lawsuit against a shipping company or any of its employees.

They do not apply, however, if injury, loss or damage is deliberate, or caused recklessly with a knowledge of the probable result. Then there is no limit to what a court might award.

A passenger has only 2 years in which to start legal proceedings. Written notice of a claim must be given immediately, if loss or damage is apparent, or otherwise within 15 days of leaving the ship.

SEARCH

When the police may search you or your property

The POLICE have no general power to search a member of the public. They may do so only if a person agrees to be searched or in circumstances where the law allows a search to be made.

For example, if the police lawfully detain or arrest someone, they may search him. *See:* ARREST; DETENTION

The police are also legally entitled to stop a person – or a vehicle in which he is travelling – and make a search without a warrant if:

- They suspect that he is carrying DRUGS.
- They suspect that he is carrying a GUN or other OFFENSIVE WEAPON.
- They suspect that he has been involved in TERRORISM.
- They suspect that he is carrying STOLEN GOODS.

If none of these circumstances apply, the police may ask a sheriff to issue them with a search warrant. To obtain the warrant, the police must state in writing the reasons why the warrant is required. It will only be issued if the sheriff is satisfied that it is reasonable to do so.

If the police search a person illegally, they commit an ASSAULT.

However, if a person refuses to be searched when the police are entitled to do so, he may be charged with OBSTRUCTION. The police may use reasonable force to carry out the lawful search.

SEASONAL WORKER

The rights of people who take seasonal work

A seasonal worker is someone who takes a short-term job that is available only at a certain time of the year – for example, a job as a raspberry or potato picker or as a summer worker in a hotel or restaurant.

Some seasonal workers, particularly those with a skilled trade, may work a few hours a week for several people and be SELF-EMPLOYED. Others, such as fruit pickers, may work full-time for one person until the job is done, and be employed.

Seasonal workers who are employed have an EMPLOYMENT CONTRACT just like any other employee, although often there is nothing in writing. In such cases, the contract's terms and conditions can be derived from the oral agreement between employer and employee or from custom and practice.

Seasonal workers have few statutory EMPLOYMENT PROTECTION rights because their period of CONTINUOUS EMPLOYMENT is not long enough to acquire them. However, if a seasonal worker is hired full-time for an unspecified period and serves more than 1 month, he must give or be given one week's NOTICE before leaving. This rule does not apply to employment under a contract to do a specific job that is not expected to last more than 3 months, unless it does in fact last for longer than that.

The rules on HEALTH AND SAFETY AT WORK apply to all workers, whether full or part-time, including those hired for a season. If a seasonal worker is injured in the course of his job because of NEGLIGENCE by his employer or a fellow employee, he can sue the employer for damages.

If a seasonal worker is an employee, his employer is obliged to deduct INCOME TAX and NATIONAL INSURANCE CONTRIBUTIONS from his wages, provided that these are sufficiently high for such deductions to be made.

SEAT BELTS

When you must ensure your own safety

As a general rule, all drivers and front-seat passengers must wear seat belts while the car is travelling forwards. There are, however, some exceptions. For example:

- People using vehicles constructed or adapted for delivering goods or mail, while they are making local rounds of deliveries – for example, milkmen and postmen.
- Drivers who are performing a manoeuvre which includes reversing.
- Holders of a valid medical certificate, signed by a doctor (fee payable), to the effect that it is inadvisable on medical grounds for them to wear a seat belt. The medical certificate must be produced to the police constable when the motorist is stopped, or within 5 days at a specified police station.

The maximum penalty for not wearing a seat belt when required is a £100 fine.

PROTECTING CHILDREN

Any driver who, without reasonable excuse, allows a child under 14 to travel in the front seat of a vehicle without wearing a seat belt or appropriate restraining device commits an offence.

The maximum penalty on conviction is a £100 fine.

SECONDHAND GOODS

Protection even for the buyer of used goods

No one expects secondhand goods to be as good as new, but that does not mean that dealers in secondhand goods are legally entitled to sell worthless junk.

The Sale of Goods Act 1979 applies to sales of secondhand goods as much as to sales of new goods. So secondhand goods, like new goods, must be of merchantable quality, and must be fit for any particular purpose known to the seller, provided the seller sells them in the course of a business. *See:* DEFECTIVE GOODS

'Merchantable quality' means that the goods should be as fit for the purpose or purposes for which goods of that kind are commonly bought as it is reasonable to expect in the circumstances. In deciding what it is reasonable to expect, regard must be had to the description applied to the goods, and the price may also be relevant.

The fact that goods are sold as secondhand will therefore be taken into account in deciding whether they are merchantable. But even secondhand goods must be fit for use, and a secondhand car, for example, that is not roadworthy because of a serious defect will not be of merchantable quality.

SELF-EMPLOYED

The rights and duties of those who work for themselves

Anyone who does paid work on his own account as an independent contractor is, in law, self-employed so far as that work is concerned.

Self-employment need not be his only or main source of income. A bus driver who supplements his earnings by giving driving lessons or acting as a mail-order agent is self-employed in those activities, although he remains an employee in his main job.

The relationship between a self-employed person and his customers or clients is governed by a 'contract for services' rather than by the 'contract of service' (meaning the employment contract) that exists between employer and employee. Both types of agreement, whether oral or written, are subject to the general law on contracts, but someone who is self-employed has far fewer rights in the course of his work than an employee. *See:* EMPLOYED PERSON

The self-employed are not entitled to the benefit of the EMPLOYMENT PROTECTION laws. If their work ends, they are not entitled to a period of NOTICE unless that is specifically provided for in the contract. They cannot claim a REDUNDANCY payment or compensation for UNFAIR DISMISSAL. Nor are they entitled to statutory sick pay or maternity pay. *See:* MATERNITY; SICKNESS

YOUR RIGHT TO CONTRIBUTORY BENEFITS

Self-employed people who have paid sufficient national insurance contributions are, with one exception, entitled to the same contributory benefits as employed people.

They are therefore entitled to claim sickness benefit, maternity allowance, widow's benefit, retirement pension, child's special allowance and death grant.

The exception is unemployment benefit. A self-employed person who loses his job, or whose business ceases, is not entitled to unemployment benefit under any circumstances. It is only available to employees who have paid Class 1 national insurance contributions.

Paying national insurance

A man between 16 and 65 (or a woman between 16 and 60), who is self-employed and earns more than the LOWER EARNINGS LIMIT must pay flat-rate Class 2 national insurance contributions. He or she may also have to pay earnings-related Class 4 contributions on profits or gains chargeable to income tax under Schedule D.

Even if a person has a job for which he pays Class 1 contributions, he is still liable for Class 2 and perhaps Class 4 contributions on his self-employed income. *See:* NATIONAL INSURANCE CONTRIBUTIONS

Paying tax

Self-employed people do not have their INCOME TAX deducted at source like employed people. Usually they produce a profit and loss account for the inspector of taxes and pay under Schedule D in two half-yearly instalments. Often they also have to pay VALUE ADDED TAX.

There are considerable tax advantages in being self-employed. It is usually worth employing an accountant to see that you derive full advantage from the rules regarding the expenses that you can claim. The accountant's fee is allowed against tax. *See:* EXPENSES

Setting up a business There are special tax concessions to help you establish your own business. These enable you to set early losses against income of previous years.

There are also allowances to help you to buy any capital equipment that you need for your business – for example, a typewriter or a computer. Office furniture and filing cabinets are also allowable.

If you want to buy a car to run a taxi service or a driving school, you can claim a full capital allowance in the same way. But if you want it only as a means of transport in connection with your business, you can write off only 25 per cent a year on a car costing up to £8,000. The method of writing off is slightly different for cars costing more than £8,000.

In either case, the inspector may allow you only a proportion of the write-off if you are also using the car privately.

SENTENCE

How the courts pass sentence on offenders

Criminal courts have a wide range of possible sentences that they can impose on convicted offenders – from an absolute discharge to a heavy fine or a long term of imprisonment.

It is generally accepted that any punishment imposed on an offender must be fair and broadly in proportion to the seriousness of the offence. Punishment for its own sake is not the only objective a court will have in mind when imposing a sentence.

A court will usually select a sentence which:

- Protects society. Violent criminals and persistent sex offenders are always likely to be imprisoned.
- Rehabilitates the offender. Guidance from a probation supervision officer or hospital treatment might help him to change his ways.
- Deters other offenders. Sometimes sentences are increased for crimes that have suddenly become more prevalent – for example, gang fights.

Before deciding on a sentence, the court may order a social inquiry report into the offender's background and personal circumstances. In some cases – for example, where a person may be sentenced to imprisonment for the first time – the court must order a report.

The report will attempt to set out why the offender committed the offence – there might be a drinking problem, marital trouble or a financial crisis – and suggest how he might respond to various sentences. The report is usually prepared by the social work department of the regional or islands council.

A court may impose a custodial or non-custodial sentence.

Custodial sentence

The custodial sentence that can be imposed depends upon the offender's age.

Prison Imprisonment is the only custodial sentence for offenders aged 21 or over. A court must not pass a sentence of imprisonment on any person who has not been previously sentenced to imprisonment (or detention) by a court in any part of the UK, unless it considers that there is no other appropriate method of dealing with him.

Detention The only custodial sentence for offenders who are 16 or over, but under 21, is detention. Detention can be imposed where – but for the age of the offender – the court would have power to impose imprisonment.

If a court imposes detention on a male offender for a period of at least 28 days but not exceeding 4 months, the court must order that the detention be in a detention centre. In any other case it must order that the detention be in a young offenders' institution. *See:* YOUNG OFFENDERS

Maximum sentences The High Court of Justiciary has unlimited powers of imprisonment and detention.

The sheriff court, when dealing with a case under solemn procedure, can impose a maximum period of imprisonment or detention of 2 years – but the sheriff has power to remit the case to the High Court for a longer sentence. Under summary procedure, the sheriff can imprison an offender for up to 3 months (increased to 6 months for a subsequent offence involving dishonesty or personal violence).

The district court can imprison an offender for up to 60 days. *See:* CRIMINAL PROCEEDINGS

Non-custodial sentences

There is a variety of non-custodial sentences available to the courts.

- FINE. A financial penalty. The High Court and sheriff court, under solemn procedure, have unlimited power to fine. The sheriff court, under summary procedure, can fine an offender up to £2,000. In the district court the maximum fine is £1,000.
- PROBATION order. Supervision by a social worker. A probation order may last for not less than one year and not more than three. It can be made only if the offender agrees to it.
- COMMUNITY SERVICE ORDER. Unpaid community work. The order may be made as an alternative to a custodial sentence in respect of an offender aged 16 or over who is convicted of an offence punishable by imprisonment. The duration of community service must be not less than 40 hours, and not more than 240 hours. Such an order can be made only if the offender agrees to it.
- CRIMINAL COMPENSATION ORDER. Compensation to a victim for personal injury, loss or damage caused by the offence. In the High Court and sheriff court, under solemn procedure, there is no limit to the amount the offender can be required to pay by the order. In the sheriff court, under summary procedure, the maximum is £2,000. In the district court the limit of a compensation order is £1,000.
- DEFERRED SENTENCE. Postpone-

ment of sentence for whatever period and on such conditions as the court may decide.

- Caution for good behaviour. The offender or cautioner (the person acting as a guarantor) will forfeit money if the offender misbehaves.

The sheriff court, under summary procedure, can require an offender to find caution (pronounced 'kayshun') of up to £2,000 for any period up to 12 months.

In the district court the maximum is caution of up to £1,000 for up to 6 months. This sentence is not available in other courts.

- Forfeiture order. Property used by an offender to commit any crime can be confiscated and disposed of as the court may direct.
- ADMONITION. A warning delivered by the court.
- ABSOLUTE DISCHARGE. No punishment imposed or warning given.

Children

Children under the age of 16 are rarely prosecuted in the criminal courts unless their offence is very serious. Instead they are usually referred to the REPORTER to the children's panel, who may decide to refer their case to a CHILDREN'S HEARING.

If a child is prosecuted and found guilty, the court may (and in some circumstances must) send the case to a children's hearing for advice. After considering the advice given, the court can dispose of the case itself or send it to the hearing for disposal.

If the court decides to dispose of the case itself, it has the following powers in dealing with a child under 16:

Custodial disposal A child convicted of MURDER must be sentenced by the High Court to be detained without limit of time.

Apart from that, a child who is convicted under solemn procedure can be sentenced to be detained for a specified period.

A child who is convicted under summary procedure in the sheriff court can be ordered to be committed for up to 2 years to undergo residential training.

Non-custodial disposal A child can be dealt with by means of a fine, probation order, admonition or absolute discharge, Alternatively, the court can defer making an order.

SEPARATION

When a husband and wife split up

When a marriage breaks down, one or both marriage partners may decide to separate and live apart from the other. To do so, they do not necessarily have to move to separate houses – they may be considered to be living apart if, for instance, one partner insists on living separately in one part of the house and refuses to eat meals or take part in family life with the other partner.

If both partners agree to separate, they can make their own arrangements about finance, property and the care of children. Alternatively either partner can apply to court for a decree of judicial separation, but only where certain legal grounds exist (see below).

Following a separation, either partner can apply to court for maintenance – called ALIMENT – to be paid by the other. But unless the partner claiming maintenance had reasonable grounds for living apart, it is a defence to the claim that the other partner is willing to resume married life. A wife will be ordered to support her husband only if he is unable to support himself and her income is more than enough for her own needs.

Aliment can also be claimed for children of the marriage living with one partner. This can be done separately or in an action of judicial separation.

A court can be asked to decide any dispute concerning the CUSTODY OF CHILDREN, either separately or in an action of judicial separation or DIVORCE.

Separation by agreement

A married couple can agree to a voluntary separation and make their own arrangements for the custody of (and access to) children, the division of property that is jointly owned, and the payment of maintenance. To make sure that there is no doubt about what has been agreed, the couple should consider having a formal separation agreement drawn up, outlining the details of their agreement. It is best to have this document drawn up by a solicitor.

Apart from the value of certainty, a formal separation agreement provides certain tax advantages which are not available to couples who make a purely verbal agreement. *See:* DIVORCE

A separation agreement should be made only if a couple have separated or are on the point of separating. An agreement drawn up because a couple think they might want to separate in the future would probably not be given effect to by the courts.

A separation agreement is a legally binding CONTRACT. Both parties are bound by it as long as they want to continue the separation. The courts cannot vary the terms of the agreement but they can be asked to enforce it if one partner breaks its terms – for example, by failing to pay aliment or by failing to return a child to the parent whom it was agreed should have custody.

If one partner decides that he or she wants to end the separation and resume married life, and the other partner refuses, the separation agreement comes to an end. However, the partner who wishes the separation to continue may have grounds for a judicial separation or divorce (see below).

A separation agreement can never prevent either partner from seeking a judicial separation or divorce – even though it contains a term expressly forbidding such legal proceedings. If decree of separation or divorce is obtained, the court can make new financial arrangements and decide who should care for the children.

Judicial separation

Either partner can apply to the court (almost always the sheriff court) for a decree of judicial separation. This is

SEPARATED, BUT NOT APART

A couple who decide to separate do not have to move from their common home.

often combined with a claim for aliment. In an action of judicial separation, or separation and aliment, the court can also deal with matters involving children – their custody, their maintenance, and access to them by the partner without custody.

It is not necessary to apply for a judicial separation in order to allow the court to decide on arrangements for maintenance and for the care of children. These matters can be dealt with by the sheriff, in separate actions. However, a judicial separation may appeal to a partner who has religious or other objections to divorce but wishes to have the marriage breakdown formally acknowledged. Unlike divorce, judicial separation does not end the marriage in law.

The grounds on which a judicial separation can be granted are the same as for a divorce – that is, adultery, desertion, unreasonable behaviour, or separation for 2 or 5 years. *See:* DIVORCE

The court can order one partner to pay aliment but it cannot order the payment of any lump sum. Nor can it order either partner to transfer property to the other. But it does have power to transfer the tenancy of the family home from one partner to the other.

Once granted, an order of judicial separation continues in force indefinitely, unless the couple divorce or one of them dies.

Getting a divorce

Separation for 2 years is a ground of divorce, provided both partners consent. If one partner refuses consent, the other partner can apply for a divorce once the separation has lasted for 5 years. *See:* DIVORCE

Financial help for a wife

A wife who is separated from her husband can claim supplementary benefit in the same way as a single woman. Any benefit received includes an amount to cover the needs of any children under 16, or still at school, who are living with her. *See:* SUPPLEMENTARY BENEFIT

If she is working full-time, she cannot claim supplementary benefit. But she may be entitled to family income supplement if she is supporting a child who is under 16 or still at school. *See:* FAMILY INCOME SUPPLEMENT

SERVICES

When a customer pays for care and skill

Anyone who charges for services in the course of a trade, business or profession has a duty to provide them with reasonable care and skill, and in a reasonable time. The standard of care and skill required is that shown by competent people in the same field.

If a customer loses money or is harmed in any other way by negligent or incompetent services, he can sue for damages.

Dissatisfied customers and clients can often get help from trade or professional associations, which try to uphold suitable standards among their members. Some associations have disciplinary powers over their members, and some have funds out of which compensation is paid in cases of incompetent service.

False or misleading statements

It is an offence under the TRADE DESCRIPTIONS Act for anyone providing a service as part of a trade or business to make a false statement about the nature or quality of that service.

For example, it is an offence to claim that a repair service is available at all hours if it is not, or to imply that an aftersales service has the endorsement of a manufacturer when it does not.

The prosecution must show that the person making the statement knew it to be false, or made it recklessly without caring whether it was true or not.

Maximum penalty 2 years' imprisonment and an unlimited fine.

NOTHING BUT THE TRUTH

It is an offence for a business to make a false statement, knowingly or recklessly, about the service that it offers.

SEX DISCRIMINATION

Your right to fair treatment regardless of your sex

The Sex Discrimination Act 1975 provides that it is unlawful to discriminate against someone on the ground of sex, in the areas of employment, education, provision of goods and services, housing and advertising.

These provisions are complemented by the Equal Pay Act 1970, which provides that men and women doing the same or broadly similar jobs, or jobs of equal value, are entitled to equal terms and conditions of work – including equal pay. *See:* PAY

Anyone who wants to bring a complaint of sex discrimination or of unequal terms and conditions of work against an employer must do so by applying to an INDUSTRIAL TRIBUNAL. In other cases of sex discrimination, legal action must be taken in the sheriff court.

The Sex Discrimination Act lays down 4 types of unlawful discrimination:

- Direct discrimination. This occurs where a person is treated less favourably simply because of his or her sex – for example, where an employer turns down a woman for a job because he wants to employ men only.
- Indirect discrimination. This occurs where the same requirement or condition is applied to both sexes, but is detrimental to one of them. An example would be where an employer required applicants for a job not to be responsible for looking after very young children – a condition which is likely to affect more women than men.
- Discrimination against married people in employment. This occurs where an employer discriminates – directly or indirectly – against someone because he or she is married. For instance, an employer may refuse to employ a married person for a job that involves unsocial hours, or may pay removal expenses for single employees only.

It is not unlawful for someone to discriminate against a person on the

HOW TO COMPLAIN ABOUT SEX DISCRIMINATION

If you think you have been unfairly treated because of your sex, write to the Equal Opportunities Commission, 249 West George Street, Glasgow (or its head office at Overseas House, Quay Street, Manchester M3 3HN).

The Commission was established under the Sex Discrimination Act 1975. Its job is to help eliminate discrimination, to promote sex equality and to monitor the working of the Sex Discrimination and Equal Pay Acts.

It will be able to advise you on what to do about your complaint. If the case is complicated, the Commission may help you to present it before an industrial tribunal (if it concerns employment) or a sheriff court (if it concerns education, housing or goods and services).

Employment discrimination

After seeking advice, complain through your grievance procedure. Consult your union if you belong to one.

If you are still dissatisfied about the treatment you have received, you can apply to an INDUSTRIAL TRIBUNAL within 3 months of the act complained of. To do so, fill in an application form (this can be obtained from the local industrial tribunal office, from a job centre or unemployment benefit office) and send it to the Central Office of the Industrial Tribunals in Glasgow. The ADVISORY, CONCILIATION AND ARBITRATION SERVICE may then contact you and your employer in order to attempt a reconciliation.

If your complaint is not resolved, it will be heard by an industrial tribunal. In order to help your case, special forms are available from the Equal Opportunities Commission on which questions may be put to the employer about his conduct. The employer is not obliged to reply, but if he does, you may use his replies in evidence before the tribunal.

If your complaint comes before a tribunal, it is up to you to prove, to the tribunal's satisfaction, that you have been discriminated against unfairly. However, if your employer claims that your job is exempt from the Act, it is up to him to prove that.

Once the tribunal has heard your complaint, it can do one or more of the following:

- Find the case proved and order the employer to pay compensation for loss of earnings, or injury to feelings, up to a maximum of £7,500.
- Find the case proved and recommend that the employer carry out a certain course of action. For example, if your complaint was that you had been passed over for promotion because you were a woman, the tribunal can recommend that the employer implement that promotion. If he unreasonably fails to do so, the tribunal may order him to pay compensation (subject to the £7,500 limit).
- Make an order declaring the rights of the parties.
- Dismiss the complaint.

If the complaint is dismissed, you can appeal to the EMPLOYMENT APPEAL TRIBUNAL, but only on a point of law.

Equal pay If your complaint is about equal pay, you can also complain to an industrial tribunal. *See:* PAY

Education discrimination

If you believe that you have been treated unfairly by a college because of your sex, or your children have been treated unfairly by a school, complain first of all to the principal or head teacher of the establishment involved.

If no action is taken, write to the education authority or the governors involved. If you are still dissatisfied, write to the Secretary of State for Scotland outlining your complaint – address it to the Secretary, Scottish Education Department, New St. Andrew's House, Edinburgh EH1 3SY.

The Secretary of State has 2 months in which to take action or inform you of his decision. If he takes no action or you disagree with his decision, you may then raise a legal action in the sheriff court. You can do so up to 8 months after the discrimination complained of.

Housing, goods and services discrimination

Any complaint about housing, goods and services must be made to a sheriff court within 6 months of the incident complained of.

Advertising discrimination

Complaints about advertising being discriminatory should be made to the Equal Opportunities Commission. Individuals cannot take action. The Commission can apply to the sheriff court for an order to prevent further discrimination.

Taking court action

If you take a case to the sheriff court and lose, you may have to pay the winner's expenses.

If the sheriff finds in your favour, he can order the person against whom the complaint was made not to commit discrimination in the future, or to pay damages, depending on the circumstances. Either party can appeal against the decision to the sheriff principal or the Court of Session.

Non-discrimination notices

If discrimination is alleged, the Equal Opportunities Commission can carry out a formal investigation. It may then serve a 'non-discrimination notice', requiring the person concerned to stop discriminating. That person can appeal to an industrial tribunal or sheriff within 6 weeks against any requirement of the notice.

If the person persists in discriminating during the 5 years following the notice, the Commission can apply to the sheriff court for an order to prevent him from doing so.

ground that he or she is unmarried.

- Victimisation. This occurs where someone is discriminated against for making allegations of unlawful discrimination, or for bringing or being involved in proceedings under the Sex Discrimination and Equal Pay Acts. It is not unlawful to discriminate against someone who dishonestly makes false allegations.

Discrimination in employment

It is generally unlawful for an employer to discriminate against men or women when recruiting new staff, or to treat an employee less favourably because of his or her sex.

So if an employer instructed an employment agency to interview only men for a job, he would be discriminating. He would also be discriminating if he refused promotion to a woman because of her sex.

The law also covers discrimination in respect of any arrangements or benefits that are made available to employees – for instance, company cars or special mortgages. An employer who provided these benefits to male employees, but not to female employees doing the same job, would be discriminating.

Apart from employers, it is also unlawful for vocational training bodies – such as industrial training boards or the Manpower Services Commission – or employment agencies or trade unions to discriminate on the grounds of sex.

Employees who are not protected The sex discrimination laws do not apply to certain types of employee:

- An employee in a firm that employs 5 or fewer employees.
- Someone employed in a private household.
- An employee employed wholly or mainly outside Great Britain. However, someone employed on a ship registered at a British port, or on an aircraft or hovercraft registered in Britain and operated by someone who is resident there, is covered by the Act unless he works wholly abroad.
- A member of the ARMED FORCES.
- A minister of religion employed by a religious body whose doctrine stipulates ministers of one sex only.

The police are not exempt from the Act, but are entitled to make different rules for male and female officers about height, equipment and types of uniform. The prison service can also make different rules about height.

Genuine qualifications In certain other cases, an employer is entitled to stipulate that he wants to employ men or women only. To do so, he must be able to show that the person's sex is a 'genuine occupational qualification' for the job. The jobs to which this exception applies are:

- A job that requires a man or woman for authenticity – for example, acting or modelling.
- A job that requires either a man or a woman as a matter of decency – for example, a lavatory attendant.
- A job that entails living on premises occupied by people of one sex where there are no facilities for the opposite sex – for example, a trawler. The employer must be able to show that it would be unreasonable to expect him to provide separate facilities.
- A job in a men-only or women-only establishment – for example, a prison – where supervision is required.
- A job that involves looking after people's welfare and education and can best be done by someone of one particular sex – for example, some social work jobs.
- A job that must be held by a man because of the law restricting women's working hours – for example, a factory job that requires night work.
- A job that requires frequent visits to a foreign country whose laws and customs would make it difficult for a woman to do it effectively – for example, a job in some Moslem countries.
- A job that is one of two to be held by a married couple – for example, where the jobs of caretaker and housekeeper are offered to a married couple.

A genuine occupational qualification cannot be used to exclude one sex where an employer already has sufficient employees of the opposite sex to do the job concerned.

THE WIFE WHO WAS ASKED FOR HER HUSBAND'S SIGNATURE

Companies that insist on having a wife's hire-purchase or other credit agreement guaranteed by the husband commit unlawful sex discrimination unless they have similar rules for men.

Mrs Quinn, who was a part-time worker, went to buy a three-piece suite from a furniture store.

Before the sale of the furniture could be completed, she was asked to obtain the signature of her husband to guarantee the credit arrangement. She claimed that this amounted to sex discrimination.

DECISION

Mrs Quinn succeeded in her complaint of sex discrimination. The appeal court said that the company had discriminated against her by insisting, requiring or even suggesting that her husband should sign a guarantee. They would not have asked a married man to obtain his wife's signature.

Discrimination in education

Anyone applying to or attending a school, further education college, polytechnic or university must not receive less favourable treatment on the ground of his or her sex.

So a school that admits pupils of both sexes cannot refuse pupils of one sex on the ground that there are too many of that sex already. Nor can a school refuse to allow a girl to attend woodwork classes, or a boy domestic science classes, because of their sex. If a school makes it less favourable to do so – for instance, by refusing a pupil permission to take an O grade in that subject – it is discriminating unlawfully.

Single-sex schools Schools that take pupils of one sex only are exempt from the sex discrimination laws. This is so even if they take some pupils of the opposite sex, so long as this is exceptional or a small number only are taken for particular courses of instruction. An example would be a private boys' school that allowed girls from other schools to attend some 6th-year classes.

Discrimination against consumers

It is unlawful for anyone providing goods or services to the public to treat a man or woman less favourably because of his or her sex, regardless of whether the goods or services are paid for or free. Anyone who does so can be sued for damages in the sheriff court.

For example, it would be unlawful for a hotel to refuse a woman accommodation because of her sex; or for a publican to refuse her drink on the same ground.

Unlawful discrimination includes imposing special conditions on one sex only. For example, a bank would be discriminating if it required a woman to give details of her husband's occupation when opening an account, but did not require a husband to give details of his wife's work. So would a credit company that required the signature of a husband or guarantor before granting credit to a woman, but imposed no such condition on a man.

Voluntary bodies The discrimination laws do not apply to non-profit making voluntary bodies that restrict membership and benefits or facilities to one sex – for example, women's rural institutes. Nor do they apply to political parties that make provision for separate women's groups.

Discrimination in housing

Anyone – including a public body – who lets or sells a house or business premises must not discriminate against one sex by:

- Imposing stricter terms for members of that sex.
- Refusing an application or offer by members of that sex.
- Giving members of that sex lower priority on a housing waiting list.
- Restricting the benefits or facilities

available to members of that sex.

However, there are exceptions.

Anyone who owns and occupies a house can discriminate when he sells it, if he does not use an estate agent or advertise the sale publicly, for example, in a newspaper or on a public notice-board. And anyone who lets out part of his home is generally entitled to discriminate by stipulating whether a male or female tenant is sought.

Discrimination when placing advertisements

If a person places an advertisement in a newspaper, offering a job, he must not stipulate that only a man or woman need apply, unless the job requires a man or woman as a genuine occupational qualification. For example, 'Man wanted for nightshift' may be lawful; but 'Waitress wanted' is not.

It is unlawful to publish a discriminatory advertisement. But the publisher will not be liable if he reasonably relied on a statement by the person who placed the advertisement that it was not unlawful.

If that statement was false, and was made knowingly or recklessly, the person placing the advertisement would commit an offence. The maximum penalty is a fine of £2,000.

When discrimination is lawful

In certain circumstances the sex discrimination laws do not apply, and it is not unlawful to make different rules for men and women.

Tax, social security and citizenship law, for instance, are not affected by the Sex Discrimination Act. It is therefore lawful to have different retirement ages for men and women, or to impose stricter conditions for women, including married women.

There are other situations in which discrimination is lawful. For example:

- A charity is entitled to provide benefits to one sex only.
- An insurance company can charge different premiums and give different benefits, so long as the differences are reasonable and are based on acceptable actuarial data.
- Special rules can be made for sportswomen if they would be at a disadvantage because of their strength or stamina.

SHAREHOLDER

Your rights if you own shares in a company

Both private and public companies issue shares that confer on their holders certain rights.

Generally speaking, these include the right to:

- Receive dividends, but only when a dividend is declared by the directors.
- A proportion of the company's remaining assets on winding up after creditors have been paid.
- Attend general meetings of the company, to speak there and to vote.

In addition to these rights, which are usually laid down in a company's memorandum and articles of association, the Companies Acts give shareholders the right to:

- Receive a copy of the annual accounts, and the auditors' and directors' reports.
- Appoint a representative, known as a proxy, to attend general meetings.
- Combine with other shareholders, owning not less than one-tenth of the company's paid-up capital, to compel the directors to hold an extraordinary general meeting to discuss the way the company is being managed.

Shareholders of public companies can sell or give away their shares at any time.

The right of shareholders of private companies to dispose of their shares is usually limited by the company's articles.

Responsibilities of shareholders

Shareholders in a limited company are not liable for the debts of the company. Once they have paid in full for their shares, their financial responsibility is at an end.

Any shareholder who controls the general meeting because of the size of his holding must use his controlling powers for the benefit of the shareholders as a whole rather than in his own interest.

Majority shareholders must not act unfairly to minority shareholders. In a small company, which is really an incorporated partnership, any shareholder can apply to have the company wound up if the other shareholders act unfairly towards him.

SHERIFF COURT

The all-purpose Scottish court

The sheriff court is the most comprehensive type of court to be found in Scotland. It deals with the widest range of legal matters, both civil and criminal, and handles the largest number of cases.

Scotland is divided into 6 sheriffdoms: Glasgow and Strathkelvin; Grampian, Highland and Islands; Lothian and Borders; North Strathclyde; South Strathclyde, Dumfries and Galloway; Tayside, Central and Fife. These sheriffdoms coincide largely with the corresponding local authority areas.

Each sheriffdom is divided into a varying number of sheriff court districts, 49 in all. Courts are held in the main cities and towns.

Each sheriffdom is headed by a full-time sheriff principal. It is his job to ensure that business in the courts is conducted speedily and efficiently. He also hears some appeals (but not in criminal cases) from the decisions of the individual sheriffs who sit as judges in the courts of the sheriffdom.

The number of sheriffs who sit in each district varies, depending on the amount of business. In rural areas one sheriff may sit in 2 or 3 courts; in Glasgow, on the other hand, 20 sheriffs are attached to the one sheriff court.

The powers of the sheriff court

The sheriff court deals with both civil and criminal cases.

Civil cases Although a sheriff has an extraordinarily wide range of powers, most of his civil business falls into a few categories. Much of the work concerns actions for debt and breach of contract. A sheriff can deal with claims of any value, however, high, and he is the only judge who can hear cases involving claims of £500 or less. Claims for £1,000 or less are dealt with under a short form of procedure, known as 'summary cause' procedure.

In May, 1984, a sheriff was for the first time given power to grant a DIVORCE. This power is shared with the Court of Session. A sheriff already has power to grant a SEPARATION to a husband or wife.

APPOINTING THE JUDGES

Sheriffs and sheriffs principal are full-time salaried judges who are appointed by the Crown.

A sheriff principal's task is to administer his sheriffdom as well as to hear appeals from decisions of sheriffs (but not in criminal cases).

Sheriffs and sheriffs principal are chosen from among advocates or solicitors who have been qualified in these professions for at least 10 years. Sheriffs principal are now usually appointed from the ranks of sheriffs.

Sheriffs are appointed to particular sheriffdoms and usually to a particular district within that sheriffdom. But in rural areas, one sheriff may sit in two or even three districts. There are also a few 'floating sheriffs' who can be sent anywhere in Scotland where the pressure of work requires.

In addition there are around 30 temporary sheriffs who sit part-time. They are legally qualified and relieve sheriffs who are, for instance, on holiday or ill. They are paid a daily fee.

Appointment as a temporary sheriff is often used as a training ground for permanent sheriffs.

There are also honorary, unpaid sheriffs, who are appointed by the sheriff principal to a particular court. They need not be legally qualified and are used in some places to deal with matters within the scope of their qualification and experience.

A sheriff also deals with matters such as CUSTODY OF CHILDREN, ADOPTION, claims for ALIMENT, actions involving land, claims for DAMAGES for negligence, and actions for the EVICTION of tenants – public and private. (Eviction is also dealt with under summary cause procedure.)

In civil matters there is usually a right of appeal to the sheriff principal or the Court of Session from the decision of a sheriff.

Criminal cases Minor and moderately serious cases are dealt with by the sheriff, sitting alone, under what is known as summary procedure.

The maximum sentence that a sheriff can impose under this procedure is a fine of £2,000 or 3 months in custody (but 6 months for a second or subsequent offence of dishonesty or personal violence).

If a case is serious, but does not deserve to be tried by the HIGH COURT OF JUSTICIARY, the sheriff sits with a jury of 15, under what is known as solemn procedure.

The maximum sentence the sheriff can impose in these circumstances is an unlimited fine or 2 years in custody. If he thinks a heavier penalty is needed, he can send the offender to the High Court to be sentenced.

The maximum penalties mentioned above are those that a sheriff can impose except when a particular ACT OF PARLIAMENT provides for a greater or lesser penalty. *See:* CRIMINAL PROCEEDINGS

Administrative duties

Sheriffs also have many administrative duties which only occasionally lead to disputes.

For instance, at each sheriff court there is a commissary department, where wills are lodged and executors confirmed in office and appointed. *See:* CONFIRMATION; WILL

Sheriffs also exercise general supervision over BANKRUPTCY and the liquidation of companies. They deal too with the registration of clubs and hear appeals from licensing boards. *See:* LICENSED PREMISES

Fatal accidents Sheriffs are also responsible for conducting inquiries into the deaths of people who have died in unusual or unexplained circumstances. *See:* FATAL ACCIDENT INQUIRY

SHERIFF OFFICER

The officer who enforces sheriff court decrees

A sheriff officer is an official of the sheriff court. His job is to serve official papers in cases coming before that court and to enforce civil decrees (orders) made by it.

However, he is not an employee of the court. Sheriff officers – there are around 140 of them in Scotland – are either partners or employees in private firms. Each is personally appointed by the sheriff principal for the sheriffdom in which he is allowed to work. *See:* SHERIFF COURT

When enforcing court decrees, sheriff officers do not act on behalf of the court, but on behalf of the person who has been granted the decree. If a person wishes to enforce a court order – for instance, one ordering payment of a debt – he (or his solicitor) must approach a sheriff officer and ask him to do so.

The sheriff officer charges fees which are laid down in rules made by the Court of Session. The person against whom the decree has been pronounced will have to pay the sheriff officer's fee for enforcing it.

Much of a sheriff officer's work concerns the enforcement of debt decrees. If a debtor fails to pay after a sheriff court has ordered him to do so, the creditor (or his solicitor) can ask a sheriff officer to arrest part of his wages, or select and auction some of his possessions, in order to clear the debt. *See:* DEBT

Sheriff officers also carry out the removal of tenants who have failed to leave following a sheriff court order for their EVICTION.

If you have a complaint about the conduct of a sheriff officer, write to the sheriff principal of the sheriffdom – you can get his address from the local sheriff court. He is responsible for ensuring that sheriff officers carry out their duties properly.

Messengers-at-arms The majority of sheriff officers also hold appointments as 'messengers-at-arms'. They are officers of the COURT OF SESSION in Edinburgh, and enforce the decrees of that court. Complaints about their conduct should be addressed to the Lord Lyon King of Arms, New Register House, Edinburgh EH1 3YT.

SHOPS

The rights of shopkeepers and shoppers

A shop is not obliged to serve every customer who comes in. The shopkeeper can refuse to serve anyone without giving a reason for his refusal. But a customer must not be refused service on the ground of his or her race or sex. *See:* RACIAL DISCRIMI-

NATION; SEX DISCRIMINATION

The display of an article in a shop window or on a shelf does not commit the shopkeeper to sell it. But if he does sell it, it is a criminal offence to charge more than the price displayed.

Responsible for quality

A shopkeeper is responsible for the quality of the goods that he sells. They must be of merchantable quality and, if the shopkeeper knows the purpose for which they are bought, they must be fit for that purpose. Where the goods normally have only one purpose, it will be implied that they are fit for that purpose.

These principles apply even when the goods have been made by someone else and when they are obtained by the shopkeeper in a sealed pack that he cannot or does not open before selling.

If the goods are not of merchantable quality or reasonably fit for their purpose, the customer may be entitled to his MONEY BACK, or to damages.

If you damage something

If you carelessly drop something or knock something over in a shop, you will be liable for any damage caused by your negligence. However, if the accident was not your fault but was caused by – for instance – an unstable display, you will not be liable.

If your child causes damage in a shop, you are responsible if you are with him and have failed to supervise him properly – but not if the child goes into a shop on his or her own.

Opening hours

Some shops are limited in the hours they can open for business, but others can open and close whenever they like. The exact position depends on the local BYELAWS in each area. There are special regulations for shops that sell liquor under an OFF-SALE LICENCE.

SHORT TENANCY

A form of tenancy with limited security

The Tenants' Rights (Scotland) Act 1980 allowed a *private* landlord to create a new kind of tenancy, called a 'short tenancy'. Although the tenant is fully protected by the Rent (Scotland) Act during the period of a short tenancy, the landlord can recover possession of the house when the period expires.

What is a short tenancy?

For there to be a short tenancy, the following conditions must all be met:

- The tenancy must be protected under the Rent (Scotland) Act. For information about those tenancies that are not protected, see EVICTION.
- The period of the tenancy must be at least 1 year, but not more than 5 years.
- The tenancy agreement must only allow the landlord to end the tenancy before the period expires if the tenant has broken a term of the agreement – for instance, if he has failed to pay the rent.
- Before the tenancy begins, the landlord must give the tenant a notice telling him that the tenancy is a short tenancy. The notice *must* be in writing and in the form set out by law. If it is not, it is invalid.

  The form of the notice can be found in a booklet called 'Short Tenancies', available from rent registration offices and citizens' advice bureaux.
- A fair rent must be registered for the house. If no fair rent has been registered, the landlord must obtain a certificate of fair rent from the rent officer and apply, within 14 days from the start of the tenancy, for the rent contained in the certificate to be registered. *See:* RENT PROTECTION

Protected tenant If your tenancy is already protected under the Rent (Scotland) Act, and is not a short tenancy, your landlord cannot remove your security by getting you to agree to convert it into a short tenancy. Any document that claims to create such a tenancy will have no effect.

Your rights under a short tenancy

During the tenancy, your rights are the same as those of any protected tenant. Subject to what is said below, you can only be evicted on the grounds set out in the Rent (Scotland) Act. And your rent can only be increased under fixed legal rules. *See:* EVICTION; RENT PROTECTION

Ending a short tenancy

Unlike other protected tenants, a tenant under a short tenancy can be evicted when the period of the tenancy expires. His landlord need give no other reason for evicting him. So if the tenancy is for one year, the landlord is legally entitled to recover possession of the house at the end of that year.

However, if the tenant refuses to leave, the landlord must obtain a court order before he can evict him. It is an offence to evict any tenant unlawfully. *See:* HARASSMENT

What a landlord must do To end a short tenancy, the landlord must serve a notice to quit on the tenant. This must be in writing, give the tenant at least 4 weeks' notice and contain information required by law. If these conditions are not met, the notice will be invalid. *See:* NOTICE TO QUIT

If no (or no valid) notice to quit is served before the tenancy expires, it will be renewed automatically for a further year.

If the tenant leaves at the expiry of the notice to quit, no legal proceedings are necessary to evict him. But if the landlord wishes to safeguard his right to take such proceedings, he must also serve a written notice – sometimes called a Case 15 notice – on the tenant telling him of his intention to apply for an eviction order.

Eviction proceedings can only be started between 3 and 6 months after this notice has been served on the tenant. So if the landlord wants to start proceedings as soon as the tenancy ends, he must serve the notice between 3 and 6 months before that date.

The landlord is entitled to serve a Case 15 notice up to 3 months after a short tenancy expires. So long as he has also served a valid notice to quit, he can start eviction proceedings – but only between 3 and 6 months after serving the Case 15 notice.

If the landlord fails to serve a Case 15 notice either before the tenancy expires or within 3 months of that date, the tenancy is automatically renewed. The period of renewal is 12 months from the date that the short tenancy expired. This automatic renewal will occur every 12 months until the landlord serves a valid Case 15 notice and a valid notice to quit.

What the court must do If the sheriff court is satisfied there is a short tenancy, and that it has been ended by a valid notice to quit, it must grant an order allowing the landlord to repossess the house and (if necessary) evict the tenant.

The court can grant the order even if the landlord has failed to register a fair rent or to give the tenant a notice telling him that the tenancy is a short tenancy. But the court must first be satisfied that it would be just and equitable to ignore these failures.

The court can delay the date when its order takes effect – it will not usually do so for more than 3 or 4 weeks.

When a tenant wants to leave

A tenant must give notice to the landlord if he wishes to leave before his short tenancy expires. He should give:

- One months' notice if the tenancy is for 2 years or less.
- Three months' notice if the tenancy is for more than 2 years. *See:* LANDLORD AND TENANT

SICKNESS

Your right to be paid when off work through illness

Most employees are entitled to a minimum amount of sick pay – called statutory sick pay (SSP) – from their employer when they are off work through sickness or injury. That includes sickness or injury contracted at work. SSP is payable for up to 8 weeks in each tax year.

Employees who are not entitled to SSP, or whose entitlement has run out, can claim SICKNESS BENEFIT from the state. (Industrial injury benefit, which used to be paid to employees whose illness or injury was contracted at work, was abolished in April, 1983.)

However, the great majority of employees are also entitled to contractual sick pay under sick pay schemes that are incorporated into their employment contracts. These schemes are negotiated with trade unions or arranged independently by employers.

Informing employees Within 13 weeks of starting work, an employee should be provided with written information about the terms of his contract, or directed to a document where the information can be found. By law, the information must include any arrangements – including sick pay – that the employer makes for employees who are off sick. If there are no such arrangements, the employer must say so. *See:* EMPLOYMENT CONTRACT

If you receive no written information, or you are told nothing about sick pay, you can apply to an INDUSTRIAL TRIBUNAL. It can decide what the arrangements are (if any).

Your right to statutory sick pay

Most employees who are off work through sickness or injury are entitled to be paid statutory sick pay (SSP) by any one employer for a maximum of 8 weeks in any tax year (April 6 to April 5). SSP is treated like normal earnings, and INCOME TAX and NATIONAL INSURANCE CONTRIBUTIONS are payable on it in the usual way. If necessary, contribution credits can be given.

Employers can recover the cost of paying SSP by deducting it from their National Insurance contributions.

An employee who is not eligible for SSP (see page 609) can get SICKNESS BENEFIT instead, so long as he satisfies the contribution and other conditions. Like employees who are eligible for SSP, he may also be entitled to sick pay under the terms of his contract.

If you receive SSP for 8 weeks, but are still unable to return to work, you

THE EMPLOYEE WHO THOUGHT HE SHOULD GET SICK PAY

The law will not presume that wages remain payable during sickness in the absence of sufficient evidence to the contrary in an employee's contract. A court must approach each case with an open mind.

Mr Mears was a security guard. Soon after starting work in 1978, he was given some written information about the terms of his employment. Nothing was said about sick pay and Mr Mears never asked.

Mr Mears was off sick for 2 periods totalling 7 months, and received state sickness benefit. He neither asked for nor received sick pay from his employer. During his illness he was told by fellow employees that he would not get sick pay.

Mr Mears applied to an industrial tribunal for a decision on the information he should have received about payment of wages during sickness. The tribunal decided, on the basis of previous cases, that there was a legal presumption that wages remained payable during sickness unless there was sufficient evidence to the contrary in an employee's contract.

Mr Mears's employer had failed to produce sufficient evidence and the tribunal therefore decided that he was entitled to sick pay, less the sickness benefit he had received.

On appeal, the Employment Appeal Tribunal disagreed. In their view there was plenty of evidence that Mr Mears was *not* contractually entitled to sick pay. They also said that there was no presumption that wages remained payable during sickness. Mr Mears appealed.

DECISION

The appeal court agreed with the Employment Appeal Tribunal. Sick pay was either payable or not payable and the job of a court was to look at all the facts, with an open mind, before deciding what the correct term was. In Mr Mears's case, it was that he had no contractual right to be paid.

WHEN WORK IS SUSPENDED ON HEALTH GROUNDS

Certain employees are entitled to be paid weekly wages for up to 26 weeks if they are suspended from work because it is dangerous to their health to continue working.

The employees covered are those who work with processes involving chemicals, rubber, lead, radiation and radioactive substances. A nuclear power station worker, for instance, would be entitled to be paid if he was sent home because the radiation level had become too high.

An employee will not be entitled to be paid unless he has been continuously employed for at least 1 month. Nor will he be entitled to payment if he unreasonably refuses suitable alternative work, or is unable to work because he is sick (he can then claim sick pay or sickness benefit).

CLAIMING STATUTORY SICK PAY

Most employees are entitled to statutory sick pay (SSP) from any one employer for up to 8 weeks in any tax year. But certain employees are not eligible and must usually rely on sickness benefit. They include:

- Male employees aged 65 or over and female employees aged 60 or over.
- Employees who become sick during a stoppage of work due to a trade dispute at their place of work – unless they are neither involved in, nor directly interested in the dispute.
- Employees earning less than the LOWER EARNINGS LIMIT for national insurance contributions – £34 in 1984–5.
- Pregnant women, if sick during the period of entitlement to maternity allowance.
- Employees entitled to sickness benefit, maternity allowance, invalidity (including non-contributory) pension, severe disablement allowance, and sometimes unemployment benefit, in the past 8 weeks.
- Employees whose contracts are for 3 months or less – for instance, a SEASONAL WORKER – unless they actually work longer than that.

When SSP is payable

To be entitled to any SSP, an eligible employee must be incapable of work because of physical or mental illness or disablement, for *at least* 4 consecutive days (including Sundays). If this condition is satisfied, SSP can be paid for the 4th day onwards, but not for the first 3 days – called 'waiting days'.

Where an employee suffers 2 periods of illness no more than 2 weeks apart, they are treated as 1 period for SSP purposes. So if he is off sick for 2 days in one week (too short a period for SSP to be payable), and then for 2 days during the following week, he is entitled to SSP for the 4th day of illness (the first 3 days are waiting days).

If you are getting SSP, and you resign or are dismissed, your SSP ends on the same day as your employment contract.

How SSP is calculated

SSP is paid at a flat-rate for each day of incapacity. There are no increases for dependants. The amount depends on the employee's 'normal weekly earnings' – that is, his average, gross weekly earnings over the previous 8 weeks (2 months, if paid monthly):

Normal weekly earnings	Weekly rate of SSP
Less than £34	Nil
£34–£50.49	£28.55
£50.50–£67.99	£35.45
£68 or more	£42.25

These figures are for the tax year 1984–5. The earnings levels and weekly rates are reviewed annually.

How to claim

If you are off sick, you must notify your employer. If you do not, he can withhold any SSP to which you are entitled.

The employer can decide how he is to be notified – for example, he may require notice to be in writing and to be given within so many days. However, he cannot require you to give notice personally if you are unable to do so; nor require notice in the form of medical evidence.

The employer can also decide what evidence he wishes about your illness. For instance, he may require a 'self-certificate' for absences that last between 4 to 7 days – in that case, you must state the nature of your illness yourself. For absences lasting longer than a week, he may require a doctor's statement. *See:* MEDICAL CERTIFICATE

After 8 weeks

If you have received SSP for 8 weeks and are likely to continue to be off work, you can transfer to the state sickness benefit scheme. Sickness benefit will be payable for up to 20 weeks; thereafter invalidity benefit is payable.

The transfer is carried out by your employer filling in form SSP 1 (T) during the 7th week of illness and sending it to you. To claim sickness benefit, you must complete the form and send it to your local social security office.

If you are refused SSP

Your employer may refuse to pay SSP because he thinks you are not eligible or not really ill. If this happens, you can apply to your local social security office for a decision by an adjudication officer on whether or not you should be paid.

If the adjudication officer decides against you, you can appeal within 28 days to a social security appeal tribunal. A further right of appeal lies to a Social Security Commissioner. *See:* SOCIAL SECURITY APPEALS; SOCIAL SECURITY COMMISSIONERS

can claim sickness benefit for a further 20 weeks. Thereafter, you qualify for long-term INVALIDITY BENEFIT.

Self-employed people A self-employed person is not entitled to SSP, but he can claim sickness benefit if he has paid sufficient Class 2 contributions.

An employee's right to contractual sick pay

Apart from their right to SSP, most employees are entitled to sick pay under the terms of their employment contract. Entitlement is either based on negotiated sick pay agreements or on private arrangements made by the employer concerned. Occasionally, sick pay is only paid at the employer's discretion; if it is refused, the employee can do nothing about it.

The amount and duration of sick pay vary enormously. Some employees are entitled to basic pay for only a few weeks. Others are entitled to average or full pay for as long as 6 months – and perhaps to half-pay for a further 3 to 6 months. Some sick pay schemes require employees to serve a qualifying period before being eligible; and some allow sick pay to be increased for length of service.

Your right to contractual sick pay is not affected by any right you have to SSP. But you cannot receive both full SSP entitlement and your full contractual entitlement when you are sick. Any contractual sick pay you receive will be treated as part of your SSP entitlement, and vice versa.

Deduction of benefit Most sick pay schemes require any sickness benefit for which the employee is eligible to be deducted from his sick pay entitlement. In some cases, only the basic rate of benefit is deducted; in others, increases for dependants are also deducted.

When your contract is 'silent' If you receive neither a written employment contract nor any written information about its terms, and you are told nothing about your rights during sickness, you may still be entitled to contractual sick pay. There may be other evidence that is sufficiently conclusive to justify including a right to sick pay as part of your contract.

For instance, there may be evidence that your employer has customarily paid sick pay to employees in the past. If the evidence is strong enough, that custom will be treated as a term of your employment contract.

If you believe you are entitled to contractual sick pay – or an industrial tribunal has said you are – but your employer refuses it, you can apply to court for an order requiring him to pay it. The court will look at all the circumstances in deciding whether or not you have any entitlement. It will not presume that you are entitled to be paid merely because your contract is not clear about what is to happen during sickness.

When a sick employee is dismissed

If a sick employee is given NOTICE when he is off work, he can claim UNFAIR DISMISSAL. He must have been employed for at least a year (2 years if no more than 20 have been employed during those 2 years).

To avoid having to pay compensation, the employer would have to convince the industrial tribunal that he acted reasonably. Each case is decided on its own facts. The tribunal would take into account the employee's job and length of service, as well as the nature of his illness. However, it would probably be considered unreasonable for an employer to:

- Dismiss a sick employee without consulting him.
- Fail to find out the true medical position before dismissing the employee.
- Fail to offer any suitable alternative job that is available. The employer is not expected to create a new job for the employee.

When 'frustration' occurs

If an employee's illness is so severe that he is unlikely to be able to return to his job for a long time, or to do the same work, his employment contract may be treated as 'frustrated'.

This means that the law treats it as having ended automatically, without any dismissal by the employer.

If frustration occurs, and the employer does dismiss, the employee has no right to compensation for unfair dismissal. However, an employee should not take his employer's word that frustration has occurred. He should make a complaint of unfair dismissal to an industrial tribunal and let it decide the matter.

When considering whether a contract is frustrated, the tribunal will look at the illness and how long it is likely to last, the nature of the job, the employee's length of service and the length of time for which he is entitled to sick pay.

SICKNESS BENEFIT

Your right to payment by the state when you are off sick

An employee who is unable to work because he is sick or disabled can get sickness benefit during the first 28 weeks of illness – but he will not usually be entitled to receive benefit for the first 8 weeks. A self-employed person who is unable to work because of illness can claim sickness benefit from the first week. In both cases, entitlement usually depends on an adequate national insurance contribution record.

Since April 1983, most employees have lost their entitlement to sickness benefit during the first 8 weeks of illness. They are entitled to statutory sick pay (SSP) from their employer instead. Their right to sickness benefit – for up to 20 weeks – and thereafter to INVALIDITY PENSION, starts to run from the 9th week of illness. However, employees who are not eligible for SSP can receive sickness benefit from the first week of their illness. *See:* SICKNESS

The contribution conditions

To be eligible for sickness benefit, a contributor must satisfy 2 conditions:

1. His contributions, in any one tax year (April 6 to April 5) since 1975, must amount to at least 25 times the contributions payable on the LOWER EARNINGS LIMIT for that year. Employees who paid 26 flat-rate Class 1 contributions before 1975 will be treated as meeting this condition.

2. To obtain full benefit, the contributor must, in the tax year *before* the year in which he claims benefit, have paid or been credited with contributions amounting to at least 50 times the contributions payable on the lower earnings limit for that year. Each self-employed (Class 2) and credited contribution counts as a contribution on earnings at the lower earnings limit. (Contributions are credited during spells of unemployment and sickness.)

For example, if someone claims benefit in 1984, he must have paid sufficient contributions between April 6, 1982 and April 5, 1983.

However, if someone becomes ill within 8 weeks of being out of work through a previous illness, the relevant contribution year is the same as for his

HOW TO CLAIM SICKNESS BENEFIT

If you are off work because of sickness, and you are entitled to sickness benefit, you should claim *without delay*. If you do not, you may lose benefit.

You do not need a doctor's statement (a 'sick note') for the first week of illness. But to claim benefit for that period, you must fill in a 'self-certificate' – called form SC1. You can get this from your doctor's surgery, a hospital, or your local social security office.

You should complete this form immediately, stating when you became sick and the nature of your illness. Then send it to the social security office via your employer.

If your illness lasts for more than a week, you must obtain a doctor's statement detailing the nature of your illness and the period for which you should refrain from working. (If your illness is likely to last for more than a week, your doctor may give you this statement when he first examines you.) Send this to the social security office. If you are still unable to work at the end of the period stated by your doctor, you must get another statement to continue claiming benefit.

If you have been receiving statutory sick pay, a different procedure applies. Before the 8-week period expires, your employer must give you a form to complete and send to the social security office. But you will need a self-certificate or a doctor's statement as evidence of your illness. *See:* SICKNESS

If benefit is refused If you are refused sickness benefit because you are considered to be capable of work, or you are disqualified for receiving it for up to 6 weeks, you can appeal within 28 days to a social security appeal tribunal.

previous illness. For instance, if he falls ill in January, 1985, after being off work through illness in December, 1984, payment of benefit is governed by his contributions between April 6, 1982 and April 5, 1983 – as it was for his December illness.

If a contributor has paid less than 50 – but at least 25 – times the contributions payable on the lower earnings limit for the year, he may get reduced benefit.

No contribution conditions need be satisfied if benefit is claimed because of illness or injury contracted at work.

A person who pays voluntary (Class 3) contributions, or a woman or widow who pays reduced contributions, is not entitled to sickness benefit. *See:* NATIONAL INSURANCE CONTRIBUTIONS

When benefit is paid

A contributor can claim sickness benefit for any period when he is incapable of work because of illness or injury – including mental illness and illness or injury contracted during work. (INDUSTRIAL INJURY BENEFIT was abolished in April, 1983.) Someone who is under observation because he is suspected of carrying or having been in contact with an INFECTIOUS DISEASE may be treated as incapable of work and entitled to benefit.

An employee's right to sickness benefit is not affected by any contractual sick pay that he gets. However, sick pay will usually be paid net of any sickness benefit received. *See:* SICKNESS

Sickness benefit is not payable for a single day off work. A contributor must be off work for at least 4 consecutive days (not counting Sunday). He can then receive benefit for the 4th and subsequent days, but *not* for the first 3 days – known as 'waiting days'.

Two periods of incapacity for work separated by not more than 8 weeks are treated as one period for sickness benefit purposes. So if a contributor has served the necessary waiting days during the first period, he does not have to serve them again before getting benefit.

Someone coming off statutory sick pay after 8 weeks can get sickness benefit immediately, without serving any waiting days.

When you can work Provided your doctor agrees and you tell your local social security office, you can do some 'therapeutic' work to help your recovery. If the social security office is satisfied that the work is of such a nature, you can earn up to £22.50 a week (in 1983–4) without your sickness benefit being affected. Certain expenses, such as fares, are not counted in this total.

The amount you get The basic rate of sickness benefit is £25.95 a week (in 1983–4). If the contributor has reached pension age (65 for a man, 60 for a woman) the rate is £32.60 – the same as invalidity pension.

A contributor may be entitled to additional benefit for a DEPENDANT – £16 a week for an adult and 15p (to be abolished in November, 1984) a week for a child. If the contributor has reached pension age, the increases are £19.55 and £7.60 respectively.

Sickness benefit is not taxable.

When you can be disqualified

You can be disqualified for receiving sickness benefit for up to 6 weeks if:

- Your sickness is due to misconduct (contracting venereal disease is not counted as misconduct).
- You fail, without good reason, to undergo medical examination by a regional medical officer when this is required – for instance, when there is doubt about the nature of your illness.
- You indulge in behaviour that delays your recovery.
- You do non-therapeutic work.

For more information about sickness benefit, see leaflet NI 16, available from your local social security office.

SKIP

When a permit is needed for a builder's skip

Someone who intends to carry out works that involve the construction, repair, maintenance or demolition of any building may want to hire a builder's skip for dumping materials.

If the skip is to be placed on a public or private road – but not if it is to be placed on private land – a permit must first be obtained from the district or islands council (the regional council in the Highland, Borders, and Dumfries and Galloway regions).

The council is not obliged to give consent for the skip to be left on the highway, but will usually do so if it is of an approved type. Since the council must check with the highway authority that the skip will not cause an obstruction, the intending hirer may be asked to submit a plan showing its proposed location.

The council may attach various conditions to a skip permit – concerning, for instance, where it is to be parked and how long it can remain. As the hirer must ensure that the skip is not a danger to the public, he may be required to have it adequately lit at night.

It is also the hirer's responsibility to ensure that any footpath next to the skip is regularly swept to keep it clear of mud and debris.

Breaking the rules

A person responsible for building works will be guilty of an offence if he parks a skip on a road without permission. He will also be guilty of an offence if he breaches any of the conditions attached to a permit.

It is a defence to a charge of breaking permit conditions that due care was exercised and all reasonable precautions were taken to comply with the permit. For example, it would be a defence to show that skip lights had been provided but vandals had damaged them.

If the permit conditions are broken by someone other than the person responsible for the building works – for instance, a contractor or one of his workmen – he can be prosecuted. It is a defence for him to show that he was unaware of the breach and that it was due to a mistake or because he was acting on instructions from the permit holder or his employer.

Maximum penalty £400 fine.

SMUGGLING

A smuggled souvenir can be expensive

Anybody who avoids paying CUSTOMS DUTY on goods from abroad is guilty of smuggling. The penalty, however, depends on all the circumstances and the amount of duty being evaded. If the amount involved was small – or if the Customs officer thinks there could have been a genuine mistake – he is empowered to impose an

SOMETHING TO DECLARE

Because the penalties for evading Customs duty are very high, it is always advisable to declare everything – even if you believe that there is no reason to pay duty.

on-the-spot penalty, extra duty and/or confiscate the goods.

The officer can seize the goods and then offer to sell them back as well as imposing a penalty. In more serious cases the offender would be prosecuted. The maximum penalties are a £2,000 fine or a fine three times the value of the smuggled goods – whichever is the greater – and 2 years' imprisonment.

Any vehicle or vessel carrying smuggled goods can be seized and confiscated by a Customs officer. For example, a car with a concealed compartment containing smuggled goods can be forfeited – even if it does not belong to the person trying to smuggle the goods.

SOCIAL SECURITY APPEALS

What you can do if you dispute a decision on your benefit claim

If your claim for a social security benefit is rejected, or you dispute the amount awarded, you can usually appeal to an independent local tribunal.

Until 1984 appeals about contributory benefits (and others such as child benefit, non-contributory invalidity pension and invalid care allowance) were heard by national insurance local tribunals. Appeals about supplementary benefit or family income supplement were heard by local supplementary benefit appeal tribunals.

However in April, 1984, these tribunals were merged and renamed social security appeal tribunals. These tribunals now hear all the appeals mentioned above. They consist of a legally qualified chairman and two lay members selected to represent people living or working in the area.

Certain matters – for instance, whether a person is an employed earner or whether contribution conditions are satisfied – cannot be referred to social security tribunals. They are decided instead by the Secretary of State for Social Services.

You cannot appeal to a social security tribunal against a refusal by the Attendance Allowance Board to pay ATTENDANCE ALLOWANCE. But you can ask the Board to review its decision. *See:* NATIONAL INSURANCE LOCAL TRIBUNAL; SUPPLEMENTARY BENEFIT

Medical matters Certain medical questions relating to DISABLEMENT BENEFIT and MOBILITY ALLOWANCE are decided initially by one or more specially-appointed adjudicating doctors. You can appeal to a medical appeal tribunal – which consists of a legally qualified chairman and 2 doctors – against their decision.

How to appeal

You can appeal against a benefit decision by writing to your local social security office or by filling in a form available from that office. You need only say that you wish to appeal, and briefly state your reasons.

You should appeal to a social security appeal tribunal within 28 days of the decision of an adjudicating officer; and to a medical appeal tribunal within 3 months of the decision of one or more adjudicating doctors.

However, a late appeal may be heard if there is a good reason for the delay.

A request to the Attendance Allowance Board to review its decision must be made within 3 months of the decision.

LEGAL AID is not available to pay for legal representation before tribunals. But a solicitor can give you advice under the LEGAL ADVICE and Assistance scheme.

It does not cost you anything to make your appeal. You will be able to get your travelling expenses and a sum to cover any loss of earnings.

If you are not satisfied

If the decision of a tribunal or the Attendance Allowance Board does not satisfy you, you may be able to appeal to a social security commissioner. *See:* SOCIAL SECURITY COMMISSIONERS

If you are not satisfied with the Secretary of State's decision on a question of law decided by him, you can refer the matter to the Court of Session if he does not do so himself. Legal aid may be available for this.

SOCIAL SECURITY COMMISSIONERS

Appealing against the decision of a social security tribunal

If you appeal to a social security or medical appeal tribunal and you are not satisfied with its decision, you can appeal to a social security commissioner. You can also appeal to him against a refusal by the Attendance Allowance Board to review a decision about attendance allowance. *See:* SOCIAL SECURITY APPEALS

If you are appealing against the decision of a social security tribunal, you can ask the commissioner to look at the evidence – including new evidence – again, as well as to consider any points of law you wish to raise.

However, if your appeal is about supplementary benefit or family income supplement, or is from a decision of a medical appeal tribunal or the Attendance Allowance Board, it is restricted to points of law only.

For instance, you can claim that the tribunal has misinterpreted the law or ignored NATURAL JUSTICE, or that no reasonable tribunal would have reached such a decision.

How to appeal

When you receive the decision of the tribunal (or Board), you should also be given information about your right to appeal. You should appeal within 3 months of the decision, although late applications can be accepted if there is a good reason for the delay. An appeal form is available from the local social security office.

If you want to appeal against the

unanimous decision of a social security tribunal, or any decision of a medical appeal tribunal, you must get permission from the chairman or a commissioner.

Where your appeal is about supplementary benefit, family income supplement, or a decision of the Attendance Allowance Board, only a commissioner can grant permission.

An appeal does not cost you anything and you are entitled to reasonable expenses to enable yourself (and any witnesses) to attend. You can be represented by anyone you choose, including a lawyer – but you cannot get LEGAL AID to cover the lawyer's fees.

Before deciding to appeal, get advice from a lawyer or from an advice agency such as a Citizens Advice Bureau.

What the commissioner does

Most appeals to a social security commissioner are decided without a hearing, on the written evidence supplied in the appeal papers – although the commissioner may write asking for further details. If you ask for a hearing so that you can put your case in person, the commissioner will grant your request unless he thinks that a hearing is unnecessary.

Once the commissioner has considered your case, his decision – and the reasons for it – will be posted to you. If you are still dissatisfied, you can appeal to the COURT OF SESSION against the commissioner's decision, but only on a point of law.

THE SOCIAL SECURITY JUDGES

The social security commissioners are full-time judges who deal solely with social security appeals. They are headed by a Chief Social Security Commissioner.

Like social security tribunals, they are independent of the Department of Health and Social Security. Only advocates (barristers in England and Wales) or solicitors of at least 10 years' standing can be appointed as commissioners.

There are 2 commissioners in Scotland (based in Edinburgh), 12 in England (based in London) and 1 in Wales (based in Cardiff). Each can hear cases from anywhere in Britain – the Scottish commissioners, for instance, deal with cases from the North of England.

If a case is important or of special difficulty, it may be heard by a Tribunal of commissioners – that is, 3 commissioners sitting together.

SOLICITING

When a prostitute seeks clients

Although PROSTITUTION – offering sex for money – is not itself an offence, a prostitute can be arrested if she approaches men in a public place. A policeman can arrest any woman whom he suspects of loitering or soliciting in a public place for the purpose of prostitution.

KEEPING PROSTITUTES OFF THE STREETS

The police can arrest any woman they suspect is loitering or soliciting for the purpose of prostitution in a public place.

'Public place' can mean doorways and entrances of any buildings abutting on a street, and a prostitute can be arrested for calling to men from a balcony. It is not soliciting, however, when she advertises in a shop window. Nor can she be prosecuted for displaying her telephone number in a public place.

A man who approaches women for immoral purposes – for example, by kerb-crawling – cannot be arrested for soliciting. At most, he can be charged with behaviour likely to cause a BREACH OF THE PEACE.

The penalty for soliciting is a fine of up to £400.

Pimps and male prostitutes A pimp – a man who solicits others on behalf of a prostitute – or a male homosexual prostitute who seeks clients in a public place is guilty of importuning. The maximum penalty is up to 2 years' imprisonment and an unlimited fine.

SOLICITOR

The rules that apply to professional legal advisers

No one can practise as a solicitor who has not obtained passes in the university legal examinations or their professional equivalents. An intending solicitor must also obtain the diploma in legal practice from one of the Scottish university law schools and complete a contract of training with a firm of solicitors (or central or local government).

After one year of training, trainees can become qualified solicitors, but there are certain restrictions on what they can do. They cannot, for instance, practise on their own until they complete a further period as a trainee.

To practise, a solicitor must hold a practising certificate, renewable annually, from the LAW SOCIETY OF SCOTLAND, the solicitors' governing body.

To obtain that certificate, solicitors must pay their annual dues to the Law Society and, if practising on their own account or in partnership, contribute to the Guarantee Fund – a fund which is administered by the Law Society and which pays compensation to people who have suffered financial loss through a solicitor's dishonesty.

If practising on their own account or in partnership, they must also have paid the premium for their insurance against being sued for negligence and have had their accounts audited by an accountant.

Money held by solicitors for their clients must be placed in a special bank or building society account. If any of this money is lost due to the dishonesty of a solicitor, the client will be reimbursed from the Guarantee Fund.

The solicitor's monopoly

With minor exceptions, the law gives solicitors an exclusive right to charge fees for:

- Drawing up deeds relating to the

sale or transfer of property. *See:* CONVEYANCE

- Obtaining authority to administer a dead person's ESTATE.
- Providing representation in court or instructing an ADVOCATE to provide such representation.

LEGAL ADVICE can be obtained from a wide range of organisations, some of whom will also provide lay representation before tribunals and in summary cause actions in the SHERIFF COURT. But anyone seeking help under the Legal Aid or Legal Advice and Assistance schemes must go to a solicitor.

Finding a solicitor

Solicitors are not permitted to advertise or to attract clients in other ways that are considered unfair by the profession. A full list of the solicitors in a given area is contained in the Yellow Pages of the telephone directory.

However, to identify which solicitors operate the Legal Aid and Legal Advice schemes, or to discover which solicitors normally handle certain types of case, it is necessary to consult the Directory of General Services or the Solicitors' Referral List, or, better still, to consult a legal advice agency in your area.

Paying your solicitors' bill

A solicitor's bill is made up of two elements – fees, which are the solicitor's charges for handling the case; and outlays, which are the expenses he incurs on the client's behalf. For further information, see LEGAL EXPENSES.

Complaining about a solicitor

If you have a complaint about how your solicitor has dealt with your case, you should address it to the Law Society of Scotland. The action taken will depend on the nature of the complaint.

If you are dissatisfied with the way in which the Society has handled your complaint, contact the Lay Observer, 20 Walker Street, Edinburgh. *See:* LAW SOCIETY OF SCOTLAND

SPECIAL EDUCATION

Helping children with learning difficulties

Local education authorities have a duty to make provision for children in their area who have special educational needs. Children are classed as having special educational needs if:

- They experience significantly greater learning difficulties than the majority of children of their age; or
- They suffer from a disability that makes it difficult or impossible for them to make use of the educational facilities available.

Education authorities must also find out which children of school age have special educational needs that are 'pronounced, specific or complex' and require continuing review. A special record – called a 'record of needs' – must be kept for such a child.

Assessing and recording children

An education authority cannot open a record of needs for a child unless he or she has undergone a process of assessment. This includes medical and psychological examinations and obtaining a report from the child's teacher.

The parents have to be told about the arrangements for these examinations and also about their right to be present when they are carried out. A parent who fails, without reasonable excuse, to arrange for his child to attend for examination will be liable to prosecution and to a fine of up to £100.

The notice telling parents about the medical and psychological examinations must also invite them to write to the authority giving *their* views on the special educational needs of their child. The authority must take account of these views when it makes its decision about the child.

Recording a child If the education authority decides that a child has 'pronounced, specific or complex' educational needs and that those require to be continually reviewed, it will open a 'record of needs' for the child. This is a document that sets out the nature of the child's impairment, his or her educational needs and the action proposed to meet those needs.

The parents must be informed about the decision to record the child, the reasons for it and the proposed contents of the record of needs. A parent again has the opportunity to express his views. If he remains unhappy about the authority's final decision, he has the right to refer the matter to an appeal committee. He should do this within 28 days of receiving the decision. *See:* SCHOOL

The appeal can be against:

- The decision of the authority to record the child or, following a review (see below), to continue to record him or her.
- The contents of the record of needs.
- The authority's decision about the school to be attended by the child.
- The decision of the authority to refuse a school placing request on behalf of the child. *See:* SCHOOL

The appeal committee can refer the matter to the Secretary of State for Scotland in certain circumstances. Even if the committee decides against the parent, he has a further right of appeal to the sheriff.

Once a child has been recorded under this procedure, there are opportunities for reviewing the authority's decision. The parent can insist on a review so long as the original decision or a subsequent review has not taken place in the preceding 12 months. The authority can decide on a review at any time and has a duty to keep the cases of all recorded children under consideration.

Educating children with special needs

Disabled children and those with

PLANNING FOR THE FUTURE

An education authority must consider what provision would benefit any recorded child in its area after the child ceases to be of school age – that is, after he or she reaches 16. The authority must prepare a report on this question at least 9 months and not more than 2 years before the child becomes 16.

The report has to include a recommendation on whether the child would benefit from further school education after the age of 16.

The report may be sent to the local social work department, the area health board and – if the parent agrees – to any other body that may be able to help.

A recorded child who continues at school after reaching 16 can insist that his or her record of needs be discontinued. A parent can also insist on this if the child is thought incapable of doing so.

learning difficulties can be educated in special schools, in ordinary schools or in special units attached to ordinary schools, in hospital schools, at home or by other individual tuition.

Special education can be given in ordinary schools so long as suitable arrangements can be made which do not affect the education of other children or make the school less efficient.

It may be necessary for children to go to boarding school because there is no local day school catering for their type of disability.

The education authority must make adequate provision for children with special educational needs without requiring payment of fees. An authority can pay for handicapped children to go to private schools regarded as suitable by the Secretary of State, and must do so if an appeal committee so requires.

Choice of school In theory, the parents of children who need special education have the same right as all parents to choose their child's school. But in practice there is little choice because of the shortage of suitable places.

SPEED LIMIT

Rules that vary with the road and the vehicle

Traffic on all public roads in Britain is subject to maximum speed limits which vary according to the type of road. Vehicles other than cars and motor cycles can be governed by lower limits, which vary according to the type of vehicle.

The normal speed limit on any road can be lowered in an emergency, or because road works are being carried out. The highway authority responsible – the Secretary of State for Scotland for trunk roads, and the regional or islands council for the other roads – can make an order at short notice. If new limits are signposted, a driver is bound by them.

Advisory signs If 'advisory' notices suggest a lower speed – for example, in fog or before sharp bends – a driver who exceeds it commits no speeding offence. However, he may be charged with careless or reckless driving.

Speed limits do not apply to police, ambulance and fire brigade vehicles on emergency calls. But the driver of an emergency vehicle must still exercise proper care for other road users.

VEHICLES THAT ARE RESTRICTED

Lower speed limits may apply to goods vehicles, vehicles fitted to carry more than 7 passengers, and to any vehicle when it is towing a trailer or caravan.

Type of vehicle	Motorway mph	Other unrestricted road mph
Car with trailer or caravan	50	50
Goods vehicle up to 30 cwt unladen	70	50
Goods vehicle over 30 cwt unladen	70 (over 3 tons, 60 – dual carriageway, 60)	40
Goods vehicle and trailer (by weight)	40/50	30/40/50
Bus or coach	70 (dual carriageway, 60)	50
Other vehicle fitted for over 7 passengers –		
up to 30 cwt unladen	70	50
over 30 cwt unladen	70	40
Invalid carriage	-	20
Vehicle without pneumatic tyres	–	20

How the speed limit varies

On motorways and dual carriageways – where traffic flowing in opposite directions is separated – the normal speed limit is 70 mph. On other roads it is never more than 60 mph, and if the road is 'restricted' the permanent limit is 30 mph unless another limit is signposted.

WHEN A DRIVER IS CAUGHT

The maximum fine for exceeding a speed limit on a public road is £1,000 for a motorway offence, or £400 on other roads, including dual carriageways that are not designated as motorways.

An offender's licence is endorsed and he can be disqualified from driving – even for a first offence.

A driver who is caught speeding must be warned by the police at the time of the offence that he may be prosecuted, or within 14 days receive a NOTICE OF INTENDED PROSECUTION or a SUMMARY COMPLAINT (a court summons).

When a road is restricted

If street lighting is provided by lamps placed not more than 200 yards apart, that indicates what is commonly called a 'built-up area', and in most cases it is automatically a restricted road.

However, a road may be restricted by highway authority order provided that

WHEN THE SPEED LIMIT DOES NOT APPLY

Speed limits do not apply to fire brigade, ambulance or police vehicles on emergency calls.

signs indicating the beginning and end of speed limits are shown.

If the lamps on a restricted road are more than 200 yards apart, it must also have illuminated or reflecting 'repeater' speed limit signs at frequent intervals.

If a road is automatically restricted under the 200-yard rule, it is no defence for a speeding driver to say that a limit sign was obscured, or not seen for some other reason. A driver in doubt about such an area should assume that the limit is 30 mph.

SQUATTER

When empty property is occupied without permission

Squatters – people who set up house in unoccupied premises without the owner's consent – can be prosecuted for criminal TRESPASS. So can those who camp on private land without permission. There is no need to break in by force or cause damage for the offence to be committed.

However, prosecutions for criminal trespass are uncommon – the maximum penalty is only a £50 fine. A squatter is much more likely to be prosecuted for causing, or being likely to cause, a BREACH OF THE PEACE; or for malicious mischief or VANDALISM if he damages the house or any property in it.

Evicting a squatter

It is lawful for an owner to use reasonable force to evict a squatter. But that may be unwise.

The best course of action may be to seek an eviction order in the sheriff court. You can ask for the normal periods of notice to be shortened. If the court agrees, the squatter need not be given the chance to answer the application for his eviction, the court order can be issued immediately and it can be put into effect without warning.

Sometimes squatters are given permission to stay in premises by the person who owns them. In that case, they can generally only be removed by a court order. Any attempt to remove them by force would amount to HARASSMENT. *See:* LICENCE TO OCCUPY

THE RIGHT TO AN ENERGY SUPPLY?

Electricity and gas authorities have a duty to supply energy to occupiers of premises. *See:* ELECTRICITY SUPPLY; GAS SUPPLY

However squatters who are living in premises without the consent of the owner are not treated as 'occupiers', because their entry was unlawful. The fuel authorities will refuse to give them an energy supply if they know the occupation is unlawful.

STAMP DUTY

The tax that must be paid on many legal documents

If a legal document or deed is not properly stamped, it cannot be relied on in any legal action. Deeds which ought to have been stamped can usually be stamped late, but an extra charge is made for doing so.

The cost of stamping the document – at the government stamp office at 16 Picardy Place, Edinburgh – varies according to the type of document. The amount paid is embossed on the document.

Duty on a house purchase

The stamp duty paid on a house purchase is calculated on the price paid for the property. Up to £30,000 no duty is payable. Above £30,000, the duty payable is 1 per cent of the whole amount.

So if the price is £30,100, duty of £301 is payable. But if the parties were to agree that £100 of that price was for moveable items such as carpets and curtains, that would bring the purchase price for the house itself below the exemption limit.

To qualify for the exemption for purchases up to £30,000 or less, a CONVEYANCE will include special wording – 'It is certified that the transaction hereby effected does not form part of a larger transaction or series of transactions in respect of which the amount or value, or the aggregate amount or value of the consideration exceeds…' That means that putting a false or over-inflated price on fixtures or fittings, so reducing the true price of the house, is illegal.

If you fail to stamp a CONVEYANCE correctly, it cannot be recorded in the REGISTER OF SASINES or the LAND REGISTER.

Duty on a lease

The stamp duty paid on a lease is a percentage of the annual rent:

Length of lease	%
7 years or indefinite	1
Over 7 and under 35 years	2
Over 35 and under 100 years	12
Over 100 years, but not indefinite	24

Reduced rates apply to leases with an annual rent of less than £500.

Duty on stocks and shares

No duty is payable when you buy government stocks, but you are liable to pay 2 per cent duty on all other transfers.

Duty on gifts

Deeds of gift are stamped on the value of the gift as if that was the price paid. If land is involved, its value must be agreed with the district valuer and if shares are involved the value must be settled with the Shares Valuation Department of the Inland Revenue. *See:* GIFT

STANDARD-FORM CONTRACT

When the same conditions apply to everyone

The conditions of many types of CONTRACT are printed on forms that are standard for all transactions of the same kind.

In some cases there is no provision for signing your agreement to the conditions. You are simply given a form containing them – or they may be included or referred to in a ticket or receipt.

Conditions printed on the face of such a document, or referred to there, are usually legally binding on you if the document is received as part of the transaction and the conditions are clearly set out on it, or if it is one that could reasonably be expected to contain conditions – for example, a railway ticket or a cloakroom receipt.

However, a document that you receive only after the contract is made – for instance, a ticket dispensed by a machine after you have parked your car in a car park – is not binding on you, unless it can be shown that you knew of the conditions – for example, if you had read and agreed to them on previous occasions.

Signing a standard contract

If you do sign a standard-form contract, you will be bound by its terms unless:

- There has been FRAUD or MISREPRESENTATION by the other party, or
- There are terms that a court considers unreasonable. *See:* UNFAIR CONTRACT

Conditions you cannot see

You may be shown, and perhaps asked to sign, a document that does not set out the standard terms of the contract itself. It may refer to terms set out in a notice displayed on the premises, or in another document you have not seen.

Courts usually regard such terms as binding if the customer has a reasonable opportunity to read them. If not, they are invalid.

STATUTORY INSTRUMENT

When Parliament delegates its powers

An ACT OF PARLIAMENT need not contain all the details of the law that it is creating. To ease the burden on its time, Parliament delegates some of its law-making powers.

It does so by passing Acts that outline the basic principles of a law and specifically enable a government minister – in practice, civil servants acting on his behalf – to draw up rules and orders that fill in the details. These rules and orders, known as statutory instruments, are no less law than are Acts of Parliament.

For example, many Acts covering such matters as road traffic, employment, social security and consumer protection provide only a framework which is filled out later by detailed regulations. Matters such as changing financial limits (for instance the rates of social security benefits), procedures for making applications, and methods of dealing with disputes are often dealt with in this way.

Once made, statutory instruments may be frequently altered or replaced by later instruments as circumstances change.

Statutory instruments are also used to bring Acts into operation. An Act may be brought into force by one instrument or in stages by several instruments.

What Parliament does

A statutory instrument must normally be laid before Parliament, but very few are debated and voted on. Most are automatically approved if they are not challenged within 40 days. Some, however, must be voted on before they become law.

The Joint Committee on Statutory Instruments, a committee of both Houses of Parliament, inspects all statutory instruments that have to be laid before Parliament, to make sure that they are technically correct. A House of Commons Select Committee on Statutory Instruments (in practice one half of the joint committee) also considers those instruments that have only to be laid before the Commons.

Keeping within the limits

A statutory instrument must not go beyond the powers laid down in its parent Act. If it does so, it can be challenged in court on the ground that it is ultra vires – that is, beyond the powers given to the minister by the Act.

When a statutory instrument is being made, any requirements laid down in the parent Act must also be observed. For example, in the case of instruments dealing with social security matters, the Social Security Advisory Committee may first have to be consulted.

STERILISATION

A means of permanent birth control

Sterilisation – of men as well as women – is the most reliable and permanent means of preventing childbirth.

The operation is available free on the National Health Service – if a doctor agrees to perform it. It may be carried out for medical reasons or simply because a couple decide that they do not wish to have any more children.

The male operation (vasectomy) is simpler, and can be done on an outpatient basis under a local anaesthetic. Female sterilisation is more complex and requires a general anaesthetic and a stay in hospital.

When sterilisation can be carried out

If a woman risks injury or death by becoming pregnant, her doctor may advise sterilisation. But the operation cannot be performed without her consent. A doctor who did so could be sued for DAMAGES, as could any health board that employed him.

Sterilisation can also be carried out if a couple decide that they do not wish to have children. This may be because they already have all the children they want and feel unable to cope with more, or because the woman has been advised against using an oral contraceptive (the 'pill') for medical reasons. It is for the couple to decide which partner should be sterilised.

When a doctor is negligent

If a doctor refused a request for sterilisation to prevent a pregnancy that he knew might harm a woman's health, or delayed a sterilisation operation that was urgently needed, he could be sued

WHAT YOU SHOULD DO

If you are considering being sterilised, consult your doctor or visit your local family planning clinic. They will be able to tell you about the male and female operation and help you come to a decision.

You have no right to be sterilised on the National Health Service – although a doctor would be negligent if he refused to operate when it was medically necessary. You may be advised against sterilisation if it is felt that you are too young or have given insufficient thought to the matter.

The hospital will usually ask your partner to give his or her written consent to your being sterilised – although this is not legally necessary. However, it is done in order to ensure that both of you appreciate the consequences of what you are doing (sterilisation is generally irreversible) and have discussed it together.

for NEGLIGENCE (as could the area health board, if he was employed by it).

If, when carrying out a sterilisation operation, a doctor failed to take reasonable care, and injury resulted, he (and the area health board) could be sued. It would also be possible to sue if a pregnancy resulted because the operation was not carried out properly. *See:* DOCTOR AND PATIENT; MEDICAL NEGLIGENCE

STOLEN GOODS

Keeping goods from their true owner

If a person knowingly retains stolen goods, with the intention of keeping them from their true owner, he is guilty of the crime of RESET.

STRIKE

Your rights during a dispute at work

A worker who withdraws his labour by going on strike is almost always breaking the terms of his EMPLOYMENT CONTRACT. If he is dismissed as a result, he *may* be able to bring an unfair dismissal claim (see below).

But provided that the strike is in support of a 'trade dispute' – a conflict between workers and their employer that is wholly or mainly about terms and conditions of employment or other workplace matters – strike organisers are generally immune from legal proceedings for certain legal wrongs that can arise from organising strikes, or threatening to do so.

Strikers – like other citizens – receive no immunity for criminal acts committed in the course of a dispute. If they damage property, obstruct the police, cause a BREACH OF THE PEACE or threaten violence to other workers, they are liable to be prosecuted.

Taking action against a union

Until 1982, a person whose business was affected by industrial action could not sue any TRADE UNION that had instructed the action to be taken. He could only sue the union's officials or shop stewards, or employees involved in organising the action.

However, the Employment Act 1982 now allows an employer to sue a trade union as well as its officials and workplace representatives. But before proceedings can be taken against the union it must be shown to have authorised or approved the strike action. This can only be done by:

- The union's executive committee, president or general secretary (whether or not they follow the union's rules).
- An employed union official, or any committee that he regularly reports to.

In this case the union will not be liable if its rules prevent the official or committee from giving authorisation or approval.

Nor will it be liable if the executive committee, president or general secretary disown the action (in writing) as soon as possible after they learn of it – provided that they then do nothing inconsistent with their decision, such as paying strike pay.

- Any person authorised by the union's rules.

If a union can be held responsible, employers are likely to take action against it rather than against officials or employees. Unlike individuals, unions are much better placed to pay damages and fines. But the amount of damages that can be awarded against a union is restricted to:

- £10,000, if the union has less than 5,000 members.
- £50,000, if it has 5,000 or more, but less than 25,000 members.
- £125,000, if it has 25,000 or more, but less than 100,000 members.
- £250,000, if it has 100,000 or more members.

Taking action against employees

An employer may decide to dismiss any employee who goes on strike. If this happens, the employee can make a complaint of UNFAIR DISMISSAL to an industrial tribunal.

However, provided that the employee is dismissed *during* the strike, the tribunal can only hear his complaint if there has been discrimination. It must first be satisfied that:

- At least one other employee at the same workplace, who was taking part in the strike at the date of the complainant's dismissal, was not dismissed; or
- At least one other such employee who was also dismissed has been offered re-engagement within 3 months of his dismissal, and no offer has been made to the complainant.

If the employee is dismissed after the employer knows the strike is over, the tribunal can hear the employee's complaint of unfair dismissal even if there has been no discrimination.

Where the tribunal does hear the case, it will deal with it in the same way as any other complaint of unfair dismissal. If the employee can show that he has been discriminated against, this will be taken into account in deciding whether the employer acted fairly in dismissing him. *See:* UNFAIR DISMISSAL

Suing for breach of contract An employer whose employees go on strike could sue each one for breach of his employment contract. But this rarely happens because of the damage it would do to industrial relations.

An employer who did sue could claim damages from each employee to cover the net value of that person's lost production, or the cost of a substitute worker.

Wages An employer is not required to pay any employees who are on strike. But in practice some return-to-work agreements contain a clause under which the employer pays the wages he withheld during the strike.

Discipline An employer can take disciplinary action – such as demotion or suspension without pay – against a striker if that is expressly or implicitly authorised by his employment contract. If it is not, a striker who resigns in protest can claim unfair dismissal (subject to what is said above). *See:* CONSTRUCTIVE DISMISSAL

Non-striking employees A non-striking employee is not entitled to any statutory guaranteed pay if he is laid off because of a strike involving employees of his employer or an associated employer. He will often not be entitled to be paid any guaranteed wages under his contract either. *See*: LAY-OFF

If the strike causes him to be made redundant, he may be entitled to a REDUNDANCY PAYMENT.

Giving strike notice

Since a strike involves a withdrawal of labour, it is almost always a breach of the strikers' employment contracts,

FINANCIAL SUPPORT FOR WORKERS DURING A STRIKE

Workers are not usually paid wages while on strike, and are entitled to only a limited amount of state assistance.

If a strike is official (recognised by a trade union) members of the union may receive strike pay – a weekly amount falling well below normal earnings – under the union's rules. The payment is made from union funds.

Your right to unemployment benefit

Strikers are not entitled to UNEMPLOYMENT BENEFIT, however justified their cause. Workers who are laid off because others have gone on strike are entitled to unemployment benefit only if they can prove that they are not participating in, or directly interested in, the dispute.

A worker will be treated as participating in a dispute if, for instance, he refuses to cross a picket line. He will be treated as directly interested in the dispute if its outcome will affect him automatically – for instance, he will benefit from any wage increase being sought (even if by another group of workers).

Your right to supplementary benefit

A worker who is disqualified for unemployment benefit is not entitled to SUPPLEMENTARY BENEFIT to meet his *own* needs. But he can claim supplementary benefit for his wife and children. He can also get help with housing costs and certain extra expenses.

A worker cannot get benefit for his dependants until he has exhausted his last payment of wages. For example, he must wait a week if he is paid weekly; or a month if he is paid monthly. If wages during the week (or the last week where the pay period is longer than a week) are more than two and a half times the family's needs under the normal supplementary benefit rules, the excess is treated as income for the following week.

When calculating the worker's entitlement to supplementary benefit, the following rules apply:

- No benefit is paid for the striker's own needs.
- The non-householder rate of benefit (£21.45 in 1983–4) is payable for his wife.
- The normal payments are made for children (£13.70 for a child aged 11–15, £9.15 for a child aged 10 or under).
- The weekly benefit payable is *automatically* reduced by £15 (in 1983–4). This is the amount of strike pay that the union is expected to provide. The deduction is made even though no strike pay is paid.

If the worker does receive strike pay, the first £15 will be ignored in calculating his income for benefit purposes.

- HOUSING BENEFITS (but not housing benefit supplement) are payable by the local housing department to cover rent and rates. Additional supplementary benefit can be paid to cover other housing costs, such as MORTGAGE interest payments.
- Additional benefit is payable only in respect of heating costs, special diets, hospital fares and blindness.

The rules regarding the calculation of income (apart from the £15 deduction) and the treatment of savings are the same as for ordinary claimants. *See:* SUPPLEMENTARY BENEFIT

Benefit for women Since November 1983 a married woman who is on strike can claim benefit for her husband and children in the same way as a married man.

A single or divorced woman who has dependent children can claim supplementary benefit for them while she is on strike.

Strikers without dependants A striker who has no dependants is not entitled to any benefit during a strike.

Dealing with hardship In certain limited circumstances, a striker may be able to obtain benefit to meet an urgent need. The circumstances include:

- Fire, flood or other disaster. Any benefit paid may have to be repaid.
- An exceptionally expensive diet that has been medically prescribed.
- Paying fares to visit an ill relative.
- The need to provide immediate necessities for a new-born baby (only if the strike has lasted at least 11 weeks).

On resuming work, a striker – whether married or single – can claim benefit (in the form of a loan) if he receives insufficient wages and cannot get an adequate advance from his employer. Benefit can be paid for up to 15 days. In calculating entitlement, earnings are taken fully into account. If the benefit payable is less than £3 in any week, no payment is made.

The social security office notifies the employer of the loan and he repays it by making deductions from the worker's wages. The social security office calculates the worker's 'protected earnings' by working out his basic weekly requirements, adding £8 and subtracting any CHILD BENEFIT payable. No deduction can be made which reduces the worker's weekly earnings below his protected earnings.

Up-to-date information on supplementary benefit and trade disputes can be obtained in leaflet SB2, available from your local social security office.

---

whether or not the striker give notice beforehand.

If strike notice is given, it should be carefully worded, making it clear that the workers are only striking – not terminating their employment.

If a strike notice was construed as a notice of resignation, the workers would lose their right to claim redundancy payments or unfair dismissal. They would also break their continuity of employment, on which many of their EMPLOYMENT PROTECTION rights depend.

When there is a lock-out

In the course of a trade dispute, an employer may close a place of work or suspend employment there. This is known as a 'lock-out'. Non-striking employees dismissed during a lock-out can claim unfair dismissal – unless all employees with a direct interest in the dispute have been dismissed, and none has been taken back within 3 months.

When workers 'sit-in'

If workers occupy their workplace without the consent or permission of their employer, they can be charged with criminal TRESPASS. The maximum penalty is a fine of £50.

They can also be charged with 'besetting' their employer's place of business. The maximum penalty is a fine of £400 or imprisonment for 3 months.

Civil liability Occupying a workplace is an infringement of the employer's property rights and he can seek an INTERDICT (a court order) to prohibit it. If an interdict is granted, ordering a sit-in to end, it is CONTEMPT OF COURT to refuse to obey it. Doing so may result in a fine or even imprisonment.

When unions and officials have immunity

A number of civil wrongs, or delicts, can be committed in the course of strike action. The most important are:

WHEN TAX IS REPAID

If a strike extends beyond the end of a tax year, or lasts longer than a few weeks, a striker may be entitled to a refund of income tax – as the deductions under PAYE while he was working did not take into account a period when he would not be earning. The payment of any tax refund will be deferred until the strike is over.

The refund, if due, may be made automatically by the employer under the PAYE system, or repaid direct by the Inland Revenue after the end of the tax year.

If the strike is short, the striker may still be owed some overpaid tax. But he does not need to make a claim: it is refunded by his employer adjusting his PAYE deductions when he returns to work.

1. Inducing employees to break or interfere with employment or commercial contracts.
2. Threatening to break or interfere with such contracts, or to induce employees to do so.

These wrongs will be committed by unions, union officials or shop stewards who instruct members to withdraw their labour, or threaten to do so.

An employer who alleges that a union or individual is committing one of these wrongs against him can apply to court for an INTERDICT prohibiting it. Failure to obey an interdict is contempt of court. In addition, the employer can seek damages.

However, as a general rule neither interdict nor damages can be obtained if the court considers the union or individual to be acting 'in contemplation or futherance of a trade dispute'. They are then immune from any liability for the wrong.

The court will therefore refuse an application for interdict if it thinks that this defence is likely to succeed in any subsequent proceedings for damages. The case will then go no further (unless the employer appeals against the decision).

'Trade dispute' For there to be a trade dispute, there must be a conflict between workers and their employer. The conflict must relate wholly or mainly to terms and conditions of employment, or other employment matters. If it does not, there is no trade dispute.

So there will be no trade dispute if strike action is taken primarily for political or personal reasons – for instance, to protest against the policies of a British or foreign government, or in pursuit of a grudge. Those who organise the action will be fully liable.

'In contemplation or furtherance' A union or individual is not immune from civil liability merely because there is a trade dispute. There is immunity only if the industrial action is taken 'in contemplation or furtherance' of that dispute.

Action is taken 'in contemplation' of a dispute if:

- A dispute is likely to arise in the immediate future, and
- The action is done in connection with that likely dispute.

For instance, a union acts in contemplation of a dispute if it issues circulars to its branches about the industrial action to be taken following the expected breakdown of wage negotiations.

Action is taken 'in furtherance' of a dispute if:

- A dispute exists, and
- The action is done with the intention of giving support to the dispute.

For instance, a union acts in furtherance of a dispute if it instructs its members to strike following the breakdown of wages negotiations.

Strike ballots In 1984 a Bill was before Parliament to withdraw immunity from an *official* strike that is not preceded by a secret ballot of the union members involved. Immunity will also be lost unless the strike takes place within 4 weeks of the ballot.

Provided that a ballot is held, immunity will not be lost merely because the strike is called in defiance of the ballot result.

MAINTAINING ESSENTIAL SUPPLIES

If the nation's essential supplies of fuel and food are threatened, the Government can advise the Queen to declare a state of emergency, which allows the armed forces to be called in to distribute vital commodities.

WHEN A STRIKE IS ILLEGAL

Certain groups are not allowed to strike. The only lawful way they may stop work is by giving proper notice of resignation, waiting until it expires and leaving their job. And even this course of action is not available to servicemen.

- Members of the armed forces may not strike. If a soldier stopped work he would, in effect, be disobeying an order and would be disciplined by a military tribunal. Nor may servicemen join a trade union or organise union activities. Someone who was a union member before he joined the forces can remain a member, however, provided he does not take an active part in the union.
- The police are not allowed to join a trade union (the Scottish Police Federation is not a union). Nor can they lawfully strike, as it is an offence for them to wilfully absent themselves from work or neglect their duty.

Inducing strike action is also unlawful, as it is an offence to 'cause disaffection' amongst the police (or attempt to do so), or to induce them to break discipline or withhold their services.

- Merchant seamen who disobey an order at sea, or who prevent a ship from sailing by being absent, are committing a criminal offence, for which the maximum penalty is a £2,000 fine. They are allowed to strike only when their ship is safely moored in a UK port and after they have given 2 days' notice of termination of their employment.
- It is a criminal offence for post office workers wilfully to delay or detain mail; the maximum penalty for doing so is an unlimited fine and 2 years' imprisonment.

When there is no immunity for 'secondary' action

Industrial action can be 'primary', meaning that it is directed against the employer with whom a dispute exists; or it can be 'secondary', meaning that it is

THE THREAT TO THE CUP FINAL

If the purpose of industrial action is mainly political, it will not be a 'trade dispute'. Those who organise it will not be protected from legal action by the employer.

The English FA Cup Final is a great international sporting occasion. Pictures of it are transmitted by satellite all over the world. In 1977, South Africa was among the countries scheduled to receive coverage of the final between Liverpool and Manchester United, transmitted by the BBC.

The Association of Broadcasting Staff, the union to which most of the BBC's staff belonged, threatened that the entire transmission would be stopped unless the BBC agreed not to transmit pictures to South Africa. The union objected to South Africa's apartheid policy.

The BBC sought a court order to require the union's general secretary to desist from calling on the BBC's technicians to interrupt the transmission. The order was refused, as the judge considered the case to be a trade dispute. The BBC appealed.

DECISION

On appeal the order was granted. It was decided that the issue was not a trade dispute with the BBC as an employer, but a political gesture directed against the South African government.

The broadcast went ahead as scheduled.

HOW A SIT-IN WAS ENDED

Refusing to obey a court order can result in workers being fined.

In the course of a demarcation dispute, 66 workers occupied the factory of Bestobell Insulation Ltd. in Glasgow.

Bestobell successfully obtained an INTERDICT (a court order) to stop the occupation, which amounted to a trespass. But when officers of the court attempted to deliver copies of the court order to those taking part in the sit-in, they would not accept them.

The court then ordered the workers to appear in court to explain their conduct. The workers failed to comply and the court issued warrants for their arrest.

DECISION

The shop steward was fined £150, and the other workers £100 each, for contempt of court in refusing to observe the court order.

When the workers were appearing in court, the employers were able to regain possession.

directed against other persons – such as customers or suppliers of that employer – who are not parties to the dispute.

Secondary action against an employer with whom no dispute exists usually involves an actual or threatened strike by his workers, or some other action – such as blacking goods – which is a breach of the workers' contracts.

If it does, any union or individual organising the action will have *no* immunity against being sued – even if acting in contemplation or furtherance of a trade dispute – unless the following conditions are all met:

- The action is against an employer who *directly* supplies goods or services to, or buys them from, the employer with whom the dispute exists. So there is no immunity if, for example, the action is directed against a competitor, or someone who supplies the employer in dispute indirectly through another supplier.
- The main purpose of the action is directly to prevent or interfere with the supply of goods and services between the supplier or customer and the employer with whom the dispute exists. So if the main purpose is, for example, to penalise the supplier or customer for publicly supporting the employer in dispute, there will be no immunity.
- The action is likely to prevent or interfere with the supply of goods and services.

When workers picket

Workers cannot generally be sued for picketing their *own* place of work, if their purpose is only to peacefully persuade others not to work or provide information on the dispute. Nor can their union be sued.

But there is no immunity if workers picket at a place of work *other* than their own; or if they picket their own place of work in support of certain disputes involving employers other than their own. Nor is there any immunity from being charged with a criminal offence. *See:* PICKETING

Taking emergency powers

When essential services are disrupted by an industrial dispute, the government can advise the Queen to declare a 'state of emergency', in which the armed forces and the police are called in to ensure the supply and distribution of food, fuel and other essential commodities.

Under its emergency powers, the government cannot abolish the freedom to strike or introduce conscription, but it can severely restrict a strike's effectiveness. *See:* EMERGENCY POWERS

STUDENT

How people are helped to gain higher qualifications

People who reach the required academic standard at school (or by taking adult education classes) can usually receive higher education with the aid of a government grant. However, there is no automatic right to a university or college place – and certainly not to the place of your choice.

The application form of the Universities Central Council on Admissions allows qualified candidates to choose up to 5 university courses. If you are not accepted for any of those, there is a clearing scheme which enables you to apply to other universities which still have vacancies for the coming year.

Teacher-training course applications are dealt with in a similar way, by a central register and clearing house. Art and design courses also have a central register. For other courses at polytechnics and colleges, you apply direct to the institution of your choice.

How grants are awarded

Student grants to applicants ordinarily resident in Scotland on the June 30 preceding the start of the course are made by the Scottish Education Department, Haymarket House, Clifton Terrace, Edinburgh EH12 5DT. Grants to persons resident in England and Wales are made by their local authority. In each case the grant may be for education in another country.

An applicant for a Scottish grant, as well as being resident in Scotland, must also normally have been resident in the British Islands for the previous 3 years.

As soon as you are unconditionally accepted for a place at a university, polytechnic or college, you should ask the Scottish Education Department for a grant application form. A delay in applying may mean that the grant is not paid until after the term starts.

When grants are paid Scottish grants are paid for:

- A full-time degree course at a university, college or polytechnic. With exceptions, grants are not awarded for second 'first degree' or comparable courses, nor to improve existing qualifications.
- Other full-time and sandwich courses approved by the Scottish Education Department – for example, teacher or other specialist training.
- Short postgraduate courses of professional or vocational training – for instance, teacher or social work training.

How much The standard rates of a maintenance grant for 1984–5 are:

- £2,050 for students in London, not living at home.
- £1,725 for students elsewhere, not living at home.
- £1,325 for students living at home.

The tuition fees are also paid.

Additional allowances are payable for courses requiring attendance for more than 30 weeks a year, for travel costs over £50 and in certain other prescribed circumstances.

The amount of maintenance grant actually paid to a student is calculated by deducting from the standard rates a sum to take account of the resources of the student and parents.

A grant will be reduced if the student's income (ignoring vacation earnings and up to £540 of scholarship income) exceeds £375 (in 1983–4).

If a student is under 25 and has not been self-supporting for 3 years, the parents' gross income for the tax year which ended in the previous April is assessed, and deductions for dependants and mortgage, insurance and pension payments are allowed. The parents are then expected to make a contribution to the student's upkeep, depending on the amount of their net income. In 1983–4, parents with a residual income of £7,100 or lower, after allowances had been deducted, were assumed to pay a contribution of £20.

A minimum grant is paid to any eligible student, regardless of parents' income. In 1984–5 the minimum will be reduced to £205 plus fees.

Mature students A student who is over 25, or who has been supporting himself for 3 years, can claim extra allowances for a dependent spouse or child, so long as he or she married not later than the August 31 before the start of the course.

There are also special allowances for the dependants of widows, widowers and divorced people, and additions for students over 26. For information on these, consult the current *Guide to Students' Allowances*, obtainable from the Scottish Education Department, universities and colleges.

Education authority help Local education authorities can make grants at their discretion to enable people over school age and resident in their areas to take advantage of educational facilities above school level, whether in Scotland or elsewhere.

Your right to benefits

Full-time students are not entitled to SUPPLEMENTARY BENEFIT during term-time – they are treated as not being available for work.

This does not apply to a student who is a single parent or severely disabled; or to a cohabiting student supporting his or her partner's child. In these cases benefit may be payable during term-time, depending on income.

Vactions Students can claim supplementary benefit during vacations. But single students who go home to their parents are not usually eligible for benefit during the Christmas and Easter vacations – the grant includes an amount (£24.55 in 1983–4) for maintenance during those periods.

Housing costs Students can claim HOUSING BENEFITS to help pay their rent. But during term-time £14.70 (1983–4) is deducted from the weekly rent on which benefit is calculated.

Students who are owner-occupiers can claim supplementary benefit during vacations to help with mortgage interest payments and other housing costs.

Part-time courses people doing a part-time school or college course, or a part-time training course, may still be eligible for supplementary benefit.

The course must not involve more than 21 hours of instruction and study a week (excluding unsupervised study periods and meal breaks). Claimants must also have been on unemployment, sickness or supplementary benefit, or a YTS course, throughout the 3 months

PAYING NATIONAL INSURANCE CONTRIBUTIONS

Most social security benefits – for example, unemployment benefit, sickness benefit (usually) and retirement pension – can be obtained only when certain contribution conditions are satisfied. These conditions can be satisfied by the student either having paid contributions or having paid and been credited with contributions. *See:* NATIONAL INSURANCE CONTRIBUTIONS.

Someone who stays on at school after 16 is credited with contributions – that is, treated as having paid them. In the tax years in which he becomes 16, 17 and 18, he will be credited with Class 3 credits to help with entitlement to long-term benefits such as retirement pension. And he will be credited with Class 1 credits in the tax years in which he is 16 or 17, to help with entitlement to short-term benefits – unemployment benefit, sickness benefit and maternity allowance.

To help with entitlement to unemployment benefit, sickness benefit and maternity allowance after he starts work, a student who starts a course of full-time education *before* the age of 21 is credited with contributions. The credits are for the tax year before the year in which he claims benefit, if he was still studying during that tax year.

However, as well as being credited with contributions, anyone claiming unemployment and sickness benefit, or maternity allowance, must also have *paid* a certain amount of contributions in any one tax year. *See:* NATIONAL INSURANCE CONTRIBUTIONS

A student who is on a sandwich course will have to pay Class 1 contributions if his employer continues to pay his wages.

Holiday work A student who takes a job during vacations will have to pay Class 1 national insurance contributions if he earns more than the LOWER EARNINGS LIMIT in any week (£34 in 1984–5).

before starting the course – or, if they worked during this period, for at least 3 out of the previous 6 months.

Special cases Special rules apply to students who are married or cohabiting, or who are single parents or disabled. In these cases, unpaid parental contributions are not taken into account in assessing income for supplementary benefit purposes. In addition, the first £2 per week of the student grant is ignored (but in the case of a married or unmarried couple, only if they have a child).

SUB-CONTRACTOR

When work you ordered is farmed out

If you engage a contractor to do work for you, it is worth making clear whether, under the contract between you, he is entitled to employ subcontractors.

If the work depends on his personal skill – for example, painting a mural – he is not allowed to do so. If the work involves a more general skill, however, such as painting your house, he can do so unless you both agree a contract stipulating specifically that he cannot.

When a contractor employs a subcontractor, he is responsible for paying him. You are responsible only to the main contractor for payment. Similarly, it is the contractor, not the subcontractor, who is responsible to you for the work being carried out properly.

However, if the sub-contractor damages your property through his negligence, he is personally liable – though if the contractor retained overall control, he will be liable also.

SUB-TENANCY

The position where a tenant sub-lets a house

A sub-tenant is someone who rents all or part of a house or flat from an existing tenant. If the sub-tenancy is lawful – that is, if it is allowed by the tenancy agreement or the landlord has consented to it – the existing tenant becomes the sub-tenant's landlord and the sub-tenant becomes, in law, his tenant. The existing tenant, however, remains the tenant of his own landlord.

The rules about sub-letting, and the rights of sub-tenants, depend on whether the existing tenant rents from a private landlord or from a public body.

Private sector tenancies

Under common law, a tenant who rents an unfurnished house or flat (but not a furnished one) from a private landlord has the power to sub-let all or part of it unless he is prohibited from doing so. In practice, however, most tenancy agreements contain a clause expressly forbidding subletting, either totally or except with the landlord's consent. If the tenant ignores such a clause, any sub-tenancy will be unlawful, and the landlord can apply for a court order to evict the tenant.

If a sub-tenancy is lawful, the subtenant has all the rights of a tenant. Depending on the circumstances, he may be protected by the Rent (Scotland) Act 1984 and therefore be entitled to security of tenure and to have a fair rent fixed by a rent officer. *See:* EVICTION; RENT PROTECTION

Protected tenancies If a tenant who is protected by the Rent (Scotland) Act creates a sub-tenancy that is also protected, he must give his landlord written details of the sub-tenancy – including the rent charged – within 14 days of its creation. This is unnecessary if he has supplied the information previously and the terms on which he sub-lets remain unchanged.

Any tenant who, without reasonable cause, fails to provide this information commits an offence. The maximum penalty is a £50 fine.

Public sector tenancies

Tenants of district and islands councils, new town development corporations, the Scottish Special Housing Association, registered housing associations, and housing co-operatives have the right to sub-let so long as they obtain their landlord's consent. They must make a written application to the landlord, enclosing details of the proposed sub-tenancy.

The landlord must not refuse consent unreasonably. A tenant who alleges that this has happened can apply to the sheriff for an order requiring the landlord to consent. If the sheriff thinks that the landlord's refusal is reasonable – because, for instance, an extra person occupying part of the house would lead to OVERCROWDING – he will not grant the order.

No application can be made to the sheriff if the landlord refuses consent because it considers that the tenant intends to charge an unreasonable rent or ask for an illegal payment in addition to the rent. *See:* KEY MONEY

A sub-tenant in the public sector has no security of tenure and no right to have a fair rent registered. However, the tenant must inform the landlord of any proposed increase in the rent payable by a sub-tenant. There can be no increase if the landlord objects to it.

When the tenancy ends

If a tenant leaves or is evicted, the rights of any lawful sub-tenant living in the house depend on the nature of the main tenancy.

If the tenancy was protected by the Rent (Scotland) Act, the sub-tenancy continues to exist. The sub-tenant automatically becomes the landlord's tenant, on the same terms as before. However, where the tenancy was unfurnished but the sub-tenancy is furnished and protected by the Rent Act, these terms do not include an obligation on the landlord's part to provide furniture and services – so long as the landlord informs the sub-tenant of this within 6 weeks of the tenancy ending.

If the tenancy was not protected by the Rent Act, or was a public sector

WHEN A SUB-TENANCY IS UNLAWFUL

If a tenant – whether private or public – sub-lets without his landlord's consent, and his tenancy agreement gives him no power to do so or forbids sub-letting (either totally or without his landlord's consent), he is in breach of the terms of his tenancy. His landlord can then apply to the sheriff court for an eviction order.

The sheriff can grant the order if he thinks it is reasonable to do so. If the tenant is not protected, he must grant the order.

If a sub-tenancy is unlawful, the 'sub-tenant' is not entitled to remain in the house unless the landlord agrees. He has no more rights than a SQUATTER and can be evicted – either by reasonable force or by a court order.

tenancy, the sub-tenancy comes to an end at the same time as the tenancy. The landlord can then either allow the sub-tenant to stay on as his tenant or evict him if he refuses to leave. For an eviction to be lawful, the landlord must obtain an eviction order from the sheriff court.

SUICIDE

Intentionally taking one's own life

Suicide is the deliberate taking of one's own life.

It is not a criminal offence to commit suicide. Nor is attempted suicide a specific crime, although in some circumstances it might be prosecuted as a BREACH OF THE PEACE.

Anyone who persuades another person to commit suicide may be guilty of MURDER or CULPABLE HOMICIDE. However, a doctor who gives a patient drugs to relieve suffering is not guilty of any crime even if the drugs also hasten the patient's death. *See:* EUTHANASIA

Suicide pacts The survivor of a genuine suicide pact – in which one person agrees to kill first the other person and then himself – will probably be guilty of culpable homicide (and not murder), so long as he made a genuine attempt on his own life in fulfilment of the agreement.

SUMMARY COMPLAINT

Detailing the criminal charges against a person

A summary complaint is the document that sets out the criminal charges against someone who is to be prosecuted in the sheriff or district court under summary CRIMINAL PROCEEDINGS – that is, before a judge sitting without a jury.

Only less serious crimes are prosecuted on summary complaint. More serious crimes are prosecuted on INDICTMENT.

When a summary complaint is served on an accused person, he will also be

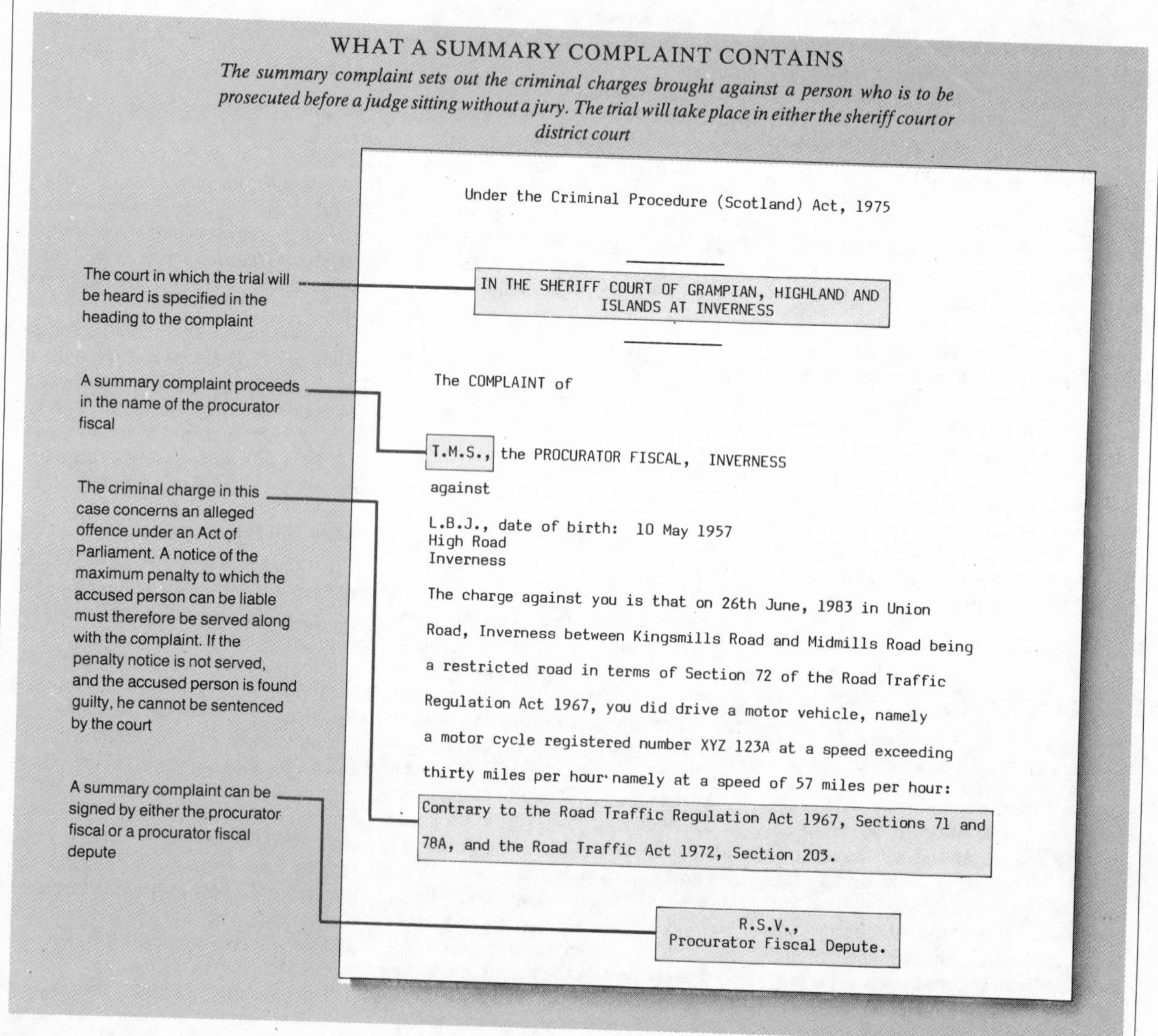

WHAT A SUMMARY COMPLAINT CONTAINS

The summary complaint sets out the criminal charges brought against a person who is to be prosecuted before a judge sitting without a jury. The trial will take place in either the sheriff court or district court

Under the Criminal Procedure (Scotland) Act, 1975

IN THE SHERIFF COURT OF GRAMPIAN, HIGHLAND AND ISLANDS AT INVERNESS

The COMPLAINT of

T.M.S., the PROCURATOR FISCAL, INVERNESS

against

L.B.J., date of birth: 10 May 1957
High Road
Inverness

The charge against you is that on 26th June, 1983 in Union Road, Inverness between Kingsmills Road and Midmills Road being a restricted road in terms of Section 72 of the Road Traffic Regulation Act 1967, you did drive a motor vehicle, namely a motor cycle registered number XYZ 123A at a speed exceeding thirty miles per hour namely at a speed of 57 miles per hour: Contrary to the Road Traffic Regulation Act 1967, Sections 71 and 78A, and the Road Traffic Act 1972, Section 203.

R.S.V.,
Procurator Fiscal Depute.

given a list of any previous convictions that the prosecutor intends to put before the court in the event of a guilty verdict.

In addition, where someone is charged with an offence under an Act of Parliament – such as an offence under the Road Traffic Act – the complaint will be served along with a notice of the maximum penalty under the Act for that offence.

Serving a complaint

When the accused receives the complaint, he will either be under ARREST and in custody, or at liberty. An accused who is in custody will have the complaint served on him before his appearance in court – usually not later than the day following his arrest.

The police do not always arrest persons suspected of an offence. For instance, a driver who commits a less serious road traffic offence will not usually be arrested. Instead the police will warn him that a report will be made to the procurator fiscal, with a view to his prosecution.

In such a case, the procurator fiscal will usually send a summary complaint to the accused person by recorded delivery post. The complaint will order the accused to appear in either the sheriff or district court to answer the charge. It is an offence for an accused to fail to appear without reasonable excuse.

SUMMONS

The document that starts a civil court action

A summons is the document that starts many legal actions in the COURT OF SESSION and certain actions in the SHERIFF COURT.

The document is lodged in court by the person taking legal action (the 'pursuer') and a copy of it is served on the person against whom the action is raised (the 'defender'). Service is usually by recorded delivery post.

The Court of Session summons

A Court of Session summons may be served in a variety of different cases – for instance, in actions where damages are claimed for breach of contract or for personal injury caused by someone's negligence; and in DIVORCE actions. But regardless of the type of case, the summons takes the same form.

The summons starts by naming the pursuer and defender, and telling the defender that he has a stated time – usually 14 days – in which to inform the court whether he intends to defend the action.

There then follows a section called the 'Conclusion', which sets out the remedy that the pursuer wants the court to give him. For example, in an action for damages the pursuer might conclude 'For payment by the defender to the pursuer of the sum of FIFTEEN THOUSAND POUNDS (£15,000) STERLING with interest thereon at the rate of eleven per cent per annum from 25 February 1983 until payment'. The pursuer will also ask the court to order the defender to pay his (the pursuer's) expenses.

The main part of the summons is the 'Condescendence'. This contains, in short numbered paragraphs, the pursuer's version of the relevant facts of the case. For instance, in a case involving personal injury the condescendence will set out how the injury occurred, its extent and consequences, and will allege that it was caused by the defender's negligence.

The last section is called the 'Pleas-in-law'. This sets out, again in short numbered paragraphs, the legal reasons why the court should grant the remedy that the pursuer seeks. For instance, if the pursuer is suing the defender for causing him injury by his negligent driving, one of the pleas will be: 'The pursuer having suffered loss, injury and damage through the fault and negligence of the defender is entitled to reparation therefor'.

The sheriff court summons

A sheriff court summons starts legal actions that are dealt with under a shortened form of court procedure, called 'summary cause' procedure. (Actions under ordinary procedure are started by a document called an INITIAL WRIT.)

The most important actions that are dealt with under summary cause procedure are those for payment of debts up to £1,000 and for the eviction of tenants. *See:* DEBT; EVICTION

The summons is lodged in court and signed by the sheriff clerk. A copy is then served on the defender, normally by recorded delivery post.

The exact form of the summons depends on the type of action. For instance, if the pursuer is seeking repayment of an alleged debt, the summons is a 'Summons for Payment'; but if the pursuer is a landlord seeking to evict a tenant, it is a 'Summons for Recovery of Possession of Heritable Property'.

In all cases the summons will set out the pursuer's claim, the place where, and the date and time when the case will first be heard in court. In actions for payment of money, the summons will also specify a 'Return Day' – this is the date by which the defender should tell the court whether he wishes to appear in court, defend the action, or admit the claim and perhaps make an offer to pay by instalments.

If you receive a summons

If you receive a summons and you wish to defend it or to appear in court, you should take LEGAL ADVICE as soon as possible. If you do nothing, the court can still make an order against you in your absence.

SUNDAY TRADING

When a trader may open for business on a Sunday

Unlike their counterparts in England and Wales, shopkeepers in Scotland are not denied the right to open on a Sunday by any Act of Parliament.

However, it is possible that local byelaws in some areas prohibit all, or some, forms of trading on a Sunday. Any shopkeeper who wishes to open for business on that day should therefore check the position with either the local authority or the local chamber of commerce.

Sunday markets have become a permanent feature of the Scottish retail industry in recent years. They are governed by the same rules of contract, the same trading standards and the same consumer protection laws as traditional shops and stores.

Hairdressers It is an offence for a hairdresser or a barber to carry on business on a Sunday. The maximum penalty for doing so is a fine of £1,000. However this does not prevent him from cutting the hair of someone who is too infirm to get to his shop.

SUPERIOR

The feudal system in Scotland

The feudal system of landownership was introduced to Scotland in the Middle Ages. The Crown, the original holder of all land, granted feus to its supporters – known as vassals. Holding a feu entitled the vassal to occupy the land in exchange for certain services, usually of a military nature.

Often the vassals granted sub-feus of all or part of the land to their own supporters. However, the owner of the land continued to be the Crown. The vassal merely had the right of feu, which could be ended in certain circumstances.

In theory, a modified version of this system continues to apply today. The person popularly regarded as owner of a house or land is, strictly speaking, just the holder of a feu.

He may be the direct vassal of the Crown, but more commonly he will be the vassal of another person – known as the 'superior' – who will himself be the vassal of the Crown. Sometimes there are several superiors between the last vassal and the Crown. The Crown is the superior at the very top of the feudal chain.

In practice, the last vassal can be regarded as if he was outright owner, except that:

- He may have to pay his superior FEU DUTY.
- The CONVEYANCE that created his feu may contain conditions that must be complied with. For example, he may be prohibited from using his house for business purposes.
- If he fails to pay feu duty for 5 years, or fails to comply with the conditions, the superior is often entitled to 'irritate' the feu – that is, to evict the vassal and reclaim possession of the land. This is very rarely done.

Only the last vassal has the right actually to occupy the land or live in the house. The main benefit of being a superior is the right to collect feu duty from the vassal, and for this reason superiors are often companies rather than private individuals.

The feudal system is very complicated and it has very few defenders. It will probably be replaced by a simple system of outright ownership in the not-too-distant future.

THE FEUDAL SYSTEM IN ACTION

510 GREENSHIELDS ROAD, GLASGOW

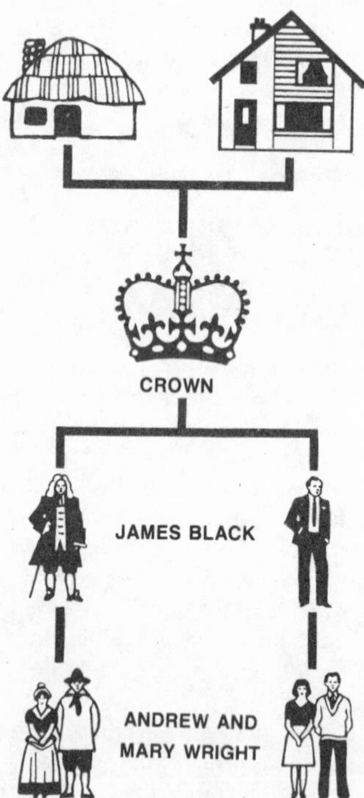

In practice the Wrights are treated as the owners of the house. In strict legal theory they are the vassals of James Black. James Black is the superior of the Wrights and vassal of the Crown.

SUPERVISION REQUIREMENT

Keeping control of children in trouble

If a CHILDREN'S HEARING decides that a child is in need of 'compulsory measures of care', it will impose a supervision requirement on the child. This is an order which places the child in the care of the regional (or islands) council.

The order can take two forms. The child may be required to live in a named institution – usually a LIST D SCHOOL – or may be subjected to some other form of control. Most often this will mean that he will have a social worker assigned to him and will meet that worker at regular intervals. He will have to promise to be of good behaviour and may have to meet certain conditions, such as living at a certain address, attending a club and going to school regularly. He may be required to live with foster parents.

Sometimes the control may take a more intensive form – called 'intermediate treatment'. Once or twice a week and at week-ends the child attends an activity centre. There he is involved in a wide range of activities – sporting, vocational and educational – by which the social workers try to influence him away from delinquency.

Reviewing the order The child and his parents can each ask for the supervision requirement to be reviewed by the children's hearing after 3 months (or 6 months if the last review continued the requirement without change). The requirement must be reviewed within a year from the time when it was made or last continued, otherwise it lapses.

When a requirement has been reviewed or continued, the child and parents can each appeal to the sheriff against the decision within 21 days.

SUPPLEMENTARY BENEFIT

Money for people whose income is less than their needs

Supplementary benefit is a social security benefit paid to people who are not in full-time work, if their income and savings are below a certain level. To qualify for benefit, a claimant must be 16 or over and living in Great Britain.

If a claimant is under retirement age – 65 for men, 60 for women – benefit is known as supplementary *allowance*. If he or she has reached retirement age, it is called supplementary *pension*.

Full-time work People who are in full-time work are not normally entitled to supplementary benefit. A person is treated as working full-time if he or she normally works, on average, at least 30 hours a week – 35 hours a week for disabled people whose earnings are reduced by 25 per cent or more.

However, someone who returns to full-time work after claiming supplementary benefit can still receive it for up to a fortnight (and sometimes longer), to cover the period before wages are paid.

A person who is working full-time may be entitled to FAMILY INCOME SUPPLEMENT if he or she is looking after at least 1 child.

School leavers School leavers aged 16 to 18 cannot claim benefit in their own right until after the *end* of the school holiday following the date they leave. So someone who leaves school in July cannot claim benefit until the beginning of September.

Students Full-time students are normally unable to claim benefit during term-time – they are treated as not being available for work (see below). But students on part-time courses – for not more than 21 hours a week – can claim benefit. *See:* STUDENT

Claiming benefit

Most people who claim supplementary allowance (but not pension) have to sign on as available for work in order to get it. Those under 18 must also register for work at a Job Centre or local authority careers office.

But certain people do not have to sign on. They include:

- Single parents looking after children under 16.
- Men aged 60 or over.
- People who cannot work, or whose work is restricted, because of physical or mental disablement.
- People caring for someone who is entitled to ATTENDANCE ALLOWANCE; or who have to look after a child or partner who is temporarily sick.
- Pregnant women who are either incapable of work or expecting a baby within 11 weeks (15 weeks if no suitable employment is available).
- People who are within 10 years of retirement, have not worked (or signed on for work) in the past 10 years and have no prospect of a job.

When couples claim When a couple are living together, only one of them can claim benefit. The partner who claims must either:

1. Be entitled to retirement pension on his or her own contributions, or have retired at 65 (60 for women) or in the five years before then; or

2. Have satisfied one of the following conditions in the previous 6 months (breaks totalling no more than 3 weeks are ignored). The claimant must:

- Have signed on as available for work.
- Have been employed for at least 8 hours a week.
- Be unable to work because of illness, disablement or a trade dispute.
- Be a single parent with a child under 16.
- Be receiving invalid care allowance; looking after someone who is severely disabled; or caring for a child or partner who is temporarily sick.
- Be in full-time education, or receiving a MSC training allowance.
- Be a prisoner, or outside the UK.

If a couple are receiving family income supplement, the partner whose work record entitled them to the supplement must be the claimant.

If both partners qualify, they can choose who is to claim. If they do not, the DHSS will decide. It is possible to swop over at a later date.

How benefit is calculated

For benefit purposes, a claimant and his or her dependants (if any) are treated as a single unit – called an 'assessment unit'. The amount of benefit payable is usually the difference between the income and capital of the unit (its 'resources') and the needs of the unit's members (its 'requirements').

A claimant's dependants are his or her marriage partner (or cohabitee) and any *dependent* children – that is:

- Children under 16.
- Children aged 16 to 18 who are still at school or college full-time. 19 year olds are included if they were still 18 at the start of the school or college year.

Other members of the claimant's household – such as a grand-parent or adult child – are *not* included as part of the assessment unit and their income and needs are ignored. But they may be expected to contribute to housing costs. *See:* HOUSING BENEFITS

How resources are worked out

Three different types of resources are taken into account in deciding entitlement to benefit: income, 'notional' income, and capital.

Income The social security office will want information from a claimant about his or her weekly earnings from part-time work, as well as any weekly unearned income – for instance, social security benefits.

Earnings are broadly defined and include not only normal wages but also bonuses, advances, wages in lieu of notice, and holiday pay (but not sick pay). The earnings of the claimant's partner or cohabitee are included, but those of dependent children are not.

Only net earnings are taken into account in deciding entitlement to benefit. That means gross earnings less income tax, occupational pension and national insurance contributions, reasonable travel expenses, the cost of child-minding, 15p for each meal for which no luncheon voucher is provided, and any other reasonable expenses.

Once net earnings are worked out, a final earnings figure is calculated by disregarding the first £4 of the claimant's net earnings and the first £4 of a partner's or cohabitee's net earnings. If the claimant is a single parent, half of his or her net earnings between £4 and £20 is *also* disregarded – a maximum of £12.

Apart from earnings, all other income belonging to members of the assessment unit must be taken into account in full – with certain exceptions. This income includes:

- All contributory social security benefits – for instance, retirement pension, unemployment and sickness benefit and maternity allowance.
- Non-contributory benefits such as child benefit, non-contributory invalidity pension/severe disablement allowance and invalid care allowance. However, mobility allowance, attendance allowance and certain other disability payments are ignored.
- Any occupational pension.
- Sick pay (including statutory sick pay). *See:* SICKNESS
- Student grant. If the student is a single parent, one of a married or unmarried couple with a child, or disabled, £2 a week of the grant is ignored.
- Maintenance payments, or periodical allowance (paid following a divorce). Any regular payments – for example those paid by a father to a mother to

help feed and clothe their children – will be taken into account as income, even though they are not made under a court order. *See:* ALIMENT; DIVORCE

- Any other income – including tax refunds, disablement and industrial death benefits, and voluntary payments from relatives, friends or charities. The first £4 of such income is ignored. Voluntary payments are ignored completely if they are intended to pay for leisure items – for instance, television rental – or for items not covered by supplementary benefit, such as a holiday or a major piece of furniture.

Also ignored in calculating income are occasional gifts up to £100 and the first £7.50 of a SCHOOL GRANT paid for a child over 16.

Notional income For supplementary benefit purposes, the income of a claimant and his or her dependants can include money that they do not actually have. Included is:

- Money (including capital) that the assessment unit deliberately deprives itself of to obtain or increase benefit.
- Money owed to the assessment unit, or available on application – if it is reasonable to include it.
- A sum to represent the wages that should have been paid for any unpaid or underpaid work done by a member of the assessment unit.
- The parental contribution taken into account when calculating a student grant – but not if the student is a single parent, disabled or one of a married or unmarried couple.

Capital If the claimant and his or her dependants have capital of more than £3,000 (in 1983–4), *no* supplementary benefit is payable until this is reduced to £3,000 or less.

'Capital' includes all savings, investments (such as shares and premium bonds) and property owned by the claimant or by dependants. It also includes redundancy payments, bequests, maternity and death grants, and the surrender value of life assurance or endowment policies.

However, some forms of capital are ignored – in particular:

- The value of the claimant's home.
- Personal possessions – unless they are an investment (such as a painting or antique) or have been deliberately bought to reduce capital and so obtain benefit. Possessions will also be treated as capital if it would be unreasonable to ignore them – an example might be an expensive car or a fur coat.
- The first £1,500 of the surrender value of life assurance policies.
- Savings to pay regular bills.
- Arrears of housing benefit.
- Any capital belonging to dependent children, but *only* if ignoring it would reduce total capital to £3,000 or less.

If a child's capital is ignored, it will be treated as an income equal to that child's weekly needs (see below).

How requirements are worked out

The amount of benefit to which a claimant and his or her dependants are entitled is usually the difference between their total net income – calculated as above – and their total needs.

These needs (known as 'requirements') are worked out by reference to fixed sums of money set out in regulations. These sums are increased each November, along with other social security benefits.

There are three kinds of needs, or requirements: normal requirements, additional requirements, and housing requirements. These, when added together, represent the assessment unit's total needs.

Normal requirements

Fixed sums of money – often called 'scale rates' – are laid down which are supposed to cover the assessment unit's weekly expenditure on all normal living expenses. These include food, fuel, clothing and footwear, laundry, travel costs, small household items such as soap and toilet paper, the replacement of small household goods such as crockery and cooking utensils, and leisure items such as television or tobacco. Housing costs are not included.

SPECIAL RULES FOR BOARDERS AND PEOPLE IN HOMES

Boarders, and people living in homes for the elderly or handicapped, have their needs (but not incomes) assessed in a different way from other claimants.

Boarders

A boarder is someone who:

- Pays a commercial charge for lodgings and at least some meals. If the accommodation and meals are provided by a close relative (a parent, child, brother or sister) or on a non-commercial basis, the claimant is treated as a non-householder.
- Lives in a hostel, lodging-house, hotel, guest house or similar establishment.
- Lives in a refugee reception centre.

The ordinary basic and long-term rates do not apply to boarders. Nor do the rules about housing costs. Instead their needs are assessed as follows:

1. The weekly board and lodging charge is met, up to a limit fixed for suitable board and lodgings in the area. In 1983–4 these local limits ranged from £56 to £91. The limit is doubled for a couple, with further increases for dependent children. It is also increased for pensioners, sick or disabled people or those entitled to long-term personal expenses (see below).

2. The cost of meals is met, if not included in the board and lodging charge. If meals are eaten out, a fixed amount is paid – up to £1 for breakfast, £1.45 for lunch and £1.45 for an evening meal.

3. An amount is paid to cover weekly personal expenses (including those of dependants). In 1983–4 the rate for a couple was £17.70, and for a single person, £8.85. Higher amounts (£19.70 and £9.85 respectively) are paid where a claimant (or partner) is 60 or more, or has been on benefit for a year without having to be available for work.

The rates for dependent children are £2.95 (under 11), £4.55 (11 to 15), £5.30 (16–17) and £8.85 (18–19).

4. Any additional needs are met in the same way as those of other claimants.

People in homes

Claimants living in local authority homes for the elderly or handicapped (or in private homes under financial arrangements made with the local authority) are entitled to an amount of benefit equal to the basic retirement pension for a single person – £34.05 (doubled for a couple). Of this, 80 per cent is to cover the minimum charge for the accommodation and 20 per cent is for personal expenses.

People who live in private homes with which the local authority has made no financial arrangements are treated as boarders. So are those who live in private nursing homes with which the health board has made no arrangements. Local limits are again laid down for both these types of home.

There are 2 scale rates to cover normal living expenses:

1. A 'basic' rate. This applies to claimants *under* retirement age who:

- Have to be available for work. These claimants can never qualify for the long-term rate (see below).
- Do not have to be available for work. These claimants can qualify for the long-term rate after 1 year.

2. A 'long-term' rate that is higher than the basic rate. This applies to:

- Claimants who have reached – or whose partners have reached – the age of 60.
- Claimants under 60 who have been on benefit for 1 year (breaks of 8 weeks or less are ignored), so long as they do not have to be available for work. People who have received invalidity benefit, non-contributory invalidity pension or unemployability supplement (paid with disablement benefit) for at least 1 year also qualify.

The scale rates for dependent children remain the same, whether the claimant is entitled to the basic or long-term rate.

The basic and long-term rates are different for couples (married or unmarried), single householders, joint householders and single non-householders:

- Couples. The scale rates for married and cohabiting couples are the same, whether they live on their own or in

CLAIMING A SINGLE PAYMENT

If you are receiving (or are entitled to) supplementary benefit, you may be able to get a lump sum – called a 'single payment' (SP, for short) – to pay for occasional needs that your benefit is not meant to cover. The amount that you get is reduced by any capital (such as savings) that you have over £500 (in 1983–4).

The needs that can be met by a lump sum are set out in regulations. Some needs can *never* be met in this way: these include educational and training needs, distinctive school uniform, television and radio, holidays and payment of fines.

The need must exist at the time you claim. So if, for example, you borrow money from a friend to buy bedding or furniture, you will not be able to get a SP for that, even though you have to repay the money.

A SP cannot be made if you already possess a suitable alternative item. Nor can it be made if you (or your partner) are involved in – or directly interested in – a strike or other industrial action.

The needs that you can claim for

The most common needs for which a SP can be made are:

- Maternity. A SP can be made to cover all essential baby items that you do not possess – for instance, baby clothes, a pram, a cot, blankets and nappies. The amount you get is reduced by £25 if you receive the MATERNITY grant – unless you spend the grant on an item for which a SP could have been made.
- Funerals. A SP can be made to pay for the funeral of a household member or a close relative. Only essential costs (such as a coffin, flowers and undertakers' fees) will be paid for, and a deduction may be made if there are other close relatives (for instance, brothers or sisters) who can afford to share the cost. The DEATH GRANT will be deducted from the sum paid.
- Clothes and footwear. The normal scale rates of benefit are meant to cover the cost of new or replacement clothes and footwear. So a SP is only made for these items if the need arises *otherwise* than through normal wear and tear – for instance, because of pregnancy, rapid weight loss or gain, heavy wear and tear caused by illness or disablement, admission to hospital, or accidental loss, damage or destruction. No payment can be made for clothes or shoes that need replacing because a child has grown out of them in the normal course of events.
- Bedclothes. A payment is made to bring the stock of bed-clothes up to 3 blankets (or 2 plus a terylene quilt) and 3 sheets per bed, and 1 pillow (plus 2 pillowcases) per person. These are the quantities considered adequate, but more can be allowed on the grounds of ill health or physical disability.
- Fuel bills. A SP to help pay a fuel bill is only made in very limited circumstances. *See:* FUEL BILL
- Removal expenses. A removal to another house can be paid for in certain circumstances – such as marriage break-up, bad housing, a new job or ill health.
- Essential furniture and household equipment. If you or your partner have recently become the owner or tenant of an unfurnished or partly furnished house, you may be able to get a SP to pay for basic furniture and household equipment – for instance, beds, chairs, a table, a cooker, curtains and floor coverings – where you do not have these items or those you do have are not worth repairing. Where there is a special need, a washing machine, refrigerator and vacuum cleaner can be paid for. But to get a SP, you must satisfy one of the following conditions:

1. Be able to meet the conditions for getting a SP for removal expenses.
2. Have a dependent child, or someone in your assessment unit who is a pensioner, chronically ill, pregnant or handicapped.
3. Have been on benefit for 6 months and have no immediate job prospects.
4. Have left prison or institutional accommodation, or have been in hospital continuously for at least a year.

Where **3** or **4** applies, there must be no suitable alternative furnished accommodation available.

Even if you have not recently moved, you can get a SP for essential items if conditions **2** or **3** (above) apply, or if you need a cooker or heating appliance.

You can also claim a SP to cover the cost of essential repairs to these items, or to clear outstanding hire purchase payments on them.

- Repairs and redecoration. A SP can be made to pay for essential house repairs – but only if the bill is not more than £325. If it is, the interest on any money borrowed for the purpose can be added to the weekly benefit payments. A SP can also be made for essential interior decoration (materials, not labour) if you have lived in your home for at least a year.
- Travel costs. A SP can be made for fares and, where necessary, overnight accommodation if you, or your partner, or a dependant have to make certain essential journeys – for instance, to visit a close relative in hospital, to attend a funeral, to look for a job or attend a job interview.
- Starting work. A SP can be made for necessary expenses, such as basic tools or working clothes and footwear.
- Voluntary repatriation. A SP can be made to enable an immigrant and his family to return to his country of birth or one in which he previously stayed for a long period. He must intend to settle there.
- Unclaimed benefit. If you are unable to pay for your basic needs – for instance, fuel or rent – because you failed to claim benefit to which you were entitled, or you spent money on an item for which a SP could have been made, you can get a SP to pay for these basic needs.

Discretionary payments A SP can be made in circumstances not provided for in the regulations if it is the *only* way to prevent serious damage or serious risk to the health or safety of a claimant or dependant.

someone else's household.

- Single householders. A single householder is someone who is neither married nor cohabiting, and is solely responsible for his household's housing costs – usually a tenant or owner-occupier who is responsible for rent, rates, mortgage payments or insurance.
- Joint householders. People who share responsibility for their household's housing costs are treated as joint householders. An example would be people in a house or flat who all share responsibility for the rent.

Joint householders are entitled to the non-householder scale rates *plus* an amount equal to the difference between the householder and non-householder rates (basic or long-term) divided by the number of people who share responsibility.

- Single non-householders. A single claimant who is not responsible for his household's housing costs is called a 'non-householder'. The best example is an adult child living in his or her parents' house.

The scale rates In 1982–3, the scale rates for all these claimants were:

	Basic	Long-term
Married and unmarried couples	£43.50	£54.55
Single householder	£26.80	£34.10
Single non-householder aged		
18 and over	£21.45	£27.25
16–17	£16.50	£20.90
Dependent children aged		
under 11	£9.15	—
11–15	£13.70	—
16–17	£16.50	—
18 and over	£21.45	—

Special situations Different rules apply to people who pay a commercial charge for board and lodgings or who live in sheltered and residential accommodation (see p. 628).

Special rules apply to claimants who go into hospital, or to prison. *See:* HOSPITAL; PRISON

Additional requirements

The weekly scale rates set out above can be increased to take account of expenses that are not meant to be covered by these rates or which, although covered, are higher than normal. These increases are referred to as 'additional requirements'.

The most common additional requirements are:

- Heating. Increases ranging from £2.05 to £5.05 (in 1983–4) are paid where extra heating is required because of old age, young children, illness or accommodation that is centrally heated or difficult to heat. *See:* FUEL BILL
- Special diet. A weekly increase is paid if the claimant or a dependant needs a special diet because he or she:

1. Suffers from diabetes, ulcers, ulcerative colitis, or any other illness that requires a similar diet. The weekly increase (1983–4) is £3.35.

2. Suffers from any other illness that requires a diet involving extra cost. The weekly increase is £1.45. If the extra cost is much more than £3.35, the weekly cost of the diet will be paid.

3. Is convalescing after a major illness or operation and requires a diet involving extra cost. The weekly increase is £1.45.

4. Is being treated on a kidney machine. The weekly increase is £9.60.

- Blindness. A weekly increase of £1.25 is paid for a claimant or dependant aged 16 or over who is so blind that he or she is unable to do work requiring eyesight. Blind non-householders aged 18 and over also get an amount to bring their scale rate up to that of a householder.
- Age addition. A weekly increase of 25p is paid for a claimant or partner who is 80 or over (50p if both are).
- Laundry. A weekly increase can be paid to cover laundry or launderette costs (apart from the first 45p). This will only be paid if:

1. All the adults in the house are ill or disabled; or

2. There are no suitable washing or drying facilities; or

3. The amount of laundry is greater than normal – for instance, because of incontinence.

- Baths. If a claimant or dependant needs more than 1 bath a week on medical grounds, a weekly increase of 25p is paid for each extra bath.

Apart from these additions, weekly increases can also be paid for needs such as domestic help, the cost of looking after a seriously ill or disabled person who has not served the qualifying period for ATTENDANCE ALLOWANCE, hire purchase payments for essential furniture and household equipment, and fares to visit relatives or household members. The amount is based on the actual or estimated cost incurred in each case.

Claimants on long-term rates The long-term rates include an amount to cover additional needs. So someone receiving the long-term rate of benefit will have the first 50p of any additional requirement deducted – unless it is for heating, blindness, people aged 80 or over, or for most of the additional needs of children.

Housing requirements

Apart from his normal and additional needs, a claimant will usually have some housing costs to meet – rent, rates, mortgage payments, insurance and payments for maintenance or repairs.

Rent and rates are not usually met by supplementary benefit – they are dealt with separately (see below). Other housing costs – called 'housing requirements' – are paid for by further increases in the weekly rate of benefit.

Rent and rates Someone who successfully claims supplementary benefit is entitled to HOUSING BENEFITS from the local housing department (or SSHA) to meet the cost of rent and rates (excluding water rates). The claim for supplementary benefit is treated as a claim for housing benefits, without any more formalities.

Claimants who are boarders or crofters are not entitled to housing benefits. All their housing costs, including rent or rates, are met out of supplementary benefit. Non-householders are not entitled to housing benefits either – they receive a fixed amount to cover their housing costs (see below).

The local social security office provides the housing department with a certificate showing the claimant's entitlement to supplementary benefit. A copy is included for the rating authority (the regional or islands council). The claimant will then be entitled to housing benefits – that is, to a 100 per cent rate

PAYING BENEFIT IN EMERGENCIES

Supplementary benefit – weekly as well as lump sum payments – can be paid in an emergency, when financial help is needed immediately to pay for living expenses or essential purchases. The payments are known as 'urgent need payments' (UNP). However, there are only a few situations in which help can be given, and the benefit must usually be repaid.

It is not only people on supplementary benefit who can claim a UNP. *People who are not entitled to benefit – for instance, those in full-time work – can also claim.*

No help is given if funds are readily available from the claimant's own resources – including any income or capital that is normally ignored when entitlement to ordinary benefit is being worked out. Nor is help given if it is readily available from elsewhere – from friends or relatives, credit facilities, local authorities or voluntary organisations.

Living expenses

The normal rules for working out income and needs do not apply. *All* income and capital is taken into account. Where a claimant's capital is more than £3,000, no UNP is payable if any of this capital is readily realisable. For the first fortnight of any claim, the needs of a claimant (plus partner) are cut to 75 per cent of the basic scale rates and the lowest scale rate is paid for each dependent child, regardless of age. After a fortnight, needs revert to the normal level.

The situations in which day-to-day living expenses can be paid include:

- Emergencies. Benefit can be paid (normally for 14 days) to a claimant affected by a fire, flood or similar disaster.
- Loss of money. A UNP can be paid to a claimant who has no money because his or her wages or savings – but not social security payments – have been lost, stolen or destroyed.
- Before benefit is paid. A claimant who is entitled to benefit, but has not yet received it, can claim a UNP to tide him or her over.
- On starting work. A UNP can be claimed if no wages have been paid after a fortnight back at work (normal benefit can be paid for the first fortnight).
- Cohabitation. A woman with children whose benefit is withdrawn because she is cohabiting with a man may be able to claim a UNP. *See:* COHABITATION
- Failure to maintain. If a husband fails to maintain his wife, she can claim a UNP to meet her own needs and those of any children. *See:* ALIMENT

Lump sum payments

A claimant can get a lump sum to help pay for some basic items or expenses. The payment is reduced by any income or capital that is ignored when normal benefit is being worked out.

The items and expenses that a lump sum can help to pay for include:

- Items and expenses caused by an emergency (see above) – clothing, footwear, travelling expenses, essential furniture and household equipment, removal expenses and fuel.
- Urgent travel expenses – to visit a critically ill relative, for instance.
- Travel expenses for a stranded person.
- A deposit to secure accommodation for a homeless person.

Discretionary payments

The social security office can pay a UNP to someone who would not otherwise qualify, if payment is the only way to prevent serious risk to the health or safety of the claimant, or the claimant's family.

Strikers

People who lose wages because of a strike or other industrial action cannot get a UNP – except in emergencies or to pay for special diets, school transport costs of disabled children, maternity needs, essential household equipment and fares to visit someone who is ill.

Recovery of payments

In general, a UNP is a loan and must be repaid unless it is small (£10 or less) or the claimant's income is too low.

But sometimes the money need not be repaid – for instance, when it is paid to one of a cohabiting couple or to someone entitled to benefit but has not yet received it.

rebate and rent rebate (or rent allowance if he or she rents from a private landlord). If there are any sub-tenants or non-dependants in the household, the rebate or allowance will be reduced.

A claimant who is awarded a rent or rate rebate pays neither rent nor rates. A claimant who is awarded a rent allowance is given an amount to meet the rent paid to the landlord.

The rebate or allowance can be reduced if the housing authority thinks that the claimant's house is too large or (if the claimant is a private tenant) that the rent is too high. But this cannot be done if no suitable cheaper accommodation is available in the area, or it is unreasonable to expect the claimant to move – because of, for instance, age, health or employment. *See:* RATES; RENT ALLOWANCE; RENT REBATE

Housing benefit supplement A claimant who is otherwise eligible for supplementary benefit may not be able to get it because his income is more than his requirements.

However, a special payment of supplementary benefit – called housing benefit supplement (HBS) – can be paid if his income, plus any housing benefit payable, is insufficient to cover both rent and rates and the needs that are met by supplementary benefit. (People who are ineligible for supplementary benefit do not usually get their *full* rent and rates met by housing benefit.)

When the claim for supplementary benefit is turned down, the local social security office works out the claimant's 'excess income' – the amount by which income exceeds needs. The figure is entered on the housing benefit claim form given to the claimant. This must be completed and sent to the housing department.

The housing department then works out whether the claimant is entitled to HBS. It does this by comparing the claimant's 'excess income' with the amount that he or she still has (or will still have) to put towards the rent and rates after getting housing benefits.

For instance, if the claimant's rent and rates come to £16 (assuming that there are no sub-tenants or non-dependants in the house) and housing benefits total £10, the amount that the claimant has to pay towards his or her housing costs is £6. If the 'excess income' figure is less than this amount (say, £4), the difference – £2 – is paid to the claimant as housing benefit supplement. If the 'excess income' figure is the same as, or more than this amount, no HBS is paid.

HBS is paid by increasing the claimant's rent rebate (or allowance) and rate rebate. Because HBS is actually supplementary benefit, housing and rating authorities are reimbursed by the Department of Health and Social Security for the money that they pay out.

A claimant will be told in writing that HBS is being paid. Because it is supplementary benefit, he or she is also entitled to apply for lump-sum payments to meet special needs and may become eligible for the long-term rate of benefit after 1 year. He or she is also entitled to the usual 'passport' benefits such as free milk, school meals, prescriptions and dental treatment.

HBS is not paid to someone who is involved in a trade dispute.

If you are receiving housing benefit, are not in full-time work and have not applied for supplementary benefit, you should find out whether you are entitled to HBS. Ask at your local social security office, Citizens Advice Bureau or other advice agency, or contact a welfare rights officer if there is one in your region (you can do this through the regional council). Do not delay: you can only get HBS from the time you claim supplementary benefit.

Other housing costs Certain other costs are met, not by housing benefit, but by an increase in the weekly rate of supplementary benefit. These are:

- Non-householder's housing costs. A non-householder – such as an adult child living with parents – does not receive benefit to cover actual housing costs, no matter how much he or she contributes. However, non-householders aged 21 or over are entitled to a flat-rate increase (£3.10 in 1983–4) to put towards their housing expenses.
- Mortgage payments by owner occupiers. Only *interest* payments are covered: repayments of *capital* are not.
- Repairs and insurance. Owner occupiers and tenants or others who are responsible for insuring or repairing their homes are entitled to a weekly increase of £1.70 to cover insurance and routine maintenance costs.
- Loans for repairs and improvements. Any capital over £500 is deducted from the loan, and weekly benefit entitlement is increased to cover the *interest* on the balance.
- Miscellaneous housing costs. Weekly benefit can be increased to cover FEU DUTY, service charges (such as those made for the maintenance and cleaning of common passages and stairs) and other similar outgoings. Water rates are included – in the case of council tenants, these are paid direct to the rating authority by the DHSS.

Paying benefit to a third party

Part – and sometimes all – of a claimant's benefit can be paid to someone else, either at the claimant's request or because the local social security office decides to do so. Before this can happen, the social security office must usually be satisfied that it is necessary to protect the interests of the claimant and his or her dependants.

Benefit can be paid to a third party in the following situations:

- Housing debts. If the claimant is receiving a rent rebate or allowance, but owes his landlord at least 4 weeks' rent, £1.35 a week can be deducted from his benefit and paid to the landlord to clear the arrears. This cannot be done if the arrears are less than the amount that any non-dependant is expected to contribute to the rent.

Where the arrears cover at least 13 weeks, the deduction must be made if the landlord requests it.

If a deduction is made, the claimant's rent allowance can also be paid direct to the landlord.

A deduction of £1.35 a week can be made to clear other housing debts – such as mortgage payments. Current payments can also be deducted and paid direct.

- Fuel debts. If a claimant owes at least £27 for gas or electricity, £2.70 a week (up to £4.05 if there is any disregarded income) can be deducted and paid direct to the gas or electricity authority to clear the debt. The estimated weekly cost of gas and electricity will also be deducted (unless the claimant has a prepayment meter) and this can continue even after the debt is cleared. *See:* FUEL BILL

If a claimant has fuel and housing debts, the maximum amount that can normally be deducted for all of them is £4.05 a week. Rent and mortgage debts are given priority over fuel debts.

- Failure to maintain. If a claimant fails to support his or her partner and children, all or part of the benefit can be paid to the partner or to some other responsible person. (An alternative solution is for a partner who is eligible to apply to be the claimant instead.)
- Incapacity. If a claimant is unable to act for himself or herself – for instance, because of illness or senility – the benefit can be paid to someone over 18, to be used on the claimant's behalf.
- Paying third parties. Lump sum payments (including urgent need payments) can be paid direct to a third party. For example, payments for furniture, funeral and removal expenses are usually made by sending the claimant a girocheque made out to the supplier or contractor.

Employment and supplementary benefit

Some special rules apply to claimants who are unemployed or who are temporarily laid off work because of industrial action.

Voluntary unemployment An employee can be disqualified from receiving unemployment benefit for up to six weeks if he or she is dismissed for misconduct; or leaves a job voluntarily or refuses suitable employment (in both cases, without good reason). Supplementary benefit can be paid instead, but the amount is reduced by 40 per cent (sometimes 20 per cent) of the single householder rate. *See:* UNEMPLOYMENT BENEFIT

Failing to take work A claimant who is required to be available for work can have his or her supplementary benefit withdrawn for failing (without good reason) to apply for or take a suitable job.

Industrial action An employee who is involved in (or directly interested in) a strike or other industrial action cannot get unemployment benefit to cover any loss of earnings. Nor can supplementary benefit be paid to meet the employee's personal needs.

However, the employee may be able to get supplementary benefit to meet the needs of any dependants. The rules are explained in leaflet SB2, available from the local social security office. *See:* STRIKE

How to claim benefit

If you are unemployed, ask for a postal claim form – form B1 – at the unemployment benefit office. Fill in the form and send it to your local social security office. An interview will not be necessary.

If you are not unemployed, you should fill in the claim form attached to leaflet SB1, which you can get from a post office or the local social security office. However, you do not have to fill in an official form. A letter stating 'I claim supplementary benefit', signed by you, and giving your name and address, will be enough. An officer from the DHSS may then visit you or ask you to call for an interview. He will want information to work out your benefit.

If you are urgently in need of money, take the form – together with any benefit books you have, evidence of rent or mortgage payments and recent wage packets or pay slips – to the social security office. Benefit can be posted to you on the same day – or the next day.

Unless you are required to be available for work, your benefit will normally be paid by a book of orders, cashable each week at the post office. If you get retirement pension, your supplementary pension will be paid with it in one book of orders.

If you are required to be available for work, you will normally be sent a fortnightly girocheque by the unemployment benefit office. This will include any unemployment benefit that you are receiving.

How to appeal against a decision

If you do not agree with a decision made by a DHSS adjudication officer about your entitlement to benefit (including housing benefit supplement), you can ask him to review his decision. If he refuses, you can usually appeal to a social security appeal tribunal. You can also appeal to the tribunal against the officer's decision, without asking for a review. *See:* SOCIAL SECURITY APPEALS

Your appeal should be in writing and lodged within 28 days of the decision (or the refusal to review). A later appeal can be heard if the chairman agrees.

You can get an appeal form (attached to leaflet NI 246) from your local social security office or you can write a letter. You do not have to give full reasons for the appeal. You need only say 'I appeal against the refusal to pay me supplementary benefit' – or whatever you are appealing against. However it is usually better to state your case as fully as possible.

At the tribunal The appeal tribunal is an independent local body consisting of a chairman (from 1984, only lawyers can be appointed as chairmen) and two other members. The members represent people living or working in the area and are chosen for their knowledge or experience of local conditions.

The hearing is held locally. You do not have to attend but you have a better chance of succeeding if you do. You can claim your fares and any loss of earnings from the clerk of the tribunal.

Your local Citizens Advice Bureau (or other local advice agency) can advise you about preparing and presenting your case. They may be prepared to represent you before the tribunal. Claimants' unions exist in some areas and they also offer free help and advice.

You can ask at the social security office to see the relevant regulations, and the guidance issued to adjudication officers by the DHSS – but note that this guidance is not binding on the tribunal. You can also ask to see any decisions quoted by the adjudication officer.

Tribunal hearings are private and informal – the press and public are not allowed in. Besides the tribunal members, there is an official from the Department of Health and Social Security. He is known as the presenting officer and puts forward the adjudication officer's views.

Another official from the Department acts as clerk of the tribunal. He arranges the hearing but should not intervene in the proceedings unless asked to do so by the chairman.

You can take witnesses to support your case and you (or whoever presents your case) have the right to put questions to the presenting officer and any witnesses called by him. Members of the tribunal and the presenting officer can put questions to you and your witnesses.

If new evidence is produced during the hearing which you need time to consider or rebut, you can ask the tribunal chairman for an adjournment. If this is granted, however, it may mean several weeks' delay before another hearing is arranged.

Decision When the hearing is over, the tribunal considers its decision, which must be sent to you in writing together with the reasons for it. Sometimes a tribunal will give you its decision orally before you leave.

If you disagree with the decision, you can apply to a social security commissioner for leave to appeal to him – but on a point of law only. The application must normally be made within 3 months of the date the decision was sent to you. *See:* SOCIAL SECURITY COMMISSIONERS

If you are thinking about appealing against the tribunal's decision, take advice from a solicitor, Citizens Advice Bureau or other local advice agency.

Finding out more

If you are receiving supplementary benefit, you are automatically entitled to a number of other benefits free of charge – prescriptions, school meals, dental treatment, milk and vitamins, legal aid and legal advice.

Basic information on supplementary benefit can be found in leaflets SB8 (for all claimants except the unemployed), SB9 (for the unemployed), SB16 (on single payments) and SB19 (on additions to weekly benefit). These are available from a post office or your local social security office.

For more detailed information, you can consult the Supplementary Benefits Handbook – an official guide prepared by the DHSS. You may find a copy in a library or Citizens Advice Bureau.

You can also consult the National Welfare Benefits Handbook (published by the Child Poverty Action Group). This is revised each year and contains the most recent changes in the law. You may also find this at your local library or Citizens Advice Bureau.

TATTOOING

Leaving a permanent colour mark on someone's skin

It is an offence to tattoo anyone under the age of 18 – even at his or her request – except for medical reasons. The maximum penalty is a fine of up to £200. The only defence is that the person performing the tattoo reasonably believed his client to be over the age of 18.

If someone under 18 has to be tattooed for medical reasons – for example, someone suffering from epilepsy or diabetes or someone with a rare blood group might be tattooed with identifying information for use in emergency – the operation must be performed by a doctor or by someone directed by him.

A tattooist who tattooes a person without permission can also be prosecuted for ASSAULT.

Anyone who is harmed as a result of tattooing – someone, for example, who contracts jaundice because of dirty equipment – can sue the tattooist for NEGLIGENCE.

TAXI

When a car is licensed to carry fare-paying passengers on demand

A taxi is a vehicle that has been licensed to carry fare-paying passengers and to be available on demand, either by travelling through the streets indicating it is for hire or by standing at a taxi rank waiting for a passenger. A vehicle that has not been licensed in this way cannot ply for hire. *See:* MINICAB

Applications for a licence are made to the district or islands council, which can charge a fee. If the council refuses to issue a licence or the applicant wishes to object to any of the conditions attached to a licence, an appeal can be made to the sheriff.

The council has a duty to inspect the vehicle and ensure it is fit for the purpose for which it is licensed. A licence will only be granted if the vehicle is of a suitable type, size and design and is properly insured. The council can refuse to issue (or can suspend) a licence if it considers that the driver of the taxi is not fit to hold one. For example, he may be physically unfit or have convictions for driving offences.

The council may supply a licence plate for the taxi and require that it be displayed on the vehicle. In addition, a sign may be carried indicating the vehicle is for hire. It is an offence, with a maximum penalty of a £400 fine, to drive a car with such a sign if it is not actually a taxi.

The council has the power to establish taxi ranks on roads in its area, on its own land, or on other land with the consent of the owner. Before doing so, it must advertise the proposed site and take account of written objections made within 28 days.

IF YOU HAVE A COMPLAINT

If you are dissatisfied with a taxi driver's behaviour – if, for instance, you think you were overcharged or were not taken on the most direct route, or you consider that the taxi was unroadworthy or dirty – you can complain to the council, which has the power to vary or suspend the licence. Give the licence number of the taxi and any other details that will assist identification.

Fixing fares

Taxi fares are fixed by the council after consultation with local bodies and organisations representing taxi interests. The fares are metered – with a meter in a place where the passenger can see it – and the driver must not charge more than the amount shown. If there has been a recent fare increase, the new tariff must be displayed in the taxi.

A passenger is under no legal obligation to give a taxi driver a tip.

If a passenger wants a taxi to take him outside the driver's area, he should agree a fare in advance with the driver. Otherwise, the fare payable is whatever is shown on the meter.

Penalties A taxi operator or driver working without the appropriate licence or charging more than the fixed fare can be fined up to £400. An operator or driver who tampers with the taxi meter can face a similar fine or 60 days' imprisonment, or both.

TELEPHONE

The state-owned telephone and telecommunications service

The telephone service is run by a state-owned corporation, British Telecommunications (British Telecom). In 1984 a Bill was before Parliament to transfer British Telecom to private ownership but to retain some state control through an Office of Telecommunications (OFTEL).

At present British Telecom has the exclusive privilege of running all telecommunications systems – that is, all electric, magnetic or similar systems for conveying visual or audible signals, or signals that activate machinery or in any way impart any other matter. However, the 1984 Bill proposes to abolish this privilege.

It is an offence to infringe the exclusive privilege. The penalty is a fine of £2,000 under summary proceedings and an unlimited fine on indictment. But the privilege is not infringed by:

- BROADCASTING under licence.
- Purely visual systems.
- Systems contained on a single set of premises.
- Systems under one person's control and used for domestic purposes, such as a baby alarm.
- Systems used by businesses for their own purposes and not as a service to others.
- Systems using apparatus supplied by British Telecom.
- Systems operating under licence from the Secretary of State or British Telecom. (Licensing of competing telecommunications systems began in 1982.)

Obtaining a telephone

No one has a legal right to a telephone, but a request for one will normally be met if the local exchange has spare lines. There is also no right to a private line (rather than one that is shared), though the service tries to provide individual lines, particularly if the telephone is for business use.

All users must have a telephone supplied by British Telecom (from the range they stock), but if they have one or more extensions, these can be purchased privately, provided the equipment is approved. All wiring for extensions must be provided by and rented from British Telecom.

When a telephone is first installed, a connection charge of up to £75 (plus VAT) is made to residential users. Users who have been disconnected in the past because of non-payment of bills may be asked for a deposit.

Once the telephone is installed, you can add equipment such as a telephone-answering machine, provided it is of a type approved for use with the telephone service. You should contact British Telecom to arrange the provision of a connection point for such equipment. Use of unauthorised equipment may result in the service being disconnected.

How the bill is calculated

Telephone bills are normally calculated every 3 months, and are made up of a quarterly rental for use of the service over the next 3 months, and tariff charges for calls made over the last 3 months. Direct dialled calls are recorded on a meter in the local telephone exchange. Operator-connected calls are recorded separately, and are individually listed on your bill (or on a supporting statement) with a total.

Non-payment of bills will result in disconnection; and the subscriber has no right to reminders.

When you want to complain

If you get a faulty call or wrong number, call the operator, who will ensure that you do not pay for it. For other faults, telephone the local faults repair service (the number is in your dialling code information).

If you rent your telephone from British Telecom, faults will be repaired free of charge (unless you are responsible for the damage or require repair outside normal working hours).

If you have bought the telephone from British Telecom, it will be covered by a one year guarantee. Should the telephone become faulty outside the guarantee period, you will have to pay for its repair unless you have opted for 'Phonecare' service. The basis of 'Phonecare' is that in return for a quarterly payment in advance (which varies according to the apparatus) replacement parts and labour will be provided without further cost.

Complaints about bills, directory entries or otherwise should be made to the local telephone area office (its address and number are in your telephone directory).

If you are dissatisfied with the response to your complaint by the area office, you can refer it to the regional headquarters, and, if that fails, the matter can be taken to an independent complaints panel set up under the Code of Practice for Telecommunications Services (revised in 1983). A small fee is payable, but it will be refunded if you are successful. The Post Office Users Council for Scotland, 45 Waterloo Street, Glasgow G2 6AT can give you advice and help with your complaint.

Liability for faults

If you have a special directory entry, or hire telephone equipment, the British Telecommunications Act 1981 provides that there is a deemed contract even though no contract was entered into between British Telecom and you. The terms and conditions of the deemed contract are those contained in the Telecommunications Scheme (copies are available from the telephone area office).

If you buy equipment from British Telecom, there is an ordinary contract of sale. However, the majority of British Telecom services are provided under statutory schemes and, by statute, British Telecom is not liable for any loss or damage caused by service faults or failure, or by directory errors or omissions.

Nevertheless it is British Telecom policy to allow a pro rata rebate if your phone is continuously out of order for more than two days after the fault has been reported. In the case of directory errors, British Telecom may provide printed cards for you to send out, or in special cases allow an ex-gratia payment of up to a year's rental.

Misusing a telephone

It is an offence to use a telephone to send a grossly offensive, indecent, obscene or menacing message, or to send a false message for the purpose of causing annoyance, inconvenience or needless anxiety. The maximum penalty is a £400 fine.

Anyone who uses a telephone dishonestly, with intent to avoid payment, commits an offence. The maximum penalty on summary conviction is 6 months' imprisonment or a £2,000 fine, or both. On indictment the maximum penalty is 2 years' imprisonment or an unlimited fine, or both.

Tapping It is an invasion of privacy for anyone to tap your telephone, whether or not he is acting under the authority of a government minister. *See:* TELEPHONE TAPPING

TELEPHONE TAPPING

When your calls may not be private

Telephone tapping is the practice of listening to – and frequently also recording – telephone conversations.

The Home Secretary and the Secretary of State for Scotland sometimes issue warrants for the police or security service to listen in to private telephone conversations if they are investigating a crime, alleged espionage or subversive activities.

In relation to espionage or subversive activities – whether in Scotland or in England and Wales – a warrant for telephone tapping will be issued by the Home Secretary only. The Secretary of State for Scotland will issue such a warrant only for the purpose of investigating crime in Scotland.

Telephone tapping – whether by the police, security service or any other person – is not authorised by the law. This is the case even where a warrant has been issued by the Home Secretary or Secretary of State for Scotland – there is no legal authority for the issue of such warrants.

Listening in to telephone conversations is an invasion of privacy, and in some circumstances the user may have a remedy under the 'actio iniuriarum'. *See:* PRIVACY

Telephone tapping is contrary to article 8 of the European Convention of HUMAN RIGHTS, which protects citizens against intrusions on their privacy.

TELEVISION LICENCE

When you must buy a licence for a television

Every television receiver in use must be licensed, but it is not necessary to have a separate licence for each set. The licence covers all sets in one household.

A licence holder can use his television at a temporary address when he is away from home. However, if he has two sets and the one at home is being used at the same time, he must have a second licence.

Special rules for hotels and old people's homes

In rented accommodation it is the user of a television set who must ensure he is licensed for that use, even if the set is provided by the landlord.

A tenant who shares living accommodation with his landlord may be covered by the landlord's licence. Anyone not sure of his position can contact the National TV Licence Records Office, Bristol BS98 1TL, who will give advice.

A landlord who installs a television set in a holiday home for his guests needs to buy a licence to cover the act of installation. But the licence need not be renewed if the set is not being used. A guest who uses it must ensure he is licensed. If his home set is licensed he will be covered, so long as simultaneous use does not occur.

A hotel proprietor's ordinary licence covers his own private set and those of his own family, and of the domestic staff resident with him in the premises for which the licence was granted.

At present, hotels of any size can take out a single licence to cover sets in a stated number of guest rooms that would otherwise need separate licences. But from January 1, 1985, hotels with sets in more than 15 rooms will need an additional licence for every 5 rooms above that number.

A group concessionary licence may be available to old people living in homes and sheltered housing – and, from January 1, 1985, to physically disabled or mentally disordered people in similar accommodation. The fee is 5p per person per year. Application should be made to NTVLRO by the owners or administrators of the property.

Blind people can obtain a reduction of £1.25 in the licence fee on producing evidence of their disability.

Refunds of licence fees

No refund can be made on television licences except when:

- An unexpired black-and-white licence is exchanged for a colour one. The refund depends on how long the black-and-white licence has been used.
- A licence has been duplicated. The full amount is refunded.
- A person takes out or renews a television licence and decides he does not need it, provided that he returns the licence within 28 days of issue. Any refund given amounts to eleven-twelfths of the original licence fee.

The retailer's responsibility

When a retailer sells or hires a set, he must advise the NTVLRO of the name and address of his customer. If he does not do so he can be fined up to £400.

If a person is convicted of not having a licence, he may be fined up to £400 in summary proceedings and he will have to pay any licence fee due.

TENANTS' ASSOCIATION

Forming a group to fight for tenants' rights

There are about 650 tenants' and residents' groups in Scotland. A list of them and the persons to contact can be obtained from the Tenants Participation Advisory Service, 266 Clyde Street, Glasgow.

Most groups have been formed to protect the interests of tenants in council and other public authority housing schemes. But in some areas private tenants have banded together to press for environmental improvements, or to safeguard tenants' interests where a HOUSING ACTION AREA has been declared.

Tenants' groups have campaigned effectively about dampness in multistorey flats in Glasgow – by withholding rent – and have urged defensive measures against vandals. They have also negotiated improvements in draft leases for public authority housing. Glasgow District Council and the Scottish Special Housing Association have allowed tenants' groups to form housing cooperatives which manage all the houses in certain schemes.

For more information contact the Scottish Tenants Organisation, 53 St. Vincent Crescent, Glasgow G3 8NQ.

TERRORISM

Emergency powers to combat political violence

Emergency powers to combat terrorism – meaning the use of violence for political ends – are granted under the Prevention of Terrorism (Temporary Provisions) Act 1984.

The Act runs until March, 1989, and its provisions require to be renewed annually by STATUTORY INSTRUMENT. It is aimed mainly at the IRA, but can be used to detain someone suspected of involvement in terrorism carried out by *any* group.

In the case of Northern Ireland affairs, the Act allows the government to ban an organisation suspected of terrorism, making it an offence to belong to or support that organisation. In 1984 the only banned organisations were the

Irish Republican Army and the Irish National Liberation Army.

An individual suspect, even if he is a British Citizen, can be the subject of an exclusion order prohibiting him from being in, or entering, mainland Britain or Northern Ireland. Someone who is not a British Citizen can be excluded from any part of the UK.

A suspect has no right of appeal against an exclusion order. But if he objects, he can ask to be heard by a government-appointed adviser who will report to the Secretary of State.

General provisions The police can SEARCH premises without a warrant if they think that the national interest requires immediate action.

If they believe that someone has committed certain offences connected with terrorism, they can arrest him without a warrant. He can then be detained for up to 48 hours – or up to 7 days on the instruction of the Secretary of State – without being charged or appearing in court. The police must believe that he:

- Is concerned in terrorist acts or plans.
- Is withholding information about terrorism or terrorists connected with Northern Irish affairs.
- Belongs to or seeks support (including financial support) for a banned organisation – the IRA or INLA.
- Is involved in raising funds to support acts of terrorism connected with Northern Irish affairs.
- Is under an exclusion order keeping him out of mainland Britain – or, if he is not a British Citizen, out of the UK.
- Has helped or given shelter to someone who is under an exclusion order.

The maximum penalty for any of these offences is 6 months' imprisonment and a £2,000 fine under summary proceedings. Under solemn proceedings it is 5 years' imprisonment and an unlimited fine.

It is also an offence for someone to wear clothes or display articles in public that suggest he is a member of a banned organisation. The maximum penalty is 6 months' imprisonment and a £2,000 fine.

Immigration law Someone suspected of terrorist activities can also be excluded from the UK under IMMIGRATION law if he is not a British Citizen and the Home Secretary considers that his exclusion is 'conducive to the public good'.

THEFT

Dishonestly taking someone else's property

Theft is the unlawful taking of someone else's goods without his consent.

Usually, it must be shown that the alleged thief intended to deprive the owner permanently of his goods: taking or 'borrowing' something – such as a friend's bicycle – with the intention of returning it will not normally be theft. However, in exceptional cases someone who intends all along to return the goods may still be guilty of theft.

Borrowed motor cars

Because taking away an article temporarily is not usually theft, there is a special offence to cover 'joy-riders' who borrow cars. This is the offence of taking and driving away a motor vehicle without the owner's consent.

The maximum penalty is 12 months' imprisonment and an unlimited fine. The offender's licence must be endorsed and he can be disqualified from driving at the court's discretion.

If someone is convicted of stealing a motor car, his driving licence is likely to be endorsed and he may be disqualified from driving for a period.

Taking something temporarily

The rule that an intention to deprive someone temporarily of his goods can be sufficient for theft is a recent development.

Because of this, the courts have not yet worked out all the cases to which the rule applies.

However, if a person dishonestly takes someone's property with the intention of returning it, and this causes loss or prejudice to the owner, a prosecution for theft may be possible. For example:

- A person who engages in industrial espionage by removing documents for photographing and then returning them could be convicted of the theft of the documents.
- It would be theft to borrow someone else's property and pawn it, intending to redeem it later and return it to him.
- It may be theft to take someone else's property temporarily, with the result that he suffers a substantial loss of use of it.

AN 'HONEST' THIEF

Someone who borrows another person's property without permission, meaning to return it, could be guilty of theft if the owner suffers substantial prejudice through being unable to use it.

Theft by finding

Lost property still belongs to its original owner. A person who finds it and decides to keep it is guilty of theft.

However, it is not theft if the finder merely keeps the property with the intention of tracing the owner or handing it into the police – though if he later decides to keep it, he will be guilty of theft.

Abandoned property – for instance, items put out for REFUSE COLLECTION into the ownership of the Crown, and a person who takes it without permission could be prosecuted for theft. In practice, however, such prosecutions are rare.

The crime of embezzlement

Embezzlement is a crime that is closely related to theft. The distinction between the two crimes is unclear, but the charge will usually be embezzlement, not theft, if:

- The goods are initially in the hands of the accused with the owner's permission; and
- The subsequent dishonest taking of the goods involves a breach of trust against the owner.

For example, a person may put money into the hands of a stockbroker and instruct him to invest it on his behalf. If the stockbroker later ignores his instructions and uses the money for his own benefit, he is guilty of embezzlement.

Penalty The penalty for theft and embezzlement is at the discretion of the court, within its sentencing limits.

TIED ACCOMMODATION

When accommodation goes with a job

Around 70–80,000 households in Scotland live in 'tied' accommodation – that is, accommodation provided by an employer for an employee. Employers who provide accommodation include farmers, the police and fire services, the armed forces, local authorities, the National Health Service, the National Coal Board, the Forestry Commission and British Rail.

The rights of someone who lives in a house provided by his employer depend on whether he is required to live in the house so that he can do his job properly. If he is, he is not a tenant, but is a 'service occupier' (even if he pays rent). If he is not, and pays rent, he is a 'service tenant'.

The rights of service occupiers

An employee who lives in a house provided by his employer does not become a service occupier merely because his employer makes living in the house a condition of providing the job, or insists that he lives there. The employee is a service occupier only if he is required to live in the house in order to do his job properly. (In technical language, living in the house must be 'ancillary and necessary' to the performance of his duties under his employment contract.)

So a caretaker may be required to live in a house on or near the premises that he looks after, to deal with any emergencies that might arise. Or a farm worker may be required to live on the farm so that he can tend livestock satisfactorily.

Because of this rule, it cannot be assumed that an employee is a service occupier merely because of the nature of his employment. A farm worker, for example, may live in a cottage on the farm but that does not prevent him being a service tenant. In each case, the question whether he is a tenant or merely an occupier can be answered only by looking at all the circumstances.

A service occupier who rents from a private employer has no security of tenure and no right to have a fair rent registered. He merely has a permission or LICENCE TO OCCUPY the house while his employment continues. When he leaves his job, or is dismissed, he loses his right to remain in the house.

If he refuses to leave, however, his employer can only lawfully evict him by obtaining an eviction order from the sheriff court. It is an offence to evict him without such an order, or to harass him in order to force him to leave. *See:* HARASSMENT

Temporary security Service occupiers who rent from a private employer and whose rent includes a payment for furniture or services provided by the employer may be able to have their eviction delayed by the sheriff for up to 3 months. (If the occupation began before December 1, 1980, the employee can ask a rent assessment committee to delay eviction for up to 6 months.) *See:* LICENCE TO OCCUPY

Public tenants People who rent their homes from district, regional or islands councils, new town development corporations, registered housing associations and the Scottish Special Housing Association have no security of tenure under the Tenants' Rights (Scotland) Act if they are employed by their landlord and are required to live in the house for the better performance of their duties. *See:* COUNCIL TENANCY

SPECIAL RULES FOR FARM COTTAGES

In certain circumstances, a sheriff court *must* grant an eviction order to a landlord who wants to replace a tenant who is not an agricultural worker with one who is – even though the tenant is protected by the Rent (Scotland) Act.

The court must make an eviction order if the following conditions are all met:

1. The house was previously occupied by an agricultural employee.
2. The present tenant is not (and never has been) employed by the landlord.
3. The tenant is not the widow of a former employee.
4. The landlord informed the tenant in writing, before the tenancy began, that he might want the house for an agricultural worker.
5. The court is satisfied that the landlord wants the house for that purpose.

These rules could be used by, for instance, a farmer who lets a farm cottage to a non-employee and then wants the cottage back for a full-time or part-time worker.

The rights of service tenants

With one important exception, a service tenant has the same rights and obligations as any other tenant. If he is a private tenant who is protected by the Rent (Scotland) Act, he will have security of tenure and also be entitled to have a fair rent fixed by a rent officer. If he is a public sector tenant, he will have security of tenure under the Tenants' Rights (Scotland) Act.

The exception applies to service tenants in the private sector who have security of tenure under the Rent (Scotland) Act. Even though a tenant is protected, his employer can ask the court to evict him on the ground that he reasonably requires the house for another full-time employee of his (or a full-time employee of one of his tenants). The sheriff can grant an eviction order if he thinks it is reasonable to do so and either:

- The house was let to the tenant because of his employment and that employment has ended; or
- The Secretary of State for Scotland has certified that the employee who is to be given the house works (or will work) on a rented farm, or as a handyman on rented farms that form part of an estate.

If the employer obtains an eviction order by lying to or misleading the court, and this is subsequently discovered, the court can award the evicted employee compensation for any loss that he suffered as a result.

TIME OFF WORK

When an employee can be away from work

An employee is expected to work the hours required by his EMPLOYMENT CONTRACT. His employer is not normally obliged to give him time off unless this is provided for in the contract. Nor, if he does, is he obliged to pay any wages.

In practice, most contracts make provision for unavoidable absence as a result of accident or illness, and grant employees a paid HOLIDAY ENTITLEMENT to be taken at a time agreed with the employer. Agricultural workers and employees in trades covered by WAGES COUNCILS have a statutory right to be paid during their holidays.

Many employers are also prepared to give employees additional time off for urgent personal matters – for example, to attend a funeral or a medical examination. But if an employee is absent without permission, his employer has the right to discipline him. If his unauthorised absences persist, they may justify dismissal. *See:* DISCIPLINE AT WORK

When an employer must grant time off

In certain circumstances, an employer must grant time off – sometimes with pay – even if it is not provided for in the contract. Most full-time employees have this right, but many part-time workers generally do not. *See:* PART-TIME WORKER

Public duties Most full-time employees are entitled to time off *without* pay to serve as a JUSTICE OF THE PEACE, or as a member of a LOCAL AUTHORITY, tribunal, area health board, river purification board, school or college council, or the governing body of a central institution or college of education.

There is no fixed rule on how much time must be granted, but it must be 'reasonable in all the circumstances', taking into account the needs of the business, the effect on it of the employee's absence, the nature of the employee's public duties and time off allowed for other purposes.

Redundancy Most full-time employees who are dismissed as redundant and who have been with their employer for 2 years or more are entitled to reasonable time off *with* pay – a maximum of two-fifths of a week's pay – during the NOTICE period to look for a new job or to make arrangements to undergo retraining. *See:* REDUNDANCY

Trade union duties and activities Most full-time employees who are officers of unions recognised by an employer for COLLECTIVE BARGAINING – such as shop stewards or branch chairmen – can take reasonable time off *with* pay to carry out their industrial relations duties and undergo relevant training.

Members of a recognised union are entitled to reasonable time off *without* pay to participate in union activities – for example, to vote in elections. These activities do not include taking industrial action, such as STRIKE action.

When deciding what is reasonable time off, regard must be had to the Code of Practice, *Time off for Trade Union Duties and Activities,* issued by the ADVISORY, CONCILIATION AND ARBITRATION SERVICE (ACAS).

Safety duties Safety representatives appointed by recognised trade unions are entitled to any necessary time off *with* pay to perform their duties and to undergo relevant training. *See:* HEALTH AND SAFETY AT WORK

Ante-natal care An employee – including a part-time employee – is entitled to time off *with* pay to keep an appointment for ante-natal care arranged by a doctor, midwife or health visitor. Except for the first appointment, she must produce a certificate of pregnancy and an appointment card if her employer requests them. *See:* MATERNITY

When an employer refuses

If an employer refuses time off, or pay, to an employee who is entitled to it, the employee can complain to an INDUSTRIAL TRIBUNAL. He should do so within 3 months, otherwise his complaint may not be heard.

If the complaint is successful, the tribunal can award compensation for the employer's failure and for any loss suffered by the employee as a result. It can also order the employer to pay any wages that are due.

In redundancy cases, the compensation payable is up to two-fifths of a week's pay. In ante-natal cases, it is the wages the employee would have got had time off not been refused.

TOUR OPERATOR

When something goes wrong with the holiday arrangements

When you book a holiday with a tour operator, you enter into a CONTRACT. Your rights – what you are entitled to under the contract and what happens if things go wrong – depend to a large extent on its terms.

Most holiday brochures and booking forms contain conditions to which you agree when you sign the booking form. These form part of your contract with the tour operator.

If a passenger is killed or injured as a result of someone's negligence, the conditions cannot take away the right of compensation. If the tour operator's negligence causes loss or damage of any other kind, the conditions will protect him only if they are fair and reasonable. *See:* UNFAIR CONTRACT

If the tour operator does not provide the holiday described in the brochure he will have broken his contract. The holidaymaker can claim compensation for loss of enjoyment.

Codes of conduct

If a tour operator is also a member of ABTA, the Association of British Travel Agents, he will be bound by the ABTA codes of conduct – ensuring that:

- Booking conditions are easily read and understood.
- Booking conditions do not include clauses purporting to exclude the agent's responsibility for misrepresentations, or purporting to exclude a tour operator's responsibility to exercise diligence in making arrangements for his clients, or for consequential loss following from breach of this duty.
- Brochures indicate prominently the circumstances in which clients can be asked to pay surcharges on their holiday costs.
- If a holiday has to be cancelled, clients are offered the choice of an alternative holiday if available or a prompt refund of all money paid.

If the cancellation is for reasons outside the tour operator's control, however, he may keep the amount of his reasonable expenses.

- Retail agents advise clients of the necessary passport, visa and health requirements for the journey.

Complaints If you have a complaint that is not dealt with to your satisfaction by your travel agent or tour operator, send details of the complaint to ABTA at 55–57 Newman Street, London W1P 4AH.

The Association offers free concilia-

HOLIDAY MISERY

The tour operator must provide the holiday described in his brochure. If he fails to do so, he is liable to pay compensation.

In November 1970 Mr Jackson booked a 4 week package holiday in Ceylon for himself, his wife and his two small children at a cost of £1,200.

The holiday brochure described the hotel as having mini golf, a swimming pool, a beauty salon, hairdressers, a gift shop and also an excellent restaurant.

When Mr Jackson booked he had specially asked that the children's room should have a connecting door with the parents' room. This was not provided.

Apart from that, the children's room was black with mildew, the toilet and shower were dirty and there was no bath.

They complained and were moved, but that was still unsatisfactory. In addition, most of the facilities advertised did not exist. Finally they moved to a better hotel where building work was still going on.

On returning home Mr Jackson sued the tour operators for damages and was awarded £1,100. The tour operators admitted breach of contract but contested the amount of damages. They appealed.

DECISION

The English Court of Appeal confirmed the award. The family had a right to £600, half the cost of the holiday, and £500 for the inconvenience and disappointment.

tion facilities and also an independent arbitration scheme. Members are obliged to go to arbitration and to accept the arbiter's decision.

When you can be surcharged

Once a booking has been made and confirmed, the tour operator can make a surcharge only if the booking conditions allow him to do so.

Most booking conditions do contain something like: 'We reserve the right to charge you any increase due to fluctuations in the costs on which our prices are based.'

When you cancel

If the customer cancels a holiday, he normally loses any deposit he has paid. In addition, the booking conditions may require him to make an extra payment as a cancellation charge. Most tour operators require the full purchase price to be paid several weeks in advance. How much they will refund on late cancellations will often depend on a sliding scale, depending on the length of notice of cancellation, and this can vary from operator to operator.

Arranging insurance

Many travel agents offer insurance cover against holiday cancellations, medical expenses, accidents and loss of luggage. It is always advisable to have insurance cover: make sure always that you disclose any existing medical problem in case the policy excludes cover.

It is also possible to take out insurance against extra expenses incurred due to delays – such as those caused by strikes or bad weather – or cancellation due to delays.

Sometimes this is included in the cover offered by the travel agent. You should check when booking.

If an agent becomes bankrupt

If a travel agent or tour operator to whom money has been paid becomes insolvent, holidaymakers on package tours may have special protection in certain circumstances.

The Civil Aviation Authority operates a licence system known as ATOL, Air Travel Organisers Licence. Before a licence is issued by the Authority, the financial position of the organiser is checked. Holders of a licence must take out a bond, usually a percentage of their annual turnover.

Members of ABTA also have a bonding system. If a member goes bankrupt they either refund the holidaymaker's money or arrange for the holiday to be taken over by another tour operator.

If the tour operator is not a member of ABTA, the holidaymaker should contact the Air Travel Reserve Fund, 20 Manvers Street, Bath, BA1 1LX. This has power to make good certain losses suffered by people travelling by air overseas, through the failure of an operator other than an airline.

TRADE DESCRIPTIONS

The right to be told the truth about what you pay for

Anyone in the business of selling goods or providing services is under a legal obligation to avoid giving false or misleading information about these to prospective customers.

Any kind of misleading information or indication – spoken, written or pictorial – constitutes a false trade description under the Trade Descriptions Act 1968.

The maximum penalty for applying a false description to goods or services is a £2,000 fine in summary proceedings or 2 years' imprisonment and an unlimited fine if there were a trial by jury.

The law applies, however, only to information provided in the course of a trade or business, not to private transactions.

What must be described accurately

Trade descriptions, in relation to goods, cover any information about all the important details of an article – its size and quality, when, how and by whom it was produced, whether it has been tested or approved by any person or authority, and any other history of use or previous ownership.

With services, accommodation and facilities, the Act covers any information about their nature and provision,

HONESTY IS THE BEST POLICY

It is an offence for a trader to give false information to a customer about the goods he is selling.

THE CASE OF THE UNFINISHED HOTEL

It is an offence to issue a brochure that contains false information. Even if the information is supplied by someone else, it is up to the person issuing the brochure to check that it is correct.

A large Scottish package-holiday company issued a brochure advertising holidays at a 'brand new' Spanish hotel. It was to open in April 1970 and to have excellent facilities, including bedrooms with private showers, large cocktail bars, and a swimming pool.

By March, the holiday company knew that the hotel would not be completed by April. Nevertheless – without making any further enquiries – they continued to take bookings. In July, a party of Glaswegians arrived at the hotel. They were horrified to find it unfinished. One of them said 'the place was a shambles', another that 'it was like a builder's yard'. The swimming pool was not complete, there were no lifts and for several days there was no water in the bedrooms.

On their return from a very disappointing holiday, a number of the holidaymakers complained to the local trading standards department. The holiday company and their manager were prosecuted in Glasgow Sheriff Court for making reckless statements in the brochure about the accommodation and facilities available, contrary to the Trade Descriptions Act 1968.

DECISION

The company and their manager were convicted. It was not a sufficient excuse that they had been misinformed by their Spanish agent. It was up to them to take reasonable precautions to make sure the information was correct, and this they had not done.

when, how and by whom they are provided, and whether they have been examined or approved by anyone. The location and amenities of any accommodation must be accurately described.

Proving an offence

Anyone who thinks he has been misled by a false trade description should complain to the trading standards or consumer protection department of his regional council. It is the department's job to enforce the Act and to report the circumstances to the PROCURATOR FISCAL for possible prosecution.

Goods If goods were falsely described by the trader himself, it is not necessary to prove that he knew the description was misleading. The falsity in itself renders him liable, if it is material.

However, no matter whether the falsehood relates to goods or services, it is a defence to show that it arose by accident or by mistake, or by relying on information supplied by someone else; and that all reasonable precautions were taken to avoid the offence.

In addition, a person charged with making a false description of goods can plead that he did not know (and could not reasonably be expected to know) that they did not fit the description.

Services In a prosecution brought for misleading information about services, accommodation, or facilities, it is necessary to show that the accused either knew the information was false or provided it recklessly.

TRADE MARK

How the law protects a brand name or symbol

Many companies and businesses adopt a special name or symbol as a trade mark to identify their goods or services. A trade mark can be a valuable commercial asset and, because of that, there are laws to prevent one trader using another's trade mark.

A trade mark owner has two ways of preventing someone else using it:

- He can register it and take legal action for any infringement.
- He can rely on the general law which prevents anyone from representing his goods or business as being the goods or business of someone else.

Registering a trade mark

To register a trade mark for goods, an application must be made to the Trade Marks Registry, 25 Southampton Buildings, Chancery Lane, London, WC2. A trade mark cannot be registered for services, such as banking, but in 1984 a Bill was before Parliament to allow this.

Not all trade marks are approved by the registry. A mark must not be so like an existing mark that it causes confusion. A new oil company, for example, could not register the symbol of a shell which resembled that used by the Shell Company.

It is not usually possible to register a surname, unless it is written in a special way – for example, a replica of the trader's signature. A surname may also be registered if it has already been used as an unregistered name for a number of years and has become identified with a particular product.

A place name cannot be registered if it indicates where the goods originated from. But a place name that obviously has nothing to do with where the goods come from can be – for example, North Pole could be registered as a trade name for bananas.

Common words of praise, such as 'splendid', 'superb' or 'perfection' cannot be registered, as others may legitimately want to use them to describe their products.

Invented words can be registered – for example, Kodak. But a word that is deliberately misspelt may be rejected if the word, correctly spelt, could not be registered, or if it creates a misleading impression of the goods.

The registry will refuse a mark if its use might be dangerous – for example, if a poisonous disinfectant is given a trade name that makes it sound like a drink.

Removing a trade mark Even after a

BY ROYAL APPOINTMENT

Any company that has been a supplier to the Queen or a member of the Royal Family for 3 consecutive years is entitled to state that its product is 'by appointment' and use the Royal Arms on the product. To do so, the company must apply to the Lord Chamberlain.

If the company stops supplying the Royal Family, the use of the Royal Arms must be withdrawn.

Anyone who falsely claims that goods or services are supplied to or approved by any member of the Royal Family is guilty of an offence. The maximum penalty is a fine of £2,000 under summary proceedings and an unlimited fine and 2 years' imprisonment under solemn proceedings.

trade mark has been registered, the owner must make use of it to keep the registration alive. If the trade mark is not used for 5 years, it can be removed from the register.

It can also be removed if it becomes widely accepted as a descriptive term. For example, 'petrol', 'linoleum' and 'gramophone' were once trade marks but are now descriptive words.

Trade mark infringements

Anyone who falsely states that a trade mark has been registered can be fined up to £50 in summary criminal proceedings.

Once a trade mark has been registered, its owner is entitled to sue anyone who uses a similar mark for the same type of goods and he may seek an INTERDICT to prevent any further infringements.

However, it is not usually an infringement to use someone else's trade mark on goods that are so different that no confusion could reasonably arise.

Unregistered marks

A trade name that is not registered is still protected by the law that prevents anyone representing his goods or business as being the goods or business of someone else. A trader who does so risks being sued for what is known as 'passing off'. Passing off may also be committed if goods are packaged in a manner distinctive of another trader.

When a descriptive trade name is used, it may be difficult to establish it as being distinctive of one particular person's goods or business. A court will not allow that person to monopolise a description and prevent others using similar names. But they may be prevented from using the same name.

For example, a company calling itself 'Office Cleaning Services' could not prevent a rival calling itself the 'Office Cleaning Association'.

TRADE SECRET

How commercial information can be protected

Most businesses possess information, techniques or processes that they wish to keep confidential – such as special production methods, recipes for food or drink products, lists of customers, and marketing techniques. The law recognises the value of these trade secrets and helps to preserve their confidentiality.

Many contracts of employment contain a clause – or restrictive covenant – forbidding an employee from using or disclosing his employer's trade secrets. But even if there is no such clause, there is an implied contractual obligation on the employee to maintain confidentiality. *See:* RESTRAINT ON EMPLOYMENT

When an employee changes jobs

An employee who changes jobs is quite entitled to use the skill and knowledge that he acquired while working for his former employer. But his obligation – whether expressly stated or implied – not to divulge any confidential information obtained from that employer may prevent him from disclosing trade secrets even after he leaves.

If an ex-employee does divulge trade secrets, or threatens to do so, his former employer can seek an INTERDICT (a court order) to prohibit him from doing this and to prohibit the person to whom the secret is disclosed from making use of the information. He is also entitled to claim DAMAGES for breach of contract from the ex-employee.

PROTECTING CONFIDENTIAL NEGOTIATIONS

The law will prevent confidential information being disclosed to others.

An industrial consultant had conducted research into the commercial production of fructose from dahlias, artichokes and chicory. In negotiations with Caledonian Produce (Holdings) Ltd., he disclosed the results of experiments and reports he had commissioned.

The consultant later maintained that the company had disclosed the information to others.

DECISION

At a preliminary hearing, the court ruled that the consultant would be entitled to damages if he could prove that there was an agreement that the information would be treated as confidential and that the company had disclosed it, or had used it for a purpose which the consultant had not agreed to.

Inventors' secrets

Someone who is unable to exploit his own invention through lack of money may ask a manufacturer to consider a joint venture. If the negotiations break down, the manufacturer is not entitled to go ahead on his own. If he does so, he can be stopped by an interdict from using any information given to him in confidence by the inventor.

Industrial espionage

Secret information may be stolen from a business or obtained by bribing one of its employees. If it discovers this, the business can seek an interdict to prohibit the person or company to whom the secret has been passed from making use of it.

TRADE UNION

The rights of union members

The law does not prevent a worker from belonging to a trade union, or taking part in its normal activities, unless he is a member of the police or the armed forces. Nor does it require a worker to join a union – though an employer may do so (see below).

Provided that the union is 'independent' – accepted by the government-appointed Certification Officer as being free from control or influence, real or potential, by an employer – it is unfair to dismiss an employee for being (or planning to be) a union member, or for taking part in union activities at an appropriate time. It will also usually be unfair to dismiss him for refusing to become or remain a union member.

In addition, an employee has a right not to have action short of dismissal taken against him for doing any of these things.

These rights apply only to employees, not to job applicants. Someone who is refused employment because he is – or refuses to become – a union member has no redress.

The rights of 'recognised' unions

Members and elected officers of an independent trade union gain additional legal rights if their union is recognised

YOUR RIGHTS IF YOU ARE DISMISSED FOR UNION REASONS

It is unfair for an employer to dismiss an employee if the main reason for doing so was that the employee:

- Was (or planned to become) a member of an independent trade union; or
- Had taken part (or planned to take part) in union activities.

'Union activities' include such things as recruiting members, collecting subscriptions, distributing union literature and attending meetings – so long as these activities take place outside working hours, or at a time within working hours that the employer has agreed to or impliedly accepted. However, if the action taken in support of union activities is wholly unreasonable or malicious, the dismissal may be treated as fair.

Dismissal for refusal to join a union

With one exception, it is unfair to dismiss an employee for refusing to become or remain a union member. The exception is where there is a union membership or 'closed shop' agreement between an employer and a union, and the employer's practice is to require his employees to be members of that union. In that case it is fair (subject to what is said below) to dismiss any employee who refuses to become or remain a member.

After November 1, 1984, this exception will only apply if the closed shop agreement has been approved by a secret ballot of affected employees in the 5 years immediately before notice of dismissal is given. Approval will have to be given by at least 80 per cent of those entitled to vote (or at least 85 per cent of those voting if the agreement was previously approved by the employees or took effect before August 14, 1980).

That apart, the exception does not apply – and the dismissal will be *unfair* – if the employee can show one of the following:

- He genuinely objects on grounds of conscience or other deeply-held personal conviction to belonging to any trade union or to the particular union in question.
- He worked for the employer before the agreement took effect, and has not since joined the union.
- He was entitled to vote in a secret ballot on an agreement that took effect after August 14, 1980 (whether or not he actually voted), and has not since joined the union.
- At the time notice of dismissal was given, he had obtained (or applied for) a declaration from an industrial tribunal that the union had unreasonably excluded or expelled him (see p. 644). The employee cannot rely on this rule if, following his application to the tribunal, his non-membership is solely due to his failure to apply or reapply for membership, or his refusal to accept it.

When you can claim unfair dismissal

If you believe that you have been unfairly dismissed because of your union membership or activities, or because of your refusal to become or remain a union member, the usual rules about making a complaint of unfair dismissal to an industrial tribunal do not apply. Unlike other dismissed employees, you can make your complaint even though you are over normal retiring age or have not been employed for at least 1 year. *See:* UNFAIR DISMISSAL

Making a complaint of unfair dismissal

If you are dismissed because of your union membership (or proposed membership) or activities, or your refusal to join a union, you can make your complaint of unfair dismissal to an industrial tribunal in the normal way. It will then be dealt with like any other complaint of unfair dismissal.

However, if you are dismissed for these reasons, you can apply to the tribunal for what is called 'interim relief'. This is a special procedure which is intended to lessen the risk of the dismissal developing into a major industrial dispute.

You must apply for interim relief within 7 days of leaving your job. To do so, you should state, in answer to Question 1 on the tribunal application form (which asks what you want the tribunal to decide), 'whether I was unfairly dismissed', and add: 'I claim interim relief on the ground that I was dismissed because of my union membership/non-membership/activities'.

Except where you are dismissed for refusing to join a union, you must send with your application form a certificate from your union (or the one you were planning to join) stating that there are reasonable grounds for believing that the main reason for your dismissal was a union reason.

If, following the preliminary hearing, the tribunal decides that you are likely to win your case at a full hearing later, it will ask your employer whether he will give you your old job (or an acceptable alternative job) back temporarily until the full hearing takes place.

If he refuses, or the tribunal considers any alternative job offered to be unacceptable, it will order your contract of employment to continue in force until the case is finally decided. You do not need to turn up for work, but you must be paid your wages and you will keep your pension and seniority rights.

Once interim relief has been granted, the claim proceeds as a normal unfair dismissal.

Getting extra compensation

If you are unfairly dismissed for union reasons, you are entitled to a higher level of compensation than normal. Your 'basic award' must be at least £2,000, and you are entitled to a 'special' award on top of your basic and compensatory awards.

The amount of this special award is £10,000 or 104 weeks' pay, whichever is greater, up to a maximum of £20,000. If your employer fails to obey a tribunal order to take you back, the amount is £15,000 or 156 weeks' pay, whichever is greater. You must first have asked the tribunal for reinstatement or re-engagement. *See:* UNFAIR DISMISSAL

When the union must pay

Either you or your employer can request the tribunal to order any trade union or individual who put pressure on your employer to dismiss you – by threatening or organising industrial action – to be brought into the proceedings. The tribunal must grant a request made before the hearing begins; and may grant one made thereafter, but before the making of any award.

If the request is granted, the union or individual can be required to pay some or all of your compensation.

---

by an employer for the purposes of COLLECTIVE BARGAINING.

The recognition does not have to be set out formally in writing; it can be implicit in the relationship between employer and union – for example, if the two of them meet regularly to negotiate on matters affecting the workforce.

Once a union is recognised by an employer, it is entitled to demand:

- Information about his business that is needed for collective bargaining.
- Advance warning of proposed redundancies.
- Time off work for union representatives, members and union-appointed health and safety representatives to perform their duties and activities.
- Consultation about changes in occupational pension schemes.

Disclosure of information Guidance on the information that an employer is expected to give to a recognised union for the purposes of collective bargaining is given in *Code of Practice 2: Disclosure of Information to Trade Unions for Collective Bargaining Purposes,* prepared by the ADVISORY, CONCILIATION AND ARBITRATION SERVICE (ACAS).

The code is not legally binding, but employers are expected to pay attention to its provisions and it is admissible as evidence in legal proceedings. A trade union is entitled to complain to the CENTRAL ARBITRATION COMMITTEE that relevant information has not been disclosed. If the dispute is not resolved by ACAS, the Committee can take the code into account in deciding whether information should be given and what it should be.

If the Committee decides that the information should be given, it fixes a set time in which the employer ought to do so. If he does not, the union can complain to the Committee and present a claim for improved employment terms for the employees concerned. The employer is legally bound by any new terms that are agreed by the Committee.

The code suggests five broad areas in which information should be provided – pay and benefits, conditions of service, manpower, performance, and finances (see p. 645). However, an employer need give details only if they are required for negotiations that would be significantly impeded without them, and if disclosure would be good industrial relations practice.

He is not expected to provide information if to do so would be against the interests of national security or would be a breach of confidence. Nor is he required to provide information that was obtained for legal proceedings or concerns an individual who has not agreed to its disclosure.

An employer can also refuse to give information if disclosure would cause substantial injury to his business – though not merely because it would strengthen the union's bargaining position – or if the cost and effort of getting the information is out of reasonable proportion to its value.

The information need only be given to a union representative authorised to carry on collective bargaining, not to individual members or to those not directly involved. It should be set out so that it can be easily understood, but an employer is not obliged to provide copies of the documents from which it is drawn, nor to allow access to his files.

Redundancies An employer who recognises an independent trade union must consult it if he is planning to make any of its members redundant or is planning redundancies among non-union members in job categories for which the union is recognised. *See:* REDUNDANCY

Time off Officials of recognised unions are entitled to reasonable time off work, with pay, to carry out their union duties. Union members are entitled to reasonable time off to take part in normal union activities during working hours, but they have no right to be paid. *See:* TIME OFF WORK

Pensions An employer who recognises an independent trade union must give it at least 3 months' notice if he intends to contract out of the state occupational pension scheme. He must then consult with the union about the private pension scheme that he proposes to introduce. *See:* OCCUPATIONAL PENSION; RETIREMENT PENSION

Complaints against a union

Where a closed shop agreement is in force, requiring an employee to be or become a union member, that employee has the right not to be unreasonably refused membership of the union, and not to be unreasonably expelled from it. So has someone seeking employment.

If this right is infringed, the person affected can complain to an industrial tribunal – whether or not he has lost or failed to obtain employment as a result. This should be done within 6 months of the refusal or expulsion.

The tribunal will decide whether the union acted reasonably. The fact that the union was acting in accordance with its own rules does not necessarily mean

HOLDING MEETINGS IN COMPANY TIME

Sometimes it is reasonable for a union to hold a meeting in working hours because of the urgency of the matter to be discussed. If so, union members must be given time off to attend – but they do not have to be paid.

WHAT TO DO IF YOU ARE PENALISED FOR UNION REASONS

You have a right not to have action short of dismissal taken against you by your employer to:

- Prevent or deter you from joining or being a member of an independent trade union; or to penalise you for doing so.
- Prevent or deter you from taking part in that union's activities at an appropriate time; or to penalise you for doing so.
- Force you to join a union – whether independent or not. If there is a closed shop agreement requiring you to join, you have no such right unless the action taken against you would have been unfair had it been a 'closed shop' dismissal (see p. 643).

The action that an employer might take against you could be: suspension without pay, unfair selection for dirty or unpopular jobs, demotion, or harassment.

Complaining to a tribunal If your employer takes such action against you, you can make a complaint to an industrial tribunal. You should do this within 3 months of the action complained of.

Your employer must say why he took action against you. But it is up to you to prove that the reason was your union activities, membership (or lack of it).

If your complaint is successful, the tribunal can order your employer to pay compensation. The amount will depend on the seriousness of the employer's action and on whether you lost earnings or other benefits because of the action.

Your employer cannot avoid being liable to pay compensation by arguing that he was forced to take action against you because of pressure of industrial action by a trade union or individual. But either you or your employer can ask the tribunal to order the union (or individual) to pay some or all of the compensation.

that it acted reasonably. Nor does a breach of those rules mean that it acted unreasonably – though in this case an action for breach of contract might be brought against the union in the sheriff court or Court of Session (see below).

If the tribunal finds that the union acted unreasonably, it will make a declaration to that effect. If the union does not then admit or readmit the employee, he can ask the EMPLOYMENT APPEAL TRIBUNAL to order the union to pay him compensation. Even if he is admitted to membership, he can ask for compensation, but on this occasion he must apply to an industrial tribunal.

Applications for compensation must be made not earlier than 4 weeks and not later than 6 months from the tribunal's declaration. The amount of compensation depends on how much the applicant has lost and whether he was in any way to blame – up to £11,850 in the industrial tribunal and £19,390 in the Employment Appeal Tribunal.

TUC machinery If there is a closed shop, and someone loses a job because of expulsion or refusal of membership by a union affiliated to the TUC, he can complain to the TUC's Independent Review Committee.

It can recommend that the union should admit or readmit the person, but cannot order it to do so. Following its decision, it may offer conciliation to help the person find a job.

THE INFORMATION EMPLOYERS ARE EXPECTED TO GIVE

The ADVISORY, CONCILIATION AND ARBITRATION SERVICE has issued a Code of Practice suggesting a wide range of information that employers should be prepared to disclose to union representatives if they want it for collective bargaining. The ACAS list is intended only as a guide – the information needed by unions may vary according to the size of a firm and the nature of its business.

Pay

The structure and principles of payment systems, including the way in which employees are graded.

Employees' earnings and hours worked, analysed by work group, grade, plant, sex, department or company, including the way in which earnings are made up.

Details of fringe benefits and non-wage labour costs.

Conditions of service

Policies on recruitment, redeployment, redundancy, training, promotion and equal opportunity.

Health, safety and welfare matters.

Job evaluation and appraisal systems.

Manpower

Numbers employed, analysed by grades, departments, location, age and sex.

Labour turnover and absenteeism.

Overtime and short-time working.

Proposed organisational or technical changes.

Manpower *continued*

Manning levels.

Manpower and investment plans

Performance

Productivity and efficiency data.

Savings from increased productivity and output.

Return on capital invested.

Sales and the state of the order book.

Finances

Cost structures.

Gross and net profits.

Sources of earnings.

Assets and liabilities.

Allocation of profits.

Details of any governmental financial assistance being received.

Transfer prices to companies within the same group.

Loans to associated companies and interest charged.

Contracts for union or non-union labour

A clause in a contract is void if it requires work under the contract to be done by union – or non-union – labour only. Anyone who suffers loss because of it – by, for instance, being excluded from a list of suppliers or tenderers because he employs non-union labour – can sue the person or body excluding him – such as a local authority or nationalised industry.

A trade union that organises strike action against an employer for contracting with someone employing non-union labour will have no immunity against being sued. *See:* STRIKE

How union rules affect members' rights

Every trade union has a rule book that forms the basis of a CONTRACT between itself and its members. If the union does not follow its own rules – for example, if it expels a member without going through the procedure laid down – it is in breach of contract, and the member affected can ask a civil court to declare the union's decision invalid and prevent it being implemented.

A court can over-ride any union rule that does not comply with the rules of NATURAL JUSTICE – because, for instance, it does not allow a member facing disciplinary action time to prepare his case or obtain a fair hearing.

A union rule that states that no union decision can be appealed against in the courts is invalid. So are rules that provide for automatic loss of membership or prevent a member from leaving – though a condition that arrears of contributions must be paid may be upheld.

Unions are not allowed to discriminate against members or applicants on grounds of sex or race, or because they are nationals of another country in the EUROPEAN COMMUNITIES.

Discrimination against members who refuse to contribute to a union's 'political fund' – money to be used for political purposes – is forbidden. A member who is affected can complain to the Certification Officer. (In 1984 a Bill was before Parliament requiring unions wanting to continue to operate a political fund to obtain their members' approval through a secret ballot.)

Trade unions and strikes

In certain circumstances an employer can successfully sue a trade union that has authorised strike action to be taken against him. The employer may be able to obtain an INTERDICT and damages. *See:* STRIKE

TRADING STANDARDS

Enforcing consumer laws

Regional and islands councils are responsible for enforcing many CONSUMER PROTECTION laws through their trading standards or consumer protection departments.

Trading standards officers are specially trained in the requirements of the WEIGHTS AND MEASURES Acts, the TRADE DESCRIPTIONS Act, the CONSUMER SAFETY Act, and some parts of the CONSUMER CREDIT Act.

The address of your local department can be found in the telephone directory under the listing for your regional (or islands) council.

Enforcement of the FOOD and Drugs (Scotland) Act and the food hygiene regulations is the responsibility of the environmental health departments of district or islands councils.

TRAFFIC SIGN

Instructions that the road user must obey

Anyone driving a vehicle on the road must obey traffic signs. Failure to do so is not only an offence in itself, but can be the basis for prosecution on more serious driving charges. It can also be an important factor in civil actions for damages.

Signs at junctions

Stop signs at junctions with major roads are used in conjunction with two solid transverse lines marking where the major road begins, reinforced with the word 'stop' painted on the roadway.

Drivers must stop and not pass the line nearest to the major road. If the lines are not visible, they must not enter the major road so as to be likely to endanger a vehicle on the major road or make the driver change his speed or swerve to avoid an accident.

A give-way sign indicates that the driver must be ready to let traffic on the major road go first. An octagonal or triangular sign is used in conjunction with two broken transverse lines and a triangle painted on the road. The broken lines must be crossed in the same way as the solid lines at a stop sign, but the driver need not necessarily stop his vehicle.

Hatching on the road surface has no legal force in itself; it indicates that the driver should not normally use that part of the road surface. But using the hatching may be evidence of careless or RECKLESS DRIVING

Traffic lights

The significance of the sequence of traffic lights is:

Red	Stop and wait behind the stop line.
Red and amber	Stop and wait behind the stop line.
Green	Go if the road is clear.
Amber alone	Do not go beyond the stop line – or, if there is no stop line visible, beyond the signal – except when in a vehicle which, when the light first appears, is so close to the line or signals that it cannot safely be stopped.

Flashing red lights on motorways indicate that vehicles in the relevant lane must not go beyond the signal.

At Pelican crossings motorists must stop on red, but they may drive on when the amber light resumes flashing – provided that any pedestrian already on the crossing is given precedence.

Roadworks and other signs

It is an offence not to stop for a hand-operated 'stop' sign where roadworks are blocking one carriageway. It is not an offence in itself to ignore flags used for the same purpose but a driver could still be charged with careless or reckless driving.

Circular signs with red circles are mostly prohibitive and it is an offence to contravene them. Circular blue signs give a positive instruction and are also compulsory.

Double continuous white lines require vehicles travelling in either direction to keep to the nearside of the nearest continuous line. Where there is a continuous white line with a broken white line, drivers must not cross or straddle a nearside, continuous white line, except for access to premises or to pass a parked vehicle. But if the nearer line is broken it may be crossed or straddled if it is safe to do so.

Census signs

Contravention of a traffic direction for the purpose of an approved traffic census is an offence.

Penalties

The maximum fine for a traffic sign offence is £400, but an offender can have his driving licence endorsed only if he ignores:

- A red signal on automatic traffic signs.
- Flashing red lights on motorways.
- Red signals at level crossings and roadworks.
- Double white lines and stop signs.

TRAFFIC WARDEN

The extra 'police' force for parking and traffic control

Traffic wardens are appointed by the local POLICE authority and act under the direction of the Chief Constable. They form an auxiliary force, with powers only to direct traffic and enforce parking regulations.

Wardens can issue a fixed-penalty notice, or 'ticket', for a PARKING offence, for leaving a car without lights or for failing to display a valid excise licence. For offences where there is no fixed penalty procedure – for example, causing unnecessary obstruction – a warden's report can still lead to prosecution. Wardens cannot order the towing-away of an illegally parked car, but they can 'cause' its removal by reporting it to the police.

When you must obey

A traffic warden can exercise his powers only if he is in uniform.

If he is controlling traffic, or if he signals a driver to move to prevent a road obstruction, any motorist who disobeys his signal commits the same offence as if he had ignored the signal of a

TOO LATE! TOO LATE!

You are entitled to try to dissuade a traffic warden from issuing a parking ticket. But if he has started to write the ticket, he has no power to cancel it.

policeman. The maximum fine is £400.

If you are in charge of a car that is illegally parked, you must give your name and address to a warden if required to do so. But he has no power to make you show your driving licence – except to identify yourself if you reclaim a car from a pound.

What you can do if you object

A motorist is entitled to try to dissuade a traffic warden from issuing an offence notice. But once a warden has started to write out the 'ticket', there is no point. The warden cannot cancel it.

A motorist who believes he has a good excuse for a parking infringement, or thinks he has been treated too harshly, should write to the chief constable.

If a motorist objects to a fixed penalty notice and does not pay it within 21 days, either he or the registered owner of the vehicle will receive a 'notice to owner' of the offence. If the owner ignores the notice and fails to pay the penalty or fails to name the driver of the vehicle at the time of the offence, he may be prosecuted and fined up to £400.

TRANSPLANT

When one person's organs are removed to help another

When someone dies in hospital or is dead on arrival there, the local health board has legal possession of the body. Otherwise, the EXECUTOR of the dead person's estate has legal possession.

Either can authorise a surgeon to remove parts of the body –for example, kidneys – for transplanting into another person, or for research.

The law, however, lays down special rules to govern the removal of any human tissue.

Whoever authorises the taking of a dead person's organs has a duty to ensure that the person, when alive, never raised an objection to such a practice, and that close relatives also have no objection.

If the dead person expressed a positive wish to donate organs – in a will, by carrying a donor card, or orally in the presence of 2 witnesses – relatives usually have no legal right to be consulted.

If a death is reported to the PROCURATOR FISCAL and he orders a POST-MORTEM examination of the body, nothing can be removed without his permission.

When a donor is alive

Anyone over the age of 18 who is capable of giving a valid consent – not, for example, someone who is mentally subnormal or disordered – can participate as a donor in transplant surgery.

If a proposed donor is under 18 but over 12 (girls) or 14 (boys), the consent of parents or a legal guardian is also required.

In the case of children under 12 (girls) or 14 (boys), the consent would have to come from the parent or guardian and would be legally acceptable only if the operation was in the child's own interests – for example, to save the life of a brother or sister whose death would greatly distress the donor.

When the recipient of a transplant is a child

The consent of parents or a legal guardian must be sought before an organ is transplanted into anyone under the age of 16.

If consent is refused unreasonably, however – for example, where there is an immediate risk of the child's death or permanent disablement – a hospital authority may be justified in ignoring parental opposition.

TRAVELLING PEOPLE

Finding suitable sites for encampments

Under legislation passed in 1960, local authorities have power to license certain sites as CARAVAN sites and also to provide such sites themselves.

However, this legislation took little account of the special needs of travelling people or gypsies: that is, those who – by whatever name they are known – live by choice in caravans or tents, and are nomadic for all or part of the year.

Travellers' traditional sites were often refused site licences because they lacked proper facilities, and unofficial sites were often closed. This forced travellers to go to even more unsatisfactory sites – sites where they had no security of tenure and from which they were often driven by pressure from the settled community.

At first, local authorities did little to provide special sites for travellers – again sometimes because of pressure from the settled community.

However, in 1968 Parliament placed a duty on local authorities in England and Wales to provide adequate sites for gypsy encampments. Once an area has been designated as having adequate gypsy accommodation, gypsies are only allowed to camp on authorised sites.

There is no equivalent legislation in Scotland. Instead, central government has sought to persuade (rather than compel) local authorities to provide a network of suitable sites with facilities such as water, sanitation and 'hard-standings'.

A number of special sites for travelling people have been provided across the country, and since 1980 central government has made 100 per cent grants towards the capital cost of caravan sites. These sites, however, are not protected by the Mobile Homes Act. *See:* MOBILE HOME

Central government has also encouraged education authorities to pay special attention to the needs of travellers' children; has asked housing authorities to keep the needs of travellers in mind when drawing up housing allocation policies; and has said that it hopes there will be no harassment of travellers pending the provision of a sufficient number of permanent sites.

Preventing unlawful activities

Travellers who set up camp on private property can be evicted by the owner or tenant of the land.

The law of NUISANCE can be used to end unsightly activities such as car-breaking and to prevent noise, smell or insanitary conditions.

TREASON

Acting as an enemy of the state

Anyone who owes allegiance to the Crown commits treason by:

- Showing his intention to kill the sovereign.
- Taking part in an insurrection against the sovereign's authority, even if there is in fact no conflict with the armed forces.
- Giving aid and comfort to the enemy in time of war – for example, by becoming an enemy citizen in wartime.

Allegiance is owed, not only by British subjects, but also by an ALIEN who is voluntarily on British territory and who is neither a diplomat nor a member of an invading or occupying force.

An alien who leaves British territory with a British passport, which he still has at the time he commits a treasonable act, is guilty of treason. That is why William Joyce (Lord Haw-Haw) was guilty of treason when he broadcast from Germany during the Second World War, although he was a United States citizen.

Treason is an offence for which someone may still be hanged in Britain.

NO NEED TO BE BRITISH

Giving 'aid and comfort' to the enemy – by, for example, assisting his propaganda effort – is treason.

TREASURE TROVE

The Crown's right to valuable objects

Any gold, silver, plate, coin, bullion or other valuable objects found abandoned belong to the Crown. This is true whether the 'find' is a collection of Roman coins or a modern engagement ring.

If the articles have been lost rather than abandoned, they do not fall to the Crown but continue to belong to the original owner. *See:* LOST PROPERTY.

When someone unearths buried treasure

Anyone who finds valuables, such as a bag of gold coins or box of silver plate, either by accident – say, while ploughing – or while searching should tell the police.

THE ST. NINIAN'S TREASURE

In Scotland, unlike in England, the Crown is entitled to all abandoned property, even if it has not been hidden and is of little value.

In 1958 an excavation team from Aberdeen University found a number of valuable articles on St. Ninian's Isle in the Shetland Islands. They included silver brooches and bowls and a porpoise bone.

The excavators challenged the right of the Crown to this treasure. They argued that the Crown would have to show that the treasure had been deliberately hidden, and that a porpoise bone was in any case not valuable enough to count as treasure.

DECISION

The Court decided that as long as the property was abandoned, it belonged automatically to the Crown. Its value, or whether or not it was hidden, did not make any difference.

The police pass the goods on to the PROCURATOR FISCAL who acts as local representative of the Queen's and Lord Treasurer's Remembrancer. The finder can normally expect a reward. If the goods are of little value he may be allowed to keep them.

Anyone who does not report a find of treasure trove and simply keeps it for himself is guilty of THEFT.

Special rules apply to objects that have been washed ashore. *See:* WRECK

TREE

When it is illegal to fell a tree

Trees upon which a tree PRESERVATION ORDER has been placed are subject to special regulations.

Where a tree is subject to a preservation order, a substantial fine (related to the tree's value) can be imposed on anyone who, without authority, 'cuts down, or wilfully destroys' the tree, or 'tops or lops' it in such a way that he is likely to destroy it.

In a conservation area it is an offence to cut down any tree without first giving 6 weeks' notice to the planning authority. This gives the authority an opportunity to consider whether or not to make a tree preservation order. *See:* CONSERVATION AREAS

Obtaining a licence to fell an unwanted tree

A landowner or tenant wishing to fell growing trees on his land must obtain a felling licence from the regional office of the Forestry Commission, except when:

- The trees are less than 3 in. in diameter or, in the case of coppice or underwood, not more than 6 in. in diameter; or, when the object is to improve the growth of other trees, not more than 4 in. in diameter.
- They are fruit trees, or trees in orchards, gardens, churchyards or public places.
- The felling does not exceed 825 cu. ft. of timber in any calendar quarter and not more than 150 cu. ft. is to be sold.
- Hedges are trimmed and laid, or when trees are dangerous or topped or lopped in normal circumstances.

WHEN A NEIGHBOUR'S TREE OVERHANGS YOUR GARDEN

If you own a house or land, you also own the AIR SPACE immediately above it. So if the branches of a neighbour's tree or bush overhang your property, you are entitled to cut them down. But you would be well advised to first write to your neighbour asking him to remove them, and keep a copy of the letter.

Any branches that you cut off – including any fruit that may be on them – belong to your neighbour and you should return them to him whether he asks for them or not.

If the offending branches are so high that you cannot reach them, ask your neighbour to arrange to have them removed at his own expense. If he refuses, you could, if you thought it worthwhile, apply to the sheriff court for a court order requiring him to do so.

A felling licence may sometimes be issued only on condition that replanting takes place.

A felling licence granted after a tree preservation order has been made is authority enough for the felling. In this situation, however, the Forestry Commission will usually refer any application for a licence to the planning authority, which may decide to take it over as an application for consent to fell under the order.

An owner who is responsible for felling trees without first obtaining a licence can be fined.

When tree roots cause damage to neighbouring property

If the roots of a tree damage a neighbouring property owner's land or buildings, he may be able to claim compensation from the owner of the tree. It is no valid defence for the tree owner to say that his tree was there before the neighbour's damaged property.

A difficult area of dispute is where the tree is growing on a grass verge outside private property and the local council refuses to accept that it is the owning occupier of the verge.

If you are affected by such a tree, take professional legal advice about suing the council.

TRESPASS

What you do about unwelcome visitors

Trespassing on someone else's land or property is a DELICT (a civil wrong).

However, in Scotland a trespasser can normally be sued for compensation in the courts only if he actually causes damage to the land or property – if, for instance, he damages crops or trees or breaks windows. There is no question of 'token damages' in order to decide a property dispute, as in England.

So provided you avoid crops, it is unlikely that the law of trespass will hinder your country walks. However, if you make a habit of being on private property even though the owner has made it clear that he objects, a court might grant an INTERDICT to prevent your crossing the land in future.

Criminal trespass

Apart from being a civil wrong, trespassing on someone's land or property can sometimes also be a crime.

For example, it is an offence under the Trespass (Scotland) Act 1865 to camp on someone's land or squat in someone's house without permission. The people who can be prosecuted for this offence include squatters who take over empty houses, demonstrators whose protest involves camping on private land and employees who engage in a 'sit-in' – that is, an occupation of their employer's work premises or offices. The maximum penalty is a fine of £50.

However, it is not a crime simply to walk across someone's land without permission. So hill-walkers and ramblers need not fear signs that say: 'Trespassers will be prosecuted'.

To protect people's safety, it is an offence under the railway laws to trespass on railway lines.

What trespass requires

The essence of trespass – whether civil or criminal – is that entry is without the owner's consent. The postman and newspaper boy, for instance, have implied consent to walk up the front path, but they are trespassing if they go into the garage or the greenhouse.

A 'No hawkers, no canvassers' sign at the gate shows that such people do not have implied permission to come in. They are trespassing if they do so.

Someone may become a trespasser if consent to be on the property is revoked. For instance, a policeman has implied consent to come to the door to make inquiries, but if he does not have a warrant and refuses a request to leave, he becomes a trespasser. Similarly, employees have implied permission to be on their employer's property, but this may be withdrawn if they stage a 'sit-in' – they then become trespassers.

Preventing trespass

Every householder or property owner has a right to take reasonable steps to keep out trespassers, but not to instal hidden devices designed to injure those who do trespass. A barbed-wire fence, or even broken glass embedded in a wall, is reasonable; an electric fence carrying sufficient charge to kill anyone who touches it is not.

A trespasser who is injured by a guard DOG may or may not be entitled to compensation, depending on whether it was reasonable for the owner to keep the dog as protection.

An owner may order a trespasser to leave. If the trespasser refuses and is causing damage or being violent or violently abusive, the owner can use reasonable force to throw him off the land. He can also do so if the trespasser is a housebreaker. *See:* HOUSEBREAKING

In other cases of trespass, the owner can probably also resort to reasonable

WHEN FORCE MUST BE NO MORE THAN REASONABLE

Householders and property owners have a legal right to keep trespassers out, but they must use only reasonable force to do so.

force if the trespasser refuses to leave.

The amount of force that may legally be used depends on the circumstances. If someone camps on your property and refuses to leave, it is not reasonable to strike him with a spade or other heavy implement. But a householder about to be attacked by armed intruders would be justified in firing a shot-gun in their direction.

However, even a trespasser has rights. If a property owner injures a trespasser deliberately – rather than accidentally while evicting him – he commits a crime and, in addition, can be sued for damages.

The owner must also avoid unreasonable disregard for the safety of trespassers known to be on his property. A company that fails to fence off a poison dump knowing that children play there can be sued if a young trespasser comes to harm.

TRIBUNAL

Dispensing justice without the legal trimmings

A major development in the administration of justice in Britain has been the growth of administrative tribunals for settling disputes without having to go to formal courts of law such as the Court of Session or a sheriff court.

Special tribunals decide claims over a wide range of issues – for instance:

Employment Industrial tribunals and the Employment Appeal Tribunal deal with most employment claims – in particular, unfair dismissal and redundancy claims.

Social security An appeal about social security benefits may, depending on the benefit, go to a social security appeal tribunal, a medical appeal tribunal or a pensions appeal tribunal.

From the first two of these a further appeal lies to an independent social security commissioner, who is in law a tribunal.

Housing Rent assessment committees consider appeals against fair rents fixed by rent officers for privately rented accommodation.

Children Children's hearings consider cases of children who are at risk and who are thought to need compulsory care.

LEGAL AID is not generally available to pay for legal representation before tribunals. But a solicitor may be able to give advice – or even prepare a case – under the Legal Advice and Assistance Scheme. *See:* LEGAL ADVICE

The tribunal's watchdog

The Council on Tribunals is appointed by the Lord Chancellor to keep under review the constitution and working of most tribunals and important kinds of public inquiry. It has a Scottish Committee, which keeps Scottish tribunals under review.

The Council inquires into complaints from the public that the working of tribunals and inquiries is unsatisfactory, or proper procedures have not been followed, or procedures are inherently unfair. But it does not hear appeals against tribunal decisions. These go to the special appeal tribunals or to the ordinary courts.

If you have a complaint, write to the Secretary, Council on Tribunals, St Dunstan's House, Fetter Lane, London EC4A 1HD. If your complaint concerns a Scottish matter, write to the Secretary, Council on Tribunals (Scottish Committee), 22 Melville Street, Edinburgh EH3 7NS.

TRUST

How property can be held by one person for another's benefit

A trust exists when property, such as land or investments, is held by one person or group of persons – the trustee(s) – for the benefit of others.

A trust can be set up, for example, to:

- Benefit someone who is incapable of conducting his or her own affairs.
- Protect family assets from extravagance or bankruptcy – for example, to allow a beneficiary to get only the income instead of the capital to squander.
- Hold and look after land given or left by will to a child. A PUPIL can own property himself but unless there is a trust only his parents or guardians can administer it on his behalf.
- Keep property for people not yet born – such as any grandchildren who might later exist.
- Provide a widow with income from her husband's estate and then allow his children to inherit it on her death.
- Benefit people unnamed by the person setting up the trust. He can leave that decision to his trustees – in what is called a discretionary trust.
- Benefit charitable institutions – for example, to provide scholarships to a particular school or to provide benefits for the poor of a community.
- Hold the assets and finances of a club or society.

Many trusts are set up to obtain tax benefits – by reducing liability to pay INCOME TAX and CAPITAL TRANSFER TAX, for example.

HOW TO CHOOSE TRUSTEES

Anyone who agrees can be appointed a trustee, except a pupil. But it would often be unwise to choose a minor, a person of unsound mind, a bankrupt or a person convicted of a serious crime. Trustees are unpaid unless the trust deed states otherwise.

Any number of trustees can be appointed. It is not wise to have too many, but there should be at least two to guard against the death of one of them.

The people chosen should be reliable and businesslike; ideally they should have a working knowledge of property or be experienced in dealing with stocks and shares. It is helpful if they also know the family background.

If the trust is complicated and is likely to continue for a long time, it may be worthwhile to appoint a bank as the trustee, or to have a professional person (such as the family solicitor) as one of the trustees. Banks and professional trustees will require to be paid.

Once the trust has been set up and the trustees appointed, the assets involved must be properly transferred and the trustees must be registered as the owners.

How to set up a trust

A trust should be in writing otherwise it may be impossible to prove it exists. Because trust law and tax rules are complex, it is wise to set out your intentions and wishes with the help of a solicitor.

The document should state what the trust is to be called and list the assets to be administered by the trustees, who should be named.

It should then name the beneficiaries or describe them – for example, 'all the children of my sons and daughters'.

You should then set out any conditions – for instance:

- How the trust is to be operated.
- Where the assets should be invested.
- Who is to get the income (if any) and when and how the capital is to be divided.

You cannot set up a perpetual family trust. If you give a LIFERENT to someone not born when the trust comes into operation, he can demand his share of the trust assets when he reaches 18.

Restricting investment

If the creator of a trust makes no conditions about how the trust funds are to be invested, the trustees are governed by the Trustee Investment Act 1961. That allows them to invest in Defence Bonds, National Savings and bank deposit accounts without taking advice from a bank, solicitor or stockbroker. But it bars them from investing more than half of a trust's assets in stocks and shares, unit trusts or building societies and even then advice must be obtained before selecting investments.

Trustees are liable for losses on improper investments, unless the court is prepared to excuse them.

What are the tax gains of establishing a trust?

Taxation can often be reduced when assets and income are transferred to a trust.

Payments made to a beneficiary are taxed as personal investment income, and trustees usually deduct the basic rate of tax before handing over the money.

When a parent makes a trust in favour of his or her own unmarried children under 18 years of age, the income from the trust is treated for tax purposes as part of his own income and is taxed accordingly.

Most transfers of assets into or out of a trust will be subject to capital gains tax and capital transfer tax.

Ending or varying a trust

A trust can be brought to an end if all the beneficiaries agree; for example, a widow can give up her liferent. Usually she gets in exchange a lump sum from the children, who receive their money immediately instead of after her death.

The conditions of a trust can be varied but that usually requires an application to the court.

TUTOR

The person who looks after the interests of young children

'Tutor' is the Scottish legal expression for the guardian of a PUPIL child – that is, a girl under 12 or a boy under 14. The parents of a legitimate or adopted child are automatically his or her tutors. Each can act without the consent of the other.

If a child has no tutor – because both parents have died and have not named a guardian – the courts can be asked to appoint one.

An illegitimate child has no tutor but a court can be asked to appoint one if necessary. *See:* GUARDIAN; PUPIL

UNBORN CHILD

A new-born baby can have rights that pre-date its birth

Once a child is conceived, he or she begins to have rights. But birth must occur for these rights to have effect. Until then, no court action can be raised on the child's behalf.

This is why a father cannot ask a court to stop an ABORTION on the ground that it is not in the interests of the unborn child.

Once born, a child can sue in the courts to make his or her rights effective. This must be done through someone else – normally the child's parents. *See:* GUARDIAN

For instance, a child could succeed in an action for DAMAGES against someone who had negligently injured him or her in the womb. This might be a car driver who had negligently caused a crash that injured a mother and her unborn child. It could even be the mother herself, if she was responsible for the injury.

A doctor could also be sued if he negligently injured a child in the mother's womb during an operation. But he could probably not be sued by the child if he negligently failed to suggest that a mother who had contracted German measles should have her pregnancy terminated, and the child was born damaged as a result.

If the parent of an unborn child is killed in circumstances where someone is legally liable for the death, the child may sue once he or she is born. The child's rights are the same as those of any other child.

THE SUCCESSION RIGHTS OF AN UNBORN CHILD

When a man dies, he may leave an unborn child. If he has made a will providing for his children to inherit, the unborn child will be treated as one of these children.

However, the bequest does not take effect until after birth. So if the child is stillborn, the bequest does not pass to whoever would have been entitled to succeed to the child's property. It goes instead to those entitled to succeed to the father's property.

If a man dies leaving an unborn child and property that is not dealt with in a will, the child, after birth, can probably take a share of this property on the same basis as any other child. But this point has not been clearly decided by the courts.

UNCOLLECTED GOODS

When you fail to collect goods on time

If you leave goods for repair, valuation or storage, you are responsible for collecting them unless delivery to you has been agreed.

When you fail to collect goods, the repairer, valuer or warehouseman can sell them if that was agreed between you. There will usually be a term about this on the receipt or ticket that you get in exchange for the goods. But if the agreement says nothing about what should happen when the goods are not collected, the law is not clear.

If the goods remained uncollected for a considerable time, the person holding them would be justified in regarding them as abandoned. However, abandoned property belongs to the Crown and this rule probably applies even when the owner is known. So the person holding the goods would have no right to sell them – though this happens.

UNEMPLOYMENT BENEFIT

Financial help for someone who is out of work

Someone who is out of work may be entitled to unemployment benefit if he has paid enough Class 1 (employees) national insurance contributions while in work. Class 2 contributions (paid by the self-employed) and Class 3 contributions (paid voluntarily) do not count for the purposes of unemployment benefit. Nor do reduced rate contributions paid by some married women and widows. *See:* NATIONAL INSURANCE CONTRIBUTIONS

Someone who is temporarily laid off work – for instance, because of lack of work or a strike – may also be entitled to unemployment benefit.

Contribution conditions Anyone claiming full unemployment benefit must satisfy two contribution conditions:

- He must have paid Class 1 contributions on earnings of at least 25 times the weekly LOWER EARNINGS LIMIT in any single tax year since April 6 1975. Someone who paid 26 flat-rate Class 1 contributions before that date will be treated as meeting this condition.
- He must have paid or been credited with Class 1 contributions on earnings of at least 50 times the weekly lower earnings limit in the tax year (April 6 to April 5) *before* the year in which he claims benefit.

So if he claims benefit in 1984, his entitlement depends on contributions paid or credited between April 6, 1982 and April 5, 1983. Students who claim benefit during the Christmas or Easter vacations must also *pay* such contributions in one of the last 2 tax years before the year they claim benefit.

If he is out of work within 8 weeks of a previous period of unemployment, his entitlement will depend on the same contribution year as for that previous period. For example, if he was out of work and claimed benefit at the end of December 1984, then returned to work and claimed benefit again at the end of January 1985, his entitlement to benefit would depend on his contributions during the 1982–83 tax year, as it did for his claim in December.

Benefit is reduced if contributions are paid or credited on earnings of less than 50 times the weekly lower earnings limit. If the figure is at least 37.5, the reduction is 25 per cent; if it is at least 25, the reduction is 50 per cent.

If the figure is less than 25, no benefit is payable.

How much?

The full rate of unemployment benefit (in 1983–4) is £27.05 a week. A married man can claim an extra £16.70 for his wife, or a cohabitee looking after his child, if neither earns more than that; and an extra 15p for each child (this payment will stop after November 1984). A married woman can claim increases for her husband and children if her husband is not earning more than £16.70 a week.

Pensioners A person who does not retire at 65 (60 if a woman), but is entitled to retirement pension on eventual retirement, can claim unemployment benefit of £34.05 a week, plus £20.45 for a spouse (or female cohabitee) and £7.60 for each child.

Taxation of benefit Unemployment benefit has been taxable since July 5, 1982, and is treated as part of a claimant's income for the tax year (tax is not directly deducted from the benefit). Any tax refund due as a result of the period of unemployment will not be paid until benefit ends, or the end of the tax year, whichever comes first.

When benefit is payable

Unemployment benefit is calculated on a daily basis. It is paid to those who experience at least 2 days of unemployment – which do not need to be consecutive – in a period of 6 consecutive days (excluding Sundays). So someone who experiences isolated days of unemployment more than a week apart cannot get benefit.

Benefit is not paid for the first 3 days of unemployment – called 'waiting days'. Two periods of unemployment separated by not more than 8 weeks count as *one* period for benefit purposes. So someone who has 2 days of unemployment, then returns to work and becomes unemployed again 6 weeks later, need serve only one more waiting day before being entitled to benefit.

Benefit can be paid for a maximum of 312 days (not counting Sundays). After that time, a person is not entitled to claim benefit again until he has worked as an employed person for at least 13 weeks. In each week he must work at least 16 hours.

A claimant who is still unemployed when his entitlement to unemployment benefit ends can claim supplementary benefit. He must usually continue to be available for full-time work. *See:* SUPPLEMENTARY BENEFIT

When benefit is not payable

Unemployment benefit is not payable for certain days, even though the claimant has satisfied the contribution conditions and is out of work. These days include:

- Any day on which the claimant is not capable of, or available for, work. Someone who puts unreasonable restrictions on the nature, hours, rate of pay, locality or other conditions of employment that he is prepared to accept will not get unemployment benefit. The reasonableness of the restrictions is determined in the light of a claimant's health, period of unemployment and

CLAIMING SUPPLEMENTARY BENEFIT WHEN UNEMPLOYED

An unemployed person may be entitled to receive SUPPLEMENTARY BENEFIT if:

- His period of entitlement to unemployment benefit has ended (after 1 year).
- His unemployment benefit and any other resources that he has are not enough to meet his needs as calculated under the supplementary benefit rules.
- He is disqualified from receiving unemployment benefit.
- He does not qualify for unemployment benefit because he has not paid any, or enough, contributions.

Availability for work

Someone who has had to be available for work in order to draw unemployment benefit will usually have to meet the same condition when he goes on to supplementary benefit.

However, certain unemployed claimants are not required to be available for work in order to claim supplementary benefit. They include:

- Single parents who are looking after children under 16.
- Men aged 60 or over.
- People caring for someone who is entitled to attendance allowance, or who have to look after a child or partner who is temporarily sick.

Claimants who have to be available for work do not qualify for the higher, 'long-term' rates of supplementary benefit, however long they are on benefit.

When supplementary benefit is reduced

The amount of supplementary benefit payable is reduced if the claimant has been disqualified from receiving unemployment benefit for up to 6 weeks because:

- He left his job voluntarily, without good reason.
- He lost his job through misconduct.
- He failed, without good reason, to apply for or accept a suitable job.

The cut in supplementary benefit is made even if the claimant has not made a claim for unemployment benefit, if he would have been disqualified for up to 6 weeks had he applied. It is also made pending a decision on whether the claimant should be disqualified from receiving unemployment benefit.

For couples and single householders the reduction is 40 per cent of the ordinary rate for a single householder – £10.70 a week in 1983–4. For non-householders it is 40 per cent of the ordinary non-householder rate – £8.60 a week.

However, the reduction is 20 per cent of these rates if both the following conditions are satisfied:

- The claimant's capital – for instance, savings – is not more than £100.
- A member of the family – the claimant, his wife or a dependent child – is seriously ill or pregnant.

Appealing Anyone whose supplementary benefit is reduced can appeal to a social security appeal tribunal. *See:* SUPPLEMENTARY BENEFIT

THE TEACHER WHO RETIRED EARLY

An employee who retires early, without good reason, may be disqualified for unemployment benefit for the first 6 weeks of retirement.

Mr Ernest Crewe was a 61 year old schoolteacher. He decided to take advantage of an early retirement scheme offered by his employers, the local education authority.

The purpose of the scheme was to reduce the number of older teachers, to encourage the employment of younger ones and to save money. It offered considerable financial inducements, including a pension almost equal to the one paid on normal retirement.

Mr Crewe retired under the scheme and applied for unemployment benefit. He was disqualified from obtaining it for the first 6 weeks because he had voluntarily left his employment 'without just cause'.

Mr Crewe appealed unsuccessfully to a national insurance local tribunal and to a Social Security Commissioner. He then appealed to the English Court of Appeal, on the ground that he had acted reasonably and in the public interest in retiring early and therefore had just cause for leaving his job.

DECISION

The court dismissed his appeal on the ground that he had no just cause for leaving his job.

The court said that it was not enough for Mr Crewe to prove that it was reasonable for him to leave his job. He had to show that it was fair and just to ask the national insurance fund to support him.

Since Mr Crewe had obtained financial benefit from early retirement and did not intend to seek other work, it was unreasonable to ask the national insurance fund to pay for his first 6 weeks' retirement.

the nature of his usual occupation.

• Any day for which a guarantee payment or guaranteed wages are payable. *See:* LAY-OFF

• Any day for which the claimant receives wages in lieu of notice.

• Any day on which the claimant earns more than £2 from part-time work. Even if the claimant earns £2 or less, he can only get benefit if he is available for full-time work and his part-time work is not in his usual main occupation.

A claimant will still be treated as available for work if as a volunteer he is away for up to a fortnight attending some project run by a charity or a local authority – such as a boy's camp – or is working with an organised group during an emergency – for instance, a flood.

• Any day, within a year of dismissal, for which the claimant has received UNFAIR DISMISSAL compensation in respect of future wage loss.

• Any day on which the claimant is on holiday from work, even if no holiday pay is given by the employer. There are, however, exceptions. *See:* HOLIDAY ENTITLEMENT.

When you are disqualified from receiving benefit

In certain circumstances, a disqualification from benefit can be imposed for *up to* 6 weeks at the discretion of the adjudication officer. Disqualification will occur if a person:

• Voluntarily leaves employment without 'just cause' – that is, without having an acceptable reason for doing so.

An employee who leaves because he does not like his job or is dissatisfied with his wages does not have any just cause for leaving. Nor does an employee who takes early retirement solely for financial reasons, even if it is in his employer's interests.

However an employee may have just cause for leaving if his employer is in serious breach of his EMPLOYMENT CONTRACT – if, for instance, the employer fails to provide safe working conditions or orders the employee to perform a job that he was not employed to do. He will also have just cause if he gives up work because of illness or pressing family responsibilities – for instance, to look after a seriously ill or disabled member of his family.

• Is dismissed for misconduct – for example, absenteeism, unpunctuality, refusing to obey reasonable orders or incompetent work.

• Refuses to apply for or accept a suitable job; or to avail himself of government-approved training facilities. A suitable job would normally be one in the claimant's usual occupation; but after a reasonable time other work could be regarded as suitable.

During the period of disqualification, the claimant can apply for supplementary benefit. But the amount he receives will be reduced by 40 per cent (sometimes 20 per cent) of the scale rate payable to a single householder or non-householder (see p. 653).

Industrial disputes An employee who is temporarily out of work because of a STRIKE or other industrial action at his workplace will not get unemployment benefit if:

• He is taking part in the industrial action; or

• He is directly interested in the dispute – for instance, his wages will be increased automatically as a result of it, even though he is not taking part in it himself.

An employee who is disqualified from receiving unemployment benefit for this reason can claim supplementary benefit for his family (subject to restrictions), but not for himself. *See:* SUPPLEMENTARY BENEFIT

Appealing A claimant who feels that he has been unfairly disqualified from receiving unemployment benefit can appeal to a social security appeal tribunal. *See:* SOCIAL SECURITY APPEALS.

Claimants receiving occupational pension

If a claimant is 60 or over, and is receiving an OCCUPATIONAL PENSION, his unemployment benefit may be affected. For every 10p that his occupational pension is over £35 a week (gross), his unemployment benefit is cut by 10p. For more information, see leaflet NI 230, available from local social security offices.

How to claim

If you want to claim unemployment benefit, visit your local unemployment benefit office on the first day of unemployment. Take your P.45 income tax form and also a note of your national insurance number. If you live more than 10 miles away, you can claim by post – the address is in the telephone book.

If you delay in claiming, you will lose benefit for the days that have elapsed unless there is a good reason for the delay. Make your claim even if you cannot find your P.45 form.

UNFAIR CONTRACT

How people are protected against unfair clauses in contracts

Under the Unfair Contract Terms Act 1977, conditions in many contracts can be challenged in legal proceedings if they attempt to remove some important legal rights from a person. These include the right to compensation for death or injury caused by negligence and the right to compensation for breach of contract.

Under the 1977 Act, some conditions are automatically void – meaning that they are completely ineffective. Other conditions are valid provided a court considers them to be fair and reasonable.

The contracts that are covered

The 1977 Act applies to the following contracts – so long as they were made on or after February 1, 1978:

- Contracts for the sale of goods – including goods bought under HIRE PURCHASE or CREDIT SALE agreements.
- Contracts for the hire of goods, including cars and television sets.
- Employment contracts – including apprenticeship contracts.
- Contracts for services – for instance, the services provided by a solicitor, accountant, architect, builder, electrician, laundry, shoe repairer or car parking company.
- Contracts involving the liability of an occupier of land or property to those entering it. That would include the contracts you enter into when you buy tickets for a cinema, theatre, fairground or zoo.

A major gap in the Act is that it does not apply to INSURANCE contracts or to leases of land or buildings.

Conditions that are automatically void

A condition in a contract mentioned above is automatically void if it attempts to:

- Exclude or restrict one person's right to compensation for death or personal injury caused by another person's negligence in the course of his business or on his business premises.
- Evade or weaken a trader's obligation to see that the goods he sells or hires (or part-exchanges) are of suitable quality and fitness. This applies only to consumer transactions – not to trade deals or to goods bought at a trade rate.

Guarantees Any condition in a manufacturer's guarantee or warranty document is automatically void if it attempts to restrict or exclude the manufacturer's liability for loss or damage – including death or personal injury – caused by defective goods, except where the goods were bought for exclusively business purposes. *See:* GUARANTEE

Conditions that must be fair and reasonable

Other contractual conditions that limit or exclude liability for negligence, or for breach of the terms of a consumer or 'standard form' contract, are only valid if they are considered to be 'fair and reasonable'. If not, they are void.

The sort of conditions that are covered include any that attempt to limit or exclude liability for:

- Property loss or damage through negligence.
- Failure to provide the service promised.
- Loss or damage to goods entrusted to a carrier.

When deciding whether a condition is fair and reasonable, and therefore valid, the courts must apply a 'reasonableness' test. The condition will be valid if it was fair and reasonable to include it, having regard to the circumstances that were known or contemplated (or should have been) by the parties at the time the contract was made.

When considering conditions in contracts for the supply of goods which the Act makes subject to the 'reasonableness' test, the courts must also take account of circumstances such as the relative bargaining strengths of the parties and whether the customer knew (or ought to have known) of the condition and its extent.

Fixed limits If a condition limits liability to a fixed sum of money, the courts must take into account the trader's financial resources and how far he could have covered himself by insurance, when deciding whether the condition is fair and reasonable.

The burden of proof The burden of proving in court that a condition is fair and reasonable rests on the party who asserts that it is.

UNFAIR DISMISSAL

How the law protects those who lose their jobs

Most full-time employees who have completed 1 year's service with their employer – 2 years if the employer has at no time during the period of service employed more than 20 – are entitled to apply to an INDUSTRIAL TRIBUNAL for compensation if they are unfairly dismissed. Sometimes they may be able to get their old job back, or to obtain a new one with the same employer.

These rights do not apply to certain employees. The most important are:

- Part-time workers who are normally employed for less than 16 hours a week (unless normally employed for at least 8 hours a week for a continuous period of 5 years). *See:* PART-TIME WORKER
- Employees over the normal retiring age in the firm – or, if there is no such age, 65 for a man and 60 for a woman.
- Employees who normally work outside Great Britain.
- Policemen and policewomen.

However, an employee who is dismissed for trade union reasons can bring a claim for unfair dismissal even if he has not been continuously employed for a year (or 2 years), or is over retirement age. *See:* TRADE UNION

An employee claiming unfair dismissal must satisfy the tribunal that he was dismissed and did not resign of his own free will. If the employer disputes the dismissal and the employee fails to prove it, his claim will be rejected.

Once dismissal has been established, the *employer* has to prove that he dismissed the employee for a fair reason (see below). If he does, the tribunal then has to decide whether the employer acted reasonably or unreasonably in treating it as a sufficient reason for dismissal, and in the way he carried out the dismissal.

Misconduct, for example, may not

justify dismissal if it is not very serious, or if the employer acted without a proper investigation of the facts.

Was the employee dismissed?

Most dismissals are straightforward. The employee is told, verbally or in writing, that his employment will end. Having served his NOTICE, or received wages in lieu, he then leaves. In such a case there will be no problem in satisfying the tribunal that he was dismissed; the employer will usually admit the dismissal and make proof of it unnecessary.

But some dismissals are less clear-cut:

Constructive dismissal An employee who leaves because of a gross breach of his EMPLOYMENT CONTRACT by his employer – for example, a refusal to pay agreed wages – is said to have been 'constructively' dismissed. Constructive dismissals are nearly always unfair. *See:* DISMISSAL

An employee who is constructively dismissed does not need to give notice. However, he should write to his employer, keeping a copy of the letter, to make it clear that he is not resigning, but leaving because of the employer's breach of contract.

Leaving while under notice An employee who is given notice of dismissal and then himself gives notice that he is leaving on an earlier date – for example, to start a new job – has still been dismissed and does not forfeit his right to claim unfair dismissal.

Fixed-term contracts If an employee has worked under a 'fixed-term' contract – that is, a contract for a specific

HOW TO CLAIM UNFAIR DISMISSAL

If you have been dismissed – or constructively dismissed – and you want to make a complaint of unfair dismissal to an industrial tribunal, you should:

- Write to your employer as soon as possible after dismissal and ask him to put the reasons for your dismissal in writing. An employer normally has to reply to such a request within 14 days (see p. 659).
- Visit your local Job Centre, unemployment benefit office or Citizens Advice Bureau and ask for form IT1 (Scot) – the application form for the industrial tribunal.
- Before completing the form, seek advice if possible from a trade union official, Citizens Advice Bureau or solicitor on how to fill it in. You will have to set out – briefly – the grounds of your application. If you wish, you can also state why you think you were dismissed.

You can be represented at the hearing by anyone you choose. If you choose a solicitor, you will have to pay the cost yourself – LEGAL AID is not available to pay for legal representation before tribunals.

- Send the completed form to the Secretary of the Tribunals, Central Office of the Industrial Tribunals (Scotland), St. Andrew House, 141 West Nile Street, Glasgow G1 2RU. You must normally do so within 3 months of your dismissal.

When the application is made

When your application form is received by the Central Office, a copy is sent to your employer. He will be asked to state – on form IT3 – whether he intends to resist your claim and what he considers to be the reason for your dismissal. A copy of this form will be sent to you.

After an application has been made, a conciliation officer from the Advisory, Conciliation and Arbitration Service may contact you and your employer to try to reach a settlement before a hearing. If this does not happen, either you or your employer can ask a conciliation officer to intervene. Although neither party is required to co-operate with the officer, it is advisable to do so as he may be able to negotiate a suitable compromise.

If you and your employer agree to a settlement before a hearing, it is only binding if it is reached with the help of a conciliation officer. In that case, the terms of the settlement are recorded on an official form (COT3), signed by you and your employer. You cannot thereafter ask the tribunal to consider your complaint.

If you reach a settlement without the help of a conciliation officer, you are entitled to change your mind and proceed with your claim before the tribunal. You are entitled to do so even if you sign an agreement with your employer that states that the agreement is a final settlement. If a claimant wins his case after making such an agreement, the tribunal usually reduces any award by the amount he has already received from his employer.

Preparing for a hearing

Where no settlement is reached, your claim will be heard by an industrial tribunal in your area. The procedure is relatively informal, but if you are representing yourself you will be expected to provide sufficient evidence to support your claim that you were unfairly dismissed. You should therefore prepare your case in advance.

- If your employer has any documents that you think might support your case – for example, your personal file or a copy of the firm's disciplinary rules and procedures – you can ask the employer for copies of them.

If he refuses to supply the information, write to the Secretary of the Tribunals and ask for an order to be made requiring the employer to supply the information. If he still fails to do so after an order has been made, he can be fined up to £400.

- When preparing your case, study your employment contract and any disciplinary rules that apply to you. If your employer has not followed the rules or has not observed the correct procedures, the tribunal may decide that he did not act 'reasonably' in dismissing you.
- Take with you to the tribunal evidence of your previous earnings – such as wage slips – and also of your attempts to find another job. Take also any documents relating to social security benefits received
- You may want to ask some of your colleagues to be witnesses for you at the hearing. For instance, one of them may have been in the same situation as you but was not dismissed. Or one of them may be prepared to testify that you were dismissed because a member of the management took a dislike to you.

If someone does not wish to be a witness, you can write to the Secretary of the Tribunals and ask for a witness order to be made. You must give the name and address of the person you want to attend. If the order is granted, the witness can be fined up to £400 if he fails to attend the hearing.

Expenses

If you win your claim, you will usually have to pay your own legal expenses – including the expense of being represented by a solicitor. But if you lose, you will not usually have to pay your employer's expenses.

This is because a tribunal will only award expenses against an unsuccessful party if he is considered to have acted 'frivolously', 'vexatiously' or 'unreasonably' in bringing or conducting the proceedings. So long as you believe that you have good reason to bring or defend a claim, you should not be affected by this rule.

period – and this is not renewed, he is treated as dismissed. If the contract – or a succession of contracts – ran continuously for at least 1 year (sometimes 2 years), he can claim unfair dismissal.

However, where the fixed-term contract is for 1 year or more, the employer is entitled to ask the employee to agree in writing to waive his right to claim unfair dismissal. If the employee does so – by, for example, signing a contract containing a clause to that effect – he will not be able to claim unfair dismissal if his contract is not renewed.

After maternity leave A woman who is not allowed to resume her old job after childbirth may, depending on the circumstances, be treated as having been dismissed on the day she would have returned. She can then claim unfair dismissal. *See:* MATERNITY

When there is no dismissal

An employee who resigns of his own free will has not been dismissed. Nor has an employee who is suspended with pay from his job. *See:* RESIGNATION

An employee whose job ends because his employer dies has not been dismissed. *See:* EMPLOYER, Death of

If some event – such as illness – prevents an employee from working for a prolonged period, or makes it impossible for him to do his job, his employment contract may be held to be 'frustrated'.

If a contract is frustrated, it ends automatically and there is *no* dismissal. *See:* SICKNESS

A contract is not frustrated if the inability to fulfil it is due to the fault of either party – as when an employee is sent to prison.

The five 'fair' reasons

Under the unfair dismissal rules, there are five 'fair' reasons for dismissing an employee:

- Lack of capacity or qualifications for doing the job.
- Misconduct by the employee.
- Redundancy.
- Where continued employment would amount to a breach of the law.
- Other 'substantial' reasons justifying dismissal.

If the employer cannot prove that he dismissed an employee for one of these reasons, the dismissal will be treated as unfair.

Was the employee's dismissal 'reasonable'?

Once the employer has shown that he dismissed an employee for a fair reason, the industrial tribunal must decide whether the employer acted reasonably in dismissing the employee for that reason, and in the way he dismissed. If he did, the dismissal is fair; if he did not, the dismissal is unfair.

When considering whether an employer acted reasonably, the tribunal must look at all the circumstances – including the size and administrative resources of the employer's firm. The circumstances vary depending on the reason for the dismissal, but the most important ones are:

- Whether the employee had in the past been given warnings that he might be dismissed.
- Whether the employer followed the correct procedure.
- Whether the employer investigated the case sufficiently before dismissing the employee.
- Whether suitable alternative work should have been found for the employee.

Incapability and lack of qualifications

An employee who lacks the capability to do his job can be fairly dismissed on those grounds. Capability is assessed by reference to skill, aptitude, health or any other physical or mental quality. To satisfy the tribunal, the employer must provide sufficient evidence of his employee's incapability.

Generally, the longer an employee has been in his job, the more difficult it is for his employer to show that he was incapable of doing it.

However, in highly technical jobs a trial period of more than 1 year may be necessary, because the capability of new employees cannot be assessed until they have undergone lengthy training. Tribunals take that into account in deciding whether a dismissal for incapability is fair.

If an employee's work is not satisfactory, a reasonable employer would normally be expected to give him a warning, or advice on how he might improve, before proceeding to dismiss him. Failure to do this in appropriate cases could make the dismissal unfair.

MISINFORMED ABOUT HER PROGRESS

An employee who has been warned of possible dismissal for poor work must be given a reasonable opportunity to improve and be kept accurately informed of his or her progress.

Mrs Mughal was employed by the Post Office on a year's probation. She received three written warnings about the poor quality of her work and was told that unless it got better she would be dismissed.

Her supervisor eventually told her that her clerical tasks had come up to standard, but her telephone work still had to improve. Soon afterwards, and with no further warning, she was dismissed by the area sales manager, who did not know about the supervisor's comments. Mrs Mughal claimed unfair dismissal.

DECISION

The dismissal was unfair. It was the employer's duty to keep Mrs Mughal informed and the decision to sack her should only have been taken when all the relevant facts – in this case, the supervisor's opinion – had been assessed.

It may be reasonable for an employer to dismiss an employee who suffers frequent bouts of ill-health. This depends on the illness, the employer's need for the employee's services and the length of the absences.

Lack of qualifications An employee may be fairly dismissed if he lacks the required qualifications – meaning any relevant degree, diploma or other academic, technical or professional qualification.

It would normally be reasonable for an employer to dismiss an employee who claimed, on recruitment, that he held qualifications essential for the job, but was later discovered not to possess them. It would also normally be reasonable to dismiss an employee who failed to pass a required test or examination, provided that he was told he was expected to do so when he was hired.

Misconduct by the employee

It may be fair to dismiss an employee because of his behaviour – for instance, bad timekeeping, persistent absenteeism, refusing to obey reasonable orders, dishonesty and showing violence to fellow employees.

The steps that an employer should normally follow if there is alleged misconduct are set out in the ADVISORY, CONCILIATION AND ARBITRATION SERVICE (ACAS) Code of Practice, *Disciplinary Practice and Procedures in Employment.* The Code is not legally binding but failure to follow it could lead to a finding by a tribunal that an employer acted unreasonably in dismissing an employee for misconduct.

The Code states that no disciplinary action should be taken until an allegation of misconduct has been properly investigated. The employee should be interviewed and allowed to put his side of the case. If there is a formal disciplinary procedure, it should be carefully followed.

Except for gross misconduct – which might justify summary dismissal – no employee should be dismissed for a first breach of discipline. The Code recommends an oral or, in more serious cases, a written warning. Further misconduct should normally result in a final written warning that dismissal will take place for any recurrence. Before dismissing, the employer should also consider the employee's work record and any other relevant factors.

The fact that an employee has been convicted of a criminal offence should not be treated as an automatic reason for dismissal. The employer should consider whether the offence makes the employee unsuitable for his work or unacceptable to other employees.

THE EMPLOYEE WHO WAS ACCUSED OF STEALING PORK CHOPS

If an employer suspects an employee of dishonesty, he should investigate the matter thoroughly and give the employee an opportunity to explain. Failure to do so could result in any subsequent dismissal being unfair.

Mrs M was employed as a supervisor in an Oban store. One day the store manager found two unwrapped packets of pork chops lying on a beer box. He assumed they belonged to Mrs M but said nothing to her.

By the following morning Mrs M had not paid for the chops and the manager accused her of stealing them. She said that she had intended to pay for them but had forgotten to do so. The manager did not accept her explanation and dismissed her instantly.

An industrial tribunal decided that the dismissal was unfair. The employers appealed to the Employment Appeal Tribunal.

DECISION

The Tribunal dismissed the employer's appeal.

They said that a reasonable employer would have given Mrs M an earlier opportunity to explain the situation and would not have leaped to the immediate conclusion that she had stolen the chops or did not intend to pay for them. Since the employers had not acted reasonably, the dismissal was unfair.

DISMISSED – AFTER 5 YEARS AS A PROBATIONER

A probationary employee who is required to pass a test before his appointment becomes permanent and who fails to do so can be fairly dismissed.

Mr Blackman was recruited by the Post Office as a probationary post and telegraph officer in 1968. After 5 years and three attempts, he had still not passed the compulsory aptitude test needed to confirm his appointment as permanent. He was dismissed, but claimed the dismissal was unfair.

DECISION

Mr Blackman lost his claim. Passing the aptitude test was a condition of his employment.

When an employee is made redundant

Redundancy is a fair reason for dismissal and the employee who loses his job because of it cannot normally claim compensation beyond any redundancy payment to which he is entitled. However, the redundancy must be genuine – if someone else is appointed to the same job there is no redundancy and the employee may succeed in a claim for unfair dismissal.

Even though an employee is genuinely redundant, his employer must still act reasonably in the manner in which he carries out the redundancy. If he does not – if, for instance, he gives an employee insufficient warning of redundancy – the dismissal may be unfair.

A dismissal is automatically unfair if an employee is selected for redundancy for trade union reasons (see p. 643); or in contravention of any rules normally applied in selecting employees for redundancy – unless there were special reasons for this. *See:* REDUNDANCY

When the law would be broken

An employer may be able to dismiss someone fairly if keeping him in his job would amount to a breach of the law. An example would be a van or lorry driver who loses his driving licence.

However, the tribunal must be satisfied that the employer acted reasonably before it will find the dismissal fair. It will therefore consider all the surrounding circumstances – including, in the example given, the proportion of the employee's duties occupied by driving, and the length of the ban.

Other 'substantial' reasons

Parliament has provided no definition of other 'substantial' reasons justifying dismissal. Because of this, industrial tribunals assess each case according to the circumstances. Reasons that have been held to be substantial include:

- The expiry of a genuinely temporary employment contract – for instance, a one year contract as a lecturer or teacher.
- Essential business reorganisation.
- Unreasonable refusal to agree to a change in employment terms.
- Violent behaviour to fellow employees during epileptic fits.
- Homosexual tendencies in an employee working with children.

Parliament has expressly declared one reason for dismissal to be substantial: the dismissal of a temporary replacement for a pregnant employee or an employee temporarily suspended on medical grounds, to allow that employee to return. The dismissed employee must have been told in writing when he or she started work that the job was temporary.

In all these cases, the tribunal must be satisfied that the employer acted reasonably before it finds the dismissal to be fair.

Obtaining the reasons for dismissal

Most employees who have been continuously employed for at least 6 months are entitled to ask their employers to state in writing the reasons for which they were dismissed. If an employer fails to provide written reasons within 14 days of being asked to do so, or provides reasons that are inadequate or untrue, he can be ordered by an industrial tribunal to pay compensation of up to two weeks' pay.

An employee who is entitled to bring a claim of unfair dismissal should therefore consider asking his employer to give reasons for his dismissal in writing.

An employer who has refused to supply written reasons to a dismissed employee is unlikely to be treated sympathetically at any subsequent unfair dismissal hearing. If he refuses to give the reason for dismissal at the hearing itself, he will lose his case.

Special rules

Special rules apply to dismissal for:

- Trade union membership, non-membership or activities. *See:* TRADE UNION
- Taking part in a strike or other industrial action. *See:* STRIKE
- Pregnancy. *See:* MATERNITY

When an employee wins his claim

An employee who wins an unfair dismissal claim has three possible remedies.

First of all, the tribunal must ask him if he wants to be reinstated in his old job; or re-engaged by the same employer in a new job.

If he wants either of these, the tribunal considers whether it would be practicable for the employer to take him back. Where the employee was partly to blame for his own dismissal, the tribunal also considers whether it would be just to order reinstatement or re-engagement.

Few orders for reinstatement or re-engagement are made. When they are, the tribunal will require the employer to pay the employee any benefit – including arrears of pay – that he lost through the dismissal. The tribunal will also set out the rights – including seniority and pension rights – that must be restored to the employee.

If an employee is reinstated or re-engaged, but the employer fails to comply fully with the terms of the order, the tribunal can award the employee compensation for any financial loss that he suffers – up to a maximum of £7,500.

If the employer refuses to reinstate or re-engage, or the tribunal decides against it, or the employee asks for neither, the tribunal will award financial compensation – the usual remedy for an unfair dismissal.

How compensation is calculated

Financial compensation for unfair dismissal is normally made up of two separate sums:

1 A 'basic' award, linked to the employee's age and length of service.

2 A 'compensatory' award to offset losses incurred as a result of the dismissal.

In certain cases, two other sums may also be awarded:

- An 'additional' award, payable where an employer has failed to comply with an order for reinstatement or re-engagement.
- A 'special' award, payable where an employee is dismissed for reasons relating to trade union membership, non-membership or activities.

The basic award

The basic award is calculated according to the same formula as that for redundancy payments. The employee will get:

- $\frac{1}{2}$ × his last normal weekly pay for each year of service with the employer between the ages of 16 and 21.
- 1 week's pay for each year of service between the ages of 22 and 40.
- $1\frac{1}{2}$ weeks' pay for each year of service in which the employee was aged 41 or over.

However, for these purposes a week's pay – including normal overtime – is limited to a maximum of £145 and service beyond 20 years is not taken into account. So the most an employee can receive as a basic award is 20 × $1\frac{1}{2}$ weeks' pay = £4,350.

Where an employee is unfairly dismissed because of trade union membership, non-membership or activities (or unfairly selected for redundancy on those grounds), the basic award (before deductions) must be at least £2,000.

The tribunal can reduce the amount of the basic award because of any conduct of the employee before being dis-

THE EPILEPTIC EMPLOYEE WHO WAS DISMISSED

If an employee's illness is a source of danger to his colleagues, it may be fair for an employer to dismiss him on the ground of incapability.

Mr Harper, who was epileptic, had worked for the National Coal Board since 1958. He suffered three epileptic fits between 1977 and 1979, during which, quite unknowingly, he attacked other employees. After the last fit Mr Harper was advised to apply for ill-health retirement under the mineworkers' pension scheme. He refused and was dismissed.

An industrial tribunal decided that the dismissal was fair. It was either on the ground of Mr Harper's incapacity or for some other 'substantial' reason and the NCB had acted reasonably in dismissing him.

Mr Harper appealed to the Employment Appeal Tribunal. He argued that there was no evidence that his epilepsy affected his ability to do his job.

DECISION

The Tribunal rejected his appeal and held his dismissal to be fair.

Although there was no evidence that Mr Harper was unable to do his actual work as a dust mask cleaner, the Tribunal decided that the fact that he was a source of danger to fellow employees reflected upon his capability for doing the job that he was employed to do.

The Tribunal also decided that even if the dismissal was not due to incapability, the reason for it could be treated as some other 'substantial' reason sufficient to justify dismissal.

missed (except in the case of redundancy for reasons other than trade union membership, non-membership or activities). It can also reduce the award if the employee unreasonably refuses an offer of reinstatement.

If the employee has already received a redundancy payment, the amount must be deducted from his basic award.

The compensatory award

The purpose of the compensatory award is to compensate the employee for the financial loss that he has suffered because of the dismissal. The maximum amount that can be awarded is £7,500.

In deciding the amount of the award, the tribunal considers the wages that he has lost (and will lose in the future) as well as any additional expenses incurred as a result of the dismissal. It also takes into account loss of benefits, pension rights and EMPLOYMENT PROTECTION rights.

Current wage loss The tribunal takes into account the net earnings – after allowances for tax, national insurance contributions and other deductions – lost by the employee between his dismissal and the tribunal hearing. That includes regular overtime and bonus payments. It also includes any wage increase or sick pay that he would have been entitled to had he remained at work.

Any UNEMPLOYMENT BENEFIT or SUPPLEMENTARY BENEFIT paid to the employee is not deducted – although the Department of Employment may recover this out of the award (see below). But SICKNESS BENEFIT received will be deducted, provided it would have been deducted from any sick pay received by the employee had he remained at work.

Future wage loss If the employee has not already found another job, the tribunal will also take into account his future wage loss – that is, the wages he is likely to lose before he finds another job. It takes into account his age, health, qualifications, experience and the general employment situation in the area, and makes allowances for the likely loss of fringe benefits – for example, a company car or luncheon vouchers.

If the employee has found other work, but at lower pay, his future wage loss is the difference between his net earnings in his old and new jobs.

Expenses Any expenses arising from the dismissal may be included in calculating the compensatory award if they represent a significant amount – for example, the cost of travelling or moving to try to find a new job. Postal and telephone expenses can also be included if they are substantial. But the legal expenses of the employee's claim to the tribunal are not included.

An employee who is claiming expenses will have to produce receipts or other evidence to support his claim.

Reducing the compensatory award

An industrial tribunal can reduce the amount of a compensatory award if it is not convinced that the employee has done all he can to mitigate, or cut, his losses – particularly by trying to find a new job. As evidence of his efforts, the employee should take to the tribunal copies of job application letters and a record of the dates on which he went for interviews or to a job centre.

If an employee's behaviour caused or contributed to his dismissal to any extent, his compensatory award can be reduced.

The additional award

If a tribunal orders an employer to reinstate or re-engage an employee, but the employer fails to do so, the tribunal

WHEN A DISMISSAL FOR REDUNDANCY CAN BE UNFAIR

Dismissal for redundancy is normally fair. But if an employee is selected for redundancy in contravention of an agreed procedure, the dismissal will be unfair.

Mr Cameron, a heavy goods vehicle driver, was dismissed for redundancy in accordance with the 'last in, first out' procedure agreed between his employer and the union.

The choice had been between Mr Cameron and another driver, Mr Boyle. Mr Boyle's total period of employment was 18 months longer than Mr Cameron's.

However, Mr Boyle had left the job 4 years previously and had returned after a month. Although he was in fact the 'last man in', the employers felt obliged to treat his employment as continuous and to make Mr Cameron redundant.

Mr Cameron complained to an industrial tribunal, which decided that his dismissal was unfair. The employers appealed to the Employment Appeal Tribunal.

DECISION

The Tribunal decided that the dismissal was unfair.

The Tribunal said that 'last in, first out' meant exactly what it said. What counted was the length of continuous employment, not the length of total employment.

Since Mr Cameron's length of continuous employment was greater than Mr Boyle's, he should not have been treated as the last man in. Making him redundant was therefore in contravention of the agreed procedure.

THE BODIES THAT WERE IN THE WRONG COFFINS

Even if a dismissal is unfair, an employee's compensation can be reduced if he or she was partly to blame.

Miss Coulter was employed by a firm of funeral directors as a receptionist. One of her duties was to check that the right body was in the right coffin before burial. She was not responsible for actually putting the bodies in the coffins.

Two bodies were placed in the wrong coffins, causing distress to the relatives. Miss Coulter said that she did not know how it had happened.

Although it was the first time she had made a mistake, she was dismissed.

An industrial tribunal decided that her dismissal was unfair, but it reduced her compensation by 50 per cent on the ground that she had contributed to the dismissal by her mistake.

Miss Coulter appealed to the Employment Appeal Tribunal against the cut in her compensation.

DECISION

The Tribunal decided that the cut was too great, given that it was her first mistake and that it was unintentional. It substituted a cut of 25 per cent.

AN EMPLOYEE'S RIGHT TO AN EXPLANATION

An employee who is eligible to claim unfair dismissal is usually entitled to be given his employer's reasons for sacking him within 14 days.

can increase the amount of compensation payable to the employee.

In that situation the employee is entitled not only to a basic and compensatory award but also to an 'additional' award – unless the employer can show that it was not practicable for him to reinstate or re-engage the employee.

The additional award is between 13 and 26 weeks' pay – up to a maximum of £3,770. If the dismissal amounted to unlawful discrimination on the ground of race or sex, the award is between 26 and 52 weeks' pay – up to a maximum of £7,540.

The special award

If an employee is unfairly dismissed or selected for redundancy because of trade union membership, non-membership or activities, the tribunal can order the employer to pay extra compensation – called a 'special' award – on top of the basic and compensatory awards. The tribunal can only do this if the employee asks to be reinstated or re-engaged.

If the tribunal decides against reinstatement or re-engagement and awards compensation instead, the special award is 104 weeks' pay or £10,000, whichever is greater – up to a maximum of £20,000.

If the tribunal orders reinstatement or re-engagement, but the employer fails to comply, the special award is 156 weeks' pay or £15,000, whichever is the greater. The additional award (see above) is not payable in this case.

The tribunal can reduce the special award because of the employee's conduct before the dismissal. It can also do so if the employee unreasonably refused an offer of reinstatement by the employer.

When unemployment or supplementary benefit is paid

An employee will usually receive some unemployment or supplementary benefit (or both) between his dismissal and the tribunal hearing. If compensation is awarded, the Department of Employment can recover some or all of the benefit by having it deducted from the part of the compensation representing loss of earnings up to the date of the hearing or conciliation settlement.

The tribunal will explain the procedure to the employee. Briefly, the Department recovers the benefit by serving a 'recoupment notice' on the employer after the hearing. This orders the employer to deduct part of the compensation due to the employee and pay it across to the Department.

No unemployment benefit If the compensation includes a sum representing loss of wages for a future period, no unemployment benefit is payable for that period (unless it is more than a year from the date of dismissal). *See:* INDUSTRIAL TRIBUNAL; EMPLOYMENT APPEAL TRIBUNAL

UNMARRIED COUPLE

Limited rights for people who live together

When two people live together without getting married, they have few of the legal rights given to a married couple. Neither has any legal duty to maintain the other; and if one of them owns or rents the home, the other has no automatic OCCUPANCY RIGHTS. *See:* COHABITATION

However, where a couple who are both free to marry have lived together for some time as husband and wife, without getting married, a court may be prepared to declare that they are lawfully married by 'cohabitation with habit and repute'. *See:* COMMON LAW MARRIAGE

Even though a couple are unmarried, the man has a duty along with the woman to maintain any children of the relationship. *See:* AFFILIATION AND ALIMENT

UNSOLICITED GOODS

When you receive goods that you have not ordered

If someone sends you goods – such as books or records – that you have not ordered, intending that you should buy them, you do not have to pay for them. Nor do you have to send them back.

When you keep goods without paying for them, there are two ways in which they can become your property – allowing you then to use or dispose of them as you think fit.

1 You can keep the goods for 6 months. If you do not unreasonably prevent the sender from collecting them during that time, they will automatically belong to you when the 6-month period expires.

2 You can write to the sender at any time within 5 months of receiving the goods, stating that they are unsolicited and asking him to collect them within 30 days. If he does not do so, they will automatically belong to you when the 30-day period expires. You must supply the sender with your name and the address where the goods can be collected.

Seeking payment for unsolicited goods

It is an offence for anyone in the course of business to demand, without reasonable cause, payment for any goods that he knows to have been sent to you without your asking. Anyone who does so can be fined up to £1,000.

If that person threatens to take legal action, invokes some other method of debt-collecting, or threatens to do so, he can be fined up to £2,000.

Any document seeking payment for unsolicited goods must state in red, in the top left-hand corner of each page where payment is mentioned:

THIS IS NOT A DEMAND FOR PAYMENT
THERE IS NO OBLIGATION TO PAY

It must also state in red, diagonally across the page:

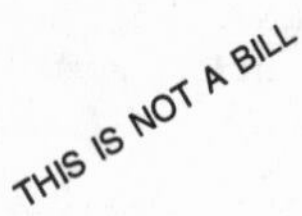

If it does not do so, the request for payment is illegal. *See:* OBSCENE PUBLICATIONS

UPPER EARNINGS LIMIT

Earnings on which national insurance contributions are not payable

The maximum weekly, monthly or yearly amount of earnings on which Class 1 (employees) NATIONAL INSURANCE CONTRIBUTIONS are payable is known as the upper earnings limit. It is also the upper level of earnings on which each year's additional RETIREMENT PENSION is calculated.

The upper earnings limit is about seven times the LOWER EARNINGS LIMIT. It goes up in April of each year, when the lower limit also rises.

In the tax year 1984–5 the upper earnings limit was:

- £250 a week for those paid weekly.
- £1,083.33 a month for those paid monthly.
- £12,999.96 a year for those paid annually.

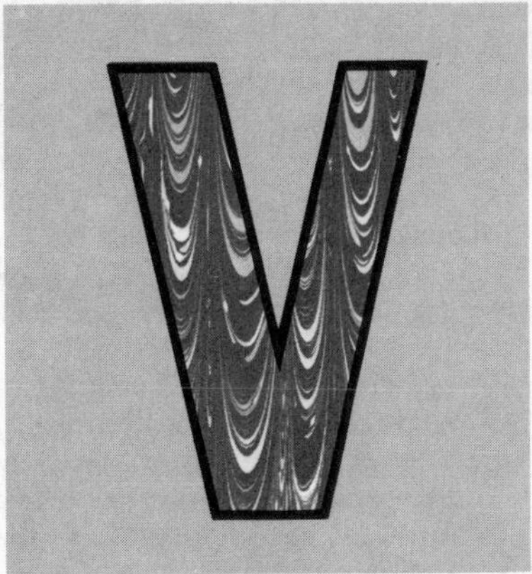

VACCINE DAMAGE

Compensation for people severely disabled by vaccination

Anyone who is severely disabled as a result of being vaccinated may be entitled to receive a tax-free lump sum of £10,000 under the Vaccine Damage Payments Scheme. If the disabled person has died, the money can be paid to his personal representatives.

To qualify, a claimant must be at least 80 per cent disabled, as defined in the assessment of benefit for people disabled by industrial injury. *See:* DISABLEMENT BENEFIT

The vaccine that caused the disablement must be one which was given against diphtheria, tetanus, whooping cough, tuberculosis, poliomyelitis, measles, German measles (rubella) or smallpox.

Several other conditions must also be met. A claimant must:

- Have been vaccinated in the UK or Isle of Man. Members of the armed forces or their families are eligible even if the vaccination was given outside the UK, provided it was part of the service's medical facilities.
- Have been vaccinated before his 18th birthday – except in the case of vaccination against polio or German measles or when the vaccination was given during an outbreak in the UK or Isle of Man of any of the prescribed diseases.
- Be over the age of two.

Time limit Until May, 1984, a claim could be accepted if it resulted from a vaccination given on or after July 5, 1948 (or before August 1, 1971 in the case of a smallpox vaccination).

From May 9, 1984, a claim will only be accepted if it is made within 6 years of the date of the vaccination or the claimant's 2nd birthday.

How to claim

A claimant should complete the form attached to the Department of Health and Social Security leaflet HB3, which is obtainable from the Vaccine Damage Payments Unit, DHSS, North Fylde Central Offices, Norcross, Blackpool FY5 3TA.

The completed form should be returned to that address with any supporting evidence that exists. Do not delay in sending the claim because some of the evidence or information required is temporarily unavailable. The Payments Unit will obtain copies of any relevant medical evidence from the doctor or hospital concerned and may require the disabled person to undergo a medical examination.

If the claimant is under 18, his parents or guardian should complete the form. An adult claimant who is unable to complete the form can get someone else to do so. If the person who was vaccinated has died, his personal representatives can make the claim.

The claimant will be told in writing of the result of his claim. When it is turned down on the ground that the disability is not sufficiently severe, or was not due to vaccination, the case can be reviewed, on request, by an independent medical tribunal.

WHEN A THIRD PARTY CAN CLAIM

In two situations, a lump sum payment of £10,000 can be made to someone who is severely disabled as a result of a vaccination given to another person.

1. It can be paid to someone who is severely disabled through a vaccination given to his mother before he was born.

2. It can be paid to someone who is severely disabled through contracting polio from another person who was vaccinated orally against the disease. He must have been looking after (or have been looked after together with) the person vaccinated, and the contact must have occurred within 9 weeks of the vaccination being given.

In both cases, no claim can be made unless the person who was vaccinated was under 18 at the time the vaccination was given – unless the vaccination was against polio or German measles or was given during an outbreak of one of the prescribed diseases.

The successful claimant will receive a lump sum of £10,000. If he is under 18 or is unable to manage his own affairs, the money will be paid to trustees appointed by the Secretary of State for Social Services. If he lives with his parents, they can be made the trustees. Where the person vaccinated has died, the money will be paid to his personal representatives.

Other claims A claim under the Vaccine Damage Payments Scheme does not prevent the bringing of a separate court action for DAMAGES. However, a payment made under the Scheme will be taken fully into account when assessing the level of damages.

A payment will also be taken into account as capital if SUPPLEMENTARY BENEFIT is claimed.

VALUE ADDED TAX

How traders collect revenue for the Government

When you buy goods or services and have to pay an extra percentage for value added tax – VAT – your payment is usually just the last in a chain. The tax is chargeable on each business transaction involved in producing and supplying those goods and services.

It is a consumption tax, however, and you as the consumer are normally the only one who loses money. Each trader further back in the chain of manufacture and supply has to pay the tax when he buys, but he generally recovers his cost by charging tax when he sells.

Because a trader sells at a higher price – called 'added value' – he automatically receives more VAT than he pays. He has to account to a Customs and Excise office for his VAT transactions, and pay over the extra amounts he receives. In effect, each trader acts as a collector for part of the tax.

Paying the tax

A trader does not actually have to calculate the amount owing to Customs and Excise from each transaction. His accounts are assessed for VAT every 3 months, simply by charging a percentage on the total of his taxable sales, and reducing that figure by the total of VAT charges that he paid in the same period.

If a trader's quarterly sales are £100,000, for example, he should have invoiced his customers for £115,000 in order to collect VAT at a rate of 15 per cent. He holds the extra £15,000 on behalf of the Government, but pays over only what is left after deducting all the VAT charges on the goods and services that he had to buy for his business.

If his taxable purchases at the 15 per cent rate totalled £40,000, he should have been invoiced by his suppliers for a total of £46,000. His debt to Customs and Excise is the difference between the extra £15,000 that he received and the extra £6,000 that he had to pay. So he hands over £9,000.

It does not matter what else a trader has to spend – staff wages, for example – to create the added value of what he sells. VAT is not a tax on income or profit. Even a business that runs at a loss has to collect VAT if it sells taxable goods or services.

However, if a business pays more VAT to its suppliers than it receives from its customers in the same period, the difference is refunded.

How VAT rates can vary

The Government sets VAT percentage rates in the same way that it fixes income tax rates.

It has the power to introduce different rates for particular goods or services – higher rates for luxuries, for example, or lower rates for second-hand goods.

The government also decides which goods can be 'zero rated', so that they attract no VAT, or which traders can be exempted, so that they do not have to account for VAT transactions.

Zero rating If a product or service is zero-rated, the trader selling it does not charge VAT. He may still be registered for VAT, however, which means that although he receives no tax payments on what he sells – called output tax – he can still claim credit for VAT payments to his suppliers – called input tax. So his payments will be refunded.

Exported goods are zero-rated. So are some sold locally – food and books, for example. But the zero rating does not apply until the product is in its final form, which is why VAT is often collected at earlier stages and has to be refunded. For example, the paper, ink, glue and so on that go into a book all incur VAT charges when a printer buys them.

Exemption VAT exemption means that a trader does not have to register and account for his VAT transactions. He is outside the VAT system altogether. A trader whose turnover is less than £18,700 a year does not need to register. Nor do traders whose whole output consists of exempted goods or services. They can, however, register voluntarily.

Some services are automatically exempt – notably health care, education, insurance and finance.

Exemption offers a trader freedom from the need to be involved in VAT administrative and accounting procedures. He is at a disadvantage, however, if his business requires him to pay VAT on purchases. He has no right to reclaim those costs. In fact, he is in the same position as a consumer paying VAT on retail goods – he is at the end of the trading chain for VAT purposes.

Second-hand trading VAT regulations are modified for second-hand trading in cars, motor cycles, caravans, boats, outboard motors, works of art and antiques. The tax is charged only on the dealer's profit margin – not on the full sale price.

If you sell your own car or other personal possessions, you do not charge VAT because the transaction is not part of a business.

Coping with the paperwork

About 2 million trading organisations, professional people and self-employed businessmen are registered for VAT because they sell taxable goods or services and their sales exceed £18,700 a year. Each is allocated a VAT reference number.

Every taxable person or organisation must keep 3-monthly accounts in enough detail to show how much VAT is payable to the Government or refundable from it. They must be available for Customs and Excise inspection at any time. The maximum penalty for failing to keep such accounts is a fine of £400, plus £10 for each day on which the failure continues.

The key to VAT accounting is a special 'tax invoice' which a trader must issue to his customer when he charges VAT. It shows the date, the price, the VAT charge and the supplier's VAT reference number.

If the customer is also registered for VAT, he uses tax invoices as proof of his payments, so that he can offset them against his VAT receipts. But he must not offset the tax paid on any goods or services bought for private purposes.

At the end of each 3 month period the trader makes a return of VAT payments and receipts to the Customs and Excise VAT central office. If his receipts are higher than his payments, he has 1 further month in which to pay the excess amount to the Government.

Evasion Fraudulent evasion of VAT is a criminal offence. The maximum penalty in summary proceedings is 6 months' imprisonment and a £2,000 fine or three times the amount of tax involved, whichever is greater.

Disputes Arguments over the amount of VAT payable to or refundable by the Government, or arguments over registration, rating or exemption, are first referred to the Commissioners of Customs and Excise.

Someone who is dissatisfied with a decision by the Commissioners has a right of appeal to a regional Value Added Tax Appeal Tribunal.

Public complaints If a consumer believes that a trading organisation is overcharging for VAT, or charging the tax when it has no right to, he should complain either to the trading standards or consumer protection department of his local authority or to a Customs and Excise office.

VANDALISM

A new word for an old crime

Destroying or damaging someone else's property – whether intentionally or recklessly – is the crime of malicious mischief.

Until February 1981 this was the offence for which vandals were normally prosecuted. However, on that date the government introduced a new offence called vandalism. This is also committed when a person intentionally or recklessly destroys or damages someone else's property.

Since vandalism is the same as malicious mischief, it adds nothing to the powers that were previously available to deal with vandals. But it has been justified on the ground that the term 'vandalism' more accurately reflects the nature of the offence than the term 'malicious mischief'.

Since malicious mischief remains an offence, prosecutors now have the choice of prosecuting alleged vandals for malicious mischief or vandalism. Most choose vandalism.

Maximum penalty The maximum penalty for vandalism is a £2,000 fine and 3 months' imprisonment – increased to 6 months' imprisonment for any subsequent offence.

Malicious mischief is usually prosecuted under summary CRIMINAL PROCEEDINGS, where it carries a maximum penalty of a £2,000 fine and 3 months' imprisonment.

Depending on the circumstances, a vandal may be charged with other offences such as FIRE-RAISING or BREACH OF THE PEACE.

VEHICLE EXCISE LICENCE

The disc that shows when road tax is due

The disc on a car windscreen is a vehicle licence receipt showing that the owner has paid excise duty – commonly known as the road-fund tax.

Regulations provide that the licence disc must be displayed on or adjacent to the nearside lower corner of the windscreen so that all particulars are clearly visible by daylight from the nearside of the road.

Licence discs, which also show an expiry date, can be bought for 6 or 12 months, unless the annual rate is £18 or less. Then, only a 12 month licence is available.

If any motor vehicle on a public road – driven, parked, towed or pushed – does not display a current disc, the owner can be fined up to £50. He can also be prosecuted for unlicensed use and fined up to £400 or five times the annual rate of duty, whichever is the greater, plus any back duty. The maximum fine for fraudulently using a vehicle licence is £2,000.

Forgery – for example, altering a licence to deceive a police officer – carries a maximum penalty of a £2,000 fine under summary criminal proceedings.

In practice, a car can be put on the road without a current disc provided that one has been applied for. A 14 day period of grace is customarily allowed, after a previous licence has expired, in which an owner can apply for renewal.

Licensing a new car

A new car is usually licensed before you take delivery. The dealer makes the application on your behalf, using the same form on which he arranges the car's registration.

If your dealer has not applied for a tax disc, make sure that he gives you an application form.

Licensing a used car

The current licence on a used car is often included as part of the deal when it is sold. But the seller is not obliged to pass on the licence – he can choose to claim a refund instead.

If you buy a used car that has no current tax disc, you must obtain one as soon as possible. Application form V10 is available from post offices. Take or send the completed form to a main post office (only certain designated post offices deal with this business) – with:

- The car registration document.
- A certificate of insurance or cover note.
- A current vehicle test certificate if the car is more than 3 years old.
- Your excise duty payment, at the rate shown on the application form.

Renewing a licence

A reminder notice is usually sent about 2 weeks before your licence expires. It works as a simplified application form for renewal.

If the details on it are correct, complete the form and take it with your payment to a post office. Your new disc is issued immediately.

If the notice details are not up to date, you can still use it for renewal but you will have to take or post it to a local vehicle licensing office – not a post office.

No reminder Licensing renewal is the responsibility of the car owner. So if he does not receive a reminder, he must make a full application on form V10, as if he were licensing the car for the first time.

If you lose a disc

If a vehicle licence is lost, stolen or destroyed, whoever is shown as the registered keeper can obtain a duplicate after a check of registration and licensing records. Application forms are available at local vehicle licensing offices. A fee of £2 is payable.

Someone who needs a duplicate licence more urgently – for example, because the car is about to be sold – may be issued with a temporary one by his local licensing office if he shows the registration document.

Claiming a refund

If you decide to sell your car without its current licence, or to take your car off the road for a long period, you can surrender the licence disc and claim a refund of unused excise duty.

Application forms are available at local vehicle licensing offices. Leave your disc there, with the completed application, and your refund will be sent by post.

Refund periods are counted only in full calendar months, and a month is counted only if the application is made on or before the last day of the preceding month.

Stolen car If a stolen car is not found quickly, the owner is entitled to a refund of unused excise duty. Local vehicle licensing offices have a special form for that purpose.

VENEREAL DISEASE

Treatment is easy to get and strictly confidential

Most hospitals have special clinics for diagnosing and treating venereal disease – now commonly called sexually transmitted disease, or STD.

Anyone who suspects that he or she might have STD can simply go along to one of these clinics, without any introductory letter from a doctor, and be assured of confidential treatment.

Symptoms of STD After sexual contact with a partner, any pain when passing urine, a discharge from the penis or vagina, swelling of glands in the groin or a rash in the genital area must lead to a suspicion of STD.

The principal sexually transmitted diseases are gonorrhoea, herpes genitalis, non-specific urethritis and syphilis. The latter, if left untreated, can lead to serious brain or heart damage and can damage a foetus in the womb.

How to find a STD clinic To find a specific clinic treating STD, telephone the main hospital in your area, a general practitioner or the local health board.

Health authorities try to ensure that any information that might lead to a STD patient being identified is kept strictly confidential. The name of the patient can only be disclosed to a doctor involved in treating the disease or preventing its spread, or to someone working under the doctor's direction in tracing possible contacts.

Someone being treated may be asked for the names of contacts, but is under no obligation to give any information.

VIDEO RECORDING

How the law controls videos

Video recordings as such, whether on tape or disc, are not protected by the law of copyright. But they may embody works of copyright, such as a film or play, which are protected. *See:* COPYRIGHT

It is a breach of copyright to make a video recording of a film less than 50 years old, even though the film is shown on television. But if the recording is for private use only, the copyright owner is unlikely to sue if he finds out about it.

'Pirate' videos are videos made by copying films without the permission of the film copyright owner. It is a criminal offence to make, sell or possess pirate videos for trade purposes. The maximum penalty is a £400 fine or 2 months' imprisonment.

It is also an offence under the TRADE DESCRIPTIONS Act to sell a pirate video under the trade name of the copyright owner.

It is not in itself a breach of copyright to make a video recording of television broadcasts other than broadcasts of cinema films. However the recording will infringe copyright if the broadcast embodies another copyright work, such as music or a play.

Controlling video 'nasties'

In 1984 a Bill was before Parliament to control the supply of violent or pornographic video recordings.

Under the Bill video recordings – with exceptions, such as educational, musical or sports recordings – will be given a classification certificate by the British Board of Film Censors. The Board will use the classification system that it applies to films. *See:* FILM CENSORSHIP

It will be an offence to sell or hire out video recordings, or even to possess them for such purposes, if they have not been given a certificate by the Board because they are considered to be too violent or pornographic. The maximum penalty will be a £20,000 fine.

It will also be an offence to supply a video recording in breach of the classification given to it – for instance, to sell an '18' (adults only) video to someone under 18. The maximum penalty will be a £2,000 fine.

Restricted 18 videos Videos that are given a 'Restricted 18' classification will only be available from sex shops licensed by the district or islands council. It will be an offence for anyone else to supply them, or even to possess them for that purpose. The maximum penalty will be a fine of £2,000.

Obscenity It is already an offence to sell or have for sale an obscene video recording. *See:* OBSCENE PUBLICATIONS

VISA

Documentation required to enter a country

People travelling abroad require permission to enter some countries. Permission may be granted before departure by means of a stamp or slip of paper fixed into the traveller's PASSPORT. This stamp (or paper) is usually called a visa.

In certain cases, a visa states how long a person is permitted to stay in the country.

If someone wants to stay longer than the visa permits, he must visit the country's immigration officials and ask for an extension of stay.

However, there are countries where a visitor from the United Kingdom is not required to have a visa.

For example, citizens of the EEC countries do not require a visa when visiting other member countries. They are permitted to enter, provided that they produce their identification card or, in the case of a British Citizen, a passport.

If you are planning travel abroad, check with your travel agent, or the embassy of the country you are visiting, what the visa requirements are. *See:* EMIGRATION

For example, someone travelling to the United States may have to produce evidence that he has a job to return to in the UK before a visa is granted.

Visitors to the UK

Visitors to the United Kingdom from certain foreign countries – for example, East European countries – need a visa authorising an IMMIGRATION official to allow them to enter the country.

Other foreign nationals can obtain a visa or a Home Office letter of consent, to facilitate their entry. COMMONWEALTH CITIZENS may, or in some cases must, obtain an 'entry certificate' which has the same function. *See:* IMMIGRATION

Holders of any of these sorts of entry clearance cannot normally be refused entry.

However, visitors from other countries, such as an EEC country, do not need a visa to enter the UK.

WAGES COUNCILS

Statutory bodies that fix minimum conditions for around 3 million workers

Wages councils set statutory minimum pay rates, holiday entitlements and other employment conditions for around 2.75 million workers in industries in which union organisation is weak – chiefly, the retail trade, hotels and catering, clothing and textile manufacturing and hairdressing.

A wages council consists of equal numbers of employers' and union representatives, supplemented by up to three independent members – often lawyers – appointed by the Secretary of State for Employment. Councils can be abolished by the Secretary of State – 13 have been since 1973. They can also be converted into Statutory Joint Industrial Councils, but so far none have been.

There are 27 wages councils, each of which is responsible for a particular industry – for example, the Hairdressing Undertakings Wages Council covers women's hairdressing and barbers. Two industries – aerated waters, and dress-making and women's light clothing – have separate wages councils for Scotland.

What employers must do

Under the Wages Councils Act 1979, each council regularly issues, through a central Office of Wages Councils based in the Department of Employment, wages orders that are binding on all employers in the industry that it covers.

Every employer to whom a wages order applies must grant his employees at least the pay rates and holidays that the order lays down. He must also observe any other minimum conditions laid down by the order – for instance, minimum pay rates during holidays and periods of LAY-OFF.

An employer who breaks the provisions of an order can be fined up to £400 for each offence.

In addition, if the offence is related to pay, he can be compelled by the court to pay to the employee up to 2 years' arrears. Prosecutions, however, are extremely rare.

All employers covered by a wages order must display a copy of it where it can easily be read by their employees. An employer who fails to do so can be fined up to £400.

The work of wages inspectors

Department of Employment wages inspectors, organised in 15 regional inspectorates, are responsible for ensuring that wages orders are enforced. They can demand to see wage records to check that employees are not being underpaid and to obtain the evidence required for any prosecution.

Although employers are rarely prosecuted, they frequently pay arrears to employees following investigation of their records by a wages inspector.

An employee who believes his employer is not obeying a wages order can ask a wages inspector, in confidence, to investigate.

Any local employment office has the address of the nearest inspectorate.

WAR PENSIONS

The country's debt to its military casualties

A man or a woman who is disabled – and the widow of a man who dies – as a result of service in the armed forces is normally entitled to a pension from the state.

In cases of special hardship or need, disablement pensions can be supplemented by one or more of a number of allowances, and widows may be entitled to allowances for their children and to other financial help, if required.

How a claim is made

The war pensions scheme is run by the Department of Health and Social Security, Norcross, Blackpool, FY5 3TA. Claims, complaints and appeals should be addressed to the Controller, Central Office (War Pensions) there.

A disabled serviceman is examined by a medical board before being invalided out. His service pay continues while the board sends a report to the Department for the pension entitlement to be worked out.

There is no time limit on an application. An ex-serviceman, whether or not he has been invalided out, can claim at any time for a disablement that he considers to be a result of his service.

If a man dies during service, the Ministry of Defence provides his widow with the claim forms. If a discharged serviceman dies – and his death is connected with his service – his widow should apply directly to the local Department office.

Assessing a disablement pension

The amount of a disablement pension is based on the degree of the disablement and on the rank held by the applicant.

Disablement below 20 per cent commands a lump-sum payment, but no pension. From 20 per cent, the disability is assessed in steps of 10 per cent up to 100 per cent – but the maximum does not necessarily imply total incapacity.

For example, a 100 per cent pension is paid for the loss of both hands or both legs and for the complete loss of sight or hearing. The loss of an arm brings 90 per cent, a thumb 30 per cent and two fingers 20 per cent.

The rate for such specific disablement is fixed. But when it is more difficult to assess the damage – for example, in cases of facial disfigurement – the pension is worked out individually.

Rank The applicant's rank is also taken into account on a sliding scale. A major-general assessed as 100 per cent disabled received, in 1983–4, a pension of £3,204 per year; a private received £55.60 per week. The same men on a 20 per cent pension received £641 per year and £11.12 per week respectively.

When extra help is available

Special allowances are payable to ex-servicemen whose disability has seriously affected their finances.

A man who requires regular personal help, for example, or whose job prospects have suffered, may qualify for one of a number of allowances on top of his pension. They include allowances for:

- Constant attendance, available to pensioners who are 100 per cent disabled, where at least 80 per cent of that disablement is from military service.
- Exceptionally severe disablement, paid to pensioners with a permanent disablement of exceptional severity.
- Unemployability – a supplement for someone so severely disabled that he is unable to get a job. There is also an extra allowance for a wife and children.

A partially disabled man, unable to take up the work he did before his military service or work of a similar standard, also qualifies for an allowance. But the allowance and pension together must not exceed the 100 per cent rate.

Mobility supplement War disablement pensioners may be entitled to a special mobility supplement – £21.15 in 1983/4 – if they are unable or virtually unable to walk. The supplement is similar to MOBILITY ALLOWANCE.

War widows' pensions

A woman is entitled to a war widow's pension if her husband:

- Died as the result of service in the 1914–18 war or service after September 2, 1939.
- Was a civilian and his death was the result of a 1939–45 war injury.
- At the time of his death was receiving a war pension constant attendance allowance (see above).

Rank There are two levels of war widow's pension – standard and lower rate. Their amounts vary with rank.

The standard rate is paid automatically to the widow of an officer above the rank of major. It is also paid to a widow who is aged:

- 40 or more.
- Under 40, but eligible for a child allowance (see below).
- Under 40, but unable to support herself because of prolonged ill-health.
- Under 40, and expecting a baby by her late husband.

The amount of the pension ranges, in 1983–4, from £10.22 per week at the lower rate for a private's widow who is childless, under 40 and capable of supporting herself, to £2,567 per year for the widow of a major-general.

An allowance is payable for a war widow's offspring until the child reaches the age of 16 or leaves school. Help with education and rent may also be available in cases of extreme hardship.

War widows' pensions are not taxable.

How war pensions are paid

Disabled officers and the widows and dependants of officers are normally paid monthly or quarterly in arrears. The Department of Health and Social Security sends them a voucher which has to be presented through a bank.

With other ranks, pensions are paid weekly in advance by books of orders that can be cashed at named post offices.

If a pensioner does not collect his or her pension for a year, it will probably be cancelled. But payment may be resumed from the date of reapplication if there was a good reason for the failure to collect it.

Appeals Anyone whose application for a war pension is turned down or who is dissatisfied with the amount awarded can appeal to an independent pensions appeal tribunal. The relevant appeal form is available from local social security offices. *See:* DISABILITY PENSION

WARRANT

The authority to carry out a court order

A warrant is a written authority that allows a person – for example, a police officer or SHERIFF OFFICER – to do some act. The most common forms of warrant are:

- Arrest warrant. This is issued by a magistrate and allows the police to arrest a suspect. *See:* ARREST
- Search warrant. This is usually issued by a magistrate to allow the police to search named premises. *See:* SEARCH

WARRANT SALE

When possessions can be sold to clear a debt

If a court orders a debtor to pay money that he owes, and he fails to do so, his creditor can ask a SHERIFF OFFICER to 'poind' – that is, select and value – some of his possessions. Once the possessions have been poinded, the debtor must not dispose of them.

If payment is still not made, the sheriff officer can ask a sheriff for authority, or warrant, to hold a public sale of the poinded possessions – usually at the debtor's home. If this is granted, the sale can then be advertised locally – though most newspapers refuse to carry warrant sale notices.

The proceeds of the warrant sale go to clear the debt. However, the cost of a poinding and sale will usually have to be met by the debtor.

Although there are thousands of 'poindings' every year, very few warrant sales actually take place. *See:* DEBT; RATES

WARRANTY

When you may have more rights – but never less

Warranty is another name sometimes given to a GUARANTEE, especially in the motor trade.

It can promise any protection or benefit that a manufacturer or trader sees fit – but not at the expense of a customer's rights under general law or under recently enacted consumer protection legislation.

A warranty document must state that the buyer's statutory rights are not affected by its terms.

See: DEFECTIVE GOODS; UNFAIR CONTRACT

WATER SUPPLY

Your right to have water but not to waste it

The water in your taps is supplied by your regional or islands council, which is the water authority for its area.

The main legal duty of the water authority is to provide a piped supply of wholesome water to every part of its area where water is needed for 'domestic purposes' – that is, for washing, cooking, drinking, central heating and sanitation.

The authority must lay water supply pipes to points that will enable any building requiring a supply to be connected at a reasonable cost to the owner.

However, the authority is only obliged to do whatever is practicable and can be done at a reasonable cost. If there is a dispute about practicability or reasonableness of cost, 10 or more local government electors can refer the matter to the Secretary of State for Scotland for a decision.

Every new house must have a piped water supply. The owner of an existing house that has no sufficient supply of wholesome water must provide a piped supply unless it is not reasonably practicable to do so. The district or islands council may be prepared to make a contribution to the cost.

The water authority may require some premises to be provided with a cistern with a ballcock and stopcock. In the case of houses built after May 1968, the cistern must be capable of giving 24 hours' supply to the premises.

Fluoride At present a water authority has no right to add fluoride – believed to prevent tooth decay – to the water supply. Strathclyde Regional Council's decision to do so was successfully challenged in the Court of Session in 1983. However the government are to legislate to allow fluoridation on the recommendation of the local health board.

Non-domestic purposes The water authority must, when requested to do so, provide water on reasonable terms and conditions for non-domestic purposes – provided this can be done at reasonable cost and without endangering the supply of water for domestic purposes. In this way water is supplied for industry and agriculture.

Cutting off the supply A water authority must give reasonable notice of its intention to cut off the water supply, except in an emergency.

Paying for water

Domestic consumers pay for water by means of the water rate, collected along with the rest of the general rate.

However, trade, business, manufacturing and agricultural establishments, as well as other premises that use greater than normal quantities of water – for instance, hotels – can be charged directly for the water they actually use. The water authority can insist on a metered water supply in these cases.

Paying the penalty for wasting water

Byelaws can make it an offence for water to be wasted or contaminated because of failure to repair pipes or fittings. The owner of property can be ordered to carry out repairs and the water authority may be entitled to carry out the necessary work itself.

The water authority is entitled to test water fittings and can forbid the use of those that cause waste. It can also forbid the use of water for certain purposes – for instance, the use of a hosepipe to water lawns or wash cars in a drought.

An official of a water authority is authorised to enter premises to check meters, to see if any offence is being committed or to carry out any necessary works. But he must produce some evidence of his authority if the occupier asks him to do so. If he is refused entry, he can ask a sheriff or justice of the peace for a warrant allowing him to enter, by force if necessary *See:* ENTRY, Right of.

WEIGHTS AND MEASURES

You can insist on getting full weight for your money

Giving short weight is a criminal offence. The maximum penalty is a fine of £2,000.

A sheriff court can order an offender to pay up to £2,000 compensation to anyone who has suffered loss or damage arising from the offence. *See:* CRIMINAL COMPENSATION ORDER

Weighed or pre-packed

If the goods are weighed in your presence, it is an offence to give you less than you are supposed to receive or less than you should get for the price.

If the goods are pre-packed, each package is marked with its nominal quantity. Any single package may contain less than the stated amount, but the average weight of a group of packages must not be less that the nominal quantity. Not more than a certain proportion of the packages may be underweight.

Where to complain

Weights and measures legislation is enforced by trading standards or consumer protection officers, who are employed by regional and islands councils. If you have a complaint about weights and measures, get in touch with them.

WIDOWED MOTHER'S ALLOWANCE

Long-term benefit for widows witn children

After receiving WIDOW'S ALLOWANCE for the first 26 weeks following her husband's death, a woman may be entitled to widowed mother's allowance if:

- She has at least one child under 19 who normally lives with her or for whom she is receiving CHILD BENEFIT; or
- She is expecting her late husband's baby.

To get the allowance, her husband must have paid sufficient NATIONAL INSURANCE CONTRIBUTIONS. (Her contributions do not count.) The contribution rules are the same as for RETIREMENT PENSION. If her husband has not paid enough for her to qualify for the full rate of allowance, she may be paid a reduced amount.

The Department of Health and Social Security can pay the allowance to a woman who has not gone through a marriage ceremony, if it considers her to have been married by 'cohabitation with habit and repute'. *See:* COMMON LAW MARRIAGE

In 1983–4, the widowed mother's allowance is £34.05 a week. In addition, a woman receives an extra £7.60 a week for each child for whom child benefit is payable. That can include a child of a previous marriage.

Widowed mother's allowance is taxable and should be included in an income tax return.

Additional pension A woman whose husband died on or after April 6, 1979, may be entitled to an additional pension based on his earnings from April 6, 1978. This is paid in addition to widowed mother's allowance. The amount of any additional pension is reduced if the widow is receiving a pension from her husband's employer. *See:* OCCUPATIONAL PENSION; RETIREMENT PENSION.

How to claim

If you are receiving widow's allowance, you do not have to claim widowed mother's allowance. You will be told whether you are entitled to it and should receive it automatically after the first 26 weeks of bereavement.

The allowance can be paid in the form of a book of weekly orders that you can cash at a post office of your choice. Alternatively, it can be paid every 4 or 13 weeks directly into your bank or National Girobank account, or into an investment account with the National Savings Bank or a building society.

When the allowance ceases to be paid

Widowed mother's allowance ceases when a woman no longer has any child under 19 living with her. If she is under 40 when this happens, she is entitled to no more widow's benefit. If she is 40 or over, she receives a WIDOW'S PENSION

Widowed mother's allowance also ceases if a woman remarries, or lives with a man as his wife without being married to him. If the couple stop living together, she can receive the allowance again. *See:* COHABITATION

WIDOW'S ALLOWANCE

Financial help during bereavement

For the first 26 weeks after a married man dies, his widow is entitled to a widow's allowance, provided he paid enough NATIONAL INSURANCE CONTRIBUTIONS. For his widow to get the allowance, he must have:

- Paid Class 1 contributions in any one tax year since April 6, 1975, on earnings of at least 25 times the LOWER EARNINGS LIMIT for that year; or
- Paid 25 Class 2 or 3 contributions in any one tax year since April 6, 1975; or
- Paid at least 25 Class 1, 2 or 3 contributions before April 6, 1975.

The allowance – £47.65 a week in 1983–4 – is paid to widows under 60 and to those aged 60 or over whose husbands were not receiving retirement pensions when they died. It can also be paid to a woman who has not gone through a marriage ceremony, if the DHSS considers her to have been married by 'cohabitation with habit and repute'. *See:* COMMON LAW MARRIAGE

If you are 60 or over, you may also be entitled to GRADUATED PENSION and additional RETIREMENT PENSION. Account can be taken of your own contributions as well as those of your late husband.

If you have children for whom you receive CHILD BENEFIT, your allowance will be increased by £7.60 (in 1983–4) for each child.

Widow's allowance stops if a widow remarries, or lives with a man as his wife without being married to him. If they stop living together, she can receive the allowance again. *See:* COHABITATION

How to claim widow's allowance

When you have registered your husband's death, complete the form on the back of the free DEATH certificate that you are given, and take or send it to the local office of the Department of Health and Social Security. Post offices supply free stamped and addressed envelopes.

You will be sent form BW1, which you should complete and return at once. If you can, enclose your birth and marriage certificates. If there is any difficulty, do not delay sending the claim form until you have the certificates. You can send them on later.

The allowance is paid by means of a book containing orders that you can cash each week. Each order should be cashed within 3 months.

Tax Widow's allowance is taxable and should be included on your income tax return. *See:* RETIREMENT PENSION; WIDOWED MOTHER'S ALLOWANCE; WIDOW'S PENSION

WIDOW'S INDUSTRIAL DEATH BENEFIT

What you may claim if your spouse dies from an industrial accident or disease

A woman whose husband dies as a result of an accident at work or a recognised industrial disease – of which there are about 50 – can claim death benefit under the industrial injuries scheme. In certain circumstances, a widower and other dependent relatives can also receive benefit. The government plan to phase out these payments soon. *See:* INDUSTRIAL DEATH BENEFIT.

Widows

A woman can claim industrial death benefit if she was living with her husband at the time of his death. If they were separated, she can claim benefit provided she was receiving maintenance of at least 25p a week from him, or was entitled to it under a court order or agreement and had taken reasonable steps to enforce payment.

A woman who receives industrial death benefit cannot receive national insurance widow's benefit as well.

There are three rates of industrial death benefit. For the first 26 weeks following the husband's death, the rate (in 1983–4) is £47.65 a week. After the 26 weeks are over, either a higher rate of £34.60 or a lower rate of £10.22 is payable.

The higher rate is paid if the woman meets any of the following conditions:

- She is entitled to an additional allowance for a child (see below).
- She has a child under 19 living with her for whom she is not entitled to a child allowance, but her husband was entitled to CHILD BENEFIT for the child at his death (or would have been had the child not left school).
- She is over 40 when she no longer satisfies either of the above conditions.
- She was over the age of 50 when her husband died.
- She was permanently incapable of supporting herself at the time her husband died.
- She is pregnant by her late husband.

The lower rate is paid to a woman who does not meet any of these conditions – for instance, someone who is self-supporting, under 50 and has no children.

When death benefit may stop

If a woman receiving an industrial death benefit remarries, the benefit stops, but she will receive a gratuity (lump sum) equal to one year's benefit.

If she lives with a man as his wife, but does not marry him, she loses her right to the benefit (though payment can resume if the couple separate).

Widowers

A man whose wife dies because of an accident at work or a recognised industrial disease can get death benefit if he satisfies *both* the following conditions:

- He was permanently unable to support himself at the time of her death.
- His wife was contributing more than half the cost of maintaining him.

If he meets these conditions, he will receive benefit at the higher rate of £34.60 a week. There are no rules about remarriage or cohabitation.

Children

If a woman who is receiving industrial death benefit is entitled to child benefit for any dependent children, she is also entitled to an additional allowance of £7.60 a week for each child. The allowance is payable for a child of her husband born after his death.

A husband receiving widower's benefit is entitled to an additional allowance of 15p a week for each child. That is also the amount that a widow will receive if her benefit ceases because of remarriage. This allowance will be abolished in November, 1984.

Other relatives

In certain circumstances, parents and other relatives – such as grandparents, brothers, sisters and parents-in-law – can claim industrial death benefit if the deceased was contributing to their maintenance. For more details, see leaflet NI 10, available from local social security offices.

How to claim the benefit

When the death is registered, the widow or widower will receive a certificate of application. That must be completed and sent to the local social security office, which will then send another form on which to make the claim for benefit.

The claim should be made within 3 months of the death, otherwise some benefit may be lost.

WIDOW'S PENSION

The long-term benefit for widows without children to support

If a woman is under 40 when her husband dies and she has no children, she receives no more widow's benefit after the 26 weeks in which she receives WIDOW'S ALLOWANCE. If she does have children, she will get WIDOWED MOTHER'S ALLOWANCE.

However, if she is 40 or over but under 65 when her husband dies or when she ceases to qualify for widowed mother's allowance, she is entitled to a widow's pension – provided her husband paid sufficient national insurance contributions. (The contribution conditions are the same as for RETIREMENT PENSION.)

The pension can be paid to a woman who has not gone through a marriage ceremony, if the DHSS considers her to have been married by 'cohabitation with habit and repute'. *See:* COMMON LAW MARRIAGE

There are two kinds of pension:

- An age-related pension, payable to women between the ages of 40 and 49.
- A standard pension, payable to women who are 50 and over when they become eligible.

In 1983–4 the age-related pension varied from £10.22 a week at 40 to £31.67 at 49. The pension is pegged to the age at which a widow became eligible for it; she does not get an increased pension with each year that passes.

In 1983–4 the standard pension was £34.05 a week.

A widow's pension is taxable and should be included in her income tax return.

A widow's pension ceases if a widow remarries or lives with a man as his wife. If she lives with a man, but later leaves him, her pension can be restored.

Retirement If a widow retires at 60, widow's pension is replaced by retirement pension of at least the same amount.

If she does not retire at 60, she can continue to receive widow's pension until she retires or reaches 65. The advantage in doing this is that there is no earnings rule for widow's pension, as there is for retirement pension. *See:* RETIREMENT PENSION

Additional pension Since April 1979, an additional pension may be paid with widow's pension. This is the additional, earnings-related part of the retirement pension that the husband was entitled to. *See:* RETIREMENT PENSION

When there is an occupational pension

An employer who has an approved OCCUPATIONAL PENSION scheme can contract his employees out of the additional pension payable under the state retirement pension scheme. When an employee dies, his widow is entitled to be paid half the guaranteed minimum pension her husband would have been entitled to had he retired at the time of his death.

This amount is deducted from the additional pension due to the widow under the state scheme, so that she receives:

- Her basic widow's pension.
- The guaranteed minimum from her husband's private pension scheme.
- Some additional pension from the state.

How a pension can be paid

A widow's pension can be paid by means of a book of weekly orders, cashable at a named post office.

Alternatively, the Department of Health and Social Security can be asked to pay the pension every 4 or 13 weeks directly into a bank or National Girobank account or into an investment account with a building society or the National Savings Bank.

WIDOW'S TAX

How a widow's pension alters her tax liability

A widow is treated as a single woman for tax purposes and therefore qualifies for the single person's allowance. If she is 65 or over she usually qualifies for the higher single person's age allowance. *See:* INCOME TAX

In the year she is widowed, she may qualify for:

- A full year's single person's or age

allowance from the date of widowhood even though she is only a widow for part of that tax year.

- Widow's bereavement allowance, which is equal to the difference between the married and single person's allowances. Again, she gets a full year's allowance even though she may only be a widow for part of that tax year.
- If she has a child to look after she may also get the full additional allowance equal to the difference between the married and single person's allowances (the same amount as the widow's bereavement allowance). She gets this in addition to the single and widow's bereavement allowances.

A widow's pension is taxable income, but on its own may not exceed or only slightly exceed the tax-free personal allowance. Therefore there should normally only be a considerable amount of tax payable by a widow when she receives other income (a wage or bank interest, for example) as well as the pension.

If a widow gets a job she should let her inspector of taxes know that she is receiving a pension so that her PAYE deductions can be calculated on her total income. If she does not inform the Inland Revenue about her pension, she may subsequently find herself having to meet a demand for the back taxes. War widows' pensions are not taxable.

WILL

Deciding what will happen to your possessions after your death

Any male aged 14 or over and any female aged 12 or over can make a will, provided that he or she is of sound mind and is capable of understanding it.

The object of making a will is to state what you want to happen to your possessions after your death, who you want to wind up your affairs and, if necessary, who you want to be the GUARDIAN of your children. You can also express your wishes about such matters as your FUNERAL and your burial or cremation.

Through making a will, someone with considerable property may also be able to minimise the amount of CAPITAL TRANSFER TAX that his heirs have to pay.

A will can be either witnessed or 'holograph' – meaning that it is written entirely in the handwriting of the person making the will (called the testator) and signed by him – or 'adopted as holograph'. *See:* HOLOGRAPH WRITINGS

If a will is witnessed, there must be at least 2 witnesses, each of whom must see the testator sign or hear him acknowledge his signature. Where the will runs to more than one page, each page must be signed at the foot by the person making the will, but the witnesses need only sign at the end.

The witnesses need not be told the terms of the will and they are not disqualified merely because they are beneficiaries (but it is better, if possible, to have witnesses who do not benefit under the will).

Alterations are often wrongly made in home-made wills. If a mistake has been made, type or write a new copy. Do not try to alter the old copy. Later alterations to a completed will should be made only by an entirely new will or a CODICIL.

A person who is blind or unable to sign can still make a will. A solicitor or Church of Scotland minister can sign on his behalf in the presence of the testator and 2 witnesses. In this case the will must be read over and the testator be seen to agree to its terms before it is signed by the solicitor or parish minister and the witnesses.

If the will is not made correctly, the law treats the estate as though no will had been made. *See:* INTESTACY

Choosing an executor

The person you choose to wind up your affairs is called the EXECUTOR. If you are leaving the bulk of your estate to one person, it is often best to make that person the executor. However, if you know that person is likely to find it a worry, it might be better to appoint someone else who is close to him or her.

If a TRUST is to be set up under the will, you must appoint trustees as well. Executors can also be trustees.

Appointing guardians You can appoint a guardian (or guardians) for your young children in your will. All that is needed is a statement such as: 'I appoint A.B. and C.D. to be the tutors and curators of my children'. The guardians can also be executors or trustees. *See:* CURATOR; TUTOR

Deciding what to do

Unless you intend to make only the simplest of wills, it is essential that you take professional advice about what to do. It will often be safer to ask a solicitor to draw up the document for you.

When considering what you want to happen to your possessions, ask:

- What do I own?
- What do I owe?
- What, including insurance policies, am I likely to own when I die?
- Who can claim 'legal rights'? *See:* DISINHERITANCE
- What do I want to happen to any gift if the person I name dies before me?

In many cases, a simple will leaving 'my whole estate' to the husband or wife is best. This may be suitable for a family with young children. Where the children are grown-up, they can be left legacies – either money, specific items or the residue of the estate.

Once he has left his whole estate to his wife, a husband has no say in what is to pass to his children. That is for his wife to decide in her will. But he could set up a trust in his will, whereby his wife only receives a LIFERENT of his estate, which will then pass to his children on her death. Such an arrangement is normally advisable only if the estate is a big one or the wife has adequate money of her own.

Leaving a legacy If you are making your own will, describe any legacy and the person to whom it is given as clearly as possible. For people, put their full names and either their addresses or their relationship to you. For gifts, remember that a description which seems satisfactory when you make your will can become ambiguous. So be as precise as you can.

For example, a vintage-car enthusiast may decide to leave an old friend his highly prized Lagonda. If it is his only car and he refers to it in his will as 'my car', it is clear what he means at the time of writing.

When he dies, however, he may be running one or more other cars. It is no longer clear what he meant and the gift can be disputed. The testator should be more specific and refer to 'my vintage Lagonda car'.

Your home Where the title to your home is in your name and that of another person – such as your husband

HOW TO MAKE A WILL WITHOUT A LAWYER

Taking every precaution to ensure that your intentions are completely clear

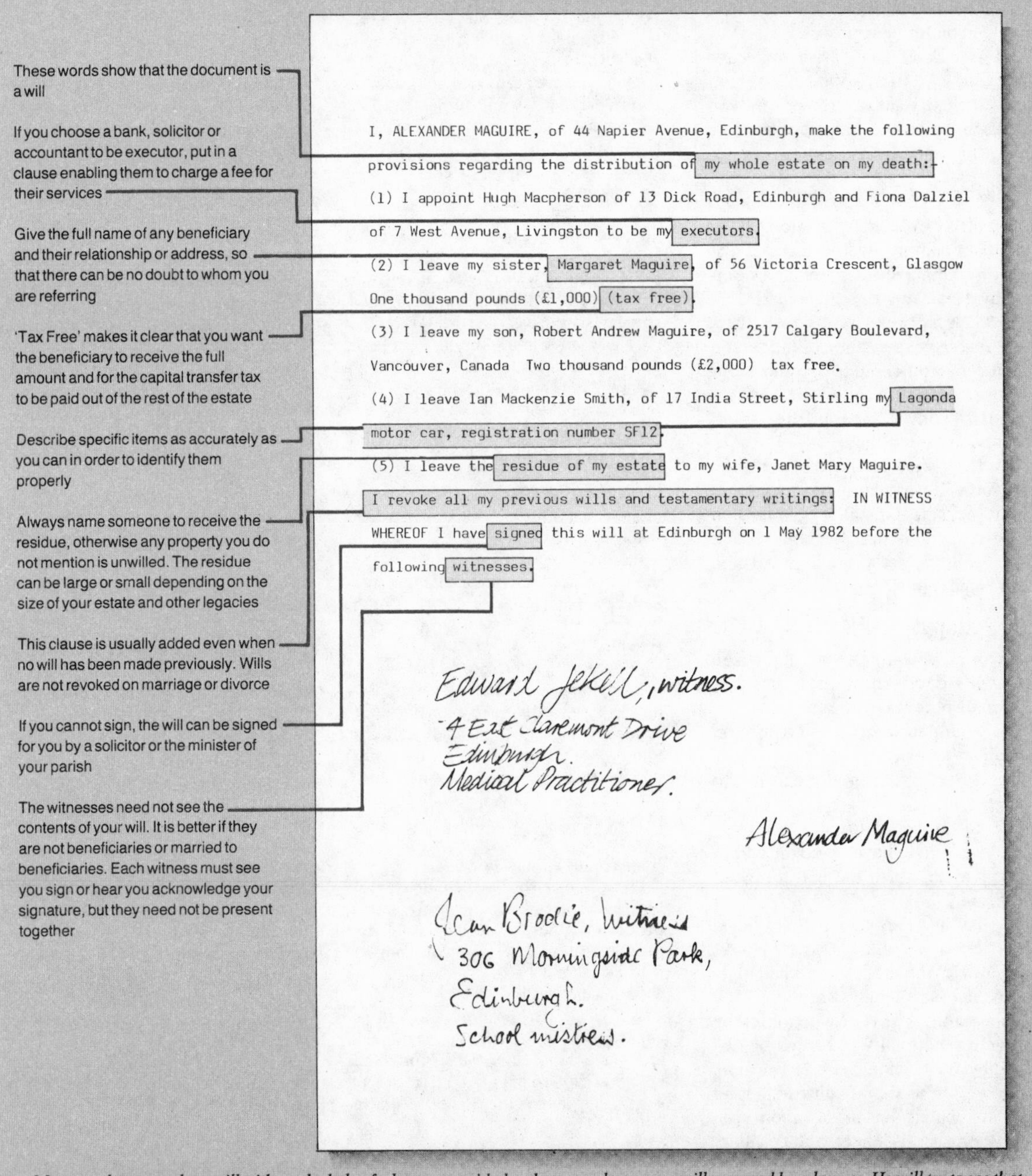

I, ALEXANDER MAGUIRE, of 44 Napier Avenue, Edinburgh, make the following provisions regarding the distribution of my whole estate on my death:-

(1) I appoint Hugh Macpherson of 13 Dick Road, Edinburgh and Fiona Dalziel of 7 West Avenue, Livingston to be my executors.

(2) I leave my sister, Margaret Maguire, of 56 Victoria Crescent, Glasgow One thousand pounds (£1,000) (tax free).

(3) I leave my son, Robert Andrew Maguire, of 2517 Calgary Boulevard, Vancouver, Canada Two thousand pounds (£2,000) tax free.

(4) I leave Ian Mackenzie Smith, of 17 India Street, Stirling my Lagonda motor car, registration number SF12.

(5) I leave the residue of my estate to my wife, Janet Mary Maguire.

I revoke all my previous wills and testamentary writings: IN WITNESS WHEREOF I have signed this will at Edinburgh on 1 May 1982 before the following witnesses.

Edward Jekell, witness.
4 East Claremont Drive
Edinburgh.
Medical Practitioner.

Alexander Maguire

Jean Brodie, witness
306 Morningside Park,
Edinburgh.
School mistress.

Most people can make a will without the help of a lawyer provided their wishes are straightforward. Avoid 'will forms' sold by stationers; even if they are in Scottish form, the accompanying advice is often based on English law.

Simply write or type your wishes on an ordinary piece of paper. (If you type them, remember to put 'adopted as holograph' above your signature.) If your family situation or wishes are at all complicated, however, have your will prepared by a lawyer. He will try to see that there are no ambiguities, so that your wishes are not misinterpreted.

If, for example, you wish to ensure that your children inherit your property when your widow(er) dies, the lawyer can help to set up a trust in your will to provide for your widow(er) throughout life, and hand everything on to the children eventually. If you are well-off he can also help to keep capital transfer tax to the minimum.

or wife – you can leave your share to whoever you please. But if the title is in the name of yourself, your spouse *and the survivor*, you cannot usually leave your share to anyone else. Do not forget this when planning your will.

Charities You may wish to leave money to charities, especially if you have no close relatives. Make sure you put down the correct name and address – many have similar names.

Revoking a will

A will is revoked by a later will or codicil, or simply by the testator (or someone acting on his behalf) intentionally destroying it.

A will is *not* revoked by the subsequent marriage or divorce of the person making it. You should therefore consider making a new will when this happens. It is in any case a good opportunity to review your affairs.

Children born to the testator soon after the will was made may be able to have it set aside if it makes no provision for them. But it may be better for a young child to let the will stand and claim 'legal rights'.

How to dispute a will

Anyone who thinks he has been wrongfully deprived by the terms of a will can dispute:

- The genuineness of the signature on the will.
- The testator's mental capacity to make the will.
- The testator's ability to act freely when he is said to have made the will.
- The way in which the will has been interpreted.

He may also be able to claim 'legal rights'. *See:* DISINHERITANCE

Whatever the basis of a challenge, legal advice is generally essential.

False signature Anyone who thinks the signature on a will was forged or obtained by a trick should enter a warning, or caveat, at the sheriff court so that he is told when an application for CONFIRMATION is lodged and can start an action to set aside the will. As a criminal offence would almost certainly be involved, the matter should also be reported to the police.

Fitness to sign The yardstick of whether a person is mentally qualified to make a will is that he or she must be able to understand:

- The nature and size of the estate.
- The identity of all those who might have a moral claim to benefit under the will.
- What the provisions of the will achieve.

The person must also not be suffering from delusions – for example, that his family living with him are dead. Doctors and nurses are usually unwilling to give a professional opinion on a patient's competence to make a will.

Undue influence A will can be set aside if it is proved that the testator was improperly dominated by someone else when he made it.

LEAVING YOUR BODY TO SCIENCE

If you want all or part of your body to be used for medical purposes after your death, you can make that request during your lifetime, but there is no guarantee that it will be carried out.

Once you are dead, your body does not form part of your property. Your widow(er), nearest relative, executor or the hospital (or other place) where death took place is the lawful custodier of it. An undertaker has no rights to it.

The request may be made orally during your last illness in the presence of at least two witnesses. However, it is more likely to be observed if you set it out in writing and give copies to your executor, spouse or nearest relative. The written request may be inserted into your will, but to avoid delay – for example, in transplanting a kidney – you should draw it up as a separate document.

A suitable statement, which you can prepare for yourself, could say:

'I (name)..
of (address)..
request that after my death my body/the following parts of my body.......................
....
should be used for therapeutic purposes under the Human Tissue Act 1961 or the Anatomy Act 1832, whichever is more suitable.'

(You must sign and date the statement.)

Some medical research organisations – for example, the Royal National Institute for the Blind and the Kidney Research Fund – issue bequest cards to potential donors. Surgeons will not normally use a dead person's kidneys unless he is known to have held a donor's card.

Bequeathing a whole body

If the dead person has requested that his body should be used for medical research, the doctor or hospital should be informed as soon as possible after death. They will then make the necessary arrangements with a medical school.

The medical school will take into account the cause of death, the condition of the body and its current need for bodies before deciding whether or not to accept. It may not accept the body if death resulted from a ravaging disease such as cancer. Bodies are normally refused if a post-mortem examination has been carried out, or if any major organs have been removed.

The widow(er) or the dead person's nearest relatives can object and require the body to be buried or cremated, even if a bequest to medical research has been made. If the PROCURATOR FISCAL is investigating the death, his permission must be obtained before the body is offered to a medical school.

The medical school can keep a body for up to 2 years. When it has finished with it, it must arrange for burial or cremation.

Any funeral should be carried out before the body is handed over, because the medical school does not notify the dead person's family when it has finished with the body. The medical school accepting a body will pay for a simple funeral, but sometimes the family are allowed to make private arrangements.

Using parts of a body

If the dead person requested that parts of his body should be used for medical purposes, action is necessary immediately after death. Kidneys, for example, must be removed within half an hour, so cannot normally be used if the death occurred at home. Tell the doctor or hospital of the request and they will make the arrangements.

The family have no legal right to object to the removal of parts from the body of a person who requested removal. But parts are unlikely to be removed by a hospital if relatives object in time. No parts may be removed without the permission of the procurator-fiscal, if he is investigating the death.

Where the dead person did not make any request, the surviving spouse or nearest relatives may be asked by the hospital authorities for permission to use parts of the body for transplant purposes. Parts may not be used if the dead person, when alive, had expressed an objection.

Once the parts have been removed, the body is returned to the family for burial or cremation.

Simply influencing him by way of advice, as a solicitor, doctor, priest or close relative might properly do, is not enough to prove undue influence.

What did he mean? A beneficiary under a will, or anyone who thinks he should be one, can bring a legal action if he thinks the EXECUTOR is failing to carry out the terms of the will or misinterpreting them.

For example, if there is an ambiguity in the will about how a property should be divided, the executor might read it one way and a beneficiary another.

Ambiguities in a will mean not only a danger that it may not be interpreted as intended; they can also create a great deal of ill-feeling in the family.

Legal proceedings are expensive and should be avoided if possible. A compromise may be better than the chance of the whole estate being swallowed up in legal fees.

WITNESS

When you are asked to give evidence as a witness

Even the most law-abiding person can find himself asked to give evidence in court if he witnesses an accident or a crime.

For example, if someone out walking witnesses an accident in which a cyclist is injured by a car, he can be asked to:

- Make a statement to the police immediately after the accident.
- Make a statement to the PROCURATOR FISCAL if the driver is to be prosecuted.
- Give evidence in a criminal court during the driver's trial.
- Give evidence in a civil court if the driver is sued for DAMAGES by the cyclist in compensation for his injuries.
- Make a statement to the solicitors acting for the driver and the cyclist.

Making statements

If a police constable reasonably suspects that a crime has been committed at any place, he can require anyone found there who he believes has information about the crime to give his name and address. The police constable must tell the witness of his suspicions and the general nature of the crime suspected, as well as of his belief that the witness has information relating to it.

It is an arrestable offence for a witness to fail or refuse to give his name and address without reasonable excuse. The penalty is a fine of up to £400.

When a person is driving a motor vehicle on a public road, he is obliged to give his name and address (and, if different, the name and address of the owner of the vehicle) to a police officer who asks for the information. The police can also require the same information from someone they reasonably believe was driving a motor vehicle at a time when an accident occurred owing to that vehicle's presence on the road. Failure to give the required information is an offence punishable by a fine of up to £400.

In other cases, a witness is not legally obliged to make a statement to the police; he does not even have to give his name and address. He cannot be prosecuted for obstructing the police by refusing to answer police questions.

Most people, however, do help and make a statement to the police if required.

When a witness is cited

A witness can be ordered to make a statement. The order is called a citation.

When the procurator fiscal is preparing a case for prosecution and a witness refuses to make a statement, the fiscal can apply to the court for a warrant to cite, or order, the accused to give a statement. Failure to obey the order can be contempt of court.

The accused person in a case can also apply to the court for a warrant to order a witness to give a statement to the lawyers for the defence.

A witness can also be ordered to attend court to give evidence. He will be given conduct money to enable him to travel to court.

Many witnesses are willing to give evidence without being ordered to attend court, but it may be best to insist on a formal citation to attend court for this purpose. Many employers insist that a citation be produced before they will release an employee from work to attend court.

If a witness ignores a citation, he can be arrested and brought to court to explain why he disobeyed it. He may be fined or, in exceptional cases, imprisoned. *See:* CONTEMPT OF COURT

Appearing in court as a witness

When you arrive at the court, show your citation to a court officer who will tell you in which court the case is being heard.

Try at once to find the solicitor who requested your attendance to tell him you have arrived.

That person is your reference point and should be able to keep you informed of the progress of the case. If you have any queries, put them to him.

Ask a solicitor for a copy of your own statement so that you can refresh your memory of events that may have happened many months ago.

A witness is not usually allowed in court before he is to give evidence, in case he is influenced by what earlier witnesses say. So inevitably you will find yourself waiting in corridors or waiting rooms for some time. If you want to go for a coffee or a walk, let the court officer or solicitor know, in case you are due to be called.

When you are called to give evidence, you will be shown to the witness box, usually in front of the court, and will be asked to swear or affirm. *See:* OATH

You will be taken through your evidence first by the advocate or solicitor representing the party who asked you to attend. Then you will be cross-examined by the representative of the opposing side. The lawyer will probably try to weaken your evidence by finding ambiguities in it or suggesting you may have been mistaken. He may even be rude or aggressive to confuse you into contradicting yourself.

Be prepared to spend a long time giving your evidence. Lawyers go through it very slowly to enable the judge to make very full notes.

A witness must not refuse to answer a question if ordered to do so by a judge or he will be in contempt of court. If he answers questions untruthfully he commits PERJURY.

After giving your evidence, do not assume you can go home. The citation requires you to attend for the duration of the trial. You may be recalled later to give further evidence or to clarify something you said.

Ask whether you can be released. If the lawyers for both parties do not need you any more, the judge will probably agree to let you go.

Send a list of the losses and expenses you incurred by attending court to the solicitor who requested your presence. You may, however, not be able to recover the full amount. Most courts lay down a maximum that can be paid to witnesses. *See:* EVIDENCE

WORK PERMIT

The system that restricts employment of outsiders

Few people outside Britain can take up permanent employment in this country unless they qualify:

- For settlement, under the rules of IMMIGRATION.
- For unrestricted entry, under the rules of CITIZENSHIP.
- For freedom of movement as workers or businessmen, under the rules of the EUROPEAN COMMUNITIES.

But if a foreign worker not qualified in one of these ways has qualifications for a particular job, and a prospective employer can show that he has been unable to find a British resident suitable for the job, the employer may succeed in obtaining a Department of Employment work permit.

It is a document that allows an immigrant to enter Britain in order to take up a certain job with a certain employer – not a general permission to work.

The rules for issuing permits differ according to the occupation concerned. Leaflets giving details can be obtained from your local Department of Employment office. The Department's decision is final and there can be no appeal to a court or appeal tribunal.

Permits are normally granted only for jobs requiring special professional or trade skills. The permit system also covers resident domestic servants – but not AU PAIR visitors.

Generally, the worker must have at least 5 years' experience of the work for which he is required, and the employer has to prove that he has tried, by advertising, to find a British resident who meets the requirements.

Certain jobs are 'permit-free employment', so do not require work permits. Otherwise they are controlled in the same way. These jobs include doctors, nurses and representatives of overseas firms with no UK office.

Work-permit holders are not given unrestricted entry to Britain. Normally their passports are stamped for stays of 12 months at a time, subject to their remaining in the same employment. However, the permit is renewable if the job is still open, for up to three more periods of 12 months.

A permit holder is not absolutely bound to stay in his first job, but he must have Department of Employment approval to start a new one. Consent is not given unless his new employment would also have qualified him for a permit.

It is not an offence to employ someone who does not have a work permit, but the employee may well not be given permission to stay here.

After 4 years of control, the conditions on a work-permit holder's stay may be lifted. He can then take any employment, stay in Britain and qualify eventually for citizenship.

Work-permit control is also imposed on employees of foreign companies who are sent to Britain for training, and on professional entertainers and sportsmen under contract to British companies, who are often given short-term work permits. Their permits do not lead to permanent residence.

WHEN A WORK PERMIT IS NOT NEEDED

Work permits are not required for foreign employees in the following categories:

- Doctors and dentists who have been appointed to British posts.
- Ministers, missionaries and members of religious orders, including teachers.
- People appointed to British Government positions – for example, scientists – with Department of Employment approval.
- Staff of overseas governments serving in Britain – for example, trade representatives – or of international organisations of which Britain is a member.
- Private servants of diplomats.
- Representatives of overseas companies that have no branch, subsidiary or other representative in Britain.
- Press and broadcasting representatives.
- Teachers and language assistants under approved exchange schemes.
- Seamen under contract to join ships.
- Airline operational staff.
- Agricultural workers admitted under approved schemes to meet seasonal demands – for example, harvesting.

WORKMEN'S COMPENSATION

Special help for people disabled before 1948

Employees who had an accident at work or contracted an industrial disease before July 5, 1948 (when workmen's compensation was replaced by the industrial injuries scheme) may qualify for a supplement to their workmen's compensation.

If the accident happened or the industrial disease was contracted before January 1, 1924, the employee may be entitled to a basic allowance of £2 per week and to either a major or lesser incapacity allowance, depending on the degree of his incapacity.

If the accident or disease happened after January 1, 1924, he can get only the major or lesser allowance.

The major allowance is paid to someone who is totally incapable of work. The rate during 1983–4 is £55.60 a week (the same as DISABLEMENT BENEFIT) less the weekly workmen's compensation and any basic allowance.

The lesser allowance is paid to someone who is partially incapacitated. The maximum weekly rate is £20.45. Any workmen's compensation over £2 a week is deducted from the allowance.

Other allowances payable under the industrial injuries scheme – constant attendance allowance, exceptionally severe disablement allowance or unemployability supplement – can be paid to someone who gets these allowances. *See:* DISABLEMENT BENEFIT

For more information about the allowances, write to the DHSS, Workmen's Compensation (Supplementation) Branch, Norcross, Blackpool FY5 3TA.

WRECK

When property found on the beach must be reported to the Receiver of Wrecks

Any object of value, identifiable as belonging to someone, that is washed up on the foreshore or found in territorial waters is known technically as 'wreck'. This includes not just a wrecked ship, but any cargo that was being carried by a ship.

If wreck is not claimed by its owner, it falls to the Crown like other abandoned property. *See:* BEACHCOMBING; TREASURE TROVE.

Anyone finding any wreck must give it or report it to the local Receiver of Wrecks – usually a local Customs officer. Failure to report wreck is an offence carrying a maximum fine of £1,000.

The Secretary of State for Scotland has power to make an order protecting any shipwrecked vessel inside territorial waters that is of historical importance. It is an offence to dive for or interfere with any wreck for which an order has been issued unless you obtain a special licence first.

WRONGFUL DETENTION

Compensation for being unlawfully detained

Every citizen is entitled to his freedom. The law sometimes allows this freedom to be taken away, but only in certain carefully defined circumstances. Examples are the lawful ARREST or DETENTION of someone who is suspected of a crime, or the compulsory treatment given to some people who are suffering from serious MENTAL DISORDER.

If you think that anyone has deprived you of your freedom unlawfully, you can sue for damages for being wrongfully detained. To succeed, you must normally prove that you were intentionally deprived of your liberty, without any lawful authority.

There is, however, an exception in the case of the police, because of the importance of what they do in the public interest. To get damages for being unlawfully arrested or detained by a policeman, you will have to show not only that he had no legal authority to arrest or detain you, but also that he did so out of malice or because of a grudge that had nothing to do with the matter for which you were arrested.

It may be presumed that a policeman acted from malice or a grudge if no reasonable person would have believed that there was a power to arrest or detain in the circumstances, or if it was done with unnecessary violence or insults.

THE LADY WHO WANTED AN APOLOGY

If you are unlawfully detained by anyone, you may be able to bring an action for damages.

Mrs Robertson and Mrs Mackenzie were staying at a hydropathic hotel. They quarrelled. Mrs Robertson went to the manager and complained that Mrs Mackenzie had slammed a door in her face.

The manager invited Mrs Mackenzie to come to his room. When she entered, she found Mrs Robertson and her husband there. The manager then shut the door and the Robertsons stood against it. The manager told Mrs Mackenzie that she would not be able to leave until she had apologised to Mrs Robertson. Mrs Mackenzie was detained against her will for 15 minutes.

Mrs Mackenzie later sued the hotel for £400, because of the action of the manager in illegally detaining her.

DECISION

The court decided that it was possible for such an action to be raised and allowed the case to go ahead.

WRONGFUL DISMISSAL

When an employer dismisses without notice

An employee who is dismissed must normally be allowed to work a period of NOTICE or be given wages for that period – called wages in lieu of notice. The only exception is where the employee himself has forfeited his right to notice by misconduct so serious that it justifies instant, or summary, dismissal – for example, by theft from the employer or serious assault on a fellow employee.

If an employee is instantly dismissed and is not given wages in lieu of notice, he can sue his employer for damages for breach of the EMPLOYMENT CONTRACT, to recover the wages he is owed. He does not have to have been with his employer for any specified time. Nor does it matter that he is part-time or on a fixed-term contract.

The employee's claim , for 'wrongful dismissal', may be brought in the sheriff court or Court of Session. It can be brought up to 5 years from the date on which dismissal took place. LEGAL AID may be available to pay some or all of the cost of being legally represented. If the claim is successful, the court will usually order the employer to pay the expenses.

If the employer can show that the employee was guilty of misconduct that justified instant dismissal, the court will reject the claim.

How damages are assessed

Damages in wrongful dismissal cases are generally limited to the net value of the wages that should have been paid during the notice period, but the employee may also seek compensation for the loss, during that period, of fringe benefits – for instance, a car or free board and lodging.

Courts expect dismissed employees to do all they can to reduce their losses, in particular by trying to find another job as soon as possible.

If an employee takes new employment during what would have been his notice period, his earnings from it are deducted from his damages. If he has not found another job, and the court feels he has not made a reasonable effort to do so, it can reduce his damages by the amount it estimates he could have earned. Because of this, the employee should keep, as evidence of his efforts, a careful record of applications sent, interviews attended and the total time spent job-hunting.

The amount of damages is also reduced by the value of any UNEMPLOYMENT BENEFIT received during what should have been the notice period, and by the INCOME TAX and NATIONAL INSURANCE CONTRIBUTIONS the employee would have had to pay. SUPPLEMENTARY BENEFIT may be deducted too, as well as any REDUNDANCY payment received.

Damages cannot be awarded for injured feelings or for the way in which the dismissal was carried out. But they could be awarded for any illness – for instance, severe depression – that the employee suffers as a result.

Awards for wrongful dismissal are not taxable unless they exceed £25,000.

Other dismissal claims

Wrongful dismissal claims are based on the law of contract and are not connected with the statutory rules on EMPLOYMENT PROTECTION. An employee who receives damages from a court for wrongful dismissal does not forfeit his rights to apply to an industrial tribunal for compensation for UNFAIR DISMISSAL or for a redundancy payment.

These rights are not affected even if, in settling the wrongful dismissal claim, the employee signs a declaration provided by his employer stating that the payment of damages is 'in full and final settlement of all claims I may have arising out of the termination of my employment'.

X-RAYS

When medical treatment involves radiation

If someone is harmed through exposure to x-rays – particularly during radiotherapy – because reasonable care and precautions were not taken, he has a right to claim damages for negligence. *See:* MEDICAL NEGLIGENCE

A foetus damaged in the womb in these circumstances would also be able to claim. *See:* UNBORN CHILD

Because x-rays involve the use of radiation, there are stringent safeguards to protect patients during radiotherapy. For example, protective clothing may be provided to protect certain areas of the body from exposure. The heads of young children should not be subjected to x-rays unless it is absolutely necessary. Similarly, a pregnant woman should be subjected to x-rays only in an emergency, such as a road accident.

HOW TO READ PICTURES

Most x-rays are taken by qualified radiographers and are then interpreted by radiologists.

Who can take an x-ray?

Any doctor may take an x-ray and dental x-rays are normally taken by dentists.

However, most x-rays are taken in a hospital or clinic by someone who is a qualified radiographer. The results are exposed on film and are then interpreted by a specialist doctor called a radiologist.

When immigrants may be x-rayed

X-rays are generally used only in connection with medical treatment. However, intending immigrants may be required to have an x-ray to determine their age, if this is in dispute and their right to enter Britain is affected as a result.

YOUNG OFFENDERS

How the law deals with young people who commit serious offences

Offenders between the ages of 16 and 21 are known as young offenders. Young offenders cannot be sentenced to imprisonment in Scotland. There are, however, separate custodial arrangements for them.

Trial and sentence

While on REMAND awaiting trial or sentence, inmates of all ages may be kept together (although Longriggend Institution near Airdrie holds only remand prisoners who are under 21).

No young offender can be given a custodial sentence unless the court considers that imprisonment would be an appropriate sentence for an adult in similar circumstances and no other sentence is appropriate. Before reaching this conclusion, the court must obtain a background report on the offender, usually from the regional social work department. This report may include medical and psychiatric assessments.

All courts must state the reasons why it is considered that a custodial sentence is appropriate.

Where young offenders can be sent

Until 1983, the courts had a choice of three different custodial sentences for young offenders: detention centre (for male offenders only), borstal or young offenders institution. Detention was a 3 month sentence, subject to remission. Borstal was a 2 year sentence with release at the discretion of the institution, usually after 9 months or so.

In November, 1983, borstal training was abolished as a sentence. All former borstal institutions have now become young offenders institutions. Friarton, a former young offenders institution in Perth, has now become a detention centre.

All female young offenders sentenced to be detained now serve their time in a young offenders institution at Cornton Vale, near Stirling. This is beside the female prison, but both groups of inmates are kept separately.

Male young offenders are divided between detention centre and young offenders institution on the simple basis of length of sentence.

Those sentenced to between 28 days and 4 months go to a detention centre. Those sentenced to less than 28 days or more than 4 months go to a young offenders institution. Transfers between the two regimes can be authorised by the Scottish Home and Health Department.

There are detention centres at Glenochil and Friarton, Perth. Young offenders institutions are at Dumfries, Glenochil, Polmont, Castle Huntly and Noranside. Dumfries takes long term offenders, Glenochil medium term offenders and security risks, and Polmont short term offenders. Castle Huntly and Noranside are 'open' institutions.

The purpose of a detention centre is to provide offenders with a "short, sharp shock". As a result there is strong emphasis on physical training and tight discipline. Young offenders institutions, on the other hand, are more relaxed and in effect operate as junior prisons.

An inmate of a young offenders institution who becomes 21 may be transferred to an adult prison and must be transferred, at the latest, on his 23rd birthday.

Discipline

Young offenders are subject to the same disciplinary rules as adult prisoners. They also have the same rights to make requests to the Governor and Visiting Committee and to petition the Secretary of State.

Visiting Committees for institutions for under 21s are appointed by the Secretary of State, not by local authorities as in the case of adult institutions.

Children

Offenders under the age of 16 can only be detained in penal institutions under special circumstances.

Following conviction on INDICTMENT, a court may, if it feels that there is no other appropriate disposal open to it, order the child to be detained for a period in a place directed by the Secretary of State. Such a place may, but need not, be a penal institution.

Equally, following a summary conviction, a sheriff court may order a period of residential training of up to 2 years. Again the place is determined by the Secretary of State. Very few children are detained under this provision.

The only other circumstances in which a child can be detained in a penal institution are when he is certified as being 'unruly' or detained for 'contempt of court'.

Parole and after-care

All young offenders have the same entitlement to remission and consideration for PAROLE as adult offenders.

Compulsory after-care is provided for all young offenders who have served a sentence of over 6 months. During the period of after-care – 6 months for those with sentences of up to 18 months, and 1 year for those with sentences above 18 months – the offender can be recalled to custody for a maximum of 3 months. Compulsory after-care ends on the offender's 23rd birthday.

Sentence on conviction for murder

Young offenders convicted of murder are not sentenced to life imprisonment, though the effect of the sentence is generally the same.

Offenders under 18 are sentenced 'to be detained without limit of time' in a place chosen by the Secretary of State. This place may be a young offenders' institution, but need not be. Offenders aged between 18 and 21 are kept in young offenders' institutions and are 'liable to be detained for life'.

Release of both categories will only be on licence and the Parole Board must be consulted by the Secretary of State before any such inmate is released.

Non-custodial sentences for young offenders

The courts have available to them the same range of non-custodial sentences for young offenders as they have for adult offenders. So absolute discharge, admonition, probation, fine and community service orders are all appropriate sentences.

While courts make strenuous attempts to find non-custodial disposals for young offenders, 3,034 such offenders were nonetheless directly received into custody in 1982. (This figure excludes remand inmates and those imprisoned because of failure to pay fines.)

ZEBRA CROSSING

The cross-traffic 'precinct' for pedestrians

Zebra crossings were designed and are recognised in law as a protected area for pedestrians wishing to cross a street.

Under most circumstances drivers must give way to anyone setting foot on a 'zebra'. Unlike pelican crossings, they are not controlled by lights, but they must have flashing amber Belisha beacons. *See:* PEDESTRIAN CROSSING

Index

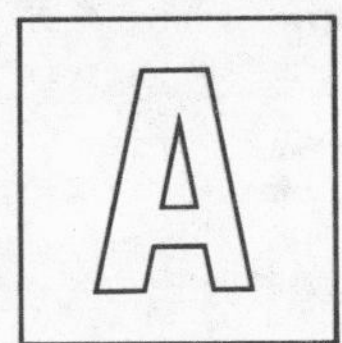

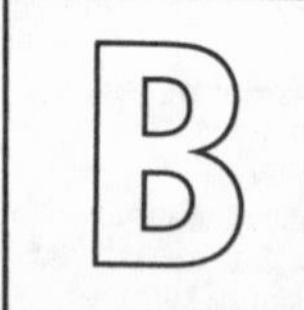

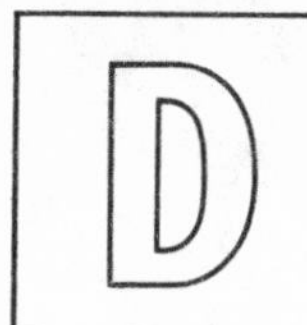

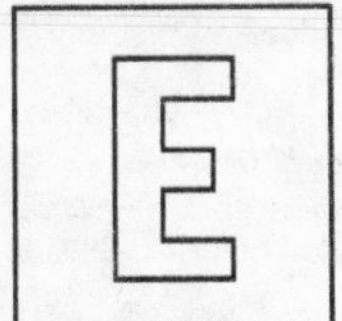

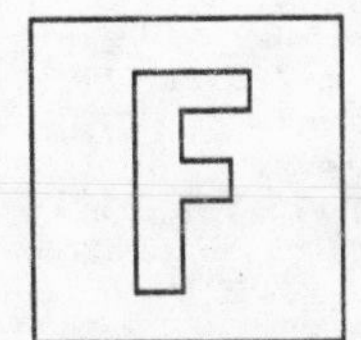

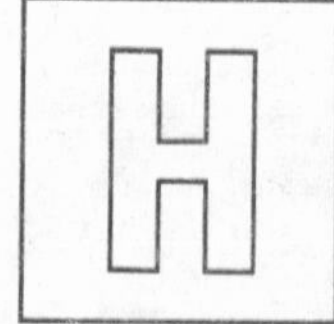

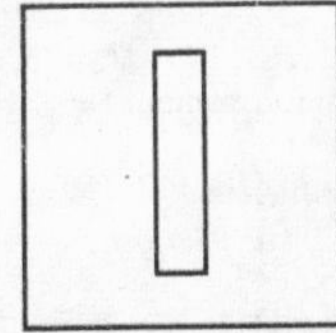

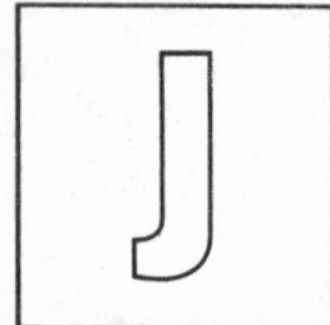

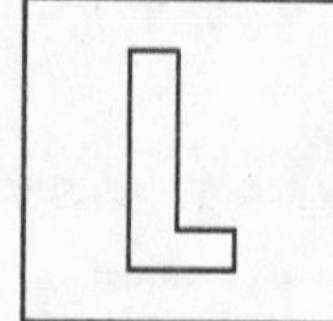

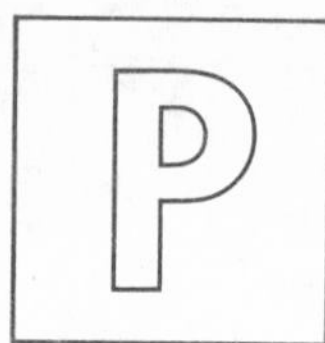

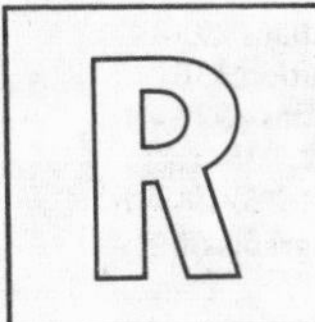

S

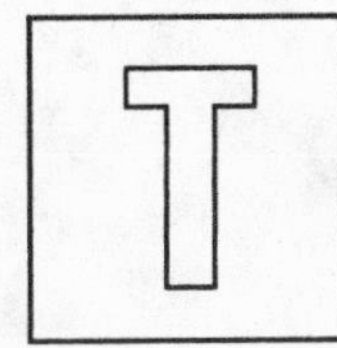

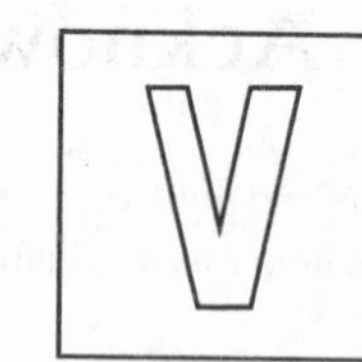

Acknowledgments

The editors and publishers are indebted to the many individuals and organisations whose help was invaluable during the preparation of this book, including:

Peter Anderson: Automobile Association: Bank of Scotland: T. St. John Bates: Anne Black: British Board of Film Censors: British Broadcasting Corporation: British Medical Association: British Rail: British Railways Board Solicitor (Scotland): British Telecom: British Transport Police, Waverley Office: Douglas Brodie: City of Edinburgh District Council: Peter Clarke: Eric Clive: Commissary Office, Linlithgow: Commission of European Communities: Countryside Commission for Scotland: Crown Office: Department of Agriculture and Fisheries for Scotland: Department of Health and Social Security: Helen Dignan: Divisional Veterinary Office: Gavin Douglas: Driver and Vehicle Licensing Centre, Swansea: Eagle Star Insurance: Edinburgh Assay Office: Electoral Registration Office, Lothian Regional Council: Environmental Health Department, City of Edinburgh District Council: Carol Ervine: Family Fund: Betty Ferguson: General Accident Fire and Life Assurance Corporation: General Register Office, Edinburgh: Donal Giltinan: Richard Girdwood: N. R. Grieve, J & J Gray Ltd., Dundee: Mike Groushko: The Housing Corporation: Norma Jones: Law Society of Scotland: Robert Leslie: Lord Lyon King of Arms: A. T. McIntosh, Registrar, City of Dundee: Motability: National Television Licence Records Office: The Performing Right Society Limited: Peterkin & Kidd, W. S.: Phillips in Scotland: Rent Registration Office, Edinburgh: Royal National Lifeboat Institution: Royal Society for the Protection of Birds: Malcolm Schaffer: Scottish Development Department: Scottish Certificate of Education Examination Board: Gas Consumers' Council for Scotland: Scottish Home and Health Department: Sheriff Clerk, Linlithgow: Sheila Smith: Society of Fine Arts: A. A. Steele, Sheriff Clerk, Dundee: Moyra Taylor: Elizabeth Thomson: Lindsey Turnbull: Fran Wasoff: Hazel Young

The following individuals and organisations provided assistance during the preparation of *You and Your Rights* (England and Wales edition):

Abbey National Building Society: Advisory, Conciliation and Arbitration Service (ACAS): Alcoholics Anonymous: American Express: Arts Council of Great Britain: Association of British Adoption and Fostering Agencies: Association of British Launderers and Cleaners: Association of British Travel Agents: Association of County Councils: Association of District Councils: Association of Metropolitan Authorities: Association of Optical Practitioners: Automobile Association

Back Pain Association: Bank of England: Banking Information Service: Barclays Bank Limited: Board of Inland Revenue: Rodney Brazier, LL.B: British Association for Early Childhood Education: British Board of Film Censors: British Broadcasting Corporation: British Dental Association: British Hotels, Restaurants and Caterers Association: British Insurance Association: British Insurance Brokers' Association: British Medical Journal: The British Petroleum Company Limited: British Property Federation: British Railways Board: British Safety Council: British Standards Institution: British Waterways Board: Building Societies Association

Professor Harry Calvert: Car & Medical Instrument Co. Ltd.: Central Criminal Court: Central Office of the Industrial Tribunals (England and Wales): Central Office of Information: Central Statistical Office: Certificated Bailiffs Association: Charity Commission: Chartered Institute of Arbitrators: Chartered Insurance Institute: Chingford Quarantine and Boarding Kennels: Church of England Information Office: Civil Aviation Authority: Michele Clarke, BA: College of Arms: Commercial Union Assurance: Commission for Racial Equality: Commons Open Spaces and Footpaths Preservation Society: Anne Comyn: Consumer Credit Trade Association: Continental Tyre and Rubber Company Limited: Elaine Cook: CORGI: Council of Co-ownership Housing Societies Limited: Council for Places of Worship: Countryside Commission: Court of the Lord Lyon: Criminal Injuries Compensation Board

Department of Education and Science: Department of Employment: Department of Energy: Department of Health and Social Security: Department of Industry: Department of Trade: Department of Transport: The Disabled Living Foundation: Domestic Coal Consumers' Council: Draegar Safety

Electoral Reform Society of Great Britain and Ireland: Electricity Council: Environmental Health Officers' Association: Equal Opportunities Commission: European Commission: European Parliament Fish Traders' Gazette: Fishmongers Company: Forestry Commission

Gaming Board for Great Britain: General Dental Council: General Medical Council: General Register Office: Gingerbread: Granada Television Limited: Grant Simmonds and Company Limited: Greater London Council: Greater Manchester Council: Guardian Royal Exchange Assurance: Guide Dogs for the Blind Association

Halifax Building Society: Hampshire County Council: Hampstead and Highgate Express: Ronald Harris: Health and Safety Executive: Health Education Council: Health Visitors Association: Peter A. Heims: Help the Aged: Hendon Times Group of Newspapers: Patricia Hewitt: HM Customs and Excise: HM Land Registry: HM Stationery Office: Brenda Hoggett: Home Office: Horserace Totalisator Board: Housing Corporation: Howard League for Penal Reform

Independent Broadcasting Authority: Independent Schools Information Service: Industrial Relations Europe: Industrial Society: Inner London Education Authority: Institute of Directors: Institute of Fisheries Management: Institute of Patent Agents: Institute of Practitioners in Advertising: Institute of Taxation: International Voluntary Service

Emyr Wyn Jones: Michel Kallipetis: Keep Britain Tidy Group: K. R. Lack, ARIBA: Laker Airways: Law and Commercial Enquiries Limited: Law Officers' Department: Law Society: Life Offices' Association: Lion Laboratories Ltd.: London Borough of Barnet: London Borough of Camden: London Borough of Hammersmith and Fulham: London Electricity Board: London Rape Crisis Centre: The London Small Claims Court: London Transport Executive: Lord Chamberlain's Office

Magistrates' Association: Manpower Services Commission: Medical Defence Union: Mental After Care Association: Metrication Board: Milk Marketing Board: MIND (National Association for Mental Health): Ministry of Agriculture, Fisheries and Food: Moorgate Marketing Consultants Limited: Motor Agents Association Limited

National Association for the Care and Resettlement of Offenders: National Bus Company: National Caravan Council: National Coal Board: National Consumer Council: National Council for One Parent Families: National Economic Development Office: National Federation of Housing Associations: National Federation of Old Age Pensioners' Associations (Pensioners' Voice): National Girobank: National House-Building Council: National Marriage Guidance Council: National Society for Clean Air: National Society for the Prevention of Cruelty to Children: National Trust: National TV Licence Records Office: National Union of Ratepayers Association: National Westminster Bank Limited: North Thames Gas: Northern Ireland Office: North-west Transport Users' Consultative Committee: Norwich Union Insurance Group

Office of Fair Trading: Office of the National Insurance Commissioners: Office of Parliamentary Commissioner and Health Service Commissioners: Office of Population, Censuses and Surveys

Partially Sighted Society: Passport Office: Patent Office: Patients Association: Paymaster General's Office: Performing Right Society: Pharmaceutical Society of Great Britain: Plant Variety Rights Office and Seeds Division: Post Office: Post Office Users' National Council: Pre-School Playgroups Association: Principal Registry of the Family Division: Privy Council Office: Public Analyst: Public Carriage Office

Registrar General: Rowntree Memorial Trust: Royal Association for Disability and Rehabilitation: Royal Institute for the Deaf: Royal National Lifeboat Institution: Royal Society for the Prevention of Accidents: Royal Society for the Prevention of Cruelty to Animals: Royal Society for the Protection of Birds: The Royal Warrant Holders Association

Salvation Army: Schools Council for Curriculum and Examinations: Scottish Anti-Vivisection Society: Scottish Office: Securicor Limited: SHAC, The London Housing Aid Centre: Shaftesbury Society: Jack Smith, LL.B: Society for the Protection of Ancient Buildings: The Solicitors' Law Stationery Society, Limited: Spastics Society: Sports Council

Tattersalls Committee: Telephone Users' Association: Thames Water Authority: Town and Country Planning Association: The Treasury

Universities Central Council on Admissions (UCCA): Victoria and Albert Museum: Wandsworth County Court: A. P. Watt Limited: Welsh Office: Westminster City Council: Westminster Coroner's Court: William Hill Organization: Woman's Royal Voluntary Service: F. W. Woolworth and Company Limited: The Worshipful Company of Goldsmiths: K. L. Wyld

Sanctissimo patri in Christo ac domino domino Johanni diuina prouidencia Sacrosancte Romane et

[illegible] Ranulphi Comes Morauie dominus Mannie et vallis Anandie. Patricius de Dumbar Comes Marchie

Magnus Comes Cathanie et Orcadie et Willelmus Comes Sutherlandie. Walterus Senescallus

[illegible] de Brechyn. David de Graham. Ingeramus de Umfrauill. Johannes de Menetethe Custos

[illegible] David de Lindesay. Willelmus Olifaunt. Patricius

[illegible] Fergusius de Ardrossan [illegible] Willelmus de Monte alto. Alanus

[illegible]

... Scotorum ... Residens a nullis quamuis barbaris ... Pictis omnino deletis ...

[illegible]

... consuetudines ... regno nostro ... pugnamus ...

[illegible]

... Rex Anglorum cum sufficiat ...

... effectum ...

Ecclesie in aliqua sui parte eclipsim aut scandalum vos videritis ...

... in omnibus ... debellan[...]

Anglorum nos in pace dimittere ...

... in ipsius confessionem ...

... in omnibus complacere ...

... hostes nostros ...

Aprilis. Anno gracie Millesimo Trescentesimo vicesimo. Anno vero Regni Regis nostri supradicti ...